Lecture Notes in Computer Science 13696

More information about this series at https://link.springer.com/bookseries/558

Shai Avidan · Gabriel Brostow ·
Moustapha Cissé · Giovanni Maria Farinella ·
Tal Hassner (Eds.)

Computer Vision – ECCV 2022

17th European Conference
Tel Aviv, Israel, October 23–27, 2022
Proceedings, Part XXXVI

 Springer

Editors
Shai Avidan
Tel Aviv University
Tel Aviv, Israel

Gabriel Brostow 🆔
University College London
London, UK

Moustapha Cissé
Google AI
Accra, Ghana

Giovanni Maria Farinella 🆔
University of Catania
Catania, Italy

Tal Hassner 🆔
Facebook (United States)
Menlo Park, CA, USA

ISSN 0302-9743   ISSN 1611-3349 (electronic)
Lecture Notes in Computer Science
ISBN 978-3-031-20058-8   ISBN 978-3-031-20059-5 (eBook)
https://doi.org/10.1007/978-3-031-20059-5

This Springer imprint is published by the registered company Springer Nature Switzerland AG
The registered company address is: Gewerbestrasse 11, 6330 Cham, Switzerland

Foreword

Organizing the European Conference on Computer Vision (ECCV 2022) in Tel-Aviv during a global pandemic was no easy feat. The uncertainty level was extremely high, and decisions had to be postponed to the last minute. Still, we managed to plan things just in time for ECCV 2022 to be held in person. Participation in physical events is crucial to stimulating collaborations and nurturing the culture of the Computer Vision community.

There were many people who worked hard to ensure attendees enjoyed the best science at the 16th edition of ECCV. We are grateful to the Program Chairs Gabriel Brostow and Tal Hassner, who went above and beyond to ensure the ECCV reviewing process ran smoothly. The scientific program includes dozens of workshops and tutorials in addition to the main conference and we would like to thank Leonid Karlinsky and Tomer Michaeli for their hard work. Finally, special thanks to the web chairs Lorenzo Baraldi and Kosta Derpanis, who put in extra hours to transfer information fast and efficiently to the ECCV community.

We would like to express gratitude to our generous sponsors and the Industry Chairs, Dimosthenis Karatzas and Chen Sagiv, who oversaw industry relations and proposed new ways for academia-industry collaboration and technology transfer. It's great to see so much industrial interest in what we're doing!

Authors' draft versions of the papers appeared online with open access on both the Computer Vision Foundation (CVF) and the European Computer Vision Association (ECVA) websites as with previous ECCVs. Springer, the publisher of the proceedings, has arranged for archival publication. The final version of the papers is hosted by SpringerLink, with active references and supplementary materials. It benefits all potential readers that we offer both a free and citeable version for all researchers, as well as an authoritative, citeable version for SpringerLink readers. Our thanks go to Ronan Nugent from Springer, who helped us negotiate this agreement. Last but not least, we wish to thank Eric Mortensen, our publication chair, whose expertise made the process smooth.

October 2022

Rita Cucchiara
Jiří Matas
Amnon Shashua
Lihi Zelnik-Manor

Preface

Welcome to the proceedings of the European Conference on Computer Vision (ECCV 2022). This was a hybrid edition of ECCV as we made our way out of the COVID-19 pandemic. The conference received 5804 valid paper submissions, compared to 5150 submissions to ECCV 2020 (a 12.7% increase) and 2439 in ECCV 2018. 1645 submissions were accepted for publication (28%) and, of those, 157 (2.7% overall) as orals.

846 of the submissions were desk-rejected for various reasons. Many of them because they revealed author identity, thus violating the double-blind policy. This violation came in many forms: some had author names with the title, others added acknowledgments to specific grants, yet others had links to their github account where their name was visible. Tampering with the LaTeX template was another reason for automatic desk rejection.

ECCV 2022 used the traditional CMT system to manage the entire double-blind reviewing process. Authors did not know the names of the reviewers and vice versa. Each paper received at least 3 reviews (except 6 papers that received only 2 reviews), totalling more than 15,000 reviews.

Handling the review process at this scale was a significant challenge. To ensure that each submission received as fair and high-quality reviews as possible, we recruited more than 4719 reviewers (in the end, 4719 reviewers did at least one review). Similarly we recruited more than 276 area chairs (eventually, only 276 area chairs handled a batch of papers). The area chairs were selected based on their technical expertise and reputation, largely among people who served as area chairs in previous top computer vision and machine learning conferences (ECCV, ICCV, CVPR, NeurIPS, etc.).

Reviewers were similarly invited from previous conferences, and also from the pool of authors. We also encouraged experienced area chairs to suggest additional chairs and reviewers in the initial phase of recruiting. The median reviewer load was five papers per reviewer, while the average load was about four papers, because of the emergency reviewers. The area chair load was 35 papers, on average.

Conflicts of interest between authors, area chairs, and reviewers were handled largely automatically by the CMT platform, with some manual help from the Program Chairs. Reviewers were allowed to describe themselves as senior reviewer (load of 8 papers to review) or junior reviewers (load of 4 papers). Papers were matched to area chairs based on a subject-area affinity score computed in CMT and an affinity score computed by the Toronto Paper Matching System (TPMS). TPMS is based on the paper's full text. An area chair handling each submission would bid for preferred expert reviewers, and we balanced load and prevented conflicts.

The assignment of submissions to area chairs was relatively smooth, as was the assignment of submissions to reviewers. A small percentage of reviewers were not happy with their assignments in terms of subjects and self-reported expertise. This is an area for improvement, although it's interesting that many of these cases were reviewers hand-picked by AC's. We made a later round of reviewer recruiting, targeted at the list of authors of papers submitted to the conference, and had an excellent response which helped provide enough emergency reviewers. In the end, all but six papers received at least 3 reviews.

The challenges of the reviewing process are in line with past experiences at ECCV 2020. As the community grows, and the number of submissions increases, it becomes ever more challenging to recruit enough reviewers and ensure a high enough quality of reviews. Enlisting authors by default as reviewers might be one step to address this challenge.

Authors were given a week to rebut the initial reviews, and address reviewers' concerns. Each rebuttal was limited to a single pdf page with a fixed template.

The Area Chairs then led discussions with the reviewers on the merits of each submission. The goal was to reach consensus, but, ultimately, it was up to the Area Chair to make a decision. The decision was then discussed with a buddy Area Chair to make sure decisions were fair and informative. The entire process was conducted virtually with no in-person meetings taking place.

The Program Chairs were informed in cases where the Area Chairs overturned a decisive consensus reached by the reviewers, and pushed for the meta-reviews to contain details that explained the reasoning for such decisions. Obviously these were the most contentious cases, where reviewer inexperience was the most common reported factor.

Once the list of accepted papers was finalized and released, we went through the laborious process of plagiarism (including self-plagiarism) detection. A total of 4 accepted papers were rejected because of that.

Finally, we would like to thank our Technical Program Chair, Pavel Lifshits, who did tremendous work behind the scenes, and we thank the tireless CMT team.

October 2022

Gabriel Brostow
Giovanni Maria Farinella
Moustapha Cissé
Shai Avidan
Tal Hassner

Organization

General Chairs

Rita Cucchiara   University of Modena and Reggio Emilia, Italy
Jiří Matas   Czech Technical University in Prague, Czech
Republic
Amnon Shashua   Hebrew University of Jerusalem, Israel
Lihi Zelnik-Manor   Technion – Israel Institute of Technology, Israel

Program Chairs

Shai Avidan   Tel-Aviv University, Israel
Gabriel Brostow   University College London, UK
Moustapha Cissé   Google AI, Ghana
Giovanni Maria Farinella   University of Catania, Italy
Tal Hassner   Facebook AI, USA

Program Technical Chair

Pavel Lifshits   Technion – Israel Institute of Technology, Israel

Workshops Chairs

Leonid Karlinsky   IBM Research, Israel
Tomer Michaeli   Technion – Israel Institute of Technology, Israel
Ko Nishino   Kyoto University, Japan

Tutorial Chairs

Thomas Pock   Graz University of Technology, Austria
Natalia Neverova   Facebook AI Research, UK

Demo Chair

Bohyung Han   Seoul National University, Korea

Social and Student Activities Chairs

Tatiana Tommasi   Italian Institute of Technology, Italy
Sagie Benaim   University of Copenhagen, Denmark

Diversity and Inclusion Chairs

Xi Yin   Facebook AI Research, USA
Bryan Russell   Adobe, USA

Communications Chairs

Lorenzo Baraldi   University of Modena and Reggio Emilia, Italy
Kosta Derpanis   York University & Samsung AI Centre Toronto,
                               Canada

Industrial Liaison Chairs

Dimosthenis Karatzas   Universitat Autònoma de Barcelona, Spain
Chen Sagiv   SagivTech, Israel

Finance Chair

Gerard Medioni   University of Southern California & Amazon,
                               USA

Publication Chair

Eric Mortensen   MiCROTEC, USA

Area Chairs

Lourdes Agapito   University College London, UK
Zeynep Akata   University of Tübingen, Germany
Naveed Akhtar   University of Western Australia, Australia
Karteek Alahari   Inria Grenoble Rhône-Alpes, France
Alexandre Alahi   École polytechnique fédérale de Lausanne,
                               Switzerland
Pablo Arbelaez   Universidad de Los Andes, Columbia
Antonis A. Argyros   University of Crete & Foundation for Research
                               and Technology-Hellas, Crete
Yuki M. Asano   University of Amsterdam, The Netherlands
Kalle Åström   Lund University, Sweden
Hadar Averbuch-Elor   Cornell University, USA

Hossein Azizpour   KTH Royal Institute of Technology, Sweden
Vineeth N. Balasubramanian   Indian Institute of Technology, Hyderabad, India
Lamberto Ballan   University of Padova, Italy
Adrien Bartoli   Université Clermont Auvergne, France
Horst Bischof   Graz University of Technology, Austria
Matthew B. Blaschko   KU Leuven, Belgium
Federica Bogo   Meta Reality Labs Research, Switzerland
Katherine Bouman   California Institute of Technology, USA
Edmond Boyer   Inria Grenoble Rhône-Alpes, France
Michael S. Brown   York University, Canada
Vittorio Caggiano   Meta AI Research, USA
Neill Campbell   University of Bath, UK
Octavia Camps   Northeastern University, USA
Duygu Ceylan   Adobe Research, USA
Ayan Chakrabarti   Google Research, USA
Tat-Jen Cham   Nanyang Technological University, Singapore
Antoni Chan   City University of Hong Kong, Hong Kong, China
Manmohan Chandraker   NEC Labs America, USA
Xinlei Chen   Facebook AI Research, USA
Xilin Chen   Institute of Computing Technology, Chinese
                                   Academy of Sciences, China
Dongdong Chen   Microsoft Cloud AI, USA
Chen Chen   University of Central Florida, USA
Ondrej Chum   Vision Recognition Group, Czech Technical
                                   University in Prague, Czech Republic
John Collomosse   Adobe Research & University of Surrey, UK
Camille Couprie   Facebook, France
David Crandall   Indiana University, USA
Daniel Cremers   Technical University of Munich, Germany
Marco Cristani   University of Verona, Italy
Canton Cristian   Facebook AI Research, USA
Dengxin Dai   ETH Zurich, Switzerland
Dima Damen   University of Bristol, UK
Kostas Daniilidis   University of Pennsylvania, USA
Trevor Darrell   University of California, Berkeley, USA
Andrew Davison   Imperial College London, UK
Tali Dekel   Weizmann Institute of Science, Israel
Alessio Del Bue   Istituto Italiano di Tecnologia, Italy
Weihong Deng   Beijing University of Posts and
                                   Telecommunications, China
Konstantinos Derpanis   Ryerson University, Canada
Carl Doersch   DeepMind, UK

Ivan Laptev	Inria Paris, France
Laura Leal-Taixé	Technical University of Munich, Germany
Erik Learned-Miller	University of Massachusetts, Amherst, USA
Gim Hee Lee	National University of Singapore, Singapore
Seungyong Lee	Pohang University of Science and Technology, Korea
Zhen Lei	Institute of Automation, Chinese Academy of Sciences, China
Bastian Leibe	RWTH Aachen University, Germany
Hongdong Li	Australian National University, Australia
Fuxin Li	Oregon State University, USA
Bo Li	University of Illinois at Urbana-Champaign, USA
Yin Li	University of Wisconsin-Madison, USA
Ser-Nam Lim	Meta AI Research, USA
Joseph Lim	University of Southern California, USA
Stephen Lin	Microsoft Research Asia, China
Dahua Lin	The Chinese University of Hong Kong, Hong Kong, China
Si Liu	Beihang University, China
Xiaoming Liu	Michigan State University, USA
Ce Liu	Microsoft, USA
Zicheng Liu	Microsoft, USA
Yanxi Liu	Pennsylvania State University, USA
Feng Liu	Portland State University, USA
Yebin Liu	Tsinghua University, China
Chen Change Loy	Nanyang Technological University, Singapore
Huchuan Lu	Dalian University of Technology, China
Cewu Lu	Shanghai Jiao Tong University, China
Oisin Mac Aodha	University of Edinburgh, UK
Dhruv Mahajan	Facebook, USA
Subhransu Maji	University of Massachusetts, Amherst, USA
Atsuto Maki	KTH Royal Institute of Technology, Sweden
Arun Mallya	NVIDIA, USA
R. Manmatha	Amazon, USA
Iacopo Masi	Sapienza University of Rome, Italy
Dimitris N. Metaxas	Rutgers University, USA
Ajmal Mian	University of Western Australia, Australia
Christian Micheloni	University of Udine, Italy
Krystian Mikolajczyk	Imperial College London, UK
Anurag Mittal	Indian Institute of Technology, Madras, India
Philippos Mordohai	Stevens Institute of Technology, USA
Greg Mori	Simon Fraser University & Borealis AI, Canada

Vittorio Murino	Istituto Italiano di Tecnologia, Italy
P. J. Narayanan	International Institute of Information Technology, Hyderabad, India
Ram Nevatia	University of Southern California, USA
Natalia Neverova	Facebook AI Research, UK
Richard Newcombe	Facebook, USA
Cuong V. Nguyen	Florida International University, USA
Bingbing Ni	Shanghai Jiao Tong University, China
Juan Carlos Niebles	Salesforce & Stanford University, USA
Ko Nishino	Kyoto University, Japan
Jean-Marc Odobez	Idiap Research Institute, École polytechnique fédérale de Lausanne, Switzerland
Francesca Odone	University of Genova, Italy
Takayuki Okatani	Tohoku University & RIKEN Center for Advanced Intelligence Project, Japan
Manohar Paluri	Facebook, USA
Guan Pang	Facebook, USA
Maja Pantic	Imperial College London, UK
Sylvain Paris	Adobe Research, USA
Jaesik Park	Pohang University of Science and Technology, Korea
Hyun Soo Park	The University of Minnesota, USA
Omkar M. Parkhi	Facebook, USA
Deepak Pathak	Carnegie Mellon University, USA
Georgios Pavlakos	University of California, Berkeley, USA
Marcello Pelillo	University of Venice, Italy
Marc Pollefeys	ETH Zurich & Microsoft, Switzerland
Jean Ponce	Inria, France
Gerard Pons-Moll	University of Tübingen, Germany
Fatih Porikli	Qualcomm, USA
Victor Adrian Prisacariu	University of Oxford, UK
Petia Radeva	University of Barcelona, Spain
Ravi Ramamoorthi	University of California, San Diego, USA
Deva Ramanan	Carnegie Mellon University, USA
Vignesh Ramanathan	Facebook, USA
Nalini Ratha	State University of New York at Buffalo, USA
Tammy Riklin Raviv	Ben-Gurion University, Israel
Tobias Ritschel	University College London, UK
Emanuele Rodola	Sapienza University of Rome, Italy
Amit K. Roy-Chowdhury	University of California, Riverside, USA
Michael Rubinstein	Google, USA
Olga Russakovsky	Princeton University, USA

Mathieu Salzmann	École polytechnique fédérale de Lausanne, Switzerland
Dimitris Samaras	Stony Brook University, USA
Aswin Sankaranarayanan	Carnegie Mellon University, USA
Imari Sato	National Institute of Informatics, Japan
Yoichi Sato	University of Tokyo, Japan
Shin'ichi Satoh	National Institute of Informatics, Japan
Walter Scheirer	University of Notre Dame, USA
Bernt Schiele	Max Planck Institute for Informatics, Germany
Konrad Schindler	ETH Zurich, Switzerland
Cordelia Schmid	Inria & Google, France
Alexander Schwing	University of Illinois at Urbana-Champaign, USA
Nicu Sebe	University of Trento, Italy
Greg Shakhnarovich	Toyota Technological Institute at Chicago, USA
Eli Shechtman	Adobe Research, USA
Humphrey Shi	University of Oregon & University of Illinois at Urbana-Champaign & Picsart AI Research, USA
Jianbo Shi	University of Pennsylvania, USA
Roy Shilkrot	Massachusetts Institute of Technology, USA
Mike Zheng Shou	National University of Singapore, Singapore
Kaleem Siddiqi	McGill University, Canada
Richa Singh	Indian Institute of Technology Jodhpur, India
Greg Slabaugh	Queen Mary University of London, UK
Cees Snoek	University of Amsterdam, The Netherlands
Yale Song	Facebook AI Research, USA
Yi-Zhe Song	University of Surrey, UK
Bjorn Stenger	Rakuten Institute of Technology
Abby Stylianou	Saint Louis University, USA
Akihiro Sugimoto	National Institute of Informatics, Japan
Chen Sun	Brown University, USA
Deqing Sun	Google, USA
Kalyan Sunkavalli	Adobe Research, USA
Ying Tai	Tencent YouTu Lab, China
Ayellet Tal	Technion – Israel Institute of Technology, Israel
Ping Tan	Simon Fraser University, Canada
Siyu Tang	ETH Zurich, Switzerland
Chi-Keung Tang	Hong Kong University of Science and Technology, Hong Kong, China
Radu Timofte	University of Würzburg, Germany & ETH Zurich, Switzerland
Federico Tombari	Google, Switzerland & Technical University of Munich, Germany

James Tompkin	Brown University, USA
Lorenzo Torresani	Dartmouth College, USA
Alexander Toshev	Apple, USA
Du Tran	Facebook AI Research, USA
Anh T. Tran	VinAI, Vietnam
Zhuowen Tu	University of California, San Diego, USA
Georgios Tzimiropoulos	Queen Mary University of London, UK
Jasper Uijlings	Google Research, Switzerland
Jan C. van Gemert	Delft University of Technology, The Netherlands
Gul Varol	Ecole des Ponts ParisTech, France
Nuno Vasconcelos	University of California, San Diego, USA
Mayank Vatsa	Indian Institute of Technology Jodhpur, India
Ashok Veeraraghavan	Rice University, USA
Jakob Verbeek	Facebook AI Research, France
Carl Vondrick	Columbia University, USA
Ruiping Wang	Institute of Computing Technology, Chinese Academy of Sciences, China
Xinchao Wang	National University of Singapore, Singapore
Liwei Wang	The Chinese University of Hong Kong, Hong Kong, China
Chaohui Wang	Université Paris-Est, France
Xiaolong Wang	University of California, San Diego, USA
Christian Wolf	NAVER LABS Europe, France
Tao Xiang	University of Surrey, UK
Saining Xie	Facebook AI Research, USA
Cihang Xie	University of California, Santa Cruz, USA
Zeki Yalniz	Facebook, USA
Ming-Hsuan Yang	University of California, Merced, USA
Angela Yao	National University of Singapore, Singapore
Shaodi You	University of Amsterdam, The Netherlands
Stella X. Yu	University of California, Berkeley, USA
Junsong Yuan	State University of New York at Buffalo, USA
Stefanos Zafeiriou	Imperial College London, UK
Amir Zamir	École polytechnique fédérale de Lausanne, Switzerland
Lei Zhang	Alibaba & Hong Kong Polytechnic University, Hong Kong, China
Lei Zhang	International Digital Economy Academy (IDEA), China
Pengchuan Zhang	Meta AI, USA
Bolei Zhou	University of California, Los Angeles, USA
Yuke Zhu	University of Texas at Austin, USA

Technical Program Committee

Yang Bai
Yuanchao Bai
Ziqian Bai
Sungyong Baik
Kevin Bailly
Max Bain
Federico Baldassarre
Wele Gedara Chaminda
    Bandara
Biplab Banerjee
Pratyay Banerjee
Sandipan Banerjee
Jihwan Bang
Antyanta Bangunharcana
Aayush Bansal
Ankan Bansal
Siddhant Bansal
Wentao Bao
Zhipeng Bao
Amir Bar
Manel Baradad Jurjo
Lorenzo Baraldi
Danny Barash
Daniel Barath
Connelly Barnes
Ioan Andrei Bârsan
Steven Basart
Dina Bashkirova
Chaim Baskin
Peyman Bateni
Anil Batra
Sebastiano Battiato
Ardhendu Behera
Harkirat Behl
Jens Behley
Vasileios Belagiannis
Boulbaba Ben Amor
Emanuel Ben Baruch
Abdessamad Ben Hamza
Gil Ben-Artzi
Assia Benbihi
Fabian Benitez-Quiroz
Guy Ben-Yosef
Philipp Benz
Alexander W. Bergman

Urs Bergmann
Jesus Bermudez-Cameo
Stefano Berretti
Gedas Bertasius
Zachary Bessinger
Petra Bevandić
Matthew Beveridge
Lucas Beyer
Yash Bhalgat
Suvaansh Bhambri
Samarth Bharadwaj
Gaurav Bharaj
Aparna Bharati
Bharat Lal Bhatnagar
Uttaran Bhattacharya
Apratim Bhattacharyya
Brojeshwar Bhowmick
Ankan Kumar Bhunia
Ayan Kumar Bhunia
Qi Bi
Sai Bi
Michael Bi Mi
Gui-Bin Bian
Jia-Wang Bian
Shaojun Bian
Pia Bideau
Mario Bijelic
Hakan Bilen
Guillaume-Alexandre
    Bilodeau
Alexander Binder
Tolga Birdal
Vighnesh N. Birodkar
Sandika Biswas
Andreas Blattmann
Janusz Bobulski
Giuseppe Boccignone
Vishnu Boddeti
Navaneeth Bodla
Moritz Böhle
Aleksei Bokhovkin
Sam Bond-Taylor
Vivek Boominathan
Shubhankar Borse
Mark Boss

Andrea Bottino
Adnane Boukhayma
Fadi Boutros
Nicolas C. Boutry
Richard S. Bowen
Ivaylo Boyadzhiev
Aidan Boyd
Yuri Boykov
Aljaz Bozic
Behzad Bozorgtabar
Eric Brachmann
Samarth Brahmbhatt
Gustav Bredell
Francois Bremond
Joel Brogan
Andrew Brown
Thomas Brox
Marcus A. Brubaker
Robert-Jan Bruintjes
Yuqi Bu
Anders G. Buch
Himanshu Buckchash
Mateusz Buda
Ignas Budvytis
José M. Buenaposada
Marcel C. Bühler
Tu Bui
Adrian Bulat
Hannah Bull
Evgeny Burnaev
Andrei Bursuc
Benjamin Busam
Sergey N. Buzykanov
Wonmin Byeon
Fabian Caba
Martin Cadik
Guanyu Cai
Minjie Cai
Qing Cai
Zhongang Cai
Qi Cai
Yancheng Cai
Shen Cai
Han Cai
Jiarui Cai

Bowen Cai
Mu Cai
Qin Cai
Ruojin Cai
Weidong Cai
Weiwei Cai
Yi Cai
Yujun Cai
Zhiping Cai
Akin Caliskan
Lilian Calvet
Baris Can Cam
Necati Cihan Camgoz
Tommaso Campari
Dylan Campbell
Ziang Cao
Ang Cao
Xu Cao
Zhiwen Cao
Shengcao Cao
Song Cao
Weipeng Cao
Xiangyong Cao
Xiaochun Cao
Yue Cao
Yunhao Cao
Zhangjie Cao
Jiale Cao
Yang Cao
Jiajiong Cao
Jie Cao
Jinkun Cao
Lele Cao
Yulong Cao
Zhiguo Cao
Chen Cao
Razvan Caramalau
Marlène Careil
Gustavo Carneiro
Joao Carreira
Dan Casas
Paola Cascante-Bonilla
Angela Castillo
Francisco M. Castro
Pedro Castro

Luca Cavalli
George J. Cazenavette
Oya Celiktutan
Hakan Cevikalp
Sri Harsha C. H.
Sungmin Cha
Geonho Cha
Menglei Chai
Lucy Chai
Yuning Chai
Zenghao Chai
Anirban Chakraborty
Deep Chakraborty
Rudrasis Chakraborty
Souradeep Chakraborty
Kelvin C. K. Chan
Chee Seng Chan
Paramanand Chandramouli
Arjun Chandrasekaran
Kenneth Chaney
Dongliang Chang
Huiwen Chang
Peng Chang
Xiaojun Chang
Jia-Ren Chang
Hyung Jin Chang
Hyun Sung Chang
Ju Yong Chang
Li-Jen Chang
Qi Chang
Wei-Yi Chang
Yi Chang
Nadine Chang
Hanqing Chao
Pradyumna Chari
Dibyadip Chatterjee
Chiranjoy Chattopadhyay
Siddhartha Chaudhuri
Zhengping Che
Gal Chechik
Lianggangxu Chen
Qi Alfred Chen
Brian Chen
Bor-Chun Chen
Bo-Hao Chen

Bohong Chen
Bin Chen
Ziliang Chen
Cheng Chen
Chen Chen
Chaofeng Chen
Xi Chen
Haoyu Chen
Xuanhong Chen
Wei Chen
Qiang Chen
Shi Chen
Xianyu Chen
Chang Chen
Changhuai Chen
Hao Chen
Jie Chen
Jianbo Chen
Jingjing Chen
Jun Chen
Kejiang Chen
Mingcai Chen
Nenglun Chen
Qifeng Chen
Ruoyu Chen
Shu-Yu Chen
Weidong Chen
Weijie Chen
Weikai Chen
Xiang Chen
Xiuyi Chen
Xingyu Chen
Yaofo Chen
Yueting Chen
Yu Chen
Yunjin Chen
Yuntao Chen
Yun Chen
Zhenfang Chen
Zhuangzhuang Chen
Chu-Song Chen
Xiangyu Chen
Zhuo Chen
Chaoqi Chen
Shizhe Chen

Xiaotong Chen
Xiaozhi Chen
Dian Chen
Defang Chen
Dingfan Chen
Ding-Jie Chen
Ee Heng Chen
Tao Chen
Yixin Chen
Wei-Ting Chen
Lin Chen
Guang Chen
Guangyi Chen
Guanying Chen
Guangyao Chen
Hwann-Tzong Chen
Junwen Chen
Jiacheng Chen
Jianxu Chen
Hui Chen
Kai Chen
Kan Chen
Kevin Chen
Kuan-Wen Chen
Weihua Chen
Zhang Chen
Liang-Chieh Chen
Lele Chen
Liang Chen
Fanglin Chen
Zehui Chen
Minghui Chen
Minghao Chen
Xiaokang Chen
Qian Chen
Jun-Cheng Chen
Qi Chen
Qingcai Chen
Richard J. Chen
Runnan Chen
Rui Chen
Shuo Chen
Sentao Chen
Shaoyu Chen
Shixing Chen

Shuai Chen
Shuya Chen
Sizhe Chen
Simin Chen
Shaoxiang Chen
Zitian Chen
Tianlong Chen
Tianshui Chen
Min-Hung Chen
Xiangning Chen
Xin Chen
Xinghao Chen
Xuejin Chen
Xu Chen
Xuxi Chen
Yunlu Chen
Yanbei Chen
Yuxiao Chen
Yun-Chun Chen
Yi-Ting Chen
Yi-Wen Chen
Yinbo Chen
Yiran Chen
Yuanhong Chen
Yubei Chen
Yuefeng Chen
Yuhua Chen
Yukang Chen
Zerui Chen
Zhaoyu Chen
Zhen Chen
Zhenyu Chen
Zhi Chen
Zhiwei Chen
Zhixiang Chen
Long Chen
Bowen Cheng
Jun Cheng
Yi Cheng
Jingchun Cheng
Lechao Cheng
Xi Cheng
Yuan Cheng
Ho Kei Cheng
Kevin Ho Man Cheng

Jiacheng Cheng
Kelvin B. Cheng
Li Cheng
Mengjun Cheng
Zhen Cheng
Qingrong Cheng
Tianheng Cheng
Harry Cheng
Yihua Cheng
Yu Cheng
Ziheng Cheng
Soon Yau Cheong
Anoop Cherian
Manuela Chessa
Zhixiang Chi
Naoki Chiba
Julian Chibane
Kashyap Chitta
Tai-Yin Chiu
Hsu-kuang Chiu
Wei-Chen Chiu
Sungmin Cho
Donghyeon Cho
Hyeon Cho
Yooshin Cho
Gyusang Cho
Jang Hyun Cho
Seungju Cho
Nam Ik Cho
Sunghyun Cho
Hanbyel Cho
Jaesung Choe
Jooyoung Choi
Chiho Choi
Changwoon Choi
Jongwon Choi
Myungsub Choi
Dooseop Choi
Jonghyun Choi
Jinwoo Choi
Jun Won Choi
Min-Kook Choi
Hongsuk Choi
Janghoon Choi
Yoon-Ho Choi

Yukyung Choi
Jaegul Choo
Ayush Chopra
Siddharth Choudhary
Subhabrata Choudhury
Vasileios Choutas
Ka-Ho Chow
Pinaki Nath Chowdhury
Sammy Christen
Anders Christensen
Grigorios Chrysos
Hang Chu
Wen-Hsuan Chu
Peng Chu
Qi Chu
Ruihang Chu
Wei-Ta Chu
Yung-Yu Chuang
Sanghyuk Chun
Se Young Chun
Antonio Cinà
Ramazan Gokberk Cinbis
Javier Civera
Albert Clapés
Ronald Clark
Brian S. Clipp
Felipe Codevilla
Daniel Coelho de Castro
Niv Cohen
Forrester Cole
Maxwell D. Collins
Robert T. Collins
Marc Comino Trinidad
Runmin Cong
Wenyan Cong
Maxime Cordy
Marcella Cornia
Enric Corona
Huseyin Coskun
Luca Cosmo
Dragos Costea
Davide Cozzolino
Arun C. S. Kumar
Aiyu Cui
Qiongjie Cui

Quan Cui
Shuhao Cui
Yiming Cui
Ying Cui
Zijun Cui
Jiali Cui
Jiequan Cui
Yawen Cui
Zhen Cui
Zhaopeng Cui
Jack Culpepper
Xiaodong Cun
Ross Cutler
Adam Czajka
Ali Dabouei
Konstantinos M. Dafnis
Manuel Dahnert
Tao Dai
Yuchao Dai
Bo Dai
Mengyu Dai
Hang Dai
Haixing Dai
Peng Dai
Pingyang Dai
Qi Dai
Qiyu Dai
Yutong Dai
Naser Damer
Zhiyuan Dang
Mohamed Daoudi
Ayan Das
Abir Das
Debasmit Das
Deepayan Das
Partha Das
Sagnik Das
Soumi Das
Srijan Das
Swagatam Das
Avijit Dasgupta
Jim Davis
Adrian K. Davison
Homa Davoudi
Laura Daza

Matthias De Lange
Shalini De Mello
Marco De Nadai
Christophe De
    Vleeschouwer
Alp Dener
Boyang Deng
Congyue Deng
Bailin Deng
Yong Deng
Ye Deng
Zhuo Deng
Zhijie Deng
Xiaoming Deng
Jiankang Deng
Jinhong Deng
Jingjing Deng
Liang-Jian Deng
Siqi Deng
Xiang Deng
Xueqing Deng
Zhongying Deng
Karan Desai
Jean-Emmanuel Deschaud
Aniket Anand Deshmukh
Neel Dey
Helisa Dhamo
Prithviraj Dhar
Amaya Dharmasiri
Yan Di
Xing Di
Ousmane A. Dia
Haiwen Diao
Xiaolei Diao
Gonçalo José Dias Pais
Abdallah Dib
Anastasios Dimou
Changxing Ding
Henghui Ding
Guodong Ding
Yaqing Ding
Shuangrui Ding
Yuhang Ding
Yikang Ding
Shouhong Ding

Haisong Ding
Hui Ding
Jiahao Ding
Jian Ding
Jian-Jiun Ding
Shuxiao Ding
Tianyu Ding
Wenhao Ding
Yuqi Ding
Yi Ding
Yuzhen Ding
Zhengming Ding
Tan Minh Dinh
Vu Dinh
Christos Diou
Mandar Dixit
Bao Gia Doan
Khoa D. Doan
Dzung Anh Doan
Debi Prosad Dogra
Nehal Doiphode
Chengdong Dong
Bowen Dong
Zhenxing Dong
Hang Dong
Xiaoyi Dong
Haoye Dong
Jiangxin Dong
Shichao Dong
Xuan Dong
Zhen Dong
Shuting Dong
Jing Dong
Li Dong
Ming Dong
Nanqing Dong
Qiulei Dong
Runpei Dong
Siyan Dong
Tian Dong
Wei Dong
Xiaomeng Dong
Xin Dong
Xingbo Dong
Yuan Dong

Samuel Dooley
Gianfranco Doretto
Michael Dorkenwald
Keval Doshi
Zhaopeng Dou
Xiaotian Dou
Hazel Doughty
Ahmad Droby
Iddo Drori
Jie Du
Yong Du
Dawei Du
Dong Du
Ruoyi Du
Yuntao Du
Xuefeng Du
Yilun Du
Yuming Du
Radhika Dua
Haodong Duan
Jiafei Duan
Kaiwen Duan
Peiqi Duan
Ye Duan
Haoran Duan
Jiali Duan
Amanda Duarte
Abhimanyu Dubey
Shiv Ram Dubey
Florian Dubost
Lukasz Dudziak
Shivam Duggal
Justin M. Dulay
Matteo Dunnhofer
Chi Nhan Duong
Thibaut Durand
Mihai Dusmanu
Ujjal Kr Dutta
Debidatta Dwibedi
Isht Dwivedi
Sai Kumar Dwivedi
Takeharu Eda
Mark Edmonds
Alexei A. Efros
Thibaud Ehret

Max Ehrlich
Mahsa Ehsanpour
Iván Eichhardt
Farshad Einabadi
Marvin Eisenberger
Hazim Kemal Ekenel
Mohamed El Banani
Ismail Elezi
Moshe Eliasof
Alaa El-Nouby
Ian Endres
Francis Engelmann
Deniz Engin
Chanho Eom
Dave Epstein
Maria C. Escobar
Victor A. Escorcia
Carlos Esteves
Sungmin Eum
Bernard J. E. Evans
Ivan Evtimov
Fevziye Irem Eyiokur
    Yaman
Matteo Fabbri
Sébastien Fabbro
Gabriele Facciolo
Masud Fahim
Bin Fan
Hehe Fan
Deng-Ping Fan
Aoxiang Fan
Chen-Chen Fan
Qi Fan
Zhaoxin Fan
Haoqi Fan
Heng Fan
Hongyi Fan
Linxi Fan
Baojie Fan
Jiayuan Fan
Lei Fan
Quanfu Fan
Yonghui Fan
Yingruo Fan
Zhiwen Fan

Zicong Fan
Sean Fanello
Jiansheng Fang
Chaowei Fang
Yuming Fang
Jianwu Fang
Jin Fang
Qi Fang
Shancheng Fang
Tian Fang
Xianyong Fang
Gongfan Fang
Zhen Fang
Hui Fang
Jiemin Fang
Le Fang
Pengfei Fang
Xiaolin Fang
Yuxin Fang
Zhaoyuan Fang
Ammarah Farooq
Azade Farshad
Zhengcong Fei
Michael Felsberg
Wei Feng
Chen Feng
Fan Feng
Andrew Feng
Xin Feng
Zheyun Feng
Ruicheng Feng
Mingtao Feng
Qianyu Feng
Shangbin Feng
Chun-Mei Feng
Zunlei Feng
Zhiyong Feng
Martin Fergie
Mustansar Fiaz
Marco Fiorucci
Michael Firman
Hamed Firooz
Volker Fischer
Corneliu O. Florea
Georgios Floros

Wolfgang Foerstner
Gianni Franchi
Jean-Sebastien Franco
Simone Frintrop
Anna Fruehstueck
Changhong Fu
Chaoyou Fu
Cheng-Yang Fu
Chi-Wing Fu
Deqing Fu
Huan Fu
Jun Fu
Kexue Fu
Ying Fu
Jianlong Fu
Jingjing Fu
Qichen Fu
Tsu-Jui Fu
Xueyang Fu
Yang Fu
Yanwei Fu
Yonggan Fu
Wolfgang Fuhl
Yasuhisa Fujii
Kent Fujiwara
Marco Fumero
Takuya Funatomi
Isabel Funke
Dario Fuoli
Antonino Furnari
Matheus A. Gadelha
Akshay Gadi Patil
Adrian Galdran
Guillermo Gallego
Silvano Galliani
Orazio Gallo
Leonardo Galteri
Matteo Gamba
Yiming Gan
Sujoy Ganguly
Harald Ganster
Boyan Gao
Changxin Gao
Daiheng Gao
Difei Gao

Chen Gao
Fei Gao
Lin Gao
Wei Gao
Yiming Gao
Junyu Gao
Guangyu Ryan Gao
Haichang Gao
Hongchang Gao
Jialin Gao
Jin Gao
Jun Gao
Katelyn Gao
Mingchen Gao
Mingfei Gao
Pan Gao
Shangqian Gao
Shanghua Gao
Xitong Gao
Yunhe Gao
Zhanning Gao
Elena Garces
Nuno Cruz Garcia
Noa Garcia
Guillermo
    Garcia-Hernando
Isha Garg
Rahul Garg
Sourav Garg
Quentin Garrido
Stefano Gasperini
Kent Gauen
Chandan Gautam
Shivam Gautam
Paul Gay
Chunjiang Ge
Shiming Ge
Wenhang Ge
Yanhao Ge
Zheng Ge
Songwei Ge
Weifeng Ge
Yixiao Ge
Yuying Ge
Shijie Geng

Zhengyang Geng
Kyle A. Genova
Georgios Georgakis
Markos Georgopoulos
Marcel Geppert
Shabnam Ghadar
Mina Ghadimi Atigh
Deepti Ghadiyaram
Maani Ghaffari Jadidi
Sedigh Ghamari
Zahra Gharaee
Michaël Gharbi
Golnaz Ghiasi
Reza Ghoddoosian
Soumya Suvra Ghosal
Adhiraj Ghosh
Arthita Ghosh
Pallabi Ghosh
Soumyadeep Ghosh
Andrew Gilbert
Igor Gilitschenski
Jhony H. Giraldo
Andreu Girbau Xalabarder
Rohit Girdhar
Sharath Girish
Xavier Giro-i-Nieto
Raja Giryes
Thomas Gittings
Nikolaos Gkanatsios
Ioannis Gkioulekas
Abhiram
  Gnanasambandam
Aurele T. Gnanha
Clement L. J. C. Godard
Arushi Goel
Vidit Goel
Shubham Goel
Zan Gojcic
Aaron K. Gokaslan
Tejas Gokhale
S. Alireza Golestaneh
Thiago L. Gomes
Nuno Goncalves
Boqing Gong
Chen Gong

Yuanhao Gong
Guoqiang Gong
Jingyu Gong
Rui Gong
Yu Gong
Mingming Gong
Neil Zhenqiang Gong
Xun Gong
Yunye Gong
Yihong Gong
Cristina I. González
Nithin Gopalakrishnan
  Nair
Gaurav Goswami
Jianping Gou
Shreyank N. Gowda
Ankit Goyal
Helmut Grabner
Patrick L. Grady
Ben Graham
Eric Granger
Douglas R. Gray
Matej Grcić
David Griffiths
Jinjin Gu
Yun Gu
Shuyang Gu
Jianyang Gu
Fuqiang Gu
Jiatao Gu
Jindong Gu
Jiaqi Gu
Jinwei Gu
Jiaxin Gu
Geonmo Gu
Xiao Gu
Xinqian Gu
Xiuye Gu
Yuming Gu
Zhangxuan Gu
Dayan Guan
Junfeng Guan
Qingji Guan
Tianrui Guan
Shanyan Guan

Denis A. Gudovskiy
Ricardo Guerrero
Pierre-Louis Guhur
Jie Gui
Liangyan Gui
Liangke Gui
Benoit Guillard
Erhan Gundogdu
Manuel Günther
Jingcai Guo
Yuanfang Guo
Junfeng Guo
Chenqi Guo
Dan Guo
Hongji Guo
Jia Guo
Jie Guo
Minghao Guo
Shi Guo
Yanhui Guo
Yangyang Guo
Yuan-Chen Guo
Yilu Guo
Yiluan Guo
Yong Guo
Guangyu Guo
Haiyun Guo
Jinyang Guo
Jianyuan Guo
Pengsheng Guo
Pengfei Guo
Shuxuan Guo
Song Guo
Tianyu Guo
Qing Guo
Qiushan Guo
Wen Guo
Xiefan Guo
Xiaohu Guo
Xiaoqing Guo
Yufei Guo
Yuhui Guo
Yuliang Guo
Yunhui Guo
Yanwen Guo

Akshita Gupta
Ankush Gupta
Kamal Gupta
Kartik Gupta
Ritwik Gupta
Rohit Gupta
Siddharth Gururani
Fredrik K. Gustafsson
Abner Guzman Rivera
Vladimir Guzov
Matthew A. Gwilliam
Jung-Woo Ha
Marc Habermann
Isma Hadji
Christian Haene
Martin Hahner
Levente Hajder
Alexandros Haliassos
Emanuela Haller
Bumsub Ham
Abdullah J. Hamdi
Shreyas Hampali
Dongyoon Han
Chunrui Han
Dong-Jun Han
Dong-Sig Han
Guangxing Han
Zhizhong Han
Ruize Han
Jiaming Han
Jin Han
Ligong Han
Xian-Hua Han
Xiaoguang Han
Yizeng Han
Zhi Han
Zhenjun Han
Zhongyi Han
Jungong Han
Junlin Han
Kai Han
Kun Han
Sungwon Han
Songfang Han
Wei Han

Xiao Han
Xintong Han
Xinzhe Han
Yahong Han
Yan Han
Zongbo Han
Nicolai Hani
Rana Hanocka
Niklas Hanselmann
Nicklas A. Hansen
Hong Hanyu
Fusheng Hao
Yanbin Hao
Shijie Hao
Udith Haputhanthri
Mehrtash Harandi
Josh Harguess
Adam Harley
David M. Hart
Atsushi Hashimoto
Ali Hassani
Mohammed Hassanin
Yana Hasson
Joakim Bruslund Haurum
Bo He
Kun He
Chen He
Xin He
Fazhi He
Gaoqi He
Hao He
Haoyu He
Jiangpeng He
Hongliang He
Qian He
Xiangteng He
Xuming He
Yannan He
Yuhang He
Yang He
Xiangyu He
Nanjun He
Pan He
Sen He
Shengfeng He

Songtao He
Tao He
Tong He
Wei He
Xuehai He
Xiaoxiao He
Ying He
Yisheng He
Ziwen He
Peter Hedman
Felix Heide
Yacov Hel-Or
Paul Henderson
Philipp Henzler
Byeongho Heo
Jae-Pil Heo
Miran Heo
Sachini A. Herath
Stephane Herbin
Pedro Hermosilla Casajus
Monica Hernandez
Charles Herrmann
Roei Herzig
Mauricio Hess-Flores
Carlos Hinojosa
Tobias Hinz
Tsubasa Hirakawa
Chih-Hui Ho
Lam Si Tung Ho
Jennifer Hobbs
Derek Hoiem
Yannick Hold-Geoffroy
Aleksander Holynski
Cheeun Hong
Fa-Ting Hong
Hanbin Hong
Guan Zhe Hong
Danfeng Hong
Lanqing Hong
Xiaopeng Hong
Xin Hong
Jie Hong
Seungbum Hong
Cheng-Yao Hong
Seunghoon Hong

Yi Hong
Yuan Hong
Yuchen Hong
Anthony Hoogs
Maxwell C. Horton
Kazuhiro Hotta
Qibin Hou
Tingbo Hou
Junhui Hou
Ji Hou
Qiqi Hou
Rui Hou
Ruibing Hou
Zhi Hou
Henry Howard-Jenkins
Lukas Hoyer
Wei-Lin Hsiao
Chiou-Ting Hsu
Anthony Hu
Brian Hu
Yusong Hu
Hexiang Hu
Haoji Hu
Di Hu
Hengtong Hu
Haigen Hu
Lianyu Hu
Hanzhe Hu
Jie Hu
Junlin Hu
Shizhe Hu
Jian Hu
Zhiming Hu
Juhua Hu
Peng Hu
Ping Hu
Ronghang Hu
MengShun Hu
Tao Hu
Vincent Tao Hu
Xiaoling Hu
Xinting Hu
Xiaolin Hu
Xuefeng Hu
Xiaowei Hu

Yang Hu
Yueyu Hu
Zeyu Hu
Zhongyun Hu
Binh-Son Hua
Guoliang Hua
Yi Hua
Linzhi Huang
Qiusheng Huang
Bo Huang
Chen Huang
Hsin-Ping Huang
Ye Huang
Shuangping Huang
Zeng Huang
Buzhen Huang
Cong Huang
Heng Huang
Hao Huang
Qidong Huang
Huaibo Huang
Chaoqin Huang
Feihu Huang
Jiahui Huang
Jingjia Huang
Kun Huang
Lei Huang
Sheng Huang
Shuaiyi Huang
Siyu Huang
Xiaoshui Huang
Xiaoyang Huang
Yan Huang
Yihao Huang
Ying Huang
Ziling Huang
Xiaoke Huang
Yifei Huang
Haiyang Huang
Zhewei Huang
Jin Huang
Haibin Huang
Jiaxing Huang
Junjie Huang
Keli Huang

Lang Huang
Lin Huang
Luojie Huang
Mingzhen Huang
Shijia Huang
Shengyu Huang
Siyuan Huang
He Huang
Xiuyu Huang
Lianghua Huang
Yue Huang
Yaping Huang
Yuge Huang
Zehao Huang
Zeyi Huang
Zhiqi Huang
Zhongzhan Huang
Zilong Huang
Ziyuan Huang
Tianrui Hui
Zhuo Hui
Le Hui
Jing Huo
Junhwa Hur
Shehzeen S. Hussain
Chuong Minh Huynh
Seunghyun Hwang
Jaehui Hwang
Jyh-Jing Hwang
Sukjun Hwang
Soonmin Hwang
Wonjun Hwang
Rakib Hyder
Sangeek Hyun
Sarah Ibrahimi
Tomoki Ichikawa
Yerlan Idelbayev
A. S. M. Iftekhar
Masaaki Iiyama
Satoshi Ikehata
Sunghoon Im
Atul N. Ingle
Eldar Insafutdinov
Yani A. Ioannou
Radu Tudor Ionescu

Umar Iqbal
Go Irie
Muhammad Zubair Irshad
Ahmet Iscen
Berivan Isik
Ashraful Islam
Md Amirul Islam
Syed Islam
Mariko Isogawa
Vamsi Krishna K. Ithapu
Boris Ivanovic
Darshan Iyer
Sarah Jabbour
Ayush Jain
Nishant Jain
Samyak Jain
Vidit Jain
Vineet Jain
Priyank Jaini
Tomas Jakab
Mohammad A. A. K.
    Jalwana
Muhammad Abdullah
    Jamal
Hadi Jamali-Rad
Stuart James
Varun Jampani
Young Kyun Jang
YeongJun Jang
Yunseok Jang
Ronnachai Jaroensri
Bhavan Jasani
Krishna Murthy
    Jatavallabhula
Mojan Javaheripi
Syed A. Javed
Guillaume Jeanneret
Pranav Jeevan
Herve Jegou
Rohit Jena
Tomas Jenicek
Porter Jenkins
Simon Jenni
Hae-Gon Jeon
Sangryul Jeon

Boseung Jeong
Yoonwoo Jeong
Seong-Gyun Jeong
Jisoo Jeong
Allan D. Jepson
Ankit Jha
Sumit K. Jha
I-Hong Jhuo
Ge-Peng Ji
Chaonan Ji
Deyi Ji
Jingwei Ji
Wei Ji
Zhong Ji
Jiayi Ji
Pengliang Ji
Hui Ji
Mingi Ji
Xiaopeng Ji
Yuzhu Ji
Baoxiong Jia
Songhao Jia
Dan Jia
Shan Jia
Xiaojun Jia
Xiuyi Jia
Xu Jia
Menglin Jia
Wenqi Jia
Boyuan Jiang
Wenhao Jiang
Huaizu Jiang
Hanwen Jiang
Haiyong Jiang
Hao Jiang
Huajie Jiang
Huiqin Jiang
Haojun Jiang
Haobo Jiang
Junjun Jiang
Xingyu Jiang
Yangbangyan Jiang
Yu Jiang
Jianmin Jiang
Jiaxi Jiang

Jing Jiang
Kui Jiang
Li Jiang
Liming Jiang
Chiyu Jiang
Meirui Jiang
Chen Jiang
Peng Jiang
Tai-Xiang Jiang
Wen Jiang
Xinyang Jiang
Yifan Jiang
Yuming Jiang
Yingying Jiang
Zeren Jiang
ZhengKai Jiang
Zhenyu Jiang
Shuming Jiao
Jianbo Jiao
Licheng Jiao
Dongkwon Jin
Yeying Jin
Cheng Jin
Linyi Jin
Qing Jin
Taisong Jin
Xiao Jin
Xin Jin
Sheng Jin
Kyong Hwan Jin
Ruibing Jin
SouYoung Jin
Yueming Jin
Chenchen Jing
Longlong Jing
Taotao Jing
Yongcheng Jing
Younghyun Jo
Joakim Johnander
Jeff Johnson
Michael J. Jones
R. Kenny Jones
Rico Jonschkowski
Ameya Joshi
Sunghun Joung

Felix Juefei-Xu
Claudio R. Jung
Steffen Jung
Hari Chandana K.
Rahul Vigneswaran K.
Prajwal K. R.
Abhishek Kadian
Jhony Kaesemodel Pontes
Kumara Kahatapitiya
Anmol Kalia
Sinan Kalkan
Tarun Kalluri
Jaewon Kam
Sandesh Kamath
Meina Kan
Menelaos Kanakis
Takuhiro Kaneko
Di Kang
Guoliang Kang
Hao Kang
Jaeyeon Kang
Kyoungkook Kang
Li-Wei Kang
MinGuk Kang
Suk-Ju Kang
Zhao Kang
Yash Mukund Kant
Yueying Kao
Aupendu Kar
Konstantinos Karantzalos
Sezer Karaoglu
Navid Kardan
Sanjay Kariyappa
Leonid Karlinsky
Animesh Karnewar
Shyamgopal Karthik
Hirak J. Kashyap
Marc A. Kastner
Hirokatsu Kataoka
Angelos Katharopoulos
Hiroharu Kato
Kai Katsumata
Manuel Kaufmann
Chaitanya Kaul
Prakhar Kaushik

Yuki Kawana
Lei Ke
Lipeng Ke
Tsung-Wei Ke
Wei Ke
Petr Kellnhofer
Aniruddha Kembhavi
John Kender
Corentin Kervadec
Leonid Keselman
Daniel Keysers
Nima Khademi Kalantari
Taras Khakhulin
Samir Khaki
Muhammad Haris Khan
Qadeer Khan
Salman Khan
Subash Khanal
Vaishnavi M. Khindkar
Rawal Khirodkar
Saeed Khorram
Pirazh Khorramshahi
Kourosh Khoshelham
Ansh Khurana
Benjamin Kiefer
Jae Myung Kim
Junho Kim
Boah Kim
Hyeonseong Kim
Dong-Jin Kim
Dongwan Kim
Donghyun Kim
Doyeon Kim
Yonghyun Kim
Hyung-Il Kim
Hyunwoo Kim
Hyeongwoo Kim
Hyo Jin Kim
Hyunwoo J. Kim
Taehoon Kim
Jaeha Kim
Jiwon Kim
Jung Uk Kim
Kangyeol Kim
Eunji Kim

Daeha Kim
Dongwon Kim
Kunhee Kim
Kyungmin Kim
Junsik Kim
Min H. Kim
Namil Kim
Kookhoi Kim
Sanghyun Kim
Seongyeop Kim
Seungryong Kim
Saehoon Kim
Euyoung Kim
Guisik Kim
Sungyeon Kim
Sunnie S. Y. Kim
Taehun Kim
Tae Oh Kim
Won Hwa Kim
Seungwook Kim
YoungBin Kim
Youngeun Kim
Akisato Kimura
Furkan Osman Kınlı
Zsolt Kira
Hedvig Kjellström
Florian Kleber
Jan P. Klopp
Florian Kluger
Laurent Kneip
Byungsoo Ko
Muhammed Kocabas
A. Sophia Koepke
Kevin Koeser
Nick Kolkin
Nikos Kolotouros
Wai-Kin Adams Kong
Deying Kong
Caihua Kong
Youyong Kong
Shuyu Kong
Shu Kong
Tao Kong
Yajing Kong
Yu Kong

Zishang Kong
Theodora Kontogianni
Anton S. Konushin
Julian F. P. Kooij
Bruno Korbar
Giorgos Kordopatis-Zilos
Jari Korhonen
Adam Kortylewski
Denis Korzhenkov
Divya Kothandaraman
Suraj Kothawade
Iuliia Kotseruba
Satwik Kottur
Shashank Kotyan
Alexandros Kouris
Petros Koutras
Anna Kreshuk
Ranjay Krishna
Dilip Krishnan
Andrey Kuehlkamp
Hilde Kuehne
Jason Kuen
David Kügler
Arjan Kuijper
Anna Kukleva
Sumith Kulal
Viveka Kulharia
Akshay R. Kulkarni
Nilesh Kulkarni
Dominik Kulon
Abhinav Kumar
Akash Kumar
Suryansh Kumar
B. V. K. Vijaya Kumar
Pulkit Kumar
Ratnesh Kumar
Sateesh Kumar
Satish Kumar
Vijay Kumar B. G.
Nupur Kumari
Sudhakar Kumawat
Jogendra Nath Kundu
Hsien-Kai Kuo
Meng-Yu Jennifer Kuo
Vinod Kumar Kurmi

Yusuke Kurose
Keerthy Kusumam
Alina Kuznetsova
Henry Kvinge
Ho Man Kwan
Hyeokjun Kweon
Heeseung Kwon
Gihyun Kwon
Myung-Joon Kwon
Taesung Kwon
YoungJoong Kwon
Christos Kyrkou
Jorma Laaksonen
Yann Labbe
Zorah Laehner
Florent Lafarge
Hamid Laga
Manuel Lagunas
Shenqi Lai
Jian-Huang Lai
Zihang Lai
Mohamed I. Lakhal
Mohit Lamba
Meng Lan
Loic Landrieu
Zhiqiang Lang
Natalie Lang
Dong Lao
Yizhen Lao
Yingjie Lao
Issam Hadj Laradji
Gustav Larsson
Viktor Larsson
Zakaria Laskar
Stéphane Lathuilière
Chun Pong Lau
Rynson W. H. Lau
Hei Law
Justin Lazarow
Verica Lazova
Eric-Tuan Le
Hieu Le
Trung-Nghia Le
Mathias Lechner
Byeong-Uk Lee

Chen-Yu Lee
Che-Rung Lee
Chul Lee
Hong Joo Lee
Dongsoo Lee
Jiyoung Lee
Eugene Eu Tzuan Lee
Daeun Lee
Saehyung Lee
Jewook Lee
Hyungtae Lee
Hyunmin Lee
Jungbeom Lee
Joon-Young Lee
Jong-Seok Lee
Joonseok Lee
Junha Lee
Kibok Lee
Byung-Kwan Lee
Jangwon Lee
Jinho Lee
Jongmin Lee
Seunghyun Lee
Sohyun Lee
Minsik Lee
Dogyoon Lee
Seungmin Lee
Min Jun Lee
Sangho Lee
Sangmin Lee
Seungeun Lee
Seon-Ho Lee
Sungmin Lee
Sungho Lee
Sangyoun Lee
Vincent C. S. S. Lee
Jaeseong Lee
Yong Jae Lee
Chenyang Lei
Chenyi Lei
Jiahui Lei
Xinyu Lei
Yinjie Lei
Jiaxu Leng
Luziwei Leng

Jan E. Lenssen
Vincent Lepetit
Thomas Leung
María Leyva-Vallina
Xin Li
Yikang Li
Baoxin Li
Bin Li
Bing Li
Bowen Li
Changlin Li
Chao Li
Chongyi Li
Guanyue Li
Shuai Li
Jin Li
Dingquan Li
Dongxu Li
Yiting Li
Gang Li
Dian Li
Guohao Li
Haoang Li
Haoliang Li
Haoran Li
Hengduo Li
Huafeng Li
Xiaoming Li
Hanao Li
Hongwei Li
Ziqiang Li
Jisheng Li
Jiacheng Li
Jia Li
Jiachen Li
Jiahao Li
Jianwei Li
Jiazhi Li
Jie Li
Jing Li
Jingjing Li
Jingtao Li
Jun Li
Junxuan Li
Kai Li

Kailin Li
Kenneth Li
Kun Li
Kunpeng Li
Aoxue Li
Chenglong Li
Chenglin Li
Changsheng Li
Zhichao Li
Qiang Li
Yanyu Li
Zuoyue Li
Xiang Li
Xuelong Li
Fangda Li
Ailin Li
Liang Li
Chun-Guang Li
Daiqing Li
Dong Li
Guanbin Li
Guorong Li
Haifeng Li
Jianan Li
Jianing Li
Jiaxin Li
Ke Li
Lei Li
Lincheng Li
Liulei Li
Lujun Li
Linjie Li
Lin Li
Pengyu Li
Ping Li
Qiufu Li
Qingyong Li
Rui Li
Siyuan Li
Wei Li
Wenbin Li
Xiangyang Li
Xinyu Li
Xiujun Li
Xiu Li

Xu Li
Ya-Li Li
Yao Li
Yongjie Li
Yijun Li
Yiming Li
Yuezun Li
Yu Li
Yunheng Li
Yuqi Li
Zhe Li
Zeming Li
Zhen Li
Zhengqin Li
Zhimin Li
Jiefeng Li
Jinpeng Li
Chengze Li
Jianwu Li
Lerenhan Li
Shan Li
Suichan Li
Xiangtai Li
Yanjie Li
Yandong Li
Zhuoling Li
Zhenqiang Li
Manyi Li
Maosen Li
Ji Li
Minjun Li
Mingrui Li
Mengtian Li
Junyi Li
Nianyi Li
Bo Li
Xiao Li
Peihua Li
Peike Li
Peizhao Li
Peiliang Li
Qi Li
Ren Li
Runze Li
Shile Li

Sheng Li
Shigang Li
Shiyu Li
Shuang Li
Shasha Li
Shichao Li
Tianye Li
Yuexiang Li
Wei-Hong Li
Wanhua Li
Weihao Li
Weiming Li
Weixin Li
Wenbo Li
Wenshuo Li
Weijian Li
Yunan Li
Xirong Li
Xianhang Li
Xiaoyu Li
Xueqian Li
Xuanlin Li
Xianzhi Li
Yunqiang Li
Yanjing Li
Yansheng Li
Yawei Li
Yi Li
Yong Li
Yong-Lu Li
Yuhang Li
Yu-Jhe Li
Yuxi Li
Yunsheng Li
Yanwei Li
Zechao Li
Zejian Li
Zeju Li
Zekun Li
Zhaowen Li
Zheng Li
Zhenyu Li
Zhiheng Li
Zhi Li
Zhong Li

Zhuowei Li
Zhuowan Li
Zhuohang Li
Zizhang Li
Chen Li
Yuan-Fang Li
Dongze Lian
Xiaochen Lian
Zhouhui Lian
Long Lian
Qing Lian
Jin Lianbao
Jinxiu S. Liang
Dingkang Liang
Jiahao Liang
Jianming Liang
Jingyun Liang
Kevin J. Liang
Kaizhao Liang
Chen Liang
Jie Liang
Senwei Liang
Ding Liang
Jiajun Liang
Jian Liang
Kongming Liang
Siyuan Liang
Yuanzhi Liang
Zhengfa Liang
Mingfu Liang
Xiaodan Liang
Xuefeng Liang
Yuxuan Liang
Kang Liao
Liang Liao
Hong-Yuan Mark Liao
Wentong Liao
Haofu Liao
Yue Liao
Minghui Liao
Shengcai Liao
Ting-Hsuan Liao
Xin Liao
Yinghong Liao
Teck Yian Lim

Che-Tsung Lin
Chung-Ching Lin
Chen-Hsuan Lin
Cheng Lin
Chuming Lin
Chunyu Lin
Dahua Lin
Wei Lin
Zheng Lin
Huaijia Lin
Jason Lin
Jierui Lin
Jiaying Lin
Jie Lin
Kai-En Lin
Kevin Lin
Guangfeng Lin
Jiehong Lin
Feng Lin
Hang Lin
Kwan-Yee Lin
Ke Lin
Luojun Lin
Qinghong Lin
Xiangbo Lin
Yi Lin
Zudi Lin
Shijie Lin
Yiqun Lin
Tzu-Heng Lin
Ming Lin
Shaohui Lin
SongNan Lin
Ji Lin
Tsung-Yu Lin
Xudong Lin
Yancong Lin
Yen-Chen Lin
Yiming Lin
Yuewei Lin
Zhiqiu Lin
Zinan Lin
Zhe Lin
David B. Lindell
Zhixin Ling

Zhan Ling
Alexander Liniger
Venice Erin B. Liong
Joey Litalien
Or Litany
Roee Litman
Ron Litman
Jim Little
Dor Litvak
Shaoteng Liu
Shuaicheng Liu
Andrew Liu
Xian Liu
Shaohui Liu
Bei Liu
Bo Liu
Yong Liu
Ming Liu
Yanbin Liu
Chenxi Liu
Daqi Liu
Di Liu
Difan Liu
Dong Liu
Dongfang Liu
Daizong Liu
Xiao Liu
Fangyi Liu
Fengbei Liu
Fenglin Liu
Bin Liu
Yuang Liu
Ao Liu
Hong Liu
Hongfu Liu
Huidong Liu
Ziyi Liu
Feng Liu
Hao Liu
Jie Liu
Jialun Liu
Jiang Liu
Jing Liu
Jingya Liu
Jiaming Liu

Jun Liu
Juncheng Liu
Jiawei Liu
Hongyu Liu
Chuanbin Liu
Haotian Liu
Lingqiao Liu
Chang Liu
Han Liu
Liu Liu
Min Liu
Yingqi Liu
Aishan Liu
Bingyu Liu
Benlin Liu
Boxiao Liu
Chenchen Liu
Chuanjian Liu
Daqing Liu
Huan Liu
Haozhe Liu
Jiaheng Liu
Wei Liu
Jingzhou Liu
Jiyuan Liu
Lingbo Liu
Nian Liu
Peiye Liu
Qiankun Liu
Shenglan Liu
Shilong Liu
Wen Liu
Wenyu Liu
Weifeng Liu
Wu Liu
Xiaolong Liu
Yang Liu
Yanwei Liu
Yingcheng Liu
Yongfei Liu
Yihao Liu
Yu Liu
Yunze Liu
Ze Liu
Zhenhua Liu

Zhenguang Liu
Lin Liu
Lihao Liu
Pengju Liu
Xinhai Liu
Yunfei Liu
Meng Liu
Minghua Liu
Mingyuan Liu
Miao Liu
Peirong Liu
Ping Liu
Qingjie Liu
Ruoshi Liu
Risheng Liu
Songtao Liu
Xing Liu
Shikun Liu
Shuming Liu
Sheng Liu
Songhua Liu
Tongliang Liu
Weibo Liu
Weide Liu
Weizhe Liu
Wenxi Liu
Weiyang Liu
Xin Liu
Xiaobin Liu
Xudong Liu
Xiaoyi Liu
Xihui Liu
Xinchen Liu
Xingtong Liu
Xinpeng Liu
Xinyu Liu
Xianpeng Liu
Xu Liu
Xingyu Liu
Yongtuo Liu
Yahui Liu
Yangxin Liu
Yaoyao Liu
Yaojie Liu
Yuliang Liu

Yongcheng Liu
Yuan Liu
Yufan Liu
Yu-Lun Liu
Yun Liu
Yunfan Liu
Yuanzhong Liu
Zhuoran Liu
Zhen Liu
Zheng Liu
Zhijian Liu
Zhisong Liu
Ziquan Liu
Ziyu Liu
Zhihua Liu
Zechun Liu
Zhaoyang Liu
Zhengzhe Liu
Stephan Liwicki
Shao-Yuan Lo
Sylvain Lobry
Suhas Lohit
Vishnu Suresh Lokhande
Vincenzo Lomonaco
Chengjiang Long
Guodong Long
Fuchen Long
Shangbang Long
Yang Long
Zijun Long
Vasco Lopes
Antonio M. Lopez
Roberto Javier
    Lopez-Sastre
Tobias Lorenz
Javier Lorenzo-Navarro
Yujing Lou
Qian Lou
Xiankai Lu
Changsheng Lu
Huimin Lu
Yongxi Lu
Hao Lu
Hong Lu
Jiasen Lu

Juwei Lu
Fan Lu
Guangming Lu
Jiwen Lu
Shun Lu
Tao Lu
Xiaonan Lu
Yang Lu
Yao Lu
Yongchun Lu
Zhiwu Lu
Cheng Lu
Liying Lu
Guo Lu
Xuequan Lu
Yanye Lu
Yantao Lu
Yuhang Lu
Fujun Luan
Jonathon Luiten
Jovita Lukasik
Alan Lukezic
Jonathan Samuel Lumentut
Mayank Lunayach
Ao Luo
Canjie Luo
Chong Luo
Xu Luo
Grace Luo
Jun Luo
Katie Z. Luo
Tao Luo
Cheng Luo
Fangzhou Luo
Gen Luo
Lei Luo
Sihui Luo
Weixin Luo
Yan Luo
Xiaoyan Luo
Yong Luo
Yadan Luo
Hao Luo
Ruotian Luo
Mi Luo

Tiange Luo
Wenjie Luo
Wenhan Luo
Xiao Luo
Zhiming Luo
Zhipeng Luo
Zhengyi Luo
Diogo C. Luvizon
Zhaoyang Lv
Gengyu Lyu
Lingjuan Lyu
Jun Lyu
Yuanyuan Lyu
Youwei Lyu
Yueming Lyu
Bingpeng Ma
Chao Ma
Chongyang Ma
Congbo Ma
Chih-Yao Ma
Fan Ma
Lin Ma
Haoyu Ma
Hengbo Ma
Jianqi Ma
Jiawei Ma
Jiayi Ma
Kede Ma
Kai Ma
Lingni Ma
Lei Ma
Xu Ma
Ning Ma
Benteng Ma
Cheng Ma
Andy J. Ma
Long Ma
Zhanyu Ma
Zhiheng Ma
Qianli Ma
Shiqiang Ma
Sizhuo Ma
Shiqing Ma
Xiaolong Ma
Xinzhu Ma

Gautam B. Machiraju
Spandan Madan
Mathew Magimai-Doss
Luca Magri
Behrooz Mahasseni
Upal Mahbub
Siddharth Mahendran
Paridhi Maheshwari
Rishabh Maheshwary
Mohammed Mahmoud
Shishira R. R. Maiya
Sylwia Majchrowska
Arjun Majumdar
Puspita Majumdar
Orchid Majumder
Sagnik Majumder
Ilya Makarov
Farkhod F.
   Makhmudkhujaev
Yasushi Makihara
Ankur Mali
Mateusz Malinowski
Utkarsh Mall
Srikanth Malla
Clement Mallet
Dimitrios Mallis
Yunze Man
Dipu Manandhar
Massimiliano Mancini
Murari Mandal
Raunak Manekar
Karttikeya Mangalam
Puneet Mangla
Fabian Manhardt
Sivabalan Manivasagam
Fahim Mannan
Chengzhi Mao
Hanzi Mao
Jiayuan Mao
Junhua Mao
Zhiyuan Mao
Jiageng Mao
Yunyao Mao
Zhendong Mao
Alberto Marchisio

Diego Marcos
Riccardo Marin
Aram Markosyan
Renaud Marlet
Ricardo Marques
Miquel Martí i Rabadán
Diego Martin Arroyo
Niki Martinel
Brais Martinez
Julieta Martinez
Marc Masana
Tomohiro Mashita
Timothée Masquelier
Minesh Mathew
Tetsu Matsukawa
Marwan Mattar
Bruce A. Maxwell
Christoph Mayer
Mantas Mazeika
Pratik Mazumder
Scott McCloskey
Steven McDonagh
Ishit Mehta
Jie Mei
Kangfu Mei
Jieru Mei
Xiaoguang Mei
Givi Meishvili
Luke Melas-Kyriazi
Iaroslav Melekhov
Andres Mendez-Vazquez
Heydi Mendez-Vazquez
Matias Mendieta
Ricardo A. Mendoza-León
Chenlin Meng
Depu Meng
Rang Meng
Zibo Meng
Qingjie Meng
Qier Meng
Yanda Meng
Zihang Meng
Thomas Mensink
Fabian Mentzer
Christopher Metzler

Gregory P. Meyer
Vasileios Mezaris
Liang Mi
Lu Mi
Bo Miao
Changtao Miao
Zichen Miao
Qiguang Miao
Xin Miao
Zhongqi Miao
Frank Michel
Simone Milani
Ben Mildenhall
Roy V. Miles
Juhong Min
Kyle Min
Hyun-Seok Min
Weiqing Min
Yuecong Min
Zhixiang Min
Qi Ming
David Minnen
Aymen Mir
Deepak Mishra
Anand Mishra
Shlok K. Mishra
Niluthpol Mithun
Gaurav Mittal
Trisha Mittal
Daisuke Miyazaki
Kaichun Mo
Hong Mo
Zhipeng Mo
Davide Modolo
Abduallah A. Mohamed
Mohamed Afham
   Mohamed Aflal
Ron Mokady
Pavlo Molchanov
Davide Moltisanti
Liliane Momeni
Gianluca Monaci
Pascal Monasse
Ajoy Mondal
Tom Monnier

Aron Monszpart
Gyeongsik Moon
Suhong Moon
Taesup Moon
Sean Moran
Daniel Moreira
Pietro Morerio
Alexandre Morgand
Lia Morra
Ali Mosleh
Inbar Mosseri
Sayed Mohammad
    Mostafavi Isfahani
Saman Motamed
Ramy A. Mounir
Fangzhou Mu
Jiteng Mu
Norman Mu
Yasuhiro Mukaigawa
Ryan Mukherjee
Tanmoy Mukherjee
Yusuke Mukuta
Ravi Teja Mullapudi
Lea Müller
Matthias Müller
Martin Mundt
Nils Murrugarra-Llerena
Damien Muselet
Armin Mustafa
Muhammad Ferjad Naeem
Sauradip Nag
Hajime Nagahara
Pravin Nagar
Rajendra Nagar
Naveen Shankar Nagaraja
Varun Nagaraja
Tushar Nagarajan
Seungjun Nah
Gaku Nakano
Yuta Nakashima
Giljoo Nam
Seonghyeon Nam
Liangliang Nan
Yuesong Nan
Yeshwanth Napolean

Dinesh Reddy
    Narapureddy
Medhini Narasimhan
Supreeth
    Narasimhaswamy
Sriram Narayanan
Erickson R. Nascimento
Varun Nasery
K. L. Navaneet
Pablo Navarrete Michelini
Shant Navasardyan
Shah Nawaz
Nihal Nayak
Farhood Negin
Lukáš Neumann
Alejandro Newell
Evonne Ng
Kam Woh Ng
Tony Ng
Anh Nguyen
Tuan Anh Nguyen
Cuong Cao Nguyen
Ngoc Cuong Nguyen
Thanh Nguyen
Khoi Nguyen
Phi Le Nguyen
Phong Ha Nguyen
Tam Nguyen
Truong Nguyen
Anh Tuan Nguyen
Rang Nguyen
Thao Thi Phuong Nguyen
Van Nguyen Nguyen
Zhen-Liang Ni
Yao Ni
Shijie Nie
Xuecheng Nie
Yongwei Nie
Weizhi Nie
Ying Nie
Yinyu Nie
Kshitij N. Nikhal
Simon Niklaus
Xuefei Ning
Jifeng Ning

Yotam Nitzan
Di Niu
Shuaicheng Niu
Li Niu
Wei Niu
Yulei Niu
Zhenxing Niu
Albert No
Shohei Nobuhara
Nicoletta Noceti
Junhyug Noh
Sotiris Nousias
Slawomir Nowaczyk
Ewa M. Nowara
Valsamis Ntouskos
Gilberto Ochoa-Ruiz
Ferda Ofli
Jihyong Oh
Sangyun Oh
Youngtaek Oh
Hiroki Ohashi
Takahiro Okabe
Kemal Oksuz
Fumio Okura
Daniel Olmeda Reino
Matthew Olson
Carl Olsson
Roy Or-El
Alessandro Ortis
Guillermo Ortiz-Jimenez
Magnus Oskarsson
Ahmed A. A. Osman
Martin R. Oswald
Mayu Otani
Naima Otberdout
Cheng Ouyang
Jiahong Ouyang
Wanli Ouyang
Andrew Owens
Poojan B. Oza
Mete Ozay
A. Cengiz Oztireli
Gautam Pai
Tomas Pajdla
Umapada Pal

Simone Palazzo
Luca Palmieri
Bowen Pan
Hao Pan
Lili Pan
Tai-Yu Pan
Liang Pan
Chengwei Pan
Yingwei Pan
Xuran Pan
Jinchan Pan
Xinyu Pan
Liyuan Pan
Xingang Pan
Xingjia Pan
Zhihong Pan
Zizheng Pan
Priyadarshini Panda
Rameswar Panda
Rohit Pandey
Kaiyue Pang
Bo Pang
Guansong Pang
Jiangmiao Pang
Meng Pang
Tianyu Pang
Ziqi Pang
Omiros Pantazis
Andreas Panteli
Maja Pantic
Marina Paolanti
Joao P. Papa
Samuele Papa
Mike Papadakis
Dim P. Papadopoulos
George Papandreou
Constantin Pape
Toufiq Parag
Chethan Parameshwara
Shaifali Parashar
Alejandro Pardo
Rishubh Parihar
Sarah Parisot
JaeYoo Park
Gyeong-Moon Park

Hyojin Park
Hyoungseob Park
Jongchan Park
Jae Sung Park
Kiru Park
Chunghyun Park
Kwanyong Park
Sunghyun Park
Sungrae Park
Seongsik Park
Songhyun Park
Sungjune Park
Taesung Park
Gaurav Parmar
Paritosh Parmar
Alvaro Parra
Despoina Paschalidou
Or Patashnik
Shivansh Patel
Pushpak Pati
Prashant W. Patil
Vaishakh Patil
Suvam Patra
Jay Patravali
Badri Narayana Patro
Angshuman Paul
Sudipta Paul
Rémi Pautrat
Nick E. Pears
Adithya Pediredla
Wenjie Pei
Shmuel Peleg
Latha Pemula
Bo Peng
Houwen Peng
Yue Peng
Liangzu Peng
Baoyun Peng
Jun Peng
Pai Peng
Sida Peng
Xi Peng
Yuxin Peng
Songyou Peng
Wei Peng

Weiqi Peng
Wen-Hsiao Peng
Pramuditha Perera
Juan C. Perez
Eduardo Pérez Pellitero
Juan-Manuel Perez-Rua
Federico Pernici
Marco Pesavento
Stavros Petridis
Ilya A. Petrov
Vladan Petrovic
Mathis Petrovich
Suzanne Petryk
Hieu Pham
Quang Pham
Khoi Pham
Tung Pham
Huy Phan
Stephen Phillips
Cheng Perng Phoo
David Picard
Marco Piccirilli
Georg Pichler
A. J. Piergiovanni
Vipin Pillai
Silvia L. Pintea
Giovanni Pintore
Robinson Piramuthu
Fiora Pirri
Theodoros Pissas
Fabio Pizzati
Benjamin Planche
Bryan Plummer
Matteo Poggi
Ashwini Pokle
Georgy E. Ponimatkin
Adrian Popescu
Stefan Popov
Nikola Popović
Ronald Poppe
Angelo Porrello
Michael Potter
Charalambos Poullis
Hadi Pouransari
Omid Poursaeed

Shraman Pramanick
Mantini Pranav
Dilip K. Prasad
Meghshyam Prasad
B. H. Pawan Prasad
Shitala Prasad
Prateek Prasanna
Ekta Prashnani
Derek S. Prijatelj
Luke Y. Prince
Véronique Prinet
Victor Adrian Prisacariu
James Pritts
Thomas Probst
Sergey Prokudin
Rita Pucci
Chi-Man Pun
Matthew Purri
Haozhi Qi
Lu Qi
Lei Qi
Xianbiao Qi
Yonggang Qi
Yuankai Qi
Siyuan Qi
Guocheng Qian
Hangwei Qian
Qi Qian
Deheng Qian
Shengsheng Qian
Wen Qian
Rui Qian
Yiming Qian
Shengju Qian
Shengyi Qian
Xuelin Qian
Zhenxing Qian
Nan Qiao
Xiaotian Qiao
Jing Qin
Can Qin
Siyang Qin
Hongwei Qin
Jie Qin
Minghai Qin

Yipeng Qin
Yongqiang Qin
Wenda Qin
Xuebin Qin
Yuzhe Qin
Yao Qin
Zhenyue Qin
Zhiwu Qing
Heqian Qiu
Jiayan Qiu
Jielin Qiu
Yue Qiu
Jiaxiong Qiu
Zhongxi Qiu
Shi Qiu
Zhaofan Qiu
Zhongnan Qu
Yanyun Qu
Kha Gia Quach
Yuhui Quan
Ruijie Quan
Mike Rabbat
Rahul Shekhar Rade
Filip Radenovic
Gorjan Radevski
Bogdan Raducanu
Francesco Ragusa
Shafin Rahman
Md Mahfuzur Rahman
  Siddiquee
Hossein Rahmani
Kiran Raja
Sivaramakrishnan
  Rajaraman
Jathushan Rajasegaran
Adnan Siraj Rakin
Michaël Ramamonjisoa
Chirag A. Raman
Shanmuganathan Raman
Vignesh Ramanathan
Vasili Ramanishka
Vikram V. Ramaswamy
Merey Ramazanova
Jason Rambach
Sai Saketh Rambhatla

Clément Rambour
Ashwin Ramesh Babu
Adín Ramírez Rivera
Arianna Rampini
Haoxi Ran
Aakanksha Rana
Aayush Jung Bahadur
  Rana
Kanchana N. Ranasinghe
Aneesh Rangnekar
Samrudhdhi B. Rangrej
Harsh Rangwani
Viresh Ranjan
Anyi Rao
Yongming Rao
Carolina Raposo
Michalis Raptis
Amir Rasouli
Vivek Rathod
Adepu Ravi Sankar
Avinash Ravichandran
Bharadwaj Ravichandran
Dripta S. Raychaudhuri
Adria Recasens
Simon Reiß
Davis Rempe
Daxuan Ren
Jiawei Ren
Jimmy Ren
Sucheng Ren
Dayong Ren
Zhile Ren
Dongwei Ren
Qibing Ren
Pengfei Ren
Zhenwen Ren
Xuqian Ren
Yixuan Ren
Zhongzheng Ren
Ambareesh Revanur
Hamed Rezazadegan
  Tavakoli
Rafael S. Rezende
Wonjong Rhee
Alexander Richard

Christian Richardt
Stephan R. Richter
Benjamin Riggan
Dominik Rivoir
Mamshad Nayeem Rizve
Joshua D. Robinson
Joseph Robinson
Chris Rockwell
Ranga Rodrigo
Andres C. Rodriguez
Carlos Rodriguez-Pardo
Marcus Rohrbach
Gemma Roig
Yu Rong
David A. Ross
Mohammad Rostami
Edward Rosten
Karsten Roth
Anirban Roy
Debaditya Roy
Shuvendu Roy
Ahana Roy Choudhury
Aruni Roy Chowdhury
Denys Rozumnyi
Shulan Ruan
Wenjie Ruan
Patrick Ruhkamp
Danila Rukhovich
Anian Ruoss
Chris Russell
Dan Ruta
Dawid Damian Rymarczyk
DongHun Ryu
Hyeonggon Ryu
Kwonyoung Ryu
Balasubramanian S.
Alexandre Sablayrolles
Mohammad Sabokrou
Arka Sadhu
Aniruddha Saha
Oindrila Saha
Pritish Sahu
Aneeshan Sain
Nirat Saini
Saurabh Saini

Takeshi Saitoh
Christos Sakaridis
Fumihiko Sakaue
Dimitrios Sakkos
Ken Sakurada
Parikshit V. Sakurikar
Rohit Saluja
Nermin Samet
Leo Sampaio Ferraz
   Ribeiro
Jorge Sanchez
Enrique Sanchez
Shengtian Sang
Anush Sankaran
Soubhik Sanyal
Nikolaos Sarafianos
Vishwanath Saragadam
István Sárándi
Saquib Sarfraz
Mert Bulent Sariyildiz
Anindya Sarkar
Pritam Sarkar
Paul-Edouard Sarlin
Hiroshi Sasaki
Takami Sato
Torsten Sattler
Ravi Kumar Satzoda
Axel Sauer
Stefano Savian
Artem Savkin
Manolis Savva
Gerald Schaefer
Simone Schaub-Meyer
Yoni Schirris
Samuel Schulter
Katja Schwarz
Jesse Scott
Sinisa Segvic
Constantin Marc Seibold
Lorenzo Seidenari
Matan Sela
Fadime Sener
Paul Hongsuck Seo
Kwanggyoon Seo
Hongje Seong

Dario Serez
Francesco Setti
Bryan Seybold
Mohamad Shahbazi
Shima Shahfar
Xinxin Shan
Caifeng Shan
Dandan Shan
Shawn Shan
Wei Shang
Jinghuan Shang
Jiaxiang Shang
Lei Shang
Sukrit Shankar
Ken Shao
Rui Shao
Jie Shao
Mingwen Shao
Aashish Sharma
Gaurav Sharma
Vivek Sharma
Abhishek Sharma
Yoli Shavit
Shashank Shekhar
Sumit Shekhar
Zhijie Shen
Fengyi Shen
Furao Shen
Jialie Shen
Jingjing Shen
Ziyi Shen
Linlin Shen
Guangyu Shen
Biluo Shen
Falong Shen
Jiajun Shen
Qiu Shen
Qiuhong Shen
Shuai Shen
Wang Shen
Yiqing Shen
Yunhang Shen
Siqi Shen
Bin Shen
Tianwei Shen

Xi Shen
Yilin Shen
Yuming Shen
Yucong Shen
Zhiqiang Shen
Lu Sheng
Yichen Sheng
Shivanand Venkanna
    Sheshappanavar
Shelly Sheynin
Baifeng Shi
Ruoxi Shi
Botian Shi
Hailin Shi
Jia Shi
Jing Shi
Shaoshuai Shi
Baoguang Shi
Boxin Shi
Hengcan Shi
Tianyang Shi
Xiaodan Shi
Yongjie Shi
Zhensheng Shi
Yinghuan Shi
Weiqi Shi
Wu Shi
Xuepeng Shi
Xiaoshuang Shi
Yujiao Shi
Zenglin Shi
Zhenmei Shi
Takashi Shibata
Meng-Li Shih
Yichang Shih
Hyunjung Shim
Dongseok Shim
Soshi Shimada
Inkyu Shin
Jinwoo Shin
Seungjoo Shin
Seungjae Shin
Koichi Shinoda
Suprosanna Shit

Palaiahnakote
    Shivakumara
Eli Shlizerman
Gaurav Shrivastava
Xiao Shu
Xiangbo Shu
Xiujun Shu
Yang Shu
Tianmin Shu
Jun Shu
Zhixin Shu
Bing Shuai
Maria Shugrina
Ivan Shugurov
Satya Narayan Shukla
Pranjay Shyam
Jianlou Si
Yawar Siddiqui
Alberto Signoroni
Pedro Silva
Jae-Young Sim
Oriane Siméoni
Martin Simon
Andrea Simonelli
Abhishek Singh
Ashish Singh
Dinesh Singh
Gurkirt Singh
Krishna Kumar Singh
Mannat Singh
Pravendra Singh
Rajat Vikram Singh
Utkarsh Singhal
Dipika Singhania
Vasu Singla
Harsh Sinha
Sudipta Sinha
Josef Sivic
Elena Sizikova
Geri Skenderi
Ivan Skorokhodov
Dmitriy Smirnov
Cameron Y. Smith
James S. Smith
Patrick Snape

Mattia Soldan
Hyeongseok Son
Sanghyun Son
Chuanbiao Song
Chen Song
Chunfeng Song
Dan Song
Dongjin Song
Hwanjun Song
Guoxian Song
Jiaming Song
Jie Song
Liangchen Song
Ran Song
Luchuan Song
Xibin Song
Li Song
Fenglong Song
Guoli Song
Guanglu Song
Zhenbo Song
Lin Song
Xinhang Song
Yang Song
Yibing Song
Rajiv Soundararajan
Hossein Souri
Cristovao Sousa
Riccardo Spezialetti
Leonidas Spinoulas
Michael W. Spratling
Deepak Sridhar
Srinath Sridhar
Gaurang Sriramanan
Vinkle Kumar Srivastav
Themos Stafylakis
Serban Stan
Anastasis Stathopoulos
Markus Steinberger
Jan Steinbrener
Sinisa Stekovic
Alexandros Stergiou
Gleb Sterkin
Rainer Stiefelhagen
Pierre Stock

Ombretta Strafforello
Julian Straub
Yannick Strümpler
Joerg Stueckler
Hang Su
Weijie Su
Jong-Chyi Su
Bing Su
Haisheng Su
Jinming Su
Yiyang Su
Yukun Su
Yuxin Su
Zhuo Su
Zhaoqi Su
Xiu Su
Yu-Chuan Su
Zhixun Su
Arulkumar Subramaniam
Akshayvarun Subramanya
A. Subramanyam
Swathikiran Sudhakaran
Yusuke Sugano
Masanori Suganuma
Yumin Suh
Yang Sui
Baochen Sun
Cheng Sun
Long Sun
Guolei Sun
Haoliang Sun
Haomiao Sun
He Sun
Hanqing Sun
Hao Sun
Lichao Sun
Jiachen Sun
Jiaming Sun
Jian Sun
Jin Sun
Jennifer J. Sun
Tiancheng Sun
Libo Sun
Peize Sun
Qianru Sun

Shanlin Sun
Yu Sun
Zhun Sun
Che Sun
Lin Sun
Tao Sun
Yiyou Sun
Chunyi Sun
Chong Sun
Weiwei Sun
Weixuan Sun
Xiuyu Sun
Yanan Sun
Zeren Sun
Zhaodong Sun
Zhiqing Sun
Minhyuk Sung
Jinli Suo
Simon Suo
Abhijit Suprem
Anshuman Suri
Saksham Suri
Joshua M. Susskind
Roman Suvorov
Gurumurthy Swaminathan
Robin Swanson
Paul Swoboda
Tabish A. Syed
Richard Szeliski
Fariborz Taherkhani
Yu-Wing Tai
Keita Takahashi
Walter Talbott
Gary Tam
Masato Tamura
Feitong Tan
Fuwen Tan
Shuhan Tan
Andong Tan
Bin Tan
Cheng Tan
Jianchao Tan
Lei Tan
Mingxing Tan
Xin Tan

Zichang Tan
Zhentao Tan
Kenichiro Tanaka
Masayuki Tanaka
Yushun Tang
Hao Tang
Jingqun Tang
Jinhui Tang
Kaihua Tang
Luming Tang
Lv Tang
Sheyang Tang
Shitao Tang
Siliang Tang
Shixiang Tang
Yansong Tang
Keke Tang
Chang Tang
Chenwei Tang
Jie Tang
Junshu Tang
Ming Tang
Peng Tang
Xu Tang
Yao Tang
Chen Tang
Fan Tang
Haoran Tang
Shengeng Tang
Yehui Tang
Zhipeng Tang
Ugo Tanielian
Chaofan Tao
Jiale Tao
Junli Tao
Renshuai Tao
An Tao
Guanhong Tao
Zhiqiang Tao
Makarand Tapaswi
Jean-Philippe G. Tarel
Juan J. Tarrio
Enzo Tartaglione
Keisuke Tateno
Zachary Teed

Ajinkya B. Tejankar
Bugra Tekin
Purva Tendulkar
Damien Teney
Minggui Teng
Chris Tensmeyer
Andrew Beng Jin Teoh
Philipp Terhörst
Kartik Thakral
Nupur Thakur
Kevin Thandiackal
Spyridon Thermos
Diego Thomas
William Thong
Yuesong Tian
Guanzhong Tian
Lin Tian
Shiqi Tian
Kai Tian
Meng Tian
Tai-Peng Tian
Zhuotao Tian
Shangxuan Tian
Tian Tian
Yapeng Tian
Yu Tian
Yuxin Tian
Leslie Ching Ow Tiong
Praveen Tirupattur
Garvita Tiwari
George Toderici
Antoine Toisoul
Aysim Toker
Tatiana Tommasi
Zhan Tong
Alessio Tonioni
Alessandro Torcinovich
Fabio Tosi
Matteo Toso
Hugo Touvron
Quan Hung Tran
Son Tran
Hung Tran
Ngoc-Trung Tran
Vinh Tran

Phong Tran
Giovanni Trappolini
Edith Tretschk
Subarna Tripathi
Shubhendu Trivedi
Eduard Trulls
Prune Truong
Thanh-Dat Truong
Tomasz Trzcinski
Sam Tsai
Yi-Hsuan Tsai
Ethan Tseng
Yu-Chee Tseng
Shahar Tsiper
Stavros Tsogkas
Shikui Tu
Zhigang Tu
Zhengzhong Tu
Richard Tucker
Sergey Tulyakov
Cigdem Turan
Daniyar Turmukhambetov
Victor G. Turrisi da Costa
Bartlomiej Twardowski
Christopher D. Twigg
Radim Tylecek
Mostofa Rafid Uddin
Md. Zasim Uddin
Kohei Uehara
Nicolas Ugrinovic
Youngjung Uh
Norimichi Ukita
Anwaar Ulhaq
Devesh Upadhyay
Paul Upchurch
Yoshitaka Ushiku
Yuzuko Utsumi
Mikaela Angelina Uy
Mohit Vaishnav
Pratik Vaishnavi
Jeya Maria Jose Valanarasu
Matias A. Valdenegro Toro
Diego Valsesia
Wouter Van Gansbeke
Nanne van Noord

Simon Vandenhende
Farshid Varno
Cristina Vasconcelos
Francisco Vasconcelos
Alex Vasilescu
Subeesh Vasu
Arun Balajee Vasudevan
Kanav Vats
Vaibhav S. Vavilala
Sagar Vaze
Javier Vazquez-Corral
Andrea Vedaldi
Olga Veksler
Andreas Velten
Sai H. Vemprala
Raviteja Vemulapalli
Shashanka
    Venkataramanan
Dor Verbin
Luisa Verdoliva
Manisha Verma
Yashaswi Verma
Constantin Vertan
Eli Verwimp
Deepak Vijaykeerthy
Pablo Villanueva
Ruben Villegas
Markus Vincze
Vibhav Vineet
Minh P. Vo
Huy V. Vo
Duc Minh Vo
Tomas Vojir
Igor Vozniak
Nicholas Vretos
Vibashan VS
Tuan-Anh Vu
Thang Vu
Mårten Wadenbäck
Neal Wadhwa
Aaron T. Walsman
Steven Walton
Jin Wan
Alvin Wan
Jia Wan

Jun Wan

Xiaoyue Wan

Fang Wan

Guowei Wan

Renjie Wan

Zhiqiang Wan

Ziyu Wan

Bastian Wandt

Dongdong Wang

Limin Wang

Haiyang Wang

Xiaobing Wang

Angtian Wang

Angelina Wang

Bing Wang

Bo Wang

Boyu Wang

Binghui Wang

Chen Wang

Chien-Yi Wang

Congli Wang

Qi Wang

Chengrui Wang

Rui Wang

Yiqun Wang

Cong Wang

Wenjing Wang

Dongkai Wang

Di Wang

Xiaogang Wang

Kai Wang

Zhizhong Wang

Fangjinhua Wang

Feng Wang

Hang Wang

Gaoang Wang

Guoqing Wang

Guangcong Wang

Guangzhi Wang

Hanqing Wang

Hao Wang

Haohan Wang

Haoran Wang

Hong Wang

Haotao Wang

Hu Wang

Huan Wang

Hua Wang

Hui-Po Wang

Hengli Wang

Hanyu Wang

Hongxing Wang

Jingwen Wang

Jialiang Wang

Jian Wang

Jianyi Wang

Jiashun Wang

Jiahao Wang

Tsun-Hsuan Wang

Xiaoqian Wang

Jinqiao Wang

Jun Wang

Jianzong Wang

Kaihong Wang

Ke Wang

Lei Wang

Lingjing Wang

Linnan Wang

Lin Wang

Liansheng Wang

Mengjiao Wang

Manning Wang

Nannan Wang

Peihao Wang

Jiayun Wang

Pu Wang

Qiang Wang

Qiufeng Wang

Qilong Wang

Qiangchang Wang

Qin Wang

Qing Wang

Ruocheng Wang

Ruibin Wang

Ruisheng Wang

Ruizhe Wang

Runqi Wang

Runzhong Wang

Wenxuan Wang

Sen Wang

Shangfei Wang

Shaofei Wang

Shijie Wang

Shiqi Wang

Zhibo Wang

Song Wang

Xinjiang Wang

Tai Wang

Tao Wang

Teng Wang

Xiang Wang

Tianren Wang

Tiantian Wang

Tianyi Wang

Fengjiao Wang

Wei Wang

Miaohui Wang

Suchen Wang

Siyue Wang

Yaoming Wang

Xiao Wang

Ze Wang

Biao Wang

Chaofei Wang

Dong Wang

Gu Wang

Guangrun Wang

Guangming Wang

Guo-Hua Wang

Haoqing Wang

Hesheng Wang

Huafeng Wang

Jinghua Wang

Jingdong Wang

Jingjing Wang

Jingya Wang

Jingkang Wang

Jiakai Wang

Junke Wang

Kuo Wang

Lichen Wang

Lizhi Wang

Longguang Wang

Mang Wang

Mei Wang

Min Wang
Peng-Shuai Wang
Run Wang
Shaoru Wang
Shuhui Wang
Tan Wang
Tiancai Wang
Tianqi Wang
Wenhai Wang
Wenzhe Wang
Xiaobo Wang
Xiudong Wang
Xu Wang
Yajie Wang
Yan Wang
Yuan-Gen Wang
Yingqian Wang
Yizhi Wang
Yulin Wang
Yu Wang
Yujie Wang
Yunhe Wang
Yuxi Wang
Yaowei Wang
Yiwei Wang
Zezheng Wang
Hongzhi Wang
Zhiqiang Wang
Ziteng Wang
Ziwei Wang
Zheng Wang
Zhenyu Wang
Binglu Wang
Zhongdao Wang
Ce Wang
Weining Wang
Weiyao Wang
Wenbin Wang
Wenguan Wang
Guangting Wang
Haolin Wang
Haiyan Wang
Huiyu Wang
Naiyan Wang
Jingbo Wang

Jinpeng Wang
Jiaqi Wang
Liyuan Wang
Lizhen Wang
Ning Wang
Wenqian Wang
Sheng-Yu Wang
Weimin Wang
Xiaohan Wang
Yifan Wang
Yi Wang
Yongtao Wang
Yizhou Wang
Zhuo Wang
Zhe Wang
Xudong Wang
Xiaofang Wang
Xinggang Wang
Xiaosen Wang
Xiaosong Wang
Xiaoyang Wang
Lijun Wang
Xinlong Wang
Xuan Wang
Xue Wang
Yangang Wang
Yaohui Wang
Yu-Chiang Frank Wang
Yida Wang
Yilin Wang
Yi Ru Wang
Yali Wang
Yinglong Wang
Yufu Wang
Yujiang Wang
Yuwang Wang
Yuting Wang
Yang Wang
Yu-Xiong Wang
Yixu Wang
Ziqi Wang
Zhicheng Wang
Zeyu Wang
Zhaowen Wang
Zhenyi Wang

Zhenzhi Wang
Zhijie Wang
Zhiyong Wang
Zhongling Wang
Zhuowei Wang
Zian Wang
Zifu Wang
Zihao Wang
Zirui Wang
Ziyan Wang
Wenxiao Wang
Zhen Wang
Zhepeng Wang
Zi Wang
Zihao W. Wang
Steven L. Waslander
Olivia Watkins
Daniel Watson
Silvan Weder
Dongyoon Wee
Dongming Wei
Tianyi Wei
Jia Wei
Dong Wei
Fangyun Wei
Longhui Wei
Mingqiang Wei
Xinyue Wei
Chen Wei
Donglai Wei
Pengxu Wei
Xing Wei
Xiu-Shen Wei
Wenqi Wei
Guoqiang Wei
Wei Wei
XingKui Wei
Xian Wei
Xingxing Wei
Yake Wei
Yuxiang Wei
Yi Wei
Luca Weihs
Michael Weinmann
Martin Weinmann

Congcong Wen
Chuan Wen
Jie Wen
Sijia Wen
Song Wen
Chao Wen
Xiang Wen
Zeyi Wen
Xin Wen
Yilin Wen
Yijia Weng
Shuchen Weng
Junwu Weng
Wenming Weng
Renliang Weng
Zhenyu Weng
Xinshuo Weng
Nicholas J. Westlake
Gordon Wetzstein
Lena M. Widin Klasén
Rick Wildes
Bryan M. Williams
William Williem
Ole Winther
Scott Wisdom
Alex Wong
Chau-Wai Wong
Kwan-Yee K. Wong
Yongkang Wong
Scott Workman
Marcel Worring
Michael Wray
Safwan Wshah
Xiang Wu
Aming Wu
Chongruo Wu
Cho-Ying Wu
Chunpeng Wu
Chenyan Wu
Ziyi Wu
Fuxiang Wu
Gang Wu
Haiping Wu
Huisi Wu
Jane Wu

Jialian Wu
Jing Wu
Jinjian Wu
Jianlong Wu
Xian Wu
Lifang Wu
Lifan Wu
Minye Wu
Qianyi Wu
Rongliang Wu
Rui Wu
Shiqian Wu
Shuzhe Wu
Shangzhe Wu
Tsung-Han Wu
Tz-Ying Wu
Ting-Wei Wu
Jiannan Wu
Zhiliang Wu
Yu Wu
Chenyun Wu
Dayan Wu
Dongxian Wu
Fei Wu
Hefeng Wu
Jianxin Wu
Weibin Wu
Wenxuan Wu
Wenhao Wu
Xiao Wu
Yicheng Wu
Yuanwei Wu
Yu-Huan Wu
Zhenxin Wu
Zhenyu Wu
Wei Wu
Peng Wu
Xiaohe Wu
Xindi Wu
Xinxing Wu
Xinyi Wu
Xingjiao Wu
Xiongwei Wu
Yangzheng Wu
Yanzhao Wu

Yawen Wu
Yong Wu
Yi Wu
Ying Nian Wu
Zhenyao Wu
Zhonghua Wu
Zongze Wu
Zuxuan Wu
Stefanie Wuhrer
Teng Xi
Jianing Xi
Fei Xia
Haifeng Xia
Menghan Xia
Yuanqing Xia
Zhihua Xia
Xiaobo Xia
Weihao Xia
Shihong Xia
Yan Xia
Yong Xia
Zhaoyang Xia
Zhihao Xia
Chuhua Xian
Yongqin Xian
Wangmeng Xiang
Fanbo Xiang
Tiange Xiang
Tao Xiang
Liuyu Xiang
Xiaoyu Xiang
Zhiyu Xiang
Aoran Xiao
Chunxia Xiao
Fanyi Xiao
Jimin Xiao
Jun Xiao
Taihong Xiao
Anqi Xiao
Junfei Xiao
Jing Xiao
Liang Xiao
Yang Xiao
Yuting Xiao
Yijun Xiao

Yao Xiao
Zeyu Xiao
Zhisheng Xiao
Zihao Xiao
Binhui Xie
Christopher Xie
Haozhe Xie
Jin Xie
Guo-Sen Xie
Hongtao Xie
Ming-Kun Xie
Tingting Xie
Chaohao Xie
Weicheng Xie
Xudong Xie
Jiyang Xie
Xiaohua Xie
Yuan Xie
Zhenyu Xie
Ning Xie
Xianghui Xie
Xiufeng Xie
You Xie
Yutong Xie
Fuyong Xing
Yifan Xing
Zhen Xing
Yuanjun Xiong
Jinhui Xiong
Weihua Xiong
Hongkai Xiong
Zhitong Xiong
Yuanhao Xiong
Yunyang Xiong
Yuwen Xiong
Zhiwei Xiong
Yuliang Xiu
An Xu
Chang Xu
Chenliang Xu
Chengming Xu
Chenshu Xu
Xiang Xu
Huijuan Xu
Zhe Xu

Jie Xu
Jingyi Xu
Jiarui Xu
Yinghao Xu
Kele Xu
Ke Xu
Li Xu
Linchuan Xu
Linning Xu
Mengde Xu
Mengmeng Frost Xu
Min Xu
Mingye Xu
Jun Xu
Ning Xu
Peng Xu
Runsheng Xu
Sheng Xu
Wenqiang Xu
Xiaogang Xu
Renzhe Xu
Kaidi Xu
Yi Xu
Chi Xu
Qiuling Xu
Baobei Xu
Feng Xu
Haohang Xu
Haofei Xu
Lan Xu
Mingze Xu
Songcen Xu
Weipeng Xu
Wenjia Xu
Wenju Xu
Xiangyu Xu
Xin Xu
Yinshuang Xu
Yixing Xu
Yuting Xu
Yanyu Xu
Zhenbo Xu
Zhiliang Xu
Zhiyuan Xu
Xiaohao Xu

Yanwu Xu
Yan Xu
Yiran Xu
Yifan Xu
Yufei Xu
Yong Xu
Zichuan Xu
Zenglin Xu
Zexiang Xu
Zhan Xu
Zheng Xu
Zhiwei Xu
Ziyue Xu
Shiyu Xuan
Hanyu Xuan
Fei Xue
Jianru Xue
Mingfu Xue
Qinghan Xue
Tianfan Xue
Chao Xue
Chuhui Xue
Nan Xue
Zhou Xue
Xiangyang Xue
Yuan Xue
Abhay Yadav
Ravindra Yadav
Kota Yamaguchi
Toshihiko Yamasaki
Kohei Yamashita
Chaochao Yan
Feng Yan
Kun Yan
Qingsen Yan
Qixin Yan
Rui Yan
Siming Yan
Xinchen Yan
Yaping Yan
Bin Yan
Qingan Yan
Shen Yan
Shipeng Yan
Xu Yan

Yan Yan
Yichao Yan
Zhaoyi Yan
Zike Yan
Zhiqiang Yan
Hongliang Yan
Zizheng Yan
Jiewen Yang
Anqi Joyce Yang
Shan Yang
Anqi Yang
Antoine Yang
Bo Yang
Baoyao Yang
Chenhongyi Yang
Dingkang Yang
De-Nian Yang
Dong Yang
David Yang
Fan Yang
Fengyu Yang
Fengting Yang
Fei Yang
Gengshan Yang
Heng Yang
Han Yang
Huan Yang
Yibo Yang
Jiancheng Yang
Jihan Yang
Jiawei Yang
Jiayu Yang
Jie Yang
Jinfa Yang
Jingkang Yang
Jinyu Yang
Cheng-Fu Yang
Ji Yang
Jianyu Yang
Kailun Yang
Tian Yang
Luyu Yang
Liang Yang
Li Yang
Michael Ying Yang

Yang Yang
Muli Yang
Le Yang
Qiushi Yang
Ren Yang
Ruihan Yang
Shuang Yang
Siyuan Yang
Su Yang
Shiqi Yang
Taojiannan Yang
Tianyu Yang
Lei Yang
Wanzhao Yang
Shuai Yang
William Yang
Wei Yang
Xiaofeng Yang
Xiaoshan Yang
Xin Yang
Xuan Yang
Xu Yang
Xingyi Yang
Xitong Yang
Jing Yang
Yanchao Yang
Wenming Yang
Yujiu Yang
Herb Yang
Jianfei Yang
Jinhui Yang
Chuanguang Yang
Guanglei Yang
Haitao Yang
Kewei Yang
Linlin Yang
Lijin Yang
Longrong Yang
Meng Yang
MingKun Yang
Sibei Yang
Shicai Yang
Tong Yang
Wen Yang
Xi Yang

Xiaolong Yang
Xue Yang
Yubin Yang
Ze Yang
Ziyi Yang
Yi Yang
Linjie Yang
Yuzhe Yang
Yiding Yang
Zhenpei Yang
Zhaohui Yang
Zhengyuan Yang
Zhibo Yang
Zongxin Yang
Hantao Yao
Mingde Yao
Rui Yao
Taiping Yao
Ting Yao
Cong Yao
Qingsong Yao
Quanming Yao
Xu Yao
Yuan Yao
Yao Yao
Yazhou Yao
Jiawen Yao
Shunyu Yao
Pew-Thian Yap
Sudhir Yarram
Rajeev Yasarla
Peng Ye
Botao Ye
Mao Ye
Fei Ye
Hanrong Ye
Jingwen Ye
Jinwei Ye
Jiarong Ye
Mang Ye
Meng Ye
Qi Ye
Qian Ye
Qixiang Ye
Junjie Ye

Sheng Ye
Nanyang Ye
Yufei Ye
Xiaoqing Ye
Ruolin Ye
Yousef Yeganeh
Chun-Hsiao Yeh
Raymond A. Yeh
Yu-Ying Yeh
Kai Yi
Chang Yi
Renjiao Yi
Xinping Yi
Peng Yi
Alper Yilmaz
Junho Yim
Hui Yin
Bangjie Yin
Jia-Li Yin
Miao Yin
Wenzhe Yin
Xuwang Yin
Ming Yin
Yu Yin
Aoxiong Yin
Kangxue Yin
Tianwei Yin
Wei Yin
Xianghua Ying
Rio Yokota
Tatsuya Yokota
Naoto Yokoya
Ryo Yonetani
Ki Yoon Yoo
Jinsu Yoo
Sunjae Yoon
Jae Shin Yoon
Jihun Yoon
Sung-Hoon Yoon
Ryota Yoshihashi
Yusuke Yoshiyasu
Chenyu You
Haoran You
Haoxuan You
Yang You

Quanzeng You
Tackgeun You
Kaichao You
Shan You
Xinge You
Yurong You
Baosheng Yu
Bei Yu
Haichao Yu
Hao Yu
Chaohui Yu
Fisher Yu
Jin-Gang Yu
Jiyang Yu
Jason J. Yu
Jiashuo Yu
Hong-Xing Yu
Lei Yu
Mulin Yu
Ning Yu
Peilin Yu
Qi Yu
Qian Yu
Rui Yu
Shuzhi Yu
Gang Yu
Tan Yu
Weijiang Yu
Xin Yu
Bingyao Yu
Ye Yu
Hanchao Yu
Yingchen Yu
Tao Yu
Xiaotian Yu
Qing Yu
Houjian Yu
Changqian Yu
Jing Yu
Jun Yu
Shujian Yu
Xiang Yu
Zhaofei Yu
Zhenbo Yu
Yinfeng Yu

Zhuoran Yu
Zitong Yu
Bo Yuan
Jiangbo Yuan
Liangzhe Yuan
Weihao Yuan
Jianbo Yuan
Xiaoyun Yuan
Ye Yuan
Li Yuan
Geng Yuan
Jialin Yuan
Maoxun Yuan
Peng Yuan
Xin Yuan
Yuan Yuan
Yuhui Yuan
Yixuan Yuan
Zheng Yuan
Mehmet Kerim Yücel
Kaiyu Yue
Haixiao Yue
Heeseung Yun
Sangdoo Yun
Tian Yun
Mahmut Yurt
Ekim Yurtsever
Ahmet Yüzügüler
Edouard Yvinec
Eloi Zablocki
Christopher Zach
Muhammad Zaigham
    Zaheer
Pierluigi Zama Ramirez
Yuhang Zang
Pietro Zanuttigh
Alexey Zaytsev
Bernhard Zeisl
Haitian Zeng
Pengpeng Zeng
Jiabei Zeng
Runhao Zeng
Wei Zeng
Yawen Zeng
Yi Zeng

Yiming Zeng
Tieyong Zeng
Huanqiang Zeng
Dan Zeng
Yu Zeng
Wei Zhai
Yuanhao Zhai
Fangneng Zhan
Kun Zhan
Xiong Zhang
Jingdong Zhang
Jiangning Zhang
Zhilu Zhang
Gengwei Zhang
Dongsu Zhang
Hui Zhang
Binjie Zhang
Bo Zhang
Tianhao Zhang
Cecilia Zhang
Jing Zhang
Chaoning Zhang
Chenxu Zhang
Chi Zhang
Chris Zhang
Yabin Zhang
Zhao Zhang
Rufeng Zhang
Chaoyi Zhang
Zheng Zhang
Da Zhang
Yi Zhang
Edward Zhang
Xin Zhang
Feifei Zhang
Feilong Zhang
Yuqi Zhang
GuiXuan Zhang
Hanlin Zhang
Hanwang Zhang
Hanzhen Zhang
Haotian Zhang
He Zhang
Haokui Zhang
Hongyuan Zhang

Hengrui Zhang
Hongming Zhang
Mingfang Zhang
Jianpeng Zhang
Jiaming Zhang
Jichao Zhang
Jie Zhang
Jingfeng Zhang
Jingyi Zhang
Jinnian Zhang
David Junhao Zhang
Junjie Zhang
Junzhe Zhang
Jiawan Zhang
Jingyang Zhang
Kai Zhang
Lei Zhang
Lihua Zhang
Lu Zhang
Miao Zhang
Minjia Zhang
Mingjin Zhang
Qi Zhang
Qian Zhang
Qilong Zhang
Qiming Zhang
Qiang Zhang
Richard Zhang
Ruimao Zhang
Ruisi Zhang
Ruixin Zhang
Runze Zhang
Qilin Zhang
Shan Zhang
Shanshan Zhang
Xi Sheryl Zhang
Song-Hai Zhang
Chongyang Zhang
Kaihao Zhang
Songyang Zhang
Shu Zhang
Siwei Zhang
Shujian Zhang
Tianyun Zhang
Tong Zhang

Tao Zhang
Wenwei Zhang
Wenqiang Zhang
Wen Zhang
Xiaolin Zhang
Xingchen Zhang
Xingxuan Zhang
Xiuming Zhang
Xiaoshuai Zhang
Xuanmeng Zhang
Xuanyang Zhang
Xucong Zhang
Xingxing Zhang
Xikun Zhang
Xiaohan Zhang
Yahui Zhang
Yunhua Zhang
Yan Zhang
Yanghao Zhang
Yifei Zhang
Yifan Zhang
Yi-Fan Zhang
Yihao Zhang
Yingliang Zhang
Youshan Zhang
Yulun Zhang
Yushu Zhang
Yixiao Zhang
Yide Zhang
Zhongwen Zhang
Bowen Zhang
Chen-Lin Zhang
Zehua Zhang
Zekun Zhang
Zeyu Zhang
Xiaowei Zhang
Yifeng Zhang
Cheng Zhang
Hongguang Zhang
Yuexi Zhang
Fa Zhang
Guofeng Zhang
Hao Zhang
Haofeng Zhang
Hongwen Zhang

Hua Zhang	Zhizhong Zhang	Bowen Zhao
Jiaxin Zhang	Qilong Zhangli	Pu Zhao
Zhenyu Zhang	Bingyin Zhao	Bingchen Zhao
Jian Zhang	Bin Zhao	Borui Zhao
Jianfeng Zhang	Chenglong Zhao	Fuqiang Zhao
Jiao Zhang	Lei Zhao	Hanbin Zhao
Jiakai Zhang	Feng Zhao	Jian Zhao
Lefei Zhang	Gangming Zhao	Mingyang Zhao
Le Zhang	Haiyan Zhao	Na Zhao
Mi Zhang	Hao Zhao	Rongchang Zhao
Min Zhang	Handong Zhao	Ruiqi Zhao
Ning Zhang	Hengshuang Zhao	Shuai Zhao
Pan Zhang	Yinan Zhao	Wenda Zhao
Pu Zhang	Jiaojiao Zhao	Wenliang Zhao
Qing Zhang	Jiaqi Zhao	Xiangyun Zhao
Renrui Zhang	Jing Zhao	Yifan Zhao
Shifeng Zhang	Kaili Zhao	Yaping Zhao
Shuo Zhang	Haojie Zhao	Zhou Zhao
Shaoxiong Zhang	Yucheng Zhao	He Zhao
Weizhong Zhang	Longjiao Zhao	Jie Zhao
Xi Zhang	Long Zhao	Xibin Zhao
Xiaomei Zhang	Qingsong Zhao	Xiaoqi Zhao
Xinyu Zhang	Qingyu Zhao	Zhengyu Zhao
Yin Zhang	Rui Zhao	Jin Zhe
Zicheng Zhang	Rui-Wei Zhao	Chuanxia Zheng
Zihao Zhang	Sicheng Zhao	Huan Zheng
Ziqi Zhang	Shuang Zhao	Hao Zheng
Zhaoxiang Zhang	Siyan Zhao	Jia Zheng
Zhen Zhang	Zelin Zhao	Jian-Qing Zheng
Zhipeng Zhang	Shiyu Zhao	Shuai Zheng
Zhixing Zhang	Wang Zhao	Meng Zheng
Zhizheng Zhang	Tiesong Zhao	Mingkai Zheng
Jiawei Zhang	Qian Zhao	Qian Zheng
Zhong Zhang	Wangbo Zhao	Qi Zheng
Pingping Zhang	Xi-Le Zhao	Wu Zheng
Yixin Zhang	Xu Zhao	Yinqiang Zheng
Kui Zhang	Yajie Zhao	Yufeng Zheng
Lingzhi Zhang	Yang Zhao	Yutong Zheng
Huaiwen Zhang	Ying Zhao	Yalin Zheng
Quanshi Zhang	Yin Zhao	Yu Zheng
Zhoutong Zhang	Yizhou Zhao	Feng Zheng
Yuhang Zhang	Yunhan Zhao	Zhaoheng Zheng
Yuting Zhang	Yuyang Zhao	Haitian Zheng
Zhang Zhang	Yue Zhao	Kang Zheng
Ziming Zhang	Yuzhi Zhao	Bolun Zheng

Haiyong Zheng
Mingwu Zheng
Sipeng Zheng
Tu Zheng
Wenzhao Zheng
Xiawu Zheng
Yinglin Zheng
Zhuo Zheng
Zilong Zheng
Kecheng Zheng
Zerong Zheng
Shuaifeng Zhi
Tiancheng Zhi
Jia-Xing Zhong
Yiwu Zhong
Fangwei Zhong
Zhihang Zhong
Yaoyao Zhong
Yiran Zhong
Zhun Zhong
Zichun Zhong
Bo Zhou
Boyao Zhou
Brady Zhou
Mo Zhou
Chunluan Zhou
Dingfu Zhou
Fan Zhou
Jingkai Zhou
Honglu Zhou
Jiaming Zhou
Jiahuan Zhou
Jun Zhou
Kaiyang Zhou
Keyang Zhou
Kuangqi Zhou
Lei Zhou
Lihua Zhou
Man Zhou
Mingyi Zhou
Mingyuan Zhou
Ning Zhou
Peng Zhou
Penghao Zhou
Qianyi Zhou

Shuigeng Zhou
Shangchen Zhou
Huayi Zhou
Zhize Zhou
Sanping Zhou
Qin Zhou
Tao Zhou
Wenbo Zhou
Xiangdong Zhou
Xiao-Yun Zhou
Xiao Zhou
Yang Zhou
Yipin Zhou
Zhenyu Zhou
Hao Zhou
Chu Zhou
Daquan Zhou
Da-Wei Zhou
Hang Zhou
Kang Zhou
Qianyu Zhou
Sheng Zhou
Wenhui Zhou
Xingyi Zhou
Yan-Jie Zhou
Yiyi Zhou
Yu Zhou
Yuan Zhou
Yuqian Zhou
Yuxuan Zhou
Zixiang Zhou
Wengang Zhou
Shuchang Zhou
Tianfei Zhou
Yichao Zhou
Alex Zhu
Chenchen Zhu
Deyao Zhu
Xiatian Zhu
Guibo Zhu
Haidong Zhu
Hao Zhu
Hongzi Zhu
Rui Zhu
Jing Zhu

Jianke Zhu
Junchen Zhu
Lei Zhu
Lingyu Zhu
Luyang Zhu
Menglong Zhu
Peihao Zhu
Hui Zhu
Xiaofeng Zhu
Tyler (Lixuan) Zhu
Wentao Zhu
Xiangyu Zhu
Xinqi Zhu
Xinxin Zhu
Xinliang Zhu
Yangguang Zhu
Yichen Zhu
Yixin Zhu
Yanjun Zhu
Yousong Zhu
Yuhao Zhu
Ye Zhu
Feng Zhu
Zhen Zhu
Fangrui Zhu
Jinjing Zhu
Linchao Zhu
Pengfei Zhu
Sijie Zhu
Xiaobin Zhu
Xiaoguang Zhu
Zezhou Zhu
Zhenyao Zhu
Kai Zhu
Pengkai Zhu
Bingbing Zhuang
Chengyuan Zhuang
Liansheng Zhuang
Peiye Zhuang
Yixin Zhuang
Yihong Zhuang
Junbao Zhuo
Andrea Ziani
Bartosz Zieliński
Primo Zingaretti

Nikolaos Zioulis
Andrew Zisserman
Yael Ziv
Liu Ziyin
Xingxing Zou
Danping Zou
Qi Zou

Shihao Zou
Xueyan Zou
Yang Zou
Yuliang Zou
Zihang Zou
Chuhang Zou
Dongqing Zou

Xu Zou
Zhiming Zou
Maria A. Zuluaga
Xinxin Zuo
Zhiwen Zuo
Reyer Zwiggelaar

Contents – Part XXXVI

Making the Most of Text Semantics to Improve Biomedical Vision–Language Processing

Benedikt Boecking⬤, Naoto Usuyama⬤, Shruthi Bannur⬤,
Daniel C. Castro⬤, Anton Schwaighofer⬤, Stephanie Hyland⬤,
Maria Wetscherek, Tristan Naumann⬤, Aditya Nori, Javier Alvarez-Valle⬤,
Hoifung Poon⬤, and Ozan Oktay[✉]⬤

Microsoft Health Futures, Redmond, USA
ozan.oktay@microsoft.com

Abstract. Multi-modal data abounds in biomedicine, such as radiology images and reports. Interpreting this data at scale is essential for improving clinical care and accelerating clinical research. Biomedical text with its complex semantics poses additional challenges in vision–language modelling compared to the general domain, and previous work has used insufficiently adapted models that lack domain-specific language understanding. In this paper, we show that principled textual semantic modelling can substantially improve contrastive learning in self-supervised vision–language processing. We release a language model that achieves state-of-the-art results in radiology natural language inference through its improved vocabulary and novel language pretraining objective leveraging semantics and discourse characteristics in radiology reports. Further, we propose a self-supervised joint vision–language approach with a focus on better text modelling. It establishes new state of the art results on a wide range of publicly available benchmarks, in part by leveraging our new domain-specific language model. We release a new dataset with locally-aligned phrase grounding annotations by radiologists to facilitate the study of complex semantic modelling in biomedical vision–language processing. A broad evaluation, including on this new dataset, shows that our contrastive learning approach, aided by textual-semantic modelling, outperforms prior methods in segmentation tasks, despite only using a global-alignment objective.

Keywords: Self-supervision · Multi-modal · Weak supervision · Radiology

---

B. Boecking and N. Usuyama contributed equally—Work conducted during Benedikt Boecking's internship at Microsoft Research.

Supplementary Information The online version contains supplementary material available at https://doi.org/10.1007/978-3-031-20059-5_1.

S. Avidan et al. (Eds.): ECCV 2022, LNCS 13696, pp. 1–21, 2022.
https://doi.org/10.1007/978-3-031-20059-5_1

1   Introduction

Advances in deep learning have enabled automated diagnosis systems that operate near or above expert-level performance, paving the way for the use of machine learning systems to improve healthcare workflows, for example by supporting fast triaging and assisting medical professionals to reduce errors and omissions [9,20,54,72]. A major hurdle to the widespread development of these systems is a requirement for large amounts of detailed ground-truth clinical annotations for supervised training, which are expensive and time-consuming to obtain. Motivated by this challenge, there has been a rising interest in multi-modal self-supervised learning [31,45] and cross-modal weak supervision [19,21,33,72,76] (using partial and imperfect labels derived from the auxiliary modality), in particular for paired image–text data. Such data is collected routinely during clinical practice, and common examples are X-ray images [19,33,76] or computed tomography (CT) scans [9,19,21,72] paired with reports written by medical experts. Importantly, while many remain private, some paired clinical datasets [3,15,34] have been released to the research community such as MIMIC-CXR [34].

This article focuses on self-supervised vision–language processing (VLP) for paired image and text data in the biomedical domain. The goal is to jointly learn good image and text representations that can be leveraged by downstream applications such as zero-/few-shot image classification, report generation and error detection, and disease localisation. Self-supervised VLP has several advantages over supervised learning, not just because it does not require laborious manual annotations, but also because it does not operate on a fixed number of predetermined conditions or object categories, since the joint latent space is learned from raw text. However, in contrast to the general domain setting, self-supervised VLP with biomedical data poses additional challenges. Take radiology as an example, publicly available datasets [3,15,34] are usually smaller, on the order of a few hundred thousand pairs rather than millions in general-domain vision–language processing (e.g. [61] collected 400M text–image pairs on the Internet for self-supervision). Furthermore, linguistic challenges are different in biomedical settings, including common usage of negations, expressions of uncertainty, long-range dependencies, more frequent spatial relations, the use of domain-specific modifiers, as well as scientific terminology rarely found in the general domain. Taking negation as an example, "there is no dog in this picture" would be a highly unusual caption on social media, but "there is no evidence of pneumonia in the left lung" or "there are no new areas of consolidation to suggest the presence of pneumonia" are descriptions commonly found in radiology reports. Moreover, pretrained models including object detectors often used in general domain visual grounding are typically unavailable or under-perform in domain-specific applications (see also Supp. in [31]). Additionally, imbalance in underlying latent entities of interest (e.g., pulmonary findings) can cause larger numbers of false negatives in contrastive learning objectives that sample at random, which can lead models to degrade and memorise irrelevant text and image aspects. For example, radiology images and text reports with normal findings occur much more frequently compared to exams that reveal abnormal conditions

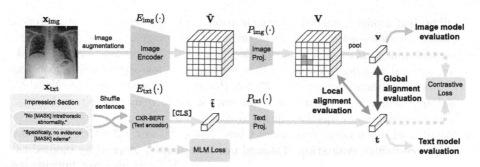

Fig. 1. BioViL leverages our radiology-specific text encoder (CXR-BERT), text augmentation, regularisation, and maintains language model quality via a masked language modelling (MLM) loss. We conduct a broad evaluation of models and representations that includes zero-shot classification, phrase grounding, and natural language inference.

such as pneumonia or pneumothorax (also see [11]). Supp. B.1 provides further discussion of these challenges.

Related self-supervised VLP work [30,31,45,56,85] has achieved impressive downstream classification and zero-shot classification performance. However, our study reveals that suboptimal text modelling due to insufficient vocabulary adjustment, fine-tuning, and language grounding appears to have gone unnoticed, all of which are shown to degrade the quality of joint latent representations. In particular, a more thorough benchmarking of the text, image, and shared embeddings, across a multitude of downstream benchmarks, reveals that large improvements in performance are possible by taking care to build highly specialised text models and by maintaining their performance during joint training. Free-text image descriptions provide a semantically dense learning signal compared to image-only contrastive methods and supervised classification [16]. Further, extracting shared semantics of images and text pairs is easier for text, as the modality is already discretised. Thus, making the most of text modelling before and during joint training can lead to large improvements in not just the text model, but also of the image model and joint representations. We present the following contributions in this work:

1. We introduce and release a new chest X-ray (CXR) domain-specific language model, CXR-BERT[1] (Fig. 2). Through an improved vocabulary, a novel pre-training procedure, regularisation, and text augmentation, the model considerably improves radiology natural language inference [54], radiology masked token prediction [17,48], and downstream VLP task performance.
2. We propose and release a simple but effective self-supervised VLP approach for paired biomedical data, which we name BioViL (See footnote 1)[2] (Fig. 1), and evaluate in the radiology setting. Through improvements in text mod-

---

[1] Pretrained models available on HuggingFace: https://aka.ms/biovil-models.
[2] Code can be found at: https://aka.ms/biovil-code.

elling, text model grounding, augmentation, and regularisation, the approach yields new state-of-the-art performance on a wide range of public downstream benchmarks. Our large-scale evaluation (see Table 2) includes phrase grounding, natural language inference [54], as well as zero-/few-shot classification and zero-shot segmentation via the RSNA Pneumonia dataset [66,76]. Notably, our approach achieves improved segmentation performance despite only using a global alignment objective during training.

3. We also release a Local Alignment Chest X-ray dataset, MS-CXR[3], to encourage reproducible evaluation of shared latent semantics learned by biomedical image-text models. This large, well-balanced phrase grounding benchmark dataset contains carefully curated image regions annotated with descriptions of eight radiology findings, as verified by board-certified radiologists. Unlike existing chest X-ray benchmarks, this challenging phrase grounding task evaluates joint, local image-text reasoning while requiring real-world language understanding, e.g. to parse domain-specific location references, complex negations, and bias in reporting style.

2   Making the Most of Free-Text Supervision

We assume that we are given a set $\mathcal{D}$ of pairs of radiology images and reports $(\mathbf{x}_{\text{img}}, \mathbf{x}_{\text{txt}})$. Let $\mathbf{w} = (w_1, \ldots, w_T)$ denote a vector of T (sub-)word tokens of a text document $\mathbf{x}_{\text{txt}}$ (after tokenisation). Recall that a BERT [73] encoder E_{txt} outputs a feature vector for each input token w_t as well as a special global [CLS] token used for downstream classification. Let $\tilde{\mathbf{t}} = [E_{\text{txt}}(\mathbf{w})]_{\text{[CLS]}}$ denote the [CLS] token prediction by E_{txt} based on input $\mathbf{w}$, and $\mathbf{t} = P_{\text{txt}}(\tilde{\mathbf{t}})$ its lower-dimensional projection by a model P_{txt}.

2.1   CXR-BERT: Domain-Specific Language Model Pretraining

We introduce CXR-BERT (Fig. 2), a specialised chest X-ray (CXR) language model with an adjusted vocabulary, pretrained in three phases to capture dense semantics in radiology reports [4]. To achieve this specialisation to the CXR report domain despite limited data availability, our approach includes pretraining on larger data from closely related domains. The phases proceed as follows: **(I)** First, we construct a custom WordPiece [80] vocabulary of 30k tokens from PubMed

Table 1. Vocabulary comparison of common radiology terms with ClinicalBERT (Wiki/Book, cased), PubMedBERT (PubMed, uncased), and CXR-BERT (PubMed+MIMIC-III/CXR, uncased). ✓ marks that a word appears in the vocabulary, otherwise its sub-tokens are shown.

Full word	ClinicalBERT	PubMedBERT	CXR-BERT
Pneumonia	✓	✓	✓
Opacity	op-acity	✓	✓
Effusion	e-ff-usion	✓	✓
Pneumothorax	p-ne-um-oth-orax	✓	✓
Atelectasis	ate-lect-asis	ate-le-ct-asis	✓
Cardiomegaly	card-io-me-gal-y	cardio-me-gal-y	✓
Bibasilar	bi-bas-ila-r	bib-asi-la-r	✓

---

[3] The MS-CXR dataset can be found on PhysioNet https://aka.ms/ms-cxr.

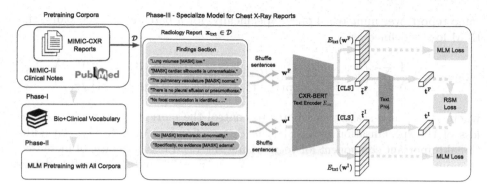

Fig. 2. The proposed CXR-BERT text encoder has three phases of pretraining and uses a domain-specific vocabulary, masked language modelling (MLM) and radiology section matching (RSM) losses, regularisation, and text augmentations.

abstracts[4] (15 GB), MIMIC-III [35] clinical notes (3.5 GB), and MIMIC-CXR radiology reports (0.1 GB). With this custom vocabulary, our model produces fewer sub-word breakdowns (Table 1). **(II)** Second, we pretrain a randomly initialised BERT model via Masked Language Modelling (MLM) on the PubMed + MIMIC-III + MIMIC-CXR corpora. We largely follow RoBERTa [48] pretraining configurations, i.e. dynamic whole-word masking for MLM and packing of multiple sentences into one input sequence. This phase aims to build an initial domain-specific BERT model in the biomedical and clinical domains. **(III)** Third, we continue pretraining on MIMIC-CXR only to further specialise our CXR-BERT to the CXR domain. Here, we also add a novel sequence prediction task to the objective to obtain better sequence representations, as explained below.

Note that a raw radiology report $\mathbf{x}_{\text{txt}}$ typically consists of several sections, including a 'FINDINGS' section that details clinical observations, and an 'IMPRESSION' section summarising the clinical assessment [74,77]. Our sequence prediction objective of phase (III) aims to take advantage of this structure. Specifically, we continually run MLM pretraining on MIMIC-CXR radiology reports and propose to add a radiology section matching (RSM) pretraining task, formulated to match IMPRESSION to FINDINGS sections of the same study.

Let θ denote the weights of our language model and $m \subset \{1, \ldots, T\}$ denote mask indices for M masked tokens, randomly sampled for each token vector $\mathbf{w}$ at every iteration. Given a batch $\mathcal{B}$ of token vectors $\mathbf{w} = (w_1, \ldots, w_T)$, we write the MLM loss as the cross-entropy for predicting the dynamically masked tokens: $\mathcal{L}_{\text{MLM}} = -\frac{1}{|\mathcal{B}|} \sum_{\mathbf{w} \in \mathcal{B}} \log p_\theta(\mathbf{w}_m \mid \mathbf{w}_{\setminus m})$. Further, let $(\tilde{\mathbf{t}}_i^{\text{F}}, \tilde{\mathbf{t}}_i^{\text{I}})$ denote a pair of [CLS] tokens corresponding to the FINDINGS and IMPRESSION sections of the same i^{th} report, and let $(\mathbf{t}_i^{\text{F}}, \mathbf{t}_i^{\text{I}})$ denote the pair projected to a lower dimension via a two-layer perceptron P_{txt}. We introduce a contrastive loss on the text modality that favours IMPRESSION and FINDINGS text pair from the

---

[4] Obtained via https://pubmed.ncbi.nlm.nih.gov/download/.

same report over unmatched ones. Specifically, for a batch of N such pairs, the RSM loss is defined as:

$$\mathcal{L}_{\text{RSM}} = -\frac{1}{N} \sum_{i=1}^{N} \left(\log \frac{\exp(\mathbf{t}_i^{\text{F}} \cdot \mathbf{t}_i^{\text{I}} / \tau_1)}{\sum_{j=1}^{N} \exp(\mathbf{t}_i^{\text{F}} \cdot \mathbf{t}_j^{\text{I}} / \tau_1)} + \log \frac{\exp(\mathbf{t}_i^{\text{I}} \cdot \mathbf{t}_i^{\text{F}} / \tau_1)}{\sum_{j=1}^{N} \exp(\mathbf{t}_i^{\text{I}} \cdot \mathbf{t}_j^{\text{F}} / \tau_1)} \right), \quad (1)$$

where $\tau_1 > 0$ is a scaling parameter to control the margin. The resulting total loss of the specialisation phase (III) is $\mathcal{L}_{\text{III}} = \mathcal{L}_{\text{RSM}} + \lambda_{\text{MLM}} \mathcal{L}_{\text{MLM}}$. An additional important component for regularising the RSM loss is the use of increased dropout (25%), including on attention. We set $\tau_1 = 0.5$ and $\lambda_{\text{MLM}} = 0.1$, determined by a limited grid-search measuring $\mathcal{L}_{\text{GA}}$ (Eq. 2) of the joint model on a validation set. We also note that similar losses to the RSM loss, over the same or separate text segments, have been explored successfully for sentence representation learning [23,50] in other settings. As such, we empirically observed that an objective as in [23] using masked FINDINGS to FINDINGS matching can achieve similar performance and may be an appropriate replacement in other biomedical settings with differing text structure.

Text Augmentation. As domain-specific datasets are often quite small, effective text augmentation can induce large benefits. In the radiology domain, the sentences of the FINDINGS and IMPRESSION sections, which contain the detailed description and summary of the radiological findings, are usually permutation-invariant on the sentence level (cf. [60]). We thus find that randomly shuffling sentences within each section is an effective text-augmentation strategy for both pretraining of CXR-BERT as well as during joint model training.

2.2   BioViL: Vision-Language Representation Learning

We now introduce BioViL, a simple but effective self-supervised VLP setup for the biomedical domain (Fig. 1), which we study in a chest X-ray (CXR) application setting. BioViLuses a convolutional neural network (CNN) [38] image encoder E_{img}, our CXR-BERT text encoder E_{txt}, and projection models P_{img} and P_{txt} to learn representations in a joint space. The CNN model allows us to obtain a grid of local image embeddings $\hat{\mathbf{V}} = E_{\text{img}}(\mathbf{x}_{\text{img}})$, which is fine-grained enough to be useful for segmentation (e.g. 16×16). Each encoder is followed by a modality-specific two-layer perceptron projection model P, which projects the encoded modality to a joint space of 128 dimensions (e.g., $\mathbf{V} = P_{\text{img}}(\tilde{\mathbf{V}})$) where the representation is ℓ_2-normalised. Note that projection should be applied to local embeddings before mean-pooling $\mathbf{v} = \text{pool}(P_{\text{img}}(\tilde{\mathbf{V}}))$, which gives us the global image embedding $\mathbf{v}$. The text branch uses the IMPRESSION section's projected [CLS] token $\mathbf{t}^{\text{I}}$ as the text representation in the joint space, as it contains a succinct summary of radiological findings. To align the representations and learn a joint embedding, we propose to use two loss terms. For a batch of size N, a symmetric contrastive loss [58] for *global alignment* of the image and text projections helps us learn the shared latent semantics:

$$\mathcal{L}_{\text{GA}} = -\frac{1}{N} \sum_{i=1}^{N} \left(\log \frac{\exp(\mathbf{v}_i \cdot \mathbf{t}_i^{\text{I}}/\tau_2)}{\sum_{j=1}^{N} \exp(\mathbf{v}_i \cdot \mathbf{t}_j^{\text{I}}/\tau_2)} + \log \frac{\exp(\mathbf{t}_i^{\text{I}} \cdot \mathbf{v}_i/\tau_2)}{\sum_{j=1}^{N} \exp(\mathbf{t}_i^{\text{I}} \cdot \mathbf{v}_j/\tau_2)} \right). \quad (2)$$

where $\tau_2 > 0$ is a scaling parameter. Further, we maintain the $\mathcal{L}_{\text{MLM}}$ loss during joint training, resulting in the final joint loss $\mathcal{L}_{\text{joint}} = \lambda_{\text{GA}}\mathcal{L}_{\text{GA}} + \mathcal{L}_{\text{MLM}}$. We set $\tau_2 = 0.5$ and $\lambda_{\text{GA}} = 0.5$, determined by a limited grid search measuring $\mathcal{L}_{\text{GA}}$ on a validation set.

Augmentations, Regularisation, and Image Encoder Pretraining. Due to the small dataset sizes expected in biomedical applications, we use image and text augmentations to help learn known invariances. We use a ResNet-50 [29] architecture as our image encoder and pretrain the model on MIMIC-CXR images using SimCLR [6] with domain-specific augmentations as detailed in Sect. 4.1. For text, we use the same sentence-shuffling augmentation as in pretraining of CXR-BERT (see Sect. 4.1 for details). Furthermore, as in phase (III) of CXR-BERT training, we apply higher text encoder dropout (25%) than in standard BERT settings [17,73]. We find that the combination of all these components, including continuous MLM optimisation, is important to improve downstream performance across the board (see ablation in Table 4).

Zero-Shot Classification. After joint training, we use text prompts to cast the zero-shot classification problem into an image–text similarity task as in [31,61,62]. For C classes, subject-matter experts design C text prompts representing the target labels $c \in \{1, \ldots, C\}$, e.g. for presence or absence of pneumonia (see Sect. 4.5). Each class prompt is represented as a vector of tokens $\mathbf{w}^c$ and passed to the text encoder and projector of BioViL to obtain ℓ_2-normalised text features $\mathbf{t}^c = P_{\text{txt}}(E_{\text{txt}}(\mathbf{w}^c)) \in \mathbb{R}^{128}$. For each input image $\mathbf{x}_{\text{img}} \in \mathbb{R}^{H \times W}$, we use the image encoder and projection module to obtain patch embeddings $\mathbf{V} = P_{\text{img}}(E_{\text{img}}(\mathbf{x}_{\text{img}})) \in \mathbb{R}^{\frac{H}{16} \times \frac{W}{16} \times 128}$ for segmentation tasks or the pooled embedding $\mathbf{v} = \text{pool}(\mathbf{V}) \in \mathbb{R}^{128}$ for instance-classification. We use dilated convolutions [82] to obtain higher-resolution feature maps. Probabilities for classes/regions can then be computed via a softmax over the cosine similarities between the image (or region) and prompt representations.

Few-Shot Tasks with BioViL. To further assess the representation quality, linear probing is applied to local ($\mathbf{V}$) and global ($\mathbf{v}$) image representations, by learning $\boldsymbol{\beta} \in \mathbb{R}^{128 \times C}$ weights and a bias term. Unlike [31,85], we leverage the pretrained projectors and class text embedding $\mathbf{t}^c$ from the zero-shot setting by using them for initialisation, which leads to improved performance and further reduces the need for manual label collection. Specifically, in few-shot classification settings, the weights and bias are initialised with $\boldsymbol{\beta} = [\mathbf{t}^1, \ldots, \mathbf{t}^C]$ and zeros, respectively.

3   Evaluating Self-supervised Biomedical VLP

Accurate local alignment between modalities is an important characteristic of successful joint image-text training in healthcare, in particular since image and

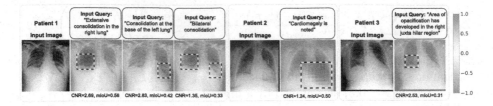

Fig. 3. Examples from the newly released MS-CXR phrase grounding dataset with BioViL latent vector similarity for different input text queries superimposed as heatmaps. Dashed boxes are ground-truth annotations by radiologists. X-ray images are mirrored horizontally.

report samples often contain multiple clinical findings, each of which correspond to distinct image regions. Standard global-alignment approaches may attain high classification accuracy by overfitting to spurious image features for a given finding (e.g., chest tubes in images correlating with mentions of pneumothorax in reports). Image classification, the most frequently evaluated downstream task in related work [31,45,56,85], requires only scene-level labels, hence a less sophisticated understanding of natural-language image descriptions. Image classification tasks can largely be solved by simply detecting a small set of words and maintaining some understanding of negation, as exemplified by the development of automated, rule-based text-labellers such as CheXpert [33]. Instance-level image-text retrieval tasks address some evaluation limitations, but do not require the level of language reasoning needed to solve local correspondence between phrases and image regions. Existing public CXR benchmark datasets to evaluate local aspects of VLP have one or more of the following limitations (see Sect. 5 and Supp. C, D for more details): bounding boxes without corresponding free text descriptions, a limited number of samples, a limited number of abnormalities, and non-curated phrases impacting evaluation quality.

With this motivation in mind, we design MS-CXR, a radiology visual-grounding benchmark that has domain-specific language (e.g., paraphrasing and negations) and forms a more challenging real-world image-text reasoning task compared to existing evaluation datasets. To name just a few challenges, the phrase grounding task requires the ability to parse domain specific location modifiers, the ability to deal with reporting style biases, and understanding of complex negations, all while relating the correct findings to specific image regions.

3.1   MS-CXR – A Chest X-Ray Phrase Grounding Benchmark

We publicly release MS-CXR, a new dataset containing image bounding box labels paired with radiology text descriptions, annotated and verified by two board-certified radiologists (see examples in Figs. 3 and C.1). MS-CXR provides 1153 image–sentence pairs of bounding boxes and corresponding phrases, collected across eight different cardiopulmonary radiological findings, with an approximately equal number of pairs for each finding (see Table C.1). It is curated to ensure gold-standard evaluation of phrase grounding. The phrases in MS-CXR are

Table 2. Comparing evaluations conducted in recent CXR image-text alignment studies.

Downstream task	Used in ref.*	Image encoder	Text encoder	Phrase reasoning	Findings localisation	Latent alignment	Annotation availability
Natural language inference	[B]	-	✓	✓	–	–	Scarce
Phrase grounding	[B]	✓	✓	✓	✓	✓	Scarce
Image classification	[B,C,G,L,M]	✓	–	–	–	–	High
Zero-shot image classif	[B,G]	✓	✓	–	–	✓	Moderate
Dense image prediction (e.g. segmentation)	[B,G,L]	✓	–	–	✓	–	High
Global image–text retrieval	[C,G]	✓	✓	–	–	✓	High

*B, BioViL (Proposed); C, ConVIRT [85]; G, GLoRIA [31]; L, LoVT [56]; M, Local MI [45].

not simple short captions, but genuine descriptions of radiological findings from original radiology reports [34] and dictated transcripts [37]. Thus, compared to existing evaluation datasets, the proposed benchmark is a more challenging real-world image-text reasoning task.

All the benchmark samples are chosen from the public MIMIC-CXR dataset [24,34]. To collect a set of bounding-box labels, we first select samples from a set of studies with pre-existing image annotations (e.g., ellipses) [37,71] and verify their correctness. To link each image region with candidate phrases, we sampled sentences from the report of each study by extracting the highest matching sentences to the annotated labels using scores of the CheXbert classifier [69], and also used transcriptions of dictations when available [37]. Next, to better balance findings, we sampled additional studies at random as well as the ones used in the ImaGenome dataset [79], the latter being a dataset of annotations of anatomical regions. Note that these sampled studies do not have preexisting region proposals. Radiologists then manually reviewed separate sets of candidates. If a bounding box was not available, the radiologists manually annotated the corresponding region(s) in the image with new bounding boxes. Radiologists rejected studies where no correct phrase candidates were available and where existing bounding boxes were placed incorrectly (e.g., covering too large an area). To ensure a high quality, consistent benchmark, the phrase-image samples that do not adhere to our guidelines (see Supp. C.1) were filtered out, such as phrases containing multiple abnormalities in distinct lung regions.

4   Experiments

We conduct a comprehensive evaluation of our CXR-BERT language model as well as the proposed BioViL self-supervised VLP approach, and compare both to state-of-the art counterparts. Table 2 shows how our evaluation coverage compares to recent related studies. We begin by demonstrating CXR-BERT's superior performance and improved vocabulary, including on a radiology-specific NLI benchmark. Next, we assess joint image-and-text understanding of BioViL on our new MS-CXR benchmark, which evaluates grounding of phrases describing radiological findings to the corresponding image regions. We also investigate zero-shot classification and fine-tuning performance of BioViL on image- and pixel-level prediction tasks via the RSNA pneumonia dataset [66,76].

4.1   Setup

Datasets. We conduct experiments on the MIMIC-CXR v2 [24,34] chest radiograph dataset, which provides 227,835 imaging studies with associated radiology reports for 65,379 patients, all collected in routine clinical practice. We only use frontal view scans (AP and PA) and also discard studies without an IMPRESSION section. From this data, we establish a training set of 146.7k samples and a set of 22.2k validation samples, ensuring that all samples used for the different downstream evaluations are kept in a held-out test set. We emphasise that no labels are used during pretraining; for early stopping only a loss on validation data is tracked. For evaluation, we use RadNLI [54] to assess the proposed CXR-BERT text model in isolation, the new MS-CXR assesses joint image–text understanding via phrase grounding, and the RSNA Pneumonia dataset [66,76] to test zero-shot segmentation, as well as zero-shot and fine-tuned classification performance.

Image and Text Pre-processing. We downsize and centre crop images to a resolution of 512×512 whilst preserving image aspect ratios. We perform image augmentations during training including: random affine transformations, random colour jitter, and horizontal flips (only for image fine-tuning tasks). For text model pre-training we utilise the 'FINDINGS' and 'IMPRESSION' sections of reports, while joint training is performed using only the latter. During training, we perform sentence shuffling within sections as text-augmentation. Additionally, we perform limited automatic typo correction as in [5].

Comparison Approaches. The proposed CXR-BERT text model is compared to the other specialised PubMedBERT [26] and ClinicalBERT [2] models. Note that ClinicalBERT was used in most related studies [31,45,56,85]. We compare BioViL to the closely related, state-of-the-art ConVIRT [85], LoVT [56] and GLoRIA [31] approaches (see Sect. 5). Lastly, we create BioViL-L by extending BioViL with the local loss term introduced in [31] to illustrate the complementary role of proposed pre-training strategy to recent advances in biomedical VLP.

Metrics. We report segmentation results via mean intersection over union (mIoU) and contrast-to-noise ratio (CNR), and report the Dice score [10] to compare to [56]. We first compute the cosine similarity between a projected phrase embedding $\mathbf{t}$ and local image representations $\mathbf{V}$, resulting in a grid of scores between $[-1, 1]$. The similarities are later thresholded to compute mIoU and Dice score. The mIoU is defined as an average over the thresholds $[0.1, 0.2, 0.3, 0.4, 0.5]$. The CNR measures the discrepancy between scores inside and out of the bounding box region, without requiring hard thresholds. This evaluation of local similarities is important as some clinical downstream applications may benefit from heatmap visualisations as opposed to discrete segmentations. For CNR, let A and $\overline{A}$ denote the interior and exterior of the bounding box, respectively. We then compute $\mathrm{CNR} = |\mu_A - \mu_{\overline{A}}|/(\sigma_A^2 + \sigma_{\overline{A}}^2)^{\frac{1}{2}}$, where μ_X and σ_X^2 are the mean and variance of the similarity values in region X.

Table 3. Evaluation of text encoder intrinsic properties and fine-tuning for radiology natural language inference: (1) RadNLI fine-tuning scores (average of 5 runs); (2) Mask prediction accuracy on MIMIC-CXR val. set; (3) Vocabulary comparison, number of tokens vs. original number of words in FINDINGS, increase shown as percentage.

	RadNLI accuracy (MedNLI transfer)	Mask prediction accuracy	Avg. # of tokens after tokenization	Vocabulary size
RadNLI baseline [54]	53.30	-	-	-
ClinicalBERT	47.67	39.84	78.98 (+38.15%)	28,996
PubMedBERT	57.71	35.24	63.55 (+11.16%)	28,895
CXR-BERT (after Phase-III)	60.46	77.72	58.07 (+1.59%)	30,522
CXR-BERT (after Phase-III + Joint Training)	65.21	81.58	58.07 (+1.59%)	30,522

4.2 Text Model Evaluation

Natural Language Understanding. We use the RadNLI benchmark [54] to evaluate how well the proposed CXR-BERT text model captures domain-specific semantics. The dataset contains labelled hypothesis and premise pairs, sourced from MIMIC-CXR radiology reports, with the following label categories: (1) entailment, i.e. the hypothesis can be inferred from the premise; (2) contradiction, i.e. the hypothesis cannot be inferred from the premise; and (3) neutral, i.e. the inference relation is undetermined. RadNLI provides expert-annotated development and test sets (480 examples each), but no official training set. Thus, following [54], we use MedNLI [67] for training, which has 11k samples sourced from MIMIC-III discharge summaries, with equally distributed NLI labels. We fine-tune the language models up to 20 epochs and use early stopping by monitoring accuracy scores on the RadNLI development set. Table 3 summarises the NLI evaluation, masked token prediction, and subword tokenisation results. Using only MedNLI training samples, our model achieves a good accuracy of 65.21%, and far outperforms fine-tuned ClinicalBERT, PubMedBERT, and the score reported in RadNLI [54]. Another important result is that RadNLI accuracy improves after joint training with images (last row of Table 3).

Mask Prediction Accuracy. While mask prediction accuracy does not always translate to downstream application performance, it is an auxiliary metric that captures important aspects of a language model's grasp of a target domain. We report Top-1 mask prediction accuracy on radiology reports in the MIMIC-CXR validation set (Table 3), and follow the standard masking configuration (15% masking probability). Despite being trained on closely related data, our CXR-BERT displays a much better mask prediction accuracy compared to ClinicalBERT (trained on MIMIC-III, which includes radiology reports) and PubMedBERT (trained on biomedical literature text). This suggests that radiology text significantly differs from other clinical text or biomedical literature text, highlighting the need for specialised text encoder models.

Ablation. We also conduct an ablation of the various aspects of CXR-BERT, measuring the impact after joint training. Table 4 shows that all components of CXR-BERT contribute to improved downstream and NLI performance, both in terms of alignment between related sentences (entailments) and of discrimination of contradictions. In particular, note the substantial improvement on these scores due to keeping the MLM objective during joint finetuning.

Table 4. CXR-BERT ablation. CNR and mIoU are macro averages of BioViL performance on all categories of MS-CXR. *Syn. sim.* denotes the average cosine similarity between RadNLI entailments. *Cont. gap* is the average similarity gap of RadNLI entailment and contradiction pairs. CXR-BERT is the combination of all components below the first row.

	RadNLI		Grounding	
Model or pretraining stage	Syn. sim	Cont. gap	mIoU	CNR
ClinicalBERT	.657	.609	.182	0.791
Pretrain & Vocab (I–II)	.749	.646	.194	0.796
+ MLM loss added to joint training	.871	.745	.209	0.860
+ Use of attention drop-out (III)	.893	.802	.217	0.945
+ RSM Pretrain (III)	.877	.779	.220	1.012
+ Sentence shuffling (CXR-BERT)	.884	.798	.220	1.031

4.3   Local Alignment Evaluation – Phrase Grounding

We perform a phrase grounding evaluation of the pretrained BioViL model on the MS-CXR dataset. For each image–phrase pair, the image is passed to the CNN image encoder and projected to obtain a grid of image representations $\mathbf{V}$ in the joint space. Similarly, the phrase is embedded via the text encoder and projected to the joint space to obtain $\mathbf{t}$. Cosine similarity between $\mathbf{t}$ and elements of $\mathbf{V}$ produces a similarity grid, which is evaluated against the ground-truth bounding boxes. Table 5 shows the superior phrase grounding results achieved by BioViL across radiological findings and further shows that the addition of local losses as in our BioViL-L can improve phrase grounding performance for almost all findings. Moreover, the ablation in Table 4 demonstrates that there are clear gains to be had in visual grounding performance by improving the text model.

Table 5. Contrast-to-noise ratio (CNR) obtained on the newly released MS-CXR dataset, averaged over four runs with different seeds. The results are collected using different text encoder and training objectives (e.g., G&L: Global and local loss).

Method	Objective	Text encoder	Atelectasis	Cardiomegaly	Consolidation	Lung opacity	Edema	Pneumonia	Pneumothorax	Pl. effusion	Avg
Baseline	Global	ClinicalBERT	0.70±.03	0.53±.04	1.15±.07	0.75±.12	0.83±.04	0.85±.09	0.29±.01	1.05±.05	0.769±.02
Baseline	Global	PubMedBERT	0.72±.08	0.64±.05	1.22±.07	0.69±.07	0.80±.04	0.91±.09	0.21±.07	0.99±.03	0.773±.05
ConVIRT [85]	Global	ClinicalBERT	0.86±.04	0.64±.06	1.25±.06	0.78±.07	0.68±.07	1.03±.05	0.28±.08	1.02±.03	0.818±.01
GLoRIA [31]	G&L	ClinicalBERT	0.98±.04	0.53±.31	1.38±.03	1.05±.04	0.66±.03	1.18±.04	0.47±.02	1.20±.04	0.930±.03
BioViL	Global	CXR-BERT	1.02±.06	0.63±.08	1.42±.02	1.05±.06	0.93±.03	1.27±.04	0.48±.06	1.40±.06	1.027±.02
BioViL-L	G&L	CXR-BERT	1.17±.04	0.95±.21	1.45±.03	1.19±.05	0.96±.05	1.19±.01	0.74±.05	1.50±.03	1.142±.04

Table 6. RSNA Pneumonia zero-shot and fine-tuned classification. We compare to GLoRIA scores reported in [31] which outperforms ConVIRT [85] (see [31]). Training size: GLoRIA ($N = 186k$, private dataset), BioViL ($N = 146.7k$ of MIMIC-CXR).

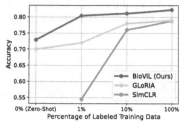

Method	Type	Text model	Loss	% of labels	Acc.	F1	AUROC
SimCLR [6]	Image only	-	Global	1%	0.545	0.522	0.701
				10%	0.760	0.639	0.802
				100%	0.788	0.675	0.849
GLoRIA [31]	Joint	ClinicalBERT	Global & local	Zero shot	0.70	0.58	-
				1%	0.72	0.63	0.861
				10%	0.78	0.63	0.880
				100%	0.79	0.65	0.886
Baseline	Joint	ClinicalBERT	Global	Zero-shot	0.719	0.614	0.812
BioViL	Joint	CXR-BERT	Global	Zero-shot	0.732	0.665	0.831
				1%	0.805	0.723	0.881
				10%	0.812	0.727	0.884
				100%	0.822	0.733	0.891

4.4 Global Alignment Evaluation – Zero-Shot and Linear Probing

To measure global alignment quality, the joint models are also benchmarked on zero-/few-shot binary pneumonia classification problems (image-level) using the external RSNA dataset [66]. Fine-tuning is done via linear probing, i.e. only a last linear layer is trained. The evaluation is conducted on $\mathcal{D}_{\text{test}} = 9006$ images as in [31] (30% eval./70% train.) using the dataset's ground-truth labels. We define two simple text prompts for BioViL, representing presence/absence of pneumonia: "Findings suggesting pneumonia" and "No evidence of pneumonia". The image encoders are utilised and fine-tuned as described in Sect. 2.2.

The zero-shot and fine-tuned results in Table 6 show that our focus on better text modelling results in improved joint modelling of shared latent information between text-image pairs. Note that, to achieve its superior performance here and in Sect. 4.5, BioViL does not require extensive human expert text-prompt engineering (see Supp. A.1 for a sensitivity analysis) as for example conducted in GLoRIA [31], where variations over severity and/or location were created.

4.5 Local Alignment Evaluation – Semantic Segmentation

We evaluate models on an RSNA pneumonia segmentation task, using grid-level image representations in the joint latent space. We use the same text prompts as in the previous section for all models, and evaluate against ground-truth bounding boxes of the RSNA pneumonia dataset ($|\mathcal{D}_{\text{train}}| = 6634$ and $|\mathcal{D}_{\text{test}}| = 2907$). Table 7 shows that BioViL significantly reduces the need for dense annotations as compared to similar multi-modal and image-only pretraining approaches, outperforming them when using the same number of labelled data points. Note that

Table 7. RSNA pneumonia segmentation, showing *Zero-shot* and *linear probing* results. Related work is reproduced in the same experimental setup except for LoVT [56].

Method	% of Labels	Supervision	IoU	Dice	CNR
LoVT [56]	100%	Lin. prob.	–	0.518	–
ConVIRT [85]	–	Zero-shot	0.228	0.348	0.849
GLoRIA [31]	–	Zero-shot	0.245	0.366	1.052
BioViL	–	Zero-shot	0.355	0.496	1.477
SimCLR [6]	5%	Lin. prob.	0.382	0.525	1.722
SimCLR [6]	100%	Lin. prob.	0.427	0.570	1.922
BioViL	5%	Lin. prob.	0.446	0.592	2.077
BioViL	100%	Lin. prob.	0.469	0.614	2.178

our proposed modelling framework BioViL (Fig. 1), uses neither a local loss term [31,56], nor a separate object detection [63] or segmentation network [65]. Further, while Table 7 shows results using two simple queries, we find that BioViL continues to outperform related work even when more prompts are used for all models as in [31]. Dice and IoU are computed using the same threshold of 0.6 on predictions scaled between [0, 1].

5   Related Work

We refer the reader to Supp. D for a more detailed review of related work.

Biomedical Vision–Language Processing. Multiple studies explore joint representation learning for paired image and text radiology data [30,31,45,56,85]. [85] follow a contrastive learning formulation for instance-level representation learning, while [31,56] introduce approaches that combine instance-level radiology image–report learning with local terms. An alternative, local-only objective is explored by [45], approximating the mutual information between local image features and sentence-level text features. While most related approaches use no ground truth, [5] study a semi-supervised edema severity classification setting, and [28] assume sets of seen and unseen labels towards CXR zero-shot classification.

Related medical VLP work commonly uses publicly available contextual word embedding models including BioBERT [39], ClinicalBERT [2], BioClinicalBERT [2], or PubMedBERT [26]. The models are either trained from scratch or fine-tuned via continual pretraining using an MLM objective. Additional objectives such as adversarial losses [47] are added infrequently. The specialised corpora these models use include PubMed abstracts and PubMed Central full texts (see [2]), as well as MIMIC-III [35] clinical notes.

Local Alignment Datasets. Presently, no datasets exist that allow for phrase grounding of radiology findings, but some enable different forms of local image evaluations. VinDr [57], RSNA Pneumonia [66], and the NIH Chest X-ray Dataset [76] provide bounding-box annotations, but lack free-text descriptions. REFLACX [37] provides gaze locations (ellipses) captured with an eye tracker, dictated reports, and some ground truth annotations for gaze locations, but no full phrase matches to image regions. Phrase annotations for MIMIC-CXR data released in [71] are of small size (350 studies), only contain two abnormalities, and for some samples have shortened phrases that were adapted to simplify the task. The ground-truth set of ImaGenome [79] only contains 500 studies, bounding-box regions annotate anatomical regions rather than radiological findings, and its sentence annotations are not curated for grounding evaluation.

6   Conclusion

We show that careful attention to text modelling can lead to large benefits for all learned models in self-supervised vision language processing (VLP) frameworks for medical applications. We introduce a novel pretraining procedure and publicly release a radiology domain-specific language model: CXR-BERT. It has an improved vocabulary and understanding of radiology sentences, contributing to improved downstream performance for all aspects of VLP approaches, e.g., the superior performance on a radiology natural language inference benchmark.

We also present BioViL, as a simple yet effective baseline for self-supervised multi-modal learning for paired image–text radiology data, with a focus on improved text modelling. The approach displays state-of-the-art performance on a large number of downstream tasks evaluating global and local aspects of the image model, text model, and joint latent space. On zero-shot tasks, the model does not require extensive text-prompt engineering compared to prior work. Notably, it outperforms related work on segmentation without requiring a local loss term or an additional vision model to produce region proposals. In that regard, it is complementary to local contrastive losses, and the combination of the two yields improved phrase grounding performance (Table 5).

To support the research community in evaluating fine-grained image–text understanding in the radiology domain, we also publicly release a chest X-ray phrase grounding dataset called MS-CXR. It presents a more challenging benchmark for joint image–text understanding compared to existing datasets, requiring reasoning over real-world radiology language and scans to ground findings in the correct image locations. Limitations of the proposed joint approach include that it does not explicitly deal with false negatives in the contrastive losses. Furthermore, co-occurrence of multiple abnormalities could enable contrastive methods to focus only on a subset to match pairs, e.g. pneumothorax and chest tubes commonly occur together [25]. Amongst its failure cases (see Supp. A.2 for more), we have seen that the approach struggles with very small structures, likely due to image resolution limits. Future work will expand the evaluated radiological findings, and explore using larger image resolution.

Acknowledgements. We would like to thank Dr Javier González and Fernando Pérez-García for their valuable feedback and contributions, Hannah Richardson for helping with the compliance review of the datasets, and Dr Matthew Lungren for their clinical input and data annotations provided to this study.

References

1. Akbari, H., Karaman, S., Bhargava, S., Chen, B., Vondrick, C., Chang, S.F.: Multi-level multimodal common semantic space for image-phrase grounding. In: Proceedings of the IEEE Conference on Computer Vision and Pattern Recognition, CVPR 2019, Long Beach, CA, USA, 16–20 June 2019, pp. 12476–12486. Computer Vision Foundation/IEEE (2019). https://doi.org/10.1109/CVPR.2019.01276

2. Alsentzer, E., et al.: Publicly available clinical BERT embeddings. In: Proceedings of the 2nd Clinical Natural Language Processing Workshop, pp. 72–78. Association for Computational Linguistics, Minneapolis, Minnesota (2019). https://doi.org/10.18653/v1/W19-1909, https://aclanthology.org/W19-1909

3. Bustos, A., Pertusa, A., Salinas, J.M., de la Iglesia-Vayá, M.: PadChest: a large chest X-ray image dataset with multi-label annotated reports. Med. Image Anal. **66**, 101797 (2020)

4. Casey, A., et al.: A systematic review of natural language processing applied to radiology reports. BMC Med. Inf. Decis. Making **21**(1), 1–18 (2021)

5. Chauhan, G., et al.: Joint modeling of chest radiographs and radiology reports for pulmonary edema assessment. In: Martel, A.L., et al. (eds.) MICCAI 2020. LNCS, vol. 12262, pp. 529–539. Springer, Cham (2020). https://doi.org/10.1007/978-3-030-59713-9_51

6. Chen, T., Kornblith, S., Norouzi, M., Hinton, G.: A simple framework for contrastive learning of visual representations. In: III, H.D., Singh, A. (eds.) Proceedings of the 37th International Conference on Machine Learning, ICML 2020, 13–18 July 2020, Virtual Event. Proceedings of Machine Learning Research, vol. 119, pp. 1597–1607. PMLR (13–18 Jul 2020), http://proceedings.mlr.press/v119/chen20j.html

7. Chen, Y.-C.: UNITER: universal image-text representation learning. In: Vedaldi, A., Bischof, H., Brox, T., Frahm, J.-M. (eds.) ECCV 2020. LNCS, vol. 12375, pp. 104–120. Springer, Cham (2020). https://doi.org/10.1007/978-3-030-58577-8_7

8. Chen, Z., Song, Y., Chang, T.H., Wan, X.: Generating radiology reports via memory-driven transformer. In: Proceedings of the 2020 Conference on Empirical Methods in Natural Language Processing (EMNLP). Association for Computational Linguistics (2020). https://doi.org/10.18653/v1/2020.emnlp-main.112, https://aclanthology.org/2020.emnlp-main.112

9. Chilamkurthy, S., et al.: Deep learning algorithms for detection of critical findings in head CT scans: a retrospective study. Lancet **392**(10162), 2388–2396 (2018)

10. Crum, W.R., Camara, O., Hill, D.L.: Generalized overlap measures for evaluation and validation in medical image analysis. IEEE Trans. Med. Imaging **25**(11), 1451–1461 (2006)

11. Dai, S., Wang, Q., Lyu, Y., Zhu, Y.: BDKG at MEDIQA 2021: system report for the radiology report summarization task. In: Proceedings of the 20th Workshop on Biomedical Language Processing, pp. 103–111. Association for Computational Linguistics (2021). https://doi.org/10.18653/v1/2021.bionlp-1.11, https://aclanthology.org/2021.bionlp-1.11

12. Datta, S., Sikka, K., Roy, A., Ahuja, K., Parikh, D., Divakaran, A.: Align2Ground: weakly supervised phrase grounding guided by image-caption alignment. In: Proceedings of the IEEE/CVF International Conference on Computer Vision, ICCV 2019, Seoul, Korea (South), 27 October–2 November 2019, pp. 2601–2610. IEEE (2019). https://doi.org/10.1109/ICCV.2019.00269

13. Datta, S., Roberts, K.: A hybrid deep learning approach for spatial trigger extraction from radiology reports. In: Proceedings of the Third International Workshop on Spatial Language Understanding, vol. 2020, pp. 50–55. Association for Computational Linguistics (2020). https://doi.org/10.18653/v1/2020.splu-1.6, https://aclanthology.org/2020.splu-1.6

14. Datta, S., Si, Y., Rodriguez, L., Shooshan, S.E., Demner-Fushman, D., Roberts, K.: Understanding spatial language in radiology: representation framework, annotation, and spatial relation extraction from chest X-ray reports using deep learning. J. Biomed. Inf. **108**, 103473 (2020)

15. Demner-Fushman, D., et al.: Preparing a collection of radiology examinations for distribution and retrieval. J. Am. Med. Inf. Assoc. **23**(2), 304–310 (2016)

16. Desai, K., Johnson, J.: VirTex: learning visual representations from textual annotations. In: Proceedings of the IEEE/CVF Conference on Computer Vision and Pattern Recognition, pp. 11162–11173 (2021)

17. Devlin, J., Chang, M.W., Lee, K., Toutanova, K.: BERT: pre-training of deep bidirectional transformers for language understanding. In: Proceedings of the 2019 Conference of the North American Chapter of the Association for Computational Linguistics: Human Language Technologies, Volume 1 (Long and Short Papers), pp. 4171–4186. Association for Computational Linguistics, Minneapolis, Minnesota (2019). https://doi.org/10.18653/v1/N19-1423, https://aclanthology.org/N19-1423

18. Dligach, D., Bethard, S., Becker, L., Miller, T., Savova, G.K.: Discovering body site and severity modifiers in clinical texts. J. Am. Med. Inf. Assoc. **21**(3), 448–454 (2014)

19. Dunnmon, J.A., et al.: Cross-modal data programming enables rapid medical machine learning. Patterns **1**(2), 100019 (2020)

20. Esteva, A., et al.: Dermatologist-level classification of skin cancer with deep neural networks. Nature **542**(7639), 115–118 (2017)

21. Eyuboglu, S., et al.: Multi-task weak supervision enables anatomically-resolved abnormality detection in whole-body FDG-PET/CT. Nature Commun. **12**(1), 1–15 (2021)

22. Fang, H., et al.: From captions to visual concepts and back. In: IEEE Conference on Computer Vision and Pattern Recognition, CVPR 2015, Boston, MA, USA, 7–12 June 2015, pp. 1473–1482. IEEE Computer Society (2015). https://doi.org/10.1109/CVPR.2015.7298754

23. Gao, T., Yao, X., Chen, D.: SimCSE: simple contrastive learning of sentence embeddings. In: Proceedings of the 2021 Conference on Empirical Methods in Natural Language Processing, pp. 6894–6910 (2021)

24. Goldberger, A.L., et al.: PhysioBank, PhysioToolkit, and PhysioNet: components of a new research resource for complex physiologic signals. Circulation **101**(23), e215–e220 (2000)

25. Graf, B., et al.: Pneumothorax and chest tube classification on chest X-rays for detection of missed pneumothorax. Machine Learning for Health (ML4H) NeurIPS Workshop: Extended Abstract (2020). https://arxiv.org/abs/2011.07353

26. Gu, Y., et al.: Domain-specific language model pretraining for biomedical natural language processing. ACM Trans. Comput. Healthc. (HEALTH) **3**(1), 1–23 (2021)

27. Gupta, T., Vahdat, A., Chechik, G., Yang, X., Kautz, J., Hoiem, D.: Contrastive learning for weakly supervised phrase grounding. In: Vedaldi, A., Bischof, H., Brox, T., Frahm, J.-M. (eds.) ECCV 2020. LNCS, vol. 12348, pp. 752–768. Springer, Cham (2020). https://doi.org/10.1007/978-3-030-58580-8_44

28. Hayat, N., Lashen, H., Shamout, F.E.: Multi-label generalized zero shot learning for the classiffcation of disease in chest radiographs. In: Machine Learning for Healthcare Conference, pp. 461–477. PMLR (2021)

29. He, K., Zhang, X., Ren, S., Sun, J.: Deep residual learning for image recognition. In: Proceedings of the IEEE Conference on Computer Vision and Pattern Recognition, pp. 770–778. IEEE Computer Society (2016). https://doi.org/10.1109/CVPR.2016.90

30. Hsu, T.M.H., Weng, W.H., Boag, W., McDermott, M., Szolovits, P.: Unsupervised multimodal representation learning across medical images and reports. Machine Learning for Health (ML4H) NeurIPS Workshop (2018). https://arxiv.org/abs/1811.08615

31. Huang, S.C., Shen, L., Lungren, M.P., Yeung, S.: GLoRIA: a multimodal global-local representation learning framework for label-efficient medical image recognition. In: Proceedings of the IEEE/CVF International Conference on Computer Vision, pp. 3942–3951 (2021)

32. Ioffe, S., Szegedy, C.: Batch normalization: Accelerating deep network training by reducing internal covariate shift. In: International Conference on Machine Learning, pp. 448–456. PMLR (2015)
33. Irvin, J., et al.: CheXpert: a large chest radiograph dataset with uncertainty labels and expert comparison. In: Thirty-Third AAAI Conference on Artificial Intelligence, pp. 590–597. AAAI Press (2019). https://doi.org/10.1609/aaai.v33i01.3301590
34. Johnson, A., Pollard, T., Berkowitz, S., Mark, R., Horng, S.: MIMIC-CXR database (version 2.0.0). PhysioNet (2019)
35. Johnson, A.E., et al.: MIMIC-III, a freely accessible critical care database. Sci. Data **3**(1), 1–9 (2016)
36. Joulin, A., van der Maaten, L., Jabri, A., Vasilache, N.: Learning visual features from large weakly supervised data. In: Leibe, B., Matas, J., Sebe, N., Welling, M. (eds.) ECCV 2016. LNCS, vol. 9911, pp. 67–84. Springer, Cham (2016). https://doi.org/10.1007/978-3-319-46478-7_5
37. Lanfredi, R.B., et al.: REFLACX, a dataset of reports and eye-tracking data for localization of abnormalities in chest x-rays. arXiv preprint arXiv:2109.14187 (2021). https://doi.org/10.13026/e0dj-8498
38. LeCun, Y., et al.: Backpropagation applied to handwritten zip code recognition. Neural Comput. **1**(4), 541–551 (1989)
39. Lee, J., et al.: BioBERT: a pre-trained biomedical language representation model for biomedical text mining. Bioinf. **36**(4), 1234–1240 (2020)
40. Li, A., Jabri, A., Joulin, A., Van Der Maaten, L.: Learning visual n-grams from web data. In: IEEE International Conference on Computer Vision, ICCV 2017, Venice, Italy, 22–29 October 2017, pp. 4183–4192. IEEE Computer Society (2017). https://doi.org/10.1109/ICCV.2017.449, http://doi.ieeecomputersociety.org/10.1109/ICCV.2017.449
41. Li, G., Duan, N., Fang, Y., Gong, M., Jiang, D.: Unicoder-VL: a universal encoder for vision and language by cross-modal pre-training. In: The Thirty-Fourth AAAI Conference on Artificial Intelligence, AAAI 2020, The Thirty-Second Innovative Applications of Artificial Intelligence Conference, IAAI 2020, The Tenth AAAI Symposium on Educational Advances in Artificial Intelligence, EAAI 2020, New York, NY, USA, 7–12 February 2020, vol. 34, no. 7, pp. 11336–11344. AAAI Press (2020). https://aaai.org/ojs/index.php/AAAI/article/view/6795
42. Li, L.H., Yatskar, M., Yin, D., Hsieh, C.J., Chang, K.W.: VisualBERT: a simple and performant baseline for vision and language. arXiv preprint arXiv:1908.03557 (2019)
43. Li, Y., et al.: Supervision exists everywhere: a data efficient contrastive language-image pre-training paradigm. arXiv preprint arXiv:2110.05208 (2021)
44. Li, Y., Wang, H., Luo, Y.: A comparison of pre-trained vision-and-language models for multimodal representation learning across medical images and reports. In: 2020 IEEE International Conference on Bioinformatics and Biomedicine (BIBM), pp. 1999–2004. IEEE (2020)
45. Liao, R., et al.: Multimodal representation learning via maximization of local mutual information. In: de Bruijne, M., et al. (eds.) MICCAI 2021. LNCS, vol. 12902, pp. 273–283. Springer, Cham (2021). https://doi.org/10.1007/978-3-030-87196-3_26
46. Liu, G., et al.: Clinically accurate chest X-ray report generation. In: Machine Learning for Healthcare Conference, pp. 249–269. PMLR (2019)
47. Liu, X., et al.: Adversarial training for large neural language models. arXiv preprint arXiv:2004.08994 (2020)

48. Liu, Y., et al.: RoBERTa: a robustly optimized bert pretraining approach. arXiv preprint arXiv:1907.11692 (2019)
49. Liu, Y., Wan, B., Ma, L., He, X.: Relation-aware instance refinement for weakly supervised visual grounding. In: Proceedings of the IEEE/CVF Conference on Computer Vision and Pattern Recognition, pp. 5612–5621 (2021)
50. Logeswaran, L., Lee, H.: An efficient framework for learning sentence representations. In: 6th International Conference on Learning Representations, ICLR 2018, Vancouver, BC, Canada, 30 April - 3 May 2018, Conference Track Proceedings. OpenReview.net (2018). https://openreview.net/forum?id=rJvJXZb0W
51. Loshchilov, I., Hutter, F.: Decoupled weight decay regularization. In: International Conference on Learning Representations (2018). https://openreview.net/forum?id=Bkg6RiCqY7
52. Lu, J., Batra, D., Parikh, D., Lee, S.: ViLBERT: pretraining task-agnostic visiolinguistic representations for vision-and-language tasks. In: Advances in Neural Information Processing Systems, vol. 32: Annual Conference on Neural Information Processing Systems 2019, NeurIPS 2019 (December), pp. 8–14 (2019). Vancouver, BC, Canada, pp. 13–23 (2019). https://proceedings.neurips.cc/paper/2019/hash/c74d97b01eae257e44aa9d5bade97baf-Abstract.html
53. Mao, J., Huang, J., Toshev, A., Camburu, O., Yuille, A.L., Murphy, K.: Generation and comprehension of unambiguous object descriptions. In: Proceedings of the 2016 IEEE Conference on Computer Vision and Pattern Recognition, CVPR 2016, Las Vegas, NV, USA, 27–30 June 2016, pp. 11–20. IEEE Computer Society (2016). https://doi.org/10.1109/CVPR.2016.9
54. Miura, Y., Zhang, Y., Tsai, E., Langlotz, C., Jurafsky, D.: Improving factual completeness and consistency of image-to-text radiology report generation. In: Proceedings of the 2021 Conference of the North American Chapter of the Association for Computational Linguistics: Human Language Technologies, pp. 5288–5304. Association for Computational Linguistics (2021). https://doi.org/10.18653/v1/2021.naacl-main.416, https://aclanthology.org/2021.naacl-main.416
55. Mu, Z., Tang, S., Tan, J., Yu, Q., Zhuang, Y.: Disentangled motif-aware graph learning for phrase grounding. In: AAAI (2021)
56. Müller, P., Kaissis, G., Zou, C., Rückert, D.: Joint learning of localized representations from medical images and reports. arXiv preprint arXiv:2112.02889 (2021)
57. Nguyen, H.Q., et al.: VinDr-CXR: an open dataset of chest X-rays with radiologist's annotations. arXiv preprint arXiv:2012.15029 (2020). https://doi.org/10.13026/3akn-b287
58. Oord, A.v.d., Li, Y., Vinyals, O.: Representation learning with contrastive predictive coding. arXiv preprint arXiv:1807.03748 (2018)
59. Plummer, B.A., Wang, L., Cervantes, C.M., Caicedo, J.C., Hockenmaier, J., Lazebnik, S.: Flickr30k entities: collecting region-to-phrase correspondences for richer image-to-sentence models. In: Proceedings of the IEEE international conference on computer vision, pp. 2641–2649 (2015)
60. Preechakul, K., Piansaddhayanon, C., Naowarat, B., Khandhawit, T., Sriswasdi, S., Chuangsuwanich, E.: Set prediction in the latent space. In: Advances in Neural Information Processing Systems, vol. 34 (2021)
61. Radford, A., et al.: Learning transferable visual models from natural language supervision. In: International Conference on Machine Learning, pp. 8748–8763. PMLR (2021)
62. Rao, Y., et al.: DenseCLIP: language-guided dense prediction with context-aware prompting. arXiv preprint arXiv:2112.01518 (2021)

63. Redmon, J., Farhadi, A.: YOLOv3: an incremental improvement. arXiv preprint arXiv:1804.02767 (2018)
64. Ren, S., He, K., Girshick, R., Sun, J.: Faster R-CNN: Towards real-time object detection with region proposal networks. In: Advances in Neural Information Processing Systems, vol. 28: Annual Conference on Neural Information Processing Systems 2015(December), pp. 7–12, 2015. Montreal, Quebec, Canada 28, pp. 91–99 (2015). https://proceedings.neurips.cc/paper/2015/hash/14bfa6bb14875e45bba028a21ed38046-Abstract.html
65. Ronneberger, O., Fischer, P., Brox, T.: U-Net: convolutional networks for biomedical image segmentation. In: Navab, N., Hornegger, J., Wells, W.M., Frangi, A.F. (eds.) MICCAI 2015. LNCS, vol. 9351, pp. 234–241. Springer, Cham (2015). https://doi.org/10.1007/978-3-319-24574-4_28
66. Shih, G., et al.: Augmenting the national institutes of health chest radiograph dataset with expert annotations of possible pneumonia. Radiol.: Artif. Intell. 1(1), e180041 (2019)
67. Shivade, C.: MedNLI - A natural language inference dataset for the clinical domain. PhysioNet (2019)
68. Simard, P., Steinkraus, D., Platt, J.: Best practices for convolutional neural networks applied to visual document analysis. In: Seventh International Conference on Document Analysis and Recognition, 2003. Proceedings, pp. 958–963. IEEE (2003)
69. Smit, A., Jain, S., Rajpurkar, P., Pareek, A., Ng, A.Y., Lungren, M.: Combining automatic labelers and expert annotations for accurate radiology report labeling using BERT. In: Proceedings of the 2020 Conference on Empirical Methods in Natural Language Processing (EMNLP), pp. 1500–1519. Association for Computational Linguistics (2020). https://doi.org/10.18653/v1/2020.emnlp-main.117, https://aclanthology.org/2020.emnlp-main.117
70. Su, W., et al.: VL-BERT: pre-training of generic visual-linguistic representations. In: 8th International Conference on Learning Representations, ICLR 2020, Addis Ababa, Ethiopia, 26–30 April 2020. OpenReview.net (2019). https://openreview.net/forum?id=SygXPaEYvH
71. Tam, L.K., Wang, X., Turkbey, E., Lu, K., Wen, Y., Xu, D.: Weakly supervised one-stage vision and language disease detection using large scale pneumonia and pneumothorax studies. In: Martel, A.L., et al. (eds.) MICCAI 2020. LNCS, vol. 12264, pp. 45–55. Springer, Cham (2020). https://doi.org/10.1007/978-3-030-59719-1_5
72. Titano, J.J., et al.: Automated deep-neural-network surveillance of cranial images for acute neurologic events. Nat. Med. 24(9), 1337–1341 (2018)
73. Vaswani, A., et al.: Attention is all you need. In: Advances in Neural Information Processing Systems, vol. 30, pp. 5998–6008 (2017). https://proceedings.neurips.cc/paper/2017/hash/3f5ee243547dee91fbd053c1c4a845aa-Abstract.html
74. Wallis, A., McCoubrie, P.: The radiology report-are we getting the message across? Clin. Radiol. 66(11), 1015–1022 (2011)
75. Wang, Q., Tan, H., Shen, S., Mahoney, M., Yao, Z.: MAF: multimodal alignment framework for weakly-supervised phrase grounding. In: Proceedings of the 2020 Conference on Empirical Methods in Natural Language Processing (EMNLP), pp. 2030–2038. Association for Computational Linguistics, Online (2020). https://doi.org/10.18653/v1/2020.emnlp-main.159, https://aclanthology.org/2020.emnlp-main.159
76. Wang, X., Peng, Y., Lu, L., Lu, Z., Bagheri, M., Summers, R.M.: ChestX-Ray8: hospital-scale chest X-ray database and benchmarks on weakly-supervised classification and localization of common thorax diseases. In: 2017 IEEE Conference

on Computer Vision and Pattern Recognition, CVPR 2017, Honolulu, HI, USA, 21–26 July 2017, pp. 2097–2106. IEEE Computer Society (2017). https://doi.org/10.1109/CVPR.2017.369

77. Wilcox, J.R.: The written radiology report. Appl. Radiol. **35**(7), 33 (2006)
78. Wolf, T., et al.: Huggingface's transformers: state-of-the-art natural language processing. arXiv preprint arXiv:1910.03771 (2019)
79. Wu, J.T., et al.: Chest ImaGenome dataset for clinical reasoning. In: Thirty-fifth Conference on Neural Information Processing Systems Datasets and Benchmarks Track (Round 2) (2021)
80. Wu, Y., et al.: Google's neural machine translation system: bridging the gap between human and machine translation. arXiv preprint arXiv:1609.08144 (2016)
81. You, Y., Gitman, I., Ginsburg, B.: Large batch training of convolutional networks. arXiv preprint arXiv:1708.03888 (2017)
82. Yu, F., Koltun, V.: Multi-scale context aggregation by dilated convolutions. In: Bengio, Y., LeCun, Y. (eds.) 4th International Conference on Learning Representations, ICLR 2016, San Juan, Puerto Rico, 2–4 May 2016, Conference Track Proceedings (2016). http://arxiv.org/abs/1511.07122
83. Yu, T., et al.: Cross-modal omni interaction modeling for phrase grounding. In: MM 2020: The 28th ACM International Conference on Multimedia, Virtual Event/Seattle, WA, USA, 12–16 October 2020, pp. 1725–1734 (2020). https://doi.org/10.1145/3394171.3413846
84. Zhang, Y., Ding, D.Y., Qian, T., Manning, C.D., Langlotz, C.P.: Learning to summarize radiology findings. In: Proceedings of the Ninth International Workshop on Health Text Mining and Information Analysis, pp. 204–213. Association for Computational Linguistics (2018). https://doi.org/10.18653/v1/W18-5623, https://aclanthology.org/W18-5623
85. Zhang, Y., Jiang, H., Miura, Y., Manning, C.D., Langlotz, C.P.: Contrastive learning of medical visual representations from paired images and text. arXiv preprint arXiv:2010.00747 (2020)
86. Zhang, Z., Zhao, Z., Lin, Z., He, X., et al.: Counterfactual contrastive learning for weakly-supervised vision-language grounding. Adv. Neural. Inf. Process. Syst. **33**, 18123–18134 (2020)

Generative Negative Text Replay for Continual Vision-Language Pretraining

Shipeng Yan[1,2,3], Lanqing Hong[4], Hang Xu[4(✉)], Jianhua Han[4],
Tinne Tuytelaars[5], Zhenguo Li[4], and Xuming He[1,6(✉)]

[1] ShanghaiTech University, Shanghai, China
yanshp@shanghaitech.edu.cn
[2] Shanghai Institute of Microsystem and Information Technology,
Chinese Academy of Sciences, Beijing, China
[3] University of Chinese Academy of Sciences, Beijing, China
[4] Huawei Noah's Ark Lab, Hong Kong, China
{honglanqing,xu.hang,xuchunjing,
hanjianhua4,li.zhenguo}@huawei.com
[5] KU Leuven, Leuven, Belgium
tinne.tuytelaars@kuleuven.be
[6] Shanghai Engineering Research Center of Intelligent Vision and Imaging,
Shanghai, China
hexm@shanghaitech.edu.cn

Abstract. Vision-language pre-training (VLP) has attracted increasing attention recently. With a large amount of image-text pairs, VLP models trained with contrastive loss have achieved impressive performance in various tasks, especially the zero-shot generalization on downstream datasets. In practical applications, however, massive data are usually collected in a streaming fashion, requiring VLP models to continuously integrate novel knowledge from incoming data and retain learned knowledge. In this work, we focus on learning a VLP model with sequential chunks of image-text pair data. To tackle the catastrophic forgetting issue in this multi-modal continual learning setting, we first introduce pseudo text replay that generates hard negative texts conditioned on the training images in memory, which not only better preserves learned knowledge but also improves the diversity of negative samples in the contrastive loss. Moreover, we propose multi-modal knowledge distillation between images and texts to align the instance-wise prediction between old and new models. We incrementally pre-train our model on the both instance and class incremental splits of Conceptual Caption dataset, and evaluate the model on zero-shot image classification and image-text retrieval tasks. Our method consistently outperforms the existing baselines with a large margin, which demonstrates its superiority. Notably, we realize an average performance boost of 4.60% on image-classification downstream datasets for class incremental split.

Supplementary Information The online version contains supplementary material available at https://doi.org/10.1007/978-3-031-20059-5_2.

Keywords: Vision-language pretraining · Continual learning

1   Introduction

Vision-and-language pre-training (VLP) [24,34] seeks to learn a generalizable multi-modal representations from large-scale image-text data. Recently, VLP models, such as CLIP [34], have demonstrated promising performance especially on the zero-shot generalization for a variety of downstream vision-language tasks including zero-shot image classification and image-text retrieval [19]. However, training a CLIP model typically requires a large amount of image-text pairs (400 million), which is particularly burdensome for the traditional off-line training strategy as all the data need to be available during the entire training process. Moreover, for practical applications, it is critical for a VLP model to continuously integrate novel knowledge in a dynamic environment, e.g., from streaming data crawled from the Internet. On the other hand, as shown in Fig. 1, a naive fine-tuning strategy for VLP using only the incoming new data suffers from a large performance degradation compared to the off-line training strategy. Consequently, it is essential to address this continual learning problem for large-scale VLPs, a topic that has received little attention in the past.

Traditional continual learning methods mostly focus on the issue of stability-plasticity dilemma [18,45], where a model is prone to forgetting the previously learned knowledge when adapting to new data. As such, much effort has been devoted to preserving discriminative features for the known classes [13]. For the VLP models, however, the pre-trained multi-modal representations need to be transferred to unseen downstream tasks. In this case, what knowledge should be retained and how it is preserved is less obvious. In addition, the forgetting

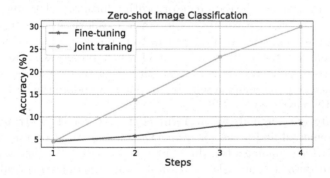

Fig. 1. Illustration of continual vision-and-language pre-training on CC2M dataset. The dataset is split into four data chunks with 0.5 million image-text pairs in each chunk. In fine-tuning, a new data chunk arrives at each step to update the pre-training model without previous data. In joint training, all data are accessible and shuffled during the whole training process. The figure shows significant performance gap between the fine-tuning and the joint training strategies on downstream zero-shot classification task.

problem in continual multi-modal learning involves the representation of visual and language inputs, as well as the multi-modal correspondence between the two modalities, which further complicates the problem.

Most state-of-the-art approaches [30] in traditional class incremental setting rely on the memory replay of representative old training samples [13]. Nevertheless, unlike the supervised class incremental learning [7] which typically trains a model to classify on a closed set of categories, VLP models learn an open set of visual concepts from natural language descriptions. Consequently, the majority of existing memory-based continual learning strategies would be rendered ineffective. In particular, those methods [47,52] aiming to alleviate class imbalance are not applicable to the continual learning of VLP models as there are no class-level supervision for VLP. In addition, the feature-based distillation methods [15] are usually designed for uni-modal CNNs and rarely take into account the characteristics of transformer-based multi-modal pre-training, and the model inversion [51] aims to generate images as positive examples for certain classes using a frozen copy of trained models, which remains challenging for high-resolution images and may introduce biases to the generated training data [46].

In this work, we propose a novel replay-based continual learning framework, named as IncCLIP, to address the above challenges for the VLP tasks. To this end, based on CLIP [34], we introduce a conditional data generation process that extracts the 'dark' knowledge from the previous-step model in a form of pseudo texts for replay, and adopt multi-modal knowledge distillation loss to further overcome catastrophic forgetting. Specifically, our model architecture is a two-stream encoder composed of separate visual and text encoders. At each incremental stage, in order to learn generic and transferable visual-linguistic representation, we adopt a contrastive loss that requires the model to predict the pairing between images and texts. Given the importance of negative instances in contrastive learning, we introduce a pseudo text generation technique via model inversion [51] to augment the data memory with informative data and replay the generated texts as negative examples. Moreover, to alleviate catastrophic forgetting, we design a knowledge distillation loss to minimize the output discrepancy between current and the previous-step model, which preserves the knowledge on cross-modal correspondence. It is also worth noting that after the incremental training of each step, we adopt reservoir sampling to update the memory for the rehearsal in the next step.

To validate our method, we perform continual model pre-training on an instance incremental and a class incremental split for the Conceptual Caption dataset [40], which simulates two different real scenarios. We then evaluate our model on two downstream tasks: zero-shot image classification and zero-shot image-text retrieval. The experimental results demonstrate the superiority of our approach, which is then further analyzed via the detailed ablation study. Notably, we outperform previous approaches by 4.6% in accuracy on the downstream image classification task with four-step class incremental split. In summary, the main contributions of our work are three-fold:

- To our best knowledge, this is the first work to tackle the problem of continual vision-language pre-training with streaming image-text pairs.
- To achieve better stability-plasticity trade-off, we propose the IncCLIP framework to augment the contrastive learning with the negative pseudo texts and adopt a multi-modal knowledge distillation loss between images and texts to preserve the learned cross-modal correspondence.
- Our proposed method consistently outperforms previous CL baselines such as UCIR in standard continual vision-language pre-training benchmarks.

2   Related Works

Vision-Language Pre-training. Vision-language pre-training learns transferable joint image-text embeddings from large-scale image-text pairs, which has been shown to be effective for a variety of vision-language (VL) tasks [11,27,31]. The majority of existing works fall into two categories based on model architectures: single-stream and dual-stream models. Single-stream models [10,24,31] introduce powerful encoders such as Transformer [44] to model the cross-modal interaction between image and text. As such, they perform well on VL tasks like VQA [2], which requires complex reasoning between image and text. However, they typically use an external object detector to generate visual region descriptions as the input to the multi-modal encoder [10,11], which can be computationally expensive. Moreover, it is difficult to apply them to certain VL tasks such as image-text retrieval, which requires feeding all potential image-text pairs into the multi-modal encoder and hence is inefficient.

On the other hand, dual-stream models [23,34] adopt a dual-encoder architecture to encode images and texts, respectively. CLIP [34] and ALIGN [23] perform pre-training on large-scale noisy data collected from the Internet. Especially, CLIP provides a flexible zero-shot classifier rather than parametric task-specific classifiers, and demonstrates impressive zero-shot generalization ability on many downstream tasks, such as zero-shot image classification and zero-shot image-text retrieval. It is a significant step towards flexible and practical zero-shot classifiers for computer vision tasks. Nevertheless, current dual-stream VLP models are trained in a joint-training manner using data prepared in advance, without the ability to continuously adapt to new data from a dynamic environment. In this work, we concentrate on the continual vision-language representation learning based on dual-stream models like CLIP.

Continual Learning. Continual learning [13,43,48,54] aims to integrate novel knowledge in a sequential fashion where old data are usually unavailable. Existing literature focuses mostly on supervised continual learning [41,50,53], which mainly falls into the following four groups. The first is the regularization methods [16,25], which penalize changes on significant weights of previously learned models. The second group is the distillation methods [28], which aim at retaining the output of the network on available data. The third is the structure methods [39,49], which keep old parameters fixed while growing and allocating weights for learning new data. The last is the pseudo rehearsal methods [42,51], which usually train a generative model to generate visual images of previously learned categories and train the classifier with the combination of real data and pseudo data to reduce forgetting. Our method combines the distillation method and the pseudo rehearsal method. However, previous pseudo rehearsal methods adopt either generative adversarial networks or variational auto-encoders, which are not easy to address their data degeneration issue, especially when dealing with complex scenarios such as high-resolution images or images of the similar classes. Our method circumvents this problem by "inverting" the model of last step to synthesize hard negative texts in the token embedding space, since token embedding has much lower dimensions and generating negative data points is easier. This is inspired by DeepInversion [51], but they do not consider generating negative data points and it is designed for the convolution network with Batch Normalization.

Recently, there also have been some efforts [8,22,36] to explore continual representation learning with unlabeled streaming data. CURL [36] proposes a continual unsupervised representation learning method, which learns a task-specific representation based on a set of share parameters and also trains a generative model to avoid forgetting. Co^2L [8] introduces a self-supervised knowledge distillation method for self-supervised continual learning. However, previous methods are designed for continual learning problems with a single modality and do not consider the properties of multi-modal representation learning. To the best of our knowledge, our work is the first to explore continual learning in the self-supervised multi-modality representation learning.

3   Methods

In this section, we describe our approach, as sketched in Fig. 2, to address the continual vision-language representation learning problem, with the goal of improving stability-plasticity trade-off. Concretely, we combine contrastive loss and multi-modal knowledge distillation and supplement the training with pseudo texts to enhance the generalization ability for the representation. Below, we first present the overview of problem setup and model architecture in Sect. 3.1, followed by the introduction of text generation in Sect. 3.2. Then we detail the training loss in Sect. 3.3.

3.1   Problem Setup and Model Architecture

Problem Setup. We first introduce the problem setup of **continual vision-language pre-training**. During sequential pre-training, the model observes a sequence of data chunks $\mathcal{D}_t$ for each step t. Particularly, the dataset $\mathcal{D}_t = \{(x_i^I, x_i^T)\}_{i=1}^{|\mathcal{D}_t|}$ is composed of image-text pairs at step t, where x_i^I means the input image, and x_i^T represents the corresponding text describing the image. We assess the transferability of learned representation to downstream tasks after the training at each chunk. In this work, all methods including our method and the

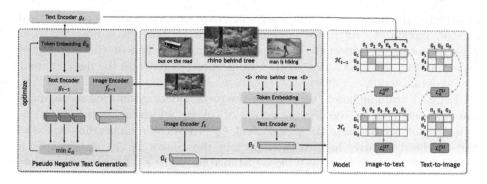

Fig. 2. The illustration of our method. The left panel illustrates the pseudo negative text generation process. We optimize pseudo texts $\bar{e}_k$ in the token embedding space by minimizing the loss $\mathcal{L}_G$. As middle panel shows, for a sampled mini-batch, we first extract the images features $\tilde{u}_i$ and language features $\tilde{v}_i$ through the corresponding encoder f_t and g_t. The right panel shows the calculation of training loss. We compute the similarity matrix S between image features $\tilde{u}_i$ and language features $\tilde{v}_i$. Then we apply the contrastive loss $\mathcal{L}_c^{\text{I2T}}$, $\mathcal{L}_c^{\text{T2I}}$ and distillation loss $\mathcal{L}_d^{\text{I2T}}$, $\mathcal{L}_d^{\text{T2I}}$ from both image to text and text to image. Note that $\bar{v}_i$ is the deep feature of the pseudo token embedding $\bar{e}_i$, which is used as negative examples in the training loss.

comparison methods are based on the rehearsal strategy, which stores a subset of observed data in memory $\mathcal{M}_t = \{(\boldsymbol{x}_i^I, \boldsymbol{x}_i^T)\}$ for future training.

Model Architecture. Like CLIP [34], we adopt a dual-stream encoder structure where the model $\mathcal{H}_t$ with parameters θ_t has independent visual encoder $f(\cdot)$ and text encoder $g(\cdot)$. Concretely, given an image $\boldsymbol{x}_i^I$ and a text $\boldsymbol{x}_j^T$, we first compute the normalized image embedding $\tilde{u}_i$ and normalized linguistic embedding $\tilde{v}_j$, and then compute the similarity score $s_i j$.

Concretely, to encode the image, we adopt ResNet as visual backbone, which extracts the features $\tilde{u}_i = f(\boldsymbol{x}_i^I)$ from image $\boldsymbol{x}_i^I$, and normalize the feature $\tilde{u}_i = \tilde{u}_i / \|\tilde{u}_i\|_2$ onto unit-sphere. To encode the text, we firstly tokenize the sequence into a sequence of word tokens $\boldsymbol{e}_i^T$ where we use the lower-cased byte pair encoding (BPE) [38] with a vocabulary size of 49,408 to tokenize the text. We adopt Transformer [44] as text encoder and encode these tokens into normalized linguistic embedding $\tilde{v}_j = g(\boldsymbol{x}_j^T)/\|g(\boldsymbol{x}_j^T)\|_2$. Finally, we compute the similarity score $s_{ij} = \tilde{u}_i^\top \tilde{v}_j$ between i-th image $\boldsymbol{x}_i^I$ and j-th text $\boldsymbol{x}_j^T$.

3.2   Pseudo Negative Text Generation

In this subsection, we introduce the pseudo text generation via model inversion to distill the knowledge of last step model $\mathcal{H}_{t-1}$ for solving the catastrophic forgetting. Due to the distribution shift between synthetic and real examples, the model is frequently biased if regarding them as positive examples [42]. We bypass this issue via generating negative texts which do not guide the model incorrectly. Having access to informative negative samples is known to be critical for the success of contrastive learning [20]. Furthermore, it is observed that negative examples, especially hard negative examples, benefit the learning of representation [37]. Motivated by this, we propose to generate the negative text via model inversion as follows.

For each training batch, we perform the pseudo data generation to augment the mini-batch. Given the discrete nature of tokens, which makes the optimization difficult, we optimize the pseudo text $\bar{e}_k$ in the token embedding space to find the hard negative texts with respect to the images x_i^I. e_k should keep a moderate distance from x_i^I as a close distance indicates e_k is a positive sample and a remote distance means e_k is easy to be distinguished.

Specifically, to generate the pseudo texts, we firstly sample a mini-batch $\mathcal{B} = \{(x_i^I, x_i^T)\}_{i=1}^B$ from memory $\mathcal{M}_t$. We initialize the token embedding $\bar{e}_k = \beta e_i^T + (1 - \beta)e_j^T$ where $\bar{e}_k$ are k-th generated text, β is uniformly sampled from the interval $[0, 1]$, i, j are indices randomly sampled from 1 to batch size B, and e_i^T, e_j^T are the corresponding token embeddings. It is worth noting that $\bar{e}_k$ takes the value of a real token embedding as initialization when $\beta = 0$ or $\beta = 1$. Given the current pseudo token embedding $\bar{e}_k$, we compute the cosine similarity scores s_{ik} with the images features $\tilde{u}_i$. Then we generate the data in the token embedding space which is continuous and easy to optimize compared to discrete tokenization space. The naive text generation via model inversion is to directly minimize the cosine similarity, which are calculated by the inner product between the generated token sequences $\bar{e}_k$ and the sampled image features $\tilde{u}_i$. However, to improve data efficiency, we require the generated token embedding $\bar{e}_k$ to be hard negative examples which means they are difficult to be distinguished from positive examples. To achieve this, we adopt margin loss as follows

$$\mathcal{L}_G = \frac{1}{B} \sum_{i=1}^B \max(0, s_{\min} - s_{ik}) + \max(0, s_{ik} - s_{\max}), \tag{1}$$

where $s_{\min}$ and $s_{\max}$ are the hyper-parameters representing the minimum and maximum score, respectively. The maximum score guarantees the generated example to be negative examples. The minimum score requires the generated examples to be hard negative examples. We adopt SGD to minimize the loss $\mathcal{L}_G$ with respect to the variable $\bar{e}_k$ for a constant number of iterations.

3.3   Training Loss

We now describe the details of our continual pre-training objective. For pre-training, we adopt a contrastive learning task to learn a generic and transferable visual-linguistic representation, which has proven to be efficient and effective in previous works [27]. To preserve the knowledge in the model, we maintain the relation of instances by introducing the knowledge distillation. With the above generated texts $\bar{e}_k$, we use it in both contrastive learning and multi-modal knowledge distillation, which helps the contrastive learning on novel data and improves the regularization of distillation loss.

During continual learning, we learn the model on the union of incoming data, memory and pseudo texts. In detail, we sample a mini-batch of image-text pairs $\{(\boldsymbol{x}_i^I, \boldsymbol{x}_i^T)\}_{i=1}^{B}$ from incoming data $\mathcal{D}_t$ and memory $\mathcal{M}_t$ where B denotes the batch size, and sample a mini-batch of token embedding $\{\boldsymbol{e}_k^T\}_{k=1}^{\hat{B}}$ of negative texts with batch size $\hat{B}$. We denote the text batch size in total as $B_T = B + \hat{B}$. The linguistic embedding for the sampled texts $\boldsymbol{x}_i^T$ and the token embedding $\boldsymbol{e}_k^T$ of negative texts are denoted as $\{\tilde{\boldsymbol{v}}_j\}_{j=1}^{B_T}$, and the visual embedding are $\{\tilde{\boldsymbol{u}}_i\}_{i=1}^{B}$. We can compute the classification probability $P_{I2T}(y_i|\tilde{\boldsymbol{u}}_i, \{\tilde{\boldsymbol{v}}_j\}_{j=1}^{B_T}), y_i \in \{1, 2, \ldots, B_T\}$, from image to texts to determine which text corresponds to the given image as follows

$$P_{I2T}(y_i = k|\tilde{\boldsymbol{u}}_i, \{\tilde{\boldsymbol{v}}_j\}_{j=1}^{B_T}; \tau) = \frac{\exp(s_{ik}/\tau)}{\sum_{j=1}^{B_T} \exp(s_{ij}/\tau)}, \tag{2}$$

where τ is the temperature parameter to control the smoothness of the Softmax function, and $P_{I2T}(y_i = k|\tilde{\boldsymbol{u}}_i, \{\tilde{\boldsymbol{v}}_j\}_{j=1}^{B_T}; \tau)$ means the chance of i-th image being paired with k-th text. Similarly, we can compute the classification probability $P_{T2I}(y_j|\tilde{\boldsymbol{v}}_j, \{\tilde{\boldsymbol{u}}_i\}_{i=1}^{B})$ from text to images, i.e. the chance of j-th text being paired with k-th image, as follows

$$P_{T2I}(y_j = k|\tilde{\boldsymbol{v}}_j, \{\tilde{\boldsymbol{u}}_i\}_{i=1}^{B}; \tau) = \frac{\exp(s_{kj}/\tau)}{\sum_{i=1}^{B} \exp(s_{ij}/\tau)}. \tag{3}$$

Contrastive Loss. We adopt bi-directional contrastive loss to learn generalized image representations from natural language supervision. We jointly train an image encoder and a text encoder to predict the correct pairings of a batch of image-text pairs. Concretely, for an image $\boldsymbol{x}_i^I$, we regard its corresponding language description $\boldsymbol{x}_i^T$ as a positive example whereas the other $B_T - 1$ texts are considered negative examples. Therefore, the image-to-text loss is as follows

$$\mathcal{L}_c^{I2T} = -\frac{1}{B} \sum_{i=1}^{B} \log P_{I2T}(y_i|\tilde{\boldsymbol{u}}_i, \{\tilde{\boldsymbol{v}}_j\}_{j=1}^{B_T}; \tau), \tag{4}$$

where the ground truth $y_i \in \{1, 2, \ldots, B\}$. The text-to-image loss $\mathcal{L}_c^{T2I}$ is defined on the texts $\{\boldsymbol{x}_i^T\}_{i=1}^{B}$ in a similar way as follows

$$\mathcal{L}_c^{T2I} = -\frac{1}{B} \sum_{i=1}^{B} \log P_{T2I}(y_j|\tilde{\boldsymbol{v}}_j, \{\tilde{\boldsymbol{u}}_i\}_{i=1}^{B}; \tau), \tag{5}$$

where we only compute the loss on real texts because the pseudo texts lack a paired image. In total, the overall contrastive loss $\mathcal{L}_c$

$$\mathcal{L}_c = \alpha \mathcal{L}_c^{I2T} + (1-\alpha)\mathcal{L}_c^{T2I}, \tag{6}$$

where hyper-parameter α is the loss weighting coefficient.

Cross-Modal Knowledge Distillation. To prevent catastrophic forgetting, knowledge distillation is introduced to keep the instance-wise prediction between current model $\mathcal{H}_t$ and the model $\mathcal{H}_{t-1}$ learned at last task. Concretely, we retain an image's relationships with texts by employing the knowledge distillation loss $\mathcal{L}_d^{I2T}$ with KL-divergence as follows

$$
\mathcal{L}_d^{I2T} = \frac{1}{B} \sum_{i=1}^{B} \mathrm{KL}\Big(P_{I2T}(y_i|\tilde{\boldsymbol{u}}_i, \{\tilde{\boldsymbol{v}}_j\}_{j=1}^{B_T}; \theta_t, \tau) \|
$$

$$
P_{I2T}(y_i|\tilde{\boldsymbol{u}}_i', \{\tilde{\boldsymbol{v}}_j'\}_{j=1}^{B_T}; \theta_{t-1}, \tau_{old}^d) \Big),
$$

(7)

where $\tilde{\boldsymbol{u}}_i', \tilde{\boldsymbol{v}}_j'$ are the features extracted the model $\mathcal{H}_{t-1}$, τ_{old}^d represents the temperatures of last model for distillation. Similarly, for a text $\boldsymbol{x}_j^T$, $1 \leq j \leq B$, we also apply distillation loss on the prediction probabilities from text to image as follows

$$
\mathcal{L}_d^{T2I} = \frac{1}{B} \sum_{j=1}^{B} \mathrm{KL}\Big(P_{T2I}(y_j|\tilde{\boldsymbol{u}}_j, \{\tilde{\boldsymbol{v}}_i\}_{i=1}^{B}; \theta_t, \tau) \|
$$

$$
P_{T2I}(y_j|\tilde{\boldsymbol{u}}_j', \{\tilde{\boldsymbol{v}}_i'\}_{i=1}^{B}; \theta_{t-1}, \tau_{old}^d) \Big).
$$

(8)

Therefore, the knowledge distillation loss

$$
\mathcal{L}_d = \eta \mathcal{L}_d^{I2T} + (1 - \eta)\mathcal{L}_d^{T2I},
$$

(9)

where the hyper-parameter η is the loss weight.

Overall Loss. Finally, we combine the contrastive loss $\mathcal{L}_c$ and distillation loss $\mathcal{L}_d$, and obtain the final loss as follows

$$
\mathcal{L}_{overall} = \mathcal{L}_c + \lambda \mathcal{L}_d,
$$

(10)

where λ is the loss coefficient to control the tradeoff between losses.

Notably, we find that the weight norm often increases over different steps, which hampers the generalization ability of the pretrained model and causes negative forward transfer. The same phenomenon is also observed in recent works [3]. Empirically, we adopt the trick of weight norm clipping. Concretely, at the end of each training iteration, if the weight norm at layer-l is higher than δ_l, we clip the weight norm to δ_l when keeping the direction of the weight W_l unchanged. In practice, $\delta_l = \gamma \|W\|_{init}$ where the initial weight norm are denoted as $\|W\|_{init}$. After the training of step t, we follow the practices [1,9] to update the memory by adopting reservoir sampling to select samples from the avaiable data to save.

4   Experiments

In this section, we conduct exhaustive experiments to validate the effectiveness of our method. Concretely, we first describe the experimental setup and implementation details in Sect. 4.1, followed by the evaluation results on class incremental

Table 1. Results on class incremental CC2M dataset at final step: The top-1 accuracy over various downstream datasets on zero-shot image classification task.

#Tasks	Methods	ImageNet	CIFAR-10	CIFAR-100	Caltech101	SUN397	Food101	Flowers102	DTD	Average
	Joint	29.97	51.94	26.04	65.2	31.79	23.71	19.44	12.82	32.61
4	ER [9]	14.45	23.56	7.84	35.93	16.83	12.59	10.17	8.94	16.29
	UCIR [21]	13.24	25.56	8.47	35.14	17.13	13.05	9.97	**9.84**	16.55
	Co^{2}L [8]	14.73	26.46	10.51	34.58	17.54	12.16	11.41	7.3	16.84
	GeoDL [41]	14.24	27.48	9.49	35.93	17.01	12.94	9.87	8.99	17.00
	IncCLIP	**18.85**	**28.31**	**13.23**	50.32	**23.38**	**16.19**	**13.08**	9.20	**21.57**
8	ER [9]	9.59	14.23	3.85	26.80	11.95	7.24	8.98	5.48	11.02
	UCIR [21]	9.89	12.69	4.42	23.56	12.95	9.53	9.33	7.02	11.17
	Co^{2}L [8]	10.99	18.34	5.51	29.1	13.52	9.01	8.56	5.9	12.62
	GeoDL [41]	10.86	14.88	5.11	30.56	14.2	10.17	8.09	7.18	12.64
	IncCLIP	**13.93**	**22.68**	**10.45**	**43.39**	**19.27**	**11.91**	**9.57**	7.38	**17.24**

split in Sect. 4.2. Then we introduce the experimental results on the instance incremental split in Sect. 4.3. Finally, we perform ablation study and analysis to validate the effectiveness of components and provide more insights in Sect. 4.4.

4.1 Experiment Setup and Implementation Details

Benchmark Protocol. Conceptual 12M (CC12M) [40] is a dataset collected from the Internet including 12 million image-text pairs for vision-language pre-training. In this section, we show results on both the class incremental and instance incremental split, corresponding to large and insignificant distribution shift in real world, respectively. Considering that the image labels are not provided, we adopt an approximate strategy to build our class incremental split. Specifically, we first generate a pseudo class label for each image and then partition ImageNet1k dataset into four chunks with 250 classes per chunk. Here the pseudo labels are the most confident predictions from the BEiT [4] model pretrained on ImageNet1k. For the instance incremental split, it models a real-world scenario in which data chunks are continuously collected in the same environment [22]. In particular, we build the split via randomly selecting 2M image-text pairs from CC12M and then randomly split them into 4 identically distributed chunks with 0.5M image-text pairs each chunk. Note that the 2M image-text pairs used for instance incremental setting here is different with image-text pairs of the class incremental split for verifying the robustness of algorithm. For completeness, we provide experiments for instance incremental split on same 2M image-text pairs with class incremental split in appendix. The splits will be released in the future. We allow the algorithms to store fixed-size instances in memory.

Comparison Methods. To demonstrate the efficacy of our method, we adopt ER [9], UCIR [21], GeoDL [41] as comparison methods. Notably, we replace the cross entropy loss with contrastive loss to train a VLP model for ER, UCIR and

Table 2. Image-text retrieval performance at final step: zero-shot image-text retrieval on MSCOCO and Flickr30k datasets with various methods. R@K means top-K recall.

| #Tasks | Methods | Flickr30K | | | | | | MSCOCO | | | | | |
| | | Image-to-text | | | Text-to-image | | | Image-to-text | | | Text-to-image | | |
		R@1	R@5	R@10	R@1	R@5	R@10	R@1	R@5	R@10	R@1	R@5	R@10
	Joint	35.7	62.4	71.8	25.16	50.52	62.36	18.8	41.82	52.94	13.14	30.74	41.78
4	ER [9]	17.5	39.8	51.3	11.18	28.68	38.18	9.6	24.72	35.34	6.41	17.76	25.61
	GeoDL [41]	18.1	40.4	51.1	11.96	29.94	39.4	9.64	25.58	35.78	6.26	18.02	26.01
	UCIR [21]	18.3	41.9	52.9	12.10	30.32	40.28	9.72	25.88	36.16	6.64	18.58	26.83
	Co^{2}L [8]	19.7	42.5	53.1	12.24	29.34	39.54	10.1	25.16	35.24	6.78	18.30	26.59
	IncCLIP	**24.1**	**49.5**	**61.9**	**17.14**	**37.96**	**48.96**	**12.38**	**29.96**	**40.6**	**8.49**	**22.55**	**31.90**
8	ER [9]	9.7	27.3	38.5	6.54	19.16	27.7	6.47	16.84	24.48	4.22	13.01	19.05
	GeoDL [41]	12.5	33.3	42.1	8.40	21.9	30.44	6.42	18.08	27.32	4.64	14.02	20.58
	UCIR [21]	10.1	28.7	40.1	7.16	20.54	29.14	7.00	17.58	25.22	4.38	13.13	19.83
	Co^{2}L [8]	12.9	32.3	41.9	8.43	21.76	30.41	6.22	18.68	26.58	4.49	13.29	20.24
	IncCLIP	**16.0**	**37.7**	**49.2**	**10.92**	**28.26**	**38.60**	**9.52**	**24.18**	**33.60**	**6.29**	**17.41**	**26.08**

Table 3. Ablation study: W.N.C means the weight norm cliping, H.N.T.G means hard negative text generation and Dist. means the knowledge distillation loss on image classification and image-to-text retrieval task. Below results on image-to-text retrieval tasks are top-1 recall.

| W.N.C | Dist. | H.N.T.G | ImageNet | Flickr30K | | MSCOCO | |
				I2T	T2I	I2T	T2I
✓	✗	✗	16.01	21.3	14.06	10.89	7.52
✓	✓	✗	17.67	22.8	15.10	11.55	8.02
✓	✓	✓	**18.85**	**24.1**	**17.14**	**12.38**	**8.49**

GeoDL. Besides, we also provide the joint-training(Joint) as an upper bound which makes use of all observed data to update the model.

Implementation Details. Following CLIP [34], all methods including comparison methods and our method IncCLIP adopt Transformer [44] as the text backbone with the architecture modifications described in [35]. Particularly, we use 12-layer 512-wide transformer with 8 attention heads and modified ResNet-50 [34]. The results on zero-shot image classification are reported using the prompt ensemble technique [34]. For each mini-batch, the size of sampled negative text $B_{aug} = 256$. The loss coefficient $\lambda = 5$. $\alpha = 0.5$, $\eta = 0.5$, $\tau_{old}^d = 0.01$. The following experiments are conducted with 10% dataset as memory except otherwise stated. To train our model, we adopt 8 Nvidia V100 GPUs with batch size 512 per GPU. For each step, we train the model for 15 epochs on CC2M. We adopt LAMB optimizer with learning rate 0.003 and weight decay 0.003. We begin by performing a linear warmup at each incremental step and then decay it using a cosine learning rate schedule. More details can be found in appendix.

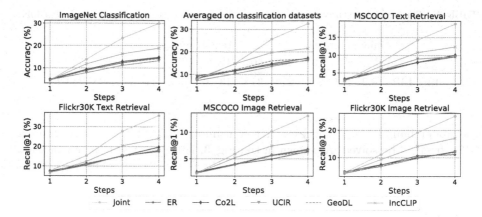

Fig. 3. The downstream task performance over time. For image classification task, the accuracy is determined by averaging accuracies of all downstream datasets.

Table 4. The sensitive study of memory size for image classification task. 'Average' means the average accuracy over all downstream image classification datasets.

	ImageNet					Average				
	1%	5%	10%	20%	50%	1%	5%	10%	20%	50%
IncCLIP	12.82	16.68	18.95	23.61	28.29	16.90	20.16	21.82	24.92	30.61

4.2   Class Incremental Split

Zero-Shot Image Classification. We conduct experiments to evaluate the algorithm's zero-shot generalization ability on image classification task. Concretely, we evaluate models on eight representative datasets including CIFAR-10 [26], CIFAR-100 [26], Caltech101 [17], Oxford 102 Flower(Flowers102) [32], Food101 [6], SUN397 [5], Describable Textures Dataset (DTD) [12], and ImageNet [14]. Like CLIP [34], we adopt prompt template, embed the class name to acquire the prediction score for each class, then use the class with the highest score as the prediction label during inference.

Table 1 summarizes the final step performance of CC2M dataset with 4 and 8 steps. We can see that our method regularly surpasses other methods with a significant margin at different downstream datasets. Specifically, our method improves the accuracy from 19.7 to 24.1(+**4.4**%) under the 4 step split on ImageNet. It is observed that when the number of steps increases, the average gain from our method increases as well. In spite of the fact that traditional methods like UCIR, Co^{2}L are better than ER, it can be seen that the improvement is limited compared to ER, indicating that their direct application can not fix the problem well. Moreover, although our method achieves obvious gain, the large gap between our method and Joint(Upper bound) indicates that continual vision-language pre-training is challenging to be solved. Furthermore, despite the clear increase achieved by our method, the wide gap between our method and

Table 5. The sensitive study on memory size for image-to-text retrieval on Flickr30K.

	image-to-text					text-to-image				
	1%	5%	10%	20%	50%	1%	5%	10%	20%	50%
IncCLIP	18.2	21.6	24.1	27.2	31.6	13.16	15.58	17.14	18.38	23.62

the upper bound 'Joint' suggests that continuous vision-language pre-training is far from to be solved. As shown in the Fig. 3, it is observed that our method consistently outperforms the comparison methods at different steps.

Zero-Shot Image-Text Retrieval. The image-text retrieval task consists of two sub-tasks: image-to-text retrieval and text-to-image retrieval. In particular, we employ MSCOCO [29] and Flickr30K [33] datasets to assess the representation transferability of pretrained representation on image-text retrieval task. Table 2 demonstrates the image-text retrieval results on 4-step split of CC2M. We can see that our method consistently outperforms the other methods in both image-to-text and text-to-image retrieval tasks. Particularly, our method improves from 10.1% to 12.38% for top-1 text recall on MSCOCO dataset at final step. As the number of steps increases from 4 to 8, our method's performance on all metrics falls, indicating that the continuous vision-language pre-training task becomes more difficult for longer sequences.

4.3   Instance Incremental Split

As Table 6 shows, we evaluate the methods on instance incremental split, and our method consistently outperforms than other methods on both classification and retrieval tasks, showing the superiority and the robustness of our method. Our method achieves 2.12% improvement on ImageNet classification task.

4.4   Ablation Study and Analysis

Ablation Study. We conduct exhaustive ablation study to evaluate the influence of each component used in our method. As shown in Table 3, we can see that the generalization performance is improved when weight norm clipping is applied. Moreover, it is observed that the introduction of knowledge distillation loss gains 1.66% improvement on classification accuracy on ImageNet. Finally, with the addition of negative text replay, we can further obtain 1.3% top-1 text recall performance gain on Flickr30K dataset for text retrieval task.

Sensitive Study on Memory Size. We conduct sensitive study on memory size and report the results in Table 4 and 5. '%x' indicates that we set the memory size to be x percents of the total size of the dataset. We can find that the performance on all tasks consistently improves as the memory size increases, which demonstrates the effectiveness of replay strategy once more.

Table 6. Results on instance incremental split of 2M image-text pairs at final step: 'Average' means the accuracy averaged on eight classification datasets. Moreover, we report the top-1 recall on both MSCOCO and Flickr30K dataset.

Methods	ImageNet	Average	Flickr30K		MSCOCO	
			I2T	T2I	I2T	T2I
Joint	20.20	24.58	27.20	19.02	14.58	9.90
ER [9]	10.74	14.38	16.3	10.74	8.50	5.49
UCIR [21]	10.57	14.91	16.7	11.34	9.14	6.11
GeoDL [41]	10.85	14.16	16.4	10.82	8.62	5.65
Co^{2}L [8]	11.12	15.33	18.3	10.86	8.58	5.69
IncCLIP	**13.24**	**17.97**	**26.5**	**17.18**	**13.46**	**8.60**

Table 7. The forgetting analysis on various methods.

Methods	ER	UCIR	Co^{2}L	GeoDL	IncCLIP
BWT	−31.93	−28.68	−30.83	−31.41	−18.48

Forgetting Analysis. Additionally, we conduct experiments to analyze the algorithm's resistance to forgetting. To measure the forgetting in the continual vision-language pre-training, we define the backward transfer(BWT) as the accuracy changes on each training chunk. Detailedly, $\text{BWT} = \frac{1}{N-1} \sum_{i=2}^{N} \frac{1}{i} \sum_{j=1}^{i} A_j^i - A_j^j$ where A_j^i means the accuracy of step i model $\mathcal{H}_i$ on chunk $j \leq i$. The model has forgotten part of knowledge it acquired in chunk j when $A_j^i - A_j^j \leq 0$. As Table 7 shows, we can see that our method is less prone to catastrophic forgetting, which indicates the superiority of our method.

5 Conclusions

In this work, we have proposed a novel continual learning problem to learn generic and transferable vision-language representation. To overcome the catastrophic forgetting, we develop a replay-based framework with two main contributions. First, we perform model inversion to generate hard negative texts in token embedding space conditioned on the available images, and then use them to augment training. Second, we adopt contrastive learning as our pre-training objective and introduce the knowledge distillation on the similarity scores between images and texts. We conduct extensive experiments on Conceptual Caption dataset, and show that our learning strategy outperforms previous methods. While the performance of our method is promising, the text generation module requires extra training time, which can be improved in future work.

Acknowledgements. This work was supported by Shanghai Science and Technology Program 21010502700, and Shanghai Frontiers Science Center Program. This work was done when Shipeng Yan was intern at Noah's Ark Lab. Hang Xu and Xuming He are equal corresponding authors. We gratefully acknowledge the support of MindSpore, CANN (Compute Architecture for Neural Networks) and Ascend AI Processor used for this research.

References

1. Aljundi, R., et al.: Online continual learning with maximal interfered retrieval. In: NeurIPS
2. Antol, S., et al.: VQA: visual question answering. In: ICCV (2015)
3. Ash, J., Adams, R.P.: On warm-starting neural network training. In: NeurIPS (2020)
4. Bao, H., Dong, L., Wei, F.: Beit: bert pre-training of image transformers. arXiv:2106.08254 (2021)
5. Barriuso, A., Torralba, A.: Notes on image annotation. arXiv:1210.3448 (2012)
6. Bossard, L., Guillaumin, M., Van Gool, L.: Food-101 – mining discriminative components with random forests. In: Fleet, D., Pajdla, T., Schiele, B., Tuytelaars, T. (eds.) ECCV 2014. LNCS, vol. 8694, pp. 446–461. Springer, Cham (2014). https://doi.org/10.1007/978-3-319-10599-4_29
7. Castro, F.M., Marín-Jiménez, M.J., Guil, N., Schmid, C., Alahari, K.: End-to-end incremental learning. In: ECCV (2018)
8. Cha, H., Lee, J., Shin, J.: Co2l: contrastive continual learning. In: CVPR (2021)
9. Chaudhry, A., et al.: On tiny episodic memories in continual learning. arXiv:1902.10486 (2019)
10. Chen, Y.-C., Li, L., Yu, L., El Kholy, A., Ahmed, F., Gan, Z., Cheng, Yu., Liu, J.: UNITER: universal image-text representation learning. In: Vedaldi, A., Bischof, H., Brox, T., Frahm, J.-M. (eds.) ECCV 2020. LNCS, vol. 12375, pp. 104–120. Springer, Cham (2020). https://doi.org/10.1007/978-3-030-58577-8_7
11. Cho, J., Lei, J., Tan, H., Bansal, M.: Unifying vision-and-language tasks via text generation. arXiv:2102.02779 (2021)
12. Cimpoi, M., Maji, S., Kokkinos, I., Mohamed, S., Vedaldi, A.: Describing textures in the wild. In: CVPR (2014)
13. Delange, M., et al.: A continual learning survey: defying forgetting in classification tasks. TPAMI **44**(7), 3366–3385 (2021)
14. Deng, J., Dong, W., Socher, R., Li, L.J., Li, K., Fei-Fei, L.: Imagenet: a large-scale hierarchical image database. In: CVPR (2009)
15. Douillard, A., Cord, M., Ollion, C., Robert, T., Valle, E.: PODNet: pooled outputs distillation for small-tasks incremental learning. In: Vedaldi, A., Bischof, H., Brox, T., Frahm, J.-M. (eds.) ECCV 2020. LNCS, vol. 12365, pp. 86–102. Springer, Cham (2020). https://doi.org/10.1007/978-3-030-58565-5_6
16. Ebrahimi, S., Elhoseiny, M., Darrell, T., Rohrbach, M.: Uncertainty-guided continual learning with bayesian neural networks. In: ICLR (2019)
17. Fei-Fei, L., Fergus, R., Perona, P.: One-shot learning of object categories. TPAMI **28**(4), 594–611 (2006)
18. Grossberg, S.: Adaptive resonance theory: how a brain learns to consciously attend, learn, and recognize a changing world. Neural Netw. **37**, 1–47 (2013)
19. Han, Z., Fu, Z., Chen, S., Yang, J.: Contrastive embedding for generalized zero-shot learning. In: CVPR (2021)
20. He, K., Fan, H., Wu, Y., Xie, S., Girshick, R.: Momentum contrast for unsupervised visual representation learning. In: CVPR (2020)

21. Hou, S., Pan, X., Loy, C.C., Wang, Z., Lin, D.: Learning a unified classifier incrementally via rebalancing. In: CVPR (2019)
22. Hu, D., et al.: How well self-supervised pre-training performs with streaming data? In: ICLR (2022)
23. Jia, C., et al.: Scaling up visual and vision-language representation learning with noisy text supervision. arXiv:2102.05918 (2021)
24. Kim, W., Son, B., Kim, I.: Vilt: vision-and-language transformer without convolution or region supervision. In: ICML (2021)
25. Kirkpatrick, J., et al.: Overcoming catastrophic forgetting in neural networks. In: Proceedings of the National Academy of Sciences (PNAS) (2017)
26. Krizhevsky, A., Hinton, G.: Learning multiple layers of features from tiny images. Technical report (2009)
27. Li, J., Selvaraju, R.R., Gotmare, A.D., Joty, S., Xiong, C., Hoi, S.: Align before fuse: vision and language representation learning with momentum distillation. In: NeurIPS (2021)
28. Li, Z., Hoiem, D.: Learning without forgetting. TPAMI **40**(12), 2935–2947 (2017)
29. Lin, T.Y., et al.: Microsoft COCO: common objects in context. In: Fleet, D., Pajdla, T., Schiele, B., Tuytelaars, T. (eds.) ECCV 2014. LNCS, vol. 8693, pp. 740–755. Springer, Cham (2014). https://doi.org/10.1007/978-3-319-10602-1_48
30. Liu, Y., Schiele, B., Sun, Q.: Meta-aggregating networks for class-incremental learning. arXiv:2010.05063 (2020)
31. Liu, Y., Wu, C., Tseng, S.Y., Lal, V., He, X., Duan, N.: Kd-vlp: improving end-to-end vision-and-language pretraining with object knowledge distillation. arXiv preprint. arXiv:2109.10504 (2021)
32. Nilsback, M.E., Zisserman, A.: Automated flower classification over a large number of classes. In: Computer Graphics and Image Processing (2008)
33. Plummer, B.A., Wang, L., Cervantes, C.M., Caicedo, J.C., Hockenmaier, J., Lazebnik, S.: Flickr30k entities: collecting region-to-phrase correspondences for richer image-to-sentence models. In: IJCV (2017)
34. Radford, A., et al.: Learning transferable visual models from natural language supervision. In: ICML (2021)
35. Radford, A., Wu, J., Child, R., Luan, D., Amodei, D., Sutskever, I., et al.: Language models are unsupervised multitask learners. OpenAI Blog **1**(8), 9 (2019)
36. Rao, D., Visin, F., Rusu, A., Pascanu, R., Teh, Y.W., Hadsell, R.: Continual unsupervised representation learning. In: NeurIPS (2019)
37. Robinson, J.D., Chuang, C.Y., Sra, S., Jegelka, S.: Contrastive learning with hard negative samples. In: ICLR (2021)
38. Sennrich, R., Haddow, B., Birch, A.: Neural machine translation of rare words with subword units. arXiv:1508.07909 (2015)
39. Serra, J., Suris, D., Miron, M., Karatzoglou, A.: Overcoming catastrophic forgetting with hard attention to the task. In: ICML (2018)
40. Sharma, P., Ding, N., Goodman, S., Soricut, R.: Conceptual captions: A cleaned, hypernymed, image alt-text dataset for automatic image captioning. In: ACL (2018)
41. Simon, C., Koniusz, P., Harandi, M.: On learning the geodesic path for incremental learning. In: CVPR (2021)
42. Smith, J., Hsu, Y.C., Balloch, J., Shen, Y., Jin, H., Kira, Z.: Always be dreaming: a new approach for data-free class-incremental learning. arXiv:2106.09701 (2021)
43. Thrun, S.: Lifelong learning algorithms. In: Pratt, L. (ed.) Learning to Learn. Springer, Boston (1998). https://doi.org/10.1007/978-1-4615-5529-2_8

44. Vaswani, A., et al.: Attention is all you need. In: NeurIPS (2017)
45. Wang, L., Yang, K., Li, C., Hong, L., Li, Z., Zhu, J.: OrdisCo: effective and efficient usage of incremental unlabeled data for semi-supervised continual learning. In: CVPR (2021)
46. Wang, S.Y., Wang, O., Zhang, R., Owens, A., Efros, A.A.: CNN-generated images are surprisingly easy to spot... for now. In: CVPR (2020)
47. Wu, Y., et al.: Large scale incremental learning. In: CVPR (2019)
48. Xie, J., Yan, S., He, X.: General incremental learning with domain-aware categorical representations. In: CVPR (2022)
49. Yan, S., Xie, J., He, X.: DER: dynamically expandable representation for class incremental learning. In: CVPR (2021)
50. Yan, S., Zhou, J., Xie, J., Zhang, S., He, X.: An em framework for online incremental learning of semantic segmentation. In: ACM MM (2021)
51. Yin, H., et al.: Dreaming to distill: data-free knowledge transfer via deepinversion. In: CVPR (2020)
52. Zhao, B., Xiao, X., Gan, G., Zhang, B., Xia, S.T.: Maintaining discrimination and fairness in class incremental learning. In: CVPR (2020)
53. Zhao, H., Qin, X., Su, S., Fu, Y., Lin, Z., Li, X.: When video classification meets incremental classes. In: ACM MM (2021)
54. Zhao, H., Wang, H., Fu, Y., Wu, F., Li, X.: Memory efficient class-incremental learning for image classification. In: TNNLS (2021)

Video Graph Transformer for Video Question Answering

Junbin Xiao[1,2,3], Pan Zhou[1], Tat-Seng Chua[2,3(✉)], and Shuicheng Yan[1]

[1] Sea AI Lab, Singapore, Singapore
junbin@comp.nus.edu.sg, {zhoupan,yansc}@sea.com
[2] Sea-NExT Joint Lab, Singapore, Singapore
dcscts@nus.edu.sg
[3] Department of Computer Science, National University of Singapore, Singapore, Singapore

Abstract. This paper proposes a Video Graph Transformer (VGT) model for Video Question Answering (VideoQA). VGT's uniqueness are two-fold: 1) it designs a dynamic graph transformer module which encodes video by explicitly capturing the visual objects, their relations, and dynamics for complex spatio-temporal reasoning; and 2) it exploits disentangled video and text Transformers for relevance comparison between the video and text to perform QA, instead of entangled cross-modal Transformer for answer classification. Vision-text communication is done by additional cross-modal interaction modules. With more reasonable video encoding and QA solution, we show that VGT can achieve much better performances on VideoQA tasks that challenge dynamic relation reasoning than prior arts in the pretraining-free scenario. Its performances even surpass those models that are pretrained with millions of external data. We further show that VGT can also benefit a lot from self-supervised cross-modal pretraining, yet with orders of magnitude smaller data. These results clearly demonstrate the effectiveness and superiority of VGT, and reveal its potential for more data-efficient pretraining. With comprehensive analyses and some heuristic observations, we hope that VGT can promote VQA research beyond coarse recognition/description towards fine-grained relation reasoning in realistic videos. Our code is available at https://github.com/sail-sg/VGT.

Keywords: Dynamic visual graph · Transformer · VideoQA

1 Introduction

Since the 1960s, the very beginning of Artificial Intelligence (AI), long efforts and steady progresses have been made towards machine systems that can demonstrate their understanding of the dynamic visual world by responding to humans'

Supplementary Information The online version contains supplementary material available at https://doi.org/10.1007/978-3-031-20059-5_3.

natural language queries in the context of videos which directly reflect our physical surroundings. In particular, since 2019 [11], we have been witnessing a drastic advancement in such multi-disciplinary AI where computer vision, natural language processing as well as knowledge reasoning are coordinated for accurate decision making. This advancement stems, in part from the success of *multimodal pretraining* on web-scale vision-text data [8,21,31,34,38,44,52–54,63], and in part from the unified deep neural network that can well model both vision and natural language data, *i.e.*, *transformer* [55]. As a typical multi-disciplinary AI task, Video Question Answering (VideoQA) has benefited a lot from these developments which helps to propel the field steadily forward over the use of purely conventional techniques [14,16,20,23,28,60,71].

Despite the excitement, we find that the advances made by such *transformer*-style models mostly lie in answering questions that demand the holistic recognition or description of video contents [30,48,62–64,68,72]. The problem of answering questions that challenge real-world visual relation reasoning, especially the causal and temporal relations that feature video dynamics [20,59], is largely under-explored. Cross-modal pretraining seems promising [29,67,70]. Yet, it requires the handling of prohibitively large-scale *video*-text data [15,70], or otherwise the performances are still inferior to the state-of-the-art (SoTA) conventional techniques [29,47,67]. In this work, we reveal two major reasons accounting for the failure: 1) **Video encoders are overly simplistic.** Current video encoders are either 2D neural networks (CNNs [18,45] or Transformers [13]) operated over sparse frames or 3D neural networks [5,37,61] operated over short video segments. Such networks encode the videos holistically, but fail to explicitly model the fine-grained details, *i.e.*, spatio-temporal interactions between visual objects. Consequently, the resulting VideoQA models are weak in reasoning and require large-scale video data for learning to compensate for such weak forms of input. 2) **Formulation of VideoQA problem is sub-optimal**. Often, in multi-choice QA, the video, question, and each candidate answer are appended (or fused) into one holistic token sequence and fed to a cross-modal Transformer to gain a global representation for answer classification [29,72]. Such a global representation is weak in disambiguating the candidate answers, because the video and question portions are the same and large, which may overwhelm the short answer and dominate the overall representation. In open-ended QA (popularly formulated as a multi-class classification problem [62]), answers are treated as class indexes and their word semantics (which are helpful for QA.) are ignored. The insufficient information modelling exacerbates the data-hungry issue and leads to sub-optimal performance as well.

To improve visual relation reasoning and also reduce the data demands for video question answering, we propose the Video Graph Transformer (VGT) model. VGT addresses the aforementioned problems and advances over previous *transformer*-style VideoQA models mainly in two aspects: 1) For video encoder, it designs a dynamic graph transformer module which explicitly captures the objects and relations as well as their dynamics to improve visual reasoning in dynamic scenario. 2) For problem formulation, it exploit *separate* vision and text transformers to encode video and text respectively for similarity (or relevance) comparison instead of using a single cross-modal transformer to fuse the vision and text information for answer classification. Vision-text communication is done by additional cross-modal interaction modules. Through more sufficient video information modelling and more reasonable QA problem solution, we show that VGT can achieve much better performances on benchmarks featuring dynamic relation reasoning than previous arts including those pretrained on million-scale vision-text data. Such strong performance comes even without using external data to pretrain. When pretraining VGT with a small amount of data, we can observe further and non-trivial performance improvements. The results clearly demonstrate VGT's effectiveness and superiority in visual reasoning, as well as its potential for more data-efficient[1] video-language pretraining.

To summarize our contributions: 1) We propose Video Graph Transformer (VGT) that advances VideoQA from shallow description to in-depth reason. 2) We design a dynamic graph transformer module which shows strength for visual reasoning. The module is task-agnostic and can be easily applied to other video-language tasks. 3) We achieve SoTA results on NExT-QA [59] and TGIF-QA [20] that task visual reasoning of dynamic visual contents. Also, our structured video representation gives a promise for data-efficient video-language pretraining.

2 Related Work

Conventional Techniques for VideoQA. Prior to the success of Transformer for vision-language tasks, various techniques, e.g., cross-modal attention [20,22,33], motion-appearance memory [14,16,36], and graph neural networks [23,35,41], have been proposed to model informative videos contents for answering questions. Yet, most of them leverage frame- or clip-level video representations as information source. Recently, graphs constructed over object-level representations [19,36,47,60] have demonstrated superior performance, especially on benchmarks that emphasize visual relation reasoning [20,49,50,59]. However, these graph methods either construct monolithic graphs that do not disambiguate between relations in 1) space and time, 2) local and global scopes [19,57], or build static graphs at frame-level without explicitly capturing the temporal dynamics [36,42,60]. The monolithic graph is cumbersome to long videos where multiple objects interact in space-time. Besides, the static graphs may lead to incorrect relations (e.g., **hug** vs. **fight**) or fail to capture dynamic relations (e.g., **take away**). In this work, we model video as a local-to-global dynamic visual graph, and design graph transformer module to explicitly model the objects, their relations, and dynamics, for exploiting object and relations in adjacent frames to calibrate the spurious relations obtained at static frame-level. Importantly, we also integrate strong language models and explore cross-modal pretraining techniques to learn the structured video representations in a self-supervised manner.

---

[1] The model demands on less training data to achieve good performance.

Transformer for VideoQA. Pioneer works [32,48,63,64,72] learn generalizable representations from HowTo100M [40] by either applying various proxy
tasks [72], or curating more tailored-made supervisions (e.g., future utterance
[48] and QA pairs [64]) for VideoQA. However, they focus on answering questions that demand the holistic recognition [62] or shallow description [68], and
their performances on visual relation reasoning [20,59] remains unknown. Furthermore, recent works [3,70] reveal that these models may suffer from performance lose on open-domain questions due to the heavy noise [1,39] and limited
data scope of HowTo100M. Recent efforts tend to use open-domain vision-text
data for end-to-end learning. ClipBERT [29] takes advantage of image-caption
data [7,27] for pretraining, but it only has limited performance improvement
on temporal reasoning tasks [20], as the temporal relations are hard to learn
from static images. In addition, ClipBERT relies on human annotated descriptions which are expensive to annotate and hard to scale up. More recent works
[15,70] collect million-scale user-generated (vastly abundant on the Web) vision-
text data [3,51,70] for pretraining, but suffers from huge computational cost
to train on such large-scale datasets. Two latest works [6,12] reveal the potential of Transformers for learning on the target datasets (relatively small scale).
While promising, they either target at revealing the single-frame bias of benchmark datasets by using image-text pretrained features (e.g. from CLIP [44]), or
only demonstrate the model's effectiveness on synthesized data [65]. Overall, the
poor-dynamic-reasoning and *data-hungry* problems in existing *transformer*-style
video-language models largely motivate this work. To alleviate these problems,
we explicitly model the objects and relations for dynamic visual reasoning and
incorporate structure priors (or relational inductive bias [4]) into transformer
architectures to reduce the demand on data.

Graph Transformer. The connection between graph neural networks and
Transformer has earned increasing attention [56,66,69]. Nonetheless, the major
advancements are made in modelling natural graph data (e.g. social connections)
by either incorporating graph expertise (e.g., node degrees) into self-attention
block of Transformer [66], or designing *transformer*-style convolution blocks to
fuse information from heterogeneous graphs [69]. A recent work [17] combines
graphs and Transformers for video dialogues. Yet, it simply applies global transformer over pooled graph representations built from static frames and does not
explicitly encode object and relation dynamics. Our work differs from it by
designing and learning dynamic visual graph over video objects and using transformers to capture the temporal dynamics at both local and global scopes.

3   Method

3.1   Overview

Given a video v and a question q, VideoQA aims to combine the two stream
information v and q to predict the answer a. Depending on the task settings, a
can be given in multiple choices along with each question for multi-choice QA,

or it is given in a global answer set for open-ended QA. In this work, we handle both types of VideoQA by optimizing the following objective:

$$a^* = \arg\max_{a \in \mathcal{A}} \mathcal{F}_W(a|q, v, \mathcal{A}), \tag{1}$$

in which $\mathcal{A}$ can be $\mathcal{A}_{mc}$ corresponding to the candidate answers of each question in multi-choice QA, or $\mathcal{A}_{oe}$ corresponding to the global answer set in open-ended QA. $\mathcal{F}_W$ denotes the mapping function with learnable parameters W.

To solve the problem, we design a video graph transformer (VGT) model to perform the mapping $\mathcal{F}_W$ in Eq. (1). As illustrated in Fig. 1, at the visual part (Orange), VGT takes as input visual object graphs, and drives a global feature f^{qv} with the integration of textual information, to represent the query-relevant video content. At the textual part (Blue), VGT extracts the feature representations $F^{\mathcal{A}}$ for all the candidate

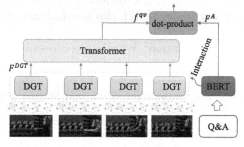

Fig. 1. Overview of video graph transformer (VGT) for VideoQA. (Color figure online)

answers via a language model (e.g., BERT [11]). The final answer a^* is determined by returning the candidate answers with maximal similarity (relevance score) between f^{qv} and $f^a \in F^{\mathcal{A}}$ via dot-product. At the heart of the model is the dynamic graph transformer module (DGT). The module clip-wisely reasons over the input graphs, and aggregates them into a sequence of feature representations F^{DGT} which are then fed to a global transformer to achieve f^{qv}. During training, the whole framework is end-to-end optimized with Softmax cross-entropy loss. For pretraining with weakly-paired video-text data, we adopt cross-modal matching as the major proxy task and optimize the model in a contrastive manner [44] along with masked language modelling [11].

3.2 Video Graph Representation

Given a video, we sparsely sample l_v frames in a way analogous to [60]. The l_v frames are evenly distributed into k clips of length $l_c = \frac{l_v}{k}$. For each sampled frame (see Fig. 2), we extract n RoI-aligned features as object appearance representations $F_r = \{f_{r_i}\}_{i=1}^n$ along with their spatial locations $B = \{b_{r_i}\}_{i=1}^n$ with a pretrained object detector [2,45], where r_i represents the i-th object region in a frame.

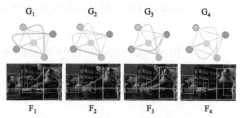

Fig. 2. Illustration of graph construction in a short video clip of $l_c = 4$ frames. The nodes of same color denote same object.

Additionally, we obtain an image-level feature $F_I = \{f_{I_t}\}_{t=1}^{l_v}$ for all the sampled frames with a pretrained image classification model [18]. F_I serve as global contexts to augment the graph representations aggregated from the local objects.

To find the same object across different frames within a clip, we define a linking score s by considering their appearance and spatial location:

$$s_{i,j} = \psi(f_{r_i}^t, f_{r_j}^{t+1}) + \lambda * \text{IoU}(b_i^t, b_j^{t+1}), \quad t \in \{1, 2, \ldots, l_c - 1\}, \tag{2}$$

where ψ denotes the cosine similarity between two detected objects i and j in adjacent frames. Intersection-over-union (IoU) computes the location overlap of objects i and j. Our experiments always set λ as one. The n detected objects in the first frame of each clip are designated as anchor objects. Detected objects in consecutive frames are then linked to the anchor objects by greedily maximizing s frame by frame[2]. By aligning objects within a clip, we ensure the consistency of the node and edge representations for the graphs constructed at different frames.

Next, we concatenate the object appearance f_r and location f_{loc} representations and project the combined feature into the d-dimensional space via

$$f_o = \text{ELU}(\phi_{W_o}([f_r; f_{loc}])), \tag{3}$$

where $[;]$ denotes feature concatenation and f_{loc} is obtained by applying a 1×1 convolution over the relative coordinates as in [60]. The function ϕ_{W_o} denotes a linear transformation with parameters W_o. With $F_o = \{f_{o_i}\}_{i=1}^n$, the relations in the t-th frame can be initialized as pairwise similarities:

$$R_t = \sigma(\phi_{W_{ak}}(F_{o_t})\phi_{W_{av}}(F_{o_t})^\top), \quad t \in \{1, 2, \ldots, l_v\}, \tag{4}$$

where $\phi_{W_{ak}}$ and $\phi_{W_{av}}$ denote linear transformations with parameters W_{ak} and $W_{av} \in \mathbb{R}^{d \times \frac{d}{2}}$ respectively. We use different transformations to reflect the asymmetric nature of real-world subject-object interactions [26,58]. For symmetric relations, we expect that the learned parameters W_{ak} and W_{av} are quite similar. σ is the Softmax operation that normalizes each row. For brevity, we use $G_t = (F_{o_t}, R_t)$ to denote the graph representation of the t-th frame where F_o are node representations and R are edge representations of the graph.

3.3   Dynamic Graph Transformer

Our dynamic graph transformer (DGT) takes as input a set of visual graphs $\{G_t\}_{t=1}^{L_v}$ clip-wisely, and outputs a sequence of representations $F^{DGT} \in \mathbb{R}^{d \times k}$ by mining the temporal dynamics of objects and their spatial interactions. To this end, we sequentially operate a temporal graph transformer unit, a spatial graph convolution unit and a hierarchical aggregation unit as detailed below.

Temporal Graph Transformer. As illustrated in Fig. 3, the temporal graph transformer unit takes as input a set of graphs G_{in} and outputs a new set of graphs G_{out} by mining the temporal dynamics among them via a node transformer (NTrans) and an edge transformer (ETrans). For completeness, we briefly

---

[2] We assume that the group of objects do not change in a short video clip.

recap the self-attention in Transformer [55]. It uses a multi-head self-attention (MHSA) to fuse a sequence of input features $X_{in} = \{x_{in}^t\}_{t=1}^l$:

$$X_{out} = \text{MHSA}(X_{in}) = \phi_{W_c}([h_1; h_2; \ldots, h_e]), \tag{5}$$

where ϕ_{W_c} is a linear transformation with parameters W_c, and

$$h_i = \text{SA}(\phi_{W_{i_q}}(X_{in}), \phi_{W_{i_k}}(X_{in}), \phi_{W_{i_v}}(X_{in})), \tag{6}$$

where $\phi_{W_{i_q}}$, $\phi_{W_{i_k}}$ and $\phi_{W_{i_v}}$ denote the linear transformations of the query, key, and value vectors of the i-th self-attention (SA) head respectively. e denotes the number of self-attention heads, and SA is defined as:

$$\text{SA}(X_q, X_k, X_v) = \sigma\left(X_k X_q^\top / \sqrt{d_k}\right) X_v, \tag{7}$$

in which d_k is the dimension of the key vector. Finally, a skip-connection with layer normalization (LN) is applied to the output sequence $X = LN(X_{out} + X_{in})$. X can undergo more MHSAs depending on the number of transformer layers.

In temporal graph transformer, we apply H self-attention blocks to enhance the node (or object) representations by aggregating information from other nodes of the same object from all adjacent frames within a clip:

$$F_{o_i}' = \text{NTrans}(F_{o_i}) = \text{MHSA}^{(H)}(F_{o_i}), \tag{8}$$

in which $F_{o_i} \in \mathbb{R}^{l_c \times d}$ denotes a sequence of feature representations corresponding to object i in a video clip of length l_c. Our motivation behind the node transformer is that it models the change of single object behaviours and thus infer the dynamic actions (e.g. **bend down**). Also, it is helpful in improving the objects' appearance feature in the cases where the object at certain frames suffer from motion blur or partial occlusion.

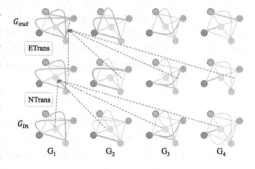

Fig. 3. Illustration of temporal graph transformer in a short video clip.

Based on the new nodes $F_o' = \{F_{o_i}'\}_{i=1}^n$, we update the relation matrix R via Eq. (4). Then, to explicitly model the temporal relation dynamics, we apply an edge transformer on the updated relation matrices:

$$\mathcal{R}' = \text{ETrans}(\mathcal{R}) = \text{MHSA}^{(H)}(\mathcal{R}), \tag{9}$$

where $\mathcal{R} = \{R_t\}_{t=1}^l \in \mathbb{R}^{l_c \times d_n}$ $(d_n = n^2)$ is the l_c adjacency matrices that are row-wisely expanded. Our motivation is that the relations captured at static frames may be spurious, trivial or incomplete. The edge transformer can help to calibrate the wrong relations and recall the missing ones. For brevity, we refer to the temporally contextualized graph at the t-th frame as $G_{out_t} = (F_{o_t}', R_t')$.

Spatial Graph Convolution. The temporal graph transformer focuses on temporal relation reasoning. To reason over the object spatial interactions, we apply a U-layer graph attention convolution [25] on all the l_v graphs:

$$F_o'^{(u)} = \text{ReLU}((R' + I)F_o'^{(u-1)}W^{(u)}), \tag{10}$$

where $W^{(u)}$ is the graph parameters at the u-th layer. I is the identity matrix for skip connections. $F_o'^{(u)}$ are initialized by the output node representations F_o' as aforementioned. The index t is omitted for brevity. A last skip-connection: $F_{o_{out}} = F_o' + F_o'^{(U)}$ is used to obtain the final node representations.

Hierarchical Aggregation. The node representations so far have explicitly token into account the objects' spatial and temporal interactions. But such interactions are mostly atomic. To aggregate these atomic interactions into higher-level video elements, we adopt a hierarchical aggregation strategy in Fig. 4.

First, we aggregate the graph nodes at each frame by a simple attention:

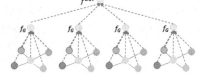

$$f_G = \sum_{i=1}^{N} \alpha_i F_{o_{out_i}}, \quad \alpha = \sigma(\phi_{W_G}(F_{o_{out}})), \tag{11}$$

Fig. 4. Hierarchical aggregation.

where ϕ_{W_G} is linear transformation with parameters $W_G \in \mathbb{R}^{d \times 1}$. The graph representation f_G captures a local object interactions. It may lose sight of a global picture of a frame, especially since we only retain n objects and cannot guarantee that they include all the objects of interest in that frame. As such, we complement f_G with the frame-level feature f_I by concatenation:

$$f_G = \text{ELU}(\phi_{W_m}([\phi_{W_f}(f_I); f_G])) \tag{12}$$

in which ϕ_{W_m} and ϕ_{W_f} are linear transformations with parameters $W_m \in \mathbb{R}^{2d \times d}$ and $W_f \in \mathbb{R}^{2048 \times d}$ respectively. We next pool the local interactions to obtain a sequence of clip-level feature representations via:

$$f^{\text{DGT}} = \text{MPool}(F_G) = \frac{1}{l_c} \sum_{t=1}^{l_v} f_{G_t} \tag{13}$$

The set of k clips are finally represented by $F^{\text{DGT}} = \{f_c^{\text{DGT}}\}_{c=1}^{k}$.

3.4   Cross-Modal Interaction

To find the informative visual contents with respect to a particular text query, a cross-model interaction between the visual and textual nodes is essential. Given a set of visual nodes denoted by X^v, we integrate textual information $X^q = \{x_m^q\}_{m=1}^{M}$ into the visual nodes via a simple cross-modal attention:

$$x^{qv} = x^v + \sum_{m=1}^{M} \beta_m x_m^q, \quad \text{where} \quad \beta = \sigma(x^v(X^q)^{\top}), \tag{14}$$

where M is the number of tokens in the text query. In principle, the X^v can be visual representations from different levels of the DGT module. In our experiment, we explore performing the cross-modal interaction with visual representations at the object-level (F_O in Eq. (3)), frame-level (F_G in Eq. (12)), and clip-level (F^{DGT} in Eq. (13)). We find that the results vary among different datasets. As a default, we perform cross-modal interaction at the clip-level outputs (*i.e.*, the outputs of the DGT module $X^v := F^{DGT}$), since the number of nodes at this stage is much smaller, and the node representations have already absorbed the information from the preceding layers. For the text node X^q, we obtain them by a simple linear projection on the token outputs of a language model [11]:

$$X^q = \phi_{W_Q}(\mathrm{BERT}(Q)), \tag{15}$$

where $W_Q \in \mathbb{R}^{768 \times d}$. The text query Q can be questions in open-end QA or QA pairs in multi-choice QA. Note that in multi-choice QA, we max-pool the obtained query-aware visual representations with respect to different QA pairs to find the one that is mostly relevant to the video.

3.5 Global Transformer

The aforementioned DGT module pays attention to extract informative visual clues from video clips. To capture the temporal dynamics between these clips, we employ another H-layer transformer over the cross-modal interacted clip feature (*i.e.* F^{DGT}), and add learnable sinusoidal temporal position embeddings [11]. Finally, the transformer's outputs are mean-pooled to obtain the global representation $f^{qv} \in \mathbb{R}^d$ for the entire video, which is defined as follows:

$$f^{qv} = \mathrm{MPool}(\mathrm{MHSA}^{(H)}(F^{DGT})). \tag{16}$$

The global transformer has two major advantages: 1) It retains the overall hierarchical structure which progressively drives the video elements at different granularity as in [60]. 2) It improves the feature compatibility of vision and text, which may benefit cross-modal comparison.

3.6 Answer Prediction

To obtain a global representation for a particular answer candidate, we mean-pool its token representations from BERT by $f^A = \mathrm{MPool}(X^A)$, where X^A denotes a candidate answer's token representations, and is obtained in a way analogous to Eq. (15). Its similarity with the query-aware video representation f^{qv} is then obtained via a dot-product. Consequently, the candidate answer of maximal similarity is returned as the final prediction:

$$s = f^{qv}(F^A)^\top, \quad a^* = \arg\max(s), \tag{17}$$

in which $F^A = \{f_a^A\}_{a=1}^{|\mathcal{A}|} \in \mathbb{R}^{|\mathcal{A}| \times d}$, and $|\mathcal{A}|$ denotes the number of candidate answers. Additionally, for open-ended QA, we follow previous works [60] and enable a video-absent QA by directly computing the similarities between the question representation f^q (obtained in a way similar to f^A) and the answer representations F^A. As a result, the final answer can be a joint decision:

$$s = f^{qv}(F^A)^\top \odot f^q(F^A)^\top \tag{18}$$

in which $\odot$ is element-wise product. During training, we maximize the $\langle VQ, A \rangle$ similarity corresponding to the correct answer of a given sample by optimizing the Softmax cross entropy loss function. $\mathcal{L} = -\sum_{i=1}^{|\mathcal{A}|} y_i \log s_i$, where s_i is the matching score for the i-th sample. $y_i = 1$ if the answer index corresponds to the i-th sample's ground-truth answer and 0 otherwise.

3.7   Pretraining with Weakly-Paired Data

For cross-model matching, we encourage the representation of each video-text interacted representation f^{qv} to be closer to that of its paired description f^q and be far away from that of negative descriptions which are randomly collected from other video-text pairs in each training iteration. This is formally achieved by maximizing the following contrastive objective:

$$\sum_i \log\left(\frac{\exp\left(f_i^{qv}(f_i^q)^\top\right)}{\exp\left(f_i^{qv}(f_i^q)^\top\right) + \sum_{(f^{qv}, f^q) \in \mathcal{N}_i} \exp\left(f^{qv}(f^q)^\top\right)}\right), \tag{19}$$

where $\mathcal{N}_i$ denotes the representations of all the negative video-description pairs of the i-th sample. The parameters to be optimized are hidden in the process of calculating f^{qv} and f^q as introduced above. For negative sampling, we sample them from the whole training set at each iteration. For masked language modelling, we only corrupt the positive description of each video for efficiency.

4   Experiment

4.1   Dataset and Configuration

We conduct experiments on benchmarks whose QAs feature temporal dynamics: 1) NExT-QA [59] is a manually annotated dataset that features causal and temporal object interaction in space-time. 2) TGIF-QA [20] features short GIFs; it asks questions about repeated action recognition, temporal state transition and frame QA which invokes a certain frame for answer. For better comparison, we also experiment on MSRVTT-QA [62] which challenges a holistic visual recognition or description. Other data statistics are presented in Appendix A.

We decode the video into frames following [60], and then sparsely sample $l_v = 32$ frames from each video. The frames are distributed into $k = 8$ clips whose length $l_c = 4$. For each frame, we detect and keep $N = 20$ regions of high confidence for NExT-QA (Top-5 are used in the pretraining-free experiments, refer to our analysis in Appendix C.2), and $N = 10$ for the other datasets, using the object detection model provided by [2]. The dimension of the models'

Table 1. Results on NExT-QA [59]. (Acc@C, T, D: Accuracy for Causal, Temporal and Descriptive questions respectively. *: Results reproduced with the official code.)

Method	CM-pretrain	NExT-QA Val				NExT-QA Test			
		Acc@C	Acc@T	Acc@D	Acc@All	Acc@C	Acc@T	Acc@D	Acc@All
HGA [23]	–	46.26	50.74	59.33	49.74	48.13	49.08	57.79	50.01
IGV [35]	–	–	–	–	–	48.56	51.67	59.64	51.34
HQGA [60]	–	48.48	51.24	61.65	51.42	_49.04_	**52.28**	59 43	_51.75_
P3D-G [9]	–	_51.33_	_52.30_	62.58	_53.40_	–	–	–	–
VQA-T* [64]	–	41.66	44.11	59.97	45.30	42.05	42.75	55.87	44.54
VQA-T* [64]	How2VQA69M	49.60	51.49	_63.19_	52.32	47.89	50.02	_61.87_	50.83
VGT (Ours)	–	**52.28**	**55.09**	**64.09**	**55.02**	**51.62**	_51.94_	**63.65**	**53.68**

hidden states is $d = 512$. The default number of layers and self-attention heads in transformer are $H = 1$ and $e = 8$ ($e = 5$ for edge transformer in DGT) respectively. Besides, the number of graph layers is $U = 2$. For training, we use Adam optimizer with initial learning rate 1×10^{-5} of a cosine annealing schedule. The batch size is set to 64, and the maximum epoch varies from 10 to 30 among different datasets. Our pretraining data ($\sim$0.18M) are collected from WebVid [3]. More details are presented in Appendix B.

4.2   Sate-of-the-Art Comparison

In Table 1, we compare VGT with the prior arts on NExT-QA [60]. The results show that VGT surpasses the previous SoTAs by clear margins on both the val and test sets, improving the overall accuracy by 1.6% and 1.9% respectively. VGT even outperforms a latest work ATP [6] which is based on CLIP features [44] (VGT vs. ATP: 55.02% vs. 54.3%), and thus sets the new SoTA results. In particular, we note that such strong results come without considering large-scale cross-modal pretraining. When pretraining VGT with (relatively) small amount of data, we can further increase the results to 56.9% and 55.7% on NExT-QA val and test sets respectively (refer to our analysis of Table 5 in Sect. 4.4).

Compared with VQA-T [64] which also formulates VideoQA as problem of similarity comparison instead of classification, VGT outperforms it almost in all metrics. The strong results could be due to that VGT explicitly models the object interactions and dynamics for visual reasoning, instead of holistically encoding video clips with S3D [39,61]. For a better analysis, we further replace the S3D encoder in VQA-T with our DGT module. As shown in Table 2 (S3D → DGT), our DGT encoder significantly improves VQA-T's result by 4.7%, in which most of the improvements are from answering reasoning type of questions. Aside from the DGT module, we encode the candidate answers in the context of the corresponding question with a single language model, whereas VQA-T encodes Q and A independently with two language models [46]. Our method improves answer encoding with contexts and reduces the model size (or parameters), as shown in Table 2 (VGT (DistilBERT)). Finally, VQA-T adopts cross-modal transformer to fuse the video-question pair, whereas we design light-weight cross-modal interaction module. The module is more parameter efficient but has little impact on the performances (CMTrans→CM in Table 2).

Compared with other graph based methods [9, 23, 60], VGT enjoys several advantages: 1) It explicitly model the temporal dynamics of both objects and their interactions. 2) It solves VideoQA by explicit similarity comparison between the video and text instead of classification.

Table 2. Detailed comparison with VQA-T [64]. CMTrans: Cross-Modal Transformer.

Models	Size (M)	NExT-QA Val			
		Acc@C	Acc@T	Acc@D	Acc@All
VQA-T [64]	600	41.66	44.11	59.97	45.30
S3D→DGT	641	47.53	48.08	62.42	50.02
CMTrans→CM	573	42.27	44.29	58.17	45.40
VGT (DistilBERT)	346	50.71	51.67	66.41	53.46
VGT (BERT)	511	52.28	55.09	64.09	55.02

3) It represents both visual and textual data with Transformers which may improve the feature compatibility and benefit cross-modal interaction and comparison [11]. 4) VGT uses much few frames for training and inference (e.g., VGT vs. HQGA [60]: 32 vs. 256), which benefits efficiency for video encoding. The detailed analyses are given in Sect. 4.3.

In Table 3, we compare VGT with previous arts on the TGIF-QA and MSRVTT-QA datasets. The results show that VGT performs pretty well on the tasks of repeating action recognition and state transition that feature temporal dynamics, surpassing the previous pretraining-free SoTA results significantly by 10.6% (VGT vs. MASN [47]: 95.0% vs. 84.4%) and 6.8% (VGT vs. MHN [43]: 97.6% vs. 90.8%) respectively. It even beats the pretraining SoTA (*i.e.* MERLOT [70]) by about 1.0%, yet without using external data for cross-modal pretraining. On TGIF-QA-R [42] which is curated by making the negative answers in TGIF-QA more challenging, we can also observe remarkable improvements. Besides, VGT also achieves competitive results on normal descriptive QA tasks as defined in FrameQA and MSRVTT-QA though they are not our focus.

Table 3. Results on TGIF-QA and MSVTT-QA. † denotes TGIF-QA-R [42] whose multiple choices for repeated action and state transition are more challenging. We grey out the results reported in [42] regarding these two sub-tasks, because the candidate answers are slightly different as we have further rectified the redundant choices.

Models	CM-pretrain	TGIF-QA					MSRVTT-QA
		Action	Transition	FrameQA	Action†	Transition†	
LGCN [19]	–	74.3	81.1	56.3	–	–	–
HGA [23]	–	75.4	81.0	55.1	–	–	35.5
HCRN [28]	–	75.0	81.4	55.9	55.7	63.9	35.6
B2A [41]	–	75.9	82.6	57.5	–	–	36.9
HOSTR [10]	–	75.0	83.0	58.0	–	–	35.9
HAIR [36]	–	77.8	82.3	60.2	–	–	36.9
MASN [47]	–	84.4	87.4	59.5	–	–	35.2
PGAT [42]	–	80.6	85.7	61.1	58.7	65.9	38.1
HQGA [60]	–	76.9	85.6	61.3	–	–	38.6
MHN [43]	–	83.5	90.8	58.1	–	–	38.6
ClipBERT [29]	VG+COCO Caption	82.8	87.8	60.3	–	–	37.4
SiaSRea [67]	VG+COCO Caption	79.7	85.3	60.2	–	–	41.6
MERLOT [70]	Youtube180M, CC3M	94.0	96.2	69.5	–	–	43.1
VGT (Ours)	–	95.0	97.6	61.6	59.9	70.5	39.7

4.3   Model Analysis

DGT. The middle block of Table 4 shows that removing the DGT module (w/o DGT) (i.e. directly summarizing the object representations in each clip) leads to clear performance drops (∼2.0%) on all tasks that challenge spatio-temporal reasoning. We then study the temporal graph transformer module (w/o TTrans) by removing both NTrans and ETrans. It shows better results than removing the whole DGT module. Yet, its performances on tasks featuring temporal dynamics are still weak. We further ablate the temporal graph transformer module to investigate the independent contribution of the node transformer (NTrans) and edge transformer (ETrans). The results (w/o NTrans and w/o ETrans) demonstrate that both transformers benefit temporal dynamic modelling. Finally, the ablation study on the global frame feature F_I reveals its vital role to DGT.

Similarity Comparison *vs.* Classification. We study a model variant by concatenating the outputs of the DGT module with the token representations from BERT in a way analogous to ClipBERT [29]. The formed text-video representation sequence is fed to a cross-modal transformer for information fusion.

Table 4. Study of model components

Models	TGIF-QA		NExT-QA Val			
	Action	Trans	Acc@C	Acc@T	Acc@D	Acc@All
VGT	**95.0**	**97.6**	**52.28**	**55.09**	64.09	**55.02**
w/o DGT	89.6	95.4	50.10	52.85	64.48	53.22
w/o TTrans	94.0	97.6	50.86	53.04	64.86	53.74
w/o NTrans	94.5	97.4	50.79	54.22	63.32	53.84
w/o ETrans	94.8	97.4	51.25	54.34	64.48	54.30
w/o F_I	93.5	97.0	50.44	53.97	63.32	53.58
Comp→CLS	70.1	79.9	42.96	46.96	53.02	45.82

Then, the output of the '[CLS]' token is fed to a $|\mathcal{A}|$-way classifier in open-ended QA or a 1-way classifier for binary relevance in multi-choice QA following [20,28,60]. As can be seen from the bottom part of Table 4, this classification model variant (Comp → CLS) leads to drastic performance drops. To be complete, we also conduct additional experiments on the FrameQA task which is set as open-ended QA. Again, we find that the accuracy drops from 61.6% to 56.9%. A detailed analysis of the performances on the training and validation sets (see Appendix C.1) reveals that the CLS-model suffers from serious over-fitting on the target datasets. The experiment demonstrates the superiority of solving QA by relevance comparison instead of answer classification.

Cross-Modal Interaction. Figure 5 investigates several implementation variants of the cross-modal interaction module as depicted in Sect. 3.4. The results suggest that it is better to integrate textual information at both the frame- and clip-level outputs (CM-CF) for TGIF-QA, while our default interaction at the clip-level outputs (CM-C) brings the optimal results on NExT-QA. Compared with the baselines that do not use cross-modal interaction, all three kinds of interactions improve the performances. We notice that the cross-modal interaction improves the accuracy on TGIF-QA by

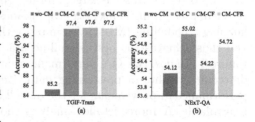

Fig. 5. Study of cross-modal interaction.

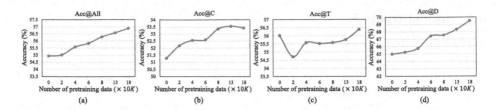

Fig. 6. Results of pretraining with different amounts of data.

Table 5. Study of cross-model pretraining. Results on NExT-QA are with 20 regions.

Methods	TGIF-QA		NExT-QA Val				NExT-QA Test			
	Action†	Trans†	Acc@C	Acc@T	Acc@D	Acc@All	Acc@C	Acc@T	Acc@D	Acc@All
VGT	59.9	70.5	51.29	56.02	64.99	54.94	50.82	52.29	63.27	53.51
VGT (FT w/ QA)	60.2	71.0	**53.93**	56.20	**70.14**	**57.19**	51.73	53.78	67.05	54.88
VGT (FT w/ QA & MLM)	**60.5**	**71.5**	53.43	**56.39**	69.50	56.89	**52.78**	**54.54**	**67.26**	**55.70**

more than 10%. A possible reason is that the GIFs are trimmed short videos that only contain the QA-related visual contents. This greatly eases the challenge in spatial-temporal grounding of the positive answers, especially when most of the negative answers are not presence in the short GIFs. Thus, the cross-modal interaction performs more effectively on this dataset. The videos in NExT-QA are not trimmed, thereby the improvements are relatively smaller. Base on these observations, we perform cross-modal interaction at both the frame- and clip-level outputs for the temporal reasoning tasks in TGIF-QA, and keep the default implementation for other datasets.

4.4   Pretraining and Finetuning

Table 5 presents a comparison between VGT with and without pretraining. We can see that pretraining can steadily boost the QA performance, especially on NExT-QA. The relatively smaller improvements on TGIF-QA could be due to that TGIF-QA dataset is large, and has enough annotated data for fine-tuning. As such, pretraining helps little [73]. Besides, we find that finetuning with masked language modelling (MLM) can improve the generalization from val to test set, and thus achieves the best overall accuracy (*i.e.* 55.7%) on NExT-QA test set. Figure 6 studies the QA performances on NExT-QA val set with respect to different amounts of pretraining data. Generally, there is a clear tendency of performance improvements for the overall accuracy (Acc@All) when more data is available. A more detailed analysis shows that these improvements mostly come from a stronger performance in answering causal (Acc@C) and descriptive (Acc@D) questions. For temporal questions, it seems that pretraining with more data does not help much. Therefore, to boost performance, it is promising to add more data or explore a better way to handle temporal languages.

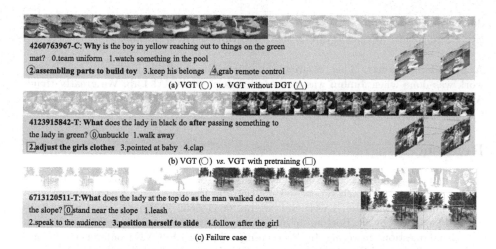

4260763967-C: Why is the boy in yellow reaching out to things on the green mat? 0.team uniform 1.watch something in the pool 2.assembling parts to build toy 3.keep his belongs 4.grab remote control

(a) VGT (○) vs. VGT without DGT (△)

4123915842-T: What does the lady in black do after passing something to the lady in green? 0.unbuckle 1.walk away 2.adjust the girls clothes 3.pointed at baby 4.clap

(b) VGT (○) vs. VGT with pretraining (□)

6713120511-T:What does the lady at the top do as the man walked down the slope? 0.stand near the slope 1.leash 2.speak to the audience 3.position herself to slide 4.follow after the girl

(c) Failure case

Fig. 7. Result visualization on NExT-QA [59]. The ground-truth answers are in green. (Color figure online)

4.5   Qualitative Analysis

In Fig. 7, we qualitatively analyze the benefits of both dynamic graph transformer and pretraining. The example in (a) shows that the model without the DGT module is prone to predicting atomic or contact actions (e.g. 'grab') that can be captured at static frame-level. (b) shows that the model without pretraining fails to predict the answer that is highly abstract (e.g. 'adjust'). Finally, we show a failure case in (c). It indicates that our model tends to predict distractor answers that are semantically close to the questions when the object of interests in the video are small and the detector fails to detect it. Keeping more detected regions could be helpful, but one needs to carefully balance the graph complexity as well as the inference efficiency. Another alternative is to perform modulated detection as in [24], we leave it for future exploration.

5   Conclusions

We presented video graph transformer which explicitly exploits the objects, their relations, and dynamics, to improve visual reasoning and alleviate the data-hungry issue for VideoQA. Our extensive experiments show that VGT can achieve superior performances as compared with previous SoTA methods on tasks that challenge temporal dynamic reasoning. The performance even surpasses those methods that are pretrained on large-scale vision-text data. To study the learning capacity of VGT, we further explored pretraining on weakly-paired video-text data and obtained promising results. With careful and comprehensive analyses of the model, we hope this work can encourage more efforts in designing effectiveness models to alleviate the burden of handling large-scale data, and also promote VQA research that goes beyond a holistic recognition/description to reason about the fine-grained video details.

Acknowledgements. This research is supported by the Sea-NExT joint Lab. Major work was done when Junbin was a research intern at Sea AI Lab. We greatly thank Angela Yao as well as the anonymous reviewers for their thoughtful comments towards a better work.

References

1. Amrani, E., Ben-Ari, R., Rotman, D., Bronstein, A.: Noise estimation using density estimation for self-supervised multimodal learning. In: AAAI Conference on Artificial Intelligence (AAAI), vol. 35, pp. 6644–6652 (2021)
2. Anderson, P., et al.: Bottom-up and top-down attention for image captioning and visual question answering. In: Proceedings of the IEEE/CVF Conference on Computer Vision and Pattern Recognition (CVPR), pp. 6077–6086 (2018)
3. Bain, M., Nagrani, A., Varol, G., Zisserman, A.: Frozen in time: a joint video and image encoder for end-to-end retrieval. In: Proceedings of the IEEE/CVF International Conference on Computer Vision (ICCV), pp. 1728–1738 (2021)
4. Battaglia, P.W., et al.: Relational inductive biases, deep learning, and graph networks. arXiv preprint arXiv:1806.01261 (2018)
5. Bertasius, G., Wang, H., Torresani, L.: Is space-time attention all you need for video understanding? In: ICML, pp. 813–824. PMLR (2021)
6. Buch, S., Eyzaguirre, C., Gaidon, A., Wu, J., Fei-Fei, L., Niebles, J.C.: Revisiting the "video" in video-language understanding. In: Proceedings of the IEEE/CVF Conference on Computer Vision and Pattern Recognition (CVPR), pp. 2917–2927 (2022)
7. Chen, X., et al.: Microsoft coco captions: data collection and evaluation server. arXiv preprint arXiv:1504.00325 (2015)
8. Chen, Y.C., et al.: UNITER: UNiversal image-TExt representation learning. In: Vedaldi, A., Bischof, H., Brox, T., Frahm, J.-M. (eds.) ECCV 2020. LNCS, vol. 12375, pp. 104–120. Springer, Cham (2020). https://doi.org/10.1007/978-3-030-58577-8_7
9. Cherian, A., Hori, C., Marks, T.K., Le Roux, J.: (2.5+ 1) d spatio-temporal scene graphs for video question answering. In: Proceedings of the AAAI Conference on Artificial Intelligence, vol. 36, pp. 444–453 (2022)
10. Dang, L.H., Le, T.M., Le, V., Tran, T.: Hierarchical object-oriented spatio-temporal reasoning for video question answering. In: IJCAI (2021)
11. Devlin, J., Chang, M.W., Lee, K., Toutanova, K.: Bert: pre-training of deep bidirectional transformers for language understanding. In: NAACL (2019)
12. Ding, D., Hill, F., Santoro, A., Reynolds, M., Botvinick, M.: Attention over learned object embeddings enables complex visual reasoning. Adv. Neural Inf. Process. syst. (NeurIPS) **34**, 9112–9124 (2021)
13. Dosovitskiy, A., et al.: An image is worth 16×16 words: transformers for image recognition at scale. In: International Conference on Representation Learning (ICLR) (2020)
14. Fan, C., Zhang, X., Zhang, S., Wang, W., Zhang, C., Huang, H.: Heterogeneous memory enhanced multimodal attention model for video question answering. In: Proceedings of the IEEE/CVF Conference on Computer Vision and Pattern Recognition (CVPR), pp. 1999–2007 (2019)

15. Fu, T.J., et al.: Violet: end-to-end video-language transformers with masked visual-token modeling. In: arXiv preprint arXiv:2111.12681 (November 2021)
16. Gao, J., Ge, R., Chen, K., Nevatia, R.: Motion-appearance co-memory networks for video question answering. In: Proceedings of the IEEE/CVF Conference on Computer Vision and Pattern Recognition (CVPR), pp. 6576–6585 (2018)
17. Geng, S., et al.: Dynamic graph representation learning for video dialog via multi-modal shuffled transformers. In: AAAI Conference on Artificial Intelligence (AAAI) (2021)
18. He, K., Zhang, X., Ren, S., Sun, J.: Deep residual learning for image recognition. In: Proceedings of the IEEE/CVF Conference on Computer Vision and Pattern Recognition (CVPR), pp. 770–778 (2016)
19. Huang, D., Chen, P., Zeng, R., Du, Q., Tan, M., Gan, C.: Location-aware graph convolutional networks for video question answering. In: AAAI Conference on Artificial Intelligence (AAAI), vol. 34, pp. 11021–11028 (2020)
20. Jang, Y., Song, Y., Yu, Y., Kim, Y., Kim, G.: TGIF-QA: toward spatio-temporal reasoning in visual question answering. In: Proceedings of the IEEE/CVF Conference on Computer Vision and Pattern Recognition (CVPR), pp. 2758–2766 (2017)
21. Jia, C., et al.: Scaling up visual and vision-language representation learning with noisy text supervision. In: ICML. pp, 4904–4916. PMLR (2021)
22. Jiang, J., Chen, Z., Lin, H., Zhao, X., Gao, Y.: Divide and conquer: question-guided spatio-temporal contextual attention for video question answering. In: AAAI Conference on Artificial Intelligence (AAAI), vol. 34, pp. 11101–11108 (2020)
23. Jiang, P., Han, Y.: Reasoning with heterogeneous graph alignment for video question answering. In: AAAI Conference on Artificial Intelligence (AAAI) (2020)
24. Kamath, A., Singh, M., LeCun, Y., Synnaeve, G., Misra, I., Carion, N.: MDETR-modulated detection for end-to-end multi-modal understanding. In: Proceedings of the IEEE/CVF International Conference on Computer Vision (ICCV), pp. 1780–1790 (2021)
25. Kipf, T.N., Welling, M.: Semi-supervised classification with graph convolutional networks. In: International Conference on Representation Learning (ICLR) (2017)
26. Krishna, R., Chami, I., Bernstein, M., Fei-Fei, L.: Referring relationships. In: Proceedings of the IEEE/CVF Conference on Computer Vision and Pattern Recognition (CVPR), pp. 6867–6876 (2018)
27. Krishna, R., et al.: Visual genome: connecting language and vision using crowd-sourced dense image annotations. IJCV **123**(1), 32–73 (2017). https://doi.org/10.1007/S11263-016-0981-7
28. Le, T.M., Le, V., Venkatesh, S., Tran, T.: Hierarchical conditional relation networks for video question answering. In: Proceedings of the IEEE/CVF Conference on Computer Vision and Pattern Recognition (CVPR), pp. 9972–9981 (2020)
29. Lei, J., et al.: Less is more: ClipBERT for video-and-language learning via sparse sampling. In: Proceedings of the IEEE/CVF Conference on Computer Vision and Pattern Recognition (CVPR), pp. 7331–7341 (2021)
30. Lei, J., Yu, L., Bansal, M., Berg, T.L.: TVQA: localized, compositional video question answering. In: Empirical Methods in Natural Language Processing (EMNLP) (2018)
31. Li, J., Selvaraju, R., Gotmare, A., Joty, S., Xiong, C., Hoi, S.C.H.: Align before fuse: Vision and language representation learning with momentum distillation. In: Advances in Neural Information Processing Systems (NeurIPS), vol. 34 (2021)
32. Li, L., Chen, Y.C., Cheng, Y., Gan, Z., Yu, L., Liu, J.: Hero: hierarchical encoder for video+ language omni-representation pre-training. In: Proceedings of the 2020

Conference on Empirical Methods in Natural Language Processing (EMNLP), pp. 2046–2065 (2020)

33. Li, X., et al.: Beyond RNNs: positional self-attention with co-attention for video question answering. In: AAAI Conference on Artificial Intelligence (AAAI), pp. 8658–8665 (2019)

34. Li, X., et al.: OSCAR: object-semantics aligned pre-training for vision-language tasks. In: Vedaldi, A., Bischof, H., Brox, T., Frahm, J.-M. (eds.) ECCV 2020. LNCS, vol. 12375, pp. 121–137. Springer, Cham (2020). https://doi.org/10.1007/978-3-030-58577-8_8

35. Li, Y., Wang, X., Xiao, J., Ji, W., Chua, T.S.: Invariant grounding for video question answering. In: Proceedings of the IEEE/CVF Conference on Computer Vision and Pattern Recognition (CVPR), pp. 2928–2937 (2022)

36. Liu, F., Liu, J., Wang, W., Lu, H.: Hair: hierarchical visual-semantic relational reasoning for video question answering. In: Proceedings of the IEEE/CVF International Conference on Computer Vision (ICCV), pp. 1698–1707 (2021)

37. Liu, Z., et al.: Video swin transformer. In: Proceedings of the IEEE/CVF Conference on Computer Vision and Pattern Recognition (CVPR), pp. 3202–3211 (2022)

38. Lu, J., Batra, D., Parikh, D., Lee, S.: ViLBERT: pretraining task-agnostic visiolinguistic representations for vision-and-language tasks. In: Advances in Neural Information Processing Systems (NeurIPS), pp. 13–23 (2019)

39. Miech, A., Alayrac, J.B., Smaira, L., Laptev, I., Sivic, J., Zisserman, A.: End-to-end learning of visual representations from uncurated instructional videos. In: Proceedings of the IEEE/CVF Conference on Computer Vision and Pattern Recognition (CVPR), pp. 9879–9889 (2020)

40. Miech, A., Zhukov, D., Alayrac, J.B., Tapaswi, M., Laptev, I., Sivic, J.: Howto100m: learning a text-video embedding by watching hundred million narrated video clips. In: Proceedings of the IEEE/CVF International Conference on Computer Vision (ICCV), pp. 2630–2640 (2019)

41. Park, J., Lee, J., Sohn, K.: Bridge to answer: structure-aware graph interaction network for video question answering. In: Proceedings of the IEEE/CVF Conference on Computer Vision and Pattern Recognition (CVPR), pp. 15526–15535 (2021)

42. Peng, L., Yang, S., Bin, Y., Wang, G.: Progressive graph attention network for video question answering. In: ACM MM, pp. 2871–2879 (2021)

43. Peng, M., Wang, C., Gao, Y., Shi, Y., Zhou, X.D.: Multilevel hierarchical network with multiscale sampling for video question answering. In: IJCAI (2022)

44. Radford, A., et al.: Learning transferable visual models from natural language supervision. In: ICML, pp. 8748–8763. PMLR (2021)

45. Ren, S., He, K., Girshick, R., Sun, J.: Faster R-CNN: towards real-time object detection with region proposal networks. Adv. Neural Inf. Process. Syst. (NeurIPS) **28**, 1–9 (2015)

46. Sanh, V., Debut, L., Chaumond, J., Wolf, T.: DistilBERT, a distilled version of BERT: smaller, faster, cheaper and lighter. In: 5th Workshop on Energy Efficient Machine Learning and Cognitive Computing - NeurIPS 2019

47. Seo, A., Kang, G.C., Park, J., Zhang, B.T.: Attend what you need: motion-appearance synergistic networks for video question answering. In: ACL, pp. 6167–6177 (2021)

48. Seo, P.H., Nagrani, A., Schmid, C.: Look before you speak: visually contextualized utterances. In: Proceedings of the IEEE/CVF Conference on Computer Vision and Pattern Recognition (CVPR), pp. 16877–16887 (2021)

49. Shang, X., Di, D., Xiao, J., Cao, Y., Yang, X., Chua, T.S.: Annotating objects and relations in user-generated videos. In: Proceedings of the 2019 on International Conference on Multimedia Retrieval (ICMR), pp. 279–287 (2019)
50. Shang, X., Xiao, J., Di, D., Chua, T.S.: Relation understanding in videos: a grand challenge overview. In: Proceedings of the 27th ACM International Conference on Multimedia (MM), pp. 2652–2656 (2019)
51. Sharma, P., Ding, N., Goodman, S., Soricut, R.: Conceptual captions: a cleaned, hypernymed, image alt-text dataset for automatic image captioning. In: ACL, pp. 2556–2565 (2018)
52. Su, W., et al.: VL-BERT: pre-training of generic visual-linguistic representations. In: International Conference on Representation Learning (ICLR) (2020)
53. Sun, C., Myers, A., Vondrick, C., Murphy, K., Schmid, C.: VideoBERT: a joint model for video and language representation learning. In: Proceedings of the IEEE/CVF International Conference on Computer Vision (ICCV), pp. 7464–7473 (2019)
54. Tan, H., Bansal, M.: LXMERT: learning cross-modality encoder representations from transformers. In: EMNLP, pp. 5100–5111 (2019)
55. Vaswani, A., et al.: Attention is all you need. In: Advances in Neural Information Processing Systems (NeurIPS), vol. 30 (2017)
56. Wang, L., et al.: TCL: transformer-based dynamic graph modelling via contrastive learning. arXiv preprint arXiv:2105.07944 (2021)
57. Wang, X., Gupta, A.: Videos as space-time region graphs. In: European Conference on Computer Vision (ECCV), pp. 399–417 (2018)
58. Xiao, J., Shang, X., Yang, X., Tang, S., Chua, T.-S.: Visual relation grounding in videos. In: Vedaldi, A., Bischof, H., Brox, T., Frahm, J.-M. (eds.) ECCV 2020. LNCS, vol. 12351, pp. 447–464. Springer, Cham (2020). https://doi.org/10.1007/978-3-030-58539-6_27
59. Xiao, J., Shang, X., Yao, A., Chua, T.S.: Next-QA: next phase of question-answering to explaining temporal actions. In: Proceedings of the IEEE/CVF Conference on Computer Vision and Pattern Recognition (CVPR), pp. 9777–9786 (2021)
60. Xiao, J., Yao, A., Liu, Z., Li, Y., Ji, W., Chua, T.S.: Video as conditional graph hierarchy for multi-granular question answering. In: Proceedings of the AAAI Conference on Artificial Intelligence (AAAI), pp. 2804–2812 (2022)
61. Xie, S., Sun, C., Huang, J., Tu, Z., Murphy, K.: Rethinking spatiotemporal feature learning: speed-accuracy trade-offs in video classification. In: European Conference on Computer Vision (ECCV), pp. 305–321 (2018)
62. Xu, D., et al.: Video question answering via gradually refined attention over appearance and motion. In: ACM MM, pp. 1645–1653 (2017)
63. Xu, H., et al.: Videoclip: contrastive pre-training for zero-shot video-text understanding. In: EMNLP, pp. 6787–6800 (2021)
64. Yang, A., Miech, A., Sivic, J., Laptev, I., Schmid, C.: Just ask: learning to answer questions from millions of narrated videos. In: Proceedings of the IEEE/CVF International Conference on Computer Vision (ICCV), pp. 1686–1697 (2021)
65. Yi, K., et al.: CLEVRER: collision events for video representation and reasoning. In: International Conference on Learning Representations (ICLR) (2019)
66. Ying, C., et al.: Do transformers really perform badly for graph representation? Adv. Neural Inf. Process. Syst. (NeurIPS) **34**, 28877–28888 (2021)
67. Yu, W., et al.: Learning from inside: self-driven siamese sampling and reasoning for video question answering. Adv. Neural Inf. Process. Syst. (NeurIPS) **34**, 26462–26474 (2021)

68. Yu, Y., Kim, J., Kim, G.: A joint sequence fusion model for video question answering and retrieval. In: European Conference on Computer Vision (ECCV), pp. 471–487 (2018)
69. Yun, S., Jeong, M., Kim, R., Kang, J., Kim, H.J.: Graph transformer networks. Adv. Neural Inf. Process. Syst. (NeurIPS) **32**, 1–11 (2019)
70. Zellers, R., et al.: Merlot: multimodal neural script knowledge models. In: Advances in Neural Information Processing Systems (NeurIPS), vol. 34 (2021)
71. Zhong, Y., Ji, W., Xiao, J., Li, Y., Deng, W., Chua, T.S.: Video question answering: datasets, algorithms and challenges. arXiv preprint arXiv:2203.01225 (2022)
72. Zhu, L., Yang, Y.: ActBERT: learning global-local video-text representations. In: Proceedings of the IEEE/CVF Conference on Computer Vision and Pattern Recognition (CVPR), pp. 8746–8755 (2020)
73. Zoph, B., et al.: Rethinking pre-training and self-training. In: Advances in Neural Information Processing Systems (NeurIPS), vol. 33, pp. 3833–3845 (2020)

Trace Controlled Text to Image Generation

Kun Yan[1]([✉])[iD], Lei Ji[2], Chenfei Wu[2], Jianmin Bao[2], Ming Zhou[3], Nan Duan[2], and Shuai Ma[1]

[1] SKLSDE Lab, Beihang University, Beijing, China
{kunyan,mashuai}@buaa.edu.cn
[2] Microsoft Research Asia, Beijing, China
{leiji,chewu,jianbao,nanduan}@microsoft.com
[3] Langboat Technology, Beijing, China
zhouming@chuangxin.com

Abstract. Text to Image generation is a fundamental and inevitable challenging task for visual linguistic modeling. The recent surge in this area such as DALL·E has shown breathtaking technical breakthroughs, however, it still lacks a precise control of the **spatial** relation corresponding to semantic text. To tackle this problem, mouse trace paired with text provides an interactive way, in which users can describe the imagined image with natural language while drawing traces to locate those they want. However, this brings the challenges of both controllability and compositionality of the generation. Motivated by this, we propose a Trace Controlled Text to Image Generation model (TCTIG), which takes trace as a bridge between semantic concepts and spatial conditions. Moreover, we propose a set of new technique to enhance the controllability and compositionality of generation, including trace guided re-weighting loss (TGR) and semantic aligned augmentation (SAA). In addition, we establish a solid benchmark for the trace-controlled text-to-image generation task, and introduce several new metrics to evaluate both the controllability and compositionality of the model. Upon that, we demonstrate TCTIG's superior performance and further present the fruitful qualitative analysis of our model.

Keywords: Controllable text to image generation · Mouse trace · Diffusion decoder

1 Introduction

Human beings always imagine about how a different world could look like even it may not ever exists. For humans, imagining is a kind of creation, a kind of deconstruction and reconstruction of the external environment. Artists can easily "create" the imagined images precisely on what, where as well the actual size,

---

Supplementary Information The online version contains supplementary material available at https://doi.org/10.1007/978-3-031-20059-5_4.

color, shape etc. However, it is quite challenging to ask the current AI agent to create the images human imagined due to 1) lack of natural interaction between human and AI agents and 2) the technique barrier of decoupling semantics concepts and then composing them into image. Although the emerging research works on text to image generation has made great progress, it is still far from satisfaction.

Controllable image generation aims to create image with fine-grained conditions and plays a key role in both research and industrial applications. These advanced works can be categorized into three types depending on the controllable signals as *layout-to-image*, *text-to-image*, and *multimodal-to-image*. We argue that only layout or text is not enough for precise image generation. Although layout can represent the spatial relation accurately, *layout-to-image* works rely on predefined object categories and are infeasible in describing open-domain objects, attribute and relations. Additionally, *text-to-image* works rely only on text to describe the image, which are complicated to describe the detailed texture and spatial etc.

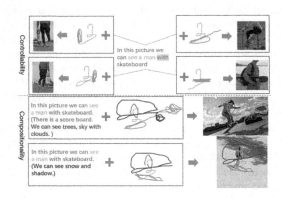

Fig. 1. The task showcases. Both controllability and compositionality are crucial to image generation.

To tackle these limitations, *multimodal-to-image* [20,21,41] generation empowers both text and layout as multimodal inputs. In this paper, we mainly investigate this task, specifically, taking text and mouse traces for image generation, as traces provide a more natural and interactive way than layouts to ground the text into the corresponding position of the image. **Also, in many advanced HCI scenarios, our fingers and eye-sight movement is also trace alike instead of layout alike.** Localized Narrative [29] is such a dataset, where each image is labeled with the detailed narration while simultaneously hovering their mouse pointer over the region they are describing. Thus each word in the narration is grounded into a sequence of traces-points in the image. Upon this, the correspondence between mouse traces and text for an image is the key for trace-controlled text to image generation.

There are two key characteristics for the trace-controlled text to image generation: 1) the narration is open domain natural language description with various types of objects, attributes, and relations; 2) the traces and text are manually grounded and aligned. Figure 1 presents several showcases of the tasks, and demonstrates the two major challenges. On one hand, **controllability** consists of both semantic condition and spatial condition, specifically object-level, sentence-level semantics, and spatial correspondence. As shown in the case, the text "man with skateboard" correlates to various appearances with different poses between the man and the skateboard, while each appearance can be specified by the mouse traces. On the other hand, **compositionality** is the generalization capability of different combination between context objects as well as various scales. In the showcase, "man with skateboard" coupled with different contexts of "tree" or "snow" aims to generate distinct correlated background.

To deal with these challenges, we first propose a novel mouse trace controlled text to image generation (TCTIG) model with two-stage training of visual discrete tokenization as the first stage and visual generation model as the second stage. In details, we design a module regarding trace as the bridge between the semantic concepts in the natural language description and spatial conditions in the image together with a trace guided re-weighting loss to improve the controllability. Besides, the segment-aligned augmentation strategy are promoted to enrich the compositionality. Furthermore, the existing evaluation metrics only focus on image quality or semantic relevance, we introduce a new evaluation metric Spatial Semantic CLIP Score (SSCP) to evaluate both the controllability and compositionality of the model. Lastly, experimental results on the LN-COCO dataset [28] present the effectiveness of our method on all these existing and the new SSCP evaluation metrics.

2   Related Work

2.1   Text to Image Generation

The text-to-image generation works can be divided into two categorizes: end-to-end and two-stage methods. Previous methods mainly adopt the conditional generative adversarial networks(GAN) [30, 34, 38, 40]. The literature [1, 10] presents a review for adversarial text-to-image generation. Recent works investigated the Denoising Diffusion Model [12, 19, 23], which demonstrate the capability of high quality image generation and beat GAN based method [6]. Although the diffusion models are capable of generating photorealistic images, it still cannot compose complex semantic and needs several pass of re-editing to make up all needed semantics as mentioned in [23]. Another research direction is the two-stage method, which is a new paradigm for pretraining with web-scale image and text pairs. They demonstrated the pretrained models are effective in generalizing high semantically related open-domain images, which first adopt VQVAE [24]/VAGAN [8] to tokenize images into discrete tokens and then generates these visual tokens for further decoding to real images [7, 32, 41]. However, these methods always produce blurred images with artifacts more or less. Motivated by the superior performance of these models, we propose a novel two-stage model with carefully designed module for trace as another controlled signal. Specifically, our model takes advantages of both high-quality capability of diffusion model and semantics relevance of the two-stage model.

2.2   Conditioned Image Generation

Besides the text-controlled image generation, there are also other conditions including explicit conditions like a semantic mask [5,9,26], layout [36,42], scene graph [17], trace [20], and implicit conditions like style [18,27]. Recently hybrid conditions for image [20,21,41] generation are emerging in the research community by combining text with layout/style inputs. *TRECS* [20] *is the only work for text and mouse traces to image generation, which retrieved and composed a mask for a further mask-to-image generation.* However, TRECS heavily relied on the object/thing categories predefined in the COCO-STUFF [3] dataset and is hard to scale to open-domain text with fine-grained attributes and long-tail objects. Besides, the grounding of the description to the trace is another challenge for generating both semantically and spatially matched images. To deal with these, we propose a novel trace-controlled text-to-image generation (TCTIG) model by leveraging the advantage of open-domain text-to-image methods, and a semantically aligned regularization for grounding.

2.3   Trace Related Image Tasks

Trace is a natural way of spatial input for humans to interact with images for image-related tasks. With the release of the Localized narrative [28] dataset, several trace related image tasks are proposed including image and trace to caption generation [22,28,39], image and text to trace generation [22], image to caption with trace generation [22], trace and text to image generation [20], multimodal queries for image retrieval [4], as well as Panoptic narrative grounding [11]. Those tasks elicit more challenges for this research direction, such as fine-grained semantics and dense grounding, and further prompt many real applications for multimodal cognition. In this work, we mainly study the problem of trace and text to image generation, one of the most challenging task.

3   Method

3.1   Preliminaries

Problem Formulation. The task is defined as, given text and mouse trace, output the synthesized image. The text is defined as a sequence of word tokens and the trace is defined as a sequence of tracepoints. We adopt the two-stage training strategy. The *first* stage is to tokenize the image into a sequence of discrete visual tokens. The *second* stage is to train our trace controlled text to image generation (TCTIG) model for conditioned image generation by using these visual tokens.

3.2   Visual Tokenization

Specifically, Vector Quantized Variational Autoencoder (VQVAE) [24] learns discrete representations for image and then reconstruct the image by these discrete tokens with a typical encoder-decoder framework. In this paper, we directly adopt the pretrained VQGAN [9], which improves VQVAE by adversarial training.

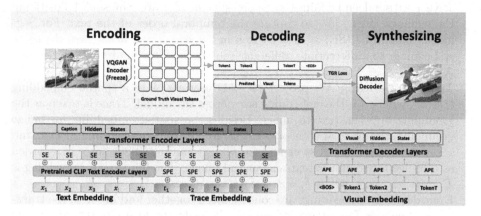

Fig. 2. Model Architecture Overview. "SE" is Segment Embedding, "SPE" is Sinusoidal Positional Embedding, and "APE" is Axial Positional Embedding.

3.3   TCTIG Model

Our TCTIG model consists of three major modules: encoding, decoding, and generation. The encoding and decoding process is streamlined with a transformer-based encoder-decoder, which mainly employs multi-head self-attention and cross attention mechanism [37]. Here, we highlight several task-oriented modifications.

Encoding

Text Preprocessing. The text description sequence is $X = \{x_1, \ldots, x_l\}$, in which x_i is the i-th token and l is the text sequence length.

Trace Preprocessing. The raw trace input is a sequence of trace-point coordinates with timestamps. We segment the trace-point sequences uniformly by the same time window τ, and then each trace segment is converted to its minimal bounding rectangle. Every bounding rectangle can be represented by a 5D vector which contains normalized coordinates of the top-left and bottom-right corners, and the area ratio with respect to the whole image. We denote the trace input as $T = \{t_1, \ldots, t_M\}$, where $t_j \in \mathbb{R}^5$, M is the number of bounding rectangles.

Text-Trace Encoder. The text X and traces T are embedded separately and then concatenated together as a single input sequence feeding into a transformer encoder.

- **Text Embedding**: Each text token x_i is embedded into $\hat{x}_i \in \mathbb{R}^d$. Then, we employ relative positional embeddings and learnable segment embeddings to represent token-level and sentence-level semantics repectively. The relative positional embeddings o_i, more specifically, are Sinusoidal Positional Embeddings (SPE) [37] to capture the temporal order of the text. For Segment Embedding (SE) s_i, every token in the same sentence shares the same embedding to differentiate different sentences. The final text embedding $\tilde{X} = \{\tilde{x}_1, \ldots, \tilde{x}_l\}$, where $\tilde{x}_i = \hat{x}_i + o_i + s_i$.
- **Trace embedding**: We project each 5D vector t_j into a spatial embedding $\hat{t}_j \in \mathbb{R}^d$, where d is the embedding size across the model. Trace is taken as the grounding between text to image. Besides the spatial embedding for image grounding, the trace also encodes the same positional embedding SPE o_j and segment embedding SE s_j as text for text grounding. Thus trace is regarded as a bridge for semantic text and spatial image. The final trace embedding is $\tilde{T} = \{\tilde{t}_1, \ldots, \tilde{t}_M\}$, where $\tilde{t}_j = \hat{t}_j + o_j + s_j$.
- **Encoder**: The embeddings are concatenated together and input to the transformer encoder for further processing. In order to leverage the pretrained model, we initiate our text encoder with the CLIP [31] weights.

$$[\bar{X}; \bar{T}] = \text{Transformer}([CLIP_{text}(\tilde{X}); \tilde{T})]). \tag{1}$$

Decoding

Visual Tokens. We use VQGAN [9] with a discrete codebook $\mathcal{Z} = \{z_k\}_{k=1}^K$ to encode every target image into a sequence of discrete image tokens $V = [v_1, \ldots, v_{h \times w}] \in \{0, \ldots, |\mathcal{Z}| - 1\}^{h \times w}$. Specifically, we adopt the VQGAN model pretrained on ImageNet with codebook size $K = 1024$, down sample factor $f = 16$ [1] Thus, for images with size of 256×256, the corresponding visual token length is $N = h \times w = 256$, where $h = 256/f, w = 256/f$.

Visual Token Decoder. Visual token decoder combines text and trace information using cross attention connected to the hidden states of Text-Trace Encoder's last layer. Each visual token v_i is embedded into $\hat{v}_i \in \mathbb{R}^d$. In order to align the spatial relation between trace and image, the input for decoder combines the visual embedding with the axial positional embedding (APE) [16]. The position embedding p_i is a linear projection of column and row axis of each visual token

---

[1] The checkpoint and model config can be found at https://heibox.uni-heidelberg.de/d/8088892a516d4e3baf92/.

in the image. The final input visual embedding is $\tilde{V} = \{\tilde{v}_1, \ldots, \tilde{v}_N\}$, where $\tilde{v}_i = \hat{v}_i + p_i$.

$$\hat{V} = \text{Transformer}(\tilde{V}, [\hat{X}; \hat{T}]). \tag{2}$$

A cross-entropy generation loss $\mathcal{L}_{gen}$ is then computed with the logits transformed from the last decoder layer's hidden states and ground truth visual token ids.

$$\mathcal{L}_{gen} = - \mathop{\mathbb{E}}_{\hat{v}_i \sim \hat{V}} \log p\left(\hat{v}_i \mid \hat{V}_{<i}, \hat{X}, \hat{T}; \theta\right). \tag{3}$$

Trace Guided Re-weighting (TGR) Loss. During self-regression training process, traditional models treat all N target image tokens equally without discrimination. But naturally the tokens corresponding to user-described objects should gain more attention and are usually hard to learn due to its high-frequency information density. In order to help the model focus on important details and better ground the description to the image, we develop a trace guided re-weighting loss (named as TGR) on top of traditional cross-entropy loss. Given a sequence of trace boxes $T = \{t_1, \ldots, t_M\}$ defined as above, we first calculate the center coordinates of each boxes, we denote the x coordinates of those centers as $T^x = \{t_1^x, \ldots, t_M^x\}$ and the y coordinates of those centers as $T^y = \{t_1^y, \ldots, t_M^y\}$, we calculate each trace-box's corresponding token position id $P = \{pid_1, \ldots, pid_M\}$ where

$$pid_i = \lfloor t_i^x * w \rfloor + \lfloor t_i^y * h \rfloor * w \tag{4}$$

We then calculate the frequency distribution of each position ids within every image

$$D = \frac{bincount(P)}{|P|} \tag{5}$$

The re-weighted loss function can be formulated as:

$$\mathcal{L}_{TGR} = - \frac{\mathop{\mathbb{E}}_{\hat{v}_i \sim \hat{V}, d_i \sim D} (1 + \alpha * d_i) \log p\left(\hat{v}_i \mid \hat{V}_{<i}, \hat{X}, \hat{T}; \theta\right)}{\mathbb{Z}} \tag{6}$$

where α is a learnable parameter to fade the weight into cross-entropy loss and $\mathbb{Z} = 1 + \frac{\alpha * \sum D}{|D|}$ is a scaling factor to keep the loss scale comparable to traditional cross entropy loss.

Synthesizing. One option of synthesizing is directly adopting the pretrained VQ-GAN decoder to synthesize the image I given the decoded discrete visual tokens V. But we find the VQ-GAN decoder brings its limitation on reconstruction quality to the whole pipeline in practical experiments. Even using ground truth tokens, the reconstruction result still has non-negligible artifacts.

In recent days, diffusion models [6] is shown to be effective in generating high-quality images and beat GANs on image synthesizing. In our work, we find using latent embedding extracted from VQ-code book as additional conditions to train an guided diffusion model dramatically improves the reconstruction quality. Specifically, we adopt similar framework as in [6]. To guided the model generate images represented by latent code, we concatenate the VQ-GAN latent code embeddings of each image to the U-Net bottle neck during diffusion steps and further train a VQ-latent conditioned diffusion model (Please find the training details in supplementary materials). Thus, at inference stage, we feed the transformer generated V's corresponding code book embeddings to the diffusion decoder, and get a high quality image I.

Training the transformer on the tokens from the VQ-GAN encoder allows us to allocate its modeling capacity to the low-frequency information that makes images visually recognizable to us. And diffusion decoder plays a good role to reconstruct high frequency, long-tailed information. By carefully combining those two methods, we reach a sweet point between efficiency and quality.

3.4   Segment Aligned Augmentation (SAA)

Traces, as a type of control signal, should be highly sensible by the model. Not only the spatial location but also the scale are essential to model. That is, when moving a trace segment spatially, the correlated semantic on the image should move along the same direction. Besides, when we enlarge or shrink the scale of a trace segment, the corresponding object should be enlarged or shrunk accordingly. An intuitive way to enhance this controllability is by employing a data-centric strategy. We design a so-called segment aligned augmentation to create more spatial-aware training cases dynamically while keeping correct alignment between text, trace, and image target.

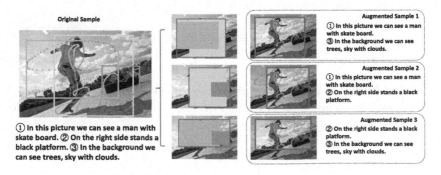

Fig. 3. Segment aligned augmentation.

As illustrated in Fig. 3, given a sample of the dataset, we first segment the caption paragraph into sentences and its corresponding traces into several pieces. For every piece of trace segment, we get its minimal bounding box. Next, we randomly sample several trace segments and reunite the corresponding bounding boxes, and thus their outer bounding forms a new cropping window. We crop the original image along those new cropping windows, and re-calculate the coordinates of the corresponding trace segments since the relative position of every tracepoint has been changed. Finally, we collect the selected sentences, re-scaled trace segments, and cropped images as a new augmented sample.

By applying this strategy, the relative scale and positions of visual objects as well as trace coordinates encoding are dynamically changed but kept aligned all along. Our experiments demonstrate this approach is crucial for preventing the model from falling into trivial biases and it also improves the overall performance significantly.

4   Experiments

4.1   Dataset

We use the annotated COCO subset of Localized Narratives [28] to evaluate our method, which is called **LN-COCO** for short. Each image has one or several pairs of the captioning paragraph and corresponding mouse traces. There are 134,272 samples in the training set and 8,573 in the validation set.

4.2   Quantitative Results

In this section, we investigate how our approach quantitatively compares to existing models and further establish metrics to assess the characteristic performance of trace-controlled image synthesis task. To measure the key components of the task including "image generation", "text to image" and "trace controlled", we evaluate the model's performance from the following three perspectives:

Table 1. Main Results. * indicates the results evaluated by us and missed in the original paper, – means to remove the module.

Dataset	Method	Fidelity		Relevance		Controllability
		$IS\uparrow$	$FID\downarrow$	$SOA-I\uparrow$	$SOA-C\uparrow$	$SSCP\uparrow$
COCO-Caption	DALL·E [32]	17.8	28	–	–	–
	CogView [7]	18.2	27.1	–	–	–
LN-COCO	Real Images	35.70	0.48	0.6608	0.6739	1.00
	AttnGAN [38]	20.80	51.80	–	–	–
	TRECS [20]	**21.3**	48.7	*0.3523*	*0.3288*	*0.862
	TCTIG(-Trace)	10.70	75.34	0.1021	0.0698	0.727
	TCTIG	17.59	**11.94**	0.2658	0.1787	**0.973**

- **Fidelity** of synthesized images
- **Semantic relevance** between text conditions and generated images
- **Controllability** of semantic arrangement and spatial composition empowered by traces

The metrics and results are presented in Table 1 and are discussed in the following paragraphs.

Fidelity

Inception Score (IS). As described in [35], Inception Score compares each image's label distribution with the whole set marginal image label distribution, encouraging models to synthesize distinguished and diverse samples.

While IS has been shown to correlate with human judgments of generated image quality, it is likely less informative as it overfits easily and can be manipulated to achieve much higher scores using simple tricks [2,40]. The other limitation of IS is that it is designed for images with salient objects which can be classified into those predefined categories. When it comes to complex scenes such as most cases in LN-COCO, the score will intrinsically drop with a large margin. To follow the traditions, we still present the IS score of our method but do not take it as a major concern.

Fréchet Inception Distance (FID) was first proposed by [14], which measures feature distribution distance between real and fake images.

From Table 1, we can see that our method achieves the best FID on trace-controlled text-to-image generation tasks. To the best of our knowledge, our approach is the first to apply the token-based two-stage image synthesis paradigm to Localized Narratives. In addition, we make a rough comparison with two-stage baseline methods on text-to-image generation including DALL·E [32] and CogView [7], which conduct evaluations on COCO-Caption. The image distribution of LN-COCO and COCO-Caption is merely identical, thus the FID comparison between our method on LN-COCO and theirs on COCO-Caption is reasonable. Compared with those models, our model is several times smaller(750M parameters compared to 3B of Cogview, 12B of DALL·E), our training data is limited (130K samples compared to 30M of Cogview and 250M of DALL·E), and the task is more challenging (Narratives are four times longer than MS-COCO captions on average with fine-grained description). From the results, we can find that although our method without trace (TCTIG(-Trace)) performs worse, our method with trace (TCTIG) achieves the lowest FID of 11.94. Thus, we demonstrate **trace is a powerful and informative signal and our design to inject trace** to build text-to-image generative models is effective and efficient.

Semantic Relevance

Semantic Object Accuracy (SOA). SOA is a score introduced by [15] to evaluate the semantic relevance of generative text-to-image models. Given the captions of the MS-COCO dataset, first generate images from the model to be evaluated. Then a pre-trained object detector YOLOv3 [33] detects whether the generated image contains the objects specified in the caption. In this paper, to adapt the SOA score calculation on LN-COCO, we use the same keywords and exclusive exceptions defined by [15] to filter all captions of the LN-COCO validation set. The metadata and statistics of each label is listed in the Appendix A.

Conclusion. We calculate the SOA score of TRECS [20] by using their released generated samples on LN-COCO. We also conduct an evaluation on reconstructed images by VQGAN decoder given ground truth images tokens. We can see that even using ground truth tokens to reconstruct, the result images still cannot surpass the TRECS, a semantic mask-based generative method, on SOA metric. TRECS are trained with exactly the same categories of objects with YOLOv3, this is beneficial to SOA scores but harmful to **generalizability**. What's more, since VQGAN cannot ensure the object shape is always kept after quantization, this indicates that YOLOv3 detects objects highly relying on shapes. The result of the reconstructed image sets an upper bound on the SOA metric for the future visual token-based method. This paper provides solid baselines for the trace-controlled visual-token-based generative method and demonstrates a way to reduce the gap to the upper bound. While to raise the aforementioned upper bound closer to real images, the image tokenization technique should be further improved to keep the shape of visual objects as efficiently as possible.

Controllability

Spatial Semantic CLIP Score (SSCP). Although the SOA can evaluate whether the semantic concepts in the text are depicted as an object in generated images, it still lacks detailed controllability evaluation. For instance, whether the objects are at the right place, whether those objects have proper relations, whether the descriptive word such as color, texture, and postures are correctly presented. All

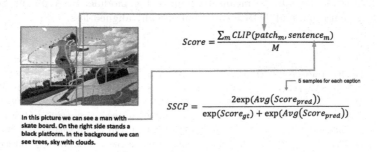

In this picture we can see a man with skate board. On the right side stands a black platform. In the background we can see trees, sky with clouds.

$$Score = \frac{\sum_m CLIP(patch_m, sentence_m)}{M}$$

5 samples for each caption

$$SSCP = \frac{2\exp(Avg(Score_{pred}))}{\exp(Score_{gt}) + \exp(Avg(Score_{pred}))}$$

Fig. 4. SSCP score calculation

those aspects can not be differentiated by the SOA score but play a critical role in the assemblage of our visual world. Recently, CLIPScore [13] and CLIP-R-Precision [25] are effective evaluation metrics using the pre-trained CLIP [31] for specific tasks. Motivated by this, we propose a novel Spatial Semantic CLIP (SSCP) score to evaluate the controllability perspective of this task.

Conclusion. The newly proposed SSCP score is to evaluate the controllability of both semantic and spatial grounding for image generation, the detailed calculation of which is presented in Fig. 4. First, we crop each generated image into four corner patches and one central patches. Next, we calculate the CLIP score between each patch with the spatially aligned sentences and average scores of these patches as $Score_{pred}$. For each caption, we generate five samples and calculate the average $Score_{pred}$ of them. Finally, together with the $Score_{gt}$ calculated for the ground truth image in the same way, we can get the SSCP score for each sample. We report the SSCP of TRECS by using their publicly released generated samples on LN-COCO and our model in Table 1. Note that, according to our metric, the SSCP score for ground truth images in the validation set is 1.0. Our TCTIG model performs significantly better than TRECS on the SSCP metric(0.973 VS 0.862), which confirms that our generated samples have more accurate spatial layouts and general flexible control over descriptive semantics.

4.3   Ablation Study

Table 2 demonstrates the ablation results including trace, trace guided reweighting loss (TGR), semantc segment augumetation (SSA) as well as the diffusion v.s. GAN synthesizing. 1) Take a closer look at the TCTIG(-Trace-SAA-TGR) which only takes text as input, we can find that the quantitative results are merely poor. This indicates that with limited caption image pair, the model can not learn enough knowledge about the correlation of linguistic and visual tokens. When we incorporate **traces** into the model, the performance boosts significantly(SSCP from 0.727 to 0.923). 2) And with the segment-aligned augmentation, our TCTIG (-TGR) significantly improve the performance with the **compositionality** and controllability. 3) By the semantic regularization

Table 2. Ablation Results. − means to remove the module, SAA means Segment Aligned Augmentation, and TGR means semantically aligned loss.

Dataset	Method		Fidelity		Relevance		Controllability
	Model	*Sythesis*	$IS \uparrow$	$FID \downarrow$	$SOA-I \uparrow$	$SOA-C \uparrow$	$SSCP \uparrow$
LN-COCO	TCTIG(-Trace-SAA-TGR)	GAN	10.70	75.34	0.1021	0.0698	0.727
	TCTIG(-SAA-TGR)	GAN	14.80	29.58	0.1320	0.0728	0.923
	TCTIG (-TGR)	GAN	15.02	26.50	0.2200	0.1565	0.955
	TCTIG	GAN	16.65	19.54	0.2593	0.1609	0.962
	GT Image	GAN	18.74	12.74	0.3501	0.3463	0.989
	TCTIG	Diffusion	**17.59**	**11.94**	**0.2658**	**0.1787**	**0.973**
	GT Image	Diffusion	21.17	8.62	0.4058	0.3636	0.994

(TGR) supervision, the grounding between the caption and image with mouse traces are learned to improve the **controllability**. 4) Lastly, the VQ based diffusion model further enhance the performance especially on the **image quality**, which achieves the best results. Those ablations are strong evidence of the effectiveness of our method.

4.4 Human Evaluation

As mentioned in [7], human evaluation is much more persuasive than these automatic evaluation metrics on text-to-image generation. We conduct a similar human evaluation through a side-by-side comparison between TRECS and TCTIG model on 1000 randomly selected images. For each case, we ask the annotators to evaluate the generated images from three perspectives including image quality, semantic relevance, and spatial grounding. Figure 5 presents the results, from which we can see that TCTIG performs better especially on spatial grounding. For semantics, we found that TRECS is good at generating predefined popular objects, while TCTIG is more general on open-domain concepts.

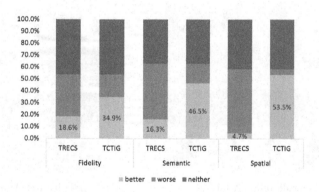

Fig. 5. Human evaluation. "neither" means both methods are equally good or poor to compare.

4.5 Qualitative Analysis

Comparison with Related Methods. Figure 6 lists the results of these samples reported in TRECS [20], and we add our results as well. The baseline AttGAN tends to generate images with semantically relevant textures, while TRECS rely on scene mask to generate more accurate predefined objects. Our model is able to generate open-domain semantically and spatially relevant images.

Fig. 6. Qualitative study with related methods

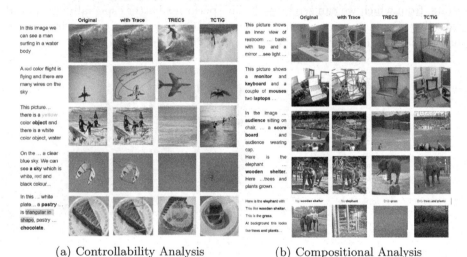

(a) Controllability Analysis　　　　　(b) Compositional Analysis

Fig. 7. Qualitative study on controllability and compositional

Controllablity. Figure 7a presents the synthesized images with the relatively simple scene with fine-grained attributes and appearance descriptions. We validate the controllability on both semantics and spatial perspectives. As shown in the first case, both TRECS and our model are able to generate accurate images. These cases present several findings. (1) As expected, with the trace, TRECS and our model are sensitive to the **spatial position**, and the generated objects are in the corresponding spatial position of the image. (2) TRECS model relies on the predefined 181 objects and things in COCO-Stuff for object generation, which is hard to deal with **open-domain** ambiguous and long-tailed objects like "object" in case 3, and "chocolate" in case 6. Our model with an open-domain text encoder is able to generate more accurate semantically related images. (3)

Our model is sensitive to the **color attribute** . From cases 2 to 4, the color is explicitly mentioned in the text and the objects in the image should be painted with the right color. Our model can generate the colored objects with the trace position as the patches of the area have the corresponding color. (4) All models are infeasible to learn the **shape attribute** but prefer to ground to the shape of the trace, like case 5. Although it is mentioned "triangular" shape, both TRECS and our model generate trace-shaped objects.

Compositionality. Figure 7b presents the synthesized images with composed and complex scenes. From these results, we can see that: (1) TRECS model rely on a composed mask for image generation, and thus would like to generate **composed** images by gathering all objects and lacks a smooth and consistent transition between boundaries as shown in case 1 and case 2. (2) The trace is important for our model to **ground** the objects to the corresponding spatial position in the image, e.g. "mirror ", "laptop", "shelter", and "audience" in the showcases. Our model is able to generate a similar layout to the ground truth image. (3) from the last row, we randomly select sentences from the last example to generate the corresponding image to present the **compositionality**.

5   Conclusion

In this work, we propose a Trace Controlled Text to Image Generation model (TCTIG) to provide a straightforward and natural solution tackling the controllability problem of text to image generation. We establish a solid benchmark for the trace-controlled text-to-image generation task. Upon that, we further demonstrate TCTIG's superior performance by detailed quantitative results and analyze the controllability and compositionality by qualitative studies.

Acknowledgement. This work is supported in part by NSFC 61925203.

References

1. Agnese, J., Herrera, J., Tao, H., Zhu, X.: A survey and taxonomy of adversarial neural networks for text-to-image synthesis. Wiley Interdis. Rev. Data Min. Knowl. Discovery **10**(4), e1345 (2020)
2. Barratt, S., Sharma, R.: A note on the inception score (2018)
3. Caesar, H., Uijlings, J., Ferrari, V.: Coco-stuff: thing and stuff classes in context. In: Computer Vision and Pattern Recognition (CVPR), 2018 IEEE conference on. IEEE (2018)
4. Changpinyo, S., Pont-Tuset, J., Ferrari, V., Soricut, R.: Telling the what while pointing to the where: multimodal queries for image retrieval. arXiv preprint arXiv:2102.04980 (2021)
5. Chen, Q., Koltun, V.: Photographic image synthesis with cascaded refinement networks. In: Proceedings of the IEEE International Conference on Computer Vision, pp. 1511–1520 (2017)

6. Dhariwal, P., Nichol, A.: Diffusion models beat gans on image synthesis. Adv. Neural Inf. Process. Syst. **34** (2021)
7. Ding, M., et al.: Cogview: mastering text-to-image generation via transformers. arXiv preprint arXiv:2105.13290 (2021)
8. Esser, P., Rombach, R., Ommer, B.: Taming transformers for high-resolution image synthesis. In: Proceedings of the IEEE/CVF Conference on Computer Vision and Pattern Recognition, pp. 12873–12883 (2021)
9. Esser, P., Rombach, R., Ommer, B.: Taming transformers for high-resolution image synthesis (2020)
10. Frolov, S., Hinz, T., Raue, F., Hees, J., Dengel, A.: Adversarial text-to-image synthesis: a review. arXiv preprint arXiv:2101.09983 (2021)
11. González, C., Ayobi, N., Hernandez, I., Hernández, J., Pont-Tuset, J., Arbelaez, P.: Panoptic narrative grounding. In: Proceedings of the IEEE/CVF International Conference on Computer Vision, pp. 1364–1373 (2021)
12. Gu, S., et al.: Vector quantized diffusion model for text-to-image synthesis. arXiv preprint arXiv:2111.14822 (2021)
13. Hessel, J., Holtzman, A., Forbes, M., Bras, R.L., Choi, Y.: Clipscore: a reference-free evaluation metric for image captioning. arXiv preprint arXiv:2104.08718 (2021)
14. Heusel, M., Ramsauer, H., Unterthiner, T., Nessler, B., Hochreiter, S.: Gans trained by a two time-scale update rule converge to a local nash equilibrium. In: NIPS (2017)
15. Hinz, T., Heinrich, S., Wermter, S.: Semantic object accuracy for generative text-to-image synthesis. IEEE Trans. Pattern Anal. Mach. Intell. **PP** (2020)
16. Ho, J., Kalchbrenner, N., Weissenborn, D., Salimans, T.: Axial attention in multi-dimensional transformers (2019)
17. Johnson, J., Gupta, A., Fei-Fei, L.: Image generation from scene graphs. In: Proceedings of the IEEE Conference on Computer Vision and Pattern Recognition, pp. 1219–1228 (2018)
18. Karras, T., Laine, S., Aila, T.: A style-based generator architecture for generative adversarial networks. In: 2019 IEEE/CVF Conference on Computer Vision and Pattern Recognition (CVPR), pp. 4396–4405 (2019). https://doi.org/10.1109/CVPR.2019.00453
19. Kim, G., Ye, J.C.: Diffusionclip: text-guided image manipulation using diffusion models. arXiv preprint arXiv:2110.02711 (2021)
20. Koh, J.Y., Baldridge, J., Lee, H., Yang, Y.: Text-to-image generation grounded by fine-grained user attention. In: Winter Conference on Applications of Computer Vision (WACV) (2021)
21. Li, B., Qi, X., Torr, P.H., Lukasiewicz, T.: Image-to-image translation with text guidance. arXiv preprint arXiv:2002.05235 (2020)
22. Meng, Z., et al.: Connecting what to say with where to look by modeling human attention traces. In: Proceedings of the IEEE/CVF Conference on Computer Vision and Pattern Recognition, pp. 12679–12688 (2021)
23. Nichol, A., Dhariwal, P., Ramesh, A., Shyam, P., Mishkin, P., McGrew, B., Sutskever, I., Chen, M.: Glide: towards photorealistic image generation and editing with text-guided diffusion models. arXiv preprint arXiv:2112.10741 (2021)
24. van den Oord, A., Vinyals, O., kavukcuoglu, k.: Neural discrete representation learning. In: Guyon, I., Luxburg, U.V., Bengio, S., Wallach, H., Fergus, R., Vishwanathan, S., Garnett, R. (eds.) Advances in Neural Information Processing Systems. vol. 30. Curran Associates, Inc. (2017). https://proceedings.neurips.cc/paper/2017/file/7a98af17e63a0ac09ce2e96d03992fbc-Paper.pdf

25. Park, D.H., Azadi, S., Liu, X., Darrell, T., Rohrbach, A.: Benchmark for compositional text-to-image synthesis (2021)
26. Park, T., Liu, M.Y., Wang, T.C., Zhu, J.Y.: Semantic image synthesis with spatially-adaptive normalization. In: Proceedings of the IEEE/CVF Conference on Computer Vision and Pattern Recognition, pp. 2337–2346 (2019)
27. Patashnik, O., Wu, Z., Shechtman, E., Cohen-Or, D., Lischinski, D.: Styleclip: text-driven manipulation of stylegan imagery. In: Proceedings of the IEEE/CVF International Conference on Computer Vision, pp. 2085–2094 (2021)
28. Pont-Tuset, J., Uijlings, J., Changpinyo, B., Soricut, R., Ferrari, V.: Connecting vision and language with localized narratives. In: ECCV (2020). https://arxiv.org/abs/1912.03098
29. Pont-Tuset, J., Uijlings, J., Changpinyo, S., Soricut, R., Ferrari, V.: Connecting vision and language with localized narratives. In: Vedaldi, A., Bischof, H., Brox, T., Frahm, J.-M. (eds.) ECCV 2020. LNCS, vol. 12350, pp. 647–664. Springer, Cham (2020). https://doi.org/10.1007/978-3-030-58558-7_38
30. Qiao, T., Zhang, J., Xu, D., Tao, D.: Mirrorgan: learning text-to-image generation by redescription. In: Proceedings of the IEEE/CVF Conference on Computer Vision and Pattern Recognition, pp. 1505–1514 (2019)
31. Radford, A., et al.: Learning transferable visual models from natural language supervision. arXiv preprint arXiv:2103.00020 (2021)
32. Ramesh, A., et al.: Zero-shot text-to-image generation. ArXiv abs/2102.12092 (2021)
33. Redmon, J., Farhadi, A.: Yolov3: an incremental improvement (2018)
34. Reed, S., Akata, Z., Yan, X., Logeswaran, L., Schiele, B., Lee, H.: Generative adversarial text to image synthesis. In: International Conference on Machine Learning, pp. 1060–1069. PMLR (2016)
35. Salimans, T., Goodfellow, I.J., Zaremba, W., Cheung, V., Radford, A., Chen, X.: Improved techniques for training gans. In: NIPS (2016)
36. Sun, W., Wu, T.: Image synthesis from reconfigurable layout and style. In: Proceedings of the IEEE/CVF International Conference on Computer Vision, pp. 10531–10540 (2019)
37. Vaswani, A., et al.: Attention is all you need. In: Guyon, I., Luxburg, U.V., Bengio, S., Wallach, H., Fergus, R., Vishwanathan, S., Garnett, R. (eds.) Advances in Neural Information Processing Systems. vol. 30. Curran Associates, Inc. (2017). https://proceedings.neurips.cc/paper/2017/file/3f5ee243547dee91fbd053c1c4a845aa-Paper.pdf
38. Xu, T., Zhang, P., Huang, Q., Zhang, H., Gan, Z., Huang, X., He, X.: Attngan: fine-grained text to image generation with attentional generative adversarial networks. In: 2018 IEEE/CVF Conference on Computer Vision and Pattern Recognition, pp. 1316–1324 (2018)
39. Yan, K., Ji, L., Luo, H., Zhou, M., Duan, N., Ma, S.: Control image captioning spatially and temporally. In: Proceedings of the 59th Annual Meeting of the Association for Computational Linguistics and the 11th International Joint Conference on Natural Language Processing (Volume 1: Long Papers), pp. 2014–2025 (2021)
40. Zhang, H., Koh, J.Y., Baldridge, J., Lee, H., Yang, Y.: Cross-modal contrastive learning for text-to-image generation. In: CVPR (2021)
41. Zhang, Z., et al.: M6-ufc: unifying multi-modal controls for conditional image synthesis. arXiv preprint arXiv:2105.14211 (2021)
42. Zhao, B., Meng, L., Yin, W., Sigal, L.: Image generation from layout. In: Proceedings of the IEEE/CVF Conference on Computer Vision and Pattern Recognition (CVPR) (2019)

Video Question Answering with Iterative Video-Text Co-tokenization

AJ Piergiovanni[✉], Kairo Morton, Weicheng Kuo, Michael S. Ryoo,
and Anelia Angelova

Google Research, New York, USA
ajpiergi@google.com

Abstract. Video question answering is a challenging task that requires understanding jointly the language input, the visual information in individual video frames, as well as the temporal information about the events occurring in the video. In this paper, we propose a novel multi-stream video encoder for video question answering that uses multiple video inputs and a new video-text iterative co-tokenization approach to answer a variety of questions related to videos. We experimentally evaluate the model on several datasets, such as MSRVTT-QA, MSVD-QA, IVQA, outperforming the previous state-of-the-art by large margins. Simultaneously, our model reduces the required GFLOPs from 150–360 to only 67, producing a highly efficient video question answering model (Code: https://sites.google.com/view/videoqa-cotokenization).

Keywords: Video question answering · Video-text joint learning · Video understanding · Efficient vision models

1 Introduction

Video Question and Answering (VideoQA) [30,38,49,82,97] targets the challenging problem of answering a variety of questions about a video, which requires both natural language understanding and understanding of the video content, including reasoning about activities, objects, sequence of events, and interactions within the video. VideoQA is the video counterpart of Visual Question and Answering (VQA) [2,14,25,33], a long-standing task in computer vision of answering questions towards an image. VideoQA is a very important multi-modal visual-language task for natural interaction with videos, aiming to understand what is happening in a video with the help of text-based specification (Fig. 1). It can satisfy information needs from videos and allow for rich user engagement such as searching for highlights, events, objects, or specific scenes in a video, e.g., "Where is the first goal scored in the game?", "How many goals were scored?" "Why was the umpire ruling considered controversial?".

Supplementary Information The online version contains supplementary material available at https://doi.org/10.1007/978-3-031-20059-5_5.

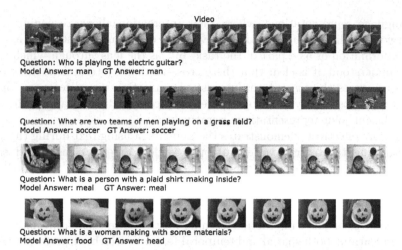

Fig. 1. We consider the challenging task of Video Question Answering which is a multi-modal information-seeking task, where natural language questions or tasks specifications are issued towards a video. The answers are in natural language open-vocabulary text. Example VideoQA outputs of our model are shown.

VideoQA has the inherent challenges of VQA tasks: it needs to understand the visual and language inputs and how they relate to each other. Additionally, VideoQA, needs to address multiple challenging video understanding tasks, such as action recognition, action detection and segmentation [9,44,62], but unlike them, needs to work in the open-set domain[1], where questions can be issued about unseen object categories or unknown activities. VideoQA needs a deeper understanding of the video input to begin with, which requires adequate spatio-temporal understanding.

VideoQA faces other challenges too: it requires the ability to process larger visual inputs e.g., 30−100x the number of frames than VQA, and to answer much harder questions, for example, why a certain event is happening, or what has happened before a certain action, where the timeframes might span small or large portions of the video. Furthermore, VideoQA inherits the efficiency challenges of video processing, which very few of the prior approaches have addressed.

The visual question and answering problem has been explored by many in the image and video research domains [2,3,46,86]. However, many previous works with regards to this problem utilize multiple backbone feature extractors for individual image frames, for the video input and for the text input separately and apply cross-attention between modalities as an after thought following feature extraction [47,86]. However, we believe, and will show in this paper, that the interaction between these modalities during the visual feature extraction process is key in attempting to solve this problem. We propose to jointly learn the video

---

[1] Unlike standard video understanding tasks, e.g., action recognition, action segmentation, where the set of action classes is pre-defined and known, the open-set VideoQA involves answering natural questions about novel or unseen actions and/or objects.

and language representations, where their interaction allows reasoning across these two modalities. Furthermore, by viewing question text not just as additional information or as a part of the task, but as the lens through which visual data is understood, it is clear that these cross-modality interactions must occur at various stages throughout the process of extracting visual features. Specifically, we propose a novel video-text iterative co-tokenization approach which learns efficient joint representations iteratively[2].

Our work effectively demonstrates the benefits of using text during the video understanding tasks for a variety of open ended VideoQA tasks and shows improvements over the state-of-the-art (SOTA) on MSVD-QA [82], MSRVTT-QA [35], and IVQA [86] datasets. Extensive ablation experiments confirm the benefit of each component. Our paper makes the following contributions:

- Novel video-language interaction learning for videos and text, especially focusing on learning both spatial and temporal features, which outperforms several SOTA on several VideoQA datasets.
- Novel multi-stream video encoder with iterative video-text co-tokenization which uses multiple inputs and iteratively selects efficient features
- An efficient approach, greatly reducing the FLOPs over baselines, which is important to save compute for video methods and allows scalability.

2   Related Work

Video Understanding. Video understanding is a fundamental visual recognition task, conducted in video inputs [8,9,20,29,31,40,51,63–65,70,71,79,81,94, 100]. What makes it challenging is the joint processing of spatial and temporal information and the sheer volume and diversity of visual inputs. Video understanding tasks include action classification, action detection, object segmentation in videos, etc. Text is not used in the training and recognition process.

Video and Language. Using language alongside videos [12,45] has opened several interesting problems in multi-modal video-language learning and language-guided video understanding, for example, VideoQA [30,97], video captioning [15, 28,41,96], text-to-video retrieval [6,32,35,45,61,76,95], referring expression comprehension for videos [7,26,37] and others [23,26,74]. In addition to the challenges of the video understanding tasks, video+language tasks bring in their own challenges of understanding text in the context of video, analyzing the video content according to the text input, or in some tasks, natural language text generation.

Previous video-language methods use pre-training from separate video models and text models which are typically pre-trained on disjoint datasets [21, 47,52,58,66,87,98]. Pre-training video and text jointly has been shown to be very beneficial to a number of downstream tasks [57,98]. End-to-end joint training with multi-modal inputs from the target datasets is also gaining popularity recently [45]. In the above-mentioned approaches, Transformer-based models [73], adapted to videos are often used to join the two modalities [66,98], e.g.,

---

[2] We consider video inputs of 32 frames which spans up to 10 s of video.

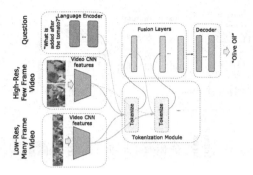

Fig. 2. Main architecture. Video features interact with text features. This is done efficiently using multi-stream video encoder to learn spatial and temporal features fusion with text features. Iterative co-tokenization fusion module learns a reduced number of useful tokens by progressively using the fused video-language representation to affect the next tokenization (red arrows). This results in a very efficient approach as compact tokenized representations are learned throughout. The decoder, which produces the answer, is a standard text-generation decoder. (Color figure online)

with masked-learning or other objectives [54,96]; in other works, standard representations e.g., I3D, S3D [9,81] for video and word2vec embeddings for text, have also been explored for joint training [57].

VideoQA. Video Question and Answering covers a broad range of questions towards a video which require both understanding of the video input and the input text [3,3,24,30,38,46,48,49,55,68,75,80,82,83,86,89,92,97,99]. Several research methods have been developed for VideoQA [4,10,18,27,34,39,42,43,49, 59,69,72,85,88,97]. Large-data pre-training is commonly used for VideoQA [57, 98]. ClipBert [45] propose end-to-end learning of video and language tasks, which are typically tested on text-to-video retrieval and VideoQA [30]. Kim et al. [38] propose multi-modal question and answering where additionally a text input such as captioning can be included in the input.

Video-Language Cross-Modal Learning. Image-language cross-modal learning has been developed for cross-modality retrieval, e.g., initially for images and text [16,91] and for videos and text [17,84]. These approaches are followed by using the popular transformer architecture [73] to encode separately each modality into a joint space, applied to both image-text [56] and to video-text retrieval [56,58,66]. A similar transformer-based architecture is commonly used for learning jointly image and language features via joint attention or cross-modal co-attention modules [11,50,54,67,77,90] This is also common in video-language joint learning, e.g., [45,98]. In the context of VideoQA, Zhu et al. [98] use the transformer architecture with pre-computed bounding boxes from an object detector, the features of which are fed to transformer layers. Hero [47] propose cross-modal transformer for multi-modal fusion based on Uniter [11]. Fan et al. [18] also propose a multimodal fusion layer. In complement to these cross-modal approaches, ours specifically learns efficient representations to reflect

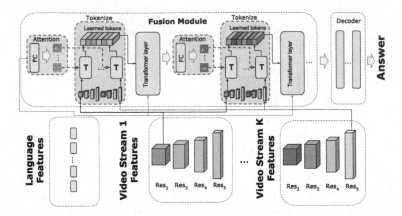

Fig. 3. Illustration of the iterative fusion module in detail. The features are used to generate N attention maps, which are applied to each stream and (optionally) scale of the video features. This results in a fixed number of tokens for the K streams and S scales (K and S are typically very small). The tokens are fed through a transformer layer, generating a new feature, which is used to generate new attention maps. This processes is repeated multiple times. The yellow boxes (denoted as 'T') represent the application of an attention map to a feature map. (Color figure online)

the interactions of these modalities at each level of abstraction of feature learning. Our multistream formulation is also conceptually related to SlowFast [20] for videos and multi-stream object detection networks for object understanding, where different network streams were utilized to look at different resolutions.

3   Approach

3.1   Multi-stream Video Encoder Overview

Our approach to the challenging VideoQA task, is video-language learning where early visual and language features are jointly learned. Specifically, we propose a multi-stream video encoder that is capable of efficiently learning both spatial and temporal features, and a new fusion method that can adaptively combine the video and text features. Our multi-stream encoder features the following components: First, the video features are extracted forming multiple learnable video representation inputs (Sect. 3.2); the text input is also preliminarily encoded. Secondly, a condensed representation for each input stream is learned via learned tokenization (Sect. 3.3). Importantly, the features are combined by an iterative video-text co-tokenization fusion mechanism which learns the most appropriate compact feature representations iteratively based on the previous features (Sect. 3.4). Figure 2 gives an overview of the main architecture.

At a high-level, our approach can be thought of as an encoder-decoder structure, however here the multi-stream video encoder is tasked with interdependent, video-language feature learning, which produces compact and efficient features. A text generation decoder directly outputs natural language free-form text.

3.2   Video Understanding at Different Timeframes

Actions and events in videos span a wide range of timeframes. Questions about videos also require different time scales. For example, 'What color is the apple?' only requires understanding a single frame, while 'What happens after cutting the apple?' requires localizing two specific actions segments in the video in order to answer, and 'What is being made in the video?' requires understanding the entire video. Being able to answer all these questions, with a model that is computationally efficient is a challenge, as, unlike images, the model must consider features of large video inputs with multiple spatial and temporal resolutions.

To address this, we propose a multi-stream approach with fusion, that extracts video features at various time and space scales. We consider them jointly together, as well as with the text/question input.

Video Features Sub-inputs. The video encoder, V, takes a video as input, e.g., a $x = T \times H \times W$ tensor where T is the number of frames and H and W are height/width of the image frame. It processes the video, producing the output features f_v. The baseline model uses a single video input, while the multi-stream model takes the video at different space- and time-scales as input. For example, one stream can take many frames at low spatial resolution, while another stream can take few frames at high spatial resolution. We can here use any number of video streams, each learning different spatio-temporal features. Importantly, subsequent components of the multi-stream visual encoder will enable learning various inter-relations of these inputs. This is critical for VideoQA, since the question can refer to the full video or specific spatial or temporal segments in it, or require the comprehension of events or actions in the video across different duration timeframes, or be very specifically pinpointed in time and space.

The features from the multi-stream visual encoder can further be mutli-scale, taking features from different points in the network, e.g., after each residual block in X3D. We denote the output(s) of the multi-stream encoder as $f_v = V(x)$, where f_v in general a set of multi-scale features over multiple feature levels: $f_v = \{f_{vi}\}_{i=1}^{S}$ where S is the total number of video features from different streams.

3.3   Learning to Tokenization

One important aspect for fusing multi-modal models is to achieve effective representations of each modality but also do so efficiently. A possible naive approach is to apply either global average pooling, reducing the entire vision stream to a single representation, or concatenate many frames together. The first averages all the spatio-temporal information into a single representation, while the latter maintains a lot of redundant information and is computationally expensive.

Instead, we here first 'compress' each modality by learning to tokenize, based on TokenLearner [63]. The advantage is that it learns to select a small set of tokens, conditioned on the inputs. This greatly reduces the number of spatio-temporal tokens, while learning to maintain the needed information. Due to its adaptive nature, it can change the tokens based on the video and text inputs, allowing it to focus on the most important information.

We modify the TokenLearner approach to better suit the problem here, since in [63] it is only applied to single image frames. In our case, we also have both videos and text as our inputs, and videos are of multiple resolutions. We here enable both video and text to condition how video tokens are learned. Intuitively, this will allow TokenLearner to better select important spatio-temporal regions in the video not only based on visual information itself but also based on the text, and adaptively tokenize such regions.

Specifically, we learn to tokenize by first taking the input representation r with shape $L \times F$, where L is the length of the sequence and F is the feature dimension. This initially is the text feature, $r = f_t$. We also take a specific video feature f_{vi}, where i is one of the multi-scale, multi-stream features which has shape $T \times H \times W \times C$. Given r, we learn $\phi(r)$ (implemented with a linear layer in our version), to produce a $L \times (T \cdot H \cdot W)$ tensor where $T \cdot H \cdot W$ is the temporal and spatial size of the video feature. Another linear layer is used to make the feature have shape $C \times (T \cdot H \cdot W)$. This is reshaped and added with the video feature: $f = \phi(r) + f_{vi}$. Next, the function $\psi(\cdot)$ (implemented with convolutional layers) is applied to convert f into a feature with shape $T \times H \times W \times N$, where N is the number of desired tokens. A softmax function (σ) is applied over this, along the N-axis, selecting the spatio-temporal features for each token. Enabling the spatial attention mechanism, this is multiplied with the video representation, f_{vi}. More specifically, the attention mask $\sigma(\psi(\phi(r) + f_{vi}))$ is transposed to shape $N \times T \times H \times W$, and is tensor-dot-producted with f_{vi} while treating $T \times H \times W$ as the dimensions to contract. Overall, this can be expressed as:

$$f_0^i = \sigma(\psi(\phi(r) + f_{vi})) \cdot f_{vi} \tag{1}$$

The resulting feature representation f_0^i will have a shape of $N \times C$, abstracting the entire video as a set of N tokens per each video feature f_{vi}.

This allows the tokenizations to reduce many video streams into a few tokens. Generally, for our multi-stream, multi-scale inputs, the final feature representation f_0 is obtained by concatenating all f_0^i in the first axis, forming a representation with shape of $(NS) \times C$ where S is the number of scales and streams that are used. Importantly, these adaptive tokens are learned according to the optimization loss of the final task, which aims to improve accuracy of the produced outputs or answers. These tokens are then fused with a learning mechanism described in the below subsections.

3.4   Video-Text Iterative Co-tokenization

We here describe how we apply the above-mentioned joint tokenization approach iteratively at various levels of feature abstraction. We utilize self-attention transformer layers to combine the text and video features. Different from previous works, we will use the features of the transformer layers to produce a few informative tokens from the data (blue arrows on Fig. 2), which are fed to the next transformer fusion layer (red arrows on Fig. 2). Importantly, we use the token learning mechanism presented above at every layer; This allows the model to change its (video feature) selections differently at different layers.

To do this, we start by using tokenization to select NS visual tokens from the video input, as described above, initially using the text feature. These are then concatenated with the encoded text representation: $[f_t, f_0]$ along the token axis. These are then passed through 1 transformer layer (H), $r_1 = H([f_t, f_0])$. The outputs, r_1 are then used as input to Eq. 1 to generate NS new tokens, f_1, which are again concatenated with the text representation, added to the previous encoded, and passed through the next transformer layer: $r_l = H([f_t, f_{l-1}] + r_{l-1})$ for $l > 1$. The tokenziation is done for each of the multi-stream, multi-scale features f_{vi}, and is repeated L times, where L is the number of transformer layers (Fig. 3).

This approach allows the model to adaptively and iteratively select different visual features, from multiple scales and streams, refining the input to best align with the text. It results in a highly efficient method, due to the iterative tokenization.

3.5   Implementation Details

For better comparison to SOTA, we use standard model components, the T5 language model [60], and for video, we use popular video representations: 3D ResNets, 2D ResNets + temporal pooling, and X3D [19]. The encoded text and video features (learnable end-to-end) are entered into the multi-stream video encoder for learning the interaction between these features. A language-based decoder, again T5 [60], then takes the fused features to generate the output text. We set $N = 8, S = 4, C = 768; K = 3$

Video Preprocessing: To preprocess the video data, each individual frame is resized a fixed size, e.g., 224 by 224 pixels, and normalized such that the value for each pixel ranges from -1 to 1. We sample T frames from each video, evenly spaced across the video, i.e., the frames-per-second per video varies to maximize the temporal extent. In the multi-stream setting, T and $H \times W$ are different for each stream. We describe these settings for the models below.

Text Preprocessing: The text is tokenized using T5's standard 32k word vocabulary, with a max length of 32 tokens per example for both input and output. The model is trained to minimize the output per-token cross-entropy.

4   Experiments

We conduct experiments across different VideoQA datasets in order to determine the benefits of the approach, pretraining, efficiency and scaling.

4.1   Datasets

IVQA. The IVQA dataset [86] is a new, human annotated dataset for VideoQA consisting of 'how-to' videos. It has 10k clips with 1 question and 5 answers per question. It follows an evaluation metric similar to the VQA2.0 dataset [2], where its accuracy is computed for 5 choose 4 ground-truth (GT) answers.

Table 1. MSRVTT-QA [35] and MSVD-QA [82] datasets. Accuracy (%).

Model	MSRVTT-QA	MSVD-QA	GFLOPs
ST-VQA [30]	31.3	30.9	–
Co-Mem [22]	31.7	32.0	–
AMU [82]	32.0	32.5	–
HME [18]	33.7	33.0	–
HRA [13]	34.4	35.1	–
HCRN [43]	36.1	35.6	–
ClipBERT [45] 8 × 2	37.4	–	–
OCRL+LOGNet [53]	38.2	36.0	–
VQA-T [86] with HowTo100M	40.4	43.5	75+
VQA-T [86] with HowToVQA69M	41.5	46.3	75+
SiaSamRea [87]	41.6	45.5	–
MERLOT [93] with YT-Temporal-180M* [93]	43.1	–	–
Ours with HowTo100M	**45.7**	**48.6**	67

Table 2. Results comparing to SOTA approaches on the IVQA [86] dataset.

Model	Pre-training dataset	Accuracy (%)	GFLOPs
VQA-T [86]	HowTo100M	28.1	–
VQA-T [86]	HowToVQA69M	35.4	–
Ours	HowTo100M	**38.2**	67

MSRVTT-QA. [82] is based on the MSRVTT descriptions dataset [35], with automatically generated QA pairs from the descriptions. It has 243k VideoQA pairs and is evaluated by answer accuracy.

MSVD-QA. [82] is based on the MSVD datasets with automatically generated QA pairs. It has 50k VideoQA pairs and is evaluated by answer accuracy.

TGIF-QA. [30] consists of short GIF video clips with accompanying questions and answers related to the video. There are four types of questions ranging from questions about objects in still frames, to activities, repetition counting and sequences of events. TGIF-QA is evaluated in the multiple-choice answer setting, which we show is trivial for a strong (and language-only) model (see supp.). Instead, we use TGIF-QA in an open-vocabulary generative setting to study the effects of our approach on both single-frame and temporal-based questions.

4.2   Evaluation Setup

We follow the standard metrics for each dataset, described above. Since our model is generative, we use three different evaluation settings. (1) Open-ended generation, where the text decoder is used as-is with beam search [78], and generates any text. We then check string equality of the generated text to the GT

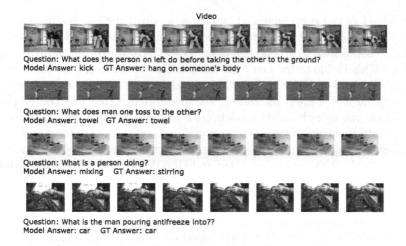

Fig. 4. Example results of our method.

answer. (2) Vocabulary-specific fully-connected (FC) layer, where we use the target vocabulary for each dataset from [86], and train a new FC layer on top of the final language features to classify the answer. (3) Masked-vocabulary generation, where we keep the text decoder from the model, but mask out tokens not in the target vocabulary. This lets us preserve the learned token embedding, but restrict the vocabulary to that of previous works, so as to be directly comparable.

5   Experimental Results

We compare our model with the SOTA approaches (Sect. 5.1) and then examine the model in a number of ablations. Section 5.4, reports on model efficiency.

5.1   VideoQA Results. Comparison to SOTA

Table 1 shows our results comparing to the MSRVTT-QA and MSVD-QA datasets, which are commonly used for VideoQA evaluation. As seen, our results outperform the SOTA, even though our pretraining is done on the weaker captioning dataset (HowTo100M), instead of the VideoQA counterpart, How-ToVQA69M, which has been shown to be superior for VideoQA tasks [86].

Table 2 compares our approach on the challenging new IVQA dataset. As seen, our results outperform SOTA with both HowToVQA69M and HowTo100M. Importantly, with the same pre-training HowTo100M, our approach outperforms the SOTA by more than 10% in absolute values.

In Table 1 of the supp. material, we show a surprising but instructive result on TGIF-QA, where our method, using a medium size pretrained text model T5 (T5-Base) [60], is able to accomplish close to 100% results on the multiple choice questions. This is due to the fact that the limited selection of answers is easy to guess even without video (it performs randomly for the action counting category as it needs the video input for these). We acknowledge that this contemporary text model is stronger than text models used previously, but is important to note that the multiple-choice setting is too easy. We experiment with the harder open-vocabulary setting in our ablations. The datasets evaluated above, MSRVTT-QA, MSVD-QA, IVQA are open-ended and thus do not suffer from this problem.

Visualizations. In Fig. 4 we show example results of the approach. In Fig. 5, we visualize the learned attention maps for different types of questions. In Fig. 6, we see a set of attention maps for each transformer layer. These figures show that the model is adapting the tokens based on both the video and text.

5.2   Open-Vocabulary Answer Generation

In the previous SOTA results (as presented in Sect. 5.1), prior approaches still use a limited vocabulary of answers, e.g., 4000 answers [86]. However in real-life scenarios, it is desirable that the generated answers are free-form text. In this section we show that generating open-vocabulary answers is a much more challenging setting for VideoQA. With our experiments, we would like to encourage future results to report this setting, as well.

In Table 3 we compare the open-ended, vs. FC vocabulary vs. masked vocabulary. The open vocabulary is the most challenging, as it requires the model to generate (in free form) the exact sequence of tokens to match the GT word. The FC vocabulary is restricted to 4k tokens, matching [86] vocabulary, but this model throws away the learned token embeddings, losing information. The masked vocabulary preserves all the token information, but removes the unneeded tokens, closely matching the previous settings, while maintaining the learned features.

Table 3. Comparing the performance of the same model with a fixed vocabulary (as reported in SOTA) and with open vocabulary, which is more challenging.

Vocabulary/Dataset	IVQA	MSRVTT-QA	MSVD-QA
Open 32k vocabulary	21.4	33.7	32.5
Fixed 4k vocabulary (FC)	37.4	42.9	45.9
Fixed 4k vocabulary (Masked)	**38.2**	**45.7**	**48.6**

5.3   Fusion Techniques

We conduct ablations on the multi-stream video encoder itself and its fusion mechanisms. Table 4 has the results – open vocabulary and no pre-training are used in these experiments. We see that each of the components of multi-stream video encoder contribute, where we note large collective contributions of the novel tokenization-based fusion techniques and also improvements compared to a single-stream model. Our approach is also very efficient, despite being multi-stream, due to the iterative tokenization approach and efficient backbones. Note that multiple frame models hurt the single-frame QA setting, but greatly benefit the time-based questions. Further, we see the most gains from the approach in the multi-frame questions, showing the benefit of the approach.

5.4   Video Multi-stream Encoder Model Efficiency

In Table 5 we experiment with the effect of scaling the model to more streams and larger models and see that our approach is much more efficient, in addition to being accurate, even with more than one streams. Our multi-stream approach, with only 67 GFLOPs, allows using various model sizes to improve performance and save FLOPs/params. We also note that to our estimates, the popular video vision transformer-based model ViViT [5] requires 2010 GFLOPs if adapted to VideoQA with T5, which would be infeasible both for training or inference (ViViT does not report VideoQA results). We used 64 TPUs for 72 h to pretrain (4608 TPU hours) and 4 TPUs for 8 h to finetune (32 TPU hours). Overall, this is fairly modest, e.g., compared to MERLOT [93] which used 1024 TPUs for 30 h (30k TPU hours) for pretraining.

Table 4. Ablations on multi-stream video encoder and fusion techniques. These models are trained from scratch and in the open-vocab generative setting. The ablations are cumulative, e.g., the last row uses 2-stream + Tok + MS + Co-Tok. Adding each component benefits. Tokenization reduces FLOPs notably and brings small performance improvements, whereas multi-scale and iterative co-tokenization bring larger improvements for very modest additional FLOPs. These models were trained with 32 frames, 224×224 images. The two streams are $32 \times 224 \times 224$ and $32 \times 128 \times 128$.

Model	GFLOPs	TGIF Frame-QA Single frame	TGIF Action (What happens X times?)	TGIF Trans (What happens after X?)	IVQA	MSRVTT QA
Single-frame	–	24.4	0.7	1.5	8.4	7.2
Single-stream	150	21.5	8.2	9.2	14.2	24.8
2-stream	47	24.2	8.8	9.2	14.5	24.7
+ Transformer	49	24.5	9.1	10.9	14.4	25.3
+ Tokenization	40	24.7	9.7	11.6	14.9	25.5
+ Multi-Scale	41	26.2	11.5	12.2	15.2	26.2
+ Iterative Co-Tok.	42	**27.3**	**11.8**	**12.5**	**15.5**	**27.6**

Table 5. Efficiency comparisons. While we use multiple streams, they take much fewer FLOPs. They also outperform the strongest X3D-XL model. Open vocabulary setting, no pre-training. 2-str (X3D-S $8 \times 224 \times 224$, X3D-M $16 \times 112 \times 112$), 3-str (X3D-S $8 \times 224 \times 224$, X3D-M $16 \times 112 \times 112$, X3D-M $32 \times 64 \times 64$), 3-str (3x X3D-L $8 \times 224 \times 224$, $16 \times 112 \times 112$, $32 \times 64 \times 64$). Note that these models use fewer frames than the ones in Table 4.

Model	IVQA	MSRVTT-QA	MSVD-QA	GFLOPS	Params
X3D-S	9.4	24.8	22.4	82	311M
X3D-XL	10.3	27.8	23.2	150	380M
2D-RN-50	2.2	6.4	6.5	306	332M
3D-RN-50	8.9	24.4	23.2	362	341M
2-stream (X3D-S, X3D-M)	9.2	25.3	23.5	40	321M
3-stream (X3D-S, X3D-M, X3D-M)	10.3	28.2	23.8	42	335M
3-stream (3x X3D-L)	**12.4**	**30.5**	**25.7**	67	345M

5.5   Pretraining

In Table 6 we explore different versions of pretraining (PT): contrastive, generative, Kinetics [36] classification, etc. for the VideoQA task. The models are pretrained using either HowTo100M with the automatic captions, YouTube8M [1] with automatic captions (when YouTube8M is split into 5 s clips, similar to HowTO100M clip duration, it has 250M clips, about 2x the size of HowTo100M). We pretrain the models using contrastive training (e.g., [58]) or language-generative training, in a completion setting where half the caption is used as input and half used as the target text. We also compare to Kinetics 600 classification pretraining of the video model and using the pretrained T5 model [60] for text. We find HowTo100M to be strongest of these pretrainings, and for our model, the generative training was better than contrastive. Both were generally better than independent Kinetics + T5 pretraining.

Table 6. Comparing different pretrianing methods for the VideoQA task. All use the single-stream baseline X3D-M model.

Method	IVQA	MSRVTT-QA	MSVD-QA
Random init	7.2	8.3	4.8
Kinetics-600 + T5	10.8	26.8	23.2
Contrastive (YouTube8M)	10.8	25.8	26.2
Contrastive (HowTo100M)	11.0	26.2	25.5
Generative (YouTube8M)	15.2	27.8	28.2
Generative (HowTo100M)	**15.6**	**29.4**	**28.6**

5.6   Exploring the Effects of Temporal Features

In Table 7 we compare the effects of temporal features on TGIF-QA and
MSRVTT-QA, IVQA. We compare the ResNet 1-frame, 16-frame and 32-frame
model, as well as the X3D video models. We can see that, for single frame questions, the 2D ResNet does better. However, for temporal questions, X3D is far
superior. This further confirms the benefit of multi-stream models for VideoQA
tasks.

Table 7. Comparing temporal features. Here the ResNet is pretrained on image-text
data, e.g., CC12M. We find that single-frame PT ResNet does very well on the single
frame QAs, but quite poorly on the temporal questions. Adding frames help, but in
general, we find that learning video specific features helps the most. 2D ResNets are
shown in the top half and X3D-M in the bottom.

Model	TGIF Frame-QA (Single frame)	TGIF Action (What happens X times?)	TGIF Transition (What happens after X?)	IVQA	MSRVTT-QA
1 frame	37.4	0.8	2.9	12.7	22.3
16 frame	35.4	2.5	3.5	18.6	23.5
32 frame	36.2	3.3	3.9	19.3	23.9
16 frame	26.2	12.4	13.4	13.5	24.5
32 frame	25.5	13.1	15.4	14.2	24.8

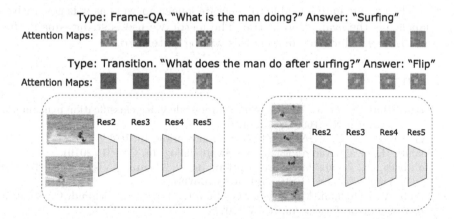

Fig. 5. Visualization of the learned attentions for two different types of questions. We
can see it learns to select the spatial stream for the "Frame-QA" type of question,
where temporal information is not needed, but for the "Transition" question, it focuses
more heavily on the stream with many frames.

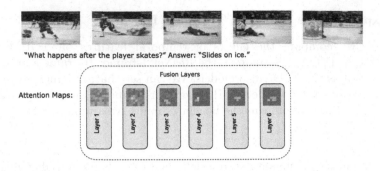

"What happens after the player skates?" Answer: "Slides on ice."

Fig. 6. Attention maps changing after each layer they are applied to. The first one focuses over the whole video, each after focuses on more specific regions. In this example, it captures the hockey player falling and sliding on the ice.

6 Conclusions

In this paper we propose a novel multi-stream video text encoder with iterative video-text co-tokenization, which efficiently extracts and fuses information from video and text inputs. We demonstrate its benefits to challenging VideoQA tasks, outperforming SOTA on the standard benchmarks and metrics and also report results in the more challenging open-vocabulary setting. Our approach is efficient taking only 67 GFLOPs. One limitation of the approach is for longer answer. Though our model is able to generate longer answers as it is generative, the challenge is the evaluation metric. The metric we use is string equality for accuracy. However, for long answers this will be quite hard.

References

1. Abu-El-Haija, S., et al.: Youtube-8m: a large-scale video classification benchmark. arXiv preprint arXiv:1609.08675 (2016)
2. Agrawal, A., et al.: VQA: visual question answering. In: ICCV (2015)
3. Alamri, H., et al.: Audio-visual scene-aware dialog. In: CVPR (2019)
4. Rohrbach, A., et al.: Movie description. Int. J. Comput. Vis. **123**(1), 94–120 (2017). https://doi.org/10.1007/s11263-016-0987-1
5. Arnab, A., Dehghani, M., Heigold, G., Sun, C., Lucic, M., Schmid, C.: Vivit: a video vision transformer. In: ICCV (2021)
6. Bain, M., Nagrani, A., Varol, G., Zisserman, A.: Frozen in time: a joint video and image encoder for end-to-end retrieval. In: ICCV (2021)
7. Bellver, M., et al.: Refvos: a closer look at referring expressions for video object segmentation (2020). https://arxiv.org/abs/2010.00263
8. Bertasius, G., Wang, H., Torresani, L.: Is space-time attention all you need for video understanding? (2021)
9. Carreira, J., Zisserman, A.: Quo vadis, action recognition? a new model and the kinetics dataset. In: CVPR (2017)
10. Chadha, A., Arora, G., Kaloty, N.: iPerceive: applying common-sense reasoning to multi-modal dense video captioning and video question answering. In: WACV (2021)

11. Chen, Y.-C., et al.: UNITER: UNiversal image-TExt representation learning. In: Vedaldi, A., Bischof, H., Brox, T., Frahm, J.-M. (eds.) ECCV 2020. LNCS, vol. 12375, pp. 104–120. Springer, Cham (2020). https://doi.org/10.1007/978-3-030-58577-8_7

12. Chen, Z., Ma, L., Luo, W., Wong, K.Y.K.: Weakly-supervised spatio-temporally grounding natural sentence in video. In: Proceedings 57th Annual Meeting of the Association for Computational Linguistics (2019)

13. Chowdhury, M.I.H., Nguyen, K., Sridharan, S., Fookes, C.: Hierarchical relational attention for video question answering. In: 25th IEEE International Conference on Image Processing (ICIP)

14. Das, A., et al.: Visual dialog. In: CVPR (2017)

15. Deng, C., Chen, S., Chen, D., He, Y., Wu, Q.: Sketch, ground, and refine: top-down dense video captioning. In: CVPR (2021)

16. Donahue, J., et al.: Long-term recurrent convolutional networks for visual recognition and description. In: CVPR (2015)

17. Dong, J., et al.: Dual encoding for zero-example video retrieval. In: CVPR (2019)

18. Fan, C., Zhang, X., Zhang, S., Wang, W., Zhang, C., Huang, H.: Heterogeneous memory enhanced multimodal attention model for video question answering. In: CVPR (2019)

19. Feichtenhofer, C.: X3D: expanding architectures for efficient video recognition. In: CVPR (2020)

20. Feichtenhofer, C., Fan, H., Malik, J., He, K.: Slowfast networks for video recognition. In: ICCV (2019)

21. Gabeur, V., Sun, C., Alahari, K., Schmid, C.: Multi-modal transformer for video retrieval. In: Vedaldi, A., Bischof, H., Brox, T., Frahm, J.-M. (eds.) ECCV 2020. LNCS, vol. 12349, pp. 214–229. Springer, Cham (2020). https://doi.org/10.1007/978-3-030-58548-8_13

22. Gao, J., Ge, R., Chen, K., Nevatia, R.: Motion appearance co-memory networks for video question answering. In: CVPR (2018)

23. Gao, J., Sun, C., Yang, Z., Nevatia, R.: Tall: temporal activity localization via language query. In: ICCV (2017)

24. Garcia, N., Otani, M., Chu, C., Nakashima, Y.: Knowit VQA: answering knowledge-based questions about videos. In: AAAI (2020)

25. Goyal, Y., Khot, T., Summers-Stay, D., Batra, D., Parikh, D.: Making the V in VQA matter: elevating the role of image understanding in visual question answering. In: CVPR (2017)

26. Hendricks, L.A., Wang, O., Shechtman, E., Sivic, J., Darrell, T., Russell, B.: Localizing moments in video with natural language. In: ICCV (2017)

27. Hori, C., et al.: End-to-end audio visual scene-aware dialog using multimodal attention-based video features. In: ICASSP (2019)

28. Huang, G., Pang, B., Zhu, Z., Rivera, C., Soricut, R.: Multimodal pretraining for dense video captioning. In: AACL-IJCNLP (2020)

29. Hussein, N., Gavves, E., Smeulders, A.W.: Timeception for complex action recognition. In: CVPR (2019)

30. Jang, Y., Song, Y., Yu, Y., Kim, Y., Kim, G.: TGIF-QA: toward spatio-temporal reasoning in visual question answering. In: CVPR (2017)

31. Ji, S., Xu, W., Yang, M., Yu, K.: 3D convolutional neural networks for human action recognition 35(1), 221–231 (2013)

32. Jianfeng Dong, X.L., Xu, C., Yang, X., Yang, G., Wang, X., Wang, M.: Dual encoding for video retrieval by text. In: T-PAMI (2021)

33. Jiang, H., Misra, I., Rohrbach, M., Learned-Miller, E., Chen, X.: In defense of grid features for visual question answering. In: CVPR (2020)
34. Jiang, P., Han, Y.: Reasoning with heterogeneous graph alignment for video question answering. In: AAAI (2020)
35. Xu, J., Mei, T., Yao, T., Rui, Y.: MSR-VTT: a large video description dataset for bridging video and language. In: CVPR (2016)
36. Kay, W., et al.: The Kinetics human action video dataset. arXiv preprint arXiv:1705.06950 (2017)
37. Khoreva, A., Rohrbach, A., Schiele, B.: Video object segmentation with language referring expressions. In: 14th Asian Conference on Computer Vision (ACCV) (2018)
38. Kim, J., Ma, M., Pham, T., Kim, K., Yoo, C.D.: Modality shifting attention network for multi-modal video question answering. In: CVPR (2020)
39. Kim, K.M., Choi, S.H., Kim, J.H., Zhang, B.T.: Multimodal dual attention memory for video story question answering. In: ECCV (2018)
40. Korbar, B., Tran, D., Torresani, L.: Scsampler: sampling salient clips from video for efficient action recognition. In: ICCV (2019)
41. Krishna, R., Hata, K., Ren, F., Fei-Fei, L., Niebles, J.C.: Dense-captioning events in videos. In: ICCV (2017)
42. Kim, K.M., Heo, M.O., Choi, S.H., Zhang, B.T.: Deepstory: video story QA by deep embedded memory networks. In: IJCAI (2017)
43. Le, T.M., Le, V., Venkatesh, S., Tran, T.: Hierarchical conditional relation networks for video question answering. In: CVPR (2020)
44. Lea, C., Flynn, M.D., Vidal, R., Reiter, A., Hager, G.D.: Temporal convolutional networks for action segmentation and detection. In: CVPR (2017)
45. Lei, J., et al.: Less is more: clipbert for video-and-language learning via sparse sampling. In: CVPR (2021)
46. Lei, J., Yu, L., Bansal, M., Berg, T.L.: TVQA: localized, compositional video question answering. In: EMNLP (2018)
47. Li, L., Chen, Y.C., Cheng, Y., Gan, Z., Yu, L., Liu, J.: Hero: hierarchical encoder for video+ language omni-representation pre-training. In: EMNLP (2020)
48. Li, L., et al.: Value: a multi-task benchmark for video-and-language understanding evaluation. In: 35th Conference on Neural Information Processing Systems (NeurIPS 2021) Track on Datasets and Benchmarks (2021)
49. Li, X., et al.: Beyondrnns: positional self-attention with co-attention for video question answering. In: AAAI (2020)
50. Li, X., et al.: OSCAR: object-semantics aligned pre-training for vision-language tasks. In: Vedaldi, A., Bischof, H., Brox, T., Frahm, J.-M. (eds.) ECCV 2020. LNCS, vol. 12375, pp. 121–137. Springer, Cham (2020). https://doi.org/10.1007/978-3-030-58577-8_8
51. Lin, J., Gan, C., Han, S.: TSM: temporal shift module for efficient video understanding. In: ICCV (2019)
52. Lin, X., Bertasius, G., Wang, J., Chang, S.F., Parikh, D.: Vx2text: end-to-end learning of video-based text generation from multimodal inputs. In: CVPR (2021)
53. Dang, L.H., Le, T.M., Le, V., Tran, T.: Object-centric representation learning for video question answering. In: IJCNN (2021)
54. Lu, J., Batra, D., Parikh, D., Lee, S.: Vilbert: pretraining task-agnostic visiolinguistic representations for vision-and-language tasks. In: CVPR (2019)
55. Maharaj, T., Ballas, N., Rohrbach, A., Courville, A., Pal, C.: A dataset and exploration of models for understanding video data through fill-in-the blank question-answering. In: CVPR (2017)

56. Miech, A., Alayrac, J.B., Laptev, I., Sivic, J., Zisserman, A.: Thinking fast and slow: efficient text-to-visual retrieval with transformers. In: CVPR (2021)
57. Miech, A., Alayrac, J.B., Smaira, L., Laptev, I., Sivic, J., Zisserman, A.: End-to-end learning of visual representations from uncurated instructional videos. In: CVPR (2020)
58. Miech, A., Zhukov, D., Alayrac, J.B., Tapaswi, M., Laptev, I., Sivic, J.: Howto100m: learning a text-video embedding by watching hundred million narrated video clips. In: ICCV (2019)
59. Park, J., Lee, J., Sohn, K.: Bridge to answer: structure-aware graph interaction network for video question answering. In: CVPR (2021)
60. Raffel, C., et al.: Exploring the limits of transfer learning with a unified text-to-text transformer. J. Mach. Learn. Res. **21**(140), 1–67 (2020)
61. Rohrbach, A., Rohrbach, M., Tandon, N., Schiele, B.: A dataset for movie description. In: CVPR (2015)
62. Rohrbach, M., Amin, S., Andriluka, M., Schiele, B.: A database for fine grained activity detection of cooking activities. In: CVPR (2012)
63. Ryoo, M.S., Piergiovanni, A., Arnab, A., Dehghani, M., Angelova, A.: Token-learner: adaptive space-time tokenization for videos (2021)
64. Ryoo, M.S., Piergiovanni, A., Tan, M., Angelova, A.: AssembleNet: searching for multi-stream neural connectivity in video architectures. In: ICLR (2020)
65. Simonyan, K., Zisserman, A.: Two-stream convolutional networks for action recognition in videos. In: NeurIPS, pp. 568–576 (2014)
66. Sun, C., Myers, A., Vondrick, C., Murphy, K., Schmid, C.: Videobert: a joint model for video and language representation learning. In: ICCV (2019)
67. Tan, H., Bansal, M.: Lxmert: learning cross-modality encoder representations from transformers. In: EMNLP (2019)
68. Tapaswi, M., Zhu, Y., Rainer Stiefelhagen, A.T., Urtasun, R., Fidler, S.: MovieQA: understanding stories in movies through questionanswering. In: CVPR (2016)
69. Le, T.M., Le, V., Venkatesh, S., Tran, T.: Neural reasoning, fast and slow, for video question answering. In: IJCNN (2020)
70. Tran, D., Bourdev, L.D., Fergus, R., Torresani, L., Paluri, M.: C3D: generic features for video analysis. CoRR, abs/1412.0767 **2**(7), 8 (2014)
71. Tran, D., Wang, H., Torresani, L., Ray, J., LeCun, Y., Paluri, M.: A closer look at spatiotemporal convolutions for action recognition. In: CVPR, pp. 6450–6459 (2018)
72. Tsai, Y.H.H., Divvala, S., Morency, L.P., Salakhutdinov, R., Farhadi, A.: Video relationship reasoning using gated spatio-temporal energy graph. In: CVPR (2019)
73. Vaswani, A., et al.: Attention is all you need. In: NeurIPS (2017)
74. Wang, J., Ma, L., Jiang, W.: Temporally grounding language queries in videos by contextual boundary-aware prediction. In: AAAI (2020)
75. Wang, X., Wu, J., Chen, J., Li, L., Wang, Y.F., Wang, W.Y.: Vatex: a large-scale, high-quality multilingual dataset for video-and-language research. In: ICCV (2019)
76. Wang, Z., Wu, Y., Narasimhan, K., Russakovsky, O.: Multi-query video retrieval. In: ArXiv:2201.03639 (2022)
77. Su, W., et al.: Vl-bert: pre-training of generic visual-linguistic representations. In: ICLR (2020)
78. Wiseman, S., Rush, A.M.: Sequence-to-sequence learning as beam-search optimization. In: EMNLP (2016)

79. Wu, C.Y., Krahenbuhl, P.: Towards long-form video understanding. In: CVPR (2021)
80. Xiao, J., Shang, X., Yao, A., Chua, T.S.: NExT-QA: next phase of question-answering to explaining temporal actions. In: CVPR (2021)
81. Xie, S., Sun, C., Huang, J., Tu, Z., Murphy, K.: Rethinking spatiotemporal feature learning: speed-accuracy trade-offs in video classification. In: ECCV, pp. 305–321 (2018)
82. Xu, D., et al.: Video question answering via gradually refined attention over appearance and motion. In: ACM Multimedia (2017)
83. Xu, L., Huang, H., Liu, J.: SUTD-TrafficQA: a question answering benchmark and an efficient network for video reasoning over traffic events. In: CVPR (2021)
84. Xu, R., Xiong, C., Chen, W., Corso, J.J.: Jointly modeling deep video and compositional text to bridge vision and language in a unified framework. In: AAAI (2015)
85. Xue, H., Chu, W., Zhao, Z., Cai, D.: A better way to attend: attention with trees for video question answering. In: IEEE Transactions on Image Processing (2018)
86. Yang, A., Miech, A., Sivic, J., Laptev, I., Schmid, C.: Just ask: learning to answer questions from millions of narrated videos. In: ICCV (2021)
87. Yu, W., et al.: Learning from inside: self-driven siamese sampling and reasoning for video question answering. Adv. Neural. Inf. Process. Syst. **34**, 26462–26474 (2021)
88. Yu, Y., Kim, J., Kim, G.: A joint sequence fusion model for video question answering and retrieval. In: ECCV (2018)
89. Yu, Z., et al.: Activitynet-QA: a dataset for understanding complex web videos via question answering. In: AAAI (2019)
90. Yu, Z., Yu, J., Cui, Y., Tao, D., Tian, Q.: Deep modular co-attention networks for visual question answering. In: CVPR (2019)
91. Gong, Y., Wang, L., Hodosh, M., Hockenmaier, J., Lazebnik, S.: Improving image-sentence embeddings using large weakly annotated photo collections. In: Fleet, D., Pajdla, T., Schiele, B., Tuytelaars, T. (eds.) ECCV 2014. LNCS, vol. 8692, pp. 529–545. Springer, Cham (2014). https://doi.org/10.1007/978-3-319-10593-2_35
92. Zadeh, A., Chan, M., Liang, P.P., Tong, E., Morency, L.P.: Social-IQ: a question answering benchmark for artificial social intelligence. In: CVPR (2019)
93. Zellers, R., et al.: Merlot: multimodal neural script knowledge models (2021)
94. Zhou, B., Andonian, A., Oliva, A., Torralba, A.: Temporal relational reasoning in videos. In: ECCV, pp. 803–818 (2018)
95. Zhou, L., Xu, C., Corso, J.J.: Towards automatic learning of procedures from web instructional videos. In: AAAI
96. Zhou, L., Zhou, Y., Corso, J.J., Socher, R., Xiong, C.: End-to-end dense video captioning with masked transformer. In: CVPR (2018)
97. Zhu, L., Xu, Z., Yan, Y., Hauptmann, A.G.: Uncovering the temporal context for video question answering. In: IJCV (2018)
98. Zhu, L., Yang, Y.: Actbert: learning global-local video-text representations. In: CVPR (2020)
99. Zhukov, D., Alayrac, J.B., Cinbis, R.G., Fouhey, D., Laptev, I., Sivic, J.: Cross-task weakly supervised learning from instructional videos. In: CVPR (2019)
100. Zolfaghari, M., Singh, K., Brox, T.: Eco: efficient convolutional network for online video understanding. In: ECCV (2018)

Rethinking Data Augmentation
for Robust Visual Question Answering

Long Chen[1], Yuhang Zheng[2], and Jun Xiao[2(✉)]

[1] Columbia University, New York, USA
zjuchenlong@gmail.com
[2] Zhejiang University, Hangzhou, China
itemzhang@zju.edu.cn, junx@cs.zju.edu.cn

Abstract. Data Augmentation (DA) — generating extra training samples beyond the original training set — has been widely-used in today's unbiased VQA models to mitigate language biases. Current mainstream DA strategies are synthetic-based methods, which synthesize new samples by either editing some visual regions/words, or re-generating them from scratch. However, these synthetic samples are always unnatural and error-prone. To avoid this issue, a recent DA work composes new augmented samples by randomly pairing pristine images and other human-written questions. Unfortunately, to guarantee augmented samples have reasonable ground-truth answers, they manually design a set of heuristic rules for several question types, which extremely limits its generalization abilities. To this end, we propose a new **K**nowledge **D**istillation based **D**ata **Aug**mentation for VQA, dubbed **KDDAug**. Specifically, we first relax the requirements of reasonable image-question pairs, which can be easily applied to any question type. Then, we design a knowledge distillation (KD) based answer assignment to generate pseudo answers for all composed image-question pairs, which are robust to both *in-domain* and *out-of-distribution* settings. Since KDDAug is a model-agnostic DA strategy, it can be seamlessly incorporated into any VQA architecture. Extensive ablation studies on multiple backbones and benchmarks have demonstrated the effectiveness and generalization abilities of KDDAug.

Keywords: VQA · Data augmentation · Knowledge distillation

1   Introduction

Visual Question Answering (**VQA**), *i.e.*, answering any natural language questions about the given visual content, is regarded as the holy grail of a human-like vision system [21]. Due to its multi-modal nature, VQA has raised unprecedented attention from both CV and NLP communities, and hundreds of VQA models

---

L. Chen and Y. Zheng—Co-first authors with equal contributions.
Codes: https://github.com/ItemZheng/KDDAug.

Supplementary Information The online version contains supplementary material available at https://doi.org/10.1007/978-3-031-20059-5_6.

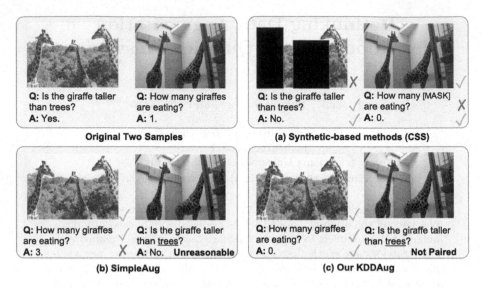

Fig. 1. Comparisons between different DA methods for VQA. (a) **Synthetic-based methods**: Take CSS [16] as an example, it masks some regions or words in the original samples. (b) **SimpleAug** [31]: It pairs images with some specific types of questions, and obtains pseudo labels by predefined heuristic rules. (c) **KDDAug**: It pairs image with any types of questions, and use a KD-based model to predict pseudo answers. Question "is ..." is not a reasonable question for the right image as it contains "trees".

have been developed in recent years. Although current VQA models can achieve really "decent" performance on standard benchmarks, numerous studies have revealed that today's models tend to over-rely on the superficial linguistic correlations between the questions and answers rather than multi-modal reasoning (*a.k.a.*, **language biases**) [3,4,24,28,54]. For example, blindly answering "2" for all counting questions or "tennis" for all sport-related questions can still get a satisfactory performance. To mitigate these bias issues and realize robust VQA, a recent surge of VQA work [2,7–9,16,18,22,23,29,30,32,46,51] resort to different data augmentation techniques (*i.e.*, generating extra training samples beyond original training set), and achieve good performance on both the in-domain (ID) (*e.g.*, VQA v2 [24]) and out-of-distribution (OOD) datasets (*e.g.*, VQA-CP [4]).

Currently, mainstream Data Augmentation (DA) strategies for robust VQA are **synthetic-based** methods. As shown in Fig. 1(a), from modality viewpoint, these synthetic-based DA methods can be categorized into two groups: 1) *Visual-manipulated*: They usually edit some visual regions in original images [16,18,32], or re-generate counterfactual/adversarial images with generative networks [2,22] or adversarial attacks [46]. 2) *Textual-generated*: They edit some words in original questions [16,18,32] or re-generate the sentence from scratch with back translation [30,46] or visual question generation (VQG) methods [51]. Although these synthetic-based methods have dominated the performance on OOD benchmarks (*e.g.*, VQA-CP), and significantly improved VQA models' interpretability and consistency, there are several inherent weaknesses: 1) Photo-realistic image generation or accurate sentence generation themselves are still open problems, *e.g.*, a significant portion of the generated questions have grammatical errors [46]. 2) They always need extra human annotations to assign reasonable answers [22].

To avoid these unnatural and synthetic training samples, a recent work SimpleAug [31] starts to compose new training samples by randomly pairing images and questions. As the example shown in Fig. 1(b), they pair the left image and human-written questions from the right image (*i.e.*, "How many giraffes are eating?") into a new image-question (VQ) pair. To obtain "reasonable" pseudo ground-truth answers for these new VQ pairs, they manually design a set of heuristic rules for several specific question types, including "Yes/No", "Color", "Number", and "What" type questions. Although SimpleAug avoids the challenging image/sentence generation procedures, there are still several drawbacks: 1) These predefined rules for answer assignment are fallible (*e.g.*, the human-check accuracy for "Yes/No" type questions is only 52.20%, slightly higher than a random guess.) 2) Due to the limitations of these rules, it only covers several specific types of answers, and it is difficult to extend to other question types[1]. 3) It still relies on some human annotations (*e.g.*, object annotations in COCO).

In this paper, we propose a **K**nowledge **D**istillation based **D**ata **Aug**mentation (**KDDAug**) strategy for robust VQA, which can avoid all the mentioned weaknesses in existing DA methods. Specifically, we first relax the requirement for reasonable VQ pairs by only considering the object categories in the images and nouns in the questions. As illustrated in Fig. 1(c), question "how many giraffes are eating" is a reasonable question for the left image which contains "giraffe" objects. To avoid extra human annotations, we only utilize an off-the-shelf object detector to detect objects[2].

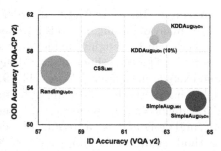

Fig. 2. Performance of SOTA DA methods. Circle sizes are in proportion to the number of their augmented samples (see footnote 3).

After obtaining all the reasonable VQ pairs, we design a multi-teacher knowledge distillation (KD) based answer assignment to generate corresponding pseudo ground-truth answers. We first pretrain two teacher models (ID and OOD teacher) with the original training set, and then utilize these teacher models to predict a "soft" answer distribution for each VQ pair. Last, we combine the predicted distributions (*i.e.*, knowledge) from both teachers, and treat them as the pseudo answers for augmented VQ pairs. Benefiting from our designs, KDDAug achieves the best trade-off results on both ID and OOD settings with even fewer samples (Fig. 2)[3].

---

[1] VQA datasets typically have much more question types (*e.g.*, 65 for VQA v2 [24]).

[2] Since all the compared state-of-the-art VQA models follow UpDn [5] and use VG [33] pretrained detector to extract visual features, we don't use extra annotations.

[3] CSS & RandImg dynamically generate different samples in each epoch, their sizes are difficult to determine. Here, their sizes are for illustration (larger than SimpleAug).

Extensive ablation studies have demonstrated the effectiveness of KDDAug. KDDAug can be seamlessly incorporated into any VQA architecture, and consistently boost their performance. Particularly, by building on top of some SOTA debiasing methods (*e.g.*, LMH [19], RUBi [11], and CSS [16]), KDDAug consistently boost their performance on both ID and OOD benchmarks.

In summary, we make three main contributions in this paper:

1. We systematically analyze existing DA strategies for robust VQA, and propose a new KDDAug that can avoid all the weaknesses of existing solutions.
2. We use multi-teacher KD to generate pseudo answers, which not only avoids human annotations, but also is more robust to both ID and OOD settings.
3. KDDAug is a model-agnostic DA method, which empirically boosts multiple different VQA architectures to achieve state-of-the-art performance.

2   Related Work

Language Biases in VQA. In order to overcome the language biases issues in VQA, many debiasing methods have been proposed recently. Specifically, existing methods can be roughly divided into two groups: 1) Ensemble-based debiasing methods. These methods always design an auxiliary branch to explicit model and exclude the language biases [11,19,25,26,35,38,40,45,52]. 2) Model-agnostic debiasing methods. These methods mainly include balancing datasets [24,54], data augmentation by generating augmented training samples [1,16,18,22,30, 31], and designing extra training objectives [22,36,56]. Almost existing debiasing methods significantly improve their OOD performance, but with the cost of ID performance drops. In this paper, we deeply analyze existing DA methods, and propose a new DA strategy to achieve a decent trade-off between ID & OOD performance.

Data Augmentation in VQA. In addition to the mainstream synthetic-based methods, there are other DA methods: some existing methods generate negative samples by randomly selecting images or questions [48,56], or compose reasonable image-question (VQ) pairs as new positive training samples [31]. For these generated VQ pairs, they utilize manually pre-defined rules to obtain answers, which are designed for some specific question types. However, these DA methods almost either suffer a severe ID performance drop [16,18,32,48] or their answer assignment mechanisms rely on human annotations and lack generality [7,22,23,29,31]. Instead, our KDDAug overcomes all these weaknesses.

Knowledge Distillation. KD is a method that helps the training process of a smaller student network under the supervision of a larger teacher network [49]. The idea of KD has been applied to numerous vision tasks, *e.g.*, object detection [12,50] or visual-language tasks [34,42,55]. Recently, Niu *et.al.* [41] began to study KD for VQA and propose a KD-based method to generate "soft" labels in training. Inspired by them, we propose to use a multi-teacher KD to generate robust pseudo ground-truth labels for all new composed VQ pairs.

3 KDDAug: A New DA Framework for VQA

Following same conventions of existing VQA works, VQA task is typically formulated as a multi-class classification problem. Given a dataset $\mathcal{D}_{\text{orig}} = \{I_i, Q_i, a_i\}_i^N$ consisting of triplets of images $I_i \in \mathcal{I}$, questions $Q_i \in \mathcal{Q}$ and ground-truth answers $a_i \in \mathcal{A}$, VQA model learns a multimodal mapping: $\mathcal{I} \times \mathcal{Q} \to [0,1]^{|\mathcal{A}|}$, which produces an answer distribution given an image-question (VQ) pair.

To reduce the language biases, a surge of data augmentation (DA) methods have been proposed for VQA. Specifically, given the original training set $\mathcal{D}_{\text{orig}}$, DA methods generate an augmented training set $\mathcal{D}_{\text{aug}}$ automatically. Then, they can train any VQA architectures with both two training sets ($\mathcal{D}_{\text{orig}} \cup \mathcal{D}_{\text{aug}}$).

In this section, we first compare proposed KDDAug with existing DA methods in Sect. 3.1. Then, we introduce details of KDDAug, including image-question pair composition in Sect. 3.2, and KD-based answer assignment in Sect. 3.3.

3.1 KDDAug vs. Existing da Pipelines

Synthetic-Based Methods. For each human-labeled sample $(I_i, Q_i, a_i) \in \mathcal{D}_{\text{orig}}$, the synthetic-based methods (*e.g.*, CSS [16]) always synthesize one corresponding augmented sample by either editing the image I_i or question Q_i, denoted as $\hat{I}_i$ or $\hat{Q}_i$. Then, original image I_i and its synthesized question $\hat{Q}_i$ compose a new VQ pair $(I_i, \hat{Q}_i)$ (similar for VQ pair $(\hat{I}_i, Q_i)$ and $(\hat{I}_i, \hat{Q}_i)$). Lastly, different answer assignment mechanisms are designed to generate pseudo answers for these augmented VQ pairs, and these samples constitute the augmented set $\mathcal{D}_{\text{aug}}$. As discussed in Sect. 1, these new synthetic VQ pairs are unnatural and error-prone.

SimpleAug [31]. Unlike synthetic-based methods, SimpleAug tries to compose new VQ pairs by randomly sampling an image $I_i \in \mathcal{I}$ and other possible question $Q_j \in \mathcal{Q}$, *i.e.*, (I_i, Q_j). This simple strategy can make sure both image I_i and question Q_j are always pristine. Not surprisingly, there is no free lunch — this arbitrary composition strategy significantly increases the difficulty of pseudo answers assignment. To this end, SimpleAug proposes a set of heuristic rules for only four types of questions ("Yes/No", "Number", "What", and "Color"), which limits its diversity and generalization ability.

Proposed KDDAug. To solve all the weaknesses in existing DA methods (*i.e.*, both synthetic-based methods and SimpleAug), we take two steps to generate the augmented set $\mathcal{D}_{\text{aug}}$: 1) We randomly compose image $I_i \in \mathcal{I}$ and all reasonable questions $Q_j \in \mathcal{Q}$ without limiting question types. 2) We utilize a knowledge distillation (KD) based answer assignment to automatically generate "soft" pseudo answers for each VQ pair. Next, we detailed introduce these two steps.

3.2 Image-Question Pair Composition

To extremely increase the diversity of the new augmented training set $\mathcal{D}_{\text{aug}}$, we relax the requirements for *reasonable* VQ pairs by only considering the object

Fig. 3. Example of three randomly composed VQ pairs. (a) **Unreasonable pair**: The question contains noun "trunk" which are not in the image. (b) **Reasonable pair**: All nouns in the question ("girl" and "sock") are in the image. (c) **Reasonable pair**: Although the question contains "hat" which are not in the image, it is still reasonable.

categories in the images and nouns in the questions. By "reasonable", we mean that: 1) The question is suitable for the image content. 2) There are some ground-truth answers for this VQ pair. For example, as shown in Fig. 3(a), the question "Why is the suitcase in the trunk?" is not a reasonable question for the image, because "truck" does not appear in the image. Therefore, we treat question Q_j as a reasonable question for image I_i as long as all the meaningful nouns in Q_j appear in I_i. For example in Fig. 3(b), questions only containing "girl" and "sock" are all reasonable questions for this image[4].

Thus, similar to other DA methods [16, 18, 31], we first extract these meaningful nouns from all questions $\mathcal{Q}$. We utilize the spaCy POS tagger [27] to extract all nouns and unify their singular and plural forms[5]. We ignore the nouns such as "picture" or "photo". We remove all the questions without any meaningful nouns (the proportion is small, $e.g.$, $\approx 9\%$ in VQA-CP v2). For all images $\mathcal{I}$, we leverage an off-the-shelf object detector to detect all proposals in each image, and predict their object categories. Lastly, we compose all possible reasonable VQ pairs by traversing all the questions and images in the original training set.

Since the number of "Yes/No" questions is quite large ($e.g.$, $\approx 42\%$ in VQA-CP v2), to prevent creating too many "Yes/No" samples, we group all "Yes/No" questions with the same set of nouns into one group, and randomly select three questions per group for new sample compositions.

CLIP-Based Filtering. One potential weakness for our VQ pair composition strategy is the excessive training samples, which may increase the training times. To achieve a good trade-off between efficiency and effectiveness, we can utilize a pretrained visual-language model CLIP [43] to filter out less-efficient augmented samples. By "less-efficient", we mean that the improvements provided by these training samples are marginal. This filtering design is based on the observation

---

[4] Some questions containing extra nouns may also be reasonable questions, especially for "Yes/No" questions ($cf.$ example in Fig. 3(c)). However, almost all VQ pairs that meet this more strict requirement are always reasonable.

[5] We tried to use WordNet to map between nouns' synsets, lemmas or hypernyms ($e.g.$, "dog" and "animal"). But empirically, the VQA performance is quite similar.

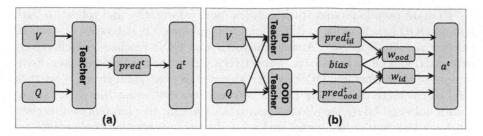

Fig. 4. Pipelines of single-teacher KD (a) and multi-teacher KD (b) answer assignment.

that people tend to ask questions about salient objects in the image, *i.e.*, the nouns mentioned in questions should appear prominently in the image. Specifically, we firstly use the template "a photo of <NOUN>" to generate prompts for each meaningful noun in the question and utilize CLIP to calculate the similarity score between the image and all corresponding prompts. Then, we use the average similarity score over all meaningful nouns to get the relevance score between the question and the image. We sort all composed VQ pairs according to the relevance score and only the $\alpha\%$ samples with the top highest relevance scores are reserved (See Table 5 for more details about influence of different α).

Advantages. Compared with existing VQ pair composition strategies, ours has several advantages: 1) Our definition for "reasonable" simplifies the composition step and further improves the diversity of the VQ pairs. 2) Our strategy gets rid of human annotations, which means it can be easily extended to other datasets.

3.3   KD-Based Answer Assignment

Given the original training set $\mathcal{D}_{\text{orig}}$ and all new composed reasonable VQ pairs ($\{I_i, Q_j\}$), we use a KD-based answer assignment to generate pseudo answers.

Single-Teacher KD for Answer Assignment. Inspired by existing KD work for pseudo labeling [41,44], we begin to shift our gaze from manual rules to KD. A straightforward KD-based strategy is training a *teacher* VQA model with the original training set $\mathcal{D}_{\text{orig}}$, and then using the pre-trained teacher model to predict answer distributions $pred^t$ for each composed VQ pair. And the $pred^t$ is treated as the pseudo answer for this VQ pair (*cf.* Fig. 4(a)). Obviously, the quality of assigned answers is determined by the performance of the teacher model, and the biases learned by the teacher model are also included in $pred^t$.

Multi-teacher KD for Answer Assignment. To generate more accurate and robust pseudo answers, an extension is merging knowledge from multiple teachers. Given N pre-trained teacher models, and each trained model can predict an answer distribution $\{pred_i^t\}$, and the pseudo answer is:

$$a^t = \sum_{i=1}^{N} w_i * pred_i^t, \quad w.r.t \ \sum_{i=1}^{N} w_i = 1, \tag{1}$$

where w_i denotes the weight of i-th teacher model.

To make pseudo ground-truth answers more informative and robust to both ID and OOD benchmarks, in KDDAug, we adopt two expert teacher models: *ID teacher* and *OOD teacher*. Among them, ID and OOD teachers can effectively extract ID and OOD knowledge, respectively. Given the predicted answer distributions of ID teacher and OOD teacher (denoted as $pred_{id}^t$ and $pred_{ood}^t$), we then need to calculate the weights for the two teachers. Following Niu *et.al.* [41], to obtain unbiased labels, we also assign a smaller weight to a more biased teacher. Since we lack any human-annotated ground-truth answers for these composed VQ pairs, we directly measure the bias degree of each teacher by calculating the cross-entropy (XE) loss between question-type bias (*bias*) and their predictions:

$$c_{id} = \frac{1}{\texttt{XE}(bias, pred_{id}^t)}, \quad c_{ood} = \frac{1}{\texttt{XE}(bias, pred_{ood}^t)}, \tag{2}$$

where *bias* is the statistical answer distribution of each question type, which is calculated from the original training set $\mathcal{D}_{\mathrm{orig}}$. Obviously, if the prediction is more closer to *bias*, the teacher is more like to be biased. Then, we obtain:

$$w_{id} = c_{ood}/(c_{id} + c_{ood}), \quad w_{ood} = c_{id}/(c_{id} + c_{ood}). \tag{3}$$

Lastly, we obtain pseudo answers a^t by Eq. (1) for each VQ pair (*cf.* Fig. 4(b)).

Benefiting from Rule-Based Initial Answers. Based on Eq. (2), our answer assignment can be easily extended to further benefit from high-quality rule-based initial answers (*i.e.*, replacing *bias* with high-quality initial answers). We denote these initial pseudo ground-truth answers as a^{init}. Following SimpleAug [31], we consider three types of questions with a single noun:

1) **"Color" questions.** For each paired image, the detector may output some color attributes. We assign the color of the noun in the question as a^{init}.
2) **"Number" questions.** For each paired image, we assign the count of detected objects which are same as the noun in the question as a^{init}.
3) **"What" questions.** For each original sample (I_i, Q_i, a_i), and new paired image I_j for Q_i, if a_i is in I_j's object labels, we assign a_i as the initial answer for VQ pair (I_j, Q_i). For example, if original sample is "What is near the fork? Knife." If paired image contains "knife", we assign "knife" as a^{init}.

We refer the readers to SimpleAug paper [31] for more details. After obtaining a^{init}, we can replace *bias* to a^{init} in these question types. Then, Eq. (2) becomes:

$$c_{id} = \frac{1}{\texttt{XE}(a^{init}, pred_{id}^t)}, \quad c_{ood} = \frac{1}{\texttt{XE}(a^{init}, pred_{ood}^t)}. \tag{4}$$

Considering that the initial answer a^{init} is more accurate than the $pred_{id}^t$ *e.g.*, ID teacher's ID performance is only 63.01% (*cf.* Table 6), we follow [41] and use a^{init} as ID knowledge, *i.e.*, $a^t = w_{id} * a^{init} + w_{ood} * pred_{ood}^t$.

Advantages. Compared with the existing answer assignment mechanism, our solution gets rid of heuristic rules and human annotations. Meanwhile, it can be easily extended to generate better answers with more advanced teacher models. Besides, it is more general, which can theoretically be applied to any VQ pair.

Why KDDAug Can Work? KDDAug improves performance from two aspects: 1) It composes new samples to increase the diversity of the training set, which implicitly mitigates the biases with more balanced data. 2) It assigns more robust and informative answers for *new* samples.

4   Experiments

4.1   Experimental Settings and Implementation Details

Evaluation Datasets. We evaluated the proposed KDDAug on two datasets: the ID benchmark **VQA v2** [24] and OOD benchmark **VQA-CP v2** [4]. For model accuracies, we followed the standard VQA evaluation metric [6]. Meanwhile, we followed [40] and used Harmonic Mean (**HM**) to evaluate the trade-off between ID and OOD evaluations. More details are left in the appendix.

VQA Models. Since KDDAug is an architecture-agnostic DA method, we evaluated the effectiveness of KDDAug on multiple different VQA models: UpDn [5], LMH [19], RUBi [11] and CSS [16,18]. Specifically, UpDn is a simple but effective VQA model, which always serves as a backbone for other advanced VQA models. LMH, RUBi, and CSS are SOTA ensemble-based VQA models for debiasing. For each specific VQA baseline, we followed their respective configurations (*e.g.*, hyperparameter settings) and re-implemented them using the official codes.

ID & OOD Teachers. The ID and OOD teachers were from a same LMH-CSS [16] model with different architectures [40,41]. Since LMH-CSS is an ensemble-based debiasing model, we took the whole ensemble model (VQA w/ bias-only model) as ID teacher, and the bare VQA model as OOD teacher (original for debiasing). Benefiting from the different architectures, they can extract ID and OOD knowledge, respectively. We used the official LMH-CSS codes to train ID and OOD teachers simultaneously *on a same dataset*, *e.g.*, for VQA-CP evaluation, both teachers were trained on the VQA-CP training set.

Two Augmented Dataset Versions. Due to the huge amount of all reasonable composed VQ pairs, and to keep fair comparisons with existing DA methods (especially SimpleAug), we constructed two versions of augmented sets: 1) $D_{\text{aug}}^{\text{basic}}$: It only contains the same four types of questions as SimpleAug. Meanwhile, it also contains a same set of extra training samples by paraphrasing[6]. Thus, $D_{\text{aug}}^{\text{basic}}$ can clearly demonstrate the effectiveness of our proposed KD-based answer assignment strategy. 2) $D_{\text{aug}}^{\text{extra}}$: It contains all possible question types. Obviously, all VQ pairs from paraphrasing(see footnote 6) are a subset of $D_{\text{aug}}^{\text{extra}}$.

---

[6] Paraphrasing is an supplementary DA tricks proposed by SimpleAug [31]. Specifically, for each original sample (I_i, Q_i, a_i), if question Q_j is similar to Q_i (predicted by pre-trained BERT [20]), they construct a new augmented training sample (I_i, Q_j, a_i).

Table 1. Accuracies (%) on VQA-CP v2 and VQA v2 of different VQA architectures. * indicates the results from our reimplementation using official codes.

Base	Models	VQA-CP v2 test				VQA v2 val				HM
		All	Y/N	Num	Other	All	Y/N	Num	Other	
UpDn [5]	Baseline	39.74	42.27	11.93	46.05	63.48	81.18	42.14	55.66	48.88
	Baseline*	39.85	42.66	12.18	45.98	**63.30**	**81.06**	**42.46**	**55.32**	48.91
	KDDAug	**60.24**$_{+20.39}$	**86.13**	**55.08**	**48.08**	62.86$_{-0.44}$	80.55	41.05	55.18	**61.52**$_{+12.61}$
LMH [19]	Baseline	52.05	—	—	—	—	—	—	—	—
	Baseline*	53.87	73.31	44.23	46.33	61.28	76.58	**55.11**	40.69	57.24
	KDDAug	**59.54**$_{+5.67}$	**86.09**	**54.84**	**46.92**	**62.09**$_{+0.81}$	**79.26**	40.11	**54.85**	**60.79**$_{+3.55}$
RUBi [11]	Baseline	44.23	—	—	—	—	—	—	—	—
	Baseline*	46.84	70.05	44.29	11.85	52.83	54.74	**41.56**	**54.38**	49.66
	KDDAug	**59.25**$_{+12.41}$	**84.16**	**54.12**	**47.61**	**60.25**$_{+7.42}$	**74.97**	40.29	54.35	**59.75**$_{+10.09}$
CSS$^+$ [18]	Baseline	59.54	83.37	52.57	**48.97**	59.96	73.69	40.18	**54.77**	59.75
	Baseline*	59.19	83.54	51.29	48.59	58.91	71.02	39.76	**54.77**	59.05
	KDDAug	**61.14**$_{+1.95}$	**88.31**	**56.10**	48.28	**62.17**$_{+3.26}$	**79.50**	**40.57**	54.71	**61.65**$_{+2.60}$

To decrease the number of augmented samples, we applied the CLIP-based filtering (*cf.* Sect. 3.2) to keep top 10 % samples. In the following experiments, we denote the model trained with D_{aug}^{basic} and D_{aug}^{extra} as **KDDAug** and **KDDAug$^+$**, respectively. Meanwhile, unless otherwise specified, we used the rule-based initial answers for D_{aug}^{basic}.

Training Details & KDDAug Settings. Details are left in the appendix.

4.2   Architecture Agnostic

Settings. Since KDDAug is a model-agnostic data augmentation method, it can seamlessly incorporated into any VQA architectures. To validate the generalization of KDDAug, we applied it to multiple different VQA models: UpDn [5], LMH [19], RUBi [11] and CSS$^+$ [18]. All the results are shown in Table 1.

Results. Compared to these baseline models, KDDAug can consistently improve the performance for all architectures, and push all models' performance to the state-of-the-art level. Particularly, the improvements are most significant in the baseline UpDn model (*e.g.*, 12.61% absolute performance gains on HM). Furthermore, when KDDAug is applied to another DA-based model CSS$^+$, KDDAug can still improve the performance on both OOD and ID benchmarks, and achieve the best performance (*e.g.*, 61.65% on HM).

4.3   Comparisons with State-of-the-Arts

Settings. We incorporated the KDDAug into model UpDn [5], LMH [19] and CSS$^+$ [18], and compared them with the SOTA VQA models both on VQA-CP v2 and VQA v2. According to the model framework design, we group them into:

Table 2. Accuracies (%) on VQA-CP v2 and VQA v2 of SOTA models. "**DA**" denotes the data augmentation methods. * indicates the results from our reimplementation. "MUTANT[†]" denotes MUTANT [22] only trained with XE loss.

Models	DA	VQA-CP v2 test				VQA v2 val				HM
		All	Y/N	Num	Other	All	Y/N	Num	Other	
UpDn [5]$_{\text{CVPR'18}}$		39.74	42.27	11.93	46.05	63.48	81.18	42.14	55.66	48.88
+AReg [45]$_{\text{NeurIPS'18}}$		41.17	65.49	15.48	35.48	62.75	79.84	42.35	55.16	49.72
+MuRel [10]$_{\text{CVPR'19}}$		39.54	42.85	13.17	45.04	—	—	—	—	—
+GRL [25]$_{\text{ACL'19}}$		42.33	59.74	14.78	40.76	51.92	—	—	—	46.64
+CF-VQA [40]$_{\text{CVPR'21}}$		53.55	91.15	13.03	44.97	63.54	82.51	43.96	54.30	58.12
+GGE-DQ [26]$_{\text{ICCV'21}}$		57.32	87.04	27.75	49.59	59.11	73.27	39.99	54.39	58.20
+D-VQA [52]$_{\text{NeurIPS'21}}$		61.91	88.93	52.32	50.39	64.96	82.18	44.05	57.54	63.40
+CVL [1]$_{\text{CVPR'20}}$	✓	42.12	45.72	12.45	48.34	—	—	—	—	—
+Unshuffling [47]$_{\text{ICCV'21}}$	✓	42.39	47.72	14.43	47.24	61.08	78.32	42.16	52.81	50.05
+CSS [16]$_{\text{CVPR'20}}$	✓	41.16	43.96	12.78	47.48	—	—	—	—	—
+CSS$^+$ [18]$_{\text{arXiv'21}}$	✓	40.84	43.09	12.74	47.37	—	—	—	—	—
+RandImg [48]$_{\text{NeurIPS'20}}$	✓	55.37	83.89	41.60	44.20	57.24	76.53	33.87	48.57	56.29
+SSL [56]$_{\text{IJCAI'20}}$	✓	57.59	86.53	29.87	50.03	63.73	—	—	—	60.50
+MUTANT[†] [22]$_{\text{EMNLP'20}}$	✓	50.16	61.45	35.87	50.14	—	—	—	—	—
+SimpleAug [31]$_{\text{EMNLP'21}}$	✓	52.65	66.40	43.43	47.98	**64.34**	**81.97**	**43.91**	**56.35**	57.91
+KDDAug	✓	**60.24**	**86.13**	**55.08**	48.08	62.86	80.55	41.05	55.18	**61.52**
LMH* [19]$_{\text{EMNLP'19}}$		53.87	73.31	44.23	46.33	61.28	76.58	55.11	40.69	57.24
+IntroD [41]$_{\text{NeurIPS'21}}$		51.31	71.39	27.13	47.41	62.05	77.65	40.25	55.97	56.17
+CSS+CL [36]$_{\text{EMNLP'20}}$		59.18	86.99	49.89	47.16	57.29	67.27	38.40	54.71	58.22
+CSS+IntroD [41]$_{\text{NeurIPS'21}}$		60.17	89.17	46.91	48.62	62.57	78.57	41.42	56.00	61.35
+CSS [16]$_{\text{CVPR'20}}$	✓	58.95	84.37	49.42	48.21	59.91	73.25	39.77	55.11	59.43
+CSS$^+$ [18]$_{\text{arXiv'21}}$	✓	59.54	83.37	52.57	48.97	59.96	73.69	40.18	54.77	59.75
+SimpleAug [31]$_{\text{EMNLP'21}}$	✓	53.70	74.79	34.32	47.97	**62.63**	79.31	**41.71**	**55.48**	57.82
+ECD [32]$_{\text{WACV'22}}$	✓	59.92	83.23	52.29	**49.71**	57.38	69.06	35.74	54.25	58.62
+KDDAug	✓	59.54	86.09	54.84	46.92	62.09	79.26	40.11	54.85	60.79
+CSS$^+$+KDDAug	✓	**61.14**	**88.31**	**56.10**	48.28	62.17	**79.50**	40.57	54.71	**61.65**

1) *Non-DA Methods*: UpDn [5], AReg [45], MuRel [10], GRL [25], CF-VQA [40], GGE-DQ [26], D-VQA [52], IntroD [41], CSS+CL [36], and LMH [19]. 2) *DA Methods*: CVL [1], Unshuffling [47], CSS [16], CSS$^+$ [18], RandImg [48], SSL [56], MUTANT [22], SimpleAug [31], and ECD [32]. All results are reported in Table 2. **Results.** Compared with all existing DA methods, KDDAug achieves the best OOD and trade-off performance on two datasets. For UpDn backbone, KDDAug improves the OOD performance of UpDn with a 20% absolute performance gain (60.24% vs. 39.74%) and improves accuracies on all different question categories. For LMH backbone, KDDAug boosts the performance on both ID and OOD benchmarks. Compared with other non-DA methods, KDDAug still outperforms most of them. It is worth noting that our KDDAug can also be incorporated into these advanced non-DA models to further boost their performance.

Table 3. Accuracies (%) on different augmented subsets. * indicates our reimplementation. For fair comparisons, SimpleAug* didn't leverage human annotation and didn't remove examples that can be answered. ⁻ denotes without "Yes/No" questions.

Models	VQA-CP v2 test				VQA v2 val				HM
	All	Yes/No	Num	Other	All	Yes/No	Num	Other	
UpDn [5]	39.74	42.27	11.93	46.05	63.48	81.18	42.14	55.66	48.88
+SimpleAug [31]	52.65	66.40	43.43	47.98	64.34	81.97	43.91	56.35	57.91
+SimpleAug*	48.56	58.83	35.41	46.78	60.67	75.65	40.45	54.65	54.57
+SimpleAug⁻ (100%)	45.38	45.59	37.63	47.40	62.62	80.49	40.68	54.85	52.62
+SimpleAug⁻ (↑ 50%)	46.35	47.72	39.36	47.55	62.51	80.64	40.08	54.67	53.23
+SimpleAug⁻ (↓ 50%)	45.06	44.84	38.44	46.99	62.49	80.38	40.24	54.78	52.36
+KDDAug	60.24	86.13	55.08	48.08	62.86	80.55	41.05	55.18	61.52
+KDDAug⁻ (100%)	59.96	84.95	54.98	48.23	62.72	80.07	40.90	55.30	61.31
+KDDAug⁻ (↑ 50%)	59.94	84.78	54.70	48.36	62.67	79.86	41.06	55.32	61.27
+KDDAug⁻ (↓ 50%)	59.97	85.11	55.13	48.13	62.60	80.13	40.78	55.04	61.26

Table 4. Accuracies (%) on VQA-CP v2 test set and VQA v2 valset of different δ.

	Baseline	KDDAug										
	(UpDn)	0%	10%	20%	30%	40%	50%	60%	70%	80%	90%	100%
VQA-CP v2	39.74	53.99	54.37	54.98	56.17	57.51	58.80	59.27	59.68	60.02	60.19	60.24
VQA v2	63.48	63.26	63.24	63.20	63.20	63.19	63.10	63.08	63.04	63.01	62.83	62.86
HM	48.88	58.26	58.47	58.80	59.48	60.22	60.87	61.12	61.31	61.48	61.48	61.52

4.4   Ablation Studies

We validate the effectiveness of each component of KDDAug by answering the following questions: **Q1**: Does KDDAug assign more robust answers than existing methods? **Q2**: Does KDDAug mainly rely on the rule-based initial answers? **Q3**: Does KDDAug only benefit from much more training samples? **Q4**: Does the multi-teacher design help to improve pseudo ground-truth answers quality? **Q5**: Is the diversity of question types important for the data augmentation model?

KDDAug vs. SimpleAug [31] (Q1). To answer **Q1**, we compared the answers assigned by KDDAug and SimpleAug. Due to different composition strategies for "Yes/No" questions, we firstly removed the "Yes/No" questions from $D_{\text{aug}}^{\text{basic}}$. We use a pretrained CLIP [43] (denoted as $\text{CLIP}_{\text{rank}}$ and more details are left in the appendix.) to rank the quality of all SimpleAug assigned answers. For more comprehensive comparisons, we divided the augmented samples into three subsets according to the ranks: 1) All augmented samples (100%), 2) Top-50% samples (↑ 50%), and 3) Bottom-50% samples (↓ 50%). We compared KDDAug and SimpleAug on these three subsets, and results are in Table 3.

Results for Q1. From Table 3, we can observe: 1) The performance of SimpleAug on three subsets varies significantly, *e.g.*, bottom-50% samples lead to a

Table 5. Accuracies (%) of different α in CLIP-based filtering. SimpleAug* is the same as Table 3. "#Samples" denotes the number of total training samples.

Models (α%)	VQA-CP v2 test					VQA v2 val					HM
	All	Y/N	Num	Other	#Samples	All	Y/N	Num	Other	#Samples	
UpDn [5]	39.74	42.27	11.93	46.05	438K	63.48	81.18	42.14	55.66	444K	48.88
+KDDAug (100%)	60.24	86.13	55.08	48.08	+4,088K	62.86	80.55	41.05	55.18	+2,279K	61.52
+KDDAug (90%)	60.19	86.09	55.13	48.00	+3,679K	62.83	80.53	41.14	55.12	+2,051K	61.48
+KDDAug (70%)	60.12	85.96	55.09	47.96	+2,861K	62.82	80.52	40.99	55.14	+1,595K	61.44
+KDDAug (50%)	60.13	86.18	54.81	47.94	+2,044K	62.71	80.41	40.98	55.00	+1,139K	61.39
+KDDAug (30%)	59.92	86.06	54.74	47.64	+1,226K	62.51	80.35	40.56	54.76	+684K	61.19
+KDDAug (10%)	59.41	85.81	54.85	46.82	+409K	62.37	80.47	40.98	54.28	+228K	60.85
+SimgpleAug [31]	52.65	66.40	43.43	47.98	+3,081K	64.34	81.97	43.91	56.35	—	57.91
+SimgpleAug*	48.56	58.83	35.41	46.78	+4,702K	60.67	75.65	40.45	54.65	+2,358K	54.57

Table 6. Effects of different teachers on pseudo answer assignment. "OOD W." denotes w_{ood}, and "dynamic" denotes w_{ood} is dynamically calculated by our strategy.

Models	OOD W.	VQA-CP v2 test				VQA v2 val				HM
		All	Y/N	Num	Other	All	Y/N	Num	Other	
UpDn [5] (baseline)		39.74	42.27	11.93	46.05	63.48	81.18	42.14	55.66	48.88
ID-Teacher		36.93	36.56	12.82	43.73	63.01	80.76	42.30	55.01	46.57
OOD-Teacher		58.07	82.47	52.03	46.93	60.21	74.19	40.32	54.86	59.12
Simple Avg	0.5	53.06	63.89	50.72	48.03	**63.45**	**81.33**	**42.48**	**55.41**	57.79
ID-distill	0.0	43.10	42.33	29.34	47.28	62.90	81.10	41.05	54.84	51.15
OOD-distill	1.0	58.40	82.27	53.16	47.33	61.50	77.08	41.62	54.92	59.91
KDDAug (Ours)	dynamic	**60.24**	**86.13**	**55.08**	**48.08**	62.86	80.55	41.05	55.18	**61.52**

huge drop in HM (-0.87%). 2) In contrast, KDDAug on different subsets achieves similar decent performance. 3) With the same augmented image-question pairs, KDDAug consistently outperforms the corresponding SimpleAug by a significant margin (over 8% on HM), which proves the robustness of our answers.

Influence of Rule-Based Initial Answers (Q2). To evaluate the quality of directly automatically assigned answers, we again used CLIP_{rank} to divide the augmented samples (except "Yes/No" samples) into two parts. The augmented samples with top-δ% ranks use rule-based initial answers (*cf.* Eq. (4)) and left samples use question-type *bias* (*cf.* Eq. (2)). All results are shown in Table 4.

Results for Q2. From the results, we can observe that KDDAug achieves consistent gains against the baseline (UpDn) on all proportions. The performance is best when all samples use rule-based initial samples. Even if all the samples' answers are assigned without any initial answers, KDDAug still gains significant improvement gains (58.26% vs. 48.88% on HM), and is better than SimpleAug.

Influence of Number of Augmented Samples (Q3). We set different α values in the CLIP-based filtering to control the number of augmented samples.

Fig. 5. Visualization results of some augmented samples by our KDDAug.

Table 7. Accuracies (%) on VQA-CP v2 and VQA v2. ‡ denotes using $\mathcal{D}_{\text{aug}-}^{\text{basic}}$. "**Extra**" denotes using $\mathcal{D}_{\text{aug}}^{\text{extra}}$.

Models (α%)	Extra	VQA-CP v2 test				VQA v2 val				HM
		All	Y/N	Num	Other	All	Y/N	Num	Other	
UpDn [5]		39.74	42.27	11.93	46.05	63.48	81.18	42.14	55.66	48.88
+KDDAug‡ (100%)		53.03	**86.55**	**17.30**	45.26	61.59	80.43	42.33	52.36	56.99
+KDDAug+‡ (100%)	✓	**53.76**	86.41	17.10	**46.70**	**62.58**	**80.51**	**42.43**	**54.28**	**57.84**
+KDDAug‡ (50%)		52.91	85.59	17.01	45.64	62.01	80.42	41.98	53.31	57.10
+KDDAug+‡ (50%)	✓	**53.76**	**86.57**	**17.86**	46.42	**62.64**	80.35	**42.25**	**54.56**	**57.86**
+KDDAug‡ (10%)		51.26	82.28	17.13	44.37	62.03	80.47	**41.41**	53.47	56.13
+KDDAug+‡ (10%)	✓	**52.53**	**83.16**	**17.76**	**46.01**	**62.71**	**80.76**	41.34	**54.63**	**57.17**

Results for Q3. From the results in Table 5, we have several observations: 1) When more samples are used, the model performs better, which reflects the robustness of generated pseudo answers. 2) Even if a small number of samples are used (*e.g.*, α% = 10%), KDDAug still achieves decent performance, and is better than SimpleAug (60.85% vs. 57.91%). 3) By adjusting the value of α, we can easily achieve a trade-off between training efficiency and model performance.

Effects of Different Teachers (Q4). To show the effectiveness of multi-teacher KD strategy, we compared three teachers with different ID teacher weight w_{id} and OOD teacher weight w_{ood}: 1) *Averaged Teacher* (Simple Avg.): $w_{id} = w_{ood} = 0.5$. 2) *Only ID Teacher* (ID-distill.): $w_{id} = 1, w_{ood} = 0$. 3) *Only OOD Teacher* (OOD-distill.): $w_{id} = 0, w_{ood} = 1$. All results are shown in Table 6.

Results for Q4. From Table 6, we have several observations: 1) Learning from all teachers can improve the performance over baseline. 2) Learning from fixed-weight teachers (*i.e.*, single-teacher KD) can't achieve good performance on both ID and OOD settings simultaneously, *e.g.*, "OOD-distill." obtains OOD performance gains (+18.66%) while suffering from a significant drop on ID performance (-1.98%). 3) In contrast, our dynamic multi-teacher strategy increases OOD performance by 20.50% while ID performance drops slightly by 0.62%, and achieves the best trade-off performance, which proves its effectiveness.

Effects of Augmentation Diversity (Q5). To explore the effects of more diverse augmentation types, we compared KDDAug and KDDAug$^+$ with D_{aug}^{basic} and D_{aug}^{extra}. For fair comparison, we didn't use initial answers and removed all paraphrasing samples from D_{aug}^{basic} (denoted as $D_{aug^-}^{basic}$) since they are a subset of $\mathcal{D}_{extra}$. Meanwhile, we sampled same number of samples of the "Other" cateogry samples with $D_{aug^-}^{basic}$ from D_{aug}^{extra}[7]. We compared them on different size of samples (different α values in CLIP-based filtering). Results are shown in Table 7.

Results for Q5. From the results, we can observe that with more diverse augmented samples, KDDAug can consistently improve both ID and OOD performance for all different α, especially on "Other" category (e.g., $> 0.78\%$ gains). In particular, even if we don't rely on any rule-based answers, KDDAug surpasses the baseline UpDn model on all categories on VQA-CP v2 when $\alpha = 50$ or 100.

4.5   Visualization Results

We show some augmented samples by KDDAug in Fig. 5. From Fig. 5, we can observe that our KDDAug can compose potential reasonable VQ pairs and assign satisfactory pseudo labels. Take the third question "What garnish is on the pizza?" as an example, there are multiple garnishes on the pizza, and KDDAug cleverly assigns multiple answers: "pepperoni", "peppers" and "cheese", which demonstrates the superiority of the "soft" pseudo labels generated by KDDAug.

5   Conclusions and Future Work

In this paper, we proposed a model-agnostic Knowledge Distillation based Data Augmentation (KDDAug) for VQA. KDDAug relaxes the requirements for pairing reasonable image-question pairs, and utilizes a multi-teacher KD to generate robust pseudo labels for augmented samples. KDDAug can consistently improve both ID and OOD performance of different VQA baselines. We validated the effectiveness of KDDAug through extensive experiments. Moving forward, we are going to 1) extend the KDDAug-like DA strategy to other visual-language tasks (e.g., captioning [13,17,39] or grounding [14,15,37,53]); 2) design some specific training objectives (e.g., contrastive loss) to further benefit from these augmented samples. 3) further improve the generalization ability of VQA models by incorporating other available large-scale datasets.

Acknowledgement. This work was supported by the National Key Research & Development Project of China (2021ZD0110700), the National Natural Science Foundation of China (U19B2043, 61976185), Zhejiang Natural Science Foundation (LR19F020002), Zhejiang Innovation Foundation(2019R52002), and the Fundamental Research Funds for the Central Universities (226-2022-00087).

---

[7] $D_{aug^-}^{basic}$ and D_{aug}^{extra} have same "Yes/No" and "Number" category samples.

References

1. Abbasnejad, E., Teney, D., Parvaneh, A., Shi, J., Hengel, A.V.D.: Counterfactual vision and language learning. In: CVPR (2020)
2. Agarwal, V., Shetty, R., Fritz, M.: Towards causal vqa: reveling and reducing spurious correlations by invariant and covariant semantic editing. In: CVPR (2020)
3. Agrawal, A., Batra, D., Parikh, D.: Analyzing the behavior of visual question answering models. In: EMNLP (2016)
4. Agrawal, A., Batra, D., Parikh, D., Kembhavi, A.: Don't just assume; look and answer: overcoming priors for visual question answering. In: CVPR (2018)
5. Anderson, P., et al.: Bottom-up and top-down attention for image captioning and visual question answering. In: CVPR (2018)
6. Antol, S., et al.: Vqa: visual question answering. In: ICCV, pp. 2425–2433 (2015)
7. Askarian, N., Abbasnejad, E., Zukerman, I., Buntine, W., Haffari, G.: Inductive biases for low data vqa: a data augmentation approach. In: WACV, pp. 231–240 (2022)
8. Bitton, Y., Stanovsky, G., Schwartz, R., Elhadad, M.: Automatic generation of contrast sets from scene graphs: probing the compositional consistency of GQA. In: NAACL, pp. 94–105 (2021)
9. Boukhers, Z., Hartmann, T., Jürjens, J.: Coin: counterfactual image generation for vqa interpretation. arXiv (2022)
10. Cadene, R., Ben-Younes, H., Cord, M., Thome, N.: Murel: multimodal relational reasoning for visual question answering. In: CVPR (2019)
11. Cadene, R., Dancette, C., Ben-younes, H., Cord, M., Parikh, D.: Rubi: reducing unimodal biases in visual question answering. In: NeurIPS (2019)
12. Chen, G., Choi, W., Yu, X., Han, T., Chandraker, M.: Learning efficient object detection models with knowledge distillation. In: NeurIPS (2017)
13. Chen, L., Jiang, Z., Xiao, J., Liu, W.: Human-like controllable image captioning with verb-specific semantic roles. In: CVPR, pp. 16846–16856 (2021)
14. Chen, L., Lu, C., Tang, S., Xiao, J., Zhang, D., Tan, C., Li, X.: Rethinking the bottom-up framework for query-based video localization. In: AAAI, pp. 10551–10558 (2020)
15. Chen, L., Ma, W., Xiao, J., Zhang, H., Chang, S.F.: Ref-nms: breaking proposal bottlenecks in two-stage referring expression grounding. In: AAAI, pp. 1036–1044 (2021)
16. Chen, L., Yan, X., Xiao, J., Zhang, H., Pu, S., Zhuang, Y.: Counterfactual samples synthesizing for robust visual question answering. In: CVPR, pp. 10800–10809 (2020)
17. Chen, L., Zhang, H., Xiao, J., Nie, L., Shao, J., Liu, W., Chua, T.S.: Sca-cnn: spatial and channel-wise attention in convolutional networks for image captioning. In: CVPR, pp. 5659–5667 (2017)
18. Chen, L., Zheng, Y., Niu, Y., Zhang, H., Xiao, J.: Counterfactual samples synthesizing and training for robust visual question answering. arXiv (2021)
19. Clark, C., Yatskar, M., Zettlemoyer, L.: Don't take the easy way out: ensemble based methods for avoiding known dataset biases. In: EMNLP (2019)
20. Devlin, J., Chang, M., Lee, K., Toutanova, K.: BERT: pre-training of deep bidirectional transformers for language understanding. In: NAACL, pp. 4171–4186 (2019)
21. Geman, D., Geman, S., Hallonquist, N., Younes, L.: Visual turing test for computer vision systems. PNAS 112(12), 3618–3623 (2015)

22. Gokhale, T., Banerjee, P., Baral, C., Yang, Y.: Mutant: a training paradigm for out-of-distribution generalization in visual question answering. In: EMNLP (2020)
23. Gokhale, T., Banerjee, P., Baral, C., Yang, Y.: VQA-LOL: visual question answering under the lens of logic. In: Vedaldi, A., Bischof, H., Brox, T., Frahm, J.-M. (eds.) ECCV 2020. LNCS, vol. 12366, pp. 379–396. Springer, Cham (2020). https://doi.org/10.1007/978-3-030-58589-1_23
24. Goyal, Y., Khot, T., Summers-Stay, D., Batra, D., Parikh, D.: Making the v in VQA matter: elevating the role of image understanding in visual question answering. In: CVPR, pp. 6904–6913 (2017)
25. Grand, G., Belinkov, Y.: Adversarial regularization for visual question answering: strengths, shortcomings, and side effects. In: ACLW (2019)
26. Han, X., Wang, S., Su, C., Huang, Q., Tian, Q.: Greedy gradient ensemble for robust visual question answering. In: ICCV (2021)
27. Honnibal, M., Montani, I.: spacy 2: natural language understanding with bloom embeddings, convolutional neural networks and incremental parsing (2017). (To appear)
28. Johnson, J., Hariharan, B., van der Maaten, L., Fei-Fei, L., Lawrence Zitnick, C., Girshick, R.: Clevr: a diagnostic dataset for compositional language and elementary visual reasoning. In: CVPR (2017)
29. Kafle, K., Yousefhussien, M., Kanan, C.: Data augmentation for visual question answering. In: INLG, pp. 198–202 (2017)
30. Kant, Y., Moudgil, A., Batra, D., Parikh, D., Agrawal, H.: Contrast and classify: training robust VQA models. In: ICCV, pp. 1604–1613 (2021)
31. Kil, J., Zhang, C., Xuan, D., Chao, W.L.: Discovering the unknown knowns: turning implicit knowledge in the dataset into explicit training examples for visual question answering. In: EMNLP (2021)
32. Kolling, C., More, M., Gavenski, N., Pooch, E., Parraga, O., Barros, R.C.: Efficient counterfactual debiasing for visual question answering. In: WACV, pp. 3001–3010 (2022)
33. Krishna, R., et al.: Visual genome: connecting language and vision using crowd-sourced dense image annotations. In: IJCV, pp. 32–73 (2017)
34. Li, X., Chen, L., Ma, W., Yang, Y., Xiao, J.: Integrating object-aware and interaction-aware knowledge for weakly supervised scene graph generation. In: ACM MM (2022)
35. Liang, Z., Hu, H., Zhu, J.: LPF: a language-prior feedback objective function for de-biased visual question answering. In: ACM SIGIR, pp. 1955–1959 (2021)
36. Liang, Z., Jiang, W., Hu, H., Zhu, J.: Learning to contrast the counterfactual samples for robust visual question answering. In: EMNLP (2020)
37. Lu, C., Chen, L., Tan, C., Li, X., Xiao, J.: Debug: a dense bottom-up grounding approach for natural language video localization. In: EMNLP, pp. 5144–5153 (2019)
38. Mahabadi, R.K., Belinkov, Y., Henderson, J.: End-to-end bias mitigation by modelling biases in corpora. In: ACL, pp. 8706–8716 (2020)
39. Mao, Y., et al.: Rethinking the reference-based distinctive image captioning. In: ACM MM (2022)
40. Niu, Y., Tang, K., Zhang, H., Lu, Z., Hua, X.S., Wen, J.R.: Counterfactual VQA: a cause-effect look at language bias. In: CVPR (2021)
41. Niu, Y., Zhang, H.: Introspective distillation for robust question answering. In: NeurIPS (2021)
42. Pan, B., et al.: Spatio-temporal graph for video captioning with knowledge distillation. In: CVPR, pp. 10870–10879 (2020)

43. Radford, A., et al.: Learning transferable visual models from natural language supervision. In: ICML, pp. 8748–8763 (2021)
44. Radosavovic, I., Dollár, P., Girshick, R., Gkioxari, G., He, K.: Data distillation: towards omni-supervised learning. In: CVPR, pp. 4119–4128 (2018)
45. Ramakrishnan, S., Agrawal, A., Lee, S.: Overcoming language priors in visual question answering with adversarial regularization. In: NeurIPS (2018)
46. Tang, R., Ma, C., Zhang, W.E., Wu, Q., Yang, X.: Semantic equivalent adversarial data augmentation for visual question answering. In: Vedaldi, A., Bischof, H., Brox, T., Frahm, J.-M. (eds.) ECCV 2020. LNCS, vol. 12364, pp. 437–453. Springer, Cham (2020). https://doi.org/10.1007/978-3-030-58529-7_26
47. Teney, D., Abbasnejad, E., Hengel, A.V.D.: Unshuffling data for improved generalization. In: ICCV (2021)
48. Teney, D., Kafle, K., Shrestha, R., Abbasnejad, E., Kanan, C., Hengel, A.V.D.: On the value of out-of-distribution testing: an example of Goodhart's law. In: NeurIPS (2020)
49. Wang, L., Yoon, K.J.: Knowledge distillation and student-teacher learning for visual intelligence: a review and new outlooks. IEEE TPAMI (2021)
50. Wang, T., Yuan, L., Zhang, X., Feng, J.: Distilling object detectors with fine-grained feature imitation. In: CVPR, pp. 4933–4942 (2019)
51. Wang, Z., Miao, Y., Specia, L.: Cross-modal generative augmentation for visual question answering. In: BMVC (2021)
52. Wen, Z., Xu, G., Tan, M., Wu, Q., Wu, Q.: Debiased visual question answering from feature and sample perspectives. In: NeurIPS (2021)
53. Xiao, S., et al.: Boundary proposal network for two-stage natural language video localization. In: AAAI, pp. 2986–2994 (2021)
54. Zhang, P., Goyal, Y., Summers-Stay, D., Batra, D., Parikh, D.: Yin and yang: balancing and answering binary visual questions. In: CVPR (2016)
55. Zhang, Z., et al.: Object relational graph with teacher-recommended learning for video captioning. In: CVPR, pp. 13278–13288 (2020)
56. Zhu, X., Mao, Z., Liu, C., Zhang, P., Wang, B., Zhang, Y.: Overcoming language priors with self-supervised learning for visual question answering. In: IJCAI (2020)

Explicit Image Caption Editing

Zhen Wang[1], Long Chen[2], Wenbo Ma[1], Guangxing Han[2], Yulei Niu[2], Jian Shao[1], and Jun Xiao[1(✉)]

[1] Zhejiang University, Hangzhou, China
zju_wangzhen@zju.edu.cn, junx@cs.zju.edu.cn
[2] Columbia University, New York, USA
zjuchenlong@gmail.com

Abstract. Given an image and a reference caption, the image caption editing task aims to correct the misalignment errors and generate a refined caption. However, all existing caption editing works are *implicit* models, *i.e.*, they directly produce the refined captions without explicit connections to the reference captions. In this paper, we introduce a new task: Explicit Caption Editing (ECE). ECE models explicitly generate a sequence of *edit operations*, and this edit operation sequence can translate the reference caption into a refined one. Compared to the implicit editing, ECE has multiple advantages: 1) Explainable: it can trace the whole editing path. 2) Editing Efficient: it only needs to modify a few words. 3) Human-like: it resembles the way that humans perform caption editing, and tries to keep original sentence structures. To solve this task, we propose the first ECE model: `TIger`. It is a non-autoregressive transformer-based model, consisting of three modules: Tagger$_{del}$, Tagger$_{add}$, and Inserter. Specifically, Tagger$_{del}$ decides whether each word should be preserved or not, Tagger$_{add}$ decides where to add new words, and Inserter predicts the specific word for adding. To further facilitate ECE research, we propose two ECE benchmarks by re-organizing two existing datasets, dubbed COCO-EE and Flickr30K-EE, respectively. Extensive ablations on both two benchmarks have demonstrated the effectiveness of `TIger`.

Keywords: Image captioning · Caption editing · Explicit editing

1 Introduction

Image caption generation (*a.k.a.*, image captioning), is the task of generating natural language captions for given images. Due to its multimodal nature and numerous downstream applications (*e.g.*, human-machine interaction [7], content-based image retrieval [29], and assisting visually-impaired people [24]), caption generation has raised unprecedented attention from both CV and NLP

Zhen Wang and Long Chen are co-first authors with equal contributions.
Codes: https://github.com/baaaad/ECE.

Supplementary Information The online version contains supplementary material available at https://doi.org/10.1007/978-3-031-20059-5_7.

Reference Cap:
a wooden bench is sitting
on a beach near the waves

(a) Caption Generation

Input: image
Output: a dog sitting on a beach near the beach

(b) Implicit Caption Editing

Input: image, reference caption
Output (Refined Cap): a dog is sitting on a beach

(c) Explicit Caption Editing

Input: image, reference caption
Output: KEP DEL DEL ADD(dog) KEP KEP KEP KEP KEP KEP KEP DEL ADD(ocean)
Refined Cap: a ~~wooden bench~~ dog is sitting on a beach near the
~~waves~~ ocean (a dog is sitting on a beach near the ocean)

Fig. 1. Comparisons between our proposed ECE task (c) and existing caption generation (a) and implicit caption editing (b). The outputs are from the SOTA models [3,35].

communities. Thanks to the development of encoder-decoder frameworks (*e.g.*, CNN+ RNN [38] or Transformer [36]), current state-of-the-art image caption generation models can generate "reasonable" captions from scratch and achieve satisfactory performance. However, numerous studies [34,35] have revealed that these SOTA models always suffer from severe bias issues and overlook some content details (*e.g.*, gender bias [14], object hallucination [33]). As shown in Fig. 1(a), given the input image, a SOTA captioning model [3] generates "a dog sitting on a beach near the beach". Thus, SOTA models can indeed generate a coherent sentence structure for the image (*i.e.*, "a __ on a __ near the __"), but fail to properly predict the correct details and even repeat the main object "beach".

To mitigate these problems and make the generated captions focus more on visually-grounded content details (beyond sentence structures), some pioneering works [34,35] have proposed a new task: Image Caption Editing (ICE). Different from captioning models which generate captions from scratch, ICE directly edits another reference caption and pays more attention to the misaligned details. For example in Fig. 1(b), ICE model takes an extra reference caption "a wooden bench is sitting on a beach near the waves" as input, and aims to generate a refined caption. Unfortunately, all existing ICE works are *implicit* editing models. By "implicit", we mean that they directly produce final refined captions, without explicit connections (editing process) to the reference captions.

Although ICE models can significantly improve the captions qualities, it is worth noting that there are still several drawbacks for this implicit manner: 1) **Unexplainable**: they fail to explain whether these words are copied from the reference caption or regenerated, and whether they truly recognize and modify errors or simply generate words by language priors [23]. 2) **Inefficient**: All words are regenerated, which is more like rewriting or re-captioning instead of editing. 3) **Structure-breaking**: They are easy to break the sentence structures of reference captions without focusing on details. For example in Fig. 1(b), the model roughly deletes part of the structure (*e.g.*, "near the __").

In this paper, we introduce a new image caption editing task: **Explicit Caption Editing** (ECE). By "explicit", we mean that ECE models explicitly generate a sequence of *edit operations*, and these edit operations translate the reference captions into the refined captions. Typically, the edit operations consist of ADD,

DELETE, and KEEP[1]. As shown in Fig. 1(c), for each input word in the reference caption, the ECE model predicts KEEP or DELETE to decide whether this word needs to be preserved or not, and predicts ADD to add extra specific words. The predicted edit operation sequence is mainly composed with KEEP to preserve the main sentence structure and few DELETE/ADD to fix misalignment errors. Compared to existing implicit caption editing works, ECE avoids all mentioned weaknesses: 1) ECE traces the whole editing path, which is used to translate reference captions (**Explainable**). 2) ECE only needs to modify a few words (**Explicit Editing Efficient**). 3) ECE resembles the way that humans perform editing, and tries to keep the original sentence structures (**Structure-preserving**).

To solve this new task, we propose the first ECE model, a non-autoregressive transformer-based ECE model: TIger (**T**agger and **I**nserter). Specifically, TIger consists of three modules: $Tagger_{del}$, $Tagger_{add}$, and Inserter. All three modules are built on top of the multimodal BERT architecture [22]. Given an input image and a reference caption, $Tagger_{del}$ decides whether each word should be preserved or not by predicting KEEP and DELETE. Then, $Tagger_{add}$ decides whether a new word should be added after each input word by predicting KEEP and ADD. A special token [Mask] is placed for each position with the ADD prediction. Subsequently, Inserter predicts the specific word for each [Mask] token. Since $Tagger_{add}$ only adds one new word after each input word once a time, we iteratively execute $Tagger_{add}$ and Inserter multiple rounds to guarantee enough words adding.

To further facilitate ECE research, we also propose two new ECE benchmarks by re-organizing MSCOCO [20] and e-SNLI-VE [17,44], dubbed **COCO-EE** and **Flickr30K-EE**, respectively. Particularly, we pair each reference caption with one ground-truth caption by several criteria and rules. Each ECE instance consists of an image, a reference caption, and a ground-truth caption. Compared to existing implicit editing works [34,35] which use machine-generated captions as reference captions, ours are all human-written sentences, *i.e.*, they are more natural and have no grammatical errors. Besides, we propose two supplementary metrics for ECE: Editing Steps (ES) and Gains Per Step (GPS), which consider not only the quality of captions, but also the efficiency of editing models.

In summary, we make three main contributions: 1) We propose a new visual-language task: ECE, *i.e.*, the caption editing model explicitly generates a set of edit operations on the reference captions. 2) For reliable benchmarking, we propose two new ECE datasets (COCO-EE and Flickr30K-EE), and new metrics for ECE evaluation. 3) We propose the first ECE model TIger. Extensive ablations have demonstrated the effectiveness of TIger. Moreover, TIger can serve as an off-the-shelf model to improve the quality of machine-generated captions.

2   Related Work

Image Caption Generation. With the release of advanced encoder-decoder frameworks, NN-based [16,27,38] methods have risen to prominence. They typ-

---

[1] These are the most common edit operations in numerous text explicit editing tasks, such as simplification [9,26], fusion [25]. Of course, different ECE models can design or propose other edit operations, *e.g.*, REORDER. More discussion are left in appendix.

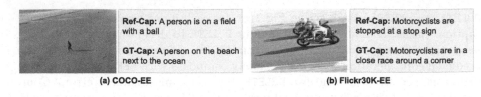

Fig. 2. Two examples from proposed ECE benchmarks: COCO-EE and Flickr30K-EE.

ically use an encoder to extract image features and a decoder to generate all words. Recent advances in captioning works focus on stronger architectures and better training procedures. To encoder visual context, numerous attention mechanisms are proposed to boost the performance [3,6,15,21,28,39,41,43], and they tend to focus on specific local features in the image when predicting each word in the caption. On the other side, current caption generation performance is dominated by reinforcement learning (RL) based methods [31,32,42], which directly optimize the sequence-level caption quality. Besides, to accelerate the decoding process, non-autoregressive methods [10,11,13] are proposed, which simultaneously generate words by discarding the sequential dependencies within sentence.

Image Caption Editing. ICE, *i.e.*, editing the existing reference caption paired with an image for refinement instead of re-generating from scratch, was first proposed by Sammani *et. al.* [34]. Specifically, they use a pre-trained deep averaging network to encode the reference caption, and design a gate mechanism to help the decoder to generate refined captions. Later, Sammani *et. al.* [35] proposed a new method for caption editing, which designs a selective copy memory attention to better encode the reference caption. As discussed above, they are all *implicit* caption editing models. In this paper, we propose the new explicit editing task, which can avoid the weaknesses in existing implicit works.

Explicit Text Editing. Explicit text editing, explicitly labeling the input reference caption with a sequence of edit operations, has been widely applied in different text editing tasks, such as text simplification [1,9], sentence fusion [25,26], grammatical error correction [4] and text generation [12]. Besides the basic edit operations like insertion and deletion, they tend to design different edit operations and edit mechanisms for their specific downstream tasks. In this paper, we extend three explicit text editing models (EditNTS [9], LaserTagger [26], and Felix [25]) into ECE, and compare them with our TIger. Specifically, Edit-NTS predicts edit operations by an LSTM sequentially. LaserTagger and Felix are all Transformer-based models, where LaserTagger predicts the edit operations restricted to a fixed phrase vocabulary and Felix uses extra reordering operations.

3   ECE and Benchmarks

3.1   Task Definition: Explicit Caption Editing (ECE)

In this section, we first formally define the ECE task. Given an image and a reference caption (Ref-Cap), ECE models aim to explicitly predict a sequence of edit operations (*e.g.*, KEEP/DELETE/ADD) on the Ref-Cap, which can translate the Ref-Cap close to the ground-truth caption (GT-Cap). Typically, Ref-Cap is slightly misaligned with the image. This task hopes the captioning models not only focus more on the visually-grounded content details, but also perform more explainable, explicit editing efficient[2], and human-like editing. As the example shown in Fig. 2(b), given Ref-Cap "Motorcyclists are stopped at a stop sign", the ECE models aim to explicitly predict a edit operation sequence: "KEEP$_{\text{Motorcyclists}}$ KEEP$_{\text{are}}$ DELETE$_{\text{stopped}}$ DELETE$_{\text{at}}$ ADD$_{\text{in}}$ KEEP$_{\text{a}}$ DELETE$_{\text{stop}}$ DELETE$_{\text{sigh}}$ ADD$_{\text{close}}$ ADD$_{\text{race}}$ ADD$_{\text{around}}$ ADD$_{\text{a}}$ ADD$_{\text{corner}}$"[3].

3.2 Explicit Caption Editing Benchmarks

Criteria. Based on the task definition of ECE and essential requirements of each ECE instance, each reference caption (Ref-Cap) and its corresponding ground-truth caption (GT-Cap) should be selected reasonably for each image. We argue that there are several criteria in developing high-quality ECE datasets:

c1. **Human Annotated Captions.** Both Ref-Cap and GT-Cap should be written by humans to avoid grammatical errors.

c2. **Image-Caption Similarity.** The scene described by the Ref-Cap should be similar to the scene in the image.

c3. **Caption Similarity.** Paired Ref-Cap and GT-Cap should have a certain degree of overlap and similar caption structure to avoid completely regenerating the whole sentence or roughly breaking the structure of Ref-Cap.

c4. **Caption Differences.** To ensure necessary editing operations, the differences between the Ref-Cap and GT-Cap shouldn't be just one (or few) words, which can be easily corrected by only language bias.

Existing ICE work [34,35] simply uses machine-generated captions as their Ref-Caps, which may mislead editing models to focus more on grammatical errors instead of content details. Meanwhile, each image has five GT-Caps, and these GT-Caps may have potential differences (caption structures or described events [5]). These training samples may confuse the editing model to break the sentence structures of Ref-Caps. To this end, we constructed two high-quality ECE benchmarks based on the aforementioned criteria. Details are as follows:

COCO-EE. We built COCO-EE based on dataset MSCOCO [20], which contains 123,287 images, and 5 ground-truth captions for each image. To ensure *c1*, we selected all Ref-Caps and GT-Caps in COCO-EE from MSCOCO captions. Since each image is labeled with 5 captions, we regard all 5 ground-truth captions as the GT-Cap candidates and filter Ref-Cap candidates from the rest captions

---

[2] We emphasize efficient from the perspective of "explicit editing efficiency", as realizing more performance gains with less meaningful editing steps, which differs from other efficiency metrics (inference time and FLOPs). More details are left in appendix.

[3] Based on different basic edit operations used in each ECE model, the GT edit operation sequence can be different. This example uses KEEP/DELETE/ADD as operations.

Table 1. Statistical summary of the COCO-EE and Flickr30K-EE benchmarks.

Dataset	COCO-EE			Flickr30K-EE		
	Train	Val	Test	Train	Val	Test
#Editing instances	97,567	5,628	5,366	108,238	4,898	4,910
#Images	52,587	3,055	2,948	29,783	1,000	1,000
Mean reference caption length	10.3	10.2	10.1	7.3	7.4	7.4
Mean ground-truth caption length	9.7	9.8	9.8	6.2	6.3	6.3
Mean edit distance	10.9	11.0	10.9	8.8	8.8	8.9
Vocabulary	11,802	3,127	3,066	19,124	4,178	4,183

based on image-caption similarity score to ensure $c2$. We then calculated several caption similarity scores to further filter the Ref-Cap candidates to ensure $c3$ and $c4$. Finally, for each filtered Ref-Caps candidate, we selected the caption with the shortest edit distance[4] from corresponding GT-Caps candidates to form a Ref-GT caption pair. Following the above steps[5], we constructed COCO-EE, and divided it into training, val, and test sets following the "Karpathy" split [16]. The statistical summary about COCO-EE is shown in Table 1.

Flickr30K-EE. We built Flickr30K-EE based on dataset e-SNLI-VE [17]. e-SNLI-VE is a visual entailment dataset using the same image set as the image captioning dataset Flicrk30K [44]. For each image in e-SNLI-VE, there are three sentences (hypothesis), which have different relations with the image (premise): entailment, neutral, and contradiction. For each image and its textual hypotheses in e-SNLI-VE, we selected the contradiction and entailment hypothesis as a Ref-GT caption pair if they have the same text premise, which ensures $c2$. Since the paired contradiction and entailment hypothesis are human-annotated ($c1$) and have the same text premises, they tend to have a certain textual similarity ($c3$) while maintaining visual differences ($c4$) at the same time. Together with the image, each ECE instance contains one image from Flickr30K and one human-annotated Ref-Cap and GT-Cap pair. Finally, we obtained the Flickr30K-EE (see footnote 5). Similarly, we divided it into training, val, and test sets based on e-SNLI-VE splits. The statistical summary about Flickr30K-EE is shown in Table 1.

4 Proposed Approach

Overview. In this section, we introduce the proposed TIger for the ECE task. Specifically, the design of the TIger is inspired from the manner in which humans conduct caption editing, *i.e.*, *our humans would like to delete all the irrelevant or wrong words in the reference caption first, and then gradually add the missing words or details till enough.* Based on this motivation, we design three modules

---

[4] The shortest edit distance is the minimum number of edit operations (except the KEEP operation) to translate one sentence to the target sentence.

[5] More details about the dataset construction steps are left in the appendix.

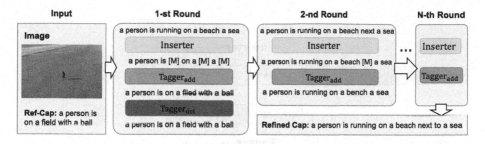

Fig. 3. Overview of the whole TIger pipeline. Tagger_del is only used in the first round, Tagger_add and Inserter are used in all rounds. In the first editing round, TIger aims to fix the main errors. Then, in the following rounds, TIger tries to add more details to generate more coherent and reasonable captions. [M] denotes the special [MASK] token.

in TIger: **Tagger_del**, **Tagger_add**, and **Inserter**. The overview of the pipeline of the TIger is illustrated in Fig. 3, and the function of each module is as follows:

1) Tagger_del: The Tagger_del aims to predict whether to keep or delete each input word. For example in Fig. 3 (1-st Round), the words "field", "with" and "ball" in the reference caption ("a person is on a filed with a ball") are not related to the image content, and we hope the Tagger_del module can predict "DELETE" for these words, and "KEEP" for the rest of the words.

2) Tagger_add: The Tagger_add aims to decide which words need to be added with a new word after them, and a special token [Mask] will be placed after these words. For example, given the input caption ("a person is on a a"), Tagger_add thinks a new word should be added after "is", "a", and "a", *i.e.*, the output of Tagger_add is "a person is [Mask] on a [Mask] a [Mask]".

3) Inserter: Given the output of Tagger_add, the Inserter aims to predict a specific word for each [Mask] token, *i.e.*, "running", "beach", and "sea".

Since the Tagger_add and Inserter can only add one new word at each position for each round, we can easily run Tagger_add and Inserter iteratively for multiple rounds to guarantee enough words adding. Instead, for the Tagger_del, we hope it directly detects all the wrong or unsuitable words in the first round.

4.1 Multimodal Feature Extraction

As shown in Fig. 4, all three modules Tagger_del, Tagger_add, and Inserter are all built on top of the multi-modal BERT [18,22], which applies a series of transformer blocks and co-attention layers to learn better multi-modal features of the images and texts. The input for each module is a sequence of multimodal tokens.

Visual Token Representations. For the given image, we first generate a set of image region features by extracting proposals and their corresponding visual features from a pre-trained object detector. We also encode the spatial location features of each proposal into a 5-d vector (normalized top-left and bottom-right coordinates, and fraction of the region area covered). A visual token feature is

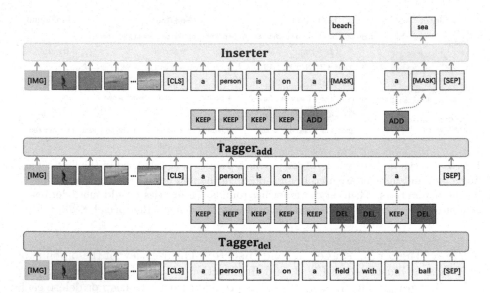

Fig. 4. Illustration of the input visual-language token sequences for each module. We take the first editing rounds in as the example.

the sum of a region proposal feature and its spatial location feature. In addition, a special [IMG] token is placed at the beginning of the visual token sequence to represent the entire image. The token feature of [IMG] is the mean-pooled visual feature with a spatial encoding corresponding to the entire image.

Textual Token Representations. For the given reference caption, we first convert it into a sequence of tokens by tokenization [8]. Then, we put special [CLS] and [SEP] tokens at the start and end of textual token sequence, respectively. Meanwhile, for Inserter, another token [MASK] is used to indicate the position for new words adding. Same as [22], a textual token representation is the sum of token-specific learned embedding [40], position encoding, and segment encoding.

Multimodal Input Token Sequence. Given the image and reference caption, we first encoder them into a sequence of visual tokens $\{v_1, \ldots, v_K\}$ and textual tokens $\{w_1, \ldots, w_L\}$, respectively. K and L is the number of visual and textual tokens, respectively. Then, the input token sequence for the three modules is $\{[\text{IMG}], v_1, \ldots, v_K, [\text{CLS}], w_1, \ldots, w_L, [\text{SEP}]\}$. The output representations for the visual and textual tokens are $\{h_{v_1}, \ldots, h_{v_K}\}$ and $\{h_{w_1}, \ldots, h_{w_L}\}$, respectively.

4.2   Model Description

Tagger$_{\text{del}}$ & Tagger$_{\text{add}}$ Modules. As shown in Fig. 4, given the visual-textual token sequence, Tagger$_{\text{del}}$ and Tagger$_{\text{add}}$ tag each textual token with a specific edit operation z. For each textual token, both Tagger$_{\text{del}}$ and Tagger$_{\text{add}}$ conduct a binary classification, *i.e.*, $z \in \{\text{KEEP}, \text{DELETE}\}$ for Tagger$_{\text{del}}$ and

$z \in \{\texttt{KEEP}, \texttt{ADD}\}$ for $\text{Tagger}_{\text{add}}$. We pass the final representation of each textual token $\{h_{w_1}, h_{w_2}, \ldots, h_{w_L}\}$ into a two-layer MLP to make the binary prediction, i.e., $z_{w_i} = \arg\max f(h_{w_i})$. Thus, the entire output of $\text{Tagger}_{\text{del}}$ and $\text{Tagger}_{\text{add}}$ is a sequence of edit operations corresponding to the sequence of input tokens, represented as $\{z_{w_1}, z_{w_2}, \ldots, z_{w_L}\}$. The output textual token sequence can be translated from the input textual token sequence and predicted edit operations.

Inserter Module. As shown in Fig. 4, the input tokens fed into the Inserter is a sequence of tokens including the word tokens and the [MASK] tokens, which is constructed from the $\text{Tagger}_{\text{add}}$ module. Given the image and the input tokens, the Inserter finishes the insertion by predicting the specific word from the vocabulary for each [MASK] token based on the observed tokens and visual information. Specifically, we pass the final representation of each [MASK] token $h_{w_{mask}}$ into a linear layer, mapping it to a distribution over the vocabulary. Lastly, all [MASK] tokens can be replaced with the predicted word, and the output textual token sequence can be formed with the rest word tokens for following the procedures.

Multi-rounds Editing. As the specific editing process shown in Fig. 4, TIger resembles the way that humans might perform caption editing, i.e., considering what to keep, where to add, and what to add. By tracing these edit operations, the whole editing process is explainable and efficient. Meanwhile, since $\text{Tagger}_{\text{add}}$ only adds one new word after each input word once a time, there might not be enough details if we only apply $\text{Tagger}_{\text{add}}$ once. Thanks to this modular design, we can seamlessly use $\text{Tagger}_{\text{add}}$ and Inserter iteratively for multi-rounds to guarantee enough details. Instead, if we make the $\text{Tagger}_{\text{add}}$ can add more than one word once a time, it also needs to predict the number of new words to add at the same time. Meanwhile, the Inserter needs to predict words for multiple [MASK] tokens that may be placed consecutively. This significantly increases the difficulty of training, and empirically this single-round solution gets worse results.

4.3 Training Objectives

The $\text{Tagger}_{\text{del}}$ and $\text{Tagger}_{\text{add}}$ are essentially solving a binary classification task, and the Inserter is essentially solving a masked language modeling task. Thus, we train all three modules with the cross-entropy (XE) loss. Due to the modular nature, we train the three modules separately. In our experiments, we also emphasize the importance of predicting relative more KEEP operation. Specifically, for $\text{Tagger}_{\text{del}}$, it can preserve more words in the caption for the whole following editing process. For $\text{Tagger}_{\text{add}}$, it can offer more context words with relative fewer [MASK] tokens for Inserter, which makes the edit operation prediction much easier. Thus, We use different XE loss weights for the KEEP tokens and other tokens (DELETE or ADD). The loss weight ratio λ denotes the XE loss weights of edit token KEEP/DELETE for training $\text{Tagger}_{\text{del}}$ and KEEP/ADD for training $\text{Tagger}_{\text{add}}$, respectively. More detailed influence of λ is discussed in Sect. 5.3.

Table 2. Performance of our model and other state-of-art models on COCO-EE. "Ref-Caps" denotes the quality of given reference captions. "D" and "A" denotes the number of editing step of DELETE and ADD operations, respectively.

	Model	Quality evaluation							Efficiency evaluation			
		B-1	B-2	B-3	B-4	R	C	S	ES	GPS(C)	D	A
	Ref-Caps	50.0	37.1	27.7	19.5	48.2	129.9	18.9	—	—	—	—
	UpDn [3]	49.9	35.3	25.5	18.8	48.3	159.2	31.2	—	—	—	—
ICE	UpDn-E [3]	54.0	40.1	30.2	22.9	52.8	182.0	33.2	19.22	2.71	10.14	9.08
	MN [34]	50.2	35.8	26.0	19.4	48.9	163.9	31.6	19.08	1.78	10.14	8.94
	ETN [35]	53.8	40.5	23.8	23.8	53.3	190.5	32.1	18.96	3.20	10.14	8.82
ECE	V-EditNTS [9]	49.2	36.5	27.4	20.5	49.8	149.0	26.2	5.90	3.24	3.76	2.14
	V-Felix [25]	36.9	28.2	21.6	16.2	49.7	139.5	25.3	5.51	1.74	4.57	0.94
	V-LaserTagger [26]	42.0	30.5	22.4	16.0	46.8	127.1	24.1	4.11	-0.68	3.54	0.57
	TIger (Ours)	**54.8**	**42.0**	**32.4**	**24.7**	**54.3**	**194.8**	**33.3**	7.74	**8.38**	4.59	3.15

5 Experiments

5.1 Experimental Setup

Evaluation Datasets and Metrics. We evaluated our TIger on both COCO-EE and Flickr30K-EE datasets (cf. Sect. 3.2). For the caption quality evaluation, we followed existing caption generation works, and used four prevalent evaluation metrics: BLEU-N (B-N) (1-to 4-grams) [30], ROUGE-L (R) [19], CIDEr-D (C) [37] and SPICE (S) [2]. Particularly, we evaluated generated captions against its single ground-truth caption. Meanwhile, to evaluate the explicit editing efficiency of editing, we propose two supplementary metrics: Editing Steps (**ES**), and Gains Per Step (**GPS**). ES is the total number of meaningful editing steps, and GPS is the average performance gains per meaningful editing step, *i.e.*, we hope ECE models realize the most performance gains with the least number of meaningful editing steps. In this paper, since all baselines apply the same set of edit operations (*i.e.*, KEEP, DELETE, and ADD), we regard the sum of DELETE and ADD operations as ES. Meanwhile, since CIDEr-D is regarded as the most important metric for caption evaluation as to its high agreements with humans, we use the improvements of CIDEr-D score to calculate GPS, denoted as GPS(C).

Baselines. We compared our TIger against state-of-the-art image caption editing models. Specifically, we compared three strong implicit caption editing models: **UpDn-E** [3], **MN** [34], and **ETN** [35]. They are all built on top of the widely-used UpDn architecture [3], and propose some extra modules to encode the reference caption. Meanwhile, for more complete comparisons, we further extended three text explicit editing models (EditNTS [9], LaserTagger [26], and Felix [25]) into ECE, denoted as **V-EditNTS**, **V-LaserTagger**, and **V-Felix**, respectively. For all these three models, their basic editing operations are KEEP, DELETE and ADD. Specifically, V-EditNTS predicts the edit operation sequence iteratively by an LSTM. V-LaserTagger and V-Felix are one-round Transformer-

Table 3. Performance of our model and other state-of-art models on Flickr30K-EE. "Ref-Caps" denotes the quality of given reference captions. "D" and "A" denotes the number of editing step of `DELETE` and `ADD` operations, respectively.

	Model	Quality evaluation							Efficiency evaluation			
		B-1	B-2	B-3	B-4	R	C	S	ES	GPS(C)	D	A
	Ref-Cap	34.7	24.0	16.8	10.9	36.9	91.3	23.4	—	—	—	—
	UpDn [3]	25.6	16.1	10.4	6.3	30.1	71.0	21.4	—	—	—	—
ICE	UpDn-E [3]	33.9	24.7	18.3	12.5	41.1	129.1	29.8	12.00	3.15	7.41	4.59
	MN [34]	30.0	20.0	13.6	8.6	34.9	91.1	25.2	12.09	-0.02	7.41	4.69
	ETN [35]	34.8	25.9	19.6	13.7	41.8	143.3	31.3	12.06	4.31	7.41	4.65
ECE	V-EditNTS [9]	38.0	27.6	20.1	13.8	40.2	129.1	28.7	5.48	6.90	3.59	1.89
	V-Felix [25]	21.1	16.7	13.5	10.1	38.0	127.4	27.8	5.54	6.51	4.92	0.62
	V-LaserTagger [26]	30.8	20.8	15.0	10.5	34.9	104.0	27.3	3.37	3.77	3.35	0.02
	TIger (Ours)	**38.3**	**28.1**	**21.1**	**14.9**	**42.7**	**148.3**	**32.0**	6.65	**8.58**	4.63	2.02

based editing models, which directly predict multiple `ADD` operations simultaneously. More details about these baselines are left in the appendix.

Implementation Details. The implementation details are left in appendix.

5.2 Comparisons with State-of-the-Arts

Settings. We evaluated `TIger` on COCO-EE and Flickr30K-EE by comparing with state-of-the-art methods. Since our target is to propose the ECE task and the first ECE model, we first compared `TIger` with simple ECE baselines which were extended by text explicit editing models (V-EditNTS, V-Felix, and V-LaserTagger). For completeness, we also reported the results of all existing ICE models (UpDn-E, ETN, and MN). Since all implicit models are built on top of the widely-used UpDn architecture, we only reported the results of the UpDn captioning model rather than all other SOTA captioning models (e.g., VLP [45]) as they actually don't belong to the caption editing task. Since V-Felix and V-LaserTagger are also Transformer-based architectures, we used the same ViLBERT pretrained weights as `TIger`. For the other baselines, we converted all the words in each dataset to lower cases and built their respective vocabulary. All baselines were trained with XE loss. Since implicit models do not explicitly predict edit operations, we suppose they delete all the words in the reference caption first and add new words from scratch to output caption, *i.e.*, ES is calculated as the sum of words in reference and output caption. Meanwhile, we mainly focused on the efficiency evaluation of ECE models, so we have used gray font for efficiency evaluation of ICE methods. Results on COCO-EE and Flickr30K-EE are reported in Table 2 and Table 3, respectively.

Results on COCO-EE. From Table 2, we can observe: 1) For the quality evaluation, our model achieves the largest performance gains on all metrics (*e.g.*, 194.8 vs. 190.5 in ETN on CIDEr-D). 2) For efficiency evaluation, SOTA implicit models always outperform their explicit counterparts, but they require more

Table 4. Performance on COCO-EE and Flickr30K-EE with different XE loss weights λ.

	λ	B-1	B-4	R	C	S
COCO	1.0	54.1	24.0	53.9	190.0	33.4
	1.2	54.4	24.1	54.0	190.9	33.4
	1.5	**54.8**	**24.7**	**54.3**	**194.8**	**33.3**
	2.0	54.6	24.6	54.1	193.9	33.1
Flickr30K	1.0	34.2	13.4	41.2	137.0	30.9
	1.2	34.3	14.1	41.7	144.0	31.4
	1.5	**38.3**	**14.9**	**42.7**	**148.3**	**32.0**
	2.0	37.2	14.9	42.7	148.0	31.5

Table 5. Influence of different modules with weighted XE loss ($\lambda = 1.5$). "T_{del}" and "T_{add}" denote Tagger$_{del}$ and Tagger$_{add}$, respectively.

	T_{del}	T_{add}	B-1	B-4	R	C	S
COCO			54.1	24.0	53.9	190.0	33.4
	✓		55.0	24.7	54.3	193.7	33.1
		✓	54.1	24.1	54.0	191.2	33.7
	✓	✓	**54.8**	**24.7**	**54.3**	**194.8**	**33.3**
Flickr30K			34.2	13.4	41.2	137.0	30.9
	✓		34.9	14.3	42.0	144.9	34.6
		✓	34.3	13.7	41.4	140.9	31.2
	✓	✓	**38.3**	**14.9**	**42.7**	**148.3**	**32.0**

editing steps. Instead, our model achieves the best GPS(C) score by predicting more ADD operations, instead of simply deleting or keeping the words in the reference captions. It also shows our ability to detect and fix detailed errors.

Results on Flickr30K-EE. From Table 3, we can observe: 1) For the quality evaluation, similar with COCO-EE, our model achieves the largest performance gains on all metrics (*e.g.*, 148.3 vs. 143.3 in ETN on CIDEr-D). 2) For efficiency evaluation, our model achieves the best GPS(C) score (*e.g.*, 8.58 vs. 6.90 in V-EditNTS). Compared to the weaknesses of implicit models (need more editing steps) and explicit models (marginal performance gains), our model achieves a decent balance between performance gains and editing steps, *i.e.*, we improved the quality of reference captions with quite a few meaningful editing steps.

5.3 Ablation Studies

In this section, we run a set of ablation studies to analyze the influence of different hyperparameter settings, and the influence of pre-trained ViLBERT weights.

Influence of Weighted XE Loss. As mentioned in Sect. 4.3, we used weighted XE loss for training. To explore the influence of different loss weights, we first run ablations by setting different loss weight ratios $\lambda \in \{1.0, 1.2, 1.5, 2.0\}$ on both Tagger$_{del}$ and Tagger$_{add}$. Results are reported in Table 4. Then, we explored the influence of weighted XE loss to a single Tagger module, *i.e.*, we run ablations by setting one of the Tagger with $\lambda > 1.0$, and the other with $\lambda = 1.0$. The results are reported in Table 5. Note that all Inserters were trained with $\lambda = 1.0$.

Results. From Table 4, we have several observations: 1) For both the COCO-EE and Flickr30K-EE, TIger with weighted XE loss training always gets better performance than the baseline ($\lambda = 1.0$). 2) The model trained with $\lambda = 1.5$ gets the best performance, *i.e.*, it boosts the CIDEr-D score from 190.0 to 194.8 for COCO-EE and from 137.0 to 148.3 for Flickr30K-EE. This demonstrates the effectiveness of paying more attention to predicting the KEEP operation. We then used $\lambda = 1.5$ to train TIger in all experiments. From Table 5, we can observe

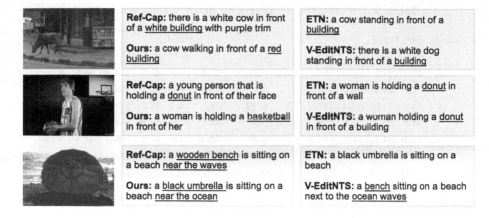

Ref-Cap: there is a white cow in front of a <u>white building</u> with purple trim

Ours: a cow walking in front of a <u>red building</u>

ETN: a cow standing in front of a <u>building</u>

V-EditNTS: there is a white dog standing in front of a <u>building</u>

Ref-Cap: a young person that is holding a <u>donut</u> in front of their face

Ours: a woman is holding a <u>basketball</u> in front of her

ETN: a woman is holding a <u>donut</u> in front of a wall

V-EditNTS: a woman holding a <u>donut</u> in front of a building

Ref-Cap: a <u>wooden bench</u> is sitting on a beach <u>near the waves</u>

Ours: a <u>black umbrella</u> is sitting on a beach <u>near the ocean</u>

ETN: a black umbrella is sitting on a beach

V-EditNTS: a <u>bench</u> sitting on a beach next to the <u>ocean waves</u>

Fig. 5. Visualization results of our model compared to baselines in COCO-EE.

that: 1) `TIger` with only one of the Tagger modules trained with $\lambda = 1.5$ alone can still achieve better performance than baseline. 2) The weighted XE loss has more impact on Tagger_{del} than Tagger_{add}. The possible reason is that `TIger` only applies Tagger_{del} once, which determines the basic caption for further adding.

Different Editing Rounds. Since `TIger` iteratively use Tagger_{add} and Inserter multiple rounds to add words, we run ablations to analyse the effect of different edit rounds. The maximum number of editing rounds was set to 5.

Results. From Table 6, we can observe that: 1) For COCO-EE, the performance of `TIger` keeps improving in the first 3 editing rounds. Then, the quality evaluation metrics reach the best scores and keep unchanged or even slightly drop with more editing rounds. For example, BLEU-1 keeps increasing with more editing rounds, CIDEr-D reaches the best score 194.8 in the 4-th round and drops to 194.6 in the 5-th round. Since most metrics reach their best scores in the 4-th round, considering the trade-off between model performance and editing efficiency, we used 4 editing rounds for the COCO-EE. 2) For Flickr30K-EE, the performance of `TIger` keeps improving in the first 3 editing rounds. Most quality evaluation metrics reach the best score in the 3-rd round, and then keep unchanged (14.9 for BLEU-4 and 148.3 for CIDEr-D) or drop slightly (SPICE) with more editing rounds. Thus, we used 3 editing rounds for the Flickr30K-EE.

Influence of the Pre-trained Weights. Since we took advantage of the pre-trained weights to train `TIger`, we further ran ablations to examine the influence of the pre-trained ViLBERT weights. The results are reported in Table 7.

Results. From Table 7, we can observe that for both datasets, as the first ECE model, both TIger models with and w/o pre-trained weights all outperform other ECE baselines with same pre-trained weights in both quality and efficiency evaluation. Meanwhile, `TIger` trained with pretraind weight achieves better performance than the model trained from scratch. For example, in CIDEr-D, the pre-trained weights improve score from 178.1 to 194.8 for COCO-EE.

Table 6. Performance of TIger with different editing rounds.

# Rounds	COCO-EE						Flickr30K-EE					
	B-1	B-4	R	C	S	GPS(C)	B-1	B-4	R	C	S	GPS(C)
1	49.3	22.2	54.2	180.2	31.6	8.01	33.5	13.9	42.2	142.8	31.0	8.79
2	52.8	23.8	54.3	189.8	32.7	8.41	36.8	14.8	42.5	148.1	31.9	**8.88**
3	54.2	24.5	**54.4**	193.9	33.1	**8.49**	38.3	**14.9**	42.7	**148.3**	**32.0**	8.58
4	54.8	**24.7**	54.3	**194.8**	**33.3**	8.38	38.4	14.9	**42.8**	148.3	31.9	8.45
5	**55.0**	24.7	54.3	194.6	33.3	8.26	**38.6**	14.9	42.8	148.3	31.9	8.42

Table 7. The Influence of the pretraind ViLBERT weight.

Models	COCO-EE					Flickr30K-EE				
	B-1	B-4	R	C	S	B-1	B-4	R	C	S
TIger w/o pretrain	53.6	23.3	52.8	178.1	31.1	35.0	14.0	41.7	140.8	30.9
TIger	**54.8**	**24.7**	**54.3**	**194.8**	**33.3**	**38.3**	**14.9**	**42.7**	**148.3**	**32.0**

5.4   Transfering to Machine-Generated Captions

As mentioned before, machine-generated captions may be semantic coherent but suffer from severe bias issues, such as overlooking some content details and producing incorrect or repetitive content. To evaluate the generalization ability on machine-generated captions, we directly use the trained TIger to edit machine-generated captions without extra fine-tuning. To guarantee fairness and avoid data leakage, we first trained TIger and the ECE baselines on the same COCO-EE (and Flickr30K-EE) training set. Then, we apply the trained TIger to directly edit the captions generated from these ECE baselines (*i.e.*, as reference captions) on the test set. The results are reported in Table 8.

Results. As shown in Tabel 8, we can observe that: 1) For COCO-EE, our proposed TIger can significantly improve the quality of all the captions generated by ECE baselines (*e.g.*, CIDEr-D score from 149.0 to 172.7 for V-EditNTS). 2) For Flickr30K-EE, the average improvements are still remarkable (*e.g.*, 135.8 vs. 129.1 in V-EditNTS on CIDEr-D score). This also demonstrates the robustness of TIger when given different reference captions (*e.g.*, these ECE baselines generated captions may erroneously delete or preserve some words).

5.5   Qualitative Evaluation

Figure 5 shows some results generated by TIger compared to baselines (ETN [35] and V-EditNTS [9]). The three examples demonstrate that our model is capable of recognizing and correcting incorrect details (*i.e.*, "white" to "red", "donut" to "basketball", and "bench" to "umbrella"), while the baselines simply delete the wrong word "white" or fail to correct the object errors "donut" and 'umbrella". Meanwhile, the last example demonstrates that our model can add

Table 8. The result of extending TIger for ECE baselines

Models	COCO-EE					Flickr30K-EE				
	B-1	B-4	R	C	S	B-1	B-4	R	C	S
V-EditNTS	49.2	20.5	49.8	149.0	26.2	38.0	13.8	40.2	129.1	28.7
V-EditNTS+Ours	**51.9**	**21.6**	**51.7**	**172.7**	**32.3**	36.2	13.6	**40.9**	**135.8**	**30.3**
V-Felix	36.9	16.2	49.7	139.5	25.3	21.1	10.1	38	127.4	27.8
V-Felix+Ours	**51.2**	**21.7**	**51.9**	**175.3**	**32.3**	**30.2**	**12.8**	**39.6**	**133.8**	**29.5**
V-LaserTagger	42.0	16.0	46.8	127.1	24.1	30.8	10.5	34.9	104.0	27.3
V-LaserTagger+Ours	**50.7**	**20.4**	**50.9**	**166.4**	**31.7**	**32.4**	**10.9**	**36.7**	**110.4**	27.2

new details to the captions, like attributes (color) of main objects (*e.g.*, black), while baselines may overlook them. Furthermore, our model can fix these details without breaking the structure of the caption (*e.g.*, near the ocean).

6   Conclusions and Future Work

In this paper, we proposed a new visual-language task: Explicit Caption Editing (ECE). To facilitate the ECE research, we also proposed two benchmarks by reorganizing two existing datasets MSCOCO and e-SNLI-VE, dubbed as COCO-EE and Flickr30K-EE, respectively. Meanwhile, we proposed the first ECE model TIger. We validate the effectiveness of TIger through extensive comparative and ablative experiments. Moving forward, we are going to 1) design stronger ECE models by introducing some advanced edit operations; 2) try to bridge the gap between explicit and implicit editing, and propose a unified model for both tasks.

Acknowledgement. This work was supported by the National Key Research & Development Project of China (2021ZD0110700), the National Natural Science Foundation of China (U19B2043, 61976185), Zhejiang Natural Science Foundation (LR19F020002), Zhejiang Innovation Foundation (2019R52002), and the Fundamental Research Funds for the Central Universities (226-2022-00051).

References

1. Alva-Manchego, F., Bingel, J., Paetzold, G., Scarton, C., Specia, L.: Learning how to simplify from explicit labeling of complex-simplified text pairs. In: IJCNLP, pp. 295–305 (2017)
2. Anderson, P., Fernando, B., Johnson, M., Gould, S.: SPICE: semantic propositional image caption evaluation. In: Leibe, B., Matas, J., Sebe, N., Welling, M. (eds.) ECCV 2016. LNCS, vol. 9909, pp. 382–398. Springer, Cham (2016). https://doi.org/10.1007/978-3-319-46454-1_24
3. Anderson, P., et al.: Bottom-up and top-down attention for image captioning and visual question answering. In: CVPR, pp. 6077–6086 (2018)
4. Awasthi, A., Sarawagi, S., Goyal, R., Ghosh, S., Piratla, V.: Parallel iterative edit models for local sequence transduction. arXiv (2019)

5. Chen, L., Jiang, Z., Xiao, J., Liu, W.: Human-like controllable image captioning with verb-specific semantic roles. In: CVPR, pp. 16846–16856 (2021)
6. Chen, L., et al.: Sca-cnn: spatial and channel-wise attention in convolutional networks for image captioning. In: CVPR, pp. 5659–5667 (2017)
7. Das, A., et al.: Visual dialog. In: CVPR, pp. 326–335 (2017)
8. Devlin, J., Chang, M.W., Lee, K., Toutanova, K.: Bert: pre-training of deep bidirectional transformers for language understanding. arXiv (2018)
9. Dong, Y., Li, Z., Rezagholizadeh, M., Cheung, J.C.K.: Editnts: an neural programmer-interpreter model for sentence simplification through explicit editing. In: ACL (2019)
10. Fei, Z.C.: Fast image caption generation with position alignment. arXiv (2019)
11. Gao, J., et al.: Masked non-autoregressive image captioning. arXiv (2019)
12. Gu, J., Wang, C., Zhao, J.: Levenshtein transformer. In: NeurIPS 32 (2019)
13. Guo, L., Liu, J., Zhu, X., He, X., Jiang, J., Lu, H.: Non-autoregressive image captioning with counterfactuals-critical multi-agent learning. arXiv (2020)
14. Hendricks, L.A., Burns, K., Saenko, K., Darrell, T., Rohrbach, A.: Women also snowboard: overcoming bias in captioning models. In: ECCV, pp. 771–787 (2018)
15. Huang, L., Wang, W., Chen, J., Wei, X.Y.: Attention on attention for image captioning. In: ICCV, pp. 4634–4643 (2019)
16. Karpathy, A., Fei-Fei, L.: Deep visual-semantic alignments for generating image descriptions. In: CVPR. pp. 3128–3137 (2015)
17. Kayser, M., et al.: e-vil: a dataset and benchmark for natural language explanations in vision-language tasks. arXiv (2021)
18. Li, G., Duan, N., Fang, Y., Gong, M., Jiang, D.: Unicoder-vl: a universal encoder for vision and language by cross-modal pre-training. In: Proceedings of the AAAI Conference on Artificial Intelligence, pp. 11336–11344 (2020)
19. Lin, C.Y.: Rouge: a package for automatic evaluation of summaries. In: Text Summarization Branches Out, pp. 74–81 (2004)
20. Lin, T.-Y., Maire, M., Belongie, S., Hays, J., Perona, P., Ramanan, D., Dollár, P., Zitnick, C.L.: Microsoft COCO: common objects in context. In: Fleet, D., Pajdla, T., Schiele, B., Tuytelaars, T. (eds.) ECCV 2014. LNCS, vol. 8693, pp. 740–755. Springer, Cham (2014). https://doi.org/10.1007/978-3-319-10602-1_48
21. Liu, A.A., Zhai, Y., Xu, N., Nie, W., Li, W., Zhang, Y.: Region-aware image captioning via interaction learning. In: IEEE Transactions on Circuits and Systems for Video Technology (2021)
22. Lu, J., Batra, D., Parikh, D., Lee, S.: Vilbert: pretraining task-agnostic visiolinguistic representations for vision-and-language tasks. In: NeurIPS (2019)
23. Lu, J., Xiong, C., Parikh, D., Socher, R.: Knowing when to look: adaptive attention via a visual sentinel for image captioning. In: CVPR, pp. 375–383 (2017)
24. MacLeod, H., Bennett, C.L., Morris, M.R., Cutrell, E.: Understanding blind people's experiences with computer-generated captions of social media images. In: Proceedings of the 2017 CHI Conference on Human Factors in Computing Systems, pp. 5988–5999 (2017)
25. Mallinson, J., Severyn, A., Malmi, E., Garrido, G.: Felix: flexible text editing through tagging and insertion. arXiv (2020)
26. Malmi, E., Krause, S., Rothe, S., Mirylenka, D., Severyn, A.: Encode, tag, realize: High-precision text editing. arXiv (2019)
27. Mao, J., Xu, W., Yang, Y., Wang, J., Huang, Z., Yuille, A.: Deep captioning with multimodal recurrent neural networks (m-rnn). arXiv (2014)
28. Mao, Y., Chen, L., Jiang, Z., Zhang, D., Zhang, Z., Shao, J., Xiao, J.: Rethinking the reference-based distinctive image captioning. In: ACMMM (2022)

29. Ordonez, V., Han, X., Kuznetsova, P., Kulkarni, G., Mitchell, M., Yamaguchi, K., Stratos, K., Goyal, A., Dodge, J., Mensch, A., Daumé, H., Berg, A.C., Choi, Y., Berg, T.L.: Large scale retrieval and generation of image descriptions. Int. J. Comput. Vis. **119**(1), 46–59 (2015). https://doi.org/10.1007/s11263-015-0840-y

30. Papineni, K., Roukos, S., Ward, T., Zhu, W.J.: Bleu: a method for automatic evaluation of machine translation. In: ACL, pp. 311–318 (2002)

31. Ren, Z., Wang, X., Zhang, N., Lv, X., Li, L.J.: Deep reinforcement learning-based image captioning with embedding reward. In: CVPR, pp. 290–298 (2017)

32. Rennie, S.J., Marcheret, E., Mroueh, Y., Ross, J., Goel, V.: Self-critical sequence training for image captioning. In: CVPR, pp. 7008–7024 (2017)

33. Rohrbach, A., Hendricks, L.A., Burns, K., Darrell, T., Saenko, K.: Object hallucination in image captioning. In: EMNLP (2018)

34. Sammani, F., Elsayed, M.: Look and modify: modification networks for image captioning. arXiv (2019)

35. Sammani, F., Melas-Kyriazi, L.: Show, edit and tell: a framework for editing image captions. In: CVPR, pp. 4808–4816 (2020)

36. Vaswani, A., et al.: Attention is all you need. In: NeurIPS 30 (2017)

37. Vedantam, R., Lawrence Zitnick, C., Parikh, D.: Cider: consensus-based image description evaluation. In: CVPR, pp. 4566–4575 (2015)

38. Vinyals, O., Toshev, A., Bengio, S., Erhan, D.: Show and tell: a neural image caption generator. In: CVPR, pp. 3156–3164 (2015)

39. Wang, Y., Xu, N., Liu, A.A., Li, W., Zhang, Y.: High-order interaction learning for image captioning. In: IEEE Transactions on Circuits and Systems for Video Technology (2021)

40. Wu, Y., et al.: Google's neural machine translation system: bridging the gap between human and machine translation. arXiv (2016)

41. Xu, K., et al.: Show, attend and tell: Neural image caption generation with visual attention. In: ICML, pp. 2048–2057 (2015)

42. Xu, N., et al.: Multi-level policy and reward-based deep reinforcement learning framework for image captioning. TMM **22**(5), 1372–1383 (2019)

43. Yang, Z., He, X., Gao, J., Deng, L., Smola, A.: Stacked attention networks for image question answering. In: CVPR, pp. 21–29 (2016)

44. Young, P., Lai, A., Hodosh, M., Hockenmaier, J.: From image descriptions to visual denotations: new similarity metrics for semantic inference over event descriptions. TACL **2**, 67–78 (2014)

45. Zhou, L., Palangi, H., Zhang, L., Hu, H., Corso, J., Gao, J.: Unified vision-language pre-training for image captioning and vqa. In: AAAI, vol. 34, pp. 13041–13049 (2020)

Can Shuffling Video Benefit Temporal Bias Problem: A Novel Training Framework for Temporal Grounding

Jiachang Hao, Haifeng Sun[✉], Pengfei Ren, Jingyu Wang[✉], Qi Qi, and Jianxin Liao

State Key Laboratory of Networking and Switching Technology, Beijing University of Posts and Telecommunications, Beijing, China
{haojc,hfsun,rpf,wangjingyu,qiqi8266}@bupt.edu.cn

Abstract. Temporal grounding aims to locate a target video moment that semantically corresponds to the given sentence query in an untrimmed video. However, recent works find that existing methods suffer a severe temporal bias problem. These methods do not reason the target moment locations based on the visual-textual semantic alignment but over-rely on the temporal biases of queries in training sets. To this end, this paper proposes a novel training framework for grounding models to use shuffled videos to address temporal bias problem without losing grounding accuracy. Our framework introduces two auxiliary tasks, cross-modal matching and temporal order discrimination, to promote the grounding model training. The cross-modal matching task leverages the content consistency between shuffled and original videos to force the grounding model to mine visual contents to semantically match queries. The temporal order discrimination task leverages the difference in temporal order to strengthen the understanding of long-term temporal contexts. Extensive experiments on Charades-STA and ActivityNet Captions demonstrate the effectiveness of our method for mitigating the reliance on temporal biases and strengthening the model's generalization ability against the different temporal distributions. Code is available at https://github.com/haojc/ShufflingVideosForTSG.

Keywords: Temporal grounding · Temporal bias · Video and language

1 Introduction

Temporal grounding [11,16] aims to localize the relevant video moment of interest semantically corresponding to the given sentence query in an untrimmed video, as illustrated in Fig. 1a. Due to its vast potential applications in video captioning, video question answering, and video retrieval, this task has attracted

---

Supplementary Information The online version contains supplementary material available at https://doi.org/10.1007/978-3-031-20059-5_8.

S. Avidan et al. (Eds.): ECCV 2022, LNCS 13696, pp. 130–147, 2022.
https://doi.org/10.1007/978-3-031-20059-5_8

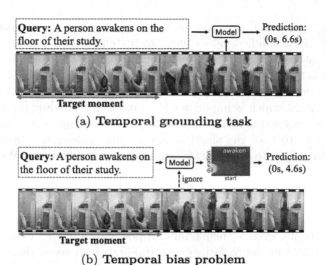

Fig. 1. (a) Temporal grounding is to localize a moment with the start point (0 s) and end point (6.6 s) in the video for the query. (b) An example of temporal bias problem: a model ignores the visual input and uses the memorized temporal bias of the word 'awaken' in the training set of Charades-STA to make the prediction.

increasing interest over the last few years. However, this task suffers a temporal bias problem [37,51,52], which severely hinders the development of the temporal grounding task.

Temporal bias problem refers to that a method reasons the target moment locations not based on the visual-textual semantic matching but over-relies on the temporal biases of queries in training set [37]. As illustrated in Fig. 1b, a grounding model ignores visual inputs and takes a shortcut to directly exploit the memorized temporal biases of the given query in training set to reason the location of the target video moment. The temporal bias problem severely hinders the development of temporal grounding [37,51]. Because when we give a sentence query, we wish the target moment to be localized based on the query semantics wherever the target moment is. [37,52] found that many state-of-the-art methods [11,34,53–55,58,60] suffer this problem and perform poor generalization ability against the different temporal distributions. Some methods [53,60] even do not make any use of the visual input during reasoning. To this end, this paper aims to mitigate the excessive reliance on temporal biases and strengthen the model's generalization ability against the different temporal distributions.

Video-query pairs in existing datasets have high correlations between queries and ground-truth temporal positions of target moments, making it possible for a grounding model to take a shortcut [37,51]. So we ask *whether we can shuffle videos to break these correlations to address the temporal bias problem*. We can shift randomly target moments to other temporal positions in videos to dilute the temporal bias of the corresponding query in training set. Thus the shortcut of memorizing temporal biases will be ineffective, and the model has to turn the attention back to the visual contents semantically matching queries. However, directly using these shuffled videos as training samples is not appropriate. On the one hand, these shuffled videos may not match the real situation, causing a poor generalization ability of the grounding model. On the other hand, shuffling videos disturbs the long-term temporal contexts within videos. These incorrect contexts may weaken the perception ability of grounding models for long-term temporal relations, which is important for temporal grounding [17,60].

To this end, instead of using the shuffled videos as augmented training samples, we propose to take the shuffled and original videos as paired input and design auxiliary tasks to promote the grounding model training. We design two auxiliary tasks, cross-modal matching and temporal order discrimination, to mine the cross-modal semantic relevance from the paired videos and mitigate the reliance on temporal biases. The cross-modal matching task requires that the model predicts as consistent frame-level cross-modal relevance as possible for target moments, even if their temporal positions change. This task encourages the grounding model to focus on spatial and short-term visual contents to semantically match queries. The temporal order discrimination task is to discriminate whether the video moment sequence is in correct temporal order. This task guides the grounding model to learn the correct temporal contexts and thus strengthens the perception ability on long-term temporal relations.

We propose a span-based framework to handle the temporal grounding and two auxiliary tasks. And our method can be easily transferred to other grounding models. To sum up, the main contributions of our work are as follows:

(1) We propose a novel training framework for temporal grounding models to use shuffled videos to address the temporal bias problem.
(2) Our cross-modal matching task can mitigate the model's reliance on temporal biases and turn the attention back to the visual-textual semantic matching, and the temporal order discrimination task can strengthen the understanding of long-term temporal relations.
(3) Extensive experiments on Charades-STA and ActivityNet Captions demonstrate the effectiveness of our method for mitigating the grounding model's reliance on temporal biases and strengthening the generalization ability against the different temporal distributions. And we achieve state-of-the-art on the re-divided splits for temporal bias problem.

2   Related Work

Temporal Grounding. Temporal grounding, also known as temporal sentence grounding in video and video moment retrieval, was first proposed by [11,16]. Proposal-based methods formulate this task as a ranking task to find the best matching video proposal for a given sentence query. These methods first generate the candidate video segments by slide windows [11,30,31] or a proposal network [6,25,48,50] or predefined anchors [1,3,22–24,26–29,56,62], and then semantically match each candidate with the sentence query. However, the proposal generation and semantic matching for all the proposals are resource-consuming and inefficient. To discard proposals, proposal-free methods encode the video modality only once and directly interact each video frame with the sentence query.

Specifically, regression-based methods [5,7,8,32,54] regress the temporal coordinates of the localized video moment from a compact representation. Span-based methods [4,13,14,18,35,39,57,61] predict the probabilities of each frame being the start/end of the location.

Temporal Bias Problem. [37] first proposed the temporal bias problem. They found that the popular datasets for temporal grounding task include significant biases through explicit statistics about temporal locations of the top-50 verbs in datasets. Then they verified that some state-of-the-art models did not achieve cross-modal alignment but exploited dataset biases instead. To correctly evaluate grounding performance, [52] re-divided the splits of two popular datasets, Charades-STA and ActivityNet Captions, to make the training and test sets have different temporal distributions of queries. To address the temporal bias problem, DCM [51] disentangles temporal position information from each proposal feature via a constraint loss and then leverages causal intervention to fairly consider all candidate proposals. To evaluate the effectiveness, DCM [51] simulated the out-of-distribution test samples by inserting a sequence of generated video features at the beginning of the original video feature sequence. However, this simulation is not much convincing. On the one hand, the inserted features are generated from a normal distribution so that these features may not contain any meaningful content. On the other hand, the length of the inserted video sequence is too short to change the temporal biases significantly. In this paper, we use the re-divided splits [52] to evaluate performance and generalization ability.

Temporal Relation Modeling. Temporal relation modeling is a fundamental problem in video understanding. Typical methods apply RNN [36], 3D-CNN [2,19,42] to capture the short-term temporal relations and non-local [47], Transformer [43], TDN [46] to capture the long-term ones. However, due to the black box of neural networks, it is uncertain whether the features learned from the aforementioned mechanism contain the temporal relations or other information like scene, appearance, and temporal bias. Therefore, some works [9,10,21,33,49] attempt to explicitly strengthen video representation learning in temporal relations by using auxiliary tasks. Temporal order verification is one of the most frequently used tasks because it does not require extra annotations. This task aims to determine whether a sequence of frames from a video is in the correct temporal order. Inspired by that, we design two auxiliary tasks for temporal grounding models to promote the visual-textual matching features mining.

3 Methods

3.1 Problem Formulation

Given an untrimmed video V and a sentence query Q, temporal grounding aims to determine the start and end timestamps (τ^s, τ^e) of specific video moment semantically corresponding to the sentence query. The video V is represented as $V = \{v_t\}_{t=1}^T$ frame-by-frame, and the query is represented as $Q = \{q_n\}_{n=1}^N$ word-by-word, where T and N are the number of frames and words, respectively.

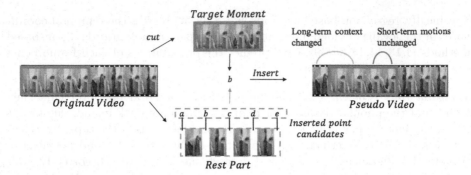

Fig. 2. An illustration of the generation of pseudo videos. The inserted point is randomly sampled from the candidates.

3.2 Input Construction

We first introduce how we shuffle videos to construct the input of our framework. For each video-query pair in the training set, we first cut out the target moment from the video and then insert the cut moment into a random temporal position of the rest of the video, as shown in Fig. 2. We name the shuffled videos pseudo videos. The pseudo videos have three characteristics: 1) temporal positions of target moments do not match the temporal biases of queries; 2) spatial contents and short-term temporal motions within target moments are consistent with original videos; 3) long-term temporal contexts around target moments are disturbed. Leveraging the three characteristics of pseudo videos, we design two auxiliary tasks to suppress the effect of temporal biases on the final reasoning and strengthen the grounding model's perception ability on visual contents.

Formally, for each video-query pair (V, Q) in the training set, we construct a triplet $(V, \bar{V}, Q)$ as the input. $\bar{V} = \{\bar{v}_t\}_{t=1}^{T}$ denotes the generated pseudo video and the corresponding timestamps of the target moment is $(\bar{\tau}^s, \bar{\tau}^e)$. Pseudo video $\bar{V}$ has the same length as original video V.

3.3 Framework Architecture

As shown in Fig. 3, our model consists of a grounding model, a cross-modal semantic matching module, and a temporal order discriminator. The grounding model predicts the locations of target moments. The latter two modules aim to address two auxiliary tasks, cross-modal matching and temporal order discrimination, respectively. The cross-modal semantic matching module predicts the relevance to the query for each video frame. And the predicted frame-level relevance scores will be used to gate the encoded video features in the span predictor. The temporal order discriminator predicts whether the input video is in correct order. The three modules share a video encoder so that the auxiliary tasks can promote the grounding model training.

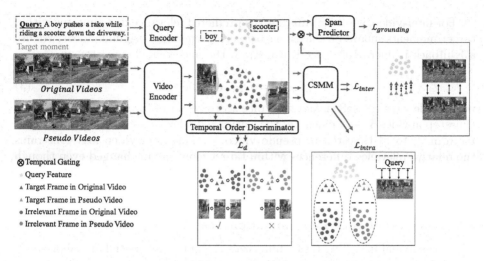

Fig. 3. An overview of our proposed framework with two auxiliary tasks. Video and query encoder encodes video and language modalities, respectively. The span predictor predicts the boundary scores for each frame. CSMM denotes the cross-modal semantic module, which predicts the relevance to the query for each video frame. We constrain the predict scores for both intra- and inter-video to deeply mine the visual-textual semantics relevance. Temporal order discriminator classifies whether the video moment sequence is in correct order.

3.4 Cross-Modal Matching Task

The cross-modal matching task aims to strengthen the visual-textual matching based on the content consistency between pseudo and original videos. We design two losses to constrain the predicted relevance scores for intra- and inter-video, respectively. For intra-video, the cross-modal semantic matching module should discriminate which frames are semantically related to the query for both pseudo and original videos. We implement this through two binary cross-entropy losses,

$$\mathcal{L}_{\mathrm{BCE}}(\boldsymbol{V}) = -\sum_{\boldsymbol{v}_t}^{V} p(\boldsymbol{v}_t)\log(c(\boldsymbol{v}_t)) + (1 - p(\boldsymbol{v}_t))\log(1 - c(\boldsymbol{v}_t)), \qquad (1)$$

$$\mathcal{L}_{intra} = \frac{1}{2}(\mathcal{L}_{\mathrm{BCE}}(\boldsymbol{V}) + \mathcal{L}_{\mathrm{BCE}}(\bar{\boldsymbol{V}})), \qquad (2)$$

where $p(\boldsymbol{v}_t)$ is set to 1 if frame $\boldsymbol{v}_t$ is within the target moments and 0 for otherwise, $c(\boldsymbol{v}_t)$ denotes the predicted cross-modal relevance scores for frame $\boldsymbol{v}_t$ with sigmoid activation. For the same query, target frames in pseudo and original videos may be at different temporal positions. Thus the model has to mine visual contents semantically matching the query. Since the long-term temporal context in videos may be incorrect, this loss encourages the model to reason cross-modal relevance more based on spatial contents and short-term temporal motions.

For inter-video, we constrain that the predicted relevance distributions within target moments should be consistent between pseudo and original videos. We use a Kullback-Leibler divergence to constrain the fine-grained consistency,

$$\mathcal{L}_{inter} = D_{\mathrm{KL}}(\boldsymbol{c} \parallel \bar{\boldsymbol{c}}), \tag{3}$$

where $\boldsymbol{c}$ denotes the softmaxed relevance score vector of frames $\boldsymbol{v}_t$ from τ^s to τ^e timestep in video $\boldsymbol{V}$ and $\bar{\boldsymbol{c}}$ denotes the softmaxed relevance score vector of frames $\bar{\boldsymbol{v}}_t$ from $\bar{\tau}^s$ to $\bar{\tau}^e$ timestep in pseudo video $\bar{\boldsymbol{V}}$. This inter-video loss constrains the relative relevance differences within target moments unchanged even though the external temporal context is changed. Thus this loss further emphasizes the impact of spatial and short-term temporal motion features.

3.5   Temporal Order Discrimination Task

The cross-modal matching task emphasizes the impact of spatial and short-term temporal motion features in final prediction, but we wish the grounding model is capable of understanding the long-term temporal contexts, which is important for temporal grounding task [17,44,59,60]. However, some methods [12,17,45, 60] learn the potential temporal position information during context capturing and thus suffer the temporal bias problem [37,51]. To this end, we introduce a temporal order discrimination task to guide explicitly the learning of long-term temporal contexts. This task aims to discriminate whether the input video is in correct temporal order. Unlike the existing temporal order tasks [10,49] that focus on the order of frames sampled from a short-span action, we design a task to focus on the long-term temporal context. Specifically, given a video-query pair, we divide the video into three parts: the target moment, the moment before the target moment, and the moment after the target moment, and ask whether the three moments are correctly ordered. We determine the supervision for this task based on the video type, i.e., we suppose that the orders of the original videos are correct and the ones of the pseudo videos are incorrect. This task is trained by a cross-entropy loss, which is denoted as $\mathcal{L}_d$.

$$L_d = -\sum_{c=1}^{C} y_{V,c} \log o_c(V) - \sum_{c=1}^{C} y_{\bar{V},c} \log o_c(\bar{V}) \tag{4}$$

where C denotes the video categories (original or pseudo), y is groundtruth label and $o_c(V)$ denotes the softmaxed prediction score of video V for category c.

3.6   Span-Based Grounding Model

We apply a span-based grounding model [14] as our baseline model. It applies a typical span-based architecture, consisting of a query encoder, a video encoder, and a span predictor[1]. Query encoder models the sentence query with multi-layered bidirectional LSTM with pre-trained language model (GloVe [38])

---

[1] As the grounding model is not our key contribution, more details about the grounding network and inference stage are provided in our supplementary material.

embeddings as input. The encoded word-level embeddings and sentence-level representation are denoted as $W = \{\dot{w}_n\}_{n=1}^{N}$ and s, respectively. The video encoder is guided by the query to encode video features over time. Different from [14], we only use the word-level features W to guide the video encoding.

$$W, s = \text{QueryEncoder}(Q), \quad \dot{V} = \text{VideoEncoder}(V, W). \tag{5}$$

Each encoded frame feature $\dot{v}$ is concatenated with the sentence representation s and gated by the cross-modal relevance score $c(v_t)$ before feed forward to the span predictor. The span predictor predicts the boundary scores $S_{start}(t)$, $S_{end}(t)$ for each frame.

$$\begin{aligned} S_{start}(t) &= \text{StartPredictor}(c(v_t)(\dot{v}_t||s)), \\ S_{end}(t) &= \text{EndPredictor}(c(v_t)(\dot{v}_t||s)). \end{aligned} \tag{6}$$

The start and end scores are normalized with SoftMax to obtain $P_{start}(t)$, $P_{end}(t)$, and trained using negative log-likelihood loss:

$$\mathcal{L}_g = -\log(P_{start}(t^s)) - \log(P_{end}(t^e)), \tag{7}$$

where t^s, t^e are the ground-truth start and end frame indices for the original video, respectively. The ground-truth frame indices (t^s, t^e) are mapped from the ground-truth time values (τ^s, τ^e).

3.7 Cross-Modal Semantic Matching Module

The cross-modal semantic matching module predicts the relevance to the query for each video frame. The module is implemented by a multi-layered perceptron (MLP) with relu activation in hidden layers. We also use concatenation as the cross-model interaction method,

$$c(v_t) = W_2^c \text{relu}(W_1^c(\dot{v}_t||s) + b_1^c) + b_2^c, \tag{8}$$

where W_1^c, W_2^c, b_1^c and b_2^c are the learnable parameters of MLP and shared across all time steps. We also apply a temporal gating on the encoded video features using the predicted relevance scores to highlight the impact of the matching results on the final reasoning, as shown in Eq. (6).

3.8 Temporal Order Discriminator

Given a moment tuple $(M_1 = \{\dot{v}_1, \cdots, \dot{v}_{\tau^s-1}\}, M_2 = \{\dot{v}_{\tau^s}, \cdots, \dot{v}_{\tau^e}\}, M_2 = \{\dot{v}_{\tau^e+1}, \cdots, \dot{v}_T\})$, we first obtain the moment-level representations for these moments by average pooling the encoded frame features within the moments,

$$m_1 = \text{pooling}(M_1), \quad m_2 = \text{pooling}(M_2), \quad m_3 = \text{pooling}(M_3). \tag{9}$$

We mainly focus on the contexts around the target moment (M_2) to reason the order correctness. We concatenate the paired moment representations and use two parallel fully-connected layers with shared parameters to obtain the context information h_1, h_2, respectively,

$$h_1 = \text{relu}(W_1^o(m_1||m_2 + b_1^o)), \quad h_2 = \text{relu}(W_1^o(m_2||m_3 + b_1^o)). \quad (10)$$

Then we concatenate the context information with the target moment representation and predict the classification scores,

$$o(V) = W_2^o(m_2||h_1||h_2) + b_2^o, \quad (11)$$

where W_1^o, W_2^o, b_1^o and b_2^o are the learnable parameters of fully-connected layers and shared across videos. To prevent the learning of temporal biases, we reason the order correctness only based on the content relevance and do not introduce any global temporal position information. The position information contained in the encoded frame features is diluted by the average-pooling operation.

3.9   Training Objective

The final training loss is the weighted summarization of the loss of each module,

$$\mathcal{L} = \mathcal{L}_g + \lambda_1 \mathcal{L}_{intra} + \lambda_2 \mathcal{L}_{inter} + \lambda_3 \mathcal{L}_d. \quad (12)$$

4   Experiments

4.1   Datasets

Charades-STA. Charades-STA is built on Charades dataset [40] by [11]. The videos in this dataset are mainly about indoor activities. The average length of videos and annotated moments are 30s and 8s, respectively.

ActivityNet Captions. ActivityNet Captions is built on ActivityNet [15], which is a large-scale dataset of human activities based on YouTube videos. The average length of videos and the annotated moments are 117 s and 36 s, respectively.

4.2   Dataset Splits

In the original splits of the two datasets, the training and test sets have similar temporal biases. Thus the methods that learn the temporal biases in the training set could also perform well on the test set [37,52]. To eliminate the impact of temporal bias problem on evaluation performance, we perform experiments on the re-divided splits[2] proposed by [52]. In the re-divided splits, each dataset is re-divided into four sets: training, validation(val), test-iid, and test-ood. The temporal locations of all samples in the training, val, and test-iid satisfy the independent and identical distribution, and the samples in test-ood are out-of-distribution. Therefore, it is useless to exploit the temporal biases in training

---

[2] https://github.com/yytzsy/grounding_changing_distribution.

Table 1. The statistics of the number of videos and query-moment pairs in different datasets and splits.

Dataset	Original splits			Re-divided splits		
	Split	Videos	Pairs	Split	Videos	Pairs
Charades-STA	Training	5,338	12,408	Training	4,564	11,071
	Test	1,334	3,720	Val	333	859
				Test-iid	333	823
				Test-ood	1,442	3,375
ActivityNet captions	Training	10,009	37,421	Training	10,984	51,415
	Val	4,917	17,505	Val	746	3,521
	Test	4,885	17,031	Test-iid	746	3,443
				Test-ood	2,450	13,578

set to make predictions on test-ood set. The test-ood sets on both datasets have similar vocabulary distributions to the training set, which means that the difference of the temporal distribution between the training and test-ood sets is the main challenge of the re-divided splits. The sample statistics of the two splits are reported in Table 1.

4.3 Experimental Settings

Metrics. Following the conventions, we adopt R@n, IoU $= \theta$ and mIoU as evaluation metrics. R@n, IoU $= \theta$ represents the percentage of testing samples having at least one result whose IoU with ground truth is larger than θ in top-n localized results. mIoU represents the average IoU over all testing samples. Following previous works [13,45,58], we use $n = 1$ and $\theta \in \{0.3, 0.5, 0.7\}$.

Implementation. For natural language, we use 300d Glove [38] vectors as word embeddings. For the words not in the vocabulary of Glove, we generate their embeddings randomly. For video modality, we use 1024d I3D feature pre-trained on Kinetics dataset [2] or 500d C3D feature [41] pre-trained on Sports-1M dataset [20] as the initial frame features, and downsample the videos at a frame rate of 1 frame per second. For each training epoch, we will re-generate a pseudo video for each video-query pair. We train the model with a batch size of 32 for 30 epochs for all datasets using Adam optimizer with an initial learning rate of 0.001. We set λ_1, λ_2 and λ_3 in Eq. 12 to 1, 1, 1, respectively. More details are provided in supplementary material.

4.4 Comparison with State-of-the-Arts

We compare our methods with the recently state-of-the-art methods and our baseline, which only contains a span-based grounding model [14] and is only supervised by the grounding loss $\mathcal{L}_g$. We first analyze the competitors' performance on the re-divided splits. Then we follow [37] and perform a test to check whether the competitors suffer the temporal bias problem. We also show the performance comparison on the original splits.

Table 2. Comparison on Charades-CD split using I3D features.

Model	Test-iid				Test-ood			
	IoU = 0.3	IoU = 0.5	IoU = 0.7	mIoU	IoU = 0.3	IoU = 0.5	IoU = 0.7	mIoU
2D-TAN [60]	60.15	49.09	26.85	42.73	52.79	35.88	13.91	34.22
LG [34]	64.52	51.28	28.68	45.16	59.32	42.90	19.29	39.43
DRN [55]	53.22	42.04	23.32	28.21	45.87	31.11	15.17	23.05
VSLNet [58]	61.48	43.26	28.43	42.92	54.61	34.10	17.87	36.34
DCM [51]	67.27	55.81	37.30	48.74	60.89	45.47	22.70	40.99
Baseline	66.34	50.55	34.26	46.81	58.96	38.22	20.50	39.52
Ours	**70.72**	**57.59**	**37.79**	**50.93**	**64.95**	**46.67**	**27.08**	**44.30**

Table 3. Comparison on ActivityNet-CD split using I3D features.

Model	test-iid				test-ood			
	IoU = 0.3	IoU = 0.5	IoU = 0.7	mIoU	IoU = 0.3	IoU = 0.5	IoU = 0.7	mIoU
2D-TAN [60]	60.56	46.59	30.55	44.99	40.13	22.01	10.34	28.31
LG [34]	61.63	46.41	29.28	44.62	40.78	23.85	10.96	28.46
VSLNet [58]	62.71	47.81	29.07	46.33	38.30	20.03	10.29	28.18
DCM [51]	60.15	47.26	31.97	45.20	39.39	22.32	11.22	28.08
Baseline	60.56	44.58	27.42	44.28	38.78	21.39	10.86	28.41
Ours	**63.29**	**48.07**	**32.15**	**47.03**	**42.08**	**24.57**	**13.21**	**30.45**

Comparison on the Re-divided Splits. Table 2 and Table 3 summarize the results on the splits Charades-CD and ActivityNet-CD, respectively. For a fair comparison, all methods use the same pre-trained visual features. Best results are in **bold** and second-best underlined. Observed that all methods have a significant performance drop on the test-ood compared to the test-iid on both datasets. The change of the temporal distribution on the test-ood set challenges the model's generalization ability. Compared with the state-of-the-art methods, our method performs best over all evaluation metrics on both test sets and on both datasets. Particularly, our method outperforms all methods by clear margins on the test-ood splits, especially in the metrics IoU = 0.7 and mIoU. It shows that our method has a stronger generalization ability against the temporal distributions. Besides, observed that our method improves the baseline on both test sets, but we achieve more relative improvements on test-ood set than test-iid set, e.g., 22.11% v.s. 13.93% in IoU = 0.5 on Charades-CD and 14.87% v.s. 7.83% on ActivityNet-CD. It shows the effectiveness of our method on strengthening the model's generalization ability against the different temporal distributions.

Sanity Check on Visual Input. Suffering temporal bias problem, a model can ignore the visual input but perform well on the evaluation metrics on the original splits. Thus, same as [37], we perform a test on some state-of-the-art competitors[3] to show how much these models take input videos into account for prediction. Specifically, we divide input videos into short segments and randomly reorder them before evaluating the models. This randomization messes up the correspondence between input videos and ground truth temporal locations. If

---

[3] We used the models with trained parameters provided by their authors if available.

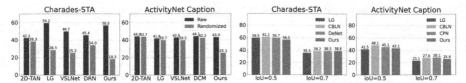

(a) R@1 (IoU=0.5) scores for competitors when the raw input videos and randomized ones are fed into these models.

(b) Comparison with the state-of-the-arts on the original splits of Charades-STA and ActivityNet Captions.

Fig. 4. Sanity check on visual input (a) and comparison on the original splits (b)

Table 4. Comparison of different usage of pseudo videos on test-ood sets.

Methods	Charades-CD				ActivityNet-CD			
	IoU = 0.3	IoU=0.5	IoU = 0.7	mIoU	IoU = 0.3	IoU = 0.5	IoU = 0.7	mIoU
Baseline	58.96	38.22	20.50	39.52	38.78	21.39	10.86	28.41
Baseline+DataAug	58.61	37.40	19.82	39.06	40.74	22.27	12.16	29.59
Baseline+CSMM+DataAug	59.22	38.45	21.41	39.84	28.42	13.36	6.13	20.29
Ours	64.95	46.67	27.08	44.30	42.08	24.57	13.21	30.45

a model makes the prediction based on visual input, the performance should drop significantly by the randomization; otherwise, we can conclude that the model doesn't make use of the visual input during reasoning. Figure 4a shows the results for the competitors and our method. On Charades-STA, all state-of-the-arts except 2D-TAN [60] and DRN [55] show significant performance drops for randomized videos. Among all competitors, our method performs the most significant drop, which demonstrates the effectiveness of our method for addressing temporal bias problem on this dataset. On ActivityNet Captions, all state-of-the-arts including DCM [51] achieve similar performance using randomized videos to the raw ones, which shows that these methods actually do not use the visual input and over-rely on the temporal biases. Our method performs a clear drop in this test on ActivityNet Captions, which validates that our method can make the model focus more on the visual content and mitigate the reliance on the temporal biases on this dataset.

Comparison on the Original Splits. We also compare our method with the state-of-the-arts [26,34,63,64] on the original splits of the two datasets. For a fair comparison, our method uses i3d features on Charades-STA and c3d on ActivityNet Captions. As shown in Fig. 4b, our method achieves competitive performance to the state-of-the-arts on both datasets, which shows that our method can address the temporal bias problem without loss in grounding accuracy.

4.5   Ablation Study

Pseudo Videos. We study the effect of the pseudo videos. We first test applying the data augmentation strategy based on the baseline, i.e., treating the pseudo

Table 5. Ablation study of loss terms on test-ood sets.

Row	Loss Terms				Charades-CD				ActivityNet-CD			
	$\mathcal{L}_g$	$\mathcal{L}_{intra}$	$\mathcal{L}_{inter}$	$\mathcal{L}_d$	IoU = 0.3	IoU = 0.5	IoU = 0.7	mIoU	IoU = 0.3	IoU = 0.5	IoU = 0.7	mIoU
1	✓				55.03	28.91	14.08	35.05	37.30	20.30	10.42	26.75
2	✓	✓			62.34	44.60	25.41	42.66	40.39	22.45	11.51	29.77
3	✓		✓		55.39	33.13	17.23	36.36	34.85	15.80	7.66	26.27
4	✓			✓	55.91	6.16	2.79	30.47	34.84	15.65	7.95	26.43
5	✓	✓		✓	62.96	45.36	26.73	43.40	41.49	23.12	12.55	30.04
6	✓	✓	✓		62.79	44.23	25.90	42.93	41.33	23.28	12.53	30.04
7	✓	✓	✓	✓	64.95	46.67	27.08	44.30	42.08	24.57	13.21	30.45

and original videos equally as training samples. Then we add the cross-modal matching module and use the frame-level relevance scores to temporally gating the encoded video features. The relevance scores are supervised by Eq. (1). As shown in Table 4, after applying data augmentation, there are slight improvements from the baseline on ActivityNet-CD while the performance is inferior to the baseline on Charades-CD. After adding CSMM, there are slight improvements on Charades-CD but a significant performance drop on ActivityNet-CD. On the contrary, our method improves the performance from the baseline with clear margins on both datasets. The comparisons validate the infeasibility of shuffled videos as augmented training samples and the superiority of our method.

Loss Terms. We analyze the impact of each loss term and their combinations. Table 5 summarizes the results, and some reveal points are listed as follows.

(1) $\mathcal{L}_{intra}$ leads to the main performance boosts on test-ood sets (comparing Rows 1, 2 and 7). It validates our design of using the content consistency between shuffled and original videos to mitigate the reliance on temporal biases.

(2) Without $\mathcal{L}_{intra}$, the improvement of adding $\mathcal{L}_{inter}$ is limited (comparing Rows 1 and 3). It means that only constraining the relative relevance differences within target moments cannot highlight the target moment from the entire video. The combination of $\mathcal{L}_{intra}$ and $\mathcal{L}_{inter}$ can further improve the performance (comparing Rows 2 and 6), which validates the effectiveness of our design of contraining the cross-modal relevance scores between shuffled and original videos.

(3) Only adding $\mathcal{L}_d$ leads to performance drops on both datasets, especially on the high IoU (comparing Rows 1 and 4). The baseline over-relies on memorizing temporal biases but the temporal order discrimination task restricts the learning of temporal position information. So the baseline model degrades to predict long-span predictions[4]. After adding the cross-modal matching task, the supervision guides the model to focus on the short-term visual contents semantically matching queries and thus leads to performance boosts (Rows 5 and 7).

---

[4] The length distribution of predictions can be found in our supplementary material.

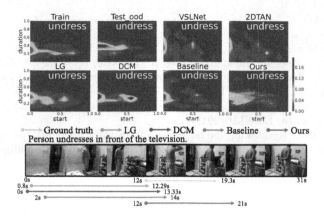

Fig. 5. Top is the temporal distribution comparison of the word 'undress' on Charades-CD. Color represents value of probability. Bottom is an example of grounding results for a query containing the word 'underss'.

Visualization. We show a qualitative example on Charades-CD to show how models suffer the temporal bias problem and the effect of our method in Fig. 5. We first show the temporal distribution comparison of the word 'undress' between the training/test_ood sets and the prediction results of grounding models on test_ood set. Observed that the competitor models have significant and similar biases to the training set while our model does not. Then we show a test samples of the word 'undress' and the grounding results of different methods. In this sample video, groundtruth target moment does not start at the beginning. But most models (LG [34], DCM [51], and our baseline) still make the predictions fitting the biases in training set. With the training of our framework, we can effectively mitigate the baseline's reliance on biases and turn the model's attention back to visual contents to make correct predictions. We provide more qualitative examples in our supplementary material.

5 Conclusion

This paper proposes a novel training framework for temporal grounding models to leverage shuffled videos to address the temporal bias problem. We propose two auxiliary tasks to suppress the effect of temporal biases and strengthen the model's perception ability on visual contents. Extensive experiments on Charades-STA and ActivityNet Captions demonstrate the effectiveness of our method on strengthening the generalization ability of the grounding model and mitigating the reliance on temporal biases.

Acknowledgement. This work was supported in part by the National Natural Science Foundation of China under Grants (62071067, 62001054, 62101064, 62171057), in part by the Ministry of Education and China Mobile Joint Fund (MCM20200202), China Postdoctoral Science Foundation under Grant 2022M710468, Beijing University of Posts and Telecommunications-China Mobile Research Institute Joint Innovation Center.

References

1. Cao, M., Chen, L., Shou, M.Z., Zhang, C., Zou, Y.: On pursuit of designing multimodal transformer for video grounding. In: EMNLP, pp. 9810–9823 (2021)
2. Carreira, J., Zisserman, A.: Quo vadis, action recognition? A new model and the kinetics dataset. In: CVPR (2017)
3. Chen, J., Chen, X., Ma, L., Jie, Z., Chua, T.: Temporally grounding natural sentence in video. In: EMNLP (2018)
4. Chen, L., et al.: Rethinking the bottom-up framework for query-based video localization. In: Proceedings of the AAAI Conference on Artificial Intelligence, vol. 34, pp. 10551–10558 (2020)
5. Chen, S., Jiang, W., Liu, W., Jiang, Y.-G.: Learning modality interaction for temporal sentence localization and event captioning in videos. In: Vedaldi, A., Bischof, H., Brox, T., Frahm, J.-M. (eds.) ECCV 2020. LNCS, vol. 12349, pp. 333–351. Springer, Cham (2020). https://doi.org/10.1007/978-3-030-58548-8_20
6. Chen, S., Jiang, Y.: Semantic proposal for activity localization in videos via sentence query. In: AAAI (2019)
7. Chen, S., Jiang, Y.-G.: Hierarchical visual-textual graph for temporal activity localization via language. In: Vedaldi, A., Bischof, H., Brox, T., Frahm, J.-M. (eds.) ECCV 2020. LNCS, vol. 12365, pp. 601–618. Springer, Cham (2020). https://doi.org/10.1007/978-3-030-58565-5_36
8. Chen, Y.W., Tsai, Y.H., Yang, M.H.: End-to-end multi-modal video temporal grounding. In: NIPS 34 (2021)
9. Choi, J., Sharma, G., Schulter, S., Huang, J.: Shuffle and attend: video domain adaptation. In: Computer Vision - ECCV 2020–16th European Conference, Glasgow, UK, 23–28 August 2020, Proceedings, Part XII, pp. 678–695 (2020). https://doi.org/10.1007/978-3-030-58610-2_40
10. Fernando, B., Bilen, H., Gavves, E., Gould, S.: Self-supervised video representation learning with odd-one-out networks. In: Proceedings of the IEEE Conference on Computer Vision and Pattern Recognition, pp. 3636–3645 (2017)
11. Gao, J., Sun, C., Yang, Z., Nevatia, R.: TALL: temporal activity localization via language query. In: ICCV (2017)
12. Gao, J., Xu, C.: Fast video moment retrieval. In: ICCV, pp. 1523–1532 (2021)
13. Ghosh, S., Agarwal, A., Parekh, Z., Hauptmann, A.G.: Excl: extractive clip localization using natural language descriptions. In: NAACL (2019)
14. Hao, J., Sun, H., Ren, P., Wang, J., Qi, Q., Liao, J.: Query-aware video encoder for video moment retrieval. Neurocomputing **483**, 72–86 (2022)
15. Heilbron, F.C., Escorcia, V., Ghanem, B., Niebles, J.C.: Activitynet: a large-scale video benchmark for human activity understanding. In: CVPR (2015)
16. Hendricks, L.A., Wang, O., Shechtman, E., Sivic, J., Darrell, T., Russell, B.C.: Localizing moments in video with natural language. In: ICCV (2017)
17. Hendricks, L.A., Wang, O., Shechtman, E., Sivic, J., Darrell, T., Russell, B.C.: Localizing moments in video with temporal language. In: EMNLP (2018)
18. Hou, Z., Ngo, C.W., Chan, W.: Conquer: contextual query-aware ranking for video corpus moment retrieval (2021). In: ACM MM, pp. 20–24 (2021)
19. Ji, S., Xu, W., Yang, M., Yu, K.: 3d convolutional neural networks for human action recognition. In: Proceedings of the 27th International Conference on Machine Learning (ICML-10), 21–24 June 2010, Haifa, Israel, pp. 495–502 (2010)
20. Karpathy, A., Toderici, G., Shetty, S., Leung, T., Sukthankar, R., Li, F.: Large-scale video classification with convolutional neural networks. In: CVPR, pp. 1725–1732 (2014)

21. Lee, H., Huang, J., Singh, M., Yang, M.: Unsupervised representation learning by sorting sequences. In: IEEE International Conference on Computer Vision, ICCV 2017, Venice, Italy, 22–29 October 2017, pp. 667–676 (2017)
22. Lin, Z., Zhao, Z., Zhang, Z., Zhang, Z., Cai, D.: Moment retrieval via cross-modal interaction networks with query reconstruction. In: IEEE TIP (2020)
23. Liu, B., Yeung, S., Chou, E., Huang, D., Fei-Fei, L., Niebles, J.C.: Temporal modular networks for retrieving complex compositional activities in videos. In: ECCV (2018)
24. Liu, D., Qu, X., Di, X., Cheng, Y., Xu, Z., Zhou, P.: Memory-guided semantic learning network for temporal sentence grounding. arXiv preprint arXiv:2201.00454 (2022)
25. Liu, D., Qu, X., Dong, J., Zhou, P.: Adaptive proposal generation network for temporal sentence localization in videos. In: EMNLP, pp. 9292–9301 (2021)
26. Liu, D., et al.: Context-aware biaffine localizing network for temporal sentence grounding. In: CVPR, pp. 11235–11244 (2021)
27. Liu, D., Qu, X., Liu, X.Y., Dong, J., Zhou, P., Xu, Z.: Jointly cross-and self-modal graph attention network for query-based moment localization. In: ACM MM (2020)
28. Liu, D., Qu, X., Zhou, P.: Progressively guide to attend: an iterative alignment framework for temporal sentence grounding. In: EMNLP, pp. 9302–9311 (2021)
29. Liu, D., Qu, X., Zhou, P., Liu, Y.: Exploring motion and appearance information for temporal sentence grounding. arXiv preprint arXiv:2201.00457 (2022)
30. Liu, M., Wang, X., Nie, L., He, X., Chen, B., Chua, T.: Attentive moment retrieval in videos. In: SIGIR (2018)
31. Liu, M., Wang, X., Nie, L., Tian, Q., Chen, B., Chua, T.: Cross-modal moment localization in videos. In: ACM MM (2018)
32. Lu, C., Chen, L., Tan, C., Li, X., Xiao, J.: DEBUG: a dense bottom-up grounding approach for natural language video localization. In: EMNLP (2019)
33. Misra, I., Zitnick, C.L., Hebert, M.: Shuffle and learn: unsupervised learning using temporal order verification. In: European Conference on Computer Vision, pp. 527–544. Springer (2016). https://doi.org/10.1007/978-3-319-46448-0_32
34. Mun, J., Cho, M., Han, B.: Local-global video-text interactions for temporal grounding. In: CVPR (2020)
35. Nan, G., et al.: Interventional video grounding with dual contrastive learning. In: CVPR, pp. 2765–2775 (2021)
36. Ng, J.Y., Hausknecht, M.J., Vijayanarasimhan, S., Vinyals, O., Monga, R., Toderici, G.: Beyond short snippets: deep networks for video classification. In: CVPR, pp. 4694–4702 (2015)
37. Otani, M., Nakashima, Y., Rahtu, E., Heikkilä, J.: Uncovering hidden challenges in query-based video moment retrieval. In: BMVC (2020)
38. Pennington, J., Socher, R., Manning, C.D.: Glove: Global vectors for word representation. In: EMNLP (2014)
39. Rodriguez, C., Marrese-Taylor, E., Saleh, F.S., Li, H., Gould, S.: Proposal-free temporal moment localization of a natural-language query in video using guided attention. In: WACV (2020)
40. Sigurdsson, G.A., Varol, G., Wang, X., Farhadi, A., Laptev, I., Gupta, A.: Hollywood in homes: crowdsourcing data collection for activity understanding. In: ECCV (2016)
41. Tran, D., Bourdev, L.D., Fergus, R., Torresani, L., Paluri, M.: Learning spatiotemporal features with 3d convolutional networks. In: ICCV, pp. 4489–4497 (2015)

42. Tran, D., Wang, H., Torresani, L., Ray, J., LeCun, Y., Paluri, M.: A closer look at spatiotemporal convolutions for action recognition. In: CVPR, pp. 6450–6459 (2018)
43. Vaswani, A., et al.: Attention is all you need. In: NIPS (2017)
44. Wang, H., Zha, Z.J., Li, L., Liu, D., Luo, J.: Structured multi-level interaction network for video moment localization via language query. In: CVPR, pp. 7026–7035 (2021)
45. Wang, J., Ma, L., Jiang, W.: Temporally grounding language queries in videos by contextual boundary-aware prediction. In: AAAI (2020)
46. Wang, L., Tong, Z., Ji, B., Wu, G.: TDN: temporal difference networks for efficient action recognition. In: IEEE Conference on Computer Vision and Pattern Recognition, CVPR 2021, virtual, 19–25 June 2021, pp. 1895–1904 (2021)
47. Wang, X., Girshick, R.B., Gupta, A., He, K.: Non-local neural networks. In: 2018 IEEE Conference on Computer Vision and Pattern Recognition, CVPR 2018, Salt Lake City, UT, USA, 18–22 June 2018, pp. 7794–7803 (2018)
48. Xiao, S., et al.: Boundary proposal network for two-stage natural language video localization. In: Thirty-Fifth AAAI Conference on Artificial Intelligence, AAAI 2021, Thirty-Third Conference on Innovative Applications of Artificial Intelligence, IAAI 2021, The Eleventh Symposium on Educational Advances in Artificial Intelligence, EAAI 2021, Virtual Event, 2–9 February 2021, pp. 2986–2994 (2021)
49. Xu, D., Xiao, J., Zhao, Z., Shao, J., Xie, D., Zhuang, Y.: Self-supervised spatiotemporal learning via video clip order prediction. In: IEEE Conference on Computer Vision and Pattern Recognition, CVPR 2019, Long Beach, CA, USA, 16–20 June 2019, pp. 10334–10343 (2019)
50. Xu, H., He, K., Plummer, B.A., Sigal, L., Sclaroff, S., Saenko, K.: Multilevel language and vision integration for text-to-clip retrieval. In: AAAI (2019)
51. Yang, X., Feng, F., Ji, W., Wang, M., Chua, T.: Deconfounded video moment retrieval with causal intervention. In: SIGIR 2021: The 44th International ACM SIGIR Conference on Research and Development in Information Retrieval, Virtual Event, Canada, 11–15 July 2021, pp. 1–10 (2021)
52. Yuan, Y., Lan, X., Chen, L., Liu, W., Wang, X., Zhu, W.: A closer look at temporal sentence grounding in videos: datasets and metrics. CoRR **abs/2101.09028** (2021). https://arxiv.org/abs/2101.09028
53. Yuan, Y., Ma, L., Wang, J., Liu, W., Zhu, W.: Semantic conditioned dynamic modulation for temporal sentence grounding in videos. In: NIPS (2019)
54. Yuan, Y., Mei, T., Zhu, W.: To find where you talk: temporal sentence localization in video with attention based location regression. In: AAAI (2019)
55. Zeng, R., Xu, H., Huang, W., Chen, P., Tan, M., Gan, C.: Dense regression network for video grounding. In: CVPR (2020)
56. Zhang, D., Dai, X., Wang, X., Wang, Y., Davis, L.S.: MAN: moment alignment network for natural language moment retrieval via iterative graph adjustment. In: CVPR (2019)
57. Zhang, H., Sun, A., Jing, W., Zhen, L., Zhou, J.T., Goh, R.S.M.: Natural language video localization: a revisit in span-based question answering framework. In: IEEE Transactions on Pattern Analysis and Machine Intelligence (2021)
58. Zhang, H., Sun, A., Jing, W., Zhou, J.T.: Span-based localizing network for natural language video localization. In: ACL (2020)
59. Zhang, M., et al.: Multi-stage aggregated transformer network for temporal language localization in videos. In: CVPR, pp. 12669–12678 (2021)
60. Zhang, S., Peng, H., Fu, J., Luo, J.: Learning 2d temporal adjacent networks for moment localization with natural language. In: AAAI (2020)

61. Zhang, Z., Zhao, Z., Zhang, Z., Lin, Z., Wang, Q., Hong, R.: Temporal textual localization in video via adversarial bi-directional interaction networks. In: IEEE TMM (2020)
62. Zhang, Z., Lin, Z., Zhao, Z., Xiao, Z.: Cross-modal interaction networks for query-based moment retrieval in videos. In: Proceedings of the 42nd International ACM SIGIR Conference on Research and Development in Information Retrieval, SIGIR 2019, Paris, France, 21–25 July 2019, pp. 655–664 (2019)
63. Zhao, Y., Zhao, Z., Zhang, Z., Lin, Z.: Cascaded prediction network via segment tree for temporal video grounding. In: CVPR, pp. 4197–4206 (2021)
64. Zhou, H., Zhang, C., Luo, Y., Chen, Y., Hu, C.: Embracing uncertainty: decoupling and de-bias for robust temporal grounding. In: CVPR, pp. 8445–8454 (2021)

Reliable Visual Question Answering: Abstain Rather Than Answer Incorrectly

Spencer Whitehead[1(✉)], Suzanne Petryk[1,2(✉)], Vedaad Shakib[2],
Joseph Gonzalez[2], Trevor Darrell[2], Anna Rohrbach[2], and Marcus Rohrbach[1]

[1] Meta AI, Menlo Park, USA
srw5@meta.com, spetryk@meta.com
[2] UC Berkeley, Berkeley, USA

Abstract. Machine learning has advanced dramatically, narrowing the accuracy gap to humans in multimodal tasks like visual question answering (VQA). However, while humans can say *"I don't know"* when they are uncertain (i.e., *abstain* from answering a question), such ability has been largely neglected in multimodal research, despite the importance of this problem to the usage of VQA in real settings. In this work, we promote a problem formulation for *reliable VQA*, where we prefer abstention over providing an incorrect answer. We first enable abstention capabilities for several VQA models, and analyze both their *coverage*, the portion of questions answered, and *risk*, the error on that portion. For that, we explore several abstention approaches. We find that although the best performing models achieve over 71% accuracy on the VQA v2 dataset, introducing the option to abstain by directly using a model's softmax scores limits them to answering less than 8% of the questions to achieve a low risk of error (i.e., 1%). This motivates us to utilize a multimodal selection function to directly estimate the correctness of the predicted answers, which we show can increase the coverage by, for example, 2.4× from 6.8% to 16.3% at 1% risk. While it is important to analyze both coverage and risk, these metrics have a trade-off which makes comparing VQA models challenging. To address this, we also propose an *Effective Reliability* metric for VQA that places a larger cost on incorrect answers compared to abstentions. This new problem formulation, metric, and analysis for VQA provide the groundwork for building effective and reliable VQA models that have the self-awareness to abstain if and only if they don't know the answer. Code and Models: https://github.com/facebookresearch/reliable_vqa.

1 Introduction

Visual Question Answering (VQA) is an important task and one core application of VQA is to provide a multimodal assistant, such as one that can answer questions to help with daily tasks for a user with visual impairments [3,24].

S. Whitehead and S. Petryk—Equal Contribution.

Supplementary Information The online version contains supplementary material available at https://doi.org/10.1007/978-3-031-20059-5_9.

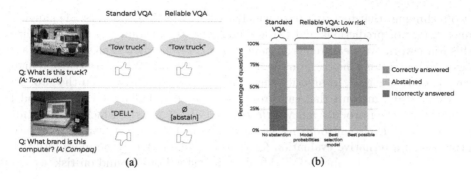

Fig. 1. In the standard VQA problem, a model must answer all questions, even if it is likely to produce errors that could mislead a user, e.g., (a). A reliable VQA model, on the other hand, operates at *low risk* by having the option to abstain from answering if uncertain. In (b), at 1% risk of error, a SoTA model [55] can answer only ~7% of questions when using vanilla model probabilities to choose when to abstain. Using a learned, multimodal selection function to estimate confidences can more than double the amount of questions answered, yet there remains much room for improvement (best possible, i.e., perfect abstention).

To provide such utility, users must be able to trust the output of these tools as they may be basing decisions or actions on the output [4,22,44,46]. While improving the accuracy of approaches may be an important factor for trusting models, models are imperfect and will inevitably produce some incorrect answers. In many scenarios, there is a price associated with a model giving an inaccurate answer as it may mislead the user and cause them to make a mistake that could be anywhere from mildly inconvenient to very serious. This is especially true for the example of helping users with visual impairments, since they likely do not have a method of verifying the outputs themselves.

One way to avoid providing incorrect information and misleading users is to *abstain* from making a prediction, as in the framework of selective prediction [10, 15,18,19]. Consider Fig. 1(a): when a model is correct, we naturally would like it to give us an answer. However, when it is unable to do so (e.g., cannot "read" the brand name) or is very uncertain, in many application we may prefer if the model communicated "*I don't know.*", i.e., abstain [25,37]. We say that VQA models are reliable, if they make highly accurate predictions when they choose to answer. Ideally, reliable models should also abstain as little as possible to be effective. Although reliability is often critical for the usage of VQA in real settings, this aspect has not received direct attention in the VQA literature aside from efforts to recognize difficult, unanswerable, or false premise questions [8,24,33,52,58]. Moreover, past efforts on selective prediction have not focused on the multimodal setting, where both an image and a question can be valid or in-distribution when considered independently, yet challenging in tandem.

In this work, we formalize and explore the notion of reliability in VQA. We propose to frame the task as a selective prediction problem [10,15] in which models must either predict an answer or abstain from answering. This requires two techniques that have not been widely explored for VQA models: (1) gauging uncertainty of predictions and (2) learning when to abstain. To operationalize this framework, we measure performance with *coverage* (how many questions are answered) and *risk* (the error on these questions) [15,35]. While low risk and high coverage are the goal, in practice there often is a trade-off between the two. To provide a scalar measure that captures this trade-off and allows for clearer model comparisons, we introduce a new *Effective Reliability* metric, which accounts for abstention while also introducing a cost for giving an incorrect answer. This also provides an alternative evaluation for domains where it may be more intuitive to specify the penalty for an individual error instead of a bound on risk.

Under this framework, we first show that existing VQA approaches leave much room for improvement. In particular, we demonstrate that, for a number of models, the common approach of using the maximum probability to determine abstention [27,35] (by thresholding the softmax scores) limits the model to answering a small fraction of questions with a low risk of error (e.g., answering less than 8% of questions at 1% risk of error), despite having high standard VQA accuracy. This inability to answer a larger number of questions at low risk indicates low utility of the existing VQA models.

To address this, we explore two other approaches: calibration and training a multimodal selection function. We find that calibration often leads to a better risk-coverage trade-off compared to using the original model probabilities. We improve beyond this by training a multimodal selection function that can better learn to predict if a the model's answer is correct, based on intermediate representations as well as the answer from the VQA model. This selection function consistently improves the coverage of different VQA models across varying risks of error, particularly for low levels of risk. However, we show that there is still room to improve the effectiveness of these models (see Fig. 1(b)). Finally, we evaluate VQA models with our new Effective Reliability metric, and see that it correlates with risk/coverage in a meaningful way – the user-defined cost of an error impacts the risk at which the model operates.

In summary, our contributions are: (1) we are the first to analyze and operationalize reliability for multimodal VQA models; (2) we expose the issue of low coverage in VQA models when asked to operate at low risk levels; (3) we explore several methods for incorporating abstention, showing that a simple yet effective multimodal selection function outperforms other methods; (4) we propose a novel *Effective Reliability* metric for this problem, establishing a new benchmark for effective and reliable VQA models.

2   Related Work

VQA Methods. Visual Question Answering (VQA) is a popular task with a plethora of methods proposed in recent years [2,3,7,16,17,30,31,40,42,43,55, 64–66]. To the best of our knowledge, there are no VQA models with a built-in abstention mechanism (i.e., they predict an answer for every image and question pair). We discuss a few exceptions with a non-standard problem statement in the following. Our work analyzes VQA models' reliability by introducing the ability to abstain into several prominent VQA models [31,40,43,55].

Detecting Intrinsic Difficulty. Some prior work on VQA involves the categorization and detection of questions that are intrinsically difficult to answer, regardless of model ability. For example, the VizWiz VQA dataset contains labels for questions which are unanswerable [24] and reasons for annotation entropy, such as low image quality or question ambiguity [5]. [12] define a similar categorization of unanswerable questions in VQA. [58] compute precision/recall based on VQA model confidences and show that these can be reflective of the ambiguities of the ground truth answers. Other work focuses on detecting whether the question incorrectly describes the visual semantics [33,41,45,52]. Identifying intrinsically difficult examples has important implications in active learning, where such examples can stifle the ability of different methods to select useful examples to train on [36]. In this work, we focus on predicting uncertainty specific to a model as opposed to the intrinsic difficulty from data itself. However, in Sect. 5.5, we find that a subset of questions on which a model abstains from answering are ambiguous or unanswerable.

Calibration. In classification settings, calibration typically refers to probabilistic calibration, where the predicted confidence for a given class should be representative of the probability of the prediction being correct [23,27,39,48,49]. One popular parametric method is Platt scaling [49], in which a logistic regression model is trained on classifier outputs on the validation set to return calibrated probabilities. In our work, we explore the effectiveness of vector scaling, a multiclass extension of Platt scaling, for improving selective prediction performance.

Selective Prediction. This refers to when models have the option to abstain from providing a prediction. It is also known as sample rejection [9,10] or selective classification [15]. [13,29,59] propose various related evaluation metrics. [13] assigns cost coefficients to misclassified, abstained, and correctly classified samples. Concurrently with our work, [59] defines reliability as out-of-the-box performance for large-scale pretrained models across many unimodal vision or language tasks, including selective prediction. Other works integrate abstention in multi-stage networks or ensembles [6,11,38,50,61]. [32,63] study selective prediction and transformer uncertainty within NLP tasks. [21,35,60] explore selective prediction performance on out-of-distribution data. [35] focuses on selective prediction for text-based question answering. However, they show that their method does not generalize to questions from the same domain which are intrinsically unanswerable, whereas this represents an important portion of difficult VQA samples. [18,19] optimize selective models for specific coverage levels in image classification. We explore learned selection functions, but in the multimodal VQA setting, where the complex interaction between modalities must be modeled and more than one output may be considered correct to varying degrees. In the multimodal space, [26] addresses gender bias in image captioning, where the model can "abstain" by predicting gender-neutral words when it is uncertain. With our proposed metric, the cost of error (e.g., misclassifying gender) can be user-defined and potentially be made class-specific.

3   Visual Question Answering with Abstention

Visual question answering is currently formulated and evaluated in the literature [3,20,24,28] as *always* predicting an answer from the answer space, $\mathcal{A}$, annotated in the dataset. So, a model $f : \mathcal{X} \mapsto \mathcal{A}$ predicts an answer $a \in \mathcal{A}$ for each input $x = (v, q) \in \mathcal{X}$, with image v and question q. This problem formulation forces the model to answer even if it is likely wrong, thus providing unreliable answers. To address this, we propose to extend the VQA problem formulation so that a model is given the option to *abstain* from answering a question (i.e., effectively saying "*I don't know*"). Outside VQA, this formulation has also been referred to as "*classification with a reject option*" [9,13,19,25,50] or "*selective prediction/classification*" [15,18]. We first discuss the problem definition in Sect. 3.1, and then the metrics to evaluate this problem in Sect. 3.2.

3.1   Problem Definition

We extend the standard VQA formulation to the setting where a model can either provide an answer from $\mathcal{A}$ or choose to abstain (denoted by $\emptyset$): $h : \mathcal{X} \mapsto \mathcal{A} \cup \{\emptyset\}$. We refer to h as a *selective model*.

One way to formulate and achieve this is by decomposing h into two functions, f and g, which jointly comprise a selective model [15,18,19]. f denotes the VQA model that predicts answers and $g : \mathcal{X} \mapsto \{0, 1\}$ is the selection function that determines whether the model answers or abstains from answering:

$$h(x) = (f, g)(x) = \begin{cases} f(x) & \text{if } g(x) = 1, \\ \emptyset & \text{if } g(x) = 0. \end{cases} \tag{1}$$

Given an input x, the selective model yields an output from f when the selection function predicts that an answer should be given, or abstains if the selection function predicts that the model should not answer. One straightforward way to formulate the selection function g is based on a threshold γ, where the function $g' : \mathcal{X} \mapsto [0, 1]$ predicts a confidence in the correctness[1] of the model $f(x)$ [35]:

$$g(x) = \begin{cases} 1 & \text{if } g'(x) \geq \gamma, \\ 0 & \text{if } g'(x) < \gamma. \end{cases} \tag{2}$$

In general, a good function $g'(x)$ for abstention should yield high values when $f(x)$ is correct and low values when it is incorrect. In Sect. 4, we will further discuss how to define $g'(x)$.

3.2   Evaluation Metrics

To evaluate a VQA model with an ability to abstain, we consider two types of evaluation and discuss how we adapt them for VQA: first, *coverage* and *risk* [15] and, second, a cost-based metric for balancing the two.

---

[1] While we define the output space of g' as $[0, 1]$ as is the case for the common softmax, one can similarly define an output space which covers, e.g., all real values $\mathbb{R}$.

Risk and Coverage. *Coverage* is the portion of questions that the model opted to answer, while *risk* is the error on that portion of questions [15]. Ideally, a reliable model should exhibit high coverage at low levels of risk, meaning it answers many questions with high accuracy and abstains on others. Concretely, coverage for dataset $\mathcal{D}$ with inputs x_i and ground truth answers y_i is given by:

$$C(g) = \frac{1}{|\mathcal{D}|} \sum_{(x_i, y_i) \in \mathcal{D}} g(x_i), \tag{3}$$

and risk is defined as:

$$\mathcal{R}(f, g) = \frac{\frac{1}{|\mathcal{D}|} \sum_{(x_i, y_i) \in \mathcal{D}} \ell(f(x_i), y_i) \cdot g(x_i)}{C(g)}, \tag{4}$$

where ℓ is a cost function that measures the error between the predicted answer $f(x_i)$ and the corresponding ground truth answer y_i. Assuming g follows Eq. 2, if the threshold γ decreases, coverage will increase, but risk will increase as well. Hence, there is a risk-coverage trade-off that models can aim to optimize.

Applying this to VQA, the composite function (f, g) becomes our selective VQA model, where f produces an answer and g decides whether to abstain. However, the open-ended nature of the VQA task requires careful consideration for designing the risk-coverage metrics. A given question might have multiple possible answers which could all be considered correct to varying degrees. As a result, the error for a prediction on a given input is not necessarily binary.

When calculating risk, we must use a cost function that accurately represents this multi-class nature. We follow [3] to define VQA accuracy for a given model answer $f(x)$ as $Acc(f(x), y) = \min\left(\frac{\# \text{ annotations that match } f(x)}{3}, 1\right)$ and average these accuracies over all 10 choose 9 subsets of human annotated answers for the input question, similar to other VQA evaluations [20,24,57]. Under this, an answer is considered fully correct if it matches at least four of the human annotations, and receives partial credit for predicting an answer with one, two, or three humans in agreement. Thus, our risk measurement becomes:

$$\mathcal{R}(f, g) = \frac{\frac{1}{|\mathcal{D}|} \sum_{(x_i, y_i) \in \mathcal{D}} (1 - Acc(f(x_i), y_i)) \cdot g(x_i)}{C(g)}. \tag{5}$$

In practice, the level of risk in model predictions that a user is willing to tolerate depends highly on the scenario. Therefore, we evaluate by computing coverage at a range of risk levels ($C@\mathcal{R}$), such as coverage at 1% or 10% risk. We can also summarize this over the distribution of risk levels by plotting coverage versus corresponding risk, and computing the area under this risk-coverage curve (AUC) [35]. Moreover, for an evaluation that controls for how the threshold γ for g is chosen, we compute the maximum coverage for each risk level, allowing for a more direct comparison of the selection function design.

Effective Reliability. Recall the trade-off between risk and coverage: a standard VQA model may have high risk at 100% coverage, but a reliable model may have low risk yet abstain on a large portion of questions (see Fig. 1(b)). In practice, for a model to be reliable and effective, it should ideally achieve both low risk and high coverage. To jointly measure these two desirable qualities, we define a metric which assigns a reward to questions that are answered correctly, a penalty to those answered entirely incorrectly, and zero reward to those abstained on. We refer to this as *Effective Reliability*, or Φ_c for a given penalty c, inspired by the "effectiveness function" introduced by [13].

Formally, we define Effective Reliability for an input x as $\Phi_c(x)$ (Eq. 6), where c is the cost for answering incorrectly, g is the selection function, and *Acc* is a measure of a model's correctness. In this case, *Acc* is the VQA accuracy [3].

$$
\Phi_c(x) = \begin{cases} Acc(x) & \text{if } g(x) = 1 \text{ and } Acc(x) > 0, \\ -c & \text{if } g(x) = 1 \text{ and } Acc(x) = 0, \\ 0 & \text{if } g(x) = 0. \end{cases} \tag{6}
$$

We define the total score $\Phi_c = \frac{1}{n}\sum_x \Phi_c(x)$, a mean over all n samples x. This formulation assigns a reward to answers which are at least partially correct (i.e., $Acc(x) > 0$) – an important property of the VQA accuracy, where the correctness of answers can vary based on the number of human annotators in agreement. The choice of c depends on the deployment-specific cost of providing an incorrect answer. In Sect. 5.3, we report Φ_c with cost values of 1, 10, and 100 (Φ_1, Φ_{10}, Φ_{100}). While [13] suggest setting $\Phi_c(x) < 0$ for $g(x) = 0$, we set $\Phi_c(x) = 0$ (i.e., a score of 0 when abstaining). This enables our formulation to have the clear upper bound for models which abstain perfectly (Lemma 1). We provide a simple proof for this in Appendix K. It is also confirmed in our experiments in Table 2.

Lemma 1. *The Effective Reliability score is equal to the VQA Accuracy* $(\Phi_c(x) = Acc(x))$ *if a model abstains* $(g(x) = 0)$ *iff it is incorrect* $(Acc(x) = 0)$.

In our experiments, we choose a threshold γ which optimizes Φ_c on a validation set to compute a model's Effective Reliability with the form of the selection function g defined in Eq. 2. Additionally, the Effective Reliability score Φ_c can be evaluated for any model, even those which do not incorporate the option to abstain from providing a prediction (i.e., $g(x)$ is always 1).

Beyond its connection to VQA Accuracy (Lemma 1), Effective Reliability has several other advantages. We show that it meaningfully correlates with risk-coverage (Table 2), yet provides a single metric to compare models. This offers simpler comparisons that can be used to rank approaches (e.g., evaluating on a challenge server). It also provides an alternative evaluation for settings where it may be easier or more intuitive to define a cost for an incorrect answer as opposed to a target level of risk.

4   Selection Functions

We investigate three promising directions to extend VQA models to abstain by exploring different options for $g'(x)$ introduced in Sect. 3.1. Additional implementation details for the selection functions can be found in Appendix I.2.

MaxProb. Without any additional training, a model can be extended to abstain by defining g' as the softmax probability of the model's predicted class (i.e., maximum probability) and is thus refered to as MaxProb [27,35,39]. Essentially, MaxProb trusts that if the model gives a high probability to one class, it is quite certain that the answer is correct and should be given: $g'_{\text{MaxProb}}(x) = \max(f'(x))$, where $f'(x)$ represents the answer probabilities.

Calibration. Calibration techniques tune the absolute confidence values [49] to make the predicted probability for an output representative of the likelihood of that output being correct. Selective prediction has more to do with relative confidence rankings [15], but, nevertheless, a poorly calibrated model might also imply poor confidence rankings [35]. Temperature scaling [23,49] is a popular calibration method, but it does not change the confidence rankings between examples and has no effect on the risk-coverage curve. Thus, we do not consider it in this work, but instead use vector scaling [23,49] to calibrate the model logits. We then apply MaxProb on top of these calibrated logits. Appendix G has evaluations of how well the scores are calibrated.

Multimodal Selection Function: Selector. Vector scaling essentially trains an additional component on top of the VQA model to refine the model confidences. We move beyond this by training a component (Selector) to predict whether the answer is correct [14,35,49]. Different from prior work on confidence estimation in other tasks [14,19,35,61], the multimodal nature of VQA presents unique challenges where the model must consider the interaction between the image, question, and answer. To model this, we extract the image v, question q, multimodal r, and answer $f'(x)$ representations from the VQA model and input these to the Selector, which gives it access to representations of both the answer itself as well as the evidence on which the answer is based. The Selector is a multi-layered perceptron that takes these representations as input and predicts the correctness of an answer with respect to the image-question pair. To train this component, the simplest method may be to treat this as a binary classification problem (correct or incorrect). However, this does not account for answers that may be partially correct, or where one answer may be more correct than another, as is the case with VQA. Therefore, we propose to treat correctness prediction as a regression task where the target value is the VQA accuracy, allowing us to scale confidence scores with correctness.

5   Experiments

5.1   Data and Models

We experiment on the VQA v2 dataset [20] and require annotations for evaluation. As annotations for the test-dev and test-std sets of VQA v2 are not publicly available, we use questions from the official validation split for our evaluation as is common [1,53,62]. As a reminder, under our selective prediction setup, the VQA model is the function f, the selection function is g, and the composition of the two form a selective model h. We train the VQA models (f) on the training

Table 1. Risk-coverage metrics for different selection functions. For coverage at risk ($C@R$) and VQA Acc., higher is better. For AUC, lower is better. All in %.

Model f	Selection function g	VQA Acc. ↑	$C@R$ ↑ $R = 1\%$	$R = 5\%$	$R = 10\%$	$R = 20\%$	AUC ↓
	MaxProb	66.17	6.00	24.71	40.99	71.45	13.88
Pythia [31]	Calibration	66.45	6.50	25.07	41.95	**73.44**	13.52
	Selector	66.17	**8.79**	**26.92**	**43.24**	73.40	**13.30**
	Best Possible (C)	66.17	62.67	68.41	73.52	82.71	6.68
	MaxProb	69.20	7.51	29.01	47.99	79.89	11.78
ViLBERT [43]	Calibration	69.16	10.07	30.15	48.75	79.96	11.62
	Selector	69.20	**11.82**	**32.44**	**50.20**	**79.97**	**11.31**
	Best Possible (C)	69.20	65.66	71.67	76.89	86.50	5.49
	MaxProb	70.18	6.85	30.78	50.46	81.78	11.21
VisualBERT [40]	Calibration	70.02	9.78	32.09	51.14	81.92	11.21
	Selector	70.18	**11.47**	**34.14**	**52.53**	**82.04**	**10.75**
	Best Possible (C)	70.18	66.70	72.76	77.98	87.73	5.13
	MaxProb	71.75	6.78	34.69	55.72	85.13	10.23
CLIP-ViL [55]	Calibration	71.71	13.12	37.06	56.06	85.23	9.91
	Selector	71.75	**16.34**	**39.48**	**58.16**	**85.37**	**9.52**
	Best Possible (C)	71.75	68.49	74.55	79.72	89.69	4.58

set of VQA v2. Meanwhile, we split the 214k examples in the VQA v2 validation set into three subsets: a split with 86k examples (40%) for validating VQA models as well as training selection functions (g), another with 22k examples (10%) for validating the selection functions, and a held out test split of 106k examples (50%) that we use strictly for evaluating the full models (h).

We benchmark the selection functions introduced in Sect. 4 in combination with VQA models with varying architectures and performance (test-std VQA v2 accuracy in parentheses): **Pythia** [31] (70.24%), an optimization of the widely used bottom-up top-down VQA model [2]; **ViLBERT** [43] (70.92%), a two-stream transformer, and **VisualBERT** [40] (71.00%), a single-stream transformer, both of which use multimodal pretraining [56]; **CLIP-ViL** [55] (74.17%), which is the MoVie+MCAN [47] model with a visual encoder from CLIP [51].

In Table 1, Table 2, and Fig. 2, we report mean results over 10 random seeds for Pythia and CLIP-ViL (standard deviations in Appendix J), while we report single runs for ViLBERT and VisualBERT using existing pretrained and fine-tuned models. All other results are single runs from the same randomly chosen seed. Details of data and model setups are in Appendix H and Appendix I.

5.2 Benchmarking Risk and Coverage

As discussed in Sect. 3.2, we measure the maximum coverage for a given risk ($C@R$) as well as AUC for the risk-coverage curves and overall accuracy for each model. We include the best possible performance on these metrics for each model, which would be a selective model that abstains only when the prediction is incorrect. Results are reported on the test test.

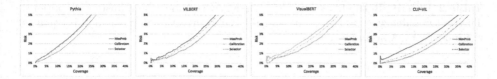

Fig. 2. Risk-coverage plots for each model up to 5% risk.

Selector Outperforms Other Methods. From Table 1, we see that adding the Selector consistently outperforms MaxProb in coverage for all risk tolerances as well as AUC. The strongest improvements occur at lower risk tolerances (e.g., 1% and 5%), becoming smaller as the tolerance increases (e.g., 10% and 20%). Notably, CLIP-ViL with Selector can improve $\mathcal{C}$@1% to 2.4× that of CLIP-ViL with MaxProb. Figure 2 illustrates how, for low risk levels, the addition of the selector maintains noticeably better risk as coverage increases compared to Max-Prob. It generally appears that the more accurate a model is overall, the more it may potentially improve in coverage at low risk tolerances when using Selector. For instance, when adding the Selector, we observe the largest improvements in $\mathcal{C}$@1% and $\mathcal{C}$@5% with CLIP-ViL (9.56% and 4.79%, respectively), which also has the highest accuracy. Meanwhile, Pythia has the lowest accuracy and exhibits the smallest improvements with the Selector at these tolerances (2.79% and 2.21%, respectively). Figure 2 depicts this between 0–5% risk, where the gap between MaxProb and Selector appears to widen as we move to more accurate models (left to right). Lastly, we observe that Calibration can improve coverage beyond MaxProb as well, but largely less so than the Selector, especially at low risk tolerances (e.g., 1%, 5%), and not as consistently. Because Calibration modifies the output logits, it also slightly changes model accuracy.

Better Accuracy $\nRightarrow$ Better Coverage at Low Risk. While accuracy appears to positively correlate with a better risk-coverage trade-off, the results in Table 1 also imply that higher accuracy does not guarantee better coverage at low risk. For example, CLIP-ViL has 2.55% higher accuracy than ViLBERT, but, with default MaxProb, ViLBERT has 0.73% higher $\mathcal{C}$@1% than CLIP-ViL. Appendix B also shows that augmenting the VQA model training data with the selection function training data and using MaxProb still has worse coverage at low risk than when using this data for Selector training, despite having higher accuracy. These results imply that improving upon the risk-coverage trade-off requires not only building more accurate models but also learning better abstention policies.

Still Room for Improvement. Though the evidence presented in Table 1 and Fig. 2 show that coverage at different risk tolerances can be improved, these approaches still fall short of the best possible. For example, in Table 1, the difference in $\mathcal{C}$@1% between each model with Selector and their respective best possibles is still >50%. Although achieving the best possible may not be realistic, more work is needed to have reliable models with high accuracy and wide coverage that shrink this gap further.

Table 2. Effective Reliability Φ_c for VQA models with and without abstention options. The best possible Φ_c is computed by only selecting correct predictions, and is equal to the model's VQA accuracy. All in %.

Model f	Selection function g	$c=1$			$c=10$			$c=100$		
		Φ_1 ↑	$\mathcal{R}$ ↓	$\mathcal{C}$ ↑	Φ_{10} ↑	$\mathcal{R}$ ↓	$\mathcal{C}$ ↑	Φ_{100} ↑	$\mathcal{R}$ ↓	$\mathcal{C}$ ↑
Pythia [31]	—	38.49	33.83	100	-210.62	33.83	100	−2701.68	33.83	100
	MaxProb	47.28	21.62	76.03	15.15	5.24	25.62	2.27	0.85	4.89
	Calibration	48.06	21.21	76.18	15.23	5.85	28.06	2.19	0.94	5.88
	Selector	**48.16**	20.67	74.84	**17.12**	5.99	30.16	**3.84**	0.94	8.23
	Best Possible (Φ_c)	66.17	8.51	72.32	66.17	8.51	72.32	66.17	8.51	72.32
ViLBERT [43]	—	44.57	30.80	100	−177.05	30.80	100	−2393.23	30.80	100
	MaxProb	52.41	20.01	79.92	18.00	6.26	34.50	1.67	1.33	10.18
	Calibration	52.51	19.53	78.93	18.29	6.10	34.24	2.92	1.12	10.47
	Selector	**52.65**	19.37	78.60	**21.02**	5.56	34.57	**5.41**	0.90	11.06
	Best Possible (Φ_c)	69.20	8.20	75.38	69.20	8.20	75.38	69.20	8.20	75.38
VisualBERT [40]	—	46.49	29.82	100	−166.77	29.82	100	−2299.33	29.82	100
	MaxProb	53.72	19.09	79.83	19.29	5.63	33.64	2.49	1.02	6.89
	Calibration	53.80	19.07	79.84	19.96	5.57	34.37	3.83	0.87	8.42
	Selector	**54.12**	18.72	79.34	**22.04**	5.13	34.61	**4.82**	1.00	11.34
	Best Possible (Φ_c)	70.18	8.02	76.30	70.18	8.02	76.30	70.18	8.02	70.18
CLIP-ViL [55]	—	49.41	28.25	100	-151.70	28.25	100	-2162.80	28.25	100
	MaxProb	55.82	19.22	83.45	22.03	5.59	37.67	2.85	0.96	6.97
	Calibration	56.03	18.30	81.61	23.24	4.95	36.82	5.30	0.73	9.97
	Selector	**56.45**	17.44	80.09	**26.06**	5.03	39.59	**8.01**	0.55	11.38
	Best Possible (Φ_c)	71.75	7.60	77.66	71.75	7.60	77.66	71.75	7.60	77.66

Thresholds Generalize to Test-Time. Thus far, we have evaluated the maximum coverage at an exact risk level. In practice, however, a threshold γ must be chosen, e.g., on a validation set, and used at test-time. We evaluate how close the actual test-time risk is to the target risk when using the validation threshold with VisualBERT, with results in Appendix F. We find relatively small differences in risk, showing that the thresholds generalize reasonably well. This aligns with prior findings on other tasks [19]. However, since the actual risks are now slightly different between models, we can no longer compare the corresponding coverages directly. This motivates Effective Reliability, which compares models based on a predefined cost for wrong answers as opposed to an exact risk level.

5.3   Effective Reliability

We evaluate Effective Reliability (Φ_c) defined in Sect. 3.1, which assigns a cost to incorrect predictions, a reward to correct predictions, and zero to questions on which a model abstained from answering. This provides a single measure to jointly consider reliability (i.e., low risk) and effectiveness (i.e., high coverage). In Table 2, we choose cost values c of 1, 10, and 100, to observe how models compare when the consequences for providing an incorrect prediction become high. Additionally, we can now directly compare to the original VQA formulation, where models do not have an option to abstain, denoted by a null selection function g. We also include Φ_c for the best possible g, where a model abstains exactly on those inputs which would result in incorrect predictions. As discussed in Sect. 3.1, this is equivalent to the model accuracy. Results are reported on the test set, with an abstention threshold selected to optimize Φ_c on the validation set. We include the corresponding risk and coverage for the selected threshold.

Selector Still Outperforms Other Methods. The Selector produces the highest Effective Reliability scores across all models and cost levels. As the penalty for wrong answers increases, the gap between the performance of Selector and the next best model generally increases as well. For example, the improvement of Selector over MaxProb for ViLBERT is 0.24% for Φ_1, yet it is 3.74% for Φ_{100}. Further, the gap between Selector and MaxProb for Φ_{100} generally increases as the VQA model itself has higher accuracy (or best possible performance). We observe a similar effect in Fig. 2, where more accurate models have larger gaps in risk between Selector and MaxProb at a given coverage.

Cost Implicitly Controls Risk and Coverage. When the penalty for a wrong answer is high, one might expect a selective model to operate in the low-risk regime. This is indeed reflected in Table 2, where the range of risk levels for selective models at Φ_{100} ($\mathcal{R} \approx 0.5\text{--}1.3\%$) is much lower than the range of risk at Φ_1 ($\mathcal{R} \approx 17\text{--}22\%$). This directly translates to a similar trend in coverage, where selective models answer about 5–11% of questions at Φ_{100}, and about 76–83% of questions at Φ_1. This shows that Effective Reliability behaves intuitively around the influence of a user-selected cost on model risk and coverage.

Human Evaluation Shows Noise has Little Effect Even with High Cost Values. For high costs (e.g., $c = 100$), models are strongly penalized for producing incorrect predictions. Given these strict penalties on errors, it becomes pertinent to ask to what degree noise in the annotations might be contributing to these penalties, though the potential impact of noise is certainly not unique to our evaluations and is a challenging problem in VQA [3,34,54]. To see if our results for Φ_{100} are significantly affected by annotation noise, in Appendix C, we manually examine each sample where the model predictions were marked incorrect (and thus heavily penalized when computing Φ_{100}). We annotate cases where models may have been unfairly penalized and recompute Φ_{100} when removing this penalty. We find that vast majority of incorrect predictions that contribute to these penalties are properly marked as incorrect. We also see that label noise does slightly change the Effective Reliability scores at high cost, but the rankings between models and selection functions are preserved.

All Models Without an Abstention Option Perform Poorly. When the cost of a wrong answer is equal to the reward of getting an answer entirely correct ($c = 1$), all models without a selection function g underperform their selective model counterparts. As c increases, this gap widens dramatically, with non-abstaining models reaching Φ_c values firmly in the negative range. Meanwhile, all selective models reach a positive Φ_c, even at high cost, illustrating the necessity of the abstention option for building models which are reliable and effective.

5.4 Selection Function Ablations

Table 3 provides ablations for the selection function design. In the following, we distill the main observations. Additional discussion is in Appendix A.

Table 3. Ablations of Selector with CLIP-ViL [55] on our selection function validation set. The overall best performance is in bold and second best is underlined. $f'(x)$,
q, $\tilde{v}$, and r are the answer, question, image, and multimodal representations, respectively. Note, v is a question conditioned image representation that is not unimodal (see
Appendix A for details). All in %.

Features	Unimodal	Loss	$\mathcal{C}@\mathcal{R}$ ↑				AUC ↓	Φ_c ↑		
			$\mathcal{R}=1\%$	$\mathcal{R}=5\%$	$\mathcal{R}=10\%$	$\mathcal{R}=20\%$		$c=1$	$c=10$	$c=100$
$\tilde{v}$	✓	Regression	0.00	0.00	0.00	16.09	23.23	48.83	0.00	0.00
q	✓	Regression	0.02	11.03	35.88	79.70	13.39	52.99	10.36	1.33
$f'(x)$		Regression	5.24	36.10	56.30	84.79	10.08	56.03	23.14	5.88
v		Regression	11.60	36.43	53.74	83.51	10.32	54.84	23.91	6.10
r		Regression	**13.42**	34.69	53.90	82.95	10.43	54.35	22.34	**7.77**
$f'(x)+\tilde{v}$		Regression	3.67	36.40	56.33	84.79	10.07	55.97	23.63	4.60
$f'(x)+q$		Regression	10.67	37.41	56.95	84.76	9.86	56.01	24.35	5.32
$f'(x)+r$		Regression	12.02	37.44	<u>57.68</u>	<u>84.93</u>	9.81	56.07	24.28	5.51
$f'(x)+v$		Regression	13.24	**38.51**	57.44	84.92	<u>9.76</u>	**56.20**	**25.11**	7.03
$f'(x)+q+v+r$		Classification	6.64	35.80	57.29	84.18	10.06	55.61	23.23	4.36
$f'(x)+q+v+r$		Regression	<u>13.32</u>	<u>38.02</u>	**58.16**	**85.03**	**9.73**	<u>56.09</u>	<u>24.85</u>	<u>7.32</u>

Selector Requires Multimodal Input. Table 3 shows the importance of using
multimodal information for coverage at low risk levels. When using each representation in isolation, we see that multimodal representations (r, v, and $f'(x)$)
yield much stronger $\mathcal{C}@1\%$, $\mathcal{C}@5\%$, Φ_{10}, and Φ_{100} than unimodal representations
(image $\tilde{v}$ or question q). For highly reliable models ($\mathcal{C}@1\%$, Φ_{100}), unimodal
selection functions fail (coverage $\leq 0.02\%$, $\Phi_{100} < 2\%$), suggesting that building
reliable and effective VQA models is a truly multimodal problem. Combining all
representations generally performs best, so we use this setup in all experiments.

Regressing to VQA Accuracy is Important. We find that formulating the
objective as a regression of the answer accuracy, rather than classifying whether
the answer is correct, offers significant improvements (Table 3), especially at
low risk. This is likely because predicting the fine-grained accuracy allows the
model to account for partially correct answers and learn to rank answers that are
more correct higher, as opposed to classification where the distinction between
partially correct answers is lost.

Selector Architecture. Appendix A presents results using different Selector
architectures, where a less complex architecture can degrade performance, but a
more complex one does not necessarily improve it. Together with Table 3, we find
that, rather than the network layout, the *input* to the Selector and optimization
target are more critical to the performance when using the Selector.

5.5   Qualitative Analysis

Figure 3 visualizes MaxProb and Selector decisions with CLIP-ViL for several
examples on the test set (more in Appendix E). The abstention threshold is
chosen to maximize Φ_{100} on validation. Figure 3 (left) shows an example of a

Fig. 3. Qualitative test set examples with CLIP-ViL selective model predictions.

question that requires commonsense reasoning to answer that the VQA model may not be certain of (and gets wrong), so Selector abstains. Similarly, in Fig. 3 (middle), we see a false premise question [52] where Selector abstains again as the question does not make sense for the image, while MaxProb yields an incorrect answer. Figure 3 (right) presents an example with synonymous answers where the model is correct yet MaxProb chooses to abstain and Selector chooses to answer. In a classification-based VQA model, synonyms can split the maximum softmax score used by MaxProb, whereas the Selector can potentially learn these answer similarities and adjust the confidence. These examples contribute to the higher coverage at low risk observed quantitatively in our experiments. We also find that MaxProb chooses to answer many simple questions, while Selector additionally chooses to answer more difficult, multimodal ones as well (see Appendix D).

6   Conclusion

The standard VQA formulation does not include an option for models to abstain from answering if they are uncertain. However, for many applications, it is important that the model only provides an answer if there is a low risk of error. In this work, we promote a problem formulation for VQA which includes an option to abstain and discuss how to evaluate this, including a metric that rewards correct predictions but expects models to abstain if they are incorrect. We benchmark several VQA models in combination with approaches for abstention. If we want a reliable model with 1% risk of error, we find that a state-of-the-art VQA model [55] only answers less than 7% of the questions when using its softmax probabilities as estimates of model confidence. Using calibration can improve this, but we find that the best results are consistently achieved by training a multimodal selection function to estimate correctness directly. This increases the coverage from 6.78% to 16.34%. While this is a marked improvement, one has to consider that this model achieves 71.75% standard VQA accuracy on the same set of data. With our *Effective Reliability* metric, the performance drops from 71.75% (for perfect abstention) to 8.01% (our best abstention baseline) with high penalties for wrong answers. We believe this new framework and metric for VQA will encourage the community to build VQA models which are both reliable and effective, as well as offer an opportunity for many exciting directions to improve the self-awareness of models.

Acknowledgements. We thank Anastasios Angelopoulos and Kurt Shuster for helpful discussions. Authors, as part of their affiliation with UC Berkeley, were supported in part by the NSF CISE Expeditions Award CCF-1730628; DoD, including DARPA's LwLL, PTG, and/or SemaFor programs; the Berkeley Artificial Intelligence Research (BAIR) industrial alliance program as well as gifts from Amazon Web Services, Ant Group, Ericsson, Facebook, Futurewei, Google, Intel, Microsoft, Scotiabank, and Mware.

References

1. Agrawal, A., Batra, D., Parikh, D., Kembhavi, A.: Don't just assume; look and answer: overcoming priors for visual question answering. In: CVPR (2018)
2. Anderson, P., et al.: Bottom-up and top-down attention for image captioning and visual question answering. In: Proceedings of the IEEE Conference on Computer Vision and Pattern Recognition, pp. 6077–6086 (2018)
3. Antol, S., et al.: VQA: visual question answering. In: Proceedings of the IEEE International Conference on Computer Vision, pp. 2425–2433 (2015)
4. Asan, O., Bayrak, A.E., Choudhury, A., et al.: Artificial intelligence and human trust in healthcare: focus on clinicians. J. Med. Internet Res. **22**(6), e15154 (2020)
5. Bhattacharya, N., Li, Q., Gurari, D.: Why does a visual question have different answers? In: Proceedings of the IEEE/CVF International Conference on Computer Vision, pp. 4271–4280 (2019)
6. Black, E., Leino, K., Fredrikson, M.: Selective ensembles for consistent predictions. In: International Conference on Learning Representations (2022)
7. Chen, Y.C., et al.: UNITER: UNiversal Image-TExt Representation Learning. In: Vedaldi, A., Bischof, H., Brox, T., Frahm, J.-M. (eds.) ECCV 2020. LNCS, vol. 12375, pp. 104–120. Springer, Cham (2020). https://doi.org/10.1007/978-3-030-58577-8_7
8. Chiu, T.Y., Zhao, Y., Gurari, D.: Assessing image quality issues for real-world problems. In: Proceedings of the IEEE/CVF Conference on Computer Vision and Pattern Recognition, pp. 3646–3656 (2020)
9. Chow, C.: On optimum recognition error and reject tradeoff. IEEE Trans. Inf. Theory **16**(1), 41–46 (1970)
10. Chow, C.K.: An optimum character recognition system using decision functions. IRE Trans. Electron. Comput. EC **6**(4), 247–254 (1957)
11. Corbière, C., Thome, N., Bar-Hen, A., Cord, M., Pérez, P.: Addressing failure prediction by learning model confidence. In: Advances in Neural Information Processing Systems, vol. 32 (2019)
12. Davis, E.: Unanswerable questions about images and texts. Front. Artif. Intell. **3**, 51 (2020)
13. De Stefano, C., Sansone, C., Vento, M.: To reject or not to reject: that is the question-an answer in case of neural classifiers. IEEE Trans. Syst. Man, Cybern. Part C (Applications and Reviews) **30**(1), 84–94 (2000). https://doi.org/10.1109/5326.827457
14. Dong, L., Quirk, C., Lapata, M.: Confidence modeling for neural semantic parsing. In: Proceedings of the 56th Annual Meeting of the Association for Computational Linguistics (Volume 1: Long Papers), pp. 743–753. Association for Computational Linguistics, Melbourne, Australia (2018). https://doi.org/10.18653/v1/P18-1069, https://aclanthology.org/P18-1069

15. El-Yaniv, R., Wiener, Y.: On the foundations of noise-free selective classification. J. Mach. Learn. Res. **11**, 1605–1641 (2010)
16. Fukui, A., Park, D.H., Yang, D., Rohrbach, A., Darrell, T., Rohrbach, M.: Multimodal compact bilinear pooling for visual question answering and visual grounding. In: EMNLP (2016)
17. Gao, P., et al.: Dynamic fusion with intra-and inter-modality attention flow for visual question answering. In: CVPR (2019)
18. Geifman, Y., El-Yaniv, R.: Selective classification for deep neural networks. In: Advances in Neural Information Processing Systems, vol. 30 (2017)
19. Geifman, Y., El-Yaniv, R.: SelectiveNet: a deep neural network with an integrated reject option. In: International Conference on Machine Learning, pp. 2151–2159. PMLR (2019)
20. Goyal, Y., Khot, T., Summers-Stay, D., Batra, D., Parikh, D.: Making the V in VQA matter: elevating the role of image understanding in visual question answering. In: Proceedings of the IEEE Conference on Computer Vision and Pattern Recognition, pp. 6904–6913 (2017)
21. Guillory, D., Shankar, V., Ebrahimi, S., Darrell, T., Schmidt, L.: Predicting with confidence on unseen distributions. In: Proceedings of the IEEE/CVF International Conference on Computer Vision (2021)
22. Gulshan, V., et al.: Development and validation of a deep learning algorithm for detection of diabetic retinopathy in retinal fundus photographs. JAMA **316**(22), 2402–2410 (2016). https://doi.org/10.1001/jama.2016.17216
23. Guo, C., Pleiss, G., Sun, Y., Weinberger, K.Q.: On calibration of modern neural networks. In: International Conference on Machine Learning, pp. 1321–1330. PMLR (2017)
24. Gurari, D., et al.: VizWiz grand challenge: answering visual questions from blind people. In: Proceedings of the IEEE Conference on Computer Vision and Pattern Recognition, pp. 3608–3617 (2018)
25. Hanczar, B., Dougherty, E.R.: Classification with reject option in gene expression data. Bioinformatics **24**(17), 1889–1895 (2008)
26. Hendricks, L.A., Burns, K., Saenko, K., Darrell, T., Rohrbach, A.: Women also snowboard: overcoming bias in captioning models. In: Proceedings of the European Conference on Computer Vision (ECCV), pp. 771–787 (2018)
27. Hendrycks, D., Gimpel, K.: A baseline for detecting misclassified and out-of-distribution examples in neural networks. In: Proceedings of International Conference on Learning Representations (2017)
28. Hudson, D.A., Manning, C.D.: GQA: a new dataset for real-world visual reasoning and compositional question answering. In: Proceedings of the IEEE/CVF Conference on Computer Vision and Pattern Recognition, pp. 6700–6709 (2019)
29. Jiang, H., Kim, B., Guan, M., Gupta, M.: To trust or not to trust a classifier. In: Bengio, S., Wallach, H., Larochelle, H., Grauman, K., Cesa-Bianchi, N., Garnett, R. (eds.) Advances in Neural Information Processing Systems. vol. 31. Curran Associates, Inc. (2018), https://proceedings.neurips.cc/paper/2018/file/7180cffd6a8e829dacfc2a31b3f72ece-Paper.pdf
30. Jiang, H., Misra, I., Rohrbach, M., Learned-Miller, E., Chen, X.: In defense of grid features for visual question answering. In: Proceedings of the IEEE/CVF Conference on Computer Vision and Pattern Recognition, pp. 10267–10276 (2020)
31. Jiang, Y., Natarajan, V., Chen, X., Rohrbach, M., Batra, D., Parikh, D.: Pythia v0.1: the winning entry to the VQA challenge 2018. arXiv preprint arXiv:1807.09956 (2018)

32. Kadavath, S., et al.: Language models (mostly) know what they know. arXiv preprint arXiv:2207.05221 (2022)
33. Kafle, K., Kanan, C.: An analysis of visual question answering algorithms. In: ICCV (2017)
34. Kafle, K., Kanan, C.: Visual question answering: Datasets, algorithms, and future challenges. Comput. Vis. Image Underst. **163**, 3–20 (2017)
35. Kamath, A., Jia, R., Liang, P.: Selective question answering under domain shift. In: Proceedings of the 58th Annual Meeting of the Association for Computational Linguistics, pp. 5684–5696. Association for Computational Linguistics, Online (2020). https://doi.org/10.18653/v1/2020.acl-main.503, https://aclanthology.org/2020.acl-main.503
36. Karamcheti, S., Krishna, R., Fei-Fei, L., Manning, C.: Mind your outliers! investigating the negative impact of outliers on active learning for visual question answering. In: Proceedings of the 59th Annual Meeting of the Association for Computational Linguistics and the 11th International Joint Conference on Natural Language Processing (Volume 1: Long Papers), pp. 7265–7281. Association for Computational Linguistics, Online (2021). https://doi.org/10.18653/v1/2021.acl-long.564, https://aclanthology.org/2021.acl-long.564
37. Khan, J., et al.: Classification and diagnostic prediction of cancers using gene expression profiling and artificial neural networks. Nat. Med. **7**(6), 673–679 (2001)
38. Khani, F., Rinard, M., Liang, P.: Unanimous prediction for 100% precision with application to learning semantic mappings. arXiv preprint arXiv:1606.06368 (2016)
39. Lakshminarayanan, B., Pritzel, A., Blundell, C.: Simple and scalable predictive uncertainty estimation using deep ensembles. In: Advances in Neural Information Processing Systems, vol. 30 (2017)
40. Li, L.H., Yatskar, M., Yin, D., Hsieh, C.J., Chang, K.W.: VisualBERT: a simple and performant baseline for vision and language. In: Arxiv (2019)
41. Li, M., Weber, C., Wermter, S.: Neural networks for detecting irrelevant questions during visual question answering. In: Farkaš, I., Masulli, P., Wermter, S. (eds.) ICANN 2020. LNCS, vol. 12397, pp. 786–797. Springer, Cham (2020). https://doi.org/10.1007/978-3-030-61616-8_63
42. Li, X., et al.: OSCAR: object-semantics aligned pre-training for vision-language tasks. In: Vedaldi, A., Bischof, H., Brox, T., Frahm, J.-M. (eds.) ECCV 2020. LNCS, vol. 12375, pp. 121–137. Springer, Cham (2020). https://doi.org/10.1007/978-3-030-58577-8_8
43. Lu, J., Batra, D., Parikh, D., Lee, S.: ViLBERT: pretraining task-agnostic Visiolinguistic representations for vision-and-language tasks. In: Advances in Neural Information Processing Systems, vol. 32 (2019)
44. Lütkenhöner, B., Basel, T.: Predictive modeling for diagnostic tests with high specificity, but low sensitivity: a study of the glycerol test in patients with suspected meniere's disease. PLoS ONE **8**(11), e79315 (2013)
45. Mahendru, A., Prabhu, V., Mohapatra, A., Batra, D., Lee, S.: The promise of premise: harnessing question premises in visual question answering. In: EMNLP (2017)
46. Mcknight, D.H., Carter, M., Thatcher, J.B., Clay, P.F.: Trust in a specific technology: an investigation of its components and measures. ACM Trans. Manage. Inf. Syst. **2**(2), 1–25 (2011). https://doi.org/10.1145/1985347.1985353
47. Nguyen, D.K., Goswami, V., Chen, X.: Movie: revisiting modulated convolutions for visual counting and beyond. In: Proceedings of the International Conference on Learning Representations (2021)

48. Niculescu-Mizil, A., Caruana, R.: Predicting good probabilities with supervised learning. In: Proceedings of the 22nd International Conference on Machine learning, pp. 625–632 (2005)
49. Platt, J., et al.: Probabilistic outputs for support vector machines and comparisons to regularized likelihood methods. Adv. Large Margin Classifiers **10**(3), 61–74 (1999)
50. Pudil, P., Novovicova, J., Blaha, S., Kittler, J.: Multistage pattern recognition with reject option. In: Proceedings., 11th IAPR International Conference on Pattern Recognition. Vol. II. Conference B: Pattern Recognition Methodology and Systems, pp. 92–95 (1992). https://doi.org/10.1109/ICPR.1992.201729
51. Radford, A., et al.: Learning transferable visual models from natural language supervision. In: International Conference on Machine Learning, pp. 8748–8763. PMLR (2021)
52. Ray, A., Christie, G., Bansal, M., Batra, D., Parikh, D.: Question relevance in VQA: identifying non-visual and false-premise questions. In: Proceedings of the 2016 Conference on Empirical Methods in Natural Language Processing, pp. 919–924 (2016)
53. Shah, M., Chen, X., Rohrbach, M., Parikh, D.: Cycle-consistency for robust visual question answering. In: CVPR (2019)
54. Sharma, H., Jalal, A.S.: A survey of methods, datasets and evaluation metrics for visual question answering. Image Vis. Comput. **116**, 104327 (2021)
55. Shen, S., et al.: How much can clip benefit vision-and-language tasks? arXiv preprint arXiv:2107.06383 (2021)
56. Singh, A., Goswami, V., Parikh, D.: Are we pretraining it right? digging deeper into visio-linguistic pretraining. arXiv preprint arXiv:2004.08744 (2020)
57. Singh, A., et al.: Towards VQA models that can read. In: Proceedings of the IEEE Conference on Computer Vision and Pattern Recognition, pp. 8317–8326 (2019)
58. Teney, D., Liu, L., van Den Hengel, A.: Graph-structured representations for visual question answering. In: Proceedings of the IEEE Conference on Computer Vision and Pattern Recognition, pp. 1–9 (2017)
59. Tran, D., et al.: Plex: towards reliability using pretrained large model extensions (2022). https://doi.org/10.48550/ARXIV.2207.07411, https://arxiv.org/abs/2207.07411
60. Varshney, N., Mishra, S., Baral, C.: Investigating selective prediction approaches across several tasks in IID, OOD, and adversarial settings. In: Findings of the Association for Computational Linguistics: ACL 2022, pp. 1995–2002 (2022). https://doi.org/10.18653/v1/2022.findings-acl.158, https://aclanthology.org/2022.findings-acl.158
61. Wang, X., Luo, Y., Crankshaw, D., Tumanov, A., Yu, F., Gonzalez, J.E.: Idk cascades: fast deep learning by learning not to overthink. arXiv preprint arXiv:1706.00885 (2017)
62. Whitehead, S., Wu, H., Ji, H., Feris, R., Saenko, K.: Separating skills and concepts for novel visual question answering. In: Proceedings of the IEEE/CVF Conference on Computer Vision and Pattern Recognition, pp. 5632–5641 (2021)
63. Xin, J., Tang, R., Yu, Y., Lin, J.: The art of abstention: selective prediction and error regularization for natural language processing. In: Proceedings of the 59th Annual Meeting of the Association for Computational Linguistics and the 11th International Joint Conference on Natural Language Processing (Volume 1: Long Papers), pp. 1040–1051 (2021)
64. Yang, Z., He, X., Gao, J., Deng, L., Smola, A.: Stacked attention networks for image question answering. In: CVPR (2016)

65. Yu, Z., Yu, J., Cui, Y., Tao, D., Tian, Q.: Deep modular co-attention networks for visual question answering. In: Proceedings of the IEEE/CVF Conference on Computer Vision and Pattern Recognition, pp. 6281–6290 (2019)
66. Zhang, P., et al.: VinVL: revisiting visual representations in vision-language models. In: Proceedings of the IEEE/CVF Conference on Computer Vision and Pattern Recognition, pp. 5579–5588 (2021)

GRIT: Faster and Better Image Captioning Transformer Using Dual Visual Features

Van-Quang Nguyen[1(✉)], Masanori Suganuma[1,2], and Takayuki Okatani[1,2]

[1] Graduate School of Information Sciences, Tohoku University, Sendai, Japan
{quang,suganuma,okatani}@vision.is.tohoku.ac.jp
[2] RIKEN Center for AIP, Tokyo, Japan

Abstract. Current state-of-the-art methods for image captioning employ region-based features, as they provide object-level information that is essential to describe the content of images; they are usually extracted by an object detector such as Faster R-CNN. However, they have several issues, such as lack of contextual information, the risk of inaccurate detection, and the high computational cost. The first two could be resolved by additionally using grid-based features. However, how to extract and fuse these two types of features is uncharted. This paper proposes a Transformer-only neural architecture, dubbed GRIT (Grid- and Region-based Image captioning Transformer), that effectively utilizes the two visual features to generate better captions. GRIT replaces the CNN-based detector employed in previous methods with a DETR-based one, making it computationally faster. Moreover, its monolithic design consisting only of Transformers enables end-to-end training of the model. This innovative design and the integration of the dual visual features bring about significant performance improvement. The experimental results on several image captioning benchmarks show that GRIT outperforms previous methods in inference accuracy and speed.

Keywords: Image captioning · Grid features · Region features

1 Introduction

Image captioning is the task of generating a semantic description of a scene in natural language, given its image. It requires a comprehensive understanding of the scene and its description reflecting the understanding. Therefore, most existing methods solve the task in two corresponding steps; they first extract visual features from the input image and then use them to generate a scene's description. The key to success lies in the problem of how we can extract good features.

Supplementary Information The online version contains supplementary material available at https://doi.org/10.1007/978-3-031-20059-5_10.

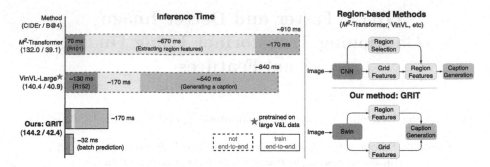

Fig. 1. Comparison of GRIT and other region-based methods for image captioning. Left: Running time per image of performing inference with beam size of five and the maximum length of 20 on a V100 GPU. Right: Their architectures

Researchers have considered several approaches to the problem. There are two primary methods, referred to as grid features [30,39,49] and region features [4]. Grid features are local image features extracted at the regular grid points, often obtained directly from a higher layer feature map(s) of CNNs/ViTs. Region features are a set of local image features of the regions (i.e., bounding boxes) detected by an object detector. The current state-of-the-art methods employ the region features since they encode detected object regions directly. Identifying objects and their relations in an image will be useful to correctly describing the image. However, the region features have several issues. First, they do not convey contextual information such as objects' relation since the regions do not cover the areas between objects. Second, there is a risk of erroneous detection of objects; important objects could be overlooked, etc. Third, computing the region feature is computationally costly, which is especially true when using a high-performance CNN-based detector, such as Faster R-CNN [38].

The grid features are extracted from the entire image, typically a high-layer feature map of a backbone network. While they do not convey object-level information, they are free from the first two issues with the region features. They may represent contextual information such as objects' relations in images, and they are free from the risk of erroneous object detection.

In this study, we consider using such region and grid features in an integrated manner, aiming to build a better model for image captioning. The underlying idea is that properly integrating the two types of features will provide a better representation of input images since they are complementary, as explained above. While a few recent studies consider their integration [32,47], it is still unclear what the best way is. In this study, we reconsider how to extract each from input images and then consider how to integrate them.

There is yet another issue with the region features, usually obtained by a CNN-based detector. At the last stage of its computation, CNN-based detectors employ non-maximum suppression (NMS) to eliminate redundant bounding boxes. This makes the end-to-end training of the entire model hard, i.e., jointly training the decoder part of the image captioning model and the detector by minimizing a single loss. Recent studies detach the two parts in training; they first train a detector on the object detection task and then train only the decoder part on image captioning. This could be a drag on achieving optimal performance of image captioning.

To overcome this limitation of CNN-based detectors and also cope with their high-computational cost, we employ the framework of DETR [6], which does not need NMS. We choose Deformable DETR [58], an improved variant, for its high performance, and also replace a CNN backbone used in the original design with Swin Transformer [29] to extract initial features from the input image. We also obtain the grid features from the same Swin Transformer. We input its last layer features into a simple self-attention Transformer and update them to obtain our grid features. This aims to model spatial interaction between the grid features, retrieving contextual information absent in our region features.

The extracted two types of features are fed into the second half of the model, the caption generator. We design it as a lightweight Transformer generating a caption sentence in an autoregressive manner. It is equipped with a unique cross-attention mechanism that computes and applies attention from the two types of visual features to caption sentence words.

These components form a Transformer-only neural architecture, dubbed GRIT (Grid- and Region-based Image captioning Transformer). Our experimental results show that GRIT has established a new state-of-the-art on the standard image captioning benchmark of COCO [28]. Specifically, in the offline evaluation using the Karpathy test split, GRIT outperforms all the existing methods without vision and language (V&L) pretraining. It also performs at least on a par with SimVLM$_{huge}$ [46] leveraging V&L pretraining on 1.8B image-text pairs.

2 Related Work

2.1 Visual Representations for Image Captioning

Recent image captioning methods typically employ an encoder-decoder architecture. Specifically, given an image, the encoder extracts visual features; the decoder receives the visual features as inputs and generates a sequence of words. Early methods use a CNN to extract a global feature as a holistic representation of the input image [20,44]. Although it is simple and compact, this holistic representation suffers from information loss and insufficient granularity. To cope with this, several studies [30,39,49] employed more fine-grained grid-based features to represent input images and also used attention mechanisms to utilize the granularity for better caption generation. Later, Anderson et al. [4] introduced the method of using an object detector, such as Faster R-CNN, to extract object-oriented features, called region features, showing that this leads to performance improvement in many V&L tasks, including image captioning and visual question answering. Since then, region features have become the de facto choice of visual representation for image captioning. Pointing out the high computational cost of the region features, Jiang et al. [18] showed that the grid features

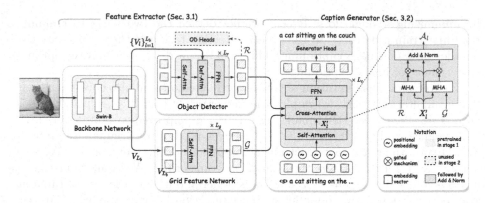

Fig. 2. Overview of the architecture of GRIT

extracted by an object detector perform well on the VQA task. RSTNet [56] has recently applied these grid features to image captioning.

2.2   Application of Transformer in Vision/Language Tasks

Transformer has long been a standard neural architecture in natural language processing [9,37,42], and started to be extended to computer vision tasks. Besides ViT [10] for image classification, it was also applied to object detection, leading to DETR [6], followed by several variants [12,41,58]. A recent study [48] applied the framework of DETR to pretraining for various V&L tasks, where they did not use it to obtain the region features.

Transformer has been applied to image captioning, where it is used as an encoder for extracting and encoding visual features and a decoder for generating captions. Specifically, Yang et al. [51] proposed to use the self-attention mechanism to encode visual features. Li et al. [25] used Transformer for obtaining the region features in combination with a semantic encoder that exploits knowledge from an external tagger. Several following studies proposed several variants of Transformer tailored to image captioning, such as Attention on Attention [16], X-Linear Attention [34], Memory-augmented Attention [7], etc. Transformer is naturally employed also as a caption decoder [13,14,32,46].

3   Grid- and Region-Based Image Captioning Transformer

This section describes the architecture of GRIT (Grid- and Region-based Image captioning Transformer). It consists of two parts, one for extracting the dual visual features from an input image (Sect. 3.1) and the other for generating a caption sentence from the extracted features (Sect. 3.2).

3.1   Extracting Visual Features from Images

Backbone Network for Extracting Initial Features. A lot of efforts have been made to apply the Transformer architecture to various computer vision tasks since ViT [10] applied it to image classification. ViT divides an input image into small patches and computes global attention over them. This is not suitable for tasks requiring spatially dense prediction, e.g., object detection since the computational complexity increases quadratically with the image resolution.

Swin Transformer [29] mitigates this issue to a great extent by incorporating operations such as patch reduction and shifted windows that support local attention. It is currently a de facto standard as a backbone network for various computer vision tasks. We employ it to extract initial visual features from the input image in our model.

We briefly summarize its structure, explaining how we extract features from the input image and send them to the components following the backbone. Given an input image of resolution $H \times W$, Swin Transformer computes and updates feature maps through multiple stages; it uses the patch merging layer after every stage (but the last stage) to downsample feature maps in their spatial dimension by the factor of 2. We apply another patch merging layer to downsample the last layer's feature map. We then collect the feature maps from all the stages, obtaining four multi-scale feature maps, i.e., $\{V_l\}_{l=1}^{L_b}$ where $L_b = 4$, which have the resolution from $H/8 \times W/8$ to $H/64 \times W/64$. These are inputted to the subsequent modules, i.e., the object detector and the network for generating grid features.

Generating Region Features. As in previous image captioning methods, ours also rely on an object detector to create region features. However, we employ a Transformer-based decoder framework, i.e., DETR [6] instead of CNN-based detectors, such as Faster R-CNN, which is widely employed by the SOTA image captioning models [4]. DETR formulates object detection as a direct set prediction problem, which makes the model free of the unideal computation for us, i.e., NMS and RoI alignment. This enables the end-to-end training of the entire model from the input image to the final output, i.e., a generated caption, and also leads to a significant reduction in computational time while maintaining the model's performance on image captioning compared with the SOTA models.

Specifically, we employ Deformable DETR [58], a variant of DETR. Deformable DETR extracts multi-scale features from an input image with its encoder part, which are fed to the decoder part. We use only the decoder part, to which we input the multi-scale features from the Swin Transformer backbone. This leads to further reduction in computational time. We will refer this decoder part as "object detector" in what follows; see Fig. 2.

The object detector receives two inputs: the multi-scale feature maps generated by the backbone, and N learnable object queries $R_0 = \{r_i\}_{i=1}^{N}$, in which $r_i \in \mathbb{R}^d$. Before forwarding them into the object detector, we apply linear transformation to the multi-scale feature maps, mapping them into d-dimensional vectors as $V_l \leftarrow W_l^r V_l$, where $\{W_l^r\}_{l=1}^{L_b}$ is a learnable projection matrix.

Receiving these two inputs, the object detector updates the object queries through a stack of L_r deformable layers, yielding $R_{L_r} \in \mathbb{R}^{N \times d}$ from the last layer; see [58] for details. We use $R_{L_r} \in \mathbb{R}^{N \times d}$ as our region features $\mathcal{R}$. We forward this to the caption generator.

Although we train it as a part of our entire model, we pretrain our "object detector" including the vision backbone on object detection before the training of image captioning. For the pretraining, we follow the procedure of Deformable DETR; placing a three-layer MLP and a linear layer on its top to predict box coordinates and class category, respectively. We then minimize a set-based global loss that forces unique predictions via bipartite matching.

Following [4,55], we pretrain the model (i.e., our object detector including the vision backbone) in two steps. We first train it on object detection following the training method of Deformable DETR. We then fine-tune it on a joint task of object detection and object attribute prediction, aiming to make it learn fine-grained visual semantics with the following loss:

$$\mathcal{L}_v(y, \hat{y}) = \sum_{i=1}^{N} [\underbrace{-\log \hat{p}_{\hat{\sigma}(i)}(c_i) + \mathbf{1}_{c_i \neq \varnothing} \mathcal{L}_{box}(b_i, \hat{b}_{\hat{\sigma}(i)})}_{\text{object detection}} \underbrace{-\log \hat{p}_{\hat{\sigma}(i)}(a_i)}_{\text{attribute prediction}}], \quad (1)$$

where $\hat{p}_{\hat{\sigma}(i)}(a_i)$ and $\hat{p}_{\hat{\sigma}(i)}(c_i)$ are the attribute and class probabilities, $\mathcal{L}_{box}(b_i, \hat{b}_{\hat{\sigma}(i)})$ is the loss for normalized bounding box regression for object i [58].

Grid Feature Network. This network receives the last one of the multi-scale feature maps from the Swin Transformer backbone, i.e., $V_{L_b} \in \mathbb{R}^{M \times d_{L_b}}$, where $M = H/64 \times W/64$. As with the input to the object detector, we apply a linear transformation with a learnable matrix $W^g \in \mathbb{R}^{d \times d_{L_b}}$ to V_{L_b}, obtaining $G_0 = W^g V_{L_b}$. We employ the standard self-attention Transformer having L_g layers. This network updates V_{L_b} through these layers, yielding our grid features $\mathcal{G}$ represented as a $M \times d$ matrix. We intend to extract contextual information hidden in the input image by modeling the spatial interaction between the grid features.

3.2   Caption Generation Using Dual Visual Features

Overall Design of Caption Generator. The caption generator receives the two types of visual features, the region features $\mathcal{R} \in \mathbb{R}^{N \times d}$ and the grid features $\mathcal{G} \in \mathbb{R}^{M \times d}$, as inputs. Apart from this, we employ the basic design employed in previous studies [14,42] that is based on the Transformer architecture. It generates a caption sentence in an autoregressive manner; receiving the sequence of predicted words (rigorously their embeddings) at time $t - 1$, it predicts the next word at time t. We employ the sinusoidal positional embedding of time step t [42]; we add it to the word embedding to obtain the input $x_0^t \in \mathbb{R}^d$ at t.

The caption generator consists of a stack of L_c identical layers. The initial layer receives the sequence of predicted words and the output from the last layer

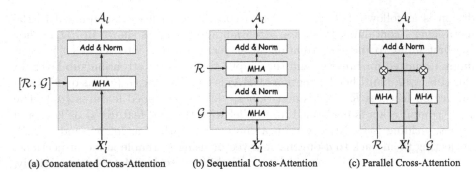

Fig. 3. Three designs of cross-attention mechanism to use dual visual features

is input to a linear layer whose output dimension equals the vocabulary size to predict the next word.

Each transformer layer has a sub-layer of masked self-attention over the sentence words and a sub-layer(s) of cross-attention between them and the visual features in this order, followed by a feedforward network (FFN) sublayer. The masked self-attention sub-layer at the l-th layer receives an input sequence $\{x_i^{l-1}\}_{i=0}^{t}$ at time step t, and computes and applies self-attention over the sequence to update the tokens with the attention mask to prevent the interaction from the future words during training.

The cross-attention sub-layer in the layer l, located after the self-attention sub-layer, fuses its output with the dual visual features by cross-attention between them, yielding $\mathcal{A}_l$. We consider the three design choices shown in Fig. 3 and described below. We examine their performance through experiments.

Cross-Attention Between Caption Word and Dual Visual Features. We show three designs of cross-attention between the word features and the dual visual features (i.e., the region features $\mathcal{R}$ and the grid features $\mathcal{G}$) as below.

Concatenated Cross-Attention. The simplest approach is to concatenate the two visual features and use the resultant features as keys and values in the standard multi-head attention sub-layer, where the words serve as queries; see Fig. 3(a).

Sequential Cross-Attention. Another approach is to perform cross-attention computation separately for the two visual features. The corresponding design is to place two independent multi-head attention sub-layers in a sequential fashion, and uses one for the grid features and the other for the region features (or the opposite combination); see Fig. 3(b). Note that their order could affect the performance.

Parallel Cross-Attention. The third approach is to perform multi-head attention computation on the two visual features in parallel. To do so, we use two multi-head attention mechanisms with independent learnable parameters. The detailed design is as follows. Let $X_{l-1} = \{x_i^{l-1}\}$ be the word features inputted to the meta-layer l containing this cross attention sub-layer. As shown in Fig. 2, they are first input to the self-attention sub-layer, converted into $X_l' = \{x_i'\}$ (layer index l omitted for brevity) and then input to this cross attention sub-layer. In this sub-layer, multi-head attention (MHA) is computed with $\{x_i'\}$ as queries and the region features $\mathcal{R}$ as keys and values, yielding attended features $\{a_i^r\}$. The same computation is performed in parallel with the grid features $\mathcal{G}$ as keys and values, yielding $\{a_i^g\}$. Next, we concatenate them with x_i' as $[a_i^r; x_i']$ and $[a_i^g; x_i']$, projecting them back to d-dimensional vector using learnable affine projections. Normalizing them with sigmoid into probabilities $\{c_i^r\}$ and $\{c_i^g\}$, respectively, we have

$$c_i^g = \text{sigmoid}(W^g[a_i^g; x_i'] + b^g), \tag{2}$$

$$c_i^r = \text{sigmoid}(W^r[a_i^r; x_i'] + b^r). \tag{3}$$

We then multiply them with $\{a_i^r\}$ and $\{a_i^g\}$, add the resultant vectors to $\{x_i'\}$, and finally feed to layer normalization, obtaining $\mathcal{A}_l = \{a_i^{(l)}\}$ as follows:

$$a_i^{(l)} = \text{LN}(c_i^g \otimes a_i^g + c_i^r \otimes a_i^r + x_i'). \tag{4}$$

Caption Generator Losses. Following a standard practice of image captioning studies, we pre-train our model with a cross-entropy loss (XE) and finetune it using the CIDEr-D optimization with self-critical sequence training strategy [39]. Specifically, the model is first trained to predict the next word x_t^* at $t = 1..T$, given the ground-truth sentence $x_{1:T}^*$. This is equal to minimize the following XE loss with respect to the model's parameter θ:

$$\mathcal{L}_{XE}(\theta) = -\sum_{t=1}^{T} \log\left(p_\theta\left(x_t^* | x_{0:t-1}^*\right)\right). \tag{5}$$

We then finetune the model with the CIDEr-D optimization, where we use the CIDEr score as the reward and the mean of the rewards as the reward baseline, following [7]. The loss for self-critical sequence training is given by

$$\mathcal{L}_{RL}(\theta) = -\frac{1}{k}\sum_{i=1}^{k}(r(\mathbf{w}^i) - b)\log p(\mathbf{w}^i), \tag{6}$$

where $\mathbf{w}^i$ is the i-th sentence in the beam; $r(\cdot)$ is the reward function; and b is the reward baseline; and k is the number of samples in the batch.

4   Experiments

4.1   Datasets

Object Detection. As mentioned earlier, we train our object detector (including the backbone) in two steps. In the first step, we train it on object detection using either Visual Genome [23] or a combination [55] of four datasets: COCO [28], Visual Genome, Open Images [24], and Object365 [40], depending on what previous methods we experimentally compare. In the second step, we train the model on object detection plus attribute prediction using Visual Genome. Note that following the standard practice, we exclude the duplicated samples appearing in the testing and validation splits of the COCO and nocaps [2] datasets to remove data contamination. See the supplementary material for more details.

Image Captioning. We conduct our experiments on the COCO dataset, the standard for the research of image captioning [28]. The dataset contains 123,287 images, each annotated with five different captions. For offline evaluation, we follow the widely adopted Karpathy split [19], where 113,287, 5,000, and 5,000 images are used for training, validation, and testing respectively.

To test our method's effectiveness on other image captioning datasets, we also report the performances on the nocaps dataset and the Artemis dataset [1]. See the supplementary material for more details.

4.2   Implementation Details

Evaluation Metrics. We employ the standard evaluation protocol for the evaluation of methods. Specifically, we use the full set of captioning metrics: BLEU@N [35], METEOR [5], ROUGE-L [27], CIDEr [43], and SPICE [3]. We will use the abbreviations, B@N, M, R, C, and S, to denote BLEU@N, METEOR, ROUGE-L, CIDEr, and SPICE, respectively.

Hyperparameters Settings. In our model, we set the dimension d of each layer to 512, the number of heads to eight. We employ dropout with the dropout rate of 0.2 on the output of each MHA and FFN sub-layer following [42]. We set the number of layers as $L_r = 6$ for the object detector, as $L_g = 3$ for the grid feature network, and as $L_c = 3$ for the caption generator. Following previous studies, we convert all the captions to lower-case, remove punctuation characters, and perform tokenization with the SpaCy toolkit [15]. We build the vocabularies, excluding the words which appear less than five times in the training and validation splits.

4.3   Training Details

First Stage. In the first stage, we pretrain the object detector with the backbone. We consider several existing region-based methods for comparison, which

Table 1. Results of ablation tests on the COCO test split. All the models are trained with the XE loss and finetuned by the CIDEr optimization.

(a)				(b)			
Factor	Choice	CIDEr	B@4	Cross Attention	Choice	CIDEr	B@4
(1) **Backbone Network**	ImageNet	135.5	41.5	(1) **Concatenated**	$\mathcal{G}$	142.1	41.7
- Training data	VG	142.3	41.9	- Visual features	$\mathcal{R}$	142.9	41.9
	4DS	**144.2**	**42.4**		$[\mathcal{G} \; ; \mathcal{R}]$	143.1	41.9
(2) **Region features**	50	141.4	41.9	(2) **Sequential**			
- Number of vectors	100	141.8	41.5	- Sequential order	$\mathcal{G} \to \mathcal{R}$	144.0	42.1
(trained on VG)	150	**142.3**	**41.9**		$\mathcal{R} \to \mathcal{G}$	143.6	42.1
(3) **Training strategy**				(3) **Parallel**			
- End-to-end training	Yes	**144.2**	42.4	- Gated activation	Sigmoid	**144.2**	**42.4**
	No	139.6	**42.7**		Identity	143.9	41.6

employ similar pretraining of an object detector but use different datasets. For a fair comparison, we consider two settings. One uses Visual Genome for training, following most previous methods. We train our detector for 150,000 iterations with a batch size of 32. The other (results indicated with † in what follows) uses the four datasets mentioned above, following [55]. We train the detector for 125,000 iterations with a batch size of 256. In both settings, the input image is resized so that the maximum for the shorter side is 800 and for the longer side is 1333. We use Adam optimizer [22] with a learning rate of 10^{-4}, decreased by 10 at iteration 120,000 and 100,000 in the first and second settings, respectively. We follow [58] for other training procedures. After this, we finetune the models on object detection plus attribute prediction using Visual Genome for additional five epochs with a learning rate of 10^{-5}, following [4,55]. The supplementary material presents the details of implementation and experimental results on object detection.

Second Stage. We train the entire model for the image captioning task in the second stage. We employ the standard method for word representation, i.e., linear projections of one-hot vectors to vectors of dimension $d = 512$. In this stage, all the input images are resized so that the maximum dimensions for the shorter side and longer side are 384 and 640 before augmented with RandAugment [8]. We train models, as explained earlier. Specifically, we train models with the cross-entropy loss $\mathcal{L}_{XE}$ for ten epochs, in which we warmp up the learning rates for the grid feature network and the caption generator from 10^{-5} to 10^{-4} in the first epoch, while we fix those for the backbone network and the object detector at 10^{-5}. Then, we finetune the model based on the CIDEr-D optimization for ten epochs, where we set the fixed learning rate to 5×10^{-6} for the entire model. We use the Adam optimizer [22] with a batch size of 128. For the CIDEr-D optimization, we use beam search with a beam size of 5 and a length of 20.

4.4 Performance of Different Configurations

Our method has several design choices. We conduct experiments to examine which configuration is the best. The results are shown in Table 1. We used an identical configuration unless otherwise noted. Specifically, we use the feature extractor pretrained on the four datasets and parallel cross-attention for fusing the region and grid features.

The first block of Table 1(a) shows the effects of different (pre)training strategies of the visual backbone on image captioning performance. The 'ImageNet' column shows the result of the model using a Swin Transformer backbone pretrained on ImageNet21K and the grid features alone; 'VG' and '4DS' indicate the models with a detector pretrained on Visual Genome and the four datasets, respectively. They show that using more datasets leads to better performance.

The second block of Table 1(a) shows the effects of the number of object queries, or equivalently region features. The performance increases as they vary as 50, 100, and 150. We also confirmed that the performance is saturated for more region features, while the computational cost and false detection increase.

The third block shows the effect of the end-to-end training of the entire model. 'Yes' indicates the end-to-end training of the entire model and 'No' indicates training the model but the vision backbone. The results show that the end-to-end training considerably improves CIDEr score (from 139.6 to 144.3) with little sacrifice of B@4. This validates our expectation about the effectiveness of the end-to-end training; it arguably helps reduce the domain gap between object detection and image captioning.

The first block of Table 1(b) shows the performances of the model employing the concatenated cross-attention and its two variants using the grid features alone or the region features alone. They show that the region features alone work better than the grid features alone, and their fusion achieves the highest performance.

The three blocks of Table 1(b) show the performances of the three cross-attention architectures explained in Sect. 3.2. The second block shows the two variants of the sequential cross-attention, and the third block shows the two variants of the parallel cross-attention with different gated activation functions, i.e., sigmoid and identity. By identity activation, we mean setting all the values of c_i^g and c_i^r in Eq. (4) to one. These results show that the parallel cross-attention with sigmoid activation function performs the best; the sequential cross-attention in the order $\mathcal{G} \to \mathcal{R}$ attains the second best result.

4.5 Results on the COCO Dataset

We next show complete results on the COCO dataset by the offline and online evaluations. We present example results in the supplementary material.

Offline Evaluation. Table 2 shows the performances of our method and the current state-of-the-art methods on the offline Karpathy test split. The compared

Table 2. Offline results evaluated on the COCO Karpathy test split. 'V. E. type' indicates the type of visual features; '# VL Data' is the number of image-text pairs used for vision-language pretraining.

Method	V. E. Type	# VL Data	Performance Metrics					
			B@1	B@4	M	R	C	S
w/ VL pretraining								
UVLP [57]	$\mathcal{R}$	3.0M	-	39.5	29.3	-	129.3	23.2
Oscar$_{base}$ [26]	$\mathcal{R}$	6.5M	-	40.5	29.7	-	137.6	22.8
VinVL$^{\dagger}_{large}$[55]	$\mathcal{R}$	8.9M	-	**41.0**	31.1	-	140.9	25.2
SimVLM$_{huge}$ [46]	$\mathcal{G}$	1.8B	-	40.6	**33.7**	-	**143.3**	**25.4**
w/o VL pretraining								
SAT [44]	$\mathcal{G}$	-	-	31.9	25.5	54.3	106.3	-
SCST [39]	$\mathcal{G}$	-	-	34.2	26.7	55.7	114.0	-
RSTNet [56]	$\mathcal{G}$	-	81.8	40.1	29.8	59.5	135.6	23.0
Up-Down [4]	$\mathcal{R}$	-	79.8	36.3	27.7	56.9	120.1	21.4
RFNet [21]	$\mathcal{R}$	-	79.1	36.5	27.7	57.3	121.9	21.2
GCN-LSTM [53]	$\mathcal{R}$	-	80.5	38.2	28.5	58.3	127.6	22.0
LBPF [36]	$\mathcal{R}$	-	80.5	38.3	28.5	58.4	127.6	22.0
SGAE [50]	$\mathcal{R}$	-	80.8	38.4	28.4	58.6	127.8	22.1
AoA [16]	$\mathcal{R}$	-	80.2	38.9	29.2	58.8	129.8	22.4
NG-SAN [13]	$\mathcal{R}$	-	-	39.9	29.3	59.2	132.1	23.3
GET [17]	$\mathcal{R}$	-	81.5	39.5	29.3	58.9	131.6	22.8
ORT [14]	$\mathcal{R}$	-	80.5	38.6	28.7	58.4	128.3	22.6
ETA [25]	$\mathcal{R}$	-	81.5	39.3	28.8	58.9	126.6	22.6
$\mathcal{M}^2$ Transformer [7]	$\mathcal{R}$	-	80.8	39.1	29.2	58.6	131.2	22.6
X-LAN [34]	$\mathcal{R}$	-	80.8	39.5	29.5	59.2	132.0	23.4
TCIC [11]	$\mathcal{R}$	-	81.8	40.8	29.5	59.2	135.4	22.5
Dual Global [47]	$\mathcal{R}+\mathcal{G}$	-	81.3	40.3	29.2	59.4	132.4	23.3
DLCT [32]	$\mathcal{R}+\mathcal{G}$	-	81.4	39.8	29.5	59.1	133.8	23.0
GRIT	$\mathcal{R}+\mathcal{G}$	-	83.5	41.9	30.5	60.5	142.2	24.2
GRIT†	$\mathcal{R}+\mathcal{G}$	-	**84.2**	**42.4**	**30.6**	**60.7**	**144.2**	**24.3**

methods are as follows: grid-based methods [39,44,54,56], region-based methods [4,7,11,13,14,16,16,17,21,25,34,36,50,53], the methods employing both grid and region features [32,47], and also the methods relying on large-scale pretraining on vision and language (V&L) tasks using a large image-text corpus [26,55,57], including SimVLM$_{huge}$, a model pretrained on an extremely large dataset (i.e., 1.8 billion image-caption pairs) [46].

For fair comparison with the region-based methods, we report the results of two variants of our model, one with the object detector pretrained on Visual Genome alone and the other (marked with †) with the object detector pretrained on the four datasets, as explained earlier. It is seen from Table 2 that our models, regardless of the datasets used for the detector's pretraining, outperform all the methods that do not use large-scale pretraining of vision and

Table 3. Online evaluation results on the COCO image captioning dataset

Method	Ensemble	B-1		B-2		B-3		B-4		M		R		C	
		c5	c40	c5	c40	c5	c40	c5	c40	c5	c40	c5	c40	c5	c40
w/ VL pretraining															
VinVL$_{large}$ [55]	✗	81.9	96.9	66.9	92.4	52.6	84.7	40.4	74.9	30.6	40.8	60.4	76.8	134.7	138.7
w/o VL pretraining															
SCST [39]	✓	78.1	93.7	61.9	86.0	47.0	75.9	35.2	64.5	27.0	35.5	56.3	70.7	114.7	116.7
Up-Down [4]	✓	80.2	95.2	64.1	88.8	49.1	79.4	36.9	68.5	27.6	36.7	57.1	72.4	117.9	120.5
HAN [45]	✓	80.4	94.5	63.8	87.7	48.8	78.0	36.5	66.8	27.4	36.1	57.3	71.9	115.2	118.2
GCN-LSTM [53]	✓	80.8	95.2	65.5	89.3	50.8	80.3	38.7	69.7	28.5	37.6	58.5	73.4	125.3	126.5
SGAE [50]	✓	81.0	95.3	65.6	89.5	50.7	80.4	38.5	69.7	28.2	37.2	58.6	73.6	123.8	126.5
AoA [16]	✓	81.0	95.0	65.8	89.6	51.4	81.3	39.4	71.2	29.1	38.5	58.9	74.5	126.9	129.6
HIP [52]	✗	81.6	95.9	66.2	90.4	51.5	81.6	39.3	71.0	28.8	38.1	59.0	74.1	127.9	130.2
$\mathcal{M}^2$Trans. [7]	✓	81.6	96.0	66.4	90.8	51.8	82.7	39.7	72.8	29.4	39.0	59.2	74.8	129.3	132.1
X-LAN [34]	✓	81.9	95.7	66.9	90.5	52.4	82.5	40.3	72.4	29.6	39.2	59.5	75.0	131.1	133.5
Dual Global [47]	✗	80.8	95.1	65.6	81.3	51.1	81.3	39.1	71.2	28.9	38.4	58.9	74.4	126.3	129.2
DLCT [32]	✓	82.4	96.6	67.4	91.7	52.8	83.8	40.6	74.0	29.8	39.6	59.8	75.3	133.3	135.4
GRIT†	✗	83.7	97.4	68.5	92.8	53.9	85.3	41.5	75.6	30.3	40.2	60.2	75.9	138.3	141.8
GRIT†	✓	**84.1**	**97.6**	**69.4**	**93.5**	**54.9**	**86.3**	**42.5**	**76.8**	**30.9**	**41.0**	**61.2**	**77.1**	**141.3**	**143.8**

language tasks (i.e., the methods in the second block entitled 'w/o VL pretraining'). Moreover, our model with the detector pretrained solely on Visual Genome (i.e., 'GRIT') performs better than those relying on large-scale V&L pretraining but SimVLM$_{huge}$. Finally, our model with the pretrained detector on multiple datasets (i.e., 'GRIT†') outperforms SimVLM$_{huge}$ leveraging large-scale V&L pretraining in CIDEr score (i.e., 144.2 vs 143.3).

Online Evaluation. We also evaluate our models (i.e., a single model and an ensemble of six models) on the 40K testing images by submitting their results on the official evaluation server. Table 3 shows the results and those of all the published methods on the leaderboard. Table 3 presents the metric scores based on five (c5) and 40 reference captions (c40) per image. We can see that our method achieves the best scores for all the metrics. Note that even our single model outperforms all the published methods that use ensembles.

4.6 Results on the ArtEmis and Nocaps Datasets

As explained above, we evaluate our method on the ArtEmis and nocaps datasets. For nocaps, we evaluate zero-shot inference performance, i.e., the performance of the model trained on COCO. For ArtEmis, we train the model in the same way as COCO except for the number of training epochs, precisely, five epochs each for the training with the XE loss and that with the CIDEr-D optimization.

Table 4. Performance on the ArtEmis and nocaps datasets

a) Performance on the ArtEmis test split

Method	V. E. Type	B@1	B@2	B@3	B@4	M	R
NN [1]	$\mathcal{H}$	36.4	13.9	5.4	2.2	10.2	21.0
ANP [1]	$\mathcal{G}$	39.6	13.4	4.2	1.4	8.8	20.2
SAT [1]	$\mathcal{G}$	53.6	29.0	15.5	8.7	14.2	29.7
$\mathcal{M}^2$Trans. [1]	$\mathcal{R}$	50.7	28.2	15.9	9.5	13.7	28.0
GRIT†	$\mathcal{R}+\mathcal{G}$	**70.1**	**40.1**	**20.9**	**11.3**	**16.8**	**33.3**

b) Performance on the nocaps validation split

Method	V.E Type	In-Domain C	In-Domain S	Out-Domain C	Out-Domain S	Overall C	Overall S
NBT [2]	$\mathcal{R}$	62.7	10.1	54.0	8.6	53.9	9.2
Up-down [2]	$\mathcal{R}$	78.1	11.6	31.3	8.3	55.3	10.1
Trans. [7]	$\mathcal{R}$	78.0	11.0	29.7	7.8	54.7	9.8
$\mathcal{M}^2$Trans. [7]	$\mathcal{R}$	85.7	12.1	38.9	8.9	64.5	11.1
GRIT†	$\mathcal{R}+\mathcal{G}$	**105.9**	**13.6**	**72.6**	**11.1**	**90.2**	**12.8**

Table 4(a) shows the results of our method on the test split of ArtEmis [1]. It also show the results of existing methods reported in [1], which are grid-based [33,44], region-based [7], and a nearest neighbor method using a holistic vector to encode images (denoted as $\mathcal{H}$). Our method outperforms all these methods by a large margin.

Table 4 shows the results on the nocaps dataset, including the baseline methods reported in [2,7]. All the models are trained on the training split of the COCO datasets and tested on the validation split of nocaps, which consists of images with novel objects and captions with unseen vocabularies. Our method surpasses all the other methods including region-based methods [4,7,31] in both in-domain and out-of-domain images. See the supplementary material for the full results.

4.7   Computational Efficiency

We measured the inference time of GRIT and two representative region-based methods, VinVL [55] and $\mathcal{M}^2$ Transformer [7]. It is the computational time per image from image input to caption generation. Specifically, we measured the time to generate a caption of length 20 with a beam size of five on a V100 GPU. The input image resolution was set to 800×1333 for VinVL and $\mathcal{M}^2$ Transformer as reported in [4,55]. We set it to 384×640 for GRIT since it already achieves higher accuracy. Figure 1 shows the breakdown of the inference time for the three methods. GRIT reduces the time for feature extraction by a factor of 10 compared with the others. Similar to $\mathcal{M}^2$ Transformer, GRIT has a lightweight caption generator and thus spends much less time than VinVL for generating a caption after receiving the visual features. GRIT can run with minibatch size up to 64 on a single V100 GPU, while others cannot afford large minibatch. With minibatch size ≥ 32, the per-image inference time decreases to about 32ms. More details are given in the supplementary material.

5   Summary and Conclusion

In this paper, we have proposed a Transformer-based architecture for image captioning named GRIT. It integrates the region features and the grid features extracted from an input image to extract richer visual information from input images. Previous SOTA methods employ a CNN-based detector to extract region features, which prevents the end-to-end training of the entire model and makes to high computational costs. Using the Swin Transformer for a backbone extracting the initial visual feature, GRIT resolves these two issues by employing a DETR-based detector. Furthermore, GRIT obtains grid features by updating the feature from the same backbone using a self-attention Transformer, aiming to extract richer context information complementing the region feature. These two features are fed to the caption generator equipped with a unique cross-attention mechanism, which computes and applies attention from the dual features on the generated caption sentence. The integration of all these components led to significant performance improvement. The experimental results validated our approach, showing that GRIT outperforms all published methods by a large margin in inference accuracy and speed.

Acknowledgments. This work was supported by JST [Moonshot Research and Development], Grant Number [JPMJMS2032] and by JSPS KAKENHI Grant Number 20H05952 and 19H01110.

References

1. Achlioptas, P., Ovsjanikov, M., Haydarov, K., Elhoseiny, M., Guibas, L.J.: Artemis: affective language for visual art. In: Proceedings of the IEEE Conference on Computer Vision and Pattern Recognition, pp. 11569–11579 (2021)
2. Agrawal, H., et al.: Nocaps: novel object captioning at scale. In: Proceedings of the IEEE International Conference on Computer Vision, pp. 8948–8957 (2019)
3. Anderson, P., Fernando, B., Johnson, M., Gould, S.: Spice: semantic propositional image caption evaluation. In: Proceedings of European Conference on Computer Vision, pp. 382–398 (2016)
4. Anderson, P., et al.: Bottom-up and top-down attention for image captioning and visual question answering. In: Proceedings of the IEEE Conference on Computer Vision and Pattern Recognition, pp. 6077–6086 (2018)
5. Banerjee, S., Lavie, A.: Meteor: an automatic metric for MT evaluation with improved correlation with human judgments. In: Proceedings of the ACL Workshop on Intrinsic and Extrinsic Evaluation Measures for Machine Translation and/or Summarization, pp. 65–72 (2005)
6. Carion, N., Massa, F., Synnaeve, G., Usunier, N., Kirillov, A., Zagoruyko, S.: End-to-end object detection with transformers. In: Vedaldi, A., Bischof, H., Brox, T., Frahm, J.-M. (eds.) ECCV 2020. LNCS, vol. 12346, pp. 213–229. Springer, Cham (2020). https://doi.org/10.1007/978-3-030-58452-8_13
7. Cornia, M., Stefanini, M., Baraldi, L., Cucchiara, R.: Meshed-memory transformer for image captioning. In: Proceedings of the IEEE Conference on Computer Vision and Pattern Recognition, pp. 10578–10587 (2020)
8. Cubuk, E.D., Zoph, B., Shlens, J., Le, Q.V.: Randaugment: practical automated data augmentation with a reduced search space. In: Proceedings of the IEEE Conference on Computer Vision and Pattern Recognition Workshops, pp. 702–703 (2020)
9. Devlin, J., Chang, M.W., Lee, K., Toutanova, K.: Bert: pre-training of deep bidirectional transformers for language understanding. arXiv:1810.04805 (2018)

10. Dosovitskiy, A., et al.: An image is worth 16x16 words: transformers for image recognition at scale. arXiv:2010.11929 (2020)
11. Fan, Z., et al.: TCIC: theme concepts learning cross language and vision for image captioning. arXiv:2106.10936 (2021)
12. Fang, Y., et al.: You only look at one sequence: rethinking transformer in vision through object detection. In: Proceedings of Advances in Neural Information Processing Systems (2021)
13. Guo, L., Liu, J., Zhu, X., Yao, P., Lu, S., Lu, H.: Normalized and geometry-aware self-attention network for image captioning. In: Proceedings of the IEEE Conference on Computer Vision and Pattern Recognition, pp. 10327–10336 (2020)
14. Herdade, S., Kappeler, A., Boakye, K., Soares, J.: Image captioning: transforming objects into words. In: Proceedings of Advances in Neural Information Processing Systems (2019)
15. Honnibal, M., Montani, I.: spaCy 2: natural language understanding with Bloom embeddings, convolutional neural networks and incremental parsing (2017, to appear)
16. Huang, L., Wang, W., Chen, J., Wei, X.Y.: Attention on attention for image captioning. In: Proceedings of the IEEE International Conference on Computer Vision, pp. 4634–4643 (2019)
17. Ji, J., et al.: Improving image captioning by leveraging intra-and inter-layer global representation in transformer network. In: Proceedings of the AAAI Conference on Artificial Intelligence, pp. 1655–1663 (2021)
18. Jiang, H., Misra, I., Rohrbach, M., Learned-Miller, E., Chen, X.: In defense of grid features for visual question answering. In: Proceedings of the IEEE Conference on Computer Vision and Pattern Recognition, pp. 10267–10276 (2020)
19. Karpathy: Karpathy/neuraltalk: Neuraltalk is a python+numpy project for learning multimodal recurrent neural networks that describe images with sentences. https://github.com/karpathy/neuraltalk
20. Karpathy, A., Fei-Fei, L.: Deep visual-semantic alignments for generating image descriptions. In: Proceedings of the IEEE Conference on Computer Vision and Pattern Recognition, pp. 3128–3137 (2015)
21. Ke, L., Pei, W., Li, R., Shen, X., Tai, Y.W.: Reflective decoding network for image captioning. In: Proceedings of the IEEE International Conference on Computer Vision, pp. 8888–8897 (2019)
22. Kingma, D.P., Ba, J.: Adam: a method for stochastic optimization. In: Proceedings of International Conference on Representation Learning (2015)
23. Krishna, R., et al.: Visual genome: connecting language and vision using crowd-sourced dense image annotations. Int. J. Comput. Vision **123**(1), 32–73 (2017). https://doi.org/10.1007/s11263-016-0981-7
24. Kuznetsova, A., et al.: The open images dataset V4: unified image classification, object detection, and visual relationship detection at scale. Int. J. Comput. Vision **128**, 1956–1981 (2020)
25. Li, G., Zhu, L., Liu, P., Yang, Y.: Entangled transformer for image captioning. In: Proceedings of the IEEE International Conference on Computer Vision, pp. 8928–8937 (2019)
26. Li, X., et al.: Oscar: object-semantics aligned pre-training for vision-language tasks. In: Proceedings of European Conference on Computer Vision, pp. 121–137 (2020)
27. Lin, C.Y.: Rouge: a package for automatic evaluation of summaries. In: Text Summarization Branches Out, pp. 74–81 (2004)
28. Lin, T.Y., et al.: Microsoft coco: common objects in context. In: Proceedings of European Conference on Computer Vision, pp. 740–755 (2014)

29. Liu, Z., et al.: Swin transformer: hierarchical vision transformer using shifted windows. In: Proceedings of the IEEE International Conference on Computer Vision, pp. 10012–10022 (2021)
30. Lu, J., Xiong, C., Parikh, D., Socher, R.: Knowing when to look: adaptive attention via a visual sentinel for image captioning. In: Proceedings of the IEEE Conference on Computer Vision and Pattern Recognition, pp. 375–383 (2017)
31. Lu, J., Yang, J., Batra, D., Parikh, D.: Neural baby talk. In: Proceedings of the IEEE Conference on Computer Vision and Pattern Recognition, pp. 7219–7228 (2018)
32. Luo, Y., et al.: Dual-level collaborative transformer for image captioning. In: Proceedings of the AAAI Conference on Artificial Intelligence, pp. 2286–2293 (2021)
33. Mathews, A., Xie, L., He, X.: Senticap: generating image descriptions with sentiments. In: Proceedings of the AAAI Conference on Artificial Intelligence, pp. 3574–3580 (2016)
34. Pan, Y., Yao, T., Li, Y., Mei, T.: X-linear attention networks for image captioning. In: Proceedings of the IEEE International Conference on Computer Vision, pp. 10971–10980 (2020)
35. Papineni, K., Roukos, S., Ward, T., Zhu, W.J.: Bleu: a method for automatic evaluation of machine translation. In: Proceedings of the Annual Meeting of the Association for Computational Linguistics, pp. 311–318 (2002)
36. Qin, Y., Du, J., Zhang, Y., Lu, H.: Look back and predict forward in image captioning. In: Proceedings of the IEEE Conference on Computer Vision and Pattern Recognition, pp. 8367–8375 (2019)
37. Radford, A., Narasimhan, K., Salimans, T., Sutskever, I.: Improving language understanding by generative pre-training. Technical report. OpenAI (2018)
38. Ren, S., He, K., Girshick, R., Sun, J.: Faster R-CNN: towards real-time object detection with region proposal networks. In: Proceedings of Advances in Neural Information Processing Systems, pp. 91–99 (2015)
39. Rennie, S.J., Marcheret, E., Mroueh, Y., Ross, J., Goel, V.: Self-critical sequence training for image captioning. In: Proceedings of the IEEE Conference on Computer Vision and Pattern Recognition, pp. 7008–7024 (2017)
40. Shao, S., et al.: Objects365: a large-scale, high-quality dataset for object detection. In: Proceedings of the IEEE International Conference on Computer Vision, pp. 8430–8439 (2019)
41. Song, H., et al.: ViDT: an efficient and effective fully transformer-based object detector. arXiv:2110.03921 (2021)
42. Vaswani, A., et al.: Attention is all you need. arXiv:1706.03762 (2017)
43. Vedantam, R., Lawrence Zitnick, C., Parikh, D.: Cider: consensus-based image description evaluation. In: Proceedings of the IEEE Conference on Computer Vision and Pattern Recognition, pp. 4566–4575 (2015)
44. Vinyals, O., Toshev, A., Bengio, S., Erhan, D.: Show and tell: a neural image caption generator. In: Proceedings of the IEEE Conference on Computer Vision and Pattern Recognition, pp. 3156–3164 (2015)
45. Wang, W., Chen, Z., Hu, H.: Hierarchical attention network for image captioning. In: Proceedings of the AAAI Conference on Artificial Intelligence, pp. 8957–8964 (2019)
46. Wang, Z., Yu, J., Yu, A.W., Dai, Z., Tsvetkov, Y., Cao, Y.: SimVLM: simple visual language model pretraining with weak supervision. arXiv:2108.10904 (2021)
47. Xian, T., Li, Z., Zhang, C., Ma, H.: Dual global enhanced transformer for image captioning. Neural Netw. **148**, 129–141 (2022)

48. Xu, H., et al.: E2E-VLP: end-to-end vision-language pre-training enhanced by visual learning. arXiv:2106.01804 (2021)
49. Xu, K., et al.: Show, attend and tell: Neural image caption generation with visual attention. In: Proceedings of International Conference on Machine Learning, pp. 2048–2057 (2015)
50. Yang, X., Tang, K., Zhang, H., Cai, J.: Auto-encoding scene graphs for image captioning. In: Proceedings of the IEEE Conference on Computer Vision and Pattern Recognition, pp. 10685–10694 (2019)
51. Yang, X., Zhang, H., Cai, J.: Learning to collocate neural modules for image captioning. In: Proceedings of the IEEE International Conference on Computer Vision, pp. 4250–4260 (2019)
52. Yao, T., Pan, Y., Li, Y., Mei, T.: Hierarchy parsing for image captioning. In: Proceedings of International Conference on Computer Vision, pp. 2621–2629 (2019)
53. Yao, T., Pan, Y., Li, Y., Mei, T.: Exploring visual relationship for image captioning. In: Proceedings of European Conference on Computer Vision, pp. 684–699 (2018)
54. Yao, T., Pan, Y., Li, Y., Qiu, Z., Mei, T.: Boosting image captioning with attributes. In: Proceedings of the IEEE International Conference on Computer Vision, pp. 4894–4902 (2017)
55. Zhang, P., et al.: VinVL: revisiting visual representations in vision-language models. In: Proceedings of the IEEE Conference on Computer Vision and Pattern Recognition, pp. 5579–5588 (2021)
56. Zhang, X., et al.: RSTNet: captioning with adaptive attention on visual and non-visual words. In: Proceedings of the IEEE Conference on Computer Vision and Pattern Recognition, pp. 15465–15474 (2021)
57. Zhou, L., Palangi, H., Zhang, L., Hu, H., Corso, J., Gao, J.: Unified vision-language pre-training for image captioning and VQA. In: Proceedings of the AAAI Conference on Artificial Intelligence, pp. 13041–13049 (2020)
58. Zhu, X., Su, W., Lu, L., Li, B., Wang, X., Dai, J.: Deformable DETR: deformable transformers for end-to-end object detection. In: Proceedings of International Conference of Learning Representations (2021)

Selective Query-Guided Debiasing for Video Corpus Moment Retrieval

Sunjae Yoon[1], Ji Woo Hong[1], Eunseop Yoon[1], Dahyun Kim[1,2], Junyeong Kim[2], Hee Suk Yoon[1], and Chang D. Yoo[1(✉)]

[1] Korea Advanced Institute of Science and Technology, Daejeon, Republic of Korea
sunjae.yoon@kaist.ac.rk, cd_yoo@kaist.ac.kr
[2] Chung-Ang University, Seoul 06974, Republic of Korea
junyeongkim@cau.ac.kr

Abstract. Video moment retrieval (VMR) aims to localize target moments in untrimmed videos pertinent to a given textual query. Existing retrieval systems tend to rely on retrieval bias as a shortcut and thus, fail to sufficiently learn multi-modal interactions between query and video. This retrieval bias stems from learning frequent co-occurrence patterns between query and moments, which spuriously correlate objects (e.g., a pencil) referred in the query with moments (e.g., scene of writing with a pencil) where the objects frequently appear in the video, such that they converge into biased moment predictions. Although recent debiasing methods have focused on removing this retrieval bias, we argue that these biased predictions sometimes should be preserved because there are many queries where biased predictions are rather helpful. To conjugate this retrieval bias, we propose a Selective Query-guided Debiasing network (SQuiDNet), which incorporates the following two main properties: (1) Biased Moment Retrieval that intentionally uncovers the biased moments inherent in objects of the query and (2) Selective Query-guided Debiasing that performs selective debiasing guided by the meaning of the query. Our experimental results on three moment retrieval benchmarks (i.e., TVR, ActivityNet, DiDeMo) show the effectiveness of SQuiDNet and qualitative analysis shows improved interpretability.

Keywords: Video moment retrieval · Retrieval bias · Selective debiasing

1 Introduction

Video streaming services (e.g., YouTube, Netflix) have rapidly grown these days, which promotes the development of video search technologies. As one of these video search technologies, video moment retrieval (VMR) [1,8] serves as essential building block to underpin many frontier interactive AI systems, including video/image captioning [26,31], video/image question answering [14,23] and visual dialog [3]. VMR aims to localize temporal moments of video pertinent to textual query. Recently, the growing interest in video searching drove this VMR

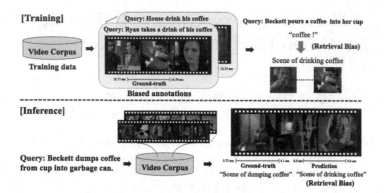

Fig. 1. VCMR training and inference. The biased annotations in training dataset make retrieval bias, which causes biased moment prediction in the inference.

to perform in a more general format of retrieval, referred to as video corpus moment retrieval (VCMR) [15]. VCMR also aims to localize a moment like VMR, but the search spaces extend to a 'video corpus' composed of the large number of videos. Therefore, given query, VCMR conducts two sub-tasks: (1) identifying relevant video in the video corpus and (2) localizing a moment in the identified video. Despite this respectful effort to generalize video retrieval, the VCMR systems still suffer from dependence on retrieval bias, which hinders the system from accurately learning multi-modal interactions. Figure 1 gives an example of incorrect moment predictions due to the retrieval bias. Given query as "Beckett dumps coffee from cup into garbage can" in inference time, current retrieval systems make incorrect moment prediction with the scene of 'drinking a coffee'. This is because annotations of training dataset include many co-occurrences between the object word 'coffee' in query and the scene of 'drinking,' which leads to biased moment prediction referred to as *retrieval bias*. This retrieval bias constrains an object (e.g., coffee) to specific scene (e.g., scene of drinking), thus the other scenes related to that object word lose chance to be searched. Recent debiasing methods [19,30] have focused on removing or mitigating this retrieval bias as they assume the bias degrades retrievals. However, we argue that these biased predictions sometimes should be preserved because there are many queries where biased prediction is rather helpful, such that selective debiasing is required.

Our experimental studies in Fig. 2 prove that retrieval bias can also be 'good'. Figure 2-(a) presents a temporal intersection of union (tIoU) scores for all queries between moment predictions and ground-truth. The predictions are from two retrieval models: (1) the current best performance model and (2) the biased retrieval model. The biased retrieval model is intended to predict biased moments for given queries. To implement this, we simply build a toy model and give it 'nouns in the query' as inputs instead of 'full query sentence'. This induces a deficiency of the original query's meaning and leads the model to depend on predicting moments where those nouns are mainly used. After that, we represent these two retrieval models' predictions in a joint-plot of tIoU scores, where it is noted that the plot shows positive correlations. This correlation stands out strong

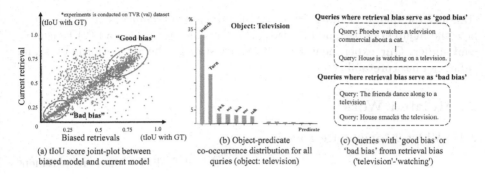

Fig. 2. (a) All predictions' tIoU score joint plot between biased model and current model shows correlations between two models, (b) object ('television')-predicate co-occurrence distribution for all queries shows predominant predicate word ('watch'), (c) exemplifies queries where the retrieval bias ('television'-'scene of watching television') serves as 'good bias' or 'bad bias' from statistics in (b).

in predictions of low and high tIoU scores, which tells that the current retrieval is both harmed and helped by the retrieval bias. Therefore, retrieval bias includes both *good bias* and *bad bias*. Then, what distinguishes good bias and bad bias? Figure 2(b) give example of our insight on this. We investigate predicates that appear together with a specific word (e.g., television) in all queries and identify that one or two predicates (e.g., watch, turn) are predominantly bound with that word. From these, we have knowledge that query sentences including object word and its most co-occurrent predicate should benefit from retrieval bias (i.e., good bias) because there are also many corresponding scenes (e.g., scene of watching television), but queries with other predicates would be degraded (i.e., bad bias) by this retrieval bias. Figure 2(c) shows query samples where the retrieval bias (i.e., television-scene of watching) serves as 'good bias' or 'bad bias'.

Intrigued by these two characteristics of retrieval bias, we propose a Selective Query-guided Debiasing network (SQuiDNet), which incorporates the following two main properties: (1) Biased Moment Retrieval (BMR) that intentionally uncovers the retrieval bias inherent in objects of the query and (2) Selective Query-guided Debiasing (SQuiD) that performs selective debiasing via disentangling 'good' and 'bad' retrieval bias according to the meaning of the query. In the overall pipeline, we first prepare two moment retrieval models: (1) Naive Moment Retrieval (NMR) and (2) Biased Moment Retrieval (BMR), where both predict the start-end-time of the moment pertinent to their input queries. The NMR is trained under the original purpose of VCMR, so it takes a video and query pair as inputs and sufficiently learns video-language alignment. However, the BMR is trained under the motivation of learning retrieval bias, so it takes a video and 'object words' in the query instead of a full query sentence. These words lose the contextual meaning of the original query, which makes the BMR difficult to properly learn a vision-language alignment, and rather, depend on the shortcut of memorizing spurious correlations that link given words to specific scenes. Based on these two retrievals, SQuiD decides whether the biased prediction of BMR is 'good bias' or 'bad bias' for the prediction of NMR via understanding the query meaning. Here, we introduce two technical contributions on how the SQuiD decides good or bad: (1) Co-occurrence table and (2) Learnable confounder. Our experimental results show state-of-the-art performances and enhanced interpretability.

2   Related Work

2.1   Video Moment Retrieval

The video moment retrieval (VMR) is the task of finding a moment pertinent to a given natural language query. The first attempts [9,11] have been made to localize the moment by giving multi-modal feature interaction between query and video. Previous VMR has focused on constructing modules that can help understand the contextual meaning of the query, including re-captioning [29] and temporal convolution [32]. With the success of natural language models [17,25], recent VMR systems are also interested in utilizing attention-based multi-modal interaction for the vision-language task. Zhang et al. [35] conjugate question answering attention model into VMR as multi-modal span-based QA by treating the video as a text passage and target moment as the answer span. Wang et al. [27] perform multi-levels of cross-modal attention coupled with content-boundary moment interaction for accurate localization of moment. Henceforth, there have been other efforts to perform a general format of video moment retrieval [6,15, 16], which finds pertinent moments from a video corpus composed of multiple videos. For this general VMR, Zhang et al. [33] suggested a hierarchical multi-modal encoder, which learns video and moment-level alignment for video corpus moment retrieval. Zhang et al. [34] utilized multi-level contrastive learning to refine the alignment of text with video corpus, which enhances representation learning while keeping the video and text encoding separate for efficiency. To advance forward general format of retrieval, we present another vulnerability as "biased retrieval" in VMR and propose novel framework of debiasing to counter the retrieval bias.

2.2   Causal Reasoning in Vision-Language

Merged with natural language processing [5,22], many high-level vision-language tasks have been introduced, including video/image captioning [26,31], video moment retrieval [1,8], and video/image question answering [14,23]. Causal reasoning has recently contributed to another growth of these high-level tasks via giving ability to reason causal effects between vision and language modalities. Wang et al. [28] first introduced observational bias in visual representation and proposed to screen out confounding effect from the bias. Recent question answering systems [20,21] have also utilized this causal reasoning to eliminate language bias in question and answer. For the moment retrieval, there have been efforts to remove the spurious correlation for correct retrieval [19,30]. In this respect, we also uncover the retrieval bias, but furthermore, perform sensible debiasing by conjugating the bias in either positive or negative way.

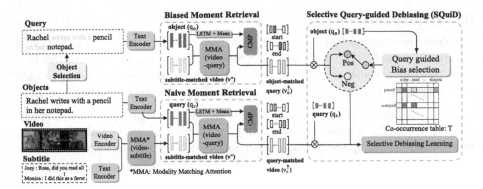

Fig. 3. SQuiDNet is composed of 3 modules: (a) BMR which reveals biased retrieval, (b) NMR which performs accurate retrieval, (c) SQuiD which removes bad biases from accurate retrieval of NMR subject to the meaning of query.

3   Method

3.1   Selective Query-Guided Debiasing Network

Figure 3 illustrates Selective Query-guided Debiasing Network (SQuiDNet). SQuiDNet prepares two moment retrievals under different motivations, where Naive Moment Retrieval (NMR) aims to perform accurate moment retrieval, while Biased Moment Retrieval (BMR) aims to explicitly reveal the retrieval bias in the training dataset. Following, Selective Query-guided Debiasing (SQuiD) conjugates the biased prediction of BMR to selectively debias NMR. Subject to the contextual meaning of the query, SQuiD decides positive or negative use of retrieval bias for contrastive learning between NMR and BMR. To this, we present two technical contributions to the decision rule in SQuiD: (1) Co-occurrence table and (2) Learnable confounder.

3.2   Input Representations

SQuiDNet takes single pair of video (i.e., video, subtitle) and query sentence as inputs, and training is performed under temporal boundary (i.e., start-end time) annotations. In inference, only video corpus and query are given, SQuiDNet predicts start-end time of moment pertinent to the query from the video corpus.

Video Representation. We use 2D and 3D feature extractors for video encoder. For 2D features, we use ResNet-101 [10] pre-trained on ImageNet [4], and for 3D features, we use SlowFast [7] pre-trained on Kinetics [12]. By concatenating the 2D and 3D features, 4352-dimensional features $\mathbf{V} = \{\mathbf{v}_i\}_{i=1}^{N_\mathbf{v}}$ are used for video frame embedding, where $N_\mathbf{v}$ is number of frames in a video. With d-dimensional embedder $\delta_\mathbf{v}$, final video features v are embedded on top of layer normalization LN [2] and positional encoding PE [25] as follows:

$$v = \mathrm{LN}(\delta_\mathbf{v}(\mathbf{V}) + \mathrm{PE}(\mathbf{V})) \in \mathbb{R}^{N_\mathbf{v} \times d}. \tag{1}$$

Text Representation. For text encoder, we use contextualized token embedding from pre-trained RoBERTa [17]. Here, we are given textual modalities as subtitle $\mathbf{S} = \{\mathbf{sub}(i)\}_i^{N_s}$ and query $\mathbf{q}$, where N_s is the number of subtitles in a video. We first tokenize all the words in subtitles and query into 5072-dimensional word tokens, so that $\mathbf{W_{sub}}(i) = \{\mathbf{w}^j_{\mathbf{sub}(i)}\}_{j=1}^{L_{s_i}}$ is word tokens in subtitle $\mathbf{sub}(i)$, where L_{s_i} is number of words in that subtitle. $\mathbf{W_q} = \{\mathbf{w}^j_{\mathbf{q}}\}_{j=1}^{L_q}$ is word token in query $\mathbf{q}$, where L_q is number of words in that query. As like the video feature v, final subtitle s_i and query q_r features are embedded by d-dimensional embedder $\delta_\mathbf{t}$:

$$s_i = \mathrm{LN}(\delta_\mathbf{t}(\mathbf{W_{sub}}_i) + \mathrm{PE}(\mathbf{W_{sub}}_i)) \in \mathbb{R}^{L_{s_i} \times d}, \qquad (2)$$

$$q_r = \mathrm{LN}(\delta_\mathbf{t}(\mathbf{W_q}) + \mathrm{PE}(\mathbf{W_q})) \in \mathbb{R}^{L_q \times d}, \qquad (3)$$

Modality Matching Attention As shown in Fig. 3, to give multi-modal interactions among input modalities (i.e., video-subtitle, video-query), we define Modality Matching Attention (MMA) founded on multi-layer attention in Transformer [24]. MMA takes video and text as inputs and produces text-matched video features. For mathematical definition of MMA, we first define d-dimensional input video feature $x = [x_1, \cdots, x_n] \in \mathbb{R}^{n \times d}$ and text features $y = [y_1, \cdots, y_m] \in \mathbb{R}^{m \times d}$, where n, m is the number of video frames and words in the text. To give interactions between x and y, we construct z by concatenating x and y along the frame and word axis, and perform self-attention on z. Here, we also add fixed token embedding $t_{<x>} \in \mathbb{R}^{n \times d}$ and $t_{<y>} \in \mathbb{R}^{m \times d}$ on x and y, so that the Transformer identifies the heterogeneity between x and y as follows:

$$x = x + t_{<x>}, y = y + t_{<y>}, \qquad (4)$$

$$z = [x||y] \in \mathbb{R}^{l \times d}, \qquad (5)$$

$$z^\star = \mathrm{Self\text{-}Attention}(z) \in \mathbb{R}^{l \times d}, \qquad (6)$$

$$x^\star = \mathrm{LN}(z^\star[: n] + x) \in \mathbb{R}^{n \times d}, \qquad (7)$$

$$\mathrm{MMA}(x, y) = x^\star, \qquad (8)$$

where $[\cdot||\cdot]$ is concatenation and $l = n + m$ is the number of frames and words. $[:]$ denotes slicing operation along the l axis, such that we take video features $z^\star[: n]$ in $z^\star$ as text-matched video features $x^\star$. Therefore, MMA produces $x^\star \in \mathbb{R}^{n \times d}$ comprehending language semantics in y. Henceforth, we introduce MMA into two types of video-text matching: (1) video-subtitle matching and (2) video-query matching for following two retrieval models (i.e., NMR and BMR).

3.3   Biased Moment Retrieval and Naive Moment Retrieval

Naive Moment Retrieval (NMR) is designed for the original purpose of moment retrieval, but Biased Moment Retrieval (BMR) aims at revealing retrieval bias. Here, shown in Fig. 3, the beauty of our proposed BMR is its model-agnostic manner, following the identical structure of NMR. In fact, NMR can be any model that performs moment retrieval (refer to experiments in Table 1), and BMR serves to remove bias inherent in that NMR. The only difference is that BMR takes object word features in query as inputs instead of full query sentence features. As these object words lose the contextual meaning of original query, BMR can only depend on the object words to find the video moment, causing it to prioritize the moment that commonly appears together with that object. To give mathematical definitions of NMR and BMR, we provide general formulations that can have variants of input text (i.e., query or object words). However, implementations of them should be independent, as they are trained for different purposes. Below, the NMR and BMR are performed in the following process: (1) video-subtitle matching, (2) video-query matching, and (3) conditional moment prediction.

Video-Subtitle Matching. Video frames and their subtitle appearing at the same time share common contextual semantics. Motivated by video-subtitle matching in [16], we also introduce MMA on video frames and their shared subtitles to give multi-modal interactions among them. For the inputs of MMA, we first reorganize video frames feature v as video clips $\mathbf{c} = \{c_i\}_{i=1}^{N_s}$ via collecting frames sharing single subtitle, where c_i collects video frames that share i-th subtitle s_i. N_s is the number of clips corresponding to the number of subtitles.

$$c_i^\star = \text{MMA}(c_i, s_i), \tag{9}$$

thus $c_i^\star$ represents i-th subtitle-matched video clip. For the following video-query matching, we perform reunion of all clips $v^\star = c_1^\star \cup \cdots \cup c_{N_s}^\star$ to reconstruct original frames and define $v^\star \in \mathbb{R}^{N_v \times d}$ as subtitle-matched video feature.

Video-Query Matching. As shown in Fig. 3, the $v^\star$ is utilized in MMA of two models (i.e., NMR, BMR) for video-query matching. But, for the input query, BMR utilizes object words instead of query sentence in order to learn retrieval bias. To this, we use nouns from the query for object words as they manly contain objects. Thus, we identify the part of speech (POS) of all words in query and sample noun words using natural language toolkit [18] like below:

$$\mathbf{W_o} = \text{Noun}(\mathbf{W_q}), \tag{10}$$

$$q_o = \text{LN}(\delta_t(\mathbf{W_o}) + \text{PE}(\mathbf{W_o})) \in \mathbb{R}^{L_{q_o} \times d}, \tag{11}$$

where Noun($\cdot$) denotes noun-filtering operation using POS tagger. The object words features $q_o \in \mathbb{R}^{L_{q_o} \times d}$ are also embedded from $\mathbf{W}_o$ like Eq. (3). The L_{q_o} is number of objects in query. Finally, we prepare query feature q_r and object feature q_o for video-query matching in NMR and BMR. Here, we define $q_x \in \{q_r, q_o\}$ for general formulation of two models in following MMA. The video-query matching is performed with q_x and subtitle-matched video $v^\star$:

$$v^{\star\star} = \text{MMA}(v^\star, q_x), \tag{12}$$

where $v^{\star\star}$ is query-matched video, redefined as $v_x^\dagger = v^{\star\star}$ for two cases in q_x. Thus, $v_x^\dagger \in \mathbb{R}^{N_v \times d}$ is our final video features for moment prediction with the query q_x.

Conditional Moment Prediction. We predict the start-time and end-time of moment for moment prediction, where we introduce conditional moment prediction (CMP) under our motivation that one prediction (e.g., start) can give causal information to the other prediction (e.g., end) rather then predicting these two independently. In details, given query feature q_x and video feature $v_x^\dagger$, CMP first, predicts start-time of moment t_{st}. In here, we use query sentence feature $\mathbf{q}_x = \text{MeanPool}(\text{LSTM}(q_x)) \in \mathbb{R}^{d \times 1}$ with lstm and mean-pooling over word axis to compute video-query similarities $v_x^\dagger \mathbf{q}_x \in \mathbb{R}^{N_v \times 1}$ in:

$$P(t_{st}|v_x^\dagger, q_x) = \text{Softmax}(\text{Conv1D}_{st}(v_x^\dagger \mathbf{q}_x)) \in \mathbb{R}^{N_v \times 1}, \tag{13}$$

where Conv1D_{st} is 1D convolution layer to embed start-time information. After that, we predict end-time t_{ed} with this prior start-time information I_{st} below:

$$I_{st} = \sigma(\text{Conv1D}_{st}(v_x^\dagger \mathbf{q}_x)) \in \mathbb{R}^{N_v \times 1}, \tag{14}$$

$$P(t_{ed}|v_x^\dagger, q_x) = \text{Softmax}(\text{Conv1D}_{ed}(v_x^\dagger \mathbf{q}_x + \alpha I_{st})) \in \mathbb{R}^{N_v \times 1}, \tag{15}$$

where $\sigma(\cdot)$ is nonlinear function like ReLU and $\alpha \in \mathbb{R}^1$ is learnable scalar. These two predictions $P(t_{st}|v_x^\dagger, q_x)$ and $P(t_{ed}|v_x^\dagger, q_x)$ are trained from ground-truth start-end labels (i.e., g_{st}, g_{ed}) using cross-entropy loss $CE(\cdot, \cdot)$ as follows:

$$\mathcal{L}_x = CE(g_{st}, P(t_{st}|v_x^\dagger, \mathbf{q}_x)) + CE(g_{ed}, P(t_{ed}|v_x^\dagger, \mathbf{q}_x)). \tag{16}$$

Depending on subscript $x \in \{r, o\}$, BMR performs biased training from $\mathcal{L}_o$ and NMR performs retrieval training from $\mathcal{L}_r$. Following SQuiD promotes selective debiasing NMR by conjugating retrieval bias in BMR.

3.4   Selective Query-Guided Debiasing

Selective Query-guided Debiasing (SQuiD) is proposed to debias moment retrieval of NMR using biased retrieval from BMR. SQuiD introduces contrastive learning to promote unbiased learning of NMR and biased learning of BMR, by contrasting the prediction of NMR as positive and BMR as negative. However, biased predictions of BMR often should be positive for NMR, depending on the meaning of the query. For example, when given a query as "person drinks a coffee.", BMR also finds the scene of "drinking coffee" in spite of input object words "person" and "coffee" due to spurious correlation between "coffee" and "drinking". SQuiD needs to be sensible in determining whether to use retrieval bias as negative or positive according to the given query. Therefore, our technical contribution is to introduce 2 different decision rules for SQuiD: (1) Co-occurrence table and (2) Learnable confounder.

Co-occurrence Table. Since we cannot directly know all the spurious correlations causing retrieval bias between 'objects' and 'scenes', we approximate these by referring to statistics of all query sentences. We assume that the 'predicate' in query would describe the 'scene' in the video, so based on top-K (e.g., K=100) frequent objects and predicates in training queries, we count the co-occurrence of predicates in query sentence for every object words. This counting builds Co-occurrence table $T_d \in \mathbb{R}^{K \times K}$ of co-occurrence between object and predicate (Co-occurrence table is illustrated in SQuiD of Fig. 3). The row in table T_d holds the co-occurrence frequency of the predicates for a specific object. Figure 2(b) shows one of the co-occurrence distributions when the object "television" is given. To determine the biased prediction of BMR as negative or positive for contrastive learning with NMR, SQuiD utilizes the prior knowledge on predominant "object-predicate" pairs in the Co-occurrence table. For input object words in BMR, SQuiD identifies top-n (e.g., n = 10) predominant predicates in the Co-occurrence table. If the top-n predicates appear in the original query sentence, SQuiD determines the prediction of BMR as positive instead of negative. For the selective debiasing learning, we used hinged loss based on video-query similarity $v_x^\dagger \mathbf{q}_x \in \mathbb{R}^{N_v}$ between NMR and BMR as follows:

$$\mathcal{L}_{hinge}^n = \max[0, \Delta_\mathbf{n} - \max(v_r^\dagger \mathbf{q}_r) + \max(v_o^\dagger \mathbf{q}_o)], \tag{17}$$

$$\mathcal{L}_{hinge}^p = \max[0, \Delta_\mathbf{p} - \max(v_r^\dagger \mathbf{q}_r) - \max(v_o^\dagger \mathbf{q}_o)]], \tag{18}$$

where $\mathcal{L}_{hinge}^n$ denotes the retrieval of BMR as negative and $\mathcal{L}_{hinge}^p$ denotes that as positive. SQuiD's decision is to select one of them. $\Delta_\mathbf{n} = 0.2$ and $\Delta_\mathbf{p} = 0.4$ is used and here, we give more margin for $\Delta_\mathbf{p}$ to promote learning of positive.

Learnable Confounder. The Co-occurrence table can be a discrete approximation of retrieval bias as it assumes predefined predicates for selective debiasing. For better approximation, we introduce learnable confounder $\mathbf{Z} \in \mathbb{R}^{K \times d}$ that can learn object-scene spurious correlation, where it consists of $\mathbf{K}$ (e.g., $\mathbf{K} = 100$) confounders with d-dimensional learnable parameters. Assuming that predicate words sufficiently contain the contextual meaning of video scenes, we predict spuriously correlated *predicate* feature $\mathbf{Y}_B$ from object words q_o and the confounder $\mathbf{Z}$. If the $\mathbf{Y}_B$ is similar to the predicate feature $\mathbf{Y}_C$ of the original query used in NMR, it means that predicate $\mathbf{Y}_B$ obtained from objects word and $\mathbf{Y}_C$ in given query have similar contextual meaning, thus, in this case, the retrieval of BMR should be used as positive.

For above, we needs to pretrain $\mathbf{Z}$ to learn spurious correlations between objects and predicates, so that generated *predicate* $\mathbf{Y}_B$ is biased predicate of the object. To train $\mathbf{Z}$, we regress $\mathbf{Y}_B$ as $\mathbf{Y}_C$, which means $\mathbf{Z}$ is trained to generate predicate features $\mathbf{Y}_B$ that commonly appears together with given object words in a query. To this, we first prepare mean-pooled objects feature $\mathbf{q}_o = \text{MeanPool}(\text{LSTM}(q_o)) \in \mathbb{R}^{1 \times d}$ over word axis. The $\mathbf{q}_o$ and confounder $\mathbf{Z}$ performs dot-product attention to make $\mathbf{Y}_B$, which regresses predicates feature $\mathbf{Y}_C$ in original query. To get $\mathbf{Y}_C$, we sample predicate words $\mathbf{W}_\mathbf{p} = \text{Pred}(\mathbf{W}_\mathbf{q})$ in original query and embed predicate words feature q_p, which is the same process in Eqs. (10, 11) and $\text{Pred}(\cdot)$ denotes predicate-filtering.

$$\mathbf{Y}_B = \text{Softmax}((\mathbf{q}_o W_o)(\mathbf{Z} W_\mathbf{z})^T)\mathbf{Z} \in \mathbb{R}^d, \tag{19}$$

$$\mathbf{Y}_C^\star = \text{MeanPool}(\text{LSTM}(q_p)) \in \mathbb{R}^d, \tag{20}$$

$$\mathcal{L}_\mathbf{z} = ||\mathbf{Y}_C^\star - \mathbf{Y}_B||_2^2 \tag{21}$$

Table 1. Performances for video corpus moment retrieval on TVR (test-public), ActivityNet and DiDeMo. ⋆: reconstruction-based results, N: NMR, B: BMR

Method	TVR			ActivityNet			DiDeMo (+ASR)		
	tIoU = 0.7			tIoU = 0.7			tIoU = 0.7		
	R@1	R@10	R@100	R@1	R@10	R@100	R@1	R@10	R@100
XML [15]	3.32	13.41	30.52	-	-	-	1.74⋆	8.31⋆	27.63⋆
HERO [16]	6.21	19.34	36.66	1.19⋆	6.33⋆	16.41⋆	1.59⋆	9.12⋆	29.23⋆
HAMMER [33]	5.13	11.38	16.71	1.74	8.75	19.08	-	-	-
ReLoCLNet [34]	4.15	14.06	32.42	1.82	6.91	18.33	-	-	-
SQuiDNet (N)	4.09	12.30	28.31	1.62	7.82	18.53	1.73	9.84	30.14
SQuiDNet (N [16], B)	8.34	28.03	35.45	3.02	10.23	22.14	2.62	10.28	31.11
SQuiDNet (N, B)	**10.09**	**31.22**	**46.05**	**4.43**	**12.81**	**26.54**	**3.52**	**12.93**	**34.03**

Table 2. Performances for single video moment retrieval (SVMR) on TVR (val) and ActivityNet and video retrieval (VR) on TVR (val).

Method	TVR				Method	ActivityNet	
	SVMR		VR			SVMR	
	R@1, tIoU = μ		-			R@1, tIoU = μ	
	$\mu = 0.5$	$\mu = 0.7$	R@1	R@10		$\mu = 0.5$	$\mu = 0.7$
XML [15]	31.11	13.89	16.54	50.41	VSLNet [35]	43.22	26.16
HERO [16]	-	4.02	30.11	62.69	IVG [19]	43.84	27.1
ReLoCLNet [34]	31.88	15.04	22.13	57.25	SMIN [27]	48.46	30.34
SQuiDNet (N,B)	**41.31**	**24.74**	**31.61**	**65.32**	**SQuiDNet**	**49.53**	**31.25**

where $W_o, W_z \in \mathbb{R}^{d \times d}$ are embedding matrices and $\mathbf{Y}_C^{\star}$ is fixed mean-pooled predicate features, which is target for L2 loss regression $\mathcal{L}_z$. After pretraining confounders $\mathbf{Z}$, SQuiD computes cosine similarity $r = \text{cosine}(\mathbf{Y}_B, \mathbf{Y}_C)$. If r is lager than 0, the retrieval from BMR is used as positive, otherwire as negative:

$$\mathcal{L}^D = \begin{cases} \mathcal{L}_{hinge}^n & \text{if } r \leq 0 \\ \mathcal{L}_{hinge}^p & \text{if } r > 0. \end{cases} \tag{22}$$

4 Experimental Results

4.1 Dataset

We validate SQuiDNet on three moment retrieval benchmarks as follows:

TV Show Retrieval. TV show Retrieval (TVR) [15] is composed of 6 TV shows across 3 genres: sitcoms, medical and crime dramas, which includes 109K queries from 21.8K multi-character interactive videos with subtitles. Each video is about 60–90 s in length. The TVR is split into 80% train, 10% val, 5% test-private, 5% test-public. The test-public is prepared for official challenge.

ActivityNet. ActivityNet Captions [13] includes 20k videos with 100k query descriptions. 10k videos are given for training and 5k for validation (val_1), where the average length of all videos is 117 s, and the average length of queries is 14.8 words. We train our SQuiDNet and evaluate on the val_1 split.

DiDeMo. The Distinct Describable Moments (DiDeMo) [1] contains 10k videos under diverse scenarios. To mitigate complexity, most videos are about 30-seconds and uniformly divided into 5-s segments, thus a single video contains 21 possible segments. DiDeMo is split into 80% train, 10% val, and 10% test.

4.2   Experimental Details

Evaluation Metric. We perform three retrieval tasks: (1) video retrieval (VR), (2) single video moment retrieval (SVMR), and (3) video corpus moment retrieval (VCMR). VR is video-level retrieval, evaluating the number of correct predictions of video, where VR measures video-query similarities of all videos to select the highest one. SVMR is moment-level retrieval in given video, evaluating the degree of overlap between predicted moments and ground-truth. VCMR is moment-level retrieval in video corpus, thus we evaluate the incidences where: (1) the predicted video matches the ground-truth video; and (2) the predicted moment has high overlap with the ground-truth moment. SQuiDNet predicts top-n (n = 10) videos first, and performs moment retrieval on them. Average recall at K (R@K) over query is used as the evaluation metric, where temporal Intersection over Union (tIoU) measures the overlap between predicted moment and the ground-truth.

4.3   Results on Benchmarks

Table 1 summarizes the best performances reported in XML [15], HERO [16], HAMMER [33], ReLoCLNet [34] on TVR, ActivityNet and DiDeMo[1]. SQuiDNet outperforms previous state-of-the-art performance. We also validate naive model without BMR, which shows large performance gap between full model of SQuiD-Net, explaining the effectiveness of selective debiasing learning. As SQuiDNet is conducted on model-agnostic manner, we replace NMR with the HERO baseline from their public code, which also shows improvement from original HERO. SQuiDNet assumes subtitle as inputs, so we can utilize audio speech recognition (ASR) for DiDeMo, which is available in [16]. We also validate results without subtitle on DiDeMo by applying video feature v instead of subtitle-matched video feature v^* in equation (9). This gives slight performance drop $-0.36\%/-0.74\%/-1.82\%$ from full model of SQuiDNet, which explains that grouping video frames based on subtitles benefits understanding of contextual scenes in video. Table 2 summarizes the results of two sub-tasks of VCMR: (1) SVMR and (2) VR on TVR and AtivityNet. SQuiDNet also shows large performance gain on the SVMR and VR, which explains that selective debiasing is effective at both moment-level and video-level. Although SQuiDNet is assumed to use subtitle, it also shows gain without subtitles in SVMR on ActivityNet.

---

[1] Please refer to Related Work and the papers for their detailed descriptions.

Table 3. Ablation on SQuiDNet variants for VCMR on TVR (val)

Model variants	tIoU = 0.7 R@1
Full SQuiDNet	8.52
w/o BMR	4.62
w/o CMP	8.17
w/ (All negative)	6.41
w/ (All positive)	6.72
w/ (Co-occurrence table)	7.91
w/ (Learnable confounder)	8.52

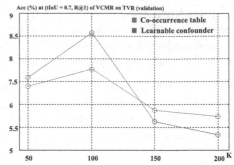

Table 4. Accuracy according to top-k objects for Co-occurrence table and variational k for Learnable confounder

4.4 Ablation Study

Table 3 presents ablation studies of our proposed components on SQuiDNet. The first section reports full model SQuiDNet for VCMR on TVR validation set. The second section shows ablative performance without Biased Moment Retrieval (BMR) and conditional moment prediction (CMP). Large performance drop is shown without BMR, which gives two interpretations: (1) retrieval datasets contain many spurious correlations and (2) selective debiasing of video moment retrieval is non-trivial. The performance gain of CMP is not as effective as that of BMR, however, it actually contributes on learning efficiency by promoting early convergence of training loss. We consider this reason to be that CMP narrows the search space with prior knowledge of start-time. Third section presents performance comparison from variants of SQuiD. To be confident of variants of SQuiD's decision rule, we first conduct ablations of giving all retrievals from BMR as negative or positive for the contrastive learning with CMR. The result shows that positive use of biased retrieval is more effective than negative, which explains why SQuiD needs discernment on selecting biased retrieval. Our proposed decision rules (i.e., Co-occurrence table, Learnable confounder) give effectiveness via selective debiasing. The Learnable confounder is more effective, but it needs additional work to train the confouder **Z**.

Figure 4 presents performances of VCMR according to the hyper-parameter **K** in Co-occurrence table and Learnable confounders. For the Co-occurrence table, **K** is the number of top-k objects, and for Learnable confounder, **K** is the number of confounders. Co-occurrence table utilizes statistics in training queries for approximating confounders while Learnable confounder learns confounder from object-predicate spurious correlations under our designed proxy learning with loss in Eq. (21), where both have similar curve. However, Learnable confounder has higher best-performance. We speculate Learnable confounder has superior control over confounders that cannot be defined in deterministic way.

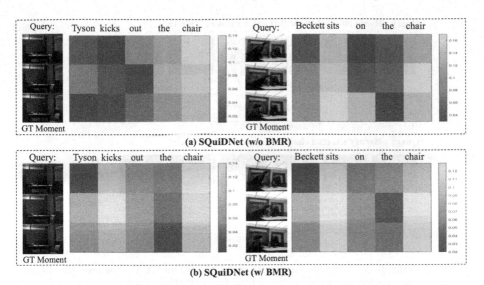

Fig. 5. Visualization of word-level query-video similarities in GT moment. Upper box is results from SQuiDNet trained without BMR and lower box is results from SQuiD-Net with BMR. It can be observed that the BMR enables the network to learn the uncommon predicate "kicks" of the object "chair" while also strengthens the learning of the spuriously correlated predicate "sits".

4.5   Qualitative Results

Figure 5 shows the word-level query-video similarities when GT moment is given to SQuiDNet when two queries are given as "Tyson kicks out the chair" and "Beckett sits on the chair". Figure 5(a) represents the similarity distributions from SQuiDNet trained without BMR, where they show high similarity in word "sit" and low in "kick". However in Fig. 5(b), the results with BMR show high similarities in both words "sit" and "kick". This explains that when one object word "chair" is given, the system without debiasing can understand the spuriously correlated predicate word "sit" but failed to learn the uncommon predicate word like "kick". In this respect, debiasing allows learning of object words' various connections with other predicate words. Furthermore, it can be observed that the system with debiasing also strengthens the understanding of the spuriously correlated predicate word by having higher similarities in more accurate moments.

Figure 6 presents moment predictions of the two models: NMR and BMR, where red box is prediction from NMR and blue box from BMR, while green box is ground-truth moment. In the right of the Figure, SQuiD's decision is shown on whether to use retrieval bias as positive or negative. When the query is "Robin rides a bicycle through a subway train car", both BMR and NMR predict the scene of person riding a bike in the video, where the SQuiD decides the prediction of BMR as positive retrieval bias. But, for the query "Barney sits

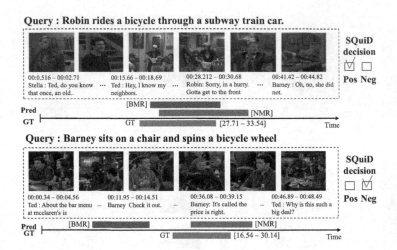

Fig. 6. Visualization of moment prediction on NMR and BMR, where the SQuiD decision is represented for using retrieval bias from BMR as positive or negative.

on a chair and spins a bicycle wheel", BMR still predicts the scene of person riding a bike, which shows the retrieval bias between "bicycle" and "riding". Here, to counter this retrieval bias, SQuiD decides the prediction of BMR as negative bias, such that NMR is trained to recede the bias prediction of BMR by contrastive learning.

5 Conclusion

This paper considers Selective Query-guided Debiasing Network for video moment retrieval. Although recent debiasing methods have focused on only removing retrieval bias, it sometimes should be preserved because there are many queries where biased predictions are rather helpful. To conjugate this retrieval bias, SQuiDNet incorporates the following two main properties: (1) Biased Moment Retrieval that intentionally uncovers the biased moments inherent in objects of the query and (2) Selective Query-guided Debiasing that performs selective debiasing guided by the meaning of the query. Our experimental results on three moment retrieval benchmarks (TVR, ActivityNet, DiDeMo) show effectiveness of SQuiDNet, while qualitative analysis shows improved interpretability.

Acknowledgemnet. This work was partly supported by Institute for Information & communications Technology Promotion(IITP) grant funded by the Korea government(MSIT) (No. 2021-0-01381, Development of Causal AI through Video Understanding) and partly supported by Institute of Information & communications Technology Planning & Evaluation(IITP) grant funded by the Korea government(MSIT) (No. 2022-0-00184, Development and Study of AI Technologies to Inexpensively Conform to Evolving Policy on Ethics).

References

1. Anne Hendricks, L., Wang, O., Shechtman, E., Sivic, J., Darrell, T., Russell, B.: Localizing moments in video with natural language. In: Proceedings of the IEEE International Conference on Computer Vision, pp. 5803–5812 (2017)
2. Ba, J.L., Kiros, J.R., Hinton, G.E.: Layer normalization. arXiv preprint arXiv:1607.06450 (2016)
3. Das, A., et al.: Visual dialog. In: Proceedings of the IEEE Conference on Computer Vision and Pattern Recognition, pp. 326–335 (2017)
4. Deng, J., Dong, W., Socher, R., Li, L.J., Li, K., Fei-Fei, L.: Imagenet: a large-scale hierarchical image database. In: 2009 IEEE Conference on Computer Vision and Pattern Recognition, pp. 248–255. IEEE (2009)
5. Devlin, J., Chang, M.W., Lee, K., Toutanova, K.: Bert: pre-training of deep bidirectional transformers for language understanding. arXiv preprint arXiv:1810.04805 (2018)
6. Escorcia, V., Soldan, M., Sivic, J., Ghanem, B., Russell, B.: Temporal localization of moments in video collections with natural language. arXiv preprint arXiv:1907.12763 (2019)
7. Feichtenhofer, C., Fan, H., Malik, J., He, K.: Slowfast networks for video recognition. In: Proceedings of the IEEE/CVF International Conference on Computer Vision, pp. 6202–6211 (2019)
8. Gao, J., Sun, C., Yang, Z., Nevatia, R.: Tall: temporal activity localization via language query. In: Proceedings of the IEEE International Conference on Computer Vision, pp. 5267–5275 (2017)
9. Gao, J., Sun, C., Yang, Z., Nevatia, R.: TALL: temporal activity localization via language query. In: IEEE International Conference on Computer Vision, ICCV 2017, pp. 5277–5285. IEEE Computer Society (2017)
10. He, K., Zhang, X., Ren, S., Sun, J.: Deep residual learning for image recognition. In: Proceedings of the IEEE Conference on Computer Vision and Pattern Recognition, pp. 770–778 (2016)
11. Hendricks, L.A., Wang, O., Shechtman, E., Sivic, J., Darrell, T., Russell, B.C.: Localizing moments in video with natural language. In: IEEE International Conference on Computer Vision, ICCV 2017, pp. 5804–5813. IEEE Computer Society (2017)
12. Kay, W., et al.: The kinetics human action video dataset. arXiv preprint arXiv:1705.06950 (2017)
13. Krishna, R., Hata, K., Ren, F., Fei-Fei, L., Carlos Niebles, J.: Dense-captioning events in videos. In: Proceedings of the IEEE International Conference on Computer Vision, pp. 706–715 (2017)
14. Lei, J., Yu, L., Bansal, M., Berg, T.L.: TVQA: localized, compositional video question answering. arXiv preprint arXiv:1809.01696 (2018)
15. Lei, J., Yu, L., Berg, T.L., Bansal, M.: TVR: a large-scale dataset for video-subtitle moment retrieval. arXiv preprint arXiv:2001.09099 (2020)
16. Li, L., Chen, Y.C., Cheng, Y., Gan, Z., Yu, L., Liu, J.: Hero: hierarchical encoder for video+ language omni-representation pre-training. arXiv preprint arXiv:2005.00200 (2020)
17. Liu, Y., et al.: Roberta: a robustly optimized bert pretraining approach. arXiv preprint arXiv:1907.11692 (2019)
18. Loper, E., Bird, S.: NLTK: the natural language toolkit. arXiv preprint CS/0205028 (2002)

19. Nan, G., et al.: Interventional video grounding with dual contrastive learning. In: Proceedings of the IEEE/CVF Conference on Computer Vision and Pattern Recognition, pp. 2765–2775 (2021)
20. Niu, Y., Tang, K., Zhang, H., Lu, Z., Hua, X.S., Wen, J.R.: Counterfactual VQA: a cause-effect look at language bias. In: Proceedings of the IEEE/CVF Conference on Computer Vision and Pattern Recognition, pp. 12700–12710 (2021)
21. Qi, J., Niu, Y., Huang, J., Zhang, H.: Two causal principles for improving visual dialog. In: Proceedings of the IEEE/CVF Conference on Computer Vision and Pattern Recognition, pp. 10860–10869 (2020)
22. Radford, A., Narasimhan, K., Salimans, T., Sutskever, I.: Improving language understanding by generative pre-training (2018)
23. Tapaswi, M., Zhu, Y., Stiefelhagen, R., Torralba, A., Urtasun, R., Fidler, S.: MovieQA: understanding stories in movies through question-answering. In: Proceedings of the IEEE Conference on Computer Vision and Pattern Recognition, pp. 4631–4640 (2016)
24. Vaswani, A., et al.: Attention is all you need. In: Advances in Neural Information Processing Systems (NIPS) (2017)
25. Vaswani, A., et al.: Attention is all you need. arXiv preprint arXiv:1706.03762 (2017)
26. Venugopalan, S., Rohrbach, M., Donahue, J., Mooney, R., Darrell, T., Saenko, K.: Sequence to sequence - video to text. In: Proceedings of the IEEE International Conference on Computer Vision (ICCV) (2015)
27. Wang, H., Zha, Z.J., Li, L., Liu, D., Luo, J.: Structured multi-level interaction network for video moment localization via language query. In: Proceedings of the IEEE/CVF Conference on Computer Vision and Pattern Recognition, pp. 7026–7035 (2021)
28. Wang, T., Huang, J., Zhang, H., Sun, Q.: Visual commonsense R-CNN. In: Proceedings of the IEEE/CVF Conference on Computer Vision and Pattern Recognition, pp. 10760–10770 (2020)
29. Xu, H., He, K., Sigal, L., Sclaroff, S., Saenko, K.: Text-to-clip video retrieval with early fusion and re-captioning. arXiv abs/1804.05113 (2018)
30. Yang, X., Feng, F., Ji, W., Wang, M., Chua, T.S.: Deconfounded video moment retrieval with causal intervention. In: Proceedings of the 44th International ACM SIGIR Conference on Research and Development in Information Retrieval, pp. 1–10 (2021)
31. Yu, H., Wang, J., Huang, Z., Yang, Y., Xu, W.: Video paragraph captioning using hierarchical recurrent neural networks. In: Proceedings of the IEEE Conference on Computer Vision and Pattern Recognition, pp. 4584–4593 (2016)
32. Yuan, Y., Ma, L., Wang, J., Liu, W., Zhu, W.: Semantic conditioned dynamic modulation for temporal sentence grounding in videos. arXiv preprint arXiv:1910.14303 (2019)
33. Zhang, B., et al.: A hierarchical multi-modal encoder for moment localization in video corpus. arXiv preprint arXiv:2011.09046 (2020)
34. Zhang, H., et al.: Video corpus moment retrieval with contrastive learning. arXiv preprint arXiv:2105.06247 (2021)
35. Zhang, H., Sun, A., Jing, W., Zhou, J.T.: Span-based localizing network for natural language video localization. arXiv preprint arXiv:2004.13931 (2020)

Spatial and Visual Perspective-Taking via View Rotation and Relation Reasoning for Embodied Reference Understanding

Cheng Shi[1] and Sibei Yang[1,2](✉)

[1] School of Information Science and Technology, ShanghaiTech University, Shanghai, China
[2] Shanghai Engineering Research Center of Intelligent Vision and Imaging, Shanghai, China
{shicheng,yangsb}@shanghaitech.edu.cn

Abstract. Embodied Reference Understanding studies the reference understanding in an embodied fashion, where a receiver requires to locate a target object referred to by both language and gesture of the sender in a shared physical environment. Its main challenge lies in how to make the receiver with the egocentric view access spatial and visual information relative to the sender to judge how objects are oriented around and seen from the sender, *i.e.*, spatial and visual perspective-taking. In this paper, we propose a **REasoning from your Perspective** (REP) method to tackle the challenge by modeling relations between the receiver and the sender as well as the sender and the objects via the proposed novel view rotation and relation reasoning. Specifically, view rotation first rotates the receiver to the position of the sender by constructing an embodied 3D coordinate system with the position of the sender as the origin. Then, it changes the orientation of the receiver to the orientation of the sender by encoding the body orientation and gesture of the sender. Relation reasoning models both the nonverbal and verbal relations between the sender and the objects by multi-modal cooperative reasoning in gesture, language, visual content, and spatial position. Experiment results demonstrate the effectiveness of REP, which consistently surpasses all existing state-of-the-art algorithms by a large margin, *i.e.*, +5.22% absolute accuracy in terms of Prec@0.5 on YouRefIt. Code is available (https://github.com/ChengShiest/REP-ERU).

Keywords: Embodied reference understanding · Referring expression comprehension · View rotation · Relation reasoning

1 Introduction

Reference understanding, recognizing referents (*e.g.*, target objects) which are referred to by interlocutors in a shared environment, helps to establish com-

S. Avidan et al. (Eds.): ECCV 2022, LNCS 13696, pp. 201–218, 2022.
https://doi.org/10.1007/978-3-031-20059-5_12

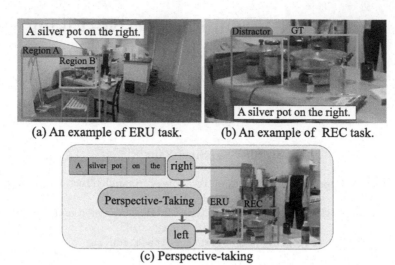

(a) An example of ERU task.   (b) An example of REC task.

(c) Perspective-taking

Fig. 1. The difference between Embodied Reference Understanding (ERU) and traditional Reference Expression Comprehension (REC). Figure (a) and (b) are two examples of ERU and REC, respectively. In (a), the person (*i.e.*, sender) in the image gives the description, while an annotator generates the description according to the image in (b). Figure (c) shows that the two tasks differ in the localization of the target objects according to the same language description due to the perspective-taking challenge. (Color figure online)

mon ground in human communication [7]. Referring Expression Comprehension (REC) [15,26,44,52,53], a reference understanding task in computer vision community, aims at learning a receiver to detect the referent from an image corresponding to a natural language sentence generated by a sender. In REC, the receiver and the sender recognize the referent of the image from the same viewpoint, *i.e.*, the camera viewpoint. An example of REC is shown in Fig. 1(b). Instead of considering cooperative communication [37] with human-in-the-scene, REC emphasizes the joint understanding of visual and language cues. To facilitate reference understanding in an embodied environment, Embodied Reference Understanding (ERU) [7] with benchmark and dataset (*i.e.*, YouRefIt) is proposed recently. ERU task mimics the referring process of human communication in an embodied manner, in which the sender and the receiver are in the same physical space but they observe the referent from different viewpoints. An example of ERU is shown in Fig. 1(a). The sender describes the "A silver pot on the right" from her perspective, and the receiver requires to locate the pot in the receiver's first-person image. Both sender's language description and gesture to the referent are included in YouRefIt [7] because people often jointly use these verbal and nonverbal forms to refer to an object.

Spatial and visual perspective-taking [8,38] is a challenging but essential factor to address ERU, where it requires the receiver to access spatial and visual information relative to the sender to judge how objects are oriented around and seen from the sender. We claim that the sender's position, gesture information, and corresponding visual cues in the 3D scene are vital to achieving spatial and visual perspective-taking. Specifically, the sender's 3D position in the physical environment and body orientation implied in visual appearance can indicate the rough area that the sender pays attention to. For example, as shown in Fig. 1(a), the "region A" facing the sender is more likely to be paid attention to by the sender. By cooperating with the gesture, we can estimate a more accurate, nonverbal-aware attention distribution of regions, *i.e.*, the "region B" around the table will be attended more. However, existing reference understanding methods [7,49,50] either neglect the perspective-taking challenge or address it by simply fusing a gesture map with visual cues, which cannot achieve satisfactory performance.

How to cooperate language cues with the perspective-taking to implement the reference understanding with verbal input serves as a crucial problem. The language descriptions in ERU usually contain two types of information, *i.e.*, the appearance of the referent and spatial relation between the referent and the sender. Therefore, we must combine both types of information with perspective-taking to perform relation reasoning from the sender's viewpoint, which is also different from the REC task with viewpoint-only compositional reasoning [46,49]. The appearance information with open-vocabulary category and attribute description helps locate the candidate objects from the attention regions. For example, two pots shown in Fig. 1(c) are figured out through the category description "pot" and attribute description "silver". Moreover, the spatial relation cues from the language description such as "front" and "right" represent the relative spatial relationship between the referent and the sender. For example, as shown in Fig. 1(c), the pot with a green bounding box will be identified because it is on the "right" of the sender from the sender's perspective.

In this paper, we propose a one-stage **REasoning from your Perspective** (**REP**) network to address the perspective-taking and multimodal cooperation challenges in ERU. REP explicitly performs the relation modeling between the receiver and the sender as well as the sender and the objects via the proposed 3D view rotation and relation reasoning modules. Specifically, (1) *REP captures the relation between the receiver and the sender via the 3D view rotation module in the following two steps.* First, it rotates the receiver into the sender's position by estimating the depth from the image and constructing an embodied 3D coordinate system with the sender's position as the origin. Second, it encodes the body orientation and gesture of the sender in the 3D coordinate system to the body language vector by fusing the visual and spatial cues, including the image, gesture, and coordinate information. The body language vector represents the orientation from the sender's viewpoint to referent in the 3D coordinate system. (2) *Next, REP performs relation reasoning between the sender and the objects by utilizing both the verbal and nonverbal cues.* First, REP obtains the spatial attention between the body language vector and the embodied 3D spatial coordinates of all the pixels in the image. The attention distribution indicates the area where the sender faces. Second, in that area, REP performs nonverbal reasoning and verbal reasoning to find the precise region where the sender points to and describes. The nonverbal reasoning models the relations among different regions and the sender via the self-attention mechanism [40], while verbal reasoning stepwisely performs language-conditional normalization [7,30,49]. Finally, REP combines both nonverbal reasoning and verbal reasoning to predict the referent.

In summary, this paper makes four major contributions:

- To the best of our knowledge, we are the first to explicitly model the relation between receiver and sender (*i.e.*, receiver-sender relation) as well as the relation between sender and objects (*i.e.*, sender-object relation) to address the spatial and visual perspective-taking and multimodal cooperation challenges in Embodied Reference Understanding (ERU).
- We propose a 3D view rotation module to rotate the receiver to sender's position and encode the direction from the sender's viewpoint to the referent for receiver-sender relation modeling, making the receiver adapts to the sender's spatial position, gesture, and body orientation.
- We propose a relation reasoning module to perform verbal and nonverbal reasoning for sender-object relation modeling, which meets the requirement of ERU for multimodal cooperation.
- Experimental results demonstrate that the proposed REP not only significantly outperforms existing state-of-the-art methods but also generates explainable visual evidence of stepwise reasoning.

2   Related Work

2.1   From Referring Expression Comprehension to Embodied Reference Understanding

Referring Expression Comprehension [26,53] aims at detecting the referent object from an image according to a natural language description. Works in referring expression comprehension can be roughly divided into two types, *i.e.*, two-stage and one-stage methods. Compared to the proposal generation and then the prediction of two-stage methods [15,23,28,41,44,45,48,52,54], one-stage methods [6,21,24,35,47,49,50] directly predict the referent by regressing coordinates of it. FAOA [50] fuses text features of the description into YOLOv3 detector [34] to make referring expression comprehension one-stage. To ground complex descriptions, ReSC [49] improves FAOA by proposing a sub-query construction to refine text-conditional visual representation recursively.

Referring expression comprehension mainly focuses on jointly understanding the vision and language, which limits the application of reference understanding in daily embodied scenes: the sender describes the referent to another people (*i.e.*, the receiver) in the shared physical space [13,42]. To extend referring expression comprehension to embodied scenes, Chen *et al.* [7] present a new challenging reference understanding task called Embodied Reference Understanding (ERU) and collect its corresponding benchmark dataset, *i.e.*, YouRefIt. In addition to language descriptions, gestural information is included in YouRefIt because people often use both natural language and gestures to refer to an object in the embodied setting. To encode the nonverbal gestural information for prediction, Chen *et al.* introduce a Part Affinity Field (PAF) heatmap [5] and a saliency heatmap [19] and fuse them with verbal language cues and visual features. Their one-stage architecture and fusion method are based on ReSC.

Although jointly encoding multiple modalities (natural language, gestures, and images) for prediction, existing state-of-the-art methods (referring expression comprehension methods [50,52] and the embodied multimodal framework [7]) fail to address a crucial challenge in ERU, *i.e.*, visual perspective-taking [3,7,33]. Visual perspective-taking is the receiver's awareness and ability to imagine how the sender sees things and describe the referent from their perspective. To solve these issues, we first transfer the receiver's perspective to the sender's one via a embodied 3D coordinate construction and body orientation estimation of the sender. Then, we perform spatial and visual reasoning between objects according to the language and gesture cues.

2.2   Single Image Depth Estimation

Single image depth estimation [12] aims at estimating a dense depth map from a single RGB image. Occlusion between objects and perspective, including size cue and texture gradient, are keys for monocular depth estimation [27], and several learning models [4,11,14] based on these cues are proposed. Apart from learning the depth estimation individually, some works jointly solve single image depth estimation task with other similar tasks such as semantic segmentation [20], surface normal estimation [31] and contour estimation [43].

Depth estimation from a single image is also introduced in vision-and-language tasks, which need depth information to reduce ambiguity in resolving scene geometry. Banerjee *et al.* [2] propose to utilize the depth information estimated by the off-the-shelf depth estimator AdaBins [4] as the weak supervision sign to help learn the relative spatial position between objects for the visual question answering task. AdaBins adopts a transformer-based architecture that divides the depth range into scene-relevant bins adaptively and estimates depth values as linear combinations of these bin centers. In this paper, we also use AdaBins to extract 3D scene geometry from a single image. Different from previous methods, we cooperate the scene geometry with gesture cues and position information of the sender to estimate spatial attention distribution and spatial relationship between the sender and objects, respectively.

2.3   Relation Reasoning in Reference Understanding

Relation reasoning, the ability to understand and perform reasoning of spatial and visual relations between visual regions, is explored in the related topics of reference understanding, such as referring expression comprehension [15,41,46,52] and visual question answering [2,16,17]. These works mainly resort to neuro-symbolic methods, attention mechanisms, or graph-based methods to perform compositional relation reasoning. Specifically, neuro-symbolic methods first extract symbolic representations and then execute neuro-symbolic programs [25,51] based on the representations, while graph-based methods capture the relation context via graph neural networks [18]. However, these methods cannot be utilized to embodied reference understanding directly. On one hand, natural language sentences on the embodied settings are much shorter than those of other reference understanding tasks, the few relation-relevant language cues should be combined with the gestures to guide the relation reasoning. On the other hand, as the sentences are described by the sender whose perspective is different from the receiver, the relation reasoning should be adaptive to the perspective-taking challenge. In this case, we convert the image coordinate to a sender-centric one and perform spatial reasoning with language and gesture cues on converted coordinates.

3   REasoning from Your Perspective

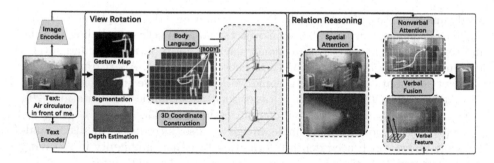

Fig. 2. An overview of our Reasoning from Your Respective (REP) model. In 3D view rotation, REP first uses the depth estimation to get the 3D coordinate map and converts it to an embodied 3D coordinate map by taking the sender's position as the origin. Then, the body language vector is encoded from the visual feature map, the gesture map and the depth estimation to represent the gesture and orientation information. In Relation Reasoning, to locate the spatial area where the sender faces, REP computes the spatial attention between the learned body language vector and spatial coordinates of all the pixels in the image. Then, in that area, REP performs the noverbal gesture attention and verbal fusion to find the precise region where the sender points to and describes. In the end, according to the precise region, REP generates a box prediction to the referent.

We propose a REasoning from your Perspective (REP) model to tackle Embodied Reference Understanding (ERU) task. As shown in Fig. 2, REP locates the referent via the 3D view rotation module and relation reasoning module. First, the 3D view rotation module (in Sect. 3.1) rotates the receiver to the sender's position by constructing an embodied 3D coordinate system and encodes the direction from the sender to the referent by learning the body language vector. Next, the relation reasoning module (in Sect. 3.2) models the relations between visual regions and the sender by cooperating with the spatial attention, nonverbal gesture reasoning and verbal fusion. Finally, we introduce the loss to train our REP in Sect. 3.3.

3.1 3D View Rotation

We model the relation between the receiver and the sender to make the receiver could access spatial and visual information relative to the sender by constructing an embodied 3D coordinate system and learning the sender's body language representation. To construct the embodied 3D coordinate system, we first combine the raw image coordinate with the estimated depth from the image to obtain the 3D spatial information and then construct the coordinate system by setting the origin as the sender's position. Next, we estimate the direction from the sender to the referent by learning the sender's body language representation from spatial, gesture, and visual information.

Embodied 3D Coordinate System Construction. As the referring action takes place in the 3D physical environment, the gesture and language cues relevant to the reference understanding and reasoning are based on the 3D scene. To better align the gesture and langauge cues with the spatial information, we thus construct a 3D coordinate system via depth estimation from the 2D image. Given an input image I with size of $H_I \times W_I$, we first obtain the normalized image coordinate map $P_I \in \mathbb{R}^{H_I \times W_I \times 2}$, where $P_I(x, y)$ is the normalized coordinate $(\frac{x}{H_I}, \frac{y}{W_I})$ of the pixel at the position (x, y) in the image. Then, we estimate the image's dense depth map $P_D \in \mathbb{R}^{H_I \times W_I}$ by using the AdaBins estimator [4] trained on the indoor dataset NYU [36] and then concatenate the normalized depth map P_D with the normalized image coordinate map P_I to get the 3D coordinate map $P \in \mathbb{R}^{H_I \times W_I \times 3}$.

In order to access scene information relative to the sender, we convert the 3D coordinate map P to a sender-centric one by taking the sender's position as the origin. First, we estimate the position $p \in \mathbb{R}^3$ of the sender by obtaining the person segmentation mask $A_{sender} \in \{0, 1\}^{H_I \times W_I \times 1}$ of the sender via U^2-Net [32] and setting the position p as the average coordinates of pixels that belong to the sender. Then, we establish the embodied 3D coordinate system by calculating the coordinates of pixels relative to the sender, and the embodied coordinate map $P_r \in \mathbb{R}^{H_I \times W_I \times 3}$ is computed as follows,

$$P_r = P - Tile(p), \tag{1}$$

where $Tile(\cdot)$ means to tile a vector to produce a map with the size of $H_I \times W_I \times 3$.

Body Language Representation. As the referent is usually in the region where the sender faces, the sender's body orientation indicates the direction from the sender to the region. To capture the body orientation, we first extract and fuse body-relevant multimodal information, including the spatial coordinate, gesture, and visual appearance, and then models the intra-relation among different parts of the sender's body. First, we extract visual feature map $S_v \in \mathbb{R}^{H \times W \times C}$ and part affinity field map $S_{gesture} \in \mathbb{R}^{H \times W \times 3}$ [5,7] from the image to encode the sender's visual appearance and gesture, respectively. Second, we fuse the visual features S_v, gesture features $S_{gesture}$, and their corresponding 3D spatial coordinates P_r to obtain the multimodal feature map $M \in \mathbb{R}^{H \times W \times C}$, which is formulated as,

$$M = Conv_{1 \times 1}([S_v; S_{gesture}; AvgPool(P_r)]), \tag{2}$$

where $AvgPool(\cdot)$ is to downsample the feature map to the size of $H \times W$ via the average pooling operation, and $[;]$ and $Conv_{1 \times 1}(\cdot)$ refers to the concatenation operation and convolutional layer with kernel size 1×1, respectively.

To force the relation modeling focus on the regions of the sender's body, we further fuse the sender's segmentation mask A_{sender} with the multimodal feature map M. The fused body feature map $M_{body} \in \mathbb{R}^{H \times W \times C}$ is computed as follows,

$$M_{body} = M \odot AvgPool(A_{sender}), \tag{3}$$

where $\odot$ is the element-wise multiplication.

Next, we capture the intra-relation among different parts of the sender's body to predict the sender's body orientation. Specifically, we flatten the multimodal feature map M_{body} into a sequence of $H \times W$ tokens $[M_{body}^{(1,1)}, M_{body}^{(1,2)}, ..., M_{body}^{(H,W)}]$ and apply a stack of transformer encoder layers [40] to build the global correlation among the tokens, where each transformer encoder layer includes a multi-head self-attention layer and an feed forward network. Inspired by ViT [10] adding an extra learnable classification token [CLS] to be taken as image representation, we make use of an additional [BODY] token to be served as an abstract representation of the body language and feed it into the transformer encoder along with other tokens. The [BODY] token is randomly initialized before training and jointly optimized with the whole model during training, and its state at the output of the transformer encoder is leveraged to predict the body language vector via a single linear layer. The body language vector $l \in \mathbb{R}^3$ is formulated as follows,

$$
\begin{aligned}
E &= Trans([[BODY], M_{body}^{(1,1)}, M_{body}^{(1,2)}, ..., M_{body}^{(H,W)}]), \\
l &= L2Norm(FC(E^{(1)})),
\end{aligned}
\tag{4}
$$

where $Trans(\cdot)$, $FC(\cdot)$ and $L2Norm(\cdot)$ represents the transformer encoder, linear layer and L2 normalization, respectively.

To facilitate the model to learn the body language vector l, we apply a regression loss $loss_{reg}$ to directly optimize the cosine distance between the body language vector and the vector from the sender to the referent, which will be introduced in Sect. 3.3.

3.2 Relation Reasoning

In this section, we perform relation reasoning between the sender and the objects from the sender's perspective by utilizing the spatial coordinates, nonverbal gesture information, and verbal cues. First, to locate the spatial area where the sender faces, we compute the **spatial attention** between the learned body language vector and spatial coordinates of all the pixels in the image. Then, in that area, we perform the **noverbal gesture attention** and **verbal fusion** to find the precise region where the sender points to and describes. Finally, according to the precise region, we generate a box prediction to the referent.

Spatial Attention. The body language vector l defined in Sect. 3.1 represents the direction from the sender to the referent, revealing an area where the referent might locate. To find and represent the region, we directly compute a spatial attention map $A_{spatial} \in \mathbb{R}^{H_I \times W_I}$ on the image via the cosine similarities between the body language vector $l \in \mathbb{R}^3$ and the spatial coordinates of pixels. The attention score $A_{spatial}(x, y)$ at the position (x, y) in the image is computed as follows,

$$A_{spatial}(x, y) = l \cdot L2Norm(P_r(x, y)), \tag{5}$$

where $P_r \in \mathbb{R}^{H_I \times W_I \times 3}$ is the embodied coordinate map defined in the Sect. 3.1. With the help of the attention map $A_{spatial}$, the noverbal gesture attention and the verbal fusion can be performed in that activated area where referent might locate.

Nonverbal Gesture Attention. Based on the sender's pointing gesture, the specific region of the referent that the sender points to can be located. To find the specific region, modeling the relations between the sender and regions in the image is not enough, we also need to model the relations among different regions. Without the modeling, the specific region cannot be differentiated from other regions on the same direction that the sender points to. Therefore, we model the relations among the sender and all the regions in the activated area. Similar to the relation modeling in Sect. 3.1, we also utilize the transformer encoder to model the relations, which is formulated as follows,

$$\begin{aligned} M_{gesture} &= M \odot ReLU(AvgPool(A_{sender} + A_{spatial})), \\ A_{gesture} &= Softmax(Trans([M_{gesture}^{(1,1)}, M_{gesture}^{(1,2)}, ..., M_{gesture}^{(H,W)}])) \end{aligned} \tag{6}$$

where A_{sender} and $A_{spatial}$ refer to the sender's region and the activated regions of spatial attention map, respectively, $ReLU(\cdot)$ is the ReLU activation function [1], M is the multimodal feature map defined in Sect. 3.1, and $Softmax(\cdot)$ is the softmax activation function. The gesture attention map $A_{gesture} \in \mathbb{R}^{H \times W \times 1}$ refers to the specific region of the referent that the sender points to. Moreover, we propose an attention loss $loss_{attn}$ to facilitate the model to learn the gesture attention map, which is given in Sect. 3.3.

Verbal Fusion. With the cooperation of gesture, which specifies the specific region of the referent, verbal cues can locate the complete referent. Verbal cues provide straightforward and informative cues and are crucial for reference understanding. Therefore, we utilize the language description to locate the referent in the activated area $A_{spatial}$. Given the language description with T words, we extract the language features $L \in \mathbb{R}^{T \times C}$ from a pretrained BERT [9] model. Then, we extract the multimodal feature map M because the informative language cues usually describe multimodal information, such as semantic category, visual appearance, and relative spatial location of the referent. Next, we fuse the language features into the multimodal feature map M to get the verbal-visual feature map $M_{verbal} \in \mathbb{R}^{H \times W \times C}$. Following ReSC [49], we use $FiLM$ module [30] as the fusion block, and the feature map M_{verbal} is computed as follows,

$$M_{verbal} = FilM(M \odot ReLU(AvgPool(A_{spatial})), Query(L)), \qquad (7)$$

where the $Query(\cdot)$ is the sub-query learner [49]. We stack three $FiLM$ blocks for verbal fusion following YouRefIt [7]. Note that the spatial attention map $A_{spatial}$ forces the verbal fusion focus on the activated area.

Finally, we fuse the nonverbal gesture attention map $A_{gesture}$ to the verbal-visual feature map M_{verbal} to predict the anchor boxes and their corresponding confidence scores. The fusion is implemented via a concatenation operation followed by a stack of convolutional layers.

3.3 Loss Function

Regression Loss. We calculate $p_{box} \in \mathbb{R}^3$ by averaging emobodied 3D coordinates of pixels in the bounding box of ground-truth referent and take it as supervision to learn the body language vector $l \in \mathbb{R}^3$. The regression loss $loss_{reg}$ is computed as follows:

$$loss_{reg} = 1 - L2Norm(p_{box}) \cdot l. \qquad (8)$$

Attention Loss. The attention loss $loss_{attn}$ is computed between the learned nonverbal gesture attention map $A_{gesture}$ and the ground-truth bounding box $box \in \mathbb{R}^{H \times W}$ as follows,

$$loss_{attn} = 1 - \sum_{x,y=1}^{H,W} A_{gesture}(x, y) * box(x, y), \qquad (9)$$

where $box(x, y) = 1$ if the position (x, y) is in the ground-truth bounding box; otherwise $box(x, y) = 0$.

Overall Loss. Following YouRefIt [7], we apply the diverse loss [49] and the YOLO's loss [34] to jointly optimize the model. Finally, our loss function can be calculated as follows,

$$loss = loss_{yolo} + loss_{div} + loss_{reg} + loss_{attn}. \tag{10}$$

The diverse loss enforces the diversity of words in different rounds. It is formulated as $loss_{div} = \left\| A^T A \odot (1 - I) \right\|_F^2$, where A is the attention score matrix in the sub-query module [49] and I is an identity matrix.

4 Experiments

4.1 Dataset and Evaluation Metric

We evaluate the proposed REP on the released indoor image benchmark YouRefIt [7] for Embodied Reference Understanding task (ERU). Note that the video version of YouRefIt is not released when this paper submits. YouRefIt[1] contains 4221 query-referent pairs with 395 object categories. It is split into train and test, which has 2970 and 1251 samples, respectively. The average length of language descriptions is 3.73 and extra nonverbal cues such as gesture and orientation are provided. The Prec@X metric is used to evaluate the performance of ERU models on different sizes of referents and the overall performance. The $Prec@X$ is the percentage of prediction bounding boxes whose IoU scores are higher than a given threshold X, where $X \in \{0.25, 0.50, 0.75\}$.

4.2 Implementation Details

Networks Architecture. For a fair comparison with previous works [7,49], we adopt Darknet-53 [34] pretrained on MSCOCO object detection dataset [22] as the visual backbone. Language features are encoded by BERT-base [9] followed by two fully connected layers. Following ReSC-large [49], we keep the ratio of height and width and resize the long edge of the input image to 512. Then, we pad the resized image to 512×512, *i.e.*, $H_I = W_I = 512$. And the H, W, and C are 32, 32 and 256, respectively. The number of transformer encoder layers are 2. For each batch, we randomly sample 16 sentences and images with random horizontal flip, random intensity, saturation change, and random affine transformation following previous works [49,50]. We Adopt the RMSProp [39] optimizer with weight decay 0.0005. The initial learning rate is set to 0.0001 and reduced by half every 10 epochs for a total of 100 epochs. The weights of each loss are set to be 1. All the experiments are implemented in PyTorch [29], with the NVIDIA GeForce RTX 3090.

---

[1] https://github.com/yixchen/YouRefIt_ERU.

Table 1. Comparison with state-of-the-art methods on YouRefIt dataset. The best performing method is marked in bold.

Model	IoU = 0.25				IoU = 0.50				IoU = 0.75			
	All	Small	Medium	Large	All	Small	Medium	Large	All	Small	Medium	Large
MAttNet$_{pretrain}$ [52]	14.2	2.3	4.1	34.7	12.2	2.4	3.8	29.2	9.1	1.0	2.2	23.1
FAOA$_{pretrain}$	15.9	2.1	9.5	34.4	11.7	1.0	5.4	27.3	5.1	0.0	0.0	14.1
ReSC$_{pretrain}$	20.8	3.5	17.5	40.0	16.3	0.5	14.8	36.7	7.6	0.0	4.3	17.5
FAOA [50]	44.5	30.6	48.6	54.1	30.4	15.8	36.2	39.3	8.5	1.4	9.6	14.4
ReSC [49]	49.2	32.3	54.7	60.1	34.9	14.1	42.5	47.7	10.5	0.2	10.6	20.1
YouRefIt$_{PAF\_only}$	52.6	35.9	60.5	61.4	37.6	14.6	49.1	49.1	12.7	1.0	16.5	20.5
YouRefIt$_{Full}$ [7]	54.7	38.5	64.1	61.6	40.5	16.3	54.4	51.1	14.0	1.2	17.2	23.2
Ours REP$_{Full}$	**58.8**	**44.7**	**68.9**	**63.2**	**45.7**	**25.4**	**57.7**	**54.3**	**18.8**	**3.8**	**22.2**	**29.9**

4.3 Comparison with State-of-the-Arts

We compare our model with baselines and state-of-the-art methods on ERU, including MattNet [52], FAOA [50], ReSC [49] and YouRefIt [7]. Experimental results are shown in Table 1. Our REP consistently outperforms all the state-of-the-art models (SOTAs) across all the indicators by large margins. REP improves the average performance of $Prec@0.25$, $Prec@0.50$ and $Prec@0.75$ achieved by the existing best method by 4.1%, 5.2% and 4.8%, respectively.

Compared with the models pretrained on traditional REC dataset [53], our REP achieves 29.4% improvements in terms of $Prec@0.50$ and 26.2% in average, which demonstrates the significant difference between REC task and ERU task. Compared with FAOA and ReSC, REP improves the $Prec@0.25$, $Prec@0.50$, and $Prec@0.75$ by 9.6%, 10.8% and 8.3%, respectively, which reveals the importance of nonverbal cues in ERU.

Our REP significantly surpasses YouRefIt by 4.7% on average of all indicators, although YouRefIt already inputs nonverbal cues (*i.e.*, part affinity field map and saliency map) for multimodal fusion. The comparison demonstrates the effectiveness of our 3D view rotation and relation reasoning for addressing the perspective-taking challenge in ERU. Note that REP improves more on the more challenging referring of small objects. Thanks to the relation reasoning of REP, it improves small objects' grounding accuracy $Prec@0.25$ and $Prec@0.50$ by 6.2% and 9.1%, respectively.

4.4 Ablation Study

We conduct an ablation study to evaluate the effectiveness of 3D view rotation and relation reasoning methods, and the results are shown in Table 2.

Baseline. Baseline model shares the same visual encoder Darknet-53 [34] and textual encoder BERT [9] with our REP and also cooperates with nonverbal and verbal cues for prediction. It first obtains the multimodal feature map by fusing the visual feature map S_v, 2D image coordinates, and part affinity field map $S_{gesture}$, and then fuses verbal representation $Query(L)$ to the multimodal

Table 2. Ablation study of 3D view rotation and relation reasoning methods. The best performing method is marked in bold.

Model	IoU = 0.25				IoU = 0.50				IoU = 0.75			
	All	Small	Medium	Large	All	Small	Medium	Large	All	Small	Medium	Large
1 Baseline	54.3	39.7	60.7	62.6	39.0	18.4	48.6	50.0	11.0	2.3	9.1	20.7
2 +depth estimation	56.4	42.1	62.0	65.1	40.8	19.6	50.4	52.5	12.3	2.8	11.1	22.4
3 +embodied coordinate	56.7	42.3	62.5	65.1	41.7	20.3	51.7	53.2	14.5	3.4	14.6	24.9
4 +body language vector	57.1	44.4	64.0	63.0	42.4	23.2	52.6	51.6	16.1	3.1	18.7	26.0
5 +verbal attention	57.7	44.0	63.3	**65.9**	44.0	23.2	54.2	**54.6**	18.0	3.8	20.0	30.0
6 +gesture attention	**58.3**	**44.7**	**68.9**	63.2	**45.7**	**25.4**	**57.7**	54.3	**18.8**	**3.8**	**22.2**	**30.0**

feature map via a stack of three FiLM layers [30,49]. REP improves $Prec@0.25$, $Prec@0.50$, and $Prec@0.75$ of baseline by 4.0%, 6.7% and 7.8%, respectively.

3D View Rotation. As shown in line 2, +depth estimation improves the grounding accuracy by 1.9%, 1.8% and 1.3% in terms of $Prec@0.25$, $Prec@0.5$, and $Prec@0.75$, respectively, which demonstrates that the depth information can help to locate the referent. The cooperation of depth estimation and embodied coordinate (line 3) improves baseline by 2.4%, 2.7% and 3.5% in terms of $Prec@0.25$, $Prec@0.50$, $Prec@0.75$, respectively, which shows the effectiveness of rotating the receiver to the position of the sender to construct the embodied 3D coordinate system. The body language vector (line 4 vs. line 3) further significantly improves average accuracy on $Prec@0.75$ by 1.6%. The reason is that the body language vector encodes the body orientation and gesture of the sender, which could indicate the rough area where the referent locates. In general, the 3D view rotation module outperforms the baseline by 2.8%, 3.4%, and 5.1% in terms of $Prec@0.25$, $Prec@0.50$, and $Prec@0.75$, respectively.

Relation Reasoning. The verbal attention aims to cooperate the spatial attention to locate the referent in the activated area where the sender faces. With verbal attention, the model (line 5 vs. line 4) improves the overall grounding accuracy $Prec@0.25$ and $Prec@0.5$ by 1.6% and 1.7%, respectively. The improvement shows that the verbal attention method helps utilize verbal cues better. The nonverbal gesture attention aims to find the specific region where the sender points to and uses the specific region to help locate the complete referent by cooperating with verbal attention. The model with nonverbal gesture attention (line 6 vs. line 5) achieves 1.7% significant improvement in terms of $Prec@0.50$, and it improves more for locating referents with small and medium sizes. In detail, with nonverbal gesture attention, the $Prec@0.5$ of the model for finding small and medium referents is improved by 2.2% and 3.5%, respectively.

4.5   Qualitative Evaluation

To better explore in-depth insights into the view rotation and relation reasoning based on the embodied 3D coordinate system, we visualize three examples along with prediction results, spatial attention, nonverbal attention, and verbal attention maps. The visualization is shown in Fig. 3. Two different verbal attention maps are visualized to show the effect of with or without the help of the spatial attention map for the verbal fusion. Following [49], we use confidence scores to represent the verbal attention scores by adopting an output head over the verbal-visual feature map at the last layer.

As shown in Fig. 3, REP can generate the explainable visual evidence of stepwise reasoning from the spatial attention to the nonverbal gesture attention and the verbal attention, and locates the referent from the sender's perspective in different kinds of challenging scenarios. (1) In the first example, REP successfully finds the activated area where the sender faces and locates the "building blocks" while excluding the distractor "bag". (2) Thanks to the view rotation, our REP precisely captures the slight differences in the sender's body orientation and generates distinct activated areas for the second and third examples. (3) With the help of spatial attention, the verbal fusion module locates the referent accurately for the novel object of "the lid on the pan". (4) The nonverbal gesture attention module and verbal fusion module can cooperate in locating the referent. The nonverbal gesture attention module finds a specific region of "the fridge in front of me", and the verbal fusion module helps to locate the referent completely.

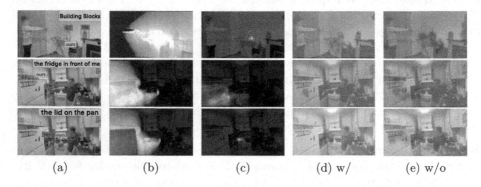

(a)   (b)   (c)   (d) w/   (e) w/o

Fig. 3. Qualitative Results showing (1) prediction results: green, yellow and red boxes are the ground-truth, our prediction result, and YouRefIt's predicted referents; (2) spatial attention; (3) gesture attention; (4) verbal fusion heatmap with the help of attention map; (5) verbal fusion headmap without the help of attention map. (Color figure online)

5   Conclusion

In this paper, we propose Reasoning from your Respective (REP) model to tackle the Embodied Reference Understanding (ERU) task. REP first rotates the receiver to the position of the sender and estimate the sender's viewpoint to the referent by constructing the embodied 3D coordinate system and learning the body language representation. Then, REP performs relation reasoning between the sender and the referent by cooperating the spatial attention, nonverbal gesture attention and the verbal fusion methods. REP not only outperforms the state-of-the-art models of ERU by a large margin but also generates explainable visual evidence of step-by-step reasoning.

Acknowledgment. This work is supported by Shanghai Pujiang Program (No. 21PJ1410900).

References

1. Agarap, A.F.: Deep learning using rectified linear units (ReLU). arXiv preprint arXiv:1803.08375 (2018)
2. Banerjee, P., Gokhale, T., Yang, Y., Baral, C.: Weakly supervised relative spatial reasoning for visual question answering. In: Proceedings of the IEEE/CVF International Conference on Computer Vision (ICCV), pp. 1908–1918 (2021)
3. Batson, C.D., Early, S., Salvarani, G.: Perspective taking: imagining how another feels versus imaging how you would feel. Pers. Soc. Psychol. Bull. **23**, 751–758 (1997)
4. Bhat, S.F., Alhashim, I., Wonka, P.: Adabins: depth estimation using adaptive bins. In: Proceedings of the IEEE/CVF Conference on Computer Vision and Pattern Recognition (CVPR), pp. 4009–4018 (2021)
5. Cao, Z., Hidalgo, G., Simon, T., Wei, S.E., Sheikh, Y.: OpenPose: realtime multiperson 2D pose estimation using part affinity fields. IEEE Trans. Pattern Anal. Mach. Intell. (TPAMI) 172–186 (2019)
6. Chen, X., Ma, L., Chen, J., Jie, Z., Liu, W., Luo, J.: Real-time referring expression comprehension by single-stage grounding network. arXiv preprint arXiv:1812.03426 (2018)
7. Chen, Y., et al.: Yourefit: embodied reference understanding with language and gesture. In: Proceedings of the IEEE/CVF International Conference on Computer Vision (ICCV), pp. 1385–1395 (2021)
8. Clinton, J.A., Magliano, J.P., Skowronski, J.J.: Gaining perspective on spatial perspective taking. J. Cogn. Psychol. 85–97 (2018)
9. Devlin, J., Chang, M.W., Lee, K., Toutanova, K.: Bert: pre-training of deep bidirectional transformers for language understanding. arXiv preprint arXiv:1810.04805 (2018)
10. Dosovitskiy, A., et al.: An image is worth 16x16 words: transformers for image recognition at scale. arXiv preprint arXiv:2010.11929 (2020)
11. Eigen, D., Fergus, R.: Predicting depth, surface normals and semantic labels with a common multi-scale convolutional architecture. In: Proceedings of the IEEE/CVF International Conference on Computer Vision (ICCV), pp. 2650–2658 (2015)
12. Eigen, D., Puhrsch, C., Fergus, R.: Depth map prediction from a single image using a multi-scale deep network. In: Advances in Neural Information Processing Systems (2014)
13. Fan, L., Qiu, S., Zheng, Z., Gao, T., Zhu, S.C., Zhu, Y.: Learning triadic belief dynamics in nonverbal communication from videos. In: Proceedings of the IEEE/CVF Conference on Computer Vision and Pattern Recognition (CVPR), pp. 7312–7321 (2021)

14. Fu, H., Gong, M., Wang, C., Batmanghelich, K., Tao, D.: Deep ordinal regression network for monocular depth estimation. In: Proceedings of the IEEE/CVF conference on Computer Vision and Pattern Recognition (CVPR), pp. 2002–2011 (2018)

15. Hu, R., Rohrbach, M., Andreas, J., Darrell, T., Saenko, K.: Modeling relationships in referential expressions with compositional modular networks. In: Proceedings of the IEEE/CVF Conference on Computer Vision and Pattern Recognition (CVPR), pp. 1115–1124 (2017)

16. Hudson, D.A., Manning, C.D.: Compositional attention networks for machine reasoning. In: International Conference on Learning Representations (2018)

17. Johnson, J., Hariharan, B., Van Der Maaten, L., Fei-Fei, L., Lawrence Zitnick, C., Girshick, R.: CLEVR: a diagnostic dataset for compositional language and elementary visual reasoning. In: Proceedings of the IEEE/CVF Conference on Computer Vision and Pattern Recognition (CVPR), pp. 2901–2910 (2017)

18. Kipf, T.N., Welling, M.: Semi-supervised classification with graph convolutional networks. In: International Conference on Learning Representations (2016)

19. Kroner, A., Senden, M., Driessens, K., Goebel, R.: Contextual encoder-decoder network for visual saliency prediction. Neural Netw. **129**, 261–270 (2020)

20. Ladicky, L., Shi, J., Pollefeys, M.: Pulling things out of perspective. In: Proceedings of the IEEE/CVF Conference on Computer Vision and Pattern Recognition (CVPR), pp. 89–96 (2014)

21. Liao, Y., et al.: A real-time cross-modality correlation filtering method for referring expression comprehension. In: Proceedings of the IEEE/CVF Conference on Computer Vision and Pattern Recognition (CVPR), pp. 10880–10889 (2020)

22. Lin, T.-Y., et al.: Microsoft COCO: common objects in context. In: Fleet, D., Pajdla, T., Schiele, B., Tuytelaars, T. (eds.) ECCV 2014. LNCS, vol. 8693, pp. 740–755. Springer, Cham (2014). https://doi.org/10.1007/978-3-319-10602-1_48

23. Liu, X., Wang, Z., Shao, J., Wang, X., Li, H.: Improving referring expression grounding with cross-modal attention-guided erasing. In: Proceedings of the IEEE/CVF Conference on Computer Vision and Pattern Recognition (CVPR), pp. 1950–1959 (2019)

24. Luo, G., et al.: Multi-task collaborative network for joint referring expression comprehension and segmentation. In: Proceedings of the IEEE/CVF Conference on Computer Vision and Pattern Recognition (CVPR), pp. 10034–10043 (2020)

25. Mao, J., Gan, C., Kohli, P., Tenenbaum, J.B., Wu, J.: The neuro-symbolic concept learner: interpreting scenes, words, and sentences from natural supervision. In: International Conference on Learning Representations (2019)

26. Mao, J., Huang, J., Toshev, A., Camburu, O., Yuille, A.L., Murphy, K.: Generation and comprehension of unambiguous object descriptions. In: Proceedings of the IEEE/CVF Conference on Computer Vision and Pattern Recognition (CVPR), pp. 11–20 (2016)

27. Mertan, A., Duff, D.J., Unal, G.: Single image depth estimation: an overview. arXiv preprint arXiv:2104.06456 (2021)

28. Nagaraja, V.K., Morariu, V.I., Davis, L.S.: Modeling context between objects for referring expression understanding. In: Leibe, B., Matas, J., Sebe, N., Welling, M. (eds.) ECCV 2016. LNCS, vol. 9908, pp. 792–807. Springer, Cham (2016). https://doi.org/10.1007/978-3-319-46493-0_48

29. Paszke, A., et al.: Pytorch: an imperative style, high-performance deep learning library. In: Advances in Neural Information Processing Systems, pp. 8026–8037 (2019)

30. Perez, E., Strub, F., De Vries, H., Dumoulin, V., Courville, A.: Film: visual reasoning with a general conditioning layer. In: Proceedings of the AAAI Conference on Artificial Intelligence (2018)
31. Qi, X., Liao, R., Liu, Z., Urtasun, R., Jia, J.: Geonet: geometric neural network for joint depth and surface normal estimation. In: Proceedings of the IEEE/CVF Conference on Computer Vision and Pattern Recognition (CVPR), pp. 283–291 (2018)
32. Qin, X., Zhang, Z., Huang, C., Dehghan, M., Zaiane, O.R., Jagersand, M.: U^2-net: going deeper with nested u-structure for salient object detection. Pattern Recognit. **106**, 107404 (2020)
33. Qiu, S., Liu, H., Zhang, Z., Zhu, Y., Zhu, S.C.: Human-robot interaction in a shared augmented reality workspace. In: Proceedings of IEEE/RSJ International Conference on Intelligent Robots and Systems (IROS) (2020)
34. Redmon, J., Farhadi, A.: Yolov3: an incremental improvement. arXiv preprint arXiv:1804.02767 (2018)
35. Sadhu, A., Chen, K., Nevatia, R.: Zero-shot grounding of objects from natural language queries. In: Proceedings of the IEEE/CVF International Conference on Computer Vision (ICCV), pp. 4694–4703 (2019)
36. Silberman, N., Hoiem, D., Kohli, P., Fergus, R.: Indoor segmentation and support inference from RGBD images. In: Fitzgibbon, A., Lazebnik, S., Perona, P., Sato, Y., Schmid, C. (eds.) ECCV 2012. LNCS, vol. 7576, pp. 746–760. Springer, Heidelberg (2012). https://doi.org/10.1007/978-3-642-33715-4_54
37. Stacy, S., Zhao, Q., Zhao, M., Kleiman-Weiner, M., Gao, T.: Intuitive signaling through an "imagined we". In: Proceedings of the Annual Meeting of the Cognitive Science Society (CogSci) (2020)
38. Surtees, A., Apperly, I., Samson, D.: Similarities and differences in visual and spatial perspective-taking processes. Cognition **129**, 426–438 (2013)
39. Tieleman, T., Hinton, G., et al.: Lecture 6.5-rmsprop: divide the gradient by a running average of its recent magnitude. COURSERA Neural Netw. Mach. Learn. **4**, 26–31 (2012)
40. Vaswani, A., et al.: Attention is all you need. In: Advances in Neural Information Processing Systems (2017)
41. Wang, P., Wu, Q., Cao, J., Shen, C., Gao, L., Hengel, A.V.D.: Neighbourhood watch: referring expression comprehension via language-guided graph attention networks. In: Proceedings of the IEEE/CVF Conference on Computer Vision and Pattern Recognition (CVPR), pp. 1960–1968 (2019)
42. Wu, Q., Wu, C.J., Zhu, Y., Joo, J.: Communicative learning with natural gestures for embodied navigation agents with human-in-the-scene. In: Proceedings of IEEE/RSJ International Conference on Intelligent Robots and Systems (IROS) (2021)
43. Xu, D., Ouyang, W., Wang, X., Sebe, N.: PAD-Net: multi-tasks guided prediction-and-distillation network for simultaneous depth estimation and scene parsing. In: Proceedings of the IEEE/CVF Conference on Computer Vision and Pattern Recognition (CVPR), pp. 675–684 (2018)
44. Yang, S., Li, G., Yu, Y.: Cross-modal relationship inference for grounding referring expressions. In: Proceedings of the IEEE/CVF Conference on Computer Vision and Pattern Recognition (CVPR), pp. 4145–4154 (2019)
45. Yang, S., Li, G., Yu, Y.: Dynamic graph attention for referring expression comprehension. In: Proceedings of the IEEE/CVF International Conference on Computer Vision, pp. 4644–4653 (2019)

46. Yang, S., Li, G., Yu, Y.: Graph-structured referring expression reasoning in the wild. In: Proceedings of the IEEE/CVF Conference on Computer Vision and Pattern Recognition (CVPR), pp. 9952–9961 (2020)

47. Yang, S., Li, G., Yu, Y.: Propagating over phrase relations for one-stage visual grounding. In: Vedaldi, A., Bischof, H., Brox, T., Frahm, J.-M. (eds.) ECCV 2020. LNCS, vol. 12364, pp. 589–605. Springer, Cham (2020). https://doi.org/10.1007/978-3-030-58529-7_35

48. Yang, S., Li, G., Yu, Y.: Relationship-embedded representation learning for grounding referring expressions. IEEE Trans. Pattern Anal. Mach. Intell. **43**(8), 2765–2779 (2020)

49. Yang, Z., Chen, T., Wang, L., Luo, J.: Improving one-stage visual grounding by recursive sub-query construction. In: Vedaldi, A., Bischof, H., Brox, T., Frahm, J.-M. (eds.) ECCV 2020. LNCS, vol. 12359, pp. 387–404. Springer, Cham (2020). https://doi.org/10.1007/978-3-030-58568-6_23

50. Yang, Z., Gong, B., Wang, L., Huang, W., Yu, D., Luo, J.: A fast and accurate one-stage approach to visual grounding. In: Proceedings of the IEEE/CVF International Conference on Computer Vision (ICCV), pp. 4683–4693 (2019)

51. Yi, K., Wu, J., Gan, C., Torralba, A., Kohli, P., Tenenbaum, J.: Neural-symbolic VQA: disentangling reasoning from vision and language understanding. In: Advances in Neural Information Processing Systems (2018)

52. Yu, L., et al.: Mattnet: modular attention network for referring expression comprehension. In: Proceedings of the IEEE/CVF Conference on Computer Vision and Pattern Recognition (CVPR), pp. 1307–1315 (2018)

53. Yu, L., Poirson, P., Yang, S., Berg, A.C., Berg, T.L.: Modeling context in referring expressions. In: Leibe, B., Matas, J., Sebe, N., Welling, M. (eds.) ECCV 2016. LNCS, vol. 9906, pp. 69–85. Springer, Cham (2016). https://doi.org/10.1007/978-3-319-46475-6_5

54. Zhang, H., Niu, Y., Chang, S.F.: Grounding referring expressions in images by variational context. In: Proceedings of the IEEE/CVF Conference on Computer Vision and Pattern Recognition (CVPR), pp. 4158–4166 (2018)

Object-Centric Unsupervised Image Captioning

Zihang Meng[1]([envelope]), David Yang[2], Xuefei Cao[2], Ashish Shah[2], and Ser-Nam Lim[2]

[1] University of Wisconsin-Madison, Madison, USA
zihangm@cs.wisc.edu
[2] Meta AI, Menlo Park, USA
{dzyang,ashishbshah,sernamlim}@fb.com

Abstract. Image captioning is a longstanding problem in the field of computer vision and natural language processing. To date, researchers have produced impressive state-of-the-art performance in the age of deep learning. Most of these state-of-the-art, however, requires large volume of annotated image-caption pairs in order to train their models. When given an image dataset of interests, practitioner needs to annotate the caption for each image in the training set and this process needs to happen for each newly collected image dataset. In this paper, we explore the task of unsupervised image captioning which utilizes unpaired images and texts to train the model so that the texts can come from different sources than the images. A main school of research on this topic that has been shown to be effective is to construct pairs from the images and texts in the training set according to their overlap of objects. Unlike in the supervised setting, these constructed pairings are however not guaranteed to have fully overlapping set of objects. Our work in this paper overcomes this by harvesting objects corresponding to a given sentence from the training set, even if they don't belong to the same image. When used as input to a transformer, such mixture of objects enables larger if not full object coverage, and when supervised by the corresponding sentence, produced results that outperform current state of the art unsupervised methods by a significant margin. Building upon this finding, we further show that (1) additional information on relationship between objects and attributes of objects also helps in boosting performance; and (2) our method also extends well to non-English image captioning, which usually suffers from a scarcer level of annotations. Our findings are supported by strong empirical results. Our code is available at https://github.com/zihangm/obj-centric-unsup-caption.

1 Introduction

Image captioning is an important task standing at the crossroad of computer vision (CV) and natural language processing (NLP) that has been widely stud-

Supplementary Information The online version contains supplementary material available at https://doi.org/10.1007/978-3-031-20059-5_13.

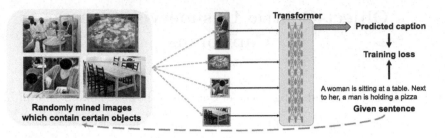

Fig. 1. Overview of our image captioning training pipeline. During training, the transformer takes the set of object regions mined from the entire image dataset as input. During test/inference, it takes in the object regions of the given image.

ied for many years. In the deep learning era, with the advent of transformer models [5,27,44], significant advances in image captioning have been made since its "humble" beginning from the early use of Convolutional Neural Networks in combination with Recurrent Neural Networks [18]. Since then, various attention mechanisms [2,41] and transformer based models [8] have been proposed with great effect. The current success has however been predicated on the availability of large amount of image-caption annotations, which is quite expensive to obtain. As a matter of fact, in [29], it was revealed that it costs 144.7 s on average for a professional full-time annotator to provide a high-quality caption for just a single image.

This has led researchers to propose methods that do not require image-caption pairings, but instead train their models on separate image and text datasets. This line of work precipitates the onset of unsupervised image captioning, with [11] making an early attempt here by utilizing policy gradient to encourage visual concepts in the predicted captions. This approach, however, only encourages the appearance of visual object words, but ignores how they should properly fit into the sentence. Later on, [22] proposed to mine pseudo image-caption pairs to train the model. Given a sentence, the algorithm searches and pairs the sentence with an image in the training set which contains overlapping visual concepts. Building on this, [16] makes further improvements by introducing a new gate function that tells the model which word in the sentence is irrelevant to the image to form higher quality pseudo image-caption pairs.

While these advances have produced state of the art performance, we found that they have a fundamental limitation. Since the image and text datasets are unpaired, it is more likely that the quality of the image-caption pairs could be sub par as measured by the number of objects in the sentence that are actually captured in the image (see Table 4 and 5 on how object coverage affects performance). Our work in this paper tries to solve this problem with a simple yet effective approach. Given a sentence in the text dataset, instead of trying to find a candidate from the image dataset, we harvest objects corresponding to the sentence. Because we do not require these objects to be from the same image, we significantly increase the chance of fully covering all the objects that appear in the sentence. Specifically, the harvested objects are fed into a transformer, which is then supervised by the corresponding sentence during training. "Surprisingly", experiments show that our approach outperforms the state-of-the-art methods by a clear margin.

To further boost performance, we note that the harvested objects do not really respect spatial relationships (e.g., the phrase "person riding a bike" requires the "person" to be above "bike"). However, when a relationship detector also becomes available, our approach naturally enables the utilization of such relationship information by feeding such information together with the objects into the transformer. Most previous works [11,14,16,22] would find the incorporation of such information challenging without making significant change to their model or training procedure.

Finally, we explore the possibility of going beyond English to generate captions in other languages. Non-English captioning tasks are expected to be one of the largest benefactors of unsupervised image captioning, simply because paired image-captions annotations are scarcely available in languages other than English, and really speaks to the importance of making advances in unsupervised image caption. We demonstrate our proposed approach on non-English captioning with convincing empirical results.

2 Related Work

Supervised Image Captioning. Supervised image captioning traditionally relies on paired image-caption data to train a generative model which creates a text description given an input image. In recent years, the research community has significantly raised the level of performance for the image captioning task [36]. Some earlier work such as [18] adopts Convolutional Neural Networks (CNNs) and Recurrent Neural Networks (RNNs) with global image feature as input, while others such as [3,41] proposed to add attention over the grid of CNN features. [2] further adds attention over visual regions to learn better feature representations. More recently, transformer-based models have been utilized with great success [8]. Other notable advances include personalized image captioning [43] that is conditioned on the learned representation of a certain user, dense image captioning [17] which localizes and describes salient image regions, and the generation of captions in a controllable way guided by speech [9], a set of bounding boxes [7] or human attention traces [27]. One recent work called CLIP [30] proposes to learn visual models using noisy image-caption pairs automatically mined from the internet. The model is not designed for captioning task but can possibly be used as a pre-trained visual and language embedding model for the captioning task.

Towards Unsupervised Image Captioning. Paired image-caption datasets are usually very expensive to obtain. To deal with this challenge, some studies have been conducted to explore the possibility of reducing the amount of paired information needed or utilizing unpaired images and sentences. [15,39] explored learning simultaneously from multiple data sources with auxiliary objectives to describe a variety of objects unseen in paired image-caption data. [12] leverages the paired information in a pivot language to train the generative model and translate the generated captions into the target language. More relevant to our work is the recent line of work in [11,13,14,16,22,26], which utilize unpaired image and text information. They assume that a pretrained object detector is available for extracting visual concepts from an image which act as the link between visual and language domain. Some of them utilize adversarial training to align the visual and language domain. [11] relies on discrete rewards to help the model generate high-quality captions. [14] trains a generator which generates a sentence from discrete words. They discard the visual information in detected object regions and only keep the visual concept words as the input to the model. [13] assumes that a pretrained scene graph detector is available, and trains a captioning model using scene graph decomposition. [22] mines pseudo image-caption pairs from existing but unpaired image and text datasets to train the captioning model. [16] improves on it by removing spurious alignments. Our work in this paper follows the same line of thoughts to mine pseudo image-caption pairs. However, unlike these existing approaches which when given a sentence look for *an* image that contains as many of the objects occurring in the sentence as possible, our method explores the possibility of harvesting these objects from different images.

Non-English Captioning. Most current works on image captioning focus on the English language. To extend captioning technology to non-English languages, we are starting to see some studies being reported. Some researchers have attempted to directly propose a captioning model on a target language while utilizing a pivot language, typically English, in which paired information is readily available [12,23,35,40]. Nevertheless, the straightforward approach remains to collect image-caption pairs in the target language (e.g., French [31], German [10], or Chinese [24]). These efforts have not been as extensive as hoped, and advances in unsupervised image captioning could have strong impact here. In this paper, we provide benchmarks showing that even in non-English captioning tasks, our proposed method surpasses or is on par with the state of the art unsupervised image captioning methods.

3   Method

Given a set of images $\mathcal{I} = \{I_1, ..., I_{N_i}\}$, and a set of sentences $\mathcal{S} = \{S_1, ..., S_{N_s}\}$, our goal is to train a model which takes an image as input and generates a caption that well describes the input image. We follow previous work on unsupervised image captioning [11] in assuming that we do not have information about the pairing between $\mathcal{I}$ and $\mathcal{S}$, but have access to a pretrained object detector (a pretrained Faster R-CNN [2]). Our overall approach is shown in Fig. 1, where we propose to mine objects from $\mathcal{I}$ without the constraint that these objects need to come from the same image. Specifically, given a sentence S_i, we first detect the set of visual concepts it contains (e.g., person, bike) as

$$\mathcal{V}_i^S = \{v_1, v_2, ..., v_k\}, \tag{1}$$

where k is the number of visual concepts in the sentence S_i. From $\mathcal{V}_i^S$, we mine a set of image regions (we use the pretrained Faster R-CNN to detect the regions and extract the visual features) given as

$$\mathcal{R}_i = \{r_1, r_2, ..., r_k\}, \tag{2}$$

where each $r_j \in \mathcal{R}_i$ is the visual feature of the object region of visual concept $v_j \in \mathcal{V}_i^S$ taken from a randomly chosen image $I \in \mathcal{I}$ which contains this visual concept. We further encode the location information by concatenating the 5-D vector representing the bounding box locations (four coordinates and the area, from the image I where the region is mined) with r_j. $\mathcal{R}_i$ forms the training pair with the given sentence S_i. We can utilize these artificially constructed $\mathcal{R}$–S pairs to train the captioning model using Cross Entropy (CE) loss:

$$L = \mathrm{CE}(f(\mathcal{R}_i), S_i), \tag{3}$$

where f represents the captioning model which predicts the caption from a set of object region features. In this work, we adopt the transformer model described in [37] as f.

3.1 Utilizing Additional Information

The flexibility of a transformer architecture means that we can also include additional information as input together with the object information. In our method described so far, we note that a part of the information is lost, being that we used the original locations of the object regions, which may be incorrect in relation to other objects as well as losing fine-grained information when we replaced the objects (e.g., face attributes). In this regard, our experiments also show that losing such information causes a drop in performance (see Table 3). To this end, we describe how we take a pretrained relationship detector and attribute detector as examples of additional information that we can add to our method.

Consider that for a given I_i, the relationship detector can detect triplets in the form of subject-relation-object,

$$\mathcal{T}_i^I = \{\mathrm{sub}_1\text{-}\mathrm{rel}_1\text{-}\mathrm{obj}_1, ..., \mathrm{sub}_{N_i^I}\text{-}\mathrm{rel}_{N_i^I}\text{-}\mathrm{obj}_{N_i^I}\}, \tag{4}$$

and for a sentence S_i, the relationship parser can detect triplets in the same form,

$$\mathcal{T}_i^S = \{\mathrm{sub}_1\text{-}\mathrm{rel}_1\text{-}\mathrm{obj}_1, ..., \mathrm{sub}_{N_i^S}\text{-}\mathrm{rel}_{N_i^S}\text{-}\mathrm{obj}_{N_i^S}\}. \tag{5}$$

Then for a given sentence S_i, we can similarly obtain $\mathcal{R}_i$ using the same strategy as that in Eq. 2. However, instead of only selecting image regions which match the visual concepts in S_i, we also add to $\mathcal{R}_i$ pairs of image regions (sub-obj) which match the triplets (sub-rel-obj) in $\mathcal{T}_i^S$:

$$\mathcal{R}_i = \{r_1, ..., r_k, pair_1, ..., pair_l\}, \tag{6}$$

where each r refers to one image region and each *pair* refers to a pair of image regions formed by the subject region and the object region from one triplet. k is the number of visual concepts in S_i and l is the number of triplets in S_i detected by the language relationship detector. The subsequent steps to construct pairs for training are the same as that in Sect. 3.

To utilize the pretrained attribute detector, we basically perform the same steps. The only difference is that instead of detecting triplets subject-relation-object, the attribute detector detects pairs in the form of attribute-object. Then when we see a certain attribute-object pair in the sentence S_i, we look for an image region that matches this attribute-object, and add this image region into $\mathcal{R}_i$. Similar procedure could be conducted when other pretrained models such as scene detector, facial expression detector, etc., are available. In this paper, we will focus on leveraging relationship and attribute detectors in addition to the objects, and leave the study of adding other detectors to future work.

3.2   Extension to Other Languages

We can also easily adapt our work to train a non-English image captioning model in an unsupervised way. Consider the same object detector pretrained on English vocabulary. We denote the English vocabulary of the object detector as

$$\text{voc}_{\text{English}} = \{\text{word}_1, ..., \text{word}_{N_{\text{English}}}\}. \tag{7}$$

Then we translate each word in the English vocabulary into the target language denoted as "Target" (although translating a whole sentence into a different language is a challenging task, translating a single word can be easily done using language dictionaries) given as

$$\text{voc}_{\text{Target}} = \{\text{word}_1, ..., \text{word}_{N_{\text{Target}}}\}, \tag{8}$$

where N_{English} may not equal to N_{Target} considering it is possible that multiple words in English are translated into the same word in the target language and vice versa. After this, we can follow the same steps in Sect. 3 to construct pairs to train a model directly in the target language.

4   Experiments

Our experiments are designed to empirically establish: (i) that our proposed method outperforms state of the art unsupervised image captioning methods, (ii) that our proposed method can easily incorporate additional information, in this case object relationships and attributes to help boost performance, (iii) the effects of swapping in objects from different images to generate training pairs, and, (iv) that our proposed method outperforms state of the art in non-English captioning tasks. We will provide the implementation details next so that we have a common ground for discussing the results.

Collecting Text Corpus from the Internet. One key advantage of unsupervised image captioning is being able to utilize text corpus directly mined from the internet. In the experiments, we use two internet-mined text corpus collected by previous works: Shutterstock (SS) [11] and Google Conceptual Captions (GCC) [34]. SS is a set of sentences collected from the Shutterstock website using the filter that each sentence should have some object words overlapped with COCO object categories. The sentences in GCC are automatically harvested from the Alt-text HTML attribute associated with web images. For some cases (described in later sections), we also utilize sentences from existing human annotated image caption datasets, mainly to demonstrate the property of our proposed method.

Implementation Details. We tokenize the text datasets and delete sentences which are shorter than 5 words or longer than a certain length, 20 for GCC and SS, and 100 for Localized Narratives [29]) and build a language vocabulary. Then we match the object words of the object detector with the language vocabulary. Our object detector is a Faster R-CNN [32] pretrained on Visual Genome [20], whose vocabulary contains 1600 object words. Next, we build a dictionary that maps an object word to a set of images which contain this object word. Finally, during training, for a randomly picked sentence, we first find all object words it contains, and for each object word, we randomly pick one image that contains this object word and crop this object region using its bounding box location. In this way, for each sentence S_i we can have a set of object regions R_i. Our captioning model is a one layer transformer [37]. The size of the hidden attention layers is 512 and that of the feed-forward layers is 2048. The input object features are extracted by the Faster R-CNN mentioned above. We train the network with a batch size of 100 using the Adam optimizer [19]. The initial learning rate is 5e-4, which decays by 0.8 every 3 epochs, for a total of 30 epochs. The same training setup is used for all experiments in this paper. Note that these hyperparameters are directly borrowed from [27] (except that we increased the batch size from 30 to 100 for faster training), and we did not utilize the validation set to further finetune the hyperparameters to ensure that we do not utilize any pairing information during training (the validation set contains pairing information).

Evaluation Datasets. For images, we follow previous work [11,16] to use the MS COCO dataset and the train/validation/test split provided by [18], and report the performance on the test split (except in Sect. 4.3, where we follow [27] to use COCO-2017 official splits). For the text, we choose the recently released Localized Narratives (LN) [29] which provides captions for four public datasets including COCO, ADE20k, Flickr30k and Open Images. We choose LN-COCO instead of COCO captions [6] because the captions in LN are longer, contain more verbs, and the overall quality is better (see our supplement or Table 2 in [29] for a comparison between LN-COCO and COCO captions). We use LN-COCO for all experiments except those on non-English languages in Sect. 4.4, where we use the annotations provided by COCO-CN [24] and Multi30k [10].

Table 1. The performance of our method and baseline methods [11,16] trained using COCO images and SS/GCC text datasets, evaluated using test split of COCO images and LN-COCO caption annotations as ground truth.

Text dataset	Method	BLEU-1	BLEU-4	METEOR	ROUGE$_L$	CIDEr	SPICE	WMD
SS	[11]	0.016	0.001	0.037	0.109	0.018	0.073	0.045
SS	[16]	0.022	0.001	0.043	0.126	0.025	0.078	0.042
SS	Ours	**0.056**	**0.003**	**0.060**	**0.127**	**0.038**	**0.102**	**0.060**
GCC	[16]	0.006	0.000	0.035	0.115	0.017	0.075	0.040
GCC	Ours	**0.062**	**0.004**	**0.062**	**0.146**	**0.032**	**0.104**	**0.055**

Table 2. The performance of utilizing only object detector and that of utilizing object detector plus relationship/attribute detector. The models are trained using COCO images and LN-OpenImages captions, and evaluated using the test split of COCO images and LN-COCO caption annotations as ground truth.

Pretrained models	BLEU-1	BLEU-4	METEOR	ROUGE$_L$	CIDEr	SPICE	WMD
Object	0.327	0.059	0.140	0.262	0.109	0.181	0.079
Object + attribute	**0.332**	0.059	0.136	0.266	0.124	0.181	0.079
Object + relationship	0.329	0.061	0.140	0.268	0.120	0.188	0.080
Object + relationship + attribute	0.329	**0.062**	**0.141**	**0.274**	**0.138**	**0.193**	**0.083**

Evaluating Metrics. We use the official COCO caption evaluation tool and report the performance in terms of BLEU-1 [28], BLEU-4, METEOR [4], ROUGE [25], CIDEr [38], SPICE [1] and WMD [21].

4.1   Comparisons with State-of-the-Art Methods

[11,16] are two state of the art methods in unsupervised image captioning. We compare our method with them using COCO images together with GCC and SS as the text datasets respectively. We use the code released by the authors to produce results on these datasets for benchmarking. It is important to note that both GCC and SS are web-crawled text datasets and help to showcase unsupervised methods' flexibility in exploiting large scale data by breaking the chain of pairing. We further note that these state of the art methods are also not transformer based.

Quantitative results are presented in Table 1. We can see that our method outperforms all baseline methods on both text datasets by a clear margin. The qualitative results are in Fig. 2. The captions generated by [11] tend to contain verbs describing the objects but make mistakes frequently (e.g., in "a person is sitting on a motorbike" the verb "sitting" matches with object "motorbike" but does not match the input image). [16] generated mostly correct captions but the captions are mainly concatenations of object names (nouns) without verbs describing the action of the objects or the relationships between objects (e.g., "a young man in a white skies"). Our method generates more comprehensive captions with mostly correct nouns and verbs and the captions are aware of

		a person is sitting on a motorbike	traditional turkish dessert baklava on a wooden background . ramadan food	a person wearing a red umbrella and a red clothing
COCO -> SS	Feng et. al. [11]			
	Honda et. al. [16]	a young man in a white skies and a red jacket	a delicious dessert of a cake with a cup of coffee and a spoon on a wooden table	a young woman in a umbrella with a umbrellas in the park
	Ours	Female skier wearing red jacket , helmet , ski pants and goggles standing with skis on snow mountain slope	colorful donuts with icing and sprinkles in a plastic tray on a light wood plank	Beautiful girl in jeans jacket shoes with umbrella standing on the road near the house with bush and graffiti sky
COCO -> LN-Open Images	Ours	In this image there is snow on the land . A man is standing on the land . He is wearing helmet , jacket , pant and shoes . He is holding ski sticks in his hand . Background there is hill . Top of the image there is sky	In this image in the center there is one table , on the table there is one plate , in that plate there are some food items , and in the plate there are some food items . And on the top of the image there is one light	In this image there are two girls standing on the road . The girl in black jacket is holding an umbrella in her hand . Beside her there is grass on the ground . In the background there are trees and sky
LN-COCO	Human Annotation	In this image we can see a person wearing goggles, helmet and gloves, and holding ski sticks and on a ski board. And there is snow. On the right side we can see hills. In the background there is sky with clouds	In this picture we can see three trays, on the right side there are some breads present in packets, in the middle we can see three doughnuts and three cake pieces, in the bottom there are two fruity boxes	In this picture there is a girl standing and holding the umbrella. At the back there are buildings, trees and vehicles. At the top there is sky. At the bottom there is a road and there is grass

Fig. 2. Qualitative results of our method and two baseline methods on COCO test split.

the interaction between objects for most part (e.g., "female skier wearing red jacket", "standing with skis on snow mountain slope").

We can also see that all methods fail to identify any color attributes, and this is a limitation of only having a pre-trained object detector with no color attribute detector. If a pre-trained color detector becomes available, our method naturally enables the utilization of this information as described in Sect. 3.1.

4.2 Utilizing Object Relationships and Attributes

In Sect. 3.1, we described how our framework naturally enables utilizing additional pretrained models when they become available. Here, we provide empirical results from adding both a relationship and attribute detector. We use the relationship and attribute detector pretrained on Visual Genome [42] for images, and the semantic parser provided by [1], which is built on [33], to find relationship triplets from sentences. Note that we only need the pretrained relationship detectors during training to construct (R_i, S_i) pairs, not test time. We train the model on COCO images, and choose LN-OpenImages as the text dataset since it contains rich semantic relationship information. Ideally, when given a pair of triplets, we would like to completely match the subject-relation-object, but we found that such complete matches are rare because the relationship detector is not 100% accurate and discrepancies between the image and sentence relationship detectors exist. So, instead, we consider two triplets a match as long as the subject-object matches between them.

The quantitative results are presented in Table 2. Row 2 shows results when a attribute detector is added while row 3 gives the results for when only a relationship detector is added. Results from row 4 come from adding both a relationship and attribute detector. We can see that adding either a relationship or attribute detector is beneficial. Interestingly, row 4 shows a slight improvement over row 3 but a much larger boost over row 2. Qualitatively, we can refer to the last row of Fig. 2. We can see that the captions are comprehensive and contain many relationship triplets in the generated captions (e.g., "he-holding-ski sticks", "he-wearing-helmet", "man-standing on-land").

4.3 Ablations

Table 3. The performance of supervised training, before and after replacing the objects with randomly mined objects of the same category (the supervised training was conducted following [27] using their provided code). Detailed interpretation of each row is in Sect. 4.3

Methods	BLEU-1	BLEU-4	METEOR	ROUGE$_L$	CIDEr	SPICE	WMD
Supervised training	0.306	0.082	0.151	0.306	0.263	0.238	0.113
After replacing objects	0.297	0.078	0.145	0.298	0.227	0.232	0.109
After replacing objects and location	0.298	0.080	0.146	0.300	0.239	0.234	0.108
Ours	0.298	0.071	0.159	0.264	0.125	0.164	0.083

Effects of Object Mining. In the set of experiments depicted in Table 3, we attempt to understand the effect of our proposal to use objects from different images. Our experiments involve a state of the art supervised image captioning method described in [27], which is a transformer based model. We adopt the same experiment settings but deleted the head for trace in their model, which the authors of [27] utilized in addition to captions and images. We took the code provided, and trained a captioning model with COCO images and LN-COCO. The resulting performance is provided in the *first row* of Table 3. Then, for each image-caption pair in the training set, we detect all object regions in the image and replace each object region with another one of the same category mined from other images in the dataset. During training, we feed the visual features of the substitute objects, together with the 5-D location vectors of the *replaced* objects into the transformer. The performance of this second model is given in the *second row* of Table 3. The third model is trained similarly as the second but with the locations taken from the images where the substitute objects come from. The result is in the *third row* of Table 3. Finally, we run our unsupervised method, which performed as given in the *last row* of Table 3. To better understand the effects of our proposed method, we highlight the difference between these four models in the following. (i) Row 1, which is the supervised model, is a transformer model as mentioned. Similar to our method, objects are fed into the model, but the key differences are, given an image-caption pair, (1) the objects are all from a single image, and (2) the objects include those that are not in the given caption, which can include background objects. (ii) Row 2 is essentially the same as row 1, but the objects are from different images. (iii) Row 3 is the same as row 2 but the locations are now from the substitute objects' locations in the images they came from. We can think of row 3 as an approximate upper bound to our method. (iv) Our method is the same as row 3 but without the benefit of the additional objects mentioned for row 1. We can see that after replacing the object regions with randomly picked objects of the same category, the performance arguably did not drop as much as expected, which empirically validates our proposal to use object regions from different images to improve object coverage. Interestingly, we can also tell by comparing the second and third rows that the location of the bounding box does not have much influence. From the last row, we can see that our *unsupervised* method performs close to the upper bound (third row) on BLEU, and even outperforms the supervised method on METEOR, while having larger than 20% relative performance drop on CIDEr and SPICE. One reasonable way to interpret the results is that our model performs relatively better on shorter n-grams (e.g., $n = 1$), and worse on longer n-grams (e.g., $n = 4$). In addition, our model performs well when synonyms are considered as correct since METEOR utilizes synonyms while CIDEr requires a stricter match of n-grams (n ranges from 1 to 4).

Table 4. Importance of object coverage. Baseline1 is the same transformer model as ours trained with pseudo (I_i, S_i) pairs. Object Coverage refers to the percent of objects in a given sentence that are captured by the corresponding image during training, averaged over all used training pairs. Our method has 100% object coverage by construction.

Text dataset	Method	BLEU-1	BLEU-4	METEOR	ROUGE$_L$	CIDEr	SPICE	WMD	Object coverage
SS	Ours	**0.058**	**0.003**	**0.060**	**0.126**	**0.039**	**0.102**	**0.060**	100%
SS	Ours-half-obj	0.056	0.002	0.055	0.117	0.036	0.082	0.055	50.0%
SS	Ours-baseline1	0.040	0.002	0.045	0.104	0.021	0.068	0.049	57.4%
GCC	Ours	**0.062**	**0.004**	**0.062**	**0.146**	**0.032**	**0.104**	**0.055**	100%
GCC	Ours-half-obj	0.057	0.003	0.054	0.140	0.025	0.080	0.050	50.0%
GCC	Ours-baseline1	0.046	0.002	0.048	0.131	0.025	0.073	0.047	68.8%

Table 5. We test the importance of object coverage by doing experiments using [16] on COCO images and SS text dataset. We change the object coverage of their method by changing the criterion of selecting training pseudo pairs from existing images and sentences. "Overlap" refers to how many objects the image and the sentence in a training pair share in common. See our supplement for the detailed explanation of how we change the object coverage. The number in the parenthesis refers to the relative performance drop compared with the first row.

BLEU-1	BLEU-4	METEOR	ROUGE$_L$	CIDEr	SPICE	WMD	Overlap	Object coverage
0.022	**0.001**	**0.042**	**0.134**	**0.026**	**0.075**	**0.042**	≥ 2	**47.5%**
0.020$_{(\downarrow 9\%)}$	0.001	0.038$_{(\downarrow 10\%)}$	0.123$_{(\downarrow 8\%)}$	0.017$_{(\downarrow 35\%)}$	0.065$_{(\downarrow 13\%)}$	0.042	≥ 1	32.6%
0.020$_{(\downarrow 9\%)}$	0.001	0.035$_{(\downarrow 17\%)}$	0.117$_{(\downarrow 13\%)}$	0.015$_{(\downarrow 42\%)}$	0.051$_{(\downarrow 32\%)}$	0.042	≥ 0	4.2%

Object Coverage. While [16] and our method all assume a pretrained object detector, a key difference is that the former mines images while our method mines objects. To demonstrate the benefit of our approach more clearly, we construct a baseline method ("Ours-baseline1") which shares all experimental settings with our method but instead of constructing (R_i, S_i) pairs, it follows [16,22] to mine pseudo pairs (I_i, S_i) from the training set. The results are in Table 4. We observe here that the practice of mining pseudo pairs performs significantly worse than our method, primarily due to the resulting lower object coverage, given as the percentage of object words in the sentence that appear in the corresponding image during training. Our method has a 100% object coverage by virtue of mining objects, while for Ours-baseline1, there is on average at least a third of the objects that are missing. To further confirm, we artificially drop half of the object coverage from our approach, and the resulting model, denoted as "Ours-half-obj", performs worse than our full approach as expected. Interestingly, Ours-half-obj performs better than Ours-baseline1 even though it has lower object coverage. We further study the importance of object coverage in Table 5, where we lower the object coverage in the current state of the art method [16]. In general, we see that object coverage plays an important role in unsupervised image captioning.

两个戴着头盔穿着滑雪服，踩着滑雪板，手拿滑雪杆的女人　　一只长颈鹿伸着脖子吃高处的草　　一列黄色引擎的火车在铁轨上　　一架飞机在多云的天空中飞行

Fig. 3. Qualitative results of our method trained on COCO images and COCO-CN (Chinese) captions.

une femme aux cheveux bruns porte une robe bleue et tenant un verre　　un homme avec une veste et un chapeau de cow-boy tient une corde　　un homme portant un casque fait du vélo sur une piste　　un homme avec un chapeau et une veste en jean est sur un skateboard devant un mur

Fig. 4. Qualitative results of our method trained on COCO images and Multi30k (French) sentences.

Table 6. Quantitative results of our method on COCO images and two text datasets of different languages (Chinese and French). "Baseline-translate" and "Baseline-existing" are defined in Sect. 4.4.

Training text	Test text	Method	BLEU-1	BLEU-4	METEOR	ROUGE$_L$	CIDEr	SPICE	WMD
COCO-CN (Chinese)	COCO-CN (Chinese)	Ours	**0.256**	**0.039**	0.121	0.228	**0.349**	**0.117**	0.272
COCO-CN (Chinese)	COCO-CN (Chinese)	[16]	0.240	0.026	**0.128**	**0.234**	0.197	0.110	**0.304**
COCO caption (English)	COCO-CN (Chinese)	Baseline-translate	0.111	0.000	0.072	0.097	0.059	0.003	0.185
COCO-CN (Chinese)	COCO-CN (Chinese)	Baseline-existing	0.176	0.020	0.119	0.189	0.108	0.047	0.259
Multi30k (French)	Multi30k (French)	Ours	**0.174**	**0.010**	**0.094**	**0.173**	**0.120**	**0.014**	**0.079**
Multi30k (French)	Multi30k (French)	[16]	0.143	0.007	0.083	0.156	0.053	0.014	0.072
Multi30k (English)	Multi30k (French)	Baseline-translate	0.104	0.000	0.053	0.092	0.099	0.006	0.056
Multi30k (French)	Multi30k (French)	Baseline-existing	0.126	0.008	0.086	0.154	0.059	0.013	0.078

4.4 Non-English Image Captioning

Due to the scarcity of annotated image-caption pairs in non-English languages, we expect unsupervised image captioning methods to have a fairly large impact in bridging the gap here. To understand how well our proposed method works for non-English image captioning, we chose Chinese and French to benchmark our method. Our aim is to demonstrate the unpairing that is made possible by our method. To do so, for the experiments in this section, we construct training pairs that are not part of any annotated pairs.

For Chinese, we use the COCO-CN [24], which provides Chinese captions on 20,342 images in COCO. We unpair the training set by training with the train split of COCO-CN captions but in conjunction with the COCO images that are not included in the 20,342 (COCO has a total of ≈123k images). Evaluation is then conducted on the test split of COCO-CN captions and the corresponding COCO images. For French, we use Multi30k [10] that provides French captions for all of Flickr30k images and 1k images from COCO. Similarly, to achieve the effect of unpairing, the model is trained on just the Flickr30k captions together with the COCO images that are not included in the 1k COCO images. Testing is subsequently conducted on the 1k image-caption COCO pairs.

Three baselines are used here. The first baseline, "Baseline-translate", is our method trained to produce English captions, which are then translated. The second baseline, "Baseline-existing", follows the same procedure of our method but instead of constructing (R_i, S_i) pairs, it mines pseudo image-caption pairs (I_s, S_i) from existing image and text datasets (similar to the "baseline1" in Sect. 4.3, but extended to non-English datasets as described in Sect. 3.2). The last baseline is the current state of the art, [16], which is extended to mine pseudo non-English image-caption pairs (Sect. 3.2). For all these baselines, we apply the same principle to unpair the training set while ensuring that the training sets for the baselines and our method are apple to apple. Therefore, all the baselines adopt the same training set described in the previous paragraph, except for "Baseline-translate", which uses the English version of the same training captions.

We present the quantitative results in Table 6. We can see that our method when trained directly on the target language performs better than "Baseline-translate", most likely because translating a full sentence accurately is much harder than translating a single object word. "Baseline-existing" performs much better but still lags behind our method as expected based on results presented in the earlier section. [16] (with modifications by us extending it to non-English) performs worse than our method on French but has a smaller gap or on par to our method on Chinese. This may be because that the training images and sentences are from the same paired dataset (COCO-CN), thus mining pairs from existing images and sentences are relatively easy. We have also observed in both the English and Chinese datasets that the captions generated by [16] usually cover most needed object words although being semantically less meaningful and comprehensive compared with our method, and the captions in COCO-CN are mostly short (like COCO captions), which favors [16] when used as the evaluation set. Qualitative results are also provided in Fig. 3 (Chinese) and Fig. 4 (French). We can see that our method generate reasonable captions in both languages.

5   Limitations and Discussions

Unsupervised image captioning is an important research area that has the potential of truly scaling up image captioning in the wild. As progress is made, the hope is that image captioning will soon take a departure from the need to laboriously annotate image-caption pairs, allowing researchers to "simply" scrape unpaired images and text from different sources, including the internet. Our work in this paper takes a step towards this goal by showing how one can mine objects from multiple images to improve object coverage. The results we presented in this paper is encouraging, perhaps even surprising that "unrelated objects" mined can produce results that surpass current state of the art. By employing a transformer architecture, we also show that our proposed approach is flexible enough to ingest additional information such as object relationships and attributes that we have shown could be immensely useful. The work is not completed yet. Unsupervised performance still lags that of supervised models, but even in that we see some encouraging signs (Table 3). Further, the current line of work in unsupervised image captioning including ours depends heavily on a pretrained object detector. The class vocabulary size of the pretrained object detector limits the range of images and text we can utilize, since the objects in the images need to be detected by the pretrained object detector, and the class vocabulary of the pretrained object detector may also act as a useful filter when we crawl sentences from the internet. One way to overcome this limitation is to employ zero-shot object detection that can identify classes not in the training set, especially some classes the practitioner is interested in, but this line of research still has some way to go in terms of maturity. Another more promising direction is for the community to continue to strengthen the performance of supervised object detection as well as broaden the classes of objects covered. Considering that the pretrained object detector has become the backbone for various vision tasks, it is expectable that we can see a much stronger object detector in the near future.

References

1. Anderson, P., Fernando, B., Johnson, M., Gould, S.: SPICE: semantic propositional image caption evaluation. In: Leibe, B., Matas, J., Sebe, N., Welling, M. (eds.) ECCV 2016. LNCS, vol. 9909, pp. 382–398. Springer, Cham (2016). https://doi.org/10.1007/978-3-319-46454-1_24
2. Anderson, P., et al.: Bottom-up and top-down attention for image captioning and visual question answering. In: Proceedings of the IEEE Conference on Computer Vision and Pattern Recognition, pp. 6077–6086 (2018)
3. Bahdanau, D., Cho, K., Bengio, Y.: Neural machine translation by jointly learning to align and translate. arXiv preprint arXiv:1409.0473 (2014)
4. Banerjee, S., Lavie, A.: Meteor: an automatic metric for MT evaluation with improved correlation with human judgments. In: Proceedings of the ACL Workshop on Intrinsic and Extrinsic Evaluation Measures for Machine Translation and/or Summarization, pp. 65–72 (2005)
5. Changpinyo, S., Pang, B., Sharma, P., Soricut, R.: Decoupled box proposal and featurization with ultrafine-grained semantic labels improve image captioning and visual question answering. In: Proceedings of the 2019 Conference on Empirical Methods in Natural Language Processing and the 9th International Joint Conference on Natural Language Processing (EMNLP-IJCNLP), pp. 1468–1474 (2019)
6. Chen, X., et al.: Microsoft coco captions: data collection and evaluation server. arXiv preprint arXiv:1504.00325 (2015)
7. Cornia, M., Baraldi, L., Cucchiara, R.: Show, control and tell: a framework for generating controllable and grounded captions. In: Proceedings of the IEEE/CVF Conference on Computer Vision and Pattern Recognition, pp. 8307–8316 (2019)
8. Cornia, M., Stefanini, M., Baraldi, L., Cucchiara, R.: Meshed-memory transformer for image captioning. In: Proceedings of the IEEE/CVF Conference on Computer Vision and Pattern Recognition, pp. 10578–10587 (2020)
9. Deshpande, A., Aneja, J., Wang, L., Schwing, A.G., Forsyth, D.: Fast, diverse and accurate image captioning guided by part-of-speech. In: Proceedings of the IEEE/CVF Conference on Computer Vision and Pattern Recognition, pp. 10695–10704 (2019)
10. Elliott, D., Frank, S., Sima'an, K., Specia, L.: Multi30k: multilingual English-German image descriptions. arXiv preprint arXiv:1605.00459 (2016)
11. Feng, Y., Ma, L., Liu, W., Luo, J.: Unsupervised image captioning. In: Proceedings of the IEEE/CVF Conference on Computer Vision and Pattern Recognition, pp. 4125–4134 (2019)
12. Gu, J., Joty, S., Cai, J., Wang, G.: Unpaired image captioning by language pivoting. In: Proceedings of the European Conference on Computer Vision (ECCV), pp. 503–519 (2018)
13. Gu, J., Joty, S., Cai, J., Zhao, H., Yang, X., Wang, G.: Unpaired image captioning via scene graph alignments. In: Proceedings of the IEEE/CVF International Conference on Computer Vision, pp. 10323–10332 (2019)
14. Guo, D., Wang, Y., Song, P., Wang, M.: Recurrent relational memory network for unsupervised image captioning. arXiv preprint arXiv:2006.13611 (2020)
15. Hendricks, L.A., Venugopalan, S., Rohrbach, M., Mooney, R., Saenko, K., Darrell, T.: Deep compositional captioning: describing novel object categories without paired training data. In: Proceedings of the IEEE Conference on Computer Vision and Pattern Recognition, pp. 1–10 (2016)

16. Honda, U., Ushiku, Y., Hashimoto, A., Watanabe, T., Matsumoto, Y.: Removing word-level spurious alignment between images and pseudo-captions in unsupervised image captioning. arXiv preprint arXiv:2104.13872 (2021)
17. Johnson, J., Karpathy, A., Fei-Fei, L.: Densecap: fully convolutional localization networks for dense captioning. In: Proceedings of the IEEE Conference on Computer Vision and Pattern Recognition, pp. 4565–4574 (2016)
18. Karpathy, A., Fei-Fei, L.: Deep visual-semantic alignments for generating image descriptions. In: Proceedings of the IEEE Conference on Computer Vision and Pattern Recognition, pp. 3128–3137 (2015)
19. Kingma, D.P., Ba, J.: Adam: a method for stochastic optimization. arXiv preprint arXiv:1412.6980 (2014)
20. Krishna, R., et al.: Visual genome: connecting language and vision using crowd-sourced dense image annotations. Int. J. Comput. Vision **123**(1), 32–73 (2017)
21. Kusner, M., Sun, Y., Kolkin, N., Weinberger, K.: From word embeddings to document distances. In: International Conference on Machine Learning, pp. 957–966. PMLR (2015)
22. Laina, I., Rupprecht, C., Navab, N.: Towards unsupervised image captioning with shared multimodal embeddings. In: Proceedings of the IEEE/CVF International Conference on Computer Vision, pp. 7414–7424 (2019)
23. Lan, W., Li, X., Dong, J.: Fluency-guided cross-lingual image captioning. In: Proceedings of the 25th ACM International Conference on Multimedia, pp. 1549–1557 (2017)
24. Li, X., et al.: COCO-CN for cross-lingual image tagging, captioning, and retrieval. IEEE Trans. Multimedia **21**(9), 2347–2360 (2019)
25. Lin, C.Y.: Rouge: a package for automatic evaluation of summaries. In: Text Summarization Branches Out, pp. 74–81 (2004)
26. Liu, F., Gao, M., Zhang, T., Zou, Y.: Exploring semantic relationships for unpaired image captioning. arXiv preprint arXiv:2106.10658 (2021)
27. Meng, Z., et al.: Connecting what to say with where to look by modeling human attention traces. In: Proceedings of the IEEE/CVF Conference on Computer Vision and Pattern Recognition, pp. 12679–12688 (2021)
28. Papineni, K., Roukos, S., Ward, T., Zhu, W.J.: Bleu: a method for automatic evaluation of machine translation. In: Proceedings of the 40th Annual Meeting of the Association for Computational Linguistics, pp. 311–318 (2002)
29. Pont-Tuset, J., Uijlings, J., Changpinyo, S., Soricut, R., Ferrari, V.: Connecting vision and language with localized narratives. In: Vedaldi, A., Bischof, H., Brox, T., Frahm, J.-M. (eds.) ECCV 2020. LNCS, vol. 12350, pp. 647–664. Springer, Cham (2020). https://doi.org/10.1007/978-3-030-58558-7_38
30. Radford, A., et al.: Learning transferable visual models from natural language supervision. In: International Conference on Machine Learning, pp. 8748–8763. PMLR (2021)
31. Rajendran, J., Khapra, M.M., Chandar, S., Ravindran, B.: Bridge correlational neural networks for multilingual multimodal representation learning. arXiv preprint arXiv:1510.03519 (2015)
32. Ren, S., He, K., Girshick, R., Sun, J.: Faster R-CNN: towards real-time object detection with region proposal networks. Adv. Neural. Inf. Process. Syst. **28**, 91–99 (2015)
33. Schuster, S., Krishna, R., Chang, A., Fei-Fei, L., Manning, C.D.: Generating semantically precise scene graphs from textual descriptions for improved image retrieval. In: Proceedings of the Fourth Workshop on Vision and Language, pp. 70–80 (2015)

34. Sharma, P., Ding, N., Goodman, S., Soricut, R.: Conceptual captions: a cleaned, hypernymed, image alt-text dataset for automatic image captioning. In: Proceedings of ACL (2018)
35. Song, Y., Chen, S., Zhao, Y., Jin, Q.: Unpaired cross-lingual image caption generation with self-supervised rewards. In: Proceedings of the 27th ACM International Conference on Multimedia, pp. 784–792 (2019)
36. Stefanini, M., Cornia, M., Baraldi, L., Cascianelli, S., Fiameni, G., Cucchiara, R.: From show to tell: a survey on image captioning. arXiv preprint arXiv:2107.06912 (2021)
37. Vaswani, A., et al.: Attention is all you need. In: Advances in Neural Information Processing Systems, pp. 5998–6008 (2017)
38. Vedantam, R., Lawrence Zitnick, C., Parikh, D.: Cider: consensus-based image description evaluation. In: Proceedings of the IEEE Conference on Computer Vision and Pattern Recognition, pp. 4566–4575 (2015)
39. Venugopalan, S., Anne Hendricks, L., Rohrbach, M., Mooney, R., Darrell, T., Saenko, K.: Captioning images with diverse objects. In: Proceedings of the IEEE Conference on Computer Vision and Pattern Recognition, pp. 5753–5761 (2017)
40. Wu, Y., Zhao, S., Chen, J., Zhang, Y., Yuan, X., Su, Z.: Improving captioning for low-resource languages by cycle consistency. In: 2019 IEEE International Conference on Multimedia and Expo (ICME), pp. 362–367. IEEE (2019)
41. Xu, K., et al.: Show, attend and tell: Neural image caption generation with visual attention. In: International Conference on Machine Learning, pp. 2048–2057. PMLR (2015)
42. Zellers, R., Yatskar, M., Thomson, S., Choi, Y.: Neural motifs: scene graph parsing with global context. In: Proceedings of the IEEE Conference on Computer Vision and Pattern Recognition, pp. 5831–5840 (2018)
43. Zhang, W., Ying, Y., Lu, P., Zha, H.: Learning long-and short-term user literal-preference with multimodal hierarchical transformer network for personalized image caption. In: Proceedings of the AAAI Conference on Artificial Intelligence, vol. 34, pp. 9571–9578 (2020)
44. Zhou, L., Palangi, H., Zhang, L., Hu, H., Corso, J., Gao, J.: Unified vision-language pre-training for image captioning and VQA. In: Proceedings of the AAAI Conference on Artificial Intelligence, vol. 34, pp. 13041–13049 (2020)

Contrastive Vision-Language Pre-training with Limited Resources

Quan Cui[1,2], Boyan Zhou[1], Yu Guo[1], Weidong Yin[1], Hao Wu[1(✉)], Osamu Yoshie[2], and Yubo Chen[1]

[1] ByteDance, Shanghai, China
cui-quan@toki.waseda.jp, wuhao.5688@bytedance.com
[2] Waseda University, Tokyo, Japan

Abstract. Pioneering dual-encoder pre-training works (*e.g.*, CLIP and ALIGN) have revealed the potential of aligning multi-modal representations with contrastive learning. However, these works require a tremendous amount of data and computational resources (*e.g.*, billion-level web data and hundreds of GPUs), which prevent researchers with limited resources from reproduction and further exploration. To this end, we propose a stack of novel methods, which significantly cut down the heavy resource dependency and allow us to conduct dual-encoder multi-modal representation alignment with limited resources. Besides, we provide a reproducible baseline of competitive results, namely ZeroVL, with only 14M publicly accessible academic datasets and 8 V100 GPUs. Additionally, we collect 100M web data for pre-training, and achieve comparable or superior results than state-of-the-art methods, further proving the effectiveness of our methods on large-scale data. We hope that this work will provide useful data points and experience for future research in contrastive vision-language pre-training. Code is available at https://github.com/zerovl/ZeroVL.

Keywords: Multi-modal representation learning · Contrastive learning · Language-image pre-training · Limited resources

1 Introduction

Large-scale representation pre-training has become the de-facto approach in vision [5,6,17,45], language [10,18,30] and vision-language [22,35] modeling tasks. In the vision-language pre-training field, most mainstream approaches fall into one of two classes: single-encoder [7,13,20,23,27–29,37,40,51] and dual-encoder [22,35]. Typical single-encoder approaches focus on learning semantic alignments between image regions and text entities with a single backbone network, greatly benefiting various downstream multi-modal tasks, *e.g.*,

Supplementary Information The online version contains supplementary material available at https://doi.org/10.1007/978-3-031-20059-5_14.

Table 1. Statistics of training resources and cross-modal retrieval RSUM scores [3, 4, 43]. "zs." and "ft." represent zero-shot and fine-tuned settings. "†" means pre-training with 100M web data.

Method	Computation		Data	MS-COCO		F30K	
	Device	Count		zs.	ft.	zs.	ft.
CLIP [35]	V100	256	400M	400.2	–	540.6	–
ALIGN [22]	TPU$_{v3}$	1,024	1800M	425.3	500.4	**553.3**	**576.0**
Baseline	V100	8	14.2M	371.6	471.9	483.3	553.0
ZeroVL	V100	8	14.2M	425.0	485.0	536.2	561.6
ZeroVL†	V100	8	100M	**442.1**	**500.5**	546.5	573.6

VQA [1,14,50], VCR [48] and NLVR [38,39], *etc.* In real-scenario applications [34], dual-encoder pre-training approach could be preferable for its flexibility. For one thing, downstream tasks of either modality can benefit from the pre-training. For another, dual-encoder approaches are more efficient than single-encoder approaches on popular multi-modal industrial applications, *e.g.*, cross-modal matching and retrieval tasks [4,21].

Recent works [22,35] have demonstrated that, by aligning visual and language representations with the contrastive loss, a simple dual-encoder architecture is able to yield state-of-the-art representation learning performances. However, we notice a significant problem which might obstruct the progress in this research direction, *i.e.*, pioneering works require a tremendous amount of vision-linguistic corpus and computational resources for training, and such heavy resource dependency prevents researchers with limited resources from reproduction and further explorations. For instance, CLIP [35] and ALIGN [22] respectively collected 400M and 1.8B web image-text pairs and trained models with 256 V100 GPUs and 1,024 TPU cores. Such experimental environments present a big challenge for the most researchers, and further lead to a lack of commonly reproducible benchmarks for dual-encoder model, making it hard to validate novel methods.

To alleviate the problems above, we design a comprehensive training pipeline with only open-source academic datasets and limited computational resources. Specifically, we propose a collection of novel methods to deal with limited data and computation, respectively. Our proposed methods boost model performances while only introducing marginal overhead to both computation and implementation. As shown in Table 1, we achieve competitive results with ∼14M academic data and 8 V100 GPUs, greatly alleviating the heavy dependency on data and computation of contrastive language-image pre-training. To further demonstrate the effectiveness of our method on large-scale data, we collect 100M web image-text images and conduct pre-training without fine-tuning hyper-parameters. Surprisingly, our method successfully outperforms CLIP and achieves comparable results with ALIGN on pre-training and fine-tuning tasks.

2   A Naive Baseline

In this section, we build up a naive baseline for stacking our methods and polishing it to a strong one. Methods are related to *training with limited data* and *training with limited computation resource*, which will be discussed in Sect. 3 and 4.

2.1   Pre-training Datasets

To ensure reproducibility, only publicly accessible academic datasets are leveraged to demonstrate the effectiveness of our methods. The statistics of collected image-text pair datasets are reported in Table 2. Four widely-used image-text pair datasets are selected for pre-training, *i.e.*, *(1) SBU Captioned Photos (SBU)* [33], *(2) Visual Genome (VG)* [25], *(3) Conceptual Captions 3M (CC3M)* [36], and *(4) Conceptual 12M (CC12M)* [2] datasets. Detailed introductions are attached in the appendix.

Table 2. The statistics of datasets for pre-training and test.

	Pre-training					Test	
	Total	SBU	VG	CC3M	CC12M	MS-COCO	F30K
#image	14.23M	0.86M	0.50M	2.81M	10.06M	5K	1K
#text	14.23M	0.86M	0.50M	2.81M	10.06M	25K	5K

2.2   Baseline Settings

Baseline settings are elaborated from the data, model, and training perspectives.

Data Preparation. Batches are comprised by randomly sampling image-text pairs from pre-training datasets. Following [22,35], each image is randomly cropped to a rectangular region with aspect ratio sampled in $[3/4, 4/3]$ and area sampled in $[60\%, 100\%]$, then resized to 224×224 resolution. Regarding the corresponding text, we use a percentage of 20% input words for processing. For each word, we mask it, replace it with a random word, or delete it with a probability of 50%, 10% and 40%, respectively. During test, images are resized to 256×256 and center cropped to 224×224, while no specific process is applied to texts.

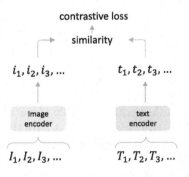

Fig. 1. Illustration of the dual-encoder model architecture.

Model Architecture. Inspired by [22,35], we employ a simple dual-encoder model to align visual and language representations of image-text pairs via a contrastive loss. The framework is illustrated in Fig. 1. Image and text encoders are ViT-B/16 [11] and BERT-Base [10], respectively. [CLS] tokens from image and text encoders are extracted and then projected to compact embeddings for calculating the contrastive loss.

Training. AdamW [24,31] optimizer is used for training and the weight decay is 1e−3. The dual-encoder model is trained for 20 epochs on 8 Nvidia V100 GPUs with a batch size of 1,024. The learning rate is initialized to 1e−4 and follows a cosine decay schedule. Notably, we set a minimum learning rate 1e−5 to avoid over-fitting. The embedding dimension for image and text representations is 512 and the trainable temperature of contrastive loss is initialized to 0.02.

2.3 Evaluations

Metrics. Typically, multi-modal retrieval tasks are assessed with the recall at K (R@K) metric, with K = $\{1, 5, 10\}$. We follow [3,4,43] to use RSUM as the metric to reveal the overall performance, which is defined as the sum of recall metrics at K = $\{1, 5, 10\}$ of both image-to-text and text-to-image retrieval tasks.

Test Datasets. Following the standard practice in [3,4,12,22,35,43], we evaluate representations of pre-trained models by carrying out *zero-shot* image-text retrieval tasks on test sets of *(1) MS-COCO Captions Karpathy's split (MS-COCO)* and *(2) Flickr 30K (F30K)* datasets. MS-COCO and F30K results are reported with 5K and 1K test images, respectively.

3 Training with Limited Data Resource

Due to the copyright or technical issues, publicly accessible image-text academic datasets are greatly limited. The common practice to construct vision-linguistic corpus is collecting datasets from multiple sources. However, it brings in the dataset bias issue, which is caused by different collection manners of these datasets. Besides, limited data could suffer from the over-fitting problem, and seldom efforts were made for creating extra data for multi-modal pre-training. In this section, we study how to take full advantages of limited data from these two perspectives, *i.e.*, (1) leveraging biased data and (2) creating extra data.

3.1 Leveraging Biased Data with Debiased Sampling

Random Sampling Brings in Dataset Bias. Random sampling is an intuitive and widely used strategy, which randomly constructs training batches with all available data, as illustrated in Fig. 2. However, when a batch is composed of samples from different datasets, models could be driven to distinguish negative samples by hacking the source information, *i.e.*, learning the dataset bias. For instance, dataset A is mainly composed of *natural scenery photos with long captions*, while dataset B is mainly comprised of *people with short captions*. To distinguish samples from A and B, models are allowed to remember the dataset bias on image contents and caption lengths. To prove this, we first carry out

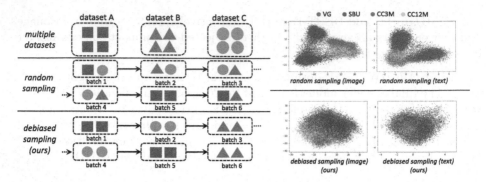

Fig. 2. Illustration of sampling strategies.

Fig. 3. Illustration of image and text embeddings.

visualizations to show the biased distribution of representations learned by random sampling. Then, we delve into the gradient of InfoNCE loss and provide evidences that data bias influences the model optimization.

Dataset Bias Leads to Biased Representation Distributions. In the upper part of Fig. 3, we visualize image and text embeddings learned with random sampling. Intra-dataset representations are closely gathered, while inter-dataset representations are separated. Representations are separated to three parts, *i.e.*, VG, SBU and "CC3M+CC12M". Since CC3M and CC12M are composed of similar image-text pairs, representations of CC3M and CC12M are slightly overlapped. It demonstrates that the model is driven to separate representations from different datasets, and, within a training batch, the model will easily distinguish negative samples.

Dataset Bias Influences the Optimization of InfoNCE. Since the dual-encoder model is optimized by InfoNCE loss, we first formulate the loss function and its gradient for further explorations:

$$\mathcal{L} = \sum_j \sum_k y_{jk} \log\left(\frac{\exp(s_{jk})}{\sum_l \exp(s_{jl})}\right), \nabla_\theta \mathcal{L} = -\sum_j \sum_k y_{jk} \nabla_\theta \log\left(\frac{\exp(s_{jk})}{\sum_l \exp(s_{jl})}\right),$$

(1)

where the similarity between the *query* j and the *key* k as s_{jk}. The ground-truth label corresponding to s_{jk} is represented by $y_{jk} \in \{0,1\}$. We omit the temperature parameter for simplification. Then, we derive the gradient item as[1]:

$$\nabla_\theta \mathcal{L} = \sum_j \sum_k \left(\frac{\exp(s_{jk})}{\sum_l \exp(s_{jl})} - y_{jk}\right) \nabla_\theta s_{jk}$$

$$= \sum_j \sum_k (\bar{p}_{jk} - y_{jk}) \nabla_\theta s_{jk}$$

(2)

---

[1] Detailed deriviations are attached in Appendix A.1.

where we could observe that the gradient term is related to the stop-gradient term $\bar{p}_{jk}$, which reflects the similarities among training samples. Negative pairs are essential for self-supervised learning methods which are based on the InfoNCE loss [32]. However, as suggested in Fig. 3, dataset bias makes the model easily separate negative samples from different data sources, resulting in the small $\bar{p}_{jk}$ and inferior gradient for negative pairs. Thus, the effectiveness of negative samples are damaged in the optimization process, especially for significant hard examples.

Debiased Sampling. Knowledge of the dataset bias is not beneficial for downstream tasks and can be even harmful for learning essential semantic concepts. To tackle the dataset bias issue, the key factor is forcing the model to focus on helpful knowledge instead of the dataset bias. Inspired by this, we propose the debiased sampling strategy, as illustrated in Fig. 2. Debiased sampling ensures instances within each batch come from the same dataset. For example, the first batch consists of samples from only SBU, and the second batch is composed of samples of only CC3M. Under this regularization, models are not allowed to hack the optimization by remembering the dataset bias. As shown in Fig. 3, the biased distributions of representations are significantly alleviated by our method, especially on the text modality. Besides, as shown in Fig. 4, it could be observed that training with debiased sampling yields larger $\bar{p}_{jk}$ of negative pairs (on all datasets) than random sampling, $i.e.$, debiased sampling successfully increases the effectiveness of negative samples. Figure 4 suggests that samples in smaller datasets could suffer from less effective gradient of negative samples, and our method alleviates this problem by increasing gradient of negative samples, especially for small datasets ($i.e.$, VG and SBU). Moreover, downstream results are remarkably improved by the debiased sampling, which will be discussed later.

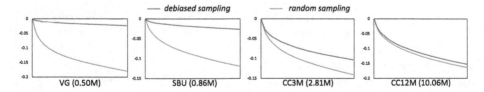

Fig. 4. $\log(\bar{p}_{jk})$ averaged over negative pairs on different datasets and scales. The larger value contributes to the larger gradient of negative samples.

3.2 Creating Extra Data with Coin Flipping Mixup

Intuitively, data augmentation is a ubiquitous method to create extra training data. With limited data resources, the augmentation plays an important rule in boosting performances. This part introduces a novel data augmentation method, which bring in little computational complexity but remarkably improve model performance.

Coin Flipping Mixup. To the best of our knowledge, mixup [15,26,42,47,49] are seldom investigated in the vision-language pre-training task. In this part, we first formulate the common mixup strategy in the dual-encoder training scheme, and reveal the label assignment dilemma when calculating contrastive loss. To solve this dilemma, we further propose a novel coin flipping mixup.

(1) Formulations and the label assignment dilemma. We follow the previous works [15,49] by applying instance-level mixup. Given a batch of N image-text pairs, the image and text of the j-th pair are denoted by I_j and T_j, respectively. Instead of randomly mixing image-text pairs within the batch, we leverage a more efficient mixing operation for easy implementations:

$$\tilde{I}_j = \lambda * I_j + (1 - \lambda) * I_{N-j},$$
$$\tilde{T}_j = \lambda * T_j + (1 - \lambda) * T_{N-j}, \tag{3}$$

where $\tilde{I}_j$ and $\tilde{T}_j$ denote the j-th mixed image and text. λ is sampled from the distribution $Beta(\alpha, \alpha)$. Therefore, the training batch after the mixing operation could be denoted by $\{(\tilde{I}_1, \tilde{T}_1), (\tilde{I}_2, \tilde{T}_2), \ldots, (\tilde{I}_N, \tilde{T}_N)\}$. However, we will encounter a label assignment dilemma. For instance, both $(\tilde{I}_j, \tilde{T}_j)$ and $(\tilde{I}_{N-j}, \tilde{T}_{N-j})$ are contained in the batch but interpolated by the same instances. It is not feasible to measure the target matching score between $\tilde{I}_j$ and $\tilde{T}_{N-j}$. Particularly, the $\tilde{I}_j$ and $\tilde{T}_{N-j}$ are written as:

$$\tilde{I}_j = \lambda * I_j + (1 - \lambda) * I_{N-j},$$
$$\tilde{T}_{N-j} = (1 - \lambda) * T_j + \lambda * T_{N-j}, \tag{4}$$

where the similarity between $\lambda * I_j$ and $(1 - \lambda) * T_j$ is not measurable based on the prior knowledge of mixup [49].

(2) Coin flipping mixup. To tackle the above problem, we propose the coin flipping mixup strategy. Briefly, mixup is applied on *one of the multiple modals* in each training batch, avoiding the above label assignment dilemma. In our implementation, by uniformly sampling γ from the range $[0, 1]$, we enable the mixup on image modal if $\gamma > 0.5$, otherwise text modal. Interestingly, as shown in Fig. 5, the strategy is similar to the coin flipping decision-making procedure, from which its name derives.

We briefly formulate the learning objective of coin flipping mixup, assuming $\gamma > 0.5$ and the mixup on

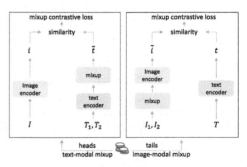

Fig. 5. Illustration of our proposed coin flipping mixup. Note that manifold mixup is applied on the text modality, since we empirically observe that interpolating sparse word embeddings could lead to significant performance drop.

Table 3. Results of stacking methods for training with limited data resource.

| | MS-COCO (5K test set) | | | | | Flickr30K (1K test set) | | | | |
| | I → T | | T → I | | | I → T | | T → I | | |
	R@1	R@10	R@1	R@10	RSUM	R@1	R@10	R@1	R@10	RSUM
Baseline	45.9	82.8	35.0	73.1	371.6	66.0	95.1	58.6	90.6	483.3
+ debiased sampling	53.2	86.4	36.7	74.1	392.3	78.8	98.2	61.2	91.9	510.1
+ coin flipping mixup	53.0	87.6	39.6	76.5	402.8	80.1	98.4	63.7	93.1	519.2

image modal is enabled. In literature [22,35], the contrastive loss could be disentangled to image-to-text and text-to-image matching parts. Correspondingly, the mixup contrastive loss of image-to-text matching is written as:

$$
\mathcal{L}_{\tilde{I}2T} = \lambda * \left(-\frac{1}{N} \sum_{j=1}^{N} \log \frac{\exp(\tilde{i}_j \cdot t_j)}{\sum_{k=1}^{N} \exp(\tilde{i}_j \cdot t_k)} \right)
$$
$$
+ (1 - \lambda) * \left(-\frac{1}{N} \sum_{j=1}^{N} \log \frac{\exp(\tilde{i}_j \cdot t_{N-j})}{\sum_{k=0}^{N-1} \exp(\tilde{i}_j \cdot t_{N-k})} \right),
$$

(5)

where $\tilde{i}_j$ and t_j respectively denote representations of the mixed image $\tilde{I}_j$ and the non-mixed text T_j. The text-to-image matching part shares similar formulations.

3.3   Experiment Results and Discussions

Main results of debiased sampling and coin flipping mixup are reported in Table 3. Overall speaking, both methods benefit performances on both F30K and MS-COCO. Note that these experiments only involve 14M academic data. Stacking these methods jointly contributes to +31.2 and +35.9 RSUM improvements on F30K and MS-COCO, respectively. Undoubtedly, properly leveraging limited data is of vital importance, and our methods are beneficial.

Effect of Debiased Sampling. Compared to the baseline, debiased sampling achieves consistent and remarkable improvements on all metrics, without any extra computational costs and hyper-parameters. It validates the effectiveness of our proposed debiased sampling, and debiased learning is a potential research direction in the contrastive language-image pre-training field.

Effect of Coin Flipping Mixup. We set the alpha value of the beta distribution to 0.1, then apply input mixup on image modal and manifold mixup on text modal. Noticeable promotions are contributed by the coin flipping mixup, especially on text-to-image (T2I) metrics, *i.e.*, text-to-image Recall@1 on F30K and MS-COCO are improved by +2.5 and +2.9.

Empirical Observations on Data Augmentation. (1) The cropping area of RandomResizeCrop should be in a relatively large range for covering main

Table 4. Results of distributed large-batch training. "baseline + data" denotes the result of stacking methods proposed in Sect. 3.

	MS-COCO (5K test set)					Flickr30K (1K test set)				
	I → T		T → I			I → T		T → I		
	R@1	R@10	R@1	R@10	RSUM	R@1	R@10	R@1	R@10	RSUM
Baseline + data	53.0	87.6	39.6	76.5	402.8	80.1	98.4	63.7	93.1	519.2
+ gradient reserved gather	55.4	88.7	42.0	78.7	415.0	81.4	98.2	66.2	93.7	524.1
+ batch = 2,048	56.4	88.5	42.7	79.2	418.0	81.5	98.6	68.2	93.7	527.5
+ batch = 4,096	58.9	89.9	43.8	79.6	425.9	82.7	98.6	68.7	94.5	531.7
+ batch = 8,192	59.0	89.5	43.7	79.5	424.4	83.1	98.7	68.5	94.6	531.8
+ batch = 16,384	59.3	89.6	44.1	70.4	425.0	85.5	98.5	69.8	94.5	536.2

objects. (2) AutoAugment [8] brings in satisfactory improvements but little computational overhead. (3) Randomly masking input words advances the model performance with no cost.

4   Training with Limited Computational Resource

In contrastive self-supervised learning [5,6], distributed large-batch training has become a standard practice, for increasing the training batch size and providing enough negative samples. Firstly, we demonstrate the remarkable benefits of distributed large-batch training in the multi-modal pre-training task; however, it relies on considerable computational resources (*e.g.*, training our model with 16,384 batch size needs 128 V100 GPUs). Then, to tackle this problem, we study how to achieve comparable results with limited computational resources (*e.g.*, 8 V100 GPUs) by proposing the decoupled gradient accumulation. Lastly, we discuss how to accelerate the training.

4.1   Large-Batch Training with Decoupled Gradient Accumulation

Benefits of Large-Batch Distributed Training. In the practical implementation of distributed InfoNCE loss, gather operations are frequently used to collect negative samples across machines. In multi-modal scenario, the InfoNCE loss could be separated into image-to-text (I2T) and text-to-image (T2I) matching parts. Similar to Eq. (2), the gradient of the I2T part is as followed[2]:

$$\nabla_\theta \mathcal{L}^{I2T} = \sum_j \sum_k \left(\bar{p}_{jk}^{I2T} - y_{jk}^{I2T} \right) \left(\bar{i}_j \nabla_\theta t_k + \bar{t}_k \nabla_\theta i_j \right), \tag{6}$$

where we place a vinculum on a value to indicate its gradient is detached. For a pair (i_j, t_k) from *different* machines, gather operations with detaching gradients would produce the following wrong gradient on the machine of sample j:

$$\tilde{\nabla}_\theta \mathcal{L}_{ij}^{I2T} = \left(\bar{p}_{jk}^{I2T} - y_{jk}^{I2T} \right) \bar{t}_k \nabla_\theta i_j. \tag{7}$$

---

[2] Due to the page limit, detailed formulations are attached in Appendix A.1.

Therefore, preserving gradients of gathered embeddings would provide valuable gradients. As reported in Table 4, by preserving gradients of gathered embeddings, noticeable gains are achieved within expectations. Concretely, +4.9 RSUM on F30K and +12.2 RSUM on MS-COCO are contributed by the gradient reversed gather, further supporting our derivations.

Previous works have demonstrated that self-supervised contrastive learning could significantly benefit from the large training batch size, which provides more negative examples to facilitate the model convergence [5]. To further analyze the impact of varying batch sizes on multi-modal contrastive pre-training, we scale the batch size from 1,024 to 16,384 and keep training epochs consistent. Besides, previous works [5,17] empirically showed that linearly scaling the initial learning rate is necessary for large-batch training. Regarding large batch experiments, up to 128 Nvidia V100 GPUs are used. As shown in Table 4, increasing the batch size from 1,024 to 16,384 leads to significant improvements on all evaluated metrics, indicating the vital importance of large-batch training. However, substantial computational resources are used for containing large batches.

Decoupled Gradient Accumulation. A common strategy to mimic large-batch training is the multi-step gradient accumulation. Concretely, a training iteration of a large batch is divided into several sub-iterations, and, in each sub-iteration, the batch size is relatively small. Gradients of multiple sub-iterations are individually calculated, accumulated and jointly back-propagated. It is a practical strategy in deep learning tasks; however, to mimic the large batch InfoNCE loss, the calculation process unavoidably involves embeddings from different training sub-iterations, which are, unfortunately, not accessible across sub-iterations. Therefore, the conventional multi-step gradient accumulation is not able to enlarge the effective batch size, greatly limiting final model performances.

We propose the decoupled gradient accumulation to make large-batch contrastive learning feasible for limited resources. According to Eq. (6), we mathematically decouple the gradient of a large batch into two parts[3]:

$$
\begin{aligned}
\nabla_\theta \mathcal{L} &= \nabla_\theta \mathcal{L}^{I2T} + \nabla_\theta \mathcal{L}^{T2I} \\
&= \sum_j \nabla_\theta \underbrace{\left(\sum_k (\bar{p}_{jk}^{I2T} - y_{jk}^{I2T} + \bar{p}_{kj}^{T2I} - y_{kj}^{T2I}) \, \bar{t}_k \right)}_{\text{stop-gradient part}} i_j \\
&\quad + \sum_k \nabla_\theta \underbrace{\left(\sum_j (\bar{p}_{jk}^{I2T} - y_{jk}^{I2T} + \bar{p}_{kj}^{T2I} - y_{kj}^{T2I}) \, \bar{i}_j \right)}_{\text{stop-gradient part}} t_k,
\end{aligned}
\tag{8}
$$

where one part of gradient is only related to embeddings within each sub-iteration, and the other part only depends on stop-gradient embeddings of the large batch, which can be obtained by forwarding the large batch for an extra

---

[3] Due to the page limit, detailed derivations are attached in Appendix A.2.

time. In this manner, we are allowed to take advantages of the large batch size by sacrificing training time.

As reported in Table 5, it empirically shows that, by sacrificing extra 40%–50% training time, our gradient accumulation successfully mimics large-batch training without damaging model performances. With 8 V100 GPUs, we are not allowed to train the model with batch sizes larger than 1,024, and thus achieved performances are relatively unsatisfactory. However, our method successfully allows us to train models with large effective batch sizes 8,192 and 16,384, achieving comparable RSUM scores with only 8 V100 GPUs.

Table 5. RSUM scores of decoupled gradient accumulation (DGA). For training with batch 8,192 and 16,384, 64 and 128 V100 GPUs are required, respectively.

Batch	DGA step	Effective batch	# GPU	GPU time (hr)	MS-COCO RSUM	F30K RSUM
1,024	–	1,024	8	~430	415.0	524.1
8,192	–	8,192	64	–	424.4	531.8
16,384	–	16,384	128	–	425.0	536.2
1,024	8	8,192	8	~600	424.1	532.2
1,024	16	16,384	8	~680	425.2	535.9

Stable Decoupled Gradient Accumulation. Note that encoders could contain modules of randomness, *e.g.*, dropout layers are widely applied in the BERT [10]. Thus, forwarding the same sample two times could produce different embeddings. To this end, we set the identical random seed for twice forwarding processes, eliminating the randomness and stabilizing the training. In Table 6, we provide an ablation study related to the stable training. It demonstrates that significant performance drops would be caused without considering the randomness. Forwarding the same sample for two times yields different embeddings results in the gradient in Eq. (8) is wrongly calculated.

Table 6. Effects of stable training. "✓" denotes setting the identical random seed for twice forwarding processes, and the achieved results correspond to Table 5.

Batch	DGA step	Effective batch	# GPU	Stable	MS-COCO RSUM	F30K RSUM
1,024	16	16,384	8	✓	425.2	535.9
1,024	16	16,384	8	–	413.4	527.1

4.2 Fast Training with TokenDrop and Auxiliary Encoders

Thus far, all methods for better performances are elaborated. For real-scenario multi-modal applications, the training efficiency and model performance are equally significant for various deployment purposes. We introduce two methods on fast training for different purposes.

TokenDrop. Inspired by the recent work [16], we randomly drop a part of input pixels to speed-up the training of image encoders. Empirically, we observe that randomly masking 25% input tokens of ViT introduces negligible performance drop, but considerably reduces training time. As shown in Table 7, enabling TokenDrop saves ~30% training time. Besides, training with TokenDrop compensates for the extra training time caused by DGA.

Table 7. Training time saved by TokenDrop.

Batch	DGA step	Token drop	# GPU	GPU time (hr)	MS-COCO RSUM	F30K RSUM
1,024	16	–	8	~680	425.2	535.9
1,024	16	✓	8	**~470**	424.8	535.5

Auxiliary Encoders. Assuming that we have trained a model with heavy encoders, we investigate how to fast obtain lightweight encoders with auxiliary heavy ones. Since the training of a dual-encoder model is driven by the InfoNCE loss, embeddings yielded by either encoder are regarded as the "learning target" of the other side. Thus, enlarging either encoder's capacity would contribute to more reliable and discriminative embeddings. Assuming that we have trained a dual-encoder model with heavy encoders, e.g., ViT-B/16 and BERT-Base, we can replace one of them to a lightweight one and re-train it with the guidance of the other one in a distillation manner [19,52]. For instance, we change the image encoder from ViT-B/16 to ViT-B/32, and then re-train it with the BERT-Base being frozen. With the guidance of the frozen encoder, the training process of the replaced encoder could be greatly accelerated, as reported in Table 8.

Table 8. Training time saved by the auxiliary encoder method. "♠" symbol denotes the model is frozen.

Training method	Encoder		GPU time (hr)	MS-COCO RSUM	F30K RSUM
	Image	Text			
Auxiliary	ViT-B/16	BERT-B	–	402.8	519.1
	ViT-B/32	BERT-B♠	~110	381.2	493.9
Baseline	ViT-B/32	BERT-B	~240	379.5	494.1

5 Comparisons with SOTA Methods

In this section, we focus on assessing the pre-training performances with cross-modal retrieval tasks, in both zero-shot and fine-tuned settings [22, 35]. We name our method as "ZeroVL", where "Zero" means the motivation for designing a strong baseline with limited resources.

5.1 Zero-Shot Cross-Modal Retrieval

Table 9. *Zero-shot* cross-modal retrieval results. "baseline" is the naive baseline in Sect. 2. "†" means training with the 100M web data.

	Computation		Data	Inputsize	Batchsize	MS-COCO (5K test set)					Flickr30K (1K test set)				
	Device	Count				I → T		T → I		RSUM	I → T		T → I		RSUM
Zero-shot						R@1	R@10	R@1	R@10		R@1	R@10	R@1	R@10	
CLIP	V100	256	400M	336	32,768	58.4	88.1	37.8	72.2	400.2	88.0	99.4	68.7	95.2	540.6
ALIGN	TPU$_{v3}$	1,024	1800M	289	16,384	58.6	89.7	45.6	78.6	425.3	88.6	99.7	75.7	96.8	553.3
Baseline	V100	8	14M	224	1,024	45.9	82.8	35.0	73.1	371.6	66.0	95.1	58.6	90.6	483.3
CLIP (our impl.)	V100	8	14M	224	1,024	51.0	85.5	38.2	75.5	392.5	80.9	97.8	63.8	92.4	518.4
CLIP (our impl.)	V100	128	14M	224	16,384	57.7	88.7	41.6	77.8	416.0	83.1	98.3	67.2	93.9	527.3
ZeroVL (ours)	V100	8	14M	224	16,384	59.3	89.6	44.1	79.5	425.0	85.5	98.5	69.8	94.5	536.2
ZeroVL† (ours)	V100	8	100M	224	16,384	**64.0**	**91.4**	**47.3**	**81.1**	**442.1**	88.0	99.2	73.5	95.7	546.5

Setup. Training implementation details are as followed. On the ground of baseline settings (*e.g.*, learning rate, training epoch, and weight decay) introduced in Sect. 2.2, we stack all proposed methods, *i.e.*, debiased sampling, coin flipping mixup, and decoupled gradient accumulation. For reproducibility, we mainly benchmark with publicly accessible academic datasets. For fair comparisons, we re-implement CLIP with 14M data to validate the performance drop caused by limited resources. Besides, CLIP and ALIGN respectively collect 400M and 1.8B image-text pairs from the web. Due to training datasets of CLIP and ALIGN are not available, we also collect ~100M web image-text pairs for validating the effectiveness of our method on large-scale data.

Main Results. In Table 9, on both F30K and MS-COCO datasets, we achieve competitive results on the basis of 14M academic publicly accessible data and 8 V100 GPUs. It is worth mentioning that our ZeroVL already exceeds CLIP on the MS-COCO dataset in both image-to-text (I2T) and text-to-image (T2I) metrics, *e.g.*, our I2T R@1 and T21 R@1 surpass CLIP by +0.9 and +6.3, respectively. Results of our implemented CLIP further validate the contribution of our efforts, *i.e.*, the performance of cross-modal retrieval would be greatly suppressed if the resources were greatly limited. In addition, although our collected 100M web images are much less than those of CLIP and ALIGN, ZeroVL still successfully outperforms CLIP trained with 400M data and ALIGN trained with 1.8B data on MS-COCO. On F30K, we perform slightly worse than ALIGN but better than CLIP, which can result from the domain of ALIGN's data is larger than ours.

Resource Costs. For computational resources, training CLIP requires 256 V100 GPUs, and training ALIGN needs 1,024 Could TPUv3 cores. Experiments in Table 9 involve 8 V100 32GB GPUs. For data resources, we mainly benchmark on 14M publicly accessible academic datasets to guarantee the reproducibility. Experiments of 100M web data demonstrate that our method is still effective on large-scale data, *i.e.*, our method fits in different data scales without tuning hyper-parameters. Additionally, only 2.4 days are required for training ZeroVL with 8 V100 and 14M academic data, which could be friendly to the most researchers.

5.2 Fine-Tuned Cross-Modal Retrieval

Table 10. *Fine-tuned* cross-modal retrieval results of representative dual-encoder methods. "RX101*" correspond to the ResNeXt-101 model pre-trained on Instagram-1B [45]. "EffNet-L2*" denotes the large CNN model EfficientNet-L2 [41,44]. "†" denotes pre-training with the 100M web data.

	Inputsize	Encoder		MS-COCO (5K test set)					Flickr30K (1K test set)				
		Image (I)	Text (T)	I → T		T → I			I → T		T → I		
Fine-tuned				R@1	R@10	R@1	R@10	RSUM	R@1	R@10	R@1	R@10	RSUM
VSE++	512	RX101*	BERT-B	57.9	92.8	44.9	84.0	439.2	80.9	98.9	65.2	93.7	524.8
GPO	512	RX101*	BERT-B	68.1	95.2	52.7	88.3	474.8	88.7	99.8	76.1	97.1	555.1
ALIGN	289	EffNet-L2*	BERT-L	77.0	96.9	**59.9**	89.8	500.4	**95.3**	**100.0**	**84.9**	**98.6**	**576.0**
baseline	224	ViT-B/16	BERT-B	69.1	94.8	51.9	86.8	471.9	90.1	99.1	75.1	96.6	553.0
CLIP (our impl. 8V100)	224	ViT-B/16	BERT-B	69.9	94.9	52.5	87.0	473.8	90.4	99.2	75.6	96.5	554.1
CLIP (our impl. 128V100)	224	ViT-B/16	BERT-B	71.7	95.8	54.0	88.1	481.3	91.1	99.5	78.5	97.7	560.7
ZeroVL (ours)	224	ViT-B/16	BERT-B	72.9	95.9	55.1	88.6	485.0	91.7	99.5	79.2	97.1	561.6
ZeroVL† (ours)	288	ViT-B/16	BERT-B	**77.2**	**97.1**	59.3	**90.2**	**500.5**	95.0	100.0	83.7	98.6	573.6

Setup. After the pre-training phase, we fine-tune the model on downstream datasets F30K and MS-COCO. Fine-tuning hyper-parameters are identical to pre-training's, except the initial learning rate, training epoch, and batch size. The is learning rate is set to 1e-5. For F30K and MS-COCO, we optimize the model for 1K and 5K steps. Batch size is set to 2,048. Similar to zero-shot experiments, we also provide fine-tuning results with both 14M and 100M data.

Main Results. In Table 10, with 14M academic pre-training data, we successfully outperforms state-of-the-art in-domain training method VSE++ [12] and GPO [4]. It is worth mentioning that GPO also involves large-scale pre-training on the image modal, *i.e.*, weakly supervised pre-training with the Instagram-1B dataset [45]. Compared with GPO, ZeroVL can achieve better results with the more efficient image encoder and smaller training input size, strongly supporting the effectiveness of our pre-training method. For experiments with 100M web data, it is worth noting that ALIGN uses (1) significantly more pre-training data, (2) heavier image and text encoders, and (3) larger pre-training resolutions than our method. Nevertheless, similar to results in zero-shot, we still achieve comparable results to ALIGN.

5.3   Linear Probing

Table 11. Linear probing results on ImageNet-1K.

	Pre-training					Linear probing		
	Computation	Data	Input size		Batch size	Backbone (#params)	Input size	Top-1 accu-
	Device	Count						racy
CLIP	V100	256	400M	224	32,768	ViT-B/16 (87M)	224	80.2
ALIGN	TPU$_{v3}$	1,024	1800M	289	16,384	EffNet-L2 (480M)	600	85.5
CLIP (our impl.)	V100	8	14M	224	1,024	ViT-B/16 (87M)	224	75.9
CLIP (our impl.)	V100	128	14M	224	16,384	ViT-B/16 (87M)	224	80.0
ZeroVL (ours)	V100	8	14M	224	16,384	ViT-B/16 (87M)	224	**80.9**

Setup. Following [22,35], we conduct the linear probing task on ImageNet-1K [9] after the pre-training phase. The batch size is set to 16,384 and learning rate is set to 6.4. We optimize the model for 90 epochs with the LARS optimizer [46], and weight decay is set to 0. To reveal the effects of our proposed methods on linear probing, we also evaluate the re-implemented CLIP as mentioned above.

Main Results. In Table 11, ZeroVL out-performs CLIP by 0.7%. However, similar to fine-tuned cross-modal retrieval, ALIGN achieves better results than ZeroVL based on heavier pre-training costs, larger model capacity, and larger image resolutions. Moreover, there are two observations on re-implemented CLIP. Firstly, we observe that training with limited computation resource (8 V100) achieves unsatisfactory top-1 accuracy 75.9%. Secondly, training CLIP with rich computation resource (128 V100) greatly improves the accuracy to 80.0%. The differences between ZeroVL and re-implemented CLIP (with 128 V100) are methods proposed in Sect. 3, validating the effectiveness of our proposed debiased sampling and coin flipping mixup. Benefits of our methods for cutting down the heavy resources dependency are further confirmed.

6   Conclusion

This work provides a training guideline for conducting dual-encoder multi-modal representation contrastive learning with limited resources. The proposed methods significantly lower computational resources, while still achieving good performance to be applied in other vision-language downstream tasks. With only 14M publicly accessible academic datasets and 8 V100 GPUs, we provide a reproducible strong baseline. In addition, we achieve comparable or superior performances than state-of-the-art methods with 100M web data. We hope our training pipeline and benchmark will be useful for future researches in the multi-modal representation learning field and benefit the community.

References

1. Antol, S., et al.: VQA: visual question answering. In: ICCV (2015)
2. Changpinyo, S., Sharma, P., Ding, N., Soricut, R.: Conceptual 12M: pushing web-scale image-text pre-training to recognize long-tail visual concepts. In: CVPR (2021)
3. Chen, H., Ding, G., Liu, X., Lin, Z., Liu, J., Han, J.: IMRAM: iterative matching with recurrent attention memory for cross-modal image-text retrieval. In: CVPR (2020)
4. Chen, J., Hu, H., Wu, H., Jiang, Y., Wang, C.: Learning the best pooling strategy for visual semantic embedding. In: CVPR (2021)
5. Chen, T., Kornblith, S., Norouzi, M., Hinton, G.: A simple framework for contrastive learning of visual representations. In: ICML (2020)
6. Chen, T., Kornblith, S., Swersky, K., Norouzi, M., Hinton, G.: Big self-supervised models are strong semi-supervised learners. In: NeurIPS (2020)
7. Chen, Y.-C., et al.: UNITER: UNiversal image-TExt representation learning. In: Vedaldi, A., Bischof, H., Brox, T., Frahm, J.-M. (eds.) ECCV 2020. LNCS, vol. 12375, pp. 104–120. Springer, Cham (2020). https://doi.org/10.1007/978-3-030-58577-8_7
8. Cubuk, E.D., Zoph, B., Mane, D., Vasudevan, V., Le, Q.V.: AutoAugment: learning augmentation strategies from data. In: CVPR (2019)
9. Deng, J., Dong, W., Socher, R., Li, L.J., Li, K., Fei-Fei, L.: ImageNet: a large-scale hierarchical image database. In: CVPR (2009)
10. Devlin, J., Chang, M.W., Lee, K., Toutanova, K.: BERT: pre-training of deep bidirectional transformers for language understanding. arXiv:1810.04805 (2018)
11. Dosovitskiy, A., et al.: An image is worth 16×16 words: transformers for image recognition at scale. In: ICLR (2021)
12. Faghri, F., Fleet, D.J., Kiros, J.R., Fidler, S.: VSE++: improving visual-semantic embeddings with hard negatives. In: BMVC (2018)
13. Gan, Z., Chen, Y.C., Li, L., Zhu, C., Cheng, Y., Liu, J.: Large-scale adversarial training for vision-and-language representation learning. In: NeurIPS (2020)
14. Goyal, Y., Khot, T., Summers-Stay, D., Batra, D., Parikh, D.: Making the V in VQA matter: elevating the role of image understanding in visual question answering. In: CVPR (2017)
15. Guo, H., Mao, Y., Zhang, R.: Augmenting data with mixup for sentence classification: an empirical study. arXiv:1905.08941 (2019)
16. He, K., Chen, X., Xie, S., Li, Y., Dollár, P., Girshick, R.: Masked autoencoders are scalable vision learners. arXiv:2111.06377 (2021)
17. He, K., Fan, H., Wu, Y., Xie, S., Girshick, R.: Momentum contrast for unsupervised visual representation learning. In: CVPR (2020)
18. He, P., Liu, X., Gao, J., Chen, W.: DeBERTa: decoding-enhanced BERT with disentangled attention. In: ICLR (2021)
19. Hinton, G., Vinyals, O., Dean, J.: Distilling the knowledge in a neural network. arXiv:1503.02531 (2015)
20. Huang, Z., Zeng, Z., Huang, Y., Liu, B., Fu, D., Fu, J.: Seeing out of the box: end-to-end pre-training for vision-language representation learning. In: CVPR (2021)
21. Jegou, H., Douze, M., Schmid, C.: Product quantization for nearest neighbor search. TPAMI **33**(1), 117–128 (2010)
22. Jia, C., et al.: Scaling up visual and vision-language representation learning with noisy text supervision. In: ICML (2021)

23. Kim, W., Son, B., Kim, I.: ViLT: vision-and-language transformer without convolution or region supervision. In: ICML (2021)
24. Kingma, D.P., Ba, J.: Adam: a method for stochastic optimization. In: ICLR (2015)
25. Krishna, R., et al.: Visual genome: connecting language and vision using crowd-sourced dense image annotations. IJCV **123**, 32–73 (2017). https://doi.org/10.1007/s11263-016-0981-7
26. Lee, K., Zhu, Y., Sohn, K., Li, C.L., Shin, J., Lee, H.: i-Mix: a domain-agnostic strategy for contrastive representation learning. In: ICLR (2021)
27. Li, J., Selvaraju, R.R., Gotmare, A.D., Joty, S., Xiong, C., Hoi, S.: Align before fuse: vision and language representation learning with momentum distillation. In: NeurIPS (2021)
28. Li, L.H., Yatskar, M., Yin, D., Hsieh, C.J., Chang, K.W.: VisualBERT: a simple and performant baseline for vision and language. arXiv:1908.03557 (2019)
29. Li, X., et al.: OSCAR: object-semantics aligned pre-training for vision-language tasks. In: Vedaldi, A., Bischof, H., Brox, T., Frahm, J.-M. (eds.) ECCV 2020. LNCS, vol. 12375, pp. 121–137. Springer, Cham (2020). https://doi.org/10.1007/978-3-030-58577-8_8
30. Liu, Y., et al.: RoBERTa: a robustly optimized BERT pretraining approach. arXiv:1907.11692 (2019)
31. Loshchilov, I., Hutter, F.: Decoupled weight decay regularization. In: ICLR (2019)
32. van den Oord, A., Li, Y., Vinyals, O.: Representation learning with contrastive predictive coding. arXiv:1807.03748 (2018)
33. Ordonez, V., Kulkarni, G., Berg, T.: Im2Text: describing images using 1 million captioned photographs. In: NeurIPS (2011)
34. Patashnik, O., Wu, Z., Shechtman, E., Cohen-Or, D., Lischinski, D.: StyleCLIP: text-driven manipulation of StyleGAN imagery. In: ICCV (2021)
35. Radford, A., et al.: Learning transferable visual models from natural language supervision. In: ICML (2021)
36. Sharma, P., Ding, N., Goodman, S., Soricut, R.: Conceptual captions: a cleaned, hypernymed, image alt-text dataset for automatic image captioning. In: ACL (2018)
37. Su, W., et al.: VL-BERT: pre-training of generic visual-linguistic representations. arXiv:1908.08530 (2019)
38. Suhr, A., Lewis, M., Yeh, J., Artzi, Y.: A corpus of natural language for visual reasoning. In: ACL (2017)
39. Suhr, A., Zhou, S., Zhang, A., Zhang, I., Bai, H., Artzi, Y.: A corpus for reasoning about natural language grounded in photographs. In: ACL (2019)
40. Sun, C., Myers, A., Vondrick, C., Murphy, K., Schmid, C.: VideoBERT: a joint model for video and language representation learning. In: ICCV (2019)
41. Tan, M., Le, Q.: EfficientNet: rethinking model scaling for convolutional neural networks. In: ICML (2019)
42. Verma, V., et al.: Manifold mixup: better representations by interpolating hidden states. In: ICML (2019)
43. Wu, H., et al.: Unified visual-semantic embeddings: bridging vision and language with structured meaning representations. In: CVPR (2019)
44. Xie, Q., Luong, M.T., Hovy, E., Le, Q.V.: Self-training with noisy student improves imagenet classification. In: CVPR (2020)
45. Yalniz, I.Z., Jégou, H., Chen, K., Paluri, M., Mahajan, D.: Billion-scale semi-supervised learning for image classification. arXiv:1905.00546 (2019)
46. You, Y., Gitman, I., Ginsburg, B.: Large batch training of convolutional networks. arXiv:1708.03888 (2017)

47. Yun, S., Han, D., Oh, S.J., Chun, S., Choe, J., Yoo, Y.: CutMix: regularization strategy to train strong classifiers with localizable features. In: ICCV (2019)
48. Zellers, R., Bisk, Y., Farhadi, A., Choi, Y.: From recognition to cognition: visual commonsense reasoning. In: CVPR (2019)
49. Zhang, H., Cisse, M., Dauphin, Y.N., Lopez-Paz, D.: Mixup: beyond empirical risk minimization. In: ICLR (2018)
50. Zhang, P., Goyal, Y., Summers-Stay, D., Batra, D., Parikh, D.: Yin and Yang: balancing and answering binary visual questions. In: CVPR (2016)
51. Zhang, P., et al.: VinVL: revisiting visual representations in vision-language models. In: CVPR (2021)
52. Zhao, B., Cui, Q., Song, R., Qiu, Y., Liang, J.: Decoupled knowledge distillation. In: CVPR (2022)

Learning Linguistic Association Towards Efficient Text-Video Retrieval

Sheng Fang[1,2], Shuhui Wang[1,3(✉)], Junbao Zhuo[1], Xinzhe Han[1,2], and Qingming Huang[1,2,3]

[1] Key Lab of Intelligent Information Processing, Institute of Computer Technology, CAS, Beijing, China
{sheng.fang,junbao.zhuo,xinzhe.han}@vipl.ict.ac.cn,wangshuhui@ict.ac.cn
[2] University of Chinese Academy of Sciences, Beijing, China
qmhuang@ucas.ac.cn
[3] Peng Cheng Laboratory, Shenzhen, China

Abstract. Text-video retrieval attracts growing attention recently. A dominant approach is to learn a common space for aligning two modalities. However, video deliver richer content than text in general situations and captions usually miss certain events or details in the video. The information imbalance between two modalities makes it difficult to align their representations. In this paper, we propose a general framework, **LIN**guistic **AS**sociation (LINAS), which utilizes the complementarity between captions corresponding to the same video. Concretely, we first train a teacher model taking extra relevant captions as inputs, which can aggregate language semantics for obtaining more comprehensive text representations. Since the additional captions are inaccessible during inference, Knowledge Distillation is employed to train a student model with a single caption as input. We further propose Adaptive Distillation strategy, which allows the student model to adaptively learn the knowledge from the teacher model. This strategy also suppresses the spurious relations introduced during the linguistic association. Extensive experiments demonstrate the effectiveness and efficiency of LINAS with various baseline architectures on benchmark datasets. Our code is available at https://github.com/silenceFS/LINAS.

Keywords: Text-video retrieval · Knowledge distillation

1 Introduction

Due to the popularity of online video sharing websites such as TikTok and YouTube, video has become one of the most informative data sources that contain rich visual content. That's the reason why video tasks attract lots of attention recently [1,3,6,9,15,33–35,42]. Especially, the explosive increase of the video data makes effective and efficient video retrieval technologies in urgent need. In

Supplementary Information The online version contains supplementary material available at https://doi.org/10.1007/978-3-031-20059-5_15.

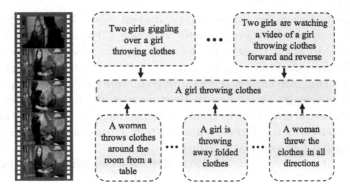

Fig. 1. Illustration of the information imbalance. The sentence in the green box is the query caption and all the other captions are relevant descriptions to the same video. The words marked in red represent the missing information. (Color figure online)

this paper, we focus on the text-video retrieval task, which aims to find the video in the candidate pool that best matches the semantics of the given natural language description, and vice versa. A general approach for text-video retrieval is to learn a similarity function on video and text that best describes their semantic relevance, so that the documents can be ranked according to the similarities. Typically, the videos and captions are encoded separately and then projected into a common embedding space, where the similarities can be calculated by dot product of their corresponding representations. The major challenge of the common latent space approach is how to align the data pairs from the two modalities, and great endeavors have been devoted in this direction [5,10,13,36,38,44].

In general situations, video delivers richer content than text. The former is a consecutive photometric record of events in a physical world, while the latter is the abstract description of the events that a person sees or experiences. So there naturally exists prominent information imbalance between video and text modalities. On the language side, it is natural for a human to describe an event with missing details of actions, attributes and objects. Moreover, different individuals may describe an event with different focuses and language habits. This further leads to the lack of information during the description process.

Figure 1 is an example for demonstrating the imbalance between video and text. In the video, two women laugh together and a video tape about a girl throwing clothes is played forward and reverse. The query caption 'A girl throwing clothes' only briefly describes the action of throwing clothes and ignores other information in the video, like 'laughing together', 'watching a video', 'forward and reverse', 'folded clothes', 'from a table', 'in all directions', *etc.* We further observe the diversity and complementarity among different language descriptions in all the associated captions of the same video in Fig. 1. This diversity is of great value for us to enrich the text representations and alleviate the imbalance between two modalities.

In this paper, we propose **LIN**guistic **AS**sociation (LINAS) framework towards efficient text-video retrieval. It includes a teacher model for aggregating the diversified captions for training and a student model for text-video retrieval without the support of extra captions for inference. First, for learning the teacher model, a support set is constructed for each caption which consists of complementary descriptions from crowdsourcing annotation or the captions of similar videos. With language cross-attention, different captions in the support set are given different weights, according to their degrees of complementarity. In this way, the teacher model learns to combine complementary semantics in different captions. Afterward, the learned enriched text representations will encourage better alignment between two modalities.

However, the teacher model requires additional captions that are inaccessible during inference. To facilitate efficient retrieval in real situations, we introduce Knowledge Distillation to train a student model with a single caption as input. The text and video embeddings of the student model are expected to be as close as possible to those of the teacher model, so the ability of linguistic association can be transfered from the teacher model to the student model without taking extra complementary descriptions at inference stage.

Moreover, the teacher model introduces some spurious correlation when aggregating additional captions, which will inevitablly confuse the student model without careful treatment. Therefore, we further propose Adaptive Distillation strategy which allows the student model to adaptively learn the relational knowledge from the teacher model. By learning the weight (or mask) on each pairwise similarity, our model gradually pays more attention to the diagonal elements of the similarity matrix, which strengthens the transfer of positive relational knowledge. The Adaptive Distillation strategy not only maintains the richness of text representations, but also suppresses the spurious relations introduced during the linguistic association. In together, LINAS achieves better performance.

Our main contributions can be summarized as follows:

- We propose a general framework LINAS for text-video retrieval that utilizes the complementarity between relevant captions. It encourages the model to learn the ability of linguistic association for better aligning two modalities.
- We introduce Knowledge Distillation to train a student model without extra input. We further propose Adaptive Distillation strategy for suppressing the spurious correlation in the teacher model.
- Consistent improvements brought by LINAS with various baseline architectures on benchmark datasets demonstrate its effectiveness. Moreover, experimental results validate the efficiency and generalization ability of the proposed LINAS.

2   Related Work

Text-Video Retrieval. Compared to text-image retrieval, text-video retrieval is more challenging and in line with the current trend of shot video. Text-video retrieval attracts growing attention recently. Early work for text-video retrieval is mostly concept-based [12,16,25,30,37,39]. The recent dominant methods are latent-space-based, which aim to project video and text into a joint embedding space for measuring similarities [5,9,10,19,23,28,29,38,43–45]. Dong *et al.* [9] compose parallel multi-level encodings, *i.e.*, mean pooling, biGRU and biGRU-CNN, for comprehensive representations. Projections into a common space are learned afterward. They further propose a hybrid common space which consists of a latent subspace and a concept subspace [10]. Wray *et al.* [44] decompose text into different parts like nouns and verbs for fined-grained action retrieval. Similarly, Chen *et al.* [5] model the text-video matching at levels of events, actions and entities. Considering the multi-modality, Mithun *et al.* [29] employ image, motion and audio modalities to obtain video representations. Liu *et al.* [23] further exploit more multi-modal cues like speech content, OCR, *etc.* Gabeur *et al.* [13] use transformer [40] to aggregate multi-modal features. Wang *et al.* [43] design a global-local alignment method with VLAD encoding. More recent work utilize BERTs or fransformers as the backbone and finetune large-scale pretrained model for cross-modal retrieval [2,17,22,24,32]. Lei *et al.* [17] propose ClipBERT by employing sparse sampling. Liu *et al.* [22] model the feature-level and semantic-level cross-modal matching through Hierarchical Transformer. Luo *et al.* [24] transfer the knowledge of the CLIP model to video-language retrieval in an end-to-end manner. In this work, we propose a general framework for learning linguistic association, which utilizes the complementarity between relevant captions to the same video. Though pretrained models have the ability of language association to a certain extent which is consistent with our method, they require large-scale data and we can capture the association with limited data.

Knowledge Distillation. Knowledge Distillation refers to the methods that train a smaller student network under the supervision of a larger teacher network. Buciluă *et al.* [4] first propose model compression for classification and regression tasks. Hinton *et al.* [14] expand this idea and transfer knowledge from the teacher model to the student model by minimizing the difference between classification logits produced by two models. Afterward, Knowledge Distillation is formalized as a pattern for downsizing a network regardless of the structural differences [41]. Park *et al.* [31] propose distance-wise and angle-wise distillation losses for transferring the mutual relations of samples from teacher model to student model instead of simply closing the outputs of them. Knowledge Distillation is widely used in various computer vision tasks such as image classification [20], object detection [18], cross-modal retrieval [26], *etc.* TeachText [7] is the most similar work to ours, which employs Knowledge Distillation for leveraging complementary cues from multiple text encoders. In our work, Knowledge Distillation is utilized to teach the student model the ability of language association. The proposed Adaptive Distillation strategy allows the student model to adaptively learn the relational knowledge from the teacher model.

3 Method

3.1 Problem Description

Due to the richness of video content, there are usually multiple captions corresponding to the same video in the crowdsourcing annotation process. Let

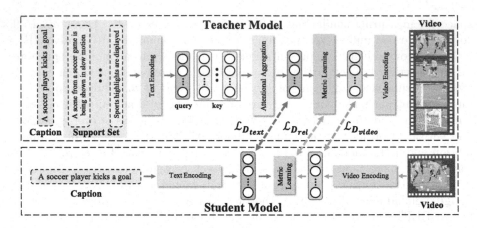

Fig. 2. Overview of LINAS.

$\mathcal{D} = \{(c_i, v_i)\}$ be a dataset where (c_i, v_i) represents a postive caption-video pair. For a video v_i, $\mathcal{C}_i$ is the set consists of all captions corresponding to v_i.

A general approach for text-video retrieval is to encode videos and captions separately. Then the similarities of their representations are measured for ranking. We summarize the framework of mainstream methods into three modules—text encoding, video encoding, and metric learning, noted as T_E, V_E, and M respectively. Metric learning here represents the module for learning similarities between two modalities. Any model that has above three modules can be used as our baseline in LINAS.

Figure 2 is an overview of our proposed LINAS framework. We first train a teacher model which takes query and support set captions as inputs. It achieves more comprehensive text embeddings through attentional aggregation. Afterward, Knowledge Distillation is used to obtain a more efficient student model whose input is a single query caption. In this approach, the student model can learn the ability of linguistic association.

We will introduce the teacher model for aggregating textual semantics in Sect. 3.2. Then the student model follows in Sect. 3.3. Section 3.4 is about the distillation process for learning linguistic association.

3.2 Teacher Model

Support Set. Before training the teacher model, we first construct a support set for each caption which can provide complementary semantics. The support set consists of descriptions belonging to the same video with the query caption. For caption c_i, N captions are selected from $\mathcal{C}_i \backslash c_i$ to compose the support set, noted as $\{s_i^n\}_{n=1}^N$. Figure 2 provides an instance of support set.

The above scheme has a premise that the videos in the training set must have multiple captions. To make our framework adaptive to datasets where each video has a unique caption, we propose an alternative approach to construct support sets. The more generalized version of LINAS will be introduced in Sect. 4.4.

Training. The three modules in our teacher model are denoted as T_E^t, V_E^t, and M^t respectively. Embeddings of query caption and support set captions are obtained by $q_i = T_E^t(c_i)$, $k_i^n = T_E^t(s_i^n)$. Since it is expected that the teacher model can aggregate the complementary semantics to the query caption, we design an attentional aggregation module for combining the representations of query caption and support set captions.

$$x_i^t = q_i + \sum_{n=1}^{N} \frac{\exp(Q(q_i)^T K(k_i^n))}{\sum_{l=1}^{N} \exp(Q(q_i)^T K(k_i^l))} k_i^n, \tag{1}$$

where Q and K are learnable linear projections. We treat the original caption as query and the support set captions as keys for cross-attention learning. Afterward, video embeddings are obtained through $y_i^t = V_E^t(v_i)$. Then the similarity matrix S^t can be achieved by $S^t(i,j) = M^t(x_i^t, y_j^t)$. The objective function for training the teacher model is the same with the original baseline, noted as $\mathcal{L}_O$.

3.3 Student Model

Training. The student model also has text encoding, video encoding, and metric learning three modules noted as T_E^s, V_E^s, and M^s, which need to train from scratch. The text embeddings, video embeddings and similarity matrix of student model can be obtained by $x_i^s = T_E^s(c_i)$, $y_i^s = V_E^s(v_i)$, $S^s(i,j) = M^s(x_i^s, y_j^s)$. Different from training the teacher model, the objective function here is

$$\mathcal{L}_S = \mathcal{L}_O + \mathcal{L}_D \tag{2}$$

where $\mathcal{L}_D$ represents the distillation loss which will be introduced in Sect. 3.4.

Inference. Only the student model is employed for inference because the support set is inaccessible while testing. Since the student model has the same structure as the chosen baseline, LINAS brings no extra computation cost but significant performance enhancement.

Efficiency. Actually, the student model does not have to be consistent with the teacher model. If we utilize a stronger teacher model for distillation and a lightweight student model for inference, LINAS will achieve efficient retrieval with the performance approaching more complex models.

3.4 Learning to Associate

Start from our motivation of learning linguistic association, we hope that the student model can imitate the teacher model. In order to make the student model to mimic the enriched text representations of the teacher model, we first propose a text distillation loss, denoted as $\mathcal{L}_{D_{text}}$. Since the main goal of text-video retrieval is to better align the two modalities, we raise a similar loss $\mathcal{L}_{D_{video}}$ for supervising the video embeddings of the student model.

$$\mathcal{L}_{D_{text}} = \sum_{i=1}^{B}(\|x_i^t - x_i^s\|_2^2), \quad \mathcal{L}_{D_{video}} = \sum_{i=1}^{B}(\|y_i^t - y_i^s\|_2^2), \tag{3}$$

where B represents the batch size.

On the other hand, retrieval is a bidirectional task which is different from classic Knowledge Distillation applications [14]. The correlation between samples is particularly important, because the essence of retrieval is ranking. Motivated by the Relational Knowledge Distillation proposed by Park *et al.* [31], we carry out a relational distillation loss $\mathcal{L}'_{D_{rel}}$. It aims to minimize the distance between the similarity matrixs of the student model and the teacher model, which is calculated by

$$\mathcal{L}'_{D_{rel}} = \sum_{i=1}^{B}\sum_{j=1}^{B} L_\delta(S^t(i,j), S^s(i,j)), \tag{4}$$

where L_δ represents the Huber loss, defined as

$$L_\delta(a,b) = \begin{cases} \frac{1}{2}(a-b)^2, & for\ |a-b| \leq \delta \\ \delta|a-b| - \frac{1}{2}\delta^2, & otherwise \end{cases} \tag{5}$$

However, there are some spurious relations in our teacher model introduced during the process of enriching textual representations. Besides, the teacher model contains extra information that the student model cannot perceive. Therefore, using all the correlation from the teacher model for supervision will confuse the student model. The experimental results are the evidence of this problem. When we use the whole similarity matrix to supervise the training of the student model with $\mathcal{L}'_{D_{rel}}$, the performance will decline (as shown in Sect. 4.3). We further propose Adaptive Distillation strategy which allows the student model to selectively learn the relational knowledge from the teacher model. In this way, the transfer of positive knowledge can be strengthened and the spurious correlation can be suppressed in the distillation process.

Adaptive Distillation. In order to enable the model to adaptively learn the required relational knowledge, we assign a weight to each element in the similarity matrix, that is

$$\mathcal{L}_{D_{rel}} = \sum_{i=1}^{B}\sum_{j=1}^{B} m(i,j)L_\delta(S^t(i,j), S^s(i,j)), \tag{6}$$

where m is a mask matrix whose elements are between 0 and 1.

Inspired by Neural Architecture Search [21], the mask m can be treated as architecture parameters for optimization. θ represents the student model parameters. Since the search space in our case is continuous, we adopt EM (Expectation-Maximization) Algorithm to iteratively optimize m and θ.

Algorithm 1 shows the overall procedure of our Adaptive Distillation strategy. For training the model parameters θ, $\mathcal{L}_{train}(\theta, m)$ is exactly the same as $\mathcal{L}_{D_{rel}}$. For optimizing the mask m, we found that the diagonal elements in S^t are relatively large. In order to reduce the numerical influence in the learning process, we reweight m in $\mathcal{L}_{val}$, that is

$$\mathcal{L}_{val}(\theta, m) = \sum_{i=1}^{B} \sum_{j=1}^{B} \frac{1}{S^t(i, j)} m(i, j) L_\delta(S^t(i, j), S^s(i, j)). \tag{7}$$

Considering that the samples of each training batch are randomly selected, we can use two values to represent the diagonal and non-diagonal elements of m respectively due to the exchange symmetry. Figure 3 is the visualization of the values in the mask during training. Note that m is normalized and uniformly initialized. When the model converges, an adaptively learned mask tends to transfer the relational knowledge from the diagonal elements from the teacher model. Finally, based on learned mask m, we retrain the student model from scratch. The whole distillation loss for learning linguistic association in our LINAS is

$$\mathcal{L}_D = \alpha * (\mathcal{L}_{D_{text}} + \mathcal{L}_{D_{video}}) + \beta * \mathcal{L}_{D_{rel}}, \tag{8}$$

where α and β are hyperparameters for balancing losses. Detailed analysis about the Adaptive Distillation strategy is available in *Supplementary Material*.

Algorithm 1: Adaptive Distillation

Create a mask m which is uniformly initialized. θ represents the model parameters.

while *not converged* **do**

  $\theta \leftarrow \theta - \eta_\theta \nabla_\theta \mathcal{L}_{train}(\theta, m)$;

  $m \leftarrow m - \eta_m \nabla_m \mathcal{L}_{val}(\theta, m)$;

end

Based on the learned mask m, retrain the model parameters θ from scratch.

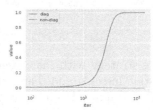

Fig. 3. Visualization of the mask learning Process.

4 Experiments

4.1 Experimental Settings

We conduct experiments on MSR-VTT, MSVD and VATEX datasets in this work. To measure the performance of retrieval models, we employ commonly used metrics including Recall at K (R@K), Median Rank (MedR) and mean Average Precision (mAP). For fair comparison, we adopt the same video features and

Table 1. Comparison on MSR-VTT.

Method	Text2Video					Video2Text					SumR
	R@1	R@5	R@10	MedR	mAP	R@1	R@5	R@10	MedR	mAP	
VSE++ [11]	5.7	17.1	24.8	65	–	10.2	25.4	35.1	25	–	118.3
Mithun et al.[29]	7.0	20.9	29.7	38	–	12.5	32.1	42.4	16	–	144.6
W2VV [8]	6.1	18.7	27.5	45	–	11.8	28.9	39.1	21	–	132.1
CE [23]	10.0	29.0	41.2	16	–	15.6	40.9	55.2	8.3	–	191.9
HGR [5]	9.2	26.2	36.5	24	–	15.0	36.7	48.8	11	–	172.4
Dual Encoding [9]	11.0	29.3	39.9	19	20.3	19.7	43.6	55.6	8	9.3	199.0
LINAS - Dual Encoding	11.9	31.0	42.1	17	21.6	22.0	46.9	59.2	6	10.4	213.1
Hybrid Space [10]	11.6	30.3	41.3	17	21.2	22.5	47.1	58.9	7	10.5	211.7
LINAS - Hybrid Space	12.3	31.6	42.8	16	22.1	22.3	47.8	60.4	6	10.6	217.2
CE+ [7]	14.4	37.4	50.2	10	–	22.7	52.6	66.3	5	–	243.6
TeachText - CE+ [7]	14.9	38.3	51.5	10	–	**24.9**	54.1	67.6	5	–	251.3
LINAS - CE+	**15.2**	**38.9**	**52.0**	10	–	24.7	**55.2**	**68.0**	4	–	**254.0**

Table 2. Comparison on MSVD.

Method	Text2Video		Video2Text	
	R@5	MedR	R@5	MedR
VSE++ [11]	39.6	9	–	–
M-Cues [29]	47.8	6	–	–
MoEE [27]	52.0	5	–	–
CE [23]	52.3	5	–	–
Support set [32]	52.8	5	50.7	5
Dual encoding [9]	32.6	13	29.4	21
LINAS - dual encoding	33.9	12	33.7	17
CE+ [7]	56.5	4	54.3	5
TeachText - CE+ [7]	56.9	4	55.0	4
LINAS - CE+	**57.6**	4	**55.7**	4

Table 3. Comparison on VATEX.

Method	Text2Video		Video2Text	
	R@5	MedR	R@5	MedR
CE [23]	68.7	–	71.0	–
W2VV++ [19]	68.2	–	75.1	–
HGR [5]	73.5	2	–	–
TeachText - CE+ [7]	**87.4**	1	–	–
VSE++ [11]	65.8	3	75.1	2
LINAS - VSE++	70.1	3	78.9	2
Dual encoding [9]	71.3	2	75.7	2
LINAS - dual encoding	72.7	2	79.1	2
Hybrid space [10]	73.6	–	75.7	–
LINAS - Hybrid Space	74.4	2	**79.4**	2

training strategy with the chosen baseline. The hyperparameters for balancing distillation losses α and β are set to be 0.2 and 1. The δ in Huber loss is set to be 1. Each caption has a support set consists of 8 corresponding descriptions in our experiments. More details are available in *Supplementary Material*.

4.2   Comparison with Existing Methods

In this section, we compare the results of our methods applied to various backbones with existing text-video retrieval methods on different datasets. We first make comparisons with methods that do not utilize pretrained large-scale model.

Results on MSR-VTT can be seen in Table 1. Note that CE+ is an improved version of CE proposed by Croitoru *et al.*, which utilizes more high-quality multimodal features and more powerful text embedding. All the methods in Table 1 are trained using only the samples from the target datasets for fair comparison. We can see that LINAS is model-agnostic and the application of LINAS on Dual Encoding, Hybrid Space and CE+ three different baseline models has significantly improved the performance. Moreover, the student model in our method

Table 4. Comparison with pretraining methods.

Method	Dataset	Text2Video				Video2Text				SumR
		R@1	R@5	R@10	MedR	R@1	R@5	R@10	MedR	
ClipBERT [17]	MSR-VTT 1k-A	22.0	46.8	59.9	6	–	–	–	–	–
MMT [13]		25.8	57.3	69.3	4	26.1	57.8	68.5	4	304.8
LINAS - MMT		27.1	59.8	71.7	4	28.3	60.3	72.0	3	319.2
Frozen in time [2]	MSVD	33.7	64.7	76.3	3	–	–	–	–	–
CLIP4Clip [24]		46.2	76.1	84.6	2	–	–	–	–	–
LINAS - CLIP4Clip		46.7	76.8	85.6	2	47.3	75.0	83.2	2	414.6

is exactly the same as the baseline, which means LINAS can improve the performance without bringing additional cost at inference. TeachText is a similar work to ours which utilizes Knolwedge Distillation for levaraging complementary cues from various text encoders, while LINAS attempts to learn the language association through relevant captions. We can draw a conclusion that, they are both effective and our LINAS can boost the performance more comprehensively. When applied on CE+, our method outperforms all the competitors in Table 1 which do not use cross-modal pretraining models. The results show the effctiveness of proposed LINAS.

The results on MSVD and VATEX are shown in Table 2 and Table 3. Note that, only a part of the results are reported for saving space. Since these two datasets are in a smaller scale compared with MSR-VTT, the performances on them are much higher than those on MSR-VTT. Nevertheless, the utilization of LINAS still improves the overall performance significantly, which illustrates the robustness of LINAS. On MSVD dataset, 'LINAS - CE+' outperforms all competitors including Support Set, which utilizes more data for training. On VATEX dataset, we apply LINAS on VSE++, which is a quite basic architecture. The consistent promising improvements show the validity of language association.[1]

Recently, pretraining methods are dominant in performance, *e.g.* MMT [13], ClipBERT [17], Frozen in time [2], *etc.* In order to better prove the generalization ability of our method, we further choose some stronger models as baselines to apply proposed LINAS. MMT utilizes transformer architecture to aggregate features from different modalities, *e.g.* OCR, Face, Speech, *etc.* Moreover, it uses a pretrained model on HowTo100M [28]. As shown in Table 4, on MSR-VTT 1k-A (another split edition of MSR-VTT dataset), LINAS further improves the performance of MMT. CLIP4Clip [24] utilizes large-scale pretrained model CLIP for text-video retrieval. Our LINAS still achieves constant gains when applied to CLIP4Clip on MSVD, which shows the effectiveness of LINAS. Actually, the pretrained model has the ability of linguistic association to some extent after scanning large-scale data, which is consistent to our motivation. However, LINAS can further improve the performance on pretraining methods and it can capture the association with limited data.

---

[1] 'TeachText-CE+' achieves the best perfomrance on VATEX. However, the authors have not provided corresponding multi-modal features of VATEX dataset.

4.3   Ablation Study

To be clear in advance, all the experiments in this section are under the same experimental settings. 'Dual Encoding' is chosen as the baseline and the experiments are conducted on MSR-VTT dataset.

Distillation Strategy. The distillation loss for training the student model in LINAS is $\mathcal{L}_D = \alpha * (\mathcal{L}_{D_{text}} + \mathcal{L}_{D_{video}}) + \beta * \mathcal{L}_{D_{rel}}$. Ablation studies on the distillation strategy are reported in Table 5. The last row shows the performance of the teacher model. We observe that the teacher model is good at text-to-video retrieval but obtains unfavorable performance in the other direction. The amazing performance at T2V is because the teacher model makes use of ground truth information to construct the support set in both training and testing stages. Meanwhile, the aggregation of captions will reduce the discrimination between texts and introduce spurious relations, which results in the reduction of performance at V2T.

We can see that $\mathcal{L}_{D_{text}}$, $\mathcal{L}_{D_{video}}$, and $\mathcal{L}_{D_{rel}}$ are all beneficial to the retrieval performance of the student model from Table 5. It shows that our poposed distillation losses are effective in the process of learning lingusitic association.

Moreover, the 6th row is trained with $\mathcal{L}'_{D_{rel}}$. The performance drop compared with the 4th row shows that using all the similarities from the teacher model for supervision is harmful. It is caused by introduced spurious correlation in the teacher model. The 7th row replaces $\mathcal{L}'_{D_{rel}}$ with $\mathcal{L}_{D_{rel}}$ which further improve the performance. It proves the validity of our Adaptive Distillation strategy. Through the mask learning procedure, we draw the conclusion that taking diagonal elements for supervision is helpful for strengthening the transfer of positive relational knowledge and suppressing the spurious correlation in the teacher model. On the other hand, the R@1 metrics at both directions of the teacher model is considerable which proves the reliability of the similarities of positive video-caption pairs. It experimentally supports the conclusion of our Adaptive Distillation strategy.

Table 5. Ablation studies on disillation loss.

	$\mathcal{L}_{D_{text}}$	$\mathcal{L}_{D_{video}}$	$\mathcal{L}_{D_{rel}}$	$\mathcal{L}'_{D_{rel}}$	Text2Video R@1	R@5	R@10	MedR	mAP	Video2Text R@1	R@5	R@10	MedR	mAP	SumR
1					10.9	29.3	39.8	20	20.2	19.5	42.8	55.8	8	9.3	199.0
2	✓				11.3	30.0	40.8	18	20.8	21.1	44.6	56.7	7	10.1	204.4
3			✓		11.3	30.1	41.1	18	20.9	20.8	44.5	58.2	7	9.8	205.9
4	✓	✓			11.7	30.6	41.6	17	21.3	21.9	45.2	58.3	7	10.2	209.3
5	✓		✓		11.5	30.2	41.1	18	21.0	20.4	45.8	57.7	7	10.2	206.7
6	✓	✓		✓	11.5	30.2	41.1	18	21.0	21.8	45.5	58.2	7	10.0	208.3
7	✓	✓	✓		**11.9**	**31.0**	**42.1**	**17**	**21.6**	**22.0**	**46.9**	**59.2**	**6**	**10.4**	**213.1**
Teacher Model					19.0	44.6	57.7	7	31.3	23.7	39.0	46.9	13	18.9	231.0

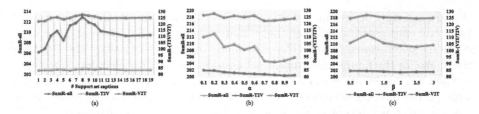

Fig. 4. The influence of support set size and hyperparameters α, β.

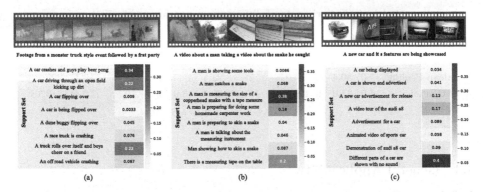

Fig. 5. Weights of support set captions in attentional aggregation.

Support Set Size. Each video in MSR-VTT has 20 relevant captions. Apart from the query caption itself, there are up to 19 captions to compose the support set. Extensive experiments are conducted to explore the impact of support set size by random sampling. The results of different support set sizes are shown in Fig. 4(a). With the increase of the number of support set captions, the performance roughly shows a trend of increasing first and then decreasing. The overall performance reaches the peak when the support set has 8 captions. When there are not enough support set captions, the model can not capture the correlation information from insufficient data. When there are too many captions, too many noise and distractive information is introduced which makes it hard to learn the linguistic association.

Loss Weight. Extensive experiments are conducted to evaluate the effects of hyperparameters α and β. The results are shown in Fig. 4(b) and (c). We can draw a conclusion that, the proper values of α and β are 0.2 and 1.

Attentional Aggregation. To validate the effectiveness of the attentional aggregation mechanism, a comparison experiment employing mean pooling for aggregation is designed. The results are shown in Table 6, which show the advantage of the attentional aggregation. Moreover, to demonstrate that the teacher model does concentrate on the complementary information through the aggregation process, we visualize some text-video pairs and the attention weights of support set captions in Fig. 5. Taking Fig. 5 (b) as an example, the original query text only expresses the message that a man catches a snake. However, the video contains more events. In the video, the man continues to measure the length of the snake. In the figure, the support set captions containing elements like 'tape', 'carpenter', 'table' are given higher attention weights as we expected. Since the aggregation module is designed for concentrating on the complementary information which is relevant to the video but not involved in the caption.

Table 6. Experiments of different aggretation mechanism.

Method	Text2Video					Video2Text					SumR
	R@1	R@5	R@10	MedR	mAP	R@1	R@5	R@10	MedR	mAP	
Mean Pooling	11.5	30.4	41.4	17	21.3	21.1	45.3	57.4	7	10.1	207.1
Attentional	11.9	31.0	42.1	17	21.6	22.0	46.9	59.2	6	10.4	213.1

4.4   General Applicability

Efficiency. We carry out a lightweight model named 'Base' in this experiment, which simply adopts mean pooling for video representations and biGRU for text representations. The 1st row in Table 7 shows the results of the 'Base' model without distillation. Then LINAS is utilized on the 'Base' model and brings significant improvement. Afterward, we utilize a more complex teacher model 'Dual Encoding' for distillation while remain the structure of the student model unchanged. We observe that the model is further improved, whose performance is comparable or even slightly surpasses that of the stronger baseline model 'Dual Encoding'. Note that the number of parameters in 'Base' (14.9M) is less than 20% of that in 'Dual Encoding' (81.4M), which results in 3× speed-up during inference. The experimental results demonstrate that LINAS can achieve efficient text-video retrieval.

Generalization. We propose an alternative approach to construct support sets for the situation where each video only has one corresponding caption. Given a trained text-video retrieval model, top-N relevant videos to the query caption can be obtained. Afterward, the support set of the query caption is composed of the corresponding captions of these N videos. For validating generalized LINAS, we construct a demo dataset by randomly choosing one caption for each video in MSR-VTT. The generalized LINAS is employed on this dataset and N is set to be 8. As shown in Table 8, the promising improvement brought by the generalized LINAS on the chosen baseline model illustrates its effectiveness. In this approach, LINAS can be extended to applications on more datasets. Visualizations of the support sets in our demo dataset can be found in *Supplementary Material.*

Table 7. Experiments of utilizing a lightweight student model.

Teacher model	Student Model	Text2Video				Video2Text				SumR
		R@1	R@5	R@10	MedR	R@1	R@5	R@10	MedR	
–	Base	9.7	26.8	37.0	23	17.7	40.0	51.7	10	182.9
Base	Base	10.3	27.9	38.9	**19**	19.3	42.9	54.1	8	193.4
Dual encoding [9]	Base	10.7	28.9	**39.9**	**19**	**20.0**	**43.9**	**56.4**	8	**199.8**
–	Dual Encoding [9]	**10.9**	**29.3**	39.8	20	19.5	42.8	55.8	8	199.0

Table 8. Experiments of generalized LINAS.

Method	Text2Video				Video2Text				SumR
	R@1	R@5	R@10	MedR	R@1	R@5	R@10	MedR	
Dual encoding [9]	4.8	17.0	25.0	55	4.7	16.4	25.3	59	91.2
Generalized LINAS - dual encoding	5.6	17.4	25.6	45	5.3	17.3	26.4	48	97.5

5 Conclusion

In this paper, we propose LINAS towards efficient text-video retrieval. A teacher model which takes extra relevant captions as inputs is trained first. It can aggregate complementary semantics of the diversified captions for text enrichment. Afterward, Knowledge Distillation is introduced to teach the student model the ability of linguistic association, which has only one query caption as input. We further design Adaptive Distillation strategy which allows the student model to adaptively learn the relational knowledge from the teacher model. It aims to strengthen the transfer of positive knowledge and suppress the spurious correlation introduced by linguistic association. LINAS can be applied to most mainstream methods and bring no extra computation cost during inference. Moreover, LINAS can achieve efficient text-video retrieval by adopting a lightweight student model. Additionally, we propose Generalized LINAS for applications on datasets where each video only has one caption. It employs an alternative scheme for constructing support sets. Extensive experimental results demonstrate the effectiveness, efficiency and generalization ability of LINAS.

Acknowledgements. This work was supported in part by the National Key R&D Program of China under Grant 2018AAA0102000, in part by National Natural Science Foundation of China: 62022083, U21B2038 and 61931008, and in part by the Fundamental Research Funds for the Central Universities.

References

1. Arnab, A., Dehghani, M., Heigold, G., Sun, C., Lucic, M., Schmid, C.: Vivit: a video vision transformer. In: 2021 IEEE/CVF International Conference on Computer Vision, ICCV 2021, Montreal, QC, Canada, 10–17 October 2021, pp. 6816–6826. IEEE (2021). https://doi.org/10.1109/ICCV48922.2021.00676

2. Bain, M., Nagrani, A., Varol, G., Zisserman, A.: Frozen in time: a joint video and image encoder for end-to-end retrieval. In: Proceedings of the IEEE/CVF International Conference on Computer Vision, pp. 1728–1738 (2021)
3. Bertasius, G., Wang, H., Torresani, L.: Is space-time attention all you need for video understanding? In: Meila, M., Zhang, T. (eds.) Proceedings of the 38th International Conference on Machine Learning, ICML 2021, 18–24 July 2021, Virtual Event. Proceedings of Machine Learning Research, vol. 139, pp. 813–824. PMLR (2021). http://proceedings.mlr.press/v139/bertasius21a.html
4. Buciluǎ, C., Caruana, R., Niculescu-Mizil, A.: Model compression. In: Proceedings of the 12th ACM SIGKDD International Conference on Knowledge Discovery and Data Mining, pp. 535–541 (2006)
5. Chen, S., Zhao, Y., Jin, Q., Wu, Q.: Fine-grained text-video retrieval with hierarchical graph reasoning. In: Proceedings of the IEEE/CVF Conference on Computer Vision and Pattern Recognition, pp. 10638–10647 (2020)
6. Chen, W., Li, G., Zhang, X., Yu, H., Wang, S., Huang, Q.: Cascade cross-modal attention network for video actor and action segmentation from a sentence. In: Proceedings of the 29th ACM International Conference on Multimedia, pp. 4053–4062 (2021)
7. Croitoru, I., et al.: Teachtext: crossmodal generalized distillation for text-video retrieval. In: Proceedings of the IEEE/CVF International Conference on Computer Vision, pp. 11583–11593 (2021)
8. Dong, J., Li, X., Snoek, C.G.: Predicting visual features from text for image and video caption retrieval. IEEE Trans. Multimedia **20**(12), 3377–3388 (2018)
9. Dong, J., et al.: Dual encoding for zero-example video retrieval. In: Proceedings of the IEEE Conference on Computer Vision and Pattern Recognition, pp. 9346–9355 (2019)
10. Dong, J., et al.: Dual encoding for video retrieval by text. IEEE Trans. Pattern Anal. Mach. Intell. **44**, 4065–4080 (2021)
11. Faghri, F., Fleet, D.J., Kiros, J.R., Fidler, S.: VSE++: improving visual-semantic embeddings with hard negatives. In: British Machine Vision Conference 2018, BMVC 2018, Newcastle, UK, 3–6 September 2018, p. 12. BMVA Press (2018). http://bmvc2018.org/contents/papers/0344.pdf
12. Foteini, M., et al.: Iti-certh participation in trecvid 2016. In: TRECVID 2016 Workshop (2016)
13. Gabeur, V., Sun, C., Alahari, K., Schmid, C.: Multi-modal transformer for video retrieval. In: Vedaldi, A., Bischof, H., Brox, T., Frahm, J.-M. (eds.) ECCV 2020. LNCS, vol. 12349, pp. 214–229. Springer, Cham (2020). https://doi.org/10.1007/978-3-030-58548-8_13
14. Hinton, G., Vinyals, O., Dean, J.: Distilling the knowledge in a neural network. arXiv preprint arXiv:1503.02531 (2015)
15. Junbao, Z., et al.: Zero-shot video classification with appropriate web and task knowledge transfer. In: Proceedings of the 30th ACM International Conference on Multimedia (2022)
16. Le, D.D., et al.: Nii-hitachi-uit at trecvid 2016. In: TRECVID, vol. 25 (2016)
17. Lei, Jet al.: Less is more: clipbert for video-and-language learning via sparse sampling. In: Proceedings of the IEEE/CVF Conference on Computer Vision and Pattern Recognition, pp. 7331–7341 (2021)
18. Li, Q., Jin, S., Yan, J.: Mimicking very efficient network for object detection. In: Proceedings of the IEEE Conference on Computer Vision and Pattern Recognition, pp. 6356–6364 (2017)

19. Li, X., Xu, C., Yang, G., Chen, Z., Dong, J.: W2vv++ fully deep learning for ad-hoc video search. In: Proceedings of the 27th ACM International Conference on Multimedia, pp. 1786–1794 (2019)
20. Li, Z., Hoiem, D.: Learning without forgetting. IEEE Trans. Pattern Anal. Mach. Intell. **40**(12), 2935–2947 (2017)
21. Liu, H., Simonyan, K., Yang, Y.: DARTS: differentiable architecture search. In: 7th International Conference on Learning Representations, ICLR 2019, New Orleans, LA, USA, 6–9 May 2019. OpenReview.net (2019). https://openreview.net/forum?id=S1eYHoC5FX
22. Liu, S., Fan, H., Qian, S., Chen, Y., Ding, W., Wang, Z.: Hit: hierarchical transformer with momentum contrast for video-text retrieval. In: Proceedings of the IEEE/CVF International Conference on Computer Vision, pp. 11915–11925 (2021)
23. Liu, Y., Albanie, S., Nagrani, A., Zisserman, A.: Use what you have: video retrieval using representations from collaborative experts. In: 30th British Machine Vision Conference 2019, BMVC 2019, Cardiff, UK, 9–12 September 2019, p. 279. BMVA Press (2019). https://bmvc2019.org/wp-content/uploads/papers/0363-paper.pdf
24. Luo, H., et al.: Clip4clip: an empirical study of CLIP for end to end video clip retrieval. CoRR abs/2104.08860 (2021). https://arxiv.org/abs/2104.08860
25. Markatopoulou, F., Galanopoulos, D., Mezaris, V., Patras, I.: Query and keyframe representations for ad-hoc video search. In: Proceedings of the 2017 ACM on International Conference on Multimedia Retrieval, pp. 407–411 (2017)
26. Miech, A., Alayrac, J.B., Laptev, I., Sivic, J., Zisserman, A.: Thinking fast and slow: efficient text-to-visual retrieval with transformers. In: Proceedings of the IEEE/CVF Conference on Computer Vision and Pattern Recognition, pp. 9826–9836 (2021)
27. Miech, A., Laptev, I., Sivic, J.: Learning a text-video embedding from incomplete and heterogeneous data. arXiv preprint arXiv:1804.02516 (2018)
28. Miech, A., Zhukov, D., Alayrac, J.B., Tapaswi, M., Laptev, I., Sivic, J.: Howto100m: learning a text-video embedding by watching hundred million narrated video clips. In: Proceedings of the IEEE/CVF International Conference on Computer Vision, pp. 2630–2640 (2019)
29. Mithun, N.C., Li, J., Metze, F., Roy-Chowdhury, A.K.: Learning joint embedding with multimodal cues for cross-modal text-video retrieval. In: Proceedings of the 2018 ACM on International Conference on Multimedia Retrieval, pp. 19–27 (2018)
30. Nguyen, P.A., et al.: Vireo@ trecvid 2017: video-to-text, ad-hoc video search, and video hyperlinking. In: TRECVID (2017)
31. Park, W., Kim, D., Lu, Y., Cho, M.: Relational knowledge distillation. In: Proceedings of the IEEE/CVF Conference on Computer Vision and Pattern Recognition, pp. 3967–3976 (2019)
32. Patrick, M., et al.: Support-set bottlenecks for video-text representation learning. In: 9th International Conference on Learning Representations, ICLR 2021, Virtual Event, Austria, 3–7 May 2021. OpenReview.net (2021). https://openreview.net/forum?id=EqoXe2zmhrh
33. Qi, Z., Wang, S., Su, C., Su, L., Huang, Q., Tian, Q.: Towards more explainability: concept knowledge mining network for event recognition. In: Proceedings of the ACM International Conference on Multimedia (ACM MM), pp. 3857–3865 (2020)
34. Qi, Z., Wang, S., Su, C., Su, L., Huang, Q., Tian, Q.: Self-regulated learning for egocentric video activity anticipation. IEEE Trans. Pattern Anal. Mach. Intell. (2021). https://doi.org/10.1109/TPAMI.2021.3059923

35. Qi, Z., Wang, S., Su, C., Su, L., Zhang, W., Huang, Q.: Modeling temporal concept receptive field dynamically for untrimmed video analysis. In: Proceedings of the ACM International Conference on Multimedia (ACM MM), pp. 3798–3806 (2020)
36. Sheng, F., et al.: Concept propagation via attentional knowledge graph reasoning for video-text retrieval. In: Proceedings of the 30th ACM International Conference on Multimedia (2022)
37. Snoek, C.G., Li, X., Xu, C., Koelma, D.C.: University of amsterdam and renmin university at trecvid 2017: searching video, detecting events and describing video. In: TRECVID (2017)
38. Song, Y., Soleymani, M.: Polysemous visual-semantic embedding for cross-modal retrieval. In: Proceedings of the IEEE/CVF Conference on Computer Vision and Pattern Recognition, pp. 1979–1988 (2019)
39. Ueki, K., Hirakawa, K., Kikuchi, K., Ogawa, T., Kobayashi, T.: Waseda_meisei at trecvid 2017: ad-hoc video search. In: TRECVID (2017)
40. Vaswani, A., et al.: Attention is all you need. Adv. Neural Inf. Process. Syst. **30**, 5998–6008 (2017)
41. Wang, L., Yoon, K.J.: Knowledge distillation and student-teacher learning for visual intelligence: a review and new outlooks. IEEE Trans. Pattern Anal. Mach. Intell. **44**, 3048–3068 (2021)
42. Wang, T., Zhang, R., Lu, Z., Zheng, F., Cheng, R., Luo, P.: End-to-end dense video captioning with parallel decoding. In: 2021 IEEE/CVF International Conference on Computer Vision, ICCV 2021, Montreal, QC, Canada, 10–17 October 2021, pp. 6827–6837. IEEE (2021). https://doi.org/10.1109/ICCV48922.2021.00677
43. Wang, X., Zhu, L., Yang, Y.: T2vlad: global-local sequence alignment for text-video retrieval. In: Proceedings of the IEEE/CVF Conference on Computer Vision and Pattern Recognition, pp. 5079–5088 (2021)
44. Wray, M., Larlus, D., Csurka, G., Damen, D.: Fine-grained action retrieval through multiple parts-of-speech embeddings. In: Proceedings of the IEEE/CVF International Conference on Computer Vision, pp. 450–459 (2019)
45. Yang, X., Dong, J., Cao, Y., Wang, X., Wang, M., Chua, T.: Tree-augmented cross-modal encoding for complex-query video retrieval. In: Huang, J., et al. (eds.) Proceedings of the 43rd International ACM SIGIR conference on research and development in Information Retrieval, SIGIR 2020, Virtual Event, China, 25–30 July 2020, pp. 1339–1348. ACM (2020). https://doi.org/10.1145/3397271.3401151

ASSISTER: Assistive Navigation via Conditional Instruction Generation

Zanming Huang, Zhongkai Shangguan(✉), Jimuyang Zhang, Gilad Bar, Matthew Boyd, and Eshed Ohn-Bar

Boston University, Boston, MA 02215, USA
{huangtom,sgzk,zhangjim,gbar,mcboyd,eohnbar}@bu.edu

Abstract. We introduce a novel vision-and-language navigation (VLN) task of learning to provide real-time guidance to a blind follower situated in complex dynamic navigation scenarios. Towards exploring real-time information needs and fundamental challenges in our novel modeling task, we first collect a multi-modal real-world benchmark with in-situ Orientation and Mobility (O&M) instructional guidance. Subsequently, we leverage the real-world study to inform the design of a larger-scale simulation benchmark, thus enabling comprehensive analysis of limitations in current VLN models. Motivated by how sighted O&M guides seamlessly and safely support the awareness of individuals with visual impairments when collaborating on navigation tasks, we present ASSISTER, an imitation-learned agent that can embody such effective guidance. The proposed assistive VLN agent is conditioned on navigational goals and commands for generating instructional sentences that are coherent with the surrounding visual scene, while also carefully accounting for the immediate assistive navigation task. Altogether, our introduced evaluation and training framework takes a step towards scalable development of the next generation of seamless, human-like assistive agents.

Keywords: Goal-driven instruction synthesis · Vision-and-language navigation · Assistive technologies · Visual impairment

1 Introduction

Embodied Vision-and-Language Navigation (VLN) tasks [5,6,64,84,85,94,105] generally *assume a sighted following agent*, i.e., a situated robot [40,54,57,78] or human [13,16,25,91] that is visually perceiving their immediate surroundings while interpreting instructions. As a result, the utility of current VLN systems in assisting *blind navigators* during complex and dynamic navigation is rarely explored, despite immense societal potential for improving the quality-of-life of blind individuals [55,58,75,96]. How well can current visually-grounded language generation methods, which are often studied in static indoor scenes

---

Z. Huang and Z. Shangguan—Equally contributed.

© The Author(s), under exclusive license to Springer Nature Switzerland AG 2022
S. Avidan et al. (Eds.): ECCV 2022, LNCS 13696, pp. 271–289, 2022.
https://doi.org/10.1007/978-3-031-20059-5_16

Fig. 1. Assistive Vision-and-Language Navigation (VLN) with a Situated Blind Walker. Our goal is to develop VLN agents that can consider the abilities of a blind walker when seamlessly providing task and safety-based contextual cues. Left: Real-world ego-centric image from the perspective of a blind participant in our dataset, with overlaid navigational instructions provided by an Orientation and Mobility (O&M) expert. Right: First-person view of a simulated pedestrian navigating an urban sidewalk with procedurally generated instructions overlaid.

with generic instructions [13,40,57], learn to consider the intricate task-driven and potentially dangerous process [12,28,51,74,79,81,95] of non-visual perception, decision-making, and exploration? Towards advancing the state-of-the-art of assistive VLN-based systems, we introduce diverse benchmarks and tools for training task and safety-critical agents that can collaborate with blind individuals (Fig. 1).

Currently, there are two key challenges hindering the scope and development of learning-based assistive navigation systems. First, the *difficulty and cost in obtaining sufficiently diverse data* for training robust assistive agents, i.e., through IRB-approved user-studies, is prohibitive. Consequently, current computer vision tasks related to navigation (e.g., human motion modeling [34,72]) provide limited insights in our context as they do not incorporate blind navigators. Constrained by practical considerations, assistive technology researchers have mostly pursued studies within constrained navigational settings [1,24,28,43,65,92] (e.g., basic navigational layouts, no dynamic pedestrians, minimal acoustic noise, etc.). Second, compared to current VLN tasks, the addition of factors related to non-visual reasoning and safety requires more *elaborate modeling of the information needs of the blind navigator* [3,9,32,42]. For example, Orientation and Mobility (O&M) experts undergo specialized training to go beyond generic instruction and effectively accommodate various needs across diverse settings [52,80]. Due to these inherent challenges, developing learning-based assistive systems for maintaining the real-time awareness of a blind agent to visual and tactile context across diverse settings remains a grand challenge [9,22,95,96,102].

Based on our survey of prior work in Sect. 2, we realized how the instructional guidance properties of assistive systems are also often manually set and hand-tuned in a somewhat cumbersome and setting-specific manner [3,9,28,31,32, 42]. Consequently, most aforementioned systems have been both developed and deployed within the same singular setting and fixed environment. In contrast, an O&M expert can flexibly provide seamless and safe guidance under arbitrary conditions, i.e., through comprehensive understanding of the needs of a blind navigator. In this work, we sought to develop a paradigm for endowing machines with similar capabilities, as described next.

Contributions: Towards facilitating robust, safe, and scalable assistive VLN systems, we make three key contributions: (1) We collect a real-world multi-modal benchmark with diverse in-situ interactions between O&M experts and blind navigators during navigation in dynamic urban settings. (2) We develop and analyze a corresponding simulation environment based on CARLA [19] that is informed by the real-world task. (3) We leverage the two benchmarks to uncover new insights regarding the instructional design space and the extent to which a state-of-the-art VLN model can learn to imitate expert sighted guides. Our benchmark and models are publicly available at https://github. com/h2xlab/ASSISTER. While we envision our findings to benefit individuals with visual impairments, our results translate towards developing expressive, safe, and less biased VLN agents that can robustly model what, when, and how guidance should be given to diverse end-users in real-time.

2   Related Work

Our goal is to understand and model the assistive VLN task in the context of navigation with blind walkers. Our work builds on recent advancements in visually-grounded language generation and assistive navigation, as described next.

Vision-and-Language Navigation: While most prior work has focused on the VLN task of instruction understanding and execution [6,11,20,21,45,47,56, 57,60,61,63,76,78,82,83,104], generic instruction generation [16,25,62,91] has recently received more attention with the introduction of suitable benchmarks (see Table 1). Recent advancements in this space aim to create more realistic instructional models, mostly set in static indoors setting [6,25,33,47,62,70,85], e.g., to find an item, or localization in outdoor environments [13,91]. Related to our work is the speaker-follower model of Fried et al. [25] where a speaker model is used for data augmentation and pragmatic selection of the most effective instructions. While relevant (our model can be interpreted as a speaker model), we learn our speaker model via imitation learning [64,67]. Moreover, our language space also includes more fine-grained obstacles and orientation directions. This enables us to empirically explore the optimal instructions to guide a blind navigator under safety-critical constraints and complex dynamic settings, i.e., beyond instruction following on the indoor R2R task [6]. In general, instructions in the aforementioned studies are also centered around visual cues, making this task inaccessible to individuals with vision impairments who may rely on spatial or tactile cues.

Table 1. Comparison with Related Benchmarks for VLN. Compared to other photo-realistic navigation-centered datasets, our datasets (UrbanWalk-Sim and UrbanWalk-Real) analyze contextual cues and guidance instructions for navigators who are blind (Blind). We also emphasize navigation involving dynamic obstacles (Dynamic) during outdoor scenarios (table marks In/Outdoor). We also note the number of samples in each dataset (Size) and source of the language annotations (Collection).

Dataset	Dynamic	In/Out	Real-World	Blind	Size	Collection
R2R [6]	✗	I	✓	✗	21,567	Crowdsourced
CVDN [85]	✗	I	✓	✗	7,000	Crowdsourced
REVERIE [70]	✗	I	✓	✗	21,702	Crowdsourced
Touchdown [13]	✓	O	✓	✗	9,326	Crowdsourced
Talk the Walk [91]	✓	O	✓	✗	10,000	Crowdsourced
RxR [48]	✗	I	✓	✗	126,069	Crowdsourced
WAY [37]	✗	I	✓	✗	6,154	Crowdsourced
UrbanWalk-Sim (Ours)	✓	O	✗	✓	399,126	Generated
UrbanWalk-Real (Ours)	✓	O	✓	✓	2,395	In-Situ

Visual Question Answering and Dialog: In Visual Question Answering (VQA), the inputted data may be a static image with a goal of understanding what is being asked through Natural Language Processing (NLP) and gathering information from visual cues to answer a specified question [7,41,71,99,100]. Recent studies have also developed two-sided dialog as an extension of VQA [17, 46,86,87]. VQA tasks have been recognized for its potential in assistive research as an aid for blind individuals [10,35,36]. While motivating to our study, our task focuses on how to navigate an individual from a current location to a target destination safely. Thus, we extend the concept of VQA to gather the visual information and communicate it via effective dialog to an individual who otherwise cannot utilize visual cues.

Orientation and Mobility Studies: In order to effectively guide blind individuals, accessibility researchers have long studied best navigational practices for people with visual impairments [96,97]. How to best support self-reliance, i.e., for everyday travel, is still an open research question [43,44,81,95]. While O&M guides can support the learning and memorization of a route [81], this is often a slow and lengthy process. Moreover, optimal real-time support in unfamiliar settings is challenging, due to factors such as cognitive load, dynamic obstacles, and ambient noise. This may explain some variability we find among the guides in our study. While there may not be universally accepted preferences among blind walkers due to various orientation and mobility skills [2,43], it is known that clock-based orientation descriptors are generally preferred [44]. We leverage such prior work when designing our instructions in simulation (Sect. 4.1) to ensure our models learn to support users' own mobility and orientation while collaborating effectively.

Assistive Navigation Technologies: There is extensive related research in designing non-AI assistive navigation technologies [24,28,30,65,68,77,92]. A relevant study is the work of Arditi et al.   [8], which demonstrates speech to be a preferred assistance modality due to the minimal initial training requirements. However, studies considering blind individuals are often performed in indoor environments with simplified route stimuli (e.g., narrow corridors, minimal obstacles, clear acoustics). Moreover, many current assistive technologies do not learn to generate instructions at all, but instead rely on extensive rule-based hand-engineered instruction, which may not generalize beyond simplified indoor environments with perfect perception and sparse route stimuli. In contrast, we aim to provide the foundations for future development of more human-like systems, i.e., systems that can seamlessly scale to operate in dynamic and real-world conditions. This goal motivates us to go beyond many prior assistive AI research tasks performed in simulation [23,69], and analyze naturalistic conditions with a real-world benchmark in Sect. 4.1 in addition to our simulation. Our study is motivated by the success of commercial real-time smartphone-based assistance apps that are based on an assistive remote human [4,59]. While very costly to use, the usability of such systems guides our real-world study design in Sect. 4.1. In particular, we outline a preliminary but highly scalable study design based on remote guidance. This design choice also supports model training from the limited perspective of a wearable assistive system.

3   Method

We introduce a task of learning to synthesize contextual and task-relevant natural language for guiding a blind follower. We emphasize that our VLN settings are inherently more complex compared to prior tasks (Table 1) which do not generally include real-time interaction with dynamic scenes. In this section, we first present our learning framework (Sect. 3.1) and novel ASSISTER model architecture (Sect. 3.2) for generating intuitive goal-conditional instructions. Subsequently, Sect. 4 introduces a novel benchmark with natural language from real-world O&M guides (Sect. 4.1) as well as procedurally generated instructions based on known information needs of blind walkers (Sect. 4.2).

3.1   Conditional Instruction Generation for Assistive Navigation

Problem Setting: We consider the task of learning instruction synthesis from observations $\mathbf{o} = [\mathbf{I}, \mathbf{p}_0, \mathbf{P}] \in \mathcal{O}$ comprising a front-view camera image $\mathbf{I}$, the current position and heading of the instruction follower $\mathbf{p}_0 \in \mathbb{R}^3$ (location and heading in map view), and a planned route $\mathbf{P} = [\mathbf{p}_1, \ldots, \mathbf{p}_K]$ specified in terms of positional waypoints towards a goal state. Our learning goal is to obtain a mapping function $f_\Theta : \mathcal{O} \rightarrow \mathcal{W}$, parameterized by $\Theta \in \mathbb{R}^l$, for generating a sequence of instructional tokens $\mathbf{w} = \{w_1, \ldots, w_M\} \in \mathcal{W}$ for guiding a follower along a planned route. In our study, we leverage ubiquitous GPS- and IMU-based localization to obtain location and heading estimates as well as employ A*

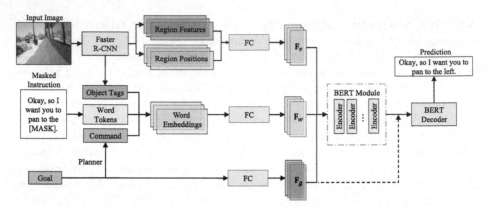

Fig. 2. ASSISTER Overview. The proposed model interlaces visual semantic, language, and goal-based features to carefully account for the immediate navigation task while maintaining situational awareness to surrounding context.

planning [38] to plan the high-level route. While our trained model should learn to account for inherent location noise in localization methods, more elaborate planning and localization schemes (e.g., SLAM [26]) are orthogonal to our study and are left for future work.

Imitating Expert Guides: As manually designing generalized assistance in dynamic and intricate real-world settings is challenging, our key insight is to leverage human-human interactions to design and train assistive VLN models. Thus, we assume access to a dataset with expert instructional guidance $\mathcal{D} = \{(\mathbf{o}_i, \mathbf{w}_i)\}_{i=1}^{N}$ in order to optimize f_Θ and generate intuitive instructions. Consequently, an instruction generation model can be trained by optimizing a behavior cloning [14,15,101,103] objective

$$\underset{\Theta}{\text{minimize}}\, \mathbb{E}_{(\mathbf{w},\mathbf{o}) \sim \mathcal{D}}\left[\mathcal{L}(\mathbf{w}, f_\Theta(\mathbf{o}))\right] \tag{1}$$

where $\mathcal{L}$ is a sequence prediction cross-entropy loss [49]. As Eq. 1 involves aligning high-dimensional vision and language semantics for task-driven navigation, it involves a challenging optimization task. In addition to leveraging supervision from expert guidance annotations, we alleviate training issues through a suitable model structure, discussed next.

3.2   Network Architecture

We introduce strong computer vision and language priors into our model architecture. The priors enable more efficient learning of integrating visual scene context with navigational and language reasoning when assisting a blind person. Our model comprises three main components: (i) a visual semantics feature extractor for obtaining an object-based embedding from an input image, (ii) a self-attention-based [89] language generation module that semantically aligns instructional language with visual context, and (iii) a goal-conditional module which integrates navigational task reasoning. The overall architecture is illustrated in Fig. 2.

Object-Based Visual Semantics Feature Extractor: Instead of optimizing f_Θ from raw images, we first extract rich object-based context using a pre-trained object detector. A Faster R-CNN [73] object detector with a ResNet-101 [39] backbone that is pre-trained on COCO [50] is used to extract and embed region features $\mathbf{F}_v \in \mathbb{R}^{50 \times 768}$ from the 50 highest scored regions in the image.

Language Generation Module: We integrate the visual embedding $\mathbf{F}_v$ with a state-of-the-art BERT language generation module [18,33,49,53]. The language module is pre-trained on a large language corpus following Li et al. [49] to facilitate natural human-like language synthesis. To further enable semantic image-language alignment, we follow [49] and extract word-based features $\mathbf{F}_w \in \mathbb{R}^{90 \times 768}$ from 30 explicit object tags, 20 commands and 40 instructional tokens for the current image. Based on BERT, the language module leverages a masked language objective where the model learns to recover masked instructional words from image and sentence context. Note that during inference the model sequentially infers instructional words, i.e., without access to ground truth instructional words.

Goal-Conditional Module: In our domain, safe and seamless navigation pivots on the ability of the model to perform extensive goal-based reasoning. To guide a blind follower in diverse settings, our instruction synthesis model must carefully consider the navigation goal to convey to blind followers only task-relevant surrounding information at any given moment. We therefore interlace goal-based features throughout the entire visually-grounded language generation process. We incorporate a goal embedding $\mathbf{F}_g \in \mathbb{R}^{768}$ computed based on a relative goal vector $\mathbf{g} \in \mathbb{R}^2$ to a near-range (five meters) waypoint along the planned route. We note that our assumption of knowledge of relative position and heading to a goal is standard when learning real-world vision-based navigation, e.g., [14,15,66].

Command-Conditional Module: In addition to the goal embedding, we propose to also leverage navigation commands generated from a *future planned path* to ease the learning of alignment among modalities. Specifically, we directly input the model with conditional navigational commands obtained via a path planner (e.g., 'turn left,' 'forward'). We input the commands as word tokens prior to computing the aligned word-based features $\mathbf{F}_w$. In this manner, the model can learn to generate natural goal-driven instructional sentences that are not only coherent with a visual scene but also account for the immediate navigation task.

4   The UrbanWalk Benchmark

Despite ample publicly available language benchmarks, there are no current datasets suitable for model training and evaluation of timely, safety-critical, and ability-aware navigation guidance to blind followers. Moreover, prior VLN tasks tend to leverage human-written instructions in simulations and not relevant instructions for providing in-situ navigation cues. Towards exploring real-time information needs and fundamental challenges in our novel modeling task, we collect the first multi-modal real-world benchmark with recorded O&M instructional guidance in dynamic urban walking navigation settings (Sect. 4.1). Subsequently, we leverage the real-world study to inform the design of a larger-scale simulation-based benchmark (Sect. 4.2) and comprehensively analyze limitations in current VLN models across diverse scenarios (e.g., harsh weathers, geographical locations, etc.). Altogether, the two datasets are used to produce complementary analysis while tackling inherent issues in safety, cost, and scalability of real-world data collection with blind participants.

4.1   Real-World Benchmark

Although VLN tasks are often studied in simulated settings, realistically simulating interactions between a blind walker, their surroundings (e.g., acoustics, objects), and an expert guide is not trivial. Hence, we pursued a real-world study to ensure our models and findings are relevant to practical navigation scenarios.

Study Design: Our IRB-approved study was kept close to others in the field in terms of participant pool and mobility aids [24]. However, we are the first to collect synchronized multi-modal camera and sensor data together with their *corresponding in-situ expert instructional guidance.* We recruited 13 participants through the mailing list of a local blind individuals services center, including 10 blind and three O&M guides (to analyze expert diversity). To train our imitation learning-based assistive agent in Sect. 3.1, we sought to collect video and sensor measurements during blind navigation in real-world urban scenes with expert guidance *from the perspective of an assistive system,* i.e., a first-person camera. Therefore, in order to capture naturalistic navigation behavior and real-world challenges associated with assistive technologies, we opted for a remote guidance solution. While the limited perspective incorporates a practical challenge, this study design choice also lends to scalability due to minimal mount configuration, ease of data collection, and ultimate large-scale deployments on commodity devices, e.g., smartphones.

Navigation Task: We asked the blind participants to navigate an unfamiliar 110m planned route through a busy business district with typical weekday traffic, including pedestrians, vehicles, and shops. We ensured control for confounding factors: participants were called on different days and on varying hours. The equipment included a 5G smartphone, an additional GoPro camera mounted to a chest harness, and a Bluetooth bone-conducting headset to provide instructions without hindering acoustic reasoning. GPS, IMU, audio, and camera data were all captured synchronously. We note that the restricted forward view provided by a chest-mounted camera rarely provided a complete view of the surroundings and potential obstacles. This necessitated crucial collaboration between the blind navigator and the guide, an interactive functionality that we wish to embody in

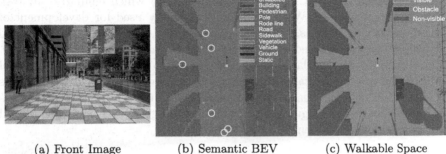

(a) Front Image   (b) Semantic BEV   (c) Walkable Space

Fig. 3. Simulation Visualization. We visualize (a) first-person view of a virtual walker, (b) corresponding BEV with semantics overlay, with a yellow square indicating the current position and heading of the walker (circles indicate surrounding pedestrians), and (c) walkable space computed from the semantic BEV. We then sample goals randomly, plan a path in walkable space, and generate contextualized instructional guidance from the path and semantic BEV objects. (Color figure online)

our assistive agent. For instance, in order to gather sufficient visual information for safe navigation the expert may ask the navigator to stop and scan the environment by rotating their torso to pan and tilt the camera. Audio transcription was performed in a semi-automatic manner, initially with Google's Speech-to-Text [29] followed by manual verification and error correction.

Dataset: We extract a total of 2,395 interactions (on average, there are 21.7 words per instruction) from the continuous data stream. Example conversational language from the dataset for supporting guidance and situational awareness include:

> *"Okay, you're going to walk directly to the street and there's going to be a detectable curb. This is a cross-walk."*

> *"Good job, You're passing some bushes on the right. You might contact those with your body."*

> *"I'm going to have you turn to the right, so I can see that area."*

In addition to route-based instructions, we find the naturalistic instructions to regularly employ cues related the spatial layout, obstacles, and information gathering.

4.2   Simulation Benchmark

In our analysis, we sought to fully capture the complexity of naturalistic real-world in-situ interaction. However, despite our attempt towards a more scalable study design, real-world data collection is inherently limited with issues of safety, cost, and data diversity. We therefore supplement our analysis by leveraging a simulation (based on the CARLA environment [19]) which emulates our task without such constraints. While CARLA is typically used for development of autonomous driving policies, we modify the environment to collect instructional guidance and a sidewalk pedestrian perspective in various weathers and towns. In particular, we use the large synthetic dataset to rigorously analyze model limitations across ample standardized data and more diverse visual conditions (e.g., new towns, harsh weathers). Nonetheless, we use the real-world navigational data (Sect. 4.1) to guide our simulation design as well as draw general conclusions among both benchmarks.

Procedural Instruction Generation: To collect a large simulation benchmark, we procedurally generate instructional guidance. We spawn navigating pedestrians and capture a first-person image perspective together with complete ground-truth information of surrounding landmarks and obstacles (i.e., 3D location of buildings, pedestrians, sidewalks, trees, etc.). Given a current walker position, a sampled goal, and a constructed Bird's-Eye-View (BEV) image, we extract walkable space and obtain a path using A* planning [38] a visualization of this process is shown in Fig. 3). We then employ the planned path to construct instructional sentences. We contextualize the instructions by extracting surrounding obstacle information from the BEV along the path and inform regarding obstacles in proximity (e.g., pedestrians, building). While this process can be used to generate standardized instructions, we leverage insights from our real-world study together with prior literature in orientation and mobility strategies [9,44,81,81,95] to consider relevant navigation strategies and immediate information needs. For instance, we leverage clock orientation to indicate turning which has been found to be more intuitive for blind users [44].

5   Experiments

Our goal is to facilitate assistive systems at scale, we emphasize model generalization across various settings and instructional guidance. In this section, we comprehensively analyze our assistive VLN task through the introduced benchmarks and task-conditional ASSISTER model.

5.1   Experimental Setup

CARLA [19] is not generally used to study instruction generation with navigators along the sidewalk. Next, we detail our data split strategy, including weather and ambient factors.

We use Town 5 of the simulation for collecting training data and Town 10 for testing. We randomly spawn pedestrians and goals in dense settings [15]. While we avoided harsh rain conditions due to safety concerns in the real-world data, it does contain natural variations in weather (including sunny weather and two sessions in slight rain conditions). While the real-world data is smaller in size, it also contains significant variability and diversity in the naturalistic instructions. We thus analyze a participant-based split. The overall event distribution

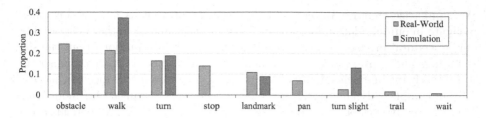

Fig. 4. Data Statistics. We cluster natural language instructions into types to present a high-level analysis of events among the two introduced datasets.

in the datasets is depicted in Fig. 4. To facilitate meaningful analysis over the conversational nature of the real-world instructions, Fig. 4 plots a distribution of clustered instructions by types.

Language-Based Metrics: We follow standard language evaluation using BLEU-4, CIDEr, and SPICE [85,90,91,104] metrics. We note that BLEU-4 is an n-gram based metric that puts equal weights to all words in a given sentences (including pronouns and connective words). Hence, it may be less relevant to our goal-driven navigation task, and is kept as reference. The recent work of Zhao et al. [104] suggests SPICE may be correlated with human wayfinding performance. However our overall navigation settings significantly differ from [104]. For instance, SPICE may be limited for our novel task due to its semantic graph which fails to properly generalize to our instructional context. Specifically, SPICE may fail to account for small but task-relevant changes in guidance, such as changing 'two,' in 'turn to two,' to 'ten.' In contrast, CIDEr identifies informative n-grams in the data from computed term-frequencies. This gives lower weight to more common n-grams, since they are likely to contain less information. Among the standard evaluation metrics we used, we qualitatively found CIDEr to produce slightly better results for our task, as it puts less emphasis on non-key words that occurs frequently appears across instructions such as 'to' and 'your,' while giving more weight to less frequent informative directional words such as 'left' and 'right.' Nonetheless, the two metrics are generally correlated based on our results.

Task-Based Interactive Evaluation: Offline language-based evaluation metrics (e.g., CIDEr, SPICE) may not fully account for our sequentially interactive assistive navigation task [104]. For instance, errors in small but critical components of an instruction (e.g., confusion of 'left' with 'right') could have large impact on the ultimate success of the navigation task. While we take a first step towards learned guidance models, several key challenges in safety and model robustness must still be tackled before real-world usability testing with ASSISTER can be performed. To provide further insights into interactive task-based model evaluation, we instead turn to our simulation environment and perform a user study with seven participants navigating routes in a blind simulation. To simulate blind navigation, only coarse orientation with noise up to 15°C and collision information is presented as participants following audio instructions.

We emphasize that **no image of the scene is shown** as human controllers navigate in our simulation in real-time. The instructions are either generated by our procedural process (i.e., employing ground truth information about the surroundings and route) or sampled from the proposed model. In this manner, we can directly evaluate the ability of the model to guide to a goal location successfully in complex, dynamic, and previously unseen test settings. Our model runs at about ten frames per second on a desktop with GeForce RTX 2080 Ti, which is sufficient given the time it takes to produce and follow instructions. Moreover, participants can also press a keyboard key in order to query the model as needed. We first familiarize the participants with the walker physics through several short training episodes where front-view image is available. We then evaluate participant route following behavior in our New Town and Weather test settings without image information. Following standard evaluation of navigation agents [19], we also timeout episodes beyond five minutes. To better understand model performance and limitations, we leverage our interactive simulation in a preliminary study which enables us to safely obtain metrics related to Success Rate (SR), Route Completion (RC), and Navigation Error (NE) [93]. We also report the average number of model queries by the human controller (per minute) and collision counts.

5.2 Results

To uncover challenges in our novel task and benchmark, we perform three main experiments. First, we evaluate the role of various inputs to the model on instruction generation and generalization in simulation. Second, we analyze model performance in the real-world data. Third, we analyze task-based performance of humans following instructions in a blind simulation.

Instruction Generation in Simulation: Table 2 analyzes model generalization across seen and unseen settings of new town and harsh weather conditions. Standard deviation results are shown over training runs. We also compare to two main baselines, OSCAR [49] and the Hard-Attention LSTM model of Xu et al. [98]. The results demonstrate the benefits of incorporating command-conditional input to the model when generating task-relevant navigational guidance. Specifically, we find our proposed conditional module to significantly outperform a goal-only ASSISTER model (only the goal vector fused into the model before and after the BERT decoder) across evaluation settings. While the trends are generally consistent across the language-based metrics, our findings demonstrate the overall challenging nature of our task. We also find weather and geographical perturbations to degrade performance of the model, in particular to unseen weathers. Given these insights, we now turn to study the models in our real-world dataset.

Instruction Generation in the Real-World: The real-world contains significantly more walker and guidance diversity due to the complex scenes and freeform instructional guidance. As shown in Table 3, this results in a significantly a challenging modeling task. While simulated data lacks realism, the

Table 2. Simulation Instruction Generation Results. Ablative results over ASSISTER model inputs, language metrics, and test conditions.

Model Input	Training Conditions			New Town			New Town and Weather		
	BLEU-4	CIDEr	SPICE	BLEU-4	CIDEr	SPICE	BLEU-4	CIDEr	SPICE
Xu et al. [98]	10.18 ± 0.03	15.46 ± 0.05	7.66 ± 0.02	6.81 ± 0.04	18.96 ± 0.05	6.39 ± 0.12	8.36 ± 0.01	15.19 ± 0.04	8.72 ± 0.06
OSCAR [49]	10.68 ± 0.04	17.63 ± 0.10	24.77 ± 0.03	9.25 ± 0.06	14.89 ± 0.07	21.30 ± 0.11	9.96 ± 0.01	11.94 ± 0.01	22.02 ± 0.16
ASSISTER (Goal Module)	10.58 ± 0.02	16.97 ± 0.03	23.98 ± 0.02	9.45 ± 0.01	14.49 ± 0.01	18.69 ± 0.07	9.97 ± 0.01	11.16 ± 0.01	19.56 ± 0.04
ASSISTER (Goal+Command Module)	**15.49 ± 0.03**	**23.58 ± 0.04**	**26.31 ± 0.01**	**12.81 ± 1.09**	**19.93 ± 0.51**	**18.63 ± 2.24**	**13.88 ± 0.61**	**19.61 ± 2.51**	**21.88 + 0.17**

Table 3. Real-World Instruction Generation Results. Ablative results over ASSISTER model variants, language metrics, and evaluation settings.

Model	Cross-Subject		
	BLEU-4	CIDEr	SPICE
Xu et al. [98]	0.00 ± 0.00	1.17 ± 0.54	1.31 ± 0.55
OSCAR [49]	2.40 ± 0.65	10.47 ± 2.09	8.89 ± 1.58
ASSISTER (Goal Module)	2.43 ± 0.36	10.42 ± 2.36	8.98 ± 1.54
ASSISTER (Goal+Command Module)	**2.50 ± 0.36**	**10.74 ± 3.47**	**9.14 ± 1.47**

resulting models suggest that our designed instructions in simulation are realistic. For instance, Table 3 shows generally similar trends to Table 2. Nonetheless, both CIDEr and SPICE are shown to be degraded, with the best performing model resulting in a 10.74 and 9.14 accuracy, respectively. There are several reasons that explain the low overall performance. First, there are natural variations among the guides when providing instructional context. Current language-based evaluation metrics cannot properly account for such variations. This challenge also motivated us to pursue a task-driven evaluation as a final experiment. Second, guides are able to accurately reason over scene acoustics and walker behavior. Integrating such information requires further study in the future. As safely generating instructions in the real-world is still beyond reach, we now turn to evaluation of the instruction generation model in simulation.

Task-Based Evaluation in Simulation: We do not deploy our models in real-world settings with blind users to generate on-policy task-based evaluation. While task-based evaluation is the most informative, current state-of-the-art VLN models cannot be safely evaluated in closed-loop real-time scenarios with blind followers. Instead, we design an interactive blind simulation experiment by removing all visual display. Such closed-loop evaluation is critical in term of assistive navigation and highlights the benefits of the introduced simulation environment. Compared with the baseline model, our ASSISTER achieves high improvement in terms of success rate, route completion and navigation errors, indicating the effectiveness of the proposed method. We note that live navigation in the simulation without any visual feedback results in a highly challenging task. We therefore also benchmark our ground truth procedural generation process. The high route completion score (98.6%) further validates our instruction generation process in simulation. We also note that the baseline model of

Table 4. Task-based Evaluation in Simulation. Navigation following performance of humans in an interactive blind simulation. We show results using ASSISTER-based and ground-truth (using our procedural BEV-based instruction generation process), highlighting the challenging nature of our task. We show the average number of queries from the human walker, per minute, as well as collision events frequency with 'D' (dynamic obstacles, pedestrians) and 'S' (static obstacles).

Model	SR↑	RC↑	NE↓	Queries/min↓	Collision-D↓	Collision-S↓
Xu et al. [98]	9.52	46.3	3.53	11.31	**1.67**	**6.0**
ASSISTER	**38.1**	**74.1**	**2.72**	**8.65**	2.14	14.0
Ground Truth	90.5	98.6	1.02	7.92	1.71	3.10

Xu et al. exhibits lower collision rates. However, this is partly due to frequent veering from the planned path to open spaces with less obstacles. Moreover, despite the low success rate for ASSISTER (38.1%), the high route completion results (74.1%) suggest generally suitable instructions are provided to the participants. However, timeouts can occur due to veering off the path as well, which partly contributes to the low success rate. Another main limitation is in the lack of realism of the walker, which can sense acoustic, motion and spatial properties in the real-world. While the process in which a blind person interprets and reacts to surrounding environmental properties and guidance cognitive load is complex [27,88], realizing such reasoning in simulation is still a current open problem and a potential future direction. While our simulation study take a first step towards robust and scalable instruction generation, future improvements can result in additional real-world validation (Table 4).

6   Conclusion

Our goal is to enable scalable assistive VLN models that can seamlessly and safely guide across diverse walkers and environments. In our study, we tackle learning-based assistive navigation systems through a novel data-driven framework, tools, and analysis. We demonstrate our novel spoken guidance task to provide a challenging setting for VLN models, both in real-world and simulated environments. As future work, transferring models trained in simulation to the real-world could further alleviate issues in cumbersome, costly, and potentially safety-critical real-world studies performed with participants who are blind. Given the potential impact of acoustic properties of the scene on navigation, a next step could explore generalization of the proposed ASSISTER model to include such inputs. While current VLN models and assistive systems do not yet consider acoustic properties, our data can facilitate such models as it was collected in busy urban settings with ambient noise. We kept such data in our experiments in order to ensure our analysis extend to real-world scenarios and usability. Finally, while the participant size is representative of the upper limit of previous studies in accessibility, future studies can replicate our scalable study design to collect data from additional locations and environments. While data can be scarce in our application context, this can facilitate further exploration into the intricate interdependence between a vision-based system and a situated blind navigator.

Acknowledgments. We thank our study participants and the support of the Department of Transportation Inclusive Design Challenge, NSF (IIS-2152077), and a Boston University CISE grant.

References

1. Ahmetovic, D., Gleason, C., Ruan, C., Kitani, K., Takagi, H., Asakawa, C.: NavCog: a navigational cognitive assistant for the blind. In: MobileHCI (2016)
2. Ahmetovic, D., Guerreiro, J., Ohn-Bar, E., Kitani, K.M., Asakawa, C.: Impact of expertise on interaction preferences for navigation assistance of visually impaired individuals. In: W4A (2019)
3. Ahmetovic, D., et al.: Achieving practical and accurate indoor navigation for people with visual impairments. In: W4A (2017)
4. Aira: aira app. https://aira.io/
5. Anderson, P., et al.: On evaluation of embodied navigation agents. arXiv (2018)
6. Anderson, P., et al.: Vision-and-language navigation: interpreting visually-grounded navigation instructions in real environments. In: CVPR (2018)
7. Antol, S., Agrawal, A., Lu, J., Mitchell, M., Batra, D., Zitnick, C.L., Parikh, D.: VQA: visual question answering. In: ICCV (2015)
8. Arditi, A., Tian, Y.: User interface preferences in the design of a camera-based navigation and wayfinding aid. J. Vis. Impairment Blindness **107**(2), 118–129 (2013)
9. Banovic, N., Franz, R.L., Truong, K.N., Mankoff, J., Dey, A.K.: Uncovering information needs for independent spatial learning for users who are visually impaired. In: ASSETS (2013)
10. Bigham, J.P., et al.: VizWiz: nearly real-time answers to visual questions. In: UIST (2010)
11. Blukis, V., Paxton, C., Fox, D., Garg, A., Artzi, Y.: A persistent spatial semantic representation for high-level natural language instruction execution. arXiv (2021)
12. Brady, E.L., Sato, D., Ruan, C., Takagi, H., Asakawa, C.: Exploring interface design for independent navigation by people with visual impairments. In: ASSETS (2015)
13. Chen, H.,et al.: Touchdown: natural language navigation and spatial reasoning in visual street environments. In: CVPR (2019)
14. Codevilla, F., Müller, M., López, A., Koltun, V., Dosovitskiy, A.: End-to-end driving via conditional imitation learning. In: ICRA (2018)
15. Codevilla, F., Santana, E., López, A.M., Gaidon, A.: Exploring the limitations of behavior cloning for autonomous driving. In: ICCV (2019)
16. Daniele, A.F., Bansal, M., Walter, M.R.: Navigational instruction generation as inverse reinforcement learning with neural machine translation. In: HRI (2017)
17. Das, A., et al.: Visual dialog. In: CVPR (2017)
18. Devlin, J., Chang, M.W., Lee, K., Toutanova, K.: BERT: pre-training of deep bidirectional transformers for language understanding. In: ACL (2018)

19. Dosovitskiy, A., Ros, G., Codevilla, F., Lopez, A., Koltun, V.: CARLA: an open urban driving simulator. In: CoRL (2017)
20. Duvallet, F., Kollar, T., Stentz, A.: Imitation learning for natural language direction following through unknown environments. In: ICRA (2013)
21. Duvallet, F., et al.: Inferring maps and behaviors from natural language instructions. In: Hsieh, M.A., Khatib, O., Kumar, V. (eds.) Experimental Robotics. STAR, vol. 109, pp. 373–388. Springer, Cham (2016). https://doi.org/10.1007/978-3-319-23778-7_25
22. Easley, W., et al.: Let's get lost: exploring social norms in predominately blind environments. In: CHI (2016)
23. Erickson, Z., Gangaram, V., Kapusta, A., Liu, C.K., Kemp, C.C.: Assistive gym: a physics simulation framework for assistive robotics. ICRA (2020)
24. Fallah, N., Apostolopoulos, I., Bekris, K., Folmer, E.: Indoor human navigation systems: a survey. Interact. Comput. 25(1), 21–33 (2013)
25. Fried, D., et al.: Speaker-follower models for vision-and-language navigation. In: NeurIPS (2018)
26. Fuentes-Pacheco, J., Ruiz-Ascencio, J., Rendón-Mancha, J.M.: Visual simultaneous localization and mapping: a survey. Artif. Intell. Rev. 43(1), 55–81 (2015). https://doi.org/10.1007/s10462-012-9365-8
27. Geruschat, D.R., Turano, K.A., Stahl, J.W.: Traditional measures of mobility performance and retinitis pigmentosa. Optom. Vis. Sci. 75(7), 525–537 (1998)
28. Giudice, N.A., Legge, G.E.: Blind navigation and the role of technology. In: The Engineering Handbook of Smart Technology for Aging, Disability, and Independence (2008)
29. Google: Google speech-to-text. https://cloud.google.com/speech-to-text
30. Granquist, C., Sun, S.Y., Montezuma, S.R., Tran, T.M., Gage, R., Legge, G.E.: Evaluation and comparison of artificial intelligence vision aids: orcam myeye 1 and seeing AI. J. Vis. Impairment Blindness 115(4), 277–285 (2021)
31. Guerreiro, J., Ahmetovic, D., Sato, D., Kitani, K., Asakawa, C.: Airport accessibility and navigation assistance for people with visual impairments. In: CHI (2019)
32. Guerreiro, J., Ohn-Bar, E., Ahmetovic, D., Kitani, K., Asakawa, C.: How context and user behavior affect indoor navigation assistance for blind people. In: W4A (2018)
33. Guhur, P.L., Tapaswi, M., Chen, S., Laptev, I., Schmid, C.: Airbert: In-domain pretraining for vision-and-language navigation. In: ICCV (2021)
34. Gupta, A., Johnson, J., Fei-Fei, L., Savarese, S., Alahi, A.: Social GAN: socially acceptable trajectories with generative adversarial networks. In: CVPR (2018)
35. Gurari, D., et al.: VizWiz-Priv: A dataset for recognizing the presence and purpose of private visual information in images taken by blind people. In: CVPR (2019)
36. Gurari, D., et al.: VizWiz grand challenge: answering visual questions from blind people. In: CVPR (2018)
37. Hahn, M., Krantz, J., Batra, D., Parikh, D., Rehg, J.M., Lee, S., Anderson, P.: Where are you? localization from embodied dialog (2020)
38. Hart, P.E., Nilsson, N.J., Raphael, B.: A formal basis for the heuristic determination of minimum cost paths. IEEE Trans. Syst. Sci. Cybern. 4(2), 100–107 (1968)
39. He, K., Zhang, X., Ren, S., Sun, J.: Deep residual learning for image recognition. In: CVPR (2016)
40. Hu, Z., Pan, J., Fan, T., Yang, R., Manocha, D.: Safe navigation with human instructions in complex scenes. IEEE Robot. Autom. Lett. 4(2), 753–760 (2019)

41. Hudson, D.A., Manning, C.D.: GQA: a new dataset for compositional question answering over real-world images. In: CVPR (2019)
42. Kacorri, H., Kitani, K.M., Bigham, J.P., Asakawa, C.: People with visual impairment training personal object recognizers: feasibility and challenges. In: CHI (2017)
43. Kacorri, H., Mascetti, S., Gerino, A., Ahmetovic, D., Takagi, H., Asakawa, C.: Supporting orientation of people with visual impairment: analysis of large scale usage data. In: ASSETS (2016)
44. Kamikubo, R., Kato, N., Higuchi, K., Yonetani, R., Sato, Y.: Support strategies for remote guides in assisting people with visual impairments for effective indoor navigation. In: CHI (2020)
45. Kollar, T., Tellex, S., Roy, D., Roy, N.: Toward understanding natural language directions. In: HRI (2010)
46. Kottur, S., Moura, J.M.F., Parikh, D., Batra, D., Rohrbach, M.: CLEV-dialog: a diagnostic dataset for multi-round reasoning in visual dialog. In: NAACL (2019)
47. Krantz, J., Gokaslan, A., Batra, D., Lee, S., Maksymets, O.: Waypoint models for instruction-guided navigation in continuous environments. In: ICCV (2021)
48. Ku, A., Anderson, P., Patel, R., Ie, E., Baldridge, J.: Room-across-room: multilingual vision-and-language navigation with dense spatiotemporal grounding (2020)
49. LI, X., et al.: OSCAR: object-semantics aligned pre-training for vision-language tasks. In: Vedaldi, A., Bischof, H., Brox, T., Frahm, J.-M. (eds.) ECCV 2020. LNCS, vol. 12375, pp. 121–137. Springer, Cham (2020). https://doi.org/10.1007/978-3-030-58577-8_8
50. Lin, T.Y., et al.: Microsoft COCO: common objects in context. In: Fleet, D., Pajdla, T., Schiele, B., Tuytelaars, T. (eds.) ECCV 2014. LNCS, vol. 8693, pp. 740–755. Springer, Cham (2014). https://doi.org/10.1007/978-3-319-10602-1_48
51. Liu, G., et al.: Tactile compass: enabling visually impaired people to follow a path with continuous directional feedback. In: CHI (2021)
52. Long, R.G., Hill, E.: Establishing and maintaining orientation for mobility. Found. Orientation Mobility, 1 (1997)
53. Lu, J., Batra, D., Parikh, D., Lee, S.: ViLBERT: pretraining task-agnostic visiolinguistic representations for Vision-and-Language Tasks. In: NeurIPS (2019)
54. Savva, M., et al.: Habitat: a platform for embodied AI research. arXiv (2019)
55. Marston, J.R., Golledge, R.G.: The hidden demand for participation in activities and travel by persons who are visually impaired. J. Vis. Impairment Blindness 97(8), 475–488 (2003)
56. Matuszek, C., FitzGerald, N., Zettlemoyer, L., Bo, L., Fox, D.: A joint model of language and perception for grounded attribute learning. In: ICML (2012)
57. Matuszek, C., Herbst, E., Zettlemoyer, L., Fox, D.: Learning to parse natural language commands to a robot control system. In: Desai, J., Dudek, G., Khatib, O., Kumar, V. (eds.) Experimental Robotics. Springer Tracts in Advanced Robotics, vol. 88, pp. 403–415, Springer, Heidelberg (2013). https://doi.org/10.1007/978-3-319-00065-7_28
58. Maunder, D., Venter, C., Rickert, T., Sentinella, J.: Improving transport access and mobility for people with disabilities. In: CILT (2004)
59. Microsoft: seeing AI app from microsoft. https://www.microsoft.com/en-us/ai/seeing-ai
60. Misra, D., Bennett, A., Blukis, V., Niklasson, E., Shatkhin, M., Artzi, Y.: Mapping instructions to actions in 3D environments with visual goal prediction. In: EMNLP (2018)

61. Misra, D.K., Sung, J., Lee, K., Saxena, A.: Tell me DAVE: context sensitive grounding of natural language to mobile manipulation instructions. In: RSS (2014)
62. Moudgil, A., Majumdar, A., Agrawal, H., Lee, S., Batra, D.: SOAT: a scene- and object-aware transformer for vision-and-language navigation. In: NeurIPS (2021)
63. Narasimhan, K., Kulkarni, T.D., Barzilay, R.: Language understanding for textbased games using deep reinforcement learning. In: EMNLP (2015)
64. Nguyen, K., Dey, D., Brockett, C., Dolan, B.: Vision-based navigation with language-based assistance via imitation learning with indirect intervention. In: CVPR (2019)
65. Ohn-Bar, E., Kitani, K., Asakawa, C.: Personalized dynamics models for adaptive assistive navigation systems. In: CoRL (2018)
66. Ohn-Bar, E., Prakash, A., Behl, A., Chitta, K., Geiger, A.: Learning situational driving. In: CVPR (2020)
67. Osa, T., Pajarinen, J., Neumann, G., Bagnell, J.A., Abbeel, P., Peters, J.: An algorithmic perspective on imitation learning. arXiv (2018)
68. Peng, H., Song, G., You, J., Zhang, Y., Lian, J.: An indoor navigation service robot system based on vibration tactile feedback. Int. J. Soc. Robot. **9**(3), 331–341 (2017)
69. Puig, X., et al.: Watch-and-help: a challenge for social perception and human-ai collaboration. In: ICLR (2021)
70. Qi, Y., Wu, Q., Anderson, P., Liu, M., Shen, C., van den Hengel, A.: Reverie: remote embodied referring expressions in real indoor environments. In: CVPR (2020)
71. Ramakrishnan, S., Agrawal, A., Lee, S.: Overcoming language priors in visual question answering with adversarial regularization. In: NeurIPS (2018)
72. Rasouli, A., Kotseruba, I., Kunic, T., Tsotsos, J.K.: Pie: A large-scale dataset and models for pedestrian intention estimation and trajectory prediction. In: ICCV (2019)
73. Ren, S., He, K., Girshick, R., Sun, J.: Faster R-CNN: towards real-time object detection with region proposal networks. In: NeurIPS (2015)
74. Rieser, J.J., Guth, D., Hill, E.: Mental processes mediating independent travel: implications for orientation and mobility. J. Vis. Impairment Blindness **76**(6), 213–218 (1982)
75. Roberts, P.W., Babinard, J.: Transport strategy to improve accessibility in developing countries (2004)
76. Roh, J., Paxton, C., Pronobis, A., Farhadi, A., Fox, D.: Conditional driving from natural language instructions. In: CoRL (2020)
77. Sato, D., Oh, U., Naito, K., Takagi, H., Kitani, K., Asakawa, C.: Navcog3: an evaluation of a smartphone-based blind indoor navigation assistant with semantic features in a large-scale environment. In: ASSETS (2017)
78. Scheutz, M., Krause, E.A., Oosterveld, B., Frasca, T.M., Platt, R.W.: Spoken instruction-based one-shot object and action learning in a cognitive robotic architecture. In: AAMAS (2017)
79. Schinazi, V.R., Thrash, T., Chebat, D.R.: Spatial navigation by congenitally blind individuals. In: Cognitive Science, Wiley Interdisciplinary Reviews (2016)
80. Soong, G.P., Lovie-Kitchin, J.E., Brown, B.: Does mobility performance of visually impaired adults improve immediately after orientation and mobility training? Optom. Vis. Sci. **78**(9), 657–666 (2001)
81. Strelow, E.R.: What is needed for a theory of mobility: direct perceptions and cognitive maps-lessons from the blind. Psychol. Rev. **92**(2), 226 (1985)

82. Tellex, S., Knepper, R.A., Li, A., Rus, D., Roy, N.: Asking for help using inverse semantics. In: RSS (2014)
83. Tellex, S., et al.: Understanding natural language commands for robotic navigation and mobile manipulation. In: AAAI (2011)
84. Thomason, J., Gordan, D., Bisk, Y.: Shifting the baseline: single modality performance on visual navigation & QA. In: NAACL (2019)
85. Thomason, J., Murray, M., Cakmak, M., Zettlemoyer, L.: Vision-and-dialog navigation. In: CoRL (2019)
86. Thomason, J., et al.: Improving grounded natural language understanding through human-robot dialog. In: ICRA (2019)
87. Thomason, J., Zhang, S., Mooney, R., Stone, P.: Learning to interpret natural language commands through human-robot dialog. In: IJCAI (2015)
88. Turano, K., Geruschat, D., Stahl, J.W.: Mental effort required for walking: effects of retinitis pigmentosa. Optom. Vis. Sci. **75**(12), 879–886 (1998)
89. Vaswani, A., et al.: Attention is all you need. In: NeurIPS (2017)
90. Vedantam, R., Zitnick, C., Parikh, D.: Cider: Consensus-based image description evaluation. In: CVPR (2015)
91. de Vries, H., Shuster, K., Batra, D., Parikh, D., Weston, J., Kiela, D.: Talk the walk: navigating New York city through grounded dialogue (2018)
92. Wang, H.C., Katzschmann, R.K., Teng, S., Araki, B., Giarré, L., Rus, D.: Enabling independent navigation for visually impaired people through a wearable vision-based feedback system. In: ICRA (2017)
93. Wang, S., et al.: Less is more: generating grounded navigation instructions from landmarks. arXiv (2021)
94. Wang, X., et al.: Reinforced cross-modal matching and self-supervised imitation learning for vision-language navigation. In: CVPR (2019)
95. Williams, M.A., Galbraith, C., Kane, S.K., Hurst, A.: "just let the cane hit it" how the blind and sighted see navigation differently. In: ASSETS (2014)
96. Williams, M.A., Hurst, A., Kane, S.K.: " pray before you step out" describing personal and situational blind navigation behaviors. In: ASSETS (2013)
97. Wong, S.: Traveling with blindness: A qualitative space-time approach to understanding visual impairment and urban mobility. Health Place **49**, 85–92 (2018)
98. Xu, K., et al.: Show, attend and tell: neural image caption generation with visual attention. In: ICML, pp. 2048–2057. PMLR (2015)
99. Yi, K., Wu, J., Gan, C., Torralba, A., Kohli, P., Tenenbaum, J.B.: Neural-symbolic VQA: disentangling reasoning from vision and language understanding. In: NeurIPS (2018)
100. Zellers, R., Bisk, Y., Farhadi, A., Choi, Y.: From recognition to cognition: visual commonsense reasoning. In: CVPR (2019)
101. Zhang, J., Ohn-Bar, E.: Learning by watching. In: CVPR (2021)
102. Zhang, J., Zheng, M., Boyd, M., Ohn-Bar, E.: X-world: accessibility, vision, and autonomy meet. In: ICCV (2021)
103. Zhang, J., Zhu, R., Ohn-Bar, E.: SelfD: self-learning large-scale driving policies from the web. In: CVPR (2022)
104. Zhao, M., et al.: On the evaluation of vision-and-language navigation instructions. ArXiv (2021)
105. Zhu, F., Zhu, Y., Lee, V., Liang, X., Chang, X.: Deep learning for embodied vision navigation: a survey. arXiv (2021)

X-DETR: A Versatile Architecture for Instance-wise Vision-Language Tasks

Zhaowei Cai[✉][iD], Gukyeong Kwon[iD], Avinash Ravichandran, Erhan Bas[iD],
Zhuowen Tu, Rahul Bhotika, and Stefano Soatto

AWS AI Labs, Seattle, USA
{zhaoweic,gukyeong,ravinash,erhanbas,ztu,bhotikar,soattos}@amazon.com

Abstract. In this paper, we study the challenging instance-wise vision-language tasks, where the free-form language is required to align with the objects instead of the whole image. To address these tasks, we propose X-DETR, whose architecture has three major components: an object detector, a language encoder, and vision-language alignment. The vision and language streams are independent until the end and they are aligned using an efficient dot-product operation. The whole network is trained end-to-end, such that the detector is optimized for the vision-language tasks instead of an off-the-shelf component. To overcome the limited size of paired object-language annotations, we leverage other weak types of supervision to expand the knowledge coverage. This simple yet effective architecture of X-DETR shows good accuracy and fast speeds for multiple instance-wise vision-language tasks, e.g., 16.4 AP on LVIS detection of 1.2K categories at ∼20 frames per second without using any LVIS annotation during training. The code is available at https://github.com/amazon-research/cross-modal-detr.

Keywords: Vision-language · Object detection · Multi-modality · Retrieval

1 Introduction

Vision-language (V+L) understanding has achieved promising progresses in the past a few years [7,8,18,24,26,32,33,42,49]. [18,42] have shown that strong vision-language alignment can be enabled by a simple dot-product between vision and language representations, with the help of large-scale image-caption pairs (hundred of millions to billions). Although they have achieved very exciting results on image-level tasks, such as open-vocabulary classification and image-text retrieval, how to develop a system for instance-wise localization based V+L tasks is still unknown, e.g., open-vocabulary object detection (OVOD) and multi-modal instance search (MMIS). OVOD detects any object categories defined by

---

Supplementary Information The online version contains supplementary material available at https://doi.org/10.1007/978-3-031-20059-5_17.

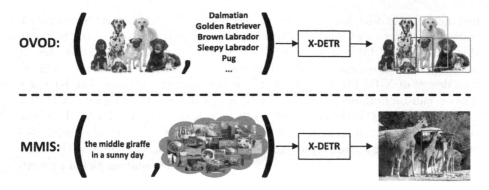

Fig. 1. The illustration for open-vocabulary object detection (OVOD) and multi-modal instance search (MMIS).

free-form language descriptions without finetuning (see Fig. 1 top), where the size of categories could span from dozens to thousands. On the other hand, MMIS retrieves the most similar object region from a database given a free-form language query (see Fig. 1 bottom), where the database size could be millions or billions for a commercial search engine.

One straightforward solution is to use a R-CNN framework [10] with a pre-trained object proposal detector, e.g., [4,5,46,61], and a pretrained V+L model, e.g., CLIP [42], denoted as R-CLIP, similar to [11]. Then the pipeline is to 1) detect object proposals, and 2) crop image regions of proposals, and 3) forward the cropped image regions through the V+L model for final vision-language alignment. However, this framework has its limitations. First, it is very slow because feature extraction is repeated in overlapped image regions. Speed is the key for applications of instance-wise V+L tasks. For example, OVOD usually requires real-time speeds (e.g., 25 frames per second), and MMIS requires instant retrieval results (e.g., in at most a few seconds) from a database of millions or billions instances. Second, the image-level representation of CLIP is suboptimal for the instance-wise V+L tasks. For example, the cropped regional representation lacks global context, which is required in some tasks. As shown in the example of locating "the middle giraffe in a sunny day" in Fig. 1 (bottom), the conditions of "middle" and "in a sunny day" require to know the relations with other giraffes and the global image context, respectively.

To resolve these issues, we propose an efficient and effective architecture for various instance-wise V+L tasks, denoted as X-DETR (cross-modal DETR). It has three major components: a visual object detector (transformer based DETR [5]), a language encoder (a RoBERTa model [31]) and alignment between the visual instance and the language description. This model is trained end-to-end, optimizing all components simultaneously. Hence, the detector is adapted to the instance-wise V+L tasks instead of as an off-the-shelf component as in the previous V+L efforts [7,26,32]. Furthermore, motivated by the success of CLIP [42], we keep the visual and language streams independent as much as possible, and align them together by a simple dot-product operation at the very end, instead of using an expensive joint-modality transformer as in [7,19,26,32]. In this sense, X-DETR can be seen as a detection counterpart of CLIP, but it overcomes the two issues of R-CLIP framework. First, thanks to the architecture design of X-DETR, the representations of multiple instances and language queries can be obtained by a single feed-forward pass. For example, X-DETR can run 20 fps for OVOD on LVIS of ~1.2K categories [12], and for MMIS, it can retrieve the object in seconds from one million of instances given a query. Second, each instance feature representation of DETR encodes the information from global image and thus can be more accurate for tasks requiring global context. For example, X-DETR is much better than R-CLIP on RefCOCO/RefCOCO+ datasets [57] requiring context information.

A cornerstone of the success of CLIP is the large-scale training data, ~400 million image-caption pairs. The paired image-caption annotation is relatively easy to collect, e.g., by crawling from the internet. However, paired object-language data usually requires human annotation and thus is very expensive. As a result, only a few datasets have this kind of annotations, i.e., Flickr30k entities [39] for grounding, RefCOCO/RefCOCO+/RefCOCOg [34,57] for referring expression comprehension (REC), VG [22] for dense captioning and GQA [17] for visual question answering (VQA). In fact, the union of them is of relatively small size, with only ~90K unique images for training, which is not enough to learn universal instance-wise V+L representations. To deal with this challenge, our framework resorts to other types of weak supervisions than the paired object-language annotation, including image-caption pairs, object bounding boxes and pseudo-labels, from datasets including COCO [28], OpenImages [21], CC [48], and LocNar [41]. This expanded combination of full and weak annotations provides broader knowledge coverage for X-DETR to learn universal representation, as will be seen in our experiments. Our contributions can be summarized as follows:

– We propose a simple yet effective architecture, X-DETR, which is end-to-end optimized for various instance-wise V+L tasks, such as OVOD, MMIS, phrase grounding, and referring expression. It also shows better transferring capacity on downstream detection tasks than other detectors.
– We have empirically shown that the CLIP-style of vision-language alignment, i.e., simple dot-product, can achieve good results with fast speeds for instance-wise V+L tasks, and the expensive cross-modality attention may not be necessary.
– We have shown that X-DETR is capable of using different weak supervisions, which are helpful to expand the knowledge coverage of the model.

2   Related Work

Vision-Language Learning is a popular interdisciplinary research topic [7, 8,24,26,32,33,42,49]. Early efforts focused on a single specific task, e.g., [35, 53] on image captioning, [1,55] on visual question answering (VQA) [2], [23,

36] on image-text retrieval and [16,56] on REC [20], etc. Recent efforts have focused on the joint pretraining of two modalities [7,24,26,32,33,49], aiming for a multi-task model that can work on multiple downstream tasks simultaneously. Although these methods do not necessarily work on detection related tasks, most of them use an off-the-shelf detector, e.g., [1,59], for more accurate visual feature representation. However, the system is not end-to-end and it is not guaranteed that the detector is optimized for the following V+L tasks. Differently, X-DETR, a versatile architecture for multiple instance-wise V+L tasks, has all components optimized end-to-end.

Uni-modal Object Detection has achieved great progresses in recent years, including the pioneering two-stage object detectors [4,10,27,46], efficient one-stage detectors [30,45], and the very recent transformer-based object detectors [5,61]. However, these uni-modal detectors are constrained to predefined categories, e.g., COCO/Objects365/OpenImages [21,28,47] of 80/365/601 classes, and they are unable to detect any categories beyond the predefined ones. In natural images, the objects are orders more diverse than the predefined categories (usually 10~1,000) in the sense of categories, attributes (e.g., colors, materials, etc.), geometric location (e.g., "man on the right"), relation to the environment ("man sitting in a couch"), etc. The traditional uni-modal object detectors are incapable of dealing with these problems.

Multi-modal Object Detection tries to detect objects with free-form language description. Previous work [15,40,54] extended traditional uni-model detection framework to accommodate the language inputs. Recently, MDETR [19], a modulated detector for multi-modal understanding, achieved state-of-the-art results on multiple datasets. However, it adopts the expensive joint-modality transformer to model the alignment between language and vision, which prevents it from being used in practical applications like OVOD and MMIS. For example, it takes 5 s per image for OVOD and hours for MMIS. OVOD [15,25,40,58,60] usually leverages language models as it is impossible to pre-define all open-vocabulary categories. It is related to zero-shot object detection (ZSOD) [3,43], where the model is trained on the seen categories and evaluated on unseen ones. X-DETR falls into the category of OVOD because it is trained on large V+L data. X-DETR shares some similarities with some concurrent OVOD works [11,25,60], but it 1) also works on other practical tasks, e.g., MMIS; 2) leverages more diverse weak supervisions; 3) has fast speeds for both OVOD and MMIS tasks.

Cross-modal Retrieval. Cross-modal (image and text) retrieval has a long research history [44]. This task is also popular in recent V+L learning efforts [36,51]. Many X-DETR tasks are related to cross-modal retrieval, but they are instance-wise. For example, OVOD [15,40,58] and MMIS [15,29,40] are to retrieve the most similar bounding boxes across the full dataset given the free-form query, and phrase grounding [39] and REC [34,57] are to retrieve the most similar bounding box in an image given a query. X-DETR aims to tackle them in an efficient and effective manner.

3   Instance-Wise Cross-modality Network

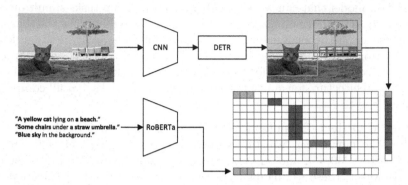

Fig. 2. Overview of our X-DETR architecture. The same color of text and object means they are aligned concepts. The matrix is the similarity matrix between text tokens and instance hypotheses, where the colored score items should be maximized but the rest should be minimized.

3.1   Overall Architecture

Figure 2 gives an overview of X-DETR architecture with its three components: a visual object detector D, a text encoder ψ and an alignment between visual instance and textual description h. The method takes an image I and a language query y as inputs and outputs the detected object o and its alignment score with the language query y. The object detector D is used to generate the instance $o = D(I)$ by processing the input image I, and the language encoder ψ is to encode the tokenized text input y into embeddings $\psi(y)$ which can be mapped to the joint space with the visual instance embeddings o. Vision-language alignment h is the key component in V+L models, aligning the visual instance o and language description y in a joint feature space, such that $h(o, \psi(y))$ is higher (lower) for paired (unpaired) visual instances and language descriptions. For example, as shown in Fig. 2, the alignment will pull the same concepts together, e.g., the detected cat (yellow bounding box) and the language description "a yellow cat", but push different concepts away, e.g., the cat and other language descriptions like "a beach", "some chairs", "blue sky", etc. In addition to the object-language alignment, X-DETR also has an image-language alignment component to leverage the weak data of image-caption pairs to learn broader knowledge coverage. The details of each component are discussed next.

3.2   Object Detection

There are many choices for the object detection component [4,5,27,30,45,61], and we are not constrained to any specific one. We chose the transformer based framework of DETR [5], because 1) it is simpler without heuristics compared

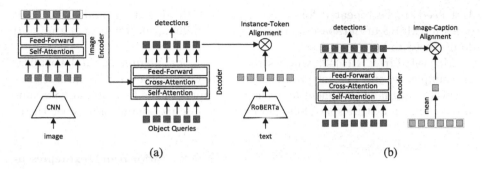

Fig. 3. (a) is the architecture of X-DETR. (b) illustrates how the encoded image-level query (red square) is aligned with the caption (yellow square). (Color figure online)

with the other popular one or two-stage frameworks [4,27,30,45], and 2) each detected instance encodes information from global image due to the attention mechanism of transformers. In DETR, a standard CNN (e.g., ResNet [14]) is applied to an image I to extract convolutional feature maps. They are then flattened into a sequence of features passed through a encoder-detector transformer architecture [50]. To detect objects, the detector also takes object queries as input, and outputs the decoded queries as the detection results o. The detection architecture of X-DETR is shown in Fig. 3 (a). Due to the slow convergence of the original DETR, we resort to Deformable DETR [61], which has faster convergence speed and better accuracy. Please refer to [5,61] for more details.

The detector in X-DETR is a stand-alone component, where the detection results are conditioned on only the image input. This is different from previous multi-modal object detection frameworks [19,54], where the detection results depend on both image and language inputs. Decoupling the vision and language streams makes the detection results independent of the queries. This is closer to a human detection system, where salient objects can be detected before being asked to detect something of interest.

3.3 Object-Language Alignment

A common and powerful strategy for image-level vision-language alignment is to leverage the interaction between two modalities by a joint-modality transformer [7,26,32], MA, as follows:

$$h(I, y) = MA(\phi(I), \psi(y)), \tag{1}$$

where ϕ is the image encoder, e.g., CNN. The joint-modality transformers could be either self-attention on concatenated vision and language features, e.g., [7,26], or cross-attention between vision and language streams, e.g., [32]. Although more cross-modal interaction could lead to stronger cross-modal representations, the computation of MA needs to be repeated if any vision or language input is changed. This is impractical for tasks such as OVOD and MMIS. For example,

MA needs to be repeated for 1.2K times for LVIS detection, and one million times for MMIS of database image size of one million, although $\phi(I)$ and $\psi(y)$ do not need to be recomputed.

Motivated by CLIP [42], where strong cross-modal alignment can be enabled by a simple and efficient dot-product operation, we adopt a similar approach, i.e., the vision-language alignment h is a linear mapping of the two modality streams into a common feature space followed by a dot-product operation between them,

$$h(o, y) = f(o) \odot g(\psi(y)), \tag{2}$$

where f and g are linear mapping for instance representation o and text representation $\psi(y)$, respectively, and $\odot$ is a dot-product operation. Since o is generated by the stand-alone object detector D, (2) can be formulated as

$$h(o, y) = f(D(I)) \odot g(\psi(y)). \tag{3}$$

Since the two modalities are coupled at the very end via an efficient dot-product, no additional computation needs to be repeated. This is a key difference with methods that use joint-modality transformers [7,19,26,32] and enables X-DETR to be used in practical tasks such as real-time OVOD and instant MMIS without sacrificing accuracy.

3.4   Image-Language Alignment

As shown in Fig. 3 (b), in addition to the queries used for object detection, an additional query is added to the query list as image query, which encodes image-level representation instead of instance-level representation like the other object queries. All queries are forwarded to the decoder with no difference. The language representation is the mean of all token representations in the sentence. Similar to CLIP, the alignment is also a simple dot-product between the encoded image query and the caption representation.

4   Training

In this section, we describe our multi-task loss design involving losses from object detection and vision-language alignment, and different types of data we used. More details about the losses can be found in the supplementary.

4.1   Class-Agnostic Object Detection

In DETR [5], object detection is a set-to-set prediction, where a set of queries is firstly mapped to a set of ground truth objects during training. Then the matched object query is learned to regress to the corresponding ground truth, with a classification loss (cross-entropy) and bounding box regression loss (generalized IoU and L1 loss). Different from the general object detection of [5,61], X-DETR does not use the class information of each object. Instead, it is class-agnostic detection: classifying a hypothesis to foreground or background. This design is similar to [11]. In total, three losses come from detection, a binary cross-entropy, a generalized IoU and L1 regression loss.

4.2   Vision-Language Alignment

We have explored different levels of vision-language alignment, including object-phrase, object-sentence and image-caption alignment. The diverse levels of alignments allow us to expand the training data, which is one of our key contributions.

Object-Phrase Alignment. In the phrase grounding dataset of Flickr30k entities [39], the ground truth is a pair of sentence phrases and objects. For example in Fig. 2, given the sentence "Some chairs under a straw umbrella.", the phrase queries are "Some chairs" and "a straw umbrella", with associated one or a few bounding boxes. We used the contrastive loss of InfoNCE [37] to optimize for the object-phrase alignment. The similarity of every potential object-token pair is computed, as shown in similarity matrix of Fig. 2, and contrastive loss is applied for each row (object-token alignment) and column (token-object alignment) of this matrix. Note that although this loss does not directly optimize the phrase-object alignment, it achieves similar results.

Object-Sentence Alignment is a special case of object-phrase alignment, where the length of the text is the full sentence, with data from REC datasets [34,57]. Contrastive loss is applied between the object query and whole sentence embedding, which is averaged from token embeddings.

Image-Caption Alignment leverages the large-scale weak data of image-caption pairs. Similar to CLIP, the loss is a cross-modality contrastive loss between the encoded image queries and the captions.

4.3   Training Efficiency

In a typical image, there are multiple objects associated multiple language descriptions. The most efficient way for training is to use all object-language pairs at a single forward-backward pass. However, this is problematic for the models with cross-modality interaction MA, e.g., [7,19,25,26], due to the reasons discussed in Sect. 3.3. As a compromise, they usually merge all independent text queries into a paragraph as a single query, and then computes MA only once. However, this violates the independence assumption of queries and queries can see each other during training, due to the property of transformer. At inference, only a single query is provided each time. On the contrary, X-DETR does not have these problems, due to the design of fully independent vision and language streams. It can take queries as many as possible at high efficiency while not violating the independence assumption, thus better performances.

4.4   Training Data

The most preferred data to learn instance-wise cross-modal representation is the paired object-language annotations, but they are very expensive and limited. X-DETR is capable of leveraging other weak supervision to cover broader knowledge.

Object-Language Data. The paired object-language data comes from Flickr30k entities [39] for grounding, RefCOCO/RefCOCO+/RefCOCOg [34,57] for REC, VG [22] for dense captioning and GQA [17] for VQA. We used the *mixed* dataset of them following MDETR [19]. Please refer to [19] for more details.

Object Detection Data. Since X-DETR has a stand-alone object detector, it can leverage data with detection annotation only. COCO [28] bounding box annotations are used because many images of the *mixed* dataset are from COCO. But category information is not used, since the detection in X-DETR is class-agnostic as described in Sect. 3.2. Instead of having an image with detection annotations only, we add COCO objects into the existing images of the *mixed* dataset, since many of them are sparsely annotated. For example, usually only 3–5 objects are annotated per image in REC datasets.

Image-Caption Data. Many datasets have image-caption annotations, e.g., Flickr30 [39], COCO Captioning [6], CC [48], SBU [38], etc. Since the *mixed* dataset already includes Flickr30k and COCO images, we added their captions into the *mixed* dataset. Beyond that, we also use the large-scale CC and Localized Narratives (LocNar) [41] (only the subset of OpenImages [21]). Note that we do not use the weak localization annotations of LocNar, i.e., the pointer tracks along narratives, because we found they are quite noisy and have no much benefit.

Pseudo-Labeled Data. We also used the pseudo labeled data generated by our X-DETR model on LocNar. Given an image and its corresponding caption, at first we use Spacy[1] to extract the noun phrases which are possible objects in the corresponding image. Then we treat the pseudo-labeling as a phrase grounding task, retrieving the bounding box that is most aligned with the noun phrase. This pseudo-labeled dataset is then used with no difference to the other object-language pairs. In addition, the OpenImages object annotations were also added to LocNar similar to COCO.

5   Experiments

In this section, we are going to show how X-DETR performs on the challenging and practical OVOD and MMIS tasks, and how it can be generalized well on the other simpler tasks, such as phrase grounding and REC.

5.1   Implementation Details

In X-DETR, we used RoBERTa-base model as the text encoder (with implementation and pretrained model from HuggingFace [52]), ResNet as the vision backbone, and Deformable DETR as the object detector. The model has been trained

---

[1] https://spacy.io/.

for 10 epochs, w.r.t. the *mixed* dataset, with class-agnostic detection, object-phrase alignment, and image-caption alignment losses introduced in Sect. 4. The object-sentence alignment loss is not used during pretraining but used in some of the downstream tasks finetuning. In each mini-batch, the batch size for fully/pseudo/weakly-annotated data is 4/2/4 for a single GPU. The image is resized such that the minimum of width and height is 600, which is smaller than the standard practice of 800 in object detection [13,27], for training cost reduction. See the supplementary for more training details. We report the results with and without finetuning. X-DETR without finetuning is a multi-task architecture for various instance-wise V+L tasks. All the compared algorithms use ResNet-101 (except R-CLIP). We do not use any prompt engineering as in CLIP [42], e.g., adding a prefix of "a photo of" to the language query.

In the baseline of R-CLIP with the pipeline introduced in Sect. 1, the proposal detector is a binary Faster R-CNN detector [27] of ResNet-50, trained on the COCO *train2017* with binary (object/non-object) annotations. Note the binary detector is not a RPN network [46]. The V+L model is a pretrained ViT-B-32 CLIP model [42]. For each image, the top 300 detection results are selected as the proposals. Since the proposals are usually tight bounding boxes, covering few context region. To include some context, we expand the proposal region by 50% on each side of the bounding box, following [11]. When using the context, the CLIP feature representations from the original and expanded regions are averaged before $L2$ normalization. This is denoted as R-CLIP+.

To evaluate the similarity between a free-form language query and an object is straightforward for R-CLIP and X-DETR. The whole sentence is forwarded through the language encoder to get feature embeddings for the input tokens. The feature embeddings corresponding to the phrase or the full sentence (excluding start and end tokens) are then averaged and $L2$-normalized as the phrase/sentence feature representation, which is then dot-producted with the $L2$-normalized object feature representation.

5.2 Open-Vocabulary Object Detection (OVOD)

First, X-DETR is evaluated on OVOD task [15,40,58]. LVIS [12], consisting of ~1.2K categories, is used for OVOD evaluation. Two settings are evaluated: 1) without finetuning and 2) finetuning with different amount (i.e., 1%/10%/100%) of LVIS annotations. The former is for OVOD and the latter is to show the transferring ability of X-DETR to other downstream detection datasets. For finetuning, the model is finetuned for 50 epochs, with the object detection and object-sentence alignment losses, learning rate dropped at 40th epoch and an image resolution of 800. For X-DETR and R-CLIP, the final score of an instance is the product between the objectness score and the classification probabilities over the categories of interest.

The results are shown in Table 1. For OVOD, R-CLIP achieves 12.7 AP even when the CLIP model is trained with image-caption annotations, and including some context information gives additional gains of 1 AP, but with 2 times slower speeds. X-DETR outperforms R-CLIP by 3.7 points and is about 100 times

Table 1. OVOD detection results on LVIS-v1 (box AP). We followed [19] to evaluate on the 5k *minival* subset. The subscript "r/c/f" of AP is for rare/common/frequent categories of LVIS. "Train Time" is the finetuning time on LVIS.

Method	Data	Train time	Test time	AP	AP50	AP_r	AP_c	AP_f
R-CLIP	0%	–	5 s	12.7	19.3	17.0	16.0	9.0
R-CLIP+	0%	–	10.6 s	13.7	20.6	18.5	17.3	9.6
MDETR [19]	0%	–	5 s	6.4	9.1	1.9	3.6	9.8
X-DETR (ours)	0%	–	0.05 s	16.4	24.4	9.6	15.2	18.8
DETR [5]	1%	0.5 h	0.05 s	4.2	7.0	1.9	1.1	7.3
MDETR [19]	1%	11 h	5 s	16.7	25.8	11.2	14.6	19.5
X-DETR (ours)	1%	1 h	0.05 s	22.8	35.0	17.6	22.0	24.4
DETR [5]	10%	3 h	0.05 s	13.7	21.7	4.1	13.2	15.9
MDETR [19]	10%	108 h	5 s	24.2	38.0	20.9	24.9	24.3
X-DETR (ours)	10%	5.2 h	0.05 s	29.5	44.7	29.4	30.6	28.6
Mask R-CNN [13]	100%	16 h	0.1 s	33.3	51.1	26.3	34.0	33.9
DETR [5]	100%	35 h	0.05 s	17.8	27.5	3.2	12.9	24.8
MDETR [19]	100%	1080 h	5 s	22.5	35.2	7.4	22.7	25.0
X-DETR (ours)	100%	45 h	0.05 s	34.0	49.0	24.7	34.6	35.1

Table 2. OVOD results on other datasets. "FT" means being finetuned on the target dataset.

Method	FT	COCO		Objects365		OpenImages	
		AP	AP50	AP	AP50	AP	AP50
Faster R-CNN [46]	✓	38.1	58.9	19.7	30.6	20.6	30.8
R-CLIP	✗	22.8	34.6	5.9	9.2	15.2	23.1
R-CLIP+	✗	24.4	36.8	6.5	10.1	16.0	24.1
MDETR [19]	✗	3.0	3.9	0.5	0.7	0.4	0.5
X-DETR (ours)	✗	26.5	38.9	5.7	8.6	4.8	6.7

faster, without using any LVIS annotations. When compared with MDETR, the recent state-of-the-art localization based V+L model, X-DETR is 10 points better. Note that X-DETR is even close to the fully-supervised vanilla DETR baseline (16.4 v.s. 17.8). These experiments support that the X-DETR can serve as an effective open-vocabulary object detector.

To evaluate the transferring ability, Mask R-CNN [13] trained on full LVIS data, using repeat factor sampling (RFS) for class imbalance, is regarded as a strong baseline, and a vanilla DETR pretrained on COCO as a transferring baseline, following [19]. The backbone for both of them is ResNet-101. When finetuning, X-DETR still has very strong improvements over MDETR, 6.1/5.3/11.5 points for 1%/10%/100% data. Using more data leads to worse

Table 3. Multi-modal instance search results. Time is evaluated per query on Ref-COCO (1,500 images) after feature indexing.

Method	FT	time	RefCOCO val			RefCOCO+ val			RefCOCOg val		
			R@5	R@10	R@30	R@5	R@10	R@30	R@5	R@10	R@30
R-CLIP	✗	~0.19 ms	5.6	8.1	14.8	7.3	10.2	17.3	21.7	29.4	42.9
R-CLIP+	✗	~0.19 ms	5.0	7.1	12.8	6.3	9.0	14.7	20.0	27.3	40.6
12-in-1 [33]	✗	~3.5 s	1.0	2.1	5.8	0.9	1.8	5.4	2.7	5.4	12.9
MDETR [19]	✗	~25 s	1.3	2.5	6.6	1.1	2.2	5.4	1.5	2.8	7.5
X-DETR (ours)	✗	~0.15 ms	21.5	30.8	47.8	14.8	22.1	37.7	23.4	33.2	52.0
UNITER [7]	✓	~1.4 s	8.1	14.3	28.9	13.5	21.0	36.0	14.5	22.1	37.7
MDETR [19]	✓	~25 s	2.0	3.7	9.0	2.5	4.4	10.9	3.5	5.9	15.3
X-DETR (ours)	✓	~0.15 ms	29.9	40.7	59.6	23.7	33.5	53.8	40.0	53.4	72.5

results in MDETR (100% v.s. 10% data), showing that MDETR does not leverage detection data very well. But X-DETR has increasing gains with more detection data, whose result using 100% data is better than the strong Mask R-CNN baseline (34.0 v.s. 33.3). Note that the X-DETR finetuning is straightforward and uses no strategy for the category imbalance issue.

In addition to OVID results on LVIS, we test X-DETR on COCO (80 classes) [28], OpenImages-v6 (601 classes) [21] and Objects365-v1 (365 classes) [47], in Table 2. Although our pretraining uses the images from COCO and OpenImages, no category information is used. X-DETR achieves relatively good results on COCO (26.5 AP), but COCO only has 80 classes, and it is possible that the pretraining data has covered those categories information in the free-form language descriptions. Since Ojbects365 and OpenImages are much more challenging, the numbers of X-DETR are relatively lower, but are still much better than MDETR. R-CLIP has close results as X-DETR on COCO and Objects365, but much better on OpenImages (~10 points gain). These have shown that OVOD is still a very challenging task and requires more research efforts.

5.3 Multi-modal Instance Search (MMIS)

Next, X-DETR is evaluated on MMIS [15,29,40]. This 1) is a practical problem, like the commercial search engines (Google, Bing, etc.), 2) is challenging, as there are tons of false positives due to the large-scale image database, and 3) requires high efficiency, i.e., instant retrieval results for millions/billions of images for commercial search engines. However, collecting MMIS datasets is very expensive, because it needs to annotate all bounding boxes in the full database for any free-form language query. This is a main reason that there is no publicly available dataset for this task yet[2].

To evaluate on this task, we converted the referred expression comprehension (REC) datasets (RefCOCO/RefCOCO+/RefCOCOg [20,34,57]), because REC

---

[2] A recent work [29] discusses this, but no data is released yet.

Table 4. Phrase grounding results on Flickr30k entities validation.

Method	FT	R@1	R@5	R@10	Method	FT	R@1	R@5	R@10
R-CLIP	✗	21.9	48.4	60.0	VisualBert [24]	✓	68.1	84.0	86.2
MDETR [19]	✗	**82.5**	92.9	94.9	VisualBert† [24]	✓	70.4	84.5	86.3
X-DETR (ours)	✗	81.4	**93.6**	**95.6**	X-DETR (ours)	✓	81.8	**93.6**	95.5

is a special (simpler) case of MMIS, which is to search the result in a single image. We changed the evaluation protocol of REC, such that the retrieval operates on the full database instead of a single image. However, only one bounding box is associated with a given query in REC datasets, which is not exclusive across the full database. For example, multiple bounding boxes from different images could correspond to a single query, especially when the query is somewhat general, e.g., "left man". Therefore, we used a loose evaluation metric, the recall @ the top {5, 10, 30} bounding boxes. The cross-modal similarity scores are used to rank and retrieve the objects for each query. The results shown in Table 3, and some MMIS examples are shown in the supplementary.

R-CLIP does not perform well for RefCOCO/RefCOCO+, because these two datasets require more context information, e.g., "left/right", which is missing in R-CLIP. Even when including the context region, it does not improve. For RefCOCOg, which focuses more on general language description, which CLIP was mainly trained on, R-CLIP shows much better results. On the contrary, X-DETR is better in all three datasets, especially on RefCOCO/RefCOCO+. When compared with 12-in-1 [33], UNITER [7] and MDETR [19], which use cross-modality transformers to model vision-language alignment and achieved very good results on REC tasks, X-DETR outperforms them by a large margin with and without finetuning. These observations are consistent with [40]: a good model for REC is not necessarily a good model for the MMIS task.

5.4   Phrase Grounding and Referring Expression Comprehension

Phrase grounding and referring expression comprehension (REC) are reduced versions of MMIS, which retrieve the targets most similar to the given query in a single image. They are simpler tasks than MMIS, which assumes that the object referred by the query definitely exists in the image.

Flickr30k entities dataset [39] is used for phrase grounding evaluation, with the train/val/test splits of [39] and Recall@{1, 5, 10} as the evaluation metrics. For finetuning, the pretrained X-DETR model was finetuned for 3 epochs on the target dataset, with the same losses as pretraining. The results are shown in Table 4. R-CLIP performs poorly on this task. Compared with MDETR [19], X-DETR only has a small gap for R@1 but better performance at R@5 and R@10, considering X-DETR does not use the much stronger transformer as the joint-modality modeling. Finetuning also helps X-DETR, but does not help MDETR as mentioned in [19].

Table 5. Comparison with state-of-the-art on REC datasets.

Method	FT	RefCOCO val			RefCOCO+ val			RefCOCOg val		
		R@1	R@5	R@10	R@1	R@5	R@10	R@1	R@5	R@10
R-CLIP	✗	21.6	52.2	68.5	24.7	57.4	72.8	36.4	72.3	86.4
R-CLIP+	✗	17.3	45.6	62.0	19.8	48.6	65.4	32.4	68.0	82.7
MDETR [19]	✗	72.4	92.2	94.7	58.3	86.3	90.5	55.9	87.0	91.8
X-DETR (ours)	✗	78.7	95.4	97.6	63.5	92.5	96.2	60.4	91.8	95.6
MAttNet [56]	✓	76.7	–	–	65.3	–	–	66.6	–	
UNITER$_L$ [7]*	✓	81.4	–	–	75.9	–	–	74.9	–	
VILLA$_L$ [9]*	✓	82.4	–	–	76.2	–	–	76.2	–	
MDETR [19]	✓	**86.8**	96.0	97.2	**79.5**	96.2	97.5	**81.6**	95.5	96.8
X-DETR (ours)	✓	86.2	**97.8**	**98.9**	77.0	**97.1**	**98.6**	80.4	**96.8**	**97.9**

RefCOCO, RefCOCO+ and RefCOCOg [20,34,57] are used for REC evaluation with Recall@{1, 5, 10} as the evaluation metrics. For finetuning, the pretrained model was finetuned for 4 epochs on the union of all three dataset (excluding all images in all three validation sets), with the object detection and object-sentence alignment losses introduced in Sect. 4. The results are shown in Table 5. Similar to grounding in Table 4, R-CLIP does not work very well for REC task. X-DETR outperforms UNITER$_L$ [7] and VILLA$_L$ [9], on all three datasets. When compared with the current state-of-the-art MDETR [19] on the finetuning setting, X-DETR is slightly worse at R@1 but better at R@5 and R@10. When the model is not finetuned, X-DETR achieves much better results than MDETR. These results have shown that X-DETR can be generalized well for simpler tasks such as phrase grounding and REC, in addition to the challenging tasks of OVOD and MMIS.

5.5   Speed Comparisons

X-DETR is an efficient architecture for both training and inference. When compared with R-CLIP, X-DETR is about 100 times faster for OVOD due to the slow R-CNN pipeline. For MMIS, X-DETR has close retrieval time with R-CLIP, since they both use the simple dot-product as the vision-language alignment and vision/language features are fully indexable. However, the indexing speed of X-DETR is about 100 times faster than R-CLIP due to the R-CNN pipeline. When compared with the state-of-the-art localization based V+L work of MDETR, X-DETR is a few times faster during training, since it can process an image with all of its queries simultaneously but MDETR needs to process the queries one by one due to the joint-modality transformer design, as discussed in Sect. 4.3. For example, finetuning on 10% LVIS, MDETR needs 108 h for 150 epochs, but X-DETR only needs 5.2 h for 50 epochs with improved results (see Table 1). At inference, for OVOD/MMIS, X-DETR is about 100/100,000 times faster than

Table 6. Ablation studies. "*" means MMIS experiments. Finetuning on LVIS is on 10% data.

Pre-training data	FT	LVIS		RefCOCOg*		Flickr	RefCOCO
		AP	AP@r	R@5	R@10	R@1	R@1
mixed	✗	11.5	6.0	16.2	24.6	79.7	63.9
*mixed**	✗	13.5	5.2	20.4	29.8	79.9	75.4
*mixed**+boxes	✗	14.7	5.1	22.4	32.4	79.9	78.0
+CC	✗	15.9	7.9	22.2	31.8	80.1	76.9
+CC+LocNar	✗	15.7	6.8	21.0	29.8	81.3	78.3
mixed	✓	20.0	13.4	34.3	45.8	80.1	83.0
*mixed**	✓	21.7	18.6	36.2	48.9	80.6	83.9
*mixed**+boxes	✓	22.8	14.8	36.5	49.4	80.3	84.1
+CC	✓	23.3	16.6	37.5	49.4	80.9	84.5
+CC+LocNar	✓	25.6	17.3	37.5	50.3	81.8	85.4

MDETR (see Table 1 and 3). Note that we have already indexed the indexable features, e.g., the ones before the joint-modality transformers for MDETR. The training (inference) speeds are reported on 8 (1) A100 GPUs.

5.6   Ablation on Pretraining Data

We ablated the effect of the pretraining data in Table 6 (with ResNet-50 for efficiency purpose). The rows are for experiments using data of 1) the original *mixed* of MDETR [19] ("*mixed*"), where all queries of an image are merged into a single paragraph, violating the independence assumption of the queries; 2) *mixed* with independent queries ("*mixed**"), by splitting the merged paragraph into independent queries; 3) adding COCO objects without category ("*mixed**+boxes"); 4) adding CC [48] weakly labeled image-caption data ("+CC"); 5) adding LocNar [41] pseudo-labeled and OpenImage [21] bounding box data ("+CC+LocNar"). It can be found that the original *mixed* dataset has a mismatch with the inference data, which leads to inferior results especially when the model is not finetuned. Independent queries of *mixed** can have significant accuracy boosts in multiple tasks. Adding COCO object data ("*mixed**+boxes") also has nontrivial improvements, showing the advantage of X-DETR to leverage detection-only data. When using CC data ("+CC"), the results of OVOD on LVIS are improved because more concepts are covered by more data, but the results on RefCOCO are decreased. When adding more LocNar pseudo-labeled data with OpenImage objects ("+CC+LocNar"), the results on Flickr30k and RefCOCO are improved over "+CC", but decreased on MMIS. The observations on finetuning settings are consistent. These ablation studies have shown that it is not enough to just use the fully annotated object-phrase annotations, and leveraging other weaker types of supervision could be helpful for instance-wise V+L learning.

6   Conclusion

In this paper, we propose a simple yet effective architecture for instance-wise vision-language tasks, which uses dot-product to align vision and language. It has shown that the expensive joint-modality transformer may not be necessary for those V+L tasks and the weak annotated data can be a big help to improve the model performances. The proposed X-DETR has shown benefits in terms of accuracy and speed, when compared to the previous V+L language state-of-the-art, on the practical and challenging tasks such as open-vocabulary detection and multi-modal instance search.

References

1. Anderson, P., et al.: Bottom-up and top-down attention for image captioning and visual question answering. In: CVPR, pp. 6077–6086 (2018)
2. Antol, S., et al.: Vqa: visual question answering. In: ICCV, pp. 2425–2433 (2015)
3. Bansal, A., Sikka, K., Sharma, G., Chellappa, R., Divakaran, A.: Zero-shot object detection. In: ECCV, pp. 384–400 (2018)
4. Cai, Z., Vasconcelos, N.: Cascade r-cnn: delving into high quality object detection. In: CVPR, pp. 6154–6162 (2018)
5. Carion, N., Massa, F., Synnaeve, G., Usunier, N., Kirillov, A., Zagoruyko, S.: End-to-end object detection with transformers. In: Vedaldi, A., Bischof, H., Brox, T., Frahm, J.-M. (eds.) ECCV 2020. LNCS, vol. 12346, pp. 213–229. Springer, Cham (2020). https://doi.org/10.1007/978-3-030-58452-8_13
6. Chen, X., Fang, H., Lin, T.Y., Vedantam, R., Gupta, S., Dollár, P., Zitnick, C.L.: Microsoft coco captions: data collection and evaluation server. arXiv preprint arXiv:1504.00325 (2015)
7. Chen, Y.-C., et al.: UNITER: UNiversal image-TExt representation learning. In: Vedaldi, A., Bischof, H., Brox, T., Frahm, J.-M. (eds.) ECCV 2020. LNCS, vol. 12375, pp. 104–120. Springer, Cham (2020). https://doi.org/10.1007/978-3-030-58577-8_7
8. Desai, K., Johnson, J.: Virtex: learning visual representations from textual annotations. In: CVPR, pp. 11162–11173 (2021)
9. Gan, Z., Chen, Y.C., Li, L., Zhu, C., Cheng, Y., Liu, J.: Large-scale adversarial training for vision-and-language representation learning. arXiv preprint arXiv:2006.06195 (2020)
10. Girshick, R.B., Donahue, J., Darrell, T., Malik, J.: Rich feature hierarchies for accurate object detection and semantic segmentation. In: CVPR, pp. 580–587. IEEE Computer Society (2014)
11. Gu, X., Lin, T.Y., Kuo, W., Cui, Y.: Open-vocabulary object detection via vision and language knowledge distillation. arXiv preprint arXiv:2104.13921 (2021)
12. Gupta, A., Dollar, P., Girshick, R.: Lvis: a dataset for large vocabulary instance segmentation. In: CVPR, pp. 5356–5364 (2019)
13. He, K., Gkioxari, G., Dollár, P., Girshick, R.: Mask r-cnn. In: ICCV, pp. 2961–2969 (2017)
14. He, K., Zhang, X., Ren, S., Sun, J.: Deep residual learning for image recognition. In: CVPR, pp. 770–778 (2016)

15. Hinami, R., Satoh, S.: Discriminative learning of open-vocabulary object retrieval and localization by negative phrase augmentation. arXiv preprint arXiv:1711.09509 (2017)
16. Hu, R., Xu, H., Rohrbach, M., Feng, J., Saenko, K., Darrell, T.: Natural language object retrieval. In: CVPR, pp. 4555–4564 (2016)
17. Hudson, D.A., Manning, C.D.: Gqa: a new dataset for real-world visual reasoning and compositional question answering. In: CVPR, pp. 6700–6709 (2019)
18. Jia, C., et al.: Scaling up visual and vision-language representation learning with noisy text supervision. In: Meila, M., Zhang, T. (eds.) ICML, vol. 139, pp. 4904–4916. PMLR (2021)
19. Kamath, A., Singh, M., LeCun, Y., Synnaeve, G., Misra, I., Carion, N.: Mdetr-modulated detection for end-to-end multi-modal understanding. In: ICCV, pp. 1780–1790 (2021)
20. Kazemzadeh, S., Ordonez, V., Matten, M., Berg, T.: Referitgame: referring to objects in photographs of natural scenes. In: EMNLP, pp. 787–798 (2014)
21. Krasin, I., et al.: openimages: a public dataset for large-scale multi-label and multi-class image classification **2**(3), 18 (2017). Dataset available from https://githubcom/openimages
22. Krishna, R., et al.: Visual genome: connecting language and vision using crowd-sourced dense image annotations. Int. J. Comput. Vis. **123**(1), 32–73 (2017)
23. Lee, K.H., Chen, X., Hua, G., Hu, H., He, X.: Stacked cross attention for image-text matching. In: ECCV, pp. 201–216 (2018)
24. Li, L.H., Yatskar, M., Yin, D., Hsieh, C.J., Chang, K.W.: Visualbert: a simple and performant baseline for vision and language. arXiv preprint arXiv:1908.03557 (2019)
25. Li, L.H., et al.: Grounded language-image pre-training. In: CVPR, pp. 10965–10975 (2022)
26. Li, X., et al.: Oscar: object-semantics aligned pre-training for vision-language tasks. In: Vedaldi, A., Bischof, H., Brox, T., Frahm, J.-M. (eds.) ECCV 2020. LNCS, vol. 12375, pp. 121–137. Springer, Cham (2020). https://doi.org/10.1007/978-3-030-58577-8_8
27. Lin, T.Y., Dollár, P., Girshick, R., He, K., Hariharan, B., Belongie, S.: Feature pyramid networks for object detection. In: CVPR, pp. 2117–2125 (2017)
28. Lin, T.-Y., et al.: Microsoft COCO: common objects in context. In: Fleet, D., Pajdla, T., Schiele, B., Tuytelaars, T. (eds.) ECCV 2014. LNCS, vol. 8693, pp. 740–755. Springer, Cham (2014). https://doi.org/10.1007/978-3-319-10602-1_48
29. Liu, S., Lin, K., Wang, L., Yuan, J., Liu, Z.: Ovis: open-vocabulary visual instance search via visual-semantic aligned representation learning. arXiv preprint arXiv:2108.03704 (2021)
30. Liu, W., et al.: SSD: single shot multibox detector. In: Leibe, B., Matas, J., Sebe, N., Welling, M. (eds.) ECCV 2016. LNCS, vol. 9905, pp. 21–37. Springer, Cham (2016). https://doi.org/10.1007/978-3-319-46448-0_2
31. Liu, Y., et al.: Roberta: a robustly optimized bert pretraining approach. arXiv preprint arXiv:1907.11692 (2019)
32. Lu, J., Batra, D., Parikh, D., Lee, S.: Vilbert: pretraining task-agnostic visiolinguistic representations for vision-and-language tasks. In: NeurIPS, pp. 13–23 (2019)
33. Lu, J., Goswami, V., Rohrbach, M., Parikh, D., Lee, S.: 12-in-1: multi-task vision and language representation learning. In: CVPR, pp. 10437–10446 (2020)
34. Mao, J., Huang, J., Toshev, A., Camburu, O., Yuille, A.L., Murphy, K.: Generation and comprehension of unambiguous object descriptions. In: CVPR, pp. 11–20 (2016)

35. Mao, J., Xu, W., Yang, Y., Wang, J., Huang, Z., Yuille, A.: Deep captioning with multimodal recurrent neural networks (m-rnn). arXiv preprint arXiv:1412.6632 (2014)
36. Miech, A., Alayrac, J.B., Laptev, I., Sivic, J., Zisserman, A.: Thinking fast and slow: Efficient text-to-visual retrieval with transformers. In: CVPR, pp. 9826–9836 (2021)
37. Oord, A.v.d., Li, Y., Vinyals, O.: Representation learning with contrastive predictive coding. arXiv preprint arXiv:1807.03748 (2018)
38. Ordonez, V., Kulkarni, G., Berg, T.L.: Im2text: describing images using 1 million captioned photographs. In: NeurIPS, pp. 1143–1151 (2011)
39. Plummer, B.A., Wang, L., Cervantes, C.M., Caicedo, J.C., Hockenmaier, J., Lazebnik, S.: Flickr30k entities: collecting region-to-phrase correspondences for richer image-to-sentence models. Int. J. Comput. Vis. **123**(1), 74–93 (2017)
40. Plummer, B.A., et al.: Revisiting image-language networks for open-ended phrase detection. IEEE Trans. Pattern Anal. Mach. Intell. **44**, 2155–2167 (2020)
41. Pont-Tuset, J., Uijlings, J., Changpinyo, S., Soricut, R., Ferrari, V.: Connecting vision and language with localized narratives. In: Vedaldi, A., Bischof, H., Brox, T., Frahm, J.-M. (eds.) ECCV 2020. LNCS, vol. 12350, pp. 647–664. Springer, Cham (2020). https://doi.org/10.1007/978-3-030-58558-7_38
42. Radford, A., et al.: Learning transferable visual models from natural language supervision. In: ICML, vol. 139, pp. 8748–8763. PMLR (2021)
43. Rahman, S., Khan, S., Porikli, F.: Zero-shot object detection: learning to simultaneously recognize and localize novel concepts. In: Jawahar, C.V., Li, H., Mori, G., Schindler, K. (eds.) ACCV 2018. LNCS, vol. 11361, pp. 547–563. Springer, Cham (2019). https://doi.org/10.1007/978-3-030-20887-5_34
44. Rasiwasia, N., et al.: A new approach to cross-modal multimedia retrieval. In: ACMMM, pp. 251–260 (2010)
45. Redmon, J., Divvala, S., Girshick, R., Farhadi, A.: You only look once: unified, real-time object detection. In: CVPR, pp. 779–788 (2016)
46. Ren, S., He, K., Girshick, R., Sun, J.: Faster r-cnn: towards real-time object detection with region proposal networks. NeurIPS **28**, 91–99 (2015)
47. Shao, S., et al.: Objects365: a large-scale, high-quality dataset for object detection. In: ICCV, pp. 8430–8439 (2019)
48. Sharma, P., Ding, N., Goodman, S., Soricut, R.: Conceptual captions: a cleaned, hypernymed, image alt-text dataset for automatic image captioning. In: ACL, pp. 2556–2565 (2018)
49. Tan, H., Bansal, M.: Lxmert: learning cross-modality encoder representations from transformers. arXiv preprint arXiv:1908.07490 (2019)
50. Vaswani, A., et al.: Attention is all you need. In: NeurIPS, pp. 5998–6008 (2017)
51. Wang, L., Li, Y., Huang, J., Lazebnik, S.: Learning two-branch neural networks for image-text matching tasks. IEEE Trans. Pattern Anal. Mach. Intell. **41**(2), 394–407 (2018)
52. Wolf, T., et al.: Huggingface's transformers: state-of-the-art natural language processing. arXiv preprint arXiv:1910.03771 (2019)
53. Xu, K., et al.: Show, attend and tell: neural image caption generation with visual attention. In: ICML, pp. 2048–2057. PMLR (2015)
54. Yang, Z., Gong, B., Wang, L., Huang, W., Yu, D., Luo, J.: A fast and accurate one-stage approach to visual grounding. In: ICCV, pp. 4683–4693 (2019)
55. Yang, Z., He, X., Gao, J., Deng, L., Smola, A.: Stacked attention networks for image question answering. In: CVPR, pp. 21–29 (2016)

56. Yu, L., et al.: Mattnet: modular attention network for referring expression comprehension. In: CVPR, pp. 1307–1315 (2018)
57. Yu, L., Poirson, P., Yang, S., Berg, A.C., Berg, T.L.: Modeling context in referring expressions. In: Leibe, B., Matas, J., Sebe, N., Welling, M. (eds.) ECCV 2016. LNCS, vol. 9906, pp. 69–85. Springer, Cham (2016). https://doi.org/10.1007/978-3-319-46475-6_5
58. Zareian, A., Rosa, K.D., Hu, D.H., Chang, S.F.: Open-vocabulary object detection using captions. In: CVPR, pp. 14393–14402 (2021)
59. Zhang, P., et al.: Vinvl: revisiting visual representations in vision-language models. In: CVPR, pp. 5579–5588 (2021)
60. Zhong, Y., et al.: Regionclip: region-based language-image pretraining. In: CVPR, pp. 16793–16803 (2022)
61. Zhu, X., Su, W., Lu, L., Li, B., Wang, X., Dai, J.: Deformable DETR: deformable transformers for end-to-end object detection. In: ICLR (2021)

Learning Disentanglement with Decoupled Labels for Vision-Language Navigation

Wenhao Cheng[1], Xingping Dong[2], Salman Khan[3], and Jianbing Shen[4(✉)]

[1] School of Computer Science, Beijing Institute of Technology, Beijing, China
[2] Inception Institute of Artificial Intelligence, Abu Dhabi, UAE
[3] Mohamed bin Zayed University of Artificial Intelligence, Abu Dhabi, UAE
[4] SKL-IOTSC, Computer and Information Science, University of Macau, Macau, China
shenjianbingcg@gmail.com

Abstract. Vision-and-Language Navigation (VLN) requires an agent to follow complex natural language instructions and perceive the visual environment for real-world navigation. Intuitively, we find that instruction disentanglement for each viewpoint along the agent's path is critical for accurate navigation. However, most methods only utilize the whole complex instruction or inaccurate sub-instructions due to the lack of accurate disentanglement as an intermediate supervision stage. To address this problem, we propose a new *Disentanglement framework with Decoupled Labels* (DDL) for VLN. Firstly, we manually extend the benchmark dataset Room-to-Room with landmark- and action-aware labels in order to provide fine-grained information for each viewpoint. Furthermore, to enhance the generalization ability, we propose a Decoupled Label Speaker module to generate pseudo-labels for augmented data and reinforcement training. To fully use the proposed fine-grained labels, we design a Disentangled Decoding Module to guide discriminative feature extraction and help alignment of multi-modalities. To reveal the generality of our proposed method, we apply it on a LSTM-based model and two recent Transformer-based models. Extensive experiments on two VLN benchmarks (i.e., R2R and R4R) demonstrate the effectiveness of our approach, achieving better performance than previous state-of-the-art methods.

Keywords: Vision-and-Language Navigation · Disentanglement · Modular network · Imitation/Reinforcement learning · LSTM and Transformer

---

W. Cheng and X. Dong—Equal contribution. Codes and annotations are available at https://github.com/cwhao98/DDL.

Supplementary Information The online version contains supplementary material available at https://doi.org/10.1007/978-3-031-20059-5_18.

S. Avidan et al. (Eds.): ECCV 2022, LNCS 13696, pp. 309–329, 2022.
https://doi.org/10.1007/978-3-031-20059-5_18

1 Introduction

Vision-and-language navigation is a challenging task that requires the agent to perceive its visual environment and understand the natural language instructions to reach the target location. Recent works have achieved remarkable progress via techniques such as pre-exploration [13,33,47,71,74], pre-training [21,23,40,41,45,48], reward shaping [56,72,73], auxiliary tasks [46,76,79], data augmentation [18,32,65] and counterfactual thinking [19,53,69].

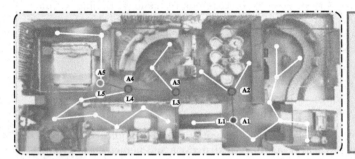

Instruction:
Go straight[A1] to the white chairs[L1].
Turn left and work forward[A2]. Pass[A3] the couches on the right[L3] and go into[A4] the room straight ahead[L4].
Wait[A5] by the bed[L5]

Fig. 1. An illustration of decoupled labels providing intermediate supervision during navigation. The superscripts in the instruction denote the landmark and action labels for each viewpoint. The decoupled labels not only contain disentangled information, but help the alignment between vision and language modalities.

The existing VLN dataset Room-to-Room [2] only provides complex human instructions which contain information about several different attributes, *e.g.*, objects, landmarks and actions. Such convoluted instructions make the agent's task more challenging. Our intuition is that disentangling these instructions can provide more accurate and clear input to improve the decisions taken by the agent. This idea is also inspired by the human concept [6], since human beings usually do orthogonal decomposition for cognition, *i.e.*, divide something into different attributes to better understand and remember. In particular, the previous works OAAM [56] and RelGraph [26] tried to disentangle the instructions into different kinds of information via attention mechanism [68]. However, the attention-based models can produce inaccurate disentangled instructions which can mislead the agent, resulting in a performance degradation.

In addition, the alignment between vision and language is also a challenging open issue in VLN. To alleviate this issue, RxR [38] provides time-aligned multilingual instruction, but without the decoupling of specific parts such as landmarks and actions. FGR2R [27] and BabyWalk [80] split the long instruction into small parts via chunking function and dynamic programming, since sub-instructions are more conducive to match visual scenes. Specifically, FGR2R utilizes a shifting module to predict the alignment between sub-instruction and navigation path. However, such a split is not fine-grained enough to provide accurate decoupled labels to achieve proper disentanglement in the VLN task.

To address the above issues and provide fine-grained guidance for VLN, we propose a novel *Disentanglement framework with Decoupled Labels* (DDL).

Our framework has three main highlights: fine-grained labels, a decoupled label speaker, and a disentangled decoding module, which we elaborate below.

Fine-Grained Labels. We enrich the benchmark R2R [2] by adding new fine-grained human annotations, and call it Landmark- and Action-aware Room-to-Room Labels (LAR2R). Specifically, as shown in Fig. 1, for each viewpoint, we annotate the specific landmark and action sub-instructions that should be highlighted to navigate correctly at the current viewpoint. Therefore, the annotated labels not only provide more precise disentangled instruction, but implicitly contain the alignment information between multi-modalities.

Decoupled Label Speaker. Most recent VLN models are trained by both Imitation Learning (IL) and Reinforcement Learning (RL), while we can only use the annotated labels during IL training since the paths in RL training phase are unknown and abundant, and it is impossible to annotate so many paths. Moreover, augmentation methods are often adopted, such as back translation augmentation [65] and random environmental mixup [44], to obtain more trajectories for training. These trajectories are also not annotated. To provide supervised signal for RL training phase and augmented data, we propose a decoupled label speaker. Taking the given instruction and visual observation along a trajectory as input, our speaker module can generate landmark and action pseudo-labels, enabling most VLN models to be trained with decoupled labels.

Disentangled Decoding Module. To make full use of the proposed fine-grained labels, we design a Disentangled Decoding Module to guide discriminative feature extraction and help the alignment of multiple modalities. Specifically, given a VLN model, we firstly design a disentanglement branch, based on its feature encoding backbone, to enable decoupling. Then, we employ a language auxiliary loss that uses the decoupled labels to regularize the landmark- and action-aware attention weights, making complex inputs easier to understand for the agent. Note that our approach is *model-agnostic* and can easily be integrated into most VLN methods. We adopt three representative algorithms: a LSTM-based navigator OAAM [56], two Transformer-based navigators VLN♢BERT [28] and HAMT [11], as baselines to show the generality of our proposed approach.

Our main contributions are summarized as follows: 1) We develop a new Disentanglement framework with Decoupled Labels (DDL) for the VLN task. DDL uses decoupled labels to guide the extraction of disentangled features and help the alignment between vision and language modalities, making the navigation more interpretable. 2) We enrich the benchmark dataset R2R [2] with landmark- and action-aware annotations. To the best of our knowledge, this is the first effort to demonstrate the effectiveness of fine-grained decoupled labels in VLN. 3) To enhance generalization ability, we further propose a decoupled label speaker to generate pseudo-labels for reinforced learning and augmented data. In addition, our speaker can be easily integrated into most VLN models to provide fine-grained labels. 4) To reveal the generality of our DDL, we apply it to both LSTM-based and Transformer-based methods. Extensive experiments on R2R [2] and R4R [32] demonstrate the improvement over three competitive baselines and state-of-the-art performance of our models.

2   Related Work

Vision-and-Language Navigation. Recently VLN has attracted significant research interest. Supported by various simulators [7,35,62], a number of tasks such as R2R [2], REVERIE [57], ALFRED [64], CVDN [67], HANNA [51], and VNLA [52] have been proposed. Many early approaches [18,33,46,46,47] for R2R are based on Imitation Learning (IL), since the agent can learn quickly from teacher actions through Behaviour Cloning [5]. Speaker-Follower [18] introduces a speaker to synthesize new instructions. Self-Monitoring [46] proposes a progress monitor for VLN agent. In addition to IL, RL-based methods have also achieved great success with strong generalization ability. RPA [74] first combines model-free and model-based deep RL for navigation. RCM [73] enforces cross-modal grounding both locally and globally. E-Drop [65] uses the environmental dropout method to generate more unseen environments. Other approaches try to improve performance by auxiliary tasks [79], reward shaping via distillation [72], active perception [71], structured scene memory [70], 3D semantic representation [66], contrastive learning [42], snapshot ensemble [59] and counterfactual cycle-consistent [69]. Due to the success of transformer [68] and BERT [14], many transformer architectures [10,12,17,39,40,48] for VLN have emerged. VLN↻BERT [28] introduces a recurrent unit within transformer to enable past information flow. HAMT [11] and E.T. [54] encode all the observation and action history within a full transformer. MTVM [43] proposes variable-length memory to encode history information. Concurrently, HOP [58] designs proxy tasks to model spatio-temporal alignment, further mining the role of historical information. SEvol [9] constructs object-level layout graph to maintain navigation state with a reinforced state evolving strategy. Apart from the above approaches that focus mainly on indoor navigation, VLN in outdoor scenes [8], continuous environments [31,36,37,60] and multilingual navigation with spatial-temporal grounding [38] have also been explored.

Disentangled Representation in VLN. Intuitively, disentangling the instruction or visual scene will help the agent better understand the complex input. Early work [29] has explored the effectiveness of grounding language to multiple modalities. Recently, OAAM [56] utilizes two learning attention modules to disentangle the object- and action-related parts in the instruction. Hong *et al.* [26] build a language and visual graph to capture the relationship of scenes, objects, and direction clues. ORIST [55] leverages object- and word-level feature representations to facilitate modality matching. CKR [20] decouples the room-type and object-entity explicitly, incorporating knowledge graph to help the entity reasoning. SOAT [50] encodes the scene feature and object reference separately in transformer which leads to performance improvement. However, the above methods are often based on attention mechanisms, which can generate inaccurate results. Although multi-head self-attention within transformers attends to information from different subspaces, it is not easily interpretable. Therefore, in this paper, we investigate the effect of decoupled labels to guide discriminative feature extraction, making VLN better interpretable.

3 Our Approach

In this section, we first formulate the VLN task in Sect. 3.1 and then briefly summarize the three baseline navigators, OAAM [56], VLN☉BERT [28] and HAMT [11], in Sect. 3.2. The Landmark- and Action-aware Room-to-Room (LAR2R) labels introduced in our work are explained in Sect. 3.3. The proposed disentanglement framework is outlined in Sect. 3.4. We further explain how to get pseudo-labels for unlabeled data in Sect. 3.5. Finally, we present the model training details in Sect. 3.6.

3.1 Problem Setup

The standard VLN task requires the agent to navigate in a connected graph to the target location following natural language instruction. Formally, given an instruction I of L words, $I = \{w_1, w_2, \ldots, w_L\}$, at each time step t, the agent obtains the surrounding environment information, which is discretized into 36 single view images $\{v_{t,i}\}_{i=1}^{36}$. Each view $v_{t,i}$ is represented by visual feature $f_{t,i}$ and orientation feature $o_{t,i} = (\cos\theta_{t,i}, \sin\theta_{t,i}, \cos\phi_{t,i}, \sin\phi_{t,i})$, where $v_{t,i}$ is an image at orientation with heading angle $\theta_{t,i}$ and elevation angle $\phi_{t,i}$. The image feature $f_{t,i}$ can be obtained by a detector [1], or ResNet [24] pretrained on Imagenet [61] or Place365 [78]. Besides, there are N_t candidate directions for the agent to select at each viewpoint, where the set of view features for each candidate direction is given by $\{c_{t,k}\}_{k=1}^{N_t}$ which are of the same type as $v_{t,i}$.

3.2 Conventional Navigation

To showcase the generality of porposed approach, we experiment on three recent navigators, OAAM [56], VLN☉BERT [28] and HAMT [11]. OAAM is a LSTM-based navigator while VLN☉BERT and HAMT [11] are transformer-based navigators. All three take natural language instruction and visual perception as input, and output the selected actions across several candidate directions at each step. However, their architectures are very different partly in language encoding, decision making, and the maintenance of internal state during navigation.

LSTM-Based Navigator. OAAM [56] is built upon EnvDrop [65], which firstly encodes the language instruction by a Bi-LSTM at the beginning of navigation, and then utilizes another LSTM to enable the entire navigation process. At each step t, the agent updates its internal state h_t by previous latent state and instruction-aware visual observation at the current viewpoint. Formally:

$$h_t = \mathrm{LSTM}(h_{t-1}, [o_t, I]) \tag{1}$$

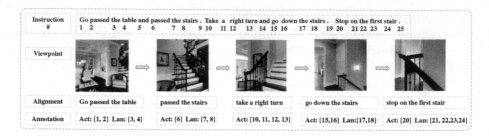

Fig. 2. Navigation with specific landmark- and action-aware sub-instructions in LAR2R. We extend the R2R dataset by providing annotations of landmark (blue) and action (green) related parts in the instruction along with each viewpoint.

where I is the instruction encoding, o_t is the perceived panoramic view feature, and [·] denotes concatenation.

In terms of the navigation decision making, OAAM adopts two learnable attention modules to highlight the corresponding object- and action-related part of the given instruction which are fed into the object-vision and action-orientation matching modules, respectively, to predict the selected direction. This is followed by an adaptive module to combine the action logits as the final decision. For more details, please refer to the supplementary materials.

Transformer-Based Navigator. VLN↻BERT [28] is a state-of-the-art agent that introduces a recurrent unit to the transformer, which enables information flow from the past to the current state during the entire navigation process. In contrast, HAMT [11] processes all historical information to enrich the current representation. The language instruction is encoded via multi-head self-attention at the beginning and the leading input token [CLS] is selected as the agent's initial state. Then, at each time step, the agent takes the language tokens and observed visual features as input, which are processed via cross-modal attention and then followed by self-attention on each candidate view to update the internal state and visual tokens. Formally, this is represented as:

$$h_t = \text{BERT}([\text{CLS}], I, o_t, p_t) \tag{2}$$

where h_t is the current agent state, [CLS] is a pre-defined classification token in the BERT model, and p_t denotes past history input that is only used in HAMT. To take the decision on next direction, attention scores over each candidate will be used as the action probability by the agent.

3.3 The LAR2R Labels

Label Collection. In order to better decouple the information of different attributes in the input instruction and to help the agent locate the specific sub-instruction part, we extend the R2R dataset with fine-grained annotations.

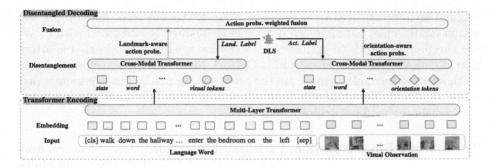

Fig. 3. Overview of the Transformer-based Disentangled Decoding Module.
The model takes language words and visual observation as input. After the transformer
encoding, two parallel cross-modal transformers are utilized to enable disentangled
decoding, supervised by our decoupled labels via a language auxiliary loss. Then the
output of two disentangled branches is fused to predict the final action of the agent.
DLS represents the decoupled label speaker (see Sect. 3.5 for details).

Specifically, as shown in Fig. 2, at each navigation step t, we annotate the landmark part L_t and action part A_t in the instruction that should be attended to
select the next action at the current viewpoint. Formally, we have:

$$L_t = [l_{t,1}, \ldots, l_{t,N_l}], \quad A_t = [a_{t,1}, \ldots, a_{t,N_a}], \tag{3}$$

where $l_{t,i}$ and $a_{t,j}$ are the index of landmark- and action-related instructions
respectively. N_l and N_a are the total number of words that should be highlighted
at the current time step. To maintain consistency and ensure accuracy, we ask
one of the annotators to mark the labels which is crosschecked by another person.
The overall process took about four months of annotation effort.

Label Statistics. For the training split, we have annotated 40,813 viewpoints for landmark-related instruction and 52,735 viewpoints for action-related
instruction, with 3.6 and 1.9 words on average for each viewpoint, respectively.
Note that some sub-instructions will cover two or more viewpoints (*e.g.*, go up
the stairs all the way), which we only annotate once at the first location. For
the validation set, the landmark-points and action-points are 6,841 and 8,732
for validation unseen, 3,058 and 3,946 for validation seen split, respectively. In
total, LAR2R provides about 1,15,000 image-text pairs.

3.4 Disentangled Decoding Module

Our method aims to use accurate labels to guide the disentangled feature extraction. Therefore, a prerequisite is that the model architecture allows feature disentanglement. Given a model without decoupling, we first propose a simple way to
achieve disentanglement, and then boost the performance using accurate annotated labels and pseudo-labels with a language auxiliary loss (LAL). Since the

original architecture of OAAM [56] uses separate streams to process object and action related cues, our approach is feasible to be directly integrated with it. We use the proposed LAL to optimize the attention weight of two learnable attention modules in parallel streams within OAAM. Next, we take Transformer-based methods as an example to illustrate the proposed approach. The overview is presented in Fig. 3. Note that the history input in HAMT is omitted for brevity. We explain the module architecture below.

Transformer Block Notation. Each Transformer block encodes features from previous block X_{l-1}, consisting of Multi-Head Self Attention (MSA) and Multi-Layer Perception (MLP) with residual connections and layer normalization. Formally, we can denote one Transformer block as:

$$H_l = \text{LN}(\text{MSA}(X_{l-1}) + X_{l-1})$$
$$Z_l = \text{MLP}(H_l)$$
$$X_l = \text{LN}(Z_l W_l + H_l) \qquad (4)$$

where LN is layer normalization [4], W_l is a learnable projection matrix, and Z_l is an intermediate output that increases the feature dimension of H_l through MLP to obtain more powerful representations.

As the term suggests, MSA in Eq. 4 captures dependencies between the tokens obtained from the input sequence elements using scaled dot-product attention (*Attn*). For MSA, the queries, keys, and values are generated from the same input i.e., $\text{MSA}(X) = Attn(W_q X, W_k X, W_v X)$ using learned projection matrices W_q, W_k, W_v. To enable Multi-head Cross-modal Attention (MCA), we denote $\text{MCA}(U, V) = Attn(W_q V, W_k U, W_v U)$. MCA uses the features V in one modality to query their correlation with the features U of another modality.

Disentanglement Branch. At each navigation step t, the agent observes k candidate directions where each view i is composed of visual feature $f_{t,i} \in \mathbb{R}^{d1}$ and orientation feature $o_{t,i} \in \mathbb{R}^{d2}$. To disentangle the observation, we design two BERT blocks to process the visual and geometry clues separately. Firstly, we have:

$$\hat{f}_{t,i} = f_{t,i} W_f \quad \hat{o}_{t,i} = o_{t,i} W_o, \qquad (5)$$

where $W_f \in \mathbb{R}^{d1 \times d}$ and $W_o \in \mathbb{R}^{d2 \times d}$ are learnable parameters to project the features into the same space as the language tokens. Meanwhile, we encode the agent state $h_t \in \mathbb{R}^d$ to get a transformed representation $\hat{h}_t$ via:

$$\hat{h}_t = \text{Tanh}(h_t W_h). \qquad (6)$$

Next, to highlight the landmark- and action-aware instruction, the refined state $\hat{h}_t \in \mathbb{R}^d$ will be concatenated with the two types of disentangled tokens respectively, and fed into the cross-modal attention block. Formally:

$$E_{lan} = \text{LN}(\text{MCA}(C_{lan}, I) + C_{lan}), \qquad (7)$$
$$E_{act} = \text{LN}(\text{MCA}(C_{act}, I) + C_{act}), \qquad (8)$$

where I is the encoded language instruction, $C_{lan} = [\hat{h}_t, \hat{f}_{t,1}, ..., \hat{f}_{t,k}] \in \mathbb{R}^{(k+1)\times d}$ and $C_{act} = [\hat{h}_t, \hat{o}_{t,1}, ..., \hat{o}_{t,k}] \in \mathbb{R}^{(k+1)\times d}$. Note that past history information will also be included here for the case of HAMT.

Subsequently, to get the intermediate action probability for each visual direction, multi-head cross attention will be performed on E_{lan} and E_{act}. The landmark-aware score $A_{lan,t} \in \mathbb{R}^k$ and action-aware score $A_{act,t} \in \mathbb{R}^k$ will be calculated by the average attention weight of all heads over each candidate token $\hat{f}_{t,i}$ and $\hat{o}_{t,i}$, respectively. At last, we perform a fusion operation where the final action probability $P_t \in \mathbb{R}^k$ for each candidate is the weighted sum over the output of two disentanglement branches:

$$P_t = \text{Softmax}([A_{lan,t}, A_{act,t}]W_s), \tag{9}$$

where $W_s = \hat{h}_t W_x$, and $W_x \in \mathbb{R}^{d\times 2}$, $W_s \in \mathbb{R}^2$ are learnable parameters, which decide the attended language component at the current position.

Language Auxiliary Loss. Given the index of landmark- and action-aware instruction, an intuitive idea is to utilize the label to regularize the attended language attention weight. Thus, we propose a language auxiliary loss (LAL) to guide more accurate disentangled feature extraction.

Considering the cross-modal attention block (Eqs. (7) and (8)), both the state token $(\hat{h}_t)$ and candidate tokens $(\hat{f}_{t,i}$ and $\hat{o}_{t,i})$ will attend to the language instruction. Instead of regularizing all attention weights of each token, we only optimize those of the state token, since the later self-attention will send the disentangled information to each candidate. Specifically, the landmark-aware language attention weight $\bar{\gamma}_{t,j}^n \in \mathbb{R}^1$ at step t is formulated by:

$$\bar{\gamma}_{t,j}^n = \frac{Q_t^n K_{t,j}^{n\mathsf{T}}}{\sqrt{d_h}}, \tag{10}$$

where d_h is the dimension of hidden state, j represents the index of a word in the instruction, n denotes the index of attention head, and Q is the query of agent state $\hat{h}_t$ while K is the key generated by each textual token. Then, to deal with the case where some states attend to more than one instruction word, a Sigmoid function is applied on the average attention weight of each head:

$$\gamma_{t,j} = \text{Sigmoid}(\frac{1}{N}\sum_{n=1}^{N}\bar{\gamma}_{t,j}^n). \tag{11}$$

Similarly, the action-aware language attention weight $\sigma_{t,j} \in \mathbb{R}^1$ can be obtained. Finally, a Binary Cross Entropy loss is enforced, as follows:

$$\mathcal{L}_{lan} = -\frac{1}{TL}\sum_{t=1}^{T}\sum_{j=1}^{L} x_{t,j}\log(\gamma_{t,j}) + (1 - x_{t,j})\log(1 - \gamma_{t,j}), \tag{12}$$

$$\mathcal{L}_{act} = -\frac{1}{TL}\sum_{t=1}^{T}\sum_{j=1}^{L} y_{t,j}\log(\sigma_{t,j}) + (1 - y_{t,j})\log(1 - \sigma_{t,j}), \tag{13}$$

where T is the number of navigation steps and L is instruction length, $\gamma_{t,j}$ and $\sigma_{t,j}$ are the predicted attention weights of landmark and action at each time step t. $x_{t,j}$ and $y_{t,j}$ are binary labels which are assigned to 1 only when the j-th word index is in L_t and A_t in Eq. (3), respectively.

3.5   Decoupled Label Speaker

Incorporating the baseline model and the Disentangled Decoding Module, we can utilize the proposed fine-grained labels to enhance the discriminative ability of the agent. However, our fine-grained label is only effective during Imitation Learning (IL) with original training data, since the exploration in Reinforcement Learning (RL) will produce abundant trajectories without fine-grained labels. Moreover, most VLN approaches use augmentation methods [44,65] to obtain more trajectories for training. These trajectories are also not annotated and can not be used by our model. A common idea is to use the baseline model to generate pseudo-labels, but this is only a by-product during the navigation. Moreover, the baseline is too large to be applied to other models. Therefore, we propose a general Decoupled Label Speaker (DLS) to provide supervised signals with landmark and action labels for these generated trajectories.

In general, as shown in Fig. 4, the DLS adopts an encoder-decoder paradigm. We first utilize two LSTM [25] to encode the observations along the path and corresponding instructions respectively, and then two cross-modal attention modules are imposed as landmark- and action-speaker to disentangle the instruction for each viewpoint.

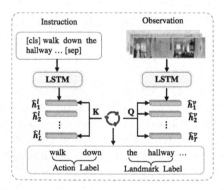

Fig. 4. Architecture of the proposed Decoupled Label Speaker (DLS). Taking the language instruction and visual observation as inputs, the DLS first encodes them using LSTMs and then employs cross-modal attention to predict landmark and action labels for each viewpoint.

Specifically, we use an external memory to store the visual observation during navigation, and then a Bi-LSTM is used to capture context information:

$$[h_1, \ldots, h_T] = \text{Bi-LSTM}(c_1, \ldots, c_T), \tag{14}$$

where T is the length of trajectory, and c_i is the view feature of selected candidate direction. Then, we attend the panoramic view o_t with the hidden state h_t:

$$z_{t,i} = \text{Softmax}_i(o_{t,i}^T W_z h_t),$$

$$h_t^v = \sum_i z_{t,i} o_{t,i},$$

$$\hat{h}_t^v = \text{Tanh}(W_v[h_t; h_t^v]), \tag{15}$$

where $\hat{h}_t^v$ is the vision-aware hidden state at each viewpoint, and W_v and W_z are trainable parameters. To get the instruction-aware hidden state, we use another encoder:

$$[\hat{h}_1^l, \ldots, \hat{h}_L^l] = \text{LSTM}(\hat{w}_1, \ldots, \hat{w}_L), \tag{16}$$

where $\hat{w}_j$ is the embedding of given instruction. Finally, we use two cross attention modules to implement landmark- and action-speaker:

$$\tilde{\gamma}_{t,j} = \text{Sigmoid}\left((W_l \hat{h}_t^v)^T \hat{h}_j^l\right),$$

$$\tilde{\sigma}_{t,j} = \text{Sigmoid}\left((W_a \hat{h}_t^v)^T \hat{h}_j^l\right), \tag{17}$$

where $\tilde{\gamma}_{t,j}$ and $\tilde{\sigma}_{t,j}$ is the probability of j-th word that belongs to landmark and action related part which should be highlighted to navigate to the next viewpoint.

To train the DLS, we use the annotated label to optimize the Binary Cross Entropy loss. The loss formulation can be obtained by replacing $\gamma_{t,j}$ in Eq. (12) and $\sigma_{t,j}$ in Eq. (13) with $\tilde{\gamma}_{t,j}$ and $\tilde{\sigma}_{t,j}$, respectively. To train our full model, we firstly train a converged DLS, and then freeze its parameters whose output will be regarded as pseudo-labels to optimize the language attention weight.

3.6 Training

The model is trained by mixed Imitation Learning (IL) and Reinforcement Learning (RL). In IL phase, the agent can learn quickly from the teacher action a_t^* at each time step t by Behaviour Cloning [5]. The IL loss is formulated by: $\mathcal{L}_{IL} = \frac{1}{T}\sum_{t=1}^T -a_t^*\log(p_t)$. In RL phase, the agent learns from the rewards by taking the action a_t^s sampled with the probability p_t. Formally: $\mathcal{L}_{RL} = \frac{1}{T}\sum_{t=1}^T -a_t^s\log(p_t)A_t$. where A_t is the advantage in A2C algorithm [49]. Overall, we jointly train our model in an end-to-end manner using the loss formulation:

$$\mathcal{L}_{loss} = \mathcal{L}_{RL} + \lambda_1\mathcal{L}_{IL} + \lambda_2\mathcal{L}_{lan} + \lambda_3\mathcal{L}_{act}. \tag{18}$$

where λ_1 manages the trade-off between IL and RL, λ_2 and λ_3 are weighting coefficients of language auxiliary loss.

4 Experiments

4.1 Experimental Setup

Evaluation Metrics. Following previous works [46,79], we use standard metrics to evaluate the navigator's performance on R2R dataset [2]. These include

Table 1. Comparison of single-run performance to the state-of-the-art methods on R2R [2]. *denotes our re-implementation. DDL provides consistent improvements.

Model	R2R Validation unseen				R2R Test unseen			
	SR↑	SPL↑	OR↑	NE↓	SR↑	SPL↑	OR↑	NE↓
Speaker-Follower [18]	36	–	45	6.62	35	28	44	6.62
RCM [73]	43	–	50	6.09	43	38	50	6.12
Self-Monitoring [46]	45	32	56	5.52	43	32	55	5.99
Regretful [47]	50	41	59	5.32	48	40	56	5.69
E-Dropout [65]	52	48	–	5.22	51	47	59	5.23
AuxRN [79]	55	50	62	5.28	55	51	62	5.15
OAAM [56]	54	50	61	–	53	50	61	–
RelGraph [26]	57	53	-	4.73	55	52	–	4.75
PREVALENT [23]	58	53	–	4.71	54	51	–	5.30
SSM [70]	62	45	73	4.32	61	46	70	4.57
VLN◯BERT [28]	63	57	–	3.93	63	57	–	4.09
HAMT [11]	66	61	–	**2.29**	65	60	–	3.93
OAAM* [56]	54.4	49.0	62.8	5.00	53.6	49.9	59.4	5.00
OAAM* + DDL	57.6	51.0	65.6	4.63	57.0	51.4	65.3	4.70
VLN◯BERT* [28]	62.2	56.5	68.3	4.09	62.2	56.7	68.6	4.04
VLN◯BERT* + DDL	64.8	58.3	71.1	3.84	64.1	58.1	70.8	3.97
HAMT* [11]	65.6	60.7	73.7	3.51	64.4	59.5	69.3	4.03
HAMT* + DDL	**67.9**	**62.2**	**76.0**	3.38	**66.3**	**61.1**	**72.4**	**3.80**

Success Rate (SR) which is a ratio of the agent whose distance between stopped position and target location is within 3 m, Success rate weighted by Path Length (SPL), Navigation Error (NE) which is the average distance in meters between the final position and the target, and Oracle Success Rate (OSR) which measures success rate at the nearest point to the goal along the entire visited path. Among these metrics, SR and SPL are the main metrics, since the SR directly quantifies the crucial notion of success rate for the VLN task, and SPL combines the path length and SR to focus on more efficient navigation. For R4R [32], additional metrics including Coverage weighted by Length Score (CLS) [32], normalized Dynamic Time Warping (nDTW) and SDTW [30] are considered to encourage the agent to stay on the path that the instruction indicates.

Implementation Details. For the decoupled label speaker, the model is trained on the proposed LAR2R dataset for 80,000 iterations with a batch size of 32. The Adam [34] optimizer is used with a learning rate of 1e−4. Then the model with the lowest loss on the validation unseen set is selected. For navigation, we set the language auxiliary loss weights to $\lambda_2 = 1.0$, $\lambda_3 = 1.0$. We keep the other settings same as the baseline [11,28,56] for fairness.

Table 2. Comparison of single-run performance to the state-of-the-art methods on R4R [32]. *denotes our re-implementation. DDL provides consistent improvements.

Model	R4R Validation seen						R4R Validation unseen					
	SR↑	SPL↑	NE↓	nDTW↑	SDTW↑	CLS↑	SR↑	SPL↑	NE↓	nDTW↑	SDTW↑	CLS↑
Speaker-Follower [18]	52	37	5.35	–	–	46	24	12	8.47	–	–	30
RCM [32]	53	31	5.37	–	–	55	26	8	8.08	–	–	35
PTA [39]	58	39	4.53	58	41	60	24	10	8.25	32	10	37
EnvDrop [65]	52	41	–	–	27	53	29	18	–	–	9	34
EGP [13]	–	–	–	–	–	–	30	–	8.00	37	18	44
OAAM* [56]	48.3	40.2	5.81	47.6	31.2	51.0	26.6	19.0	8.51	30.3	12.6	36.2
OAAM* + DDL	50.2	41.9	5.59	49.8	33.6	53.7	28.5	21.2	8.15	33.1	14.2	38.5
VLN◯BERT* [28]	60.2	50.7	4.63	48.2	36.3	49.5	39.3	29.3	6.66	35.2	19.1	39.4
VLN◯BERT* + DDL	64.4	53.6	3.97	55.6	43.1	57.6	42.4	32.7	6.43	38.5	21.0	43.6

4.2 Results and Analysis

Comparison to SoTA. The single-run setting is considered as the primary experimental setup since it can accurately reflect the agent's performance and generalizability to novel environments and instructions. Under this setting, the agent is not allowed to run multiple trials or pre-explore the test environments. As shown in Table 1, DDL brings consistent and substantial performance improvement to both the LSTM-based and BERT-based navigators, demonstrating the generality and effectiveness of our approach. For the state-of-the-art method HAMT, DDL increases the success rate by 2.3% and SPL with 1.5% on validation unseen set. On test unseen, we increase SR by 1.9%, while SPL is improved by 1.6%. Table 2 shows we can also boost the performance on R4R in terms of nDTW, SDTW and CLS, indicating that DDL can encourage the agent to stay on the path and have high instruction fidelity.

Table 3. Ablation study with OAAM showing the effect of each component on R2R. LAR2R means the annotated labels, DLS represents the pseudo-labels, and BT denotes extra augmented training data [65] without decoupled labels.

Model	Component				R2R Val seen		R2R Val unseen	
	Baseline	LAR2R	DLS	BT	SR↑	SPL↑	SR↑	SPL↑
1	✓				63.0	59.5	50.2	45.4
2	✓	✓			65.3	61.1	50.8	45.7
3	✓	✓	✓		65.2	61.4	51.5	45.9
4	✓			✓	70.7	67.1	54.4	49.0
5	✓	✓	✓	✓	70.8	66.4	**57.6**	**51.0**

Ablation Study. Table 3 presents the impact of each component in OAAM. The training process consists of two stages. In the first stage, only the original training data is used. Thus, we use the annotated labels for IL phase and pseudo-labels for RL phase. In the second stage, a large amount of augmented data is

Table 4. Performance comparison with OAAM considering different types of decoupled labels on R2R. Our fine-grained labels perform favorably against the other alternatives.

Model	R2R Val seen				R2R Val unseen			
	SR↑	SPL↑	OR↑	NE↓	SR↑	SPL↑	OR↑	NE↓
Random	53.6	50.0	60.9	5.03	47.9	44.2	55.6	5.45
Average	62.3	58.3	68.0	4.19	48.7	45.3	55.8	5.43
FGR2R* [27]	63.0	58.8	71.2	4.09	49.6	44.6	56.9	5.41
Ours (LAR2R)	**65.3**	**61.1**	**72.4**	**3.84**	**50.8**	**45.7**	**58.1**	**5.27**

added, which is unlabeled. We utilize Decoupled Label Speaker to provide intermediate supervision signals for this augmented data. As shown in Table 3, we find that when the annotated labels (model #2) are used to regularize the language attention weight in IL phase, the performance gets slight improvement. Moreover, model #3 indicates that the generalizability of the agent can be improved via providing landmark and action pseudo-labels for the reinforcement training phase. Comparing model #5 with #4, we find that the performance on validation unseen split gets significant improvement with the gains of 3.2% and 2.0% in terms of SR and SPL. This can be attributed to the fact that although Back Translation (BT) [65] brings lots of data without decoupled labels, our speaker can accurately generate landmark and action pseudo-labels for the augmented data thereby providing additional supervision signals during training.

Effectiveness of Decoupled Label. Based on the proposed LAR2R labels, initially, we only utilize the annotated label to regularize language attention weight in IL phase. Under this setting, to reveal its effectiveness, Table 4 shows the results of different types of language label. In the first column, *Random* represents the language labels $x_{t,j}$ and $y_{t,j}$ in Eqs. (12) and (13) are sampled from a uniform distribution $U[0, 1]$. *Average* means all language labels are assigned to 1. *FGR2R* means we generate the labels by Part-of-Speech tagging for each sub-instruction of FGR2R [27]. As shown in Table 4, the random label degrades the performance with the reduction of 2.3% SR and 1.2% SPL on validation unseen set compared with model #1 in Table 3 without language label. Moreover, our proposed labels have better performance than that of FGR2R, since FGR2R only focuses on the segmentation while ours is more fine-grained. These results further demonstrate the effectiveness of our decoupled labels.

Quantitative and Qualitative Analysis of Decoupled Label Speaker. Figure 5 presents an example of the distribution of landmark and action attention weights predicted by our DLS at two navigation steps. One can note that the landmark- and action-related instructions are clearly disentangled. In particular, the landmark-speaker not only focuses on the object (*e.g.*. bed), but it is also able to attend the specific position next to the object (*e.g.*. the end of the

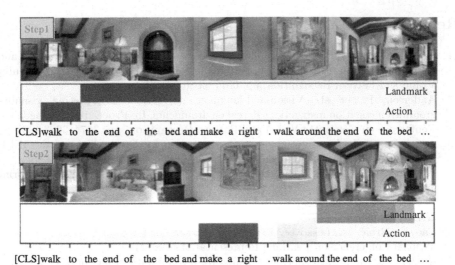

Fig. 5. Distribution of landmark and action attention weights predicted by the decoupled label speaker at the first two navigation steps in an unseen environment. Color shade represents the relative attention weight (darker is higher).

bed), which can help the agent navigate to the precise location. Notice that the example is tested in an unseen environment, demonstrating the generalizability of our model. Moreover, a quantitative analysis is presented in Supp-Figure 1. It can be noted that most pseudo-labels have high cosine similarity with the human-annotated labels, showing the effectiveness of DLS.

5   Conclusion

In this paper, we have explored the effectiveness of the decoupled instruction label on the vision-and-language navigation task. Firstly, we enrich R2R with specific landmark- and action-aware labels. We further propose a Decoupled Label Speaker to generate pseudo-labels, which are utilized to guide discriminative feature extraction in Disentangled Decoding Module. Superior performance on two VLN benchmarks demonstrates the effectiveness of our proposed approach. Although this work focuses on using the decoupled labels to provide accurate inputs for VLN, this framework can positively impact other tasks, such as visual question answering [3,63,77] and visual dialog navigation [51,52,67]. Further, new solutions for achieving disentanglement is an critical open research question in VLN, as well as other computer vision tasks, such as object tracking [15,22] and segmentation [16,75].

Acknowledgements. This work was supported partly by the Start-up Research Grant (SRG) of University of Macau. We thank the reviewers for their insightful comments.

References

1. Anderson, P., et al.: Bottom-up and top-down attention for image captioning and visual question answering. In: Proceedings of the IEEE Conference on Computer Vision and Pattern Recognition, pp. 6077–6086 (2018)
2. Anderson, P., et al.: Vision-and-language navigation: interpreting visually-grounded navigation instructions in real environments. In: Proceedings of the IEEE Conference on Computer Vision and Pattern Recognition, pp. 3674–3683 (2018)
3. Antol, S., et al.: Vqa: visual question answering. In: Proceedings of the IEEE International Conference on Computer Vision (2015)
4. Ba, J.L., Kiros, J.R., Hinton, G.E.: Layer normalization. arXiv preprint arXiv:1607.06450 (2016)
5. Bojarski, M., et al.: End to end learning for self-driving cars. arXiv preprint arXiv:1604.07316 (2016)
6. Cao, K., Brbić, M., Leskovec, J.: Concept learners for few-shot learning. In: International Conference on Learning Representations (2021)
7. Chang, A., et al.: Matterport3d: learning from rgb-d data in indoor environments. In: 7th IEEE International Conference on 3D Vision, 3DV 2017, pp. 667–676. Institute of Electrical and Electronics Engineers Inc. (2018)
8. Chen, H., Suhr, A., Misra, D., Snavely, N., Artzi, Y.: Touchdown: natural language navigation and spatial reasoning in visual street environments. In: Proceedings of the IEEE/CVF Conference on Computer Vision and Pattern Recognition, pp. 12538–12547 (2019)
9. Chen, J., Gao, C., Meng, E., Zhang, Q., Liu, S.: Reinforced structured state-evolution for vision-language navigation. In: Proceedings of the IEEE/CVF Conference on Computer Vision and Pattern Recognition (CVPR). pp. 15450–15459 (2022)
10. Chen, K., Chen, J.K., Chuang, J., Vázquez, M., Savarese, S.: Topological planning with transformers for vision-and-language navigation. In: Proceedings of the IEEE/CVF Conference on Computer Vision and Pattern Recognition, pp. 11276–11286 (2021)
11. Chen, S., Guhur, P.L., Schmid, C., Laptev, I.: History aware multimodal transformer for vision-and-language navigation. Adv. Neural Inf. Process. Syst. **34**, 1–14 (2021)
12. Chen, S., Guhur, P.L., Tapaswi, M., Schmid, C., Laptev, I.: Think global, act local: dual-scale graph transformer for vision-and-language navigation. arXiv preprint arXiv:2202.11742 (2022)
13. Deng, Z., Narasimhan, K., Russakovsky, O.: Evolving graphical planner: contextual global planning for vision-and-language navigation. In: Advances in Neural Information Processing Systems, vol. 33, pp. 20660–20672. Curran Associates, Inc. (2020)
14. Devlin, J., Chang, M., Lee, K., Toutanova, K.: BERT: pre-training of deep bidirectional transformers for language understanding. In: Proceedings of the 2019 Conference of the North American Chapter of the Association for Computational Linguistics: Human Language Technologies, volu. 1 (Long and Short Papers), pp. 4171–4186 (2019)
15. Dong, X., Shen, J., Shao, L., Porikli, F.: CLNet: a compact latent network for fast adjusting siamese trackers. In: Vedaldi, A., Bischof, H., Brox, T., Frahm, J.-M. (eds.) ECCV 2020. LNCS, vol. 12365, pp. 378–395. Springer, Cham (2020). https://doi.org/10.1007/978-3-030-58565-5_23

16. Dong, X., Shen, J., Shao, L., Van Gool, L.: Sub-markov random walk for image segmentation. IEEE Trans. Image Process. **25**(2), 516–527 (2015)
17. Fang, K., Toshev, A., Fei-Fei, L., Savarese, S.: Scene memory transformer for embodied agents in long-horizon tasks. In: Proceedings of the IEEE/CVF Conference on Computer Vision and Pattern Recognition, pp. 538–547 (2019)
18. Fried, D., et al.: Speaker-follower models for vision-and-language navigation. In: Proceedings of the 32nd International Conference on Neural Information Processing Systems, pp. 3318–3329 (2018)
19. Fu, T.-J., Wang, X.E., Peterson, M.F., Grafton, S.T., Eckstein, M.P., Wang, W.Y.: Counterfactual vision-and-language navigation via adversarial path sampler. In: Vedaldi, A., Bischof, H., Brox, T., Frahm, J.-M. (eds.) ECCV 2020. LNCS, vol. 12351, pp. 71–86. Springer, Cham (2020). https://doi.org/10.1007/978-3-030-58539-6_5
20. Gao, C., Chen, J., Liu, S., Wang, L., Zhang, Q., Wu, Q.: Room-and-object aware knowledge reasoning for remote embodied referring expression. In: Proceedings of the IEEE/CVF Conference on Computer Vision and Pattern Recognition (CVPR), pp. 3064–3073 (2021)
21. Guhur, P.L., Tapaswi, M., Chen, S., Laptev, I., Schmid, C.: Airbert: in-domain pretraining for vision-and-language navigation. In: Proceedings of the IEEE/CVF International Conference on Computer Vision, pp. 1634–1643 (2021)
22. Han, W., Dong, X., Khan, F.S., Shao, L., Shen, J.: Learning to fuse asymmetric feature maps in siamese trackers. In: Proceedings of the IEEE/CVF Conference on Computer Vision and Pattern Recognition, pp. 16570–16580 (2021)
23. Hao, W., Li, C., Li, X., Carin, L., Gao, J.: Towards learning a generic agent for vision-and-language navigation via pre-training. In: Proceedings of the IEEE/CVF Conference on Computer Vision and Pattern Recognition, pp. 13137–13146 (2020)
24. He, K., Zhang, X., Ren, S., Sun, J.: Deep residual learning for image recognition. In: Proceedings of the IEEE Conference on Computer Vision and Pattern Recognition, pp. 770–778 (2016)
25. Hochreiter, S., Schmidhuber, J.: Long short-term memory. Neural Comput. **9**(8), 1735–1780 (1997)
26. Hong, Y., Rodriguez, C., Qi, Y., Wu, Q., Gould, S.: Language and visual entity relationship graph for agent navigation. Adv. Neural Inf. Process. Syst. **33**, 1–12 (2020)
27. Hong, Y., Rodriguez, C., Wu, Q., Gould, S.: Sub-instruction aware vision-and-language navigation. In: Proceedings of the 2020 Conference on Empirical Methods in Natural Language Processing, pp. 3360–3376 (2020)
28. Hong, Y., Wu, Q., Qi, Y., Rodriguez-Opazo, C., Gould, S.: Vln bert: a recurrent vision-and-language bert for navigation. In: Proceedings of the IEEE/CVF Conference on Computer Vision and Pattern Recognition, pp. 1643–1653 (2021)
29. Hu, R., Fried, D., Rohrbach, A., Klein, D., Darrell, T., Saenko, K.: Are you looking? grounding to multiple modalities in vision-and-language navigation. arXiv preprint arXiv:1906.00347 (2019)
30. Ilharco, G., Jain, V., Ku, A., Ie, E., Baldridge, J.: General evaluation for instruction conditioned navigation using dynamic time warping. arXiv preprint arXiv:1907.05446 (2019)
31. Irshad, M.Z., Mithun, N.C., Seymour, Z., Chiu, H.P., Samarasekera, S., Kumar, R.: Sasra: semantically-aware spatio-temporal reasoning agent for vision-and-language navigation in continuous environments. arXiv preprint arXiv:2108.11945 (2021)

32. Jain, V., Magalhaes, G., Ku, A., Vaswani, A., Ie, E., Baldridge, J.: Stay on the path: instruction fidelity in vision-and-language navigation. In: Proceedings of the 57th Annual Meeting of the Association for Computational Linguistics, pp. 1862–1872 (2019)
33. Ke, L., et al.: Tactical rewind: Self-correction via backtracking in vision-and-language navigation. In: Proceedings of the IEEE/CVF Conference on Computer Vision and Pattern Recognition, pp. 6741–6749 (2019)
34. Kingma, D.P., Ba, J.: Adam: a method for stochastic optimization. In: 3rd International Conference on Learning Representations, San Diego, CA, USA, 7–9 May 2015, Conference Track Proceedings (2015)
35. Kolve, E., et al.: Ai2-thor: an interactive 3D environment for visual AI. arXiv preprint arXiv:1712.05474 (2017)
36. Krantz, J., Gokaslan, A., Batra, D., Lee, S., Maksymets, O.: Waypoint models for instruction-guided navigation in continuous environments. In: Proceedings of the IEEE/CVF International Conference on Computer Vision, pp. 15162–15171 (2021)
37. Krantz, J., Wijmans, E., Majumdar, A., Batra, D., Lee, S.: Beyond the navgraph: vision-and-language navigation in continuous environments. In: Vedaldi, A., Bischof, H., Brox, T., Frahm, J.-M. (eds.) ECCV 2020. LNCS, vol. 12373, pp. 104–120. Springer, Cham (2020). https://doi.org/10.1007/978-3-030-58604-1_7
38. Ku, A., Anderson, P., Patel, R., Ie, E., Baldridge, J.: Room-across-room: multilingual vision-and-language navigation with dense spatiotemporal grounding. In: Proceedings of the 2020 Conference on Empirical Methods in Natural Language Processing, pp. 4392–4412 (2020)
39. Landi, F., Baraldi, L., Cornia, M., Corsini, M., Cucchiara, R.: Perceive, transform, and act: multimodal attention networks for low-level vision-and-language navigation. arXiv preprint arXiv:1911.12377 (2019)
40. Li, X., et al.: Robust navigation with language pretraining and stochastic sampling. In: Proceedings of the 2019 Conference on Empirical Methods in Natural Language Processing and the 9th International Joint Conference on Natural Language Processing, pp. 1494–1499 (2019)
41. Li, X., et al.: OSCAR: object-semantics aligned pre-training for vision-language tasks. In: Vedaldi, A., Bischof, H., Brox, T., Frahm, J.-M. (eds.) ECCV 2020. LNCS, vol. 12375, pp. 121–137. Springer, Cham (2020). https://doi.org/10.1007/978-3-030-58577-8_8
42. Liang, X., Zhu, F., Zhu, Y., Lin, B., Wang, B., Liang, X.: Contrastive instruction-trajectory learning for vision-language navigation. arXiv preprint arXiv:2112.04138 (2021)
43. Lin, C., Jiang, Y., Cai, J., Qu, L., Haffari, G., Yuan, Z.: Multimodal transformer with variable-length memory for vision-and-language navigation. arXiv preprint arXiv:2111.05759 (2021)
44. Liu, C., Zhu, F., Chang, X., Liang, X., Ge, Z., Shen, Y.D.: Vision-language navigation with random environmental mixup. In: Proceedings of the IEEE/CVF International Conference on Computer Vision, pp. 1644–1654 (2021)
45. Lu, J., Batra, D., Parikh, D., Lee, S.: Vilbert: pretraining task-agnostic visiolinguistic representations for vision-and-language tasks. In: Advances in Neural Information Processing Systems, vol. 32. Curran Associates, Inc. (2019)
46. Ma, C.Y., et al.: Self-monitoring navigation agent via auxiliary progress estimation. In: Proceedings of the International Conference on Learning Representations (2019)

47. Ma, C.Y., Wu, Z., AlRegib, G., Xiong, C., Kira, Z.: The regretful agent: heuristic-aided navigation through progress estimation. In: Proceedings of the IEEE/CVF Conference on Computer Vision and Pattern Recognition, pp. 6732–6740 (2019)
48. Majumdar, A., Shrivastava, A., Lee, S., Anderson, P., Parikh, D., Batra, D.: Improving vision-and-language navigation with image-text pairs from the web. In: Vedaldi, A., Bischof, H., Brox, T., Frahm, J.-M. (eds.) ECCV 2020. LNCS, vol. 12351, pp. 259–274. Springer, Cham (2020). https://doi.org/10.1007/978-3-030-58539-6_16
49. Mnih, V., et al.: Asynchronous methods for deep reinforcement learning. In: International Conference on Machine Learning, pp. 1928–1937. PMLR (2016)
50. Moudgil, A., Majumdar, A., Agrawal, H., Lee, S., Batra, D.: Soat: a scene- and object-aware transformer for vision-and-language navigation. arXiv preprint arXiv:2110.14143 (2021)
51. Nguyen, K., Daumé III, H.: Help, anna! visual navigation with natural multimodal assistance via retrospective curiosity-encouraging imitation learning. In: Proceedings of the 2019 Conference on Empirical Methods in Natural Language Processing and the 9th International Joint Conference on Natural Language Processing, pp. 684–695 (2019)
52. Nguyen, K., Dey, D., Brockett, C., Dolan, B.: Vision-based navigation with language-based assistance via imitation learning with indirect intervention. In: Proceedings of the IEEE/CVF Conference on Computer Vision and Pattern Recognition, pp. 12527–12537 (2019)
53. Parvaneh, A., Abbasnejad, E., Teney, D., Shi, Q., van den Hengel, A.: Counterfactual vision-and-language navigation: unravelling the unseen. Adv. Neural Inf. Process. Syst. **33**, 5296–5307 (2020)
54. Pashevich, A., Schmid, C., Sun, C.: Episodic transformer for vision-and-language navigation. In: ICCV (2021)
55. Qi, Y., Pan, Z., Hong, Y., Yang, M.H., van den Hengel, A., Wu, Q.: The road to know-where: An object-and-room informed sequential bert for indoor vision-language navigation. In: Proceedings of the IEEE/CVF International Conference on Computer Vision, pp. 1655–1664 (2021)
56. Qi, Y., Pan, Z., Zhang, S., van den Hengel, A., Wu, Q.: Object-and-action aware model for visual language navigation. In: Proceedings of the European Conference on Computer Vision, Glasgow, Scotland, pp. 23–28. Springer, Heidelberg (2020)
57. Qi, Y., et al.: Reverie: Remote embodied visual referring expression in real indoor environments. In: Proceedings of the IEEE/CVF Conference on Computer Vision and Pattern Recognition, pp. 9982–9991 (2020)
58. Qiao, Y., Qi, Y., Hong, Y., Yu, Z., Wang, P., Wu, Q.: Hop: history-and-order aware pre-training for vision-and-language navigation. In: Proceedings of the IEEE/CVF Conference on Computer Vision and Pattern Recognition (CVPR), pp. 15418–15427 (2022)
59. Qin, W., Misu, T., Wijaya, D.: Explore the potential performance of vision-and-language navigation model: a snapshot ensemble method. arXiv preprint arXiv:2111.14267 (2021)
60. Raychaudhuri, S., Wani, S., Patel, S., Jain, U., Chang, A.X.: Language-aligned waypoint (law) supervision for vision-and-language navigation in continuous environments. arXiv preprint arXiv:2109.15207 (2021)
61. Russakovsky, O., et al.: Imagenet large scale visual recognition challenge. Int. J. Comput. Vision **115**(3), 211-252 (2015)

62. Savva, M., et al.: Habitat: a platform for embodied ai research. In: Proceedings of the IEEE/CVF International Conference on Computer Vision, pp. 9339–9347 (2019)
63. Shih, K.J., Singh, S., Hoiem, D.: Where to look: focus regions for visual question answering. In: Proceedings of the IEEE Conference on Computer Vision and Pattern Recognition (2016)
64. Shridhar, M., et al.: Alfred: a benchmark for interpreting grounded instructions for everyday tasks. In: Proceedings of the IEEE/CVF Conference on Computer Vision and Pattern Recognition, pp. 10740–10749 (2020)
65. Tan, H., Yu, L., Bansal, M.: Learning to navigate unseen environments: back translation with environmental dropout. In: Proceedings of the 2019 Conference of the North American Chapter of the Association for Computational Linguistics: Human Language Technologies, vol. 1 (Long and Short Papers), pp. 2610–2621 (2019)
66. Tan, S., Ge, M., Guo, D., Liu, H., Sun, F.: Self-supervised 3D semantic representation learning for vision-and-language navigation. arXiv preprint arXiv:2201.10788 (2022)
67. Thomason, J., Murray, M., Cakmak, M., Zettlemoyer, L.: Vision-and-dialog navigation. In: Conference on Robot Learning, pp. 394–406. PMLR (2020)
68. Vaswani, A., et al.: Attention is all you need. In: Proceedings of the 31st International Conference on Neural Information Processing Systems, pp. 6000–6010 (2017)
69. Wang, H., Liang, W., Shen, J., Van Gool, L., Wang, W.: Counterfactual cycle-consistent learning for instruction following and generation in vision-language navigation. In: Proceedings of the IEEE/CVF Conference on Computer Vision and Pattern Recognition, pp. 15471–15481 (2022)
70. Wang, H., Wang, W., Liang, W., Xiong, C., Shen, J.: Structured scene memory for vision-language navigation. In: Proceedings of the IEEE/CVF Conference on Computer Vision and Pattern Recognition, pp. 8455–8464 (2021)
71. Wang, H., Wang, W., Shu, T., Liang, W., Shen, J.: Active visual information gathering for vision-language navigation. In: Vedaldi, A., Bischof, H., Brox, T., Frahm, J.-M. (eds.) ECCV 2020. LNCS, vol. 12367, pp. 307–322. Springer, Cham (2020). https://doi.org/10.1007/978-3-030-58542-6_19
72. Wang, H., Wu, Q., Shen, C.: Soft expert reward learning for vision-and-language navigation. In: Vedaldi, A., Bischof, H., Brox, T., Frahm, J.-M. (eds.) ECCV 2020. LNCS, vol. 12354, pp. 126–141. Springer, Cham (2020). https://doi.org/10.1007/978-3-030-58545-7_8
73. Wang, X., et al.: Reinforced cross-modal matching and self-supervised imitation learning for vision-language navigation. In: Proceedings of the IEEE/CVF Conference on Computer Vision and Pattern Recognition, pp. 6629–6638 (2019)
74. Wang, X., Xiong, W., Wang, H., Wang, W.Y.: Look before you leap: bridging model-free and model-based reinforcement learning for planned-ahead vision-and-language navigation. In: Proceedings of the European Conference on Computer Vision, pp. 37–53 (2018)
75. Wu, D., Dong, X., Shao, L., Shen, J.: Multi-level representation learning with semantic alignment for referring video object segmentation. In: Proceedings of the IEEE/CVF Conference on Computer Vision and Pattern Recognition, pp. 4996–5005 (2022)
76. Xiang, J., Wang, X., Wang, W.Y.: Learning to stop: a simple yet effective approach to urban vision-language navigation. In: Proceedings of the 2020 Conference on Empirical Methods in Natural Language Processing: Findings, pp. 699–707 (2020)

77. Zhang, Y., Niebles, J.C., Soto, A.: Interpretable visual question answering by visual grounding from attention supervision mining. In: 2019 IEEE Winter Conference on Applications of Computer Vision, pp. 349–357. IEEE (2019)
78. Zhou, B., Lapedriza, A., Khosla, A., Oliva, A., Torralba, A.: Places: a 10 million image database for scene recognition. IEEE Trans. Pattern Anal. Mach. Intell. **40**(6), 1452–1464 (2017)
79. Zhu, F., Zhu, Y., Chang, X., Liang, X.: Vision-language navigation with self-supervised auxiliary reasoning tasks. In: Proceedings of the IEEE/CVF Conference on Computer Vision and Pattern Recognition, pp. 10012–10022 (2020)
80. Zhu, W., et al.: Babywalk: going farther in vision-and-language navigation by taking baby steps. In: Proceedings of the 58th Annual Meeting of the Association for Computational Linguistics, pp. 2539–2556 (2020)

Switch-BERT: Learning to Model Multimodal Interactions by Switching Attention and Input

Qingpei Guo[1(✉)], Kaisheng Yao[2], and Wei Chu[1]

[1] Ant Group, Hangzhou, China
{qingpei.gqp,weichu.cw}@antgroup.com
[2] Amazon AWS AI, Seattle, US
kaishey@amazon.com

Abstract. The ability to model intra-modal and inter-modal interactions is fundamental in multimodal machine learning. The current state-of-the-art models usually adopt deep learning models with fixed structures. They can achieve exceptional performances on specific tasks, but face a particularly challenging problem of modality mismatch because of diversity of input modalities and their fixed structures. In this paper, we present **Switch-BERT** for joint vision and language representation learning to address this problem. Switch-BERT extends BERT architecture by introducing learnable layer-wise and cross-layer interactions. It learns to optimize attention from a set of attention modes representing these interactions. One specific property of the model is that it learns to attend outputs from various depths, therefore mitigates the modality mismatch problem. We present extensive experiments on visual question answering, image-text retrieval and referring expression comprehension experiments. Results confirm that, whereas alternative architectures including ViLBERT and UNITER may excel in particular tasks, Switch-BERT can consistently achieve better or comparable performances than the current state-of-the-art models in these tasks. Ablation studies indicate that the proposed model achieves superior performances due to its ability in learning task-specific multimodal interactions.

Keywords: Multimodal interactions · Cross-layer interaction · Switch attention

1 Introduction

The current state-of-the-art approaches for multimodal machine learning [5,18, 19,22,25,32,34] are based on the BERT encoders [6] that use the Transformer architecture [36]. These BERT-based models follow two design paradigms for

---

Supplementary Information The online version contains supplementary material available at https://doi.org/10.1007/978-3-031-20059-5_19.

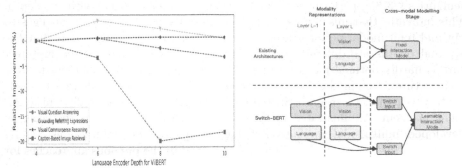

(a) Illustration of modality misalignment in VilBERT(fixed structure).

(b) Comparison between popular multi-modal architectures with Switch-BERT.

Fig. 1. (a) The text and visual encoder are separate before their interactions in Vil-BERT [25]. By varying the depth of text encoder from 4 to 10, the accuracy of VilBERT is changed relative to that from depth 4. The optimal relative improvements in accuracy are different in the four tasks. For VilBERT, the misalignment can degrade performances by approximately 20% relatively. (b) In contrast to fixed structures, Switch-BERT learns to attend outputs from various depth and has learnable layer-wise and cross-layer interactions.

intra-modal and inter-modal interactions. The first paradigm utilizes a single-stream BERT encoder to jointly encode representations from these modalities, such as those from vision and language [5, 18, 19, 22, 32]. In this case, intra-modal interactions and the implicit association between modalities are jointly modeled with the multi-head attention mechanism [36]. The second paradigm learns modal-specific representations through different BERT encoders, for instance using dual-stream BERT encoders on vision and language [25, 34]. These methods achieve inter-modal interactions via specially designed structures such as cross-attention sub-layers [14, 25, 40].

However, misalignment between modal semantics is a challenging problem for these methods. For example, the visual modality observation often is based on region-level semantic feature from detection models such as Faster R-CNN [29], whereas the text modality observation can be simply raw tokens or sub-word tokens such as word-pieces [37]. For single-stream models, these visual features with high-level semantics and text input with low-level semantics are both fed to the BERT encoder simultaneously. Given that these observations are not at the same semantic level, using a common encoding process for different modalities seems to be contradictory. The dual-stream models can ease the misalignment problem with distinct encoding process for each modality. However, the interaction between modalities of dual-stream models is restricted to specific layers that can be inflexible.

Figure 1(a) illustrates this problem by tuning the depth of a BERT-based language encoder before interaction with the visual stream in ViLBERT [25] on a set of tasks. Though with deeper encoder that usually extracts higher level semantics [23,35], performances don't reveal monotonous trend with the depth. This indicates that misalignment between modal semantics poses challenges to optimal multimodal performances. Another observation in Fig. 1(a) is that the optimal depths are different for these tasks, indicating that a fixed architecture is hardly optimal for every task. This suggests necessity for more flexible architectures. The modality misalignment problem is however not well studied.

In this paper, we propose Switch-BERT to alleviate the modality misalignment problem. As illustrated in Fig. 1(b), Switch-BERT extends the recently developed multimodal methods but has sample-specific interactions among modalities, instead of fixed architectures adopted in the previous approaches for every sample. Specifically, it introduces two modules, respectively for layer-wise switch operation in Switch-Attention Block (SAB) and cross-layer switch operation in Switch Input Block (SIB). The SAB module learns to attend to, given a sample, particular modality and choose from a set of predefined operations for interactions among modalities. The SIB module introduces sample-specific modeling of cross-layer modal representations and learns to switch inputs among representations at various depths.

We pre-train Switch-BERT on Conceptual Captions [30] to learn task independent visual and text grounding. Proxy pre-training tasks include masked language modeling with visual clues (MLM), masked region classification with KL-divergence (MRC-KL) [5] and Image-Text Matching (ITM). We evaluate Switch-BERT on three downstream tasks including visual question answering, cross-modal retrieval and referring expression comprehension, and perform experiments on VQAv2 [9], Flick30k [27] and RefCOCO+ [14] datasets. Experimental results show Switch-BERT can learn better multimodal representations, compared with previous single- and dual-stream models. We conduct ablation studies and show that Switch-BERT can learn task-specific multimodal interactions end-to-end, including layer-wise interaction selection and cross-layer input selection. This task-specificity is an advantage over other methods with fixed architectures.

2   Methodology

2.1   Preliminaries

Language BERT Encoder. BERT [6] was originally proposed for natural language processing tasks to learn semantic representations for each input token via a stack of transformers [36]. A BERT encoder consists of L transformer layers, in which representation X_l at l-th layer is obtained from the representation X_{l-1} in its lower layer as follows:

$$X_l = LN(\bar{X}_l + GeLU(\bar{X}_l W_1)W_2), \tag{1}$$
$$\bar{X}_l = LN(\hat{X}_l + X_{l-1}), \tag{2}$$
$$\hat{X}_l = MHA(Q_l, K_l, V_l) \tag{3}$$

where $MHA(\cdot)$ implements the multi-head attention mechanism [36], with query, key, and value at layer l each computed as $Q_l = X_{l-1}W^Q$, $K_l = X_{l-1}W^K$, and $V_l = X_{l-1}W^V$. LN is layer normalization [3], $GeLU$ [10] is the activation function of feed forward block. $W^Q, W^K \in R^{d \times d^q}$, $W^V \in R^{d \times d^i}$, and $W_1, W_2^\top \in R^{d \times d^f}$ are learnable matrices. The multi-head attention block and feed forward block form a transformer layer.

Multimodal BERT Encoder. Multimodal BERT [15,25] extends the language BERT with multimodal input vector sequences. For instance, for tasks that consist of image and text, the model assigns two types of inputs: image can be a sequence of vectors as $X^i = [IMG, i_1, \cdots, i_{N_i-1}] \in R^{N_i \times d_i}$ and text can be $X^t = [CLS, w_1, \cdots, w_{N_t-2}, SEP] \in R^{N_t \times d_t}$, where IMG, CLS and SEP are embeddings of special markers. Usually, we have $d_i = d_t = d$. Typical approaches include UNITER [5], in which X^i and X^t are concatenated, forming a single stream of input $X_0 = [X^i X^t]$ to compute query, key and value matrices. In contrast, ViLBERT [25] computes query from one modality but key and value from other modality, and vice versa, forming dual steams of computations.

2.2 Generalizing BERT Encoder

We would like to generalize the encoder in Eqs. (1-3) beyond the multimodal architectures described above. To this end, we first use $X \in \{X^i, X^t\}$ to denote either the image modality observation X^i or text modality observation X^t. We use $\neg X$ to denote complementary of X; e.g., $\neg X = X^i$ if $X = X^t$. Notice that X^i and X^t are for purpose of notations, and can be generalized beyond image and text modalities.

We further generalize the multi-head attention mechanism in Eq. (3) beyond linear projections on input X_{l-1}, in which query, key, and value are obtained via certain transformations. Formally, we rewrite Eq. (3) as follows:

$$\hat{X}_l = MHA(q(X_{input}), k(X_{context}), v(X_{context})), \qquad (4)$$

where $q(\cdot)$, $k(\cdot)$ and $v(\cdot)$ extract query, key and value representations, respectively. Notice that key and value operations share the input observation $X_{context}$, whereas query $q(\cdot)$ operates on X_{input}.

Table 1. Multimodal interaction mode spaces

Interaction mode	Attention mechanisms
M_0: Self-Self Attention	X & $\neg X$: Self-Attention
M_1: Self-Cross Attention	X: Self-Attention, $\neg X$: Cross-Attention
M_2: Cross-Self Attention	X: Cross-Attention, $\neg X$: Self-Attention
M_3: Joint-Attention	X & $\neg X$: Joint-Attention

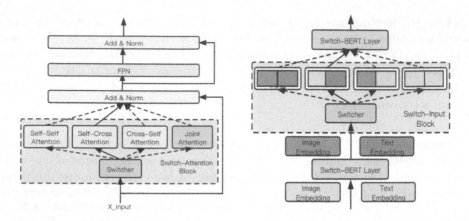

(a) Illustration of Switch-BERT layer and   (b) Illustration of Switch-Input Block.
Switch-Attention Block.

Fig. 2. (a) The Switch-BERT layer extends the Multi-head Joint Attention block in a normal transformer encoder layer with our proposed Switch-Attention Block. (b) The Switch-Input Block brings in modality representations from current and previous layers for its successive Switch-BERT layer. (best viewed in color)

Equation (4) enables us to relate the previously proposed multimodal approaches. For dual-stream models [25,34], intra-modal and inter-modal interactions are independently modeled explicitly. Using Eq. (4), Self-Attention for intra-modal interaction is modeled with $X_{input} = X_{l-1}$ and $X_{context} = X_{l-1}$. Cross-Attention for inter-modal interaction can be achieved using $X_{input} = X_{l-1}$ and $X_{context} = \neg X_{l-1}$. For single-stream models [5,18,19], intra-modal and inter-modal interactions are implicitly modeled with Joint-Attention using $X_{input} = X_{l-1}$ and $X_{context} = [X_{l-1}, \neg X_{l-1}]$, the latter is obtained via concatenation and enables attention to the whole multimodal context.

Among the above described attention mechanisms, Joint-Attention uses whole multimodal context, therefore has potential of representation of both Self-Attention and Cross-Attention. However, its multimodal context can face potential semantic misalignment between modalities, as described in Sect. 1. On the other hand, Self-Attention and Cross-Attention restrict the modal context to attend, easing semantic misalignment of modalities, but leads to limited representation to particular modality.

We therefore design a more complete space of multimodal interactions. Table 1 lists four interaction modes between X and its complementary $\neg X$. Self-Self Attention invokes self-attention on each modality. Self-Cross Attention has X use Self-Attention and $\neg X$ use Cross-Attention, and vice versa for Cross-Self Attention. Joint-Attention has both X and $\neg X$ conduct their own Joint-Attention operations. Those attention operators share the same attention weights in our setting and can be implemented with different layer-wise attention masks.

2.3   Switch Attention and Input Block

Switch-Attention Block. Unlike conventional multimodal models that limit the modality interaction between specific layers, we employ the Switch-Attention Block (SAB) to achieve learning layer-wise multimodal interaction in an end-to-end manner. As illustrated in Fig. 2 (a), SAB depends on an attention switcher module to search for an appropriate mode from the multimodal interactions described in Table 1. The search space can be formally defined as a set of operations $\{M_n\}_{n=1}^{N_a}$, where N_a indicates the number of interaction modes.

We describe in the following a switcher method to search for proper interaction. Given a holistic representation of image and text as X_l^i and X_l^t, we apply average pooling over the image and text tokens to obtain global features of each modality:

$$z_l^i = AvgPool(X_l^i), z_l^t = AvgPool(X_l^t))). \tag{5}$$

Then we define the modality "alignment degree" of the l-th layer as $d_l = z_l^i \odot z_l^t$, and apply a trainable MLP, f_{MLP} with Softmax activation to obtain the probability of the interaction modes π:

$$\pi = Softmax(f_{MLP}(d_l)). \tag{6}$$

We use Gumbel-Softmax reparameterization [12] to sample a particular interaction based on the above probability, in which probability of interaction M_n is

$$p(M_n) = \frac{\exp\left((\log(\pi_n) + g_n)/\tau\right)}{\sum_{j=1}^{N_a} \exp\left((\log(\pi_j) + g_j)/\tau\right)}, \tag{7}$$

where g_n is sampled Gumbel noise, computed as $g_n = -\log(-\log(u_n))$, with u_n sampled from uniform distribution of $Uniform(0,1)$. τ is the smooth parameter for Gumbel-Softmax distribution.

Given $X_{input} = X_l^i \cup X_l^t$, SAB performs "soft weighting" or "hard selection" of interaction modes by:

$$y_{soft} = \sum_{i \in N_a} p(M_i)M_i(X_{input})$$

$$y_{hard} = M_{n^*}(X_{input}), n^* = \underset{n}{\operatorname{argmax}}\{p(M_n)\} \tag{8}$$

For training, we start at a high temperature in Eq. 7 for small gradient variance, then anneal to a small but non-zero temperature to make the output distribution $p(M)$ approximate one-hot. We adopt "soft weighting" of attention modes during training and "hard selection" for inference.

Switch-Input Block. To ease semantic misalignment between modalities, we propose Switch-Input Block (SIB) to bring in cross-layer modal representation. SIB enables Switch-BERT layer, illustrated in Fig. 2 (a), to take input either from the output of its lower layer or from the residual connection in the lower layer, which connects to the output from the layer further below. Concretely, for l-th layer with $l \geq 2$, its input is in a set of $\{X_{l-1}{}^\neg X_{l-1}\} \cup \{X_{l-1}{}^\neg X_{l-2}, X_{l-2}{}^\neg X_{l-1}, X_{l-2}{}^\neg X_{l-2}\}$. We then apply switch operation on the set and obtain an element from the set as input X_{input} to layer l. The switcher algorithm follows Eq. 6, Eq. 7 and Eq. 8 but is trained specifically for SIB. Figure 2 (b) illustrates the Switch-Input Block.

2.4   The Switch-BERT Model

The Switch-BERT model's components are described in details below. Further details are in the supplementary material.

Visual and Text Embedding. Following [25], images are represented with detected objects. We extract the bounding box and visual feature of each object from the widely used Faster-RCNN [29] detector trained on Visual Genome [16]. We also add a type field (VisualType/TokenType) to distinguish visual and text input. The region feature, position and type field are fed into a visual embedding layer to obtain the visual embedding for Switch-Encoder. A special IMG token representing the entire image segment is also inserted at the beginning of the visual sequence. The text embedding is generated following BERT [6], in which we tokenize the input sentence and keep orders of tokens as their position ids. The token, position and type field are fed into a text embedding layer to perform embedding lookup.

Switch-Encoder. Given the pair of visual and text embedding, the Switch-Encoder learns to model layer-wise multimodal interactions. The Switch-Encoder consists of a stack of Switch-BERT layers, with Switch-Input Block inserted between consecutive Switch-BERT layers. Switch-BERT layer in Fig. 2 (a) generally follows the architecture of the Transformer encoder layer [36], but distinguishes it with the adaptive multimodal attention mechanism using Switch-Attention Block. It takes the entire representations from visual and text embedding, but selects sample-specific interactions of these representations. The Switch-Input Block routes the modality input for the following Switch-BERT layer to help alleviate semantic misalignment. The rest of the Switch-Encoder proceeds similarly as that in BERT encoder, resulting in a multimodal feature as its output.

Pretraining Tasks. Task-agnostic multimodal pre-training can help learn associations between modalities. Like previous work [19,21,22,25,26,33,41], we first pre-train Switch-BERT on proxy tasks and then adapt it to downstream tasks through finetuning. Three proxy tasks are used for pre-training. (1) Masked language modeling with visual clues (MLM). This task follows the MLM objective in BERT [6] but with the above described contextualized multimodal input. In

Table 2. Statistics of datasets for the downstream tasks

Dataset	Tasks	Train	Test	Metric
Flick30k	Image-Text Retrieval	29 k	1 k	Recall@k
RefCOCO+	Referring Expression	120 k	10.6 k	Accuracy
VQAv2	Visual Question Answering	657 k	107.3 k	VQA-score

this task, word tokens are randomly masked but with their positions preserved. The model needs to predict the token from the left visual and textual context. (2) Masked region classification with KL-divergence (MRC-KL) [5]. Similar to MLM, this task masks approximately 15% of the region features. MRC-KL then trains the model to predict the class distribution from the object detector for the region, rather than reconstructing the feature of masked regions. (3) Image-Text matching (ITM). Given paired image-and-text as positives, their negative pairs are generated by randomly replacing texts in the positive pairs with unrelated ones. The ITM task is for the model to distinguish positive pairs from negatives.

3   Experiments

3.1   Datasets and Downstream Tasks

We evaluate Switch-BERT on different types of downstream tasks including image-text retrieval, referring expressions and vocab-based VQA. Their statistics are shown in Table 2.

Image-Text Retrieval. Given images or captions, the image-text retrieval task requires the model to perform cross-modal retrieval. We conduct experiments on Flick30k [27] dataset, which has images paired with five captions. Following [25], we train models on Flick30k in a 4-way multiple-choice setting. For each image-text pair, three negatives are generated by replacing the caption with a random one and replacing the image with a random and a hard one. The model outputs similarity scores of these four image-text pairs as the ITM task. Once softmax is computed on the similarity scores, cross-entropy loss is applied to learn the models. We report Recall@1.

Referring Expressions Comprehension. This task focuses on localizing objects queried by a natural language expression. For the RefCOCO+ [14] dataset, we take the bounding boxes detected by [40] and select the top 36 regions with the highest class scores. Following the conventions in [25,32], a simple fully-connected layer is added on top to regress the matching degree, defined as the IOU with the ground truth box, with the referring expression for each input region. We train the model with binary cross-entropy loss. To evaluate, regions with matching degree above threshold of 0.5 are considered correct. We apply the accuracy score as the evaluation metric.

Visual Question Answering. Given questions about an image, this task expects the model to give correct answers. Following [1], we consider the VQA [9] task a multi-label classification problem on a closed answer pool and generate the target soft-label based on its relevance to ten human answer responses. We add two fully-connected layers to map the multimodal representation, which is the element-wise product fusion of image and text representation, to the answers' space and apply binary cross-entropy loss for training. Following the same protocol with SOTA baselines, we train models on train-val split and report VQA-score [2] on the test-dev split.

3.2   Controlled Settings

Shown in [5,25,28,34], the quality and volume of the pre-training data significantly impact the performance of multimodal BERTs. This explain most of the claimed performance differences in downstream tasks [4]. In this paper, we focus our discussion on the independent contribution of architecture design. To exclude performance influences other than architectures and enable fair comparison under limited resources, we adopt the controlled settings introduced by [4]. Specifically, we pre-train multimodal BERTs on the same subset of 2.7 M image-text pairs of Conceptual Captions [30] for 10 epochs and employ the same proxy tasks as our Switch-BERT model. We use the VOLTA[1] implementation for all state-of-the-art models for comparison in our experiments, and train these multimodal BERTs with a fixed set of hyperparameters, such as encoder dimensions, methods for modality fusion, number of MLP layers in the finetune head, to exclude possible confounds that may interfere with a fair comparison of these architectures. Models with the best validation set performance are chosen for downstream tasks evaluation[2]. Due to space constraints, more implementation details as well as hyper-parameter settings are split into the supplementary materials.

3.3   Main Results

We compare the proposed Switch-BERT against existing multimodal architectures of both single and dual-stream on three widely-used benchmark datasets. Baselines for comparison include the state-of-the-art multimodal architectures of ViLBERT [25], UNITER [5], VisualBERT [19], VL-BERT [32] and LXMERT [34]. These baselines and Switch-BERT follow the pre-train-then-finetune procedure with the controlled settings described above and have the same context for comparison.

Table 3 presents the experimental results of the model, together with results from these baselines. We observe that Switch-BERT has performances that are on par or better than the previous state-of-the-art architectures in these downstream tasks. The absolute improvements of 0.9% on RefCOCO+, 1.8% on

---

[1] https://github.com/e-bug/volta.

[2] We train with three different random seeds and report their average performances.

Table 3. Results on downstream tasks. We adopt the re-implementation from the VOLTA [4] framework for baseline models. All models perform the same controlled settings and "*" denotes models without pre-training on Conceptual Captions [30]. We report std of Switch-BERT as well as baseline models on three runs with different random seeds.

Models		Params	VQAv2	Flick30K-Retrieval		RefCOCO+
				Image Retrieval	Text Retrieval	
Single-stream (Fixed)	UNITER [5]	114.9M	68.8 ± 0.4	60.9 ± 0.7	76.4 ± 1.3	71.9 ± 0.67
	VL-BERT [32]	116.1 M	68.3 ±0.31	57.9 ± 1.1	70.9 ± 1.7	71.1 ± 0.23
	VisualBERT [19]	114.9 M	68.9 ± 0.27	61.1 ± 1.2	75.5 ± 1.8	69.7 ± 0.31
Dual-stream (Fixed)	LXMERT [34]	211.4M	67.1 ± 0.34	58.6 ± 1.4	74.9 ± 2.7	69.8 ± 0.46
	VilBERT [25]	242.1 M	68.7 ± 0.82	59.8 ± 0.8	**78.3** ± 1.6	70.8 ± 0.58
Dynamic	Switch-BERT*	130.6 M	66.7 ± 0.97	38.2 ± 1.7	57.3 ±2.3	68.9 ±0.82
	Switch-BERT		**70.7** ± 0.62	**62.2** ± 0.9	78.2 ± 1.6	**72.8** ± 0.45

VQAv2 and 1.1% on Flick30K Image Retrieval over previous SOTA[3] indicating that Switch-BERT can learn better vision and language representations that generalize better than these alternative methods to the downstream tasks. The controlled settings ensure the improvements are mainly contributed from the proposed architectures of Switch-Attention and Switch-Input blocks, which aim at easing the semantic misalignment between modalities and learning image-text modality interactions. Table 3 also includes the results of Switch-BERT without pre-training on Conceptual Captions dataset, i.e., initialized only from BERT in [6]. The degradation in performance demonstrates that the Switch-BERT benefits from pretraining as other multimodal BERTs.

3.4   Ablation Studies

Effectiveness of the Switch-Attention and Switch-Input Blocks. We start by investigating the influences of Switch-Attention and Switch-Input blocks. Following our controlled settings, we compare Switch-BERT with its three variants on downstream tasks. (i) SIB-ONLY: this variant uses normal encoder-style transformer layers instead of the Switch-BERT layer, (ii) SAB-ONLY: in this variant, we fix the input to each Switch-BERT layer to the output from its lower layer as usual. (iii) No-SIB-SAB: this variant is a normal single stream BERT encoder. All variants are evaluated following the pre-train-then-fine-tune procedure, and share the same hyperparameter setting with Switch-BERT.

Results in Table 5 clearly show better performances by Switch-BERT than its variants. Given that SIB brings cross-layer input, we conclude that the semantic-level misalignment exists in single stream models and reducing misalignment

---

[3] For overall SOTA numbers that can be achieved without the controlled settings, readers can refer to [39] for VQAv2 and Flick30K Retrieval datasets, and [13] for RefCOCO+.

Table 4. An ablation study of interaction modes. Cross-Self (Self-Cross) and Joint stand for interaction modes. Pretraining indicates whether the models are pre-trained on Conceptual Captions before adapt to RefCOCO+. The default interaction mode is Self-Self Attention for all tested models, which means no interactions between modalities.

Model			RefCOCO+
Pretraining	Cross-Self & Self-Cross	Joint	Accuracy
✓	✓		71.5
✓		✓	71.2
✓	✓	✓	**72.8**
	✓		68.3
		✓	67.5
	✓	✓	**68.9**

Table 5. An ablation study of Switch-Attention and Switch-Input blocks.

Model		Flick30K		VQAv2	RefCOCO+
SIB	SAB	IR(r@1)	TR(r@1)	VQA-score	Accuracy
		60.7	76.2	67.8	69.5
	✓	61.7	76.9	68.9	72.4
✓		60.8	77.7	68.5	71.7
✓	✓	**62.2**	**78.2**	**70.7**	**72.8**

Table 6. An ablation study on effect of models' depth.

Model	#layers	VQAv2 6 → 12	RefCOCO+6 → 12
UNITER		64.2 → 68.8	69.7 → 71.9
Switch-BERT		**65.4 → 70.7**	**70.2 → 72.8**
SAB-ONLY		65.0 → 68.9	69.4 → 72.4

between semantics of modalities results in better representations. The improvements of SAB-ONLY over the No-SIB-SAB variant also hint that our switching attention mechanism that learns to model modality associations is superior to the widely used single Joint-Attention mechanism. This bring us to the second question: Is the Joint-Attention necessary for Switch-Attention block?.

Necessity of Joint-Attention. We perform experiments on the RefCOCO+ dataset to verify the necessity for Joint-Attention. Table 4 shows the results of Switch-BERT and its variants of the attention mode space with different initialization in the upper and lower panel. Models with the Cross-Self and Self-Cross Attention show similar results (71.5 vs 71.2) to those with Joint-Attention when pre-trained. However, even with Cross-Self & Self-Cross, using Joint-Attention with negligible additional parameters consistently outperforms those without using it. Therefore, results support the necessity of Joint-Attention.

Effect of Model's Depth. We also compare transferred results from models of varying depths including Switch-BERT and UNITER. Since Switch-BERT's SIB block introduces cross-layer connections given to more sensitivity to the model's

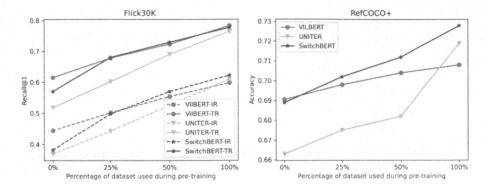

Fig. 3. Effects on scale of pre-training sets. *-IR and *-TR represents the image-to-text retrieval and text-to-image retrieval tasks, respectively. We find large performance drop with less pre-training data for UNITER - implying single-stream models with only Joint-Attention "eagers" for larger pre-training data before fully-trained.

Table 7. Computation overhead(FLOPs) and performances. Top-K routes are activated in Switch-Attention Blocks during fine-tuning.

Models	VQAv2		RefCOCO+	
	FLOPs	VQA-score	FLOPs	Accuracy
UNITER	$2.31*1e^{16}$	68.8	$3.68*1e^{15}$	71.9
VilBERT	$2.72*1e^{16}$	68.7	$4.29*1e^{15}$	70.8
Switch-BERT(K=4)	$8.02*1e^{16}$	70.7	$10.57*1e^{15}$	72.8
Switch-BERT(K=2)	$3.07*1e^{16}$	70.2	$5.27*1e^{15}$	72.1
Switch-BERT(K=1)	$1.97*1e^{16}$	68.2	$3.12*1e^{15}$	70.8

depth, we also add the SAB-ONLY variant to the comparison. As shown in Table 6, Switch-BERT of various depth show superior performance compared to its counterparts UNITER baseline. In addition, we observe meaningful improvements of Switch-BERT on the SAB-ONLY variant of fewer layers across multiple tasks evaluated, proving SIB help adapt to different tasks regardless of the model's depth.

We now turn our attention to the effect of pre-training dataset's scale on Switch-BERT's performance. For this experiment, we take random subsets of 25% and 50% from our conceptual caption dataset to pre-train models and then adapt them to various downstream tasks under our predefined controlled settings. Shown in Fig. 3, we can see that Switch-BERT benefits from increasing amounts of data as well as UNITER and VilBERT. Another observation is that larger performance gaps emerge between UNITER and VilBERT with less pre-training data on both evaluated tasks, we conjecture that UNITER(single-stream models) with only Joint-Attention eagers for larger pre-training data volumes

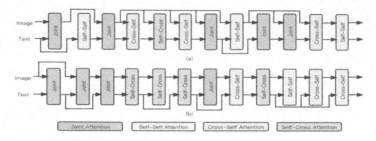

Fig. 4. Architectures Learned by Switch-BERT. (a) and (b) shows the learned architectures for referring expression comprehension and cross-modal retrieval tasks, respectively.

to get fully-trained, and Switch-BERT alleviates this problem with complete interaction mode space.

Computation Overhead of Switch-BERT. We estimate the number of floating point operations of training a model on each downstream task for static approaches. For Switch-BERT, we track its routing path and accumulate the operation count during training due to its dynamic characteristics. Results are shown in Table 7. Switch-BERT indeed requires extra computation to converge compared to traditional static models, the overhead is mainly caused by SABs that activate all paths at the beginning of training. We further investigate this with only top-K paths in SAB activated, and observe an acceptable overhead and performance balance when K=2.

3.5   Qualitative Studies

With SAB and SIB modules, Switch-BERT should be able to adapt its architecture to different multimodal tasks. To confirm this, we analyze utility of SAB and SIB on Switch-BERT fine-tuned on referring expression comprehension and cross-modal retrieval tasks. We sort the learned architectures according to their occurrence frequency on each task. Figure 4 illustrates the most frequently used architectures by Switch-BERT on the two tasks. For the referring expression comprehension task, Switch-BERT learns to use cross-layer representations more frequently for the visual modality than the text modality. On the cross-modal retrieval task, Switch-BERT uses Self-Self attention once but more frequently with other attention modes that involve interactions between modalities. The frequencies of selecting these most-frequent architectures are dominantly 48.79% and 31.09%, respectively, on the two tasks. These results indicate that Switch-BERT is able to extract task-specific architecture.

4   Related Work

Multimodal BERTs. BERT-style representations [6,7,17,24,38] have been advancing the state-of-the-art performances in natural language processing in recent years. Its success has encouraged researchers to apply them more widely to tasks including multimodality. Methods based on BERT architectures have been proposed recently and have become the dominant approaches in applications such as video captioning [33]. The works of VisualBERT [19], UNITER [5], VLBERT [32], and PixelBERT [11] employ a single-stream BERT encoder for joint modeling of interactions between modalities. The other dual-stream approach including ViLBERT [25] and LXMERT [34] has representations separately for each modality and uses cross-attention mechanism to model their interactions. The proposed method distinguishes from the above methods in using flexible Switch Attention-and-Input mechanism to select proper interaction modes and cross-layer input. It aims at alleviating the not-well-studied semantic misalignment problem. Empirically, we have confirmed its superior performances over the other methods.

Conditional Computation Models. The proposed Switch-BERT dynamically adjusts its architecture according to inputs. It is therefore in line with Mixture of Experts (MoE) methods in [8,31]. The method in [31] uses a gating function to select experts to perform computations. The method in [8] introduces the MoE layer into the Transformer architecture and applies a routing algorithm that sends tokens to their token-specific experts. Switch-BERT differs from these works in two aspects: i) instead of using MoE as a substitute of the FFN layers in [31], it selects sample-specific attention and input with the novel Switch Attention-and-Input blocks; ii) whereas MoE is conducted at token-level in [8], Switch-BERT conducts switch operations at modality-level and cross-layer. Besides, our switch input mechanism learns to "select" or "skip" a transformer layer, which shares the same spirit with variable depth in Transformer [20]. Work in [20] explores using a shared deep Transformer for multiple tasks with the learned distribution of layer selection, the learned distribution is restricted on task-level. While for Switch-BERT, the layer selection distribution is conditioned on modality inputs, such that it performs sample-specific switch operations. To our best knowledge, Switch-BERT is the first attempt to have conditional computation for multimodal learning.

5   Conclusion

In this paper, we proposed Switch-BERT to effectively alleviate the modality misalignment problem for multimodal representation learning. Switch-BERT learns to model intra- and inter-modal interactions and select interaction mode for each layer individually. It also learns to select, for each layer, the inputs that are not restricted to the current layer and therefore learns selecting inputs cross layers. We verified its effectiveness through controlled settings on multimodal tasks including visual question answering, cross-modal retrieval, and referring expression comprehension. We also carried out ablation studies to confirm that Switch-BERT is capable of learning task-specific architectures. Experimental results show that Switch-BERT dynamically adapts its structure and consistently achieve better or comparable performances than other state-of-the-art fixed architectures on a variety of multimodal tasks. In future work, we plan to explore the efficiency of variant mechanisms and reveal the internal alignment with more details.

Acknowledgments.. The authors would like to thank the anonymous reviewers for their helpful feedback that improved this work.

References

1. Anderson, P., et al.: Bottom-up and top-down attention for image captioning and visual question answering. In: Proceedings of the IEEE Conference on Computer Vision and Pattern Recognition, pp. 6077–6086 (2018)
2. Antol, S., et al.: Vqa: visual question answering. In: Proceedings of the IEEE International Conference on Computer vision, pp. 2425–2433 (2015)
3. Ba, J.L., Kiros, J.R., Hinton, G.E.: Layer normalization. arXiv preprint. arXiv:1607.06450 (2016)
4. Bugliarello, E., Cotterell, R., Okazaki, N., Elliott, D.: Multimodal pretraining unmasked: a meta-analysis and a unified framework of vision-and-language berts. Trans. Assoc. Comput. Linguist. **9**, 978–994 (2021)
5. Chen, Y.C., et al.: UNITER: universal image-text representation learning. In: Vedaldi, Andrea, Bischof, Horst, Brox, Thomas, Frahm, Jan-Michael. (eds.) ECCV 2020. LNCS, vol. 12375, pp. 104–120. Springer, Cham (2020). https://doi.org/10.1007/978-3-030-58577-8_7
6. Devlin, J., Chang, M.W., Lee, K., Toutanova, K.: Bert: pre-training of deep bidirectional transformers for language understanding. In: The North American Chapter of the Association for Computational Linguistics (2019)
7. Dong, L., et al.: Unified language model pre-training for natural language understanding and generation. In: Advances in Neural Information Processing Systems, vol. 32 (2019)
8. Fedus, W., Zoph, B., Shazeer, N.: Switch transformers: scaling to trillion parameter models with simple and efficient sparsity. J. Mach. Learn. Res. **23**(120), 1–39 (2022). http://jmlr.org/papers/v23/21-0998.html
9. Goyal, Y., Khot, T., Summers-Stay, D., Batra, D., Parikh, D.: Making the v in vqa matter: Elevating the role of image understanding in visual question answering. In: Proceedings of the IEEE Conference on Computer Vision and Pattern Recognition, pp. 6904–6913 (2017)
10. Hendrycks, D., Gimpel, K.: Gaussian error linear units (gelus). arXiv preprint. arXiv:1606.08415 (2016)
11. Huang, Z., Zeng, Z., Liu, B., Fu, D., Fu, J.: Pixel-bert: aligning image pixels with text by deep multi-modal transformers. arXiv preprint. arXiv:2004.00849 (2020)
12. Jang, E., Gu, S., Poole, B.: Categorical reparameterization with gumbel-softmax. In: International Conference on Learning Representations (2017). https://arxiv.org/abs/1611.01144

13. Kamath, A., Singh, M., LeCun, Y., Synnaeve, G., Misra, I., Carion, N.: Mdetr-modulated detection for end-to-end multi-modal understanding. In: Proceedings of the IEEE/CVF International Conference on Computer Vision, pp. 1780–1790 (2021)
14. Kazemzadeh, S., Ordonez, V., Matten, M., Berg, T.: Referitgame: referring to objects in photographs of natural scenes. In: Proceedings of the 2014 Conference on Empirical Methods in Natural Language Processing (EMNLP), pp. 787–798 (2014)
15. Kiela, D., Bhooshan, S., Firooz, H., Testuggine, D.: Supervised multimodal bitransformers for classifying images and text. arXiv preprint. arXiv:1909.02950 (2019)
16. Krishna, R., et al.: Visual genome: connecting language and vision using crowdsourced dense image annotations. Int. J. Comput. Vis. **123**(1), 32–73 (2017). https://doi.org/10.1007/S11263-016-0981-7
17. Lan, Z., Chen, M., Goodman, S., Gimpel, K., Sharma, P., Soricut, R.: Albert: a lite bert for self-supervised learning of language representations. arXiv preprint. arXiv:1909.11942 (2019)
18. Li, G., Duan, N., Fang, Y., Gong, M., Jiang, D.: Unicoder-vl: a universal encoder for vision and language by cross-modal pre-training. In: Proceedings of the AAAI Conference on Artificial Intelligence, vol. 34, pp. 11336–11344 (2020)
19. Li, L.H., Yatskar, M., Yin, D., Hsieh, C.J., Chang, K.W.: Visualbert: a simple and performant baseline for vision and language. arXiv preprint. arXiv:1908.03557 (2019)
20. Li, X., Stickland, A.C., Tang, Y., Kong, X.: Deep transformers with latent depth. In: Conference and Workshop on Neural Information Processing Systems, NeurIIPS (2020)
21. Li, X., et al.: OSCAR: object-semantics aligned pre-training for vision-language tasks. In: Vedaldi, Andrea, Bischof, Horst, Brox, Thomas, Frahm, Jan-Michael. (eds.) ECCV 2020. LNCS, vol. 12375, pp. 121–137. Springer, Cham (2020). https://doi.org/10.1007/978-3-030-58577-8_8
22. Lin, J., Yang, A., Zhang, Y., Liu, J., Zhou, J., Yang, H.: Interbert: vision-and-language interaction for multi-modal pretraining. arXiv preprint. arXiv:2003.13198 (2020)
23. Lin, Y., Tan, Y.C., Frank, R.: Open sesame: getting inside bert's linguistic knowledge. In: Proceedings of the 2019 ACL Workshop BlackboxNLP: Analyzing and Interpreting Neural Networks for NLP (2019)
24. Liu, Y., et al.: Roberta: a robustly optimized bert pretraining approach. arXiv preprint. arXiv:1907.11692 (2019)
25. Lu, J., Batra, D., Parikh, D., Lee, S.: Vilbert: pretraining task-agnostic visiolinguistic representations for vision-and-language tasks. In: Advances in Neural Information Processing systems, vol. 32 (2019)
26. Miech, A., Alayrac, J.B., Smaira, L., Laptev, I., Sivic, J., Zisserman, A.: End-to-end learning of visual representations from uncurated instructional videos. In: Proceedings of the IEEE/CVF Conference on Computer Vision and Pattern Recognition, pp. 9879–9889 (2020)
27. Plummer, B.A., Wang, L., Cervantes, C.M., Caicedo, J.C., Hockenmaier, J., Lazebnik, S.: Flickr30k entities: collecting region-to-phrase correspondences for richer image-to-sentence models. In: Proceedings of the IEEE International Conference on Computer Vision, pp. 2641–2649 (2015)
28. Qi, D., Su, L., Song, J., Cui, E., Bharti, T., Sacheti, A.: Imagebert: cross-modal pre-training with large-scale weak-supervised image-text data. arXiv preprint. arXiv:2001.07966 (2020)

29. Ren, S., He, K., Girshick, R., Sun, J.: Faster r-cnn: towards real-time object detection with region proposal networks. In: Advances in Neural Information Processing Systems, vol. 28 (2015)
30. Sharma, P., Ding, N., Goodman, S., Soricut, R.: Conceptual captions: a cleaned, hypernymed, image alt-text dataset for automatic image captioning. In: Proceedings of the 56th Annual Meeting of the Association for Computational Linguistics, (Vol. 1: Long Papers), pp. 2556–2565 (2018)
31. Shazeer, N., et al.: Outrageously large neural networks: the sparsely-gated mixture-of-experts layer. arXiv preprint. arXiv:1701.06538 (2017)
32. Su, W., et al.: Vl-bert: pre-training of generic visual-linguistic representations. arXiv preprint. arXiv:1908.08530 (2019)
33. Sun, C., Myers, A., Vondrick, C., Murphy, K., Schmid, C.: Videobert: a joint model for video and language representation learning. In: Proceedings of the IEEE/CVF International Conference on Computer Vision, pp. 7464–7473 (2019)
34. Tan, H., Bansal, M.: LXMERT: learning cross-modality encoder representations from transformers. In: Empirical Methods in Natural Language Processing, pp. 5100–5111 (2019)
35. Tenney, I., Das, D., Pavlick, E.: BERT rediscovers the classical NLP pipeline. In: Proceedings of the 57th Annual Meeting of the Association for Computational Linguistics, pp. 4593–4601. Association for Computational Linguistics, Florence, Italy (2019). https://doi.org/10.18653/v1/P19-1452, https://aclanthology.org/P19-1452
36. Vaswani, A., et al.: Attention is all you need. In: Advances in Neural Information Processing Systems, vol. 30 (2017)
37. Wu, Y., et al.: Google's neural machine translation system: bridging the gap between human and machine translation. arXiv:1609.08144 (2016)
38. Yang, Z., Dai, Z., Yang, Y., Carbonell, J., Salakhutdinov, R.R., Le, Q.V.: Xlnet: generalized autoregressive pretraining for language understanding. In: Advances in Neural Information Processing Systems, vol. 32 (2019)
39. Yu, J., Wang, Z., Vasudevan, V., Yeung, L., Seyedhosseini, M., Wu, Y.: Coca: contrastive captioners are image-text foundation models. arXiv preprint. arXiv:2205.01917 (2022)
40. Yu, L., et al.: Mattnet: modular attention network for referring expression comprehension. In: Proceedings of the IEEE Conference on Computer Vision and Pattern Recognition, pp. 1307–1315 (2018)
41. Zhou, L., Palangi, H., Zhang, L., Hu, H., Corso, J., Gao, J.: Unified vision-language pre-training for image captioning and vqa. In: Proceedings of the AAAI Conference on Artificial Intelligence, vol. 34, pp. 13041–13049 (2020)

Word-Level Fine-Grained Story Visualization

Bowen Li[✉][iD]

University of Oxford, Oxford, UK
bowen.li@cs.ox.ac.uk

Abstract. Story visualization aims to generate a sequence of images to narrate each sentence in a multi-sentence story with a global consistency across dynamic scenes and characters. Current works still struggle with output images' quality and consistency, and rely on additional semantic information or auxiliary captioning networks. To address these challenges, we first introduce a new sentence representation, which incorporates word information from all story sentences to mitigate the inconsistency problem. Then, we propose a new discriminator with fusion features and further extend the spatial attention to improve image quality and story consistency. Extensive experiments on different datasets and human evaluation demonstrate the superior performance of our approach, compared to state-of-the-art methods, neither using segmentation masks nor auxiliary captioning networks.

1 Introduction

Image generation from different-modal text descriptions with semantic alignment is a challenging task and has the potential for many applications, including art creation, computer-aided design, and image editing. Recently, due to the great progress in realistic image generation based on generative adversarial networks (GANs) [3], text-guided image generation and modification has drawn much attention [2,6,9–12,19,23,26,28,30].

Differently from text-to-image generation, story visualization aims to generate a sequence of story images given a multi-sentence story, which is more challenging, as it further requires output images to be consistent, e.g., having a similar background or objects' appearances. StoryGAN [14] first proposed a sequential conditional GAN-based framework. Using StoryGAN as the backbone, CP-CSV [24] utilized segmentation masks to keep character consistency, and DUCO [17] and VLC [16] adopted additional auxiliary captioning networks to improve text-image semantic alignment. However, all these works still struggle with the quality of output images, and may fail to generate fine-grained image regional details corresponding to different semantic words (see Fig. 1). Besides, CP-CSV requires character segmentation masks in the network, which are hard to get, and the performance of DUCO and VLC may be affected by auxiliary captioning networks. Moreover, some keywords, e.g., describing the global style of a story, do not exist in all sentences within a story. So, if keywords only

S. Avidan et al. (Eds.): ECCV 2022, LNCS 13696, pp. 347–362, 2022.
https://doi.org/10.1007/978-3-031-20059-5_20

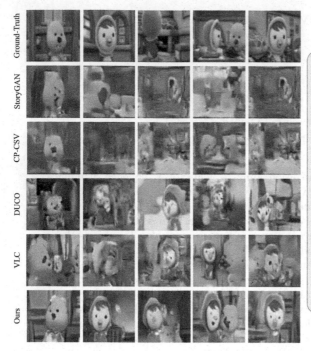

1. Loopy is in the house. Loopy holds skis in her hand. Loopy is looking around the house.

2. Petty gets surprised. Petty raises her hands. Outside the window the sky is blue and clear.

3. Petty rushes to the oven and pulls out the plate.

4. Petty and Loopy are seated beside a table. On the table there are two plates of cookies. Lots of cookies are stacked on the plate. The cookies are all burnt.

5. Petty has a plate of cookies on the table. The cookies are burnt.

Fig. 1. Examples of story visualization on different methods, with the given story sentences and ground-truth story images.

appear in some sentences, these sequential generation methods may fail to keep consistent object appearances and a global style in all synthetic images.

To tackle these problems, we first introduce a new sentence representation, where each sentence representation in a story can selectively incorporate different word information from the entire story to ensure a global consistency. Then, we propose a new discriminator with fusion features, which provides the generator with fine-grained training feedback, evaluating the quality of fusion features to examine whether all word-required attributes are generated in the story images. Finally, we further explore word-level spatial attention [26] in story visualization, which can not only highlight local word-related image regions in the generation process, but also capture long-distant correlations between regions in the current image and words from other sentences within the same story. By doing this, the generator can focus on different parts of an image to enable better regional details and also to ensure consistency over all synthetic images in a story. The main contributions are summarized as follows:

- We propose a new approach for story visualization, which contains three novel components: new sentence representation, discriminator with fusion features, and extended spatial attention, neither utilizing cost segmentation masks nor additional auxiliary captioning networks.
- Our approach builds a new state of the art on Pororo-SV, measured by different evaluation metrics with large absolute margins, and further establishes a strong benchmark on Abstract Scenes.

- We conduct extensive experiments, including a human evaluation, to demonstrate the superior performance of our approach over baselines, in terms of image quality, text-image semantic alignment, and story consistency. The code is available at https://github.com/mrlibw/Word-Level-Story-Visualization.

2 Related Work

Story visualization aims to generate a sequences of images corresponding to a multi-sentence story, and imposes consistency over output story images. Story-GAN [14] first proposed this task and also introduced a GAN-based sequential generation network. CP-CSV [24] was built on StoryGAN, and utilized segmentation masks to improve the character consistency. DUCO [17] and VLC [16] also adopted StoryGAN as the backbone, and added auxiliary captioning networks to build a text-image-text circle. However, all these methods still struggle with the quality of output images, and fail to generate fine-grained regional details. Our approach explores word-level information within the story, to ensure a high-quality image generation with good text-image semantic alignment and story consistency, neither requiring an additional supervision from segmentation masks, like CP-CSV, nor auxiliary captioning networks, like DUCO and VLC.

Text-to-image generation is closely related to our work, which generates one image from one given text description and keeps semantic alignment between image and text [6,13,21,23,25,26,29,30]. AttnGAN [26] and ControlGAN [9] introduced word-level attention to fuse text and image features. DMGAN [30] proposed a dynamic memory module to refine image features. DF-GAN [25] introduced a deep text-image fusion block to fuse text and image information. OPGAN [6] relied on additional semantic information to improve output results. XMC-GAN [27] is a contrastive-learning-based method with a single stage. DALL-E [22] proposed an transformer-based method for zero-shot text-to-image generation. Li et al. [13] proposed a semi-parametric approach via constructing a memory bank of image features, selectively fusing stored image features into the generation pipeline.

Another related work is video generation from text [1,4,15,18,20], which generates continuous frames from only one text input. Differently, story visualization does not require the frames to flow continuously, and allows synthetic story images to be discrete with different scene views.

3 Fine-Grained Story Visualization

The model aims to produce a series of story images from a given multi-sentence story, one for each, and output images should be realistic, semantically match corresponding sentences, and keep consistency. To achieve this, we propose three novel components: (1) new sentence representation that selectively fuses word information from an entire story, (2) discriminator with fusion features, and (3) extended spatial attention at story-level.

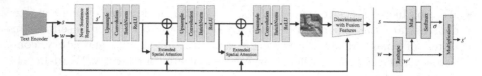

Fig. 2. Left: architecture of the proposed approach. Right: design of the proposed new sentence representation.

3.1 Architecture

Similarly, we adopt StoryGAN [14] as our basic backbone. To produce story images with fine-grained regional details and a better consistency, we propose to utilize both global sentence vectors and fine-grained word embeddings in the generation pipeline. However, there is only one discriminator, and neither segmentation masks nor auxiliary captioning networks are used in our method.

Given a multi-sentence story Z with a sequence of n story descriptions, $S_1, \ldots, S_n$, a text encoder, e.g., bi-directional LSTM [26], encodes the story sentences into a sequence of sentence vectors $s \in \mathbb{R}^{N \times D}$ with corresponding word embeddings $w \in \mathbb{R}^{N \times D \times L}$, where N is the number of sentences in a story, D is the feature dimension, and L is the number of words in a sentence. Then, we feed both sentence vectors and word embeddings into the generation pipeline using a series of upsampling blocks to produce story images at the required resolution. To generate high-quality images with fine-grained regional details, we propose to utilize word-level information in the network, including the input representation, the generator, and the discriminator.

3.2 Sentence Representation with Word Information

One problem arising in previous works [14,24] is that they feed given story sentences sequentially into the generation pipeline to produce corresponding story images. Thus, when some keywords do not appear in all sentences, the corresponding keyword-related attributes may not be generated in all story images due to the sequential generation, and then the synthetic story may fail to keep consistency across all images.

To address the issue, we propose a new sentence representation, which can selectively incorporate different word information from the entire story to mitigate the inconsistency problem. To build this sentence representation, we first reshape the word embeddings $w \in \mathbb{R}^{N \times D \times L}$ to get $w' \in \mathbb{R}^{D \times (L*N)}$. Then, we calculate the correlation weights $\sigma \in \mathbb{R}^{N \times (L*N)}$ between each sentence and all words within the story, according to applying a matrix multiplication followed by a Softmax operation between w' and a sentence vector $s \in \mathbb{R}^{N \times D}$, denoted as $\sigma = \text{Softmax}(sw')$. Then, a new sentence representation weighted by word-sentence relation can be obtained by doing $s' = \sigma(w')^T$, and is fed into the generation pipeline at the beginning. By doing this, this new sentence vectors can selectively incorporate different word information, even if they only appear in some sentences, to keep information consistency across all story images.

3.3 Discriminator with Fusion Features

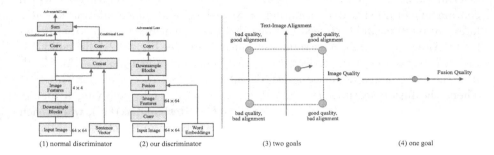

Fig. 3. Left: comparison between the normal discriminator (1) and ours (2). Right: a diagram for two goals of current methods (3) and the goal of our proposed one-way output design (4).

In this work, we propose a new discriminator with one-way output, which works on fusion features that contain both image and text information. Although DFGAN [25] also introduced an one-way output discriminator, differently, (1) our discriminator uses fine-grained word-level information and image features at the original size without information loss, while DFGAN first downsamples image features to a small size at 4×4, which may suffer a potential information loss problem, (2) our discriminator builds fusion features via applying matrix multiplication between detailed image features and word-level text representations, while DFGAN concatenates a coarse sentence vector with small-scale image features at 4×4, and may fail to comprehensively explore the correlation between image and text representations, and (3) loss objectives for our discriminator become to only check the difference of fusion features created from word representations and synthetic images and fusion features created from word representations and real images, while fusion features in DFGAN is to promote an additional gradient penalty, along with discriminator objectives.

Fusion Features. As shown in Fig. 3, (1), in current methods [9,21,26], the discriminator first extracts image features with a small size at 4×4 through a series of downsampling blocks. Then, this small-size features are used in two ways: one way is to determine whether the image is real or fake, and the other way is to concatenate this image features with the sentence vector to evaluate text-image semantic consistency. So, there are two kinds of loss computed, the unconditional loss and the conditional loss.

However, concatenating such small-size image features with the coarse sentence vector may not fully evaluate the text-image semantic alignment, because the image features at 4×4 may lose much text-matched image information, and the sentence vector is a global representation of a given text, and cannot comprehensively reflect the alignment between image and text. Based on this, to better evaluate the text-image semantic consistency, we suggest to utilize word embeddings, and combine both text and image information at a shallow layer of the discriminator, instead of at size 4×4. Here, we introduce fusion features, which contain fine-grained text information at word-level and image information at a larger resolution, and then feed this detailed fusion features into the discriminator to evaluate the text-image semantic consistency (see Fig. 3, (2)). To build this fusion features, we convert the output real/fake image features $v \in \mathbb{R}^{C \times H \times W}$ into the same semantic space as word embeddings w, to get $v' \in \mathbb{R}^{D \times (H*W)}$. Then, the fusion features $F \in \mathbb{R}^{L \times H \times W}$ are obtained by applying a matrix multiplication between v' and w, denoted as $F = \text{Reshape}((w)^T v')$, where each value in F denotes the correlation between each pixel and each word. Finally, we feed fusion features into the discriminator. Basically, checking the difference between fusion features created from word representations and synthetic images and fusion features created from word representations and real images can also reflect the realism of synthetic images, as good fusion features should be realistic and have good text-image semantic alignment, similar to real images matching the corresponding text descriptions.

One-Way Output. As mentioned above, there are two kinds of losses computed in the discriminator, unconditional loss for image quality and conditional loss for text-image semantic alignment, see Fig. 3 (1). Thus, the discriminator needs to promote the generator to achieve two goals: synthetic images should be indistinguishable from real images, and the semantic alignment between synthetic image and text should be captured similarly as the alignment between real image and text. However, there is no strong connection between these two goals, and thus the output results can be in four kinds of situations (see Fig. 3, (3)): good quality and good semantic alignment, bad quality and good semantic alignment, good quality and bad semantic alignment, bad quality and bad semantic alignment. This is because these two goals can be treated independently, and the network may fail to reach the minimum points of loss function surface for both quality and alignment at the same time. However, thanks to the implementation of fusion features in our discriminator, we can combine these two goals into one. Now, the goal of the discriminator is to promote the generator to produce better fusion features, which should be indistinguishable from the fusion features built from real images and text (see Fig. 3, (4)). Building good fusion features should have a good output image quality and effective correlation between image regions and corresponding finer word information. So, the loss functions to train our model is as follows:

$$
\begin{aligned}
\mathcal{L}_{G,I} &= -E_{F'_I \sim P_g} \left[\log(D(F'_I)) \right], \\
\mathcal{L}_{D,I} &= -E \left[\log(D(F_I)) \right] - E_{F'_I \sim P_g} \left[\log(1 - D(F'_I)) \right], \\
\mathcal{L}_{G,V} &= -E_{F'_V \sim P_g} \left[\log(D(F'_V)) \right], \\
\mathcal{L}_{D,V} &= -E \left[\log(D(F_V)) \right] - E_{F'_V \sim P_g} \left[\log(1 - D(F'_V)) \right],
\end{aligned}
\tag{1}
$$

where I denotes an image, V denotes a story with a series of images, F are real fusion features created by word representations and real image (or story) features that are sampled from the real distribution, F' are synthetic fusion features created by word representations and synthetic image (or story) features that are sampled from the model distribution.

3.4 Extended Word-Level Spatial Attention

To generate high-quality story images with finer details and a better consistency, we adopt word-level spatial attention [26], and further extend it to focus on all words and visual spatial locations in the entire story. By doing this, our extended attention not only highlights local word-related image regions in the generation process, but also captures the long-range correlation between words in the current sentence and visual spatial locations from other images within the same story, which ensures both the local image region quality and the global consistency of the whole story, tailored for the story visualization task.

First, we convert intermediate visual features $v \in \mathbb{R}^{N \times C \times H \times W}$ into a joint semantic space $\mathbb{R}^D$ via a convolution layer, and then reshape the new features to get $v' \in \mathbb{R}^{D \times (H * W * N)}$, where N is the size of a story, C is channel number, H is height of the features, and W is width. We also reshape word embeddings $w \in \mathbb{R}^{N \times D \times L}$ into $w' \in \mathbb{R}^{D \times (L * N)}$, where D is the feature dimension and L is the number of words in a sentence. Then, the extended spatial attention $\beta \in \mathbb{R}^{(H * W * N) \times (L * N)}$ focusing on capturing correlation between words and visual spatial locations across the entire story can be obtained by:

$$\beta_{i,j} = \frac{\exp(a_{i,j})}{\sum_{l=0}^{L*N-1} \exp(a_{i,l})}, \quad \text{where } a = v'^T w', \tag{2}$$

where $\beta_{i,j}$ denotes the correlation between the ith spatial location and the jth word in the story. Therefore, weighted visual features containing word information v_w can be obtained by $v_w = w' \beta^T$. By doing this, the model encourages all images within a story not only to have fine-grained regional details matching corresponding semantic words, but also share similar appearances to make the whole story more consistent.

4 Experiments

There are limited number of methods working on the same story visualization task as ours: StoryGAN [14], CP-CSV [24], DUCO [17], and VLC [16]. Story-GAN is based on generative adversarial networks, and CP-CSV, DUCO, and VLC are built on top of StoryGAN, where CP-CSV relies on character segmentation masks to provide an additional supervision, and DUCO and VLC utilized auxiliary captioning networks to keep consistency.

4.1   Datasets

We adopt Pororo-SV to evaluate our approach, which is first introduced in [14]. Pororo-SV was created from the Pororo dataset [7], which was used for video question answering. There are 13, 000 training pairs and 2, 336 test pairs. Following previous works, we consider every five consecutive images as a story.

Differently, we do not evaluate our approach on CLEVR-SV [14], as there are only 15 different words in the entire dataset, which might fail to fully explore the multi-modal story visualization task. Based on this, we adopt Abstract Scenes [31,32]. Abstract Scenes was proposed for studying semantic information, which contains over 1, 000 sets of 10 semantically similar scenes of children playing outside. The scenes are composed with 58 clip-art objects, and there are six sentences describing different aspects of a scene. Following [32], we reserve 1000 samples as the testing set and 497 samples for validation.

4.2   Implementation

Our approach is developed using PyTorch, building on top of the original StoryGAN codebase. The resolution of output images on Pororo-SV is 64×64, and on Abstract Scenes is 256×256. The text encoder is a bi-directional LSTM, pretrained to maximize the cosine similarity between matched image and text features [26]. We select the best checkpoints and tune hyperparameters by using the FID and FSD scores mentioned below. The network is trained 240 epochs on both Pororo-SV and Abstract Scenes, using the Adam optimizer [8] with learning rate 0.0002. All models were trained on a single Quadro RTX 6000 GPU.

4.3   Evaluation Metrics

To evaluate the quality of output images, the Fréchet Inception Distance (FID) [5] is our main evaluation metric, which computes the Fréchet distance between the distribution of the synthetic images and ground-truth images in the feature space of a pretrained Inception-v3 network. Besides, following [24], we adopt the Fréchet Story Distance (FSD), as FID is commonly used to evaluate the image generation task but takes only a single image into account. FSD is a redesigned evaluation matrix for story visualization, and is easier to capture the quality of the generated image sequence for a story, with respect to temporal consistency.

However, as both FID and FSD cannot reflect the semantic alignment between sentences and story images, we compute the average cosine similarity (Cosine) between pairs of sentence and synthetic image over the testing set, and further scale the value by 100.

4.4   Quantitative Evaluation

Table 1 shows quantitative comparisons between our approach and the baselines on Pororo-SV and Abstract Scenes. From the table, we can observe that our approach achieves better evaluation results against other methods on both datasets,

Table 1. Quantitative evaluation between different methods on Pororo-SV and Abstract Scenes. For FID and FSD, lower is better; for text-image cosine similarity (Cosine), higher is better.

Method	Pororo-SV dataset			Abstract dataset		
	FID↓	FSD↓	Cosine↑	FID↓	FSD↓	Cosine↑
StoryGAN [14]	78.64	94.53	0.22	135.16	55.80	3.59
CP-CSV [24]	67.76	71.51	0.32	–	–	–
DUCO [17]	95.17	171.70	0.08	142.34	49.16	3.95
VLC [16]	94.30	122.07	0.21	–	–	–
Ours	**56.08**	**52.50**	**2.98**	**72.34**	**14.86**	**4.05**

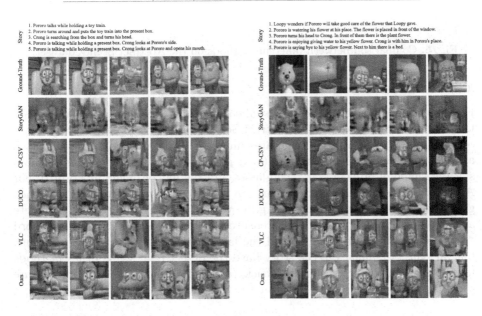

Fig. 4. Comparison between different methods on the Pororo-SV.

and builds a new state of the art. Note that differently from CP-CSV, DUCO, and VLC, our approach uses neither segmentation masks nor auxiliary captioning networks. Compared to StoryGAN, our approach achieves 28.7% improvement in FID, and 44.5% improvement in FSD on Pororo-SV; and as for Abstract Scenes, our approach achieves 46.5% improvement in FID, and 73.4% improvement in FSD. This illustrates that our approach can generate images with finer quality, achieve a better image-text semantic alignment, and keep a higher consistency across story images. Note that we do not evaluate CP-CSV and VLC on Abstract Scenes, as CP-CSV requires segmentation masks, and VLC has not released the complete code.

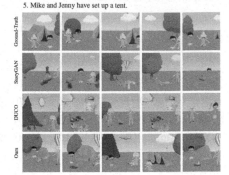

Fig. 5. Comparison between different methods on the Abstract Scenes dataset.

4.5 Qualitative Evaluation

Figures 4 and 5 show examples of visual comparisons between our approach and the baselines on Pororo-SV and Abstract Scenes, respectively. As we can observe, on Pororo-SV, our approach generates images with finer regional details, such as detained character appearances (e.g., penguin Pororo and frog Crong) and sharper shape of objects (e.g., the glasses and the hat on penguin Pororo). For Abstract Scenes, a good improvement can be also observed, where our approach generates high-quality characters (e.g., boy Mike and girl Jenny) with complete and detailed appearances, and also ensures a better consistency, e.g., the word "tent" only appears in the first and the last sentences for the second example, but all synthetic images in the story have the object tent, while other methods fails to keep the object tent in the background of all images. More samples are shown in the supplementary material.

4.6 Component Analysis

We conduct an ablation study to evaluate the effectiveness of different components proposed in the paper, and the results are shown in Table 2.

Sentence Representation with Word Information. First, we can find that the new sentence representation improves scores on all evaluation metrics. We attribute this improvement to the better representation of text that contains fine-grained word information from the entire story, which enables high-quality initial image features with finer regional details and a better consistency (e.g., better FSD score), and thus further improves final synthetic results (e.g., better FID and Cosine scores). This can be also supported by the observation found in text-to-image generation [30], where the quality of initial image features can considerably affect the quality of output images in such a sequential upsampling generation pipeline (see Fig. 2).

Table 2. Component Analysis on Pororo-SV. "Ours w/o Sentence" stands for without using the proposed new sentence representation; "Ours w/Discrimiantor" stands for using the discriminator in current story visualization methods [14,17,24]; "Ours w/o Extended Spatial Attention" stands for without adopting the proposed attention; "Ours w/Word-Level Spatial Attention" is with the implementation of word-level spatial attention [26], instead of our proposed extended spatial attention.

Method	FID	FSD	Cosine
Ours w/o New sentence representation	68.48	62.85	2.24
Ours w/Discriminator [14]	62.23	59.33	2.61
Ours w/o Extended spatial attention	83.66	78.80	2.26
Ours w/Word-level spatial attention [26]	58.26	63.39	2.54
Ours w/Pretrained BERT	52.38	49.69	3.71
Ours w/FT BERT	50.96	48.81	3.95
Ours w/BERT scratch	55.78	51.71	2.80
Ours	56.08	52.50	2.98

Discriminator with Fusion Features and Extended Word-Level Spatial Attention. A degradation can be observed when our approach does not implement the proposed discriminator. Similarly, without adopting proposed extended spatial attention, we can observe a decrease in both FID and FSD scores. We think that this is because both components are complement to each other: (1) without the proposed discriminator, although the generator tries to make use of word-level information via the proposed attention in the generation process, there is no corresponding word-level feedback from the discriminator, regarding whether word-related attributes are produced in synthetic story images, and (2) without the extended spatial attention, the fine-grained feedback from the proposed discriminator at both word- and image region-level cannot be fully utilized by the generator. Therefore, both components can work together to make a full use of word information to enable a higher-quality image generation with a better story consistency. Besides, we can find that the scores for "Ours w/o New Sentence Representation" is better than "Ours w/o Extended Spatial Attention". This shows that the fine-grained training feedback provided by our discriminator can be more utilized by the proposed extended word-level spatial attention.

Besides, we further record the number of trainable parameters in both kinds of discriminators, where our proposed single-directional discriminator only contains 10.4M trainable parameters, while the number of parameters in StoryGAN, DUCO, and VLC is 47.2M, and 70.9M for CP-CSV. So, compared to Story-GAN, our proposed discriminator reduces about 77.97% number of parameters, but achieves 28.7% improvement in FID, and 44.5% improvement in FSD on Pororo-SV, which verifies its superiority.

Moreover, we replace the extended spatial attention with word-level spatial attention [26] to verify its effectiveness. The main improvement using the

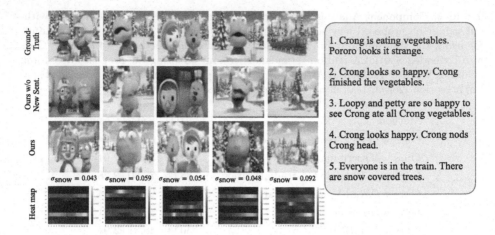

Fig. 6. Visualization of extended spatial attention and new sentence representation.

extended spatial attention is shown on the consistency of output results, especially on FSD score. This is because our proposed component focuses mainly on the whole story with multiple images and sentences, instead of only a pair of image and sentence, which coincides with the purpose of keeping the consistency across story images.

Text Encoder Using BERT. In Table 2, we use BERT to replace LSTM as the text encoder. If the BERT is trained from scratch, denoted as "w/BERT Scratch", there is no significant changes on all metrics. We think that this is because Pororo-SV is small and each caption contains limited number of words, and thus a RNN-based text encoder (e.g., LSTM) is strong enough to capture long-range dependencies between words. If we use a pretrained BERT, denoted as "w/Pretrained BERT" or further fine tune BERT on Pororo-SV, denoted as "w/FT BERT", performance improves. This is because BERT pretrained on a larger text corpus (e.g., Wikipedia) can generate better text representations.

4.7 Visualization of Extended Spatial Attention and New Sentence Representation

Capturing relations between words and image regions has been adopted in text-to-image generation [9,21,26] and image editing using text [10,12] to improve image quality and text-image semantic alignment. Our proposed extended word-level spatial attention captures relations between image regions and words from the entire story to ensure local image quality and also global consistency across story images, tailored for story visualization. In Fig. 6, we visualize the extended spatial attention using heatmap. The y axis denotes the last 10 words in the story (i.e., sentence 5: Everyone...), and x denotes image regions, where we evenly split an image into 32 regions and compute the average for each region. So, the

Table 3. Effects of our new sentence representation adopted in story visualization on Pororo-SV and text-to-image generation on CUB birds. For FID and FSD, lower is better, for IS, higher is better. "+ New Sent." means using our new representation.

Method	FID	FSD	IS
StoryGAN + New Sent.	72.81	84.06	–
CP-CSV + New Sent.	63.12	64.29	–
DUCO + New Sent.	87.82	131.83	–
VLC + New Sent.	82.19	100.94	–
AttnGAN [26]	23.98	–	4.36
AttnGAN + New Sent.	19.20	–	4.71
DFGAN [25]	14.81	–	5.10
DFGAN + New Sent.	11.98	–	5.16
Ours	56.08	52.50	–

Table 4. Results of a side-by-side human evaluation between our approach and DUCO on Pororo-SV.

Choice (%)	Ours	Tie	DUCO
Visual quality	75.3	8.3	16.4
Consistency	81.8	4.4	13.8
Relevant	72.3	5.7	22.0

heatmap shows the correlation values captured by our attention between the last 10 words and image regions in each image. The word snow ($y = 7$) is highlighted in each heatmap, and snow is also generated in all output images, which verifies that our method captures distant word-image relations and ensures consistency even when some keywords do not appear in all sentences.

Furthermore, we also visualize the proposed new sentence representation with word information by showing the σ values between "snow" and each sentence in Fig. 6. As we can see, our sentence representation learns to give high σ to keywords, without it, distant images from keywords may not keep consistency (e.g., there is no snow in the 1st image of "Ours w/o New Sent.").

4.8 General Applicability of New Sentence Representation

As shown in Table 3, we implement our new sentence representation in other story visualization methods and also text-to-image generation (e.g., AttnGAN [26] and DFGAN [25]) by feeding word information into the sentence vector without changing networks. We can observe that our sentence representation further improves these methods by having better evaluation scores. For story visualization, the improvement is mainly because our proposed sentence representation enables high-quality initial image features with finer regional details and a better consistency, and thus further improves final synthetic results. For text-to-image generation, the improvement verifies the observation shown in the work [30] that the quality of initial image features can considerably affect the quality of output images in a sequential upsampling generation pipeline.

4.9 Human Evaluation

We also conduct a human evaluation to comprehensively evaluate the performance of our approach on Pororo-SV. To do this, following [14], a side-by-side human evaluation study is conducted based on three evaluation criteria: (1) the visual image quality, (2) the consistency among story images, and (3) the semantic alignment between paired image and sentence. The study compares the synthetic image sequences from our approach and DUCO. We showed the generated story images along with the corresponding story sentences from two methods, and three options are provided: (1) the first is better, (2) two are similar, and (3) the second is better. In this evaluation, we randomly choose 200 synthetic story images, generated from corresponding story descriptions sampled from the testing dataset, and each was assigned to 5 workers to reduce human variance.

From Table 4, story images produced by our approach are more preferred by workers on three evaluate criteria, which demonstrates the effectiveness of our approach on high-quality image generation with a better text-image semantic alignment, and a better story consistency.

5   Conclusion

In this paper, we investigated the task of story visualization. We proposed a new approach by exploring fine-grained information at both word and story level, and demonstrate the effectiveness of proposed components by conducting extensive experiments. Our approach has three novel components: a new sentence representation selectively incorporates different word information from the entire story to enable a better consistency, the extended spatial attention captures relations between image regions and words across the entire story to enable the generation of higher-quality story images with better consistency, and the novel discriminator contains a smaller number of parameters, but effectively provides the generator with fine-grained training signals, evaluating the quality of fusion features to examine whether word-related image attributes are generated in story images and also their quality, and thus encouraging the generator with the proposed attention to highlight image relations corresponding to semantic words from the story. Finally, a human evaluation has been conducted to further verify the effective performance of our proposed approach.

However, there is still much space for quality improvement on different datasets, such as the images details on characters. Also, a more concise architecture design is desired, as current methods (including our approach) require a large amount of memory storage to hold and train. Also, the resolution of output images is small at 64×64, which is less practical for real-word applications.

Acknowlegments. We sincerely thank Thomas Lukasiewicz for helpful discussions and feedback. This work was supported by the Alan Turing Institute under the EPSRC grant EP/N510129/1, by the AXA Research Fund, and by the EPSRC grant EP/R013667/1. We also acknowledge the use of the EPSRC-funded Tier 2 facility JADE (EP/P020275/1) and GPU computing support by Scan Computers International Ltd.

References

1. Balaji, Y., Min, M.R., Bai, B., Chellappa, R., Graf, H.P.: Conditional gan with discriminative filter generation for text-to-video synthesis. In: IJCAI, vol. 1, p. 2 (2019)
2. Dong, H., Yu, S., Wu, C., Guo, Y.: Semantic image synthesis via adversarial learning. In: Proceedings of the IEEE International Conference on Computer Vision, pp. 5706–5714 (2017)
3. Goodfellow, I., et al.: Generative adversarial nets. In: Advances in Neural Information Processing Systems, pp. 2672–2680 (2014)
4. Gupta, T., Schwenk, D., Farhadi, A., Hoiem, D., Kembhavi, A.: Imagine this! scripts to compositions to videos. In: Proceedings of the European Conference on Computer Vision (ECCV), pp. 598–613 (2018)
5. Heusel, M., Ramsauer, H., Unterthiner, T., Nessler, B., Hochreiter, S.: GANs trained by a two time-scale update rule converge to a local nash equilibrium. In: Advances in Neural Information Processing Systems, pp. 6626–6637 (2017)
6. Hinz, T., Heinrich, S., Wermter, S.: Semantic object accuracy for generative text-to-image synthesis. arXiv preprint. arXiv:1910.13321 (2019)
7. Kim, K.M., Heo, M.O., Choi, S.H., Zhang, B.T.: Deepstory: video story qa by deep embedded memory networks. arXiv preprint. arXiv:1707.00836 (2017)
8. Kingma, D.P., Ba, J.: Adam: a method for stochastic optimization. arXiv preprint. arXiv:1412.6980 (2014)
9. Li, B., Qi, X., Lukasiewicz, T., Torr, P.: Controllable text-to-image generation. In: Advances in Neural Information Processing Systems, pp. 2063–2073 (2019)
10. Li, B., Qi, X., Lukasiewicz, T., Torr, P.: ManiGAN: text-guided image manipulation. In: Proceedings of the IEEE/CVF Conference on Computer Vision and Pattern Recognition, pp. 7880–7889 (2020)
11. Li, B., Qi, X., Torr, P., Lukasiewicz, T.: Image-to-image translation with text guidance. arXiv preprint. arXiv:2002.05235 (2020)
12. Li, B., Qi, X., Torr, P., Lukasiewicz, T.: Lightweight generative adversarial networks for text-guided image manipulation. Adv. Neural. Inf. Process. Syst. **33**, 22020–22031 (2020)
13. Li, B., Torr, P., Lukasiewicz, T.: Memory-driven text-to-image generation (2021)
14. Li, Y., Gan, Z., Shen, Y., Liu, J., Cheng, Y., Wu, Y., Carin, L., Carlson, D., Gao, J.: Storygan: a sequential conditional gan for story visualization. In: Proceedings of the IEEE/CVF Conference on Computer Vision and Pattern Recognition, pp. 6329–6338 (2019)
15. Li, Y., Min, M., Shen, D., Carlson, D., Carin, L.: Video generation from text. In: Proceedings of the AAAI Conference on Artificial Intelligence, vol. 32 (2018)

16. Maharana, A., Bansal, M.: Integrating visuospatial, linguistic and commonsense structure into story visualization. arXiv preprint. arXiv:2110.10834 (2021)
17. Maharana, A., Hannan, D., Bansal, M.: Improving generation and evaluation of visual stories via semantic consistency. arXiv preprint. arXiv:2105.10026 (2021)
18. Mahon, L., Giunchiglia, E., Li, B., Lukasiewicz, T.: Knowledge graph extraction from videos. In: 2020 19th IEEE International Conference on Machine Learning and Applications (ICMLA), pp. 25–32. IEEE (2020)
19. Nam, S., Kim, Y., Kim, S.J.: Text-adaptive generative adversarial networks: manipulating images with natural language. In: Advances in Neural Information Processing Systems, pp. 42–51 (2018)
20. Pan, Y., Qiu, Z., Yao, T., Li, H., Mei, T.: To create what you tell: generating videos from captions. In: Proceedings of the 25th ACM international conference on Multimedia, pp. 1789–1798 (2017)
21. Qiao, T., Zhang, J., Xu, D., Tao, D.: Mirrorgan: Learning text-to-image generation by redescription. In: Proceedings of the IEEE Conference on Computer Vision and Pattern Recognition, pp. 1505–1514 (2019)
22. Ramesh, A., et al.: Zero-shot text-to-image generation. In: International Conference on Machine Learning, pp. 8821–8831. PMLR (2021)
23. Reed, S., Akata, Z., Yan, X., Logeswaran, L., Schiele, B., Lee, H.: Generative adversarial text to image synthesis. arXiv preprint. arXiv:1605.05396 (2016)
24. Song, Y.-Z., Rui Tam, Z., Chen, H.-J., Lu, H.-H., Shuai, H.-H.: Character-preserving coherent story visualization. In: Vedaldi, A., Bischof, H., Brox, T., Frahm, J.-M. (eds.) ECCV 2020. LNCS, vol. 12362, pp. 18–33. Springer, Cham (2020). https://doi.org/10.1007/978-3-030-58520-4_2
25. Tao, M., et al.: DF-GAN: deep fusion generative adversarial networks for text-to-image synthesis. arXiv preprint. arXiv:2008.05865 (2020)
26. Xu, T., et al.: AttnGAN: fine-grained text to image generation with attentional generative adversarial networks. In: Proceedings of the IEEE Conference on Computer Vision and Pattern Recognition, pp. 1316–1324 (2018)
27. Zhang, H., Koh, J.Y., Baldridge, J., Lee, H., Yang, Y.: Cross-modal contrastive learning for text-to-image generation. In: Proceedings of the IEEE/CVF Conference on Computer Vision and Pattern Recognition, pp. 833–842 (2021)
28. Zhang, H., et al.: StackGAN: text to photo-realistic image synthesis with stacked generative adversarial networks. In: Proceedings of the IEEE International Conference on Computer Vision, pp. 5907–5915 (2017)
29. Zhang, H., Xu, T., Li, H., Zhang, S., Wang, X., Huang, X., Metaxas, D.N.: StackGAN++: realistic image synthesis with stacked generative adversarial networks. In: IEEE Transactions on Pattern Analysis and Machine Intelligenc, vol. 41, no.8, pp. 1947–1962 (2018)
30. Zhu, M., Pan, P., Chen, W., Yang, Y.: DM-GAN: dynamic memory generative adversarial networks for text-to-image synthesis. In: Proceedings of the IEEE Conference on Computer Vision and Pattern Recognition, pp. 5802–5810 (2019)
31. Zitnick, C.L., Parikh, D.: Bringing semantics into focus using visual abstraction. In: Proceedings of the IEEE Conference on Computer Vision and Pattern Recognition, pp. 3009–3016 (2013)
32. Zitnick, C.L., Parikh, D., Vanderwende, L.: Learning the visual interpretation of sentences. In: Proceedings of the IEEE International Conference on Computer Vision, pp. 1681–1688 (2013)

Unifying Event Detection and Captioning as Sequence Generation via Pre-training

Qi Zhang⑩, Yuqing Song, and Qin Jin$^{(\boxtimes)}$⑩

School of Information, Renmin University of China, Beijing, China
{zhangqi1996,syuqing,qjin}@ruc.edu.cn

Abstract. Dense video captioning aims to generate corresponding text descriptions for a series of events in the untrimmed video, which can be divided into two sub-tasks, event detection and event captioning. Unlike previous works that tackle the two sub-tasks separately, recent works have focused on enhancing the inter-task association between the two sub-tasks. However, designing inter-task interactions for event detection and captioning is not trivial due to the large differences in their task specific solutions. Besides, previous event detection methods normally ignore temporal dependencies between events, leading to event redundancy or inconsistency problems. To tackle above the two defects, in this paper, we define event detection as a sequence generation task and propose a unified pre-training and fine-tuning framework to naturally enhance the inter-task association between event detection and captioning. Since the model predicts each event with previous events as context, the inter-dependency between events is fully exploited and thus our model can detect more diverse and consistent events in the video. Experiments on the ActivityNet dataset show that our model outperforms the state-of-the-art methods, and can be further boosted when pre-trained on extra large-scale video-text data. Code is available at https://github. com/QiQAng/UEDVC.

Keywords: Dense video captioning · Pre-training · Sequence generation

1 Introduction

Dense Video Captioning (DVC) [22], as one of the important tasks in video understanding, aims to localize and describe multiple events in untrimmed videos. The early mainstream approaches [19,20,27,38,42] normally decompose the DVC task into two sub-tasks, event detection and event captioning, and tackle the two sub-tasks separately. However, an obvious limitation of these methods is that they ignore the association of the two sub-tasks which can benefit from each other.

Supplementary Information The online version contains supplementary material available at https://doi.org/10.1007/978-3-031-20059-5_21.

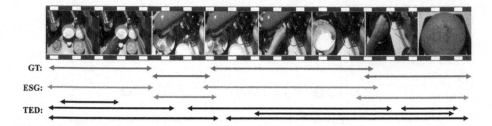

Fig. 1. Illustration of event detection results by the traditional event detection method (TED for short) and our proposed event sequence generation method (ESG for short). The TED usually predicts redundant events with a high degree of overlaps due to the lack of event relationship modeling, while our ESG can generate events sequentially with previous events as context. GT refers to the ground-truth event annotation.

To address this limitation, some recent works [8, 25, 35, 37, 43] explore to enhance the inter-task association between event detection and event captioning. For example, Deng *et al.* [8] propose a "top-down" framework which connects visual and language information to localize events or connects visual and event information to generate captions at different stages to enforce the interaction between the two sub-tasks. Wang *et al.* [37] propose to share the same intermediate features and jointly optimize the two sub-tasks. Although the mutual promotion between the two sub-tasks has been witnessed, it is not trivial to design inter-task interactions for event detection and event captioning due to the large differences in their task specific solutions, which makes them hard to fully benefit from each other.

Besides, the previous methods detect the event boundaries solely based on the video information or the hybrid knowledge of video and text, which ignores the temporal relationships between multiple events. It easily leads to redundant event detection, either producing a large number of event candidates, or having excessive overlap between events. As shown in Fig. 1, due to the lack of consideration of the temporal relationship between events, the traditional event detection methods usually detect redundant events with a high degree of overlap. In fact, there are strong temporal dependencies between events in the video. For example, in the instructional videos, events usually occur one after another, explaining each operation step.

To address the above mentioned two limitations, in this paper, we propose to define event detection as a sequence generation task, which generates the event sequence one by one conditioned on previously detected events. It can fully exploit the previous events as context to avoid generating redundant events, and unify the event detection and event captioning sub-tasks into the same framework to explore inter-task interactions in a simpler but highly effective way. Specifically, we define the event as a new modality and propose a unified video-event-text pre-training and fine-tuning framework based on the transformer architecture [32] for both the event detection and the event captioning. We employ two pre-training tasks including Masked Language Modeling

(MLM) and Masked Video Feature Regression (MVFR) to learn the video-text representation for event captioning, and propose a novel pre-training task called Masked Event Feature Modeling (MEFM) to learn the video-event representation for event detection. Since the two sub-tasks share the same model architecture and parameters, we can alternately train the unified model with the three pre-training tasks, which is a simple, natural and effective method to strengthen the association between two sub-tasks. Experimental results on the ActivityNet Captions dataset [22] show that even pre-trained on the same dataset without any extra data, our model significantly outperforms the state-of-the-art methods on both event detection and event captioning. In particular, benefiting from the new event detection framework, our model generates more diverse events similar to human annotations. When pre-training the model on extra out-of-domain captioning data, our model achieves more additional gains, which demonstrates the effectiveness of our pre-training and fine-tuning framework.

The main contributions of this work are three-fold:

- We transform the event detection sub-task into a sequence generation problem with temporal dependencies modeling between events, which makes our model directly generate an appropriate and low redundancy sequence of events for untrimmed videos.
- With the task format unification, we propose a unified video-event-text pre-training model with three pre-training tasks to effectively enhance the inter-task association between event detection and event captioning.
- Our model achieves new state-of-the-art dense video captioning results on the ActivityNet Captions dataset, and can be further promoted by pre-training on more out-of-domain video caption data.

2   Related Works

Dense Video Captioning. The dense video captioning (DVC) task is first proposed by Krishna *et al.* [22] to localize and describe rich events in long untrimmed videos. A two-stage framework is proposed, which first produces a large amount of event candidates via an event detection module, and then generates descriptions for each event. Some following works separately improve the performance of two modules by producing less redundant event proposals [27] or introducing multi-modal features to enrich event representation [19,20]. However, handling event detection and captioning independently without any association has obvious limitations. Therefore, some other following works [8,25,35,37,43] focus on enhancing the inter-task association between event detection module and event captioning module to improve the performance of DVC. Specifically, Li *et al.* [25] adopt a new descriptiveness regression component to build a bridge between event detection and captioning modules, which measures the descriptive complexity of each event proposal, and adjusts the event proposal boundaries. Deng *et al.* [8] reverse the predominant "detect-then-describe" fashion and propose a three-stage top-down framework, which first generates coarse-grained sentences, then aligns each sentence with event fragments, and finally refines the caption quality by a Dual-Path Cross Attention module. Wang *et al.* [37] extend the "Object Query" manner in DETR [4, 44] to the DVC task and decode the intermediate features and event query to produce event proposal and description simultaneously.

Although promising DVC results have been achieved in these methods, they fail to explore the temporal relationship between events for event detection, which leads to highly redundant event proposals. Furthermore, the "propose-then-select" detection manner [10, 13, 16, 29] based on a large amount of event candidates is also computationally complex. In this work, we convert the event detection task into a sequence generation problem, and unify the event detection and captioning into a unified framework, which makes the inter-task association more natural and effective.

Pre-training for V+L Tasks. The pre-training and fine-tuning paradigm has demonstrated strong potentials in V+L [5, 6, 18, 23, 24, 30] cross-modal tasks recently. Such as the Oscar [24] model, first pre-trained on large-scale image-text pairs to learn a joint representation for vision and language, and then fine-tuned on several downstream tasks, achieves the state-of-the-art results on both vision-and-language understanding tasks (*e.g.,* image-text retrieval [11], visual question answering [14]) and generation tasks (*e.g.,* image captioning [34], novel object captioning [1]). However, due to the coupling complexity of event detection and captioning, none of them have verified the effectiveness of multi-modal pre-training on the dense video captioning task.

3   Method

Our unified model for dense video captioning following the pre-training and fine-tuning paradigm is illustrated in Fig. 2. We unify the event detection and event captioning in one framework and treat the video, events and captions as three independent modalities. Three pre-training tasks are proposed for the cross-modal representation learning, including Masked Language Modeling (MLM), Masked Video Feature Regression (MVFR), and Masked Event Feature Modeling (MEFM). We first alternately pre-train the model with the three pre-training tasks and then fine-tune it for event detection and event captioning respectively.

3.1   Model Architecture

Video Representation. Given an input video, we follow previous works [8, 37] to use C3D [31] and TSN [36] to extract the raw video features in order to have a fair comparison in experimental evaluations. In addition, we also introduce semantic concept features (called CPT) to enrich the visual representation. Specifically, we employ a bidirectional LSTM [15] as a multi-class multi-label video classifier to predict concept labels for each frame, which are the nouns and verbs extracted from corresponding annotated captions. To enable the model to

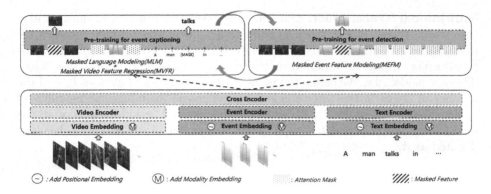

Fig. 2. Overview of our proposed model, which unifies three pre-training tasks for event detection and captioning. It contains three independent transformer encoders to capture the corresponding intra-modality context and a multi-layer cross encoder to encode the inter-modality context.

predict distinguishable fine-grained concept labels for different frames, we optimize the model with an additional event boundary prediction objective, which requires the model to predict whether the current frame is the start, middle or the end frame of an event. The hidden state from the last LSTM layer is used as the concept feature for each video frame. Finally, we concatenate the concept feature with visual appearance features from C3D or TSN to represent the video as a sequence of frame-level features $V = \{v_1, v_2, \cdots, v_N\}$, where N is the number of frames in the video. We employ a fully-connected layer to embed the video feature sequence V into the same dimensionality as the word embedding, and add a learnable modality embedding $mode_v$ to represent the video modality.

Event Representation. For an event with timestamp $[start_i, end_i]$ in the video, we convert it into a N-dimensional binary feature vector, which is expressed as $e_i = \{x_1^i, x_2^i, \cdots, x_N^i\}$, where N is the total number of video frames. The value x_t^i is set as 1 if the t-th frame is included in the event interval, otherwise it is set as 0. In this way, we represent all the events in the video as a sequence of $E = \{e_1, e_2, \cdots, e_M\}$, where M is the number of events in the current video. Similar to the video representation, we employ a fully-connected layer to embed the event sequence E into the same dimensionality as the video and text embeddings, and add a learnable modality embedding $mode_e$ to represent the event modality. Furthermore, we add positional embedding to reserve the temporal order information of events in the video.

Text Representation. For the caption text, we represent each caption with a sequence of word embeddings $T = \{t_1, t_2, \cdots, t_s\}$, where s is the total number of words. We further add the positional embedding to keep the sequential information, and add a learnable modality embedding $mode_t$ to represent the text modality.

Multimodal Transformer. Our model is based on a multi-stream architecture as illustrated in Fig. 2, where three independent transformer encoders are first applied on each modality for the intra-modality learning, and then a cross transformer encoder is employed to capture the inter-context information across different modalities. We define the number of cross encoder layers as L_c and the number of layers in the three single-modal encoders including the modality of video, event and text as L_v, L_e and L_t respectively. The hidden size of all the transformer layers is denoted as H, and the number of self-attention heads is denoted as A.

3.2 Proxy Tasks

Masked Language Modeling (MLM). To enable our model the ability for caption generation, we adopt MLM as one of the pre-training tasks like other Vision-and-Language (V+L) pre-training models [5,6,18,23,24,30]. The MLM task takes V, E and T as inputs, and predict the masked words in T according to the corresponding video content of the current event timestamps e_i. Since all the events in E are input to the model while the caption T is only corresponding to the current event, we restrict the attentions for other events $E_{\backslash i}$, so that the model can focus on the current event captioning. Specifically, we mask the cross-modal attention weights in the cross encoder for other events $E_{\backslash i}$ to make the caption generation ignores other events. Similar to the BERT [9], we randomly mask out the words in T with a probability of 15%, and replace the masked ones t_m with a special token [MASK] 80% of the time, with another random word 10% of the time and the original word 10% of the time. The goal of this task is to predict the masked words based on the context information from the whole video content, the current event boundary e_i, and the surrounding captioning words by minimizing the negative log-likelihood as follows:

$$\mathcal{L}_{\text{MLM}} = -\mathbb{E}_{(V,e_i,T)\sim\mathcal{D}} \log p(t_m | t_{\backslash m}, e_i, V; \Theta), \tag{1}$$

where Θ denotes all trainable parameters, $\mathcal{D}$ denotes the whole training set, and t_m denotes the masked words in T.

Masked Video Feature Regression (MVFR). In contrast to the MLM task which predicts the masked caption words according to the video content, we also introduce the MVFR task to reconstruct video features based on the description. The input for MVFR task is exactly the same as the MLM task. Suppose T is the description for the event e_i, we randomly choose some video frames in e_i for prediction. Specifically, we randomly mask 15% of the features from $\{V_i\}_{i=s}^e$, where v_s and v_e are the start and end video frame in e_i respectively. Each masked feature v_m is replaced by a special feature vector [MASK], which is an all-zeros vector with the same dimensionality as the original video feature $r(v_m)$. The hidden state of v_m from the cross transformer encoder is input to a FC layer to predict the original video feature denoted as $p(v_m)$, according to the remaining video features $V_{\backslash m}$ and the event description T. We adopt the L2 regression loss to reduce the distance between $p(v_m)$ and $r(v_m)$ as follows:

$$\mathcal{L}_{\text{MVFR}} = \mathbb{E}_{(V,e_i,T)\sim\mathcal{D}} FC(v_m|v_{\backslash m}, e_i, T; \Theta), \qquad (2)$$

$$FC(v_m|v_{\backslash m}, e_i, T; \Theta) = \sum_{j=1}^{N} \|p(\mathbf{v_m}^{(j)}) - r(\mathbf{v_m}^{(j)})\|_2^2, \qquad (3)$$

where N is the dimension of video features. We share the FC prediction layer with the video feature embedding layer.

Masked Event Feature Modeling (MEFM). To predict event boundaries in a sequence generation manner, we propose a new pre-training task called Masked Event Feature Modeling (MEFM). Unlike above two pre-training tasks, the MEFM task takes V, E as inputs. We randomly mask event embeddings in E with a probability of 15%, and replace the masked one e_m with a special feature vector [MASK], which is an all-zeros vector. The model is required to predict the event boundaries of e_m according to the surrounding events in E and the video content. We apply a FC layer on the output of cross transformer encoder as a N-dimensional binary classifier, where N is the length of video frame sequences. The training loss can be defined as follows:

$$\mathcal{L}_{\text{MEFM}} = \mathbb{E}_{(V,E)\sim\mathcal{D}} f(e_m|e_{\backslash m}, V; \Theta), \qquad (4)$$

$$f(e_m|e_{\backslash m}, V; \Theta) = \sum_{i=1}^{N} [l_i \log x_i + (1 - l_i) \log(1 - x_i)], \qquad (5)$$

where $l_i \in [0, 1]$ indicates whether the i-th video frame is included in the masked event e_m interval, and x_i denotes the predicted probability.

3.3   Pre-training and Fine-Turning for DVC Task

As shown in Fig. 2, we pre-train the model for event detection and event captioning in a unified framework. However, the pre-training tasks of MLM and MVFR for event captioning take three modalities (video, event, text) as input, while the MEFM task for event detection takes two modalities without the text modality as input, making it problematic to optimize the three objectives jointly. Therefore, we train the two sub-tasks alternatively. Specifically, we divide the batch data into two categories: the batch with three modalities input (for MLM, MVFR) named as B_{three}, and the batch with two modalities input (for MEFM) named as B_{two}. We introduce a hyper-parameter λ to represent the probability of choosing batch B_{three}, and thus $(1-\lambda)$ denotes the probability of choosing batch B_{two}. When the batch B_{three} is fed to the model, the training loss is defined as $\mathcal{L} = \mathcal{L}_{\text{MLM}} + \mathcal{L}_{\text{MVFR}}$, while when batch B_{two} is fed to the model, the loss is defined as $\mathcal{L} = \mathcal{L}_{\text{MEFM}}$.

After pre-training, we fine-tune the model for the event detection sub-task (called ED) and event captioning sub-task (called EC) respectively. The two downstream tasks are similar since they both follow the auto-regressive manner [7,17] for generation. Therefore, we fine-tune the model in a similar way for the two sub-tasks. Specifically, we adapt our bi-directional pre-trained model to a uni-directional generator by constraining the self-attention mask of the text/event sequence to avoid seeing future items. Similar to the MLM and MEFM pre-training tasks, we randomly choose 15% of word/event features and replace them with the [MASK] token/special all-zeros vector for prediction. Note that the event detection task is to generate event sequences with the whole video as input, while the event captioning task generates captions for the corresponding event according to the whole video and event embedding e_i. Therefore, the fine-tuning objective for ED and EC tasks can be expressed as follows:

$$\mathcal{L}_{ED} = -\mathbb{E}_{(V,E)\sim\mathcal{D}} \log p(e_m|e_{<m}, V; \Theta), \tag{6}$$

$$\mathcal{L}_{EC} = -\mathbb{E}_{(V,e_i,T)\sim\mathcal{D}} \log p(t_m|t_{<m}, e_i, V; \Theta). \tag{7}$$

In the inference phase, we follow the "detect-then-describe" pipeline. At the stage of event prediction, we first input the whole video frame sequence and a special "start event" vector to the model. Then, we start to generate the event sequence one by one via feeding a [MASK] vector and sampling the predicted event feature from the N-dimensional binary classification layer. The predicted event feature vector is then used to replace the previous [MASK] vector, and a new [MASK] vector is fed to the model for the next event generation until the special "end event" vector is predicted. Finally, following the rule that the first 1-value in the event vector is regarded as the start time of an event in the video, and the last 1-value in the event vector is regarded as the end time of the event in the video, we translate the event vector into the event timestamp format. After predicting the event sequence for the untrimmed video, we generate corresponding captions for each predicted event. We first input the whole video, the current event embedding and the start [SOS] token to the model. Then, we follow the same auto-regressive sequence generation process to generate the captions until the end [EOS] token is predicted.

4   Experiments

4.1   Experimental Settings

Dataset. We conduct experiments on the benchmark ActivityNet Captions dataset [22], which contains 19,994 videos with an average of 3.65 event proposals per video. We follow the official split with 10009/4925/5044 videos for training, validation, and test. Furthermore, to demonstrate the ability of our model to benefit from more out-of-domain captioning data, we further evaluate our model pre-trained with other non-dense video captioning datasets, including MSRVTT [41], TGIF [26] and VATEX [39] datasets.

Implementation Details. For fair comparisons with the state-of-the-art methods, we use the same video features as PDVC [37], including the C3D [31] features

Table 1. The DVC performance measured by different evaluation tools on the original results and results with four adverse operations. SODA_{old} is the old version of SODA implementation and SODA_{mr} is the new implementation with multiple references.

Operation	Avg Recall	Avg precision	Evaluator2018			SODA_{old}	SODA_{mr}
			BLEU@4	CIDEr	METEOR		
Original	59.00	60.32	1.45	26.92	7.33	5.29	7.28
Increase	59.00	60.08	1.57	25.94	7.48	5.04	6.91
Reduce	53.75	60.21	1.55	27.99	7.44	5.06	6.99
Exchange	53.75	59.99	1.66	26.45	7.58	4.81	6.61
Extreme	20.63	58.76	2.45	14.94	8.52	2.98	4.64

provided by PDVC [37] and TSN [36] features provided by MT [43]. The max length of video frames V is set as 100. We set the layer number of independent encoders $L_v = L_e = L_t = 1$, the layer number of cross encoder $L_c = 4$, the hidden size $H = 512$, and the head number $A = 8$. When pre-training the model for event detection, the hyper-parameter λ for choosing different batches is set as 1/3 on both C3D and TSN features. When pre-training the model for event captioning, it is set as 1/2 on C3D features and 3/4 on TSN features. We use Adam [21] as the optimizer and train all the model parameters from scratch.

Metrics. We evaluate our method from three aspects. **(1)** To evaluate the performance of event detection, we use the evaluation tool provided by the 2018 ActivityNet Captions Challenge[1] (called Evaluator2018), which computes the average precision and average recall against the ground-truth events across temporal IoU (tIoU) at [0.3, 0.5, 0.7, 0.9]. Moreover, we also compute the self-tIoU between the detected events to evaluate the event diversity. **(2)** To purely evaluate the event captioning ability, we report the captioning results based on the ground-truth events with classic captioning metrics, including BLEU [28], METEOR [2] and CIDEr [33]. We also use the Evaluator2018 to compute these metrics and report the results with tIoU threshold of 0.9. **(3)** To evaluate the performance of dense video captioning, the captioning performance based on the *generated* events, we use SODA[2] [12] as the evaluation metric, which is a new evaluation metric proposed for dense video captioning to overcome some of the limitations of previous metrics.

To verify that the general video captioning metrics are not appropriate enough for the dense video captioning evaluation, we carefully design an experiment to compare the classic evaluation metrics provided in Evaluator2018 with the newly proposed SODA metric. We first compute the scores of captions for events in different intervals of the video, and observe that the first event of the video usually gets higher captioning scores than other locations. Based on such observation, we propose four simple operations, including *Increase*, *Reduce*, *Exchange* and *Extreme*, to modify our dense video captioning results, and then show the variations of scores computed by different evaluation metrics. Given a

---

[1] https://github.com/ranjaykrishna/densevid_eval.
[2] https://github.com/fujiso/SODA.

Table 2. Event detection results (using C3D feature) on the ActivityNet Captions validation set. sIoU refers to self-tIoU. The best results are in bold and the second best are underlined.

Method	Recall					Precision					sIoU
	0.3	0.5	0.7	0.9	avg	0.3	0.5	0.7	0.9	avg	
MFT [40]	46.18	29.76	15.54	5.77	24.31	86.34	68.79	38.30	12.19	51.41	–
SDVC [27]	<u>93.41</u>	<u>76.40</u>	42.40	10.10	<u>55.58</u>	96.71	77.73	<u>44.84</u>	10.99	57.57	–
PDVC [37]	89.47	71.91	<u>44.63</u>	**15.67**	55.42	**97.16**	<u>78.09</u>	42.68	**14.40**	<u>58.07</u>	0.19
Ours	**94.68**	**80.95**	**47.84**	<u>12.54</u>	**59.00**	<u>96.97</u>	**80.80**	**50.15**	<u>13.37</u>	**60.32**	0.02

submission file with the best results of our model, the *Increase* operation randomly copies the first event and its corresponding caption in the submission file with 40% probability for each video. The *Reduce* operation randomly removes the i-th (where $i > 1$) event and its corresponding caption in the submission file with 15% probability. The *Exchange* operation is the combination of *Increase* and *Reduce* operations, and the *Extreme* operation removes the i-th (where $i > 1$) event and its corresponding caption with 100% probability. We run the four operations with different random seeds for three times and report the average results in Table 1. Although we intuitively expect that the above four operations should adversely affect the dense video captioning results, the scores evaluated by the Evaluator2018 surprisingly increase significantly from 7.33 to 8.52 on the METEOR metric. On the contrary, SODA correctly reflects the captioning quality with the score constantly decreased. It is because the Evaluator2018 fails to penalize redundant and non-recalled events. Therefore, simply repeating the first event caption with 40% probability can significantly improve the BLEU@4 and METEOR scores by 8% and 2% respectively, although the results actually do not have any substantial improvements. Therefore, we consider SODA as the main evaluation metric for dense video captioning. In this work, we use two versions of SODA to evaluate our DVC performance. The $SODA_{old}$ is commonly used in previous methods, which computes the score based on two references independently and reports the averaged score. The $SODA_{mr}$ however computes the score based on multiple references simultaneously, which are more accurate.

4.2   Comparison with State-of-the-Art Methods

We compare our model with both types of baseline methods, including the ones that tackle event detection and captioning separately, such as MFT [40], SDVC [27] and ECHR [38], and the state-of-the-art models that exploit interactions between the two sub-tasks, such as DCE [22], TDA-CG [35], DVC [25], MT [43], PDVC [37] and SGR [8].

Event Detection Results. As shown in Table 2, our proposed event sequence generation model outperforms previous event detection methods by a large margin. Although pre-trained on the same dataset without any extra data, our model achieves significant improvements over previous best results at most of tIoU

Table 3. Event captioning results on the ActivityNet Captions validation set. $SODA_{old}$ is the old version of SODA implementation and $SODA_{mr}$ is the new implementation with multiple references.

Method	Features	With Ground-Truth proposals			With generated proposals	
		BLEU@4	METEOR	CIDEr	$SODA_{old}$	$SODA_{mr}$
DCE [22]	C3D	1.60	8.88	25.12	–	–
TDA-CG [35]	C3D	–	9.69	–	–	–
DVC [25]	C3D	1.62	10.33	25.24	–	–
ECHR [38]	C3D	1.96	10.58	39.73	3.22	–
PDVC [37]	C3D	2.64	10.54	47.26	5.26	7.14
Ours	C3D	**2.67**	**11.01**	**52.42**	**5.29**	**7.28**
MT [43]	TSN	2.71	11.16	47.71	4.02	–
SGR [8]	TSN	–	–	–	5.29	–
PDVC [37]	TSN	**3.07**	11.27	52.53	5.44	7.42
Ours	TSN	2.90	**11.43**	**54.75**	**5.49**	**7.61**

thresholds, with the average recall score improved from 55.58% to 59.00% and the average precision score improved from 58.07% to 60.32% . Furthermore, our model generates 2.94 events per video on average with the self-tIoU of 0.02, which shows a greater improvement on reducing the event redundancy than traditional event detection methods. It is also much closer to the ground-truth events which have an average self-tIoU of 0.05. In addition to achieving much better results on the event detection accuracy and diversity, our model is also more efficient than previous methods. The PDVC [37] model needs to train an additional predictor for event prediction and SDVC [27] first adopts an extra model (SST [3]) to extract 1000 event proposals and obtains M candidate proposals with Non-Maximum Suppression. Then, SDVC selects the final proposals from the M candidates in an auto-regressive manner. On the contrary, our model directly generates an appropriate number of events from the raw input video features, which is one-stage without error accumulation and with much less computational cost.

Event Captioning Results. Table 3 reports the dense video captioning results of different models on the ActivityNet Captions validation set. To have a fair comparison with the state-of-the-art methods, we train our model with C3D and TSN visual features respectively. When inferring based on the ground-truth event proposals, our model trained by C3D features improves the BLUE@4 from 2.64 to 2.67, the METEOR from 10.58 to 11.01, and the CIDEr from 47.26 to 52.42. Similar improvement trends are obtained with the TSN features on METEOR and CIDEr as well. It demonstrates the effectiveness of our model for event captioning. When inferring based on the generated proposals, we follow the "detect-then-describe" pipeline, which first predicts the event sequence and then describes each event clip. We evaluate our model with the more appropriate

Table 4. Ablation study to demonstrate the effectiveness of different components for event captioning.

Row	Components				BLEU@4	METEOR	CIDEr
	MLM	MVFR	MEFM	CPT			
1					2.22	9.98	47.7
2	✓				2.17	10.20	49.05
3	✓	✓			2.38	10.48	51.08
4	✓	✓	✓		2.59	10.94	52.13
5	✓	✓	✓	✓	2.67	11.01	52.42

Table 5. Ablation study to demonstrate the effectiveness of different components for event detection.

Row	Components				Avg@Recall	Avg@Precision
	MEFM	MLM	MVFR	CPT		
1					54.94	57.95
2	✓				56.49	58.12
3	✓	✓			58.00	59.93
4	✓	✓	✓		58.32	59.95
5	✓	✓	✓	✓	59.00	60.32

evaluation metric SODA for dense video captioning (SODA [12]), and report two scores, including $SODA_{old}$ and $SODA_{mr}$. As shown in Table 3, our model with C3D features achieves the best $SODA_{old}$ score and $SODA_{mr}$ score, outperforming all previous methods. The performance of our model with more advanced TSN features surpasses all previous methods as well.

4.3   Ablation Studies

In this section, we ablate our model to demonstrate the effectiveness of different components for event captioning and event detection respectively.

Table 4 shows the ablation results of our model for the event captioning. To purely analyse the caption generation qualities, we use the ground-truth video events to avoid the impact of event detection quality. As shown in Table 4, the model pre-trained only with MLM task (Row 2) has outperformed the non-pretrain baseline (Row 1) even without any extra data for pre-training. When combining with other pre-training tasks, including MVFR and MVFR+MEFM (Row 3 and 4), our model achieves significant improvements on the captioning metrics, which demonstrates the effectiveness of the proposed pre-training tasks. Specifically, the improvement brought by MEFM task is the most significant, which improves the BLEU@4 from 2.38 to 2.59, the METEOR from 10.48 to 10.94 and the CIDEr from 51.08 to 52.13. It shows that the event captioning

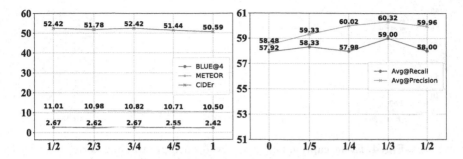

Fig. 3. Performance variations with different trade-off parameter λ. The left and right sub-figures show the event captioning and event detection results respectively.

task can benefit from the event detection task, and demonstrates the advantages of our proposed unified framework for the inter-task interaction.

The same trend can also be found in the Table 5. The pre-trained model significantly outperforms the non-pretrain baseline in Row 1. Adding the MLM and MVFR tasks in the pre-training stage greatly improves the event detection results, with the average recall improved from 56.49 to 58.32 and the average precision improved from 58.12 to 59.95. It shows that the event detection task can also benefit from the event captioning task. Besides different pre-training tasks, enhancing the video representation with semantic concept features also brings additional gains for both the event captioning and event detection tasks, as shown in Row 5 vs. Row 4 of the Table 4 and Table 5. The surprising performance improvement by the semantic concept features (short for CPT) in event detection (improved from 58.32 to 59.00 on average recall and 59.95 to 60.32 on average precision) further demonstrates that comprehensive semantic understanding of video frames can greatly help event boundary detection. This is also the reason why the event detection and event captioning can help each other, because they are both based on the semantic understanding of videos. Finally, combining all the components together in our model achieves the best performance for both event detection and event captioning (Row 5).

We also ablate the influence of the hyper-parameter λ in our model in Fig. 3. We observe that enhancing inter-task association in different degrees all outperform the model without inter-task interaction (where $\lambda = 0$ *or* 1) for both the event captioning and event detection. With gradually increasing λ from 1/2 to 1, the METEOR score continues to decline, while the CIDEr and BLUE@4 scores fluctuate slightly. We observe that modulating hyper-parameter λ to 1/2 obtains the best performance for event captioning. While when pre-training for event detection, the best performance is achieved when hyper-parameter λ is set as 1/3.

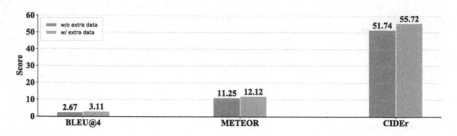

Fig. 4. Event captioning w/ and w/o extra pre-training data.

4.4 Pre-training with Out-of-Domain Data

Due to the advantage of pre-training and fine-tuning framework, our model can benefit from more out-of-domain data besides the ActivityNet dataset. Specifically, we pre-train the model with conventional non-dense video captioning datasets including MSRVTT [41], TGIF [26] and VATEX [39], which results in 676K additional video-caption pairs in total. Since the conventional video captioning datasets do not contain event annotations, we pre-train the model only with the MLM and MVFR tasks on these out-of-domain data, and fine-tune it on the ActivityNet Captions training set to adapt to the dense video captioning task. Figure 4 shows the results of our model pre-trained with extra data. Compared with the model pre-trained only on the ActivityNet dataset, the additional out-of-domain data brings significant additional gains on all the captioning metrics, e.g., improving BLEU@4, METEOR and CIDEr by more than 0.4, 0.8 and 4 points respectively. It demonstrates the merit of our unified pre-training based model framework, which enables the dense video captioning task to benefit from conventional non-dense video captioning datasets.

5   Conclusion

In this work, we define the event detection task as a sequence generation problem to fully exploit the temporal relationship between events for more accurate and diverse event detection. Benefiting from the unification of event detection and event captioning sub-tasks, we propose a unified dense video captioning model based on pre-training and fine-tuning framework. We design a new "event" modality and propose three pre-training tasks to interact the event detection and event captioning sub-tasks naturally. Experimental results on the ActivityNet Captions dataset show that our model significantly outperforms the state-of-the-art methods on both event detection and event captioning, and achieves additional gains when leveraging more out-of-domain data.

Acknowledgement. This work was partially supported by National Key R&D Program of China (No. 2020AAA0108600) and National Natural Science Foundation of China (No. 62072462).

References

1. Agrawal, H., et al.: NoCaps: novel object captioning at scale. In: Proceedings of the IEEE/CVF International Conference on Computer Vision (2019)
2. Banerjee, S., Lavie, A.: METEOR: an automatic metric for MT evaluation with improved correlation with human judgments. In: Proceedings of the ACL Workshop on Intrinsic and Extrinsic Evaluation Measures for machine translation and/or Summarization, pp. 65–72 (2005)
3. Buch, S., Escorcia, V., Shen, C., Ghanem, B., Carlos Niebles, J.: SST: single-stream temporal action proposals. In: Proceedings of the IEEE Conference on Computer Vision and Pattern Recognition (2017)
4. Carion, N., Massa, F., Synnaeve, G., Usunier, N., Kirillov, A., Zagoruyko, S.: End-to-End object detection with transformers. In: Vedaldi, A., Bischof, H., Brox, T., Frahm, J.-M. (eds.) ECCV 2020. LNCS, vol. 12346, pp. 213–229. Springer, Cham (2020). https://doi.org/10.1007/978-3-030-58452-8_13
5. Chen, Y.-C., et al.: UNITER: universal image-text representation learning. In: Vedaldi, A., Bischof, H., Brox, T., Frahm, J.-M. (eds.) ECCV 2020. LNCS, vol. 12375, pp. 104–120. Springer, Cham (2020). https://doi.org/10.1007/978-3-030-58577-8_7
6. Cho, J., Lei, J., Tan, H., Bansal, M.: Unifying vision-and-language tasks via text generation. In: International Conference on Machine Learning (2021)
7. Cornia, M., Stefanini, M., Baraldi, L., Cucchiara, R.: Meshed-memory transformer for image captioning. In: Proceedings of the IEEE/CVF Conference on Computer Vision and Pattern Recognition, pp. 10578–10587 (2020)
8. Deng, C., Chen, S., Chen, D., He, Y., Wu, Q.: Sketch, ground, and refine: Top-down dense video captioning. In: Proceedings of the IEEE/CVF Conference on Computer Vision and Pattern Recognition., pp. 234–243 (2021)
9. Devlin, J., Chang, M., Lee, K., Toutanova, K.: BERT: pre-training of deep bidirectional transformers for language understanding. In: Proceedings of the 2019 Conference of the North American Chapter of the Association for Computational Linguistics, pp. 4171–4186 (2019)
10. Escorcia, V., Caba Heilbron, F., Niebles, J.C., Ghanem, B.: DAPs: deep action proposals for action understanding. In: Leibe, B., Matas, J., Sebe, N., Welling, M. (eds.) ECCV 2016. LNCS, vol. 9907, pp. 768–784. Springer, Cham (2016). https://doi.org/10.1007/978-3-319-46487-9_47
11. Faghri, F., Fleet, D.J., Kiros, J.R., Fidler, S.: VSE++: improving visual-semantic embeddings with hard negatives. In: British Machine Vision Conference, p. 12 (2018)
12. Fujita, S., Hirao, T., Kamigaito, H., Okumura, M., Nagata, M.: SODA: story oriented dense video captioning evaluation framework. In: Vedaldi, A., Bischof, H., Brox, T., Frahm, J.-M. (eds.) ECCV 2020. LNCS, vol. 12351, pp. 517–531. Springer, Cham (2020). https://doi.org/10.1007/978-3-030-58539-6_31
13. Gao, J., Yang, Z., Chen, K., Sun, C., Nevatia, R.: Turn tap: temporal unit regression network for temporal action proposals. In: Proceedings of the IEEE International Conference on Computer Vision (2017)
14. Goyal, Y., Khot, T., Summers-Stay, D., Batra, D., Parikh, D.: Making the V in VQA matter: elevating the role of image understanding in visual question answering. In: Proceedings of the IEEE Conference on Computer Vision and Pattern Recognition (2017)

15. Graves, A., Schmidhuber, J.: Framewise phoneme classification with bidirectional LSTM and other neural network architectures. Neural Netw. **18**(5), 602–610 (2005), iJCNN 2005
16. Heilbron, F.C., Niebles, J.C., Ghanem, B.: Fast temporal activity proposals for efficient detection of human actions in untrimmed videos. In: Proceedings of the IEEE Conference on Computer Vision and Pattern Recognition (2016)
17. Huang, L., Wang, W., Chen, J., Wei, X.Y.: Attention on attention for image captioning. In: Proceedings of the IEEE/CVF International Conference on Computer Vision, pp. 4634–4643 (2019)
18. Huang, Z., Zeng, Z., Huang, Y., Liu, B., Fu, D., Fu, J.: Seeing out of the box: end-to-end pre-training for vision-language representation learning. In: Proceedings of the IEEE/CVF Conference on Computer Vision and Pattern Recognition, pp. 12976–12985 (2021)
19. Iashin, V., Rahtu, E.: A better use of audio-visual cues: Dense video captioning with bi-modal transformer. In: British Machine Vision Conference. https://arxiv.org/abs/2005.08271(2020)
20. Iashin, V., Rahtu, E.: Multi-modal dense video captioning. In: Proceedings of the IEEE/CVF Conference on Computer Vision and Pattern Recognition Workshops (2020)
21. Kingma, D.P., Ba, J.: Adam: a method for stochastic optimization. In: Bengio, Y., LeCun, Y. (eds.) International Conference on Learning Representations (2015)
22. Krishna, R., Hata, K., Ren, F., Fei-Fei, L., Carlos Niebles, J.: Dense-captioning events in videos. In: Proceedings of the IEEE International Conference on Computer Vision (2017)
23. Li, G., Duan, N., Fang, Y., Gong, M., Jiang, D.: Unicoder-vl: A universal encoder for vision and language by cross-modal pre-training. In: Proceedings of the AAAI Conference on Artificial Intelligence. pp. 11336–11344 (2020)
24. Li, X., et al.: OSCAR: object-semantics aligned pre-training for vision-language tasks. In: Vedaldi, A., Bischof, H., Brox, T., Frahm, J.-M. (eds.) ECCV 2020. LNCS, vol. 12375, pp. 121–137. Springer, Cham (2020). https://doi.org/10.1007/978-3-030-58577-8_8
25. Li, Y., Yao, T., Pan, Y., Chao, H., Mei, T.: Jointly localizing and describing events for dense video captioning. In: Proceedings of the IEEE Conference on Computer Vision and Pattern Recognition (2018)
26. Li, Y., et al.: TGIF: a new dataset and benchmark on animated gif description. In: Proceedings of the IEEE Conference on Computer Vision and Pattern Recognition (2016)
27. Mun, J., Yang, L., Ren, Z., Xu, N., Han, B.: Streamlined dense video captioning. In: Proceedings of the IEEE/CVF Conference on Computer Vision and Pattern Recognition, pp. 6588–6597 (2019)
28. Papineni, K., Roukos, S., Ward, T., Zhu, W.J.: Bleu: a method for automatic evaluation of machine translation. In: Proceedings of the 40th annual meeting of the Association for Computational Linguistics, pp. 311–318 (2002)
29. Shou, Z., Wang, D., Chang, S.F.: Temporal action localization in untrimmed videos via multi-stage CNNs. In: Proceedings of the IEEE Conference on Computer Vision and Pattern Recognition (2016)
30. Su, W., et al.: VL-BERT: pre-training of generic visual-linguistic representations. In: International Conference on Learning Representations (2020)
31. Tran, D., Bourdev, L., Fergus, R., Torresani, L., Paluri, M.: Learning spatiotemporal features with 3d convolutional networks. In: Proceedings of the IEEE International Conference on Computer Vision (2015)

32. Vaswani, A., et al.: Attention is all you need. In: Advances in Neural Information Processing Systems, pp. 5998–6008 (2017)
33. Vedantam, R., Lawrence Zitnick, C., Parikh, D.: Cider: consensus-based image description evaluation. In: Proceedings of the IEEE Conference on Computer Vision and Pattern Recognition (2015)
34. Vinyals, O., Toshev, A., Bengio, S., Erhan, D.: Show and tell: a neural image caption generator. In: Conference on Computer Vision and Pattern Recognition, pp. 3156–3164 (2015)
35. Wang, J., Jiang, W., Ma, L., Liu, W., Xu, Y.: Bidirectional attentive fusion with context gating for dense video captioning. In: Proceedings of the IEEE Conference on Computer Vision and Pattern Recognition, pp. 7190–7198 (2018)
36. Wang, L., et al.: Temporal segment networks for action recognition in videos. IEEE Trans. Pattern Anal. Mach. Intell. **41**(11), 2740–2755 (2018)
37. Wang, T., Zhang, R., Lu, Z., Zheng, F., Cheng, R., Luo, P.: End-to-end dense video captioning with parallel decoding. In: Proceedings of the IEEE/CVF International Conference on Computer Vision, pp. 6847–6857 (2021)
38. Wang, T., Zheng, H., Yu, M., Tian, Q., Hu, H.: Event-centric hierarchical representation for dense video captioning. IEEE Trans. Circuits Syst. Video Technol. **31**(5), 1890–1900 (2020)
39. Wang, X., Wu, J., Chen, J., Li, L., Wang, Y.F., Wang, W.Y.: Vatex: A large-scale, high-quality multilingual dataset for video-and-language research. In: Proceedings of the IEEE/CVF International Conference on Computer Vision, pp. 4581–4591 (2019)
40. Xiong, Y., Dai, B., Lin, D.: Move forward and tell: a progressive generator of video descriptions. In: Proceedings of the European Conference on Computer Vision, pp. 468–483 (2018)
41. Xu, J., Mei, T., Yao, T., Rui, Y.: MSR-VTT: a large video description dataset for bridging video and language. In: Proceedings of the IEEE Conference on Computer Vision and Pattern Recognition, pp. 5288–5296 (2016)
42. Yang, D., Yuan, C.: Hierarchical context encoding for events captioning in videos. In: International Conference on Image Processing, pp. 1288–1292 (2018)
43. Zhou, L., Zhou, Y., Corso, J.J., Socher, R., Xiong, C.: End-to-end dense video captioning with masked transformer. In: Proceedings of the IEEE Conference on Computer Vision and Pattern Recognition (2018)
44. Zhu, X., Su, W., Lu, L., Li, B., Wang, X., Dai, J.: Deformable DETR: deformable transformers for end-to-end object detection. In: International Conference on Learning Representations (2021)

Multimodal Transformer with Variable-Length Memory for Vision-and-Language Navigation

Chuang Lin[1]($\boxtimes$) , Yi Jiang[2] , Jianfei Cai[1] , Lizhen Qu[1] ,
Gholamreza Haffari[1] , and Zehuan Yuan[2]

[1] Monash University, Clayton, Australia
Chuang.Lin@monash.edu
[2] ByteDance, Beijing, China

Abstract. Vision-and-Language Navigation (VLN) is a task that an agent is required to follow a language instruction to navigate to the goal position, which relies on the ongoing interactions with the environment during moving. Recent Transformer-based VLN methods have made great progress benefiting from the direct connections between visual observations and language instructions via the multimodal cross-attention mechanism. However, these methods usually represent temporal context as a fixed-length vector by using an LSTM decoder or using manually designed hidden states to build a recurrent Transformer. Considering a single fixed-length vector is often insufficient to capture long-term temporal context, in this paper, we introduce Multimodal Transformer with Variable-length Memory (MTVM) for visually-grounded natural language navigation by modeling the temporal context explicitly. Specifically, MTVM enables the agent to keep track of the navigation trajectory by directly storing activations in the previous time step in a memory bank. To further boost the performance, we propose a memory-aware consistency loss to help learn a better joint representation of temporal context with random masked instructions. We evaluate MTVM on popular R2R and CVDN datasets. Our model improves Success Rate on R2R test set by 2% and reduces Goal Process by 1.5 m on CVDN test set. Code is available at: https://github.com/clin1223/MTVM.

Keywords: Vision-and-language navigation · Multimodal transformer

1 Introduction

Enabling robots to assist humans in real world has been desired so long in AI [4,11,41]. To achieve it, one crucial capability of robots is to be able to follow human instructions to navigate their environments. Vision-and-Language

---

C. Lin—This work was performed while Chuang Lin worked as an intern at ByteDance.

S. Avidan et al. (Eds.): ECCV 2022, LNCS 13696, pp. 380–397, 2022.
https://doi.org/10.1007/978-3-031-20059-5_22

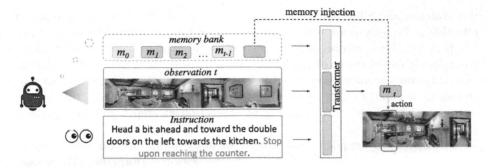

Fig. 1. In contrast to most existing methods that utilize a fixed-length vector to represent temporal context, we equip the agent with the capability to model long-term dependency. At each step t, MTVM takes all the tokens stored in the memory bank as the temporal context input. After making a decision, it adds a memory token m_t by simply reusing the output activation corresponding to the action at step t.

Navigation (VLN) is the task where an embodied agent is required to follow language instructions to navigate to a goal position. Specifically, the agent is given a detailed instruction, like *"Head a bit ahead and towards the double doors on the left towards the kitchen. Stop upon reaching the counter."* At each step, then, the agent observes the panorama view of its surrounding environment and makes a decision for the direction to move in the next step, until it reaches the desired goal position.

Recently, many methods [3,9,15,19,24,27,30,34,40,44,46,50] have been proposed for the VLN task. Most of the literature adopts the encoder-decoder framework to encode the instruction and visual observations, and then decode the action sequence. Recent VLN studies [12,13,23,31,36] have shown great performance by directly modeling cross-modal vision-language modelling with Transformer. Different from other vision and language tasks, e.g. VQA and image captioning that learn relationships between each individual image and its corresponding text, VLN aims to learn the joint representation between each instruction and a series of observations by interacting with the environment. Thus, taking the temporal context into account is the key to ground the instruction onto the observations, figuring out what has been completed, what is next, and where to go. A straightforward way is to directly encode all the past observations [35], which however misses record cross-modal history and also increases the training cost as the path grows. Further, [16] employs the recurrent hidden state to inject temporal information into Transformer and [13,36] use the encoder-decoder structure with an additional LSTM to encode the temporal context. Nevertheless, a single hidden state vector is not expressive enough to encode the whole history of interactions with environment in Transformer. It is very challenging to align such hidden state at time t with the corresponding sub-instruction for decision making.

To address this challenge, we propose a Multimodal Transformer with Variable-length Memory (MTVM) framework for VLN. Instead of using hidden states or an LSTM to encode temporal context, we find that it is simple and effective to directly reuse the cross-modal Transformer activations obtained in the previous steps. Storing past activations in an explicit memory bank allows to explicitly model the cross-modal history. Moreover, the Transformer architecture naturally accommodates variable-length memory token inputs. In this way, the agent is able to easily update the temporal context by adding the current output activation m_t, corresponding to the action at step t, into the memory bank, as shown in Fig. 1.

Thanks to the explicit cross-modal memory bank, we further design a memory-aware consistency loss to boost the navigation performance. The consistency loss aims to help cross-modal alignment by learning the relations between the previous activations and the language instruction. Specifically, we randomly mask out some instruction words and force the model output distribution to be consistent with that of the original unmasked instruction. In this way, the model avoids overfitting to the language modality with the help of the explicit memory bank.

Our contributions can be summarized as follows:

1. We propose MTVM that allows the agent to capture temporal context without distance dependency by simply reusing the previous cross-model activations corresponding to the actions.
2. We design a memory-aware consistency loss to learn strong relations between instruction and temporal context to further boost the navigation performance.
3. We conduct extensive experiments on R2R and CVDN datasets, improving Success Rate by 2% on R2R and reducing Goal Progress by 1.5 m on CVDN compared to strong baselines.

2   Related Work

Vision-and-Language Navigation. VLN [1] is a task that requires an agent to follow a nature-language instruction to navigate in a photo-realistic environment to a goal location. In this process, the given instruction describes the trajectory in detail and the embodied agent needs to move through the scene with first person views as observations. Following [1], several navigation tasks [5,33,34,37,42] have been further proposed for interactions with surrounding environments. In particular, different from [1] collecting data from an indoor environment, [5] extends the navigation environment to real-life visual urban streets. [42] introduces navigating according to several question-answering pairs in a dialog history. [20] further extends the dialog navigating task by taking the full dialogue and the whole navigation path as one instance. [34] and [33] consider object-finding tasks [25,26,38,47] by requesting and interpreting simulated human assistants. [37] requires the agent to navigate to an appropriate location and identify the target object. [21] proposes a multilingual datasets for VLN, which including more visual entities and avoiding language bias.

As a practical task in real-world applications, VLN has made incredible progress in recent years. [24] uses adversarial attacking to capture key information from long instructions for a robust navigation. The progress monitor in [30] aims to estimate the navigation progress explicitly as a multi-task learning, supervised by the normalized distance to the goal. RCM [44] enforces cross-modal grounding both locally and globally via a matching critic providing rewards for reinforcement learning.

In vision-and-language navigation setting, it is difficult to collect enough annotated data due to the large navigation space. [9] synthesizes new instructions where the speaker model helps the agent by additional route-instruction pairs to expand the limited training data. To make further advances, [46] proposes an instruction-trajectory compatibility model to improve the instruction evaluation. [40] proposes an environmental dropout method based on the view consistency to mimic novel and diverse environments. From a different perspective, REM [27] reconnect the seen scenes to generate augmented data via mixing up environments. To further understand the relations between the instructions and scenes, [15] and [36] take the objects in scenes and the corresponding words in instructions as the minimal units of encoding. AuxRN [50] introduces additional training signals including explaining actions, predicting next orientation, etc., to help acquire semantic knowledge. In contrast, our method focuses on modeling the temporal context to help the alignment between language and observations.

Multi-modal Transformers. The Transformer [43] architecture has shown great effectiveness in vision and language tasks [7, 10, 18, 22, 29, 39, 45, 49]. Most of the vision-and-language tasks focus on the joint embedding learning with individual pairs of an image and its corresponding language, such as VQA, image captioning, and text-to-image retrieval. Different from these tasks, VLN is a Markov Decision Process, which learns the joint representation between the instruction and a series of observations along the corresponding trajectory. Inspired by the success of BERT [8], PRESS [23] first introduces a large-scale pretrained language model to VLN for text representations. As cross-modal joint learning is the key for VLN task, VLN-BERT [31] and PREVALENT [13] develop Transformer-based model in a self-supervised manner on image-text pairs from the web and image-text-action triplets from R2R dataset [1], respectively. [16] and [36] adapt pre-trained V&L BERT to VLN task by leveraging the hidden state representations with the learned linear projection or LSTM. Recently, HAMT [6] and Episodic Transformer [35] also propose to model the history information explicitly by directly encoding all past observations and the actions. Our key insight is: *only explicitly modelling the history observations is not good enough; instead, explicitly modelling the history interactions between observations and the instruction is more critical since it helps figure out the progress of the navigation trajectory.*

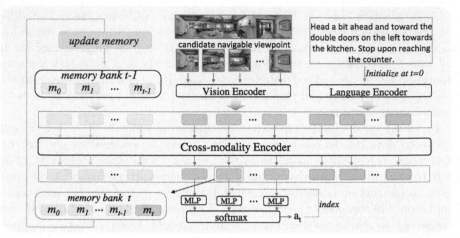

Fig. 2. The general framework of our proposed MTVM framework. At each step, we concatenate temporal context in the memory bank, together with visual features and language features as input. After making decision, we update the memory bank by storing the output activation that corresponding to the action.

3 Methods

3.1 Overview

Formally, at the beginning of each episode, the agent is given a nature language instruction $x = \langle x_1, x_2, \ldots, x_L \rangle$, where L is the length of the instruction and x_i denotes a word. VLN task requires the agent to follow the instruction to navigate from a start position to the goal location. At each step t, the agent is able to observe the surrounding environment in a panoramic view $o_t = \langle o_t^1, o_t^2, \ldots, o_t^{36} \rangle$ comprised by 36 single view images. Figure 2 gives an overview of our proposed Multimodal Transformer with Variable-length Memory (MTVM). At each step, our MTVM directly interacts with visual information, language information, and history information to make the action decision. After that, we update the memory bank by reusing the activation of the Transformer output according to the action decision. Moreover, a consistency loss is introduced to measure the distance between the output distributions of the full instruction and a randomly masked instruction to help the cross-modal alignment. Note that the instruction masking is only used in training but not in inference.

3.2 Memory-Based Multimodal Transformer

As VLN is a Markov decision process [1], an embodied agent needs to pay attention to the temporal context information during its navigation. The general Transformer is not enough to model the instruction and the observations due

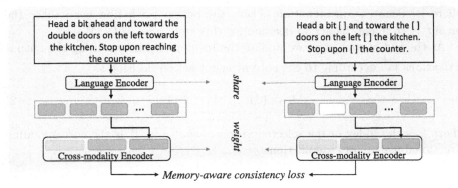

Fig. 3. The proposed memory-aware consistency loss. During training, we randomly mask out some words to help the alignment between language and temporal context, avoiding model overfitting to the language modality.

to the lack of the temporal context. At each navigation step, an agent needs to ground an instruction to which part has finished and which part is the next.

MTVM learns the cross-modal alignment to encourage matching the completed part of the instructions with the past trajectory. Our memory bank enables the agent to be aware of the navigation process by directly interacting with the previous actions so that it can ground the sub-instructions as guidance. In this way, it becomes easier for the agent to locate the sub-instruction to gain useful information to select the candidate direction from the current-step observation. We construct our model following the vision and language pretrained work [13,39], which consists of a language encoder, a vision encoder and a cross-modality encoder (Fig. 3).

Language Encoder. The language encoder is a standard multi-layer transformer with self-attention. At the beginning of an episode, we feed the instruction to the language encoder $\mathcal{S}$ to get the language representation $X = \mathcal{S}(x)$.

Vision Encoder. The vision encoder is a convolution network to encode each single view image o_t^i to a 2048-dimensional visual feature v_t^i. A 128-dimensional directional feature d_t^i by repeating the trigonometric function representation [9] is concatenated with the visual feature v_t^i to represent the orientation of each single view $V_t^i = [v_t^i; d_t^i]$. For each step, we have $V_t = \{V_t^1, V_t^2, \ldots, V_t^K\}$ as the visual representation, where K is the number of candidate directions.

Cross-Modality Encoder. In order to learn cross-modality representations, the cross-modality encoder $\mathcal{C}$ is composed of self-attention layers and cross-attention layers, where cross-attention layers treat one modality as query and the other as key and value to exchange the information and align the entities between the two modalities. In particular, we feed language representation X, vision representation V_t, and previous activations M_t to the cross-modality encoder $\mathcal{C}$ as

$$\widehat{X}, \widehat{M_t}, \widehat{V_t} = \mathcal{C}(X, [M_t; V_t]),   \tag{1}$$

where $[;]$ denotes concatenation. Then, the action prediction head takes the output $\widehat{V}_t$ to make the action decision for this step: $a_t = MLP(\widehat{V}_t)$.

At the end of each step, we update the memory bank by reusing the output activations $\widehat{V}_t^k$ according to the current agent action decision as

$$M_t \leftarrow (M_{t-1}, \left[\widehat{V}_t^k; d_t^k\right]) \tag{2}$$

where k is the index of the selected vision output and d_t^k is the corresponding directional feature of t step action.

3.3   Memory-Aware Consistency Loss

As aforementioned, the key challenge in VLN is that the embodied agent needs to be aware of the progress of the navigating trajectory by learning the cross-modal representation. However, the existing studies [1,17] show that the agent tends to overfit the instructions, which could be due to large variations in the visual modality. In order to avoid the model from overfitting a single modality, we design a memory-aware consistency loss. By randomly dropping some words in the instruction, we force the model to learn strong representations among language, vision, and temporal context from the cross-modality encoder.

Specifically, given an instruction x, we random drop some words with a fixed probability and obtain

$$x' = RandomDrop(x). \tag{3}$$

Both x and x' are then encoded by language encoder $\mathcal{S}$ to produce the instruction representations X and X', respectively. Same as the instruction feature X, X' is also fed through the cross-modality encoder $\mathcal{C}$ with the same history and vision representations as Eq. (1):

$$\widehat{X'}, \widehat{M'_t}, \widehat{V'_t} = \mathcal{C}(X', [M_t; V_t]), \tag{4}$$

Although some words are discarded, we expect the similarities between the instruction features X and X' and their corresponding outputs are preserved. Concretely, we generate the probability vectors for the outputs of the language encoder and cross-modality encoder respectively with the Softmax layer. By minimizing the bidirectional Kullback-Leibler (KL) divergence between the outputs of the full instruction and the randomly dropped instruction, the consistency loss is defined as

$$\begin{aligned}
\mathcal{L}_{consis} = \lambda_s(\mathcal{D}_{KL}(X\|X') + \mathcal{D}_{KL}(X'\|X)) \\
+ \lambda_m(\mathcal{D}_{KL}(\widehat{X'}, \widehat{M'_t}, \widehat{V'_t}\|\widehat{X}, \widehat{M_t}, \widehat{V_t}) \\
+ \mathcal{D}_{KL}(\widehat{X}, \widehat{M_t}, \widehat{V_t}\|\widehat{X'}, \widehat{M'_t}, \widehat{V'_t})),
\end{aligned} \tag{5}$$

where λ_s and λ_m are the weights to balance the distance losses. The first term aims to prevent the agent from overfitting the special words (such as route words), while the second term aims to avoid overfitting the language modality.

3.4 Training

Following the existing VLN works, we apply the mixture of Imitation Learning (IL) and Reinforcement Learning (RL) strategies [40,44]. In IL, the agent learns to follow the teacher action a_t^* of the ground-truth path at each step t by minimizing the negative log probability loss function. In RL, the agent learns from rewards by using A2C algorithm [32], where sampling the action a_t^s from the agent's action distribution a_t, the agent will get rewards if successfully arriving at the target within 3m $(t = T)$ or reducing the distance to the target after taking the action $(t < T)$. Besides, we consider the similarity of the agent path and the ground-truth path as a reward to encourage the agent follow the instruction to move closer to the target. The overall loss function can be written as:

$$\mathcal{L} = \lambda_l \mathcal{L}_{IL} + \mathcal{L}_{RL} + \mathcal{L}_{consis}$$
$$= \lambda_l \sum_{t=0}^{T-1} -a_t^* log(a_t) + \sum_{t=0}^{T-1} -a_t^s log(a_t) A_t + \mathcal{L}_{consis} \qquad (6)$$

where λ_l is a trade-off weight for IL loss, T is the length of the navigation path, and A_t is the advantage calculated by A2C algorithm [32]. We alternately train the agent with IL and RL strategies while applying the consistency loss in both.

4 Experiments

4.1 Setup

Datasets: We evaluate MTVM on the Room-to-Room dataset (R2R) [1] and Cooperative Vision-and-Dialog Navigation dataset (CVDN) [42] in 3D environments based on Matterport3D Simulator [2]. The simulated environments include 90 different housing scenes. R2R dataset provides fully specified instructions describing the steps necessary to reach the goal, while CVDN dataset provides an ambiguous and underspecified goal location and human-human dialogs to guide the agent. R2R splits the dataset into the training set consisting of 61 environments with 14,025 instructions, the seen validation set consisting of the same 61 environments with 1,020 instructions, and the unseen validation consisting of another 11 environments with 2,349 instructions, while the test consists of the remaining 18 environments with 4,173 instructions. CVDN contains 4742 training, 382 seen validation, 907 unseen validation, and 1384 unseen test instances.

Evaluation Metrics: For R2R, we use its three standard metrics: Navigation Error (NE) defined as the distance (in meters) from the stop viewpoint to the goal position, Success Rate (SR), and Success rate weighted by Path Length (SPL), where SPL is regarded as the primary metric. For CVDN, following [42], we evaluate the performance on the navigation from dialog history (NDH) task by Goal Progress, which measures how much reduction in meters the agent makes towards the goal. There are three settings depending on the supervised

Table 1. Comparisons of the VLN performance on R2R dataset in a single-run setting. The best results are in bold font. The set of methods at the bottom are Transformer based solutions, whose model parameters are initialized by the pre-trained vision-and-language BERT. The set of methods in the middle are non-Transformer based solutions.

Methods	Validation Seen			Validation Unseen			Test		
	NE↓	SR↑	SPL↑	NE↓	SR↑	SPL↑	NE↓	SR↑	SPL↑
Random	9.45	16	-	9.23	16	-	9.79	13	12
Human	-	-	-	-	-	-	1.61	86	76
Speaker-Follower [9]	3.36	66	-	6.62	35	-	6.62	35	28
Self-monitoring [30]	3.22	67	58	5.52	45	32	5.67	48	35
RCM [44]	3.53	67	-	6.09	43	-	6.12	43	38
FAST-Short [19]	-	-	-	4.97	56	43	5.14	54	41
EnvDrop [40]	3.99	62	59	5.22	52	48	5.23	51	47
DR-Attacker [24]	3.52	70	67	4.99	53	48	5.53	52	49
AuxRN [50]	3.33	70	67	5.28	55	50	5.15	55	51
RelGraph [15]	3.47	67	65	4.73	57	53	4.75	55	52
PRESS [23]	4.39	58	55	5.28	49	45	5.49	49	45
PREVALENT [13]	3.67	69	65	4.71	58	53	5.30	54	51
ORIST [36]	-	-	-	4.72	57	51	5.10	57	52
VLN↻BERT [16]	2.90	72	68	3.93	63	57	4.09	63	57
Ours	**2.67**	**74**	**69**	**3.73**	**66**	**59**	**3.85**	**65**	**59**

strategy. *Oracle* indicates the agent regarding the shortest path as ground truth and *Navigator* indicates learning from the navigator path (maybe not be the optimal navigation). *Mixed* supervision means to learn from the navigator path if it reaches the goal point; otherwise learn from the shortest path.

Implementation Details: To leverage vision and language pre-trained models, we initialize the language encoder and the cross-modality encoder by a pre-train VLN model PREVALENT [13]. Following PREVALENT [13] and VLN↻BERT [16], we train the agent on the original training data and the augmented data provided by [13]. The vision encoder is a fixed ResNet-152 [14] pre-trained on Place365 [48] provided by R2R dataset. The experiments are conducted on 3 V100 GPUs. We train the model 10,000 iterations and adopt the early stopping strategy when the model achieves the best performance on the evaluation metric. The learning rate is fixed to 5e−6 with an AdamW optimiser [28]. The parameters λ_s and λ_m are respectively set to 0.6 and 0.2 and λ_{IL} is set to 0.2. We find different levels of dropping words are all helpful, and we fix the word dropping probability to 0.5.

Table 2. Comparisons with state-of-the-art methods in terms of Goal Progress (m) on the navigation from dialog history (NDH) task on CVDN dataset [42]. 'Ora', 'Nav' and 'mix' denote the three settings, 'Oracle', 'Navigator' and 'Mixed', respectively.

Methods	Validation Unseen			Test		
	Ora	Nav	Mix	Ora	Nav	Mix
Random	1.09	1.09	1.09	0.83	0.83	0.83
Shortest Path	8.36	7.99	9.58	8.06	8.48	9.76
Seq-to-seq [42]	1.23	1.98	2.10	1.25	2.11	2.35
PREVALENT [13]	2.58	2.99	3.15	1.67	2.39	2.44
CMN [52]	2.68	2.28	2.97	2.69	2.26	2.95
ORIST [36]	3.30	3.29	3.55	2.78	3.17	3.15
SCoA [51]	1.94	2.91	2.85	2.49	3.37	3.31
DR-Attacker [24]	3.27	4.00	4.18	2.77	2.95	3.26
Ours	**4.57**	**4.80**	**5.15**	**4.23**	**4.46**	**4.82**

4.2   Comparisons with SoTA

Table 1 shows the performance comparisons of different VLN methods on R2R dataset in a single-run setting. It can be seen that our model performs the best on all the metrics under both unseen validation and test sets, suggesting the good generalizing ability. Compared with other transformer-based methods including PRESS [23], ORIST [36] and VLN◯BERT [16] which also initialize their models using the pre-trained ones [7,13], our method is at least 2% higher in terms of SPL or SR under both test and validation unseen scenarios. In addition, the lowest navigation error achieved by our model indicates that we can make the agent move closer to the target.

Table 2 shows the performance comparisons in terms of Goal Progress on CVDN dataset under the three different settings. Again, our method achieves the best performance with significant gains on both unseen validation and test sets, demonstrating the effectiveness of handling a variety of language instructions. Note that the Shortest Path Agent takes the shortest path to the supervision goal at inference, which represents the upper bound navigation performance for an agent.

4.3   Ablation Studies

Memory Bank Size. Recall that our method stores the activations at each step as history information in a memory bank. Here, we evaluate the model performance with different memory bank sizes. When the memory bank size is n, we only record the last n step activations; when the size is variable, it means we record every step. Note that the paths in R2R dataset are all around four to six steps. The results are shown in Fig. 4. In general, a larger memory size helps, and the variable-length memory gives the best performance, suggesting

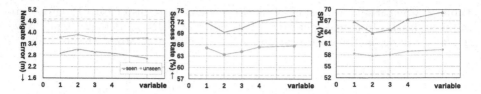

Fig. 4. Impacts of the memory bank size on seen and unseen validation sets of R2R dataset in terms of NE, SR and SPL. Solid lines are our results with different memory bank sizes, and dashed lines are the results of PREVALENT [13] from which our model is initialized.

the importance of explicitly storing the history information. In addition, we also show the performance of PREVALENT as our baseline (dashed lines) since our model is initialized from it. It can be seen that our model under most of the fixed-length memory banks outperforms the baseline.

Comparison of History Encoding Methods. We next evaluate the advantage of proposed variable-length memory bank to other baselines, including visual-only [6,35] and cross-modal interaction [16] as history encoding methods. [35] encodes oriented observations (one view of full observations) and the actions as the history information. [6] proposes a hierarchical observations and actions encoding method which is able to learning intra-panorama and inter-panorama visual information for temporal context. The experiments are under the R2R validation seen and unseen setting and measured by Success Rate (SR) and Success rate weighted by Path Length (SPL). As [35] was proposed for the ALFRED benchmark which is for household action learning from instructions and egocentric vision, we reproduce it by simply replacing our history encoding with the corresponding methods.

As shown in Table 3, we have the following observations from the results: (1) The visual-only method [35] that only encodes the past oriented views and actions obtains the worst performance. This is obvious, because only recording the oriented views may ignore significant information in the trajectory. For instance, "Go straight passing the fridge", "fridge" might not be in the oriented visual observations, which is essential for the agent to record history. (2) Compared with visual-only methods, the cross-modal history encoding methods achieves better performance in most settings, which demonstrates the effectiveness of considering the multimodal interactions as history for VLN. Only modelling history observations provides the visual information in temporal context, but is insufficient to record vision and language navigation progress. (3) Our MTVM achieves the highest SR and SPL among all history encoding methods, because of the proposed variable length memory and the memory consistency loss. Compared to the typically used recurrent state, we found that cross-modal history can be better captured by simply reusing the previous cross-model activations corresponding to the actions, which is simple but effective and non-trivial.

Table 3. Comparison of different history encoding methods in R2R setting. "Visual-only" indicates methods that encoding past observations and actions as history. "Cross-modal" indicates methods considering cross-modal interactions and actions as history.

History Encoding Methods		Val Seen		Val Unseen	
		SR↑	SPL↑	SR↑	SPL↑
Visual-only	E.T. [35] *Oriented observations*	68.1	63.6	59.0	54.5
	HAMT [6] *Hierarchical observations*	69.3	64.8	63.5	57.5
Cross-modal	VLN◐BERT [16] *Recurrent state*	72	68	63	57
	Ours	**73.7**	**69.3**	**65.7**	**59.4**

Table 4. Impacts of our proposed memory-aware consistency loss and random word dropping. "word dropping" refers to our model without using the consistency loss but with random word dropping in language instructions for data augmentation.

Methods			Validation Unseen	
Memory bank	Consistency	Word dropping	SR(%)↑	SPL(%)↑
✓			64.0	58.6
✓	✓		$65.7_{\uparrow 1.7}$	$59.4_{\uparrow 0.8}$
✓		✓	$64.5_{\uparrow 0.5}$	$57.8_{\downarrow 0.8}$

Table 5. Comparisons of training memory and computation cost on R2R dataset. We produce MTVM†* with the same cross-attention strategy as VLN◐BERT, where language is used as keys and values but not as queries. † indicates MTVM without the consistency loss. The best results are in bold and the second best results are underlined.

Methods	Params#	Memory	Validation Unseen	
			SR(%)↑	SPL(%)↑
VLN◐BERT	41.9M	8.6 GB	63.3	57.5
MTVM†*	41.6M	8.4 GB	<u>63.6</u>	<u>58.2</u>
MTVM†	68.4M	17.9 GB	**64.0**	**58.6**

Note that for HAMT [6], we report its results with Resnet-152 as the vision encoder for fair comparison.

Impacts of Consistency Loss and Random Word Dropping. Table 4 compares the results with and without our proposed consistency loss. For our MTVM model, we can see that the consistency loss significantly improves the performance. The consistency loss is designed to encourage the model to pay more attention to our explicitly modelled history tokens. Although some words are dropped during training, a lot of vision-language alignments have already been captured in the memory. It improves 1.7% and 0.8% on R2R validation unseen

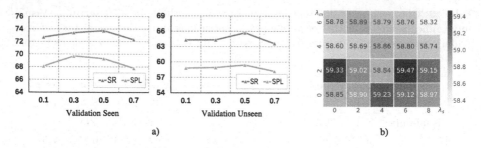

Fig. 5. a) Impact of different random word dropping rates on SR and SPL on both seen and unseen validation sets of R2R dataset. b) Sensitivity examples of the hyper-parameters in Eq. (5) to SPL metric on R2R unseen validation set. The darker the color, the better the performance.

setting with SR and SPL metric, indicating that the agent with the memory consistency loss achieves better generalize ability.

Note that our word-drop strategy for the consistency loss is similar to conventional random word dropping used for data augmentation. Thus, we make a comparison with direct word dropping for data augmentation (denoted as "memory bank" + "word dropping") in Table 4, where we fix the word dropping rate to 0.5 in all methods. It can be seen that direct word dropping as data augmentation is not as effective as ours.

We further investigate the effect of different word dropping rates on SR and SPL in both seen and unseen validation sets of R2R dataset. Here we conduct experiments by varying the word dropping rate in $\{0.1, 0.3, 0.5, 0.7\}$. As shown in Fig. 5 a), we can see that a small dropping rate (e.g., 0.1) does not perform as good as a large one (e.g., 0.5), while a too large dropping rate (e.g. 0.7) also hurts the performance. Thus, the best choice is 0.5.

Hyper-Parameter Sensitivity. We analyze the sensitivity of the hyper-parameters to SPL metric on R2R unseen validation set by using λ_s and λ_m in Eq. (5) as examples. The results are reported in Fig. 5 b). From these results, we can see that SPL is not very sensitive to the variations of λ_s and λ_m in a range around 2~8 and we find that it is a good choice to set $\lambda_s = 6, \lambda_m = 2$.

Memory and Computation Cost. Following most of the cross-modal Transformer methods [13,39], our MTVM facilitates vision-and-language interactions by bi-directional cross-attention sub-layers, where language is used as query attending to vision and vice versa. To compare with single-direction cross-modal Transformer method VLN◯BERT [16], which only considers language tokens as keys and values but not as queries, we also develop a similar version, MTVM†*. The comparison results of VLN◯BERT, MTVM†* and MTVM† in terms of Parameters and GPU Memory Cost are shown in Table 5. For a fair comparison with VLN◯BERT, all the experiments are conducted on a single V100 GPU with batch size 16. With the same cross-attention strategy, compared with VLN◯BERT, our MTVM†* archives better performance but with lower mem-

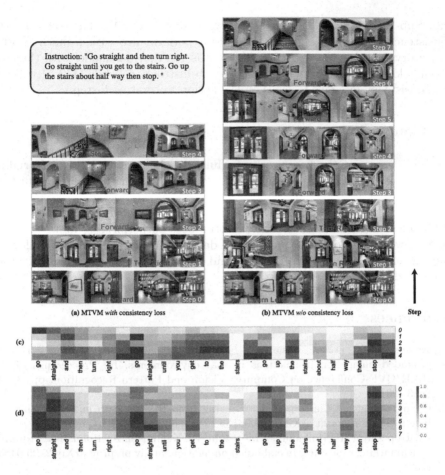

Fig. 6. Visualization examples of panoramic views and language attention weights. From sub-figures (a) and (b), it can be seen that without the consistency loss, MTVM took a longer path to reach "stairs". (c) and (d) are the language attention weights at the final layer of the cross-modality encoder corresponding to (a) and (b) at each step.

ory and computation cost. This is because VLN○BERT needs an additional small network to encode update its hidden states for temporal context while our MTVM†* directly reuses the previous activations. This demonstrates the efficiency and effectiveness of our proposed memory bank based Transformer design.

4.4 Visualization

To demonstrate the proposed consistency loss, we give a few visualization examples of panoramic views and language attention weights in Fig. 6. In R2R dataset, the agent needs to navigate following the instruction from the beginning to the end. Sub-figures (a) and (b) in Fig. 6 show that our MTVM model with the consistency loss achieves better navigation performance with a much shorter trajectory. In sub-figures (c) and (d), we observe that our model with the consistency loss is able to better ground the sub-instructions while MTVM without the consistency loss fails to focus on the action word at each step.

5   Conclusion

We have proposed the framework of Multimodal Transformer with Variable-length Memory (MTVM), which enables the agent explicitly model the history information in a simple and effective way. We have also designed the memory-aware consistency loss to improve the generalization ability of our model. Our MTVM has demonstrated strong performance, outperforming almost all the existing works on both R2R and CVDN dataset. We see the benefit of allowing long-range dependency for VLN task and we hope this idea can benefit other vision and language interaction tasks.

References

1. Anderson, P., et al.: Vision-and-language navigation: interpreting visually-grounded navigation instructions in real environments. In: Proceedings of the IEEE/CVF Conference on Computer Vision and Pattern Recognition, pp. 3674–3683 (2018)
2. Chang, A., et al.: Matterport3D: learning from RGB-D data in indoor environments. arXiv preprint arXiv:1709.06158 (2017)
3. Chattopadhyay, P., Hoffman, J., Mottaghi, R., Kembhavi, A.: RobustNav: towards benchmarking robustness in embodied navigation. arXiv preprint arXiv:2106.04531 (2021)
4. Chen, D., Mooney, R.: Learning to interpret natural language navigation instructions from observations. In: Proceedings of the AAAI Conference on Artificial Intelligence, vol. 25 (2011)
5. Chen, H., Suhr, A., Misra, D., Snavely, N., Artzi, Y.: Touchdown: natural language navigation and spatial reasoning in visual street environments. In: Proceedings of the IEEE/CVF Conference on Computer Vision and Pattern Recognition, pp. 12538–12547 (2019)
6. Chen, S., Guhur, P.L., Schmid, C., Laptev, I.: History aware multimodal transformer for vision-and-language navigation. In: Advances in Neural Information Processing Systems, vol. 34 (2021)
7. Chen, Y.-C., et al.: UNITER: UNiversal Image-TExt representation learning. In: Vedaldi, A., Bischof, H., Brox, T., Frahm, J.-M. (eds.) ECCV 2020. LNCS, vol. 12375, pp. 104–120. Springer, Cham (2020). https://doi.org/10.1007/978-3-030-58577-8_7
8. Devlin, J., Chang, M.W., Lee, K., Toutanova, K.: BERT: pre-training of deep bidirectional transformers for language understanding. arXiv preprint arXiv:1810.04805 (2018)
9. Fried, D., et al.: Speaker-follower models for vision-and-language navigation. arXiv preprint arXiv:1806.02724 (2018)

10. Gan, Z., Chen, Y.C., Li, L., Zhu, C., Cheng, Y., Liu, J.: Large-scale adversarial training for vision-and-language representation learning. arXiv preprint arXiv:2006.06195 (2020)

11. Guadarrama, S., et al.: Grounding spatial relations for human-robot interaction. In: 2013 IEEE/RSJ International Conference on Intelligent Robots and Systems, pp. 1640–1647. IEEE (2013)

12. Guhur, P.L., Tapaswi, M., Chen, S., Laptev, I., Schmid, C.: AirBERT: in-domain pretraining for vision-and-language navigation. arXiv preprint arXiv:2108.09105 (2021)

13. Hao, W., Li, C., Li, X., Carin, L., Gao, J.: Towards learning a generic agent for vision-and-language navigation via pre-training. In: Proceedings of the IEEE/CVF Conference on Computer Vision and Pattern Recognition, pp. 13137–13146 (2020)

14. He, K., Zhang, X., Ren, S., Sun, J.: Deep residual learning for image recognition. In: Proceedings of the IEEE/CVF Conference on Computer Vision and Pattern Recognition, pp. 770–778 (2016)

15. Hong, Y., Rodriguez-Opazo, C., Qi, Y., Wu, Q., Gould, S.: Language and visual entity relationship graph for agent navigation. arXiv preprint arXiv:2010.09304 (2020)

16. Hong, Y., Wu, Q., Qi, Y., Rodriguez-Opazo, C., Gould, S.: VLN BERT: a recurrent vision-and-language BERT for navigation. In: Proceedings of the IEEE/CVF Conference on Computer Vision and Pattern Recognition, pp. 1643–1653 (2021)

17. Hu, R., Fried, D., Rohrbach, A., Klein, D., Darrell, T., Saenko, K.: Are you looking? Grounding to multiple modalities in vision-and-language navigation. arXiv preprint arXiv:1906.00347 (2019)

18. Huang, Z., Zeng, Z., Liu, B., Fu, D., Fu, J.: Pixel-BERT: aligning image pixels with text by deep multi-modal transformers. arXiv preprint arXiv:2004.00849 (2020)

19. Ke, L., et al.: Tactical rewind: self-correction via backtracking in vision-and-language navigation. In: Proceedings of the IEEE/CVF Conference on Computer Vision and Pattern Recognition, pp. 6741–6749 (2019)

20. Kim, H., Li, J., Bansal, M.: NDH-full: learning and evaluating navigational agents on full-length dialogue. In: Proceedings of the 2021 Conference on Empirical Methods in Natural Language Processing, pp. 6432–6442 (2021)

21. Ku, A., Anderson, P., Patel, R., Ie, E., Baldridge, J.: Room-across-room: multilingual vision-and-language navigation with dense spatiotemporal grounding. arXiv preprint arXiv:2010.07954 (2020)

22. Li, G., Duan, N., Fang, Y., Gong, M., Jiang, D.: Unicoder-VL: a universal encoder for vision and language by cross-modal pre-training. In: Proceedings of the AAAI Conference on Artificial Intelligence, vol. 34, pp. 11336–11344 (2020)

23. Li, X., et al.: Robust navigation with language pretraining and stochastic sampling. arXiv preprint arXiv:1909.02244 (2019)

24. Lin, B., Zhu, Y., Long, Y., Liang, X., Ye, Q., Lin, L.: Adversarial reinforced instruction attacker for robust vision-language navigation. arXiv preprint arXiv:2107.11252 (2021)

25. Lin, C., Yuan, Z., Zhao, S., Sun, P., Wang, C., Cai, J.: Domain-invariant disentangled network for generalizable object detection. In: Proceedings of the IEEE/CVF International Conference on Computer Vision, pp. 8771–8780 (2021)

26. Lin, C., Zhao, S., Meng, L., Chua, T.S.: Multi-source domain adaptation for visual sentiment classification. In: Proceedings of the AAAI Conference on Artificial Intelligence, vol. 34, pp. 2661–2668 (2020)

27. Liu, C., Zhu, F., Chang, X., Liang, X., Shen, Y.D.: Vision-language navigation with random environmental mixup. arXiv preprint arXiv:2106.07876 (2021)

28. Loshchilov, I., Hutter, F.: Decoupled weight decay regularization. arXiv preprint arXiv:1711.05101 (2017)
29. Lu, J., Batra, D., Parikh, D., Lee, S.: ViLBERT: pretraining task-agnostic visiolinguistic representations for vision-and-language tasks. arXiv preprint arXiv:1908.02265 (2019)
30. Ma, C.Y., et al.: Self-monitoring navigation agent via auxiliary progress estimation. arXiv preprint arXiv:1901.03035 (2019)
31. Majumdar, A., Shrivastava, A., Lee, S., Anderson, P., Parikh, D., Batra, D.: Improving vision-and-language navigation with image-text pairs from the web. In: Vedaldi, A., Bischof, H., Brox, T., Frahm, J.-M. (eds.) ECCV 2020. LNCS, vol. 12351, pp. 259–274. Springer, Cham (2020). https://doi.org/10.1007/978-3-030-58539-6_16
32. Mnih, V., et al.: Asynchronous methods for deep reinforcement learning. In: International Conference on Machine Learning, pp. 1928–1937. PMLR (2016)
33. Nguyen, K., Daumé, H., III.: Help, anna! visual navigation with natural multi-modal assistance via retrospective curiosity-encouraging imitation learning. arXiv preprint arXiv:1909.01871 (2019)
34. Nguyen, K., Dey, D., Brockett, C., Dolan, B.: Vision-based navigation with language-based assistance via imitation learning with indirect intervention. In: Proceedings of the IEEE/CVF Conference on Computer Vision and Pattern Recognition, pp. 12527–12537 (2019)
35. Pashevich, A., Schmid, C., Sun, C.: Episodic transformer for vision-and-language navigation. arXiv preprint arXiv:2105.06453 (2021)
36. Qi, Y., Pan, Z., Hong, Y., Yang, M.H., van den Hengel, A., Wu, Q.: Know what and know where: an object-and-room informed sequential BERT for indoor vision-language navigation. arXiv preprint arXiv:2104.04167 (2021)
37. Qi, Y., et al.: REVERIE: remote embodied visual referring expression in real indoor environments. In: Proceedings of the IEEE/CVF Conference on Computer Vision and Pattern Recognition, pp. 9982–9991 (2020)
38. Ren, S., He, K., Girshick, R., Sun, J.: Faster R-CNN: towards real-time object detection with region proposal networks. In: Advances in Neural Information Processing Systems, vol. 28 (2015)
39. Tan, H., Bansal, M.: LXMERT: learning cross-modality encoder representations from transformers. arXiv preprint arXiv:1908.07490 (2019)
40. Tan, H., Yu, L., Bansal, M.: Learning to navigate unseen environments: back translation with environmental dropout. arXiv preprint arXiv:1904.04195 (2019)
41. Tellex, S., et al.: Understanding natural language commands for robotic navigation and mobile manipulation. In: Proceedings of the AAAI Conference on Artificial Intelligence, vol. 25 (2011)
42. Thomason, J., Murray, M., Cakmak, M., Zettlemoyer, L.: Vision-and-dialog navigation. In: Conference on Robot Learning, pp. 394–406. PMLR (2020)
43. Vaswani, A., et al.: Attention is all you need. In: Advances in Neural Information Processing Systems, pp. 5998–6008 (2017)
44. Wang, X., et al.: Reinforced cross-modal matching and self-supervised imitation learning for vision-language navigation. In: Proceedings of the IEEE/CVF Conference on Computer Vision and Pattern Recognition, pp. 6629–6638 (2019)
45. Wu, J., Jiang, Y., Sun, P., Yuan, Z., Luo, P.: Language as queries for referring video object segmentation. In: Proceedings of the IEEE/CVF Conference on Computer Vision and Pattern Recognition, pp. 4974–4984 (2022)
46. Zhao, M., et al.: On the evaluation of vision-and-language navigation instructions. arXiv preprint arXiv:2101.10504 (2021)

47. Zhao, S., et al.: CycleEmotionGAN: emotional semantic consistency preserved CycleGAN for adapting image emotions. In: Proceedings of the AAAI Conference on Artificial Intelligence, vol. 33, pp. 2620–2627 (2019)

48. Zhou, B., Lapedriza, A., Khosla, A., Oliva, A., Torralba, A.: Places: a 10 million image database for scene recognition. IEEE Trans. Pattern Anal. Mach. Intell. **40**(6), 1452–1464 (2017)

49. Zhou, L., Palangi, H., Zhang, L., Hu, H., Corso, J., Gao, J.: Unified vision-language pre-training for image captioning and VQA. In: Proceedings of the AAAI Conference on Artificial Intelligence, vol. 34, pp. 13041–13049 (2020)

50. Zhu, F., Zhu, Y., Chang, X., Liang, X.: Vision-language navigation with self-supervised auxiliary reasoning tasks. In: Proceedings of the IEEE/CVF Conference on Computer Vision and Pattern Recognition, pp. 10012–10022 (2020)

51. Zhu, Y., et al.: Self-motivated communication agent for real-world vision-dialog navigation. In: Proceedings of the IEEE/CVF International Conference on Computer Vision, pp. 1594–1603 (2021)

52. Zhu, Y., et al.: Vision-dialog navigation by exploring cross-modal memory. In: Proceedings of the IEEE/CVF Conference on Computer Vision and Pattern Recognition, pp. 10730–10739 (2020)

Fine-Grained Visual Entailment

Christopher Thomas$^{(\boxtimes)}$, Yipeng Zhang, and Shih-Fu Chang

Columbia University, New York, NY 10034, USA
{christopher.thomas,zhang.yipeng,sc250}@columbia.edu

Abstract. Visual entailment is a recently proposed multimodal reasoning task where the goal is to predict the logical relationship of a piece of text to an image. In this paper, we propose an extension of this task, where the goal is to predict the logical relationship of fine-grained knowledge elements within a piece of text to an image. Unlike prior work, our method is inherently explainable and makes logical predictions at different levels of granularity. Because we lack fine-grained labels to train our method, we propose a novel multi-instance learning approach which learns a fine-grained labeling using only sample-level supervision. We also impose novel semantic structural constraints which ensure that fine-grained predictions are internally semantically consistent. We evaluate our method on a new dataset of manually annotated knowledge elements and show that our method achieves 68.18% accuracy at this challenging task while significantly outperforming several strong baselines. Finally, we present extensive qualitative results illustrating our method's predictions and the visual evidence our method relied on. Our code and annotated dataset can be found here: https://github.com/SkrighYZ/FGVE.

1 Introduction

Tasks requiring multimodal understanding across vision and language have seen an explosion of interest in recent years, driven largely by their many downstream applications. Common tasks include visual question answering [1,20,41], visual commonsense reasoning [55], and visual dialog [14,15]. Moreover, tasks that had historically been studied by only the natural language processing or computer vision communities have recently received attention from both communities. For example, event extraction [10,28,57] and coreferencing [26,38], longstanding information extraction and NLP tasks, have all recently been explored multimodally.

One such task is the textual entailment task, first proposed in 2005 [13]. The task requires a system to decide whether a piece of text (the hypothesis) can be logically deduced from another piece of text accepted as true (the premise). Xie

---

C. Thomas and Y. Zhang—These two authors contributed equally.

Supplementary Information The online version contains supplementary material available at https://doi.org/10.1007/978-3-031-20059-5_23.

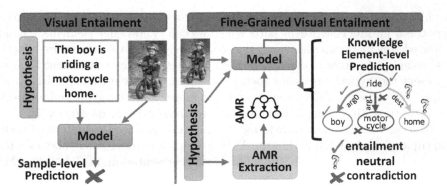

Fig. 1. In the standard visual entailment task, a model predicts the logical relationship of the entire hypothesis to an image. In our proposed task, the model predicts the relationship of each knowledge element of the hypothesis. Specifically, our model predicts a boy is present, someone is riding, the boy is riding, a motorcycle is not present, no one is riding a motorcycle, and can't conclude whether someone is riding home or not.

et al. [50] posed a multimodal variant of the task called visual entailment, which replaces the textual premise with an image. Because of the rich cross-modal reasoning required, it has become a standard benchmark for testing joint vision-and-language understanding in many recent multimodal models [12,23,31].

The standard visual entailment benchmark [50] is a three-way classification task between entailment (hypothesis is true), neutral (hypothesis could be true or false), and contradiction (hypothesis is false). Though the classification is made for the entire hypothesis, the task by its very nature requires fine-grained multimodal reasoning. For example, for a hypothesis to be labeled contradiction, the model must find at least one facet of the hypothesis that conflicts with the image. The task as posed, however does not require the model to produce fine-grained predictions which would explain its reasoning.

This lack of fine-grained predictions is significant for several important reasons. First, it limits the utility of the task to downstream applications. Fundamentally, the visual entailment task requires models to search for visual evidence necessary to make logical inferences about the text. This capability has many possible downstream use cases, from detecting image-text inconsistencies for misinformation detection [32] to ensuring answers to questions are entailed by the image [44]. However, many of these tasks require localized predictions [19], which existing methods are unable to provide. Secondly, the fine-grained predictions produced by the model naturally explain its reasoning, making its prediction interpretable.

To address the above shortcomings, we propose the **fine-grained visual entailment** task. Similar to the original visual entailment task, our goal is to predict the logical relationship of textual claims about images. But differently, we require the model to make predictions for each specific "claim" in the text.

We illustrate our task in Fig. 1. Our method works by decomposing the textual hypothesis into its constituent parts which we call "knowledge elements" (KEs). Knowledge elements are the claims that collectively constitute the entire hypothesis' meaning. In order to decompose the hypothesis into its constituent KEs, we represent the hypothesis as its abstract meaning representation (AMR) [3,25] graph. We choose AMR to represent the semantics of the hypothesis because AMR captures the semantic meaning of text irrespective of its syntax [3].

We train a multimodal transformer to make fine-grained predictions on nodes and tuples (i.e. the KEs) within the AMR graph. Our transformer takes as input visual tokens, the hypothesis, and a linearized representation [21,35] of the AMR graph. To make predictions for each KE within the AMR graph, we introduce a novel local aggregation mechanism which learns a localized contextual representation. Our contextual representation fuses the representation of the KE's AMR with its associated visual context. These representations are then used to make KE-specific predictions.

The model described above requires KE-level supervision to train, but our dataset only contains *sample*-level supervision. Rather than rely on expensive and hard to obtain AMR graph annotations, we instead propose a novel multi-instance learning (MIL) approach. Specifically, we leverage the sample-level label to impose a set of MIL constraints on our prediction function which induce a fine-grained labeling of the graph without requiring any new annotations.

While our MIL losses ensure that knowledge element-level predictions are consistent with the sample-level label, they do not ensure that they are semantically consistent with each other. Thus, we impose both top-down and bottom-up semantic structural constraints which penalize the model for semantically inconsistent knowledge element predictions. These constraints leverage the same intuition as our sample-level MIL constraints, but instead work *between* KEs at different structures within the AMR graph.

In order to benchmark performance on this task, we densely annotate AMR graphs at the knowledge element-level. We compare our method against a number of baselines across numerous metrics. Experiments show that our approach substantially outperforms all baselines for the fine-grained visual entailment task. We also include detailed qualitative results showing our method produces semantically plausible predictions at the knowledge element-level as well as examples of the "visual evidence" chosen by our model to make its predictions.

The major contributions of this paper are as follows:

- We introduce the novel task of fine-grained visual entailment and contribute a benchmark of AMR graphs densely annotated by experts.
- We propose a novel method for this task which relies on localized cross-modal contextual representations of each knowledge element.
- We develop a number of novel loss functions to train our method to make knowledge element-level predictions with only sample-level labels.
- We perform detailed experiments and ablations of our model and loss functions which clearly demonstrate the superiority of our approach. We also

present qualitative results and show the "visual evidence" used by our method.

2 Related Work

Textual Entailment. Textual entailment (predicting whether a hypothesis is entailed by a premise) has long been studied by the natural language processing [13] community. Later work such as SICK [34] and the Stanford natural language inference benchmark (SNLI) [6] expanded the task definition to allow more granular labels, i.e. by adding the neutral category. The SNLI benchmark is a large-scale benchmark of crowdsourced hypotheses written for Flickr30K [52] image captions (which served as the premises). [7] further extend the SNLI dataset with human-written free-form text explanations of the sample's label. None of these works operate multimodally or make granular predictions as we do.

Visual Entailment. Most related to this paper is past work in visual entailment. Xie et al. [50] introduced the visual entailment task which replaced the textual premise from SNLI (a Flickr30K image caption) with its corresponding image, while preserving the original label. Other work [11,30] has also explored visual entailment in the video domain. [24] observed that the visual entailment dataset contained substantial label errors caused by replacing the image caption with its image. To correct this, [24] reannotated the samples labeled neutral in the test set and proposed an automatic technique to correct some mislabeled neutral train examples. [24] also use the rationales from [7] to train a text generation method to generate free-form textual "explanations" of their predictions.

Our approach offers several significant benefits over [24]'s. First, while [24] generate explanations, there is no guarantee that the generated text truly describes the model's reasoning. Moreover, the generated text may not address specific claims (or any claims) made in the hypothesis. Unlike prior work, our method decomposes the hypothesis into its constituent KEs. Our KE-level predictions naturally cover all claims within the hypothesis which may be important for downstream applications, while inherently explaining the model's reasoning.

Explainability. Our work is also related to research in producing explainable and interpretable predictions. Common examples include as saliency-map techniques [43,58,60] as well attention mechanism visualizations [18,29]. One popular such example of the former category is Grad-CAM [40] which computes class-specific gradient heatmaps with the input. [48] produce fine-grained visual explanations of image regions which caused the model to predict a particular class. More recent work visualizes the attention maps in transformers [8,9,47]. Similar to our method, [11] produce grounded video regions as explanations for video entailment, but do not tackle the fine-grained entailment setting as we do. [19] make fine-grained predictions of image-text inconsistency using a predefined ontology, but do not consider the open domain and more granular entailment problem we do.

| Text | AMR Graph | Linearized AMR | Knowledge Elements |

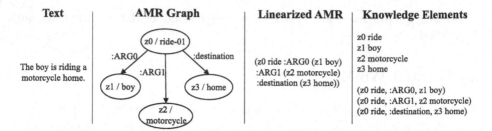

Fig. 2. Illustration of knowledge element (KE) extraction. `Arg#` tokens are role labels from PropBank [36], while `z#` tokens are IDs for nodes to facilitate node coreference. During preprocessing, we make simplifications to the linearized AMRs such as removing "/" and "−01". We include details on preprocessing and tokenization in our supplementary.

Multi-instance Learning. Our model is required to learn which knowledge elements are entailed, neutral, or contradictory from only the sample-level label. Our work is thus related to multi-instance learning (MIL) methods where a bag of samples are assigned a single label with at least one sample in the bag being the label of the bag [16]. MIL methods have recently been explored for a variety of tasks including image classification [39,49], object detection [17,51,54], scene graph generation [42], and video segment localization [33,59]. All share the goal of learning a finer-grained prediction function than directly available from the training labels. We are the first to apply MIL techniques to learn a knowledge element-level entailment prediction model.

3   Fine-Grained Visual Entailment

Given an image and a textual hypothesis about the image, our goal is to predict the logical relationship of the image to every "assertion" contained within the hypothesis. To do so, we transform the textual hypothesis into its abstract meaning representation (AMR) graph. We make predictions for each node and tuple (edge with its endpoint nodes) in the graph, which we call knowledge elements (KEs). KEs consist of assertions within the hypothesis about actions, entities (objects, people, etc.), colors, gender, count, etc. We propose a multimodal transformer which operates over the image, hypothesis, and a representation of the AMR graph. At a high level, our method works by locating KE tokens in the AMR graph, aggregating visual information to create a contextualized KE embedding, and performing predictions by a classifier trained with novel multi-instance learning and structural losses (which enforce semantic consistency).

3.1   Problem Formulation

More formally, let $\mathcal{D} = \{(i^{(1)}, h^{(1)}, y^{(1)}), \ldots, (i^{(s)}, h^{(s)}, y^{(s)}), \ldots, (i^{(n)}, h^{(n)}, y^{(n)})\}$ represent a dataset of image, hypothesis, and entailment label triples respectively, where n is the number of sample triples within the dataset. The goal of the standard visual entailment task [50] is to learn the prediction function $f_\theta(i^{(s)}, h^{(s)}) = y^{(s)}$, i.e., to predict the sample-level logical relationship of the image and hypothesis. Note that in the remainder of this text, we omit the sample index and refer to a single sample for clarity unless noted. Because we seek to make sub-hypothesis-level predictions, we first decompose each hypothesis into its constituent KEs. We denote the set of KEs extracted from h as $KE = \{kc_j\}_{j=0}^{|KE|}$. We seek a prediction function $g_\theta(i, h) = \{y_{ke_j}\}_{j=0}^{|KE|}$ where y_{ke_j} is the label of ke_j describing its specific logical relationship with the image.

3.2   Knowledge Element Extraction

We next describe more specifically how we extract KEs from the hypothesis. Let $\mathcal{G}$ be a text to AMR graph prediction method, then $\mathcal{G}(h) = G$ represents the conversion of a hypothesis into its AMR graph representation G, where $G = (V, E)$ and V and E represent the set of vertices (nodes) and edges within the graph, respectively. Each node $v \in V$ represents a simple, atomic statement about the image (e.g., "there is a car"; "something is walking"). In contrast, each edge $\vec{e} \in E$ is directed and defines the relationship type between nodes. Because edges are of ambiguous meaning without the nodes they connect, we do not consider edges independently as KEs. Instead, we consider the set of directed node-edge tuples denoted $T = (v_h, e, v_t)$ with $\{v_h, v_t\} \in V$, v_h and v_t being the head and tail nodes defined by the edge's direction, and $\vec{e}$ defining the relation type between the nodes. Each tuple thus represents a composite statement (e.g., "v_t is performing the action in v_h"; "v_t is the color of v_h"). Thus, the set of KEs extracted for a sample is $KE = \{V \cup T\} = \{ke_j\}_{j=0}^{|KE|}$. We show an example of what our AMR to KE extraction process looks like in Fig. 2.

3.3   Architecture

Figure 3 shows the architecture of our method. In this work, we use OSCAR$^+$ [56] as our multimodal encoder $\mathcal{F}$. OSCAR$^+$ achieved recent SOTA performance on several downstream vision-language tasks [56]. Given an image-hypothesis pair (i, h), a pretrained object detector first extracts a sequence of object region features $o = o_1, \ldots, o_m$ and a sequence of predicted object tags $t = t_1, \ldots, t_p$ (object labels in text form) from the image, where m and p are the number of regions and tags respectively. Let f_φ denote a graph linearization method [35], then $r = f_\varphi(\mathcal{G}(h))$ where r is h's AMR in linearized form. The linearized AMR encapsulates all KEs within the hypothesis' AMR in a string form, while retaining their semantic structure. We extract the token embeddings from the last layer of the encoder for each of the sequences: $(\mathbf{o}, \mathbf{t}, \mathbf{r}, \mathbf{h}) = \mathcal{F}(o, t, r, h)$. Although providing h to the model is not required, it provides context and we find it slightly improves sample-level performance ($\sim$2%) in practice. Our method for fine-grained KE prediction to be described does not involve or require $\mathbf{h}$.

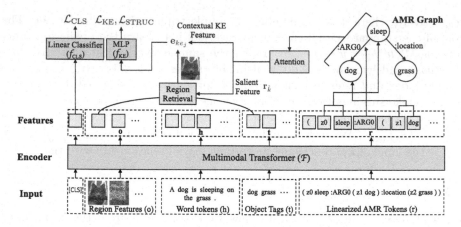

Fig. 3. Our method that makes predictions on both the sample level and the KE level. We show the processing steps for an example KE: (z0 sleep, :ARG0, z1 dog).

3.4 Knowledge Element-Contextual Aggregation

Although multimodal interactions happen naturally through self-attention in the transformer's layers, we find it beneficial to apply attention to tokens inside each KE. For example, the model might pay more attention to predicates than entity labels such as "z0". Let $\mathbf{r} = (\mathbf{r}_1, \mathbf{r}_2, \ldots, \mathbf{r}_l)$ be the full AMR embedding sequence, where $l = |r|$. Let a subset $\mathbf{r}_{ke_j} = (\mathbf{r}_{l_1}, \ldots, \mathbf{r}_{l_k}) \in \mathbb{R}^{m_j \times d}$, where d is the hidden state dimension and $\{l_1, \ldots, l_k\} \subseteq \{1, \ldots, l\}$, be the embeddings of the m_j tokens (not necessarily consecutive) that form $ke_j \in KE$. To estimate each token's importance, we learn a function f_α that takes as input $\mathbf{r}_{ke_j}$ and outputs token-wise attention weights $\mathbf{w}_j \in R^{m_j}$. In this work, $f_\alpha(\mathbf{r}_{ke_j}) = \sigma(\mathbf{r}_{ke_j} \mathbf{w}^\alpha)$, where σ is the softmax function and $\mathbf{w}^\alpha \in \mathbb{R}^d$ is a learned vector shared by all KEs. We leave exploring stronger weighting mechanisms as future work.

A challenging aspect of our task requires the model to create grounded representations for individual KEs. For a single node in the AMR graph, context information from the image space could be essential for prediction. Therefore, we propose a method to retrieve relevant image region features for each $\mathbf{r}_{ke_j}$.

We first select the most salient token $\hat{k}$ characterized by having the highest attention weight ($\hat{k} = \arg\max_k w_{j,k}$, where $w_{j,k}$ is the k-th element of $\mathbf{w}_j$). We then compare the cosine similarity between $\mathbf{r}_{\hat{k}}$ and each of the tag embeddings $\mathbf{t}_{k'}$, $\frac{\mathbf{r}_{\hat{k}} \cdot \mathbf{t}_{k'}}{\|\mathbf{r}_{\hat{k}}\| \|\mathbf{t}_{k'}\|}$, and retrieve the most similar tag $t_{\hat{k}'}$. With the correspondence given by the object detector, we can now retrieve the object region feature $\mathbf{o}_{\hat{k}''} \in \mathbb{R}^d$ that $t_{\hat{k}'}$ refers to.

The full contextualized embedding used for predicting ke_j's label is therefore obtained by:

$$\mathbf{e}_{ke_j} = \text{Concatenate}([\mathbf{r}_{ke_j}^\top \mathbf{w}_j, \mathbf{o}_{\hat{k}''}]) \in \mathbb{R}^{2d}. \tag{1}$$

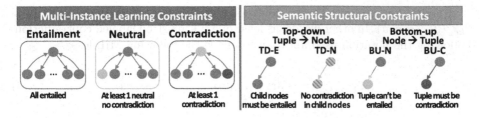

Fig. 4. Left: Our MIL constraints transfer sample-level supervision to KEs, but allow semantically inconsistent predictions (e.g. bicycle = contradiction, riding bicycle = entailed). **Right:** Structural constraints work within the graph to ensure semantically consistent predictions. Multicolor nodes/tuples indicate the KE could be either color. (Color figure online)

We denote our classifier's output for each KE as $f_{KE}\left(\mathbf{e}_{ke_j}\right) = \mathbf{z} = \left(\mathbf{z}_1, \ldots, \mathbf{z}_{|KE|}\right) = \left(f_{KE}\left(\mathbf{e}_{ke_1}\right), \ldots, f_{KE}\left(\mathbf{e}_{ke_{|KE|}}\right)\right)$, where $\mathbf{z}_i$ denotes the output logits of the classifier for ke_i and $f_{KE}(\cdot) \in \mathbb{R}^3$.

3.5 Multi-instance Learning Losses

Because we lack KE-level supervision, to train f_{KE} we leverage novel multi-instance learning (MIL) objectives which we derive from the problem semantics. Specifically, we observe that if a hypothesis is entailed by an image, all KEs within the hypothesis should themselves be entailed (denoted ent.). Formally, $(y = \text{ent}) \implies \forall_{ke_i}(y_{ke_i} = \text{ent})$. Because there is no ambiguity as to what each KE's label should be, we impose a standard cross entropy classification loss across all KEs for entailed samples:

$$\mathcal{L}_{KE_{y=\text{ent}}} = \sum_i^{|KE|} - \log \frac{\exp\left(z_{i_{\text{ent}}}\right)}{\sum_c^C \exp\left(z_{i_c}\right)} \tag{2}$$

where z_{i_c} is the classifier's predicted value for class $c \in \{\text{ent, neu, con}\}$.

For a sample to be labeled neutral, we next observe that its KEs must observe the following definition: $(y = \text{neu}) \implies (\forall_{ke_i} \neg (y_{ke_i} = \text{con}) \land \exists_{ke_i}(y_{ke_i} = \text{neu}))$. That is, no KE may be labeled contradiction (but they may be labeled either entailment or neutral) and at least one KE should be labeled neutral. We enforce these two constraints through the following MIL loss:

$$\mathcal{L}_{KE_{y=\text{neu}}} = \sum_i^{|KE|} \left(- \log \left(1 - \frac{\exp\left(z_{i_{\text{con}}}\right)}{\sum_c^C \exp\left(z_{i_c}\right)}\right)\right) - \underset{z_{i_{neu}} \in \mathbf{z}}{\arg\max} \left(\log \frac{\exp\left(z_{i_{\text{neu}}}\right)}{\sum_c^C \exp\left(z_{i_c}\right)}\right) \tag{3}$$

where $\arg\max_{z_{i_{neu}} \in \mathbf{z}}$ selects the KE whose score in the neutral dimension is the largest. Intuitively, this amounts to selecting the KE the model is most confident is neutral and treating its label as such.

Finally, for samples labeled contradiction, we note that $(y = \text{con}) \implies \exists_{ke_i} (y_{ke_i} = \text{con})$. In other words, at least one KE must be labeled contradiction. Following the notation used above, we impose the following MIL loss:

$$\mathcal{L}_{KE_{y=\text{con}}} = - \underset{z_{i_{con}} \in \mathbf{z}}{\arg\max} \left(\log \frac{\exp\left(z_{i_{con}}\right)}{\sum_c^C \exp\left(z_{i_c}\right)} \right) \tag{4}$$

which selects the KE the model is most confident is contradiction and enforces it to be so classified. We illustrate our MIL constraints for these three categories in Fig. 4 (left).

3.6 Semantic Structural Constraints

The above constraints enforce that the KE predictions are consistent with the sample-level label, but they do not ensure that the KE predictions are *internally* semantically consistent with one another. For example, a model trained with the above constraints would be free to predict the node "girl" as contradictory, but the tuple "girl on bicycle" as entailed. We call this a "bottom-up" semantic structural violation because the tuple's prediction (the parent) is inconsistent with the node's prediction (the child). Like our MIL constraints, our structural constraints flow from the semantics of the problem. We note that two types of bottom-up structural constraints should hold: BU-C) $(y_{ke_i} = \text{con}) \implies \forall_{ke_j \in \text{parent}(ke_i)} (y_{ke_j} = \text{con})$ and BU-N) $(y_{ke_i} = \text{neu}) \implies \forall_{ke_j \in \text{parent}(ke_i)} \neg (y_{ke_j} = \text{ent})$. BU-C requires that, if a node is contradiction, any parent tuple that contains it must also be contradiction. BU-N requires that if a node is neutral, no parent tuple may be entailed. We enforce BU-C and BU-N through the following two bottom-up structure preserving losses:

$$\mathcal{L}_{\text{STRUC}_{\text{BU-C}}} = \sum_{ke_i, ke_j}^{\substack{ke_i \in V \\ ke_j \in \text{parent}(ke_i)}} -\sigma\left(z_{i_{con}}\right) \log \left(\frac{\exp\left(z_{j_{con}}\right)}{\sum_c^C \exp\left(z_{j_c}\right)} \right) \cdot \mathbb{1}\left\{\hat{y}_i = \text{con}\right\} \tag{5}$$

$$\mathcal{L}_{\text{STRUC}_{\text{BU-N}}} = \sum_{ke_i, ke_j}^{\substack{ke_i \in V \\ ke_j \in \text{parent}(ke_i)}} -\sigma\left(z_{i_{neu}}\right) \log \left(1 - \frac{\exp\left(z_{j_{ent}}\right)}{\sum_c^C \exp\left(z_{j_c}\right)} \right) \cdot \mathbb{1}\left\{\hat{y}_i = \text{neu}\right\} \tag{6}$$

where σ is the sigmoid function, $\hat{y}_i$ represents ke_i's predicted label (i.e., the maximum scoring class in z_i), and $\mathbb{1}$ is the indicator function. Note that we weight each structural constraint with the confidence of the child's prediction which lessens the impact of incorrectly predicted KEs. We found that this significantly improved performance.

Similarly, two top-down constraints must also hold for their predictions to be logically consistent: TD-E) $(y_{ke_i} = \text{ent}) \implies \forall_{ke_j \in \text{child}(ke_i)} (y_{ke_j} = \text{ent})$ and TD-N) $(y_{ke_i} = \text{neu}) \implies \forall_{ke_j \in \text{child}(ke_i)} \neg (y_{ke_j} = \text{con})$. Analogous to our bottom-up constraints, we enforce our top-down constraints through the following two losses:

$$\mathcal{L}_{\text{STRUC}_{\text{TD-E}}} = \sum_{\substack{ke_i, ke_j \\ ke_j \in \text{child}(ke_i) \\ ke_i \in V}} -\sigma\left(z_{i_{\text{ent}}}\right) \log\left(\frac{\exp\left(z_{j_{\text{ent}}}\right)}{\sum_c^C \exp\left(z_{j_c}\right)}\right) \cdot \mathbb{1}\left\{\hat{y}_i = \text{ent}\right\} \quad (7)$$

and

$$\mathcal{L}_{\text{STRUC}_{\text{TD-N}}} = \sum_{\substack{ke_i, ke_j \\ ke_j \in \text{child}(ke_i) \\ ke_i \in V}} -\sigma\left(z_{i_{\text{neu}}}\right) \log\left(1 - \frac{\exp\left(z_{j_{\text{con}}}\right)}{\sum_c^C \exp\left(z_{j_c}\right)}\right) \cdot \mathbb{1}\left\{\hat{y}_i = \text{neu}\right\}. \quad (8)$$

3.7 Final Loss Formulation

In addition to our KE-level losses, we also include a standard sample-level cross-entropy loss performed on the CLS token of the transformer which we denote by $\mathcal{L}_{CLS}$. Thus, our final loss formulation is given by the summation of the previous losses: $\mathcal{L} = \beta_{\text{CLS}} * \mathcal{L}_{\text{CLS}} + \beta_{\text{KE}} * \mathcal{L}_{\text{KE}} + \beta_{\text{STRUC}} * \mathcal{L}_{\text{STRUC}}$, where β are hyperparameters controlling the relative weight of each component of the loss.

3.8 Implementation Details

All methods and baselines use a pretrained VinVL [56] multimodal transformer as our backbone architecture with the ResNeXt-152 C4 detector for visual features. We use a max length of 50 for $\mathbf{o}$ and 165 for $|\mathbf{t}| + |\mathbf{r}| + |\mathbf{h}|$, truncating $\mathbf{h}$. We use a batch size of 128, an initial learning rate of $5e^{-5}$ that linearly decreases, a weight decay of 0.05, and train for a max of 10 epochs. We use Spring [4] to extract AMR graphs from hypotheses. We use a depth-first approach for AMR linearization. We implement our model in PyTorch [37]. Training takes approximately two days on four Nvidia Titan RTX GPUs. Unless otherwise specified, we set $\beta_{\text{CLS}} = 0.5$ and $\beta_{\text{KE}} = \beta_{\text{STRUC}} = 1$. We include additional details in supplementary.

4 Experiments

We compare our method to several baselines on the new task of fine-grained visual entailment. Our results consistently demonstrate that our approach significantly outperforms these baselines on the fine-grained visual entailment task. We also include detailed ablations and analysis of various components of our method. We also present qualitative results illustrating that our method makes semantically meaningful predictions at the KE-level. Finally, we show the visual regions chosen by our method to make its predictions for each KE.

Table 1. We show KE-level accuracies at the class-level, across different types of KEs, and the overall KE-level accuracy. Finally, we show the structural constraint accuracy (see text). The best result per column is shown in bold and second best is underlined.

Method	Acc_{ent}	Acc_{neu}	Acc_{con}	Acc_{node}	Acc_{tup}	Overall Acc	Acc_{STRUC}
VE → KE	49.77	**60.00**	<u>83.33</u>	54.36	60.51	57.17	**100**
VE+AMR → KE	55.51	<u>58.06</u>	**85.10**	58.14	64.10	60.86	96.40
w/o $\mathcal{L}_{STRUC}$	**88.87**	15.48	9.57	66.88	57.17	62.44	70.26
w/o Region Retrieval	78.20	24.51	55.67	64.61	64.87	64.73	93.57
Ours	79.64	31.29	62.76	<u>69.79</u>	<u>66.02</u>	<u>68.07</u>	96.36
Ours+CLS	<u>80.35</u>	29.35	62.76	**70.01**	**66.02**	**68.18**	<u>96.98</u>

4.1   Dataset

The original visual entailment benchmark [50] was found to have a substantial (~39%) label error rate for the neutral class [24]. For training and testing, we therefore use the relabeled version presented in [24] which corrects this issue in the test set. The dataset contains 430,796 image, hypothesis, label triples in total. We use the original train/val/test splits [24].

In order to evaluate our method's on the KE-level prediction task, we require KE-level annotated data. To do so, we created an web annotation interface using LabelStudio [45]. Our interface shows annotators the image, hypothesis, and an image of the hypothesis AMR graph. Annotators annotate each node and tuple (the KEs) within the graph with the class that describes its relationship to the image. Note that we also allow annotators to "opt-out" of KEs that are of unclear meaning (which may occur from AMR prediction errors, etc.). These KEs are ignored in evaluation. Because the original sample labels are crowdsourced and still noisy, we also ask annotators to provide a new sample-level label.

Annotating AMR graphs is an intellectually demanding and laborious task, often requiring annotators to consult PropBank [36] or the AMR specifications [25] to understand the meaning of the KE. Because of the difficulty of the task, we concluded it was inappropriate for crowdsourcing. We instead employed two expert annotators who were familiar with AMR, similar to [3,5]. Collectively, our annotators annotated 1909 KEs (1113-e, 306-n, 282-c, 208-opt-out) from 300 random samples (100-e, 100-n, 100-c) from the test set. Our annotation process took ~75 h of effort. We include more details in our supplementary.

4.2   Baselines

Because we are the first to tackle the fine-grained visual entailment task, there are no standard baselines for this task. We thus formulate two baselines in order to benchmark our method's performance. VE→KE is a standard sample-level visual entailment model which takes as input the visual features and the hypothesis. We replicate the model's sample-level prediction for every KE. VE+AMR→KE is similar to the previous model but also takes as input the linearized AMR of the hypothesis. At test time, we make a prediction for each KE separately by feeding the AMR corresponding to each KE into the model.

4.3   Quantitative Results

We experimentally compare several variants of our method with the baselines described above. Ours is our full method described in Sect. 3. We also include an ablation of our method showing the performance of our method without our structural constraints (w/o $\mathcal{L}_{STRUC}$) and without our KE-specific region retrieval technique (w/o Region Retrieval). The latter can be directly applied on top of encoders not based on object features as well. Finally, we show a version of our method (Ours+CLS) that predicts all KEs as entailed when the sample-level is predicted entailed. Otherwise, it uses our KE-specific classifier.

KE-Level Performance. In Table 1 we show the performance of each method on our KE-level annotations. The first group of results shows the accuracy for each ground truth KE class (here equivalent to recall). VE→KE achieves strong performance for KEs labeled neutral and particularly contradiction. This is because contradiction KEs only appear in contradiction samples, while neutral and entailment KEs can appear in multiple categories. However, we observed that relatively few neutral KEs appear in the contradiction category, because hypotheses usually mention untrue facts (contradiction) about something truly in the image (entailment). Thus, baseline performance is also strong for the neutral category. We note that the KE classes are unbalanced by nature of our task and we seek to locate the entailment KEs in neutral and contradiction samples. To this end, our method substantially outperforms both baselines for entailment KEs which can appear in any type of sample and are thus by far the most frequent. The baseline's apparent strength is because the first group of columns don't account for the *precision* of each KE category. In our supplementary, we show that our predictions much more closely align with the ground truth KE distribution for each sample type. This performance is reflected in the node, tuple, and overall accuracies on which our method performs best.

The second group of results shows accuracies across different types of KEs. We note our method performs better on nodes than tuples. This is unsurprising because nodes represent simpler statements about the presence of objects or actions, while tuples make more complex, composite statements about nodes and are thus harder to verify for the model. While VE+AMR→KE outperforms VE→KE overall and for most metrics, their predictions are highly similar for most samples and it is significantly outperformed by our method overall.

We next measure the number of structural violations. We consider each parent-child KE relationship a separate instance and calculate the accuracy of each method at producing semantically consistent predictions across parent-child relationships. We note that while VE→KE has no structural violations (because all KEs are predicted as the sample label), it makes no fine-grained predictions. Of the methods that make such predictions, our method performs best.

Finally, we measure the performance of our ablated method and our method's variants. Without $\mathcal{L}_{STRUC}$ our method achieves the lowest overall performance of

Table 2. We show the sample-level accuracy of each method across different metrics. The best method for each metric is shown in bold and the second best is underlined.

Method	Acc_{CLS}	$\text{Acc}_{\text{KE}\rightarrow\text{CLS}}$	$\text{Acc}_{\text{CLS}}^{\text{Relab.}}$	$\text{Acc}_{\text{KE}\rightarrow\text{CLS}}^{\text{Relab.}}$	$\text{Acc}_{\text{Best}}^{\text{Relab.}}$
VE $\rightarrow$ KE	**80.37**	-	**79.73**	-	79.73
VE+AMR $\rightarrow$ KE	-	**79.15**	-	<u>80.06</u>	<u>80.06</u>
w/o $\mathcal{L}_{\text{STRUC}}$	79.78	75.17	<u>79.40</u>	79.73	79.73
w/o Region Retrieval	79.58	75.21	<u>79.40</u>	<u>80.06</u>	<u>80.06</u>
Ours	<u>79.99</u>	76.26	78.73	**80.73**	**80.73**
Ours+CLS	<u>79.99</u>	<u>77.70</u>	78.73	77.74	78.73

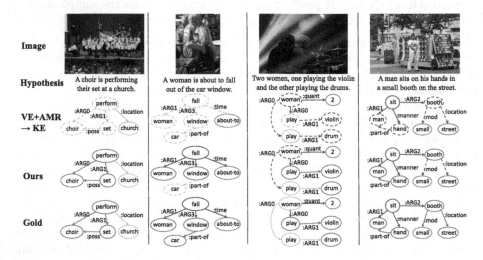

Fig. 5. Qualitative results showing our KE-level predictions on AMR graphs compared to the baseline. Nodes and edges (representing tuples) are colored based on their predicted label (ent, neu, con, opt-out). Wrong predictions are denoted by dashed lines. (Color figure online)

our method, indicating that the structural constraints work synergistically with our MIL constraints to further disambiguate the KE-level labels. We further note that without $\mathcal{L}_{\text{STRUC}}$ our model has a high rate ($\sim$30%) of structural violations within the graph. We next show that aggregating visual features into our model's contextual embedding is important. Without region retrieval our model's accuracy drops by (-3.45% acc) because our KE's embeddings lack relevant visual context (especially for nodes). Finally, we observe that ignoring our KE-level predictions for sample's predicted entailment and predicting all KEs as entailed (Ours+CLS) slightly improves performance ($+0.11\%$ acc).

Sample-Level Performance. Though not our focus, we also include the performance of sample-level label prediction in Table 2. The left side shows the performance on the labels given by the MTurkers in [24], while the right shows

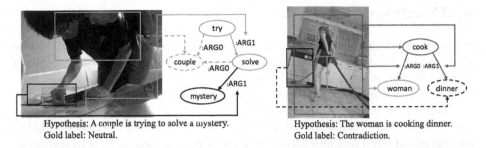

Hypothesis: A couple is trying to solve a mystery.
Gold label: Neutral.

Hypothesis: The woman is cooking dinner.
Gold label: Contradiction.

Fig. 6. We show the image region our model selects for each KE prediction. KEs are colored based on their predicted label. Wrong predictions are denoted by dashed lines. (Color figure online)

the performance on the sample labels in our expertly annotated set (Relab.). We explore two ways of predicting the sample label. The first uses the CLS token, while the second uses the logical rules defined in Sect. 3.5 to produce the sample label from the predicted KE labels. We observe a slight drop (0.38%) in the sample-level label for our method on the crowdsourced labels. Aside from label noise, one possible reason is that the model pays less attention to the sample-level task and focuses on the KE-level task (see ablation on loss weightings in our supplementary). We show that on our set of expertly annotated samples, producing the sample-level label using our KE predictions outperforms all baselines.

4.4 Qualitative Results

In this section, we present qualitative results showcasing our method's KE-level predictions. We also illustrate the visual region our method selects for each KE.

KE-Level Prediction Results. In Fig. 5, we show KE-level prediction results. We observe that the baseline often predicts many KEs the same label. In contrast, our model's predictions are more diverse and reasonable. In the first column, our model correctly concludes the location can't be determined and marks "church" neutral. In the next column, our model struggles to detect a car in the image so incorrectly marks "car" as neutral, but correctly infers that "fall" is contradictory. In the rightmost column, our model "incorrectly" says the booth is not small, but this is subjective. Similarly, our model says the booth is not located on the street, which is feasible because the booth is on the sidewalk.

Region Selection Results. In Fig. 6 we show the image regions selected by our model for each KE. We observe relevant KE→image localization results. For example, on the left we observe that "(try, :ARG1, solve)" retrieves the puzzle being assembled and "couple" retrieves the two people. On the right, the model selects the upper body of the woman for "woman" and a large region of the image to conclude the action "cook" is incorrect.

5   Conclusion

We introduced the novel problem of fine-grained visual entailment where the goal is to predict the logical relationship of knowledge elements extracted from a piece of text with an image. We proposed a model for this task which fuses relevant visual features with the representation of each knowledge element. Because of a lack of fine-grained annotations, we proposed novel multi-instance learning losses to transfer sample-level supervision to the knowledge element-level. We also proposed novel semantic structure preserving constraints. Experiments conducted on a new benchmark show that our approach significantly outperforms relevant baselines, and more importantly, produces interpretable predictions.

There are several possible directions for future work. For example, pretraining encoders with human-created AMR inputs [4,22] may better prepare encoders for our task. While we use object labels in our work, object attributes are also potentially helpful for predicting KEs that involves attributes [56]. Finally, region retrieval [2,27,53] and graph networks [46] may also be exploited.

Acknowledgements. This research is based upon work supported by DARPA SemaFor Program No. HR001120C0123. The views and conclusions contained herein are those of the authors and should not be interpreted as necessarily representing the official policies, either expressed or implied, of DARPA, or the U.S. Government. The U.S. Government is authorized to reproduce and distribute reprints for governmental purposes notwithstanding any copyright annotation.

References

1. Antol, S., et al.: VQA: visual question answering. In: Proceedings of the IEEE International Conference on Computer Vision, pp. 2425–2433 (2015)
2. Babar, S., Das, S.: Where to look?: mining complementary image regions for weakly supervised object localization. In: Proceedings of the IEEE/CVF Winter Conference on Applications of Computer Vision, pp. 1010–1019 (2021)
3. Banarescu, L., et al.: Abstract meaning representation for sembanking. In: Proceedings of the 7th Linguistic Annotation Workshop and Interoperability with Discourse, pp. 178–186 (2013)
4. Bevilacqua, M., Blloshmi, R., Navigli, R.: One SPRING to rule them both: symmetric AMR semantic parsing and generation without a complex pipeline. In: Proceedings of AAAI (2021)
5. Bonial, C., et al.: Abstract meaning representation of constructions: the more we include, the better the representation. In: Proceedings of the Eleventh International Conference on Language Resources and Evaluation (LREC 2018) (2018)
6. Bowman, S., Angeli, G., Potts, C., Manning, C.D.: A large annotated corpus for learning natural language inference. In: Proceedings of the 2015 Conference on Empirical Methods in Natural Language Processing, pp. 632–642 (2015)
7. Camburu, O.M., Rocktäschel, T., Lukasiewicz, T., Blunsom, P.: e-SNLI: natural language inference with natural language explanations. In: Advances in Neural Information Processing Systems, vol. 31 (2018)

8. Chefer, H., Gur, S., Wolf, L.: Generic attention-model explainability for interpreting bi-modal and encoder-decoder transformers. In: Proceedings of the IEEE/CVF International Conference on Computer Vision, pp. 397–406 (2021)

9. Chefer, H., Gur, S., Wolf, L.: Transformer interpretability beyond attention visualization. In: Proceedings of the IEEE/CVF Conference on Computer Vision and Pattern Recognition, pp. 782–791 (2021)

10. Chen, B., et al.: Joint multimedia event extraction from video and article. In: Findings of the Association for Computational Linguistics: EMNLP 2021, pp. 74–88 (2021)

11. Chen, J., Kong, Y.: Explainable video entailment with grounded visual evidence. In: Proceedings of the IEEE/CVF International Conference on Computer Vision (2021)

12. Chen, Y.-C., et al.: UNITER: UNiversal Image-TExt representation learning. In: Vedaldi, A., Bischof, H., Brox, T., Frahm, J.-M. (eds.) ECCV 2020. LNCS, vol. 12375, pp. 104–120. Springer, Cham (2020). https://doi.org/10.1007/978-3-030-58577-8_7

13. Dagan, I., Glickman, O., Magnini, B.: The PASCAL recognising textual entailment challenge. In: Quiñonero-Candela, J., Dagan, I., Magnini, B., d'Alché-Buc, F. (eds.) MLCW 2005. LNCS (LNAI), vol. 3944, pp. 177–190. Springer, Heidelberg (2006). https://doi.org/10.1007/11736790_9

14. Das, A., et al.: Visual dialog. In: Proceedings of the IEEE Conference on Computer Vision and Pattern Recognition (CVPR) (2017)

15. Das, A., Kottur, S., Moura, J.M., Lee, S., Batra, D.: Learning cooperative visual dialog agents with deep reinforcement learning. In: Proceedings of the IEEE International Conference on Computer Vision, pp. 2951–2960 (2017)

16. Dietterich, T.G., Lathrop, R.H., Lozano-Pérez, T.: Solving the multiple instance problem with axis-parallel rectangles. Artif. Intell. **89**(1–2), 31–71 (1997)

17. Dong, B., Huang, Z., Guo, Y., Wang, Q., Niu, Z., Zuo, W.: Boosting weakly supervised object detection via learning bounding box adjusters. In: Proceedings of the IEEE/CVF International Conference on Computer Vision, pp. 2876–2885 (2021)

18. Fukui, H., Hirakawa, T., Yamashita, T., Fujiyoshi, H.: Attention branch network: learning of attention mechanism for visual explanation. In: Proceedings of the IEEE/CVF Conference on Computer Vision and Pattern Recognition, pp. 10705–10714 (2019)

19. Fung, Y., et al.: InfoSurgeon: cross-media fine-grained information consistency checking for fake news detection. In: Proceedings of the 59th Annual Meeting of the Association for Computational Linguistics and the 11th International Joint Conference on Natural Language Processing (Volume 1: Long Papers), pp. 1683–1698 (2021)

20. Gokhale, T., Banerjee, P., Baral, C., Yang, Y.: VQA-LOL: visual question answering under the lens of logic. In: Vedaldi, A., Bischof, H., Brox, T., Frahm, J.-M. (eds.) ECCV 2020. LNCS, vol. 12366, pp. 379–396. Springer, Cham (2020). https://doi.org/10.1007/978-3-030-58589-1_23

21. Goodman, M.W.: Penman: an open-source library and tool for AMR graphs. In: Proceedings of the 58th Annual Meeting of the Association for Computational Linguistics: System Demonstrations, pp. 312–319 (2020)

22. Hinton, G., Vinyals, O., Dean, J., et al.: Distilling the knowledge in a neural network. arXiv preprint arXiv:1503.02531, vol. 2, no. 7 (2015)

23. Huang, Z., Zeng, Z., Huang, Y., Liu, B., Fu, D., Fu, J.: Seeing out of the box: end-to-end pre-training for vision-language representation learning. In: Proceedings

of the IEEE/CVF Conference on Computer Vision and Pattern Recognition, pp. 12976–12985 (2021)

24. Kayser, M., et al.: e-ViL: a dataset and benchmark for natural language explanations in vision-language tasks. In: Proceedings of the IEEE/CVF International Conference on Computer Vision, pp. 1244–1254 (2021)

25. Knight, K., et al.: Abstract meaning representation (AMR) annotation release 3.0 (2020). https://catalog.ldc.upenn.edu/LDC2020T02

26. Kong, C., Lin, D., Bansal, M., Urtasun, R., Fidler, S.: What are you talking about? Text-to-image coreference. In: Proceedings of the IEEE Conference on Computer Vision and Pattern Recognition, pp. 3558–3565 (2014)

27. Kumar, V., Namboodiri, A., Jawahar, C.: Region pooling with adaptive feature fusion for end-to-end person recognition. In: Proceedings of the IEEE/CVF Winter Conference on Applications of Computer Vision, pp. 2133–2142 (2020)

28. Li, M., et al.: Cross-media structured common space for multimedia event extraction. In: Proceedings of the 58th Annual Meeting of the Association for Computational Linguistics, pp. 2557–2568 (2020)

29. Li, Y., Zeng, J., Shan, S., Chen, X.: Occlusion aware facial expression recognition using CNN with attention mechanism. IEEE Trans. Image Process. **28**(5), 2439–2450 (2018)

30. Liu, J., et al.: VIOLIN: a large-scale dataset for video-and-language inference. In: Proceedings of the IEEE/CVF Conference on Computer Vision and Pattern Recognition, pp. 10900–10910 (2020)

31. Lu, J., Goswami, V., Rohrbach, M., Parikh, D., Lee, S.: 12-in-1: multi-task vision and language representation learning. In: Proceedings of the IEEE/CVF Conference on Computer Vision and Pattern Recognition, pp. 10437–10446 (2020)

32. Luo, G., Darrell, T., Rohrbach, A.: NewsCLIPpings: automatic generation of out-of-context multimodal media. In: Proceedings of the 2021 Conference on Empirical Methods in Natural Language Processing, pp. 6801–6817 (2021)

33. Luo, Z., et al.: Weakly-supervised action localization with expectation-maximization multi-instance learning. In: Vedaldi, A., Bischof, H., Brox, T., Frahm, J.-M. (eds.) ECCV 2020. LNCS, vol. 12374, pp. 729–745. Springer, Cham (2020). https://doi.org/10.1007/978-3-030-58526-6_43

34. Marelli, M., Menini, S., Baroni, M., Bentivogli, L., Bernardi, R., Zamparelli, R.: A sick cure for the evaluation of compositional distributional semantic models. In: Proceedings of the Ninth International Conference on Language Resources and Evaluation (LREC 2014), pp. 216–223 (2014)

35. Matthiessen, C.M., Christian, M., Bateman, J.A., Matthiessen, M.: Text Generation and Systemic-Functional Linguistics: Experiences from English and Japanese. Burns & Oates (1991)

36. Palmer, M., Gildea, D., Kingsbury, P.: The proposition bank: an annotated corpus of semantic roles. Comput. Linguist. **31**(1), 71–106 (2005)

37. Paszke, A., et al.: Pytorch: an imperative style, high-performance deep learning library. In: Advances in Neural Information Processing Systems, vol. 32 (2019)

38. Plummer, B.A., Mallya, A., Cervantes, C.M., Hockenmaier, J., Lazebnik, S.: Phrase localization and visual relationship detection with comprehensive image-language cues. In: Proceedings of the IEEE International Conference on Computer Vision, pp. 1928–1937 (2017)

39. Rymarczyk, D., Borowa, A., Tabor, J., Zielinski, B.: Kernel self-attention for weakly-supervised image classification using deep multiple instance learning. In: Proceedings of the IEEE/CVF Winter Conference on Applications of Computer Vision, pp. 1721–1730 (2021)

40. Selvaraju, R.R., Cogswell, M., Das, A., Vedantam, R., Parikh, D., Batra, D.: Grad-CAM: visual explanations from deep networks via gradient-based localization. In: Proceedings of the IEEE International Conference on Computer Vision, pp. 618–626 (2017)
41. Sheng, S., et al.: Human-adversarial visual question answering. In: Advances in Neural Information Processing Systems, vol. 34 (2021)
42. Shi, J., Zhong, Y., Xu, N., Li, Y., Xu, C.: A simple baseline for weakly-supervised scene graph generation. In: Proceedings of the IEEE/CVF International Conference on Computer Vision, pp. 16393–16402 (2021)
43. Shrikumar, A., Greenside, P., Kundaje, A.: Learning important features through propagating activation differences. In: International Conference on Machine Learning, pp. 3145–3153. PMLR (2017)
44. Si, Q., Lin, Z., Zheng, M., Fu, P., Wang, W.: Check it again: progressive visual question answering via visual entailment. In: Proceedings of the 59th Annual Meeting of the Association for Computational Linguistics and the 11th International Joint Conference on Natural Language Processing (Volume 1: Long Papers), pp. 4101–4110 (2021)
45. Tkachenko, M., Malyuk, M., Shevchenko, N., Holmanyuk, A., Liubimov, N.: Label studio: data labeling software (2020–2021). https://github.com/heartexlabs/label-studio. Open source software. https://github.com/heartexlabs/label-studio
46. Veličković, P., Cucurull, G., Casanova, A., Romero, A., Liò, P., Bengio, Y.: Graph attention networks. In: International Conference on Learning Representations (2018)
47. Voita, E., Talbot, D., Moiseev, F., Sennrich, R., Titov, I.: Analyzing multi-head self-attention: specialized heads do the heavy lifting, the rest can be pruned. In: 57th Annual Meeting of the Association for Computational Linguistics, pp. 5797–5808. ACL Anthology (2019)
48. Wagner, J., Kohler, J.M., Gindele, T., Hetzel, L., Wiedemer, J.T., Behnke, S.: Interpretable and fine-grained visual explanations for convolutional neural networks. In: Proceedings of the IEEE/CVF Conference on Computer Vision and Pattern Recognition, pp. 9097–9107 (2019)
49. Wu, J., Yu, Y., Huang, C., Yu, K.: Deep multiple instance learning for image classification and auto-annotation. In: Proceedings of the IEEE Conference on Computer Vision and Pattern Recognition, pp. 3460–3469 (2015)
50. Xie, N., Lai, F., Doran, D., Kadav, A.: Visual entailment: a novel task for fine-grained image understanding. arXiv preprint arXiv:1901.06706 (2019)
51. Yang, H., Wu, H., Chen, H.: Detecting 11k classes: large scale object detection without fine-grained bounding boxes. In: Proceedings of the IEEE/CVF International Conference on Computer Vision, pp. 9805–9813 (2019)
52. Young, P., Lai, A., Hodosh, M., Hockenmaier, J.: From image descriptions to visual denotations: new similarity metrics for semantic inference over event descriptions. Trans. Assoc. Comput. Linguist. 2, 67–78 (2014)
53. Yuan, S., et al.: Weakly supervised cross-domain alignment with optimal transport. In: Proceedings of the British Machine Vision Conference (2020)
54. Yuan, T., et al.: Multiple instance active learning for object detection. In: Proceedings of the IEEE/CVF Conference on Computer Vision and Pattern Recognition, pp. 5330–5339 (2021)
55. Zellers, R., Bisk, Y., Farhadi, A., Choi, Y.: From recognition to cognition: visual commonsense reasoning. In: Proceedings of the IEEE/CVF Conference on Computer Vision and Pattern Recognition, pp. 6720–6731 (2019)

56. Zhang, P., et al.: VinVL: revisiting visual representations in vision-language models. In: Proceedings of the IEEE/CVF Conference on Computer Vision and Pattern Recognition, pp. 5579–5588 (2021)
57. Zhang, T., et al.: Improving event extraction via multimodal integration. In: Proceedings of the 25th ACM International Conference on Multimedia, pp. 270–278 (2017)
58. Zhou, B., Bau, D., Oliva, A., Torralba, A.: Interpreting deep visual representations via network dissection. IEEE Trans. Pattern Anal. Mach. Intell. **41**(9), 2131–2145 (2018)
59. Zhou, Y., Sun, X., Liu, D., Zha, Z., Zeng, W.: Adaptive pooling in multi-instance learning for web video annotation. In: Proceedings of the IEEE International Conference on Computer Vision Workshops, pp. 318–327 (2017)
60. Zunino, A., et al.: Explainable deep classification models for domain generalization. In: Proceedings of the IEEE/CVF Conference on Computer Vision and Pattern Recognition, pp. 3233–3242 (2021)

Bottom Up Top Down Detection Transformers for Language Grounding in Images and Point Clouds

Ayush Jain[1(✉)], Nikolaos Gkanatsios[1], Ishita Mediratta[2], and Katerina Fragkiadaki[1]

[1] Carnegie Mellon University, Pittsburgh, USA
ayushj2@andrew.cmu.edu
[2] Meta AI, New York, USA

Abstract. Most models tasked to ground referential utterances in 2D and 3D scenes learn to select the referred object from a pool of object proposals provided by a pre-trained detector. This is limiting because an utterance may refer to visual entities at various levels of granularity, such as the chair, the leg of the chair, or the tip of the front leg of the chair, which may be missed by the detector. We propose a language grounding model that attends on the referential utterance and on the object proposal pool computed from a pre-trained detector to decode referenced objects with a detection head, without selecting them from the pool. In this way, it is helped by powerful pre-trained object detectors without being restricted by their misses. We call our model Bottom Up Top Down DEtection TRansformers (BUTD-DETR) because it uses both language guidance (top down) and objectness guidance (bottom-up) to ground referential utterances in images and point clouds. Moreover, BUTD-DETR casts object detection as referential grounding and uses object labels as language prompts to be grounded in the visual scene, augmenting supervision for the referential grounding task in this way. The proposed model sets a new state-of-the-art across popular 3D language grounding benchmarks with significant performance gains over previous 3D approaches (12.6% on SR3D, 11.6% on NR3D and 6.3% on ScanRefer). When applied in 2D images, it performs on par with the previous state of the art. We ablate the design choices of our model and quantify their contribution to performance. Our code and checkpoints can be found at the project website https://butd-detr.github.io.

1 Introduction

Language-directed attention helps us localize objects that our "bottom-up", task-agnostic perception may miss. Consider Fig. 1. The utterance *"bottle on top*

A. Jain and N. Gkanatsios—Equal contribution, order decided by `np.random.rand`.
I. Mediratta—Work done during an internship at CMU.

Supplementary Information The online version contains supplementary material available at https://doi.org/10.1007/978-3-031-20059-5_24.

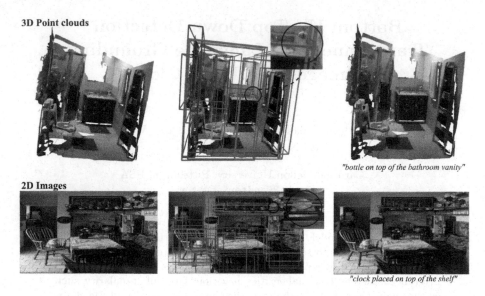

Fig. 1. Language-modulated 3D (*top*) and 2D (*bottom*) detection with BUTD-DETR. *Middle:* State-of-the-art object detectors often fail to localize small, occluded or rare objects (here they miss the clock on the shelf and the bottle on the cabinet). *Right:* Language-driven and objectness-driven attention in BUTD-DETR modulates the visual processing depending on the referential expression while taking into account salient, bottom-up detected objects, and correctly localizes all referenced objects.

of the bathroom vanity" suffices to direct our attention to the reference object, even though it is far from salient. Language-directed perception adapts the visual processing of the input scene according to the utterance. Object detectors instead apply the same computation in each scene, which can miss task-relevant objects.

Most existing language grounding models use object proposal bottlenecks: they select the referenced object from a pool of object proposals provided by the pre-trained object detector [9,11,17,20,22]. This means they cannot recover objects or parts that a bottom-up detector misses. This is limiting since small, occluded, or rare objects are hard to detect without task-driven guidance. For example, in Fig. 1 middle, state-of-the-art 2D [39] and 3D [30] detectors miss the clock on the shelf and the bottle on the bathroom vanity, respectively.

Recently, Kamath et al. [21] introduced MDETR, a language grounding model for 2D images that decodes object boxes using a DETR [3] detection head and aligns them to the relevant spans in the input utterance, it does not select the answer from a box proposal pool. The visual computation is modulated based on the input utterance through several layers of self-attention on a concatenation of language and visual features. MDETR achieves big leaps in performance in 2D language grounding over previous box-bottlenecked methods.

We propose a model for grounding referential utterances in 3D and 2D visual scenes that builds upon MDETR, which we call <u>BUTD</u>-DETR (pronounced

Beauty-DETR), as it uses both box proposals, obtained by a pre-trained detector "bottom-up" and "top-down" guidance from the language utterance, to localize the relevant objects in the scene. BUTD-DETR uses box proposals obtained by a pre-trained detector as an additional input stream to attend on; however, it is not box-bottlenecked and still decodes objects with a detection head, instead of selecting them from the input box stream. Current object detectors provide a noisy tokenization of the input visual scene that, as our experiments show, is a useful cue to attend on for multimodal reasoning. Second, BUTD-DETR augments grounding annotations by configuring annotations for object detection as detection prompts to be grounded in visual scenes. A detection prompt is a list of object category labels, e.g., *"Chair. Door. Person. Bed."*. We train the model to ground detection prompts by localizing the labels that are present in the image and learn to discard labels that are mentioned but do not correspond to any objects in the scene. Third, BUTD-DETR considers improved bounding box - word span alignment losses that reduce noise during alignment of object boxes to noun phrases in the referential utterance.

We test BUTD-DETR on the 3D benchmarks of [2,4] and 2D benchmarks of [23,47]. In 3D point clouds, we set new state-of-the-art in the two benchmarks of Referit3D [2] and ScanRefer [4] and report significant performance boosts over all prior methods (12.6% on SR3D, 11.6% on NR3D and 6.3% on ScanRefer), as well as over a direct MDETR-3D implementation of ours that does not use a box proposal stream or detection prompts during training. In 2D images, our model obtains competitive performance with MDETR on RefCOCO, RefCOCO+ and Flickr30k, and requires less than half of the GPU training time due to the cheaper deformable attention in the visual stream. We ablate each of the design choices of the model to quantify their contribution to performance.

In summary, our contributions are: **(i)** A model with SOTA performance across both 2D and 3D scenes with minor changes showing that modulated detection in 2D images can also work in 3D point clouds with appropriate visual encoder and decoder modifications. **(ii)** Augmenting supervision with detection prompts, attention on an additional input box stream and improved bounding box - word span alignment losses. **(iii)** Extensive ablations to quantify the contribution of different components of our model. We make our code publicly available at https://butd-detr.github.io.

2   Related Work

Object Detection with Transformers. Object detectors are trained to localize all instances of a closed set of object category labels in images and 3D point-clouds. While earlier architectures pool features within proposed boxes to decode objects and classify them into categories [14,28,38], recent methods pioneered by DETR [3] use transformer architectures where a set of object query vectors attend to the scene and among themselves to decode object boxes and their labels. DETR suffers from the quadratic cost of within image features self attention. D(eformable)-DETR [50] proposes deformable attention, a locally adaptive kernel that is predicted directly in each pixel location without attention to other pixel locations, thus saving the quadratic cost of pixel-to-pixel attention. Our model builds upon deformable attention for feature extraction from RGB images. [30,34] extend detection transformers to 3D point cloud input.

2D Referential Language Grounding. Referential language grounding [23] is the task of localizing the object(s) referenced in a language utterance. Most 2D language grounding models obtain sets of object proposals using pre-trained object detectors and the original image is discarded upon extraction of the object proposals [9,11,17,20,22]. Many of these approaches use multiple layers of attention to fuse information across both, the extracted boxes and language utterance [6,31,46]. Recently, a few approaches directly regress the target bounding box without using pre-trained object proposals. In [5] language and visual features cross-attend and are concatenated to predict the box of the referential object. Yang et al. [45] extends the YOLO detector [38] to referential grounding by channel-wise concatenating language, visual and spatial feature maps and then regressing a single box using the YOLO box prediction head. [42] performs a fusion similar to [45], then selects a single box from a set of anchor boxes and predicts a deformation of it, much like the Faster-RCNN object detector [39]. While previous approaches encode the whole text input into a single feature vector, [44] further improves performance by recursively attending on different parts of the referential utterance. Lastly, [8] encodes the image and utterance with within- and cross-modality transformers, and a special learnable token regresses a single box. In contrast to our method, all these works predict a single bounding box per image-utterance pair. Our work builds upon MDETR of Kamath et al. [21] that modulates visual processing through attention to the input language utterance and decodes objects from queries similar to DETR, without selecting from a pool of proposals. Both our method and MDETR can predict multiple instances being referred to, as well as ground intermediate noun phrases. Concurrent to our work, GLIP [26] shows that adding supervision from detection annotations can improve 2D referential grounding. Our work independently confirms this hypothesis in 2D and also shows its applicability on the 3D domain.

3D Referential Language Grounding has only recently gained popularity [2,4]. To the best of our knowledge, all related approaches are box-bottlenecked: they extract 3D object proposals and select one as their answer. Their pipeline can be decomposed into three main steps: i) Representation of object boxes as point features [46], segmentation masks [48] or pure spatial/categorical features [41]. ii) Encoding of language utterance using word embeddings [41,46] and/or scene graphs [10]. iii) Fusion of the two modalities and scoring of each proposal using graph networks [18] or Transformers [46]. Most of these works also employ domain-specific design choices by explicitly encoding pairwise relationships [13, 18,48] or by relying on heuristics, such as restricting attention to be local [48,49] and ignoring input modalities [41]. Such design prevents those architectures from being applicable to both the 3D and 2D domains simultaneously.

Due to the inferior performance of 3D object detectors in comparison to their 2D counterparts, popular benchmarks for 3D language grounding, such as Referit3D [2] provide access to ground-truth object boxes at test time. The proposed BUTD-DETR is the first 3D language grounding model that is evaluated on this benchmark without access to oracle 3D object boxes.

3   Method

We first describe MDETR [21] in Sect. 3.1. Then, we present BUTD-DETR's architecture in Sect. 3.2, supervision augmentation with detection prompts in Sect. 3.3 and its training objectives in Sect. 3.4.

3.1   Background: MDETR

MDETR is a 2D language grounding model that takes a referential utterance and an RGB image as input and localises in the image all objects mentioned in the utterance. MDETR encodes the image with a convolutional network [15] and the language utterance with a RoBERTa encoder [29]. It then fuses information across the language and visual features through multiple layers of self-attention on the concatenated visual and language feature sequences. In MDETR's decoder, a set of query vectors iteratively attend to the contextualized visual features and self-attend to one another, similar to the DETR's [3] decoder. Finally, each query decodes a bounding box and a confidence score over each word in the input utterance, which associates the box to a text span.

The predicted boxes are assigned to ground-truth ones using a Hungarian matching, similar to [3]. Upon matching, the following losses are computed:

- A bounding box loss between predicted boxes and the corresponding ground-truth ones. This is a combination of L1 and generalized IoU [40] losses.
- A soft token prediction loss. A query matched to a ground-truth box is trained to decode a uniform distribution over the language token positions that refer to that object. Queries not matched to ground-truth targets are trained to predict a no-object label.
- Two contrastive losses between query and language token features. The first one, called *object contrastive loss*, pulls an object query's features closer to the features of the corresponding ground-truth span's word tokens, and further than all other tokens. The second one, called *token contrastive loss*, pulls the features of a ground-truth span's token closer to the corresponding object query features, and further than all other queries.

3.2   Bottom-Up Top-Down DETR (BUTD-DETR)

The architecture of BUTD-DETR is illustrated in Fig. 2. Given a referential language utterance, e.g., "find the plant that is on top of the end table" and a visual scene, which can be a 3D point cloud or a 2D image, BUTD-DETR

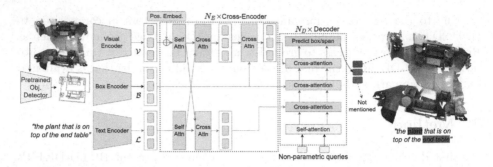

Fig. 2. BUTD-DETR architecture. Given a visual scene and a referential utterance, the model localizes all object instances mentioned in the utterance. A pre-trained object detector extracts object box proposals. The visual scene features, the language utterance and the labelled box proposals are encoded into corresponding sequences of visual, word and box tokens using visual, language and box encoders, respectively. The three streams cross-attend and finally decode boxes and corresponding spans in the language utterance that each decoded box refers to. We visualize here the model operating on a 3D point cloud; an analogous architecture is used for 2D image grounding.

is trained to localize all objects mentioned in the utterance. In the previous example, we expect one box for the "plant" and one for the "end table". The model attends across image/point cloud, language and box proposal streams, then decodes the relevant objects and aligns them to input language spans.

Within-Modality Encoder. In 2D, we encode an RGB image using a pre-trained ResNet101 backbone [16]. The 2D appearance visual features are added to 2D Fourier positional encodings, same as in [19,50]. In 3D, we encode a 3D point cloud using a PointNet++ backbone [37]. The 3D point visual features are added to learnable 3D positional encodings, same as in [30]: we pass the coordinates of the points through a small multilayer perceptron (MLP). Let $\mathcal{V} \in \mathbb{R}^{n_v \times c_v}$ denote the visual token sequence, where n_v is the number of visual tokens and c_v is the number of visual feature channels.

The words of the input utterance are encoded using a pre-trained RoBERTa [29] backbone. Let $\mathcal{L} \in \mathbb{R}^{n_\ell \times c_\ell}$ denote the word token sequence.

A pre-trained detector is used to obtain 2D or 3D object box proposals. Following prior literature, we use Faster-RCNN [39] for RGB images, pre-trained on 1601 object categories of Visual Genome [24], and Group-Free detector [30] for 3D point clouds pre-trained on a vocabulary of 485 object categories on ScanNet [7]. The detected box proposals that surpass a confidence threshold are encoded using a box proposal encoder, by mapping their spatial coordinates and categorical class information to an embedding vector each, and concatenating them to form an object proposal token. We use a pre-trained and frozen RoBERTa [29] backbone to encode the semantic categories of proposed boxes. Let $\mathcal{O} \in \mathbb{R}^{n_o \times c_o}$ denote the object token sequence.

The 3D detector is trained on ScanNet and all 3D benchmarks we use are also ScanNet-based. This creates a discrepancy in the quality of the detector's predictions between train and test time, as it is far more accurate on the training set. As a result, we find that BUTD-DETR tends to rely on the detector at training time and generalizes less at test time, where the detector's predictions are much noisier. To mitigate this, we randomly replace 30% of the detected boxes at training time with random ones. This augmentation leads to stronger generalization when the detector fails to locate the target object. Note that this is not the case in 2D, where the detector is trained on a different dataset.

All visual, word and box proposal tokens are mapped using (different per modality) MLPs to same-length feature vectors.

Cross-Modality Encoder. The visual, language and box proposals, interact through a sequence of N_E cross-attention layers. In each encoding layer, visual and language tokens cross-attend to one another and are updated using standard key-value attention. Then, the resulting language-conditioned visual tokens attend to the box proposal tokens. We use standard attention for both streams in 3D and deformable attention [50] for the visual stream in 2D.

In contrast to MDETR, BUTD-DETR keeps visual, language and box stream separate in the encoder instead of concatenating them. This enables us to employ deformable attention [50] in self and cross attention layers involving the visual stream in 2D domain. Deformable attention involves computing bilinearly interpolated features which is expensive and non-robust in discontinuous and sparse modalities like pointclouds, hence we use vanilla attention in 3D (for more details see supplementary). In our experiments, we show that concatenation versus keeping separate streams performs similarly in 3D referential grounding.

Decoder. BUTD-DETR decodes objects from contextualized features using non-parametric queries in both 2D and 3D, similar to [30,50]. Non-parametric queries are predicted by visual tokens from the current scene, in contrast to parametric queries used in DETR [3] and MDETR [21] that correspond to a learned set of vectors shared across all scenes. Specifically, the contextualized visual tokens from the last multi-modality encoding layer predict confidence scores, one per visual token. The top-K highest scoring tokens are each fed into an MLP to predict a vector which stands for an *object query*, i.e., a vector that will decode a box center and size relative to the location of the corresponding visual token, similar to D-DETR [50]. The query vectors are updated in a residual manner through N_D decoder layers. In each decoder layer, we employ four types of attention operations. First, the queries self-attend to one another to contextually refine their estimates. Second, they attend to the contextualized word embeddings to condition on the language utterance. Next, they attend to the box proposal tokens and then in the image or point visual tokens. At the end of each decoding layer, there is a prediction head that predicts a box center displacement, height and width vector, and a token span for each object query

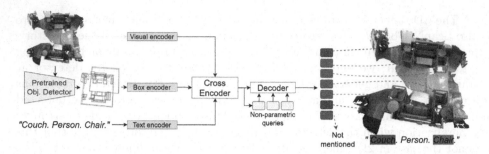

Fig. 3. Augmenting referential grounding supervision with detection prompts. A detection prompt is constructed by sequencing sampled object category labels (here *couch, person* and *chair*). The task is to localize all instances of mentioned objects and associate them with the correct span in the prompt. 50% of the sampled labels are negative, i.e., they have no corresponding object instance in the scene. The model learns not to associate these spans with predicted boxes.

that localizes the corresponding object box and aligns it with the language input. We refer the reader to our supplementary file for more implementation details.

3.3 Augmenting Supervision with Detection Prompts

Object detection is an instance of referential language grounding in which the utterance is a single word, namely, the object category label. Language grounding models have effectively combined supervision across referential grounding, caption description and question answering tasks [31,32], which is an important factor for their success. Object detection annotations have not been considered so far as candidates for such co-training.

We cast object detection as grounding of detection prompts, namely, referential utterances comprised of a list of object category labels, as shown in Fig. 3. Specifically, given the detector's vocabulary of object category labels, we randomly sample a fixed number of them—some appear in the visual scene and some do not—and generate synthetic utterances by sequencing the sampled labels, e.g., *"Couch. Person. Chair. Fridge."*, we call them detection prompts. We treat these prompts as referential utterances to be grounded: the task is to localize *all* object instances of the category labels mentioned in the prompt if they appear in the scene. The sampling of negative category labels (labels for which there are no object instances present) operates as negative training: the model is trained to not match any boxes to the negative category labels. Further details on this negative training can be found in the supplementary.

3.4 Supervision Objectives

We supervise the outputs of all prediction heads in each layer of the decoder. We follow MDETR [21] in using Hungarian matching to assign a subset of object queries to the ground-truth object boxes and then compute the bounding box, soft token prediction and contrastive losses. Our bounding box and soft token prediction losses are identical to MDETR's. However, we notice that MDETR's contrastive losses do not compare all object queries and word tokens symmetrically. Specifically, the object contrastive loss supervises only the object queries that are matched to a ground-truth object box. On the other hand, the token contrastive loss includes only the tokens that belong to positive spans, namely, noun phrases with corresponding object instances in the scene. As a result, object queries not matched to any ground-truth object box are not pulled far from non-ground-truth text spans, which means at inference object queries can be close to negative spans. We find this asymmetry to hurt performance, as we show in our experiments.

To address this, we propose a symmetric alternative where the similarities between all object queries and language tokens are considered. We append the span "not-mentioned" to all input utterances. This acts as the ground-truth text span for all object queries that are not assigned to any of the ground-truth objects. The object contrastive loss now supervises all queries and considers the similarities with all tokens. We empirically find that gathering unmatched queries to "not mentioned" is beneficial. This is similar in principle to the soft token prediction loss, where unmatched queries have to predict "no object". In fact, we find that this symmetric contrastive loss is sufficient for our model's supervision, but we observe that co-optimizing for soft token prediction results in faster convergence.

4   Experiments

We test BUTD-DETR on grounding referential utterances in 3D point clouds and 2D images. Our experiments aim to answer the following questions:

1. How does BUTD-DETR perform compared to the state-of-the-art in 3D and 2D language grounding?
2. How does BUTD-DETR perform compared to a straightforward extension of the 2D state-of-the-art MDETR [21] model in 3D?
3. How much, if at all, attending to a bottom-up box proposal stream helps performance?
4. How much, if at all, co-training for grounding detection prompts helps performance?
5. How much, if at all, the proposed contrastive loss variant helps performance?

4.1   Language Grounding in 3D Point Clouds

We test BUTD-DETR on SR3D, NR3D [2] and ScanRefer [4] benchmarks. All three benchmarks contain pairs of 3D point clouds of indoor scenes from Scan-Net [7] and corresponding referential utterances, and the task is to localize the objects referenced in the utterance. The utterances in SR3D are short and synthetic, e.g., *"choose the couch that is underneath the picture"*, while utterances in NR3D and ScanRefer are longer and more natural, e.g. *"from the set of chairs against the wall, the chair farthest from the red wall, in the group of chairs that is closer to the red wall"*. For fair comparison against previous methods, we train BUTD-DETR separately on each of SR3D, NR3D and ScanRefer. We augment supervision in each of the three datasets with ScanNet detection prompts. SR3D provides annotations for all objects mentioned in the utterance, so during training we supervise localization of all objects mentioned. In NR3D and ScanRefer, we use supervision for grounding only the referenced object.

All existing models that have been tested in SR3D or NR3D benchmarks are box-bottlenecked, namely, they are trained to select the answer from a pool of box proposals. They all use **ground-truth 3D object boxes (without category labels)** as the set of boxes to select from. We thus consider two evaluation setups:

1. **det**: where we re-train previous models using their publicly available code and provide the same 3D box proposals we use in BUTD-DETR, obtained by the Group-Free 3D object detector [30] trained to detect 485 object categories in ScanNet (Section **det** in Table 1).
2. **GT**, where we use ground-truth 3D object boxes for our model and baseline (Section **GT** in Table 1).

Alongside previous models, we also compare our model against our implementation of the MDETR model in 3D. This is similar to our model but without attention on a box stream, without co-training with detection prompts and with the original contrastive losses proposed by MDETR. We also replace MDETR's parametric object queries with non-parametric one—similar to our model—since they have been shown to be crucial for good performance in 3D [30,34]. We call this model MDETR-3D. For the sake of completeness, we do have a 3D version of MDETR that uses parametric queries in Table 2 and, as expected, it is significantly worse. MDETR does not use a pool of box proposals in any way and hence we cannot report results of MDETR-3D under GT.

We show quantitative results of our models against previous works in Table 1. We use top-1 accuracy metric, which measures the percentage of times we can find the target box with an IoU higher than the threshold. We report results with IoU@0.25 on SR3D and NR3D; and with both IoU@0.25 and IoU@0.5 on ScanRefer. Please refer to supplementary for more detailed results.

BUTD-DETR outperforms existing approaches as well as MDETR-3D by a large margin under both evaluation setups, **det** and **GT**. It also outperforms the recent SAT-2D [46] that uses additional 2D RGB image features during training. BUTD-DETR does not use 2D image features, but it can be easily extended to do so. We show qualitative results in Fig. 4. For more qualitative results, please check the supplementary file.

Ablative Analysis. We ablate all our design choices for 3D BUTD-DETR on SR3D benchmark [2] in Table 2. We compare BUTD-DETR against the following variants:

Table 1. Results on language grounding in 3D point clouds. We evaluate top-1 accuracy using ground-truth (**GT**) or detected (**det**) boxes. * denotes method uses extra 2D image features. † denotes evaluation with detected boxes using the authors' code and checkpoints. ‡ denotes re-training using the authors' code. For [49], we compare against their 3D-only version.

Method	SR3D		NR3D	ScanRefer (Val. Set)	
	Acc@0.25(det)	Acc.(GT)	Acc@0.25(det)	Acc@0.25(det)	Acc@0 5(det)
ReferIt3DNet [2]	27.7†	39.8	24.0†	26.4	16.9
ScanRefer [4]	-	-	-	35.5	22.4
TGNN [18]	-	45.0	-	37.4	29.7
3DRefTransformer [1]	-	47.0	-	-	-
InstanceRefer [48]	31.5‡	48.0	29.9‡	40.2	32.9
FFL-3DOG [10]	-	-	-	41.3	34.0
LanguageRefer [41]	39.5†	56.0	28.6†	-	-
3DVG-Transformer [49]	-	51.4	-	45.9	34.5
TransRefer3D [13]	-	57.4	-	-	-
SAT-2D [46]*	35.4†	57.9	31.7†	44.5	30.1
MDETR- [21]-3D (our impl.)	45.4	-	31.5	47.2	31.9
BUTD-DETR (ours)	**52.1**	**67.0**	**43.3**	**52.2**	**39.8**

Table 2. Ablation of design choices for BUTD-DETR on SR3D.

Model	Accuracy
BUTD-DETR	**52.1**
w/o visual tokens	41.9
w/o detection prompts	47.9
w/o box stream	51.0
with MDETR's [21] contrastive loss	49.6
w/o detection prompts; w/o box stream; (MDETR [21]-3D)	45.4
with parametric queries; w/o detection prompts; w/o box stream; (MDETR [21]-3D-Param)	33.8
with concatenated Visual, Language and Object Streams	51.3

- w/o visual tokens: an object-bottlenecked variant, which only attends to the language and box proposal streams and selects one box out of the proposals.
- w/o detection prompts: BUTD-DETR trained solely on SR3D grounding utterances.
- w/o box stream: BUTD-DETR without attention on the box stream.
- w/MDETR's contrastive loss: BUTD-DETR where we replace our modified contrastive loss with MDETR's.
- w/o detection prompts, w/o box stream, w/MDETR's contrastive loss: an MDETR [21]-3D implementation.
- w/parametric queries, w/o detection prompts, w/o box stream, w/MDETR's contrastive loss: an MDETR-3D implementation that uses parametric object queries, as in original MDETR.
- w/concatenated visual, language and box streams: instead of attending to each modality separately, we concatenate the different streams along their sequence dimension.

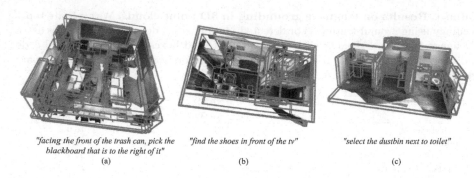

"facing the front of the trash can, pick the   "find the shoes in front of the tv"   "select the dustbin next to toilet"
blackboard that is to the right of it"
         (a)   (b)   (c)

Fig. 4. Qualitative results of BUTD-DETR in the SR3D benchmark. Predictions for the target are shown in green and for other mentioned objects in orange. The detected proposals appear in blue. (a) The variant without box stream (red box) fails to exploit the information given by the detector, but BUTD-DETR succeeds. (b) The detector misses the "shoes" and any box-bottlenecked variant fails. (c) The detector is successful in finding the "dustbin", still BUTD-DETR refines the box to get a more accurate bounding box. (Color figure online)

The conclusions are as follows:

1. **Box bottlenecks hurt:** Models such as BUTD-DETR and MDETR-3D that decode object boxes instead of selecting them from a pool of given object proposals significantly outperform box-bottlenecked variants. BUTD-DETR outperforms by 10.2% an object-bottlenecked variant, that does not attend to 3D point features and does not decode boxes.
2. **BUTD-DETR outperforms MDETR-3D by 6.7%:**
3. **Attention on a box proposal stream helps:** Removing attention on the box stream causes an absolute 1.1% drop in accuracy.
4. **Co-training with detection prompts helps:** Co-training with detection prompts contributes 4.2% in performance (from 47.9% to 52.1%).
5. **BUTD-DETR's contrastive loss helps:** Replacing our contrastive loss with MDETR's results in drop of 2.5% in absolute accuracy.
6. **Concatenating Visual, Language and Object Streams performs worse than a model that has separate streams for each modality** Our motivation is to keep separate streams in 3D cross-modality encoder and decoder to be consistent with 2D BUTD-DETR as explained in Sect. 3.2. We additionally find that having separate streams gives a boost of 0.8%.

4.2 Language Grounding in 2D Images

We test BUTD-DETR on the referential grounding datasets of RefCOCO [23], RefCOCO+ [47] and Flickr30k entities dataset [36]. We follow the pretrain-then-finetune protocol of MDETR and first pre-train on combined grounding annotations from Flickr30k [36], referring expression datasets [23,33,47], Visual Genome [24]. During pre-training the task is to detect all instances of objects

Table 3. Results on language grounding in 2D RefCOCO and RefCOCO+ Datasets on Top-1 accuracy metric using standard splits. All training times are computed using same V100 GPUs. Training epochs are written as $x + y$ where x = number of pre-training epochs and y = number of fine-tuning epochs. All reported results use ResNet101 backbone.

Method	RefCOCO			RefCOCO+			Training Epochs	Training GPU Hours
	val	testA	testB	val	testA	testB		
UNITER_L [6]	81.4	87.0	74.2	75.9	81.5	66.7	-	-
VILLA_L [12]	82.4	87.5	74.8	76.2	81.5	66.8	-	-
MDETR [21]	**86.8**	**89.6**	81.4	**79.5**	**84.1**	**70.6**	40 + 5	5560
BUTD-DETR (ours)	85.9	88.5	**81.5**	78.2	82.8	70.0	**12 + 5**	**2748**

Table 4. Results on language grounding in Flickr30k 2D images. We use Recall@k metric. All training times are computed using same V100 GPUs.

Method	Val			Test			Training Epochs	Training GPU hours
	R@1	R@5	R@10	R@1	R@5	R@10		
VisualBERT [25]	70.4	84.5	86.3	71.3	85.0	86.5	-	-
MDETR [21]	**82.5**	**92.9**	**94.9**	**83.4**	**93.5**	**95.3**	40	5480
BUTD-DETR (ours)	81.2	90.9	92.8	81.0	91.6	93.2	**12**	**2688**

mentioned in the utterance. Different than MDETR, we augment this supervision with detection prompts from the MS-COCO dataset [27]. Following MDETR, we directly evaluate our pre-trained model on Flickr30k without any further fine-tuning and fine-tune for 5 epochs on RefCOCO and RefCOCO+.

We report top-1 accuracy on the standard splits of RefCOCO and Ref-COCO+ in Table 3 and Recall metric with ANY-BOX protocol [25] on Flickr30k in Table 4. Our model and MDETR use the same 200k image-language pairs from COCO [27], Flickr30k [36] and Visual Genome [24]. VisualBERT [25] is trained on COCO captions. UNITER [6] and VILLA [12] use a larger dataset of 4.4M pairs from COCO, Visual Genome, Conceptual-Captions [43], and SBU Captions [35]. In addition, we augment our training set with detection prompts from COCO. BUTD-DETR trains two times faster than MDETR while getting comparable performance. This computational gain comes mostly from deformable attention which is much cheaper than original visual self-attention that scales quadratically with the number of visual tokens, as already reported in [50]. For qualitative results, please see the supplementary file.

Ablative Analysis. We ablate our model in RefCOCO without pre-training in Table 5, since pre-training is computationally expensive due to the size of the combined datasets. Consistent with 3D, removing detection prompts results in an accuracy drop of 2.4%. Additionally removing attention to the box proposal stream results in a drop of 3.1% in accuracy. When replacing our contrastive loss with MDETR's, the model achieves 74.2%, resulting in an additional drop of 2.1% accuracy.

Table 5. Ablation for BUTD-DETR on the RefCOCO validation set.

Model	Accuracy
BUTD-DETR	**79.4**
w/o det prompts	77.0
w/o box stream w/o det prompts	76.3
w/o box stream w/o det prompts w/MDETR's [21] contrastive	74.2

4.3 Limitations

Our work relies on language-image alignment and does not address how to ground language better and more robustly through abstraction of the visual features, e.g., the fact that *left* and *right* reverse when we change the user's viewpoint, the fact that numbers requires precise counting, or the fact that the *"chair furthest away from the door"* requires to satisfy a logical constraint which our model can totally violate when presented with out-of-distribution visual input. This limitation is a direct avenue for future work.

5   Conclusion

We present BUTD-DETR , a model for referential grounding in 3D and 2D scenes, that attends to language, visual and box proposal streams to decode objects mentioned in the referential utterance and align them to corresponding spans in the input. BUTD-DETR builds upon MDETR [21] and outperforms its straightforward MDETR-3D equivalent by a significant margin thanks to attention on labelled bottom-up box proposals, co-training with detection prompts and improved contrastive losses, setting a new state-of-the-art in two 3D language grounding benchmarks. BUTD-DETR is also the first model in 3D referential grounding that operates on the realistic setup of not having access to oracle object boxes, but rather detects them from the input 3D point cloud.

Acknowledgement. This material is based upon work supported by an Air Force grant FA95502010423, an AFOSR Young Investigator Award, DARPA Machine Common Sense, and an NSF CAREER award provided in affiliation to Carnegie Mellon University. Any opinions, findings and conclusions or recommendations expressed in this material are those of the author(s) and do not necessarily reflect the views of the United States Army or the United States Air Force. The authors would also like to thank Adam W. Harley, Leonid Keselman, Muyang Li and Rohan Choudhary for their helpful feedback.

References

1. Abdelreheem, A., Upadhyay, U., Skorokhodov, I., Yahya, R.A., Chen, J., Elhoseiny, M.: 3DRefTransformer: fine-grained object identification in real-world scenes using natural language. In: Proceedings of the WACV (2022)

2. Achlioptas, P., Abdelreheem, A., Xia, F., Elhoseiny, M., Guibas, L.: ReferIt3D: neural listeners for fine-grained 3D object identification in real-world scenes. In: Vedaldi, A., Bischof, H., Brox, T., Frahm, J.-M. (eds.) ECCV 2020. LNCS, vol. 12346, pp. 422–440. Springer, Cham (2020). https://doi.org/10.1007/978-3-030-58452-8_25

3. Carion, N., Massa, F., Synnaeve, G., Usunier, N., Kirillov, A., Zagoruyko, S.: End-to-end object detection with transformers. In: Vedaldi, A., Bischof, H., Brox, T., Frahm, J.-M. (eds.) ECCV 2020. LNCS, vol. 12346, pp. 213–229. Springer, Cham (2020). https://doi.org/10.1007/978-3-030-58452-8_13

4. Chen, D.Z., Chang, A.X., Nießner, M.: ScanRefer: 3D object localization in RGB-D scans using natural language. In: Vedaldi, A., Bischof, H., Brox, T., Frahm, J.-M. (eds.) ECCV 2020. LNCS, vol. 12365, pp. 202–221. Springer, Cham (2020). https://doi.org/10.1007/978-3-030-58565-5_13

5. Chen, X., Ma, L., Chen, J., Jie, Z., Liu, W., Luo, J.: Real-time referring expression comprehension by single-stage grounding network. arXiv abs/1812.03426 (2018)

6. Chen, Y.-C., et al.: UNITER: UNiversal Image-TExt representation learning. In: Vedaldi, A., Bischof, H., Brox, T., Frahm, J.-M. (eds.) ECCV 2020. LNCS, vol. 12375, pp. 104–120. Springer, Cham (2020). https://doi.org/10.1007/978-3-030-58577-8_7

7. Dai, A., Chang, A.X., Savva, M., Halber, M., Funkhouser, T.A., Nießner, M.: ScanNet: richly-annotated 3D reconstructions of indoor scenes. In: Proceedings of the CVPR (2017)

8. Deng, J., Yang, Z., Chen, T., Zhou, W., Li, H.: TransVG: end-to-end visual grounding with transformers. In: Proceedings of the ICCV (2021)

9. Fang, H., et al.: From captions to visual concepts and back. In: Proceedings of the CVPR (2015)

10. Feng, M., et al.: Free-form description guided 3D visual graph network for object grounding in point cloud. In: Proceedings of the ICCV (2021)

11. Fukui, A., Park, D.H., Yang, D., Rohrbach, A., Darrell, T., Rohrbach, M.: Multi-modal compact bilinear pooling for visual question answering and visual grounding. In: Proceedings of the EMNLP (2016)

12. Gan, Z., Chen, Y.C., Li, L., Zhu, C., Cheng, Y., Liu, J.: Large-scale adversarial training for vision-and-language representation learning. In: Proceedings of the NeurIPS (2020)

13. He, D., et al.: TransRefer3D: entity-and-relation aware transformer for fine-grained 3D visual grounding. In: Proceedings of the ACMMM (2021)

14. He, K., Gkioxari, G., Dollár, P., Girshick, R.B.: Mask R-CNN. In: Proceedings of the ICCV (2017)

15. He, K., Zhang, X., Ren, S., Sun, J.: Deep residual learning for image recognition. In: Proceedings of the IEEE Conference on Computer Vision and Pattern Recognition (CVPR), pp. 770–778 (2016)

16. He, K., Zhang, X., Ren, S., Sun, J.: Deep residual learning for image recognition. In: Proceedings of the CVPR (2016)

17. Hu, R., Rohrbach, M., Andreas, J., Darrell, T., Saenko, K.: Modeling relationships in referential expressions with compositional modular networks. In: Proceedings of the CVPR (2017)

18. Huang, P.H., Lee, H.H., Chen, H.T., Liu, T.L.: Text-guided graph neural networks for referring 3D instance segmentation. In: Proceedings of the AAAI (2021)

19. Jaegle, A., Gimeno, F., Brock, A., Zisserman, A., Vinyals, O., Carreira, J.: Perceiver: general perception with iterative attention. In: Proceedings of the ICML (2021)

20. Johnson, J., Karpathy, A., Fei-Fei, L.: DenseCap: fully convolutional localization networks for dense captioning. In: Proceedings of the CVPR (2016)
21. Kamath, A., Singh, M., LeCun, Y.A., Misra, I., Synnaeve, G., Carion, N.: MDETR - modulated detection for end-to-end multi-modal understanding. In: Proceedings of the ICCV (2021)
22. Karpathy, A., Fei-Fei, L.: Deep visual-semantic alignments for generating image descriptions. In: Proceedings of the CVPR (2015)
23. Kazemzadeh, S., Ordonez, V., Matten, M.A., Berg, T.L.: ReferItGame: referring to objects in photographs of natural scenes. In: Proceedings of the EMNLP (2014)
24. Krishna, R., et al.: Visual genome: connecting language and vision using crowd-sourced dense image annotations. Int. J. Comput. Vis. **123** (2016)
25. Li, L.H., Yatskar, M., Yin, D., Hsieh, C.J., Chang, K.W.: VisualBERT: a simple and performant baseline for vision and language. arXiv abs/1908.03557 (2019)
26. Li, L.H., et al.: Grounded language-image pre-training. In: Proceedings of the CVPR (2022)
27. Lin, T.-Y., et al.: Microsoft COCO: common objects in context. In: Fleet, D., Pajdla, T., Schiele, B., Tuytelaars, T. (eds.) ECCV 2014. LNCS, vol. 8693, pp. 740–755. Springer, Cham (2014). https://doi.org/10.1007/978-3-319-10602-1_48
28. Liu, W., et al.: SSD: single shot multibox detector. In: Leibe, B., Matas, J., Sebe, N., Welling, M. (eds.) ECCV 2016. LNCS, vol. 9905, pp. 21–37. Springer, Cham (2016). https://doi.org/10.1007/978-3-319-46448-0_2
29. Liu, Y., et al.: RoBERTa: a robustly optimized BERT pretraining approach. arXiv abs/1907.11692 (2019)
30. Liu, Z., Zhang, Z., Cao, Y., Hu, H., Tong, X.: Group-free 3D object detection via transformers. In: Proceedings of the ICCV (2021)
31. Lu, J., Batra, D., Parikh, D., Lee, S.: ViLBERT: pretraining task-agnostic visiolinguistic representations for vision-and-language tasks. In: Proceedings of the NeurIPS (2019)
32. Lu, J., Goswami, V., Rohrbach, M., Parikh, D., Lee, S.: 12-in-1: multi-task vision and language representation learning. In: Proceedings of the CVPR (2020)
33. Mao, J., Huang, J., Toshev, A., Camburu, O.M., Yuille, A.L., Murphy, K.P.: Generation and comprehension of unambiguous object descriptions. In: Proceedings of the CVPR (2016)
34. Misra, I., Girdhar, R., Joulin, A.: An end-to-end transformer model for 3D object detection. In: Proceedings of the ICCV (2021)
35. Ordonez, V., Kulkarni, G., Berg, T.: Im2Text: describing images using 1 million captioned photographs. In: Proceedings of the NIPS (2011)
36. Plummer, B.A., Wang, L., Cervantes, C.M., Caicedo, J.C., Hockenmaier, J., Lazebnik, S.: Flickr30k entities: collecting region-to-phrase correspondences for richer image-to-sentence models. In: Proceedings of the ICCV (2015)
37. Qi, C., Yi, L., Su, H., Guibas, L.J.: PointNet++: deep hierarchical feature learning on point sets in a metric space. In: Proceedings of the NIPS (2017)
38. Redmon, J., Divvala, S.K., Girshick, R.B., Farhadi, A.: You only look once: unified, real-time object detection. In: Proceedings of the CVPR (2016)
39. Ren, S., He, K., Girshick, R., Sun, J.: Faster R-CNN: towards real-time object detection with region proposal networks. In: Proceedings of the NIPS (2015)
40. Rezatofighi, S.H., Tsoi, N., Gwak, J., Sadeghian, A., Reid, I.D., Savarese, S.: Generalized intersection over union: a metric and a loss for bounding box regression. In: Proceedings of the CVPR (2019)
41. Roh, J., Desingh, K., Farhadi, A., Fox, D.: LanguageRefer: spatial-language model for 3D visual grounding. In: Proceedings of the CoRL (2021)

42. Sadhu, A., Chen, K., Nevatia, R.: Zero-shot grounding of objects from natural language queries. In: Proceedings of the ICCV (2019)
43. Sharma, P., Ding, N., Goodman, S., Soricut, R.: Conceptual captions: a cleaned, hypernymed, image alt-text dataset for automatic image captioning. In: Proceedings of the ACL (2018)
44. Yang, Z., Chen, T., Wang, L., Luo, J.: Improving one-stage visual grounding by recursive sub-query construction. In: Vedaldi, A., Bischof, H., Brox, T., Frahm, J.-M. (eds.) ECCV 2020. LNCS, vol. 12359, pp. 387–404. Springer, Cham (2020). https://doi.org/10.1007/978-3-030-58568-6_23
45. Yang, Z., Gong, B., Wang, L., Huang, W., Yu, D., Luo, J.: A fast and accurate one-stage approach to visual grounding. In: Proceedings of the ICCV (2019)
46. Yang, Z., Zhang, S., Wang, L., Luo, J.: SAT: 2D semantics assisted training for 3D visual grounding. In: Proceedings of the ICCV (2021)
47. Yu, L., Poirson, P., Yang, S., Berg, A.C., Berg, T.L.: Modeling context in referring expressions. In: Leibe, B., Matas, J., Sebe, N., Welling, M. (eds.) ECCV 2016. LNCS, vol. 9906, pp. 69–85. Springer, Cham (2016). https://doi.org/10.1007/978-3-319-46475-6_5
48. Yuan, Z., Yan, X., Liao, Y., Zhang, R., Li, Z., Cui, S.: InstanceRefer: cooperative holistic understanding for visual grounding on point clouds through instance multi-level contextual referring. In: Proceedings of the ICCV (2021)
49. Zhao, L., Cai, D., Sheng, L., Xu, D.: 3DVG-transformer: relation modeling for visual grounding on point clouds. In: Proceedings of the ICCV (2021)
50. Zhu, X., Su, W., Lu, L., Li, B., Wang, X., Dai, J.: Deformable DETR: deformable transformers for end-to-end object detection. In: Proceedings of the ICLR (2021)

New Datasets and Models for Contextual Reasoning in Visual Dialog

Yifeng Zhang⬤, Ming Jiang⬤, and Qi Zhao(✉)⬤

University of Minnesota, Minneapolis, MN 55455, USA
{zhan6987,mjiang}@umn.edu, qzhao@cs.umn.edu

Abstract. Visual Dialog (VD) is a vision-language task that requires AI systems to maintain a natural question-answering dialog about visual contents. Using the dialog history as contexts, VD models have achieved promising performance on public benchmarks. However, prior VD datasets do not provide sufficient contextually dependent questions that require knowledge from the dialog history to answer. As a result, advanced VQA models can still perform well without considering the dialog context. In this work, we focus on developing new datasets and models to highlight the role of contextual reasoning in VD. We define a hierarchy of contextual patterns to represent and organize the dialog context, enabling quantitative analyses of contextual dependencies and designs of new VD datsets and models. We then develop two new datasets, namely CLEVR-VD and GQA-VD, offering context-rich dialogs over synthetic and realistic images, respectively. Furthermore, we propose a novel neural module network method featuring contextual reasoning in VD. We demonstrate the effectiveness of our proposed datasets and method with experimental results and model comparisons across different datasets. Our code and data are available at https://github.com/SuperJohnZhang/ContextVD.

1 Introduction

Understanding vision and language and reasoning about both modalities is a challenging research problem. With the development of advanced machine learning techniques and large-scale datasets, recent progress in computer vision (CV) and natural language processing (NLP) has resulted in promising achievements in developing intelligent agents for various vision-language tasks [5,9,12,16,38]. A typical task is visual question answering (VQA) [5], which requires to answer an open-ended question about an image. As a step further, researchers generalize VQA to the more challenging visual dialog (VD) [12] task, which aims at holding a continuous question-answering dialog about visual contents. A unique challenge of VD is to understand the context of a question from the dialog history. Take the question *"what is the fruit to the right of it with the same color?"*

Supplementary Information The online version contains supplementary material available at https://doi.org/10.1007/978-3-031-20059-5_25.

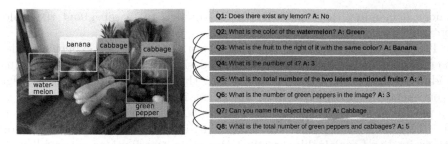

Fig. 1. An example from our GQA-VD dataset. It consists of a variety of questions that require contextual information to answer. Different from existing datasets, each GQA-VD question can refer to multiple entities (blue) or abstract concepts (red) in the dialog history, which offers a more challenging testbed for VD modeling. (Color figure online)

for example (see Fig. 1) – to answer the question, one must extract contextual information from previous questions about what *"it"* and *"same color"* refer to.

To tackle this challenge, recent VD studies have developed models to keep track of all phrases in the dialog that refer to the same entity in the image (*i.e.*, coreferences) [23]. Despite their promising results in existing VD benchmarks, it has been observed that state-of-the-art VQA models can achieve comparable or better performances in some metrics (*e.g.*, mean rank) without even considering the dialog history [29]. This suggests that existing VD benchmarks place an imbalanced emphasis on answering questions that do not depend on information from the dialog context. Therefore, further advances in VD research require to bridge three research gaps in the design of VD datasets and models: 1) the unclear definition and quantification of contextual dependencies, 2) the shortage of context-dependent questions in current datasets, and 3) the lack of model design for encoding complex dialog contexts.

In this work, we bridge the research gap with new datasets and models that focus on diverse dialog contexts. Specifically, based on linguistic theories [8], we first define a hierarchy of contextual patterns that explicitly characterize **contextual dependencies**, the general and diverse relationships across different questions in a dialog. Different from visual coreferences [23] that only focus on visual entities, contextual dependencies are more general and account for a broader range of contextual relationships.

Based on the novel definitions, we then develop two context-rich VD datasets (*i.e.*, CLEVR-VD and GQA-VD) by generating dialogs based on the popular CLEVR [21] and GQA [19] datasets. Compared with existing VD datasets [12,24], our proposed datasets consist of more diverse and balanced contexts. As shown in Fig. 1, many questions of our GQA-VD dataset depend on one or multiple previous questions. They not only refer to the previously mentioned visual entities (*e.g.*, watermelon, banana, cabbage, green pepper), but also depend on the understanding of abstract concepts (*e.g.*, number, color, *etc.*). Such general and diverse contextual dependencies lead to more challenging dialogs demanding the capabilities of VD models to reason about the dialog context.

Further, we propose a neural module network approach that explicitly models the reasoning process with a novel memory design and corresponding contextual modules to enable the attention shift among the abstract contextual knowledge. Experimental results demonstrate significant improvements of our method on the proposed datasets and existing datasets (*i.e.*, CLEVR-Dialog [24] and Vis-Dial [12]). This work pushes the state-of-the-art VD research towards a more fine-grained and explainable direction. Our main contributions are as follows:

1. Inspired by linguistic studies, we propose a novel definition of VD based on a hierarchy of contextual patterns, explicitly characterizing how dialog contexts are involved in a dialog.
2. We propose CLEVR-VD and GQA-VD, two new VD datasets offering diverse and complex dialog contexts, enabling the development of more sophisticated VD models. We also provide structured representations of a dialog (*i.e.*, primitives, compounds, and topics) as extra annotations.
3. Based on the new definition and datasets, we propose an explainable VD method that explicitly reasons about the dialog context with a novel memory mechanism and contextual modules, resulting in significantly improved performance while demonstrating model interpretability.

2   Related Works

Language Contexts in Dialog. Linguistic researches have studied language contexts in dialog [6–8,14,36] for many decades. Linguistic theories (*e.g.*, Speech Act Theory [6,36]) have been widely applied in dialogue act classification [33,34] and dialogue state tracking [27,44]. Derived from VQA [5], the task of VD [13] performs multiround question answering. To better encode language contexts, recent VD works [20,23] consider visual coreference resolution by linking phrases and pronouns across different QA rounds that refer to the same entity. However, coreference is far from sufficient to address complex dialog contexts related to abstract concepts (*e.g.*, number or color) or multiple entities (*e.g.*, watermelon and banana in Fig. 1). Aiming to represent language contexts in a formal, mathematical, and detailed manner, we revisit the VD task and introduce a hierarchy of dialog contextual patterns that clearly describe the semantics and functionalities of different language entities following the Speech Act Theory [6,36]. These patterns characterize a broad range of contextual dependencies.

Visual Dialog Datasets. VisDial [12] and CLEVR-Dialog [24] are two large-scale VD datasets for real-world and diagnostic images, respectively. To create multiround questions and answers, VisDial hires crowd workers to discuss about real-world images (*e.g.*, MSCOCO [26]), while CLEVR-Dialog leverages virtual agents to ground complete scene graphs from synthetic images (*e.g.*, CLEVR [21]). The CLEVR-Dialog has more frequent and difficult coreference cases than VisDial. We draw inspiration from CLEVR-Dialog to create our own datasets for both real-world (*e.g.*, GQA [19]) and diagnostic images (*e.g.*, CLEVR [21]). Compared to VisDial and CLEVR-Dialog, our datasets contain richer contexts in terms of both diversity and complexity. Our new datasets include a broader range of contextual dependencies other than just coreferences. The novel contextual patterns are annotated to offer detailed and structured representations that previous datasets did not provide. Another difference lies in the question generation process. Unlike CLEVR-Dialog that solely relies on two agents to implicitly include contexts, we provide a set of randomly sampled contexts to the question engine to ensure the context diversity and complexity.

Visual Dialog Models. Most VD models [12,13,20,27,32,37] follow an encoder-decoder framework to fuse dialog contexts and decode either an answer ranking or free-form response. With some researches [10,29] pointing out the importance of dialog context modeling, recent works use attention networks to solve coreferences [37], and more recently, a probabilistic treatment of dialogs using conditional variational autoencoders [30] to better encode the dialog context. All those models consider coreferences implicitly by encoding features and lack interpretability. Recent studies focus on pretraining and attention modeling (*e.g.*, VisDial-BERT [31], VD-BERT [40]) to improve model performance. Different from these methods, our proposed NDM model explicitly learns the reasoning process using neural modules that result in better explainability. It is mostly relevant to the CorefNMN [23] model that learns to infer coreferences using neural module networks. Inspired by a class of explicit VQA models [4,18,39,41,43] where an instance-specific architecture is dynamically constructed from basic building blocks representing different reasoning operations, CorefNMN stores all mentioned entities in a memory and represents coreferences as a feature extraction process with novel neural module implementations. Different from CorefNMN, we develop new modules along with a memory mechanism to reason over richer contextual dependencies and achieves significant improvements.

3   Visual Dialog Context

Visual Dialog (VD) refers to the task of answering a sequence of questions about a given image in multiple rounds [13]. Understanding the context of a dialog is essential for VD models, which helps them to answer each question based on its relationship with previous ones. Although it has been well known that extracting coreferences from the dialog history can benefit the answering of new questions [23,37], existing VD models fail to demonstrate superior performance over VQA methods, because of insufficient context representation. To promote the development of context-rich VD datasets and models, in this section, we present a more structured definition of dialog contexts. Inspired by linguistic theories [6,36] and visual reasoning studies [23,25], we define dialog contexts based on three levels of basic patterns: **primitives**, **compounds**, and **topics**.

Primitives are atomic patterns derived from the Speech Act Theory [35], which also corresponds to the atomic reasoning operations defined in visual reasoning

Table 1. Summary of all primitives. We introduce two novel primitives (Include, Exclude) that represent the knowledge inclusion and exclusion through contextual dependencies. [rel] – predicate in a subject-predicate-object triplet, [fea] – the feature type, (param) – the parameter of primitives (*i.e.*, a specific object or attribute), (att) – the intermediate attention map, [qids] – the IDs of related questions.

Primitive	Question	Example compound
Find(param)	Where is the apple?	Find(apple)-Describe[position]
Relate[rel](param)	Which object is made of metal?	Find(object)-Relate[madeOf](metal)
Filter[fea](param)	How many objects are there excluding sphere shape?	Find(object)-Filter[shape](sphere)-Count
And(att1, att2)	What is the number of blue metal objects?	Find(object)-And(Find(blue), Find(metal))-Count
Or(att1, att2)	What is the total number of apples and bananas?	Or(Find(apple), Find(banana))-Count
Not(att)	What is the number of non-blue objects?	Find(object)-Not(Find(blue))-Count
Exist	Is there any apple?	Find(apple)-Exist
Count	What is the number of apple?	Find(apple)-Count
Compare[fea](praram)	Who is larger, the watermelon or the apple	Find(watermelon)-Find(apple)-Compare[size](large)
Describe[fea]	What is the color of apple?	Find(apple)-Describe[color]
Exclude[qids][fea](param)	How many other fruits are there in the image?	Find(fruit)-Count-Exclude[qids][number](fruit)
Include[qids][fea](param)	How many mentioned fruits are there in the image?	Include[qids][name](fruit)-Find(prev)-Count

studies. For contextual reasoning in VD, we define two new primitives (*i.e.*, Include and Exclude) that represent the knowledge inclusion and exclusion through contextual dependencies. They each can refer to one or multiple concepts mentioned in previous questions, and these concepts can either be visually grounded entities or abstract ones, as specified in the parameters. Such parameters consist of 1) a list of related questions with shared knowledge, 2) the knowledge type (*e.g.*, name or number), and 3) the knowledge entity (*e.g.*, an object). In contrast, coreferences defined by previous studies (*i.e.*, visual entities that are referred to by multiple questions) can only represent a single visual entity, which is insufficient for complex contextual representation. Other primitives are defined following conventional visual reasoning operations [19], such as attention operations (*i.e.*, Find, Relate, Filter), logical operations (*i.e.*, And, Or, Not), output operations (*i.e.*, Compare, Exist, Count, Describe), *etc.* Examples of all primitives are shown in Table 1.

Compounds are contextual patterns composed of a sequence of primitives. Each compound corresponds to a question in the dialog. If a compound contains Include or Exclude primitives, it means that the corresponding question is dependent on previous questions in the dialog history. For instance, the question *"What is the fruit that shares the same color as the watermelon and banana?"* can be represented as a parameterized sequence of primitives Find(fruit)-Include[qids][color](watermelon, banana)- Describe[name]. Therefore, all previous questions about the watermelons, bananas or their colors are its contextual dependencies, because they share the same contextual knowledge with it.

Topics are contextual patterns defined as connected graphs of multiple questions and their dependencies. We represent questions as graph nodes and their dependencies as edges. Thus, different topics are represented as isolated graphs. Each dialog consists of at least one topic, while the maximum number of topics

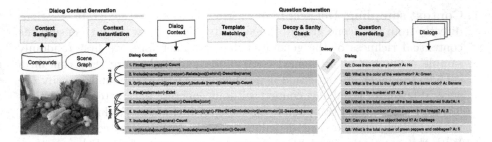

Fig. 2. An overview of the dataset generation process. First, we generate question contexts by sampling and instantiating them with parameters into a collection of topics. Next, instantiated contexts are fed into the question engine, which performs template matching, decoy and sanity check, and question reordering to generate diverse dialogs.

is the number of questions (*i.e.*, all questions are independent from each other and can be answered without knowledge from the dialog history).

The primitives, compounds, and topics defined above provide concise and informative representation of dialog contexts, which are used in Sect. 4 to ensure the contextual richness of our proposed datasets.

4   The CLEVR-VD and GQA-VD Datasets

Based on the definition in Sect. 3 and the popular visual reasoning datasets CLEVR [21] and GQA [19], we develop two novel datasets, namely CLEVR-VD and GQA-VD, featuring rich dialog contexts and questions. Both datasets offer ten-round dialogs with complex contexts and diverse questions. Compared with existing VD datasets, the diversity and complexity of CLEVR-VD and GQA-VD demonstrate great potential for developing and benchmarking VD models capable of better contextual reasoning. In this section, we first describe the process of generating dialogs, and then report the data statistics.

4.1   Dataset Generation

Previous studies [12,24] develop VD datasets by either recruiting crowd workers or developing AI agents to perform question answering. Though these datasets consist of naturally generated questions about the context, there is no explicit control over the richness of contextual dependency. Differently, we generate dialogs explicitly from a structured representation of dialog context following the definition in Sect. 3. As shown in Fig. 2, the data generation process consists of five steps: context sampling, context instantiation, template matching, decoy & sanity check, and question reordering. Following these steps, we 1) generate complex dialog contexts with a variety of primitives, compounds, and topics, and 2) develop a question engine to generate a diverse set of dialogs based on each dialog context. We summarize these data generation steps in this section. For more details, please refer to the supplementary.

1. **Context sampling.** Different from existing datasets that generate questions directly from the scene graph of images, in this work, we aim to ensure the contextual richness of the generated dialogs. Therefore, we first randomly sample a number of predefined compounds and make sure they contain a sufficient number of contextual dependencies. These compounds specify the general layout of the dialog context without concrete parameters. In particular, for each sampled compound consisting of Include or Exclude primitives, we recursively sample their dependencies, which generates complex topics. With this approach, we arrive at a preliminary layout of the dialog context. It contains a number of topics, each forming a graph with compounds as nodes and their dependencies as edges, indicating the overall contextual relationships of questions.

2. **Context instantiation.** The previous step specifies the structure of the dialog context without taking into account the visual information. Next, given the scene graph of an input image, we instantiate the dialog context by filling in the parameters. Specifically, we first randomly sample objects and attributes from the scene graph and assign them to each primitive. We then validate the compounds to makes sure that a question depending on another one must have shared parameters, but independent questions must all have different parameters. For example, when the referred object is unique in the image, a question about the object could be independent of the context. This process leads to an image-specific dialog context with rich contextual dependencies.

3. **Question templates.** From a dialog context, we can generate a variety of dialogs by choosing different question templates for each compound. For example, the questions *"Is there any watermelon?"*, *"Does there exist any watermelon?"* can be generated from the compound Find(watermelon)-Exist using different templates. We not only design 240 templates for CLEVR-VD and 360 templates for GQA-VD, but also prepare a set of synonyms to further increase the language diversity. The lists of templates are presented in the supplementary.

4. **Decoys and sanity check.** To further increase the diversity of the dialogs, we randomly replace objects or attributes in the questions with plausible decoys. The decoys do not necessarily exist in the image and they may affect the answer. After the replacement, to maintain the validity of questions, we perform sanity check based on a set of predefined rules. For example, considering the two questions *"Does there exist any watermelon?"* and *"what is the color of it?"* (see Fig. 2), with a decoy *"lemon"*, the first one may be changed to *"Does there exist any lemon?"*. Due to this change, the next question must be revised to *"What is the color of the watermelon?"* to maintain the validity of the dialog context. By making adjustments to the affected questions accordingly, these rules (see the supplementary for details) of the sanity check ensure the dialog-image integrity.

5. **Question reordering.** Although the order of questions has been determined by the dialog context, some questions in the dialog can be reordered without breaking the integrity of the context. For example, as shown in Fig. 2, inde-

Table 2. Dataset statistics of CLEVR-Dialog, CLEVR-VD, VisDial and GQA-VD. Q. – questions, A. – answers, T. – topics, C. – contextual dependencies. Note that the 1.4k unique VisDial answers are short answers extracted from the 340k long answers by removing synonyms, while the 1.8k short answers of GQA-VD can also be augmented into 840k unique long answers with the current templates.

	CLEVR-Dialog	CLEVR-VD	VisDial	GQA-VD
Image Type	Synthetic	Synthetic	Real	Real
# Images	85k	100k	123k	113k
# Questions	4.25M	2M	1.2M	5.6M
# Unique Q	73k	89k	380k	970k
# Unique A	29	76	1.4k	1.8k
Vocab Size	125	240	7k	11k
Mean Q. Length	10.6	11.2	5.1	11.9
# T. Per Dialog	6.7	4.1	7.9	4.4
# Q. Per T	2.3	2.9	1.4	2.6
# C. Per Q	1.6	2.1	0.9	1.8
% Long-term C	56	63	48	65
% Independent Q	69	36	78	39

pendent questions or topics can be randomly shuffled without affecting each other, since they do not require shared knowledge. Therefore, by shuffling the question orders we further increase the diversity of dialogs.

4.2 Dataset Analysis

Table 2 compares the overall statistics between ours and the related VisDial [13] and CLEVR-Dialog [24]. These datasets are grouped based on their image sources: VisDial and GQA-VD use COCO images, while CLEVR-Dialog and CLEVR-VD use CLEVR images. Both CLEVR-VD and GQA-VD have several unique characteristics that distinguish them from the previous ones. For example, they have larger sizes of vocabulary and unique questions. GQA-VD has 5 times more questions than VisDial and 3 times more unique questions, making it more diverse for mitigating biases. Although the total number of questions for CLEVR-VD is smaller than CLEVR-Dialog, it has more unique questions and answers. In particular, compared with CLEVR-Dialog and VisDial, our datasets have a reduced number of topics and more contextual dependencies per question. They also have more long-term contextual dependencies between non-adjacent questions and fewer independent questions. These statistics suggest that our datasets have more complex dialog contexts, with more questions being dependent on each other. In the following, we analyze the distribution of questions and answers, as well as different contextual patterns. Detailed statistics of our datasets are reported in the supplementary.

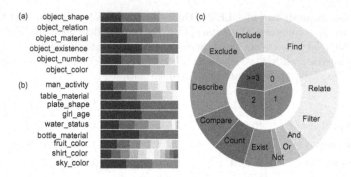

Fig. 3. Our CLEVR-VD and GQA-VD datasets maintain a balanced distribution of answers and contextual patterns. (a) Answer distribution of the six major question types of CLEVR-VD. (b) Answer distribution of the top-10 question types of GQA-VD. (c) Distribution of primitives and number of contextual dependencies.

Balanced Questions and Answers. One of the main challenges of VQA and VD is the prevalent language bias [1,2,11,15,42] that allows models to answer questions based on shallow question-answer correlations rather than reasoning over both modalities. To mitigate such bias and encourage models to focus on the learning of dialog contexts, we diversify and balance the question and answer categories in the generated dialog. Figure 3a–b show the answer distribution for the six major question categories of CLEVR-VD and the top-10 question categories of GQA-VD. As it is shown, the answers are well-balanced for each question category, which reduces the tendency of models fitting the language bias.

Diverse Contextual Patterns. The core characteristics of both CLEVR-VD and GQA-VD are their diverse contextual patterns. Figure 3c demonstrates the statistics of various patterns (*i.e.*, primitives and number of contextual dependencies) for both datasets. Although their total numbers of compounds are different, CLEVR-VD and GQA-VD maintain a similar distribution of primitives and compounds. In particular, more than half of all questions have at least two contextual dependencies, which is significantly higher than existing VD datasets. The increased number of contextual dependencies leads to more challenging benchmarks for future VD models.

5   Explainable Contextual Reasoning

To model the rich and diverse dialog contexts, we develop a Neural Dialog Modular network (NDM) for explainable contextual reasoning. In particular, we propose a memory mechanism and two contextual modules to explicitly store and transfer knowledge across different questions to tackle specific challenges in understanding dialog contexts. These novel components enable the shift of attention to multiple abstract concepts through diverse contextual dependencies rather than just a single coreference [23].

Table 3. Implementation of neural modules. Apart from common neural modules, we design two novel contextual modules (Include, Exclude) to include or exclude the memorized features from the dialog history. MLP($\cdot$) indicates a multi-layer perceptron consisting of several fully-connected and ReLU layers, $\boldsymbol{W}_h$ is the transfer matrix computed following [43], and $\boldsymbol{W}$ is a set of K matrices of learnable weights [39] that map features onto K specific fields. $\boldsymbol{a}$, $\boldsymbol{h}$, and $\boldsymbol{q}$ indicate the input attention, features, and parameters. $\boldsymbol{a}'$ and $\boldsymbol{h}'$ are the output attention and features, respectively. $\boldsymbol{a}_1$, $\boldsymbol{a}_2$ are two input attention maps for Or/And, while $\boldsymbol{h_1}$, $\boldsymbol{h_2}$ are two input features for Compare.

Modules	Category	Operation
Or	Logic	$\boldsymbol{a}' = \max(\boldsymbol{a}_1, \boldsymbol{a}_2)$
And	Logic	$\boldsymbol{a}' = \min(\boldsymbol{a}_1, \boldsymbol{a}_2)$
Not	Logic	$\boldsymbol{a}' = 1 - \boldsymbol{a}$
Find	Attention	$\boldsymbol{a}' = \mathrm{softmax}(\mathrm{MLP}(\boldsymbol{h}, \boldsymbol{q}))$
Relate	Attention	$\boldsymbol{a}' = norm(\boldsymbol{W}_h \boldsymbol{a})$
Filter	Attention	$\boldsymbol{a}' = \mathrm{And}[\boldsymbol{a}, \mathrm{Find}(\boldsymbol{q})]$
Compare	Output	$\boldsymbol{h}' = \mathrm{MLP}(\boldsymbol{W}(\boldsymbol{h}_1 - \boldsymbol{h}_2)))$
Count	Output	$\boldsymbol{h}' = \mathrm{MLP}(\mathrm{sum}(\boldsymbol{a}))$
Exist	Output	$\boldsymbol{h}' = \mathrm{MLP}(\mathrm{sum}(\boldsymbol{a}))$
Describe	Output	$\boldsymbol{h}' = \mathrm{softmax}(\mathrm{MLP}(\boldsymbol{q}))\boldsymbol{W}(\boldsymbol{a} \circ \boldsymbol{h})$
Include	Attention	Or[$\boldsymbol{a}$, softmax($Eq.$ (4))]
Exclude	Attention	And[$\boldsymbol{a}$, Not[softmax($Eq.$ (4))]]

Neural module networks are a class of explainable reasoning methods [4,39, 43]. They perform visual reasoning by first parsing the questions into a set of predefined reasoning modules to dynamically construct a network and then feeding the visual input to the network to predict an answer. Our NDM method adopts conventional question parser and VQA modules following the NMN approach [4]. Table 3 shows the implementation of our neural modules. In the following, we briefly present the design of our novel components: memory and contextual modules. More details are presented in supplementary.

Memorizing Visual and Semantic Features. Due to the complexity of dialog contexts, knowledge from the dialog history can be critical for answering questions, while simply storing features of coreferences can be insufficient. For example (see Fig. 1), to answer *"What is the total number of the two latest mentioned fruits?"*, abstract knowledge (*e.g.*, the number of watermelons) can be included from the history to help answer the question. To effectively retrieve the relevant knowledge, we propose a novel memory mechanism $\boldsymbol{M}_t$ that stores both the attended visual features $\boldsymbol{M}_t^v$ and their corresponding semantic embeddings $\boldsymbol{M}_t^p$. The memory (as shown in Fig. 4) is updated by projecting the concatenation of the previous memory $\{\boldsymbol{M}_{t-1}^v, \boldsymbol{M}_{t-1}^p\}$ and current features $\{\boldsymbol{m}_t^v, \boldsymbol{m}_t^v\}$

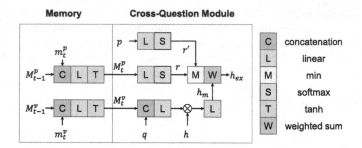

Fig. 4. The proposed memory mechanism and contextual modules that retrieve relevant knowledge h_{ex} from the dialog history. Contextual modules first find the attended features of relevant entity from image feature h (with memorized attended feature M_t^v and the parameter q), and then retrieve the relevant knowledge using a weighted combination of the features projected over different spaces (*e.g.*, name, color, number). The weights are computed by measuring the overlap between the memorized semantic embedding M_t^p and target feature name p.

$$M_t^v = tanh(W^v[M_{t-1}^v, m_t^v]) \tag{1}$$

$$M_t^p = tanh(W^p[M_{t-1}^p, m_t^p]), \tag{2}$$

where W_v, W_p are learnable parameters. m_t^v is the duplication of current attended visual features, while m_t^p describes the attended language features by encoding the dialog history into semantic embeddings with an LSTM [17].

Contextual Modules. To precisely extract relevant information from the attended visual features M^v and their semantic embeddings M^p, we also implement Include and Exclude as novel contextual modules. Different from CorefNMN [23], our contextual modules extract visual features from the memory M^v, project them into several feature spaces (*e.g.*, name, color, count) and finally produce the abstract features with a linear combination.

As shown in Fig. 4, given the memorized features M^v, the input parameter q and the image features h, we can obtain relevant features h_m from the memory

$$h_m = \text{softmax}(\text{MLP}(M^v, q)) \circ h, \tag{3}$$

where $\circ$ denotes the Hadamard product. The relevant features h_m are then projected into K spaces with the same learnable projecting matrix ($W = \{W_k\}_{k=1}^K$) as Describe. Finally, given the memorized semantic embeddings M^p and target feature name p, we measure the overlap of their probability distributions (*i.e.*, $r = \text{softmax}(\text{MLP}(M_p))$, $r' = \text{softmax}(\text{MLP}(p))$) as weights and weighted combine K projections to obtain the extracted features

$$h_{ex} = \sum_{k=1}^K \min(r_k, r_k') W_k h_m, \tag{4}$$

where r_k, r'_k are the k-th entries of r and r'. Finally, as shown in Table 3, the Include and Exclude modules process the result (h_{ex}) of Eq. (4) differently to determine the inclusion or exclusion of the retrieved knowledge.

6   Experiments

Our proposed datasets provide new opportunities for developing and benchmarking context-aware VD models. In this section, we conduct extensive experiments to demonstrate the effectiveness of our datasets and the proposed NDM method. Section 6.2 reports quantitative results in comparison with the state-of-the-art. Section 6.3 visualizes the parameters of neural modules to illustrate the contextual knowledge reasoning. Section 6.4 analyzes the effectiveness of our novel memory mechanism and contextual modules.

6.1   Models and Evaluation

We systematically evaluate NDM and a series of baselines and state-of-the-art models. First, we develop a baseline model that predicts the answers based on the prior distribution of the training data. We then compare our method with three VD models (*i.e.*, HRE-QIH [12], MN-QIH [12], CorefNMN [23]) and two VQA models (*i.e.*, NMN [4], BUTD [3]). In addition, we incorporate pretrained ViLBERT [28] features into our NDM model, and compare it (*i.e.*, NDM-BERT) with language-pretrained VD-BERT [40] and VisDial-BERT [31] methods. We train and evaluate these models on our proposed CLEVR-VD and GQA-VD datasets, as well as two public datasets: CLEVR-Dialog [24] and VisDial [12]. All the compared models are trained with default parameters, and evaluated on the validation sets. Our NDM and NDM-BERT models are optimized using the Adam [22] optimizer with a learning rate of 10^{-4} and a decay rate of 10^{-5}.

6.2   Quantitative Results

Table 4 shows quantitative results demonstrating the importance of context-rich datasets for visual dialog modeling. In general, we find that the VD models perform much better on CLEVR-VD and GQA-VD than VQA models (*i.e.*, NMN and BUTD in the top panel), suggesting that the more challenging dialogs of our datasets with complex contextual patterns cannot be handled without reasoning about contextual dependencies. Further, we find that our NDM achieves the highest accuracy among all non-pretraining methods (*i.e.*, HRE-QIH, MN-QIH, CorefNMN). The significant gains on CLEVER-VD and GQA-VD datasets demonstrate its ability to reason about rich dialog contexts, and its high performances on CLEVR-Dialog and VisDial demonstrate our model's generalizability.

Though NDM is a neural module network focusing on structured reasoning but not pretraining, Table 4 also compares it with the state-of-the-art methods based on language pretraining (the bottom panel of Table 4). The proposed NDM, without pretraining, is competitive among the state-of-the-art pretrained

Table 4. Quantitative comparison with state-of-the-art methods on CLEVR-Dialog, CLEVR-VD, VisDial, and GQA-VD datasets.

Model	CLEVR-Dialog	CLEVR-VD	VisDial	GQA-VD
Answer prior	33.42	27.52	23.55	30.06
NMN [4]	56.63	45.47	42.18	52.18
BUTD [3]	65.74	50.85	46.75	52.90
HRE-QIH [12]	63.38	57.41	42.28	55.97
MN-QIH [12]	59.65	54.96	45.55	57.75
CorefNMN [23]	68.03	56.82	50.92	56.59
NDM	**68.21**	**59.89**	**52.72**	**60.84**
VD-BERT [40]	68.12	59.67	51.63	60.67
VisDial-BERT [31]	68.20	59.78	**53.85**	60.89
NDM-BERT	**68.23**	**59.92**	52.91	**61.08**

Table 5. Average accuracy for questions with different numbers of contextual dependencies on CLEVR-VD and GQA-VD.

Model	CLEVR-VD				GQA-VD			
	0	1	2	≥3	0	1	2	≥3
Answer prior	28.75	28.24	26.53	26.65	31.99	31.71	28.23	28.34
NMN [4]	48.36	45.79	44.28	43.94	57.86	52.33	49.92	49.68
BUTD [3]	60.95	48.90	48.12	47.82	61.53	51.79	50.38	49.78
HRE-QIH [12]	**61.95**	59.85	54.67	53.49	60.62	56.88	53.74	53.30
MN-QIH [12]	60.48	55.16	52.74	52.53	**61.85**	58.52	55.60	54.69
CorefNMN [23]	60.83	58.78	54.31	53.74	60.76	59.45	53.79	52.51
NDM	60.52	**60.13**	**59.66**	**59.32**	61.28	**61.47**	**60.61**	**59.92**

models. It also consistently outperforms VD-BERT on all four datasets. Further, our pretrained NDM-BERT maintains interpretability while achieving the best performance (*i.e.*, also outperforming VisDial-BERT) on CLEVR-Dialog, CLEVR-VD, and GQA-VD. Between NDM and NDM-BERT, we only observe minor performance improvements, which suggests that the learning of contextual dependencies does not benefit significantly from pretraining.

Table 5 groups the questions into categories with different numbers of contextual dependencies and shows the average accuracy for each category. It is noteworthy that for VQA models, the performances decrease significantly with the number of contextual dependencies, while for VD models the performance drop is less significant. Our proposed NDM performs almost equally well on questions with different number of dependencies, suggesting its ability to perform contextual reasoning across multiple questions.

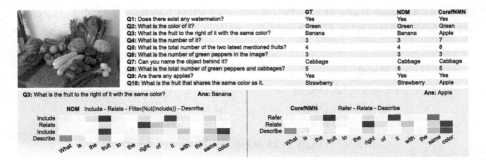

Fig. 5. A typical example on the GQA-VD dataset. Heat maps demonstrate the attention of each parameterized reasoning module when answering Q3.

6.3 Qualitative Analysis

Figure 5 shows a typical example of answering questions in a context-rich dialog, with attention maps demonstrating the reasoning processes of NDM and CorefNMN. In this dialog, NDM shifts attention to multiple abstract concepts in the contextual knowledge, while CorefNMN only focuses on visual entities. The dialog starts with questions about the existence and color of the watermelon, and both models answer correctly. However, CorefNMN fails to answer Q3 and the subsequent questions Q4 and Q5 that depend on Q3. It incorrectly answers *"apple"* that is also to the right of the watermelon, but with different colors. Differently, NDM correctly locates the banana that is both *"to the right of the watermelon"* and *"with the same color"*. It is because our NDM can acquire both the name and color of the watermelon. By memorizing this knowledge and leveraging multiple contextual dependencies, NDM performs more effectively in reasoning across questions. The ability of using multiple Include modules to infer complex contextual dependencies allows NDM to focus on the watermelon and its color in different reasoning steps, while CorefNMN fails to handle such complexity. Further qualitative results are reported in the supplementary.

6.4 Ablation Study

To analyze the contributions of different technical components, we further compare NDM variants with different combinations of conventional VQA modules, contextual modules (C) and the memory mechanism (M). Similarly, we adapt CorefNMN by keeping its original VQA neural modules but replacing its coreference modules and/or its memory mechanism with ours. Table 6 shows the results on the CLEVR-VD and GQA-VD datasets. We find that our memory and contextual modules contribute significantly to the model accuracy, leading to further improvements when they are combined. They are shown to be general, with consistent performance gains on both baselines.

Table 6. Ablation study of CorefNMN [23] and NDM baselines with different combinations of conventional VQA modules, memory (M), and contextual modules (C).

Model	CLEVR-VD	GQA-VD
CorefNMN (VQA)	54.69	54.06
CorefNMN (VQA + M)	56.45	56.24
CorefNMN (VQA + C)	56.71	56.46
CorefNMN (VQA + M + C)	**57.72**	**58.87**
NDM (VQA)	55.27	54.95
NDM (VQA + M)	57.81	57.63
NDM (VQA + C)	58.12	57.98
NDM (VQA + M + C)	**59.80**	**60.84**

7   Conclusion

Research on VD could fundamentally change the experience of human-machine interaction. However, VD studies are limited by insufficient contextual dependencies in existing datasets. To overcome this limitation, we introduce a novel definition of the dialog context with a hierarchy of contextual patterns, and construct two new VD datasets, CLEVR-VD and GQA-VD. We further propose NDM, a neural module network that performs explainable visual reasoning over the dialog context across different questions. Experimental results demonstrate that our proposed datasets offer a more general and challenging benchmark for VD models. Our NDM method also achieves promising performance by explicitly memorizing and retrieving contextual knowledge. We hope that our work will inspire future developments of interpretable and contextual reasoning methods.

Acknowledgment. This work is supported by NSF Grants 1908711 and 1849107.

References

1. Agrawal, A., Batra, D., Parikh, D.: Analyzing the behavior of visual question answering models. In: Proceedings of the 2016 Conference on Empirical Methods in Natural Language Processing, pp. 1955–1960 (2016)
2. Agrawal, A., Batra, D., Parikh, D., Kembhavi, A.: Don't just assume; look and answer: overcoming priors for visual question answering. In: Proceedings of the IEEE Conference on Computer Vision and Pattern Recognition, pp. 4971–4980 (2018)
3. Anderson, P., et al.: Bottom-up and top-down attention for image captioning and visual question answering. In: Proceedings of the IEEE Conference on Computer Vision and Pattern Recognition, pp. 6077–6086 (2018)
4. Andreas, J., Rohrbach, M., Darrell, T., Klein, D.: Neural module networks. In: Proceedings of the IEEE Conference on Computer Vision and Pattern Recognition, pp. 39–48 (2016)

5. Antol, S., et al.: VQA: visual question answering. In: Proceedings of the IEEE International Conference on Computer Vision, pp. 2425–2433 (2015)
6. Austin, J.L.: How to Do Things with Words. Oxford University Press, Oxford (1975)
7. Brooks, N.: Language and language learning, theory and practice (1964)
8. Bühler, K.: Theory of Language. The Representational Function of Language (1990)
9. Chattopadhyay, P., et al.: Evaluating visual conversational agents via cooperative human-AI games. In: Proceedings of the AAAI Conference on Human Computation and Crowdsourcing, vol. 5 (2017)
10. Chen, F., Chen, X., Meng, F., Li, P., Zhou, J.: GoG: relation-aware graph-over-graph network for visual dialog. arXiv preprint arXiv:2109.08475 (2021)
11. Das, A., Agrawal, H., Zitnick, L., Parikh, D., Batra, D.: Human attention in visual question answering: do humans and deep networks look at the same regions? Comput. Vis. Image Underst. **163**, 90–100 (2017)
12. Das, A., et al.: Visual dialog. In: Proceedings of the IEEE Conference on Computer Vision and Pattern Recognition, pp. 326–335 (2017)
13. Das, A., Kottur, S., Moura, J.M., Lee, S., Batra, D.: Learning cooperative visual dialog agents with deep reinforcement learning. In: Proceedings of the IEEE International Conference on Computer Vision, pp. 2951–2960 (2017)
14. Giles, H., Coupland, N.: Language: Contexts and Consequences. Thomson Brooks/Cole Publishing Co. (1991)
15. Goyal, Y., Khot, T., Summers-Stay, D., Batra, D., Parikh, D.: Making the V in VQA matter: elevating the role of image understanding in visual question answering. In: Proceedings of the IEEE Conference on Computer Vision and Pattern Recognition, pp. 6904–6913 (2017)
16. Guo, X., Wu, H., Cheng, Y., Rennie, S., Tesauro, G., Feris, R.: Dialog-based interactive image retrieval. In: Advances in Neural Information Processing Systems, vol. 31 (2018)
17. Hochreiter, S., Schmidhuber, J.: Long short-term memory. Neural Comput. **9**(8), 1735–1780 (1997)
18. Hudson, D., Manning, C.D.: Learning by abstraction: the neural state machine. In: Advances in Neural Information Processing Systems, vol. 32 (2019)
19. Hudson, D.A., Manning, C.D.: GQA: a new dataset for real-world visual reasoning and compositional question answering. In: Proceedings of the IEEE/CVF Conference on Computer Vision and Pattern Recognition, pp. 6700–6709 (2019)
20. Jiang, X., et al.: DualVD: an adaptive dual encoding model for deep visual understanding in visual dialogue. In: Proceedings of the AAAI Conference on Artificial Intelligence, vol. 34, pp. 11125–11132 (2020)
21. Johnson, J., Hariharan, B., Van Der Maaten, L., Fei-Fei, L., Lawrence Zitnick, C., Girshick, R.: CLEVR: a diagnostic dataset for compositional language and elementary visual reasoning. In: Proceedings of the IEEE Conference on Computer Vision and Pattern Recognition, pp. 2901–2910 (2017)
22. Kingma, D.P., Ba, J.: Adam: a method for stochastic optimization. arXiv preprint arXiv:1412.6980 (2014)
23. Kottur, S., Moura, J.M.F., Parikh, D., Batra, D., Rohrbach, M.: Visual coreference resolution in visual dialog using neural module networks. In: Ferrari, V., Hebert, M., Sminchisescu, C., Weiss, Y. (eds.) ECCV 2018. LNCS, vol. 11219, pp. 160–178. Springer, Cham (2018). https://doi.org/10.1007/978-3-030-01267-0_10

24. Kottur, S., Moura, J.M., Parikh, D., Batra, D., Rohrbach, M.: CLEVR-Dialog: a diagnostic dataset for multi-round reasoning in visual dialog. arXiv preprint arXiv:1903.03166 (2019)
25. Li, M., Moens, M.F.: Modeling coreference relations in visual dialog. In: Proceedings of the 16th Conference of the European Chapter of the Association for Computational Linguistics: Main Volume, pp. 3306–3318. Association for Computational Linguistics, April 2021. https://www.aclweb.org/anthology/2021.eacl-main.290
26. Lin, T.-Y., et al.: Microsoft COCO: common objects in context. In: Fleet, D., Pajdla, T., Schiele, B., Tuytelaars, T. (eds.) ECCV 2014. LNCS, vol. 8693, pp. 740–755. Springer, Cham (2014). https://doi.org/10.1007/978-3-319-10602-1_48
27. Liu, B., Tür, G., Hakkani-Tür, D., Shah, P., Heck, L.: Dialogue learning with human teaching and feedback in end-to-end trainable task-oriented dialogue systems. In: Proceedings of NAACL-HLT, pp. 2060–2069 (2018)
28. Lu, J., Batra, D., Parikh, D., Lee, S.: ViLBERT: pretraining task-agnostic visiolinguistic representations for vision-and-language tasks. In: Advances in Neural Information Processing Systems, vol. 32 (2019)
29. Massiceti, D., Dokania, P.K., Siddharth, N., Torr, P.H.: Visual dialogue without vision or dialogue. arXiv preprint arXiv:1812.06417 (2018)
30. Massiceti, D., Siddharth, N., Dokania, P.K., Torr, P.H.: FlipDial: a generative model for two-way visual dialogue. In: Proceedings of the IEEE Conference on Computer Vision and Pattern Recognition, pp. 6097–6105 (2018)
31. Murahari, V., Batra, D., Parikh, D., Das, A.: Large-scale pretraining for visual dialog: a simple state-of-the-art baseline. In: Vedaldi, A., Bischof, H., Brox, T., Frahm, J.-M. (eds.) ECCV 2020. LNCS, vol. 12363, pp. 336–352. Springer, Cham (2020). https://doi.org/10.1007/978-3-030-58523-5_20
32. Murahari, V., Chattopadhyay, P., Batra, D., Parikh, D., Das, A.: Improving generative visual dialog by answering diverse questions. In: Proceedings of the 2019 Conference on Empirical Methods in Natural Language Processing (2019)
33. Raheja, V., Tetreault, J.: Dialogue act classification with context-aware self-attention. In: Proceedings of the 2019 Conference of the North American Chapter of the Association for Computational Linguistics: Human Language Technologies, Volume 1 (Long and Short Papers), pp. 3727–3733 (2019)
34. Ravi, S., Kozareva, Z.: Self-governing neural networks for on-device short text classification. In: Proceedings of the 2018 Conference on Empirical Methods in Natural Language Processing, pp. 887–893 (2018)
35. Searle, J.R., Kiefer, F., Bierwisch, M., et al.: Speech Act Theory and Pragmatics, vol. 10. Springer, Dordrecht (1980). https://doi.org/10.1007/978-94-009-8964-1
36. Searle, J.R., Searle, J.R.: Speech Acts: An Essay in the Philosophy of Language, vol. 626. Cambridge University Press, Cambridge (1969)
37. Seo, P.H., Lehrmann, A., Han, B., Sigal, L.: Visual reference resolution using attention memory for visual dialog. In: Advances in Neural Information Processing Systems, vol. 30 (2017)
38. Shekhar, R., Baumgärtner, T., Venkatesh, A., Bruni, E., Bernardi, R., Fernandez, R.: Ask no more: deciding when to guess in referential visual dialogue. In: Proceedings of the 27th International Conference on Computational Linguistics, pp. 1218–1233 (2018)
39. Shi, J., Zhang, H., Li, J.: Explainable and explicit visual reasoning over scene graphs. In: Proceedings of the IEEE/CVF Conference on Computer Vision and Pattern Recognition, pp. 8376–8384 (2019)
40. Wang, Y., Joty, S., Lyu, M.R., King, I., Xiong, C., Hoi, S.C.: VD-BERT: a unified vision and dialog transformer with BERT. arXiv preprint arXiv:2004.13278 (2020)

41. Yang, Z., He, X., Gao, J., Deng, L., Smola, A.: Stacked attention networks for image question answering. In: Proceedings of the IEEE Conference on Computer Vision and Pattern Recognition, pp. 21–29 (2016)
42. Zhang, P., Goyal, Y., Summers-Stay, D., Batra, D., Parikh, D.: Yin and Yang: balancing and answering binary visual questions. In: Proceedings of the IEEE Conference on Computer Vision and Pattern Recognition, pp. 5014–5022 (2016)
43. Zhang, Y., Jiang, M., Zhao, Q.: Explicit knowledge incorporation for visual reasoning. In: Proceedings of the IEEE/CVF Conference on Computer Vision and Pattern Recognition (CVPR), pp. 1356–1365, June 2021
44. Zhong, V., Xiong, C., Socher, R.: Global-locally self-attentive encoder for dialogue state tracking. In: Proceedings of the 56th Annual Meeting of the Association for Computational Linguistics (Volume 1: Long Papers), pp. 1458–1467 (2018)

VisageSynTalk: Unseen Speaker Video-to-Speech Synthesis via Speech-Visage Feature Selection

Joanna Hong⬥, Minsu Kim⬥, and Yong Man Ro⁽✉⁾⬥

Image and Video Systems Lab, School of Electrical Engineering, KAIST,
Daejeon, South Korea
{joanna2587,ms.k,ymro}@kaist.ac.kr

Abstract. The goal of this work is to reconstruct speech from a silent talking face video. Recent studies have shown impressive performance on synthesizing speech from silent talking face videos. However, they have not explicitly considered on varying identity characteristics of different speakers, which place a challenge in the video-to-speech synthesis, and this becomes more critical in unseen-speaker settings. Our approach is to separate the speech content and the visage-style from a given silent talking face video. By guiding the model to independently focus on modeling the two representations, we can obtain the speech of high intelligibility from the model even when the input video of an unseen subject is given. To this end, we introduce speech-visage selection that separates the speech content and the speaker identity from the visual features of the input video. The disentangled representations are jointly incorporated to synthesize speech through visage-style based synthesizer which generates speech by coating the visage-styles while maintaining the speech content. Thus, the proposed framework brings the advantage of synthesizing the speech containing the right content even with the silent talking face video of an unseen subject. We validate the effectiveness of the proposed framework on the GRID, TCD-TIMIT volunteer, and LRW datasets.

Keywords: Video to speech synthesis · Speech-visage selection

1 Introduction

Imagine a subway station packed with people, and a middle-aged woman next to you appears to ask you something. It is hard for you to understand her because of the noise of an incoming subway, so you try to follow her by looking at her face and mouth movements and infer what she tries to say. Then, you can finally understand and give an answer to her. These days, people frequently encounter these kinds of situations, not only in real-time but also in silent video conferences, corrupted video messages, and even conversations with a speech-impaired person

Supplementary Information The online version contains supplementary material available at https://doi.org/10.1007/978-3-031-20059-5_26.

[3]. In order to help these situations, there has been much research, namely lip-reading, on recognizing speech from silent or audio-corrupted videos.

Video-to-speech synthesis is one of the lip-reading techniques, which reconstructs speech from silent talking face videos. It has the advantage of not requiring extra human annotations (*i.e.*, text), while other conventional text-based lip-reading techniques need them [2,37]. Nevertheless, video-to-speech synthesis is considered as challenging since it is expected to represent not only the speech content but also the identity characteristics (*e.g.*, voice) of the speaker. Thus, it is difficult to be applied in unseen, even multi-speaker, settings. There has been remarkable progresses in video-to-speech synthesis [8,9,17,22,28,33,40], especially with few speakers. While they have shown impressive performances, they have not explicitly considered the varying identity characteristics of different speakers, thus not investigated well in unseen multi-speaker setting.

To alleviate the challenge, we draw inspiration from human intuition in predicting a silent speech. When a silent talking video – seen or unseen – is given, humans firstly look at the entire appearance that represents the speaker's character (e.g., gender and age) and then predict the speech sound based on the lip movements [4]. By mimicking the human speech predicting process, we propose to learn to disentangle the lip movements (*i.e.*, speech content) and the visage appearances (*i.e.*, identities) from a silent talking face video and to predict the speech by jointly modeling the two disentangled representations. In doing so, it is promising that the model can reconstruct speech containing correct content from even unseen speaker's talking face videos.

In this paper, we introduce a novel framework for video-to-speech synthesis. It consists of speech-visage feature selection module that separates speech content and visage-style (*i.e.*, identity) from a given talking face video. The proposed module exploits a deep learning-based feature selection [14,26] with feature transformation and normalization, which is jointly trained with the entire model in an end-to-end manner. The proposed module outputs speech selective masks, each of which contains the distinctive score of the speech content information in the visual feature of a talking face video while leaving out its speaker identity attributes. From the masks, the speech content features and the identity features can be separately driven. With the obtained two distinctive features through the speech-visage feature selection module, we introduce a visage-style based synthesizer, called VS-synthesizer. Inspired by [5,21], the content features are taken into the VS-synthesizer as input, and the encoded content features are sequentially coated with the visage-styles of extracted identity features.

In order to guide the proposed framework, two learning methods are proposed: visual- and audio-identification. In visual-identification learning, we guide the network to produce the same identity features when they are from the same subject and to predict right subject identity from the identity features. Through audio-identification learning, we expect that the network well predicts the correct subject identity from the generated mel-spectrogram, even when the different identity features are coated in the original speech content features.

Through the proposed framework, the model can separately focus on modeling the speech content and generating the speech with target speaker's appearance. It brings the advantage of synthesizing speech containing the right content even if a silent talking face video of an unseen subject is given. Moreover, the proposed framework can synthesize speech with different visage-styles while maintaining the original content. Our key contributions are as follows: (1) To the best of our knowledge, it is the first time to directly tackle the challenge induced from varying visage-styles of different speakers, in video-to-speech synthesis by separating the identity and speech content. (2) We design a speech-visage feature selection for masking identity attributes from a talking face video while maintaining speech content, and vice versa. (3) To guarantee the disentanglement of speech content from identity, we propose two learning methods: visual-identification and audio-identification.

2   Related Work

Video to Speech Synthesis. Speech synthesis from silent talking faces is one of the lip-reading techniques that have been consistently studied [28,43]. The initial approach [9] presented an end-to-end CNN-based model that predicts the speech audio signal from a silent talking face video and significantly improved the performance than the methods using hand-crafted visual features [29]. Another initial work [8] proposed reconstructing the speech representation by using both video frames and dense optical flow fields for capturing the dynamics of lip movements. Lip2Audspec [1] also presented a reconstruction-based video-to-speech synthesis method with autoencoders. 1D GAN-based methods [30,40] were proposed to directly synthesize a raw waveform from the lip movements video. Lip2Wav [33] introduced a well-known sequence-to-sequence architecture into video-to-speech synthesis to capture the context. Memory [17,22] proposed to use a multi-modal memory network to associate audio modalities during the inference. Distinct from the previous methods, we try to disentangle the identity characteristics and speech content from a silent talking face video for video-to-speech synthesis.

Feature Selection. Feature selection has become a focus of many research areas that utilize huge amounts of high-dimensional data. Early works [15,24] initially surveyed feature selection and extraction techniques for improving learning performance, increasing computational efficiency, decreasing memory storage, and building better generalized models. Among a number of different techniques, deep learning-based feature selection methods are hybrid feature selection methods that ensemble different feature selection algorithms to construct a group of feature subsets [24]. Deep feature selection [25] selected features by imposing a sparse regularization term to select nonzero weights features at the input level. Another work [35] proposed a method to assess which features are more likely to contribute to the classification phase. In recent research for feature selection, attention-based feature selection [14] was proposed to build the correlation that best describes the degree of relevance of the target and features. Most recently, a feature mask module [26] is proposed that considers the relationships between the original features by applying a feature mask normalization. By adopting

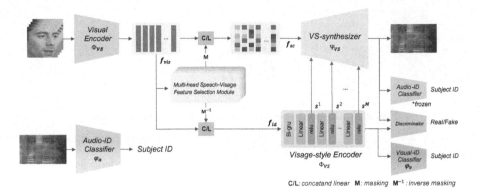

Fig. 1. Overall architecture of the proposed method, containing multi-head speech-visage feature selection and visage-style synthesizer

the feature selection concept, this paper attempts to select identity-relevant and content-relevant features from the visual representations.

3   Proposed Method

Suppose we are given a sequence of silent talking face video $x \in \mathbb{R}^{T \times H \times W \times 3}$ with length T, height H, and width W. The goal of our work is to reconstruct a mel-spectrogram $y \in \mathbb{R}^{F \times S}$ that matches the input silent talking face frames, where F and S represents the spectral dimension of the mel-spectrogram and the frame length, respectively. The main objective of our learning problem is to disentangle the speech content and the visage-style (*i.e.*, identity) from a silent talking face video, and to synthesize speech by jointly incorporating the two disentangled representations. Hence, it is for enhancing the robustness of the model to unseen speakers and bringing the advantage of generating speech of different visage-styles with fixed speech content. Figure 1 shows the overview of the proposed framework. It contains two major modules: multi-head speech-visage feature selection and visage-style based synthesizer.

3.1   Speech-Visage Feature Selection

When a silent talking face video is given, humans discriminate the entire appearances of the speaker that represent the speaker's character (*e.g.*, gender and age) and the lip movements, to associate the speech. Motivated from the human cognitive system [4], speech-visage feature selection module is designed to discriminate between human lip movements and visage-styles.

To this end, a visual encoder Φ_{VE} firstly extracts visual feature f_{vis} from a silent talking face video x with the dimension of embedding C,

$$f_{vis} = \Phi_{VE}(x) \in \mathbb{R}^{T \times C}. \tag{1}$$

From f_{vis}, the proposed speech-visage feature selection module chooses the speech content information while leaving out the identity information, by

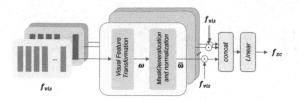

Fig. 2. Multi-head speech-visage feature selection module

producing a speech selective mask $\bar{w}$. Inspired by the modern deep feature selection method [14], the speech selective mask $\bar{w}$ is produced with two steps, non-linear transformation and normalization. Firstly, a non-linear transformation, ϕ_{trans} ($i.e.$LSTM), is applied to the visual features f_{vis} to capture the importance of each feature having on speech content,

$$w = \phi_{trans}(f_{vis}) \in \mathbb{R}^{T \times C}. \tag{2}$$

Next, mask generalization and normalization are performed to prevent the speech selective mask from being biased to the batch-wise input visual features during training [26]. This enables extracting the generalized vector from all samples. For the normalization, the softmax function is utilized to extract the importance score of the speech content of f_{vis},

$$\bar{w} = Softmax(\frac{1}{B}\sum_{i=1}^{B} w_i), \tag{3}$$

where w_i represents the transformed visual feature of i-th sample in the mini-batch size of B. Note that the generalization on mini-batch is performed during training only. Then, the speech selective mask is applied to the embedded visual feature f_{vis} to select the speech content feature as follows,

$$f_{sc} = \phi_{sc}(\bar{w} \odot f_{vis}) \in \mathbb{R}^{T \times C}, \tag{4}$$

where the ϕ_{sc} is an embedding layer, $\odot$ represents element-wise multiplication, and f_{sc} represents the selected speech content feature. Since the speech selective mask $\bar{w}$ only attends to the speech content information, making the mask opposite, $\bar{w}_c = 1 - \bar{w}$, can produce the opposite of the speech content, namely the identity feature f_{id}:

$$f_{id} = \phi_{id}(\bar{w}_c \odot f_{vis}) \in \mathbb{R}^{T \times C}, \tag{5}$$

where ϕ_{id} represents a linear layer that embeds the selected identity feature.

Multi-head Speech-Visage Feature Selection. Due to the multiple characteristics, such as gender and age, of a speaker in regard to the identity and speech content, viewing multiple aspects of the visual face features can enable a better

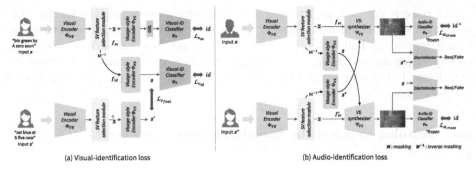

(a) Visual-identification loss   (b) Audio-identification loss

Fig. 3. Visualization of (a) visual-identification loss and (b) audio-identification loss

selection of both the speech content and identity. To enhance the feature selection procedure, the speech-visage feature selection can be employed in a multi-view fashion that produces N different speech selective masks, $\{\bar{w}^1, \ldots, \bar{w}^N\}$, as shown in Fig. 2. Similar to the multi-head attention [39], our multi-view design allows the model to jointly consider the information with different aspects (*e.g.*, gender and age). The multi-view speech-visage feature selection procedure can be written as,

$$f_{sc} = \phi_{sc}([\bar{w}^1 \odot f_{vis}, \ldots, \bar{w}^N \odot f_{vis}]), \tag{6}$$

where $[,]$ represents concatenation in the channel dimension. Similarly, we also utilize the inverse of multi-view speech selective masks to obtain the identity features,

$$f_{id} = \phi_{id}([\bar{w}_c^1 \odot f_{vis}, \ldots, \bar{w}_c^N \odot f_{vis}]). \tag{7}$$

We investigate the effect of using multiple speech selective masks in Sect. 4.3.

3.2   Visage-Style Based Synthesizer

The speech content features f_{sc} contain the correct words of speech and the identity features f_{id} have the visage-style of a certain speaker. During generation, the speech content should be maintained and only the style should be coated. Therefore, our generation objective is similar to that of style transfer [11,18,19]. For this purpose, we employ a style-based generator, namely Visage Style-based synthesizer (VS-synthesizer), which reconstructs the mel-spectrogram with respect to the speech content features f_{sc} clothed in the encoded identity features f_{id}. For the style encoder, a visage-style encoder Φ_{VS} is introduced to sequentially extract visage-style features $s = \{s^1, \ldots, s^M\}$ from the identity features f_{id}, where M represents the number of styles which will be embedded into the synthesizer through AdaIN [18,21]. The speech (*i.e.*, mel-spectrogram) $f_{mel} \in \mathbb{R}^{F \times S}$ is generated with the following equation,

$$f_{mel} = \Psi_{VS}(f_{sc}, s). \tag{8}$$

To convert the mel-spectrogram into a waveform, we utilize the Griffin-Lim algorithm [13] which is a well known method for converting linear spectrogram into a waveform. Following [42], we use a postnet that learns to convert the mel-spectrogram into a linear spectrogram which is utilized for the Griffin-Lim algorithm. It is trained with the reconstruction loss using ground-truth linear spectrograms.

3.3 Learning to Select the Speech Content

To guide the proposed speech-visage feature selection module to select the speech content feature while leaving out the identity features, we propose two identification learning methods on different modalities, visual and audio.

Visual-Identification Learning. To guide the visage-style features s obtained from the identity features $\boldsymbol{f}_{id}$ contain identity-related representation, we apply the identification loss as follows,

$$\mathcal{L}_{v_{id}} = CE(\varphi_v(\Phi_{VS}(\boldsymbol{f}_{id})), id), \tag{9}$$

where φ_v is a visual-identity classifier, CE represents the cross-entropy loss, and id is the subject identity. Therefore, both the visage-style and identity features can carry the identity-related information. In addition to the identification loss, we sample two input talking face videos with the same subject, $\boldsymbol{x}$ and $\boldsymbol{x}'$. We expect that the two extracted visage-style features from each video, s and s', to be similar, since the visage-style of the same speaker is not varying. Thus, we apply mean squared error objective function as a feature loss,

$$\mathcal{L}_{v_{feat}} = ||s - s'||_2. \tag{10}$$

Finally, to guarantee the disentanglement of speech content and identity representations, the speech content feature $\boldsymbol{f}_{sc}$ should not contain the identity representations. To achieve this, we adopt an adversarial learning concept that guides the encoder to learn to deceive a classifier. Specifically, Gradient Reversal Layer (GRL) [10] is added before the visual-identity classifier φ_v so that the gradient sign is reversed during back-propagation. The loss function of speech content feature can be written as follows,

$$\mathcal{L}_{v_{sc}} = CE(\varphi_v(grl(\Phi_{VS}(\boldsymbol{f}_{sc}))), id). \tag{11}$$

Therefore, the visual-identity classifier struggles to find the identity information from $\boldsymbol{f}_{sc}$ while the speech-visage feature selection module learns to not include the identity information into the speech content features $\boldsymbol{f}_{sc}$. Note that we only utilize the last style (*i.e.*, s^M) for the visual-identification learning instead of using all styles to reduce the computational cost. The final visual-identification loss (Fig. 3(a)) is defined as $\mathcal{L}_v = \mathcal{L}_{v_{id}} + \mathcal{L}_{v_{feat}} + \mathcal{L}_{v_{sc}}$.

Audio-Identification Learning. Although we disentangled the identity features f_{id} and speech content features f_{sc}, there is no guidance to properly incorporate the two disentangled representations for generating speech. Therefore, we additionally guide the model with a proposed audio-identification loss at the output side. To this end, a pre-trained audio-identity classifier φ_a is introduced to recognize the subject of the final synthesized mel-spectrogram,

$$\mathcal{L}_{a_{self}} = CE(\varphi_a(\Psi_{VS}(f_{sc}, s)), id). \tag{12}$$

Moreover, we design a cross speech classification learning (Fig. 3(b)); when two input talking face videos with different subjects x and x^* are given, we crossly cloth the visage-style features s and s^* into the speech content features of the different subjects, f_{sc}^* and f_{sc}, respectively. Therefore, each generated speech should contain the crossly changed visage-style (i.e., identity). This is guided with the following cross-speech classification loss,

$$\mathcal{L}_{a_{cross}} = CE(\varphi_a(\Psi_{VS}(f_{sc}, s^*)), id^*) \\ + CE(\varphi_a(\Psi_{VS}(f_{sc}^*, s)), id)). \tag{13}$$

Through the cross-speech classification loss, we can achieve both the disentanglement of speech content and identity and the ability to jointly incorporate the disentangled representations in synthesizing the desired speech. The final audio-identification loss is defined as $\mathcal{L}_a = \mathcal{L}_{a_{self}} + \mathcal{L}_{a_{cross}}$.

3.4 Total Loss Functions

Adversarial Loss. We utilize both unconditional and conditional GAN losses [12,31], where the former makes the generated mel-spectrogram realistic, and the latter guides the mel-spectrogram to match the final visage-style feature, s^M,

$$\mathcal{L}_g = logD(f_{mel}) + logD(f_{mel}, s^M), \tag{14}$$

and the discriminator loss is defined as,

$$\mathcal{L}_d = logD(y) + log(1 - D(f_{mel})) \\ + logD(y, s^M) + log(1 - D(f_{mel}, s^M)). \tag{15}$$

Reconstruction Loss. Finally, a reconstruction loss is adopted to synthesize the mel-spectrogram containing correct contents. The reconstruction loss is defined as,

$$\mathcal{L}_{recon} = ||y - f_{mel}||_2 + ||y - f_{mel}||_1. \tag{16}$$

Total Loss. The total loss function for the generator part is the sum of the pre-defined loss functions with the balancing weights α_1, α_2, α_3, and α_4,

$$\mathcal{L}_{tot} = \alpha_1 \mathcal{L}_v + \alpha_2 \mathcal{L}_a + \alpha_3 \mathcal{L}_g + \alpha_4 \mathcal{L}_{recon}. \tag{17}$$

4   Experiments

4.1   Dataset

GRID corpus [7] dataset is the most commonly used dataset for speech reconstruction tasks [1,8,9,28,30,33,40], containing 33 speakers with 6 words taken from a fixed dictionary. Since we focus on the training with a large number of subjects, we conduct experiments on two different settings: 1) multi-speaker independent (unseen) setting where the speakers in the test dataset are unseen and 2) multi-speaker dependent (seen) setting that all 33 speakers are used all training, validation, and evaluation with 90%–5%–5% split, respectively. For multi-speaker independent setting, we follow the same split as [41].

TCD-TIMIT volunteer [16] dataset has 59 speakers with about 100 phonetically rich sentences. Similar to the GRID dataset, we use two experimental settings. We utilize the officially provided data split of the TCD TIMIT dataset. Please note that it is the first time to exploit the TCD-TIMIT volunteer dataset in a video-to-speech task, which was not utilized due to its difficulties.

LRW [6] dataset contains up to 1000 utterances of 500 different words, spoken by manifold speakers. Since the original dataset does not provide identity information, we clustered and labeled the speaker information of LRW Total 17,580 speakers are labeled; train, validation, and evaluation splits are newly generated so that the subjects are completely separated among three splits (20 for test and validation, respectively, and the rest for train). It is also the first time to utilize the identity information with the multi-speaker independent (unseen) splits. The details and splits are available in supplementary materials.

4.2   Implementation Details

For both GRID and TCD-TIMIT volunteer datasets, we center-crop [44] and resize the video frames to 96×96, and 128×128 for LRW dataset. All of the audio in the dataset are resampled to 16 kHz We convert the mel-spectrogram so that the length of the mel-spectrogram is 4 times longer than that of the video frames. The architectural details of each module can be found in the supplementary materials. We use the Adam optimizer [23] with 0.0001 learning rate, discretely decaying half at step 20000, 40000, and 60000. We choose the number N of multi-head masks to 6 and 9 for multi-speaker independent setting and multi-speaker dependent setting, respectively. The number of styles is set to 3 (*i.e.*, $M = 3$). The hyperparameters α_1, α_2, α_3, and α_4 are 1.0, 1.0, 1.0, and 50.0, respectively. For computing, we use a single Titan-RTX GPU.

For the evaluation, we use three standard speech quality metrics: Short Time Objective Intelligibility (STOI) [38], Extended Short Time Objective Intelligibility (ESTOI) [20] for estimating the intelligibility and Perceptual Evaluation of Speech Quality (PESQ) [34]. To verify our generated speech, we conduct a human subjective study through mean opinion scores of naturalness, content accuracy, and voice matching.

Table 1. Performance comparison in multi-speaker independent setting on GRID

Method	STOI	ESTOI	PESQ
GAN-based [40]	0.445	0.188	1.240
Vocoder-based [28]	0.537	0.227	1.230
Lip2Wav [33]	0.522	0.251	1.284
VV-Memory [17]	0.550	0.275	1.346
End-to-end GAN [30]	0.553	0.269	1.372
Proposed model	**0.567**	**0.308**	**1.373**

Table 2. Performance comparison in multi-speaker independent setting on TCD-TIMIT volunteer dataset

Method	STOI	ESTOI	PESQ
Lip2Wav [33]	0.456	0.210	1.375
VV-Memory [17]	0.450	0.212	1.382
Proposed model	**0.478**	**0.217**	**1.410**

4.3 Experimental Results

Results in Multi-speaker Independent Setting. To verify the robustness of the proposed framework to unseen speakers, we conduct the experiments on a multi-speaker independent setting of the GRID and TCD-TIMIT volunteer datasets, where unseen subjects are utilized for testing. Table 1 elaborates the performance comparisons on the GRID dataset. We can clearly see that the proposed method outperforms the state-of-the-art performances. For the TCD-TIMIT volunteer dataset, shown in the upper part of Table 2, our proposed method achieved 0.478, 0.217, and 1.410, in STOI, ESTOI, and PESQ, respectively, outperforming the previous works [17,33].

We additionally conduct a human subjective study through mean opinion scores (MOS) for naturalness, intelligibility, and voice matching. Naturalness evaluates how natural the synthetic speech is compared to the actual human voice, and intelligibility evaluates how clear words in the synthetic speech sound compared to the actual transcription. For the above two measures, naturalness and intelligibility, we follow the exactly same protocol of the previous works [17,33]. We additionally measure voice matching part that determines how well the results of the proposed model matches the voice of the target speaker. We use 20 samples obtained from the multi-speaker independent setting of the GRID dataset and ask 16 participants to evaluate 6 different approaches and the ground truth in a 5-point scale. The mean scores with 95% confidence intervals are shown in Table 3. Our method achieves the score of 2.96, 3.35, and 3.34 for naturalness, intelligibility, and voice matching, respectively, which are the best among the state-of-the-art methods. Especially, the highest intelligibility means the proposed framework can generate speech containing the right content by

Table 3. MOS results comparison of the previous methods [22,28,30,33,40], the proposed method, and the ground truth

Method	Naturalness	Intelligibility	Voice matching
GAN-based [40]	1.94 ± 0.22	1.74 ± 0.21	1.37 ± 0.17
Vocoder-based [28]	1.98 ± 0.16	1.68 ± 0.25	1.15 ± 0.11
Lip2Wav [33]	2.71 ± 0.25	2.64 ± 0.24	2.71 ± 0.23
VV-Memory [17]	2.91 ± 0.19	2.80 ± 0.23	2.85 ± 0.26
End-to-end GAN [30]	2.68 ± 0.22	2.76 ± 0.26	2.18 ± 0.19
Proposed model	$\mathbf{2.96 \pm 0.28}$	$\mathbf{3.35 \pm 0.34}$	$\mathbf{3.34 \pm 0.27}$
Actual voice	4.28 ± 0.40	4.73 ± 0.41	–

Table 4. Performance comparison in multi-speaker dependent setting on GRID corpus

Method	STOI	ESTOI	PESQ
End-to-end GAN [30]	0.647	0.436	1.777
Proposed model	**0.667**	**0.502**	**1.868**

Table 5. Performance comparison in multi-speaker dependent setting on TCD-TIMIT volunteer dataset

Method	STOI	ESTOI	PESQ
Lip2Wav [33]	0.524	0.303	1.545
VV-Memory [17]	0.555	**0.356**	1.584
Proposed model	**0.557**	0.352	**1.587**

disentangling the speech content from the identity representations. Moreover, from the voice matching, we verify that the model can synthesize the proper voices that follow the visages of the subjects even if the subjects are not seen before.

Results in Multi-speaker Dependent Setting. To verify that the effectiveness of the proposed method in a multi-speaker dependent setting, we conduct experiments on the full data of the GRID dataset and the TCD-TIMIT volunteer dataset. Table 4 shows the comparison results on the GRID dataset with the previous state-of-the-art method [30]. The results on the TCD-TIMIT volunteer dataset are shown in Table 5. The proposed method achieves the best performances except for ESTOI, but it shows comparable performance with [17]. The results in the multi-speaker dependent setting show that the proposed method is effective not only for an unseen speaker but also for multi-speaker.

Results on Dataset with a Large Number of Subjects. We additionally conduct an experiment on LRW dataset which contains 17,580 subjects to verify the generalization of the proposed model to new large unseen speakers. Table 6 shows the performance in multi-speaker independent (unseen) setting on LRW. This even indicates the comparable performance to the results reported in Lip2Wav [33] (0.543 STOI, 0.344 ESTOI, and 1.197 PESQ) which has performed the experiments on LRW dataset with the original seen setting that contain overlapped subjects in all train, validation, and test splits. This proves

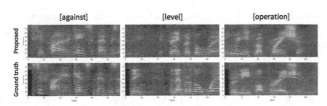

Fig. 4. Qualitative results of generated mel-spectrogram of ground truth and the proposed method on LRW

Table 6. Performance in multi-speaker independent setting on LRW

Proposed model	
STOI	0.555
ESTOI	0.305
PESQ	1.264

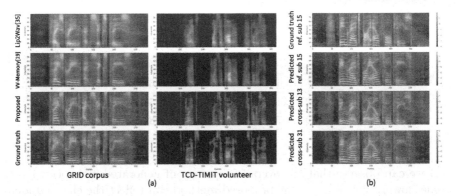

Fig. 5. Qualitative results of (a) generated mel-spectrogram of ground truth, the proposed method, [17], and [33] in multi-speaker independent setting of GRID corpus and TCD-TIMIT datasets and (b) the ground truth and the generated mel-spectrogram by changing the reference speaking-style features of subject id 15 (female) with that of subject id 13 (male), and that of subject id 31 (female)

that our model works well on dataset with a very large number of subjects with diverse vocabulary, thus generalizing our model's performance. The audio samples of the generated speech of LRW are available in supplementary materials.

Qualitative Results. We visualize the generated mel-spectrogram with the ground truth ones and those from the previous works [17,33]. Figure 5(a) indicates the generated mel-spectrogram from the multi-speaker independent setting of the GRID and TCD-TIMIT datasets, respectively. Additionally, Fig. 4 shows the generated mel-spectrogram of words *against, level,* and *operation* in LRW dataset with the ground truth ones. It is clearly shown that the generated mel-spectrograms from the proposed method are visually well-matched with the ground truth mel-spectrograms.

One of our contribution is that we can synthesize speech with different visage-styles by altering the identity features f_{id} with others. Figure 5(b) shows the results of the generated mel-spectrogram with different visage-style features, subject id 13 and 31, which are originally from the subject id 15 of the GRID corpus dataset. When we generate with male speaker's visage-style (*i.e.*, subject

Table 7. Ablation study in multi-speaker independent setting on GRID dataset

Baseline	Proposed method			STOI	ESTOI	PESQ
	$\mathcal{L}_v$	$\mathcal{L}_a$	Multi-head			
✓	✗	✗	✗	0.521	0.247	1.288
✓	✓	✗	✗	0.532	0.289	1.299
✓	✓	✓	✗	0.556	0.291	1.360
✓	✓	✓	✓	**0.567**	**0.308**	**1.373**

Table 8. Analysis on different number of speech selective masks in multi-speaker dependent setting on GRID dataset

Metric	N = 1	N = 3	N = 6	**N = 9**
STOI	0.651	0.648	0.653	**0.667**
ESTOI	0.489	0.480	0.486	**0.502**
PESQ	1.706	1.738	1.767	**1.868**

id 13) we can observe that the overall frequency of generated mel-spectrogram becomes lower, which means the proposed method can reflect the changed identity features. The audio samples are provided in the supplementary materials.

Ablation Study. We analyze the effectiveness of the proposed architecture through ablation studies. We firstly verify two proposed learning methods, visual- and audio-identification, that help to guide the speech-visage feature selection module. Then, we examine that the multi-head speech-visage feature selection technique is more beneficial than the single speech-visage feature selection. Table 7 shows the ablation results in the multi-speaker independent setting using the GRID dataset. The baseline is the model that does not apply the speech-visage feature selection, so f_{vis} are taken in to both VS-synthesizer and visage-style encoder. After applying the speech-visage feature selection, the performances increases when both visual- and audio- identification learning methods are adopted. The highest performances are obtained when multiple selections are adopted with 6 heads in the feature selection. The result shows that the multiple masks help the module to discover various attributes of the input visual features, thus yielding better separation of the speech content and identity, which are finally beneficial to reconstruct the speech of diverse speakers.

Effectiveness of Multi-heads. To analyze the effect of different number of speech selective masks from the multi-head speech-visage feature selection module, we check the performances by differing the number of heads in multi-speaker dependent setting on the GRID dataset, shown in Table 8. While the proposed method with the single speech selective mask achieves the reasonable perfor-

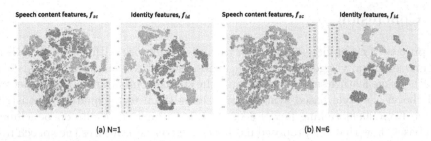

Speech content features, f_{sc} Identity features, f_{id} Speech content features, f_{sc} Identity features, f_{id}

(a) N=1   (b) N=6

Fig. 6. t-SNE [27] visualization of speech content features f_{sc} and identity features f_{id} of (a) single speech visage feature selection procedure (N = 1) and (b) multi-head speech visage feature selection procedure (N = 6) in regard to the subject ids

Table 9. The Equal Error Rate (EER) for evaluating the content-voice disentanglement quality

EER (%)	f_{id}	f_{id}
N = 1	29.44	33.84
N = 6	16.90	46.48

mance compared to [30] in Table 4, the 9 speech selective masks helps the proposed model attaining the highest performances. This means that the sufficient number of the speech selective masks enables our model to separate the speech content and identity.

We additionally visualize the representations of speech content features f_{sc} and identity features f_{id} in multi-speaker independent setting on the GRID dataset. Figure 6(a) shows t-SNE [27] visualization of two features from the single speech-visage feature selection procedure, $N = 1$, and Fig. 6(b) shows the two features from $N = 6$. Each color represents a different subject identity. We can observe that the identity feature f_{id} tends to be clustered with the same identity while the speech content feature f_{sc} does not, confirming the proposed framework is effective for disentangling the two factors. Moreover, when we increase the number of heads for the speech-visage selection module, the disentanglement is further strengthened as seen in the better-clustered identity features f_{id}.

Speaker Verification on Disentangled Features. Finally, we perform the speaker verification on the disentangled identity features f_{id} and the speech content features f_{sc} in multi-speaker independent setting on the GRID. We quantitatively evaluate the content-voice disentanglement quality using the Equal Error Rate (EER) (The lower the EER value, the higher the accuracy) which is commonly used for identity verification. Following [32], we find the EER of f_{id} to be 29.44% and that of f_{sc} to be 33.84% for $N = 1$, and 16.90% and that of f_{sc} to be 46.48% for $N = 6$, shown in Table 9. The results show that the proposed method can well disentangle the identity and speech content representations. With the greater N, the model can disentangle the two features more clearly.

5   Conclusion

We propose a novel video-to-speech synthesis framework with the speech-visage feature selection, visage-style based synthesizer, and two learning methods. The speech-visage feature selection separates the speech content and speaker identity, and the visage-style based synthesizer utilizes them to adequately reconstruct speech from silent talking face videos. The experimental results on benchmark databases show that the proposed method effectively synthesizes the speech from silent talking face videos of unseen speakers [36].

Acknowledgement. This work was supported by the National Research Foundation of Korea (NRF) grant funded by the Korea government (MSIT) (No. NRF-2022R1A2C2005529).

References

1. Akbari, H., Arora, H., Cao, L., Mesgarani, N.: Lip2Audspec: speech reconstruction from silent lip movements video. In: 2018 IEEE International Conference on Acoustics, Speech and Signal Processing (ICASSP), pp. 2516–2520. IEEE (2018)
2. Assael, Y.M., Shillingford, B., Whiteson, S., De Freitas, N.: LipNet: end-to-end sentence-level lipreading. arXiv preprint arXiv:1611.01599 (2016)
3. Burnham, D., Campbell, R., Away, G., Dodd, B.: Hearing Eye II: The Psychology of Speechreading and Auditory-Visual Speech. Psychology Press (2013)
4. Chen, T.: Audiovisual speech processing. IEEE Sig. Process. Mag. **18**(1), 9–21 (2001)
5. Chen, Y.H., Wu, D.Y., Wu, T.H., Lee, H.Y.: Again-VC: a one-shot voice conversion using activation guidance and adaptive instance normalization. In: ICASSP 2021–2021 IEEE International Conference on Acoustics, Speech and Signal Processing (ICASSP), pp. 5954–5958. IEEE (2021)
6. Chung, J.S., Zisserman, A.: Lip reading in the wild. In: Lai, S.-H., Lepetit, V., Nishino, K., Sato, Y. (eds.) ACCV 2016. LNCS, vol. 10112, pp. 87–103. Springer, Cham (2017). https://doi.org/10.1007/978-3-319-54184-6_6
7. Cooke, M., Barker, J., Cunningham, S., Shao, X.: An audio-visual corpus for speech perception and automatic speech recognition. J. Acoust. Soc. Am. **120**(5), 2421–2424 (2006)
8. Ephrat, A., Halperin, T., Peleg, S.: Improved speech reconstruction from silent video. In: Proceedings of the IEEE International Conference on Computer Vision Workshops, pp. 455–462 (2017)
9. Ephrat, A., Peleg, S.: Vid2Speech: speech reconstruction from silent video. In: 2017 IEEE International Conference on Acoustics, Speech and Signal Processing (ICASSP), pp. 5095–5099. IEEE (2017)
10. Ganin, Y., Lempitsky, V.: Unsupervised domain adaptation by backpropagation. In: International Conference on Machine Learning, pp. 1180–1189. PMLR (2015)
11. Gatys, L.A., Ecker, A.S., Bethge, M.: Image style transfer using convolutional neural networks. In: Proceedings of the IEEE Conference on Computer Vision and Pattern Recognition, pp. 2414–2423 (2016)
12. Goodfellow, I., et al.: Generative adversarial nets. In: Advances in Neural Information Processing Systems, vol. 27 (2014)

13. Griffin, D., Lim, J.: Signal estimation from modified short-time Fourier transform. IEEE Trans. Acoust. Speech Sig. Process. **32**(2), 236–243 (1984)
14. Gui, N., Ge, D., Hu, Z.: AFS: an attention-based mechanism for supervised feature selection. In: Proceedings of the AAAI Conference on Artificial Intelligence, vol. 33, pp. 3705–3713 (2019)
15. Guyon, I., Elisseeff, A.: An introduction to variable and feature selection. J. Mach. Learn. Res. **3**, 1157–1182 (2003)
16. Harte, N., Gillen, E.: TCD-TIMIT: an audio-visual corpus of continuous speech. IEEE Trans. Multimedia **17**(5), 603–615 (2015)
17. Hong, J., Kim, M., Park, S.J., Ro, Y.M.: Speech reconstruction with reminiscent sound via visual voice memory. IEEE/ACM Trans. Audio Speech Lang. Process. **29**, 3654–3667 (2021)
18. Huang, X., Belongie, S.: Arbitrary style transfer in real-time with adaptive instance normalization. In: Proceedings of the IEEE International Conference on Computer Vision, pp. 1501–1510 (2017)
19. Huang, X., Liu, M.-Y., Belongie, S., Kautz, J.: Multimodal unsupervised image-to-image translation. In: Ferrari, V., Hebert, M., Sminchisescu, C., Weiss, Y. (eds.) ECCV 2018. LNCS, vol. 11207, pp. 179–196. Springer, Cham (2018). https://doi.org/10.1007/978-3-030-01219-9_11
20. Jensen, J., Taal, C.H.: An algorithm for predicting the intelligibility of speech masked by modulated noise maskers. IEEE/ACM Trans. Audio Speech Lang. Process. **24**(11), 2009–2022 (2016)
21. Karras, T., Laine, S., Aila, T.: A style-based generator architecture for generative adversarial networks. In: Proceedings of the IEEE/CVF Conference on Computer Vision and Pattern Recognition, pp. 4401–4410 (2019)
22. Kim, M., Hong, J., Park, S.J., Ro, Y.M.: Multi-modality associative bridging through memory: speech sound recollected from face video. In: Proceedings of the IEEE/CVF International Conference on Computer Vision, pp. 296–306 (2021)
23. Kingma, D.P., Ba, J.: Adam: a method for stochastic optimization. arXiv preprint arXiv:1412.6980 (2014)
24. Li, J., et al.: Feature selection: a data perspective. ACM Comput. Surv. (CSUR) **50**(6), 1–45 (2017)
25. Li, Y., Chen, C.Y., Wasserman, W.W.: Deep feature selection: theory and application to identify enhancers and promoters. J. Comput. Biol. **23**(5), 322–336 (2016)
26. Liao, Y., Latty, R., Yang, B.: Feature selection using batch-wise attenuation and feature mask normalization. In: 2021 International Joint Conference on Neural Networks (IJCNN), pp. 1–9. IEEE (2021)
27. Van der Maaten, L., Hinton, G.: Visualizing data using t-SNE. J. Mach. Learn. Res. **9**(11), 2578–2605 (2008)
28. Michelsanti, D., Slizovskaia, O., Haro, G., Gómez, E., Tan, Z.H., Jensen, J.: Vocoder-based speech synthesis from silent videos. In: Interspeech 2020, pp. 3530–3534 (2020)
29. Milner, B., Le Cornu, T.: Reconstructing intelligible audio speech from visual speech features. In: Interspeech 2015 (2015)
30. Mira, R., Vougioukas, K., Ma, P., Petridis, S., Schuller, B.W., Pantic, M.: End-to-end video-to-speech synthesis using generative adversarial networks. arXiv preprint arXiv:2104.13332 (2021)
31. Mirza, M., Osindero, S.: Conditional generative adversarial nets. arXiv preprint arXiv:1411.1784 (2014)
32. Nagrani, A., Chung, J.S., Zisserman, A.: VoxCeleb: a large-scale speaker identification dataset. arXiv preprint arXiv:1706.08612 (2017)

33. Prajwal, K., Mukhopadhyay, R., Namboodiri, V.P., Jawahar, C.: Learning individual speaking styles for accurate lip to speech synthesis. In: Proceedings of the IEEE/CVF Conference on Computer Vision and Pattern Recognition, pp. 13796–13805 (2020)

34. Rix, A., Beerends, J., Hollier, M., Hekstra, A.: Perceptual evaluation of speech quality (PESQ)-a new method for speech quality assessment of telephone networks and codecs. In: 2001 IEEE International Conference on Acoustics, Speech, and Signal Processing. Proceedings (Cat. No. 01CH37221), vol. 2, pp. 749–752 (2001). https://doi.org/10.1109/ICASSP.2001.941023

35. Roy, D., Murty, K.S.R., Mohan, C.K.: Feature selection using deep neural networks. In: 2015 International Joint Conference on Neural Networks (IJCNN), pp. 1–6. IEEE (2015)

36. Selvaraju, R.R., Cogswell, M., Das, A., Vedantam, R., Parikh, D., Batra, D.: Grad-CAM: visual explanations from deep networks via gradient-based localization. In: Proceedings of the IEEE International Conference on Computer Vision, pp. 618–626 (2017)

37. Stafylakis, T., Tzimiropoulos, G.: Combining residual networks with LSTMs for lipreading. arXiv preprint arXiv:1703.04105 (2017)

38. Taal, C.H., Hendriks, R.C., Heusdens, R., Jensen, J.: A short-time objective intelligibility measure for time-frequency weighted noisy speech. In: 2010 IEEE International Conference on Acoustics, Speech and Signal Processing, pp. 4214–4217. IEEE (2010)

39. Vaswani, A., et al.: Attention is all you need. In: Advances in Neural Information Processing Systems, pp. 5998–6008 (2017)

40. Vougioukas, K., Ma, P., Petridis, S., Pantic, M.: Video-driven speech reconstruction using generative adversarial networks. arXiv preprint arXiv:1906.06301 (2019)

41. Vougioukas, K., Petridis, S., Pantic, M.: End-to-end speech-driven facial animation with temporal GANs. arXiv preprint arXiv:1805.09313 (2018)

42. Wang, Y., et al.: Tacotron: towards end-to-end speech synthesis. arXiv preprint arXiv:1703.10135 (2017)

43. Yadav, R., Sardana, A., Namboodiri, V.P., Hegde, R.M.: Speech prediction in silent videos using variational autoencoders. In: ICASSP 2021–2021 IEEE International Conference on Acoustics, Speech and Signal Processing (ICASSP), pp. 7048–7052. IEEE (2021)

44. Zhang, S., Zhu, X., Lei, Z., Shi, H., Wang, X., Li, S.Z.: S3FD: single shot scale-invariant face detector. In: Proceedings of the IEEE International Conference on Computer Vision, pp. 192–201 (2017)

Classification-Regression for Chart Comprehension

Matan Levy[1(✉)], Rami Ben-Ari[2], and Dani Lischinski[1]

[1] The Hebrew University of Jerusalem, Jerusalem, Israel
levy@cs.huji.ac.il
[2] OriginAI, Ramat-Gan, Israel

Abstract. Chart question answering (CQA) is a task used for assessing chart comprehension, which is fundamentally different from understanding natural images. CQA requires analyzing the relationships between the textual and the visual components of a chart, in order to answer general questions or infer numerical values. Most existing CQA *datasets* and *models* are based on simplifying assumptions that often enable surpassing human performance. In this work, we address this outcome and propose a new model that jointly learns classification and regression. Our language-vision setup uses co-attention transformers to capture the complex real-world interactions between the question and the textual elements. We validate our design with extensive experiments on the realistic PlotQA dataset, outperforming previous approaches by a large margin, while showing competitive performance on FigureQA. Our model is particularly well suited for realistic questions with out-of-vocabulary answers that require regression.

Keywords: Chart question answering · Multimodal learning

1 Introduction

Figures and charts play a major role in modern communication, help to convey messages by curating data into an easily comprehensible visual form, highlighting the trends and outliers. However, despite tremendous practical importance, chart comprehension has received little attention in the computer vision community. Documents ubiquitously contain a variety of plots. Using computer vision to parse these visualizations can enable extraction of information that cannot be gleaned solely from a document's text. Recently, with the rise of multimodal learning methods, *e.g.*, [4,6,18,21,23,25,26,30], interest in chart understanding has increased [5,13–15,20,27].

Studies on figure understanding (*e.g.*, [15,20]), commonly involve answering questions, a task known as Chart Question Answering (CQA). This task is closely

---

M. Levy—Part of this research was conducted at IBM Research AI, Israel.

Supplementary Information The online version contains supplementary material available at https://doi.org/10.1007/978-3-031-20059-5_27.

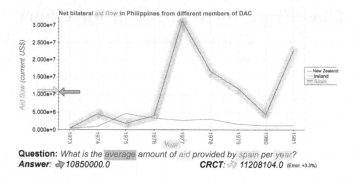

Fig. 1. Interactions marked on a sample from the PlotQA dataset [20], alongside with our CRCT prediction. We highlight the interacting parts/tokens with matching colors. Note the complexity of attention between the different modalities needed to correctly answer the question. The result predicted by CRCT and the ground truth answer are indicated by green and purple arrows. (Color figure online)

related to Visual Question Answering (VQA), which is usually applied on natural images [2,6,26,30]. VQA is typically treated as a classification task, where the answer is a category, *e.g.*, [1,2,19,30]. In contrast, answering questions about charts often requires regression. Furthermore, a small local change in a natural image typically has limited effect on the visual recognition outcome, while in a chart, the impact might be extensive. Previous works have demonstrated that standard VQA methods perform poorly on CQA benchmarks [13,20]. A chart comprehension model must consider the interactions between the question and the various chart elements in order to provide correct answers. The complexity of such interactions is demonstrated in Fig. 1. For example, failing to correctly associate a line with the correct legend text would yield an erroneous answer.

Several previous CQA studies suggest a new dataset along with a new processing model, *e.g.*, [5,13,15,20]. CQA datasets differ in several ways: (1) type and diversity of figures, (2) type and diversity of questions, (3) types of answers (*e.g.*, discrete or continuous). While previous methods have recently reached a saturation level on some datasets, *e.g.*, 94.9% on FigureQA [15], 92.2% on LEAF-QA++ [27], and 97.5% on DVQA [13], Methani *et al.* [20] attribute this to the limitations of these datasets. Hence, they propose a new dataset (PlotQA-D), which is the largest and the most diverse dataset to date, with an order of magnitude more images/figures and ×4,000 different answers. PlotQA-D further contains more challenging and realistic reasoning and data retrieval tasks, with a new model (PlotQA-M) achieving 22.5% accuracy on this dataset, while human performance reached 80.47% [20].

In this paper we further explore the cause behind the saturation of various methods on previous data sets. We argue that similarly to early stages of VQA [8], several common datasets and benchmarks suffer from bias, oversimplicity and classification oriented Q&A, allowing some methods to surpass human performance [14,27]. Next, we introduce a novel method called Classification - Regression Chart Transformer (CRCT) for CQA. We start with parsing

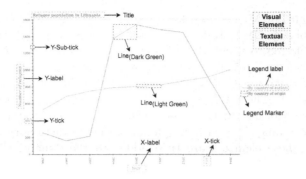

Fig. 2. Examples of object annotations in train images.

the chart with a detector that extracts all of its textual and visual elements, which are then passed, along with the question text, to a dual branch transformer for bimodal learning. Our model features the following novelties: 1) In contrast to previous methods that encode only the question, our language model jointly processes all textual elements in the chart, allowing inter and intra relations between all textual and visual elements. 2) We show high generalization by dropping the common 'string matching' practice (replacing question tokens with certain textual chart elements), and accommodating a co-transformer with pre-trained BERT [7]. 3) We introduce a new chart element representation learning, fusing multiple inputs from different domains. 4) Finally, a new hybrid prediction head is suggested, allowing unification of classification and regression into a single model. By jointly optimizing our model end-to-end for all types of questions, we further leverage the multi-task learning regime [31].

We test our model on the challenging and more realistic dataset of PlotQA-D, as well as on FigureQA. Our results show that CRCT outperforms the previous method by a large margin on PlotQA-D (76.94% vs. 53.96% total accuracy), capable of matching previous results with 10% of the training data. We further analyze our model via explainability visualizations, revealing its limitations as well as strong capabilities.

2 Related Work

In this section, we review existing CQA models, while focusing on the datasets in Sect. 3. In particular, we find that previous methods are often over-fitted to the type of datasets and corresponding questions/answers (Q&A).

Some CQA methods take the entire chart image as input to the model [13–15], while others first parse the image to extract visual elements using a detector [5,20,27]. An example of chart elements and their corresponding class name, obtained from a detector, are shown in Fig. 2.

The pioneering model of Kahou *et al.* [15] outputs binary (Yes/No) answers using a backbone pretrained on ImageNet fed into a Relation Network (RN) [24], in parallel to an LSTM [11] used for question encoding. Removing the strong limitation to binary Q&A, Kafle *et al.* [13] proposed a new dataset (DVQA) and a model referred to as SANDY. The dataset introduces new question types with *out-of-vocabulary (OOV)* answers. These answers are chart specific (*e.g.*, *Which item sold the most units in any store?*) and do not necessarily appear in the training set. The SANDY model is a classification network (SAN [30]) with DYnamic encoding. In their approach, each text element in the chart is associated with a unique token in a dynamic encoding dictionary, based on the text location. These elements are then added to the dynamic list of answer classes. Kafle *et al.* [14] later introduced PReFIL, another detector-free model with two branches: a visual branch based on DenseNet [12], and a text branch based on LSTM to encode the question. For bimodal fusion, they apply a series of 1×1 convolutions on concatenated visual and question features.

Singh and Shekar [27] introduced STL-CQA, a new detector-based approach, combining transformers followed by co-transformers [3]. Their method however, relies on replacement of tokens from the question with their string match in the chart, therefore tailored to the dataset question generator and is trained on its dictionary. As also claimed by the authors, STL-CQA is likely to fail in real cases where entities are addressed through their variations, which is the case in a reality as represented also in the PlotQA-D dataset.

All the above methods use only a classification head, without a regression capability, strongly limiting the generalization of these methods to realistic charts. OOV answers are therefore limited only to values appearing in the chart's image or *seen in train set* and added a-priori to the answer classes (see Table 1, Sect. 3). They commonly overlook the lingual relations between the chart's text, such as the relations between the content of the title, the legend, and the question. Instead, they only rely on the position of the text in the chart as a hint for its class. Nevertheless, PReFIL showed overall accuracy above 93% on FigureQA and DVQA surpassing human performance. Recent results shown in [20] imply that these datasets are strictly "forgiving" with respect to regression capability and lingual interactions between the questions and chart text (see Sect. 3).

Recently, Methani *et al.* [20] introduced a new method (PlotQA-M) and dataset (PlotQA-D). To the best of our knowledge, this is the first model to address the regression task, suggesting a solution for reasoning on realistic charts. PlotQA-M uses a visual detector and two separate pipelines. In a staging structure, a trained classifier switches between the pipelines, one handling fixed vocabulary classification, and the other for dealing with OOV and regression. In its OOV branch, PlotQA-M first converts the chart to a table and uses a standard table question-answering [22], to generate an answer. This pipeline branching complicates the model requiring each pipeline to be optimized separately and trained on a separate subset of the data, missing the impact of multi-task learning, which we further show as a strong advantage. Furthermore, PlotQA-M inter and intra visual-text interactions from the chart image are only determined through question encoding and a preprocessing stage using prior assumption on proximity between chart elements.

Table 1. CQA datasets comparison. Real world vocabulary refers to axes variables. Some datasets apply question paraphrasing (par.)

Dataset	#Plot types	#Plot images	#Q&A pairs	Avg. question length	Q&A #Templates	#Unique answers	Open vocab.	Real World Vocabulary	Semantic Relations	Bbox Ann.	Regression answers	Publicly Available
FigureQA	4	180k	2.4M	33.39	15 (no variations)	2	✗	✗ (100 colors names)	✗	✓	✗	✓
DVQA	1	300k	3.5M	55.22	26 (w\o par.)	1.5k	✓ (Strings)	✗ (1K nouns)	✗	Partial	✗	✓
LEAF-QA	5	246k	1.9M	–	35 (with par.)	12k	✓ (Strings)	✓	✓	✓	✗	✗
LEAF-QA++	5	246k	2.6M	65.65	75 (with par.)	25k	✓ (Strings)	✓	✓	✓	✗	✗
PlotQA-D1	3	224k	8.2M	78.96	74 (with par.)	1M	✓ (Strings, Floats)	✓	✓	✓	✓ (29.86%)	✓
PlotQA-D2	3	224k	29M	105.18	74 (with par.)	5.7M	✓ (Strings, Floats)	✓	✓	✓	✓ (88.84%)	✓

3 Datasets

In this section we discuss the properties of existing CQA datasets, emphasizing the bias they introduce into the models and the evaluation methodologies that were proposed. Table 1 presents various properties of these datasets that may strongly impact the realism and generalization of the results to a real world application. This is an extended version of a table shown by Methani *et al.* [20].

Probably the most popular CQA datasets/benchmarks are FigureQA [15] and DVQA [13], both of which are publicly available. FigureQA consists of line plots, bar charts, pie plots, and dot line plots, with question templates that require binary answers. The plot titles and the axes label strings are constant; the axes range is mostly in [0, 100] with low variation; and the legends are chosen from a small set of *color names* (see example in supplementary material). These properties detract from the realism of this dataset.

DVQA [13] contains a single type of charts (bar charts), but offers more complexity in Q&A. The answers are no longer only binary, and may be out of vocabulary (OOV). Questions are split to three conceptual types: **Structural, Data retrieval** and **Reasoning**. Structural questions refer to the chart's structure (*e.g., How many bars are there?*). Data retrieval questions require the retrieval of information from the chart (*e.g., What is the label of the third bar from the bottom?*). Reasoning questions demand a higher level of perceptual understanding from the chart and require a combination of several sub-tasks (*e.g., Which algorithm has the lowest accuracy across all datasets?*). Yet, this dataset suffers from lack of semantic relations between the text elements (*e.g.,* bar and legend labels are randomly selected words), and the range of values on the Y-axis is limited. About 46 out of 1.5K unique answers are numeric, consisting of integers with the same values in the train and test sets, allowing a classification head to handle data retrieval and reasoning.

Two more datasets LEAF-QA [5] and LEAF-QA++ [27], have fewer Q&A pairs than DVQA, but several types of charts, and use a real world vocabulary with semantic relations (see Table 1). However, they are both proprietary. All the mentioned datasets share a strong limitation, lack of regression Q&A, indicated by their question templates and their discrete answer set. PlotQA-D

[20] is, however, the largest and most comprehensive publicly released dataset to date. This dataset consists of charts generated from real-world data, thereby exhibiting realistic lingual relations between textual elements. The questions and answers are based on multiple crowd-sourced templates. PlotQA-D consists of three different chart types: line-plots, bar-charts (horizontal and vertical), and dot line plots. The range of the Y-axis values is orders of magnitudes larger (up to $[0, 3.5 \times 10^{15}]$) with non-integer answers generally not seen in training, resulting over 5.7M of different answers. In contrast to previous datasets, PlotQA-D often requires a regressor for correctly answering questions. Nearly 30% and 90% of questions require regression in PlotQA-D1 and PlotQA-D2 respectively (see Table 1). To the best of our knowledge, PlotQA-D is currently the most realistic publicly available dataset. PlotQA-D offers two benchmarks, the first version of the dataset PlotQA-D1, and its extended version PlotQA-D2, which contains the former as a subset (28% of the Q&A pairs on the charts). The majority of PlotQA-D2 question types require regression (see the suppl. material). We believe that saturated performance on DVQA (97.5%), probably attributed to a single plot type and having only 1.5K unique in contrast to 5.7M answers in PlotQA-D, makes it inappropriate for regression benchmarking.

4   Method

We present an overview of our CRCT architecture for CQA in Fig. 3. In our approach, the image is first parsed by a trained object detector (see object classes in Fig. 2). The output of the parsing stage are object classes, positions (bounding boxes), and visual features. All of the above are projected into a single representation per visual element, then stacked to form the *visual sequence*. Similarly, each textual element is represented by fusing its text tokens, positional encoding and class. Together with the question text tokens, we obtain the *text sequence*. The two sequences are fed in parallel to a bimodal co-attention-transformer (co-transformer). The output of the co-transformer are pooled visual and textual representations that are then fused by Hadamard product and concatenation, and fed into our unified classification-regression head. In the next sections we describe the train and test configurations in detail.

Visual Encoding: The visual branch encodes all the visual elements in the chart, *e.g.*, line segments or legend markers. For visual encoding we train a Mask-RCNN [9] with a ResNet-50 [10] backbone. Object representations are then extracted from the penultimate layer in the classification branch. In our detection scheme objects are textual elements (*e.g.*, title, xlabel) as well as visual elements (*e.g.*, plot segment) as shown in Fig. 2. We create a single representation per visual element by a learnable block as shown in Fig. 4a. This block takes as input the 4D vector describing the bounding box (normalized top-left and bottom-right coordinates), the class label and the object representation produced by the detector (encapsulating *e.g.*, the line direction), and projects them to an embedding space (1024D).

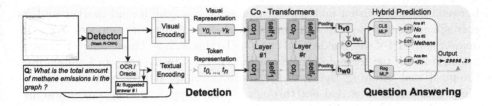

Fig. 3. Our Classification - Regression Chart Transformer (CRCT) network architecture consists of two stages of detection and question answering. The detection stage (left) provides bounding boxes and object representations of the visual and textual elements (see Fig. 2). These features, along with the question text, enable the co-transformers in the second stage (right) to fuse both visual and textual information into a pooled tuple of two single feature vectors $\{h_{v_0}, h_{w_0}\}$. Next, our hybrid prediction head containing two different MLPs, outputs a classification score and a regression result. $co_i/self_i$: co/self attention.

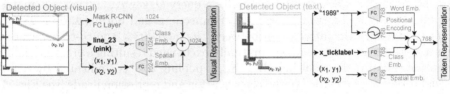

(a) Visual Representation.   (b) Textual Representation (per token).

Fig. 4. Chart element representations. The relevant information for representing each type of element is summed into a single vector.

Object colors are generally encoded in the representation output from the detector. However the actual colors are often important for linking the legend marker to the legend label (text), allowing the connection between the question and the target line or bar in the chart. Our observation shows that training the detector with decomposition of graphs to colors, boosts the performance. Finally, our visual element representations form a sequence, is denoted by $v_1, ..., v_k$. We further add the global plot representation (v_0) as [CLS] token.

Text Encoding: Raw text is handled with a pretrained BERT [7]. The textual features are derived from the question and the text contained within the chart, such as the axes labels, legends and title. In contrast to VQA where the lingual part includes only the question, in CQA there are additional text elements that are essential for chart comprehension. Text position in the chart carries important information. In this study, we encode the textual elements in a concatenated version, separated with the special [SEP] token, followed by the question and an answer with the special token [CLS] on top (t_0). In contrast to previous work [13,15,18,27,30], where only the question (or question + answer) was encoded, here the text encoder is generalized to include all textual elements enriched with their spatial location and class. This approach allows free data-driven interaction between different visual and textual elements, *e.g.*, the legend marker and its corresponding text, as well as interactions between text sub-elements, *e.g.*, the answer and *part* of the Y-axis label or title. To this end, we create a new representation from all the textual elements in the chart by fusing the word embedding, the positional encoding, the text location in the chart and the text class embedding. This fusion is carried out through a MLP layer, including projection and summation as shown in Fig. 4b.

4.1   Associating Visual and Textual Elements

For multi-modal interaction we rely on the co-attention architecture that was first suggested for machine translation in [3]. This model contains two different sequence to sequence branches: visual and textual, as shown in Fig. 3. The information in the two streams is fused through a set of attention block exchanges, called co-attention. We use a transformer with 6 blocks of two encoders with *co-* and *self-* attention. Each encoder computes a query Q, key K, and value V matrices, followed by feed-forward layer, skip connections and normalization [28]. In order to exchange the information between the modalities, the *co*-transformer's keys and values at each stream are mutually exchanged resulting a cross-modality attention. Finally, the resulting $\{h_{v_0}, h_{w_0}\}$ pooling tokens (indicated by [CLS] special token) are forwarded to the classification and regression heads (see Fig. 3). For more details, see suppl. material.

4.2   Question Answering Stage

Similar to previous work [5,13,14,20,27] and in order to allow fair comparison, we use an oracle to recognize the extracted text elements. The oracle is a perfect text recognition machine, and is used to disentangle the impact of OCR accuracy. Previous work frequently assume a perfect text detector, *e.g.*, [13,15,20,27]. In this work however, we explicitly account for inaccuracies in the detector by considering only text elements from the oracle with $IoU > 0.5$. We then create the set of possible answers for classification, composed of *in-vocabulary* (*e.g.*, Yes / No) and *out-of-vocabulary* (OOV) answers (*e.g.*, the title or specific legend label). OOV additional classes (dynamically added) allow dealing with chart specific answers that has not been seen during training. To predict the correct answer, we train the model with binary cross-entropy loss. To this end, we concatenate the answer to the question in the textual branch, pass it through the model and evaluate a score in $[0, 1]$ range (see Fig. 3). This score indicates the model's certainty whether the answer is aligned with the question (correct) or not (wrong).

4.3   Unified Prediction

Previous works frequently use only a classification head, overlooking regression [5,13,15,27], or use a totally separate pipeline for the regression task [20]. In classification based methods, the answers are restricted to discrete values, that are part of the numeric values appearing on the chart. This approach strongly limits the generalization, lacking the capability to predict unseen numeric values or charts with unseen ranges. In this work, we propose a novel hybrid prediction head allowing unified classification-regression. To this end, we add a regression soft decision flag $\langle R \rangle$ as an answer class, followed by a regressor. During training the model learns which type of questions require regression by choosing the $\langle R \rangle$ class as the correct answer. A separate and consequent regression is then applied to generate the answer (see Fig. 3). Note that during training, the loss changes dynamically from BCE loss for classification and L1 loss for regression, so the network is jointly optimized for classification and regression. During train, we vanish the regression loss when the correct class is not $\langle R \rangle$. The hybrid prediction allows joint training on all types of Q&As, leveraging multi-task learning.

4.4 Implementation Details

For training the CRCT we use two stages. We first train a Mask-RCNN [9] from which the visual features are derived, using Detectron2 [29] library. We then train the co-transformer model for 20 epochs with linear learning rate scheduler. We use binary cross entropy loss for the classification component and L1 loss for regression. For answer alignment prediction (as described in Sect. 4.2), we generate negative examples by randomly assigning wrong answers to questions. Training our model on PlotQA-D1 took 3.5 days on two Nvidia RTX-6000 GPUs. The inference computational cost is proportional to the size of candidate answers. In our experiments the inference time took 0.23 s per question. Our code and models are publicly available at https://github.com/levymsn/CQA-CRCT.

5   Evaluation

As evaluation benchmark we opted for PlotQA-D and FigureQA datasets, being fully annotated to train a detector (DVQA lacks the important annotation of legend markers). Yet, we focus our analysis on PlotQA-D for several reasons: (1) Publicly available to allow benchmarking. (2) The scale: Over ×10 larger Q&A pairs and over ×1000 more unique answers, than the predecessors (see Table 1); (3) Highly variable axis scale; (4) Having diverse and realistic questions/answers with rich vocabulary titles, legend labels, X and Y labels including initials gathered from real figures; (5) Most importantly, question types that require regression and therefore reflect a realistic case for CQA.

In terms of methods to compare with, we searched for publicly available code or assessments on the chosen datasets. To allow a fair comparison to previous methods, in addition to PlotQA-M, we further test PReFIL [14] on PlotQA-D. To this end, we trained PReFIL on PlotQA-D1. We chose PreFIL due to it's high performance on DVQA and FigureQA and as a representative candidate for previous methods that rely on classification and lack a regression capability. Since PReFIL has only a classification head we quantized the numeric values into Y-ticks and added them to the dynamic classification head in training and also at test (a common practice, also performed in PReFIL [14]). For sake of analysis and to allow a fair comparison we show the PReFIL results for numeric evaluation with various error tolerances (see Fig. 5b).

To handle the wide range of Y-axis values in PlotQA-D, we normalize values to $[-1, 1]$ (by detecting X-Y axes and their values). This improves convergence and enables scale invariant prediction. We output answers in the same range.

5.1   Results

We train our model on PlotQA-D1 dataset, that consists of one third of PlotQA-D2 in questions, while testing on both PlotQA-D1 and PlotQA-D2 test sets. We show significant improvements on both test sets. Results are shown as average accuracy over the test set and accuracy breakdown per-question category.

Comparison to previous methods: Table 2a summarizes the results on PlotQA-D1 test set. In general, we outperform PlotQA-M in all categories by a large margin. For instance, the gaps for Data Retrieval and Reasoning are 48.8% (94.52% vs. 45.68%) and 23.7% (54.87% vs. 31.20%) *absolute* points, respectively. Finally, on average we achieve 76.94% accuracy, compared to 53.96% of PlotQA-M. While outperforming PlotQA-M when trained on the same train set, in the next experiment we show the extent of train data reduction that can be allowed to match the previous results of PlotQA-M. This experiment shows that as little as 10% of training data (randomly selected) are already sufficient to reach this goal. (see CRCT-10% in Table 2a).

With respect to PReFIL, while we show comparable results on the Structural question category, containing classification type questions, CRCT is superior to PReFIL in all other categories. As expected, PReFIL performs poorly on Data Retrieval and particularly Reasoning Q&As (only 31.66% vs 54.87% for our CRCT) due to lack of regression capability. In total average accuracy we surpass both PlotQA-M and PReFIL by 23% and 19% *absolute* points, respectively. Interestingly, with our quantization scheme training of PReFIL, it outperforms PlotQA-M, in all categories.

Due to extreme computational demand for train on PlotQA-D2, in the next experiment we train PReFIL and CRCT on PlotQA-D1 train set and report the results on PlotQA-D2 test set in Table 2b. Note that for PlotQA-M we report the result from [20] with the model trained on whole PlotQA-D2. These results show that even when we train on PlotQA-D1 dataset we are able to outperform PlotQA-M trained on ×3 larger size data, in all categories, often with significant margin. Our CRCT is superior here also to PReFIL with average accuracy of 34.44% vs. 10.37%. Note the poor performance of PReFIL on Reasoning category, from which many questions require regression, reaching 3.9% comparing 25.81% in CRCT. These results show the significance of our hybrid classification-regression capability.

Regression Performance: The accuracy of regression errors are often measured by L_2 or L_1 differences or by ER-error rate. In PlotQA-D [20], a regres-

Table 2. Accuracies [%] on PlotQA test sets. Values in each column indicate average accuracy per-question category. CRCT and PReFIL are trained on the PlotQA-D1 subset. PReFIL results are reproduced. 'CRCT-10%' indicates our results with training on 10% of the PlotQA-D1 train set. S, D and R stand for Structural, Data Retrieval and Reasoning question categories, respectively

(a) Evaluation on PlotQA-D1 test set

Method	S	D	R	Overall
PlotQA-M [20]	86.31	45.68	31.2	53.96
CRCT-10%	87.15	74.71	29.19	57.75
PReFIL [14]	**96.66**	58.69	31.66	57.91
CRCT (ours)	96.13	**94.52**	**54.87**	**76.94**

(b) Evaluation on PlotQA-D2 test set

Method	S	D	R	Overall
PReFIL [14]	**96.66**	21.9	3.9	10.37
PlotQA-M [20]	75.99	58.94	15.77	22.52
CRCT (ours)	96.23	**66.65**	**25.81**	**34.44**

sion answer is considered correct if it falls within ±5% tolerance from the ground truth value. This measure, however, is proportional to the true value, vanishing (no tolerance) for true values near zero. We therefore suggest the *tick-based* error measure as more appropriate for extraction of numerical values. To this end we suggest a constant gap per-chart, defined as a fraction of units between two consecutive sub-ticks (see Fig. 2) *e.g.*, 1/4 sub-tick.

In PlotQA-D1, 29% of the questions require regression. Following PlotQA [20], we show in Fig. 5a CRCT accuracy distribution considering the error rate (ER) measure. We observe that 44.37% of the answers are within ±5% of the true value. The prevalence of errors decreases in higher tolerance ranges except the *outlier* in the tail, indicating that 11.3% of the answers were over 100% off the true value. As expected, we observe that CRCT error distribution indeed accumulates near zero true values (see suppl. material), justifying the advantage of value invariant error measure. Figure 5b shows the variation of regression accuracy with increased tolerance (as sub-tick fraction) for CRCT and PReFIL. CRCT achieves over 85% total accuracy and 78% regression accuracy for 1 sub-tick tolerance. Note the large gap w.r.t PReFIL through all the range as well as the drop in CRCT-10% that obtained similar accuracy to PlotQA-M (Fig. 5a). For visual examples of our CRCT model on regression assignment see Figs. 1, 6b and the suppl. material.

Results on FigureQA: Although our model's strength is in general Q&A with regression, we also test our model on the binary answer data set of FigureQA [15]. FigureQA's training set was generated using different 100 colors. This dataset contains two families of validation and test sets. The first family is the Val-1/Test-1 sets, that was generated using the original color schemes as in the train set. On the contrary, Val-2/Test-2 sets consist of alternate color scheme that *was not seen* in the train set at all. Table 3 presents a comparison on FigureQA dataset. CRCT shows comparable performance to SoTA on the original color scheme. While we outperform previous methods on the alternate color scheme sets, we reach an inferior performance w.r.t PReFIL. This test indicates a color sensitivity for our detector-based approach as we discuss in Sect. 8.

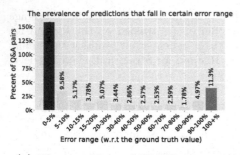
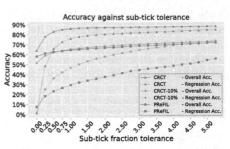

(a) The prevalence of CRCT's answers that fall in certain error range.

(b) Accuracy for different sub-tick error range (tolerance).

Fig. 5. Model regressor performances on PlotQA-D1. In a, the green column shows the "correct" answers *i.e.* fall in 5% tolerance. 11.3% of the answers (red) miss the target by more than 100%. In b, $x = 0$ indicates exact match between prediction and ground truth (zero tolerance). (Color figure online)

Table 3. Accuracy on FigureQA dataset [15]. Second place is coloured in brown

(a) Original color scheme			(b) Alternate color scheme		
Model / Acc.	Val.	Test	Model / Acc.	Val.	Test
RN [15]	–	76.52	RN [15]	72.54	72.40
LEAF-Net [5]	–	–	LEAF-Net [5]	81.15	–
Zou et al. [32]	85.48	85.37	Zou et al. [32]	82.95	83.05
CRCT (ours)	**94.61**	**94.23**	CRCT (ours)	**85.04**	**84.77**
PReFIL [14]	**94.84**	**94.88**	PReFIL [14]	**93.26**	**93.16**

6 Ablation Study

Table 4 shows an ablation study of our method using different configurations. First we examine the impact of the *legend marker* (see Fig. 2) as key element. Removing it from the input in the visual branch prevents the model to associate the question to the specific plots/bar in multi-graph chart. The results show drop in performance in all categories with total accuracy dropping from 57.75% to 50.45%. In the next two tests we show the impact of representation architecture on the end results. To this end we remove the class label embeddings from the visual and textual representation (*e.g.*, 'line_23' or 'x_ticklabel' in Fig. 4). Although noisy, these inputs derived from the detector, positively impact the results. Removing them, causes regression accuracy to drop from 20.74% to 17.35%, for visual and 15.51% for text. We observe the best classification performance is achieved without the visual class embedding. However, this embedding is just one component of the visual representation (see Fig. 4a - Class-Emb). In some cases Class-Emb is redundant to the visual representation, and removing it can slightly improve certain classification Q&As, resulting

Table 4. Ablation study with different configurations (see also Fig. 4). All models are trained on 10% of PlotQA-D1 train set, and evaluated on the entire PlotQA-D1 test set. S, D and R stand for Structural, Data Retrieval and Reasoning, respectively

Method	Regression	Classification	S	D	R	Overall
w/o Legend Marker	14.76	65.02	81.13	56.01	27.05	50.45
w/o *Textual* Class Emb.	15.51	66.86	81.75	61.73	26.96	51.98
w/o *Visual* Class Emb.	17.35	73.68	85.06	73.09	30.57	57.36
Only Bbox for *Visual* Feats.	18.66	68.68	84.97	72.94	23.75	54.19
Two Pipelines	14.80	70.19	84.49	68.65	25.16	53.64
CRCT	20.74	72.86	87.15	74.71	29.19	**57.75**

in this outcome (*e.g.*, where only textual elements are addressed). However, as Table 4 shows, the slight improvement in classification task ($\sim 1\%$) is traded with large degradation in regression accuracy ($\sim 3\%$), resulting a lower total accuracy. When removing all features except the bounding box coordinates, from the visual representation, the total accuracy drops by 3.6%. This shows the importance of all elements in our chart element representation model (see Fig. 4). Finally, we examine the importance of the multi-tasking regime inherent in our unified classification-regression network. To this end we train our classification and regression network separately (similar to [20]). Assuming an oracle for routing classification and regression type questions to the proper network, we report the outcome accuracies. We observe performance drop on all categories emphasizing the importance of combining both regression and classification in CRCT's learning process. Our detector achieved AP50 = 0.90. Testing our model with ground truth detections had a negligible effect on the accuracy.

7   Explainability

We provide visualizations for CRCT attention using the *Captum* package [16,17]. Often, relatively few units in a NN are highly influential towards a particular class [17]. Considering the true answer, we integrate over the input gradients to find the most influential features. We then color code the image to indicate the regions in the chart, visual or textual, that the network found influential in answering the posed question. Figure 6 shows such visualization maps over charts, on examples from the test set. In Fig. 6a CRCT correctly "looks" at the x-tick at the global minimum in the plot and on the corresponding x-label, when asked about the *minimum* argument. Figure 6b shows an example of a bar chart. Note that CRCT's attention is driven toward the dark-green bars due to the question asking about the *average* for a certain category (*secondary education*). As observed, CRCT attends intuitive features and spatial locations according to the questions asked. For more examples see the suppl. material.

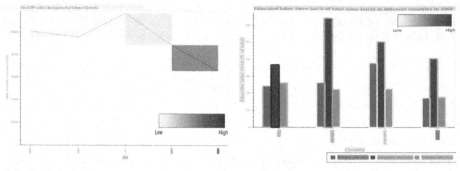

(a) Q: *In which year was the use of IMF credit in DoD minimum?*
GT: 1989, CRCT: 1989.

(b) Q: *What is the average percentage of labor force who received secondary education per country?*
GT: 48.05, CRCT: 47.91 (Error: -0.29%).

Fig. 6. Test set visualizations. Warmer box color means higher influence.

8   Summary and Discussion

In this paper we argue that the simplicity of Chart Question Answering (CQA) associated with lack of realistic chart content and question types, has lead previous methods to omit the regression task. The recent PlotQA work [20] addresses these shortcomings, suggesting a remedy via a new large scale and diverse dataset, as well as a new model. We hereby suggest a bimodal framework for CQA that leverages the natural lingual inter-relations between different chart elements and introduce a novel unified classification-regression head. Our explainability visualizations shed light on question-chart understanding of our model.

We evaluate our method on the PlotQA and FigureQA datasets, significantly outperforming the PlotQA model. We further compare our method to a previous classification based method of PReFIL, that reached SoTA results on FigureQA (also high performing on DVQA) observing a strong drop in performance when tested on more challenging datasets such as PlotQA-D. We argue that the edge of our method is not in classification but rather on the combined classification regression tasks with natural lingual relations that exist in real CQA case.

However, some limitations still remains, such as sensitivity to color combinations and non-linear axis scales. Although we reach a comparable result to PReFIL on FigureQA, we noticed deterioration in results when the test and train colors are different. We relate this limitation to the detector representation learning, including the color attributes from the charts and relying on them to distinguish between the plots in a chart. In practice, this limitation can be overcome by extending the (synthetic) dataset to contain more colors.

In future work we intend to relax the need for full chart annotations, and tackle the efficiency of the training. With PlotQA opening the door again toward chasing human performance in chart comprehension, we hope this paper will encourage researchers to take this challenge.

Acknowledgements. We thank Or Kedar and Nir Zabari for their assistance in parts of this research. We thank PlotQA [20] authors for sharing additional breakdowns. This work was supported in part by the Israel Science Foundation (grant 2492/20).

References

1. Acharya, M., Kafle, K., Kanan, C.: TallyQA: Answering Complex Counting Questions. In: AAAI (2019)
2. Antol, S., et al.: VQA: visual Question Answering. In: ICCV (2015)
3. Bahdanau, D., Cho, K., Bengio, Y.: Neural Machine Translation by Jointly Learning to Align and Translate. In: ICLR (2015)
4. Changpinyo, S., Sharma, P., Ding, N., Soricut, R.: Conceptual 12M: pushing web-scale image-text pre-training to recognize long-tail visual concepts. In: CVPR (2021)
5. Chaudhry, R., Shekhar, S., Gupta, U., Maneriker, P., Bansal, P., Joshi, A.: LEAF-QA: locate, encode & attend for figure question answering. In: WACV (2020)
6. Das, A., et al.: Visual dialog. In: CVPR (2017)
7. Devlin, J., Chang, M., Lee, K., Toutanova, K.: BERT: pre-training of deep bidirectional transformers for language understanding. In: NAACL-HLT (2019)
8. Goyal, Y., Khot, T., Summers-Stay, D., Batra, D., Parikh, D.: Making the V in VQA matter: elevating the role of image understanding in visual question answering. In: CVPR 2017 (2017)
9. He, K., Gkioxari, G., Dollár, P., Girshick, R.: Mask R-CNN. In: ICCV (2017)
10. He, K., Zhang, X., Ren, S., Sun, J.: Deep residual learning for image recognition. In: CVPR (2016)
11. Hochreiter, S., Schmidhuber, J.: Long short-term memory. Neural Comput. **9**(8), 1735–1780 (1997)
12. Huang, G., Liu, Z., Van Der Maaten, L., Weinberger, K.Q.: Densely connected convolutional networks. In: CVPR (2017)
13. Kafle, K., Cohen, S., Price, B., Kanan, C.: DVQA: understanding data visualizations via question answering. In: CVPR (2018)
14. Kafle, K., Shrestha, R., Cohen, S., Price, B., Kanan, C.: Answering questions about data visualizations using efficient bimodal fusion. In: WACV (2020)
15. Kahou, S.E., Michalski, V., Atkinson, A., Kádár, Á., Trischler, A., Bengio, Y.: FigureQA: an annotated figure dataset for visual reasoning. In: ICLRW (2018)
16. Kokhlikyan, N., et al.: PyTorch captum. https://github.com/pytorch/captum (2019)
17. Leino, K., Sen, S., Datta, A., Fredrikson, M., Li, L.: Influence-directed explanations for deep convolutional networks. In: ITC (2018)
18. Lu, J., Batra, D., Parikh, D., Lee, S.: ViLBERT: pretraining task-agnostic visiolinguistic representations for vision-and-language tasks. In: NeurIPS, pp. 13–23 (2019)
19. Malinowski, M., Fritz, M.: A multi-world approach to question answering about real-world scenes based on uncertain input. In: NeurIPS (2014)
20. Methani, N., Ganguly, P., Khapra, M.M., Kumar, P.: PlotQA: reasoning over scientific plots. In: WACV (2020)

21. Miech, A., Zhukov, D., Alayrac, J., Tapaswi, M., Laptev, I., Sivic, J.: HowTo100M: learning a text-video embedding by watching hundred million narrated video clips. In: ICCV (2019)
22. Pasupat, P., Liang, P.: Compositional semantic parsing on semi-structured tables. In: ACL (2015)
23. Radford, A., et al.: Learning transferable visual models from natural language supervision. In: Meila, M., Zhang, T. (eds.) ICML (2021)
24. Santoro, A., et al.: A simple neural network module for relational reasoning. In: NIPS (2017)
25. Schwartz, I., Yu, S., Hazan, T., Schwing, A.G.: Factor graph attention. In: CVPR (2019)
26. Singh, A., et al.: Towards VQA models that can read. In: CVPR (2019)
27. Singh, H., Shekhar, S.: STL-CQA: structure-based transformers with localization and encoding for chart question answering. In: EMNLP (2020)
28. Vaswani, A., et al.: Attention is all you need. In: NeurIPS (2017)
29. Wu, Y., Kirillov, A., Massa, F., Lo, W.Y., Girshick, R.: Detectron2. https://github.com/facebookresearch/detectron2 (2019)
30. Yang, Z., He, X., Gao, J., Deng, L., Smola, A.J.: Stacked attention networks for image question answering. In: CVPR (2016)
31. Zhang, Y., Yang, Q.: A survey on multi-task learning. IEEE Trans. Knowl. Data Eng. (2021)
32. Zou, J., Wu, G., Xue, T., Wu, Q.: An affinity-driven relation network for figure question answering. In: 2020 ICME (2020)

AssistQ: Affordance-Centric Question-Driven Task Completion for Egocentric Assistant

Benita Wong, Joya Chen, You Wu, Stan Weixian Lei, Dongxing Mao, Difei Gao, and Mike Zheng Shou[✉]

Show Lab, National University of Singapore, Singapore, Singapore
benitawong@u.nus.edu, mike.zheng.shou@gmail.com

Abstract. A long-standing goal of intelligent assistants such as AR glasses/robots has been to assist users in affordance-centric real-world scenarios, such as *"how can I run the microwave for 1 min?"*. However, there is still no clear task definition and suitable benchmarks. In this paper, we define a new task called Affordance-centric Question-driven Task Completion, where the AI assistant should learn from instructional videos to provide step-by-step help in the user's view. To support the task, we constructed AssistQ, a new dataset comprising 531 question-answer samples from 100 newly filmed instructional videos. We also developed a novel Question-to-Actions (Q2A) model to address the AQTC task and validate it on the AssistQ dataset. The results show that our model significantly outperforms several VQA-related baselines while still having large room for improvement. We expect our task and dataset to advance Egocentric AI Assistant's development. Our project page is available at: https://showlab.github.io/assistq/.

Keywords: Affordance-centric · Egocentric AI · Question-answering

1 Introduction

People often require assistance when dealing with new events. Consider the example in Fig. 1: the user comes across an unfamiliar washing machine and wants to start a cotton wash, but he does not know how to operate it. He may search for the device's instructional video, and experiment with buttons on the machine. These actions are time-consuming and may not address the user's question effectively. This example highlights the need for an intelligent assistant to help us with affordance-centric queries. The intelligent assistant should: (1) understand the user's query and view, (2) learn from instructional video/manual, (3) guide the user to achieve his goal.

B. Wong, J. Chen and Y. Wu—Equal Contribution.

Supplementary Information The online version contains supplementary material available at https://doi.org/10.1007/978-3-031-20059-5_28.

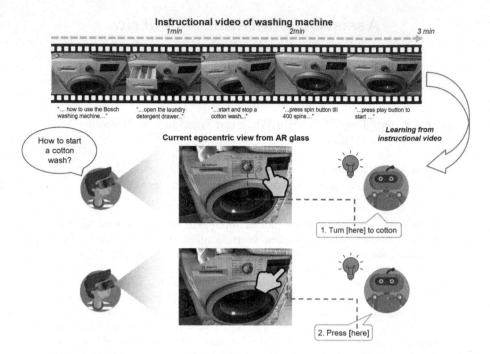

Fig. 1. An illustration of an AI assistant for affordance-centric questions. The AI assistant on AR glass can guide the user to complete the intended task.

However, few works support the development of such an assistant. First, AI assistants should deal with affordance-centric queries, while current visual question answering (VQA) benchmarks [3,17,19,23,25,33] focus on fact-based questions and answers. Second, most ground-truth answers in VQA benchmarks are single-step and textual, which fails to express detailed instructions to the user's complex question. Even though visual dialog [1,12] (VDialog) introduces sequence question answering, the answer of each dialog round is still single-step and textual. Finally, AI assistants should solve questions in users' egocentric perspective [20,28,31,37,40], which is more natural and meaningful for understanding users' situations. However, existing VQA and VDialog studies mainly comprise third-person web videos. Although embodied QA [9,41] (EQA) attempts to develop egocentric agents, they are mostly focused on virtual environments, which may be difficult to generalize to real-world scenarios, and they are also incapable of dealing with complex, affordance-centric user queries.

Hence, we propose a novel **Affordance-centric Question-driven Task Completion (AQTC)** task. It presents a unique set-up: the user asks a question in his/her view, and then the AI assistant answers in a sequence of actions. Figure 2 shows the differences between our task and VQA, VDialog, and EQA. Unlike VQA and VDialog, where the question is fact-based and the answer is a short text, our question is task-oriented and our answer is multi-modal and multi-step, which is more challenging and closer to the intelligent assistant setting. Furthermore, our task makes use of new content – real-world, egocentric

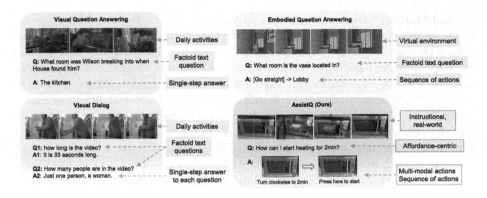

Fig. 2. The differences between VQA, VDialog, EQA, and our AQTC task.

videos – for question answering, which is more suitable for real-world applications compared to virtual environments in the EQA.

To support the AQTC task, we collected the AssistQ dataset containing 531 multiple-choice QA samples on 100 newly filmed, with an average duration of 115s egocentric videos. Participants recorded instructional videos by themselves (*e.g.,* operating microwaves, washing machine), and provided scripts of their narration. These instructional videos were used to create affordance-centric, multi-step QA samples. We also developed a Question-to-Actions (Q2A) model to address the AQTC task. It uses a context grounding module to infer from multi-modal cues (video, script, user view), and introduces a steps network to generate step-by-step answers. Experimental results show that our Q2A model is especially suitable for the AQTC task. In summary, our contributions are:

- We proposed a new task, namely Affordance-centric Question-driven Task Completion (AQTC), whereby AI assistants should learn from instructional videos to guide users step-by-step in the users' view.
- We constructed a pilot dataset for the task, comprising 531 question-answer samples derived from 100 newly filmed instructional videos.
- We developed a Question-to-Actions (Q2A) model and performed extensive experiments to show its superiority in the AQTC task.

2   Related Work

Visual Question Answering. The goal of VQA is to answer questions based on visual cues. VQA v1 and v2 [3,19] are standard benchmarks for image QA. TGIF-QA [23] is one of the earlier large-scale video QA datasets and was built from short animated videos (GIFs) taken from Tumblr. In this task, the main goal is to recognize actions and their repetitions. Similar video QA datasets [17,25,26,33] mainly illustrate daily life or story. In contrast, our task focuses on instructional videos more suitable for affordance-centric tasks.

Visual Dialog. VDialog [12] is a task to generate natural responses based on the given image/video and the dialog context. An example is Audio Visual Scene-Aware Dialog (AVSD) [1], where the agent is shown a video of indoor activity and answers multiple questions about actions and events in the video. Compared to models developed for single-step VQA tasks, VDialog models should utilize the dialog history. Some models [1,12,27,32] simply splice historical dialogs or model using RNN, while others [13,24] introduce reinforcement learning methods. Like VDialog, historical actions in our AQTC task may affect the current answer step. But their differences are apparent: Visual Dialog is more like a single-step QA problem in each round, whereas AQTC requires a sequence of actions to answer. We believe the latter is more appropriate for affordance-centric questions.

Embodied Question Answering. If we consider the instructional video in our AQTC task as the environment, then our model should explore the environment to answer the question. This is similar to EQA [9], where the agent needs to explore the scene and answer the question. Recent works try to solve or extend EQA by improving the logical reasoning [11,41], applying multi-agent cooperation [10,22,41], or creating more challenging environments [18]. However, the current setting of EQA focuses on virtual environments, while our proposed AQTC task revolves around real-world images and videos. This allows AQTC to be more readily adopted for practical applications, such as intelligent agents built in portable devices (*e.g.,* mobile phones, AR glasses).

3   Affordance-Centric Question-Driven Task Completion

In this section, we propose Affordance-centric Question-driven Task Completion (AQTC), a novel task aimed at driving the evolution of egocentric AI assistants. We begin by outlining the abilities required of an egocentric, user-helping AI assistant. The AQTC work is then formalized in accordance with these abilities. Finally, we talk about how to generalize and apply the task.

3.1   Required Abilities of Egocentric AI Assistants

Handling Multi-modal Inputs. In affordance-centric settings, the user often asks questions in both visual (*e.g.,* his/her current view) and linguistic (*e.g.,* *"how to start the microwave?"*). As a result, the egocentric AI assistant is expected to handle multimodal inputs.

Learning from Instructional Sources. It is difficult for an AI assistant to answer questions without learning anything. An acceptable way is for the AI assistant to read the instructional manual first and then teach users. We notice that there are various instructional videos available on the internet, and it would be preferable if AI assistants could utilize these data, *i.e.,* learning from instructional videos and then guide users in their situation.

Grounding Between Modalities. The different input modalities are often not grounded with respect to each other. For example, a video guide might point to

Table 1. Comparisons with VQA-related tasks.

Tasks	Property	Model input	Model output
Video QA	Factoid	Reference video	Single textual answer
Video Dialog	Factoid	Reference video	Multi textual answers
Embodied QA	Factoid	User situation	Multi actions, Single textual answer
AQTC	Affordance	Reference video, User situation	Multi <action, textual answer> pairs

a button, whereas the corresponding textural guide may say "Press this". The egocentric AI assistant should know how to link visual and language concepts.

Multi-step Interaction with Users. Interaction with the user is necessary for an egocentric AI assistant. For example, if a user inquires about *"how to start the microwave"*, the assistant should tell him/her the location of the power switch. When a user's inquiry is complex, the interaction between the user and the assistant may be held for several steps.

3.2 Task Definition of AQTC

Now we design a task for the abilities discussed in Sect. 3.1. To begin, the task should include multi-modal inputs, such as the user's egocentric view and textural question. Then, there should be a reference instructional video from which AI assistants can learn to address problems. Furthermore, rather than using different modalities independently, the grounding between them should be necessary to handle the task. Finally, the task should reflect multi-step interactions between users and assistants, such as a sequence of actions taught to users by the assistant.

With these considerations, we propose affordance-centric question-driven task completion (AQTC) task. Given an instructional video (V), the corresponding video's textural script (S_V), the user's view (U), and the question (Q_U) asked from the view, the model should answer the question by a sequence of answers ($A^1, A^2, ..., A^I$) in I ($I >= 1$) steps. Note that the question Q_U is proposed under the user view U rather than the instructional video V, so the model should ground between U and V (with S_V) to answer Q_U. Currently, we set candidate answers (A_j^i) to lower the difficulties of answering, where A_j^i denotes the j-th potential answer in the i-th step.

Comparing with existing VQA-related tasks (*e.g.*, VQA [3,25,33], VDialog [1, 12], EQA [9]), our proposed AQTC task is more suitable in supporting the affordance-centric requirements of AI assistants. We list the reasons in Table 1:

(1) Property: existing VQA-related datasets are mostly factoid, but some applications go beyond just visual facts and focus on affordance.
(2) Model Input: our work is the first to consider both reference instructional video and the video of user's current situation.

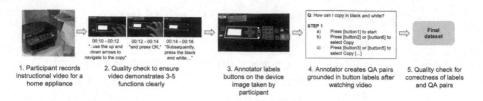

Fig. 3. Data collection pipeline for our AssistQ benchmark.

(3) Model Output: to complete the user's task, our model needs to operate across multiple steps, necessitating the model to perform an action described by textual answer at each step.

3.3   Task Application of AQTC

Our AQTC task actually proposes a typical and general AI process to assisting humans, *i.e.*, model solves a user's query depicted in text and user view image by seeking answers from the instructional video. Therefore, the task can support a wide range of applications:

(1) Life assistant: supporting AR glass to guide users in daily life, like operating home appliances, cooking dishes.
(2) Skills training: reducing the labor costs, *e.g.*,, replacing human instructors to teach bicycle repair/PC assembly.
(3) Working partner: improving people's working efficiency, such as recent DARPA's Virtual Partners program. In research, our task is also not limited in a specific scope. It can be a typical task in egocentric AI, which is a new trend in computer vision (*e.g.*, Ego4D dataset).

4   AssistQ Benchmark

We now describe our new benchmark for the AQTC task. The data collection and annotation pipeline is shown in Fig. 3. Participants would record videos of themselves operating home appliances, and then annotators would create QA pairs after watching the instructional video.

4.1   Video Collection

Videos. The recruited participants were asked to record instructional videos for home appliances. In each video, the participant demonstrated how to operate a device, such as a washing machine or oven. Participants were asked to propose the functions that they were to record to ensure that the video was sufficiently informative for meaningful question-answering. For example, filming the steps needed to change the temperature of a microwave would result in an information-rich video of interest to AssistQ, whereas filming a video about merely turning

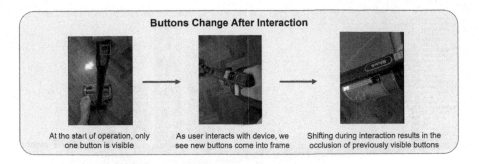

Fig. 4. Sample device (vacuum cleaner) with new buttons in the video frame.

the device on would be inadequate. Participants were also encouraged to perform at least 3–5 functions in each video and were given video samples on the recommended placement of their camera to ensure that the videos recorded are of a baseline quality. In addition, participants were required to narrate their actions in the video similar to the audio instructions that accompany product videos which were then submitted.

4.2 Query Collection

User Images and Button Annotation. For visual query, participants took front-facing pictures of their appliances. In most cases, one image was sufficient to capture all device buttons. But when there is huge change of the device state (Fig. 4), participants were asked to provide pictures of the other states to ensure that the agent has sufficient visual information about available choices at each query stage. Annotators were tasked to place bounding boxes over all visible buttons in the image(s), using Makesense.AI annotation tool.

QA Pairs. Annotators were asked to create at least 3 questions that were answerable from the video. For greater language diversity in the question set, annotators were encouraged to vary the question stems (*"How do I"*, *"How to"*, *"What to do to"*), action words (*"cook"*, *"bake"*, *"turn"*) and question type. Questions were categories as either specific functionality or pure functionality. Specific functionality questions include specific end-stage values, whereas pure functionality type questions only reference the intended functionality. For example, queries such as *"How to change timer on rice cooker to 3 min"* are specific functionality in nature as they contain a desired end-stage value (3 min), whereas queries such as *"How do I access the timer on the rice cooker"* are pure functionality.

Annotators were asked to write MCQ options grounded to labelled buttons on user image(s), creating a vision-language option space. There were no restrictions on the number of MCQ options, though there should be at least as many MCQ options as there are buttons, with each button referenced in at least one option. The structure of the MCQ options varied by question type. MCQ options for

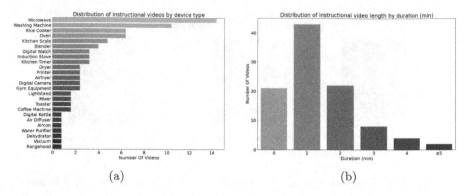

(a)   (b)

Fig. 5. Statistics of videos in AssistQ. (a) Distribution of devices by appliance types. (b) Distribution of instructional videos by length.

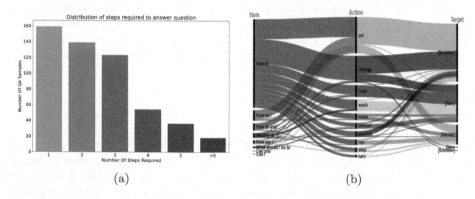

(a)   (b)

Fig. 6. Statistics of questions in AssistQ. (a) Distribution of steps required to answer generated queries. (b) Analysis of question structure by stem-action-target.

pure functionality questions were typically written as `action <button>`, such as *Press* `<button1>`. For specific functionality questions, relevant function details were appended to the option space *i.e., Press* `<button1>` *to select Defrost*. This evaluated the agent's ability to reason about the user's desired outcome. To push the model to understand the underlying semantics of QA pairs, at least one wrong MCQ option had similar instructions to the correct one.

In summary, 18 participants were engaged in video collection; over 350 man-hours were involved in recruitment, filming and liaison over a span of 6 months. 4 annotators were then engaged over another 300 man-hours to label images and create multiple-choice, multi-step QA pairs.

4.3   Dataset Statistics

100 videos with duration averaging 115 s were collected. Figure 5(b) shows the distribution of the video duration, with instructional videos spanning 1–2 min

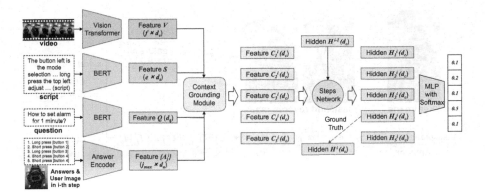

Fig. 7. Architecture of our question-to-answer (Q2A) model. It can be viewed as an encoder-decoder architecture, where the input encoders obtain feature representations for different inputs (video, script, question, answer), and the decoder modules (context grounding, steps network) estimate the answer from encodings. Best viewed in colors.

having the highest frequency in AssistQ. The videos spanned 25 common household appliances, with microwave, washing machine and oven having the highest frequencies due to their ubiquity in households (Fig. 5(a)). The devices came from a diverse pool of 53 distinct appliance brands such as Panasonic (5%), Cornell (4%), Sharp (4%), LG (4%) and Bosch (4%). Instructional videos of more complex devices such as printers (240 s) and gym equipment (216 s) have longer average duration to capture their larger variety of functions.

From the 100 instructional videos, we collected 531 multiple-choice QA pairs (Fig. 6) Of which, 251 are pure functionality questions and 278 are specific functionality questions. 70% of QA pairs require more than 2 steps in the answer sequence (Fig. 6(a)), rendering a majority of our questions multi-step. Figure 6(b) shows the alluvial chart of question stem-action-target words obtained from the generated queries. Only the top 10 most common action words were included in the alluvial chart for greater clarity. From the chart, we can see that while distributed, questions beginning with *"How to"* and *"How do I"*, actions words *set* and *change* as well as target words *[function]* and *[item]* having the highest occurrence in our dataset. Apart from diversity, this dataset also poses a large number of interesting challenges. See supplementary material for details.

5   Question-to-Actions (Q2A) Model

In this section, we propose a question-to-actions (Q2A) model for the proposed AQTC task. As shown in Fig. 7, our Q2A model is an encoder-decoder architecture including: (1) Input Encoder extracts feature from video, script, question, and answers; (2) Context Grounding Module generates context-aware feature for each question-answer pair; (3) Steps Network answers the question in the current step. Next, we describe them in detail.

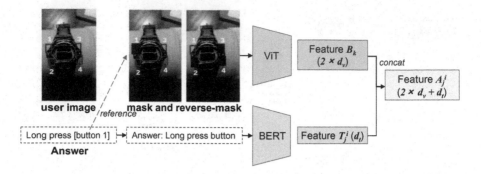

Fig. 8. The architecture of the answer encoder. This figure presents the case of visual button encoding with both mask and reverse-mask images. Note that ViT and BERT used here are the same networks shown in Fig. 7. Best viewed in colors.

5.1   Input Encoders

Video. Video encoding aims to obtain the visual location and of buttons. This not only requires the video embedding [16,34,35], but also requires some object information in video embedding [36,38,39]. For simplicity, we just use a pre-trained vision transformer (ViT) [15] to encode frames instead of a video transformer [4,6], but use a special button encoding method for user image (described latter). We encode one frame per second for the video. Suppose the video has f frames and the encoding dimension is d_v, we can obtain the feature representation V of shape $f \times d_v$.

Script. The video script describes the button's operation and function, which are the crucial cues to answer the question. We use BERT [14] for text embedding. Because the answer in a step usually corresponds to a specific sentence in the script, we transform the script into e sentences, and use the pooled outputs from BERT as sentence embeddings S ($e \times d_s$), where d_s is the feature dimension.

Question. Following the embedding way of the script, we also use the pooled output from BERT [14] as the question feature Q^1, with the dimension d_q. To keep the consistency, we leverage the same BERT used in the script (*i.e.*, $d_q = d_s$). By this way, the question feature and the script feature may have similarities, which can help answer the question. To distinguish the question from the script, we add the prefix "Question:" to each question before encoding.

The j-th Answer of the i-th Step. An answer contains both text and visual button (bounding-box in the user image), making it difficult to encode. For answer text, we still use BERT to extract the feature. Like the prefix in question, we also prefix each answer with "Answer:". The challenging part is the button representation. As shown in Fig. 8, we encode the user image U with the masked referenced button. Meanwhile, we also encode U with all buttons masked except

---

[1] Q_U in Sect. 3.2 denotes the question under user view. To simplify, we use Q here.

the referenced button. The visual button feature B_k, and text feature T_j^i are concatenated to the answer's feature A_j^i. The masked button image allows our model to utilize the appearance cues when buttons differ in their appearance, and another reverse-masked image allows our model to focus on the mutual cues (like the relative location) when buttons' appearances are similar.

Context Grounding Module. In video QA models [7,25] there are usually modules that utilize context for better question and answer representation. Following this idea, we also design a context grounding module. Consider the input feature representations V, S, Q, A_j^i (T_j^i as the text encoding, B_j^i as the button encoding), we generate context-aware question-answer pair feature C_j^i as:

$$C_j^i = MLP([T_j^i, B_j^i, At_{QA \to S}(T_j^i, S, S), At_{QA \dashrightarrow S \dashrightarrow V}(T_j^i, S, V)]) \qquad (1)$$

where $At(query, key, value)$ denotes the attention operation [5]. MLP denotes a 2-layer MLP, of which dimension is carefully adjusted to satisfy the calculation requirements. $[\cdot]$ is the concatenate operation. $QA \to S$ denotes the attention from question-answer (query) to script (key), and produces the QA-aware script feature. We also introduce a "transfer attention" ($QA \dashrightarrow S \dashrightarrow V$) here to simulate the process of finding visual cues based on text:

$$Mask_{QA \dashrightarrow S \dashrightarrow V}(T_j^i, S, V) = Mask_{QA \to S}(T_j^i, S, S) \times Mask_{S \to V}(S, V, V), \qquad (2)$$

where $Mask$ denotes the attention mask. With the attention mask, we can obtain the QA-aware video feature by $At_{QA \dashrightarrow S \dashrightarrow V} = Mask_{QA \dashrightarrow S \dashrightarrow V} \times V$.

Steps Network. Our Q2A leverages the historical steps via a steps network, which is a 2-layer MLP or a GRU. In i-th step, the steps network would use the state from $i-1$-th step to produce the state H_j^i for j-th answer. Then, the state of the ground-truth answer would be reused as the hidden state of the $i+1$ step. The initial state is a random-initialized vector with standard normal distribution if the step just begins.

Prediction Head. In each step, the hidden states generated by the steps indicate the answers' feature representations. We use a two-layer MLP followed by softmax activation to predict a score for each answer.

Training and Inference. Following common practice in Visual QA/Dialog [1, 2], BERT and ViT in the input encoder are frozen since they have a large number of parameters. Other parts are trainable. We use cross-entropy (CE) with softmax activation to calculate the loss. During inference, our Q2A model chooses the state that can yield the highest predicted score after the prediction head. In this way, the model can finish the whole multi-step answering procedure by itself.

6   Experiments

6.1   Experimental Setting

Data Splits. We randomly split 100 instructional videos of AssistQ into the training set and the validation set with a ratio of 8:2. In statistics, the training set has 80 instructional videos with 425 QA instances, and the testing set has 20 instructional videos with 106 QA instances. About 25% device types in the testing set are not present in the training set, making our AssistQ benchmark more challenging.

Evaluation Metrics. As illustrated in Sect. 4, the "multi-step" characteristic is similar to "multi-round" characteristic in visual dialog [1,12]. Therefore, it is natural to use their evaluation metrics for the proposed AssistQ task:

- **Recall@k** measures how often the ground-truth answer selected in top k choices. We report Recall@1 and Recall@3 in our experiments.
- **Mean rank (MR)** refers to mean value of the predicted ranking position of the correct answer. The model should pursue lower MR.
- **Mean reciprocal rank (MRR)** is the mean value of the reciprocal predicted ranking position of the correct answer. Higher MRR is better.

Implementation Details. We use PyTorch [30] to perform experiments. For a fair comparison, all models use the same optimizer and learning rate scheduler. Specifically, we use a momentum SGD optimizer with a batch size of 16, and a cosine annealing scheduler [29] with the learning rate 2×10^{-3}, 1 epoch for warmup, and maximum 6 training epochs.

6.2   Ablation Study

As illustrated in Sect. 5, we design an encoder-decoder architecture Q2A to solve the AQTC task. In its encoder, we encode the video, script, question, and candidate answers, where a special visual button encoding method is designed for the answer encoding. Meanwhile, in the Q2A decoder, we also specifically develop the context grounding module and utilize historical steps for better prediction. A default setting of our model is (a) encode both video and script, (b) double-mask button encoding, (c) $QA \rightarrow S \rightarrow V$ attention, (d) MLP for historical steps. Next, we perform ablation studies on the points mentioned above.

Visual Button Encoding. See Table 2(a), we analyze the encoding ways of visual button encoding. Interestingly, the model achieves the best performance when only using reverse-mask image encoding (mask $\times$ and reverse-mask $\checkmark$), with a clear margin compared to other configurations. These results demonstrate that it is better to mask the other buttons when encoding a visual button. In our opinion, both mask and reverse-mask schemes can help the model to infer the button location, but the reverse-mask scheme can help the model use the button appearance.

Table 2. Ablation studies of our proposed Q2A model on the AssistQ benchmark. (a) and (b) are for the Q2A encoder, where (a) explores the necessary input modalities and (b) studies the ways of button encoding. (c) and (d) are for the Q2A decoder, where (c) illustrates the importance of using historical steps and (d) shows different combinations for context grounding. Note $\rightarrow$ and $\dashrightarrow$ denote attention methods we described in Sect. 5.1.

(a) Ablation on button encoding

Mask	Reverse-mask	R@1 ↑	R@3 ↑	MR ↓	MRR ↑
×	×	17.9	54.8	3.8	2.5
✓	×	19.4	53.6	3.7	2.5
×	✓	**30.2**	62.3	3.2	3.2
✓	✓	21.4	59.1	3.7	2.6

(b) Ablation on input modalities

Video	Script	R@1 ↑	R@3 ↑	MR ↓	MRR ↑
×	×	23.4	57.9	3.6	2.8
✓	×	29.4	59.5	3.3	3.1
×	✓	24.6	58.7	3.6	2.9
✓	✓	**30.2**	62.3	3.2	3.2

(c) Ablation on context grounding

QA→S	S→V	QA-->S-->V	R@1 ↑	R@3 ↑	MR ↓	MRR ↑
×	×	×	19.8	52.8	3.8	2.5
✓	×	×	28.6	69.8	3.1	3.2
×	✓	×	22.6	56.0	3.6	2.6
✓	✓	×	29.0	62.7	3.2	3.2
✓	✓	✓	**30.2**	62.3	3.2	3.2

(d) Ablation on historical steps

Network	History	R@1 ↑	R@3 ↑	MR ↓	MRR ↑
MLP	×	21.4	60.7	3.5	2.7
MLP	✓	21.8	56.8	3.7	2.6
GRU	×	25.0	62.3	3.4	2.9
GRU	✓	**30.2**	62.3	3.2	3.2

Input Modalities. As shown in Table 2(b), when the model ignores some contexts (video × or script ×), it achieves much lower performance (23.4 v.s. 30.2) than the model with the full contexts (video ✓ and script ✓). We also found that the independent video (video ✓ or script ×) can lead to much better results (29.4 v.s. 24.6) than the independent script (video × or script ✓). This is because when using only script w/o video, some information in scripts might be misleading. For example, say we have two candidate answers: (a) "press here [refer to <button1> in video, but not accessible when using only script] on the microwave"; (b) "press here [refer to <button2>] to heat it up". If the script has a language context (*e.g.,* "press here to heat it up") which is similar to (b), it will mislead the model, making it more inclined to choose (b); but in fact, (a) is the ground truth option, which we can clearly tell by watching the instructional video. These results suggest that the model should fully utilize both video and script to answer questions, rather than only one of them.

Context Grounding.[2] According to Table 2(c), all parts in our proposed grounding schemes (see Sect. 5.1) can improve the performances. Among them, the model benefits less from $S \rightarrow V$ but obtains a significant gain from $QA \rightarrow S$. This is because $S \rightarrow V$ is unrelated to the question, suggesting the importance of finding the corresponding context according to the question. Moreover, based on $QA \rightarrow S$ and $S \rightarrow V$, the model would benefit from the "transfer attention" $QA \dashrightarrow S \dashrightarrow V$. We believe the "transfer attention" could link QA to V, which simulates finding the related script based on the question, and then locating the related video moment by the related script. Compared with direct $QA \rightarrow V$, the calculation cost of our "transfer attention" is much smaller since the script is shared for all candidate QA pairs.

Steps Network. Table 2(d) presents the ablation on whether to use cues from historical steps (✓ or ×) and how to use them (MLP or GRU [8]). We can

---

[2] We use the same notation of Sect. 5. V: video, S: script, Q: question, A: answer.

Table 3. Baseline comparison on the AssistQ benchmark. Benefiting from the specific design for the benchmark, Q2A achieves the highest performance on all metrics.

Baseline method	Recall@1 ↑	Recall@3 ↑	MR ↓	MRR ↑
Random guess	18.3	50.4	3.9	2.3
Multi-stream [25] (Video QA)	22.8 (+4.5)	54.8 (+4.4)	3.7 (−0.2)	3.0 (+0.7)
LateFusion [1] (Video Dialog)	19.9 (+1.6)	49.3 (−1.1)	4.1 (+0.2)	2.6 (+0.3)
PACMAN [9] (EQA)	24.6 (+6.3)	54.0 (+3.6)	3.9 (−0.0)	2.9 (+0.6)
Q2A (Ours)	**30.2 (+11.9)**	**62.3 (+11.9)**	**3.2 (−0.7)**	**3.2 (+0.9)**

find that historical information can stably improve the performances of GRU on all metrics, especially on Recall@1 (25.0 to 30.2). But for MLP with historical information, only a few gains (21.4 to 21.8) can be observed on Recall@1, while other metrics even declined. Compared to MLP, GRU has advantages in temporal modeling, which is more suitable as the steps network.

6.3 Comparison

As shown in Table 3, we compare our Q2A model with baselines in other domains on the AssistQ benchmark. Since the answers encoded in other methods are plain text (without placeholders for buttons), we simply introduce our double-mask answer encoding scheme. For all models, we use the same backbone network in the encoder for a fair comparison. We also provide the results of random guess for improvement comparison.

Video QA. Multi-stream is proposed as a baseline model for the TVQA [25] task. Like our model, it has modules similar to context grounding. However, It cannot take advantage of cues from historical steps (as video QA is a single-step task), limiting its performance on the AssistQ benchmark.

Video Dialog. [1] proposes LateFusion to solve the multi-round video dialog, which simply concatenates the historical dialog and introduces an LSTM [21] to model them. However, its performance is even worse than Multi-stream. We believe that simple late fusion leads to inferior performance as there is no module similar to context grounding. Also, its LSTM models a very long sequence of the entire script and historical dialogue, which may lose useful information.

EQA. PACMAN [9] uses an LSTM-based planner to update the agent state, with an MLP-based control planner to predict answers. This procedure is similar to our GRU-based decoder that utilizes historical steps, but PACMAN only considers the visual information for navigation. As shown in Table 3, PACMAN achieves better performance than Multi-stream and LateFusion, but still lags behind our Q2A model.

7 Conclusion

In this paper, we proposed Affordance-centric Question-driven Task Completion (AQTC) task, which enables AI assistants to guide users by learning from instructional videos. To support the task, we collected the AssistQ benchmark, consisting of 531 multiple-step QA samples derived from 100 newly filmed instructional videos, with efforts underway to continue scaling this dataset. We also present a new baseline called Question-to-Actions (Q2A) for our AQTC task, and experimental results demonstrate the effectiveness of the Q2A model on the AQTC task. We hope that our proposed AQTC and AssistQ can advance the development of AI assistants that see the world through our eyes, assisting humans in daily, real-world scenarios.

Acknowledgements. This project is supported by the National Research Foundation, Singapore under its NRFF Award NRF-NRFF13-2021-0008, and Mike Zheng Shou's Start-Up Grant from NUS. The computational work for this article was partially performed on resources of the National Supercomputing Centre, Singapore.

References

1. AlAmri, H., et al.: Audio visual scene-aware dialog. In: CVPR, pp. 7558–7567 (2019)
2. Anderson, P., et al.: Bottom-up and top-down attention for image captioning and visual question answering. In: CVPR, pp. 6077–6086 (2018)
3. Antol, S., et al.: VQA: visual question answering. In: ICCV, pp. 2425–2433 (2015)
4. Arnab, A., Dehghani, M., Heigold, G., Sun, C., Lučić, M., Schmid, C.: ViViT: a video vision transformer. In: ICCV, pp. 6836–6846 (2021)
5. Bahdanau, D., Cho, K., Bengio, Y.: Neural machine translation by jointly learning to align and translate. In: ICLR (2015)
6. Bertasius, G., Wang, H., Torresani, L.: Is space-time attention all you need for video understanding? In: ICML (2021)
7. Chadha, A., Arora, G., Kaloty, N.: iPerceive: applying common-sense reasoning to multi-modal dense video captioning and video question answering. arXiv:2011.07735 (2020)
8. Chung, J., Gülçehre, Ç., Cho, K., Bengio, Y.: Empirical evaluation of gated recurrent neural networks on sequence modeling. arXiv:1412.3555 (2014)
9. Das, A., Datta, S., Gkioxari, G., Lee, S., Parikh, D., Batra, D.: Embodied question answering. In: CVPR, pp. 1–10 (2018)
10. Das, A., et al.: TarMAC: targeted multi-agent communication. In: ICML, pp. 1538–1546 (2019)
11. Das, A., Gkioxari, G., Lee, S., Parikh, D., Batra, D.: Neural modular control for embodied question answering. In: CoRL, pp. 53–62 (2018)
12. Das, A., et al.: Visual dialog. In: CVPR, pp. 1080–1089 (2017)
13. Das, A., Kottur, S., Moura, J.M.F., Lee, S., Batra, D.: Learning cooperative visual dialog agents with deep reinforcement learning. In: ICCV, pp. 2970–2979 (2017)
14. Devlin, J., Chang, M., Lee, K., Toutanova, K.: BERT: pre-training of deep bidirectional transformers for language understanding. In: NAACL, pp. 4171–4186 (2019)

15. Dosovitskiy, A., et al.: An image is worth 16×16 words: transformers for image recognition at scale. In: ICLR (2021)
16. Feichtenhofer, C., Fan, H., Xiong, B., Girshick, R.B., He, K.: A large-scale study on unsupervised spatiotemporal representation learning. In: CVPR (2021)
17. Gao, D., Wang, R., Bai, Z., Chen, X.: Env-QA: a video question answering benchmark for comprehensive understanding of dynamic environments. In: CVPR, pp. 1675–1685 (2021)
18. Gordon, D., Kembhavi, A., Rastegari, M., Redmon, J., Fox, D., Farhadi, A.: IQA: visual question answering in interactive environments. In: CVPR, pp. 4089–4098 (2018)
19. Goyal, Y., Khot, T., Agrawal, A., Summers-Stay, D., Batra, D., Parikh, D.: Making the V in VQA matter: elevating the role of image understanding in visual question answering. Int. J. Comput. Vis. **127**(4), 398–414 (2019)
20. Grauman, K., et al: Ego4D: around the world in 3, 000 hours of egocentric video. arXiv:2110.07058 (2021)
21. Hochreiter, S., Schmidhuber, J.: Long short-term memory. Neural Comput. **9**(8), 1735–1780 (1997)
22. Jain, U., et al.: Two body problem: collaborative visual task completion. In: CVPR, pp. 6689–6699 (2019)
23. Jang, Y., Song, Y., Yu, Y., Kim, Y., Kim, G.: TGIF-QA: toward spatio-temporal reasoning in visual question answering. In: CVPR, pp. 1359–1367 (2017)
24. Kottur, S., Moura, J.M.F., Parikh, D., Batra, D., Rohrbach, M.: Visual coreference resolution in visual dialog using neural module networks. In: Ferrari, V., Hebert, M., Sminchisescu, C., Weiss, Y. (eds.) ECCV 2018. LNCS, vol. 11219, pp. 160–178. Springer, Cham (2018). https://doi.org/10.1007/978-3-030-01267-0_10
25. Lei, J., Yu, L., Bansal, M., Berg, T.L.: TVQA: localized, compositional video question answering. In: EMNLP, pp. 1369–1379 (2018)
26. Lei, J., Yu, L., Berg, T.L., Bansal, M.: TVQA+: spatio-temporal grounding for video question answering. In: Jurafsky, D., Chai, J., Schluter, N., Tetreault, J.R. (eds.) ACL, pp. 8211–8225 (2020)
27. Li, Z., Li, Z., Zhang, J., Feng, Y., Zhou, J.: Bridging text and video: a universal multimodal transformer for audio-visual scene-aware dialog. IEEE ACM Trans. Audio Speech Lang. Process. **29**, 2476–2483 (2021)
28. Lin, K.Q., et al.: Egocentric video-language pretraining. arXiv:2206.01670 (2022)
29. Loshchilov, I., Hutter, F.: SGDR: stochastic gradient descent with warm restarts. In: ICLR (2017)
30. Paszke, A., Gross, S., Massa, F.E.A.: PyTorch: an imperative style, high-performance deep learning library. In: NeurIPS, pp. 8026–8037 (2019)
31. Sax, A., et al.: Learning to navigate using mid-level visual priors. In: CoRL, pp. 791–812 (2019)
32. Schwartz, I., Schwing, A.G., Hazan, T.: A simple baseline for audio-visual scene-aware dialog. In: CVPR, pp. 12548–12558 (2019)
33. Tapaswi, M., Zhu, Y., Stiefelhagen, R., Torralba, A., Urtasun, R., Fidler, S.: MovieQA: understanding stories in movies through question-answering. In: CVPR, pp. 4631–4640 (2016)
34. Tong, Z., Song, Y., Wang, J., Wang, L.: VideoMAE: masked autoencoders are data-efficient learners for self-supervised video pre-training. arXiv:2203.12602 (2022)
35. Wang, A.J., et al.: All in one: exploring unified video-language pre-training. arXiv:2203.07303 (2022)
36. Wang, J., et al.: Object-aware video-language pre-training for retrieval. In: CVPR, pp. 3313–3322 (2022)

37. Wortsman, M., Ehsani, K., Rastegari, M., Farhadi, A., Mottaghi, R.: Learning to learn how to learn: self-adaptive visual navigation using meta-learning. In: CVPR, pp. 6750–6759 (2019)
38. Yan, R., et al.: Video-text pre-training with learned regions. arXiv:2112.01194 (2021)
39. Yan, R., Xie, L., Tang, J., Shu, X., Tian, Q.: HiGCIN: hierarchical graph-based cross inference network for group activity recognition. IEEE Trans. Pattern Anal. Mach. Intell. 1 (2020). https://ieeexplore.ieee.org/document/9241410
40. Yang, W., Wang, X., Farhadi, A., Gupta, A., Mottaghi, R.: Visual semantic navigation using scene priors. In: ICLR (2019)
41. Yu, L., Chen, X., Gkioxari, G., Bansal, M., Berg, T.L., Batra, D.: Multi-target embodied question answering. In: CVPR, pp. 6309–6318 (2019)

FindIt: Generalized Localization with Natural Language Queries

Weicheng Kuo[(✉)], Fred Bertsch, Wei Li, A. J. Piergiovanni,
Mohammad Saffar, and Anelia Angelova

Google Research, Brain Team, Mountain View, USA
weicheng@google.com

Abstract. We propose FindIt, a simple and versatile framework that
unifies a variety of visual grounding and localization tasks including
referring expression comprehension, text-based localization, and object
detection. Key to our architecture is an efficient multi-scale fusion module that unifies the disparate localization requirements across the tasks.
In addition, we discover that a standard object detector is surprisingly effective in unifying these tasks without a need for task-specific
design, losses, or pre-computed detections. Our end-to-end trainable
framework responds flexibly and accurately to a wide range of referring expression, localization or detection queries for zero, one, or multiple objects. Jointly trained on these tasks, FindIt outperforms the
state of the art on both referring expression and text-based localization, and shows competitive performance on object detection. Finally,
FindIt generalizes better to out-of-distribution data and novel categories
compared to strong single-task baselines. All of these are accomplished
by a single, unified and efficient model. The code will be released at:
https://sites.google.com/view/findit-eccv22/home.

1 Introduction

Natural language enables flexible descriptive queries about images. The interaction between text queries and images grounds linguistic meaning in the visual
world, facilitating a stronger understanding of object relationships, human inten-
tions towards objects, and interactions with the environment. The research community has studied visual grounding through tasks including phase grounding,
object retrieval and localization, language-driven instance segmentation, and
others [21,25,56,60,62,68,70,80].

Among the most popular visual grounding tasks is referring expression comprehension (REC), which localizes an object given a referring text [55,70,90].
This task often requires complex reasoning on prominent objects. A highly
related semantic localization task is object detection (DET), which seeks to

---

Supplementary Information The online version contains supplementary material
available at https://doi.org/10.1007/978-3-031-20059-5_29.

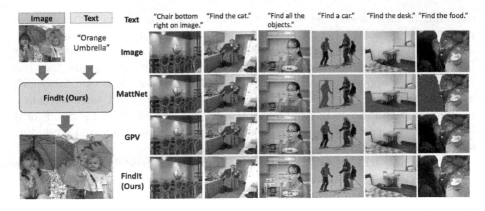

Fig. 1. FindIt is a general-purpose model for visual grounding and localization tasks (left). The input is an image-text pair specifying the objects of interest using natural language, and the outputs are a set of bounding boxes and classification scores. Specifically, FindIt addresses the following tasks (col. 1–3): referring expression comprehension (col. 1), text-based localization (col. 2), and the object detection task by an optional generic prompt e.g. "Find all the objects.", (col. 3). Furthermore, FindIt can respond accurately when the referred object is absent (col. 4), or when it is tested on out-of-distribution (OOD) images and with novel category names, e.g. "desk", where "dining table" is the closest category in the training set (col. 5). FindIt can also locate objects, referred to by novel super-category names e.g. "food" (col. 6). We compare to MattNet [89] and GPV [20] in all these scenarios. (Best viewed in color)

detect all objects from a predefined set of classes without text inputs [17,58,66, 69,75,78]. In contrast to REC, this task requires the accurate classification and localization of small, occluded objects. At the intersection of the two is text-based localization [20,23] (LOC), in which a simple category-based text query prompts the model to detect the objects of interest.

Due to their highly dissimilar task properties, REC, DET, and LOC are mostly studied through separate benchmarks with most models only dedicated to one task [20,67,87]. As a result, existing models have not adequately synthesized information from the three tasks to achieve a more holistic visual and linguistic understanding. REC models, for instance, are trained to predict one object per image, and often struggle to localize multiple objects[1], reject negative queries, or detect novel categories (see Fig. 1). In addition, DET models are unable to process text inputs, and LOC models often struggle to process complex queries such as "Chair bottom right on image" (see Fig. 1). Lastly, none of the models can generalize sufficiently well beyond the their training data and categories.

To address these limitations, we propose a unified visual localization approach which we call FindIt. Key to our architecture is a multi-level cross-modality fusion module which can perform complex reasoning for REC and simultaneously recognize small and challenging objects for LOC and DET. To unify the disparate

---

[1] Technically, many REC models can localize more than one object, but they often struggle because they are only trained to predict one object per image on REC data.

demands of these tasks, the module efficiently fuses and learns features across many levels of abstraction. Concretely, we utilize the more expressive cross-attention fusion on lower resolution features, and the more efficient product fusion on higher resolution features to combine the best of both worlds. Last but not least, we discover that a standard object detector and detection losses [67] are sufficient and surprisingly effective for REC, LOC, and DET tasks without a need for task-specific design and losses [12,20,50,54,86,87,89]. In short, FindIt is a simple, efficient, and end-to-end trainable model for unified visual grounding and object detection.

By learning REC, LOC, and DET jointly in one model, FindIt acquires a more holistic and versatile capability for visual grounding than its single-task counterparts. Notably, FindIt surpasses the state of the art on REC and LOC, and demonstrates competitive performance on DET. Moreover, unlike existing task-specific models, FindIt accomplishes these in a single model that can respond flexibly to a wide range of referring expression and localization queries, solve the standard detection task, and generalize better to novel data and classes. In summary, our contributions are:

- We propose FindIt, a simple and versatile framework for visual grounding and detection tasks. In contrast to task-specific models, a single FindIt model can respond flexibly to a wide range of referring expression and localization queries, solve the standard detection task, and generalize better to novel data and classes.
- We propose an efficient multi-scale cross-attention fusion module to unify the disparate task requirements between REC, LOC, and DET. Using the fused features, we discover that a standard detector and detection losses are surprisingly effective for all tasks without a need for task-specific design or losses.
- We surpass the state of the art on REC and LOC, and show competitive DET performance within a single, unified and efficient model.

2   Related Work

Referring Expression Comprehension (REC) and phrase grounding tasks [35,55,62,63,76,86,87,89,90] require the models to ground linguistic elements in the image. Several datasets which enable and enrich the study of these tasks have been proposed [9,30,33,55,62,70,90]. Yu et al. and Mao et al. [55,90] expand the COCO benchmark with referring expression annotations, while the Referit game [70] crowd-sources such labels through game-play. One-stage [7,12,43,54,87] and two-stage [26,49,81,85,89,92] methods have been popular for these tasks. **Object Detection (DET)** task is well established and has a plethora of approaches [17,22,45,66,67] and benchmarks [46,71]. The goal is to identify the bounding boxes of a set of pre-defined classes without prompting by text. Many recent approaches have started to study the open-set and zero-shot settings [2,14,19,82,96]. **Text-based Localization (LOC)** has been recently proposed alongside other vision and language tasks [20,23]. Text-based localization is similar to the referring expression comprehension task. The text query specifies an object class to be localized. This task is typically derived from standard detection datasets [38,46]. Early results with this tasks are presented by [20,23] where the focus has been on a single object [23]. FindIt extends this capability to localize multiple objects of any given category or detect all objects of a given vocabulary through a free-form text prompt.

Multi-modal Vision-Language Learning. Large amounts of vision and language work are present, such as visual-grounding [15,48,60,79,89,94], image captioning [1,5,6], visual question and answering (VQA) [11,32], visual reasoning [73,83,91], image-text retrieval [31,64,72], and video-text learning [11,28, 34,47]. Many approaches to vision-language learning leverage large-scale image-text pre-training or pre-computed detections [5,8,13,29,37,40,42,51,52,64,74, 84,88,95]. In particular, many methods underscore the importance of localization to increase the success of related vision-and-language understanding/reasoning tasks such as VQA and CLEVR [1,4,8,16,35,42,93].

Vision and Language Feature Fusion. Recently, the Transformer [77] and its cross-modality variants [8,36,52] have been popular fusion choices for vision-language tasks. To localize objects at various scales, existing REC works have used multi-level fusion by applying activation and product fusion [54,86] or concatenation and convolution fusion [87]. Inspired by recent works [8,12,36,52] on single-scale cross-attention, we propose multi-scale fusion to satisfy the disparate requirements of REC and detection tasks, where REC requires complex reasoning while detection requires accurate localization and recognition. The fusion module enables us to unify these tasks in a single model and surpass the state of the art on REC, LOC and maintains competitive DET performance.

Multi-task Learning for Visual Grounding and Object Localization. Existing multi-task approaches have combined grounding and localization tasks with text-generation tasks such as VQA, captioning, visual entailment [10,27,53], and have leveraged pretraining or joint training on similar localization datasets and tasks [35,41,54]. Hu et al. [27] combine a detection task with text-generation tasks. GPV [20] combines text-based localization with VQA by generating both boxes and text for each input image/text pairs. MCN [54] combines REC and RES (Referring Expression Segmentation) to show the benefits of multi-task learning for both. GLIP [41] formulates object detection as phrase grounding and combines detection, caption, and grounding datasets for zero/few-shot detection. M-DETR [35] combines many grounding datasets in a phrase grounding pretraining. Similar to MCN, FindIt unifies semantically similar tasks to study the benefits of multitask learning. Different from M-DETR and GLIP, FindIt uses only COCO and RefCOCO data to isolate the effects of additional data.

Table 1. FindIt tasks comparison. FindIt unifies the referring expression (REC), text-based localization (LOC) and detection (DET) tasks.

Task	Text Input	Output	Image Size	Loss and Architecture	Metric
REC	Expr. for one object	One box	256 [59,87]/640 [12]	Ref-specific or DETR loss/arch. [12,59,87]	Precision
LOC	Expr. for one class	Many boxes	640 [20]	DETR loss and DETR + image-text fusion [20]	AP50
DET	None/Task prompt	Many boxes/classes	1333 [18,22]	Two-stage [67], one-stage [45,66], transformer [3]	AP
FindIt	All the above	Many boxes/classes	640	Two-stage detector loss [67] + image-text fusion	All

3   Method

3.1   Overview

The goal of FindIt is to unify a family of semantically-related localization tasks: 1) referring expression comprehension (REC), 2) text-based localization (LOC), and 3) detection (DET). To accomplish this, FindIt produces a set of boxes/classes when given an RGB image and a text query (see Table 1). The architecture (Sect. 3.3) includes an image encoder, a text encoder, a fusion model, and a set of box/class prediction heads. The fusion model (Sect. 3.4) takes multi-scale features from the image encoder and fuses them with the text encoder features. The box/class heads take the fused features as input and produce a set of bounding boxes, their categories and confidence scores. All tasks share the same architecture, losses, and weights.

3.2   Task Definitions

Table 1 shows a comparison of the FindIt sub-tasks. Since these tasks are similar in nature, our goal is to unify, and consider them jointly. We define them as follows:

- **REC:** In the referring expression comprehension task, inputs are an image and a user query about a specific (often prominent) object in the image. The expected output is one bounding box around the correct object. While natural queries may invoke multiple objects, this task is limited to providing a single box as an answer. We adopt the standard precision@1 metric.
- **LOC:** In the text-based localization task, inputs are an image and a query about a category, e.g. "Find the cars" [20]. The expected output is a set of bounding boxes around all objects in that category. This task challenges the model to only predict the relevant objects based on the query. We follow the AP50 metric proposed by [20].
- **DET:** In the detection task, inputs are an image and a standard query, "Find all the objects". The expected outputs are bounding boxes around the objects of categories present in the dataset and their classes, but as we show in

Table 4, FindIt can generalize to novel categories via text-based localization. Our modification allows us to share the same vision and language interface with the other tasks. We adopt the standard mAP metric in detection [46].

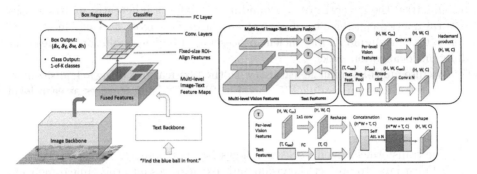

Fig. 2. (Left) Our main architecture accepts an image and a query text as inputs, and processes them separately in image/text backbones before applying the multi-level fusion. We feed the fused features to region proposal network to generate candidate regions and then extract the region features for box regression and classification. (Right) Our multi-level image-text fusion module (top-left) uses transformer fusion blocks (T), and product fusion blocks (P) at the higher/lower levels of the feature maps respectively.

3.3 Network Architecture

Our network architecture is simple and extensible: it includes an image encoder, a text encoder, a fusion model, and box/class prediction heads (Fig. 2). All parameters are shared by all tasks, i.e. there are *no task-specific parameters*. The image encoder is a ResNet backbone which yields multi-level features. The text encoder is a T5 transformer [65] model which encodes a query sentence as a series of token features. The fusion model fuses the multi-level image features with token features (Sect. 3.4). We fuse the image and text features at the image level, as it allows more flexibility to adapt visual representation to various queries. After the fusion, we apply the standard region proposer [67] and box/class decoders [67]. Our design can tackle any task that predicts multiple objects and their classes given an image and a text query (optional). Although we use FRCNN [67] in this work, our unification approach is agnostic to the choice of detectors and other detectors are also viable [3, 45, 66][2].

3.4 Multi-level Image-Text Fusion

To combine these different localization tasks, one major challenge is that they are created around different domains and with different goals (see Table 1). For

---

[2] The detector head may also be adapted from existing visual grounding models such as [12,87], but we leave this for future studies.

example, the referring expression task primarily references prominent objects in the image rather than small, occluded or faraway objects such that low resolution images would suffice. In contrast, the detection task aims to detect objects with various sizes and occlusion levels in higher resolution images. Apart from these benchmarks, the general visual grounding problem is inherently multiscale, as natural queries can refer to objects of any size. This motivates our multi-level image-text fusion model for efficient processing of higher resolution images over different localization tasks.

We fuse multi-level image features with the text features using a Transformer-based cross attention module [77] (See Fig. 2). The vision features at each level are fused with the text features. A feature pyramid [44] fuses features across resolutions by progressively up-sampling the higher level fused features to the resolution of lower level features.

The transformer fusion works as follows (see bottom right of Fig. 2). We first use a linear layer to project the vision and text features into the same dimension at each level. Next, we collapse the spatial dimension of vision features into a sequence and concatenate it with the text sequence features. We compute the relative position bias based on the total length of the concatenated sequence before applying the self-attention layers. As self-attention is intractable with large feature maps, we apply product fusion (see top right of Fig. 2) for the early high resolution feature maps (i.e. F2 and F3), and use self-attention for the smaller, higher level feature maps (i.e. F4 and F5). Ablation studies show the benefits of multi-level fusion and self-attention for handling complex queries (see Sect. 4.3). Finally, we truncate and reshape the fused features to the same spatial dimensions as the input vision features.

3.5   Task Unification and Multi-task Learning

The three localization tasks must be unified in terms of model, loss, and inputs so they can be trained together. The implications of unification are significant. First, all tasks can share the same model during both training and inference time. Second, the unification of inputs and loss enables us to efficiently train on multiple datasets. Lastly, the model can leverage information from other tasks, which allows the transfer of visual concepts and enables zero-shot applications. For example, we can learn long-tail concepts from the referring expression task and transfer them to other localization tasks.

Apart from the unified architecture (see Sect. 3.3 and 3.4), datasets are adapted to the different tasks as follows. For the localization task, detection datasets are adapted by generating a set of queries over the categories present in the image. For any present category, the text query takes the form "Find the X" where X is the category name. The objects corresponding to that category are labeled as foreground and the other objects as background. At training time, we randomly sample a text query and corresponding objects from each image. For the detection task, detection datasets are adapted by adding a static task prompt such as "Find all the objects". We found that the specific choice of prompts are not important for LOC and DET tasks (see Table 6a).

After adaptation, all tasks in consideration share the same inputs and outputs—an image input, a text query, and a set of output bounding boxes/classes. We then combine the datasets and train on the mixture. At training time, we use a mixing ratio of 1:1:1 between DET:LOC:REC tasks in each minibatch. To ensure each dataset is sampled adequately, we use a larger batch size of 256 split among the 3 tasks. To make the image size uniform across tasks (see Table 1), we adopt the LOC task's image size of 640 [20] as a middle ground. This is larger but comparable to the image size of REC task [12,86,87]. It is smaller than the size of DET task's images [22] which might limit performance on smaller objects.

Finally, we unify the losses of all tasks. The losses we use are box classification and regression loss, region proposal classification and regression loss, and weight decay. The loss formulation and relative weights follow [67] without any task-specific modification. All losses have equal weights across tasks. We note that it is unclear how to use existing grounding models out-of-the-box for task unification due to the task-specific architectures, losses, and training strategies [12, 20, 50, 54, 86, 87, 89].

3.6   Implementation Details

FindIt uses a region proposer (RPN) [67], class predictor [67] and a class-agnostic box regressor [67] shared among all tasks. The class decoder has the same number of outputs as the detection vocabulary size (i.e. 80 for COCO), as it primarily serves the detection task. We note that no pre-computed detections are used in FindIt as in many two-stage referring expression models [50, 89].

FindIt image encoder is initialized from the ResNet50 model pretrained on COCO detection. FindIt text encoder is initialized from T5-base [65] pretrained checkpoint. All other modules are trained from scratch, including the multi-level fusion model, feature pyramid network [44], the region proposal network (RPN) and the box/class decoders [67]. All hyper-parameters of the feature pyramid, RPN and box/class decoder heads follow the Faster R-CNN [18].

We set the batch size to 256 split among 3 tasks DET:LOC:REC with mixing ratio 1:1:1 in the minibatch. The ratio was chosen for simplicity and has room for further optimization. We train the model for 150k steps on a learning rate of 0.08, linear warmup of 500 steps, and a decay factor of 0.1 at 70% and 90% of the training schedule. Total training takes about 1.2 days. For the ablations, we train for 25k steps (0.25x) on the same learning rate schedule. We set the learning rate of the pretrained image encoder and text encoder to be 10% of the rest of the model which trains from scratch [12,86].

We apply random scale jittering uniformly sampled between [0.4, 2.5] for every input image. The image is padded or randomly cropped to the size of (640, 640) after the scale jittering. For the ablation studies, we reduce the scale jittering magnitude to [0.8, 1.25] due to the shorter training. For detection and text-based localization tasks we also apply random horizontal flip following the standard protocol [67]. In addition, we tokenize the text with SentencePiece [39] following T5 [65] and set the maximum expression length to 64 for all tasks.

Table 2. Comparison with state-of-the-art methods on RefCOCO including those using external data for pretraining. We outperform the state of the art on RefCOCO [90], RefCOCO+ [90] and RefCOCOg [55] with only R50 backbone. FindIt-REC is our own single task baseline. **Bold** indicates the highest non-unified training number. *Red* indicates the highest number overall, whereas *blue* the second highest. (Best viewed in color)

Models	Backbone	RefCOCO			RefCOCO+			RefCOCOg		
		val	testA	testB	val	testA	testB	val-g	val-u	test-u
Two-stage										
CMN [26]	VGG16	–	71.03	65.77	–	54.32	47.76	57.47	–	–
VC [92]	VGG16	–	73.33	67.44	–	58.40	53.18	62.30	–	–
ParalAttn [97]	VGG16	–	75.31	65.52	–	61.34	50.86	58.03	–	–
MAttNet [89]	R101	76.65	81.14	69.99	65.33	71.62	56.02	–	66.58	67.27
LGRANs [81]	VGG16	–	76.60	66.40	–	64.00	53.40	61.78	–	–
DGA [85]	VGG16	–	78.42	65.53	–	69.07	51.99	–	–	63.28
RvG-Tree [24]	R101	75.06	78.61	69.85	63.51	67.45	56.66	–	66.95	66.51
NMTree [49]	R101	76.41	81.21	70.09	66.46	72.02	57.52	64.62	65.87	66.44
CM-Att-Erase [50]	R101	78.35	83.14	71.32	68.09	73.65	58.03	–	67.99	68.67
One-stage										
SSG [7]	DarkNet-53	–	76.51	67.50	–	62.14	49.27	47.47	58.80	–
FAOA [87]	DarkNet-53	72.54	74.35	68.50	56.81	60.23	49.60	56.12	61.33	60.36
RCCF [43]	DLA-34	–	81.06	71.85	–	70.35	56.32	–	–	65.73
ReSC-Large [86]	DarkNet-53	77.63	80.45	72.30	63.59	68.36	56.81	63.12	67.30	67.20
MCN [54]	DarkNet-53	80.08	82.29	74.98	67.16	72.86	57.31	–	66.46	66.01
Transformer										
TransVG [12]	R50	80.32	82.67	78.12	63.50	68.15	55.63	66.56	67.66	67.44
TransVG [12]	R101	81.02	82.72	78.35	64.82	70.70	56.94	67.02	68.67	67.73
FindIt-REC	R50	79.45	82.43	72.94	66.01	71.13	58.62	63.91	67.73	68.77
FindIt	R50	**84.66**	**85.50**	**83.46**	**73.85**	**78.57**	**67.31**	**73.25**	**77.64**	**77.02**
Unified training										
FindIt-MIX	R50	84.92	85.54	83.44	74.31	76.93	69.91	82.77	83.17	84.11
FindIt-MIX (384)	R50	**87.09**	85.55	**86.89**	76.35	75.47	**71.85**	**89.84**	**90.40**	**91.01**
FindIt-MIX (384)	R101	87.91	86.56	88.04	**77.24**	77.42	73.12	90.58	90.97	91.72
External data										
UNITER-L [8]	R101	81.41	87.04	74.17	75.90	81.45	66.70	–	74.86	75.77
VILLA-L [16]	R101	82.39	**87.48**	74.84	76.17	**81.54**	66.84	–	76.18	76.71
MDETR [35]	R101	86.75	89.58	81.41	79.52	84.09	70.62	–	81.64	80.89

4 Experiments

We compare FindIt to the state of the art (SOTA) on REC, LOC and DET tasks (Sect. 4.1). We follow the protocols established in prior works [20,90], using only MS-COCO [46] for training and validation. In addition, we evaluate how FindIt generalizes to OOD datasets and settings (Sect. 4.2).

Here we define the family of FindIt models. *FindIt* is trained jointly on REC, LOC, and DET tasks, while *FindIt-REC, FindIt-LOC, FindIt-DET* are trained on each individual task to serve as single-task baselines. FindIt does not require more labeled data than existing REC methods, because pre-trained detector outputs [89,92] or initialization with detector weights [12,86,87] have been commonly used. Towards further unification, *FindIt-MIX* trains on all RefCOCO splits (as opposed to a single RefCOCO split used by *FindIt*), LOC, and DET together, resulting in one model for all splits instead of one model for each split, which is the case with FindIt. To our best knowledge, we are the first to report single-model unified training results on RefCOCO benchmarks. We report all FindIt-MIX (384) results as an average of five independent runs.

Table 3. Text-based Localization and Detection Benchmarks. All models in the tables use the ResNet-50 (R50) backbone.

(a) Text-based localization results on COCO. We compare with the single- and multi-task GPV [20].

Models	Multitask	Image Size	AP50
FRCNN [20,67]	✗	640	75.2
GPV [20]	✓	640	73.0
FindIt-LOC	✗	640	77.9
FindIt-MIX	✓	640	78.6
FindIt	✓	640	**79.7 ± 0.1**

(b) Detection results on COCO. We compare with the single- and multi-task baselines from [18,27]. .

Models	Multitask	Image Size	mAP
FRCNN [18]	✗	1333	37.9
UNiT [27]	✗	1333	**40.6**
UNiT [27]	✓	1333	39.0
FindIt-DET[1]	✗	1024	**40.6**
FindIt-MIX	✓	640	38.4
FindIt	✓	640	39.7 ± 0.1

4.1 Main Results

Table 2, Table 3a, and Table 3b show our results on REC, LOC and DET tasks compared to the SOTA. In each table, we compare FindIt to both single- or multi-task approaches for the corresponding task. The single-task approaches are advantaged as they are fully optimized for the task.

Table 2 compares with existing COCO-trained methods on the three popular REC benchmarks: RefCOCO [90], RefCOCO+ [90] and RefCOCOg [55]. We see that FindIt outperforms the SOTA results, including two-stage/one-stage methods and recent Transformer-based models. In particular, on the challenging splits of RefCOCO+ (no location-based information) and RefCOCOg (longer expressions), FindIt outperforms the SOTA results by a clear margin of 5–10 points. Compared to the single-task baselines, FindIt consistently improves the performance by 3–9 points across the RefCOCO splits, showing the benefits of multitask training.

We note that all results in Table 2 only use COCO box annotation and language corpus pretraining [65]. We do not pretrain on vision and language datasets or use the mask annotations in COCO [54]. Existing approaches [8,16,35] obtain SOTA performance on RefCOCO by pretraining on large vision and language datasets [5,57], visual grounding datasets [35,38,61], or graph relationships [88]. Without using external data, FindIt-MIX is on par with or better than the SOTA method [35] pre-trained with more visual grounding data. Our best-performing model on REC uses a smaller image size (384) than the rest of the paper (640).

To avoid contamination for FindIt, we remove the overlapping images of the RefCOCO val/test sets from the training sets of LOC and DET based on the RefCOCO split they are trained with. For FindIt-MIX, we carefully

Fig. 3. Visualization of FindIt on REC, LOC, and DET. Compared to existing baselines [20,89], FindIt can perform these tasks well and in a single model.

Table 4. Generalization study through text-based localization task.

(a) Generalization to novel categories.					(b) Generalization to super-categories.			
Model	REC	Base-80	Novel-285	All	Model	COCO	COCO-O365	O365
FindIt-REC	79.5	21.3	5.2	13.1	FindIt-REC	33.0	18.6	11.0
FindIt-LOC	–	56.7	15.2	33.9	FindIt-LOC	45.8	25.3	15.3
FindIt-MIX	84.9	57.8	18.7	36.4	FindIt-MIX	49.5	30.1	17.5

remove the overlapping images of all RefCOCO val/test sets from all REC, LOC, and DET training sets. The mixing ratio for FindIt-MIX is 2:2:1:1:1:1 among DET:LOC:REC:REC+:REC-g:REC-umd. The FindIt and FindIt-MIX models in Table 2 and Table 3 are the same without task-specific fine-tuning.

Table 3a compares our work on the text-based localization (LOC) task. We compare to the recent GPV method [20] which is is the best approach on this task. For FindIt, we report the mean and standard deviation over four individual RefCOCO splits. FindIt outperforms GPV in all settings. Following GPV [20], we train both LOC and DET tasks on COCO'14 train split (80k images) and report performance on COCO'14 val split (40k images) in Table 3. Table 3b shows our results on detection. We see that our approach is comparable to the full UNiT [27], which uses a detection-specific task head, larger image size, and more training images (COCO'17 vs our COCO'14). Compared to the single-task setup, FindIt shows a similar performance gap to that seen in UNiT's multitask setup. Figure 3 shows examples of FindIt on all three tasks[3].

---

[3] FindIt-DET is trained and tested on COCO 17' to match the settings of [18,27].

Table 5. Runtime benchmark with recent REC approaches.

Models	Image size	Backbone	Runtime (ms)
MattNet [89]	1000	R101	378
FAOA [87]	256	DarkNet-53	39
MCN [54]	416	DarkNet-53	56
TransVG [12]	640	R50	62
FindIt	640	R50	107
FindIt	384	R50	57

4.2   Generalization Capabilities of FindIt

We now evaluate the generalization capabilities of the FindIt model presented in Sect. 4.1. The Objects365 dataset [71] is chosen for the study, because it is independently collected and represents OOD (Out-of-Distribution) data. In addition, the dataset is large, well-annotated with high recall, and contains all of 80 COCO categories and 285 novel categories (365 in total) to assess the generalization of FindIt models. Our models acquire the linguistic knowledge of novel categories from multi-task cross-attention learning and language pretraining [65]. However, as all of our single- and multi-task models share the same language pretraining, the main differences arise from multi-task learning.

Localization on Novel Categories. Even though referring expression models are able to effectively localize objects from complex queries, we want to investigate whether they are able to handle the text-based localization task. Thus, we evaluate the single-task FindIt-REC, FindIt-LOC, and unified training FindIt-MIX models on Objects365 dataset. All FindIt models are identical to their counterparts in Table 2 and Table 3a without further fine-tuning. The FindIt-REC model was trained on the RefCOCO UNC split. Table 4a shows the results, where the column "Base-80" evaluates the 80 COCO categories; "Novel-285" evaluates the 285 non-COCO categories; "All" evaluates all 365 categories; "REC" is the performance on RefCOCO UNC. We first observe that FindIt-REC struggles on this task, despite having strong performance on REC. FindIt-LOC model performs much better because it was directly trained for this task. Compared to FindIt-LOC and FindIt-REC, FindIt generalizes better especially on the novel categories of Objects365, because it has acquired broader knowledge about objects and grounding texts through multi-task learning.

Localization on Super-Categories. By accepting text inputs, FindIt model relaxes the requirement for a pre-defined set of classes for localization and can generalize beyond the training vocabulary (i.e. COCO categories). We study this behavior by testing on COCO and Objects365 super-categories (e.g. giraffe $\in$ animal, pizza $\in$ food). The setup is identical to Table 4a except that the query category names are replaced with their corresponding super-categories. All models here are the same as in Table 4b. We present the results in Table 4a. The

Table 6. Ablations on task prompts, language model sizes, multi-level fusion architecture design, and mixing ratios.

(a) Ablations on task prompts. The first row corresponds to default FindIt.

LOC Prompt	DET Prompt	LOC	DET
"Find the X"	"Find all the objects"	78.78	38.96
"X"	"This is detection task"	79.13	38.88
GPV [20]	"Find all the objects"	78.92	38.97

(b) Ablations on language model sizes.

Language Model	DET	LOC	REC
T5-Small [65]	38.7	78.7	80.7
T5-Base [65]	38.4	78.7	81.0
T5-Large [65]	38.8	78.8	81.2

(c) Ablations on the fusion mechanism, feature dimension and the number of transformer layers.

Fusion	Dim.	# Layers	DET	LOC	REC
Concat	256	1	35.6	76.6	77.7
Product	256	1	35.4	76.6	78.9
Product	256	3	35.1	76.2	76.7
Attention	128	1	35.7	75.8	75.2
Attention	256	3	35.6	76.5	79.3
Attention	512	6	35.7	76.9	79.3
Attention	1024	12	35.7	77.1	82.1

(d) Ablations on the fusion levels, feature dimension dimensionsion and the number of transformer layers.

Levels	Dim.	# Layers	DET	LOC	REC
(5,)	256	3	35.6	76.7	78.8
(5,)	512	6	34.6	76.0	80.0
(5,)	1024	12	33.0	75.0	80.5
(4, 5)	256	3	35.6	76.5	79.3
(4, 5)	512	6	35.7	76.9	79.3
(4, 5)	1024	12	35.7	77.1	82.1

(e) Ablations on the fusion architecture for the REC tasks.

Fusion	Dim.	Layers	UNC	Plus	G	UMD
Concat.	128	1	76.1	60.4	53.2	62.4
Concat.	256	3	76.8	61.7	54.5	63.6
Concat.	512	6	77.2	61.8	57.1	64.6
Product	128	1	66.5	62.4	55.3	63.3
Product	256	3	76.0	60.9	54.6	62.6
Product	512	6	75.6	60.1	57.4	62.4
Attention	128	1	73.7	57.1	53.9	60.6
Attention	256	3	78.6	62.9	60.8	64.4
Attention	512	6	78.6	65.6	60.6	67.3

(f) Ablations on multitask mixing ratios for all tasks.

DET : LOC : REC	DET	LOC	REC
1 : 1 : 1	35.5	76.6	78.5
2 : 1 : 1	35.9	75.9	77.7
1 : 2 : 1	34.9	77.0	78.3
2 : 2 : 1	35.8	76.8	76.9

column "COCO" evaluates the COCO super-categories on COCO data; "COCO-O365" evaluates the COCO super-categories on Objects365; "O365" evaluates the Objects365 super-categories on Objects365. Despite the challenging setup, FindIt generalizes better than single-task baselines by a clear margin, showing the merits of broader grounding knowledge provided by multitask learning (see Table 1 for more examples).

4.3   Analysis and Ablations

Inference Time. We benchmark the inference times across image sizes in Table 5 on the REC task. FindIt is efficient and comparable with existing approaches, while achieving higher accuracy (See Table 2). For fair comparison, all running times are measured on one GTX 1080Ti GPU. Compared to the two-step approach [89], FindIt is more efficient because it trains end-to-end without a need for pre-computed detections.

Task Prompts. We conducted the ablations on the prompts of LOC and DET tasks in Table 6a and found the prompts have minimal effects on performance. Our LOC prompt "Find the X" is one of the prompts used by GPV [20].

Language Model Size. We conducted ablations on the language model sizes in Table 6b and found that larger models are only marginally better. In Table 6b, REC is the mean performance over all RefCOCO splits. We choose T5 base [65] as the best trade-off between performance and speed.

Multi-level Fusion Architecture. We conduct ablation studies on the fusion architecture and multitask mixing ratios. All experiments of this section are run with a 6x shorter schedule and weaker data augmentation for faster convergence. In all tables we use RefCOCO-UNC as a representative split to evaluate the REC task except for the ablation on language model size. In Table 6c we study the effect of architecture choices on the downstream tasks. We find that attention-based fusion outperforms other alternatives given the same configuration (e.g. 256 dim, 3 layers). In addition, increasing the number of attention layers and the embedding dimension both improve the performance on referring expression, but not as much on detection and localization. We explore multi-scale fusion in Table 6d, and find that using more levels is beneficial for all model sizes we study. Thus, levels (4, 5) are chosen for all experiments. Table 6e delves deeper to show the benefits of attention fusion for REC tasks. With adequate model capacity (e.g. 256 dim, 3 layers), attention fusion outperforms the other alternatives under the same configuration. On the split with the most complex queries (RefCOCO-g), we notice attention fusion performs substantially better than other alternatives. From these studies, we choose (Attention, 256 dim, 3 layers) as our model, because we find the larger alternative (Attention, 512 dim, 6 layers) to perform only marginally better with full training schedule.

Table 6f studies the sampling weight in multitask learning. We find that a simple 1:1:1 ratio achieves a good balance between DET, LOC and REC task performance. Increasing the sampling rate for one task tends to improve the performance at the expense of other tasks. We note that the mixing ratios can be further optimized to improve the performance of any constituent task. We use 256-dimension fusion features, 3 layers, and fusion levels (4, 5) in this ablation.

5   Conclusion

We present FindIt, which unifies referring expression comprehension, text-based localization, and object detection tasks. We propose multi-scale cross-attention to unify the disparate localization requirements of these tasks. Without any task-specific design, FindIt surpasses the state of the art on referring expression and text-based localization, shows competitive performance on detection, and generalizes better to out-of-distribution data and novel classes. All of these are accomplished in a single, unified and efficient model.

Acknowledgements. We would like to thank Ashish Vaswani, Prajit Ramachandran, Niki Parmar, David Luan, Tsung-Yi Lin, and other colleagues at Google Research for their advice and helpful discussion.

References

1. Anderson, P., et al.: Bottom-up and top-down attention for image captioning and visual question answering. In: CVPR (2018)
2. Bansal, A., Sikka, K., Sharma, G., Chellappa, R., Divakaran, A.: Zero-shot object detection. In: Ferrari, V., Hebert, M., Sminchisescu, C., Weiss, Y. (eds.) ECCV 2018. LNCS, vol. 11205, pp. 397–414. Springer, Cham (2018). https://doi.org/10.1007/978-3-030-01246-5_24
3. Carion, N., Massa, F., Synnaeve, G., Usunier, N., Kirillov, A., Zagoruyko, S.: End-to-end object detection with transformers (2020). https://arxiv.org/abs/2005.12872
4. Changpinyo, S., Pont-Tuset, J., Ferrari, V., Soricut, R.: Telling the what while pointing to the where: multimodal queries for image retrieval. Arxiv: 2102.04980 (2021)
5. Changpinyo, S., Sharma, P., Ding, N., Soricut, R.: Conceptual 12m: pushing web-scale image-text pre-training to recognize long-tail visual concepts. In: CVPR (2021)
6. Chen, X., et al.: Microsoft coco captions: data collection and evaluation server. Arxiv: https://arxiv.org/abs/1504.00325 (2015)
7. Chen, X., Ma, L., Chen, J., Jie, Z., Liu, W., Luo, J.: Real-time referring expression comprehension by single-stage grounding network. arXiv preprint arXiv:1812.03426 (2018)
8. Chen, Y.C., et al.: UNITER: UNiversal image-TExt representation learning. In: Vedaldi, A., Bischof, H., Brox, T., Frahm, J.-M. (eds.) ECCV 2020. LNCS, vol. 12375, pp. 104–120. Springer, Cham (2020). https://doi.org/10.1007/978-3-030-58577-8_7
9. Chen, Z., Wang, P., Ma, L., Wong, K.Y.K., Wu, Q.: Cops-ref: a new dataset and task on compositional referring expression comprehension. In: CVPR (2020)
10. Cho, J., Lei, J., Tan, H., Bansal, M.: Unifying vision-and-language tasks via text generation. Arxiv: 2102.02779 (2021)
11. Das, A., et al.: Visual dialog. In: CVPR (2017)
12. Deng, J., Yang, Z., Chen, T., Zhou, W., Li, H.: TransVG: end-to-end visual grounding with transformers. ICCV (2021)
13. Desai, K., Johnson, J.: VirTex: learning visual representations from textual annotations. In: CVPR (2021)
14. Dhamija, A.R., Gunther, M., Ventura, J., Boult, T.E.: The overlooked elephant of object detection: open set. In: WACV (2020)
15. Gan, C., Li, Y., Li, H., Sun, C., Gong, B.: VQS: linking segmentations to questions and answers for supervised attention in VQA and question-focused semantic segmentation. In: ICCV (2017)
16. Gan, Z., Chen, Y.C., Li, L., Zhu, C., Cheng, Y., Liu, J.: Large-scale adversarial training for vision-and-language representation learning. In: NeurIPS (2020)
17. Girshick, R., Donahue, J., Darrell, T., Malik, J.: Rich feature hierarchies for accurate object detection and semantic segmentation. In: CVPR (2014)
18. Girshick, R., Radosavovic, I., Gkioxari, G., Dollár, P., He, K.: Detectron (2018). https://github.com/facebookresearch/detectron

19. Gu, X., Lin, T., Kuo, W., Cui, Y.: Zero-shot detection via vision and language knowledge distillation. CoRR abs/2104.13921 (2021). https://arxiv.org/abs/2104.13921

20. Gupta, T., Kamath, A., Kembhavi, A., Hoiem2, D.: Towards general purpose vision systems. arxiv.org/abs/2104.00743 (2021)

21. Gupta, T., Vahdat, A., Chechik, G., Yang, X., Kautz, J., Hoiem, D.: Contrastive learning for weakly supervised phrase grounding. In: Vedaldi, A., Bischof, H., Brox, T., Frahm, J.-M. (eds.) ECCV 2020. LNCS, vol. 12348, pp. 752–768. Springer, Cham (2020). https://doi.org/10.1007/978-3-030-58580-8_44

22. He, K., Gkioxari, G., Dollar, P., Girshick, R.: Mask R-CNN. In: ICCV (2017)

23. Hinami, R., Satoh, S.: Discriminative learning of open-vocabulary object retrieval and localization by negative phrase augmentation. In: Proceedings of the 2018 Conference on Empirical Methods in Natural Language Processing (2018)

24. Hong, R., Liu, D., Mo, X., He, X., Zhang, H.: Learning to compose and reason with language tree structures for visual grounding. TPAMI (2019)

25. Hu, R., Rohrbach, M., Darrell, T.: Segmentation from natural language expressions. In: Leibe, B., Matas, J., Sebe, N., Welling, M. (eds.) ECCV 2016. LNCS, vol. 9905, pp. 108–124. Springer, Cham (2016). https://doi.org/10.1007/978-3-319-46448-0_7

26. Hu, R., Rohrbach, M., Andreas, J., Darrell, T., Saenko, K.: Modeling relationships in referential expressions with compositional modular networks. In: CVPR, pp. 1115–1124 (2017)

27. Hu, R., Singh, A.: Unit: multimodal multitask learning with a unified transformer. arxiv.org/abs/2102.10772 (2021)

28. Huang, G., Pang, B., Zhu, Z., Rivera, C., Soricut, R.: Multimodal pretraining for dense video captioning. In: AACL-IJCNLP (2020)

29. Huang, Z., Zeng, Z., Huang, Y., Liu, B., Fu, D., Fu, J.: Seeing out of the box: end-to-end pre-training for vision-language representation learning. In: CVPR (2021)

30. Hudson, D.A., Manning, C.D.: GQA: a new dataset for compositional question answering over realworld images. In: CVPR (2019)

31. Jia, C., et al.: Scaling up visual and vision-language representation learning with noisy text supervision. In: ICML (2021)

32. Jiang, H., Misra, I., Rohrbach, M., Learned-Miller, E., Chen, X.: In defense of grid features for visual question answering. In: CVPR (2020)

33. Johnson, J., Hariharan, B., van der Maaten, L., Fei-Fei, L., Zitnick, C.L., Girshick, R.: A diagnostic dataset for compositional language and elementary visual reasoning. In: CVPR (2017)

34. Xu, J., Mei, T., Yao, T., Rui, Y.: MSR-VTT: a large video description dataset for bridging video and language. In: CVPR (2016)

35. Kamath, A., Singh, M., LeCun, Y., Misra, I., Synnaeve, G., Carion, N.: MDETR - modulated detection for end-to-end multi-modal understanding (2021). https://arxiv.org/abs/2104.12763

36. Kant, Y., Moudgil, A., Batra, D., Parikh, D., Agrawal, H.: Contrast and classify: training robust VQA models. In: ICCV (2021)

37. Kim, W., Son, B., Kim, I.: ViLT: vision-and-language transformer without convolution or region supervision. In: ICML (2021)

38. Krishna, R., et al.: Visual genome: connecting language and vision using crowd-sourced dense image annotations (2016). https://arxiv.org/abs/1602.07332

39. Kudo, T., Richardson, J.: SentencePiece: a simple and language independent subword tokenizer and detokenizer for neural text processing. arXiv preprint arXiv:1808.06226 (2018)

40. Li, L.H., Yatskar, M., Yin, D., Hsieh, C.J., Chang, K.W.: VisualBERT: a simple and performant baseline for vision and language. Arxiv:https://arxiv.org/abs/1908.03557 (2019)
41. Li, L.H., et al.: Grounded language-image pre-training. In: CVPR (2022)
42. Li, X., et al.: Oscar: object-semantics aligned pre-training for vision-language tasks. In: Vedaldi, A., Bischof, H., Brox, T., Frahm, J.-M. (eds.) ECCV 2020. LNCS, vol. 12375, pp. 121–137. Springer, Cham (2020). https://doi.org/10.1007/978-3-030-58577-8_8
43. Liao, Y., et al.: A real-time cross-modality correlation filtering method for referring expression comprehension. In: CVPR, pp. 10880–10889 (2020)
44. Lin, T.Y., Dollár, P., Girshick, R., He, K., Hariharan, B., Belongie, S.: Feature pyramid networks for object detection. In: Proceedings of the IEEE Conference on Computer Vision and Pattern Recognition, pp. 2117–2125 (2017)
45. Lin, T.Y., Goyal, P., Girshick, R., He, K., Dollár, P.: Focal loss for dense object detection. In: Proceedings of the IEEE International Conference on Computer Vision, pp. 2980–2988 (2017)
46. Lin, T.Y., et al.: Microsoft COCO: common objects in context. In: Fleet, D., Pajdla, T., Schiele, B., Tuytelaars, T. (eds.) ECCV 2014. LNCS, vol. 8693, pp. 740–755. Springer, Cham (2014). https://doi.org/10.1007/978-3-319-10602-1_48
47. Lin, X., Bertasius, G., Wang, J., Chang, S.F., Parikh, D.: Vx2text: end-to-end learning of video-based text generation from multimodal inputs. In: CVPR (2021)
48. Liu, C., Lin, Z., Shen, X., Yang, J., Lu, X., Yuille, A.: Recurrent multimodal interaction for referring image segmentation. In: ICCV (2017)
49. Liu, D., Zhang, H., Wu, F., Zha, Z.J.: Learning to assemble neural module tree networks for visual grounding. In: ICCV, pp. 4673–4682 (2019)
50. Liu, X., Wang, Z., Shao, J., Wang, X., Li, H.: Improving referring expression grounding with cross-modal attention-guided erasing. In: Proceedings of the IEEE/CVF Conference on Computer Vision and Pattern Recognition, pp. 1950–1959 (2019)
51. Liu, Z., Stent, S., Li, J., Gideon, J., Han, S.: LocTex: learning data-efficient visual representations from localized textual supervision. In: ICCV (2021)
52. Lu, J., Batra, D., Parikh, D., Lee, S.: ViLBERT: pretraining task-agnostic visiolinguistic representations for vision-and-language tasks. In: CVPR (2019)
53. Lu, J., Goswami, V., Rohrbach, M., Parikh, D., Lee, S.: 12-in-1: multi-task vision and language representation learning. In: CVPR (2020)
54. Luo, G., et al.: Multi-task collaborative network for joint referring expression comprehension and segmentation. In: 2020 IEEE/CVF Conference on Computer Vision and Pattern Recognition (CVPR), pp. 10031–10040 (2020)
55. Mao, J., Huang, J., Toshev, A., Camburu, O., Yuille, A., Murphy, K.: Generation and comprehension of unambiguous object descriptions. In: CVPR (2016)
56. Margffoy-Tuay, E., Pérez, J.C., Botero, E., Arbeláez, P.: Dynamic multimodal instance segmentation guided by natural language queries. In: Ferrari, V., Hebert, M., Sminchisescu, C., Weiss, Y. (eds.) ECCV 2018. LNCS, vol. 11215, pp. 656–672. Springer, Cham (2018). https://doi.org/10.1007/978-3-030-01252-6_39
57. Ordonez, V., Kulkarni, G., Berg, T.L.: Im2text: describing images using 1 million captioned photographs. In: NeurIPS (2011)
58. Papageorgiou, C., Oren, M., Poggio, T.: A general framework for object detection. In: ICCV (1998)
59. Peng, J., Bu, X., Sun, M., Zhang, Z., Tan, T., Yan, J.: Large-scale object detection in the wild from imbalanced multi-labels. In: CVPR (2020)

60. Plummer, B.A., Shih, K.J., Li, Y., Xu, K., Lazebnik, S., Sclaroff, S., Saenko, K.: Revisiting image-language networks for open-ended phrase detection. TPAMI (2020)
61. Plummer, B.A., Wang, L., Cervantes, C.M., Caicedo, J.C., Hockenmaier, J., Lazebnik, S.: Flickr30k entities: collecting region-to-phrase correspondences for richer image-to-sentence models. In: Proceedings of the IEEE International Conference on Computer Vision, pp. 2641–2649 (2015)
62. Plummer, B.A., Wang, L., Cervantes, C.M., Caicedo, J.C., Hockenmaier, J., Lazebnik, S.: Flickr30k entities: collecting region-to-phrase correspondences for richer image-to-sentence models. Int. J. Comput. Vis. (2017)
63. Qiao, Y., Deng, C., Wu, Q.: Referring expression comprehension: a survey of methods and datasets. IEEE TMM **23**, 4426–4440 (2020)
64. Radford, A., et al.: Learning transferable visual models from natural language supervision. In: ICML (2021)
65. Raffel, C., et al.: Exploring the limits of transfer learning with a unified text-to-text transformer. J. Mach. Learn. Res. (JMLR) **21**, 1–67 (2020)
66. Redmon, J., Divvala, S., Girshick, R., Farhadi, A.: You only look once: unified, real-time object detection. In: CVPR (2016)
67. Ren, S., He, K., Girshick, R., Sun, J.: Faster R-CNN: towards real-time object detection with region proposal networks. In: Advances in Neural Information Processing Systems (2015)
68. Hu, R., Xu, H., Rohrbach, M., Feng, J., Saenko, K., Darrell, T.: Natural language object retrieval. In: CVPR (2016)
69. Rowley, H., Baluja, S., Kanade, T.: Human face detection in visual scenes. In: Advances in Neural Information Processing Systems (1995)
70. Kazemzadeh, S., Ordonez, V., Matten, M., Berg, T.: ReferitGame: referring to objects in photographs of natural scenes. In: EMNLP (2014)
71. Shao, S., et al.: Objects365: a large-scale, high-quality dataset for object detection. In: ICCV (2019)
72. Srinivasan, K., Raman, K., Chen, J., Bendersky, M., Najork, M.: WIT: Wikipedia-based image text dataset for multimodal multilingual machine learning. arXiv:2103.01913 (2021)
73. Suhr, A., Lewis, M., Yeh, J., Artzi, Y.: A corpus of natural language for visual reasoning. In: Proceedings of the 55th Annual Meeting of the Association for Computational Linguistics (2017)
74. Tan, H., Bansal, M.: LXMERT: learning cross-modality encoder representations from transformers. In: EMNLP (2019)
75. Vaillant, R., Monrocq, C., Cun, Y.L.: An original approach for the localization of objects in images. In: IEEE Proceedings of the Visual Image Signal Processing (1994)
76. Nagaraja, V.K., Morariu, V.I., Davis, L.S.: Modeling context between objects for referring expression understanding. In: Leibe, B., Matas, J., Sebe, N., Welling, M. (eds.) ECCV 2016. LNCS, vol. 9908, pp. 792–807. Springer, Cham (2016). https://doi.org/10.1007/978-3-319-46493-0_48
77. Vaswani, A., et al.: Attention is all you need. In: NeurIPS (2017)
78. Viola, P., Jones, M.: Robust real-time object detection. Int. J. Comput. Vis. **57**, 137–154 (2001). https://doi.org/10.1023/B:VISI.0000013087.49260.fb
79. Wang, L., Li, Y., Huang, J., Lazebnik, S.: Learning two-branch neural networks for image-text matching tasks. IEEE Trans. Pattern Anal. Mach. Intell. **41**, 394–407 (2018)

80. Wang, M., Azab, M., Kojima, N., Mihalcea, R., Deng, J.: Structured matching for phrase localization. In: Leibe, B., Matas, J., Sebe, N., Welling, M. (eds.) ECCV 2016. LNCS, vol. 9912, pp. 696–711. Springer, Cham (2016). https://doi.org/10.1007/978-3-319-46484-8_42

81. Wang, P., Wu, Q., Cao, J., Shen, C., Gao, L., Hengel, A.V.D.: Neighbourhood watch: referring expression comprehension via language-guided graph attention networks. In: CVPR, pp. 1960–1968 (2019)

82. Xian, Y., Lampert, C.H., Schiele, B., Akata, Z.: Zero-shot learning - a comprehensive evaluation of the good, the bad and the ugly. TPAMI **41**, 2251–2265 (2018)

83. Xie, N., Lai, F., Doran, D., Kadav, A.: Visual entailment: a novel task for fine-grained image understanding (2019). https://arxiv.org/abs/1901.06706

84. Xu, H., et al.: E2E-VLP: end-to-end vision-language pre-training enhanced by visual learning. In: Proceedings of the 59th Annual Meeting of the Association for Computational Linguistics and the 11th International Joint Conference on Natural Language Processing (2021)

85. Yang, S., Li, G., Yu, Y.: Dynamic graph attention for referring expression comprehension. In: ICCV, pp. 4644–4653 (2019)

86. Yang, Z., Chen, T., Wang, L., Luo, J.: Improving one-stage visual grounding by recursive sub-query construction. In: Vedaldi, A., Bischof, H., Brox, T., Frahm, J.-M. (eds.) ECCV 2020. LNCS, vol. 12359, pp. 387–404. Springer, Cham (2020). https://doi.org/10.1007/978-3-030-58568-6_23

87. Yang, Z., Gong, B., Wang, L., Huang, W., Yu, D., Luo, J.: A fast and accurate one-stage approach to visual grounding. In: ICCV, pp. 4683–4693 (2019)

88. Yu, F., et al.: ERNIE-VIL: knowledge enhanced vision-language representations through scene graph. In: AAAI (2021)

89. Yu, L., et al.: MAttNet: modular attention network for referring expression comprehension. In: CVPR (2018)

90. Yu, L., Poirson, P., Yang, S., Berg, A.C., Berg, T.L.: Modeling context in referring expressions. In: Leibe, B., Matas, J., Sebe, N., Welling, M. (eds.) ECCV 2016. LNCS, vol. 9906, pp. 69–85. Springer, Cham (2016). https://doi.org/10.1007/978-3-319-46475-6_5

91. Zellers, R., Bisk, Y., Farhadi, A., Choi, Y.: From recognition to cognition: visual commonsense reasoning. In: CVPR (2019)

92. Zhang, H., Niu, Y., Chang, S.F.: Grounding referring expressions in images by variational context. In: CVPR, pp. 4158–4166 (2018)

93. Zhang, P., et al.: VinVL: revisiting visual representations in vision-language models. In: CVPR (2021)

94. Zhao, F., Li, J., Zhao, J., Feng, J.: Weakly supervised phrase localization with multi-scale anchored transformer network. In: CVPR (2018)

95. Zhou, L., Palangi, H., Zhang, L., Hu, H., Corso, J.J., Gao, J.: Unified vision-language pre-training for image captioning and VQA. In: AAAI (2020)

96. Zhu, P., Wang, H., Saligrama, V.: Zero-shot detection. IEEE Trans. Circ. Syst. Video Technol. **30**, 998–1010 (2018)

97. Zhuang, B., Wu, Q., Shen, C., Reid, I., van den Hengel, A.: Parallel attention: a unified framework for visual object discovery through dialogs and queries. In: CVPR. pp. 4252–4261 (2018)

UniTAB: Unifying Text and Box Outputs for Grounded Vision-Language Modeling

Zhengyuan Yang[✉], Zhe Gan, Jianfeng Wang, Xiaowei Hu, Faisal Ahmed,
Zicheng Liu, Yumao Lu, and Lijuan Wang

Microsoft Cloud and AI, Bellevue, USA
{zhengyang,zhe.gan,jianfw,xiaowei.hu,fiahmed,zliu,
yumaolu,lijuanw}@microsoft.com

Abstract. We propose UniTAB that Unifies Text And Box outputs for grounded vision-language (VL) modeling. Grounded VL tasks such as grounded captioning require the model to generate a text description and align predicted words with object regions. To achieve this, models must generate desired text and box outputs together, and meanwhile indicate the alignments between words and boxes. In contrast to existing solutions that use multiple separate modules for different outputs, UniTAB represents both text and box outputs with a shared token sequence, and introduces a special <*obj*> token to naturally indicate word-box alignments in the sequence. UniTAB thus could provide a more comprehensive and interpretable image description, by freely grounding generated words to object regions. On grounded captioning, UniTAB presents a simpler solution with a single output head, and significantly outperforms state of the art in both grounding and captioning evaluations. On general VL tasks that have different desired output formats (*i.e.*, text, box, or their combination), UniTAB with a single network achieves better or comparable performance than task-specific state of the art. Experiments cover 7 VL benchmarks, including grounded captioning, visual grounding, image captioning, and visual question answering. Furthermore, UniTAB's unified multi-task network and the task-agnostic output sequence design make the model parameter efficient and generalizable to new tasks.

1 Introduction

Text sequences [5,11] and bounding boxes [39,72] are two representative output formats for image understanding tasks [11,16,39]. Text is well suited for generating image-level predictions, such as describing an image with a sentence [11] or tagging an image with keywords [20], but fails to refer to a dense image region. On the other hand, box could point to any image area [39], but alone has a limited ability to provide semantically-rich descriptions. A natural question is *can we have a single model that unifies text and box outputs, i.e.,* generating both text and box outputs while aligning predicted words with boxes. Unifying these

---

Supplementary Information The online version contains supplementary material available at https://doi.org/10.1007/978-3-031-20059-5_30.

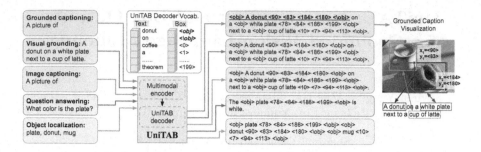

Fig. 1. We propose UniTAB that Unifies Text And Box outputs with no format-specific modules. UniTAB generates both text and box tokens in an auto-regressive manner, conditioned on the multimodal image-text inputs. The introduced $<obj>$ token naturally indicates the word-box alignments, as shown in word-box pairs of the same color in the right visualization. UniTAB thus can approach a wide range of VL tasks, including the challenging grounded captioning, with a single unified architecture. The ~~gray~~ tokens in the task-agnostic output sequence are predictions not used for downstream task evaluation, *e.g.*, box tokens in image captioning and VQA.

two output formats allows the model to better express its understanding of the image. Taking captioning as an example, such a unified model could ground all noun entities [49,78] in the caption back to aligned image regions, thus providing a more comprehensive and interpretable image description. This problem is known as grounded captioning [45,49,78,80]. Moreover, unifying output formats is one important step toward the grand vision of building task-agnostic, general-purpose vision systems [23] that are parameter efficient and well generalizable.

Recent works [13,23,45,78,80] have developed models that can generate both text and box outputs. Specifically, the system combines an online [23] or offline [13,45,78,80] object detection module that predicts boxes, with a vision-language model that generates text. The word and box alignments are then separately generated as additional predictions, such as the relevance score [23,45,78,80]. Predicting text, box, and their alignments separately weakens the benefits of a unified system. The separate modules prevent the framework from being simple and parameter efficient. Furthermore, the explicit object detection component increases the model running time [33] and potentially limits its generalization ability given the preset detector vocabulary [65], as discussed in previous VL studies [33,65]. Going beyond these successful initial explorations, we ask a bolder question: *can we unify the output formats with no separate modules?* Specifically, we explore **1)** how to have a single architecture without an explicit detector jointly generating text and box, and **2)** how to represent the word-box alignments naturally in the output to avoid the additional alignment prediction. To this end, we model both text and box predictions as an auto-regressive token generation task, and present a single encoder-decoder model that is fully shared among text, box, and alignment predictions.

Our modeling of box prediction takes inspiration from Pix2seq [10], an object detection study showing that predicting boxes in an auto-regressive manner yields good detection performance [39]. Its core idea is to quantize the four coordinates in each box into four discrete box tokens, and arrange them with a fixed order into a token sequence, $i.e.$, $[y_{min}, x_{min}, y_{max}, x_{max}]$. Box prediction can then be modeled as a multi-step classification task, instead of conventional coordinate regression [8,22,52]. The same classification modeling as in text generation [50] makes it possible to unify text and box prediction. However, Pix2seq is designed for the single-modal object detection task, and does not support open-ended text generation nor multimodal inputs and outputs. Moreover, it is unclear how the text and box alignment is intended to be presented in a unified sequence.

In this study, we propose UniTAB that unifies text and box outputs. As shown in Fig. 1, we unify open-ended text generation [50] and discrete box token prediction [10] into a single shared decoder. During the auto-regressive decoding, UniTAB switches to box tokens right after any text words to be grounded, and switches back to text tokens after predicting the box. In UniTAB, we study how to handle such text-box code-switching [67] and naturally represent word-box alignments. We introduce a special $<obj>$ token inserted before the text word to be grounded, and after the generated box tokens. The $<obj>$ token simplifies the sequence generation by providing hints of the code-switching, and naturally represents word-box alignments. That is, the words and box within a pair of $<obj>$ tokens refer to the same entity, as shown in word-box pairs of the same color in Fig. 1. With the $<obj>$ token and output sequence design, UniTAB approaches grounded VL tasks such as grounded captioning [49,78] and phrase grounding [49] with a single decoder, in contrast to separately predicting text, box, and their alignments with multiple output heads [31,45,78,80].

We further apply UniTAB on general VL tasks [5,11,46,49,72,77,78] and observe two unique properties. $First$, the unified architecture for text, box, and alignment predictions enables UniTAB to perform multi-task training [1,6,66], which learns a single set of parameters for different VL tasks without introducing task-specific heads. Multi-task training avoids task-specific model copies and thus saves the parameters to store. It also facilities the use of data in different tasks, thus boosting the performance of certain VL tasks. $Second$, as shown in Fig. 1, UniTAB's output sequence is designed to be task-agnostic and shares the same text+box design across different VL tasks. The task-agnostic output design could help UniTAB generalize to certain unseen tasks, by reformatting new tasks' desired outputs into the seen text+box sequences.

We evaluate UniTAB on 7 VL benchmarks, including grounded captioning [49,78], visual grounding [46,49,72], image captioning [11], and visual question answering [5], all with a single encoder-decoder network architecture, trained by the cross-entropy language modeling objective [50]. With a unified framework and minimum task-specific assumptions, our model achieves better or comparable performance with task-specific state of the art. In grounded captioning, UniTAB not only presents a simpler solution by eliminating separate task-specific heads [31,45,78,80], but also significantly outperforms the prior art [9,45] (from 62.5 to 69.7 in captioning CIDEr score and from 8.44 to 12.95 in grounding F1 score). Our contributions are summarized as follows.

- UniTAB is the first grounded VL model that can approach a wide range of tasks, including the challenging grounded captioning, without separate output

Table 1. Summary of unified VL models. We highlight the desired modeling in blue. *Visual Modeling:* instead of using an object detection (OD) module, we take raw "image patches" as visual input. *Text Output:* instead of using task-specific output heads [26, 29,31,42] for different VL tasks (classification or text generation heads), we use a "single output sequence" [13,23] to approach different tasks. *Box Output:* many prior models cannot predict boxes [29] or simplify it as region index prediction with detector-generated region proposals [13,23,42]. We aim to predict "box coordinates" without an explicit OD module [26,31]. *Word-box Align:* most models fail to generate either open-ended text [26,31,42] or object boxes [29], thus cannot represent word-box alignments. In contrast to the extra alignment predictions [13,23], our introduced *<obj>* token naturally indicates word-box alignments "inline" in the output sequence.

Representative models	Visual modeling	Text output	Box output	Word-box align
ViLBERT [42], OSCAR [38], UNITER [12], VinVL [74], *etc.* [35,37,43,58,59,79]	Offline OD	Task-specific Heads	Region Index	✗
PixelBERT [29], SOHO [28], ViLT [33], SimVLM [65], *etc.* [19,36,56,63,69]	Image Patches	Task-specific Heads	✗	✗
VL-T5 [13] GPV [23]	Offline OD Online OD	Single Output Seq.	Region Index	Extra Prediction
MDERT [31], UniT [26]	Image Patches	Task-specific Heads	Box Coordinate	✗
UniTAB (Ours)	Image Patches	Single Output Seq.	Box Coordinate	Inline Indicated

modules. We introduce the *<obj>* token that helps text and box outputs synergistically work together, with their alignments naturally represented.
- UniTAB achieves better or comparable performance to state of the art on 7 VL benchmarks. Its unified multi-task network and the task-agnostic output sequence design make it parameter efficient and generalizable to new tasks.

2   Related Work

Grounded Captioning. The grounded captioning task [49,78] requires the model to generate a text caption and grounds all mentioned noun phrases [49,78] to aligned image regions. The input is a single image, and the desired outputs are the caption sentence, multiple object boxes, and the word-box alignments. Existing methods [9,45,78,80] adopt separate output heads for text, box (usually with an offline detector [4,53]), and alignment predictions. In contrast, UniTAB uses a single decoding sequence to represent all desired outputs.

Vision-Language Pre-training (VLP). Large-scale VLP has become the new training paradigm for VL research. Prior works [2,12,35,37,38,42,43,58,59,79] first show the power of VLP by using region features obtained from an off-the-shelf object detector [53]. However, the region feature extraction significantly increases the model's computation cost and run time. Recent studies [29,33,36,65] shift the paradigm and show that grid features extracted from raw image patches also work well. Most studies adopt similar output architectures of either discriminative classification heads or auto-regressive text decoders. As shown in the second row of Table 1, these output structures often contain

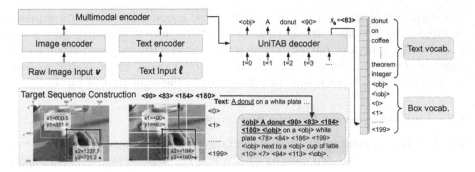

Fig. 2. UniTAB is an encoder-decoder framework that can jointly output open-ended text and box without output format specific modules. A transformer encoder-decoder takes the encoded image-text features to predict the target text+box sequence. The bottom sub-figure illustrates the output target sequence design. We introduce a special $<obj>$ token to indicate the alignments between predicted words and boxes, such as words "a donut" and the blue box. During decoding, the output sequence could seamlessly switch between text and box tokens to ground an object, if applicable. (Color figure online)

task-specific designs and do not support bounding box prediction, which is an important output format for VL tasks such as visual grounding and grounded image captioning.

Unified VL Framework. Prior works have presented successful explorations on building VL models with unified input-output formats. VL-T5 [13] and GPV [23] first represent images as object region features with an online or offline object detector [8,53]. Bounding box prediction is then simplified as index classification over the set of region candidates generated by the detector. The other threads, MDETR [31] and UniT [26], add task-specific classification heads on top of the DETR object detector [8] to perform VL tasks. However, different tasks still require different output heads. Moreover, it is unclear how to extend the framework for open-ended text generation, thus supporting VL tasks like image captioning. In this study, we aim to build a single unified framework that takes structured inputs (*i.e.*, raw image and language) in, and generates structured outputs (*i.e.*, text and boxes), with no output format specific modules.

3 The UniTAB Framework

3.1 Architecture Overview

We implement UniTAB using a transformer encoder-decoder architecture built on top of the single-modality image and text encoders, as shown in Fig. 2. For image, we use ResNet-101 [24] to encode the raw image input v, and flatten the grid features as the visual representation. For text, we use RoBERTa$_{BASE}$ [40] to encode input text l into hidden word features. The encoded image and text features are then projected into a shared embedding space. We use a 6-layer transformer encoder that takes the concatenated image and text feature sequence as input, and a 6-layer transformer decoder for output sequence generation. The decoder generates output tokens in an auto-regressive manner, similar to language modeling [50,51]. The UniTAB decoder could generate tokens from both the text and box vocabularies, as shown in the right part of Fig. 2.

3.2 UniTAB Target Output Sequence

We show how to construct ground-truth target output sequences, such that text and box can be jointly represented with word-box alignments contained inline.

Box Token Sequence. We first review the bounding box quantization approach introduced in Pix2seq [10]. As shown in the bottom part of Fig. 2, a rectangular bounding box in a 2D image can be represented by four floating-point numbers, namely $[x_{\min}, y_{\min}, x_{\max}, y_{\max}]$. The established object detection paradigm [8,52,53] predicts four continuous floating-point values to regress the coordinates in a single step. In contrast, Pix2seq quantizes each coordinate into one of the n_{bins} discrete bins, and represent each box with four tokens arranged sequentially. We adopt the similar idea and represent each box as four discrete tokens, $[<x_{\min}>, <y_{\min}>, <x_{\max}>, <y_{\max}>]$, where $<x>,<y>$ are quantized box tokens ranging from $<0>$, to $<n_{\text{bins}} - 1>$.

Unified Decoding Sequence with $<obj>$ Token. We aim to have a unified decoding sequence s that can jointly represent text and box, meanwhile indicating word-box alignments. For the former, we unify the text and box vocabularies such that a single decoder can freely generate text or box tokens at any decoding step. Specifically, UniTAB's decoding vocabulary contains both text and box tokens, and has a size of $n_{\text{text}} + n_{\text{bins}} + 2$. n_{text} and n_{bins} are the text vocabulary size and the number of coordinate bins. We use the same set of n_{bins} box tokens [10] for all four box coordinates. The output token selection at each decoding step is conducted over the entire unified vocabulary.

The remaining question is how to represent the word-box alignments in the output sequence. Instead of extra alignment score prediction [23,45,78,80], we represent word-box alignments inline with two introduced special tokens $<obj>$ and $<\backslash obj>$. Specifically, the model switches to box tokens right after any text words to be grounded, and inserts the $<obj>$ tokens before the first text word and after the last box tokens, respectively. For example, in Fig. 2, we extend the text phrase "a donut" in the text-only caption as "$<obj>$ a donut $<90>$ $<83>$ $<184>$ $<180>$ $<\backslash obj>$" in the extended target sequence, where $90, 83, 184, 180$ are the quantized box coordinates for the blue box. The word-box alignments then can be easily extracted from the predicted sequence, i.e., words and box within the pair of $<obj>$ tokens refer to the same entity, such as "a donut."

3.3 UniTAB Training

Objective. We train the model with a single language modeling objective [50], i.e., at each decoding step t, maximizing the likelihood of target token s_t conditioned on input image v, input text l, and previous target tokens $s_{<t}$:

$$\mathcal{L}_{LM}(\theta) = -\sum_{t=1}^{T} \log P_\theta(s_t|s_{<t}, v, l), \tag{1}$$

where θ denotes the model parameters, and T is the target sequence length.

Training Stages. UniTAB's unified structure facilitates the pre-training and finetuning that use the same language modeling objective. We train UniTAB with up to three stages. The first is vision-language pre-training, which leverages large-scale image-text dataset optionally with grounded box annotations. Then, we perform multi-task finetuning, where multiple downstream task datasets with supervised annotations are merged to finetune a single model for different VL tasks. Lastly, we could conduct task-specific finetuning that adapts the model to each specific task for further improvement. The three stages share the same training objective as in Eq. 1, but with different training corpus and input-output designs. We discuss the combinations of these different training stages in Sect. 4.3. We next introduce each of these three training stages.

1. Pre-training. Pre-training aims to use large-scale data loosely related to downstream tasks for general VL representation learning. We pre-train the model with a single language modeling objective to predict the target sequence s, conditioned on image v and input text l. We randomly set the input text l as an empty string or the text-only image description, with the same probability of 0.5. We train the model to generate the text+box sequence s shown in Fig. 2. The model thus learns to perform both captioning-like (with empty string input) and grounding-like (with image description input) VL tasks during pre-training.

2. Multi-task Finetuning. Multi-task finetuning [1,6,66] aims to use supervised annotations from multiple downstream task datasets to train a single model, thus avoiding task-specific model copies and further boosting the model performance. UniTAB's unified architecture and training objective facilitate the unique property of multi-task finetuning. Instead of having multiple duplicates of a pre-trained model, each optimized for a downstream task, multi-task finetuning trains a single set of parameters to perform all different VL tasks. We gather supervised data annotations from all 7 experimented VL tasks and train a single model with the language modeling objective. One major advantage of multi-task finetuning is that a single model can support multiple VL tasks, thus saving model parameters. Multi-task finetuning could also improve certain downstream tasks' performance by using annotations from different tasks.

3. Task-Specific Finetuning. UniTAB can also perform the standard task-specific finetuning as in VLP studies [12,38,42]. Furthermore, we observe that multi-task finetuning not only generates a single model that performs well in different VL tasks, but also serves as a good initialization point for a second-stage task-specific finetuning. We refer to this setting as "pre-finetuning" [1,6,66].

Inference. We use arg max sampling to obtain the sequence prediction. We then extract the text and box predictions from the sequence offline for final evaluation. For example, we discard box tokens to get the text prediction, and dequantize box tokens to get the box prediction. Finally, we evaluate the model on each downstream task with its desired output formats, e.g., text for VQA, boxes for visual grounding, or both text and boxes for grounded captioning. We show in Sect. 4.3 that the task-agnostic output sequence design could help UniTAB generalize to unseen tasks that require text or box outputs.

4   Experiments

4.1   Experiment Overview

Downstream Tasks. We evaluate UniTAB on 7 VL benchmarks (later summarized in Table 6). We start with grounded captioning [49,78] that requires the model to predict text, box, and their alignment. We then benchmark UniTAB on other representative VL tasks, including visual grounding [46,49,72], COCO image captioning [11], and VQAv2 visual question answering [5]. UniTAB approaches a wide range of VL tasks with a single unified architecture. In contrast, prior works require task-specific model designs, making it difficult to work on VL tasks with different desired output formats (text, box, or their combination).

Model Variants. In addition to the comparison with state of the art, we systematically study the following UniTAB variants with different training stages:

- **Separate-scratch** conducts task-specific finetuning without pre-training.
- **Shared-scratch** conducts multi-task finetuning without pre-training.
- **Separate** is first pre-trained and then optimized separately for each downstream task, *i.e.*, the standard pretrain-then-finetune setting in VLP [12,38, 42].
- **Shared** uses multi-task finetuning after pre-training, and shares a single set of parameters for all experimented VL tasks.
- **Pre-finetuning** adopts two-stage finetuning from a pre-trained checkpoint. The first stage is multi-task finetuning, followed by task-specific finetuning.

We take UniTAB$_{\text{Pre-finetuning}}$ as the default setting and refer to it as UniTAB. We report the main "Pre-finetuning" results in Sect. 4.2, and discuss the full results of UniTAB variants in Table 6 and Sect. 4.3.

Training Corpus. The pre-training corpus [31] aggregates images from Flickr30k Entities [49], COCO [11,39], and Visual Genome (VG) [34] datasets. Text and grounded box annotations are from the referring expression datasets [46,72], VG regions, Flickr30k Entity annotations, and the GQA dataset [30]. The corpus contains around 200K images and 1.3M image-text pairs with grounded box annotations. Optionally, we further add the image-text data with no box annotations from Conceptual Captioning [55] and SBU [47] to pre-training, with settings and results detailed in Sect. 4.3. For multi-task finetuning, we collect supervised annotations from all 7 downstream datasets [5,11,46,49,72,78] to jointly train a single model for different tasks.

Implementation Details. The transformer contains 6 encoder layers and 6 decoder layers, with 8 attention heads and a hidden dimension of 256 in each

Table 2. Grounded image captioning results on the test set of Flickr30k Entities [49]. BLEU@4 [48], METEOR [18], CIDEr [62], and SPICE [3] metrics are used for caption evaluation. $F1_{all}$ and $F1_{loc}$ metrics [78] are used for grounding evaluation. Caption scores with $\dagger$ are optimized with CIDEr [54].

Method	Caption eval.				Grounding eval.	
	B@4	M	C	S	$F1_{all}$	$F1_{loc}$
NBT [44]	27.1	21.7	57.5	15.6	–	–
GVD [78]	27.3	22.5	62.3	16.5	7.55	22.2
Cyclical [45]	26.8	22.4	61.1	16.8	8.44	22.78
POS-SCAN [80]	$30.1^{\dagger}$	$22.6^{\dagger}$	$69.3^{\dagger}$	$16.8^{\dagger}$	7.17	17.49
Chen *et al.* [9]	27.2	22.5	62.5	16.5	7.91	21.54
UniTAB	**30.1**	**23.7**	**69.7**	**17.4**	**12.95**	**34.79**

layer [8]. We use the scale and crop augmentation in DETR [8] such that the shortest side is between 480 and 800 pixels while the longest at most is 1333. We pre-train the model for 40 epochs, and finetune for 20 epochs in multi-task and task-specific settings. We use a learning rate of $1e^{-4}$ and $2e^{-5}$ for transformer layers and backbones. We train our model with AdamW [41] and adopt exponential moving average [31,61] with a decay rate of 0.9998 and a weight decay of $1e^{-4}$. More details are provided in Appendix A.

4.2 Comparison with Prior Arts

Grounded Captioning. The grounded captioning task [49,78] requires the model to generate a caption and ground all generated noun phrases to image regions. The final predictions consist of three parts, *i.e.*, the text caption, visual regions as boxes, and the grounding alignments between words and boxes. Instead of separately predicting those outputs with multiple output heads [45,78,80], UniTAB naturally represents all desired outputs with a single unified text+box output sequence. Following the established benchmarks [45,78,80] on the Flickr30k Entities dataset, we evaluate "captioning" and "grounding" separately with the caption metrics [3,18,48,62] and grounding F1 scores [78], respectively. The F1 score $F1_{all}$ evaluates grounding as a multi-label classification problem, where a correct prediction contains both the same object word as ground-truth (GT) caption and a larger than 0.5 IoU with the GT box. We also report $F1_{loc}$ that only computes the grounding score on correctly predicted object words.

Table 2 compares our method to state of the art [9,45,78,80]. We observe a significant improvement in the grounding quality, with the $F1_{all}$ score improving from 8.44 to 12.95, and $F1_{loc}$ from 22.78 to 34.79. UniTAB also achieves a better captioning quality, with the CIDEr score improving from 62.5 to 69.7, compared with prior arts [9]. By exploiting image-text data without box in pre-training, we further boost the CIDEr score from 69.7 to 74.2, as detailed in Sect. 4.3.

Table 3. The performance comparisons (Acc@0.5) on the referring expression comprehension (Refcoco, Refcoco+, Refcocog) and phrase grounding task (Flickr30k Entities).

Method	Refcoco			Refcoco+			Refcocog		Flickr30k
	val	testA	testB	val	testA	testB	val-u	test-u	Entities
MAttNet [71]	76.40	80.43	69.28	64.93	70.26	56.00	66.67	67.01	–
FAOA [70]	72.05	74.81	67.59	55.72	60.37	48.54	59.03	58.70	68.71
TransVG [17]	81.02	82.72	78.35	64.82	70.70	56.94	68.67	67.73	79.10
ViLBERT [42]	–	–	–	72.34	78.53	62.61	–	–	–
UNITER [12]	81.41	87.04	74.17	75.90	81.45	66.70	74.02	68.67	–
VILLA [21]	82.39	87.48	74.84	76.17	81.54	66.84	76.18	76.71	–
MDETR [31]	86.75	89.58	81.41	79.52	84.09	70.62	81.64	80.89	**83.8**
UniTAB$_{Separate}$	86.32	88.84	80.61	78.70	83.22	69.48	79.96	79.97	79.39
UniTAB	**88.59**	**91.06**	**83.75**	**80.97**	**85.36**	**71.55**	**84.58**	**84.70**	79.58

In addition to the performance improvement, UniTAB presents a simpler and more natural way for the grounded captioning task. Specifically, UniTAB does not require the pre-generated object regions [45,78,80] and avoids using multiple output heads. As shown in Fig. 3(a), UniTAB naturally represents text, box, and word-region alignments in a single unified output sequence. Such a simple approach better transfers the model's grounding ability to other datasets or tasks with limited box or grounding annotations, such as COCO caption [11] and ImageNet [16], as shown in Figs. 3(d, f). We hope UniTAB's new paradigm simplifies future studies on grounded VL tasks.

Visual Grounding. Visual grounding aims to ground language queries into aligned image regions. We experiment on the sub-tasks of referring expression comprehension [46,72] with Refcoco/Refcoco+/Refcocog, and phrase grounding [49] with Flickr30k Entities. Referring expression comprehension contains a query that describes a single image region and expects a single box prediction. Phrase grounding aims to ground all noun phrases in the input sentence, and requires the model to predict all referred boxes and the word-box alignments. In contrast to previous studies that do not know word-box alignments [17,70,71] or require separate alignment predictions [31], UniTAB generates a unified sequence with word-box alignments naturally represented by the special $<obj>$ token. We report the standard metric Acc@0.5 [46,49,72].

As shown in Table 3, UniTAB outperforms the state of the art, including those pre-trained on larger VL corpus [12,21,42] and methods that use carefully-designed task-specific architectures [17,70,71]. Moreover, UniTAB's unified output with both text and box presents a more natural way of visual grounding, compared to box regression [17,31,70] or region index classification [12,13,71]. UniTAB's multi-task finetuning enables the use of data from different tasks and datasets, thus boosting performance on all splits, compared with UniTAB$_{Separate}$.

Table 4. COCO image captioning results on the Karparthy test split. The "#Pretrain" column shows the number of pretraining images, if any.

Method	#Pre-train	B@4	M	C	S
Unified VLP [79]	3M	36.5	28.4	117.7	21.3
OSCAR [38]	4M	36.5	30.3	123.7	23.1
E2E-VLP [68]	180K	36.2	–	117.3	–
VL-T5 [13]	180K	34.5	28.7	116.5	21.9
VL-BART [13]	180K	35.1	28.7	116.6	21.5
UniTAB	200K	36.1	28.6	119.8	21.7

Table 5. Visual question answering results on VQAv2 [5]. We experiment on both test-dev/test-std splits, and the Karpathy test split used in VL-T5 [13].

Method	#Pre-train	Test-		Karpathy-test		
		Dev	Std	In	Out	All
UNITER [12]	4M	72.7	72.9	74.4	10.0	70.5
VL-T5 [13]	180K	–	70.3	71.4	13.1	67.9
VL-BART [13]	180K	–	71.3	72.1	13.2	68.6
UniTAB	200K	70.7	71.0	71.1	11.1	67.5

Table 6. Summary of results obtained by UniTAB and its variants. The compared methods (upper portion) use task-specific architectures and training objectives, thus could only perform a subset of VL tasks. UniTAB (bottom portion) approaches all tasks with a unified framework and obtains competitive performance. The Refcoco/Refcoco+/Refcocog numbers are on the val set. The Flickr grounding and grounded caption results are on the test set. VQAv2-KP is the VQA Karpathy split [13]. UniTAB_{Pre-finetuning} is the default setting that is also referred to as UniTAB.

Method	#Pre-train	Visual grounding				Grounded caption		COCO	VQAv2	
		Refcoco	Refcoco+	Refcocog	Flickr	Cider	F1_{all}	test-Cider	test-dev	KP-test
MDETR [31]	200K	86.75	79.52	81.64	83.8	–	–	–	70.6	–
UNITER [12]	4M	81.24	75.31	74.31	–	–	–	–	72.7	70.5
GVD [78]	–	–	–	–	–	62.3	7.55	–	–	–
VL-T5 [13]	180K	–	–	71.2	–	–	–	116.5	–	67.9
OSCAR [38]	4M	–	–	–	–	–	–	123.7	73.2	–
UniTAB Variants										
Separate-scratch	None	72.96	64.98	63.56	73.40	60.5	9.22	105.3	55.4	52.4
Shared-scratch	None	82.06	70.72	73.39	65.67	61.1	7.85	111.8	65.8	63.1
Separate	200K	86.32	78.70	79.96	79.39	65.6	11.46	119.3	69.9	66.6
Shared	200K	88.50	80.98	84.46	79.23	63.4	9.18	115.8	69.1	66.6
Pre-finetuning	200K	88.59	80.97	84.58	79.58	69.7	12.95	119.8	70.7	67.5

COCO Captioning. We benchmark UniTAB on the COCO image captioning dataset [39]. We report the results without beam search [4] or CIDEr optimization [54]. Table 4 shows the captioning results on the Karpathy test split [32]. We refer to our pre-training corpus as "200K" in the "#Pre-train" column, and introduce the corpus used by compared methods later in Appendix A.

UniTAB achieves better performance than prior arts [13,68] that use similar amounts of pre-training images, with the CIDEr score improved from 117.3 to 119.8. Meanwhile, UniTAB does not require input region proposals or object tags [13,38,79]. Using extra image-text pairs [47,55] in pre-training further boosts the CIDEr score to 123.1. We expect a further gain by scaling up the pre-training corpus, as observed in VLP studies [27,36,65,74]. Despite only being evaluated with caption metrics on COCO, UniTAB's unified output sequence could also ground generated noun phrases to image regions, as visualized in Fig. 3(d).

Visual Question Answering. UniTAB takes a generative approach to the VQA task [5], where the model generates a free-form text sequence to represent the answer. Table 5 reports the VQA results on both the official test-dev/std split [5] and the Karpathy split [32] used in VL-T5 [13]. The Karpathy test set is further split into in- and out-domain subsets, based on whether the answer is covered in the top-K (K = 3129) vocabulary [13]. The metric is the soft-voting accuracy [5]. UniTAB obtains competitive results to the state of the art, and performs better on the Karpathy out-of-domain subset than the discriminative approach [12].

4.3   Ablation and Analysis

Training Stage Ablation. We compare the variants of UniTAB to examine the influence of different pre-training and finetuning stages introduced in Sect. 3.3. The bottom portion of Table 6 summarizes the results. We first discuss the standard pretrain-then-finetune setting in VLP [12,38,42] that adopts task-specific finetuning. UniTAB$_\text{Separate}$ approaches various VL tasks with a single unified architecture, and obtains competitive results to the state of the art that has architectures tailored for each task, or uses larger-scale pre-training data. Compared with UniTAB$_\text{Separate-scratch}$ without pre-training, pre-training leads to consistent improvements on all experimented tasks.

With UniTAB's unified architecture and output modeling, we can train a single **UniTAB$_\text{Shared}$** model for all experimented VL tasks. Compared with UniTAB$_\text{Separate}$, the multi-task finetuning UniTAB$_\text{Shared}$ performs comparable or better on experimented VL tasks, while using **7** times fewer model parameters by avoiding task-specific model copies. The strong performance of UniTAB$_\text{Shared}$ indicates that we can use a single model for multiple downstream tasks, thus being *parameter efficient*. We further experiment with adding task-specific prefixes [13,66] to the input text. This variant uses a task-specific prefix such as "visual grounding:" to describe each sample's task. We observe that the task prefix has no major influence on model performance, as detailed in Appendix C.

In addition to achieving good performance with a single model, multi-task finetuning UniTAB$_\text{Shared}$ also provides a strong initialization point for further task-specific finetuning. **UniTAB$_\text{Pre-finetuning}$** further boosts the performance and achieves better or comparable performance than the state of the art on experimented VL tasks, as shown in the bottom row of Table 6.

Zero-Shot Generalization. The task-agnostic output sequence design helps UniTAB generalize to new tasks. UniTAB could perform certain tasks in a zero-shot manner by transferring the learned ability of generating text+box sequences s conditioned on image-text inputs. We next explore adapting UniTAB to ImageNet object localization [16]. Object localization [14,64,77] aims to localize an ImageNet class onto an object region. We take the words in class names as the text input, and have UniTAB generate text+box sequence s conditioned on image-text inputs. We then obtain box predictions by extracting boxes and alignments from s, similar to the phrase grounding post-processing. There

Table 7. Zero-shot object localization results on ImageNet [16]. Prior works with the weakly supervised setting use ImageNet class labels.

Method	Top-1 acc.	MaxBoxAcc	MaxBoxAccV2
CAM [77]	51.8	64.2	63.7
HaS [57]	49.9	63.1	63.4
CutMix [73]	51.5	65.4	63.3
MinMaxCAM [64]	–	66.7	65.7
UniTAB$_{Shared}$	**60.2**	**68.1**	**67.8**

Table 8. UniTAB pre-training with additional image-text pairs. "Separate[††]" uses additional 4M image-text pairs from CC [55] and SBU [47] that do not have grounded box annotations.

UniTAB	Grounded caption		COCO	VQAv2
	Cider	F1$_{all}$	Test-Cider	KP-test
Separate	65.6	11.46	119.3	66.6
Separate[††]	74.2	12.62	123.1	69.1

exist two established benchmark settings. The "GT-known" [15,57,75,76] setting aims to localize a given ground-truth class. The metrics [14] "MaxBoxAcc" and "MaxBoxAccV2" are the Top-1 accuracy with an IoU threshold of 0.5, and the average at thresholds 0.3/0.5/0.7. The second setting tries to localize a predicted class. The metric is "Top-1 accuracy" with a 0.5 IoU threshold. We use EfficientNet [60] classification result with an accuracy of 77.5% for this setting.

We experiment with UniTAB$_{Shared}$ and show ImageNet object localization results in Table 7. UniTAB achieves better performance than the state of the art without using ImageNet images or annotations. The good generalization results show the possibility of generalizing UniTAB to unseen images and tasks in a zero-shot manner. We expect larger-scale pre-training to boost such generalization ability further, as observed in the NLP community [7,66].

Pre-training with additional image-text pairs. We experiment with adding image-text pairs without boxes in UniTAB pre-training, and examine if the extra image-text data could further improve VL tasks that require text output. For image-text pair data, we pre-train the model to generate the text-only caption conditioned on image and an empty text input. The model variant is referred to as "Separate[††]", which uses 4M image-text pairs from Conceptual Captioning [55] and SBU [47]. Table 8 compares "Separate[††]" with UniTAB$_{Separate}$ on grounded captioning, COCO captioning, and VQA. We observe consistent improvements in the text output quality by using extra image-text pairs, i.e., +8.6 CIDEr score on grounded captioning [49], +3.8 CIDEr score on COCO captioning [11], and +2.5% absolute accuracy on VQA [5]. Appendix C further discusses the benefit of pre-training with other addition data, such as boxes from object detection [39].

Model and Output Sequence Design. We empirically observe that the introduced $<obj>$ token not only naturally represents the word-box alignment, but also simplifies the sequence prediction by providing hints of the text-box code-switching, thus helping the VL tasks' performance. We postpone the detailed ablation studies on model and output sequence design to Appendix B, including the effectiveness of $<obj>$ token, decoding sampling methods [4,10,25], the number of object tokens, decoding syntactic restrictions, etc.

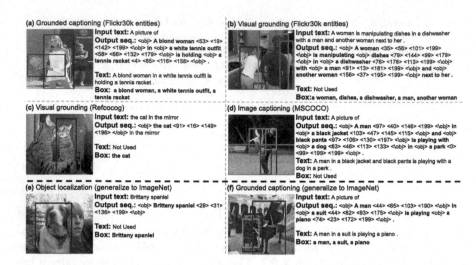

Fig. 3. Predictions made by UniTAB_Shared that uses a single model for different VL tasks. In each subfigure, we show the input text, the raw output sequence, and the extracted outputs for downstream task evaluations. Specifically, the output sequence contains an open-ended text sequence, box predictions (visualized as bounding boxes), and word-box alignments (visualized as the word-box colors). **(a–d)** UniTAB approaches a wide range of VL tasks with a single unified model and output sequence. **(e, f)** With the task-agnostic output sequence, we further generalize UniTAB to unseen images or even new tasks, with examples on ImageNet object localization and grounded captioning.

4.4   Qualitative Results

Figure 3 shows the predictions made by UniTAB_Shared on different VL tasks, where all predictions are made by a single model with the same set of parameters. On the right side of each subfigure, we show the input text and predicted output sequence. The output sequence is colored for visualization purposes only, where the text and box colors indicate the word-box alignments. We then show the extracted text and box predictions used for downstream task evaluation. For text, we discard all box tokens to obtain the text-only sequence. For boxes, we keep box tokens and dequantize them as box coordinate predictions [10].

UniTAB's task-agnostic output sequence seamlessly supports different VL tasks. Figure 3(a) shows an example of grounded captioning, where the input text is a blank string and both text and box predictions are used for evaluation. UniTAB could perform the phrase grounding task with the exact output sequence design, by replacing the blank input text with an image description, as shown in Fig. 3(b). Figure 3(c) shows a referring expression comprehension example from the Refcocog dataset [46]. The model correctly localizes the referred "cat" in the "mirror". Despite not being used by the downstream task evaluation, the model successfully aligns the predicted box with phrase "the cat".

UniTAB's unified output sequence helps the model transfer the grounded description ability to datasets or tasks with limited box or grounding annotations. As shown in Fig. 3(d), UniTAB learns grounded captioning on Flickr30k Entities and transfers such ability to COCO during multi-task finetuning. The generated caption not only has a good caption quality, as evaluated in Table 4, but also contains grounding predictions that make the description more comprehensive and interpretable. With the task-agnostic output sequence design, we further explore generalizing UniTAB to unseen images or even new tasks. Figure 3(e) shows an example of zero-shot object localization on ImageNet. The model correctly localizes the dog conditioned on the text input of ImageNet class label "brittany spaniel". Figure 3(f) shows an example of zero-shot grounded captioning on ImageNet images, where UniTAB generates a smooth caption and correctly grounds all noun phrases. More qualitative results are in Appendix D.

5 Conclusion

We have presented UniTAB that unifies text and box outputs for grounded VL modeling. With the special $<obj>$ token, UniTAB could generate both text and box predictions, with the word-box alignments naturally represented in the output sequence. Unifying text and box outputs allows the model to better approach grounded VL tasks such as grounded captioning. Furthermore, the unified multi-task network and the task-agnostic output sequence design make UniTAB parameter efficient and generalizable to new tasks. We see great potential in UniTAB, and believe it paves the way for building vision systems with stronger intelligence, such as in-context learning [7] and instruction tuning [66].

References

1. Aghajanyan, A., Gupta, A., Shrivastava, A., Chen, X., Zettlemoyer, L., Gupta, S.: Muppet: massive multi-task representations with pre-finetuning. In: EMNLP (2021)
2. Alberti, C., Ling, J., Collins, M., Reitter, D.: Fusion of detected objects in text for visual question answering. In: EMNLP (2019)
3. Anderson, P., Fernando, B., Johnson, M., Gould, S.: SPICE: semantic propositional image caption evaluation. In: Leibe, B., Matas, J., Sebe, N., Welling, M. (eds.) ECCV 2016. LNCS, vol. 9909, pp. 382–398. Springer, Cham (2016). https://doi.org/10.1007/978-3-319-46454-1_24
4. Anderson, P., et al.: Bottom-up and top-down attention for image captioning and visual question answering. In: CVPR (2018)
5. Antol, S., et al.: VQA: visual question answering. In: ICCV (2015)
6. Aribandi, V., et al.: ExT5: towards extreme multi-task scaling for transfer learning. In: ICLR (2022)
7. Brown, T.B., et al.: Language models are few-shot learners. In: NeurIPS (2020)
8. Carion, N., Massa, F., Synnaeve, G., Usunier, N., Kirillov, A., Zagoruyko, S.: End-to-end object detection with transformers. In: Vedaldi, A., Bischof, H., Brox, T., Frahm, J.-M. (eds.) ECCV 2020. LNCS, vol. 12346, pp. 213–229. Springer, Cham (2020). https://doi.org/10.1007/978-3-030-58452-8_13

9. Chen, N., et al.: Distributed attention for grounded image captioning. In: ACMMM (2021)

10. Chen, T., Saxena, S., Li, L., Fleet, D.J., Hinton, G.: Pix2seq: a language modeling framework for object detection. In: ICLR (2022)

11. Chen, X., et al.: Microsoft COCO captions: data collection and evaluation server. arXiv preprint arXiv:1504.00325 (2015)

12. Chen, Y.-C., et al.: UNITER: UNiversal image-TExt representation learning. In: Vedaldi, A., Bischof, H., Brox, T., Frahm, J.-M. (eds.) ECCV 2020. LNCS, vol. 12375, pp. 104–120. Springer, Cham (2020). https://doi.org/10.1007/978-3-030-58577-8_7

13. Cho, J., Lei, J., Tan, H., Bansal, M.: Unifying vision-and-language tasks via text generation. In: ICML (2021)

14. Choe, J., Oh, S.J., Lee, S., Chun, S., Akata, Z., Shim, H.: Evaluating weakly supervised object localization methods right. In: CVPR (2020)

15. Choe, J., Shim, H.: Attention-based dropout layer for weakly supervised object localization. In: CVPR (2019)

16. Deng, J., Dong, W., Socher, R., Li, L.J., Li, K., Fei-Fei, L.: ImageNet: a large-scale hierarchical image database. In: CVPR (2009)

17. Deng, J., Yang, Z., Chen, T., Zhou, W., Li, H.: TransVG: end-to-end visual grounding with transformers. In: ICCV (2021)

18. Denkowski, M., Lavie, A.: Meteor universal: language specific translation evaluation for any target language. In: Proceedings of the Ninth Workshop on Statistical Machine Translation (2014)

19. Dou, Z.Y., et al.: An empirical study of training end-to-end vision-and-language transformers. arXiv preprint arXiv:2111.02387 (2021)

20. Fu, J., Rui, Y.: Advances in deep learning approaches for image tagging. APSIPA Trans. Signal Inf. Process. **6** (2017)

21. Gan, Z., Chen, Y.C., Li, L., Zhu, C., Cheng, Y., Liu, J.: Large-scale adversarial training for vision-and-language representation learning. In: NeurIPS (2020)

22. Girshick, R., Donahue, J., Darrell, T., Malik, J.: Rich feature hierarchies for accurate object detection and semantic segmentation. In: CVPR (2014)

23. Gupta, T., Kamath, A., Kembhavi, A., Hoiem, D.: Towards general purpose vision systems. arXiv preprint arXiv:2104.00743 (2021)

24. He, K., Zhang, X., Ren, S., Sun, J.: Deep residual learning for image recognition. In: CVPR (2016)

25. Holtzman, A., Buys, J., Du, L., Forbes, M., Choi, Y.: The curious case of neural text degeneration. In: ICLR (2020)

26. Hu, R., Singh, A.: UniT: multimodal multitask learning with a unified transformer. In: ICCV (2021)

27. Hu, X., et al.: Scaling up vision-language pre-training for image captioning. In: CVPR (2022)

28. Huang, Z., Zeng, Z., Huang, Y., Liu, B., Fu, D., Fu, J.: Seeing out of the box: end-to-end pre-training for vision-language representation learning. In: CVPR (2021)

29. Huang, Z., Zeng, Z., Liu, B., Fu, D., Fu, J.: Pixel-BERT: aligning image pixels with text by deep multi-modal transformers. arXiv preprint arXiv:2004.00849 (2020)

30. Hudson, D.A., Manning, C.D.: GQA: a new dataset for real-world visual reasoning and compositional question answering. In: CVPR (2019)

31. Kamath, A., Singh, M., LeCun, Y., Synnaeve, G., Misra, I., Carion, N.: MDETR-modulated detection for end-to-end multi-modal understanding. In: ICCV (2021)

32. Karpathy, A., Fei-Fei, L.: Deep visual-semantic alignments for generating image descriptions. In: CVPR (2015)

33. Kim, W., Son, B., Kim, I.: ViLT: vision-and-language transformer without convolution or region supervision. In: ICML (2021)
34. Krishna, R., et al.: Visual genome: connecting language and vision using crowdsourced dense image annotations. IJCV **123**, 32–73 (2017)
35. Li, G., Duan, N., Fang, Y., Gong, M., Jiang, D., Zhou, M.: Unicoder-VL: a universal encoder for vision and language by cross-modal pre-training. In: AAAI (2020)
36. Li, J., Selvaraju, R.R., Gotmare, A.D., Joty, S., Xiong, C., Hoi, S.: Align before fuse: vision and language representation learning with momentum distillation. In: NeurIPS (2021)
37. Li, L.H., Yatskar, M., Yin, D., Hsieh, C.J., Chang, K.W.: VisualBERT: a simple and performant baseline for vision and language. arXiv preprint arXiv:1908.03557 (2019)
38. Li, X., et al.: OSCAR: object-semantics aligned pre-training for vision-language tasks. In: Vedaldi, A., Bischof, H., Brox, T., Frahm, J.-M. (eds.) ECCV 2020. LNCS, vol. 12375, pp. 121–137. Springer, Cham (2020). https://doi.org/10.1007/978-3-030-58577-8_8
39. Lin, T.-Y., et al.: Microsoft COCO: common objects in context. In: Fleet, D., Pajdla, T., Schiele, B., Tuytelaars, T. (eds.) ECCV 2014. LNCS, vol. 8693, pp. 740–755. Springer, Cham (2014). https://doi.org/10.1007/978-3-319-10602-1_48
40. Liu, Y., et al.: RoBERTa: a robustly optimized BERT pretraining approach. arXiv preprint arXiv:1907.11692 (2019)
41. Loshchilov, I., Hutter, F.: Decoupled weight decay regularization. arXiv preprint arXiv:1711.05101 (2017)
42. Lu, J., Batra, D., Parikh, D., Lee, S.: VilBERT: pretraining task-agnostic visiolinguistic representations for vision-and-language tasks. In: NeurIPS (2019)
43. Lu, J., Goswami, V., Rohrbach, M., Parikh, D., Lee, S.: 12-in-1: multi-task vision and language representation learning. In: CVPR (2020)
44. Lu, J., Yang, J., Batra, D., Parikh, D.: Neural baby talk. In: CVPR (2018)
45. Ma, C.-Y., Kalantidis, Y., AlRegib, G., Vajda, P., Rohrbach, M., Kira, Z.: Learning to generate grounded visual captions without localization supervision. In: Vedaldi, A., Bischof, H., Brox, T., Frahm, J.-M. (eds.) ECCV 2020. LNCS, vol. 12363, pp. 353–370. Springer, Cham (2020). https://doi.org/10.1007/978-3-030-58523-5_21
46. Mao, J., Huang, J., Toshev, A., Camburu, O., Yuille, A.L., Murphy, K.: Generation and comprehension of unambiguous object descriptions. In: CVPR (2016)
47. Ordonez, V., Kulkarni, G., Berg, T.L.: Im2Text: describing images using 1 million captioned photographs. In: NeurIPS (2011)
48. Papineni, K., Roukos, S., Ward, T., Zhu, W.J.: BLEU: a method for automatic evaluation of machine translation. In: ACL (2002)
49. Plummer, B.A., Wang, L., Cervantes, C.M., Caicedo, J.C., Hockenmaier, J., Lazebnik, S.: Flickr30k entities: collecting region-to-phrase correspondences for richer image-to-sentence models. In: ICCV (2015)
50. Radford, A., Narasimhan, K., Salimans, T., Sutskever, I.: Improving language understanding by generative pre-training (2018)
51. Raffel, C., et al.: Exploring the limits of transfer learning with a unified text-to-text transformer. JMLR **21**, 1–67 (2020)
52. Redmon, J., Divvala, S., Girshick, R., Farhadi, A.: You only look once: unified, real-time object detection. In: CVPR (2016)
53. Ren, S., He, K., Girshick, R., Sun, J.: Faster R-CNN: towards real-time object detection with region proposal networks. In: NeurIPS (2015)
54. Rennie, S.J., Marcheret, E., Mroueh, Y., Ross, J., Goel, V.: Self-critical sequence training for image captioning. In: CVPR (2017)

55. Sharma, P., Ding, N., Goodman, S., Soricut, R.: Conceptual captions: a cleaned, hypernymed, image alt-text dataset for automatic image captioning. In: ACL (2018)
56. Shen, S., et al.: How much can clip benefit vision-and-language tasks? In: ICLR (2022)
57. Singh, K.K., Lee, Y.J.: Hide-and-seek: forcing a network to be meticulous for weakly-supervised object and action localization. In: ICCV (2017)
58. Su, W., Zhu, X., Cao, Y., Li, B., Lu, L., Wei, F., Dai, J.: VL-BERT: pre-training of generic visual-linguistic representations. In: ICLR (2019)
59. Tan, H., Bansal, M.: LXMERT: learning cross-modality encoder representations from transformers. In: EMNLP (2019)
60. Tan, M., Le, Q.: EfficientNet: rethinking model scaling for convolutional neural networks. In: ICML (2019)
61. Tarvainen, A., Valpola, H.: Mean teachers are better role models: weight-averaged consistency targets improve semi-supervised deep learning results. In: NeurIPS (2017)
62. Vedantam, R., Lawrence Zitnick, C., Parikh, D.: CIDEr: consensus-based image description evaluation. In: CVPR (2015)
63. Wang, J., et al.: GIT: a generative image-to-text transformer for vision and language. arXiv preprint arXiv:2205.14100 (2022)
64. Wang, K., Oramas, J., Tuytelaars, T.: MinMaxCAM: improving object coverage for CAM-based weakly supervised object localization. arXiv preprint arXiv:2104.14375 (2021)
65. Wang, Z., Yu, J., Yu, A.W., Dai, Z., Tsvetkov, Y., Cao, Y.: SimVLM: simple visual language model pretraining with weak supervision. In: ICLR (2022)
66. Wei, J., et al.: Finetuned language models are zero-shot learners. In: ICLR (2022)
67. Wikipedia contributors: Code-switching—Wikipedia, the free encyclopedia (2022). https://en.wikipedia.org/w/index.php?title=Code-switching&oldid=1068820985
68. Xu, H., et al.: E2E-VLP: end-to-end vision-language pre-training enhanced by visual learning. In: ACL (2021)
69. Xue, H., et al.: Probing inter-modality: visual parsing with self-attention for vision-and-language pre-training. In: NeurIPS (2021)
70. Yang, Z., Gong, B., Wang, L., Huang, W., Yu, D., Luo, J.: A fast and accurate one-stage approach to visual grounding. In: ICCV (2019)
71. Yu, L., Lin, Z., Shen, X., Yang, J., Lu, X., Bansal, M., Berg, T.L.: MAttNet: modular attention network for referring expression comprehension. In: CVPR (2018)
72. Yu, L., Poirson, P., Yang, S., Berg, A.C., Berg, T.L.: Modeling context in referring expressions. In: Leibe, B., Matas, J., Sebe, N., Welling, M. (eds.) ECCV 2016. LNCS, vol. 9906, pp. 69–85. Springer, Cham (2016). https://doi.org/10.1007/978-3-319-46475-6_5
73. Yun, S., Han, D., Oh, S.J., Chun, S., Choe, J., Yoo, Y.: CutMix: regularization strategy to train strong classifiers with localizable features. In: CVPR (2019)
74. Zhang, P., et al.: VinVL: revisiting visual representations in vision-language models. In: CVPR (2021)
75. Zhang, X., Wei, Y., Feng, J., Yang, Y., Huang, T.S.: Adversarial complementary learning for weakly supervised object localization. In: CVPR (2018)
76. Zhang, X., Wei, Y., Kang, G., Yang, Y., Huang, T.: Self-produced guidance for weakly-supervised object localization. In: Ferrari, V., Hebert, M., Sminchisescu, C., Weiss, Y. (eds.) ECCV 2018. LNCS, vol. 11216, pp. 610–625. Springer, Cham (2018). https://doi.org/10.1007/978-3-030-01258-8_37

77. Zhou, B., Khosla, A., Lapedriza, A., Oliva, A., Torralba, A.: Learning deep features for discriminative localization. In: CVPR (2016)
78. Zhou, L., Kalantidis, Y., Chen, X., Corso, J.J., Rohrbach, M.: Grounded video description. In: CVPR (2019)
79. Zhou, L., Palangi, H., Zhang, L., Hu, H., Corso, J.J., Gao, J.: Unified vision-language pre-training for image captioning and VQA. In: AAAI (2020)
80. Zhou, Y., Wang, M., Liu, D., Hu, Z., Zhang, H.: More grounded image captioning by distilling image-text matching model. In: CVPR (2020)

Scaling Open-Vocabulary Image Segmentation with Image-Level Labels

Golnaz Ghiasi[✉], Xiuye Gu, Yin Cui, and Tsung-Yi Lin

Google Research, Mountain View, USA
{golnazg,xiuyegu,yincui}@google.com,
tsungyil@nvidia.com

Abstract. We design an open-vocabulary image segmentation model to organize an image into meaningful regions indicated by arbitrary texts. Recent works (CLIP and ALIGN), despite attaining impressive open-vocabulary classification accuracy with image-level caption labels, are unable to segment visual concepts with pixels. We argue that these models miss an important step of visual grouping, which organizes pixels into groups before learning visual-semantic alignments. We propose OpenSeg to address the above issue while still making use of scalable image-level supervision of captions. First, it learns to propose segmentation masks for possible organizations. Then it learns visual-semantic alignments by aligning each word in a caption to one or a few predicted masks. We find the mask representations are the key to support learning image segmentation from captions, making it possible to scale up the dataset and vocabulary sizes. OpenSeg significantly outperforms the recent open-vocabulary method of LSeg by +19.9 mIoU on PASCAL dataset, thanks to its scalability.

1 Introduction

Image segmentation is an important step to organize an image into a small number of regions in order to understand *"what"* and *"where"* are in an image. Each region represents a semantically meaningful entity, which can be a thing (*e.g.*, a chair) or stuff (*e.g.*, floor). Language is a natural interface to describe what is in an image. However, semantic segmentation algorithms often only learn with closed-set categories, and thus are unable to recognize concepts outside labeled datasets. Figure 1 shows examples of image segmentation driven by language. The segmentation model takes text queries as inputs and produces segmented regions accordingly. In this work, we aim to learn open-vocabulary models which can segment an image and indicate regions with arbitrary text queries.

T.-Y. Lin—Work done while at Google.

Supplementary Information The online version contains supplementary material available at https://doi.org/10.1007/978-3-031-20059-5_31.

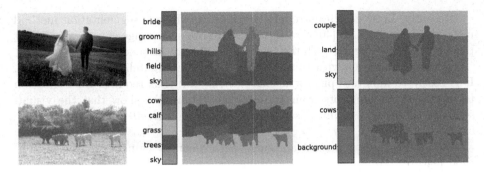

Fig. 1. Examples of image segmentation with arbitrary text queries. We propose a model, called **OpenSeg**, that can organize pixels into meaningful regions indicated by texts. In contrast to segmentation models trained with close-vocabulary categories, OpenSeg can handle arbitrary text queries. For example, the model segments out a region for 'couple' and two regions for 'bride' and 'groom'.

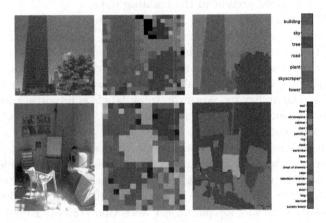

Fig. 2. ALIGN (middle) can only roughly localize text queries onto the image. In contrast, OpenSeg (right) can localize visual concepts with accurate segmentation. Moreover, ALIGN predicts more false positives not present in the image.

Recently, CLIP [40] and ALIGN [23] learn with billion-scale image-text training examples to understand *"what"* are in an image with arbitrary text queries. These models demonstrate impressive results when directly evaluated on downstream image-text retrieval or classification tasks. However, localizing text queries to understand *"where"* these visual concepts are in an image is still challenging. For example, Fig. 2 shows the segmentation predictions of a pre-trained ALIGN [23] model using class activation maps [60].

We argue that what is missing in these state-of-the-art open-vocabulary classification models are mid-level representations from visual groupings [48], which organize an image into a small set of segmentation masks. Furthermore, visual-semantic alignments should perform after grouping to align texts to segmentation regions. However, these models represent an image with a single feature vector, inevitably losing much location information.

Recently, Li *et al.* [29] introduce an open-vocabulary segmentation method using pre-trained CLIP [40] text-encoders. It trains an image encoder to predict pixel embedding aligned with the text embedding of its pixel label.

However, the issue with this approach is in the scalability of training data. It is costly to annotate pixel-wise class labels, and thus requires generalization to unseen visual concepts from limited class labels. We show that the visual-semantic alignments of image segmentation can be learned from scalable image caption labels.

In this work, we represent an image with a set of segmentation masks and their features. We implement a class-agnostic segmentation module with region-to-image cross-attention [8,10,46] and train it with class-agnostic segmentation masks. In contrast to the works using similar architectures [10,46], we do not predict the "no object" label $\varnothing$ to indicate if a predicted mask is a valid group of pixels. Considering the training data is only annotated with one possible organization of an image, we allow our model to predict other possible organizations beyond the annotations present in the training data.

Next, we learn visual-semantic alignments based on the predicted masks, which provide two major benefits in training. First, we perform mask-based feature pooling to aggregate pixels inside the predicted mask to generate location-aware region features. Second, the small number of predicted masks makes it easier to learn weakly-supervised alignments between regions to words in an image caption. The ability to learn from weak labels is important for scaling up training data and increasing vocabulary sizes. We call our method **OpenSeg**, standing for open-vocabulary image segmentation.

To evaluate our method, we measure performances on holdout image segmentation datasets. We want to promote the framework where the model is trained with a large scale supervised/weakly-supervised data to learn *generalist* models transferable to other datasets. Such a framework has been recently introduced for image classification [23,40] and object detection [18,58]. To our knowledge, OpenSeg is the first work in image segmentation to demonstrate zero-shot transfer results across datasets using language. This is in stark contrast to the existing evaluation protocol which measures performances of *specialist* models trained and tested using limited labeled data from the same dataset distribution.

In our experiments, we train the mask prediction model using class-agnostic mask annotations in the Panoptic COCO dataset [26]. We show that the model can generalize well to other datasets, reaching superior performances compared with prior works on segmentation proposals [3,33]. Then, we report mean intersection over union (mIoU) metrics for measuring both localization quality and accuracy of open-vocabulary semantic recognition. We compare OpenSeg to the recent open-vocabulary method of LSeg. Thanks to the scalability of OpenSeg, our best model significantly outperforms strongest LSeg model by 19.9 on PASCAL dataset. We also compare OpenSeg to a version of LSeg implemented in our framework, trained on a larger semantic segmentation dataset of COCO (LSeg+). OpenSeg with ResNet-101 backbone outperforms LSeg+ models with similar backbone by 2.7 mIoU on PASCAL-Context (459 categories) and 1.9

mIoU on ADE-20k (847 categories). OpenSeg achieves this improvement mainly because of its ability to make use of image caption data which enables us to train it on a larger set of vocabularies and also a larger set of training examples.

2 Related Work

Grouping for Visual Recognition: Grouping has been a core research area in mid-level visual representations. The importance of grouping for human perception was pointed out almost a hundred years ago [48]. In machine perception, early works [11,42] group pixels based on local affinities. Arbelaez *et al.* [2] find contour detection and multiscale information helpful to generate segmentation and use it to predict object candidates [3]. COB [33] improves the efficiency and performance by leveraging deep nets. These mid-level region representations are then used for semantic segmentation [33] and object detection [45]. Recently, Qi *et al.* [39] propose to segment all visual entities without considering semantic labels and show generalization to unseen domains. In contrast to [39], our work not only predicts segmentation, but also understands the semantics of segmented regions by open-vocabulary visual-semantic alignments.

Fully-Supervised Segmentation: To understand the semantics of pixels, several datasets have been developed with an increasing number of images and categories [5,7,13,35]. Models trained on these datasets can only learn to recognize the pre-defined classes, which are at most in the order of hundreds for standard benchmarks. Also, the classes across datasets are not transferable. MSeg [28] points out the ambiguity of class definitions, and manually resolves it to learn a transferable model across datasets. But the model still can not transfer to new visual concepts not present in the dataset. OpenSeg overcomes these drawbacks.

Semantic Segmentation with Less Supervisions: Weakly-supervised semantic segmentation trains with image-level labels [24,31,36,47,52], of which refining CAMs [60] is a popular techniques. Our model also adopts weak image-caption supervision, and it is different in that it has access to a set of class-agnostic segmentation annotations. Furthermore, it can transfer to arbitrary classes while these methods can not. Zero-shot semantic segmentation methods [4,6,20,30,49] aim to segment images with unseen visual concepts using language embeddings. These approaches learn with pixel-wise class labels which are expensive to scale up due to the long-tailed nature mentioned in the previous paragraph. In contrast, we leverage cheap image caption data that covers a wide range of concepts, to achieve better and more practical performance on arbitrary categories. In addition, we evaluate on datasets with much larger number of categories to verify the zero-shot transfer capability.

Open-Vocabulary Segmentation: Open-vocabulary segmentation aims to overcome the limitation of closed-set vocabulary in previous segmentation works. Zhao *et al.* [59] is the pioneering work that learns a joint pixel and word concept embedding space; however, its vocabulary and knowledge is limited to WordNet and can not take arbitrary texts as input.

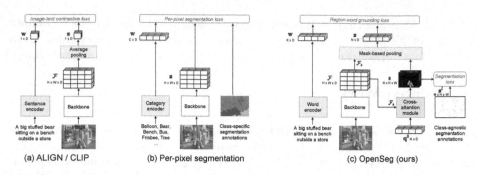

(a) ALIGN / CLIP   (b) Per-pixel segmentation   (c) OpenSeg (ours)

Fig. 3. An overview of our approach. We compare OpenSeg with ALIGN/CLIP [23, 40] and per-pixel segmentation models such as LSeg [29]. The major differences are in the image and text representations $\mathbf{z}$ and $\mathbf{w}$. ALIGN/CLIP has $\mathbf{z} \in \mathbb{R}^{1 \times D}$, losing location information. Per-pixel segmentation represents an image with $\mathbf{z} \in \mathbb{R}^{H \times W \times D}$, requiring class-specific mask annotations for training. OpenSeg represents an image with a set of N segmentation regions $\mathbf{z} \in \mathbb{R}^{N \times D}$, facilitating weakly-supervised learning using captions.

In a recent work, Li *et al.* [29] train an image encoder to encode pixel embeddings and use CLIP [40] text embeddings as the per-pixel classifier. Both Zhao *et al.* [59] and Li *et al.* [29] need per-pixel semantic supervision which is expensive to scale up. On the contrary, OpenSeg makes use of cheap image-level supervision such as captions, which allows scaling up training data. There are multiple works concurrently developed with OpenSeg: GroupVit [51] learn segmentation masks from text supervision. Zabari and Hoshen [57] use model interpretability to obtain pixel-level pseudo-labels from CLIP to supervise single-image segmentation methods; it's different from all other works as it does not need any training images, but the method is slow. Zhou *et al.* [62] adapt CLIP for segmentation, and use pseudo per-pixel labels and self-training to boost the performance; similar to Li *et al.* [29], it utilizes per-pixel semantic supervision. Xu *et al.* [53] first generate mask proposals, and then leverage CLIP for classification of the proposals. In contrast, we learn visual-semantic alignment from image captions, which is no longer limited by image classification models (*e.g.*, CLIP).

Visual Grounding: Image captioning and image text datasets [9,27,37] enable research on the interplay of captions and grounded visual concepts [14,15,19,25, 41]. However, these methods often rely on an object detector to predict object bounding boxes for grounding. Therefore, they are not able to handle stuff and can not generate a single segmentation map for everything. Our method also uses captions as semantically-rich supervision. We draw inspiration from these works and expand the model's ability to ground visual concepts of both things and stuff to pixels with our mask representations.

Referring Image Segmentation: The goal of this task is to compute a binary mask localizing a referring expression. Since there are multiple supervised datasets (*e.g.*, RefCOCO [56]) for this task, previously developed methods are usually fully supervised [12,21,22,54,55]. As a result, the training data for these methods are not scalable.

3   Method

Figure 3 shows an overview of our approach. In contrast to approaches that represent an image with a vector $\mathcal{Z} \in \mathbb{R}^{1 \times D}$ or a feature map $\mathcal{Z} \in \mathbb{R}^{H \times W \times D}$, OpenSeg represents an image with N proposal masks with their features $\mathcal{Z} \in \mathbb{R}^{N \times D}$. Our mask representations support learning precise image segmentation with image captions by weakly-supervised learning. In Sect. 3.1, we describe the learning of predicting mask proposals from an image. In Sect. 3.2, we describe the feature representations of proposal and the learning of region-word alignments. In the following sections, We use a bold symbol to indicate an array of elements $\mathbf{x} = \{x_1, x_2, ..., x_n\}$, where the first dimension indicates the number of elements.

3.1   Learning Segmentation Masks

We design a model architecture which consists of a feature pyramid network (FPN) [32] for multi-scale feature extraction and a cross-attention module for segmentation region proposal. We fuse FPN features into P_2 resolution as described in [17] to generate image features $\mathcal{F}$. From $\mathcal{F}$, we obtain $\mathcal{F}_s \in \mathbb{R}^{H \times W \times D}$ by convolution and fc layers. Then we augment image features by adding learnable position embeddings PE: $\mathcal{F}_s^{PE} = \mathcal{F}_s + PE$. We use a cross-attention module taking inputs as $\mathcal{F}_s^{PE}$ and a randomly initialized queries $\mathbf{q}^0 \in \mathbb{R}^{N \times D}$ to generate mask queries $\mathbf{q} \in \mathbb{R}^{N \times D}$. Then, we compute the dot product of mask queries and position-augmented image features to predict masks $\mathbf{s} = Sigmoid(dot(\mathbf{q}, \mathcal{F}_s^{PE})) \in \mathbb{R}^{N \times H \times W}$. This architecture is conceptually similar to Max-deeplab [46] and MaskFormer [10]. The details of the architecture are in Appendix C.

We compute Dice coefficient [34] between predicted masks $\mathbf{s}$ and class-agnostic labeled masks $\mathbf{s}^l \in \mathbb{R}^{M \times H \times W}$ and maximize the Dice coefficient of the best matched mask for each labeled mask.

$$\mathcal{L}_\mathcal{S} = \frac{1}{M} \sum_{j=1}^{M} (1 - \max_i Dice(s_i, s_j^l)) \tag{1}$$

Typically, $N > M$ for each training image. Therefore, a subset of proposal masks are optimized to best match labeled masks. The rest of proposals can still segment out unlabeled regions without being penalized. One predicted mask may match to multiple labeled masks in the early training stage when their overlaps are low. But this does not prevent learning masks that highly overlap with labeled masks in the latter training stage.

3.2   Visual-Semantic Alignment with Masks

We use a pair of image I_b and caption C_b to learn visual-semantic alignments. We break I_b into regions (Sect. 3.1) and C_b into words by extracting list of nouns and adjectives from the caption. We randomly drop each word with the probability of $1 - kp$, where kp is the keep probability of words extracted from captions. We generate image features $\mathcal{F}_z$ using the same architecture as $\mathcal{F}_s$. For each region, we compute its feature by pooling image features with the mask $z[n,d] = \sum_{ij} s[n,i,j] \cdot \mathcal{F}_z[i,j,d]$. We feed each word to a pre-trained text encoder to compute the word feature w.

We follow the grounding loss in prior works [19,58] to learn region-word alignments. We first define the notation for Softmax on an array $\mathbf{x}$ to get the normalized score at the i-th element:

$$\sigma(\mathbf{x})_i = \frac{e^{x_i/\tau}}{\sum_j e^{x_j/\tau}} \tag{2}$$

where τ is a learnable scalar for the temperature. The similarity score of a region i and a word j is defined by its cosine similarity $\langle z_i, w_j \rangle = \frac{z_i \cdot w_j}{\|z_i\|\|w_j\|}$. Then we define the similarity of all regions $\mathbf{z}$ to a word w_j as: $g(\mathbf{z}, w_j) = [\langle z_1, w_j \rangle, ..., \langle z_N, w_j \rangle] \in \mathbb{R}^{N \times 1}$. We compute the similarity of an image I_b and its caption C_b by:

$$G(I_b, C_b) = \frac{1}{K} \sum_{j=1}^{K} \sum_{i=1}^{N} \sigma(g(\mathbf{z}, w_j))_i \cdot \langle z_i, w_j \rangle \tag{3}$$

The above similarity function encourages each word to be grounded to one or a few regions. Also, it avoids penalizing regions that can not find any similar word. Next, a grounding loss is defined for a given mini-batch B, where each example contains an image-caption pair. We define the similarity scores of all images in a batch $\mathbf{I}$ to a caption C_b by $G(\mathbf{I}, C_b) = [G(I_1, C_b), ..., G(I_{|B|}, C_b)] \in \mathbb{R}^{|B| \times 1}$ and similarly $G(I_b, \mathbf{C}) = [G(I_b, C_1), ..., G(I_b, C_{|B|})] \in \mathbb{R}^{|B| \times 1}$. The grounding loss aims at maximizing the normalized score of a labeled image-caption pair $\langle I_b, C_b \rangle$ over all images and all captions in a mini-batch.

$$\mathcal{L}_\mathcal{G} = -\frac{1}{|B|} \sum_{b=1}^{|B|} \left(\log \sigma\big(G(\mathbf{I}, C_b)\big)_b + \log \sigma\big(G(I_b, \mathbf{C})\big)_b \right) \tag{4}$$

To train OpenSeg, we simply sum the two losses with a weight α:

$$\mathcal{L} = \mathcal{L}_\mathcal{G} + \alpha \mathcal{L}_\mathcal{S} \tag{5}$$

When setting $\alpha = 0$, the model learns without labeled class-agnostic segmentation, and thus needs to induce mask predictions with the visual-semantic grounding loss. We find this setting leads to a poor performance, suggesting class-agnostic mask annotations are critical for learning mask predictions.

3.3   Learning from Caption only Data

Since annotating images with segmentation is expensive, to scale up the training data we need to learn from images with only caption annotations. We follow MuST [17] and first train a teacher model on a segmentation dataset with only the segmentation loss $\mathcal{L}_\mathcal{S}$. Then we annotate a large image-text dataset with pseudo segmentation labels using the teacher model. Lastly, the OpenSeg model is trained with a mix of human and pseudo labels.

3.4 Inference

Up to this point, we learn a vision model that predicts segmentation masks $\mathbf{s} \in \mathbb{R}^{N \times H \times W}$ and corresponding features $\mathbf{z} \in \mathbb{R}^{N \times D}$. Given an evaluation segmentation dataset, we encode its categories using the text encoder. If a category is defined by more than one word, we simply include all word embeddings for that category. We obtain K word embeddings $\mathbf{w} \in \mathbb{R}^{K \times D}$ representing all categories. The region logits are obtained by taking the cosine similarity between words and regions $\langle \mathbf{w}, \mathbf{z} \rangle \in \mathbb{R}^{K \times N}$. We multiply the region logits and segmentation masks to obtain segmentation logits at each pixel $\mathbf{y} = \langle \mathbf{w}, \mathbf{z} \rangle \cdot \mathbf{s} \in \mathbb{R}^{K \times H \times W}$. Then the category prediction at each pixel is an argmax of segmentation logits along the word dimension:

$$pred[i,j] = \operatorname*{argmax}_{k} \mathbf{y}[k,i,j] \tag{6}$$

4 Experiments

4.1 Experimental Settings

Architecture. We use EfficientNet-B7 [44] (and ResNet101 in Table 2) as the backbone architecture and employ FPN [32] for multi-scale feature fusion. We use pyramid levels from P_2 to P_5 with feature dimension 640, upsample all feature levels to P_2, and then merge them by a sum operation to obtain $\mathcal{F}$. To compute $\mathcal{F}_z$ and $\mathcal{F}_s$, we apply a fc layer followed by 3 layers of 3×3 convolutions with 640 channels after $\mathcal{F}$. For text encoder we use the frozen pre-trained BERT-Large model in ALIGN [23].

Training Parameters. All models are trained with an image size of 640×640. We apply multi-scale jittering with a random scale between $[0.8, 1.2]$ (*i.e.*, small scale jittering in [16]). The weight decay is set to 1e-05 and we use a learning rate 0.005 with the cosine learning rate schedule. Unless otherwise mentioned, we initialize the backbone of the model from the ALIGN checkpoint [23]. We train OpenSeg on COCO dataset for 30k steps. For training on COCO and Localized Narrative datasets, we sample examples from the datasets with equal probability and we train the model for 60k steps. We set kp (keep probability of words extracted from captions) to 0.5. We train models with global batch size of 1024 and local batch size of 16 (we have 64 Cloud TPU v3 cores). Unless otherwise stated, for each core we compute the loss over the local batch of examples (See Appendix F for the comparison between sync and unsync contrastive loss over the cores and also comparison of training with smaller batch sizes).

Training Datasets

COCO: We use the panoptic segmentation [26] and caption [9] annotations in the 2017 splits which include 118k/5k train/val images. We utilize the panoptic segmentation annotations in a class-agnostic manner. When evaluating on

Table 1. Recall of segmentation mask proposals on COCO and PASCAL-Context datasets. All methods use 128 proposals.

	COCO			PASCAL Context-59		
	R50	R70	R90	R50	R70	R90
MCG [3]	41.1	21.4	4.6	57.8	31.7	8.7
COB [33]	46.0	24.8	4.9	62.9	37.6	12.1
OpenSeg	**68.9**	**48.1**	**16.9**	**84.5**	**65.1**	**29.1**

COCO Panoptic, we treat it as a semantic segmentation dataset and our model only predicts the semantic class for each pixel.

Localized Narrative (Loc. Narr.): Localized Narrative [38] contains detailed natural language descriptions along with mouse traces for multiple datasets (COCO, Flickr, Open Images, ADE20k). We don't train on the ADE20k portion to keep its image distribution unseen. The remaining 652k images are used for training.

Evaluation Datasets

PASCAL Context: PASCAL Context [35] includes per-pixel segmentation annotations of object and stuff on 5k/5k train/val images from various indoor and outdoor senses. The full version (PC-459) includes 459 classes. The version with the most frequent 59 classes (PC-59) is widely used in the existing literature.

PASCAL VOC: PASCAL VOC 2012 [13] includes 20 object classes and a background class with 1.5k/1.5k train/val images. Since the text "background" is ambiguous, we assign the background class to the pixels predicted as PC-59 categories that are not in PASCAL VOC.

ADE20k: ADE20k [61] includes 20k/2k train/val images with segmentation annotations and covers a wide variety of indoor and outdoor scenes. The full version has annotations in an open-vocabulary setting and includes 2693 object and stuff classes. We follow [10] and evaluate on the version with 847 classes (A-847). We also test on the widely-used version with 150 frequent categories (A-150).

4.2 Predicting Masks Across Datasets

We train the segmentation proposal model on COCO and evaluate on COCO and PC-59 with recalls at IoU 50%, 70%, and 90% as metrics. Table 1 shows performance comparisons with MCG [3] and COB [33] using their pre-computed proposals. OpenSeg shows significantly superior performances. We perform additional cross-dataset evaluation using datasets in MSeg [28] in Appendix D. Figure 4 shows 6 manually selected proposals to demonstrate our model can

Fig. 4. Examples of predicted segmentation masks in an unseen scene. OpenSeg is able to segment an image into meaningful regions. These regions may be overlapping and indicate concepts of foreground (diver and coral) *vs.* background (ocean), and whole (diver) *vs.* parts (scuba and goggles). Notably, OpenSeg is trained on COCO which does not include underwater scenes.

organize images into semantically meaningful regions. Particularly, the underwater scene is not present in our training dataset COCO, but the model can still organize pixels into regions for ocean, coral, diver, goggles, *etc.* The full 128 proposals are included in Appendix E.

4.3   Open-Vocabulary Image Segmentation

In this section, we first describe open-vocabulary baselines and our evaluation metrics. Then we discuss the experimental results with our open-vocabulary baselines and state-of-the-art open-vocabulary and zero-shot methods.

ALIGN Baseline: Although ALIGN [23] is trained for open-vocabulary classification, it can still roughly localize objects and stuff with arbitrary text queries (see Fig. 2). Since we initialize the backbone of OpenSeg from ALIGN's pretrained checkpoint, we use ALIGN as a baseline. We follow the CAM [60] method for segmentation prediction. We compute the activation map before the average pooling layer of the image encoder. Then for each spatial location we compute its cosine similarity with the text embeddings of all input categories. We assign the class with the highest similarity to each location.

LSeg Baseline: Recently, [29] introduce an open-vocabulary segmentation method which trains an image encoder to encode pixel embeddings and use CLIP [40] text embeddings as the per-pixel classifier. Figure 3(b) illustrates the model of this approach. For a fair comparison, we also construct LSeg in our codebase as follows. We add FPN and introduce a high resolution map in the same approach in Sect. 4.1. We embed class names into text embeddings using ALIGN [23] text-encoder and use them as per-pixel classifiers. We fine-tune the pre-trained image encoder and FPN layers on COCO dataset using a per-pixel cross-entropy loss to align pixel embeddings with text embeddings. We call this model LSeg+.

ALIGN w/Proposal Baseline: The ALIGN, LSeg and LSeg+ baselines are methods that perform visual-semantic alignments without explicit visual grouping. Since our method uses visual grouping, we also compare our method to

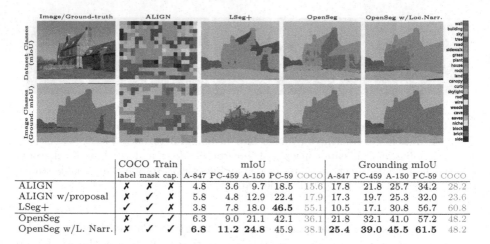

	COCO Train			mIoU					Grounding mIoU				
	label	mask	cap.	A-847	PC-459	A-150	PC-59	COCO	A-847	PC-459	A-150	PC-59	COCO
ALIGN	✗	✗	✗	4.8	3.6	9.7	18.5	15.6	17.8	21.8	25.7	34.2	28.2
ALIGN w/proposal	✗	✓	✗	5.8	4.8	12.9	22.4	17.9	17.3	19.7	25.3	32.0	23.6
LSeg+	✓	✓	✗	3.8	7.8	18.0	**46.5**	55.1	10.5	17.1	30.8	56.7	60.8
OpenSeg	✗	✓	✓	6.3	9.0	21.1	42.1	36.1	21.8	32.1	41.0	57.2	48.2
OpenSeg w/L. Narr.	✗	✓	✓	**6.8**	**11.2**	**24.8**	45.9	38.1	**25.4**	**39.0**	**45.5**	**61.5**	48.2

Fig. 5. (Bottom) The mIoU and Grounding mIoU results of ALIGN, ALIGN w/proposal, LSeg+, and OpenSeg. (Top) Segmentation predictions on an image from the ADE20k (847 categories). (First row) Predictions with all 847 classes as text queries. (Second row) Predictions with only classes in the ground-truth segmentation as text queries.

ALIGN w/proposal baseline which leverage proposals generated by OpenSeg at inference. We use the ALIGN model to classify each proposal and then similarly to OpenSeg we aggregate all proposals to compute the final segmentation map.

Evaluation Metrics: We use two metrics, *mIoU* and *Grounding mIoU*, for evaluation. Both metrics are calculated using the standard mIoU formula [13] and only differ in the text queries for each image. The mIoU is commonly used in literature. It measures the performance of image segmentation with fixed text queries, *e.g.*, 847 classes when evaluated for all images in A-847. The Grounding mIoU evaluates concept grounding. An example scenario is interactive segmentation where users can specify a set of concepts in an image for the model to segment. It only uses the ground-truth classes in an image, *e.g.*, 7 classes are used as text queries for the example in the second row of Fig. 5. We find that predictions in the mIoU and Grounding mIoU settings can look quite differently and sometimes mIoU does not correctly reflect the prediction quality due to class ambiguity. For example, building, brick, house are all correct visual concepts to describe the object in Fig. 5 but the ground-truth label is building.

Zero-Shot Transfer to ADE20k/PASCAL: We evaluate the performance of OpenSeg and the baselines on holdout image segmentation datasets whose train sets are not used for training. In Fig. 5 (bottom), we compare ALIGN, ALIGN w/proposal, LSeg+ and OpenSeg on the challenging A-847 and PC-459 datasets with large vocabularies and also on the widely used A-150 and PC-59. In the following sections we discuss our findings based on these results.

OpenSeg Significantly Outperforms Pre-trained ALIGN [23]: OpenSeg-trained on COCO outperforms ALIGN baseline on all of the benchmarks significantly. While adding proposals to ALIGN improves mIoU results. OpenSeg still performs significantly better. For example, on PC-459 OpenSeg outperforms ALIGN and ALIGN w/proposals by +5.4 and +4.2 mIoU, respectively.

Training on Limited Categories Hurts Generalization: LSeg+, which is trained with pixel-wise segmentation in COCO, outperforms ALIGN by a large margin on COCO (+39.5 mIOU) and PC-59 (+28.0 mIOU). Note COCO categories contain most of PC-59 categories. However, when we evaluate LSeg+ on A-847 which includes a larger set of vocabularies, the performance of LSeg+ is worse than ALIGN by 1.0 mIoU and 7.3 Grounding mIoU. These results demonstrate that training on the limited categories of COCO hurts the generalization of the model.

OpenSeg Improves Generalization:. While OpenSeg trained on COCO has worse mIoU on COCO and PC-59 in comparison to LSeg+, it generalizes better on all other benchmarks. OpenSeg outperforms LSeg+ by +2.5 mIoU and +11.3 Grounding mIoU on A-847 and also by +1.2 mIoU and +15.0 Grounding mIoU on PC-459. The OpenSeg uses class-agnostic masks and image-level caption supervision, while LSeg+ uses 134 per-pixel class name supervision. Although OpenSeg is trained with a weaker supervision, it has a better generalization to classes outside of COCO. These results reveal that we need open-vocabulary supervision such as captions for training a *generalist* model.

Scaling Training Data with Captions Improves Performance: To scale up training data we utilize the Localized Narrative dataset, which includes detailed narratives about the objects and stuff in each image. We train a segmentation teacher model on the COCO dataset and use it to generate segmentation pseudo labels on the Loc. Narr. dataset. By scaling training data from 118k images to 652k images, the performance of OpenSeg improves on average by 2.5 mIoU and 4.8 Grounding mIoU across 4 benchmarks (see Fig. 5). In Appendix G, we study the importance of using pseudo segmentation labels during training.

Ensembling of Text Queries and Prompt Engineering: To further improve the performance of OpenSeg we use ensembling where we include synonyms or subcategories of classes. For example, we use 'person', 'child', 'girl', 'boy', *etc.* for the class of 'person'. We ensemble the multiple text queries by taking the max score as described in the Sect. 3.4. Also, since some of the class names of the segmentation datasets are not descriptive, we add a short context to the names. *e.g.* we change 'glass' to 'drinking glass'. These improvements give us on average 2.6 mIoU gain across 4 datasets (see Table 2). See Appendix I for more details.

Compare with Existing Methods: We compare OpenSeg with previous open-vocabulary and zero-shot segmentation methods in Table 2. We initialize ResNet101 backbone of OpenSeg and LSeg+ with ImageNet pretrained weights similar to the baselines. LSeg+ significantly outperforms LSeg (and also

SPNet [49] and ZS3Net [6]) as it is trained on the larger dataset of COCO instead of PASCAL-20. In contrast to LSeg and LSeg+ which are trained on COCO class labels, OpenSeg is trained on COCO captions and as a result has a better generalization. OpenSeg outperforms LSeg+ by +1.3 mIoU on PC-459. Compared with GroupVit, OpenSeg learns visual grouping with class-agnostic segmentation, and has a superior performance. Also, by scaling up the training data from COCO to COCO+Loc. Narr. it achieves further gain of +1.4 on PC-459.

For the strongest OpenSeg (last two rows), we initialize EfficientNet-b7 backbone with ALIGN pre-trained image encoder [23]. Also we train this model with sync loss (see Appendix F for more details). This model significantly outperforms the strongest LSeg model with ViT-L backbone (+19.9 mIoU on PASCAL-20).

Table 2. The mIoU results of our model and previous open-vocabulary and zero-shot segmentation methods. Results for SPNet and ZS3Net on PASCAL-20 are reported from [29].

	Backbone	External dataset	Target dataset	A-847	PC-459	A-150	PC-59	PAS-20
LSeg [29]	ViT-L/16	✗	✓(seen classes)	–	–	–	–	52.3
SPNet [49]	ResNet101	✗	✓(seen classes)	–	–	–	24.3	18.3
ZS3Net [6]	ResNet101	✗	✓(seen classes)	–	–	–	19.4	38.3
LSeg [29]	ResNet101	✗	✓(seen classes)	–	–	–	–	47.4
LSeg+	ResNet101	COCO	✗	2.5	5.2	13.0	36.0	59.0
OpenSeg(ours)	ResNet101	COCO	✗	4.0	6.5	15.3	36.9	60.0
OpenSeg(ours)	ResNet101	COCO+Loc. Narr.	✗	4.4	7.9	17.5	40.1	63.8
GroupVit [51]	VIT-S	CC12M+YFCC	✗	–	–	–	22.4	52.3
OpenSeg(ours)	eff-b7	COCO+Loc. Narr.	✗	8.1	11.5	26.4	44.8	70.2
+prompt eng.	eff-b7	COCO+Loc. Narr.	✗	**8.8**	**12.2**	**28.6**	**48.2**	**72.2**

4.4 Ablation Experiments

Importance of Backbone Initialization: In order to save the computation, we initialize OpenSeg from the state-of-the-art ALIGN checkpoint trained on 1.8 billion examples for image-text alignments. In this section, we study the importance of initialization of the vision backbone from this checkpoint. In Table 3, we compare the performance of training OpenSeg from scratch, initializing from the NoisyStudent checkpoint [50] and initializing from the ALIGN checkpoint. For training these models, we use the same hyper-parameters, and only tune the learning rate (0.32 for scratch, 0.08 for NoisyStudent init. and 0.005 for ALIGN init.) and number of steps (180k steps for scratch and 60k for NoisyStudent and ALIGN init.). Table 3 shows that using the NoisyStudent checkpoint to initialize the backbone achieves slightly worse results (less than 0.5 mIoU on all benchmarks) compared to using the ALIGN checkpoint. This shows initializing from the ALIGN model is not necessary for good word-region alignments. However, training from scratch is still trailing behind. We may be able to reduce the gap by increasing the batch size and training with more data.

Table 3. Backbone initialization with an ALIGN pre-trained image encoder is not critical. The models use the pre-trained ALIGN text encoder and are trained on COCO and Loc. Narr. datasets.

	A-847	PC-459	A-150	PC-59
Random init.	4.5	7.6	18.6	40.6
NoisyStudent init.	6.6	10.7	24.4	**46.9**
ALIGN init.	**6.8**	**11.2**	**24.8**	45.9

Incorporating Proposals at Inference Time Improves Accuracy: We are curious about the importance of mask proposals in OpenSeg during inference. To study this problem, we take the feature map $\mathcal{F}_z$ in OpenSeg and perform per-pixel segmentation by taking the dot product of $\mathcal{F}_z$ with word embeddings $\mathbf{w}$. This method performs inference without mask proposals. In Table 4, we compare the performance of OpenSeg and its counterparts that do not use mask proposals (the above method) or using ground-truth as mask proposals. The performance of OpenSeg is much worse if not using proposals: mIoU on PC-59 drops from 42.1 to 32.1 and from 21.1 to 16.4 on A-150. Using ground-truth as proposals can be seen as an upper bound when we have perfect class-agnostic localization. The results show the room for improving localization. It also demonstrates even with perfect localization, the semantic alignment is still challenging.

Table 4. Incorporating predicted masks at inference improves mIoU accuracy. Using the ground-truth masks can be seen as the performance upper bound when segmentation masks are perfectly predicted. The model is trained on COCO.

	A-847	PC-459	A-150	PC-59
OpenSeg	6.3	9.0	21.1	42.1
cre - pred. masks	(-1.7) 4.6	(-3.1) 5.9	(-4.7) 16.4	(-10.0) 32.1
+ gt. masks	$(+2.8)$ 9.1	$(+3.3)$ 12.3	$(+6.4)$ 27.5	$(+7.2)$ 49.3

Table 5. Using all words in training captions hurts performance. Using nouns+adj for training achieves the best results. The model is trained on COCO.

Caption filter	A-847	PC-459	A-150	PC-59
All words	5.3	8.8	20.0	41.3
noun + adj. + verb	6.0	8.8	20.9	41.7
noun + adj	**6.3**	**9.0**	**21.1**	**42.1**

Importance of Text Filtering: We train OpenSeg with image captions which may include words that do not represent any regions in an image. These noises make training more challenging. We perform a simple pre-processing on the captions and extract the list of nouns and adjectives. This procedure removes conjunctions, pronouns, adverbs, verbs, *etc.* which reduces the noises. In Table 5, we study the performance of OpenSeg when using different types of filtering on the captions. Keeping only nouns and adjectives yields the best results. The worst results are from using all words, which show 0.2–1.1 worse mIoU. The small performance differences across different ways of text filtering show OpenSeg is robust to the noise in the input words to some degree.

5   Conclusion

We propose OpenSeg, an open-vocabulary image segmentation model, to organize an image into regions described with arbitrary text queries. This is in stark contrast to previous works in semantic segmentation learned to predict categories in closed vocabulary. We propose to represent an image with a set of mask regions followed by visual-semantic alignments. Such representations support weakly-supervised learning for grounding words in a caption to predicted mask proposals, and thus make the training data scalable. We are the first work to directly evaluate on holdout image segmentation datasets, attaining significant performance gains against strong baselines initialized by a pre-trained ALIGN model. We hope to encourage future works to learn a *generalist* segmentation model that can transfer across datasets using language as the interface.

References

1. Agarwal, S., Krueger, G., Clark, J., Radford, A., Kim, J.W., Brundage, M.: Evaluating clip: towards characterization of broader capabilities and downstream implications. arXiv preprint arXiv:2108.02818 (2021)
2. Arbelaez, P., Maire, M., Fowlkes, C., Malik, J.: Contour detection and hierarchical image segmentation. PAMI **33**, 898–916 (2010)
3. Arbelaez, P., Pont-Tuset, J., Barron, J.T., Marques, F., Malik, J.: Multiscale combinatorial grouping. In: CVPR (2014)
4. Baek, D., Oh, Y., Ham, B.: Exploiting a joint embedding space for generalized zero-shot semantic segmentation. In: ICCV (2021)
5. Zhou, B., et al.: Semantic understanding of scenes through the ADE20K dataset. Int. J. Comput. Vis. **127**(3), 302–321 (2018). https://doi.org/10.1007/s11263-018-1140-0
6. Bucher, M., Vu, T.H., Cord, M., Pérez, P.: Zero-shot semantic segmentation. In: NeurIPS (2019)
7. Caesar, H., Uijlings, J., Ferrari, V.: Coco-stuff: thing and stuff classes in context. In: CVPR (2018)
8. Carion, N., Massa, F., Synnaeve, G., Usunier, N., Kirillov, A., Zagoruyko, S.: End-to-end object detection with transformers. In: Vedaldi, A., Bischof, H., Brox, T., Frahm, J.-M. (eds.) ECCV 2020. LNCS, vol. 12346, pp. 213–229. Springer, Cham (2020). https://doi.org/10.1007/978-3-030-58452-8_13
9. Chen, X., et al.: Microsoft coco captions: data collection and evaluation server. arXiv preprint arXiv:1504.00325 (2015)

10. Cheng, B., Schwing, A.G., Kirillov, A.: Per-pixel classification is not all you need for semantic segmentation. arXiv preprint arXiv:2107.06278 (2021)
11. Comaniciu, D., Meer, P.: Robust analysis of feature spaces: color image segmentation. In: CVPR (1997)
12. Ding, H., Liu, C., Wang, S., Jiang, X.: Vision-language transformer and query generation for referring segmentation. In: ICCV (2021)
13. Everingham, M., et al.: The pascal visual object classes (VOC) challenge. Int. J. Comput. Vis. **88**, 303–338 (2010). https://doi.org/10.1007/s11263-009-0275-4
14. Fang, H., et al.: From captions to visual concepts and back. In: CVPR (2015)
15. Fukui, A., Park, D.H., Yang, D., Rohrbach, A., Darrell, T., Rohrbach, M.: Multimodal compact bilinear pooling for visual question answering and visual grounding. arXiv preprint arXiv:1606.01847 (2016)
16. Ghiasi, G., et al.: Simple copy-paste is a strong data augmentation method for instance segmentation. In: CVPR (2021)
17. Ghiasi, G., Zoph, B., Cubuk, E.D., Le, Q.V., Lin, T.Y.: Multi-task self-training for learning general representations. In: ICCV (2021)
18. Gu, X., Lin, T.Y., Kuo, W., Cui, Y.: Zero-shot detection via vision and language knowledge distillation. arXiv e-prints, p. arXiv–2104 (2021)
19. Gupta, T., Vahdat, A., Chechik, G., Yang, X., Kautz, J., Hoiem, D.: Contrastive learning for weakly supervised phrase grounding. In: Vedaldi, A., Bischof, H., Brox, T., Frahm, J.-M. (eds.) ECCV 2020. LNCS, vol. 12348, pp. 752–768. Springer, Cham (2020). https://doi.org/10.1007/978-3-030-58580-8_44
20. Hu, P., Sclaroff, S., Saenko, K.: Uncertainty-aware learning for zero-shot semantic segmentation. In: NeurIPS (2020)
21. Hu, R., Rohrbach, M., Darrell, T.: Segmentation from natural language expressions. In: Leibe, B., Matas, J., Sebe, N., Welling, M. (eds.) ECCV 2016. LNCS, vol. 9905, pp. 108–124. Springer, Cham (2016). https://doi.org/10.1007/978-3-319-46448-0_7
22. Hu, Z., Feng, G., Sun, J., Zhang, L., Lu, H.: Bi-directional relationship inferring network for referring image segmentation. In: CVPR (2020)
23. Jia, C., et al.: Scaling up visual and vision-language representation learning with noisy text supervision. ICML (2021)
24. Jo, S., Yu, I.J.: Puzzle-CAM: improved localization via matching partial and full features. arXiv preprint arXiv:2101.11253 (2021)
25. Kamath, A., Singh, M., LeCun, Y., Misra, I., Synnaeve, G., Carion, N.: Mdetr-modulated detection for end-to-end multi-modal understanding. arXiv preprint arXiv:2104.12763 (2021)
26. Kirillov, A., He, K., Girshick, R., Rother, C., Dollar, P.: Panoptic segmentation. In: CVPR (2019)
27. Krishna, R., et al.: Visual genome: connecting language and vision using crowd-sourced dense image annotations. IJCV **123**, 32–73 (2017) and vision using crowd-sourced dense image annotations. IJCV (2017)
28. Lambert, J., Liu, Z., Sener, O., Hays, J., Koltun, V.: MSeg: A composite dataset for multi-domain semantic segmentation. In: CVPR (2020)
29. Li, B., Weinberger, K.Q., Belongie, S., Koltun, V., Ranftl, R.: Language-driven semantic segmentation. In: ICLR (2022)
30. Li, P., Wei, Y., Yang, Y.: Consistent structural relation learning for zero-shot segmentation. In: NeurIPS (2020)
31. Li, Y., Kuang, Z., Liu, L., Chen, Y., Zhang, W.: Pseudo-mask matters in weakly-supervised semantic segmentation. In: ICCV (2021)

32. Lin, T.Y., Dollár, P., Girshick, R., He, K., Hariharan, B., Belongie, S.: Feature pyramid networks for object detection. In: CVPR (2017)
33. Maninis, K.K., Pont-Tuset, J., Arbeláez, P., Gool, L.V.: Convolutional oriented boundaries: from image segmentation to high-level tasks. TPAMI **40**, 819–833 (2018)
34. Milletari, F., Navab, N., Ahmadi, S.A.: V-Net: fully convolutional neural networks for volumetric medical image segmentation. In: 3DV (2016)
35. Mottaghi, R., et al.: The role of context for object detection and semantic segmentation in the wild. In: CVPR (2014)
36. Pinheiro, P.O., Collobert, R.: From image-level to pixel-level labeling with convolutional networks. In: CVPR (2015)
37. Plummer, B.A., Wang, L., Cervantes, C.M., Caicedo, J.C., Hockenmaier, J., Lazebnik, S.: Flickr30k entities: collecting region-to-phrase correspondences for richer image-to-sentence models. In: ICCV (2015)
38. Pont-Tuset, J., Uijlings, J., Changpinyo, S., Soricut, R., Ferrari, V.: Connecting vision and language with localized narratives. In: Vedaldi, A., Bischof, H., Brox, T., Frahm, J.-M. (eds.) ECCV 2020. LNCS, vol. 12350, pp. 647–664. Springer, Cham (2020). https://doi.org/10.1007/978-3-030-58558-7_38
39. Qi, L., et al.: Open-world entity segmentation. arXiv preprint arXiv:2107.14228 (2021)
40. Radford, A., et al.: Learning transferable visual models from natural language supervision. In: ICML (2021)
41. Rohrbach, A., Rohrbach, M., Hu, R., Darrell, T., Schiele, B.: Grounding of textual phrases in images by reconstruction. In: Leibe, B., Matas, J., Sebe, N., Welling, M. (eds.) ECCV 2016. LNCS, vol. 9905, pp. 817–834. Springer, Cham (2016). https://doi.org/10.1007/978-3-319-46448-0_49
42. Shi, J., Malik, J.: Normalized cuts and image segmentation. PAMI **22**, 888–905 (2000)
43. Shridhar, M., Manuelli, L., Fox, D.: CLIPORT: what and where pathways for robotic manipulation. In: Proceedings of the 5th Conference on Robot Learning (CoRL) (2021)
44. Tan, M., Le, Q.V.: EfficientNet: rethinking model scaling for convolutional neural networks. In: ICML (2019)
45. Uijlings, J.R.R., van de Sande, K.E.A., Gevers, T., Smeulders, A.W.M.: Selective search for object recognition. Int. J. Comput. Vis. **104**, 154–171 (2013). https://doi.org/10.1007/s11263-013-0620-5
46. Wang, H., Zhu, Y., Adam, H., Yuille, A., Chen, L.C.: MaX-DeepLab: end-to-end panoptic segmentation with mask transformers. In: CVPR (2021)
47. Wang, Y., Zhang, J., Kan, M., Shan, S., Chen, X.: Self-supervised equivariant attention mechanism for weakly supervised semantic segmentation. In: CVPR (2020)
48. Wertheimer, M.: Laws of organization in perceptual forms. In: Ellis, W. (ed.) A Source Book of Gestalt Psychology, pp. 71–88. Routledge and Kegan Paul, London (1938)
49. Xian, Y., Choudhury, S., He, Y., Schiele, B., Akata, Z.: Semantic projection network for zero-and few-label semantic segmentation. In: CVPR (2019)
50. Xie, Q., Hovy, E., Luong, M.T., Le, Q.V.: Self-training with noisy student improves ImageNet classification. In: CVPR (2020)
51. Xu, J., et al.: GroupViT: Semantic segmentation emerges from text supervision. In: CVPR (2022)

52. Xu, L., Ouyang, W., Bennamoun, M., Boussaid, F., Sohel, F., Xu, D.: Leveraging auxiliary tasks with affinity learning for weakly supervised semantic segmentation. In: ICCV (2021)
53. Xu, M., et al.: A simple baseline for zero-shot semantic segmentation with pre-trained vision-language model. arXiv preprint arXiv:2112.14757 (2021)
54. Ye, L., Rochan, M., Liu, Z., Wang, Y.: Cross-modal self-attention network for referring image segmentation. In: CVPR (2019)
55. Yu, L., et al.: MAttNet: Modular attention network for referring expression comprehension. In: CVPR (2018)
56. Yu, L., Poirson, P., Yang, S., Berg, A.C., Berg, T.L.: Modeling context in referring expressions. In: Leibe, B., Matas, J., Sebe, N., Welling, M. (eds.) ECCV 2016. LNCS, vol. 9906, pp. 69–85. Springer, Cham (2016). https://doi.org/10.1007/978-3-319-46475-6_5
57. Zabari, N., Hoshen, Y.: Semantic segmentation in-the-wild without seeing any segmentation examples. arXiv preprint arXiv:2112.03185 (2021)
58. Zareian, A., Rosa, K.D., Hu, D.H., Chang, S.F.: Open-vocabulary object detection using captions. In: CVPR (2021)
59. Zhao, H., Puig, X., Zhou, B., Fidler, S., Torralba, A.: Open vocabulary scene parsing. In: ICCV (2017)
60. Zhou, B., Khosla, A., Lapedriza, A., Oliva, A., Torralba, A.: Learning deep features for discriminative localization. In: CVPR (2016)
61. Zhou, B., et al.: Semantic understanding of scenes through the ADE20K dataset. IJCV **127**, 302–321 (2019)
62. Zhou, C., Loy, C.C., Dai, B.: DenseCLIP: extract free dense labels from clip. arXiv preprint arXiv:2112.01071 (2021)

The Abduction of Sherlock Holmes: A Dataset for Visual Abductive Reasoning

Jack Hessel[1]([✉])[ID], Jena D. Hwang[1]([✉])[ID], Jae Sung Park[2][ID], Rowan Zellers[2][ID],
Chandra Bhagavatula[1][ID], Anna Rohrbach[3][ID], Kate Saenko[4,5][ID],
and Yejin Choi[1,2][ID]

[1] Allen Institute for AI, Seattle, USA
{jackh,jenah,chandrab}@allenai.org
[2] Paul G. Allen School of Computer Science and Engineering,
University of Washington, Seattle, USA
{jspark96,rowanz,yejin}@cs.washington.edu
[3] University of California, Berkeley, USA
anna.rohrbach@berkeley.edu
[4] Boston University, Boston, USA
saenko@bu.edu
[5] MIT-IBM Watson AI, Cambridge, USA

Abstract. Humans have remarkable capacity to reason abductively and hypothesize about what lies beyond the literal content of an image. By identifying concrete visual **clues** scattered throughout a scene, we almost can't help but draw probable **inferences** beyond the literal scene based on our everyday experience and knowledge about the world. For example, if we see a "20 mph" sign alongside a road, we might assume the street sits in a residential area (rather than on a highway), even if no houses are pictured. Can machines perform similar visual reasoning?

We present **Sherlock**, an annotated corpus of 103K images for testing machine capacity for abductive reasoning *beyond* literal image contents. We adopt a free-viewing paradigm: participants first observe and identify salient clues within images (e.g., objects, actions) and then provide a plausible inference about the scene, given the clue. In total, we collect 363K (clue, inference) pairs, which form a first-of-its-kind abductive visual reasoning dataset. Using our corpus, we test three complementary axes of abductive reasoning. We evaluate the capacity of models to: i) *retrieve* relevant inferences from a large candidate corpus; ii) *localize* evidence for inferences via bounding boxes, and iii) *compare* plausible inferences to match human judgments on a newly-collected diagnostic corpus of 19K Likert-scale judgments. While we find that fine-tuning CLIP-RN50 × 64 with a multitask objective outperforms strong baselines, significant headroom exists between model performance and human agreement. Data, models, and leaderboard available at http://visualabduction.com/.

Supplementary Information The online version contains supplementary material available at https://doi.org/10.1007/978-3-031-20059-5_32.

> You know my method.
> It is founded upon the observation of trifles.

> "The Boscombe Valley Mystery", by A. C. Doyle

1   Introduction

The process of making the most plausible inference in the face of incomplete information is called *abductive reasoning,* [47] personified by the iconic visual inferences of the fictional detective Sherlock Holmes[1]. Upon viewing a scene, humans can quickly synthesize cues to arrive at abductive hypotheses that go beyond the what's captured in the frame. Concrete cues are diverse: people take into account the emotion and mood of the agents, speculate about the rationale for the presence/absence of objects, and zero-in on small, contextual details; all the while accounting for prior experiences and (potential mis)conceptions[2]. Fig. 1 illustrates: snow may imply dangerous road conditions, an Ohio licence plate may suggest the location of the accident, and a blue sign may indicate this road is an interstate. Though not all details are equally important, certain *salient* details shape our abductive inferences about the scene as a whole [56]. This type of visual information is often left unstated.

Fig. 1. We introduce **Sherlock**: a corpus of 363 K commonsense inferences grounded in 103 K images. Annotators highlight localized clues (color bubbles) and draw plausible abductive inferences about them (speech bubbles). Our models are able to predict localized inferences (top predictions are shown), but we quantify a large gap between machine performance and human agreement.

We introduce **Sherlock**, a new dataset of 363 K commonsense inferences grounded in 103 K images. **Sherlock** makes explicit typically-unstated cognitive processes: each image is annotated with at least 3 inferences which pair depicted details (called clues) with commonsense conclusions that aim to go *beyond* what

---

[1] While Holmes rarely makes mistakes, he frequently misidentifies his mostly abductive process of reasoning as "deductive" [8,39].

[2] The *correctness* of abductive reasoning is certainly not guaranteed. Our goal is to study perception and reasoning *without* endorsing specific inferences (see Sect. 3.1).

is literally pictured (called inferences). **Sherlock** is more diverse than many existing visual commonsense corpora like Visual Commonsense Reasoning [75] and VisualCOMET [44]³, due to its free-viewing data collection paradigm: we purposefully do not pre-specify the types of clues/inferences allowed, leaving it to humans to identify the most salient and informative elements and their implications. Other forms of free-viewing like image captions may not be enough: a typical caption for Fig. 1 may mention the accident and perhaps the snow, but smaller yet important details needed to comprehend the larger scene (like the blue freeway sign or the Ohio plates) may not be mentioned explicitly [5]. Dense captioning corpora [22] attempts to overcome this problem by highlighting *all* details, but it does so without accounting for which details are salient (and why).

Table 1. Comparison between **Sherlock** and prior annotated corpora addressing visual abductive reasoning from static images. **Sherlock** showcases a unique data collection paradigm, leading to a rich variety of non-human centric (i.e., not solely grounded in human references) visual abductive inferences.

Dataset	# Images	Format	bboxes?	free-viewing?	human-centric?
VCR [75]	110 K	QA	✓		✓
VisualCOMET [44]	59 K	If/Then KB	✓		✓
Visual7W [79]	47 K	QA	✓	partial	
Visual madlibs [72]	11 K	FiTB	✓	partial	✓
Abstract scenes [65]	4.3 K	KB			
Why in images [49]	792	KB			✓
BD2BB [48]	3.2 K	If/Then		✓	✓
FVQA [66]	2.2 K	QA+KB			
OK-VQA [36]	14 K	QA		✓	
KB-VQA [67]	700	QA	✓		
Sherlock	103K	Clue/inference	✓	✓	

Using our corpus, we propose three complementary tasks that evaluate different aspects of machine capacity for visual abductive reasoning:

1. *Retrieval of Abductive Inferences:* given an image+region, the algorithm scores a large set of candidate inferences and is rewarded for assigning a high score to the gold annotation.
2. *Localization of Evidence:* the algorithm selects a bounding box within the image that provides the best evidence for a given inference.
3. *Comparison of Plausibility:* the algorithm scores a small set of plausible inferences for a given image+region, and is rewarded for aligning its scores with human judgments over those sets.

In our setup, a single model undertakes all of these tasks: we ask algorithms to score the plausibility of an inference given an image and a bounding box con-

---

³ For instance, 94% of visual references in [75] are about depicted actors, and [44] even requires KB entries to explicitly regard people; see Fig. 2.

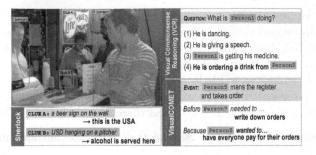

Fig. 2. Side-by-side comparison of VCR [75], VisualCOMET [44], and **Sherlock** on a representative instance. **Sherlock** showcases a wider range of (non-human centric) situational contexts.

tained within it[4]. We can directly compare models in their capacity to perform abductive reasoning, without relying on indirect generation evaluation metrics.

Model predicted inferences are given in Fig. 1. The model is a fine-tuned CLIP [51] augmented to allow bounding boxes as input, enabling users to specify particular regions for the model to make abductive inferences about. Our best model, a multitask version of CLIP RN50 × 64, outperforms strong baselines like UNITER [9] and LXMERT [61] primarily because it pays specific attention to the correct input bounding box. We additionally show that 1) for all tasks, reasoning about the full context of the image (rather than just the region corresponding to the clue) results in the best performance; 2) a text-only model cannot solve the comparison task even when given oracle region descriptions; and 3) a multi-task model fit on both clues/inferences at training time performs best even when only inferences are available at test time.

We foresee **Sherlock** as a difficult diagnostic benchmark for vision-and-language models. On our comparison task, in terms of pairwise accuracy, our best model lags significantly below human agreement (headroom also exists for retrieval and localization). We release code, data, and models at http://visualabduction.com/.

2 Related Work

Abductive Reasoning. Abduction, a form of everyday reasoning first framed byPeirce, [46,47]; involves the creating of explanatory hypothesesbased on limited evidence. Humans use abduction to reconcile seemingly disconnected observations to arrive at meaningful conclusions [56] but readily retract in presence of new evidence [1]. In linguistics, abduction for communicated meaning (in an impoverished conversational context) is systematized through conversational

---

[4] We reserve generative evaluations (e.g., BLEU/CIDEr) for future work: shortcuts (e.g., outputting the technically correct "this is a photo" for all inputs) make generation evaluation difficult in the abductive setting (see Sect. 6). Nonetheless, generative *models* can be evaluated in our setup; we experiment with one in Sect. 5.1.

maxims [15]. In images, [5] show that different object types have different like-lihoods of being mentioned in image captions (e.g., "fireworks" is always mentioned if depicted, but "fabric" is not), but that object type alone does not dictate salience for abductive inferences, e.g., a TV in a living room may not be as conceptually salient as a TV in a bar, which may signal a particular type of bar. Abductive reasoning has recently received attention in language processing tasks [6,11,45,50], proof writing [60], and discourse processing [17,42], etc.

Beyond Visual Recognition. Several tasks that go beyond image description/recognition have been proposed, including visual and analogical reasoning [3,21,43,77], scene semantics [23], commonsense interactions [49,65], temporal/causal reasoning [26,71], and perceived importance [5]. Others have explored commonsense reasoning tasks posed over videos, which usually have more input available than a single frame [12,13,19,20,31,32,34,63,74,78] (inter alia).

Visual Abductive Reasoning. Sherlock builds upon prior grounded visual abductive reasoning efforts (Table 1). Corpora like Visual Commonsense Reasoning (VCR) [75], VisualCOMET [44], and Visual7W [79] are most similar to **Sherlock** in providing benchmarks for rationale-based inferences (i.e., the why and how). But, **Sherlock** differs in format and content (Fig. 2). Instead of annotated QA pairs like in [75,79] where one option is definitively correct, free-text clue/inference pairs allow for broader types of image descriptions, lending itself to softer and richer notions of reasoning (see Sect. 4)—inferences are not definitively correct vs. incorrect, rather, they span a range of plausibility. Deviating from the constrained, human-centric annotation of [44], **Sherlock** clue/inference pairs support a broader range of topics via our open-ended annotation paradigm (see Sect. 3). **Sherlock**'s inferences can be grounded on any number of visual objects in an image, from figures central to the image (e.g., persons, animals, objects) to background cues (e.g., time, location, circumstances).

3   Sherlock Corpus

The **Sherlock** corpus contains a total of 363 K abductive commonsense inferences grounded in 81 K Visual Genome [29] images (photographs from Flickr) and 22 K Visual Commonsense Reasoning (VCR) [75] images (still-frames from movies). Images have an average of 3.5 OBSERVATION PAIRS, each consisting of:

- **clue**: an observable entity or object in the image, along with bounding box(es) specifying it (e.g., "people wearing nametags").
- **inference**: an abductive inference associated with the clue; not immediately obvious from the image content (e.g., "the people don't know each other").

Both clues and inferences are represented via free text in English; both have an average length of seven tokens; per clue, there are a mean/median of 1.17/1.0 bounding boxes per clue. We divide the 103 K annotated images into a training/validation/test set of 90 K/6.6 K/6.6 K. Further details are available in §A.

Annotation Process. We crowdsource our dataset via Amazon Mechanical Turk (MTurk). For each data collection HIT, a manually qualified worker is given an image and prompted for 3 to 5 OBSERVATION PAIRS. For each OBSERVATION PAIR, the worker is asked to write a clue, highlight the regions in the image corresponding to the clue, and write an inference triggered by the clue. To discourage purely deductive reasoning, the workers are actively encouraged to think beyond the literally depicted scene, while working within real-world expectations. Crowdworkers also self-report Likert ratings of confidence in the correctness of their abductive inferences along a scale of "definitely" = 3/3, "likely" = 2/3, and "possibly" = 1/3. The resulting inferences span this range (31%, 51%, 18%, respectively). To validate corpus quality, we run a validation round for 17K OBSERVATION PAIRS in which crowdworkers provide ratings for *acceptability* (is the annotation reasonable?), *bboxes* (are the boxes reasonably placed for the clue?), and *interestingness* (how interesting is the annotation?). We find that 97.5% of the OBSERVATION PAIRS are acceptable with 98.3% accurate box placement; and 71.9% of inferences are found to be interesting.

3.1 Dataset Exploration

Sherlock's abductive inferences cover a wide variety of real world experiences from observations about unseen yet probable details of the image (e.g., "smoke at an outdoor gathering" → "something is being grilled") to elaborations on the expected social context (e.g., "people wearing nametags" → "[they] don't know each other"). Some inferences are highly likely to be true (e.g., "wet pavement" → "it has rained recently"); others are less definitively verifiable, but nonetheless plausible (e.g., "large trash containers" → "there is a business nearby"). Even the inferences crowdworkers specify as 3/3 confident are almost always abductive, e.g., wet pavement strongly but not always indicate rain. Through a rich array of natural observations, **Sherlock** provides a tangible view into the abductive inferences people use on an everyday basis (more examples in Fig. 7).

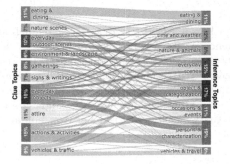

Fig. 3. Overview of the topics represented in the clues and inferences in **Sherlock**. This analysis shows that **Sherlock** covers a variety of topics commonly accessible in the natural world. Color of the connections reflect the clue topic.

Assessing Topic Diversity. To gauge the diversity of objects and situations represented in **Sherlock**, we run an LDA topic model [7] over the OBSERVATION PAIRS. The topics span a range of common everyday objects, entities, and situations (Fig. 3). Inference topics associated with the clues include within-category associations (e.g., "baked potatoes on a ceramic plate" → "this [is] a side dish") and cross-category associations (e.g., "a nametag" (attire) → "she works here" (characterization)). Many topics are not human centric; compared to VCR/VisualCOMET in which 94%/100% of grounded references are to people. A manual analysis of 150 clues reveals that only 36% of **Sherlock** OBSERVATION PAIRS are grounded on people.

Intended Use Cases. We manually examine of 250 randomly sampled OBSERVATION PAIRS to better understand how annotators referenced protected characteristics (e.g., gender, color, nationality). A majority of inferences (243/250) are not directly about protected characteristics, though, a perceived gender is often made explicit via pronoun usage, e.g., "she is running". As an additional check, we pass 30 K samples of our corpus through the Perspective API[5]. A manual examination of 150 cases marked as "most toxic" reveals mostly false positives (89%), though 11% of this sample do contain lewd content (mostly prompted by visual content in the R-rated VCR movies) or stigmas related to, e.g., gender and weight. See §A.4 for a more complete discussion.

While our analysis suggests that the relative magnitude of potentially offensive content is low in **Sherlock**, *we still advocate against deployed use-cases that*

(a) Retrieval of abductive inferences   (b) Localization of evidence   (c) Comparison of plausibility

Fig. 4. We pose three tasks over **Sherlock**: In *retrieval*, models are tasked with finding the ground-truth inference across a wide range of inferences, some much more plausible/relevant than others. In *localization*, models must align regions within the same image to several inferences written about that image. For *comparison*, we collect 19 K Likert ratings from human raters across plausible candidates, and models are evaluated in their capacity to reconstruct human judgments across the candidates. Despite intrinsic subjectivity, headroom exists between human agreement and model performance, e.g., on the *comparison* task.

---

[5] https://www.perspectiveapi.com/; November 2021 version. The API (which itself is imperfect and has biases [18,38,55]) assigns toxicity value 0–1 for a given input text. Toxicity is defined as "a rude, disrespectful, or unreasonable comment that is likely to make one leave a discussion".

run the risk of perpetuating potential biases: our aim is to *study* abductive reasoning without endorsing the correctness or appropriateness of particular inferences. We foresee **Sherlock** as 1) a diagnostic corpus for measuring machine capacity for visual abductive reasoning; 2) a large-scale resource to study the types of inferences people may make about images; and 3) a potentially helpful resource for building tools that require understanding *abductions* specifically, e.g., for detecting purposefully manipulative content posted online, it could be useful to specifically study what people *might assume* about an image (rather than what is objectively correct; more details in Datasheet (§F) [14]).

4   From Images to Abductive Inferences

We operationalize our corpus with three tasks, which we call retrieval, localization, and comparison. Notationally, we say that an instance within the **Sherlock** corpus consists of an image i, a region specified by N bounding boxes $r = \{\langle x_{1i}, x_{2i}, y_{1i}, y_{2i}\rangle\}_{i=1}^{N}$ [6], a clue c corresponding to a literal description of r's contents, and an in**F**erence f that an annotator associated with i, r, and c. We consider:

1. *Retrieval of Abductive Inferences:* For a given image/region pair (i, r), how well can models select the ground-truth inference f from a large set of candidates (~1 K) covering a broad swath of the corpus?
2. *Localization of Evidence:* Given an image i and an inference f written about an (unknown) region within the image, how well can models locate the proper region?
3. *Comparison of Plausibility:* Given an image/region pair (i, r) and a small set (~10) of relevant inferences, can models predict how humans will rank their plausibility?

Each task tests a complementary aspect of visual abductive reasoning (Fig. 4): retrieval tests across a broad range of inferences, localization tests within-images, and comparison tests for correlation with human judgement. Nonetheless, the same model can undertake all three tasks if it implements the following interface:

Sherlock Abductive Visual Reasoning Interface
- **Input:** An image i, a region r within i, and a candidate inference f.
- **Target:** A score s, where s is proportional to the plausibility that f could be inferred from (i, r).

That is, we assume a model $m : (i, r, f) \rightarrow \mathbb{R}$ that scores inference f's plausibility for (i, r). Notably, the interface takes as input inferences, but not clues: our intent is to focus evaluation on abductive reasoning, rather than the distinct setting of literal referring expressions[7]. Clues can be used for training m; as we will see in Sect. 5 our best performing model, in fact, does use clues at training time.

---

[6] As discussed in Sect. 3, N has a mean/median of 1.17/1.0 across the corpus.
[7] In §B.1, for completeness, we give results on the retrieval and localization setups, but testing on clues instead.

4.1 Retrieval of Abductive Inferences

For retrieval evaluation, at test time, we are given an (i, r) pair, and a large ($\sim$1 K)[8] set of candidate inferences $f \in F$, only one of which was written by an annotator for (i, r); the others are randomly sampled from the corpus. In the $im \to txt$ direction, we compute the mean rank of the true item (lower = better) and P@1 (higher = better); in the $txt \to im$ direction, we report mean rank (lower = better).

4.2 Localization of Evidence

Localization assesses a model's capacity select a regions within an image that most directly supports a given inference. Following prior work on literal referring expression localization [25,28,73] (inter alia), we experiment in two settings: 1) we are given all the ground-truth bounding boxes for an image, and 2) we are given only automatic bounding box proposals from an object detection model.

GT Bounding Boxes. We assume an image i, the set of 3+ inferences F written for that image, and the (unaligned) set of regions R corresponding to F. The model must produce a one-to-one assignment of F to R in the context of i. In practice, we score all possible $F \times R$ pairs via the abductive visual reasoning interface, and then compute the maximum linear assignment [30] using lapjv's implementation of [24]. The evaluation metric is the accuracy of this assignment, averaged over all images. To quantify an upper bound, a human rater performed the assignment for 101 images, achieving an average accuracy of 92.3%.

Auto Bounding Boxes. We compute 100 bounding box proposals per image by applying Faster-RCNN [54] with a ResNeXt101 [69] backbone trained on Visual Genome to all the images in our corpus. Given an image i and an inference f that was written about the image, we score all 100 bounding box proposals independently and take the highest scoring one as the prediction. We count a prediction as correct if it has IoU > 0.5 with a true bounding box that corresponds to that inference[9], and incorrect otherwise[10].

4.3 Comparison of Plausibility

We assess model capacity to make fine-grained assessments given a set of plausible inferences. For example, in Fig. 4c (depicting a group of men marching and carrying bags), human raters are *likely* to say that they are military men and that

---

[8] Our validation/test sets contain about 23 K inferences. For efficiency we randomly split into 23 equal sized chunks of about 1 K inferences, and report retrieval averaged over the resulting splits.

[9] Since the annotators were able to specify multiple bounding boxes per OBSERVATION PAIR, we count a match to any of the labeled bounding boxes.

[10] A small number of images do not have a ResNeXt bounding box with IoU > 0.5 with any ground truth bounding box: in Sect. 5.1, we show that most instances (96.2%) are solvable with this setup.

Table 2. Test results for all models across all three tasks. CLIP RN50 × 64 outperforms all models in all setups, but significant headroom exists, e.g., on Comparison between the model and human agreement.

	Retrieval			Localization	Comparison
	Im → txt (↓)	Txt → im (↓)	$P@1_{im \to txt}$ (↑)	GT-Box/Auto-Box (↑)	Val/Test human Acc (↑)
Random	495.4	495.4	0.1	30.0/7.9	1.1/−0.6
Bbox Position/Size	257.5	262.7	1.3	57.3/18.8	5.5/1.4
LXMERT	51.1	48.8	14.9	69.5/30.3	18.6/21.1
UNITER base	40.4	40.0	19.8	73.0/33.3	20.0/22.9
CLIP ViT-B/16	19.9	21.6	30.6	85.3/38.6	20.1/21.3
CLIP RN50 × 16	19.3	20.8	31.0	85.7/38.7	21.6/23.7
CLIP RN50 × 64	19.3	19.7	31.8	86.6/39.5	25.1/26.0
↳ + multitask clue learning	**16.4**	**17.7**	**33.4**	**87.2/40.6**	**26.6/27.1**
Human + (Upper Bound)	-	-	-	92.3/(96.2)	42.3/42.3

the photo was taken during WWII, and *unlikely* to see them as porters despite them carrying bags. Our evaluation assumes that a performant model's predictions should correlate with the (average) relative judgments made by humans, and we seek to construct a corpus that supports evaluation of such reasoning.

Constructing Sets of Plausible inferences. We use a performant model checkpoint fine-tuned for the Sherlock tasks[11] to compute the similarity score between all (i, r, f) triples in the validation/test sets. Next, we perform several filtering steps: 1) we only consider pairs where the negative inference received a higher score than the ground-truth according to the model; 2) we perform soft text deduplication to downsample inferences that are semantically similar; and 3) we perform hard text deduplication, only allowing inferences to appear verbatim 3x times. Then, through an iterative process, we uniquely sample a diverse set of 10 inferences per (i, r) that meet these filtering criteria. This results in a set of 10 plausible inference candidates for each of 485/472 validation/test images. More details are in §E. In a retrieval sense, these plausible inferences can be viewed as "hard negatives": i.e., none are the gold annotated inference, but a strong model nonetheless rates them as plausible.

Human Rating of Plausible inferences. Using MTurk, we collect two annotations of each candidate inference on a three-point Likert scale ranging from 1 (bad: "irrelevant"/"verifiably incorrect") to 3 (good: "statement is probably true; the highlighted region supports it".). We collect 19 K annotations in total (see §E for full details). Because abductive reasoning involves subjectivity and uncertainty, we expect some amount of intrinsic disagreement between raters[12]. We measure model correlation with human judgments on this set via pairwise accuracy. For each image, for all pairs of candidates that are rated differently on

---

[11] Specifically, a CLIP RN50 × 16 checkpoint that achieves strong validation retrieval performance (comparable to the checkpoint of the reported test results in Sect. 5.1); model details in Sect. 5.

[12] In Sect. 5.1, we show that models achieve significantly less correlation compared to human agreement.

the Likert scale, the model gets an accuracy point if it orders them consistently with the human rater's ordering. Ties are broken randomly but consistently across all models. For readability, we subtract the accuracy of a random model (50%) and multiply by two to form the final accuracy metric.

5   Methods and Experiments

Training Objective. To support the interface described in Sect. 4, we train models $m : (i, r, f) \rightarrow \mathbb{R}$ that score inference f's plausibility for (i, r). We experiment with several different V+L backbones as detailed below; for each, we train by optimizing model parameters to score truly corresponding (i, r, f) triples more highly than negatively sampled (i, r, f_{fake}) triples.

LXMERT [61] is a vision+language transformer [64] model pre-trained on Visual Genome [29] and MSCOCO [33]. The model is composed of three transformer encoders [64]: an object-relationship encoder (which takes in ROI features+locations with a max of 36, following [2]), a language encoder that processes word tokens, and a cross modality encoder. To provide region information r, we calculate the ROI feature of r and always place it in the first object token to the visual encoder (this is a common practice for, e.g., the VCR dataset [75]). We follow [9] to train the model in "image-text retrieval" mode by maximizing the margin $m = .2$ between the cosine similarity scores of positive triple (i, r, f) and two negative triples (i, r, f_{fake}) and (i_{fake}, r_{fake}, f) through triplet loss.

UNITER [9] consists of a single, unified transformer that takes in image and text embeddings. We experiment with the Base version pre-trained on MSCOCO [33], Visual Genome [29], Conceptual Captions [57], and SBU Captions [41]. We apply the same strategy of region-of-reference-first passing and train with the same triplet loss following [9].

CLIP. We finetune the ViT-B/16, RN50 × 16, and RN50 × 50 versions of CLIP [51]. Text is represented via a 12-layer text transformer. For ViT-B/16, images are represented by a 12-layer vision transformer [10], whereas for RN50 × 16/RN50 × 64, images are represented by EfficientNet-scaled ResNet50 [16,62].

We modify CLIP to incorporate the bounding box as input. Inspired by a similar process from [70,76], to pass a region to CLIP, we simply draw a bounding box on an image in pixel space—we use a green-bordered / opaque purple box as depicted in Fig. 5b (early experiments proved this more effective than modifying CLIP's architecture). To enable CLIP to process the widescreen images of VCR, we apply it twice to the input using overlapping square regions, i.e., graphically, like this: $[_1[_2]_1]_2$, and average the resulting embeddings. We finetune using InfoNCE [40,59]. We sample a batch of truly corresponding (i, r, f) triples, render the regions r in their corresponding images, and then construct all possible negative (i, r, f_{fake}) triples in the batch by aligning each inference to each (i, r). We use the biggest minibatch size possible using 8 GPUs with

48GB of memory each: 64, 200, and 512 for RN50 × 64, RN50 × 16, and ViT-B/16, respectively.

Multitask Learning. All models thus far only utilize inferences at training time. We experiment with a multitask learning setup using CLIP that additionally trains with clues. In addition to training using our abductive reasoning objective, i.e., InfoNCE on inferences, we mix in an additional referring expression objective, i.e., InfoNCE on clues. Evaluation remains the same: at test time, we do not assume access to clues. At training time, for each observation, half the time we sample an inference (to form (i, r, f), and half the time we sample a clue (to form (i, r, c)). The clue/inference mixed batch of examples is then handed to CLIP, and a gradient update is made with InfoNCE as usual. To enable to model to differentiate between clues/inferences, we prefix the texts with clue:/inference:, respectively.

Baselines. In addition to a random baseline, we consider a content-free version of our CLIP ViT-B/16 model that is given only the position/size of each bounding box. In place of the image, we pass a mean pixel value across the entire image and draw the bounding box on the image using an opaque pink box (see Sect. 5.2).

5.1 Results

Table 2 contains results for all the tasks: In all cases, our CLIP-based models perform best, with RN50 × 64 outperforming its smaller counterparts. Incorporating the multitask objective pushes performance further. While CLIP performs the best, UNITER is more competitive on comparison and less competi-

	$P@1$ (↑)	Val/Test Human (↑)
CLIP ViT-B/16	30.5	20.1/21.2
↳ Position only	1.3	5.5/1.4
↳ No Region	18.1	16.8/19.0
↳ No Context	24.8	18.1/17.8
↳ Only context	18.9	17.4/16.3
↳ Trained w/ only Clues	23.0	16.2/19.7
↳ Crop no Widescreen	27.8	23.1/21.8
↳ Resize no Widescreen	27.7	19.4/20.6
↳ Zero shot w/ prompt	12.0	10.0/9.5

(a)

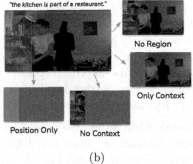

(b)

Fig. 5. We perform ablations by varying the input data, top (a), and the modeling components, bottom (a). Figure (b) depicts our image input ablations, which are conducted by drawing in pixel-space directly, following [76]. Having no context may make it difficult to situate the scene more broadly; here: neatly stacked cups could be in a bar, a hotel, a store, etc. Access only the context of the dining room is also insufficient. For modeling, bottom (a), cropping/resizing decreases performance on retrieval ($P@1$), but not comparison (Val/Test Human).

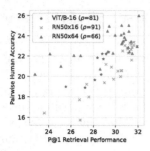

Fig. 6. Validation retrieval perf. ($P@1$) vs. comparison acc. for CLIP checkpoints.

Fig. 7. Error analysis: examples of false positives and false negatives predicted by our model on the comparison task's validation set.

tive on retrieval and localization. We speculate this has to do with the nature of each task: retrieval requires models to reason about many incorrect examples, whereas, the inferences in the comparison task are usually relevant to the objects in the scene. In §C, we provide ablations that demonstrate CLIP models outperform UNITER even when trained with a smaller batch size. Compared to human agreement on comparison, our best model only gets 65% of the way there (27% vs. 42 %).

5.2   Ablations

We perform data and model ablations on CLIP `ViT-B/16`. Results are in Fig. 5.

Input Ablations. Each part of our visual input is important. Aside from the position only model, the biggest drop-off in performance results from not passing the region as input to CLIP, e.g., $P@1$ for $im \rightarrow txt$ retrieval nearly halves, dropping from 31 to 18, suggesting that CLIP relies on the local region information to reason about the image. Removing the region's content ("Only Context") unsurprisingly hurts performance, but so does removing the surrounding context ("No Context"). That is, the model performs the best when it can reason about the clue and its full visual context jointly. On the text side, we trained a model with only clues; retrieval and comparison performance both drop, which suggests that clues and inferences carry different information (additional results in §B.1).

Model Ablations. We considered two alternate image processing configurations. Instead of doing two CLIP passes per image to facilitate widescreen processing (Sect. 5), we consider (i) center cropping and (ii) pad-and-resizing. Both take less computation, but provide less information to the model. Cropping removes the sides of images, whereas pad-and-resize lowers the resolution significantly. The bottom half of the table in Fig. 5 reports the results: both configurations lower performance on retrieval tasks, but there's less impact for comparison.

Better retrieval $\rightarrow$ better comparison. In Fig. 6, we observe a high correlation between the retrieval performance of our (single-task) CLIP model checkpoints ($P@1$) and the comparison human accuracy for the comparison task. For the smaller RN50 × 16 and ViT-B/16 models, this effect cannot simply be explained by training time; for RN50 × 16, pearson corr. between training steps and comparison performance is 81, whereas, the correlation between $P@1$ and comparison performance is 91. Overall, it's plausible that a model with higher precision at retrieval could help further bridge the gap on the comparison task.

Oracle Text-Only Models are Insufficient. One potential concern with our setup is that clues may map one-to-one onto inferences, e.g., if all soccer balls in our corpus were mapped onto "the owner plays soccer" (and vice versa). We compare to an oracle baseline that makes this pessimistic assumption (complementing our "No Context" ablation, which provides a comparable context-free *visual* reference to the clue). We give the model oracle access to the ground-truth clues. Following [6], we use T5-Large v1.1 [52] to map clues to inferences with no access to the image by fitting $P(\text{inference}|\text{clue})$ in a sequence-to-sequence fashion; training details are in §B. The resulting text-only clue → inference model, when given the clue *"chipped paint and rusted umbrella poles"*, estimates likely inferences, for example: *"the area is in a disrepair"*, *"the city does not care about its infrastructure".*, etc. The text-only oracle under-performs vs. CLIP *despite the fact that, unlike CLIP, it's given the ground-truth clue*: on comparison, it achieves 22.8/19.3 val/test accuracy; significantly lower than 26.6/27.1 that our best vision+language model achieves. This is probably because global scene context cannot be fully summarized via a local referring expression. In the prior *"chipped paint and rusted umbrella poles"* example, the true inference, *"this beach furniture does not get put inside at night"*, requires additional visual context beyond the clue—chipped paint and a rusty umbrella alone may not provide enough context to infer that this furniture is *beach* furniture.

5.3   Error Analysis

We conduct a quantitative error analysis of multitask CLIP RN50 × 64 for the comparison task. We select 340 validation images with highest human agreement, and split images into two groups: one where the model performed above average, and one where the model performed below average. We attempt to predict into which group an image will fall using logistic regression in 5-fold cross-validation. Overall, errors are difficult to predict. Surface level image/text features of the images/inferences are not very predictive of errors: relative to a 50% ROC AUC baseline, CLIP ViT-B/16 image features achieve 55%, whereas the mean SentenceBERT [53] embedding of the inference achieves 54%. While not available *a priori*, more predictive than content features of model errors are human Likert ratings: a single-feature mean human agreement model achieves 57% AUC, (more human agreement = better model performance).

Figure 7 gives qualitative examples of false positives/negatives. The types of abductive reasoning the model falls short on are diverse. In the boat example, the model fails to notice that a florist has set up shop on a ship deck; in the window example, the model misinterprets the bars over the windows as being *outside* the building versus inside and attached to a bed-frame. The model is capable of reading some simple signs, but, as highlighted by [37], reasoning about the semantics of written text placed in images remains a challenge, e.g., a "no parking" sign is misidentified as an "okay to park" sign. Overall: the difficult-to-categorize nature of these examples suggests that the **Sherlock** corpus makes for difficult benchmark for visual abductive reasoning.

6   Conclusion

We introduce **Sherlock**, a corpus of visual abductive reasoning containing 363 K clue/inference OBSERVATION PAIRS across 103 K images. Our work complements existing abductive reasoning corpora, both in format (free-viewing, free-text) and in diversity (not human-centric). Our work not only provides a challenging vision+language benchmark, but also, we hope it can serve as a resource for studying visual abductive reasoning more broadly. Future work includes:

1. Salience: in **Sherlock**, annotators specify salient clues; how/why does salience differ from other free-viewing setups, like image captioning?
2. Ambiguity: when/why do people (justifiably) come to different conclusions?
3. Generative evaluation metrics: generation evaluation in abductive setting, i.e., without definitive notions of correctness, remains a challenge.

Acknowledgments. This work was funded by DARPA MCS program through NIWC Pacific (N66001-19-2-4031), the DARPA SemaFor program, and the Allen Institute for AI. AR was additionally in part supported by the DARPA PTG program, as well as BAIR's industrial alliance program. We additionally thank the UC Berkeley Semafor group for the helpful discussions and feedback.

References

1. Aliseda, A.: The logic of abduction: an introduction. In: Magnani, L., Bertolotti, T. (eds.) Springer Handbook of Model-Based Science. SH, pp. 219–230. Springer, Cham (2017). https://doi.org/10.1007/978-3-319-30526-4_10
2. Anderson, P., et al.: Bottom-up and top-down attention for image captioning and visual question answering. In: CVPR (2018)
3. Antol, S., et al.: VQA: visual question answering. In: ICCV (2015)
4. Bender, E.M., Friedman, B.: Data statements for natural language processing: toward mitigating system bias and enabling better science. TACL **6**, 587–604 (2018)
5. Berg, A.C., et al.: Understanding and predicting importance in images. In: CVPR (2012)
6. Bhagavatula, C., et al.: Abductive commonsense reasoning. In: ICLR (2020)
7. Blei, D.M., Ng, A.Y., Jordan, M.I.: Latent dirichlet allocation. JMLR **3**, 993–1022 (2003)
8. Carson, D.: The abduction of sherlock holmes. Int. J. Police Sci. Manage. **11**(2), 193–202 (2009)

9. Chen, Y.-C., Li, L., Yu, L., El Kholy, A., Ahmed, F., Gan, Z., Cheng, Yu., Liu, J.: UNITER: UNiversal image-TExt representation learning. In: Vedaldi, A., Bischof, H., Brox, T., Frahm, J.-M. (eds.) ECCV 2020. LNCS, vol. 12375, pp. 104–120. Springer, Cham (2020). https://doi.org/10.1007/978-3-030-58577-8_7

10. Dosovitskiy, A., et al.: An image is worth 16 × 16 words: transformers for image recognition at scale. In: ICLR (2021)

11. Du, L., Ding, X., Liu, T., Qin, B.: Learning event graph knowledge for abductive reasoning. In: ACL (2021)

12. Fang, Z., Gokhale, T., Banerjee, P., Baral, C., Yang, Y.: Video2Commonsense: generating commonsense descriptions to enrich video captioning. In: EMNLP (2020)

13. Garcia, N., Otani, M., Chu, C., Nakashima, Y.: KnowIT vqa: answering knowledge-based questions about videos. In: AAAI (2020)

14. Gebru, T., et al.: Datasheets for datasets. Commun. ACM **64**(12), 86–92 (2021)

15. Grice, H.P.: Logic and conversation. In: Speech Acts, pp. 41–58. Brill (1975)

16. He, K., Zhang, X., Ren, S., Sun, J.: Deep residual learning for image recognition. In: CVPR (2016)

17. Hobbs, J.R., Stickel, M.E., Appelt, D.E., Martin, P.: Interpretation as abduction. Artif. Intell. **63**(1–2), 69–142 (1993)

18. Hosseini, H., Kannan, S., Zhang, B., Poovendran, R.: Deceiving google's perspective api built for detecting toxic comments. arXiv preprint arXiv:1702.08138 (2017)

19. Ignat, O., Castro, S., Miao, H., Li, W., Mihalcea, R.: WhyAct: identifying action reasons in lifestyle vlogs. In: EMNLP (2021)

20. Jang, Y., Song, Y., Yu, Y., Kim, Y., Kim, G.: Tgif-QA: toward spatio-temporal reasoning in visual question answering. In: CVPR (2017)

21. Johnson, J., Hariharan, B., Van Der Maaten, L., Fei-Fei, L., Lawrence Zitnick, C., Girshick, R.: Clevr: a diagnostic dataset for compositional language and elementary visual reasoning. In: CVPR (2017)

22. Johnson, J., Karpathy, A., Fei-Fei, L.: Densecap: fully convolutional localization networks for dense captioning. In: CVPR (2016)

23. Johnson, J., et al.: Image retrieval using scene graphs. In: CVPR (2015)

24. Jonker, R., Volgenant, A.: A shortest augmenting path algorithm for dense and sparse linear assignment problems. Computing **38**(4), 325–340 (1987). https://doi.org/10.1007/BF02278710

25. Kazemzadeh, S., Ordonez, V., Matten, M., Berg, T.: ReferItGame: referring to objects in photographs of natural scenes. In: EMNLP (2014)

26. Kim, H., Zala, A., Bansal, M.: CoSIm: commonsense reasoning for counterfactual scene imagination. In: NAACL (2022)

27. Kingma, D.P., Ba, J.: Adam: a method for stochastic optimization. arXiv preprint arXiv:1412.6980 (2014)

28. Krahmer, E., Van Deemter, K.: Computational generation of referring expressions: a survey. Comput. Linguist. **38**(1), 173–218 (2012)

29. Krishna, R., et al.: Visual genome: connecting language and vision using crowd-sourced dense image annotations. In: IJCV (2016). https://doi.org/10.1007/S11263-016-0981-7

30. Kuhn, H.W.: The hungarian method for the assignment problem. Naval Res. Logistics Q. **2**(1–2), 83–97 (1955)

31. Lei, J., Yu, L., Berg, T.L., Bansal, M.: TVQA+: spatio-temporal grounding for video question answering. In: ACL (2020)

32. Lei, J., Yu, L., Berg, T.L., Bansal, M.: What is more likely to happen next? video-and-language future event prediction. In: EMNLP (2020)

33. Lin, T.Y., et al.: Microsoft COCO: common objects in context. In: ECCV (2014)
34. Liu, J., et al.: Violin: a large-scale dataset for video-and-language inference. In: CVPR (2020)
35. Loshchilov, I., Hutter, F.: Decoupled weight decay regularization. In: ICLR (2019)
36. Marino, K., Rastegari, M., Farhadi, A., Mottaghi, R.: OK-VQA: a visual question answering benchmark requiring external knowledge. In: CVPR (2019)
37. Mishra, A., Shekhar, S., Singh, A.K., Chakraborty, A.: OCR-VQA: visual question answering by reading text in images. In: ICDAR (2019)
38. Mitchell, M., et al.: Model cards for model reporting. In: FAccT (2019)
39. Niiniluoto, I.: Defending abduction. Philos. Sci. **66**, S436–S451 (1999)
40. Oord, A.V.D., Li, Y., Vinyals, O.: Representation learning with contrastive predictive coding. arXiv preprint arXiv:1807.03748 (2018)
41. Ordonez, V., Kulkarni, G., Berg, T.L.: Im2text: describing images using 1 million captioned photographs. In: NeurIPS (2011)
42. Ovchinnikova, E., Montazeri, N., Alexandrov, T., Hobbs, J.R., McCord, M.C., Mulkar-Mehta, R.: Abductive reasoning with a large knowledge base for discourse processing. In: IWCS (2011)
43. Park, D.H., Darrell, T., Rohrbach, A.: Robust change captioning. In: ICCV (2019)
44. Park, J.S., Bhagavatula, C., Mottaghi, R., Farhadi, A., Choi, Y.: VisualCOMET: reasoning about the dynamic context of a still image. In: Vedaldi, A., Bischof, H., Brox, T., Frahm, J.-M. (eds.) ECCV 2020. LNCS, vol. 12350, pp. 508–524. Springer, Cham (2020). https://doi.org/10.1007/978-3-030-58558-7_30
45. Paul, D., Frank, A.: Generating hypothetical events for abductive inference. In: *SEM (2021)
46. Peirce, C.S.: Philosophical Writings of Peirce, vol. 217. Courier Corporation (1955)
47. Peirce, C.S.: Pragmatism and Pragmaticism, vol. 5. Belknap Press of Harvard University Press (1965)
48. Pezzelle, S., Greco, C., Gandolfi, G., Gualdoni, E., Bernardi, R.: Be different to be better! a benchmark to leverage the complementarity of language and vision. In: Findings of EMNLP (2020)
49. Pirsiavash, H., Vondrick, C., Torralba, A.: Inferring the why in images. Technical report (2014)
50. Qin, L., et al.: Back to the future: unsupervised backprop-based decoding for counterfactual and abductive commonsense reasoning. In: EMNLP (2020)
51. Radford, A., et al.: Learning transferable visual models from natural language supervision. arXiv preprint arXiv:2103.00020 (2021)
52. Raffel, C., et al.: Exploring the limits of transfer learning with a unified text-to-text transformer. In: JMLR (2020)
53. Reimers, N., Gurevych, I.: Sentence-bert: sentence embeddings using siamese bert-networks. In: EMNLP (2019)
54. Ren, S., He, K., Girshick, R., Sun, J.: Faster R-CNN: towards real-time object detection with region proposal networks. In: NeurIPS (2015)
55. Sap, M., Card, D., Gabriel, S., Choi, Y., Smith, N.A.: The risk of racial bias in hate speech detection. In: ACL (2019)
56. Shank, G.: The extraordinary ordinary powers of abductive reasoning. Theor. Psychol. **8**(6), 841–860 (1998)
57. Sharma, P., Ding, N., Goodman, S., Soricut, R.: Conceptual captions: a cleaned, hypernymed, image alt-text dataset for automatic image captioning. In: ACL (2018)
58. Shazeer, N., Stern, M.: Adafactor: adaptive learning rates with sublinear memory cost. In: ICML (2018)

59. Sohn, K.: Improved deep metric learning with multi-class n-pair loss objective. In: NeurIPS (2016)
60. Tafjord, O., Mishra, B.D., Clark, P.: ProofWriter: generating implications, proofs, and abductive statements over natural language. In: Findings of ACL (2021)
61. Tan, H., Bansal, M.: LXMERT: learning cross-modality encoder representations from transformers. In: EMNLP (2019)
62. Tan, M., Le, Q.: Efficientnet: rethinking model scaling for convolutional neural networks. In: ICML (2019)
63. Tapaswi, M., Zhu, Y., Stiefelhagen, R., Torralba, A., Urtasun, R., Fidler, S.: MovieQA: understanding stories in movies through question-answering. In: CVPR (2016)
64. Vaswani, A., et al.: Attention is all you need. In: NeurIPS (2017)
65. Vedantam, R., Lin, X., Batra, T., Zitnick, C.L., Parikh, D.: Learning common sense through visual abstraction. In: ICCV (2015)
66. Wang, P., Wu, Q., Shen, C., Dick, A., Van Den Hengel, A.: FVQA: fact-based visual question answering. TPAMI **40**(10), 2413–2427 (2017)
67. Wang, P., Wu, Q., Shen, C., Hengel, A.V.D., Dick, A.: Explicit knowledge-based reasoning for visual question answering. In: IJCAI (2017)
68. Wolf, T., et al.: Transformers: state-of-the-art natural language processing. In: EMNLP: System Demonstrations (2020)
69. Xie, S., Girshick, R., Dollár, P., Tu, Z., He, K.: Aggregated residual transformations for deep neural networks. In: CVPR (2017)
70. Yao, Y., Zhang, A., Zhang, Z., Liu, Z., Chua, T.S., Sun, M.: CPT: colorful prompt tuning for pre-trained vision-language models. arXiv preprint arXiv:2109.11797 (2021)
71. Yi, K., et al.: CLEVRER: collision events for video representation and reasoning. In: ICLR (2020)
72. Yu, L., Park, E., Berg, A.C., Berg, T.L.: Visual Madlibs: fill in the blank image generation and question answering. In: ICCV (2015)
73. Yu, L., Poirson, P., Yang, S., Berg, A.C., Berg, T.L.: Modeling context in referring expressions. In: Leibe, B., Matas, J., Sebe, N., Welling, M. (eds.) ECCV 2016. LNCS, vol. 9906, pp. 69–85. Springer, Cham (2016). https://doi.org/10.1007/978-3-319-46475-6_5
74. Zadeh, A., Chan, M., Liang, P.P., Tong, E., Morency, L.P.: Social-iq: a question answering benchmark for artificial social intelligence. In: CVPR (2019)
75. Zellers, R., Bisk, Y., Farhadi, A., Choi, Y.: From recognition to cognition: Visual commonsense reasoning. In: CVPR (2019)
76. Zellers, R., et al.: MERLOT: multimodal neural script knowledge models. In: NeurIPS (2021)
77. Zhang, C., Gao, F., Jia, B., Zhu, Y., Zhu, S.C.: Raven: a dataset for relational and analogical visual reasoning. In: CVPR (2019)
78. Zhang, H., Huo, Y., Zhao, X., Song, Y., Roth, D.: Learning contextual causality from time-consecutive images. In: CVPR Workshops (2021)
79. Zhu, Y., Groth, O., Bernstein, M., Fei-Fei, L.: Visual7W: grounded question answering in images. In: CVPR (2016)

Speaker-Adaptive Lip Reading with User-Dependent Padding

Minsu Kim[ID], Hyunjun Kim[ID], and Yong Man Ro[✉][ID]

Image and Video Systems Lab, School of Electrical Engineering, KAIST,
Daejeon, South Korea
{ms.k,kimhj709,ymro}@kaist.ac.kr

Abstract. Lip reading aims to predict speech based on lip movements alone. As it focuses on visual information to model the speech, its performance is inherently sensitive to personal lip appearances and movements. This makes the lip reading models show degraded performance when they are applied to unseen speakers due to the mismatch between training and testing conditions. Speaker adaptation technique aims to reduce this mismatch between train and test speakers, thus guiding a trained model to focus on modeling the speech content without being intervened by the speaker variations. In contrast to the efforts made in audio-based speech recognition for decades, the speaker adaptation methods have not well been studied in lip reading. In this paper, to remedy the performance degradation of lip reading model on unseen speakers, we propose a speaker-adaptive lip reading method, namely user-dependent padding. The user-dependent padding is a speaker-specific input that can participate in the visual feature extraction stage of a pre-trained lip reading model. Therefore, the lip appearances and movements information of different speakers can be considered during the visual feature encoding, adaptively for individual speakers. Moreover, the proposed method does not need 1) any additional layers, 2) to modify the learned weights of the pre-trained model, and 3) the speaker label of train data used during pre-train. It can directly adapt to unseen speakers by learning the user-dependent padding only, in a supervised or unsupervised manner. Finally, to alleviate the speaker information insufficiency in public lip reading databases, we label the speaker of a well-known audio-visual database, LRW, and design an unseen-speaker lip reading scenario named LRW-ID. The effectiveness of the proposed method is verified on sentence- and word-level lip reading, and we show it can further improve the performance of a well-trained model with large speaker variations.

Keywords: Visual speech recognition · Lip reading · Speaker-adaptive training · Speaker adaptation · User-dependent padding · LRW-ID

Supplementary Information The online version contains supplementary material available at https://doi.org/10.1007/978-3-031-20059-5_33.

1   Introduction

Lip reading, also known as Visual Speech Recognition (VSR), aims to predict what a person is saying based on visual information alone. It has drawn big attention with its beneficial applications, such as speech recognition under a noisy environment, extracting speech of target speaker from multi-speaker over-lapped speech, and conversation with people who cannot make a voice. With the great development of deep learning and the availability of large-scale audio-visual databases [4,10,11,13,61], many efforts have been made to improve lip reading performance. Architectural improvements of deep neural network are made by [3,9,38,47,50], pre-training schemes are introduced by [12,37], and coupling audio modal knowledge into lip reading is performed by [5,26,27,29,48,66].

It is widely known that speech recognition techniques, including both audio-based Automatic Speech Recognition (ASR) and lip reading, show degraded performance when they are applied on unseen speakers due to the mismatch between train and test data distributions [9,17,31]. Speaker adaptation technique aims to narrow this mismatch by fitting a trained speech recognition model to unseen test speakers to improve performances during test time. With its practical importance, speaker adaptation has been an important research topic in ASR for decades [7,24,31,41,42,45,59]. They attempt to optimize the speech recognition performance by transforming pre-trained models to well operate on one particular speaker or modifying the encoded features to match the pre-trained model, by using a small amount of adaptation data. For example, previous works [1,2,42,59] showed that providing speaker-specific input as hints for the input speaker to the ASR model is beneficial in adapting the trained model to an unseen speaker.

However, in contrast to the efforts in ASR, speaker adaptation methods have not been well addressed in lip reading. Since different speakers show varying lip appearances and movements, it is also important in lip reading to adaptively encode the lips of different speakers to achieve robust performance. As lip reading handles lip movement video which is higher-dimensional than audio (*i.e.*, composed of both spatial and temporal dimensions), encoding spatio-temporal information to be aware of the displacement of lips and their movement is important for accurate recognition. To this end, visual features are usually extracted using 2D or 3D Convolutional Neural Network (CNN) to achieve high recognition performance [9,46], compared to the discriminative audio features that are relatively easily obtained by transforming the raw audio into Mel-Frequency Cepstral Coefficient (MFCC) or Mel-spectrogram in ASR. Due to the different characteristics of modalities and feature extraction methods, the speaker adaptation methods of ASR might be less effective when they are directly applied to lip reading. Therefore, a speaker adaptation method suitable for lip reading, which can jointly consider the spatial information of visual features during adaptation is required. One main impediment in developing speaker-adaptive lip reading is the lack of speaker information in public databases. Usually, publicly available large-scale lip reading databases [10,11,61] have no speaker information and have overlapped speakers between train and test splits, which makes it hard to investigate the effect of speaker variations in lip reading. Therefore, a large-scale lip reading database with speaker information, beyond the constrained databases [13,65], is needed for the future research.

In this paper, we propose a speaker-adaptive training method for lip reading by introducing an additional speaker-specific input, namely user-dependent padding. The proposed user-dependent padding is for narrowing the data distribution gap between training speakers and the target test speaker. Distinct to the previous methods of using speaker-specific inputs in ASR that modified the extracted feature by introducing additional layers [1,2,42,59], the proposed user-dependent padding participates in the visual feature extraction stage so that the personal lip appearances and movements can be jointly considered during the feature encoding. Moreover, it can interact with pre-trained weights without the necessity of additional network parameters or finetuning the network. This has the advantage of simple adaptation steps of directly adaptable from a pre-trained model, while the previous works [1,2,42,59] need to train a speech recognition model that attached an adaptation network. Finally, the user-dependent padding is optimized for each target speaker, so it can achieve the optimal performance for each speaker with one pre-trained lip reading model.

Specifically, we replace the padding of convolution layers in the pre-trained lip reading model with the proposed user-dependent padding so that the additional speaker-specific input can interact with the learned convolution filter without modifying the architecture and weight parameters. By doing this, we can naturally achieve a strong regularization effect by maintaining the pre-trained weight, whereas previous works [34,63] tried with regularization loss to retain the learned model knowledge. Finally, to remedy the speaker information insufficient problem in large-scale lip reading databases, we label and provide speaker identity of a popular audio-visual dataset, LRW [11], obtained in the wild environment, and name LRW-ID to distinguish it from the original seen-speaker setting of LRW. The effectiveness of the proposed method is verified on GRID [13] and the newly designed unseen-speaker lip reading scenario of LRW-ID.

The main contributions of the paper are as follows, 1) we propose a novel speaker-adaptive lip reading framework which utilizes user-dependent padding. User-dependent padding has a negligible number of parameters compared to that of the model and can improve the lip reading performance for each target speaker, adaptively. Moreover, it does not require any additional network and finetuning of the pre-trained model, 2) to the best of our knowledge, this is the first work to investigate the speaker-adaptive lip reading on a large-scale database obtained in the wild. To this end, we label the speaker information of a well-known large-scale audio-visual database, LRW, and build a new unseen-speaker lip reading setting named LRW-ID, and 3) compared to the previous speaker-adaptive and -independent speech recognition methods, we set new state-of-the-art performances and show the proposed method is close to practical usage.

2 Related Work

2.1 Lip Reading

Lip reading is a task of recognizing speech by watching lip movements only, which is regarded as one of the challenging problems. With the great development of deep learning, many research efforts have been made to improve the performance of lip reading [23,28,43,44]. In word-level lip reading, [50] constructed an architecture consists of a 3D convolution layer and 2D ResNet [22] as a front-end and LSTM as a back-end. Some studies [56,57] proposed two-stream networks to better capture the lip movements by using the raw video and the optical flow. Recent work [38] improved the temporal encoding with Multi-Scale Temporal Convolutional Network (MS-TCN). In sentence-level lip reading, [9] proposed an end-to-end model that trained with Connectionist Temporal Classification (CTC) [20] loss. [10] developed lip reading based on Seq2Seq architecture [51]. Further architectural improvement was made by [3] using Transformer [54]. Some studies have focused on bringing audio modal knowledge into visual modality [5,27,48,66]. They successfully complemented the insufficient speech information of lip video with the rich audio knowledge. For example, [26,29] proposed Visual-Audio Memory that can recall the audio features with just using the input video. Finally, [12,37] proposed methods of pre-training the network in a self-supervised manner and showed promising results in lip reading.

Even with the successful development of the lip reading techniques, the speaker dependency of learned model has not been well studied. Since different speakers have different lip appearances and movements, applying a trained lip reading model to an unseen speaker can show degraded performance [9]. To effectively utilize the trained model without performance degradation, a method of speaker adaptation should be developed. In this paper, we investigate the speaker dependency of a pre-trained lip reading model and propose a speaker-adaptive lip reading method that can effectively adapt to an unseen speaker.

2.2 Speaker Adaptation

Speaker adaptation technique has been mainly developed in the area of audio-based Automatic Speech Recognition (ASR). [35] examined finetuning the different parts of the model how affects the performance. However, the finetuning methods are easily suffer from the overfitting problem, especially with a small number of adaptation data. To handle this, [63] tried to prevent the model from overfitting by regularizing the adaptation. Some works [33,49] tried to augments the speech recognition model with additional speaker-dependent layers. In [52], a speaker dependent vector is added to every hidden layer of the trained speech recognition model and adapted on the test speaker. In recent, using meta-learning [31] and generation [24] based methods were proposed.

In other approaches, some works proposed providing additional speaker-specific inputs to the model for adapting the trained model to unseen speakers. [42] proposed to utilize i-vectors [14] extracted at the speaker level to suppress the speaker variance. With an adaptation network, the i-vectors are converted

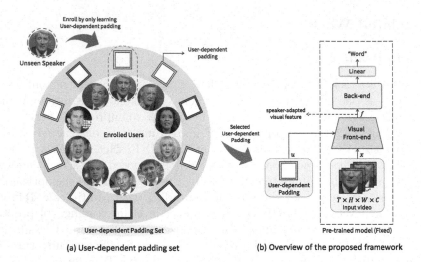

(a) User-dependent padding set   (b) Overview of the proposed framework

Fig. 1. Overview of the proposed framework. (a) When an unseen speaker is coming, the proposed framework can enroll the speaker by learning user-dependent padding only. (b) By using the user-dependent padding matched to the input speaker, lip reading model can adaptively encode the visual features and achieve improved performance

to speaker-specific shifts that will be added to the original acoustic features. In [1,2,59], they proposed speaker-specific inputs, named speaker code, which can be learned during the adaptation for each speaker. They have the advantage of adapting large-size models using only a few adaptation data. However, as they require additional layers to encode the speaker code, they need to train the additional layers using training data before performing the adaptation. Therefore, they need speaker labels for both training and adaptation data, where the training data contains many speakers compared to the adaptation data.

Compared to the research efforts in ASR, the speaker adaptation method has not been studied much in lip reading. Combination of MLLT [19] and speaker adaptation [7] is applied to lip reading in [6]. [25] proposed to utilize i-vector in lip reading. These methods are evaluated with a constrained dataset with few speakers, due to the lack of speaker labels in public lip reading databases, and they need the speaker information of whole training data which is usually large.

In this paper, we develop a speaker-adaptive lip reading that utilizes user-dependent padding as speaker-specific inputs. Different from the previous methods, the proposed method does not need any additional network and the speaker information of the entire training data that utilized for pre-training. Instead, the proposed method can participate in the visual speech extraction stage of the visual front-end without modifying the network parameters, and just need the speaker information of adaptation data which is usually small (*e.g.*, 1 min).

3   Methods

Let $\mathcal{S} = \{(\mathbf{X}^s, \mathbf{Y}^s)\} = \{(x_1^s, y_1^s), \ldots, (x_{N_s}^s, y_{N_s}^s)\}$ be a set of N_s training samples where x_i^s is the i-th lip video and y_i^s is the corresponding ground-truth label,

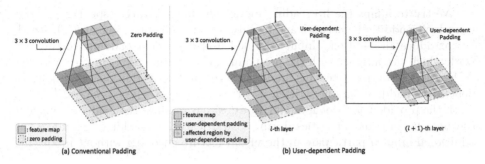

Fig. 2. Example of padded convolution with 3×3 kernel and stride 2. (a) Conventional padding such as zero, reflect, and constant padding. (b) The proposed user-dependent padding can gradually affect entire visual features as it moves to deeper layers.

$\mathcal{A}_j = \{(\mathbf{X}^{a_j}, \mathbf{Y}^{a_j})\} = \{(x_1^{a_j}, y_1^{a_j}), \ldots, (x_{N_{a_j}}^{a_j}, y_{N_{a_j}}^{a_j})\}$ be a set of N_{a_j} adaptation data of the j-th target speaker not appear in $\mathcal{S}$, and $\mathcal{T}_j = \{x_1^{t_j}, \ldots, x_{N_{t_j}}^{t_j}\}$ be a test set of the target speaker. With a pre-trained lip reading model learned on a large dataset $\mathcal{S}$ containing various speakers, our objective is to adapt the pre-trained model to the j-th unseen speaker using $\mathcal{A}_j$ containing a small number of data (*i.e.*, $N_{a_j} \ll N_s$) in a supervised manner, thus achieving improved performance on the test data $\mathcal{T}_j$ of j-th unseen speaker. Otherwise, if the adaptation data $\mathcal{A}_j$ is not available, we try to adapt the pre-trained model directly on $\mathcal{T}_j$ in an unsupervised way. The overview of the proposed framework is shown in Fig. 1.

A lip reading model is usually composed of a front-end $\mathcal{F}$ which extract visual features f of lips, and back-end $\mathcal{B}$ which encodes the dynamics and predict the speech from the encoded visual features f. The training of a lip reading model can be achieved by updating the weight parameters θ of the front-end $\mathcal{F}$ and the back-end $\mathcal{B}$ through back-propagation of the loss computed using cross-entropy or CTC loss [20] functions $\mathcal{L}(\cdot)$. It can be written as follows,

$$\theta^* = \underset{\theta}{\operatorname{argmin}} \, \mathcal{L}(\mathbf{Y}^s, \hat{\mathbf{Y}}), \quad \text{where } \hat{\mathbf{Y}} = (\mathcal{B} \circ \mathcal{F})_\theta(\mathbf{X}^s), \tag{1}$$

where θ^* is the parameters of the pre-trained lip reading model on a large dataset $\mathcal{S}$. With the pre-trained model, our goal is to encode speaker-adapted visual features f according to the input speaker for improving performance.

3.1   User-Dependent Padding

In ASR, to adapt the trained model on a new speaker, [1,2,42,59] proposed using a speaker code or i-vector [14] as an additional input to the trained model. The additional speaker-specific input is encoded with an additional network to modify the extracted acoustic features adaptively to the input speaker. However, they need to train the newly added network or fine-tune the entire network including the additional network on training data $\mathcal{S}$, before performing speaker adaptation.

We try to adapt the lip reading model on the j-th target speaker without introducing additional network and modifying the pre-trained weight θ^*. Instead, we introduce an additional input u, called user-dependent padding, to the network which can interact with the pre-trained convolution filters in the front-end $\mathcal{F}$. Predictions of the lip reading model with the proposed additional inputs, user-dependent padding, can be written as, $\hat{\mathbf{Y}} = (\mathcal{B} \circ \mathcal{F})(\mathbf{X}^{t_j}, u^j) = \mathcal{B}(\mathcal{F}(\mathbf{X}^{t_j}, u^j))$. With the provided additional inputs, our desire is to allow the model to consider the personal lip characteristics during visual feature embedding. To make the additional input u participate in the visual feature encoding without modifying the weight parameters, we utilize the region of padding in the CNN.

In CNN, for convolving the features with a kernel, padding is usually employed to maintain or control the output feature size. Conventionally used padding is zero padding, reflect padding, and constant padding. These padded region is also convolved with a learned kernel during the convolutions as shown in Fig. 2a. We utilize these potential regions to insert the additional inputs. That is, the user-dependent padding is applied for the padding before convolution, instead of the conventional padding (e.g., zeros) used during pre-training, as shown in Fig. 2b. If we assume that the pre-trained lip reading model is trained with zero padding, the optimization of a lip reading model in Eq. (1) can be re-written as,

$$\theta^* = \underset{\theta}{\operatorname{argmin}} \, \mathcal{L}(\mathbf{Y}^s, \hat{\mathbf{Y}}), \quad \text{where } \hat{\mathbf{Y}} = (\mathcal{B} \circ \mathcal{F})_\theta(\mathbf{X}^s, \mathbf{0}), \tag{2}$$

where $\mathbf{0}$ represents the zero inputs to be applied padding before the convolution operations. Now, we can provide additional inputs to the front-end by simply changing the zero inputs with the proposed user-dependent padding u, without modifying the learned weight parameters or using additional layers.

Then, with the proposed user-dependent padding u, the speaker-adaptation of a lip reading model on j-th unseen speaker using the adaptation data $\mathcal{A}_j$ can be achieved with the following equations,

$$u^{j*} = \underset{u^j}{\operatorname{argmin}} \, \mathcal{L}(\mathbf{Y}^{a_j}, \hat{\mathbf{Y}}), \quad \text{where } \hat{\mathbf{Y}} = (\mathcal{B} \circ \mathcal{F})_{\theta^*}(\mathbf{X}^{a_j}, u^j), \tag{3}$$

where u^{j*} represents the learned user-dependent padding for the j-th speaker. Please note that we only optimize the user-dependent padding u, while maintaining the learned pre-trained knowledge θ^*. Otherwise, if the adaptation data $\mathcal{A}$ is not available, the user-dependent padding also can be trained directly on $\mathcal{T}$ via any unsupervised training method such as self-training [39] and adversarial training [53] which are proven to be effective in unsupervised domain adaptation.

The user-dependent padding can affect the entire visual feature map as the layers go deeper, as shown in Fig. 2b. Therefore, different from the previous methods that modify the extracted features [1,42,59], the proposed user-dependent padding can participate in the whole visual feature encoding stages, so the personal lip appearances of the input speaker can be considered during the feature embedding. Finally, the user-dependent padding consumes small memory compared to the model, θ^*, and this makes it possible to provide customized speech recognition services. All we need is one well-trained model in a central system and user-dependent paddings that can be deployed on personal mobile devices.

3.2 LRW-ID

In order to develop and evaluate speaker-adaptive lip reading method, a dataset containing speaker information is essential. However, publicly available lip reading databases that contain speaker information are captured in a constrained environment and have a small number of speakers [13,65], which is limited in evaluating the developed speaker-adaptive lip reading method. To remedy this problem, we clustered and labeled the speaker information of a large-scale unconstrained audio-visual dataset, LRW [11]. Then, we split the train and test set without speaker overlapping which named as LRW-ID to distinguish it with the original splits of the dataset. Specifically, the speaker information of the LRW is labeled with the similar pipeline of [8] as follows,

1) **Feature Extraction.** In order to represent the speaker feature of a video, we employ a powerful face recognition system of ArcFace [16]. We employ ResNet-101 [22] model pre-trained on MS-Celeb-1M [21]. From each video in LRW composed of 29 frames, 5 frames are randomly chosen for feature extraction. Face detection and alignment are performed using RetinaFace [15]. Then, the video-level speaker representation is obtained by averaging that of 5 frames embedded through the pre-trained face recognition model.

2) **Clustering.** With the obtained video-level speaker representations, speaker clustering is performed. For this stage, we perform face identification between video and clusters. Specifically, if the cosine similarity between a given video and all clusters is lower than a threshold t_1, a new cluster is introduced for the video. Otherwise, the video is assigned to a cluster showing the highest similarity. The speaker feature representing the cluster is updated with a new assigned video, with a momentum m as, $C_k = norm(m \times C_k + (1 - m) \times f_l)$, where C_k indicates face feature of cluster k, f_l represents the normalized speaker feature of a video l that assigned to cluster k, and $norm(\cdot)$ represents l2 normalization.

3) **Face Verification.** Due to the imperfection of clustering algorithms, having false positive samples are inevitable. To minimize the error, we should remove the false positive samples that different speakers are assigned to one cluster. To this end, face verification is performed between all samples in a cluster. Specifically, samples in the same cluster are compared by using their video-level speaker representations, and the cluster is split if they are detected as not the same person (*i.e.*, the similarity is lower than a threshold t_2).

4) **Face Identification.** In this stage, we deal with the multiple clusters of one speaker which should be merged. To handle this, face identification is performed between clusters. To represent the cluster-level speaker feature, the video-level speaker representations of all videos in the cluster are averaged. Each cluster is compared with the other clusters, and it is merged with multiple top-similarity clusters above a threshold t_3.

5) **Manual Correction.** Even if we merge the clusters through the previous step, we find that there still exist multiple clusters of the same speaker. Usually, they are not merged in the previous step due to the extreme differences in illumination and pose variations of faces that result in low similarities of face representations. To handle this, we extract the candidate clusters that exist in

Table 1. Selected 20 speakers for the test from LRW-ID. '% Overlap class' represents how many word classes are overlapped between adaptation and test sets

Speaker number (Speaker ID)	S1 (#4243)	S2 (#5125)	S3 (#6003)	S4 (#7184)	S5 (#9335)	S6 (#9368)	S7 (#9438)	S8 (#9653)	S9 (#10209)	S10 (#10293)
# Tot. class	316	402	478	494	453	421	497	365	411	358
# Tot. video	1130	1486	2381	6542	4116	1900	14478	1245	1490	1477
# Adapt. video (# Word class)	565 (252)	743 (329)	1190 (425)	3271 (473)	2058 (418)	950 (346)	7239 (493)	622 (282)	745 (316)	738 (290)
# Test video (# Word class)	565 (240)	743 (313)	1191 (416)	3271 (476)	2058 (412)	950 (346)	7239 (495)	623 (290)	745 (330)	739 (294)
% Overlap class	73.3	76.7	87.3	95.6	91.5	78.3	99.2	71.4	71.2	76.9
Speaker number (Speaker ID)	S11 (#10587)	S12 (#11041)	S13 (#11777)	S14 (#11875)	S15 (#11910)	S16 (#13287)	S17 (#13786)	S18 (#15545)	S19 (#15769)	S20 (#17378)
# Tot. class	350	475	365	235	304	346	370	456	313	477
# Tot. video	1106	5480	1743	2800	950	1213	1654	4126	936	3586
# Adapt. video (# Word class)	553 (258)	2740 (455)	871 (303)	1400 (195)	476 (236)	606 (264)	827 (298)	2063 (419)	468 (237)	1793 (441)
# Test video (# Word class)	553 (268)	2740 (447)	872 (311)	1400 (191)	476 (239)	607 (263)	827 (303)	2063 (426)	468 (231)	1793 (424)
% Overlap class	65.7	95.5	80.1	79.1	71.5	68.8	76.2	91.3	67.1	91.5

the boundary by using a lower threshold t_4 than used before, and manually inspect whether the clusters are from the same person or not.

The thresholds are empirically set by examining the quality of resulted clusters by humans as 0.41, 0.63, 0.63, and 0.59 for t_1, t_2, t_3, and t_4. The total number of labeled speakers through the above pipeline is 17,580 which is large compared to the previously used data [13] for speaker adaptation. Therefore, it is very useful to evaluate the speaker-dependency of a lip reading model trained with large speaker variations. We choose 20 speakers who contain more than 900 videos to construct the test and adaptation (or validation) sets. Information of the 20 selected speakers for the test is shown in Table 1. Since the classes that appear in adaptation and test sets are not perfectly overlapped, it is important that the speaker-adaptive method not be overfitted to the adaptation dataset.

4 Experiments

We evaluate the effectiveness of the proposed user-dependent padding on both sentence- and word-level lip reading databases. Moreover, we conduct experiments in two different adaptation settings, supervised adaptation where a small amount of adaptation data (*e.g.*, under 5 min) is required and unsupervised adaptation where no supervision is required for the speaker adaptation.

4.1 Dataset

GRID corpus [13] is a popular sentence-level lip reading dataset. It is composed of sentences following the fixed grammar from 34 speakers. Videos are 3 s long, thus every 20 videos compose 1 min. We follow the unseen speaker split of [9] that speakers 1, 2, 20, and 22 are used for test and the remainder is used for training. For the supervised adaptation setting, we split half of the data (*i.e.*, about 500 videos) from each test speaker to construct the candidate dataset for adaptation and the others for the test data. For the unsupervised adaptation setting, all data

Table 2. Adaptation result using different time lengths of adaptation data on GRID

Adapt. min	S1	S2	S20	S22	Mean
Baseline	17.04	9.02	10.33	8.13	11.12
1 min	10.65	4.20	7.77	4.59	6.80
3 min	9.35	3.75	6.88	4.27	6.05
5 min	8.78	3.45	6.49	3.99	5.67

Table 3. Ablation results by using different padding layers with different amounts of adaptation data on LRW-ID

Adapt. min	5 layers	11 layers	17 layers
1 min	86.54	86.81	87.06
3 min	86.69	87.12	87.61
5 min	86.85	87.31	87.91

from the test speakers are utilized for the test. For the performance measurement, Word Error Rate (WER) in percentage is utilized.

LRW-ID is a speaker labeled version of LRW [11], a word-level lip reading dataset, as described in Sect. 3.2. Each video is 1.16 s, thus 52, 155, and 259 videos compose 1, 3, and 5 min. For the supervised adaptation, the adaptation set is used for the speaker adaptation. For the unsupervised adaptation, only the test set is used. Word accuracy (%) is utilized for the metric.

4.2 Baselines and Implementation Details

Videos are pre-processed following [26]. For LRW-ID, videos are cropped into 136×136 centered at the lip, resized into 112×112, and converted into grayscale. For GRID, the lip region is cropped and resized into a size of 64×128.

Baseline Lip Reading Model. For the sentence-level lip reading, we utilize a modified network of LipNet [9], which consists of three 3D convolutions and two 2D convolutions for the front-end, and two layered bi-GRU for the back-end. It is trained with CTC loss function [20] with word tokens, and beam search with beam width 100 is utilized for the decoding. For the word-level lip reading, we employ an architecture of [38], which consists of ResNet-18 [22] for the front-end and MS-TCN [38] for the back-end, and train the model using cross-entropy loss. AdamW optimizer [30,36] with an initial learning rate of 0.001, and batch size of 112 and 220 are utilized, respectively on GRID and LRW-ID.

Speaker-Invariant. We borrow a speaker-invariant ASR method [40] into lip reading, which trains the model via adversarial learning to suppress the speaker information from the encoded features, to compare the effectiveness of the proposed method with a speaker-invariant speech recognition model. Specifically, an additional speaker classifier is introduced which classifies the speaker identity from the encoded visual feature. The sign of gradient calculated from the speaker classifier is reversed before backpropagated through the front-end [18], thus the front-end learns to suppress the speaker information from the encoded visual feature, while the speaker classifier attempts to find the speaker information from the encoded visual feature in an adversarial manner.

Speaker Code. We bring a popular speaker-adaptation method [1] of ASR which utilizes speaker code as additional inputs with additional layers, to compare the effectiveness of the proposed method with a speaker-adaptive model.

For GRID, we use 128, 64, and 32 dimensions of speaker code with three additional fully connected layers which correspond to Adaptation Network of [1], to transform the visual feature encoded from the front-end. For LRW, 256, 128, and 64 dimensions of speaker code are utilized. The training procedures are as follows, 1) bring a pre-trained lip reading model, 2) only train Adaptation Network and the speaker code after attaching them to the pre-trained model using the training dataset S while other network parameters are fixed, and 3) perform adaptation by training speaker code only using the adaptation dataset A.

User-Dependent Padding. We utilize all padded convolutions to insert the user-dependent padding. For GRID, user-dependent padding is inserted before every 5 convolutional layers, and 17 convolutional layers for LRW-ID. The user-dependent padding is initialized with the padding used during pre-training (*i.e.*, zero) and updated with a learning rate of 0.01. As the proposed method does not need an additional adaptation network, the training procedures can be simple as follows, 1) bring a pre-trained lip reading model, and 2) perform adaptation by updating the user-dependent padding only using the adaptation dataset A.

4.3   Supervised Adaptation

Adaptation Results Using Data Under 5 min. To investigate the effectiveness of the proposed user-dependent padding, we adapt the lip reading model by using a small number of adaptation data. Specifically, we utilize 1, 3, and 5 min length of videos for adaptation, which might be relatively easily obtained in a practical situation. For reliable experimental results, each experiment is performed in 5 folds with different adaptation samples and the mean performance is reported. The results on GRID are shown in Table 2. The baseline achieves 11.12% mean WER on four unseen speakers. By using 1 min of adaptation data, the performances are significantly improved in all speakers by achieving mean WER of 6.80%. Specifically, the WER of speaker 1 (s1) is improved by about 6.4% WER from the baseline. By using adaptation data of 3 min, the mean WER is further improved to 6.05%. Finally, adapting on 5 min video achieves 5.67% WER. The adaptation results of each speaker on LRW-ID are shown in Table 4. The baseline model achieves 85.85% mean word accuracy and it is improved by 1.21% by adapting the model with 1 min of adaptation video. Using more adaptation data further improves the performance. The mean word accuracy achieves 87.61% and 87.91% with 3 and 5 min adaptation data, respectively. This shows the effectiveness of the speaker-adaptation in lip reading that even if the model is trained with various speakers over 17,000, we can still improve the performance for unseen speakers through the adaptation.

Comparison with Previous Methods. We compare the adaptation results of the proposed method with the previous methods in ASR described in Sec. 4.2. The mean WER and mean word accuracy are reported in Table 5 and the best two performances are highlighted in bold. The speaker-invariant model [40] improves the performance on both GRID and LRW-ID by suppressing the speaker variations. The speaker-adaptive method [1] which utilizes speaker code

Table 4. Adaptation result using different time lengths of adaptation data on LRW-ID

Adapt. min	S1 (#4243)	S2 (#5125)	S3 (#6003)	S4 (#7184)	S5 (#9335)	S6 (#9368)	S7 (#9438)	S8 (#9653)	S9 (#10209)	S10 (#10293)
Baseline	75.93	80.08	84.13	89.36	77.70	84.53	91.12	77.05	88.46	81.33
1min	78.94	82.15	85.14	89.39	81.68	85.07	91.57	80.06	88.46	84.00
3min	80.00	82.26	85.74	89.43	82.93	85.75	92.00	81.38	88.70	85.20
5min	81.10	82.77	85.79	89.64	83.83	86.21	92.05	81.86	88.75	85.68

S11 (#10587)	S12 (#11041)	S13 (#11777)	S14 (#11875)	S15 (#11910)	S16 (#13287)	S17 (#13786)	S18 (#15545)	S19 (#15769)	S20 (#17378)	Mean
73.78	86.83	88.07	85.79	72.69	75.95	81.74	87.01	88.25	86.67	85.85
79.96	87.07	88.14	90.60	74.83	77.33	82.01	87.30	89.87	87.52	87.06
81.88	87.60	88.17	91.54	76.89	77.86	82.06	87.44	90.17	88.20	87.61
82.10	88.04	88.56	91.76	78.19	78.48	82.44	87.42	89.74	88.66	87.91

Table 5. Performance comparisons with speaker-invariant and -adaptive methods

Method	GRID (WER ↓)			LRW-ID (ACC ↑)		
	1 min	3 min	5 min	1 min	3 min	5 min
Baseline [9, 38]	11.12	11.12	11.12	85.85	85.85	85.85
Speaker-invariant (SI) [40]	10.60	10.60	10.60	86.55	86.55	86.55
Speaker code [1]	**6.77**	6.32	6.21	85.50	86.31	86.99
Proposed method	**6.80**	**6.05**	**5.67**	**87.06**	**87.61**	**87.91**
Proposed method + SI	6.85	**6.00**	**5.80**	**87.59**	**88.14**	**88.48**

for the additional speaker-specific input also shows improved performances when the adaptation is performed, except for the 1 min adaptation on LRW-ID. Even if the 1 min adaptation on LRW-ID dataset is very challenging due to the small number of adaptation data, the proposed method robustly enhances the lip reading performances regardless of the adaptation video lengths. Moreover, we also report the performance of using the proposed user-dependent padding onto the speaker-invariant model [40] (*i.e.*, Proposed Method + SI). By jointly applying the speaker-invariant and -adaptive techniques, we can further improve the overall lip reading performance.

Adaptation Results Using More Data. In this experiment, we investigate the effectiveness of the proposed method when more adaptation data is available. Since the number of available adaptation data may be different for each individual person in practice, we perform experiments using 10, 30, 50, 70, 100% of the adaptation data of each speaker. The mean results of all test speakers on GRID are shown in the second row of Table 6. Training the user-dependent padding using more adaptation data further improves the lip reading performances. When we utilize 100% of the adaptation dataset (about 25 min), the model achieves 4.65% WER which is improved over 6.4% WER from the baseline. The last row of Table 6 shows the mean results of all test speakers on

Table 6. Adaptation result by using different rate of adaptation data

Adapt. %	0%	10%	30%	50%	70%	100%
GRID (WER ↓)	11.12	6.05	5.15	5.02	4.86	4.65
LRW-ID (ACC ↑)	85.85	87.35	88.08	88.52	88.74	88.92

LRW-ID, and it shows consistent results with the sentence-level lip reading by achieving steadily improved performances.

Comparison with Finetuning. We compare the effectiveness of the user-dependent padding with finetuning. To this end, the entire model parameters are finetuned from pre-trained lip reading model on the adaptation data of LRW-ID. This yields the total number of 20 speaker-specific lip reading models which results in a total of $20 \times 40.58M = 811.6M$ parameters. Figure 3 shows the comparison results on LRW-ID dataset. When a small amount of adaptation data is utilized (*i.e.*, less than 30%), the user-dependent padding surpasses the finetuning. This is because finetuning the entire model parameter with a small number of data can be easily overfitted to the classes that appear in adaptation data. On the other hand, the user-dependent padding largely improves the performance with just 10% of adaptation data which shows the significance of the proposed method in the small data setting. When more than 50% of the adaptation data are utilized, the finetuning shows better performance than the user-dependent padding. Please note that user-dependent paddings for 20 speakers have $20 \times 0.15M = 3M$ parameters, thus we just require $3M + 40.58M = 43.58M$ parameters including that of one pre-trained model, which is about 19 times smaller than using user-specific lip reading models (*i.e.*, 811.6M). This result shows the user-dependent padding is effective and practical even if enough adaptation data is available.

Ablation Study. Finally, we investigate the effect of the number of padding layers for user-dependent padding. To this end, we vary the number of layers for inserting the user-dependent padding from the total 17 layers of ResNet-18. We use 5, 11, and 17 layers and 1, 3, and 5 min of adaptation data for the experiments. Table 3 shows the ablation results by using different padding layers on LRW-ID. When 1 min of adaptation data is utilized, the performances are less varying by the different number of layers, and when more adaptation data is used, the performance gain by using more layers becomes larger, while that of using 5 layers is marginal. This means that we can use a small number of layers for the user-dependent padding to avoid overfitting when we have a very small amount of adaptation data, and as the adaptation data increases, we can increase the padding layers accordingly to achieve high performance.

4.4   Unsupervised Adaptation

One advantage of the user-dependent padding is that it does not depend on specific training methods. That means we can bring any unsupervised learning

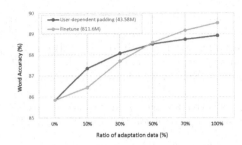

Fig. 3. Performance comparisons with fine-tuning method on LRW-ID

Table 7. Unsupervised adaptation results on GRID and LRW-ID

Method	GRID (WER ↓)	LRW-ID (ACC ↑)
MS-TCN [38]	–	85.85
CroMM-VSR [26]	–	87.30
LipNet [9]	11.12	–
TVSR-Net [60]	9.1	–
DVSR-Net [64]	7.8	–
Visual i-vector [25]	7.3	–
Proposed method	**7.2**	**87.51**

method to adapt our lip reading model on an unseen speaker when adaptation dataset $\mathcal{A}$ is not available. To verify this, we employ a self-training method [32,55,58,62] that pseudo labels the unlabeled samples with the pre-trained lip reading model before adaptation. We utilize one of the simplest form of self-training that chooses the pseudo labels by inspecting the model confidences. Specifically, we use the model predictions having approximated beam confidence larger than 0.9 for GRID and the model predictions with over 0.8 confidence for LRW-ID, as the pseudo labels to perform adaptation. Table 7 shows the mean performance of test speakers in the unsupervised adaptation setting on GRID and LRW-ID, and the comparisons with the state-of-the-art methods. The results for each speaker can be found in the supplemental material. The proposed method sets new state-of-the-art performances on both word- and sentence-level lip reading without using adaptation data $\mathcal{A}$, and this shows the effectiveness and the practicality of the proposed user-dependent padding in speaker adaptation.

5   Conclusion

In this paper, we propose a speaker adaptation method for lip reading, named user-dependent padding. The proposed user-dependent padding can cooperate with the pre-trained model without modifying the architecture and learned weight parameters. The effectiveness of the proposed method is verified on both sentence- and word-level lip reading. Through the experiment, we show that with just a few amount of adaptation data, the lip reading performance for unseen speakers can be further improved, even if the model is pre-trained with many utterances from thousands of speakers. Finally, for the future research on speaker-adaptation in lip reading, we label speaker of a popular lip reading database, LRW, and build a new unseen-speaker scenario named LRW-ID.

Acknowledgment. This work was supported by Institute of Information & communications Technology Planning & Evaluation (IITP) grant funded by the Korea government (MSIT) (No. 2022-0-00124, Development of Artificial Intelligence Technology for Self-Improving Competency-Aware Learning Capabilities).

References

1. Abdel-Hamid, O., Jiang, H.: Fast speaker adaptation of hybrid NN/HMM model for speech recognition based on discriminative learning of speaker code. In: 2013 IEEE International Conference on Acoustics, Speech and Signal Processing, pp. 7942–7946. IEEE (2013)
2. Abdel-Hamid, O., Jiang, H.: Rapid and effective speaker adaptation of convolutional neural network based models for speech recognition. In: INTERSPEECH, pp. 1248–1252 (2013)
3. Afouras, T., Chung, J.S., Senior, A., Vinyals, O., Zisserman, A.: Deep audio-visual speech recognition. IEEE Trans. Pattern Anal. Mach. Intell. (2018)
4. Afouras, T., Chung, J.S., Zisserman, A.: LRS3-TED: a large-scale dataset for visual speech recognition. arXiv preprint arXiv:1809.00496 (2018)
5. Afouras, T., Chung, J.S., Zisserman, A.: ASR is all you need: cross-modal distillation for lip reading. In: ICASSP 2020 IEEE International Conference on Acoustics, Speech and Signal Processing (ICASSP), pp. 2143–2147. IEEE (2020)
6. Almajai, I., Cox, S., Harvey, R., Lan, Y.: Improved speaker independent lip reading using speaker adaptive training and deep neural networks. In: 2016 IEEE International Conference on Acoustics, Speech and Signal Processing (ICASSP), pp. 2722–2726. IEEE (2016)
7. Anastasakos, T., McDonough, J., Makhoul, J.: Speaker adaptive training: a maximum likelihood approach to speaker normalization. In: 1997 IEEE International Conference on Acoustics, Speech, and Signal Processing, vol. 2, pp. 1043–1046. IEEE (1997)
8. Anvari, Z., Athitsos, V.: A pipeline for automated face dataset creation from unlabeled images. In: Proceedings of the 12th ACM International Conference on PErvasive Technologies Related to Assistive Environments, pp. 227–235 (2019)
9. Assael, Y.M., Shillingford, B., Whiteson, S., De Freitas, N.: LipNet: end-to-end sentence-level lipreading. arXiv preprint arXiv:1611.01599 (2016)
10. Chung, J.S., Senior, A., Vinyals, O., Zisserman, A.: Lip reading sentences in the wild. In: 2017 IEEE Conference on Computer Vision and Pattern Recognition (CVPR), pp. 3444–3453. IEEE (2017)
11. Chung, J.S., Zisserman, A.: Lip reading in the wild. In: Lai, S.-H., Lepetit, V., Nishino, K., Sato, Y. (eds.) ACCV 2016. LNCS, vol. 10112, pp. 87–103. Springer, Cham (2017). https://doi.org/10.1007/978-3-319-54184-6_6
12. Chung, J.S., Zisserman, A.: Out of time: automated lip sync in the wild. In: Chen, C.-S., Lu, J., Ma, K.-K. (eds.) ACCV 2016. LNCS, vol. 10117, pp. 251–263. Springer, Cham (2017). https://doi.org/10.1007/978-3-319-54427-4_19
13. Cooke, M., Barker, J., Cunningham, S., Shao, X.: An audio-visual corpus for speech perception and automatic speech recognition. J. Acoust. Soc. Am. **120**(5), 2421–2424 (2006)
14. Dehak, N., Kenny, P.J., Dehak, R., Dumouchel, P., Ouellet, P.: Front-end factor analysis for speaker verification. IEEE Trans. Audio Speech Lang. Process. **19**(4), 788–798 (2010)
15. Deng, J., Guo, J., Ververas, E., Kotsia, I., Zafeiriou, S.: RetinaFace: single-shot multi-level face localisation in the wild. In: Proceedings of the IEEE/CVF Conference on Computer Vision and Pattern Recognition, pp. 5203–5212 (2020)
16. Deng, J., Guo, J., Xue, N., Zafeiriou, S.: ArcFace: additive angular margin loss for deep face recognition. In: Proceedings of the IEEE/CVF Conference on Computer Vision and Pattern Recognition, pp. 4690–4699 (2019)

17. Digalakis, V.V., Rtischev, D., Neumeyer, L.G.: Speaker adaptation using constrained estimation of Gaussian mixtures. IEEE Trans. Speech Audio Process. **3**(5), 357–366 (1995)

18. Ganin, Y., Lempitsky, V.: Unsupervised domain adaptation by backpropagation. In: International Conference on Machine Learning, pp. 1180–1189. PMLR (2015)

19. Gopinath, R.A.: Maximum likelihood modeling with gaussian distributions for classification. In: Proceedings of the 1998 IEEE International Conference on Acoustics, Speech and Signal Processing, ICASSP 1998 (Cat. No. 98CH36181), vol. 2, pp. 661–664. IEEE (1998)

20. Graves, A., Fernández, S., Gomez, F., Schmidhuber, J.: Connectionist temporal classification: labelling unsegmented sequence data with recurrent neural networks. In: Proceedings of the 23rd International Conference on Machine Learning, pp. 369–376 (2006)

21. Guo, Y., Zhang, L., Hu, Y., He, X., Gao, J.: MS-Celeb-1M: a dataset and benchmark for large-scale face recognition. In: Leibe, B., Matas, J., Sebe, N., Welling, M. (eds.) ECCV 2016. LNCS, vol. 9907, pp. 87–102. Springer, Cham (2016). https://doi.org/10.1007/978-3-319-46487-9_6

22. He, K., Zhang, X., Ren, S., Sun, J.: Deep residual learning for image recognition. In: Proceedings of the IEEE Conference on Computer Vision and Pattern Recognition, pp. 770–778 (2016)

23. Hong, J., Kim, M., Park, S.J., Ro, Y.M.: Speech reconstruction with reminiscent sound via visual voice memory. IEEE/ACM Trans. Audio Speech Lang. Process. **29**, 3654–3667 (2021)

24. Huang, Y., He, L., Wei, W., Gale, W., Li, J., Gong, Y.: Using personalized speech synthesis and neural language generator for rapid speaker adaptation. In: ICASSP 2020 IEEE International Conference on Acoustics, Speech and Signal Processing (ICASSP), pp. 7399–7403. IEEE (2020)

25. Kandala, P.A., et al.: Speaker adaptation for lip-reading using visual identity vectors. In: INTERSPEECH, pp. 2758–2762 (2019)

26. Kim, M., Hong, J., Park, S.J., Ro, Y.M.: CroMM-VSR: cross-modal memory augmented visual speech recognition. IEEE Trans. Multimedia (2021)

27. Kim, M., Hong, J., Park, S.J., Ro, Y.M.: Multi-modality associative bridging through memory: speech sound recollected from face video. In: Proceedings of the IEEE/CVF International Conference on Computer Vision, pp. 296–306 (2021)

28. Kim, M., Hong, J., Ro, Y.M.: Lip to speech synthesis with visual context attentional GAN. Adv. Neural. Inf. Process. Syst. **34**, 2758–2770 (2021)

29. Kim, M., Yeo, J.H., Ro, Y.M.: Distinguishing homophenes using multi-head visual-audio memory for lip reading. In: Proceedings of the 36th AAAI Conference on Artificial Intelligence, Vancouver, BC, Canada, vol. 22 (2022)

30. Kingma, D.P., Ba, J.: Adam: a method for stochastic optimization. arXiv preprint arXiv:1412.6980 (2014)

31. Klejch, O., Fainberg, J., Bell, P., Renals, S.: Speaker adaptive training using model agnostic meta-learning. In: 2019 IEEE Automatic Speech Recognition and Understanding Workshop (ASRU), pp. 881–888. IEEE (2019)

32. Lee, D.H., et al.: Pseudo-label: the simple and efficient semi-supervised learning method for deep neural networks. In: Workshop on Challenges in Representation Learning, ICML, vol. 3, p. 896 (2013)

33. Li, B., Sim, K.C.: Comparison of discriminative input and output transformations for speaker adaptation in the hybrid NN/HMM systems. In: Eleventh Annual Conference of the International Speech Communication Association (2010)

34. Li, X., Bilmes, J.: Regularized adaptation of discriminative classifiers. In: 2006 IEEE International Conference on Acoustics Speech and Signal Processing Proceedings, vol. 1, pp. I. IEEE (2006)
35. Liao, H., McDermott, E., Senior, A.: Large scale deep neural network acoustic modeling with semi-supervised training data for YouTube video transcription. In: 2013 IEEE Workshop on Automatic Speech Recognition and Understanding, pp. 368–373. IEEE (2013)
36. Loshchilov, I., Hutter, F.: Decoupled weight decay regularization. arXiv preprint arXiv:1711.05101 (2017)
37. Ma, P., Mira, R., Petridis, S., Schuller, B.W., Pantic, M.: LiRA: learning visual speech representations from audio through self-supervision. arXiv preprint arXiv:2106.09171 (2021)
38. Martinez, B., Ma, P., Petridis, S., Pantic, M.: Lipreading using temporal convolutional networks. In: ICASSP 2020 IEEE International Conference on Acoustics, Speech and Signal Processing (ICASSP), pp. 6319–6323. IEEE (2020)
39. Mei, K., Zhu, C., Zou, J., Zhang, S.: Instance adaptive self-training for unsupervised domain adaptation. In: Vedaldi, A., Bischof, H., Brox, T., Frahm, J.-M. (eds.) ECCV 2020. LNCS, vol. 12371, pp. 415–430. Springer, Cham (2020). https://doi.org/10.1007/978-3-030-58574-7_25
40. Meng, Z., et al.: Speaker-invariant training via adversarial learning. In: 2018 IEEE International Conference on Acoustics, Speech and Signal Processing (ICASSP), pp. 5969–5973. IEEE (2018)
41. Miao, Y., Zhang, H., Metze, F.: Towards speaker adaptive training of deep neural network acoustic models. In: Fifteenth Annual Conference of the International Speech Communication Association (2014)
42. Miao, Y., Zhang, H., Metze, F.: Speaker adaptive training of deep neural network acoustic models using i-vectors. IEEE/ACM Trans. Audio Speech Lang. Process. 23(11), 1938–1949 (2015)
43. Mira, R., Haliassos, A., Petridis, S., Schuller, B.W., Pantic, M.: SVTS: scalable video-to-speech synthesis. arXiv preprint arXiv:2205.02058 (2022)
44. Mira, R., Vougioukas, K., Ma, P., Petridis, S., Schuller, B.W., Pantic, M.: End-to-end video-to-speech synthesis using generative adversarial networks. IEEE Trans. Cybern. (2022)
45. Neto, J., et al.: Speaker-adaptation for hybrid HMM-ANN continuous speech recognition system (1995)
46. Noda, K., Yamaguchi, Y., Nakadai, K., Okuno, H.G., Ogata, T.: Lipreading using convolutional neural network. In: Fifteenth Annual Conference of the International Speech Communication Association (2014)
47. Petridis, S., Stafylakis, T., Ma, P., Cai, F., Tzimiropoulos, G., Pantic, M.: End-to-end audiovisual speech recognition. In: 2018 IEEE International Conference on Acoustics, Speech and Signal Processing (ICASSP), pp. 6548–6552. IEEE (2018)
48. Ren, S., Du, Y., Lv, J., Han, G., He, S.: Learning from the master: distilling cross-modal advanced knowledge for lip reading. In: Proceedings of the IEEE/CVF Conference on Computer Vision and Pattern Recognition, pp. 13325–13333 (2021)
49. Seide, F., Li, G., Chen, X., Yu, D.: Feature engineering in context-dependent deep neural networks for conversational speech transcription. In: 2011 IEEE Workshop on Automatic Speech Recognition & Understanding, pp. 24–29. IEEE (2011)
50. Stafylakis, T., Tzimiropoulos, G.: Combining residual networks with LSTMs for lipreading. arXiv preprint arXiv:1703.04105 (2017)
51. Sutskever, I., Vinyals, O., Le, Q.V.: Sequence to sequence learning with neural networks. Adv. Neural Inf. Process. Syst. 27 (2014)

52. Swietojanski, P., Renals, S.: Learning hidden unit contributions for unsupervised speaker adaptation of neural network acoustic models. In: 2014 IEEE Spoken Language Technology Workshop (SLT), pp. 171–176. IEEE (2014)
53. Tzeng, E., Hoffman, J., Saenko, K., Darrell, T.: Adversarial discriminative domain adaptation. In: Proceedings of the IEEE Conference on Computer Vision and Pattern Recognition, pp. 7167–7176 (2017)
54. Vaswani, A., et al.: Attention is all you need. Adv. Neural Inf. Process. Syst. **30** (2017)
55. Veselý, K., Hannemann, M., Burget, L.: Semi-supervised training of deep neural networks. In: 2013 IEEE Workshop on Automatic Speech Recognition and Understanding, pp. 267–272. IEEE (2013)
56. Weng, X., Kitani, K.: Learning spatio-temporal features with two-stream deep 3D CNNs for lipreading. arXiv preprint arXiv:1905.02540 (2019)
57. Xiao, J., Yang, S., Zhang, Y., Shan, S., Chen, X.: Deformation flow based two-stream network for lip reading. In: 2020 15th IEEE International Conference on Automatic Face and Gesture Recognition (FG 2020), pp. 364–370. IEEE (2020)
58. Xie, Q., Luong, M.T., Hovy, E., Le, Q.V.: Self-training with noisy student improves ImageNet classification. In: Proceedings of the IEEE/CVF Conference on Computer Vision and Pattern Recognition, pp. 10687–10698 (2020)
59. Xue, S., Abdel-Hamid, O., Jiang, H., Dai, L., Liu, Q.: Fast adaptation of deep neural network based on discriminant codes for speech recognition. IEEE/ACM Trans. Audio Speech Lang. Process. **22**(12), 1713–1725 (2014)
60. Yang, C., Wang, S., Zhang, X., Zhu, Y.: Speaker-independent lipreading with limited data. In: 2020 IEEE International Conference on Image Processing (ICIP), pp. 2181–2185. IEEE (2020)
61. Yang, S., et al.: LRW-1000: a naturally-distributed large-scale benchmark for lip reading in the wild. In: 2019 14th IEEE International Conference on Automatic Face & Gesture Recognition (FG 2019), pp. 1–8. IEEE (2019)
62. Yarowsky, D.: Unsupervised word sense disambiguation rivaling supervised methods. In: 33rd Annual Meeting of the Association for Computational Linguistics, pp. 189–196 (1995)
63. Yu, D., Yao, K., Su, II., Li, G., Seide, F.: KL-divergence regularized deep neural network adaptation for improved large vocabulary speech recognition. In: 2013 IEEE International Conference on Acoustics, Speech and Signal Processing, pp. 7893–7897. IEEE (2013)
64. Zhang, Q., Wang, S., Chen, G.: Speaker-independent lipreading by disentangled representation learning. In: 2021 IEEE International Conference on Image Processing (ICIP), pp. 2493–2497. IEEE (2021)
65. Zhao, G., Barnard, M., Pietikainen, M.: Lipreading with local spatiotemporal descriptors. IEEE Trans. Multimedia **11**(7), 1254–1265 (2009)
66. Zhao, Y., Xu, R., Wang, X., Hou, P., Tang, H., Song, M.: Hearing lips: improving lip reading by distilling speech recognizers. In: Proceedings of the AAAI Conference on Artificial Intelligence, vol. 34, pp. 6917–6924 (2020)

TISE: Bag of Metrics for Text-to-Image Synthesis Evaluation

Tan M. Dinh[✉], Rang Nguyen, and Binh-Son Hua

VinAI Research, Hanoi, Vietnam
tan.m.dinh.vn@gmail.com

Abstract. In this paper, we conduct a study on the state-of-the-art methods for text-to-image synthesis and propose a framework to evaluate these methods. We consider syntheses where an image contains a single or multiple objects. Our study outlines several issues in the current evaluation pipeline: (i) for image quality assessment, a commonly used metric, e.g., Inception Score (IS), is often either miscalibrated for the single-object case or misused for the multi-object case; (ii) for text relevance and object accuracy assessment, there is an overfitting phenomenon in the existing R-precision (RP) and Semantic Object Accuracy (SOA) metrics, respectively; (iii) for multi-object case, many vital factors for evaluation, e.g., object fidelity, positional alignment, counting alignment, are largely dismissed; (iv) the ranking of the methods based on current metrics is highly inconsistent with real images. To overcome these issues, we propose a combined set of existing and new metrics to systematically evaluate the methods. For existing metrics, we offer an improved version of IS named IS* by using temperature scaling to calibrate the confidence of the classifier used by IS; we also propose a solution to mitigate the overfitting issues of RP and SOA. For new metrics, we develop counting alignment, positional alignment, object-centric IS, and object-centric FID metrics for evaluating the multi-object case. We show that benchmarking with our bag of metrics results in a highly consistent ranking among existing methods that is well-aligned with human evaluation. As a by-product, we create AttnGAN++, a simple but strong baseline for the benchmark by stabilizing the training of AttnGAN using spectral normalization. We also release our toolbox, so-called TISE, for advocating fair and consistent evaluation of text-to-image models.

Keywords: Language and vision · Metrics · Text-to-image synthesis

1   Introduction

The unprecedented growth of deep learning has sparked significant interest in tackling the vital vision-language task of text-to-image synthesis in recent years,

Supplementary Information The online version contains supplementary material available at https://doi.org/10.1007/978-3-031-20059-5_34.

Caption	DM-GAN	CPGAN	AttnGAN++	Real Images

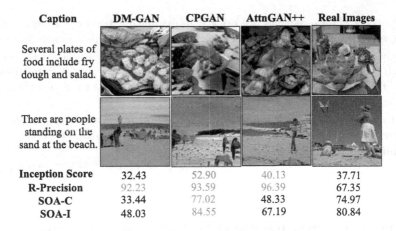

	DM-GAN	CPGAN	AttnGAN++	Real Images
Inception Score	32.43	52.90	40.13	37.71
R-Precision	92.23	93.59	96.39	67.35
SOA-C	33.44	77.02	48.33	74.97
SOA-I	48.03	84.55	67.19	80.84

Fig. 1. Evaluating the text-to-image models is a challenging task. Many existing metrics are inconsistent especially for the case when an input sentence involves multiple objects. Values in red denote inconsistent evaluations, where the quantitative results are even higher than that of real photos, despite the fact that such generated images are not perceptually real. (Color figure online)

with potential applications from computer-aided design, image editing with text-guided to image retrieval. This is a challenging task because of the wide semantic gap between two domains and the high many-to-many mapping (e.g., one text caption can correspond to many image counterparts and vice versa). Many aspects of image synthesis, such as image fidelity, object relations, object counting have to be considered for generating complex scenes from a sentence.

In the past few years, key techniques for text-to-image synthesis are largely based on the evolution of generative adversarial networks (GANs) [7]. Tremendous achievements has been obtained in many domains, e.g. from unconditional image generation [13,14] to latent space mapping and manipulation [31,32]. Most of text-to-image synthesis approaches [16,17,35,40,42,46] are built upon GANs and jointly consider text and image features in the synthesis.

Despite excellent results have been achieved on particular datasets [18,22, 39], the current evaluation pipeline is far from ideal. For single object case, image quality and text-image alignment are primary factors considered in a typical evaluation process. Some commonly evaluation metrics are Inception Score (IS) [30] and the Fréchet Inception Distance (FID) [10] for image fidelity and R-precision (RP) [40] for text-image alignment, which works well for most single-object cases. However, in complex scenes with multiple objects, adopting these metrics are not enough and causes some inconsistency issues. As can be seen in Fig. 1, the ranking of GAN models based on the current metrics is not strongly correlated to their generated image qualities. The numbers reported from several GANs are even better than the one of corresponding real images, while it is clearly seen that the quality of generated images are still far from being real. Additionally, the existing evaluation system lacks the metrics for assessing other aspects like object fidelity, positional alignment, and counting alignment, among others. These aspects are critical in evaluating the performance of text-to-image models in the multi-object case. Furthermore, the absence of a unified evaluation toolbox has resulted in inconsistent outcomes reported by different research works. These issues are also highlighted in the recent comprehensive survey [6], which raises a demand to devise a unified bag of metrics for text-to-image evaluation.

In this paper, we develop a systematic method for evaluating text-to-image synthesis approaches to tackle the challenges mentioned above. Our contributions are summarized as follows:

1. For existing metrics, we create IS* as an improved version of IS metric for image quality assessment, which alleviates the low confidence phenomenon due to miscalibrations in the pre-trained classifier used for IS. We also develop the robust versions for text relevance and object accuracy assessment (RP and SOA [11]) to mitigate their overfitting issues in multi-object case.
2. For new metrics, we develop O-IS and O-FID for object fidelity, PA for positional alignment, and CA for counting alignment to evaluate these lacking aspects in multi-object text-to-image synthesis.
3. Based on these metrics, we conduct a comprehensive, fair and consistent evaluation of the current state-of-the-art methods for both single- and multi-object text-to-image models.
4. Finally, we propose AttnGAN++, a simple but strong baseline that works well for both single- and multi-object scenarios. Our AttnGAN++ has competitive performance to current state-of-the-art text-to-image models.

On top of these contributions, we develop a *Python* assessment toolbox called **TISE** (**T**ext-to-**I**mage **S**ynthesis **E**valuation) implementing our bag of metrics in a unified way to facilitate, advocate fair comparisons and reproducible results for future text-to-image synthesis research[1].

2   Background

Text-to-Image Synthesis is a vision-language task substantially benefit from the unprecedented evolutions of generative adversarial neural networks and language models. GAN-INT-CLS [29] is the first conditional GAN [19] designed for text-to-image generation, but images generated by GAN-INT-CLS only have 64×64 resolution. StackGAN and its successor StackGAN++ [44,45] enhanced the resolution of generated images by using a multi-stage architecture. These works, however, only consider sentence-level features for image synthesis; word-level features are completely dismissed, which causes poor image details. To fix this issue, an attention mechanism can be used to provide word-level features, notably used by AttnGAN [40] and DM-GAN [46], which significantly improves the generated image quality. Beyond modifying the network architecture, improving semantic consistency between image and caption is also an

---

[1] TISE toolbox is available at https://github.com/VinAIResearch/tise-toolbox.

active research topic to gain better image quality. SD-GAN [42] and SE-GAN [35] guarantee text-image consistency by the Siamese mechanism; [24] proposes a text-to-image-to-text framework called MirrorGAN inspired by the cycle consistency, while [41,43] leverage contrastive learning in their text-to-image models. To improve the performance of model in the multi-object case, InferGAN [12] and Obj-GAN [16] introduce a two-step generation process including layout generation and image generation, while CPGAN [17] leverages the object memory features in developing the model. Regarding model scaling approach, DALL-E [26] and CogView [5] are two large scale text-to-image synthesis models with 12 and 4 billion parameters, respectively, synthesizing the image from the caption autoregressively by using a transformer [38] and VQ-VAE [27].

Evaluation. The rapid advancement of text-to-image generation necessitates the construction of a reliable and systematic evaluation framework to benchmark models and guide future research. However, assessing the quality of generative modeling tasks has proven difficult in the past [37]. Because none of the existing measures are perfect, it is usual to report many metrics, each of which assesses a different aspect. The performance assessment is even more challenging in the text-to-image synthesis task due to the multi-modal complexity of text and image, which motivates us to develop a new evaluation toolbox to compare text-to-image approaches fairly and confidently.

3   Single-Object Text-to-Image Synthesis

3.1   Existing Metrics

Most of existing metrics access the quality of model based on two aspects: image quality and text-image alignment. For assessing the image quality of the model, Inception score (IS) [30] and Fréchet Inception Distance (FID) [10] are two common metrics. These metrics originally come from traditional GAN tasks for evaluating the image quality. For evaluating text-image alignment, R-precision [40] metric is utilized popularly.

Inception Score (IS) [30] leverages a pretrained Inception-v3 network [34] for calculating the Kullback-Leibler divergence (KL-divergence) between class-conditional distribution and class-marginal distribution of the generated images. The formula of IS is defined below.

$$IS = \exp(\mathbb{E}_x D_{KL}(p(y|x) \parallel p(y))), \tag{1}$$

where x is the generated image and y is the class label. The goal of this metric is to determine whether a decent generator can generate samples under two conditions: *(i)* The object in the image should be *distinct* $\rightarrow p(y|x)$ must have low entropy; *(ii)* Generated images should have the *diversity* of object class $\rightarrow p(y)$ must have high entropy. Combining these two considerations, we expect that the KL-divergence between $p(y)$ and $p(y|x)$ should be large. Therefore, higher IS value means better image quality and diversity.

Table 1. Benchmark results for the single-object text-to-image synthesis models on the CUB dataset. In this benchmark, we only consider the methods, which have been released with officially source code and pre-trained weights by their authors. **Best** and runner-up values are marked in bold and underline.

Method	IS (↑)	FID (↓)	RP (↑)
GAN-INT-CLS [29]	2.73	194.41	3.83
StackGAN++ [45]	4.10	27.40	13.57
AttnGAN [40]	4.32	24.27	65.30
AttnGAN + CL [41]	4.45	17.96	60.82
DM-GAN [46]	4.68	15.52	<u>76.25</u>
DF-GAN [36]	<u>4.77</u>	16.46	42.95
DM-GAN + CL [41]	<u>4.77</u>	**14.57**	69.80
AttnGAN++ (ours)	**4.78**	<u>15.01</u>	**77.31**

Fréchet Inception Distance (FID) [10] calculates the Fréchet distance between two sets of images: generated and actual. To calculate FID, features from each set are firstly extracted by a pre-trained Inception-v3 network [34]. Then, these two feature sets are modeled as two *multivariate Gaussian distributions*. Finally, the Fréchet distance is calculated between two distributions.

$$\text{FID} = ||\mu_r - \mu_g||^2 + \text{trace}\left(\Sigma_r + \Sigma_g - 2(\Sigma_r\Sigma_g)^{\frac{1}{2}}\right), \tag{2}$$

where $X_r \sim \mathcal{N}(\mu_r, \Sigma_r)$ and $X_g \sim \mathcal{N}(\mu_g, \Sigma_g)$ are the features of real images and generated images extracted by a pretrained Inception-v3 model. Lower FID value means better image quality and diversity.

R-precision (RP) [40] metric is used popularly to evaluate text-image consistency. The idea of RP is to use synthesized image query again the input caption. In particular, given a ground truth text description and 99 mismatching captions sampled randomly, an image is generated from ground truth caption. Then this image is used to query again input description among 100 candidate captions. This retrieval is marked as successful if the matching score of it and ground truth caption is the highest one. The cosine similarity between image encoding vector and caption encoding vector is used as matching score. RP is the ratio of successful retrieval and higher score means better quality.

3.2 Benchmark Results

In this section, we conduct an assessment to re-evaluate existing text-to-image models in the single-object case. For simplicity, CUB dataset [39] is selected for our mini-benchmark and used to generate images with only one object from fine-grained text description. CUB dataset [39] contains $11,788$ images from 200 different bird species. We follow the same setup as mentioned in [44] to pre-process and prepare train/test data in zero-shot setting.

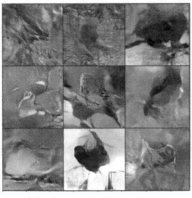 

(a) IS = 5.12; IS* = 13.05   (b) IS = 4.78; IS* = 15.13

Fig. 2. Evaluating the single-object text-to-image synthesis models can be inconsistent with the IS score. (a) Generated images from the counter model are unrealistic but the IS score of this model is high; (b) Generated images of our AttnGAN++. As can be seen, our IS* fixes well this inconsistency issue.

We suggest a new baseline approach for this benchmark based on recent breakthroughs in deep learning techniques, in addition to previous efforts. Particularly, we revise the architecture of AttnGAN [40] by adding the spectral normalization layers to the discriminator that helps stabilize the training process. We also hand-tune the hyperparameters of our baseline network, which we denote as AttnGAN++. The detail architecture and network setting of AttnGAN++ are shown in supplementary material. The quantitative results of our benchmark is reported in Table 1, which brings the following insights.

Insight 1: AttnGAN++ is a Strong Baseline. As can be seen in Table 1, our AttnGAN++ outperforms the original version (AttnGAN) with a large gap on all metrics for CUB dataset and has the comparable results with existing state-of-the-art works. It is worth noting that most of current state-of-the-art works [15,17,41,46] are built on AttnGAN. Therefore, this empirical finding would help create a very strong baseline for further improving the successor works. The qualitative results can be found in the supplementary.

Insight 2: IS Scores are Inconsistent. During the development of AttnGAN++, we discovered that it is feasible to design a generator that produces unrealistic images while yet having a high IS score, which we refer to as the *counter model*. Generated images from this counter model is shown in Fig. 2(a). Note that the images from the counter model are randomly sampled and not curated. We describe the architecture of this counter model as well as how to reproduce these results in the supplementary.

Motivated by Insight 2, we revisited the definition of IS metric, and discovered that the inconsistency is due to a pitfall when the IS score is computed in the text-to-image synthesis task. From this observation, we proposed an improved version of IS that address such limitation, as follows.

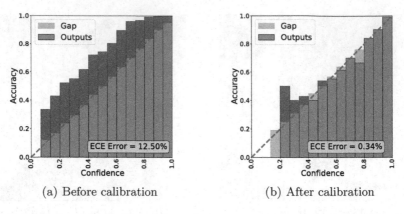

(a) Before calibration   (b) After calibration

Fig. 3. Reliability diagrams of the fine-tuned Inception-v3 network on the CUB dataset before and after calibration.

3.3   Improved Inception Score (IS*): Calibrating Image Classifiers

We found that the pretrained classifier based on the Inception network (used to calculate IS) is uncalibrated or mis-calibrated. As a result, the classifier tends to be either over-confident or under-confident. This is verified by using expected calibration error (ECE) [20] and reliability diagram [4,21]. ECE is the popular metric used to evaluate calibration whereas reliability diagram is a tool to visualize calibration quality. A classifier is well calibrated if they have a small ECE value and reliability diagram is close to identity. As can been seen in Fig. 3(a), the Inception network, pretrained by StackGAN [44] for evaluating recent text-to-image models on CUB, is under-confident. When computing the IS, this leads to inconsistency due to erroneous distance between conditional and marginal probability distributions.

To tackle this issue, we propose to calibrate the confidence score of the classifier, which we opt to apply the popular network calibration method of temperature scaling [8]. Particularly, the classifier receives an input image x and output a logit vector z. Before this logit vector z is passed to a softmax layer to obtain probability values, we calibrate z by scaling it with a positive scalar value T for all classes. The conditional probability $p(y = k \mid x)^*$ with class label $k \in \{1..K\}$ after calibration is:

$$p(y = k \mid x)^* = \sigma(z/T)_k, \tag{3}$$

where K is the number of classes, T is the temperature, and σ represents the softmax function. We use the $p(y \mid x)^*$ vector for computing the divergence in IS*. The calibrated confidence score is $\max_k p(y = k \mid x)^*$. The value of T is obtained by optimizing the negative log-likelihood loss on the validation set used to train the classifier. After calibration on CUB, we get $T = 0.598$. Figure 3(b) showed that after calibration, the under-confident issue is greatly mitigated illustrated by a significant drop in ECE error and a nearly diagonal shape of the plot. The IS* score shown in Table 2 demonstrated that the inconsistent score causing by the countermodel is also addressed by using IS* instead of IS.

Table 2. A comparison between the IS and IS* scores on the CUB dataset. Thanks to the calibration step, our IS* no longer suffers the problem of counter models being ranked high despite producing bad results.

Method	IS ($\uparrow$)	IS* ($\uparrow$))
GAN-INT-CLS [29]	2.73	7.51
StackGAN++ [45]	4.10	12.69
AttnGAN [40]	4.32	13.63
AttnGAN + CL [41]	4.45	14.42
DM-GAN [46]	4.68	15.00
DF-GAN [36]	4.77	14.70
DM-GAN + CL [41]	4.77	<u>15.08</u>
Counter model	**5.12**	13.05
AttnGAN++ (ours)	<u>4.78</u>	**15.13**
Real images	*24.16*	*46.27*

Summary. Single-object text-to-image synthesis is a relatively well-explored topic. Challenges still arise with new tasks, e.g., validating the models with novel word compositions [23]. Here we focused on the evaluation aspect and provided a unified benchmark with existing metrics and our IS* metric. Note that while both IS and FID are for image quality assessment, the benefit of IS (and our IS*) is that it does not require the distribution of real images for evaluation.

4   Multiple-Object Text-to-Image Synthesis

Evaluating text-to-image synthesis models with multiple objects is far more difficult than with a single object. The comprehensive survey by Frolov et al. [6] suggested many essential aspects for evaluating multiple-object text-to-image synthesis. We summarize these aspects in Table 3. As can be seen, simply using existing metrics as in the single-object case is insufficient because many critical aspects in the multi-object case have been implied or ignored, such as object count, relative position among objects, etc. In this section, we will describe a systematic approach for evaluating multi-object text-to-image models by revisiting and improving existing metrics and proposing new metrics for aspects that do not yet have a metric to quantify. Before we get into the specifics of the evaluation metrics, let us give an overview of the benchmark dataset that we use. Our benchmark is conducted on the MS-COCO version 2014 dataset [18], which contains photos with many objects and complex backgrounds. We choose MS-COCO since this dataset is used popularly in developing text-to-image model with multiple objects. The setup for preparing training and validation set in our experiments are same with [29]. In particular, we employ the official training set

Table 3. Demanding aspects for the evaluation of multi-object text-to-image models presented by [6] and our proposed metrics to assess the lacking criteria.

Metric	Image realism	Object fidelity	Text relevance	Object accuracy	Positional alignment	Counting alignment	Paraphrase robustness	Explainable	Automatic
IS [30]	✓								✓
FID [10]	✓								✓
RP [40]			✓						✓
SOA [11]			✓	✓					✓
O-IS (Ours)		✓							✓
O-FID (Ours)		✓							✓
PA (Ours)					✓				✓
CA (Ours)						✓			✓
Human	✓	✓	✓	✓	✓	✓	✓	✓	

of MS-COCO (approximately 80 K images) as the training set of text-to-image models, and we test models on the MS-COCO validation set (approximately 40 K images).

4.1 Existing Metrics

Image Realism. FID and our IS* can be used to analyze the photorealism of multi-object synthetic images in the same way they have been used for single object images.

Text Relevance. Current studies use RP to assess the alignment between text and the generated image. However, this metric is shown to overfit in multiple-object synthesis, having inconsistent ranking with real images, which can be seen in Fig. 1. One reason for this is that previous works have used the same image and text encoders from DAMSM [40] for training and computing RP. To alleviate this overfitting issue, we use an independent text encoder and image encoder for RP. We selected CLIP [25], a powerful text and image encoders trained on a very large-scale dataset with 400 million text-image pairs. This idea is also used by the concurrent work of Park et al. [23]. In our experiment, the overfitting problem of RP is mitigated using two new encoders, as demonstrated by the value of RP in real images have a large gap with the previous methods. A comparison between the traditional and our modified RP results can be found in supplementary material.

Object Accuracy. Semantic Object Accuracy (SOA) [11] is proposed to measure whether generate images having the objects mentioned in the caption. Specifically, the authors proposed two sub-metrics including SOA-I (average recall between images) and SOA-C (average recall between classes), which are formulated as:

$$\text{SOA-C} = \frac{1}{|C|} \sum_{c \in C} \frac{1}{|I_c|} \sum_{i_c \in I_c} \text{Object-Detector}(i_c), \tag{4}$$

$$\text{SOA-I} = \frac{1}{\sum_{c \in C} |I_c|} \sum_{c \in C} \sum_{i_c \in I_c} \text{Object-Detector}(i_c), \qquad (5)$$

where C is the object category set; I_c is a set of images belonging to category c; Object-Detector$(i_c) \in \{0,1\}$ is an pretrained object detector returning 1 if the detector detect successfully an object belong to class c in i_c.

As can be seen, SOA is a plausible metric to evaluate the object accuracy factor in the text-to-image model. However, we found that both CPGAN [17] and SOA used the same pre-trained YOLO-v3 [28] in their implementation, which can potentially lead to overfitting. Empirically, the values of SOA-I and SOA-C of CPGAN are better than those for real images despite images from CPGAN are still non-realistic (Fig. 1). To lessen the chance of overfitting, we choose Mask-RCNN [9] instead of YOLO-v3 to compute SOA. The empirical result in our experiment shows that this selection helps mitigate the inconsistency problem. A comparison between the SOA results when using YOLO-v3 and Mask-RCNN can be found in the supplementary material. In this paper, we solely report SOA values computed by Mask-RCNN.

We now turn to describe our new metrics. As shown in Table 3, several aspects in evaluating multi-object text-to-image models remain lacking. Unsolved aspects that we will tackle in this paper include *Object Fidelity*, *Positional Alignment* and *Counting Alignment*. Positional alignment measures the relative position among the objects in the image, e.g., when there is a man and a tree in an image, whether 'a man stands in front of a tree' and 'a man stands behind a tree' affects the positional alignment. Counting alignment measures the compatibility of the number of objects illustrated by the input sentence and the generated image. Object fidelity evaluates the quality of the object set extracted from generated images. In the survey by Frolov et al. [6], the authors simply provided a discussion without providing any concrete metrics for such aspects. In the following sections, we propose new metrics to address these shortcomings.

4.2 Object Fidelity

Object-centric IS (O-IS) and Object-centric FID (O-FID) are our straightforward extensions of IS and FID with the aim to measure object fidelity in the generated images. In the literature, SceneFID [33] is the closest metric that can assess this criteria and is proposed for evaluating layout-to-image models. However, SceneFID requires the ground truth object bounding boxes from the layout to extract objects in the images preventing them to apply for the text-to-image task. In this work, we replace the need of using ground truth bounding boxes by leveraging the bounding boxes predicted by an off-the-shelf object detection model. Specifically, we first use a well-trained object detector to localize and crop all object regions in each image in the generated image set. By treating all image regions as independently generated, we evaluate the fidelity by IS* and FID on the image regions, respectively. In our experiments, we used Mask-RCNN [9] pre-trained on MS-COCO as the object detector. We also fine-tune and then calibrate the Inception-v3 classifier on the object dataset cropped from the images

[TRUE caption] (SOA-C=100.0)
The cat is perched **on top of** a wood bench.

[FALSE caption] (SOA-C=100.0)
The cat is perched **under** a wood bench.

[TRUE caption] (SOA-C=100.0)
A woman riding a red motorcycle **behind** a truck.

[FALSE caption] (SOA-C=100.0)
A woman riding a red motorcycle **in front of** a truck.

Fig. 4. Accessing positional alignment of the objects in the multi-object image is critical, yet it is still mostly ignored. This example shows a flaw in the existing metrics, such as SOA, which completely ignored the evaluation of positional alignment while maintaining good object accuracy. As can be seen, the SOA values for the image with the *true* caption and with the *false* caption are the same, which demonstrates that the SOA metric skips positional alignment. This weakness leads to the appearance of our Positional Alignment (PA) metric.

in MS-COCO based on ground truth bounding boxes to obtain a classifier having 80 classes, equaling the number of classes in MS-COCO. The Inception-v3 network after fine-tuning is used for both computing O-IS and O-FID.

4.3   Positional Alignment

Text descriptions are used to describe an image and typically include phrases that convey the positioning information between objects, such as *behind, on top of, etc.* (Fig. 4). However, existing object-aware metrics like SOA do not penalize such incorrect relative object locations (e.g. generated images with inaccurate positional alignment still has high SOA scores). To tackle this issue, we propose a new metric to evaluate positional alignment, denoted by PA. First, we define the set of positional words as $W = \{$*above, right, far, outside, between, below, on top of, bottom, left, inside, in front of, behind, on, near, under*$\}$. For each word w in W, we filter the captions having word w in the evaluation set of the COCO dataset, and obtain the caption set P_w for each word w. Each caption in P_w is a matched caption, which means the image clearly explains the text. Given P_w, we build a mismatched caption by replacing w in the matched caption by its antonym and keeping other words. For example, the mismatched caption of "A man is *in front of* the blue car" is "A man is *behind* the blue car". Our evaluation begins by generating images from the matched captions in the test dataset. For each word w in W, we now have a set $D_w = \{(R_{wi}, P_{wi}, Q_{wi})\}_{i=1}^{N_w}\}$ where R_{wi} is a generated image from P_{wi}; P_{wi} is matched caption; Q_{wi} is mismatched caption of P_{wi}; N_w is the number of captions having word w. For each triplet in D_w, we use the image R_{wi} to query the input caption from the binary query set including matched caption P_{wi} and mismatched caption Q_{wi}. We mark a query as successful if the matched caption is successfully queried. The query success rate measures the positional alignment quality over all words:

$$\text{PA} = \frac{1}{|W|} \sum_{w \in W} \frac{k_w}{N_w}, \tag{6}$$

where k_w is the number of success cases, and $|W|$ is the total number of words. For image-to-text query, we use CLIP [25] as our text-image matching model.

4.4 Counting Alignment

In the multi-object case, counting alignment is an vital factor but so far disregarded in current text-to-image synthesis evaluation. Therefore, we propose a metric for counting alignment (CA metric) that measures how closely the number of objects in a generated image matches the text description.

To evaluate with CA, we first need to construct the test data by filtering from captions in MS-COCO validation set the captions mentioned counting aspect such as *a, one, two, three, four*. From these selected captions, we annotate the ground truth counting information for each one. It is worth noting that we only annotate the object types which can be counted by an object counter to avoid this metric to penalizing those object categories, which cannot be counted. For example, with a caption *"A group of seven people having a light meal and discussion at a single large table"*, the ground truth counting is { *"person": 7.0, "dining table": 1.0*}. Finally, we created a counting test set D with 1000 records. Each record has a form of (t, c), in which t is an input text description, and c is the ground truth counting information.

We use a text-to-image model to generate images from each caption and use an off-the-shelf object counting model [2] to count the number of objects for each object class from generated images. To get CA value, we compare the object count to the ground truth and measure the counting error using root mean squared error averaged over the test images:

$$\text{CA} = \frac{1}{|D|} \sum_{i=1}^{|D|} \sqrt{\frac{1}{N_{ic}} \sum_{j=1}^{N_{ic}} (\hat{c_{ij}} - c_{ij})^2}, \tag{7}$$

where c_{ij} and $\hat{c_{ij}}$ is the ground truth and predicted object count in the image i for object class j; N_{ic} is the number of ground truth object types in image i, $|D|$ is the number of test samples.

4.5 Ranking Score

To facilitate the benchmark, we propose a simple formula to compute an average score for ranking purpose. The ranking score is calculated by summing all *rankings* of the considered metrics. To the best of our knowledge, a similar approach is used in the nuScenes challenge for autonomous driving [1] that ranks object detection methods by combining metrics for different bounding box properties such as center, orientation, and dimensions. In our case, since some evaluation

Table 4. Benchmark performances of the multi-object text-to-image synthesis models on the MS-COCO dataset. The **best** and <u>runner-up</u> values are marked in bold and underline, respectively. As can be seen, our $\overline{\text{AttnGAN++}}$ gains the competitive results compared to the current state-of-the-art text-to-image synthesis methods.

Method	IS* (↑)	FID (↓)	RP(↑)	SOA-C(↑)	SOA-I (↑)	O-IS (↑)	O-FID (↓)	CA (↓)	PA (↑)	RS (↑)
GAN-CLS [29]	8.10	192.09	10.00	5.31	5.71	2.46	51.13	2.51	32.79	7.0
StackGAN [44]	15.50	53.44	9.10	9.24	9.90	3.36	29.09	2.41	34.33	11.5
AttnGAN [40]	33.79	36.90	50.56	47.13	49.78	5.04	20.92	1.82	40.08	29.0
DM-GAN [46]	45.63	28.96	66.98	55.77	58.11	5.22	17.48	1.71	42.83	41.0
CPGAN [17]	**59.64**	50.68	69.08	**81.86**	**83.83**	**6.38**	20.07	2.07	43.28	43.0
DF-GAN [36]	30.45	**21.05**	42.44	37.85	40.19	5.12	**14.39**	1.96	40.39	31.5
AttnGAN + CL [41]	36.85	26.93	57.52	47.45	49.33	4.92	19.92	1.72	43.92	37.0
DM-GAN + CL [41]	46.61	<u>22.60</u>	<u>70.36</u>	58.68	61.05	5.09	15.50	<u>1.66</u>	**49.06**	<u>51.5</u>
DALLE-mini (zero-shot) [3]	19.82	62.90	48.72	26.64	27.90	4.10	23.83	2.31	47.39	23.5
AttnGAN++ (Ours)	<u>54.63</u>	26.58	**72.48**	<u>67.83</u>	<u>69.97</u>	<u>6.01</u>	<u>15.43</u>	**1.57**	<u>47.75</u>	**56.0**
Real images	*51.25*	*2.62*	*83.54*	*90.02*	*91.19*	*8.63*	*0.00*	*1.05*	*100.0*	*65.0*

aspects could have more than one metric variant, the ranking for each aspect is the average of the ranking of the variants. We treat all metrics and aspects equally, and thus use $\frac{1}{2}$ weight for IS and FID in image realism, O-IS and O-FID in object fidelity, SOA-I and SOA-C in object accuracy; other metrics have a unit weight. Our ranking score (RS) is computed as

$$\text{RS} = \frac{1}{2}(\#\text{IS}^* + \#\text{FID}) + \frac{1}{2}(\#\text{O-IS} + \#\text{O-FID}) \qquad (8)$$

$$+ \frac{1}{2}(\#\text{SOA-I} + \#\text{SOA-C}) + \#\text{PA} + \#\text{CA} + \#\text{RP},$$

where $\#(\text{metric}) \in \{1..N\}$ denotes the ranking by a particular metric with N is the number of considered methods.

4.6   Benchmark Results

We show the benchmark results in Table 4, from which we draw some following insights. Firstly, our proposed metrics (O-IS, O-FID, CA, PA) and two improved version of existing metrics (RP, SOA), properly rank real images as the best. An exception is IS* which ranks AttnGAN++ and CPGAN better than real images. However we opt to retain this metric due to its excellent properties on the single-object case, and the ranking score is consistent to human when including IS*. Second, our AttnGAN++ is ranked top for multi-object text-to-image synthesis in terms of overall performance, demonstrating that it is a substantial strong baseline for both single-object and multiple-object instances. Third, breaking down each part of our evaluation pipeline allows us to more clearly analyze each model's flaws and strengths than earlier evaluations. For examples, CPGAN outperforms other techniques on SOA-I and SOA-C since it explicitly considers object-level information in the training phase. DM-GAN + CL is the most effective method for positional alignment. While our AttnGAN++ performs better in the remaining aspects. The details of aspect's scores for each method are included in the supplementary material.

Table 5. Human evaluation results on the MS-COCO dataset. In this table, ranking scores (RS) are recalculated using just 5 considered techniques and real photos. As can be observed, RS is well-aligned with human decisions.

Method	Ranking score ($\uparrow$)	Human score ($\uparrow$)
StackGAN [44]	6.00	28.45
AttnGAN [40]	13.5	37.40
DM-GAN [46]	20.0	41.47
CPGAN [17]	23.0	43.73
AttnGAN++ (ours)	**28.5**	**45.01**
Real images	*35.0*	*99.82*

4.7 Human Evaluation

To ensure that our evaluations are reliable, we conducted a user analysis to test the metrics against assessments done by humans. We opt for 5 methods including StackGAN, AttnGAN, DM-GAN, CPGAN, AttnGAN++ (ours), and real images to conduct our user survey. We sample 50 test captions from MS-COCO and use the above methods to generate an image for each caption. The IDs for these captions are provided in supplementary for reproducibility. We ask each human subject (40 participants in total) to score each method from 1 (worst) to 5 (best) based on two criteria: *plausibility* – whether the image is plausible based on the content of the caption (object accuracy, counting, and positional alignment, text relevance), and *naturalness* – whether the image looks natural. The score of each human subject for each method is the sum of score of 50 images and divide by 250 for normalization. The final score of each method is an average of the scores of each participant. Our evaluation result in Table 5 shows that our final ranking is well-aligned with human evaluation.

5 Conclusion

This paper performed an empirical study with benchmarks for text-to-image synthesis methods for both single-object and multiple-object scenario. The benchmark results reveal the inconsistency issues in the existing metrics, prompting us to propose the improved version of existing metrics as well as new metrics to evaluate many vital but lacking aspects in the multiple-object case. Our extensive experiments show that this bag of metrics provides a better and more consistent ranking with real images and human evaluation.

Our bag of metrics for text-to-image synthesis is by no means perfect. The proposed metrics can be further extended for complex cases, for example, to handle more positional words for positional alignment score and indefinite numeral adjectives (e.g., several, many) for counting alignment.

References

1. Caesar, H., et al.: nuscenes: a multimodal dataset for autonomous driving. In: CVPR (2020)
2. Cholakkal, H., Sun, G., Khan, F.S., Shao, L.: Object counting and instance segmentation with image-level supervision. In: CVPR (2019)
3. Dayma, B., et al.: Dall·e mini (2021). https://github.com/borisdayma/dalle-mini
4. DeGroot, M.H., Fienberg, S.E.: The comparison and evaluation of forecasters. J. R. Stat. Soc. Series D (Stat.) **32**(1–2), 12–22 (1983)
5. Ding, M., et al.: Cogview: mastering text-to-image generation via transformers. In: NeurIPS (2021)
6. Frolov, S., Hinz, T., Raue, F., Hees, J., Dengel, A.: Adversarial text-to-image synthesis: a review. In: Neural Networks (2021)
7. Goodfellow, I., et al.: Generative adversarial nets. In: NeurIPS (2014)
8. Guo, C., Pleiss, G., Sun, Y., Weinberger, K.Q.: On calibration of modern neural networks. arXiv preprint arXiv:1706.04599 (2017)
9. He, K., Gkioxari, G., Dollár, P., Girshick, R.: Mask r-cnn. In: ICCV (2017)
10. Heusel, M., Ramsauer, H., Unterthiner, T., Nessler, B., Hochreiter, S.: Gans trained by a two time-scale update rule converge to a local nash equilibrium. In: NeurIPS (2017)
11. Hinz, T., Heinrich, S., Wermter, S.: Semantic object accuracy for generative text-to-image synthesis. arXiv preprint arXiv:1910.13321 (2019)
12. Hong, S., Yang, D., Choi, J., Lee, H.: Inferring semantic layout for hierarchical text-to-image synthesis. In: CVPR (2018)
13. Karras, T., Laine, S., Aila, T.: A style-based generator architecture for generative adversarial networks. In: CVPR (2019)
14. Karras, T., Laine, S., Aittala, M., Hellsten, J., Lehtinen, J., Aila, T.: Analyzing and improving the image quality of stylegan. In: CVPR (2020)
15. Li, B., Qi, X., Lukasiewicz, T., H. S. Torr, P.: Controllable text-to-image generation. arXiv preprint arXiv:1909.07083 (2019)
16. Li, W., et al.: Object-driven text-to-image synthesis via adversarial training. In: CVPR (2019)
17. Liang, J., Pei, W., Lu, F.: Cpgan: full-spectrum content-parsing generative adversarial networks for text-to-image synthesis. arXiv preprint arXiv:1912.08562 (2019)
18. Lin, T.Y., et al.: Microsoft coco: common objects in context. In: ECCV (2014)
19. Mirza, M., Osindero, S.: Conditional generative adversarial nets. arXiv preprint arXiv:1411.1784 (2014)
20. Naeini, M.P., Cooper, G.F., Hauskrecht, M.: Obtaining well calibrated probabilities using bayesian binning. In: AAAI (2015)
21. Niculescu-Mizil, A., Caruana, R.: Predicting good probabilities with supervised learning. In: ICML (2005)
22. Nilsback, M.E., Zisserman, A.: Automated flower classification over a large number of classes. In: Proceedings of the Indian Conference on Computer Vision, Graphics and Image Processing (2008)
23. Park, D.H., Azadi, S., Liu, X., Darrell, T., Rohrbach, A.: Benchmark for compositional text-to-image synthesis. In: NeurIPS Datasets and Benchmarks Track (2021)
24. Qiao, T., Zhang, J., Xu, D., Tao, D.: Mirrorgan: learning text-to-image generation by redescription. In: CVPR (2019)

25. Radford, A., et al.: Learning transferable visual models from natural language supervision. arXiv preprint arXiv:2103.00020 (2021)
26. Ramesh, A., et al.: Zero-shot text-to-image generation. In: ICML (2021)
27. Razavi, A., van den Oord, A., Vinyals, O.: Generating diverse high-fidelity images with vq-vae-2. In: NeurIPS (2019)
28. Redmon, J., Farhadi, A.: Yolov3: an incremental improvement. arXiv preprint arXiv:1804.02767 (2018)
29. Reed, S., Akata, Z., Yan, X., Logeswaran, L., Schiele, B., Lee, H.: Generative adversarial text-to-image synthesis. In: ICML (2016)
30. Salimans, T., Goodfellow, I., Zaremba, W., Cheung, V., Radford, A., Chen, X.: Improved techniques for training gans. In: NeurIPS (2016)
31. Shen, Y., Gu, J., Tang, X., Zhou, B.: Interpreting the latent space of gans for semantic face editing. In: CVPR (2020)
32. Shen, Y., Yang, C., Tang, X., Zhou, B.: Interfacegan: interpreting the disentangled face representation learned by gans. arXiv preprint arXiv:2005.09635 (2020)
33. Sylvain, T., Zhang, P., Bengio, Y., Hjelm, R.D., Sharma, S.: Object-centric image generation from layouts. In: AAAI (2021)
34. Szegedy, C., Vanhoucke, V., Ioffe, S., Shlens, J., Wojna, Z.: Rethinking the inception architecture for computer vision. In: CVPR (2016)
35. Tan, H., Liu, X., Li, X., Zhang, Y., Yin, B.: Semantics-enhanced adversarial nets for text-to-image synthesis. In: ICCV (2019)
36. Tao, M., Tang, H., Wu, F., Jing, X.Y., Bao, B.K., Xu, C.: Df-gan: a simple and effective baseline for text-to-image synthesis. In: CVPR (2022)
37. Theis, L., Oord, A.v.d., Bethge, M.: A note on the evaluation of generative models. arXiv preprint arXiv:1511.01844 (2015)
38. Vaswani, A., et al.: Attention is all you need. In: NeurIPS (2017)
39. Welinder, P., et al.: Caltech-ucsd birds 200. Technical Report CNS-TR-2010-001. California Institute of Technology (2010)
40. Xu, T., et al.: Attngan: fine-grained text to image generation with attentional generative adversarial networks. In: CVPR (2018)
41. Ye, H., Yang, X., Takac, M., Sunderraman, R., Ji, S.: Improving text-to-image synthesis using contrastive learning. arXiv preprint arXiv:2107.02423 (2021)
42. Yin, G., Liu, B., Sheng, L., Yu, N., Wang, X., Shao, J.: Semantics disentangling for text-to-image generation. In: CVPR (2019)
43. Zhang, H., Koh, J.Y., Baldridge, J., Lee, H., Yang, Y.: Cross-modal contrastive learning for text-to-image generation (2021)
44. Zhang, H., et al.: Stackgan: text to photo-realistic image synthesis with stacked generative adversarial networks. In: ICCV (2017)
45. Zhang, H., et al.: Stackgan++: realistic image synthesis with stacked generative adversarial networks. TPAMI 41(8), 1947–1962 (2018)
46. Zhu, M., Pan, P., Chen, W., Yang, Y.: Dm-gan: dynamic memory generative adversarial networks for text-to-image synthesis. In: CVPR (2019)

SemAug: Semantically Meaningful Image Augmentations for Object Detection Through Language Grounding

Morgan Heisler[✉], Amin Banitalebi-Dehkordi, and Yong Zhang

Huawei Technologies Canada Co., Ltd., Burnaby, Canada
{morgan.lindsay.heisler,amin.banitalebi,yong.zhang3}@huawei.com

Abstract. Data augmentation is an essential technique in improving the generalization of deep neural networks. The majority of existing image-domain augmentations either rely on geometric and structural transformations, or apply different kinds of photometric distortions. In this paper, we propose an effective technique for image augmentation by injecting contextually meaningful knowledge into the scenes. Our method of semantically meaningful image augmentation for object detection via language grounding, SemAug, starts by calculating semantically appropriate new objects that can be placed into relevant locations in the image (the **what** and **where** problems). Then it embeds these objects into their relevant target locations, thereby promoting diversity of object instance distribution. Our method allows for introducing new object instances and categories that may not even exist in the training set. Furthermore, it does not require the additional overhead of training a context network, so it can be easily added to existing architectures. Our comprehensive set of evaluations showed that the proposed method is very effective in improving the generalization, while the overhead is negligible. In particular, for a wide range of model architectures, our method achieved 2–4% and 1–2% mAP improvements for the task of object detection on the Pascal VOC and COCO datasets, respectively. Code is available as supplementary.

Keywords: Semantic image augmentation · Language grounding

1 Introduction

Training a deep neural network (DNN) relies on the availability of representative datasets which contain a sufficient number of labeled examples. Collecting relevant samples and labeling them is a time consuming and costly task. In practice, various techniques are employed to improve the network accuracy given the available training data. Of these techniques, methods of artificially expanding the size of the training dataset are of especial importance. For computer vision tasks,

Supplementary Information The online version contains supplementary material available at https://doi.org/10.1007/978-3-031-20059-5_35.

Fig. 1. Examples of our method: originals (left) and semantically augmented (right).

image augmentation is a technique that is used to artificially expand the size of a training dataset by generating modified versions of the training images. Almost all modern vision-DNNs involve some form of image augmentation in training [31]. The importance of augmentation is even more pronounced for applications where training data is imbalanced (distribution of instances among categories is not uniform), when target categories are rare or uncommon in nature (e.g. detection of security threats), or when adding new object categories to datasets.

Although traditional techniques such as flipping, rotating, cropping, and altering the colour space are helpful, they are generic and all-purpose in nature. When performing visual tasks such as object detection and semantic segmentation, a more object-aware method specifically created for these tasks could improve results. To address this, [12,15] performed studies of placing objects randomly inside training images, and observed consistently better results for both object detection and semantic segmentation tasks.

Conversely, though randomly placing new object instances has an effect of generating more training samples and therefore reduces over-fitting, it is likely forcing the detector to fixate on the appearance of individual objects thereby becoming invariant to contextual information that humans find useful [11]. Intuitively, methods which preserve such context should further boost performance results. This intuition was confirmed by [10,11] that showed context-based object placement achieves higher generalization compared to random placement. However, training a context model adds a considerable overhead, making it less practical in real-world applications [14]. In addition, contextual associations in such methods are derived using data in the training dataset and therefore the potential for new associations is limited.

Contextual relationships have been an area of interest in the Natural Language Processing (NLP) world for quite some time [1,8,16,23]. In this domain, words can be represented as real-valued vectors allowing for quantitative latent space analysis. Various language models such as GloVe [29], fasttext [27], BERT [8], etc. have been trained on vast text corpora to encode the intricate relationships between words. In this paper, we present a simple and effective method for injecting contextual information using these semantic word vectors, without the overhead of training additional dataset-dependent context networks. By leveraging the semantic labels, our method can consider the context of a scene

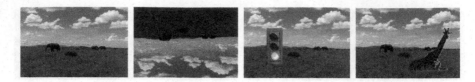

Fig. 2. Various methods of augmentation: From left to right: the original image, traditional augmentations (flip, contrast/brightness adjustment, additive noise), random object placement, and SemAug (our method). A giraffe could reasonably be found in a field with elephants, whereas a traffic light has no contextual basis in this scene.

and augment appropriately as shown in Fig. 1 through the injection of contextual knowledge. In brief, word vectors from pre-trained embeddings are used to compute the most similar objects which can then be placed in an image. A comparison to other techniques is shown in Fig. 2 where the original image consists of elephants in a field with sky above. Traditional techniques are able to globally modify the image to look different than the original, but do not add any information based on prior knowledge. Neither does the random object placement which placed a traffic light in the scene. The semantically augmented image has added a giraffe, which is contextually relevant, and added it to the scene in an appropriate location. This addition based on prior knowledge aids the network in discerning the relationships between objects in a dataset.

The main contributions of this paper are as follows:

- We present a new method of object-based contextually meaningful image augmentation for object detection. In particular, we propose a solution for the **what** and **where** problems for object instance placement. Moreover, our method allows for the introduction of new object categories into a dataset while still considering context as it is not dataset-dependent.
- Our method considers context without the overhead of training additional context models, allowing for easy adoption to existing models and training pipelines.
- Through a comprehensive set of experiments, we show that our method provides consistent improvements on standard object detection benchmarks. We show our context-based object handling is indeed more meaningful than random placements, while it does not require training additional context models.

2   Related Works

Related to our work are image augmentation methods, in particular context-based augmentations. We provide a brief overview in this section.

Traditional Augmentations: Include rotate, flip, resize, blur, added noise, color manipulations, and other geometric or photometric transformations. A typical preprocessing pipeline may include a combination of such augmentations.

Combining Image Augmentations: To address situations where traditional augmentations do not cover, several more advanced methods of mixing augmentations and their respective labels have been proposed in the recent years.

Examples include: RandAugment [7]/AutoAugment [6] (to identify suitable augmentations on each training iteration), AugMix [22] (mixing multiple random augmentations and enforcing a consistency loss), MixUp [37] (mixing training samples), CutOut [9] (cutting out a random bounding box), CutMix [36] (cut a random box from an image and paste to another), DeepAugment [21] (adding perturbation on weights and activations), FenceMask [24] (fence-shape CutOut), FMix [18] (applying binary masks from Fourier space), KeepAugment [17] (CutMix but not applying any augmentations on the pasted box), ClassMix [28] (combining segmentation masks), ComplexMix [5] (advanced version of ClassMix). These augmentations have shown to improve on the traditional augmentations, however as mentioned in the introduction section, some form of object-level augmentation specifically created for the task of object detection rather than image classification may provide a larger performance boost.

Object-Level Augmentations: The previous methods do not consider any specific object-level augmentations but rather apply some transformations over the whole image, which may not be optimal for tasks such as object detection. Recently, object-aware methods such as Copy-Paste [15] or Cut-Paste-Learn [12] have gained traction (denoted by 'random' in Fig. 2). Though these methods do increase the number of object instances in a dataset, no prior contextual knowledge is used to determine whether pasted objects would naturally be found in the scene. This is the major disadvantage because the object-aware method may learn improper associations which would not appear in test images, leading to inevitable accuracy loss in object detection.

Other than the random object pasting, some recent methods propose other approaches of object-level augmentation. InstaBoost [14] proposes to move an object within its neighborhood to create new training examples. Inpainting might be used to fill in the black pixels. PSIS [34] and COCP [35] on the other hand, switch different instances of a same object category within two images. While effective, these methods provide sub-optimal augmentation as the object categories for each image do not change. Additionally, the constraints in place for COCP [35] inhibit the number of synthetic images that can be created, especially for a smaller dataset. Our method is able to add new object categories to images, enabling stronger perturbations in the image domain, as well as add new object categories to the datasets.

Contextual Augmentations: To take context into consideration, Context-DA [10,11] and [33] proposed to train a separate model that learns the context. The main disadvantages of using an additional context model are: additional networks require extra training overhead, and are highly dataset-dependent. Our method differs as it does not model the visual context of the images, but rather leverages the availability of pre-trained language embeddings to derive semantic context from images. This allows for the injection of new knowledge not necessarily already in the given dataset, less overhead than training and inferencing an additional context network, and improved flexibility as it can be readily used in any architecture or framework.

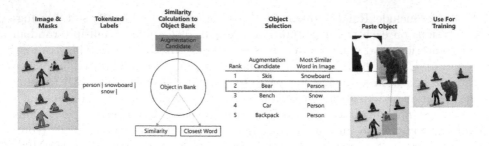

Fig. 3. Illustration of our data augmentation approach. After an image is selected for semantic augmentation, the semantic labels are converted into word vectors. The similarity between these word vectors and the word vectors of the available objects to be pasted are computed. Then one of these objects is chosen from the object bank based on a criteria such as balancing the number of objects in a dataset, or adding more instances of a poor-performing object category. The chosen object is then pasted into the image in the vicinity of the most similar label.

3   Method

In this section, we first provide a formulation of the problem. Then, we describe our method and provide insights on different aspects of our approach.

3.1   Problem Statement

Let $\mathbf{I} \in \mathbb{R}^{W \times H}$ denote a training image from the train set with width W and height H (for brevity we drop the channels dimension). The goal of SemAug is to generate a new training sample $\tilde{\mathbf{I}}$ by inserting one or more contextually relevant objects from an object bank Ω using semantic knowledge, π. This can be expressed by:

$$\tilde{\mathbf{I}} = f_\pi(\mathbf{I}, \Omega). \tag{1}$$

In this section, we present a method of language grounding as a way of extracting and matching high level semantic context π. The augmented training sample set $\{\tilde{\mathbf{I}}\}$ is then used to train the model with its original loss function. Through this injection of semantic knowledge, we strengthen the network's ability to predict objects given context.

3.2   Semantic Augmentation

An overview of SemAug is illustrated in Fig. 3 and detailed steps are summarized in Algorithm 1. In our method, we first create an object bank Ω that contains multiple instances of various objects that can be inserted into host images. The object bank can be created either from external sources such as the web, or can be created based upon an existing dataset. Due to its convenience, we opt in for the second option in this work.

Once the object bank is created, we explore the language representations associated with the objects in the bank and analyze them with respect to the objects appearing in each training image. By matching the high level semantics through the lens of language embeddings we identify what and where to insert from the bank to a host image. Details are explained in this section.

At the end, we can apply any other kind of augmentation such as the traditional image transformations to the pipeline before passing the dataset to the training engine.

Algorithm 1. The proposed semantic augmentation method

Inputs: An image dataset $\mathcal{D}$
Output: Semantically augmented images $\tilde{\mathcal{D}}$

1: **procedure** SEMAUG($\mathcal{D}$)
  \# *Object Bank Creation*
2:   **for** each $\mathbf{I}$ in $\mathcal{D}$ **do:**
3:     $\mathbf{M} \leftarrow \texttt{GetMask}(\mathbf{I})$
4:     **for** each object k in $\mathbf{I}$ **do:**
5:       $\mathbf{I}_c^k, \mathbf{M}_c^k = \texttt{crop}(\mathbf{I}^k, \mathbf{M}^k | bbox^k)$
6:       $\mathbf{L}_e = \texttt{GetLanguageEmbedding}(\mathbf{L}_w(k))$
7:       $\Omega \leftarrow \mathbf{I}_c^k, \mathbf{M}_c^k, \mathbf{L}_w, \mathbf{L}_e$
8:     $\mathbf{D} : \mathbf{L}_w \rightarrow \mathbf{L}_e$
  \# *Image Augmentation*
9:   **for** each $\mathbf{I}$ in $\mathcal{D}$ **do:**
10:     $a^*, b^* = \texttt{FindBestMatch}(\mathbf{I}, \Omega)$ from (5)
11:     $\mathbf{I}^*, \mathbf{M}^* = \texttt{PadZeros}(\mathbf{I}, a^*, b^*)$
12:     $\tilde{\mathcal{D}} \leftarrow \tilde{\mathbf{I}} = \mathbf{I} \odot (1 - \mathbf{M}^*) + \mathbf{I}^*$

Object Bank Creation. To create the object bank, we first start by generating an approximate segmentation mask $\mathbf{M}$ for each image $\mathbf{I}$ in the dataset. These masks can be generated by leveraging a static side model such as a DeepLab [4] model (later we study the impact of mask quality and observe that even rough masks are enough). For the kth object in the image, its mask can be denoted as $\mathbf{M}^k \in \{0,1\}^{W \times H}$. The mask associates a binary value where the kth object appears in the image, such that $\mathbf{M}_{x,y}^k = 1$ if the pixel at (x, y) belongs to the kth object. The object's masked image can be denoted as $\mathbf{I}^k \in \mathbb{R}^{W \times H}$. Before placing the object's image and mask in the object bank, they are first cropped according to the object's bounding box to reduce their storage space:

$$\mathbf{I}_c^k, \mathbf{M}_c^k = \texttt{crop}(\mathbf{I}^k, \mathbf{M}^k | bbox^k). \tag{2}$$

This process is done once, before training, and for all images in the training dataset. The last step of the object bank creation is to create a dictionary, $\mathbf{D}$, of all the words (or "tokens") in semantic labels, $\mathbf{L}_w$, and their corresponding word embeddings, $\mathbf{L}_e$, such that $\mathbf{D} : \mathbf{L}_w \rightarrow \mathbf{L}_e$. To this end, we leverage an existing language model to extract the embedding descriptions of the semantics.

Matching Semantics Through Word Embeddings. Once we obtain the language representations of objects, we perform a similarity analysis to identify a target object from the bank (what) and where to place it in the host image (where). We use the cosine similarity metric to measure the embedding similarity,

Fig. 4. Our method can augment different instances from the same object category. Top row: Different instances from the category airplane are inserted. Bottom row: Different instances from the category kite are inserted.

however other metrics such as a Euclidean distance can be used too. To this end, let a and b denote two word vectors we wish to compare. The cosine similarity is defined as:

$$f_{sim}(a,b) = \frac{a \cdot b}{\|a\| \cdot \|b\|} = \frac{\sum_{i=1}^{d} a_i b_i}{\sqrt{\sum_{i=1}^{d} a_i^2} \sqrt{\sum_{i=1}^{d} b_i^2}}, \tag{3}$$

where d is the word embedding dimension. Supplementary materials [2] contain ablations on the choice of the embedding dimension.

A simple strategy for object selection is to choose the object pair with the highest similarity:

$$a^*, b^* = \operatorname*{argmax}_{a \in \{\mathbf{L}_e^{\mathbf{I}}\}, b \in \{\mathbf{L}_e^{bank}\}} f_{sim}(a,b), \tag{4}$$

where $\{\mathbf{L}_e^{\mathbf{I}}\}$ and $\{\mathbf{L}_e^{bank}\}$ denote all possible embedding choices within the host image and the bank, respectively, and a random instance from the b^* object category will be inserted in the host image at the a^* location. While this strategy intuitively might make sense, it has a down-side that during different epochs, a same object category will be selected every time. To address this issue, we choose from the top N most similar embeddings, the object category with the least number of appearances so far in the current epoch. Note that the number of instance appearances is constantly being updated due to object injection and batch-wise training. Therefore, we are dynamically promoting for a better balancing of the training examples, while also choosing categories with high semantic similarity:

$$a^*, b^* = \operatorname*{argmin}_{b \in \{top\ N\ sim\}} count \left(\operatorname*{arg\text{-}top\ N}_{a \in \{\mathbf{L}_e^{\mathbf{I}}\}, b \in \{\mathbf{L}_e^{bank}\}} f_{sim}(a,b) \right). \tag{5}$$

Image Augmentation Following the semantic similarity matching strategy of (5), we obtain an object category b^* and a target host object a^*, i.e., **what** and **where**. In this section, we explain the actual image augmentation procedure

Fig. 5. Our method can augment instances of different categories. Top row: An instance from the categories truck, bus and motorcycle are inserted. Bottom row: An instance from the categories sheep, and bird are inserted. Note that objects are inserted in logical locations: vehicles on roads, birds in trees, sheep on grass.

using the selected pairs. To this end, first, we randomly select an object-image instance of type b^* from the bank (Note that different instances can be selected at different epochs, thereby presenting diversified object instances to the training algorithm). Then we scale it randomly by a factor between 5–40% of the image $\mathbf{I}$ width. The object image is scaled using linear interpolation and the mask is scaled using nearest neighbour interpolation. To ensure the pasted objects are not too small or too large, we repeat the random scaling until the resized object's area falls within some bounds (A_{min}, A_{max}). Next, the center coordinates of the incoming object (x_b, y_b) is selected at a random vicinity of the corners of the most similar object in the image, as follows:

$$x_b = x_a \pm \frac{w_a}{2} \pm \epsilon_a, \qquad\qquad y_b = y_a \pm \frac{h_a}{2} \pm \epsilon_b, \qquad (6)$$

where (x_a, y_a) is the center coordinate of the host object, (w_a, h_a) are its bounding box width and height, and ϵ_a and ϵ_b are small random values to add extra randomness in the placement. If this results in occlusions, the bounding box labels are updated accordingly.

Once the center of the object to be pasted is found, its image and mask are padded with zeros to fit the shape of the training image $\mathbf{I}$. The zero-padded image and mask are denoted as $\mathbf{I}^*$ and $\mathbf{M}^*$ respectively. To compute the final augmented image and mask $(\tilde{\mathbf{I}}, \tilde{\mathbf{M}})$ the followings are used:

$$\tilde{\mathbf{I}} = \mathbf{I} \odot (1 - \mathbf{M}^*) + \mathbf{I}^*, \qquad (7)$$

$$\tilde{\mathbf{M}} = \mathbf{M} \odot (1 - \mathbf{M}^*) + \mathbf{M}^*, \qquad (8)$$

where $\odot$ denotes the element-wise multiplication. At this point, the semantically augmented image $\tilde{\mathbf{I}}$ is ready to be used for training. Semantic augmentation examples are seen in Fig. 4, where the method pasted different instances from the same category and Fig. 5 where different categories were pasted into the image. In both figures, the pasted objects are contextually relevant to the scenes.

3.3   Computational Complexity

In its simplest form, SemAug uses a dictionary lookup to gather the word embeddings of an image, computes a similarity metric then chooses an object to be pasted based on the similarity values. The complexity of the initial creation of the dictionary is O(len(D)) where len(D) is the number of dictionary items. To get a value from the dictionary is O(1), therefore for each image it is O(obj) where obj is the number of labeled objects in the image. For cosine similarity, the overall computational complexity is O(len(D).Obj.d), where d is the dimension of the embeddings, as the similarity is being calculated for every pair of word embeddings. This negligible overhead is the extra computation that is required to take place for each image during training. For a Mask-RCNN model with ResNet-50 backbone trained on COCO, the additional FLOPs required will be 480,000 (80 objects × 20 objects × 300 dimension vector). This corresponds to only 0.000107% additional FLOPs. Inference does not incur any extra overhead as it is unchanged.

4   Experiments

This section reviews the results of experiments in support of our method, and provides discussions around them.

4.1   Setup

Architecture: For a fair comparison with existing cut-paste methods, we used Mask R-CNN [19] with ResNet [20] backbone and the publicly available MMDet toolkit [3] on the MS COCO dataset [26]. We also show that SemAug is compatible with Faster-RCNN [30] and RetinaNet [25] using this framework in addition to showing that it improves data efficiency. Otherwise, we employ an Efficientdet-d0 [32] as the backbone for some PASCAL VOC experiments. We ran the experiments on a server equipped with eight NVIDIA V100 GPUs.

Training Details: For the experiments in this paper, we choose a default N of 3, for the top 3 most similar embeddings. For (A_{min}, A_{max}) we use the values (300, 90000). Additionally, default image resolutions from MMDet/Efficientdet config files were used [3, 32].

Datasets: We evaluate SemAug on two standard benchmarks: MS COCO [26] and Pascal VOC [13]. The COCO dataset contains 118 k training, 5 k validation images, and 41 k test images over 80 object categories. The Pascal dataset is considerably smaller containing only 20 object categories. Following the standard practice, we use VOC'07+12 training set (16551 examples) for training, and evaluate the models on the VOC'07 test set (4952 images). In contrast to previous object-based approaches such as [35] and [14] which relied on accurate ground-truth segmentation masks, in our method these masks were generated with an off-the-shelf DeepLab-v2 [4] model when needed (See Sect. 4.2 for details).

For language grounding, we used the word embeddings from Glove [29] trained over a 2014 Wikipedia dump + Gigaword 5 [29] with a dimension of 300.

4.2   Results

Comparison to Cut-Paste Methods: In this subsection, we compare with state-of-the-art cut-paste methods (e.g., COCP [35], InstaBoost [14] and Context-DA [11]) using Mask R-CNN based on ResNet101 on object detection and instance segmentation tasks. The results can be seen in Table 1 where our SemAug outperforms ContextDA [11], InstaBoost [14] and COCP [35] by 2.8%, 2.1% and 1.6% on object detection, respectively ('Vanilla' refers to traditional augmentations used by default in MMdet training pipeline, and is applied for all benchmarks). On the COCO test-dev dataset, SemAug achieves 41.6% mAP, while Vanilla 39.4%, and Instaboost 39.5%. Additionally, our method sees similar performance boosts on the task of instance segmentation. Specifically, our SemAug outperforms ContextDA [11], InstaBoost [14], and COCP [35] by 2.4%, 1.7%, and 1.5%, respectively. An additional comparison to Context-DA is provided in the supplementary materials. Based on these observations, our SemAug method achieves better accuracy than other cut-paste approaches.

Table 1. Comparison to other state-of-the-art (SOTA) methods using MMdet and Mask RCNN with a Resnet 101 backbone on COCO val. Context-DA and COCP numbers taken from the COCP paper [35]. The APdet and APseg for SemAug are reported as the mean value and 95% Confidence Intervals based on 5 repeat trails.

	APdet, IOU			APdet, Area			APseg, IOU			APseg, Area		
	0.5:0.95	0.50	0.75	Sma	Med	Lar	0.5:0.95	0.50	0.75	Sma	Med	Lar
Vanilla [19]	39.6	61.4	43.5	23.1	43.8	51.5	36.0	57.9	38.7	19.0	39.7	49.5
Context-DA [11]	39.9	61.4	43.7	23.0	44.2	51.5	36.2	58.2	38.4	19.4	39.8	49.9
InstaBoost [14]	40.6	62.1	44.3	24.4	44.6	53.3	36.8	58.6	39.6	20.4	40.4	50.8
COCP [35]	41.1	62.5	45.0	23.3	44.6	52.4	37.0	58.9	39.4	19.4	40.5	50.7
SemAug	**42.7 ± 0.13**	**64.5**	**46.9**	**25.6**	**47.3**	**56.1**	**38.5 ± 0.11**	**61.3**	**41.1**	**21.7**	**42.3**	**53.4**

Results of Incorporating SemAug in Labeled Datasets and Different Architectures: Our SemAug method has been shown to work on a variety of state-of-the-art object detection architectures with different capacities as shown in Table 2. This exemplifies how our augmentation strategy considers context without the training and inference overhead of an additional context models allowing for easy adoption into existing models.

Table 2. Object detection results (%) on the COCO val benchmark with different size backbones and default parameters.

	Detector	Backbone	APdet, IOU			APdet, Area			ARdet, #Det			ARdet, Area		
			0.5:0.95	0.50	0.75	Sma	Med	Lar	1	10	100	Sma	Med	Lar
Vanilla	Faster R-CNN [30]	Resnet-50	36.5	58.4	39.5	21.7	40.2	46.8	30.5	49.3	51.9	32.8	56.2	65.2
SemAug			**38.5**	**60.7**	**41.5**	**23.9**	**42.4**	**49.5**	**31.7**	**50.4**	**53.0**	**34.8**	**57.6**	**66.7**
Vanilla	Faster-RCNN [30]	Resnet-101	38.5	60.3	41.7	22.7	42.9	49.7	31.7	50.6	53.3	34.8	57.7	66.9
SemAug			**40.5**	**62.8**	**44.4**	**26.1**	**45.1**	**52.0**	**32.8**	**52.0**	**54.8**	**37.4**	**59.6**	**68.8**
Vanilla	RetinaNet [25]	Resnet-50	35.3	55.2	37.6	19.4	39.3	46.5	30.4	49.2	52.3	31.9	56.4	66.9
SemAug			**37.4**	**57.7**	**40.3**	**22.3**	**41.4**	**49.5**	**31.7**	**50.4**	**53.6**	**33.5**	**58.3**	**68.6**
Vanilla	RetinaNet [25]	Resnet-101	37.6	57.5	40.2	20.8	42.2	49.9	31.7	50.6	53.8	33.2	58.4	69.7
SemAug			**39.6**	**60.0**	**42.4**	**23.4**	**44.6**	**52.3**	**32.9**	**51.9**	**55.2**	**35.5**	**60.3**	**71.1**
Vanilla	Mask-RCNN [19]	Resnet-50	37.8	59.5	41.0	23.2	41.4	49.4	31.7	50.6	53.3	35.1	57.5	66.8
SemAug			**39.2**	**61.4**	**42.9**	**24.8**	**43.2**	**50.9**	**32.2**	**51.2**	**53.9**	**35.8**	**58.2**	**68.1**
Vanilla	Mask-RCNN [19]	Resnet-101	39.6	61.4	43.5	23.1	43.8	51.5	32.3	51.5	54.2	34.9	58.8	68.5
SemAug			**42.7**	**64.5**	**46.9**	**25.6**	**47.3**	**56.1**	**34.2**	**54.4**	**57.3**	**38.7**	**62.1**	**71.8**

Results Using Smaller Dataset Sizes: In many real-world applications, it is difficult to collect and label data. Therefore, we evaluated the performance of our method in settings where less labeled data was available. As shown in Fig. 6, SemAug was able to provide a boost in performance even in the low data regimes using a fraction of the COCO dataset.

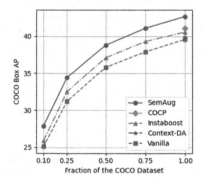

Fig. 6. Data-efficiency on the COCO val benchmark using Mask-RCNN with a Resnet-101 backbone. The results show a consistent increase of ≈3% mAP over vanilla in both the low data and high data regimes. Curves (fractional results) are shown for methods for which code was available and could run.

Ablation of Object Bank Size and Mask Qualities: As mentioned in Sect. 3.2, to create an object bank from images without given masks, we can use an off-the-shelf model for convenience such as deeplab. Note the deeplab generated masks are only being used for object bank creation, and therefore the

Object   Ground Truth Mask   DeepLab Mask

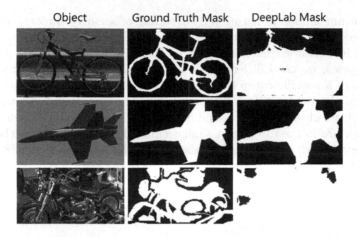

Fig. 7. Mask quality examples. Ground truth masks are much more precise than DeepLab masks.

algorithm is not sensitive to their quality. In the case of a bad quality mask (larger or smaller mask) the impact will be similar to either adding an object with more context, or an occluded (partial) object, which may in fact improve the generalization. As shown in Fig. 7, the deeplab masks were less precise than the ground truth masks which were only provided for a small subset (VOC-seg, 1464 images) of the VOC dataset. For this experiment we used Efficientdet-d0 with deeplab masks on VOC-seg as well as the whole Pascal VOC training dataset. As shown in Table 3, our method is not sensitive to the quality of the masks in the object bank. An added benefit to using deeplab masks is the ability to supplement the object bank with additional objects from previously unlabeled images. In this regard, we observe that while the deeplab masks were worse quality than the ground truth masks, they provided better performance when additional objects were added to the object bank.

Table 3. Effect of object bank mask quality on SemAug.

Method	Bank dataset	Object mask	mAP
Vanilla	—	—	73.59
SemAug	VOC-seg	DeepLab	77.19
SemAug	VOC-seg	Ground truth	77.31
SemAug	VOC-all	DeepLab	**77.35**

Results of Adding New Categories: The ability to add new categories to datasets is applicable to important real-world scenarios when target categories are rare or uncommon in nature (e.g. detection of security threats). Due to the inherent constraints of previous works [11,14,35], they are unable to add new categories in a knowledgeable manner. To demonstrate SemAug's ability to add new categories, we use Efficientdet-d0 on the Pascal VOC dataset and remove all images of a specific category. Object instances from that category are then pasted into the remaining images during training where appropriate. For this experiment, we chose an N of 5, and only paste objects from the removed category if they are in the top 5 most similar embeddings. We compare the average AP of the other 19 categories before and after the addition of a new category to show that it does not harm the other categories. We do this experiment on the first five categories of VOC, one at a time. Results are shown in Table 4. As observed, SemAug is able to add categories with decent results, while not harming the detection of existing categories in the dataset.

Table 4. Effect of removing categories from the PASCAL VOC dataset then adding them back using semantic augmentation.Top two rows are the mAP results of all categories except the newly augmented category. Results are recorded as mAP.

	Aeroplane	Bicycle	Bird	Boat	Bottle
Categories before	79.3	79.5	79.4	80.7	81.1
Categories after	79.6	79.7	79.6	80.6	80.9
New category	64.6	78.2	67.4	39.9	37.9

Additional Comparisons on Pascal VOC: In Sect. 4.2, we compared SemAug with several other SOTA methods on the COCO dataset. Here, we additionally provide a comparison with other augmentation methods on the Pascal VOC object detection task. As in previous papers [35,36], we employ a Faster-RCNN network with a Resnet-50 backbone. The results are given in Table 5. In this table, Random Paste (pasting random objects at random locations) and Co-occurrence (where we paste objects based on how often they appears together in a same image) are two naive object-based augmentation approaches that are included as additional ablation results to our method. As mentioned previously, context is important for the object selection strategy in cut and paste methods. As we can see, methods which do not consider context either degrade performance or marginally improve it; whereas, the three methods that consider context improve performance the most.

Ablation of the Effect of Scaling Objects: In this experiment, we compare the use of different scaling ranges with our method. This experiment was conducted using MMDET and the Pascal VOC dataset. Inserting an object can occlude other objects in the scene, and adding an object that is large may remove

Table 5. Comparison to other augmentation methods on the Pascal VOC dataset using Faster-RCNN and a Resnet-50 backbone. * Results taken from [36] and [35].

Augmentation Method	mAP
Baseline	75.6
Mixup* [37]	73.9 (−1.7)
Cutout* [9]	75.0 (0.6)
Random Paste	75.9 (+0.3)
CutMix* [36]	76.7 (+1.1)
COCP* [35]	77.4 (1.8)
Co-occurrence	79.3 (3.7)
SemAug	**80.7** (+5.1)

context from the image. As can be seen in Table 6, it is advantageous to scale the objects so that they are not too small as to be unrecognizable, but also not too big to be occluding other objects.

Table 6. Effect of the scaling range for objects pasted into the scene on the Pascal VOC dataset using Faster-RCNN with a Resnet 50 backbone. The objects are randomly scaled to a percentage of the image into which they are being pasted.

Scaling Range (%)	mAP
No scaling	79.9
5–40	**80.7**
10–30	80.0
15–40	80.4

Ablation on the Object Similarity Metric: In this experiment, we study the impact of object similarity methods discussed in the paper. We employ an Efficientdet-d0 [32] as the backbone, train using the VOC'07+12 training set, and evaluate the models on the VOC'07 test set. As can be seen in the results of Table 7, both euclidean distance and cosine similarity provide comparable results. As cosine similarity provided marginally better results, it was used as default in the paper.

Table 7. Effect of object similarity calculation choice on Pascal VOC.

Object similarity method	AP50
Euclidean distance	77.16
Cosine similarity	**77.35**

4.3 Limitations

As with any method, there are several limitations to the method presented. Firstly, this method uses pre-exisiting open-source word embeddings. Though this is not a core part of our method and one could choose to train their own word embeddings if necessary. Additionally, the quality of the word embeddings is related to the corpus used for training, therefore care should be taken to ensure meaningful semantic correlations exist before using for augmentation. For example, using a news-based corpora could align 'apple' more with technology than fruit. As several high quality pre-existing open-source word embeddings currently exist, this should not pose a major issue to anyone wishing to use this method. A future works section is discussed in Supplementary [2].

5   Conclusion

This paper proposes an effective technique for image augmentation by injecting contextually meaningful knowledge into training examples. Our object-level augmentation method identifies the most suitable object instances to be pasted into host images, and chooses appropriate target regions. We do that, by analyzing and matching objects and target regions through the lens of high level natural language. Our method results in consistent generalization improvements on various object detection benchmarks.

References

1. Allen, J.: Natural language understanding. Benjamin-Cummings Publishing Co., Inc. (1988)
2. Authors: SemAug: Semantically Meaningful Image Augmentations for Object Detection Through Language Grounding (2022). supplied as additional material 5739-supp.pdf
3. Chen, K., et al.: MMDetection: open mmlab detection toolbox and benchmark. arXiv preprint arXiv:1906.07155 (2019)
4. Chen, L.C., Papandreou, G., Kokkinos, I., Murphy, K., Yuille, A.L.: Deeplab: semantic image segmentation with deep convolutional nets, atrous convolution, and fully connected crfs. IEEE Trans. Pattern Anal. Mach. Intell. **40**(4), 834–848 (2017)
5. Chen, Y., Ouyang, X., Zhu, K., Agam, G.: Mask-based data augmentation for semi-supervised semantic segmentation. arXiv preprint arXiv:2101.10156 (2021)

6. Cubuk, E.D., Zoph, B., Mane, D., Vasudevan, V., Le, Q.V.: Autoaugment: Learning augmentation strategies from data. In: Proceedings of the IEEE/CVF Conference on Computer Vision and Pattern Recognition, pp. 113–123 (2019)
7. Cubuk, E.D., Zoph, B., Shlens, J., Le, Q.V.: Randaugment: practical automated data augmentation with a reduced search space. In: Proceedings of the IEEE/CVF Conference on Computer Vision and Pattern Recognition Workshops, pp. 702–703 (2020)
8. Devlin, J., Chang, M.W., Lee, K., Toutanova, K.: Bert: pre-training of deep bidirectional transformers for language understanding. In: Proceedings of the 2019 Conference of the North American Chapter of the Association for Computational Linguistics: Human Language Technologies, Volume 1 (Long and Short Papers), pp. 4171–4186 (2019)
9. DeVries, T., Taylor, G.W.: Improved regularization of convolutional neural networks with cutout. arXiv preprint arXiv:1708.04552 (2017)
10. Dvornik, N., Mairal, J., Schmid, C.: Modeling visual context is key to augmenting object detection datasets. In: Proceedings of the European Conference on Computer Vision (ECCV), pp. 364–380 (2018)
11. Dvornik, N., Mairal, J., Schmid, C.: On the importance of visual context for data augmentation in scene understanding. IEEE Trans. Pattern Anal. Mach. Intell. **43**(6), 2014–2028 (2019)
12. Dwibedi, D., Misra, I., Hebert, M.: Cut, paste and learn: surprisingly easy synthesis for instance detection. In: Proceedings of the IEEE International Conference on Computer Vision, pp. 1301–1310 (2017)
13. Everingham, M., Van Gool, L., Williams, C.K., Winn, J., Zisserman, A.: The pascal visual object classes (voc) challenge. Int. J. Comput. Vis. **88**(2), 303–338 (2010). https://doi.org/10.1007/s11263-009-0275-4
14. Fang, H.S., Sun, J., Wang, R., Gou, M., Li, Y.L., Lu, C.: Instaboost: Boosting instance segmentation via probability map guided copy-pasting. In: Proceedings of the IEEE/CVF International Conference on Computer Vision, pp. 682–691 (2019)
15. Ghiasi, G., et al.: Simple copy-paste is a strong data augmentation method for instance segmentation. arXiv preprint arXiv:2012.07177 (2020)
16. Gokhale, T., Banerjee, P., Baral, C., Yang, Y.: MUTANT: a training paradigm for out-of-distribution generalization in visual question answering. In: Proceedings of the 2020 Conference on Empirical Methods in Natural Language Processing (EMNLP), pp. 878–892. Association for Computational Linguistics (2020). https://doi.org/10.18653/v1/2020.emnlp-main.63, http://aclanthology.org/2020.emnlp-main.63
17. Gong, C., Wang, D., Li, M., Chandra, V., Liu, Q.: Keepaugment: a simple information-preserving data augmentation approach. In: Proceedings of the IEEE/CVF Conference on Computer Vision and Pattern Recognition, pp. 1055–1064 (2021)
18. Harris, E., Marcu, A., Painter, M., Niranjan, M., Hare, A.P.B.J.: Fmix: enhancing mixed sample data augmentation. arXiv preprint arXiv:2002.12047, vol. 2, no 3, p. 4 (2020)
19. He, K., Gkioxari, G., Dollár, P., Girshick, R.: Mask r-cnn. In: Proceedings of the IEEE International Conference on Computer Vision, pp. 2961–2969 (2017)
20. He, K., Zhang, X., Ren, S., Sun, J.: Deep residual learning for image recognition. In: Proceedings of the IEEE Conference on Computer Vision and Pattern Recognition, pp. 770–778 (2016)

21. Hendrycks, D., et al.: The many faces of robustness: a critical analysis of out-of-distribution generalization. In: Proceedings of the IEEE/CVF International Conference on Computer Vision, pp. 8340–8349 (2021)

22. Hendrycks, D., Mu, N., Cubuk, E.D., Zoph, B., Gilmer, J., Lakshminarayanan, B.: Augmix: a simple data processing method to improve robustness and uncertainty. arXiv preprint arXiv:1912.02781 (2019)

23. Hirschberg, J., Manning, C.D.: Advances in natural language processing. Science **349**(6245), 261–266 (2015)

24. Li, P., Li, X., Long, X.: Fencemask: a data augmentation approach for pre-extracted image features. arXiv preprint arXiv:2006.07877 (2020)

25. Lin, T.Y., Goyal, P., Girshick, R., He, K., Dollár, P.: Focal loss for dense object detection. In: Proceedings of the IEEE International Conference on Computer Vision, pp. 2980–2988 (2017)

26. Lin, T.Y., et al.: Microsoft coco: common objects in context. In: European Conference on Computer Vision (ECCV), pp. 740–755. Springer (2014). https://doi.org/10.1007/978-3-319-10602-1_48

27. Mikolov, T., Grave, E., Bojanowski, P., Puhrsch, C., Joulin, A.: Advances in pre-training distributed word representations. In: Proceedings of the International Conference on Language Resources and Evaluation (LREC 2018) (2018)

28. Olsson, V., Tranheden, W., Pinto, J., Svensson, L.: Classmix: segmentation-based data augmentation for semi-supervised learning. In: Proceedings of the IEEE/CVF Winter Conference on Applications of Computer Vision, pp. 1369–1378 (2021)

29. Pennington, J., Socher, R., Manning, C.D.: Glove: global vectors for word representation. In: Empirical Methods in Natural Language Processing (EMNLP), pp. 1532–1543 (2014). http://www.aclweb.org/anthology/D14-1162

30. Ren, S., He, K., Girshick, R., Sun, J.: Faster r-cnn: towards real-time object detection with region proposal networks. Adv. Neural. Inf. Process. Syst. **28**, 91–99 (2015)

31. Shorten, C., Khoshgoftaar, T.M.: A survey on image data augmentation for deep learning. J. Big Data **6**(1), 1–48 (2019). https://doi.org/10.1186/s40537-019-0197-0/

32. Tan, M., Pang, R., Le, Q.V.: Efficientdet: Scalable and efficient object detection. In: Proceedings of the IEEE/CVF Conference on Computer Vision and Pattern Recognition, pp. 10781–10790 (2020)

33. Volokitin, A., Susmelj, I., Agustsson, E., Van Gool, L., Timofte, R.: Efficiently detecting plausible locations for object placement using masked convolutions. In: European Conference on Computer Vision (ECCV), pp. 252–266. Springer (2020). https://doi.org/10.1007/978-3-030-66823-5_15

34. Wang, H., Wang, Q., Yang, F., Zhang, W., Zuo, W.: Data augmentation for object detection via progressive and selective instance-switching. arXiv preprint arXiv:1906.00358 (2019)

35. Wang, H., Wang, Q., Zhang, H., Yang, J., Zuo, W.: Constrained online cut-paste for object detection. In: IEEE Transactions on Circuits and Systems for Video Technology (2020)

36. Yun, S., Han, D., Oh, S.J., Chun, S., Choe, J., Yoo, Y.: Cutmix: regularization strategy to train strong classifiers with localizable features. In: Proceedings of the IEEE/CVF International Conference on Computer Vision, pp. 6023–6032 (2019)

37. Zhang, H., Cisse, M., Dauphin, Y.N., Lopez-Paz, D.: mixup: beyond empirical risk minimization. arXiv preprint arXiv:1710.09412 (2017)

Referring Object Manipulation of Natural Images with Conditional Classifier-Free Guidance

Myungsub Choi[✉][iD]

Google Research, Seoul, South Korea
cms6539@gmail.com

Abstract. We introduce the problem of referring object manipulation (ROM), which aims to generate photo-realistic image edits regarding two textual descriptions: 1) a text referring to an object in the input image and 2) a text describing how to manipulate the referred object. A successful ROM model would enable users to simply use natural language to manipulate images, removing the need for learning sophisticated image editing software. We present one of the first approach to address this challenging multi-modal problem by combining a referring image segmentation method with a text-guided diffusion model. Specifically, we propose a conditional classifier-free guidance scheme to better guide the diffusion process along the direction from the referring expression to the target prompt. In addition, we provide a new localized ranking method and further improvements to make the generated edits more robust. Experimental results show that the proposed framework can serve as a simple but strong baseline for referring object manipulation. Also, comparisons with several baseline text-guided diffusion models demonstrate the effectiveness of our conditional classifier-free guidance technique.

Keywords: Referring segmentation · Text-guided image manipulation

1 Introduction

With the surge of digital content and an ever increasing number of daily creators, there have been more and more needs for easy-to-use image/video editing tools. However, existing tools usually require expensive software or professional knowledge of editing techniques. To allow image editing to be more accessible to diverse user groups, recent works are beginning to explore image manipulation with natural language, which can serve as a highly intuitive user interface [5, 41].

Recently, the combination of large-scale vision-language models [42] and high-quality generative models [25, 38] led to interesting new text-driven applications, including text-guided image manipulation [4, 37, 41] and out-of-domain image translation [13]. However, previous methods typically modify the image globally, and fine-grained control of specific objects is not possible. A number of recent methods [4, 37, 53] also allow to use a segmentation mask as an additional input,

---

M. Choi—Now at Samsung Advanced Institute of Technology (SAIT).

S. Avidan et al. (Eds.): ECCV 2022, LNCS 13696, pp. 627–643, 2022.
https://doi.org/10.1007/978-3-031-20059-5_36

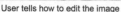

| User tells how to edit the image | 1) Identify the regions to manipulate | 2) Edit image to match the target text |

Fig. 1. Referring object manipulation problem setting. Given an image, a referring text prompt that describes which region to edit, and a target text prompt describing how to modify the specified region, our goal is to generate a photo-realistic edited image that matches all (both referring and target) textual descriptions.

so that users can specify the regions for text-guided inpainting. While providing a mask is a convenient interface for image editing, it still requires the users to draw a good mask that fully covers the regions of interest.

In this work, we introduce the new problem of *referring object manipulation*, which can provide a fully automatic user interface of image editing with natural language. The goal of this task is to generate photo-realistic image edits that follow the target text description, given an input image and a text referring to a specific region in the image. The edited output image should be different from the input image only in the referred regions, and the intended modifications should correctly reflect the attributes described in the target text. The main concept of our proposed problem setting is illustrated in Fig. 1.

To address this challenging problem for the first time, we present a simple baseline framework that combines a referring object segmentation model with text-guided image manipulation model. In particular, we leverage the pretrained models of MDETR [21] and GLIDE [37] for localizing the referring object and editing the region with textual guidance, respectively. While naive sequential combination of the two models shows plausible result, we propose three additional techniques for improvement: 1) a new conditional classifier-free guidance for better guiding the generation process in GLIDE, 2) localized ranking of multiple generations, and 3) dilation of the intermediate segmentation mask. Note that, our proposed techniques do not require any additional training or fine-tuning of the pretrained model parameters but still shows significant improvements. The experimental results and analyses demonstrate the effectiveness of the proposed framework, both qualitatively and quantitatively with a user study.

In summary, our contributions are as follows:

- We introduce a new problem of referring object manipulation, and propose a simple and effective baseline framework.
- We present conditional classifier-free guidance for improved manipulation of local image regions using a text-guided diffusion model.
- The proposed framework generates the most favorable image edits qualitatively and outperforms all compared baselines.

2   Related Works

2.1   Text-Guided Image Manipulation

Multi-modal Representation Learning Many existing works on vision and language learn a joint representation used for various downstream applications, including image captioning [28], visual question answering [3], and text-based image retrieval [22]. With the advances in Transformers [49] in the language domain, recent representation learning methods [19,42] also adopt similar architectures and train a joint embedding space with large-scale image-text data [32, 46]. Notably, CLIP [42] model, which is trained on 400 million image-text pairs with contrastive learning approach, provides a powerful representation that can be used to estimate the semantic similarity between a given image-text pair.

Text-Guided Image Generation/Manipulation. Early works on text-guided image synthesis [45,60] and manipulation [11,36,62] train a conditional GAN [35] based model with learned text embeddings. While the fidelity of the generated samples are greatly improved in the following efforts [30,54,61], images generated using these models are usually restricted to specific domains (*e.g.* flowers [50] or birds [39]), and could not be generalized to make diverse natural images.

Recently, text-guided image generation/manipulation problem [5,41,53] is gaining increased attention with the progress in large-scale multi-modal representation learning methods [19,42]. The most impressive works leverage the strong generative power of modern GANs [23–25] combined with CLIP. Notable approaches include StyleCLIP [41], which introduces three methodologies to manipulate the latent space of StyleGAN2 [25] with textual guidance using the semantic power of CLIP. Also, Bau *et al.* [5] used additional user-given mask input to perform text-guided inpainting using StyleGAN2 and CLIP. Following works develop many interesting new improvements, such as enabling out-of-domain manipulations [13], exploring robustness [34] or disentanglement [55] for better generative quality, and accelerating inference time [29]. However, GAN-based approaches are often limited to a restricted domain of their training data and require special GAN inversion techniques [1,2,64] to manipulate real images.

On the other hand, several approaches aim to use diffusion models [48] as an alternative to GANs. These efforts combines a conditional diffusion model with CLIP and demonstrate robust out-of-domain manipulation [26], capabilities for local manipulation on realistic natural images [4], and photo-realistic synthesis and editing with a large-scale model [37]. In particular, the GLIDE model of Nichol *et al.* [37] greatly improves the previous work DALL-E [43] with diffusion models and classifier-free guidance [16]. In this work, we adopt GLIDE for text-guided local image manipulation with a novel guidance scheme fitted for the new problem of referring object manipulation.

We note that Zhang *et al.* [63] introduce a similar problem setting of image manipulation by text instruction, which specifies the object or region of the input image in natural language. However, their method is only tested on synthetic datasets with constrained set of vocabularies, whereas we demonstrate the capabilities of our framework on much more challenging settings.

2.2   Referring Image Segmentation

Referring image segmentation, first introduced by Hu *et al.* [18], aims to segment a target region (object or stuff) in an image that corresponds to the given natural language expression. Standard approaches [18,31,33,47,59] first extract image features with a CNN and text features with LSTM [17]. Then, the multi-modal features are fused to estimate the segmentation mask using an image segmentation model. Recent approaches adopt Transformers [49] for extracting better text features [21,56], better fusion and localization [12,20,58], or sometimes to train a unified multi-modal model [10,57].

Current state of the recent referring image segmentation models are surprisingly good, which motivated us to directly use the results for the challenging task of referring object manipulation. Though we choose to use MDETR [21] in this paper for its good performance and code availability[1], note that any other model can take place in our framework, and we can also benefit from the developments in referring image segmentation architectures.

3   Background

In this section, we briefly review the series of developments in guided diffusion models: the baseline diffusion model [15,48], classifier guidance [9], classifier-free guidance [16], and CLIP guidance [37]. The line of works form the fundamentals of our proposed classifier-free guidance technique and are all compared in the experiments. We generally follow the notations as summarized in GLIDE [37]. For detailed mathematical derivations, we refer the readers to [15] and [9].

3.1   Diffusion Models

Given a sample from the real data distribution $x_0 \sim q(x_0)$, a diffusion process generates a Markov chain of latent variables $x_1, ..., x_T$ by adding Gaussian noise at each timestep t:

$$q(x_t|x_{t-1}) := \mathcal{N}(x_t; \sqrt{1 - \beta_t}x_{t-1}, \beta_t\mathcal{I}), \tag{1}$$

where the amount of noise is controlled by a variance schedule $\{\beta_t \in (0, 1)\}_{t=1}^{T}$. It is known that if β_t is small enough, the posterior $q(x_{t-1}|x_t)$ can be approximated by a diagonal Gaussian, and that the final variable x_T approximately follows $\mathcal{N}(0, \mathcal{I})$ with sufficiently large amount of total noise added. Since calculating the true posterior $q(x_{t-1}|x_t)$ is infeasible, an approximate model p_θ needs to be learned as follows:

$$p_\theta(x_{t-1}|x_t) := \mathcal{N}(\mu_\theta(x_t), \Sigma_\theta(x_t)). \tag{2}$$

Then, sample generation can be done by starting with a random Gaussian noise $x_T \sim \mathcal{N}(0, \mathcal{I})$ and sequentially sampling $x_{T-1}, ..., x_0$ using the learned model. In

---

[1] https://github.com/ashkamath/mdetr.

practice, Ho *et al.* [15] uses a reparameterization trick [27] and decompose the latent variable x_t into a mixture of signal x_0 and some additive noise ϵ, which is estimated by a noise approximation model $\epsilon_\theta(x_t, t)$. They also derive $\mu_\theta(x_t)$ as a function of $\epsilon_\theta(x_t, t)$, fix Σ_θ to a constant, and use a simplified mean-square error objective for practical benefits:

$$L_{\text{simple}} := E_{t \sim [1,T], x_0 \sim q(x_0), \epsilon \sim \mathcal{N}(0,\mathbf{I})}[||\epsilon - \epsilon_\theta(x_t, t)||^2]. \tag{3}$$

3.2 Guided Diffusion

Dhariwal and Nichol [9] showed that better class-conditioned samples can be generated with classifier guidance. Concretely, the mean $\mu_\theta(x_t|y)$ and variance $\Sigma_\theta(x_t|y)$ of the diffusion model is perturbed by the classifier's gradient for a target class y. The resulting *perturbed* mean $\hat{\mu}_\theta(x_t|y)$ can then be calculated as:

$$\hat{\mu}_\theta(x_t|y) = \mu_\theta(x_t|y) + s \cdot \Sigma_\theta(x_t|y)\nabla_{x_t} \log p_\phi(y|x_t), \tag{4}$$

where the coefficient s is a guidance scale that controls the trade-off between sample quality and diversity (higher s gives better quality with less diversity). One downside of classifier guidance is that it requires a separate classifier which needs to be explicitly trained on noisy input images (to simulate the latent variables x_t). This introduces notable additional complexity, since the standard pretrained classifiers (trained on clean images) cannot be used.

3.3 Classifier-Free Guidance

Classifier-free guidance (CFG), first proposed by Ho and Salimans [16], is a recent technique that removed the need for a separately trained classifier. Specifically, when training a class-conditional diffusion model $\epsilon_\theta(x_t|y)$, the class label y is randomly replaced with a null label $\emptyset$ with a fixed probability (denoted as an unconditional model, $\epsilon_\theta(x_t|\emptyset)$). Sampling is done by a linear combination of the conditional and unconditional model estimates:

$$\hat{\epsilon}_\theta(x_t|y) = \epsilon_\theta(x_t|\emptyset) + s \cdot (\epsilon_\theta(x_t|y) - \epsilon_\theta(x_t|\emptyset)), \tag{5}$$

where $s \geq 1$ is the guidance scale. Intuitively, CFG further extrapolates the output of the model along the direction of $\epsilon_\theta(x_t|y)$, moving away from $\epsilon_\theta(x_t|\emptyset)$.

GLIDE [37] used CFG with generic text prompts, which is implemented by randomly replacing the text captions with an empty sequence ($\emptyset$) during training. The generative process can then be guided towards the caption c as

$$\hat{\epsilon}_\theta(x_t|c) = \epsilon_\theta(x_t|\emptyset) + s \cdot (\epsilon_\theta(x_t|c) - \epsilon_\theta(x_t|\emptyset)). \tag{6}$$

CFG can be thought of a self-supervised way of leveraging the learned knowledge of a single diffusion model. In this work, we extend this approach to give better guidance direction when applied to a referring object manipulation problem.

3.4   CLIP Guidance

CLIP [42] is a popular method of learning joint image-text representation. The model consists of an image encoder $f(x)$ and a caption encoder $g(c)$, which is trained with a contrastive loss that encourages a high dot product for the matching image (x) - text (c) pairs and low values otherwise.

Since CLIP provides a way of measuring the semantic distance between an image and a caption, many previous works use it for designing text-guided image manipulation models using the state-of-the-art GANs [13,41]. More recently, the same idea is applied to diffusion models [4,26,37], where the noisy classifier of classifier guidance (Eq. (4)) is replaced with a CLIP model:

$$\hat{\mu}_\theta(x_t|c) = \mu_\theta(x_t|c) + s \cdot \Sigma_\theta(x_t|c) \nabla_{x_t} \left(f(x_t) \cdot g(c) \right). \tag{7}$$

Prior works [7,8] have shown that the public CLIP models are capable of guiding the diffusion models, even though they are not trained with noisy input images x_t as in [9]. However, GLIDE [37] has shown that noise-aware trained model, named as noised CLIP model, performs considerably better than the unnoised CLIP, and we use the noised version in our comparison experiments.

4   Method

4.1   Problem Setting

We formulate the problem of *Referring Object Manipulation (ROM)*, which aims to modify the referring region of interest from an input image to conform to the target text expression. Specifically, a ROM model has three inputs: an input image **I**, a referring text prompt c_{ref}, and a target text prompt c_{target}. The output is an edited image $\tilde{\mathbf{I}}$, which should successfully contain the attributes described in the target text. To achieve this goal, a model should correctly infer the local regions where c_{ref} is referring to, and then manipulate the regions according to the target c_{target}. This is a challenging task that requires full multi-modal (vision and language) understanding and high-quality generative models. The conceptual illustration is shown in Fig. 1.

Referring object manipulation problem can be decomposed into two sub-problems, referring image segmentation and text-guided image inpainting. Referring image segmentation models aim to estimate a precise segmentation mask **M**, given an input image **I** and a referring prompt c_{ref}. The goal of text-guided image inpainting models is to generate a photo-realistic edited image $\tilde{\mathbf{I}}$ given an input image **I**, a (user-given) mask specifying the regions to edit, and a target prompt c_{target}. Therefore, by substituting the user-given mask with the automatically generated mask **M**, we can build an end-to-end ROM framework.

With recent developments in both fields (referring segmentation and text-guided inpainting), a sequential combination of two models serves as a simple but strong baseline. However, due to the different focus and the evaluation metrics in each field, there exists some cases when the errors from an earlier model propagates and generates visually unpleasing outputs. In the following subsections, we propose a novel solution to make the generations more robust (Fig. 2).

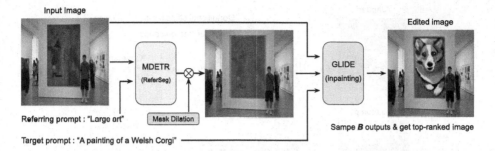

Fig. 2. Architecture overview. First, MDETR model estimates the referred-to segmentation mask given the input image and the referring text prompt. Then, using the input image, the dilated segmentation mask, and the target text prompt, GLIDE model edits the masked regions to correctly follow the target prompt. The final output is decided to be the top-ranked image *w.r.t.* our localized ranking scheme, out of $B = 24$ samples.

4.2   Architecture Overview

As a realization of the referring object manipulation framework, we combine two state-of-the-art models in each area: MDETR [21] for referring image segmentation, and GLIDE [37] for text-guided image inpainting.

MDETR is a Transformer-based text-guided detection model that can localize a specific image region given a referring textual expression. In practice, we use the extended MDETR model fine-tuned on PhraseCut dataset [51], which allows for generating pixel-level segmentation masks along with the bounding boxes.

GLIDE is a large-scale image generation and editing framework based on conditional diffusion models. We use the model specifically trained to perform image inpainting; in particular, we use the smaller open-sourced version[2] that is trained with a filtered dataset.[3]

A simple combination of MDETR and GLIDE can occasionally generate impressive output edits, but we also introduce three additional improvements for more reliable manipulation: conditional classifier-free guidance, context-aware localized output ranking, and mask dilation. Each new component will be described in detail in the following Sect. 4.3, 4.4, and 4.5, respectively.

Note that we use the pretrained models from MDETR and GLIDE *as is*, without any further training or fine-tuning. Also, any referring object segmentation model can be substituted instead of MDETR, and any conditional diffusion model can be substituted instead of GLIDE, as long as it is trained with the inpainting setting with a mask input.

---

[2] https://github.com/openai/glide-text2im.

[3] The filtered dataset aims to remove any potential bias in the data and pretrained models. This model should be denoted as GLIDE (*filt.*) following the original work [37], but we omit (*filt.*) in this paper for brevity, since all of our experiments are done with the publicly available filtered version.

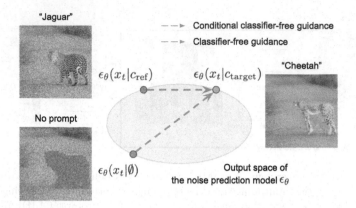

Fig. 3. Conceptual illustration of conditional classifier-free guidance. While the original classifier-free guidance (CFG) can be thought of guiding the denoising generative process from no input prompt, our conditional CFG starts from the referring prompt and can make the manipulation (empirically) easier on the noise prediction space ϵ_θ.

4.3   Conditional Classifier-Free Guidance

Inspired by StyleCLIP [41] (global direction) and StyleGAN-NADA [13], we aim to guide the generative process along the direction of the source to the target. However, unlike StyleGAN [25], which has a well-analyzed latent embedding space [52], diffusion models currently do not have such correspondent. Nevertheless, we provide an intuitive modification to the classifier-free guidance for each time step in the (reverse) diffusion process, based on its geometric interpretation of extrapolating towards the noise prediction given a target caption.

Formally, recall the classifier-free guidance towards the caption c (Eq. (6), where $c = c_{\mathrm{target}}$ in our problem setting). Instead of starting the guidance from an empty set $\emptyset$, we propose to guide the generative sampling process starting from our reference text prompt c_{ref} as follows:

$$\hat{\epsilon}_\theta(x_t|c) = \epsilon_\theta(x_t|c_{\mathrm{ref}}) + s \cdot (\epsilon_\theta(x_t|c) - \epsilon_\theta(x_t|c_{\mathrm{ref}})). \tag{8}$$

Intuitively, we can think of Eq. (8) as guiding the generative process along the direction towards the target expression *from the referring expression* on the joint (noisy) image-text embedding space, as illustrated in Fig. 3.

To align with the changes in our guidance direction, we also set the input to the inpainting model as the original input image, instead of the masked image as in the original GLIDE. We can roughly think of the original classifier-free guidance as generating a new object in a blank region (corresponding to the $\emptyset$ caption). However, since we have additional semantic information about the referring region with c_{ref} in our problem setting, conditioning on this knowledge is beneficial to the editing quality. The effects of the proposed term is more discussed in Sect. 5.3.

4.4   Localized Output Ranking with Context

Many existing works on text-guided generative models [43] first synthesize a
large number of samples and rank the generations using CLIP. Nichol *et al.* [37]
suggests that CLIP re-ranking is not necessary when a model is trained with
classifier-free guidance, but we have empirically found that the generated images
with higher rankings are perceptually better than the low-ranked images and re-
apply the output ranking scheme. Avrahami *et al.* [4] proposes to rank the final
generated outputs with a pretrained CLIP model, similarly to [43,44]. However,
they perform ranking only on the masked region, which can sometimes lead the
model to generate a plausible region by itself but does not harmonize with the
unmasked regions well. Thus, we propose to instead rank the final outputs $w.r.t.$
the bounding box enlarged by a small ratio ($\times 1.3$ in practice), for localized
ranking that also considers the surrounding context. Experimental results and
the ranking effects are more discussed in Sect. 5.3.

4.5   Dilated Mask Prediction

The main problem that arises when using an automatically generated segmentation mask is that the mask prediction can be inaccurate. Especially, we have
empirically found that the errors are much more critical when the mask does not
cover the full object, compared to when the mask is covering the region larger
than the object. Thus, we propose a simple heuristic of enlarging the predicted
segmentation mask with a dilation operator, one of morphological transformations, to ensure that the mask better covers the referred object. This problem
was not an issue for previous text-guided inpainting approaches, since a user-
generated mask almost always covers the full object.

5   Experiments

5.1   Implementation Details

We use PyTorch [40] for implementation. Since our framework does not require
additional training, all results in this paper can be obtained with a single GPU
(we used NVIDIA V100) or by simply using a hosted runtime on Colab [6].
The public GLIDE-inpainting model consists of two separate models: 64×64
inpainting diffusion model and 256×256 (inpainting-aware) upsampling model,
and our proposed improvements are only applied to the 64×64 inpainting model.
Following the setting in GLIDE, we used 100 diffusion steps in the inpainting
model for fast sampling (instead of the full 1000 steps in DDPM [15]), and
27 steps for the upsampling model. For guidance scale s, we found that the
default setting of $s = 5$ in the open-source GLIDE repository works well for the
compared GLIDE baselines, but our method typically works better for a larger
scale of $s = 15$. The code to reproduce our experimental results is publicly
released[4] to facilitate future research on referring object manipulation.

---

[4] https://github.com/google/referring-manipulation.

5.2   Comparisons

We compare the proposed framework with three baselines: 1) Blended-diffusion [4] (denote as 'Blended') and GLIDE with 2) CLIP guidance and 3) Classifier-free guidance (CFG). We use the images and captions from the PhraseCut dataset [51] for our comparisons, but occasionally modify the referring captions to a more salient object (or stuff) for better visualizations on our manipulation settings. We manually give the target text prompts to demonstrate new and interesting edits. For the compared models, the user-given mask inputs are substituted with the prediction from MDETR (and dilated). The overall qualitative results are summarized in Fig. 4.

In general, we found that CLIP-guided approach is susceptible to making adversarial examples that fool the CLIP model (as discussed in [14]). The Blended model is able to mitigate this issue by augmentations and generates high-quality edits, but sometimes shows imbalanced proportions between the masked region and the rest (also mentioned in [4]). CFG and our conditional CFG enables to remove CLIP during the diffusion steps and generates plausible edits most of the time, but the results using our conditional CFG is usually more realistic.

We also demonstrate more diverse generations *w.r.t.* each target text prompt in Fig. 5. Note that when there is no target prompt, the model performs inpainting and fills in the masked region from the surrounding context. Please refer to our supplementary materials for additional qualitative results and analyses in various different settings.

User Studies. For quantitative evaluation of the editing quality, we perform a human subjective test on 20 sample outputs, compared with Blended [4] and GLIDE (CLIP and CF-guided). In each testing case, we show the input image, the local region of interest, the target text, and 4 output edits including ours. The order of the display is randomized, and each participant is asked to rank the 4 outputs. A total of 60 users participated in this study, and the aggregated results are shown in Table 1. We found that no single model absolutely wins over the other, since all models have strong generation capabilities and give plausible outputs. However, our CCF-guided method shows the best average rank (best rank is 1, worst is 4), and our algorithm has 54.4% of winning probability when compared with the second best method of Blended, and 58.4% against the most similar baseline, CF-guided GLIDE. We report more detailed results in our supplementary document due to the page limit.

5.3   Ablation Studies

Effects of Guidance Direction. Given an input image and the segmentation mask estimated by MDETR, we compare the effects of the guidance direction of GLIDE in Fig. 6. Note that all results are obtained using *exactly the same values of the pretrained parameters* regardless of the guidance scheme. While all methods are capable of generating realistic outputs, our results tend to better keep the characteristics of the original image, while CF-guided GLIDE generates

Fig. 4. Comparison between existing methods on text-guided image manipulation using images from PhraseCut dataset [51]. All models use the same input mask given by the output of MDETR [21]. Our conditional classifier-free guidance is able to make more visually pleasing edits that correctly follow the target text.

more diverse results. This is because CF-guided GLIDE model does not know the masked-out region which our CCF-guided model knows, and each can be beneficial for its own use cases. Also, exploring which characteristic of the input image are preserved on the noise manifold of the diffusion process would make an interesting future work, which is out of scope of this paper.

Fig. 5. Qualitative example for diverse target text queries. We use the guidance scale $s = 15.0$ for all methods. Interestingly, inpainting the bananas without any condition led to generating what looks like a shrimp tempura due to the dipping sauce next to it. We could also generate many interesting objects near the horizon.

Table 1. User study results. We report the average rank (1–4) and the winning probability of a method in each row against the other models in each column.

Method	Avg. Rank↓	Winning prob. vs:			
		Blend	G-CLIP	G-CF	Ours
Blended	2.40	–	57.8%	51.4%	45.6%
GLIDE (CLIP-guided)	2.82	42.2%	–	46.6%	34.2%
GLIDE (CF-guided)	2.57	48.6%	57.4%	–	41.6%
Ours (CCF-guided)	2.20	54.4%	65.8%	58.4%	–

Effects of Localized Ranking. A qualitative comparison between the ranking method in Blended [4] and ours is shown in Fig. 7. Since the outputs are generated using the same guidance scheme with the same random seed, the total set of output images should be identical. However, the top-ranked results for the proposed localized ranking technique are usually more realistic and harmonize with the nearby context better.

Effects of Mask Dilation. We show the effects of enlarging the intermediate segmentation mask with dilation in Fig. 8. If the predicted segmentation mask does not cover fully cover the object of interest, the remaining boundaries strongly affect how the model infers nearby context. This leads to generating a similar object category or some other unpleasing artifacts instead of removing the target object.

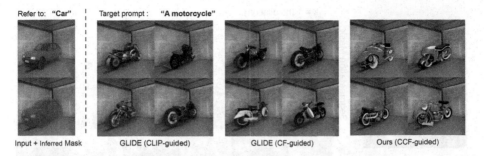

Fig. 6. The effects of different guidance methods. Four samples using different random seeds are shown for each guidance scheme. CLIP-guidance sometimes fails to generate the full object and shows only distinctive parts. While CF-guidance and Ours (CCF-guided) successfully synthesize the target object as a whole, ours tend to more keep the characteristics of the original input image, *e.g.* red color, unless otherwise guided by the target prompt. (Color figure online)

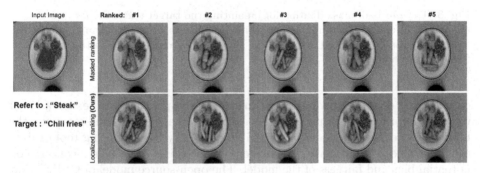

Fig. 7. The effects of different ranking mechanisms. While the set of total generated images for the first and the second rows are the same, the masked ranking tends to prefer relatively thicker potato-like objects, whereas our top-ranked outputs are thinner and match the target text better.

6   Limitations and Future Work

Although our proposed referring object manipulation framework with conditional classifier-free guidance generates plausible image edits, it still has several major limitations. First, at its current state, it cannot generate images of resolution other than 64 × 64 or 256 × 256, due to the constraint in the conditional diffusion model that we used. We believe that further research in conditional diffusion model can mitigate this issue. Second, our model cannot recover from a wrong segmentation output, because we sequentially combine the two separate models explicitly. Given the recent progress in vision-language transformers, we think that designing a fully end-to-end trainable architecture for referring object manipulation would also be an interesting direction for research. Third, the current model cannot perform very fine-grained manipulation, and the edited outputs for the referred regions are sometimes blurry. Even though we provide better

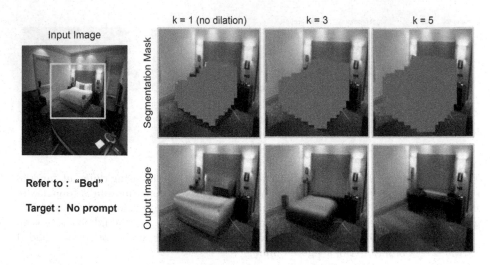

Fig. 8. The effects of mask dilation for inpainting (no target text). For $k = 1$ or $k = 3$, the model infers from the remaining white bed sheets or the bottom frame, which makes potentially unwanted artifacts. We show the enlarged region in the yellow box. (Color figure online)

conditioning on the input image and referred prompt, there still exists a lot of room for improvement in preserving the original image details and removing the boundary effects or artifacts. Also, building an easy-to-use editing tool enables even unskilled users to make fake imagery, which raises many safety concerns on potential bias and fairness of the model. The open-source model of GLIDE that we use has already considered safety issues in various aspects, but further effort will be required as a community to prevent any harmful use cases.

7 Conclusions

In this paper, we introduced a new problem of referring object manipulation and the first approach to address this task. The proposed framework combines a referring image segmentation method with a text-guided diffusion model and guides the generative diffusion process with a novel conditional classifier-free guidance scheme. We also proposed a new localized ranking method and mask dilation technique, which leads to visually more pleasing edits when combined together. As we demonstrate and analyze in the experiments, our model is capable of serving as a simple and effective baseline for referring object manipulation.

Acknowledgement. We would like to thank Tobias Weyand, Fangting Xia, and Mikhail Sirotenko for helpful discussions, comments, and proofreading this work. This work is fully supported by Google Research.

References

1. Abdal, R., Qin, Y., Wonka, P.: Image2StyleGAN: how to embed images into the StyleGAN latent space? In: ICCV (2019)
2. Abdal, R., Qin, Y., Wonka, P.: Image2StyleGAN++: how to edit the embedded images? In: CVPR (2020)
3. Antol, S., et al.: VQA: visual question answering. In: ICCV (2015)
4. Avrahami, O., Lischinski, D., Fried, O.: Blended diffusion for text-driven editing of natural images. arXiv:2111.14818 (2021)
5. Bau, D., et al.: Paint by word. arXiv:2103.10951 (2021)
6. Bisong, E.: Google colaboratory. In: Building Machine Learning and Deep Learning Models on Google Cloud Platform: A Comprehensive Guide for Beginners, pp. 59–64. Apress, Berkeley (2019). https://doi.org/10.1007/978-1-4842-4470-8_7
7. Crowson, K.: Clip guided diffusion 512×512, secondary model method(2021). https://twitter.com/RiversHaveWings/status/1462859669454536711
8. Crowson, K.: Clip guided diffusion HQ 256×256 (2021). https://colab.research.google.com/drive/12a_Wrfi2_gwwAuN3VvMTwVMz9TfqctNj
9. Dhariwal, P., Nichol, A.: Diffusion models beat GANs on image synthesis. In: NeurIPS (2021)
10. Ding, H., Liu, C., Wang, S., Jiang, X.: Vision-language transformer and query generation for referring segmentation. In: ICCV (2021)
11. Dong, H., Yu, S., Wu, C., Guo, Y.: Semantic image synthesis via adversarial learning. In: ICCV (2017)
12. Feng, G., Hu, Z., Zhang, L., Lu, H.: Encoder fusion network with co-attention embedding for referring image segmentation. In: CVPR (2021)
13. Gal, R., Patashnik, O., Maron, H., Chechik, G., Cohen-Or, D.: StyleGAN-NADA: CLIP-guided domain adaptation of image generators. arXiv:2108.00946 (2021)
14. Goh, G., et al.: Multimodal neurons in artificial neural networks. Distill (2021). https://distill.pub/2021/multimodal-neurons
15. Ho, J., Jain, A., Abbeel, P.: Denoising diffusion probabilistic models. In: NeurIPS (2020)
16. Ho, J., Salimans, T.: Classifier-free diffusion guidance. In: NeurIPS 2021 Workshop on Deep Generative Models and Downstream Applications (2021)
17. Hochreiter, S., Schmidhuber, J.: Long short-term memory. Neural Comput. **9**(8), 1735–1780 (1997)
18. Hu, R., Rohrbach, M., Darrell, T.: Segmentation from natural language expressions. In: Leibe, B., Matas, J., Sebe, N., Welling, M. (eds.) ECCV 2016. LNCS, vol. 9905, pp. 108–124. Springer, Cham (2016). https://doi.org/10.1007/978-3-319-46448-0_7
19. Jia, C., et al.: Scaling up visual and vision-language representation learning with noisy text supervision. In: ICML (2021)
20. Jing, Y., Kong, T., Wang, W., Wang, L., Li, L., Tan, T.: Locate then segment: a strong pipeline for referring image segmentation. In: CVPR (2021)
21. Kamath, A., Singh, M., LeCun, Y., Synnaeve, G., Misra, I., Carion, N.: MDETR-modulated detection for end-to-end multi-modal understanding. In: ICCV (2021)
22. Karpathy, A., Fei-Fei, L.: Deep visual-semantic alignments for generating image descriptions. In: CVPR (2015)
23. Karras, T., Aila, T., Laine, S., Lehtinen, J.: Progressive growing of GANs for improved quality, stability, and variation. arXiv:1710.10196 (2017)

24. Karras, T., Laine, S., Aila, T.: A style-based generator architecture for generative adversarial networks. In: CVPR (2019)
25. Karras, T., Laine, S., Aittala, M., Hellsten, J., Lehtinen, J., Aila, T.: Analyzing and improving the image quality of StyleGAN. In: CVPR (2020)
26. Kim, G., Ye, J.C.: DiffusionCLIP: text-guided diffusion models for robust image manipulation. arXiv:2110.02711 (2021)
27. Kingma, D.P., Welling, M.: Auto-encoding variational bayes. arXiv:1312.6114 (2013)
28. Kiros, R., Salakhutdinov, R., Zemel, R.S.: Unifying visual-semantic embeddings with multimodal neural language models. arXiv:1411.2539 (2014)
29. Kocasari, U., Dirik, A., Tiftikci, M., Yanardag, P.: StyleMC: multi-channel based fast text-guided image generation and manipulation. In: Proceedings of the IEEE/CVF Winter Conference on Applications of Computer Vision (2022)
30. Li, B., Qi, X., Lukasiewicz, T., Torr, P.H.: ManiGAN: text-guided image manipulation. In: CVPR (2020)
31. Li, R., et al.: Referring image segmentation via recurrent refinement networks. In: CVPR (2018)
32. Lin, T.-Y., et al.: Microsoft COCO: common objects in context. In: Fleet, D., Pajdla, T., Schiele, B., Tuytelaars, T. (eds.) ECCV 2014. LNCS, vol. 8693, pp. 740–755. Springer, Cham (2014). https://doi.org/10.1007/978-3-319-10602-1_48
33. Liu, C., Lin, Z., Shen, X., Yang, J., Lu, X., Yuille, A.: Recurrent multimodal interaction for referring image segmentation. In: ICCV (2017)
34. Liu, X., Gong, C., Wu, L., Zhang, S., Su, H., Liu, Q.: FuseDream: training-free text-to-image generation with improved CLIP+GAN space optimization. arXiv:2112.01573 (2021)
35. Mirza, M., Osindero, S.: Conditional generative adversarial nets. arXiv:1411.1784 (2014)
36. Nam, S., Kim, Y., Kim, S.J.: Text-adaptive generative adversarial networks: manipulating images with natural language. In: NeurIPS (2018)
37. Nichol, A., et al.: GLIDE: towards photorealistic image generation and editing with text-guided diffusion models. arXiv:2112.10741 (2021)
38. Nichol, A.Q., Dhariwal, P.: Improved denoising diffusion probabilistic models. In: ICML (2021)
39. Nilsback, M.E., Zisserman, A.: Automated flower classification over a large number of classes. In: 2008 Sixth Indian Conference on Computer Vision, Graphics & Image Processing, pp. 722–729. IEEE (2008)
40. Paszke, A., et al.: PyTorch: an imperative style, high-performance deep learning library. arXiv:1912.01703 (2019)
41. Patashnik, O., Wu, Z., Shechtman, E., Cohen-Or, D., Lischinski, D.: StyleCLIP: text-driven manipulation of StyleGAN imagery. In: ICCV (2021)
42. Radford, A., et al.: Learning transferable visual models from natural language supervision. arXiv:2103.00020 (2021)
43. Ramesh, A., et al.: Zero-shot text-to-image generation. In: ICML (2021)
44. Razavi, A., van den Oord, A., Vinyals, O.: Generating diverse high-fidelity images with VQ-VAE-2. arXiv:1906.00446 (2019)
45. Reed, S., Akata, Z., Yan, X., Logeswaran, L., Schiele, B., Lee, H.: Generative adversarial text to image synthesis. In: ICML (2016)
46. Sharma, P., Ding, N., Goodman, S., Soricut, R.: Conceptual captions: a cleaned, hypernymed, image alt-text dataset for automatic image captioning. In: ACL (2018)

47. Shi, H., Li, H., Meng, F., Wu, Q.: Key-word-aware network for referring expression image segmentation. In: Ferrari, V., Hebert, M., Sminchisescu, C., Weiss, Y. (eds.) ECCV 2018. LNCS, vol. 11210, pp. 38–54. Springer, Cham (2018). https://doi.org/10.1007/978-3-030-01231-1_3

48. Sohl-Dickstein, J., Weiss, E., Maheswaranathan, N., Ganguli, S.: Deep unsupervised learning using nonequilibrium thermodynamics. In: ICML (2015)

49. Vaswani, A., et al.: Attention is all you need. In: NeurIPS (2017)

50. Wah, C., Branson, S., Welinder, P., Perona, P., Belongie, S.: The Caltech-UCSD Birds-200-2011 dataset (2011)

51. Wu, C., Lin, Z., Cohen, S., Bui, T., Maji, S.: PhraseCut: language-based image segmentation in the wild. In: CVPR (2020)

52. Wu, Z., Lischinski, D., Shechtman, E.: StyleSpace analysis: disentangled controls for StyleGAN image generation. In: CVPR (2021)

53. Xia, W., Yang, Y., Xue, J.H., Wu, B.: TediGAN: text-guided diverse face image generation and manipulation. In: CVPR (2021)

54. Xu, T., et al.: AttnGAN: fine-grained text to image generation with attentional generative adversarial networks. In: CVPR (2018)

55. Xu, Z., et al.: Predict, prevent, and evaluate: disentangled text-driven image manipulation empowered by pre-trained vision-language model. arXiv:2111.13333 (2021)

56. Yang, S., Xia, M., Li, G., Zhou, H.Y., Yu, Y.: Bottom-up shift and reasoning for referring image segmentation. In: CVPR (2021)

57. Yang, Z., Wang, J., Tang, Y., Chen, K., Zhao, H., Torr, P.H.: LAVT: language-aware vision transformer for referring image segmentation. arXiv:2112.02244 (2021)

58. Ye, L., Rochan, M., Liu, Z., Wang, Y.: Cross-modal self-attention network for referring image segmentation. In: CVPR (2019)

59. Yu, L., et al.: MAttNet: modular attention network for referring expression comprehension. In: CVPR (2018)

60. Zhang, H., et al.: StackGAN: text to photo-realistic image synthesis with stacked generative adversarial networks. In: ICCV (2017)

61. Zhang, H., et al.: StackGAN++: realistic image synthesis with stacked generative adversarial networks. IEEE TPAMI **41**(8), 1947–1962 (2018)

62. Zhang, L., Chen, Q., Hu, B., Jiang, S.: Text-guided neural image inpainting. In: ACM MM (2020)

63. Zhang, T., Tseng, H.Y., Jiang, L., Yang, W., Lee, H., Essa, I.: Text as neural operator: image manipulation by text instruction. In: ACM MM (2021)

64. Zhu, J., Shen, Y., Zhao, D., Zhou, B.: In-domain GAN inversion for real image editing. In: Vedaldi, A., Bischof, H., Brox, T., Frahm, J.-M. (eds.) ECCV 2020. LNCS, vol. 12362, pp. 592–608. Springer, Cham (2020). https://doi.org/10.1007/978-3-030-58520-4_35

NewsStories: Illustrating Articles with Visual Summaries

Reuben Tan[1]([✉]), Bryan A. Plummer[1], Kate Saenko[1], JP Lewis[2],
Avneesh Sud[2], and Thomas Leung[2]

[1] Boston University, Boston, USA
{rxtan, bplum, saenko}@bu.edu
[2] Google Research, Mountain View, CA, USA
{jplewis, asud, leungt}@google.com

Abstract. Recent self-supervised approaches have used large-scale image-text datasets to learn powerful representations that transfer to many tasks without finetuning. These methods often assume that there is a one-to-one correspondence between images and their (short) captions. However, many tasks require reasoning about multiple images paired with a long text narrative, such as photos in a news article. In this work, we explore a novel setting where the goal is to learn a self-supervised visual-language representation from longer text paired with a set of photos, which we call *visual summaries*. In addition, unlike prior work which assumed captions have a **literal** relation to the image, we assume images only contain loose **illustrative** correspondence with the text. To explore this problem, we introduce a large-scale multimodal dataset called NEWSSTORIES containing over 31 M articles, 22 M images and 1 M videos. We show that state-of-the-art image-text alignment methods are not robust to longer narratives paired with multiple images, and introduce an intuitive baseline that outperforms these methods, e.g., by 10% on on zero-shot image-set retrieval in the GoodNews dataset. (https://github.com/NewsStoriesData/newsstories.github.io).

Keywords: Vision-and-language · Image-and-text alignment

1 Introduction

State-of-the-art image-and-text representation learning approaches generally focus on learning a one-to-one correspondence between an image and one [15,20,30] or more captions [6,32,35], such as a photo with a caption *"An airplane is flying in the sky"* (Fig. 1a). While existing datasets such as MSCOCO

R. Tan—Work done as part of an internship at Google
K. Saenko—Also affiliated with MIT-IBM Watson AI Lab.

Supplementary Information The online version contains supplementary material available at https://doi.org/10.1007/978-3-031-20059-5_37.

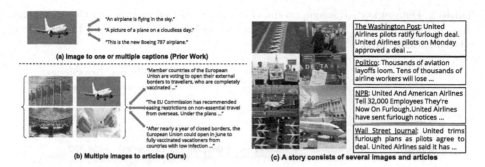

Fig. 1. Unlike prior work (a) which aligns a single image with one or more captions, we study the problem of learning the multiplicity of correspondences between an unordered set of visually diverse images and longer text sequences (b). (c) shows an example story from our NewsStories dataset. For each story, we cluster articles from different media channels and collect images that are used in the articles. In contrast to conventional **literal** caption datasets such as MSCOCO and Flickr30K, the images and text narratives in NewsStories only have **illustrative** relationships

[23] and Flickr30K [40] contain multiple captions for an image, the aforementioned approaches still learn a one-to-one correspondence between an image and a short caption that generally has a strong literal relation to it. However, this is unrealistic for longer text narratives containing multiple images (*e.g.*news articles, Wikipedia pages, blogs). To challenge such constraints, Kim *et al.* [18] first introduce the problem of retrieving image sequences based on blog posts that may be composed of multiple paragraphs, using the assumption that the image sequence and the paragraphs have the same weak temporal ordering. However, this assumption is quite restrictive due to the prevalence of long narrative texts and groups of relevant images without information about their temporal order, *e.g.*, in the news domain and Wikipedia. More importantly, they do not consider semantically related text narratives that may use similar groups of images.

Motivated by recent representation learning approaches which leverage large-scale data [15,30], we seek to address the important problem of learning visual-semantic representations from text narratives of varying lengths and groups of complementary images from publicly available data. In this paper, we address this research problem in the news domain due to the prevalence of related articles and their corresponding images on the same story from different media channels. However, this is a general problem inherent in other domains including Wikipedia and social media posts on similar events. We define a *story* as an event associated with a *visual summary* consisting of images that illustrate it and articles that describe it, or videos depicting it. In contrast to prior work, this problem requires the capability to reason about the multiplicity of correspondences between sets of complementary images and text sequences of varying lengths. For example, in (Fig. 1b), we aim to identify the story that is jointly illustrated by images of an airplane, flags of the European Union (EU) and a nurse preparing a vaccine. Here, one possibility is about traveling to the EU during a pandemic. A story could

Table 1. Dataset statistics comparison. Our NEWSSTORIES dataset is significantly larger than existing datasets with diverse media channels and story clusters that indicate related articles, images and news videos

	GoodNews [4]	NYTimes 800 K [36]	Visual news [24]	NewsStories Unfiltered	NewsStories Filtered
# Media channels	1	1	4	28,215	46
# Story clusters	–	–	–	–	350,000
# Articles	257,033	444,914	623,364	31,362,735	931,679
# Images	462,642	792,971	1,080,595	22,905,000	754,732
# Videos	0	0	0	1,020,363	333,357
Avg article length	451	974	773	446	584

contain a variety of photos that illustrate a particular concept, and conversely, stock images of an airplane or EU flags could illustrate different stories.

We formulate the problem of visual summarization as a retrieval task, where the image sets are given and the goal is to retrieve the most *relevant* and *illustrative* image set for an article. Our proposed research problem is distinguished from prior work in two ways. First, we must be able to reason about the *many-to-many* correspondences between multiple images and linguistically diverse text narratives in a story. Second, the images in our problem setting often only have *illustrative* correspondences with the text rather than *literal* connections (*e.g.* "travel" or "vacation" rather than "airplane flying"). Extracting complementary information from images and relating them to the concepts embodied by the story is a relatively under-explored problem, especially when the images and text only have loose and symbolic relationships. While existing work such as Visual Storytelling [14] aims to generate a coherent story given a set of images, the images have a temporal ordering and exhibit *literal* relations to the text.

To facilitate future work in this area, we introduce **NewsStories**, a large-scale multimodal dataset (Fig. 1-c and Table 1). It contains approximately 31 M articles in English and 22 M images from more than 28 k news sources. Unlike existing datasets, NEWSSTORIES contains data consisting of three modalities - natural language (articles), images and videos. More importantly, they are loosely grouped into *stories*, providing a rich test-bed for understanding the relations between text sequences of varying lengths and visually diverse images and videos. With an expanding body of recent work on joint representation learning from the language, visual, and audio modalities, we hope that our NEWSSTORIES dataset will pave the way for exploring more complex relations between multiple modalities.

Our primary goal is to learn robust visual-semantic representations that can generalize to text narratives of varying lengths and different number of complementary images from uncurated data. We benchmark the capabilities of state-of-the-art image-text alignment approaches to reason about such correspondences in order to understand the challenges of this novel task. Additionally, we compare them to an intuitive Multiple Instance Learning (MIL) approach that aims to maximize the mutual information between the images in a set and the sentences of a related articles. We pretrain these approaches on our NEWSSTORIES dataset before transferring the learnt representations to the downstream task of article-to-image-set retrieval on the GoodNews dataset under 3 challenging settings, without further finetuning. Importantly, we empirically demonstrate the utility of our dataset by showing that training on it improves significantly on CLIP and increases the robustness of its learnt representations to text with different numbers of images. To summarize, our contributions are as follows:

1. We propose the novel and challenging problem of aligning a story and a set of illustrative images *without temporal ordering*, as an important step towards advancing general vision-and-language reasoning, and with applications such as automated story illustration and bidirectional multimodal retrieval.
2. We introduce a large-scale news dataset NEWSSTORIES that contains over 31 M articles from 28 K media channels as well as data of three modalities. The news stories provide labels of relevance between articles and images.
3. We experimentally demonstrate that existing approaches for aligning images and text are ineffective for this task and introduce an intuitive MIL approach that outperforms state-of-the art methods as a basis for comparisons. Finally, we show that training on the NEWSSTORIES dataset significantly improves the model's capability to transfer its learned knowledge in zero-shot settings.

2   Related Work

To the best of our knowledge, there has been limited work that directly address our problem of learning *many-to-many* correspondence between images and texts. Wang et al. [38] propose to learn an alignment between image regions and its set of related captions. However, the images and captions in their setting have strong literal relationships instead of illustrative correspondences. Current vision-language models have other applications including text-based image retrieval [40], visual question answering [2,42] and visual reasoning [33], and as a tool for detection of anomalous image-text pairing in misinformation [1,34].

Recent vision-language models [15,30] demonstrate excellent zero-shot performance on various downstream tasks, sometimes exceeding the performance of bespoke models for these tasks. This advancement has relied on very large-scale datasets consisting simply of images and their associated captions. Such datasets require little or no curation, whereas the need for training labels has limited the size of datasets in the past [13]. These image-caption datasets are paired with a natural contrastive learning objective, that of associating images with their correct captions [15,30,41]. Previous work has demonstrated that improved visual representations can be learned by predicting captions (or parts of them) from images [8,16,21,31]. Captions provide a semantically richer signal [8] than the restricted number of classes in a dataset such as ImageNet – for example, a caption such as "my dog caught the frisbee" mentions two objects and an action.

Closer to our work are methods that learn one-to-many correspondences from images or videos to captions [6,32,35], or vice-versa. Polysemous Instance Embedding Networks (PVSE) [32] represents a datum from either modality with multiple embeddings representing different aspects of that instance, resulting in $n \times n$ possible matches. They use multiple instance learning (MIL) [9] align a image-sentence pair in a joint visual-semantic embedding [10,11,17] while ignoring mismatching pairs. PCME [6] explicitly generalizes the MIL formulation from a single best match to represent the set of possible mebeddings as a normal distribution, and optimize match probabilities using a soft contrastive loss [28]. In contrast to prior work, in our setting both the visual and text modalities contain semantically distinct concepts that are not appropriately represented with a unimodal probability density.

Finally, while there exist news datasets including GoodNews [4], NYT800k [36] and VisualNews [24], they are only sourced from a single (GoodNews and NYT800K) or four (VisualNews) media channels. Additionally, the VMSMO dataset [22] contains news articles and videos that are downloaded from Weibo, but it does not contain images. Compared to these datasets, our NEWSSTORIES dataset not only contains articles from over 28K sources, but also has story labels to indicate related articles and images. Related to our work, [12] released the NewSHead dataset for the task of News Story Headline generation, containing 369 k stories and 932 k articles but no images. However, ours contains a much larger corpus of stories and associated articles. Last but not least, the aforementioned datasets generally only contain either images and articles or videos and articles. In contrast, ours provides data from all 3 modalities.

3   The NewsStories Dataset

Our NEWSSTORIES dataset comprises the following modalities: 1. news articles and meta data including titles and dates 2. images 3. news videos and their corresponding audio. As mentioned above, NEWSSTORIES has three main differences from existing datasets. First, it is significantly larger in scale and consists of data from a much wider variety of news media channels. Second, unlike a significant percentage of multimodal datasets, it contains three different modalities – text, image and videos. Third, the text, images, and videos are grouped into stories. This provides story cluster labels that not only help to identify related articles but also create sets of multiple corresponding images for each story.

3.1   Data Collection

Learning the multiplicity of correspondences between groups of complementary images and related text narratives requires a dataset that contains multiple *relevant but different* images that correspond to a given text sequence and vice versa. Curating a large-scale dataset with these characteristics is an extremely expensive and time-consuming process. In contrast, the news domain provides a rich source of data due to the proliferation of online multimedia information. We collected news articles and associated media links spanning the period between October 2018 and May 2021[1]. The articles from a filtered subset (Sect. 3.2) are grouped into *stories* by performing agglomerative clustering on learned document representations [25], similar to [12], which iteratively loads articles published in a recent time window and groups them based on content similarity. We merge clusters that can possibly share similar images via a second round of clustering based on named entities. Specifically, we begin by extracting the named entities in the articles using Spacy and their contextualized representations with a pretrained named-entity aware text encoder [39]. To obtain a single vector for the story cluster, we perform average-pooling over all named entity representations across all articles. Finally, these representations are merged into a slightly smaller number of clusters. We extracted video links, however only the text and images are used for alignment in Sect. 4.

3.2   Dataset Filtering

We observed that there is a large amount of noise in the collected datasets due to the prevalence of smaller media channels. To address this, we removed articles and links that do not belong to a curated list of 46 news media channels[2] selected by an independent organization rating media biases. The list contains major news sources including BBC, CNN, and Fox News.

Curated Evaluation Set. Due to the sparsity of suitable datasets for this task, we curate a subset of the story clusters and use it as our evaluation set for the proxy task of retrieving image sets based on long narrative textual queries. Out of the 350,000 story clusters in the filtered story clusters, we randomly select 5000 clusters with at least 5 images. In the news domain it is common that articles on the same story may use similar photos. For example, different articles on the covid vaccinations may use the same image of a vaccination shot. To ensure that we can visually discriminate between two stories, we adopt a heuristic to ensure that the images are as diverse as possible. We begin by computing a set of detected entities for each image using the Google Web Detection API[3].

   To generate a visually diverse image set for a story, we compute all possible combinations of five images from the entire set of images present in the story and compute the intersection set of all detected entities over the images within a combination. Finally, we select the combination with the smallest intersection set as the ground-truth (GT) image set for a story. During training, each set of images is randomly sampled from all available images in the story cluster.

3.3   Quality of Story Clusters

To evaluate the quality of these story clusters, we use qualified human raters to judge three aspects of our NEWSSTORIES dataset. Each data sample is rated by

---

[1] CommonCrawl [7] can be used to fetch web articles.

[2] https://www.allsides.com/media-bias/media-bias-chart.

[3] https://cloud.google.com/vision/docs/detecting-web.

three humans and the rating with the most votes is selected as the final score. We provide the instructions for these evaluations in the supplementary.

Relatedness of Articles in a Story Cluster. For an approach to learn a meaningful alignment between groups of images and groups of related text, it is necessary that the articles in a story cluster are mostly relevant to each other. We randomly sample 100 stories and provide each rater with up to 10 articles from each story. A story is rated as of good quality if at least 80% of the articles are related to each other. Out of 100 randomly selected story clusters, raters determine that 82% of them are of good quality. Note that we do not try to eliminate all noise in the story clusters since we do not have ground-truth targets.

Relevance of Images in a Story Cluster. To rate the semantic relevance of the images to the story, each rater is provided with a maximum of 10 articles and 20 images from each cluster. The image set is labeled as relevant to the articles if at least 80% of the images are plausible in the context of the story. 76% of the randomly selected sets are rated as relevant. Some possible sources of irrelevant images may come from links to other articles or advertisements.

Ambiguity of ground-truth image sets in the evaluation set. A well-known problem of existing bidirectional sentence-to-image retrieval datasets is that some sentences can be relevant to other images in the dataset that are not in the ground truth, which results in inherent noise in the evaluation metrics. We use raters to determine if humans are able to discriminate between the ground-truth image set and others that can potentially be relevant. We randomly sample 150 stories and use the pretrained CLIP model to rank the image sets given the query article. A rater is provided with the GT image set as well as the top-5 sets retrieved by the CLIP model and is asked to select the most relevant image set. 86% of GT sets are selected by at least 2 out of 3 raters as the most relevant, indicating that our annotations are of high quality.

3.4   Data Statistics

We compare our NEWSSTORIES dataset to existing news datasets such as Good-News, NYT800K and VisualNews [4,24] in Table 1. We present statistics of both unfiltered and filtered sets. In contrast to existing datasets, the entire dataset contains articles from approximately 28 K news media channels, which significantly increases its linguistic diversity. Additionally, it contains over 31 M articles and 22 M images. We compute the story clusters over articles from the filtered set due to computational constraints, but we release the entire dataset. The articles, images, and videos in the final filtered set are grouped into approximately 350 K fine-grained story clusters. The number of articles per story cluster varies greatly across different clusters, ranging from a minimum of 1 to a maximum of about 44,000 (see suppl. for frequency histograms). We observe that story clusters that contain unusually high number of articles tend to come from the entertainment domain, e.g., reality television shows. These story clusters are

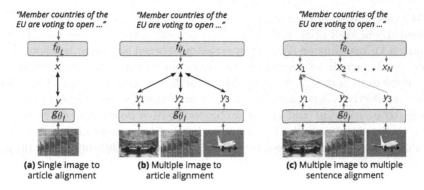

Fig. 2. Comparison of image-and-text alignment objectives. The images and text are encoded by encoders g_{θ_I} and f_{θ_L}, respectively. x and y denote the representations of the encoded article and image respectively. In (c), x is also labeled with a subscript to indicate that it is the representation for a sentence in the article

removed from the final filtered set to eliminate noise. Additionally, we observe that most story clusters contain about 1 to 20 images. This is indicative of the challenges faced in obtaining sufficient data to study the novel problem of learning multiple correspondences between images and text. Finally, please refer to the supplementary material for details on the video statistics.

4   Illustrating Articles with Visual Summaries

The primary objective of this work is to explore the problem of illustrating articles with visual summaries that comprise a varying number of images. By reasoning about the multiplicity of correspondences between longer text sequences and multiple image illustrations, we hope to jointly learn visual-semantic representations that are robust to text narratives of different lengths as well as a varying number of images. Specifically, given a set of visually different images, the goal is to learn an aggregated and contextualized representation for the images such that it is able to infer the relevant story, regardless of the exposition styles in the articles. To address this goal, we formulate the task of retrieving the most relevant set of images given a query article.

In this task, given a story consisting of a set of related articles $\mathcal{A}$, and a corresponding set of images $\mathcal{I}$, where $|\mathcal{I}| = N_I$, we aim to maximize the semantic similarity between each article $L \in \mathcal{A}$, and the entire image set $\mathcal{I}$. A language encoder f_{θ_L} is used to encode the entire text sequence L into its representation $x \in \mathbb{R}^{N_L \times D}$. Depending on the number of text segments N_L, L can be used to denote an article-level representation or a set of sentence representations. Each image is encoded to obtain its base representation y_i with an image encoder g_{θ_I} parameterized by weights θ_I, where $i \in \{1, \cdots, N_I\}$.

We describe several existing image-text alignment objectives that can be applied to our task in Sect. 4.1. We then present a Multiple Instance Learning approach for maximizing the correspondence between an image and specific sentences in the article to determine the importance of fine-grained alignment for this problem in Sect. 4.2. See Fig. 2 for a high level comparison of these objectives. An effective visual summarization of an article requires the set of retrieved images to be *coherent* and *complete*. Since negative image sets may only overlap with the story partially, we enforce coherence by constraining the models to rank them lower than the positive set for an article. Additionally, our proposed approach seeks to enforce completeness by maximizing the semantic alignment between articles and the sets of relevant images via an article-level loss.

4.1 Existing Alignment Objectives

Single Image-Text Contrastive Loss: We first explore an objective that aligns an image with a caption. Contrastive learning and its variants (InfoNCE and triplet loss) are commonly used to align an image with its corresponding text sequence by maximizing the similarity score between their respective representations [3, 15,30]. We use the popular InfoNCE [5,29] loss, formulated as $\mathcal{L}_{\text{InfoNCE}}(x, y)$:

$$-\log \frac{\exp\left(sim(x,y)/\tau\right)}{\exp\left(sim(x,y)/\tau\right) + \sum_{x'} \exp\left(sim(x',y)/\tau\right) + \sum_{y'} \exp\left(sim(x,y')/\tau\right)} \tag{1}$$

where x', y' denote the non-corresponding text and image representations with respect to a ground-truth pair in a given batch, τ is a temperature value, and $sim(.)$ is a similarity function.

Multiple Instance Learning for Noise Contrastive Estimation: The MIL-NCE formulation [27] provides a natural and intuitive extension to the regular InfoNCE objective by allowing for comparisons between a text sequence and multiple images, formulated as $\mathcal{L}_{\text{MIL-NCE}}(x, y)$:

$$-\log \frac{\sum_{i \in N_I} \exp\left(sim(x, y_i)/\tau\right)}{\exp\left(sim(x,y)/\tau\right) + \sum_{x'} \exp\left(sim(x',y)/\tau\right) + \sum_{y'} \exp\left(sim(x,y')/\tau\right)} \tag{2}$$

When evaluating with sets of images for both the InfoNCE and MIL-NCE baselines, we first compute the similarity score between the text query and each image before taking their average as the final similarity score.

Soft Contrastive Loss: PCME [6] models each image or text instance as a probability distribution. The probability that an image and a text match ($m = 1$) is computed as:

$$\frac{1}{K^2} \sum_{k}^{K} \sum_{k'}^{K} p(m | z_I^k, z_L^{k'}) \tag{3}$$

where z_I^k is the k-th sampled embedding from the image distribution and K is the number of sampled embeddings from each modality. The probability that two sampled embeddings match is computed using: $p(m|z_I^k, z_L^{k'}) = \sigma(-\alpha\|z_I^k - x_L^{k'}\| + \beta)$, where σ is the sigmoid function and α and β are learnable parameters. Finally, the loss for a given pair of image I and text L is formulated as:

$$\mathcal{L}_{\text{soft}} = \begin{cases} -\log p(m|I, L), & \text{if } I \text{ corresponds to } L \\ -\log(1 - p(m|I, L)), & \text{otherwise} \end{cases} \tag{4}$$

During training and evaluation, multiple representations are computed for each image and caption. The final similarity score between a {image, caption} pair is computed from the highest-scoring pair of image and caption representations.

4.2 Multiple Instance Learning - Sentence to Image (MIL-SIM)

Inspired by [18], we assume that each image in a given set should correspond to at least one sentence in the the article. Consequently, we adopt a Multiple Instance Learning framework where a bag of image and sentence instances is labeled as positive if most of the instances are from the same story cluster and negative otherwise. The MIL-NCE loss formulation is a smooth approximation of the max function, thus it learns an alignment between the entire article and the most representative image in a set. In contrast, MIL-SIM tries to learn the illustrative correspondence between each image and the most relevant sentence.

We segment the text article into individual sentences and encode them as $L = \{x_1, \cdots, x_{N_L}\}$. Given a positive pair of image set $I = \{I_1, \cdots, I_{N_I}\}$ and text article L, we aim to maximize the mutual information between them:

$$\max_\theta \mathbb{E}[\log \frac{p(I, L)}{p(I)p(L)}], \tag{5}$$

where $p(I)$, $P(L)$ and $P(I, L)$ are the marginal distributions for the images and articles as well as their joint distribution, respectively.

In this setting, we do not have the ground-truth target labels which indicate the sentence that a given image should correspond to. This problem is compounded by the fact that some of the images may not originate from the same text source but from related articles. Consequently, we generate pseudo-targets by selecting the best matching sentence in an article for an image (colored arrows in Fig. 2(c)). Then we use Eq. 1 to maximize the lower bound of the mutual information between them. Given an image representation y_i and an article L, we compute their similarity as $\max_l x_l^T y_i$ where l denotes the index of the sentence representation. In this formulation, multiple sentences in a corresponding article may be related to the image but will be treated erroneously as irrelevant. We circumvent this by selecting the highest-scoring sentences, with respect to the image, in articles from other clusters as negatives. Additionally, we mitigate the possibility of a different cluster containing a related sentence by reducing the weight of the image-sentence loss.

However, this may introduce a lot of noise to the learning process, especially if an image originates from a weakly-related article. To alleviate this problem, we impose an article-level loss that aims to maximize the general semantic similarity between the entire article and image set. We compute a single representation for the entire article L_f as well as image set I_f by mean-pooling over the sentence and image representations, respectively. Finally, we learn an alignment between them by minimizing the value of InfoNCE(I^f, L^f), where their similarity is computed as: $\text{sim}(I^f, Y^f) = (I^f)^T Y^f$. Our final objective function is formulated as:

$$\mathcal{L}_{\text{MIL-SIM}} = \sum_{b=1}^{B} L_{\text{InfoNCE}}(I_b^f, L_b^f) + \lambda * \sum_{b=1}^{B} \sum_{i=1}^{N_I} L_{\text{InfoNCE}}(I_{b,i}, L_b), \qquad (6)$$

where B and λ are the batch size and trade-off weight, respectively.

5   Experiments

5.1   Implementation Details

We use the visual and text encoders of CLIP [30] as a starting point and finetune them using the image-and-text alignment objectives described above. The original CLIP model is trained end-to-end using 400 million image-and-text pairs. Due to the scale of the pretraining dataset, its representations have been demonstrated to be transferable to downstream tasks without further finetuning on the target datasets. During training, we finetune the projection layers of the CLIP encoders on the train split of our NewsStories dataset. We extend the max input text length in CLIP from 77 to 256 in our experiments. We set an initial learning rate of 1e-5 and optimize the model using the Adam [19] optimizer, with a linear warm-up of 20,000 steps. The learning rate is gradually annealed using a cosine learning rate scheduler. We tune the hyperparameter settings by averaging the validation performance over 5 splits of 1000 articles that are randomly selected from the entire training set. In the MIL-SIM objective, we use the NLTK [26] library to tokenize the articles into sentences and set the value of λ to 0.1.

5.2   Evaluation Datasets and Metrics

We conduct an evaluation of article-to-image set retrieval on both our proposed NewsStories dataset and the GoodNews [4] dataset, which contains approximately 250 K articles from the New York Times. For our evaluation on the GoodNews dataset, we create three different evaluation sets of 5000 articles with 3, 4 and 5 images with no overlapping articles or images between the sets and evaluate on each separately. Note that compared to [35] which retrieves the ground-truth image from a set of five images, our evaluation setup is more challenging and arguably more realistic for real-world applications. We use two metrics: recall at top-K (R@1, R@5, R@10), where higher recall is better, and Median Rank of the correct sample, where lower is better.

Table 2. Comparison on the task of article-to-image-set retrieval on the test split of our NEWSSTORIES dataset, which contains 5000 unseen stories with image sets of size 5. Higher R@K values and lower median rank indicate more accurate retrievals

Method	Alignment type	R@1	R@5	R@10	Median rank
Pretrained CLIP [30]	Single	31.03	53.87	63.53	4
Single Image	Single	35.88	63.58	74.12	3
MIL-NCE [27]	Single	32.84	59.60	70.92	3
PCME [6]	Single	35.18	65.52	75.65	3
Transformer [37]	Multiple	50.08	78.79	86.10	2
Mean	Multiple	49.12	76.04	85.18	2
MIL-SIM	Multiple	**54.24**	**82.76**	**90.38**	**1**

Table 3. Zero-shot evaluations of article-to-image-set retrieval approaches on our test splits of the GoodNews [4] dataset. Each test split has 3, 4, or 5 images in each article

Method	R@1			R@5			R@10			Median rank		
	3	4	5	3	4	5	3	4	5	3	4	5
CLIP [30]	22.29	21.13	20.90	41.14	39.25	38.83	49.94	47.33	47.41	11	13	13
Single Image	17.27	16.27	15.61	34.84	32.57	32.55	43.94	41.47	40.95	16	19	20
MIL-NCE [27]	13.75	13.87	13.30	30.14	29.06	28.33	38.30	37.40	36.40	24	26	29
PVSE [32]	19.21	20.29	20.17	38.52	37.72	39.21	47.72	48.04	49.17	14	14	13
PCME [6]	20.08	20.65	20.14	39.36	39.72	39.91	48.12	48.56	49.03	14	14	13
Transformer [37]	29.06	28.69	29.41	51.15	**50.77**	**51.61**	59.83	59.71	60.57	5	5	5
Mean	28.73	28.01	28.77	50.22	49.11	50.24	58.80	58.64	59.39	5	6	5
MIL-SIM	**29.42**	**30.59**	**30.23**	**52.07**	49.82	51.44	**60.51**	**61.73**	**62.58**	**4**	**4**	**5**

Table 4. Evaluation of retrieval models on article-to-image-set retrieval on the Good-News dataset, where the candidate image sets do not contain a fixed number of images

Method	Alignment type	R@1	R@5	R@10	Median rank
Pretrained CLIP [30]	Single	18.43	36.59	46.92	12
Single image [30]	Single	17.14	33.77	43.56	17
MIL-NCE [27]	Single	15.50	28.96	37.60	24
PVSE	Single	18.57	37.70	47.78	12
PCME	Single	19.37	39.19	48.04	12
Mean	Multiple	21.30	41.56	51.66	9
Transformer	Multiple	20.30	40.88	49.24	11
MIL-SIM	Multiple	**25.12**	**46.17**	**56.16**	**7**

5.3 Quantitative Results

NewsStories. Table 2 reports the Recall@K retrieval accuracies and median rank on the test split of our NEWSSTORIES dataset. In this setting, each image set has a fixed size of 5 images. As demonstrated by Radford et al. [30], the learnt representations of the pretrained CLIP model transfer effectively to the GoodNews dataset without further finetuning, obtaining a R@1 accuracy of 31.03%. We observe that approaches that align a single image with a text sequence generally perform worse than variants that learn an aggregation function over the images.

In contrast to the video variant of the MIL-NCE approach [27] which reports that aligning a video clip to multiple narrations leads to better performance on downstream tasks, applying such an approach on images and text that only have loose topical relationships does not work out-of-the-box. The retrieval accuracies obtained by MIL-NCE show that maximizing the similarity between the text representation and the most representative image in the set performs worse than training with single images. Despite using a simple average-pooling function, the mean images baseline outperforms the single image and MIL-NCE baselines significantly. This suggests that context between images is crucial.

Although transformers have been shown to be effective at reasoning about context, using an image transformer to compute contextual information across the images only improves 1% over the mean baseline. This indicates that the self-attention mechanism alone is insufficient to capture the complementary relations between related but visually different images. Last but not least, the significant improvements obtained by MIL-SIM over other alignment objectives highlight the importance of maximizing the alignment between an image and the most relevant segment in an article, despite not having access to the ground-truth pairings during training. We also provide results of an ablation study over the length of the input text sequence in the supplementary.

Zero-Shot evaluation on GoodNews. Next, we compare the effectiveness of our finetuned models on the curated test splits of the GoodNews dataset without further finetuning. We verify that none of the images and articles are present in our NEWSSTORIES train split. Since GoodNews does not group articles into stories, the images in a set are obtained from the same article, instead of related articles as done in NEWSSTORIES. Similar to the evaluation results on our NEWSSTORIES dataset, Table 3 shows that the pretrained CLIP model already performs well on all 3 test splits of the GoodNews dataset, achieving an average of approximately 21% Recall@1 accuracy without any finetuning on the target dataset. Additionally, finetuning the CLIP model on NEWSSTORIES using the standard single image-and-text and MIL-NCE objectives actually leads to significant drops in performance from the pretrained CLIP model. These results suggest that learning a one-to-one correspondence is not optimal for allowing a model to reason about correspondences with multiple related images. This is corroborated by the observation that models trained to learn a one-to-one correspondences between images and text generally perform worse as the number

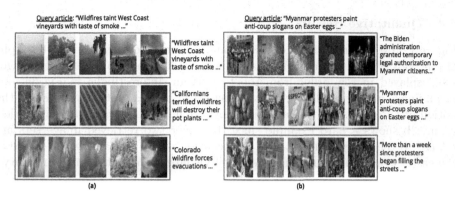

Fig. 3. Qualitative results showing the three top-ranked image sets per query on the test split of our NEWSSTORIES dataset. The ground-truth and incorrect image sets, as determined by the cluster labels, are outlined with green and red boxes, respectively (Color figure online)

of images increases. In contrast, we observe that training the models to align text with *varying* numbers of images helps them to generalize to sets of images better.

By finetuning the CLIP model on our dataset, the mean baseline shows significantly improved retrieval accuracies despite not observing any articles and images from the GoodNews dataset during training. The much improved performances obtained by the mean images and transformer approaches demonstrate the importance of understanding the complementary relationships between images even in this setting, where all ground-truth images originate from the same text narrative. Similar to the results in the first setting, the results of the best-performing MIL-SIM approach suggests that being able to learn a mapping between each image and specific parts of the text narrative is crucial during training for this research problem, even if the images and text are only weakly-related.

Zero-Shot With Multiple Set Sizes on GoodNews. Finally, we evaluate on images sets of variable size in Table 4, where the number of images in a set varies from 3 to 5. This requires a model to not only reason about the general semantic similarity between the query article and images but also determine if the number of images in a given set provides enough complementary information to discriminate one story from another. To this end, we randomly select 1500 articles from each of the above-mentioned GoodNews evaluation sets to create an evaluation split with different number of images per set.

Despite the inherent noise in obtaining positive text and image pairs using unsupervised clustering, the results suggest that aligning text narratives with varying numbers of complementary images during training is beneficial for learning more robust representations. These learnt representations are better able to discriminate between articles with different number of images.

5.4   Qualitative Results

Figure 3 provides an example of correct and incorrect retrievals on the test split of our NEWSSTORIES dataset. For each query article, the top 3 retrieved images are displayed in row order from top to bottom. Interestingly, in Fig. 3a, our mean image model is able to retrieve other set of images that are relevant to the notion of "fire", despite the fact that they belong to relatively different stories. Figure 3b shows a hard example since the other two retrieved image sets are related to the query article, with the exception of not containing the image of the easter eggs. We include more retrieval visualizations in the supplementary.

5.5   Practical Application of Retrieving Sets of Images

While we formulate the evaluation of this research problem as an article-to-image-set retrieval task, it may be impractical to find suitable images that have already been grouped into sets. Hence, we present an algorithm to find individual candidate images before grouping them into sets and ranking them using our trained models. We refer interested readers to the supplementary for more details as well as visualizations of the retrieval results.

6   Conclusion

In this work, we propose the important and challenging problem of illustrating stories with visual summarizes. This task entails learning many-to-many *illustrative* correspondences between relevant images and text. To study this problem in detail, we introduce a large-scale multimodal news dataset that contains over 31 M news articles and 22 M images. Finally, we benchmark the effectiveness of state-of-the-art image-and-text alignment approaches at learning the many-to-many correspondences between the two modalities and draw useful insights from our empirical results for future research in this direction.

Limitations and societal impact. Data and algorithms dealing with media can potentially be repurposed for misinformation. The selection of media channels in NEWSSTORIES reflects the judgment of an independent organization. Our models are trained on top of the CLIP model and may inherit its bias (if any).

Acknowledgements. This material is based upon work supported, in part, by DARPA under agreement number HR00112020054.

References

1. Aneja, S., Bregler, C., Nießner, M.: COSMOS: catching out-of-context misinformation with self-supervised learning. CoRR abs/2101.06278 (2021). https://arxiv.org/abs/2101.06278

2. Antol, S., et al.: VQA: visual question answering. In: 2015 IEEE International Conference on Computer Vision, ICCV 2015, Santiago, Chile, 7–13 December 2015, pp. 2425–2433. IEEE Computer Society (2015). https://doi.org/10.1109/ICCV.2015.279

3. Bain, M., Nagrani, A., Varol, G., Zisserman, A.: Frozen in time: a joint video and image encoder for end-to-end retrieval. CoRR abs/2104.00650 (2021). https://arxiv.org/abs/2104.00650

4. Biten, A.F., Gomez, L., Rusinol, M., Karatzas, D.: Good news, everyone! context driven entity-aware captioning for news images. In: Proceedings of the IEEE/CVF Conference on Computer Vision and Pattern Recognition, pp. 12466–12475 (2019)

5. Chen, T., Kornblith, S., Norouzi, M., Hinton, G.E.: A simple framework for contrastive learning of visual representations. In: Proceedings of the 37th International Conference on Machine Learning, ICML 2020, 13–18 July 2020, Virtual Event, pp. 1597–1607 (2020). https://proceedings.mlr.press/v119/chen20j.html

6. Chun, S., Oh, S.J., de Rezende, R.S., Kalantidis, Y., Larlus, D.: Probabilistic embeddings for cross-modal retrieval. In: IEEE Conference on Computer Vision and Pattern Recognition, CVPR 2021, virtual, 19–25 June 2021 (2021). https://openaccess.thecvf.com/content/CVPR2021/html/Chun_Probabilistic_Embeddings_for_Cross-Modal_Retrieval_CVPR_2021_paper.html

7. https://commoncrawl.org

8. Desai, K., Johnson, J.: Virtex: Learning visual representations from textual annotations. In: IEEE Conference on Computer Vision and Pattern Recognition, CVPR 2021, virtual, 19–25 June 2021, pp. 11162–11173. Computer Vision Foundation / IEEE (2021). https://openaccess.thecvf.com/content/CVPR2021/html/Desai_VirTex_Learning_Visual_Representations_From_Textual_Annotations_CVPR_2021_paper.html

9. Dietterich, T.G., Lathrop, R.H., Lozano-Pérez, T.: Solving the multiple instance problem with axis-parallel rectangles. Artif. Intell. **89**(1–2), 31–71 (1997). https://doi.org/10.1016/S0004-3702(96)00034-3

10. Faghri, F., Fleet, D.J., Kiros, J.R., Fidler, S.: VSE++: improving visual-semantic embeddings with hard negatives. In: British Machine Vision Conference 2018, BMVC 2018, Newcastle, UK, 3–6 September 2018, p. 12. BMVA Press (2018). https://doi.org/10.1016/S0004-3702(96)00034-3, https://bmvc2018.org/contents/papers/0344.pdf

11. Frome, A., Corrado, G.S., Shlens, J., Bengio, S., Dean, J., Ranzato, M., Mikolov, T.: DeViSE: a deep visual-semantic embedding model. In: Advances in Neural Information Processing Systems 26: 27th Annual Conference on Neural Information Processing Systems 2013. Proceedings of a Meeting held 5–8 December 2013, Lake Tahoe, Nevada, United States (2013). https://proceedings.neurips.cc/paper/2013/hash/7cce53cf90577442771720a370c3c723-Abstract.html

12. Gu, X., et al.: Generating representative headlines for news stories. In: Proceeding of the the Web Conference 2020 (2020)

13. Gurevych, I., Miyao, Y. (eds.): Proceedings of the 56th Annual Meeting of the Association for Computational Linguistics, ACL 2018, Melbourne, Australia, 15–20 July 2018, Volume 1: Long Papers. Association for Computational Linguistics (2018). https://aclanthology.org/volumes/P18-1/

14. Huang, T.K., et al.: Visual storytelling. CoRR abs/1604.03968 (2016). https://arxiv.org/abs/1604.03968

15. Jia, C., et al.: Scaling up visual and vision-language representation learning with noisy text supervision. In: Proceedings of the 38th International Conference on Machine Learning, ICML (2021)

16. Joulin, A., van der Maaten, L., Jabri, A., Vasilache, N.: Learning visual features from large weakly supervised data. In: Computer Vision - ECCV 2016–14th European Conference, Amsterdam, The Netherlands, 11–14 October 2016, Proceedings, Part VII (2016). https://doi.org/10.1007/978-3-319-46478-7_5

17. Karpathy, A., Fei-Fei, L.: Deep visual-semantic alignments for generating image descriptions. In: IEEE Conference on Computer Vision and Pattern Recognition, CVPR 2015, Boston, MA, USA, 7–12 June 2015, pp. 3128–3137. IEEE Computer Society (2015). https://doi.org/10.1109/CVPR.2015.7298932

18. Kim, G., Moon, S., Sigal, L.: Ranking and retrieval of image sequences from multiple paragraph queries. In: Proceedings of the IEEE Conference on Computer Vision and Pattern Recognition, pp. 1993–2001 (2015)

19. Kingma, D.P., Ba, J.: Adam: a method for stochastic optimization. In: 3rd International Conference on Learning Representations, ICLR 2015, San Diego, CA, USA, 7–9 May 2015, Conference Track Proceedings (2015). https://arxiv.org/abs/1412.6980

20. Lee, K.H., Chen, X., Hua, G., Hu, H., He, X.: Stacked cross attention for image-text matching. In: Proceedings of the European Conference on Computer Vision (ECCV), pp. 201–216 (2018)

21. Li, A., Jabri, A., Joulin, A., van der Maaten, L.: Learning visual n-grams from web data. In: IEEE International Conference on Computer Vision, ICCV 2017, Venice, Italy, 22–29 October 2017, pp. 4193–4202. IEEE Computer Society (2017). https://doi.org/10.1109/ICCV.2017.449https://doi.ieeecomputersociety.org/10.1109/ICCV.2017.449

22. Li, M., Chen, X., Gao, S., Chan, Z., Zhao, D., Yan, R.: Vmsmo: learning to generate multimodal summary for video-based news articles. arXiv preprint arXiv:2010.05406 (2020)

23. Lin, T.-Y., et al.: Microsoft COCO: common objects in context. In: Fleet, D., Pajdla, T., Schiele, B., Tuytelaars, T. (eds.) ECCV 2014. LNCS, vol. 8693, pp. 740–755. Springer, Cham (2014). https://doi.org/10.1007/978-3-319-10602-1_48

24. Liu, F., Wang, Y., Wang, T., Ordonez, V.: Visual news: benchmark and challenges in news image captioning. In: Proceedings of the 2021 Conference on Empirical Methods in Natural Language Processing, pp. 6761–6771 (2021)

25. Liu, J., Liu, T., Yu, C.: NewsEmbed: modeling news through pre-trained document representations. arXiv preprint arXiv:2106.00590 (2021)

26. Loper, E., Bird, S.: NLTK: the natural language toolkit. CoRR cs.CL/0205028 (2002). https://dblp.uni-trier.de/db/journals/corr/corr0205.html#cs-CL-0205028

27. Miech, A., Alayrac, J., Smaira, L., Laptev, I., Sivic, J., Zisserman, A.: End-to-end learning of visual representations from uncurated instructional videos. In: 2020 IEEE/CVF Conference on Computer Vision and Pattern Recognition, CVPR 2020, Seattle, WA, USA, 13–19 June 2020 (2020). https://doi.org/10.1109/CVPR42600.2020.00990, https://openaccess.thecvf.com/content_CVPR_2020/html/Miech_End-to-End_Learning_of_Visual_Representations_From_Uncurated_Instructional_Videos_CVPR_2020_paper.html

28. Oh, S.J., Murphy, K.P., Pan, J., Roth, J., Schroff, F., Gallagher, A.C.: Modeling uncertainty with hedged instance embeddings. In: 7th International Conference on Learning Representations, ICLR 2019, New Orleans, LA, USA, 6–9 May 2019 (2019). https://openreview.net/forum?id=r1xQQhAqKX

29. van den Oord, A., Li, Y., Vinyals, O.: Representation learning with contrastive predictive coding. CoRR abs/1807.03748 (2018). https://arxiv.org/abs/1807.03748

30. Radford, A., et al.: Learning transferable visual models from natural language supervision. In: Proceedings of the 38th International Conference on Machine Learning, ICML (2021)
31. Sariyildiz, M.B., Perez, J., Larlus, D.: Learning visual representations with caption annotations. In: Computer Vision - ECCV 2020–16th European Conference, Glasgow, UK, 23–28 August 2020, Proceedings, Part VIII (2020). https://doi.org/10.1007/978-3-030-58598-3_10
32. Song, Y., Soleymani, M.: Polysemous visual-semantic embedding for cross-modal retrieval. In: IEEE Conference on Computer Vision and Pattern Recognition, CVPR (2019)
33. Suhr, A., Zhou, S., Zhang, A., Zhang, I., Bai, H., Artzi, Y.: A corpus for reasoning about natural language grounded in photographs. In: Proceedings of the 57th Conference of the Association for Computational Linguistics, ACL 2019, Florence, Italy, July 28- August 2 2019, Volume 1: Long Papers (2019). https://doi.org/10.18653/v1/p19-1644
34. Tan, R., Plummer, B., Saenko, K.: Detecting cross-modal inconsistency to defend against neural fake news. In: Proceedings of the 2020 Conference on Empirical Methods in Natural Language Processing (EMNLP), pp. 2081–2106. Association for Computational Linguistics (2020). https://doi.org/10.18653/v1/2020.emnlp-main.163, https://aclanthology.org/2020.emnlp-main.163
35. Thomas, C., Kovashka, A.: Preserving semantic neighborhoods for robust cross-modal retrieval. In: Vedaldi, A., Bischof, H., Brox, T., Frahm, J.-M. (eds.) ECCV 2020. LNCS, vol. 12363, pp. 317–335. Springer, Cham (2020). https://doi.org/10.1007/978-3-030-58523-5_19
36. Tran, A., Mathews, A., Xie, L.: Transform and tell: entity-aware news image captioning. In: Proceedings of the IEEE/CVF Conference on Computer Vision and Pattern Recognition, pp. 13035–13045 (2020)
37. Vaswani, A., et al.: Attention is all you need. In: Advances in Neural Information Processing Systems, pp. 5998–6008 (2017)
38. Wang, L., Li, Y., Lazebnik, S.: Learning deep structure-preserving image-text embeddings. In: Proceedings of the IEEE Conference on Computer Vision and Pattern Recognition, pp. 5005–5013 (2016)
39. Yamada, I., Asai, A., Shindo, H., Takeda, H., Matsumoto, Y.: LUKE: deep contextualized entity representations with entity-aware self-attention. arXiv preprint arXiv:2010.01057 (2020)
40. Young, P., Lai, A., Hodosh, M., Hockenmaier, J.: From image descriptions to visual denotations: new similarity metrics for semantic inference over event descriptions. Trans. Assoc. Compu. Linguist. **2**, 67–78 (2014)
41. Zhang, Y., Jiang, H., Miura, Y., Manning, C.D., Langlotz, C.P.: Contrastive learning of medical visual representations from paired images and text. CoRR abs/2010.00747 (2020). https://arxiv.org/abs/2010.00747
42. Zhu, Y., Groth, O., Bernstein, M.S., Fei-Fei, L.: Visual7W: grounded question answering in images. In: 2016 IEEE Conference on Computer Vision and Pattern Recognition, CVPR 2016, Las Vegas, NV, USA, 27–30 June 2016, pp. 4995–5004. IEEE Computer Society (2016). https://doi.org/10.1109/CVPR.2016.540,https://doi.org/10.1109/CVPR.2016.540

Webly Supervised Concept Expansion for General Purpose Vision Models

Amita Kamath[1(✉)], Christopher Clark[1], Tanmay Gupta[1], Eric Kolve[1], Derek Hoiem[2], and Aniruddha Kembhavi[1]

[1] Allen Institute for Artificial Intelligence, Seattle, USA
amitak@allenai.org
[2] University of Illinois at Urbana-Champaign, Champaign, USA

Abstract. General Purpose Vision (GPV) systems are models that are designed to solve a wide array of visual tasks without requiring architectural changes. Today, GPVs primarily learn both skills and concepts from large fully supervised datasets. Scaling GPVs to tens of thousands of concepts by acquiring data to learn each concept for every skill quickly becomes prohibitive. This work presents an effective and inexpensive alternative: learn skills from supervised datasets, learn concepts from web image search, and leverage a key characteristic of GPVs: the ability to transfer visual knowledge across skills. We use a dataset of 1M+ images spanning 10k+ visual concepts to demonstrate webly-supervised concept expansion for two existing GPVs (GPV-1 and VL-T5) on 3 benchmarks: 5 Coco-based datasets (80 primary concepts), a newly curated series of 5 datasets based on the OpenImages and VisualGenome repositories (∼500 concepts), and the Web-derived dataset (10k+ concepts). We also propose a new architecture, GPV-2 that supports a variety of tasks — from vision tasks like classification and localization to vision+language tasks like QA and captioning, to more niche ones like human-object interaction detection. GPV-2 benefits hugely from web data and outperforms GPV-1 and VL-T5 across these benchmarks. Our data, code, and web demo are available at https://prior.allenai.org/projects/gpv2.

Keywords: General purpose vision systems · Webly supervised data

1 Introduction

General Purpose Vision systems (GPVs) [24] are designed to support a wide range of tasks without requiring architectural changes. A task is the application of skills (e.g. localization, captioning) to concepts (e.g. monkey, brown, climbing)

A. Kamath, C. Clark and T. Gupta—Equal contribution.

Supplementary Information The online version contains supplementary material available at https://doi.org/10.1007/978-3-031-20059-5_38.

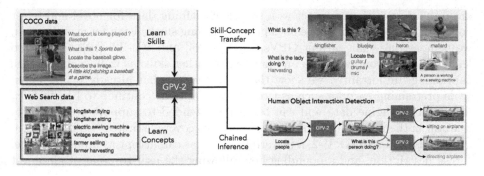

Fig. 1. Learning concepts from the web with GPV-2. We demonstrate webly-supervised concept expansion on two existing GPV architectures (GPV-1 and VL-T5) as well as our proposed GPV-2 architecture. In addition to outperforming previous architectures, GPV-2 expands the inputs to contain bounding boxes which enables support for niche tasks like Human-Object Interaction detection with multi-step inference without any architectural modifications.

in order to map from the input (image, text) to a target output (text, boxes). Given the virtually unlimited number of fine-grained and topical concepts, it is not feasible to provide a GPV with annotations for all skills on all concepts, as even large pre-collected datasets cannot anticipate every need. In this work, we ask: *Can a GPV leverage web image search and skill-concept transfer to massively and inexpensively expand its concept vocabulary across a variety of tasks?* To answer this question, we present a large-scale webly supervised dataset for learning 10k+ concepts, a new benchmark for broader concept evaluation (∼500) across 5 diverse tasks, and a new GPV architecture that improves cross-task concept transfer and outperforms existing GPVs across multiple benchmarks.

Image search engines provide remarkably good results for millions of queries by leveraging text on the accompanying web pages, visual features from images, and click data from millions of users querying and selecting relevant results each day. They often provide high-quality, decluttered, object- and action-centric images, which can be used to learn powerful visual representations for concepts. Importantly, searches scale easily and inexpensively to thousands of queries. Given the large cost of producing high-quality supervised datasets, scaling today's manually annotated datasets to support 10,000+ concepts is infeasible for many tasks. In contrast, using Bing search to create WEB10K, a dataset with 1M+ images spanning 10k nouns, 300 verbs, and 150 adjectives with thousands of noun-verb and noun-adj combinations, cost us just over $150. Moreover, while existing data sources such as ImageNet-22k and YFCC100M are valuable resources, they are static snapshots of a diverse and ever-changing world. For example, these static datasets may not represent specialized categories of interest to a downstream application such as *boysenberry* and will definitely not contain latest concepts such as *Pixel 6* or *COVID-19 home test*. On the other hand, modern web image search engines are designed to serve imagery on-demand and are uniquely positioned to act as a source of training data for novel and latest concepts. While search engine data provides strong supervision for classification, we demonstrate that current GPVs, GPV-1 [24] and VL-T5 [13], are able to learn concepts from web data and improve on other skills as well, such as image captioning. Importantly, we show that even models that already utilize large-scale pretraining corpora such as Conceptual Captions continue to benefit from using search engine data and can be easily extended to support new concepts relevant in the present day that have little or no coverage in large static corpora.

We also propose GPV-2, a powerful GPV that can accept as input an image, a task description, and a bounding box (allowing the user to point at an object or region of interest), and output boxes and text for any bounding box or for the entire image. These diverse input and output modalities enable GPV-2 to support a large spectrum of skills ranging from vision skills like classification and localization, vision-language skills like VQA and captioning, to niche ones like classification in context and human-object interaction detection. An important design principle of GPV-2 is Language-Based Localization, whereby *all* tasks are based on scoring/ranking/generation using the same text decoder applied to one or more image regions. This ensures that all tasks share the same weights and representations, ranging from the input encoders all the way to the output decoders — resulting in more effective skill-concept transfer for learning from diverse tasks' datasets. We also propose a re-calibration mechanism to down-weight scores of labels that are disproportionally represented in training, and demonstrate its effectiveness on out-of-domain test datasets for multiple tasks.

Benchmarking the diverse capabilities of large-vocabulary general purpose models is challenging. Most current datasets in computer vision are designed for single tasks. The recently proposed Coco-sce [24] benchmark is designed to test the skill-concept transfer ability and overall skill competency across five vision skills. However, it is limited to evaluate these competencies on 80 primary Coco concepts. In this work, we present a new benchmark named DCE for broader concept evaluation for the same five skills but now expanding to 492 OpenImages concepts. DCE is an evaluation-only benchmark sourced from OpenImages [38], VisualGenome [36] and NoCAPS [1] with new VQA annotations and has been sampled in a way that prevents over-representation of any single category while maximizing representation of infrequent categories.

We evaluate present day GPVs and GPV-2 on three benchmarks: (i) the Coco-sce and Coco benchmarks [24], (ii) the newly presented DCE benchmark; and (iii) the Web10k dataset consisting of *manually verified* images from Bing Image Search paired with questions and answers that covers 10,000+ concepts. Our analysis shows that all three GPVs benefit from web data. Furthermore, GPV-2 outperforms both GPV-1 and VL-T5 across these benchmarks and shows significantly large gains when using web data, particularly for captioning and classification. We also demonstrate how GPV-2 can be chained to perform niche tasks like human-object interaction detection, without any task-specific architecture modifications. Finally, we show how web data can be efficiently used to expand GPV-2's concept vocabulary to include new visual concepts that are relevant in today's world such as *COVID-19 vaccination cards* and *N95 masks*, concepts that are infrequent or non-existent in static corpora.

In summary, our main contributions include: (a) WEB10K, a new web data source to learn over 10k visual concepts with an accompanying human-verified VQA benchmark; (b) demonstration that GPVs can learn concepts from WEB10K and transfer this knowledge to other tasks; (c) DCE, a benchmark spanning 5 tasks and approximately 500 concepts to evaluate GPVs; and (d) GPV-2, an architecture that supports box and text modalities in both input and output, improves skill-concept transfer and outperforms existing GPVs. Our code and benchmarks are available at https://prior.allenai.org/projects/gpv2, along with a new tool to easily create a web dataset from a list of queries

2 Related Work

General Purpose Models. Computer vision models have progressively become more general. Specialization first gave way to multitask models which aimed at solving multiple, albeit predefined, tasks with one architecture. A common approach for building such models [27,47] is to use task-specialized heads with a shared backbone. However, adding a new head for each new task makes scaling to a large number of tasks and reuse of previously learned skills challenging. An alternative approach is to build a *general-purpose* architecture without task-specific components. This approach has become common in natural language processing via text-to-text generative models [4,51,58], and recent work in computer vision has striven towards this kind of generality [6,16,34,45].

Examples of general-purpose computer vision models include VL-T5 [13], which adapts T5 [58] to jointly train on vision+language (V+L) tasks while using a single text-generation head to produce outputs for all tasks, and GPV-1 [24], which combines a similar text-generation head with the ability to return bounding-boxes and relevance scores as output. In this work, we work with both GPV-1 and VL-T5 and extend their concept vocabulary with web data. Our proposed model, GPV-2 follows VL-T5 in its use of the T5 backbone, builds upon the vision capabilities of GPV-1, and further extends the range of tasks that can be performed by allowing a bounding-box input and introducing the ability to generate per-image-region text output. Perceiver [30] and Perceiver-rIO [29] aim to generalize the architecture beyond images and text to other modalities such as audio, video, and point cloud. However, both architectures remain to be tested for multitask learning and for learning V+L tasks such as VQA and captioning. Many other V+L models [12,43,48,66,76] can be fine-tuned on a variety of downstream tasks, but they typically use task-specific heads, while the focus of our work is on general purpose models in a multi-task setting.

Web Supervision. Image search engines provide highly relevant results, using a combination of text, image and user features. Researchers have used search data as a form of supervision to build computer vision models. Early works used noisy retrieved results with probabilistic Latent Semantic Analysis [19] and multiple instance learning [70] to build recognition systems. As web results improved, works used this data to build object detectors [10,14,42,49,64,75], attribute detectors [20], image taggers [73], large vocabulary categorization models [23,52, 77] and fine-grained recognition models [35,53], segmentation models [32,63,65], online dataset builders [40], visual reasoning systems [82] and visual knowledge bases with learnt relationships between objects [11]. More recently, massive scale web data in the form of retrieved search results and the accompanying text was employed to build the powerful CLIP family of models [56] that provide powerful visual representations for downstream tasks. While these works have shown that web data can be used to build single task models, we show that one can build GPVs with web data and importantly transfer this knowledge across skills.

Concept Transfer Across Skills. There has been considerable interest in transferring concept knowledge from classification to object detection, as classification labels are far cheaper to obtain than detection labels. Hoffman *et al.* [28] cast this problem as a domain adaptation problem, adapting classifiers to detectors. Redmon *et al.* [60] build a 9,000 class detector using Imagenet22k classification data [15] by jointly training for the two tasks. Uijlings *et al.* [67] use Multiple Instance Learning to pseudo-label data and train a large vocabulary detector. Recent works build open vocabulary detectors [22,31,79] by leveraging image caption pairs (or models like CLIP [57] which are built from the same), obtained in large quantities on the web. Even though image-captions are noisy, the resulting detectors improve as the data is scaled up.

The V+L field has leveraged object detectors as feature inputs [1,2,81], which can be considered as transferring concepts from detection to downstream tasks. Another effective approach is pre-training using image-captions [41,43,46] like Conceptual Captions [61]. CLIP [57] is a family of powerful models that are pre-trained on a massive 400M image caption paired dataset. The resulting encoders are very effective at V+L tasks [62]. These methods effectively transfer visual knowledge from caption data to tasks like VQA. Recently Whitehead *et al.* [74] disentangle the encoding of concepts and skills and build a model that can generalize to new skill-concept compositions and new concepts for VQA.

The focus of our work is to build a GPV that can transfer concepts across various skills, particularly from web data to vision and vision-and-language skills, and also provide a new test-only evaluation benchmark for the same (Fig. 2).

3   The WEB10K Dataset

Search engines can be leveraged to collect datasets with highly desirable characteristics: (1) **Diversity** — Search engines benefit from a large volume of user click data to produce high-quality results for a large vocabulary of concepts including tail concepts not frequently mentioned in annotated computer vision datasets (e.g. *hyacinth*); (2) **Freshness** — Search engines are designed to serve the freshest content on the internet, and often produce very good results for the latest queries (that may not have existed or been popular before; e.g. *COVID-19*

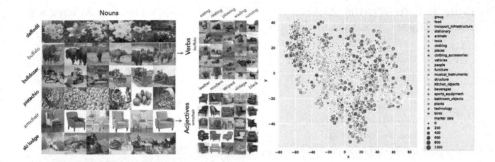

Fig. 2. Concept diversity in WEB10K. Left: Besides 10k nouns, WEB10K provides dense coverage of feasible adj-noun and verb-noun combinations to enable learning of fine-grained differences in object appearance due to attributes. **Right:** TSNE [50] plot of Phrase-BERT [71] embeddings of WEB10K nouns with bubble size indicating frequency (capped at 1000) in CC, a common large-scale pretraining dataset. WEB10K nouns cover a wide range of concept groups identified using WordNet and include many concepts which are infrequent/absent in CC.

vaccination card, 2022 winter olympics mascot) which have few/no occurences in standard vision datasets that tend to be static; and (3) **Concept focus** — The image distribution of search engine results tends to be similar to image classification data with the image centered on the queried object with few distractions, making them ideal for learning visual concept representations.

We present WEB10K, a dataset sourced from web image search data with over 10K concepts. WEB10K contains queries with nouns, adjectives and verbs. **Nouns.** We consider single and multi-word nouns. Single-word nouns are sourced from a language corpus with a list of 40,000 concrete words [5], each with a concreteness score (defined as the degree to which a word refers to a perceptible entity). From this list, we select nouns with a concreteness score > 4.0/5 and any verb or adjective with an alternate word sense as a noun (e.g. "comb") with a score > 4.5/5. These thresholds avoid more abstract or non-visual words such as "humor". Multi-word nouns are sourced from CONCEPTUAL CAPTIONS (CC) [61]. We identify candidates using POS tagging and select the most frequent 2,000, and an additional 282 where the second word of the multi-word noun is present in the concreteness dataset (e.g. "street artist", where "artist" is in concrete nouns). In total, we select 10,211 nouns. Sourcing nouns from a language corpus enables coverage of concepts not commonly covered in vision datasets: over 4,000 nouns in WEB10K are not present in CC, e.g. "wind tunnel". **Verbs.** We source verbs from a combination of vision datasets with large verb vocabularies including imSitu [78], HICO [8] and VRD [44]. We remove verbs that are either polysemous (have multiple meanings e.g. "person holding breath" vs. "person holding cup") or aren't associated with an animate agent (e.g. "snowing"). This results in 298 unambiguous and visually recognizable verbs. These verbs improve model performance on action recognition (Supplementary Sec. 8).

Table 1. Left: WEB10K statistics (Sect. 3). There are approximately 25 images per concept. **Right:** DCE val and test statistics (Sect. 5).

Type	Count
Concepts	Nouns: 10211 Adjectives: 144 Verbs: 298 Noun-adjective pairs: 18616 Noun-verb pairs: 9243 **Total: 38072** (Nouns + Pairs)
Images	Noun images: 255073 Noun-adjective images: 465146 Noun-verb images: 230224 **Total: 950443**
QAs	Templates: 26 Noun QAs: 1900886 Adjective QAs: 930292 Verb QAs: 460448 **Total: 3291626**

Subset	Skill	Samples	Images	Categories
Val	VQA	5169	2131	295
	Localization	8756	7588	463
	Classification	9485	6770	464
	Cls-in-context	9485	6770	464
	Captioning	4500	4500	–
Test	VQA	5281	2160	307
	Localization	10586	9986	476
	Classification	10888	9161	476
	Cls-in-context	10888	9161	476
	Captioning	10600	10600	–

Note: Since nocaps [1] annotations are hidden behind an evaluation server, we are unable to provide category counts for captioning.

Adjectives. We source adjectives from several datasets that have a large number of adjectives [9,18,36,37,39,54,55,61,72]. We manually filter out ones that are subjective ("beautiful"), non-visual ("loud"), or relative ("big"). This results in 144 adjectives which we group into 16 adjective types (e.g. "color", "texture").

We select noun-adj pairs and noun-verb pairs which appear at least thrice in CC: this removes nonsensical pairs, e.g. "cloudy dog". The total number of queries in WEB10K is 38,072 with roughly 10k nouns, 18k noun-adj and 9k noun-verb combinations. We feed each query into the Bing Search API and retrieve a total of 950,443 image URLs (approx. 25 per query). **Importantly, this cost us $154**, so it is inexpensive to scale further, and such data acquisition is affordable for many other research organizations. See Table 1 for detailed statistics.

Conversion into QA Data. We convert each query-image pair into multiple templated QA pairs where the answer is the noun, adjective or verb from the query. For example "What is the [noun] doing?" and "What [adj type] is this object?"; see Supplementary Sec. 3 for all question templates. The QA format has two advantages: (1) it removes ambiguity from the task (e.g., "What color is this" tells the model not to return a potentially accurate non-color attribute); and (2) it bridges the domain gap to other tasks posed as questions.

Data Splits. We split image-query pairs into train (874k), val (38k) and test (38k). We sample 5k and 10k pairs from the val and test sets and ask 3 crowd-workers to verify that the query is present in the image. We only retain unanimously verified examples (71%) resulting in: Val – 4k images (9k QAs), Test – 8k images (19k QAs). The Train set has about 3M QAs with no manual verification.

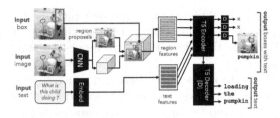

		INPUTS			OUTPUTS	
Skill	Image	Text/Prompt	Bbox		Text	Bbox+Scores
VQA	Full	Question	-		Answer	Attended regions
Cap	Full	Describe the image Caption this image	-		Caption	Attended regions
Loc	Full	Find [OBJECT] Locate instances of [OBJECT]	-		-	Localized [OBJECT] instances
Cls	Cropped	What is this thing? What object is this?	-		Category	-
ClC	Full	What is this thing? What object is this?	Region to classify		Category	-

Fig. 3. Left: GPV-2 architecture. **Right**: I/O for 5 skills in Coco and DCE.

4   GPV-2

In this section we present GPV-2, a model combining an object detector with the T5 pre-trained language model. GPV-2 supports additional input and output modalities (and thus tasks) beyond present day GPVs (GPV-1 and VL-T5). It uses the stronger VinVL [81] object detector, uses a shared language decoder (for all tasks including localization) and employs a classification re-calibration approach, which together improve generalization to unseen concepts at test time.

Model Design. GPV-2 takes an image, text, and a bounding box as input. As output, it can produce text for an individual bounding box (the input box, or boxes produced by the visual model) and for the entire image (see Fig. 3).

First, the input text is tokenized and embedded using T5-Base to get a sequence of text feature vectors. Then an object detection model is used to identify regions in the image and extract bounding boxes and features for those regions (we do not use the class labels identified by the detector) via RoI pooling. We additionally use the object detector to extract features for the input bounding box, and a learned embedding is added to those features to distinguish them from the other visual features. These sets of visual features are then converted to embeddings of the same dimensionality as the text embedding using a linear layer. We primarily use the VinVL [81] object detector for our experiments. However the GPV-2 architecture allows us to easily swap in other detectors, and we use features from DETR [6] for some of our experiments in Sect. 6.

The resulting visual and text vectors are concatenated as a sequence and used as an input to the T5-Encoder to build joint contextualized embeddings. To generate text for the entire image we use the T5-Decoder with this contextualized embedding sequence as input, and to generate text for individual boxes we run the same T5-Decoder while using the contextualized embedding that corresponds to just that box as input. The usage of a common decoder for image-based outputs and region-based outputs enables transfer of learned concepts between skills that require processing the entire image and skills that rely primarily on the representation of a single region.

Using GPV-2. GPV-2's design gives us flexibility to handle a variety of vision and vision+language tasks without needing task-specific heads. For tasks that do not have text input, we follow [24] by building appropriate text prompts for that task (e.g., "What is this object?" for classification) and selecting one at random to use as the input text. For tasks that do not have an input bounding box, we use a box around the entire image.

Decoded text from the image is used to answer questions and generate captions. For classification or limited-choice responses, answers are scored based on log-probability of generating each option, and the highest scoring answer is chosen. To localize objects, we propose Language-Based Localization (LBL) where a box is scored by first computing the log-probabilities of generating an object class or "other" from that box, and then applying a linear classifier to those scores to yield a scalar relevance score. For example, "Localize dog" is performed by computing the log-probability of "dog" and "other" for each region.

Importantly, the same text decoder is used to generate image and region text, thus *classification, question answering, captioning, localization, and all other tasks use the same encoders, decoder, and weights*. Our experiments show that this facilitates skill-concept transfer.

Even complex tasks like human-object interaction (HOI) can be performed by chaining inference steps (Fig. 1). HOI [7,8] requires localizing a person, an object and categorizing their interaction. GPV-2 performs this by first returning detections for "Locate person", then providing each person box as input with the prompt "What is this person doing?" The log-probs of generating object-interaction phrases, such as "directing the airplane" for other boxes are used to identify the most likely interaction.

Classification Re-calibration. We observe that a common issue in classification is that the model becomes biased towards classes that are common in the training data. For example, we find that if the model is trained to classify Coco objects it will almost always guess the names of Coco objects in response to the prompt "What is this object?", even if no such objects exist in the image. This can be viewed as a language bias, as has been well-studied in VQA [21,59]. To solve this issue we re-calibrate the models output prediction by reducing the log-probability of classes that were seen in the training data when doing answer re-ranking. The down-weighting amount is selected on the validation data. See Supplementary Sec. 2 for an analysis and example.

Pre-training. Recent works have shown that pre-training V+L models on large amounts of data results in large improvements [13,43,81]. We do not have the resources to fully-replicate these setups, but as a partial measure we pre-train GPV-2 for 8 epochs on the CC 3M dataset [61], which shows significant gains on our benchmarks. Since GPV-2 is generative, we pre-train it by simply learning to generate the target caption rather than using span masking or other more complex objectives [43,66]. While we use much less data than some V+L works, pre-training on CC 3M allows us to verify that GPV-2 still benefits from web data even when exposed to a broad range of concepts during pre-training.

Table 2. Concept expansion with web data. Jointly training on WEB10K + COCO shows consistent gains on DCE and WEB10K benchmarks without adversely affecting COCO performance for 3 different GPVs. GPV-1[20] refers to 20 epoch training.

Model	Web data	Coco					DCE					WEB10K			
		VQA	Cap	Loc	Cls	CiC	VQA	Cap	Loc	Cls	CiC	All	Nouns	Verbs	Adj
[a] GPV-1	no web	62.5	102.3	73.0	83.6	-	45.3	25.8	61.9	10.1	-	11.9	2.7	8.5	24.5
[b] GPV-1[20]	no web	61.2	95.7	65.3	82.3	-	44.3	23.1	60.3	9.3	-	13.1	3.1	7.7	28.4
[c] GPV-1[20]	with web	61.5	97.3	64.9	82.8	-	45.8	28.6	61.5	20.0	-	54.4	32.7	51.7	78.8
[d] VL-T5	no web	69.8	100.7	-	78.1	-	60.2	31.6	-	10.9	-	18.6	4.3	15.8	35.7
[e] VL-T5	with web	69.9	106.4	-	77.3	-	59.9	45.0	-	16.2	-	61.0	38.0	59.3	85.8
[f] GPV-2	no web	71.1	112.1	70.9	82.2	93.4	60.6	65.4	74.8	36.3	43.6	22.5	3.8	23.6	39.9
[g] GPV-2	with web	71.4	113.0	70.9	82.3	93.2	61.1	72.5	75.9	45.4	52.2	62.0	41.7	60.0	84.3

5   DCE Benchmark

The COCO benchmark focuses on 80 object categories and is insufficient for evaluating skills on a wide range of concepts. We introduce the **D**iverse **C**oncept **E**valuation (DCE) benchmark to evaluate GPV models on a large subset of the 600 OPENIMAGES categories across 5 skills: classification (Cls), classification-in-context (CiC), captioning (Cap), localization (Loc), and visual question answering (VQA). See Fig. 3 for the inputs and outputs for each task. We introduce CiC as a natural and unambiguous object classification task (similar to pointing at an object and asking what it is), providing a direct complement to localization. We source Cls, CiC and Loc samples from OPENIMAGES, VQA samples from VISUALGENOME (VG), and use the nocaps [1] benchmark for Cap evaluation. To curate the DCE benchmark, we first select a set of mutually exclusive categories from OPENIMAGES and draw samples for each of those categories according to a sampling strategy that prevents over-representation of any category while maximizing representation of tail categories. DCE is an evaluation-only benchmark and is not accompanied by a distributionally similar training set.

Category Selection. OPENIMAGES provides a total of 600 hierarchical object categories. After removing some categories due to label noise, we use the remaining 492 leaf nodes in the hierarchy as our mutually exclusive set of categories.

Sampling Strategy. For Cls, CiC and Loc, we randomly sample up to 25 samples from each of the selected categories. A sample for Cls/CiC is defined as any bounding box annotated with a category. For Loc, a sample is all bounding boxes in an image annotated with a category (we discard "group" annotations). For VQA, we first discard annotations exceeding 2 word answers after removing articles and tag each QA pair in VG with any of the selected categories mentioned in either the question or answer. Then, for each category, we sample up to 50 data points. Since each sample in VQA may consist of multiple categories, this strategy does result in more than 50 samples for some categories, but in practice it achieves the goal of preventing common categories from dominating

Table 3. Concept scaling using web data: Closed world experiment. To eliminate the effect of VinVL features and CC pretraining, we restrict GPV-2 to Coco-SCE trained DETR features. Training jointly with WEB10K still shows massive gains on DCE and WEB10K vs training with only Coco-SCE.

Model	Web data	Coco-SCE VQA Test	Sn	Unsn	Cap Test	Sn	Unsn	Loc Test	Sn	Unsn	Cls Test	Sn	Unsn	DCE VQA	Cap	Loc	Cls	WEB10K All	Noun	Verb	Adj
GPV-2	no web	59.6	60.1	48.5	88.4	91.7	55.5	62.2	**67.2**	14.0	**73.1**	77.2	**33.9**	46.9	21.1	54.9	13.6	14.0	3.3	11.6	27.1
GPV-2	with web	**59.9**	**60.3**	**49.7**	89.2	**92.1**	**58.0**	62.2	67.0	**14.8**	73.0	77.2	32.6	46.8	**33.4**	**58.7**	**26.5**	**47.0**	**25.1**	**43.0**	**73.0**

the evaluation. Finally, some of the 492 categories do not have annotations in the source datasets. The final sample, image, and category counts for each skill are in Table 1 and category frequencies are shown in Supplementary Sec. 4.

Additional VQA Annotations. VQA annotations from VG only consist of one answer per question. For each selected VQA sample, we source 9 additional answers from Amazon Mechanical Turk as in standard Coco-based VQA benchmarks [3,21]. Samples where ≥ 3 workers agreed on an answer were retained.

6   Experiments

We train models jointly on all tasks that are supported by each GPV using Coco-based datasets. In addition, each model is also trained with and without training data from WEB10K. We evaluate these models on in-domain test sets for each task as well as on the WEB10K and DCE test sets.

We now summarize the tasks and training details. See Fig. 3 for the inputs/outputs for each task and Supplementary Sec. 6 for additional experimental details. **VQA:** We train on the VQA v2 [21] train set and report results using the annotator-weighted metric from [21] on the VQA v2 test-dev set and DCE test set. **Captioning:** We train on Coco captioning and report CIDEr-D [69] on Coco test. DCE uses nocaps [1] for captioning. Due to space constraints, we only report CIDEr-D on the out-of-domain split, as performance on novel concepts is our primary interest. See Supplementary Sec. 11 for results on all splits. **Localization:** Localization training data is built from bounding box annotations in Coco images following [24]. We report mAP on the Coco val set (since the test servers do not support this task) and the DCE test set. VL-T5 does not support this task out-of-the-box since it does not have a means to rank its input boxes, so we do not train or evaluate it for this task. **Classification:** We use the classification data from [24] and report accuracy on the Coco val set and the DCE test set. Since DCE is out-of-domain we apply the recalibration method from Sect. 4 for GPV-2. **Classification-in-Context:** The same as classification, except instead of cropping images the bounding box of the target object is used as an input box. Having an input box means only GPV-2 supports this task.

Training Details. We train GPV-2 and VL-T5 for 8 epochs with a batch size of 60 and learning rate of 3e-4 that linearly warms up from 0 for 10% of the training steps then decays to 0. We stratify the data so examples from each source are proportionally represented in each batch. Since the web data is large, we shard the data into 4 parts and use 1 shard each epoch, resulting in about a third of the data in each epoch being web data. VL-T5 is initialized with a pre-trained checkpoint [13] and GPV-2 is initialized from our checkpoint after CC pre-training. We train GPV-1 to 40 epochs following [24][1].

Concept Expansion Using Web Data. Table 2 shows the performance of models when trained with and without WEB10K. On DCE, which contains a more diverse set of concepts than COCO, we find that all models benefit from web data and perform better on captioning and the two classification tasks (with large gains of +7.1, +9.1, +8.6 for GPV-2). We see modest gains of +1.0 for DCE localization. VQA shows small gains, presumably because many frequent answers such as colors or numbers are common between COCO and DCE, and adding web supervision brings little benefits for such questions. Training with web data makes little difference on COCO and, unsurprisingly, leads to large gains on WEB10K test, where models achieve over 40% accuracy on nouns and 60% on verbs despite the large number of concepts. Overall, these results show multi-tasking GPVs with web data improves performance significantly on concepts unseen in supervised data without compromising in-domain performance.

Of the three GPVs we test, we find GPV-2 to be the most effective across all three benchmarks. GPV-2 uses less pre-training data and a simpler and cheaper pre-training strategy than VL-T5. However, it uses more powerful VinVL [81] features and benefits from classifier re-calibration (See Table 4). In contrast to VL-T5, GPV-2 can also perform CiC and localization. In contrast to GPV-1, GPV-2 has more shared features and a better pre-trained language model, which help produce large gains across the benchmarks. It also trains much faster than GPV-1 as it can use pre-computed detection features (1 day on 2 GPUs vs. >3 weeks on 4 GPUs). See Supplementary Secs. 10 and 5 for more comparisons and GPV-2 efficiency metrics respectively. GPV-2 also achieves state-of-the-art on the GRIT benchmark [25] at the time of submission (Supplementary Sec. 9).

Closed World Evaluation of Web Data. Table 3 shows results for GPV-2 when it is trained on the COCO-SCE [24] dataset, a dataset that holds out different concepts from each COCO training supervised dataset (e.g., captions that mention the word "bed" are held out from the caption training data), and then evaluates whether models can still perform well on those unseen concepts by learning about them from the data in other tasks (e.g., captions with the word "bed" are in the captioning test set, and classification and localization training still include examples about beds). When GPV-2 is trained on COCO-SCE we make two notable changes: (1) We replace VinVL features with DETR [6] features trained only on the COCO-SCE training categories (this avoids leak-

---

[1] Since [24] takes a long time to train when using the web data (over 3 weeks), results for GPV-1 with and without web data are reported after 20 epochs training.

Table 4. Ablating GPV-2. The left-most columns indicate using WEB10K ('Pre.' indicates pre-training with WEB10K instead of multi-tasking), CC pre-training, classifier re-calibration (Cb), language-based localization (LBL) (see Sect. 4), and VinVL instead of the DETR detector from GPV-1. The first row shows results for GPV-2, and the lower rows show the differences in scores between ablations and GPV-2. Each component improves performance on DCE.

					Coco					DCE					WEB10K			
Web	CC	Cb	LBL	Vin.	VQA	Cap	Loc	Cls	CiC	VQA	Cap	Loc	Cls	CiC	All	Nouns	Verbs	Adj
✓	✓	✓	✓	✓	70.7	117.3	70.9	82.3	93.2	60.7	78.0	76.8	45.8	52.2	60.4	39.9	57.5	83.8
-	✓	✓	✓	✓	-0.2	-1.1	0.0	-0.1	0.2	-0.5	-8.8	-1.0	-8.5	-7.4	-37.2	-35.4	-32.5	-43.8
Pre.	✓	✓	✓	✓	-0.4	-0.6	0.0	-0.2	0.1	-0.8	-8.2	-1.3	-6.2	-5.5	-31.3	-30.4	-27.6	-35.9
✓	-	✓	✓	✓	0.4	-2.4	0.1	0.5	0.1	0.8	-13.9	-0.7	-4.3	-4.5	-2.3	-3.7	-2.4	-0.9
-	-	✓	✓	✓	0.2	-4.2	0.1	0.5	0.2	-0.2	-33.7	-4.5	-20.7	-21.1	-40.6	-37.4	-39.3	-44.9
✓	✓	-	✓	✓	0.0	0.0	0.0	0.0	0.0	0.0	0.0	0.0	-11.8	-12.8	0.0	0.0	0.0	0.0
✓	✓	✓	-	✓	-0.1	-1.4	0.0	0.3	0.0	-0.2	-2.4	-1.3	-1.3	-0.7	0.1	0.2	0.7	-0.8
✓	✓	✓	✓	-	-8.1	-15.8	6.1	-2.2	-	-9.8	-41.7	-15.0	-17.4	-	-13.8	-13.3	-16.4	-11.7

ing detection information by VinVL's broad category set); and (2) We do not pre-train with CC (this avoids leaking caption information from CC's broad vocabulary). These choices severely reduce the performance of the model, but this setup serves as a closed world evaluation to determine if GPV-2 can learn skills from COCO-SCE and concepts from WEB10K. As seen in Table 3, training with web data shows large gains across the board in this controlled experiment. In fact, we now also see gains in the unseen categories within COCO-SCE.

Ablation Analysis. We perform ablation studies on GPV-2. Table 4 shows results on the validation sets. The model that does not use LBL scores each box using a linear classifier on top of its contextualized embedding instead. On both classification tasks and captioning, we find that web data helps with and without CC pre-training, and that removing both reduces performance dramatically (>30 points for captioning). This shows that the two approaches are independently effective and complementary at helping models handle new concepts. This is also true to a more modest extent for localization. Using the web data for a second round of pre-training performed better than not using it, but was significantly worse than our multi-tasking framework. Re-calibration is critical for classification, providing a gain of up to 12 points, confirming that models tend to be overly influenced by the concept distribution observed during training. Performance on COCO remains largely unchanged, which is expected as our design choices target performance on unseen concepts. Finally, VinVL significantly outperforms DETR, as expected given its much more extensive training regime.

Human Object Interaction. To demonstrate the flexibility of GPV-2, we also employ it for human-object interaction detection [7] using the two-stage procedure described in Sect. 4. We fine-tune GPV-2 on the HICO-DET train set for 4 epochs (see Supplementary Sec. 7 for details). GPV-2 gets an AP of 20.6 on the HICO-DET benchmark, which is comparable to a number of other approaches (17.2 [26], 19.8 [68], 20.8 [83], 21.8 [17]). Although recent models [33,80,84] show

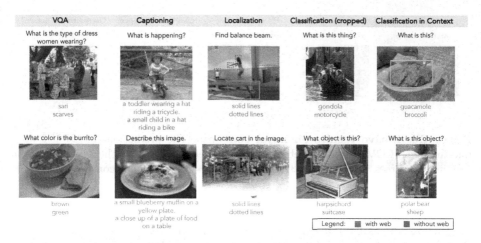

Fig. 4. Qualitative results of GPV-2 on DCE with and without WEB10K: Without web training, GPV-2 can ignore concepts rarely seen in the supervised training data (e.g., 'balance beam' top middle) or predict frequently occurring concepts that do not appear in the image (e.g., 'sheep' lower right). Web training fixes these issues and allows generalization to rare concepts like 'sari' and 'harpsichord'.

results up to 32.1 mAP [80], they require highly specialized architectures requiring up to 5 output heads (e.g. for decoding human+object boxes, interaction score, and object and interaction categories), well crafted losses (e.g. Hungarian HOI instance matching objectives), and custom post-processing steps (e.g. pairwise non-maximum suppression). GPV-2's flexibility allows us to get reasonable results by side-stepping complex model design with simple chained inference.

Qualitative Results from DCE (Fig. 4). Training on WEB10K helps GPV-2 understand rare concepts like 'sari' or 'gondola', which it is able to use across diverse skills. See Supplementary Sec. 1 for more examples.

Novel Concepts Case Study. A unique advantage of using web-search is the ability to easily and cheaply access new visual concepts that are too specialized or too recent to appear in statically-collected corpora. To demonstrate this we present qualitative results on an experiment to train GPV-2 to learn a number of COVID-19 related concepts. We collect 43 terms related to COVID-19 (e.g., N95 mask, face shield, etc.) and gather a 1000-image train set with a 100-image val set using the same automatic pipeline we used to gather WEB10K. We fine-tune GPV-2 (after it has been trained on COCO and WEB10K) on these examples mixed with a sample of 2000 examples from each COCO train set for 3 epochs.

After fine-tuning, the model achieves 71% accuracy on the new val set compared to only 4% without fine-tuning (performance is initially low since these concepts are too specialized and new to appear in CC, COCO or WEB10K). See some qualitative results in Fig. 5 that show that GPV-2 is able to use such recently-introduced concepts when applying multiple skills. Although this is a small-scale qualitative study, it shows that our approach of combining a GPV

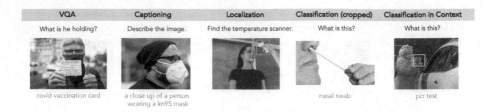

Fig. 5. Qualitative results on novel concepts: The predictions of GPV-2 after fine-tuning on COVID-related web data. The model can recognize the new concepts in new images across all skills after training on only ~20 images per concept.

and web-search data can lead to models that not only understand a wide range of concepts and skills, but can also be efficiently adapted to new visual concepts that become common in the world or that are needed due to the specialized needs of a user. We think this is an exciting avenue for future work in GPVs.

7   Discussion

Extensions. GPV-2 achieves transfer of concepts from web data to skills, but our results indicate that more work is needed, particularly for tasks like VQA or localization, through new architectures or training protocols. GPV-2 supports many tasks, but could be extended to handle more modalities (e.g., video) and outputs (e.g., segmentation). Recent work shows promise in this regard [29], potentially enabling transfer of web concepts to a wider range of tasks.

Conclusion. As the vision community builds progressively more general models, identifying efficient ways of learning a large variety of skills and concepts is of prime importance. Our work revisits the idea of webly-supervised learning in the context of GPVs and shows that learning skills from task-datasets and concepts from the web is an efficient and inexpensive option for concept expansion.

Acknowledgements. This work is partially supported by ONR award N00014-21-1-2705.

References

1. Agrawal, H., et al.: Nocaps: novel object captioning at scale. In: International Conference on Computer Vision, pp. 8947–8956 (2019)
2. Anderson, P., et al.: Bottom-up and top-down attention for image captioning and visual question answering. In: 2018 IEEE/CVF Conference on Computer Vision and Pattern Recognition, pp. 6077–6086 (2018)
3. Antol, S., et al.: VQA: visual question answering. In: ICCV (2015)
4. Brown, T., et al.: Language models are few-shot learners. ArXiv arXiv:2005.14165 (2020)

5. Brysbaert, M., Warriner, A., Kuperman, V.: Concreteness ratings for 40 thousand generally known English word lemmas. Behav. Res. Methods **46**(3), 904–911 (2013). https://doi.org/10.3758/s13428-013-0403-5
6. Carion, N., Massa, F., Synnaeve, G., Usunier, N., Kirillov, A., Zagoruyko, S.: End-to-end object detection with transformers. ECCV arXiv:2005.12872 (2020)
7. Chao, Y.W., Liu, Y., Liu, X., Zeng, H., Deng, J.: Learning to detect human-object interactions. In: Proceedings of the IEEE Winter Conference on Applications of Computer Vision (2018)
8. Chao, Y.W., Wang, Z., He, Y., Wang, J., Deng, J.: HICO: a benchmark for recognizing human-object interactions in images. In: Proceedings of the IEEE International Conference on Computer Vision (2015)
9. Chen, H., Gallagher, A., Girod, B.: Describing clothing by semantic attributes. In: Fitzgibbon, A., Lazebnik, S., Perona, P., Sato, Y., Schmid, C. (eds.) ECCV 2012. LNCS, vol. 7574, pp. 609–623. Springer, Heidelberg (2012). https://doi.org/10.1007/978-3-642-33712-3_44
10. Chen, X., Gupta, A.: Webly supervised learning of convolutional networks. In: ICCV (2015)
11. Chen, X., Shrivastava, A., Gupta, A.: NEIL: extracting visual knowledge from web data. In: ICCV (2013)
12. Chen, Y.C., et al.: Uniter: learning universal image-text representations. ArXiv arXiv:1909.11740 (2019)
13. Cho, J., Lei, J., Tan, H., Bansal, M.: Unifying vision-and-language tasks via text generation. arXiv preprint arXiv:2102.02779 (2021)
14. Divvala, S., Farhadi, A., Guestrin, C.: Learning everything about anything: webly-supervised visual concept learning. In: CVPR (2014)
15. Dong, W., Socher, R., Li-Jia, L., Li, K., Fei-Fei, L.: ImageNet: a large-scale hierarchical image database. In: CVPR (2009)
16. Dosovitskiy, A., et al.: An image is worth 16 × 16 words: transformers for image recognition at scale. ICLR arXiv:2010.11929 (2021)
17. Fang, H., Xie, Y., Shao, D., Lu, C.: Dirv: dense interaction region voting for end-to-end human-object interaction detection. In: AAAI (2021)
18. Farhadi, A., Endres, I., Hoiem, D., Forsyth, D.A.: Describing objects by their attributes. In: 2009 IEEE Conference on Computer Vision and Pattern Recognition, pp. 1778–1785 (2009)
19. Fergus, R., Fei-Fei, L., Perona, P., Zisserman, A.: Learning object categories from Google's image search. In: Tenth IEEE International Conference on Computer Vision (ICCV 2005) Volume 1 2, vol. 2, pp. 1816–1823 (2005)
20. Golge, E., Duygulu, P.: ConceptMap: mining noisy web data for concept learning. In: Fleet, D., Pajdla, T., Schiele, B., Tuytelaars, T. (eds.) ECCV 2014. LNCS, vol. 8695, pp. 439–455. Springer, Cham (2014). https://doi.org/10.1007/978-3-319-10584-0_29
21. Goyal, Y., Khot, T., Summers-Stay, D., Batra, D., Parikh, D.: Making the V in VQA matter: elevating the role of image understanding in Visual Question Answering. In: CVPR (2017)
22. Gu, X., Lin, T.Y., Kuo, W., Cui, Y.: Open-vocabulary object detection via vision and language knowledge distillation (2021)
23. Guo, S., et al.: Curriculumnet: weakly supervised learning from large-scale web images. ArXiv arXiv:1808.01097 (2018)
24. Gupta, T., Kamath, A., Kembhavi, A., Hoiem, D.: Towards general purpose vision systems: an end-to-end task-agnostic vision-language architecture. In: CVPR (2022)

25. Gupta, T., Marten, R., Kembhavi, A., Hoiem, D.: Grit: general robust image task benchmark. arXiv preprint arXiv:2204.13653 (2022)
26. Gupta, T., Schwing, A.G., Hoiem, D.: No-frills human-object interaction detection: factorization, layout encodings, and training techniques. In: 2019 IEEE/CVF International Conference on Computer Vision (ICCV), pp. 9676–9684 (2019)
27. He, K., Gkioxari, G., Dollar, P., Girshick, R.: Mask R-CNN. In: ICCV (2017)
28. Hoffman, J., et al.: LSDA: large scale detection through adaptation. In: NIPS (2014)
29. Jaegle, A., et al.: Perceiver IO: a general architecture for structured inputs & outputs. ArXiv arXiv:2107.14795 (2021)
30. Jaegle, A., Gimeno, F., Brock, A., Zisserman, A., Vinyals, O., Carreira, J.: Perceiver: general perception with iterative attention. In: ICML (2021)
31. Jia, C., et al.: Scaling up visual and vision-language representation learning with noisy text supervision. In: ICML (2021)
32. Jin, B., Segovia, M.V.O., Süsstrunk, S.: Webly supervised semantic segmentation. In: 2017 IEEE Conference on Computer Vision and Pattern Recognition (CVPR), pp. 1705–1714 (2017)
33. Kim, B., Lee, J., Kang, J., Kim, E.S., Kim, H.J.: HOTR: end-to-end human-object interaction detection with transformers. In: Proceedings of the IEEE/CVF Conference on Computer Vision and Pattern Recognition (2021)
34. Kim, W., Son, B., Kim, I.: ViLT: vision-and-language transformer without convolution or region supervision. ArXiv arXiv:2102.03334 (2021)
35. Krause, J., et al.: The unreasonable effectiveness of noisy data for fine-grained recognition. ArXiv arXiv:1511.06789 (2016)
36. Krishna, R., et al.: Visual genome: connecting language and vision using crowd-sourced dense image annotations. IJCV **123**, 32–73 (2017)
37. Kumar, N., Berg, A.C., Belhumeur, P.N., Nayar, S.K.: Attribute and simile classifiers for face verification. In: 2009 IEEE 12th International Conference on Computer Vision, pp. 365–372 (2009)
38. Kuznetsova, A., et al.: The Open Images Dataset V4: unified image classification, object detection, and visual relationship detection at scale. arXiv:1811.00982 (2018)
39. Lampert, C.H., Nickisch, H., Harmeling, S.: Learning to detect unseen object classes by between-class attribute transfer. In: 2009 IEEE Conference on Computer Vision and Pattern Recognition, pp. 951–958 (2009)
40. Li, L.J., Fei-Fei, L.: Optimol: automatic online picture collection via incremental model learning. Int. J. Comput. Vision **88**, 147–168 (2007)
41. Li, L.H., Yatskar, M., Yin, D., Hsieh, C., Chang, K.W.: Visualbert: a simple and performant baseline for vision and language. ArXiv arXiv:1908.03557 (2019)
42. Li, Q., Wu, J., Tu, Z.: Harvesting mid-level visual concepts from large-scale internet images. In: 2013 IEEE Conference on Computer Vision and Pattern Recognition, pp. 851–858 (2013)
43. Li, X., et al.: OSCAR: object-semantics aligned pre-training for vision-language tasks. In: Vedaldi, A., Bischof, H., Brox, T., Frahm, J.-M. (eds.) ECCV 2020. LNCS, vol. 12375, pp. 121–137. Springer, Cham (2020). https://doi.org/10.1007/978-3-030-58577-8_8
44. Liang, K., Guo, Y., Chang, H., Chen, X.: Visual relationship detection with deep structural ranking. In: AAAI (2018)
45. Liu, Z., et al.: Swin transformer: hierarchical vision transformer using shifted windows. ICCV arXiv:2103.14030 (2021)

46. Lu, J., Batra, D., Parikh, D., Lee, S.: Vilbert: pretraining task-agnostic visiolin-guistic representations for vision-and-language tasks. In: NeurIPS (2019)

47. Lu, J., Goswami, V., Rohrbach, M., Parikh, D., Lee, S.: 12-in-1: multi-task vision and language representation learning. In: 2020 IEEE/CVF Conference on Computer Vision and Pattern Recognition (CVPR), pp. 10434–10443 (2020)

48. Lu, J., Goswami, V., Rohrbach, M., Parikh, D., Lee, S.: 12-in-1: multi-task vision and language representation learning. In: CVPR (2020)

49. Luo, A., Li, X., Yang, F., Jiao, Z., Cheng, H.: Webly-supervised learning for salient object detection. Pattern Recognit. **103**, 107308 (2020)

50. van der Maaten, L., Hinton, G.E.: Visualizing data using t-SNE. J. Mach. Learn. Res. **9**, 2579–2605 (2008)

51. McCann, B., Keskar, N., Xiong, C., Socher, R.: The natural language decathlon: multitask learning as question answering. ArXiv arXiv:1806.08730 (2018)

52. Niu, L., Tang, Q., Veeraraghavan, A., Sabharwal, A.: Learning from noisy web data with category-level supervision. In: 2018 IEEE/CVF Conference on Computer Vision and Pattern Recognition, pp. 7689–7698 (2018)

53. Niu, L., Veeraraghavan, A., Sabharwal, A.: Webly supervised learning meets zero-shot learning: a hybrid approach for fine-grained classification. In: 2018 IEEE/CVF Conference on Computer Vision and Pattern Recognition, pp. 7171–7180 (2018)

54. Parikh, D., Grauman, K.: Relative attributes. In: 2011 International Conference on Computer Vision, pp. 503–510 (2011)

55. Patterson, G., Hays, J.: Sun attribute database: discovering, annotating, and recognizing scene attributes. In: 2012 IEEE Conference on Computer Vision and Pattern Recognition, pp. 2751–2758 (2012)

56. Radford, A., et al.: Learning transferable visual models from natural language supervision (2021)

57. Radford, A., et al.: Learning transferable visual models from natural language supervision. In: ICML (2021)

58. Raffel, C., et al.: Exploring the limits of transfer learning with a unified text-to-text transformer. J. Mach. Learn. Res. **21**, 140:1-140:67 (2020)

59. Ramakrishnan, S., Agrawal, A., Lee, S.: Overcoming language priors in visual question answering with adversarial regularization. arXiv preprint arXiv:1810.03649 (2018)

60. Redmon, J., Farhadi, A.: Yolo9000: better, faster, stronger. In: 2017 IEEE Conference on Computer Vision and Pattern Recognition (CVPR), pp. 6517–6525 (2017)

61. Sharma, P., Ding, N., Goodman, S., Soricut, R.: Conceptual captions: a cleaned, hypernymed, image alt-text dataset for automatic image captioning. In: ACL (2018)

62. Shen, S., et al.: How much can clip benefit vision-and-language tasks? ArXiv arXiv:2107.06383 (2021)

63. Shen, T., Lin, G., Shen, C., Reid, I.D.: Bootstrapping the performance of webly supervised semantic segmentation. In: 2018 IEEE/CVF Conference on Computer Vision and Pattern Recognition, pp. 1363–1371 (2018)

64. Shen, Y., et al.: Noise-aware fully webly supervised object detection. In: 2020 IEEE/CVF Conference on Computer Vision and Pattern Recognition (CVPR), pp. 11323–11332 (2020)

65. Sun, G., Wang, W., Dai, J., Van Gool, L.: Mining cross-image semantics for weakly supervised semantic segmentation. In: Vedaldi, A., Bischof, H., Brox, T., Frahm, J.-M. (eds.) ECCV 2020. LNCS, vol. 12347, pp. 347–365. Springer, Cham (2020). https://doi.org/10.1007/978-3-030-58536-5_21

66. Tan, H.H., Bansal, M.: Lxmert: learning cross-modality encoder representations from transformers. In: EMNLP/IJCNLP (2019)
67. Uijlings, J.R.R., Popov, S., Ferrari, V.: Revisiting knowledge transfer for training object class detectors. In: 2018 IEEE/CVF Conference on Computer Vision and Pattern Recognition, pp. 1101–1110 (2018)
68. Ulutan, O., Iftekhar, A.S.M., Manjunath, B.S.: Vsgnet: spatial attention network for detecting human object interactions using graph convolutions. In: 2020 IEEE/CVF Conference on Computer Vision and Pattern Recognition (CVPR), pp. 13614–13623 (2020)
69. Vedantam, R., Zitnick, C.L., Parikh, D.: Cider: Consensus-based image description evaluation. 2015 IEEE Conference on Computer Vision and Pattern Recognition (CVPR) pp. 4566–4575 (2015)
70. Vijayanarasimhan, S., Grauman, K.: Keywords to visual categories: multiple-instance learning forweakly supervised object categorization. In: 2008 IEEE Conference on Computer Vision and Pattern Recognition, pp. 1–8 (2008)
71. Wang, S., Thompson, L., Iyyer, M.: Phrase-Bert: improved phrase embeddings from Bert with an application to corpus exploration. In: EMNLP (2021)
72. Wang, S., Joo, J., Wang, Y., Zhu, S.C.: Weakly supervised learning for attribute localization in outdoor scenes. In: 2013 IEEE Conference on Computer Vision and Pattern Recognition, pp. 3111–3118 (2013)
73. Wang, X.J., Zhang, L., Li, X., Ma, W.Y.: Annotating images by mining image search results. IEEE Trans. Pattern Anal. Mach. Intell. **30**, 1919–1932 (2008)
74. Whitehead, S., Wu, H., Ji, H., Feris, R.S., Saenko, K., MIT-IBM, U.: Separating skills and concepts for novel visual question answering. In: 2021 IEEE/CVF Conference on Computer Vision and Pattern Recognition (CVPR), pp. 5628–5637 (2021)
75. Wu, Z., Tao, Q., Lin, G., Cai, J.: Exploring bottom-up and top-down cues with attentive learning for webly supervised object detection. In: 2020 IEEE/CVF Conference on Computer Vision and Pattern Recognition (CVPR), pp. 12933–12942 (2020)
76. Xu, H., Yan, M., Li, C., Bi, B., Huang, S., Xiao, W., Huang, F.: E2E-VLP: end-to-end vision-language pre-training enhanced by visual learning (2021)
77. YANG, J., et al.: Webly supervised image classification with self-contained confidence. In: Vedaldi, A., Bischof, H., Brox, T., Frahm, J.-M. (eds.) ECCV 2020. LNCS, vol. 12353, pp. 779–795. Springer, Cham (2020). https://doi.org/10.1007/978-3-030-58598-3_46
78. Yatskar, M., Zettlemoyer, L., Farhadi, A.: Situation recognition: visual semantic role labeling for image understanding. In: 2016 IEEE Conference on Computer Vision and Pattern Recognition (CVPR), pp. 5534–5542 (2016)
79. Zareian, A., Rosa, K.D., Hu, D.H., Chang, S.F.: Open-vocabulary object detection using captions. In: 2021 IEEE/CVF Conference on Computer Vision and Pattern Recognition (CVPR), pp. 14388–14397 (2021)
80. Zhang, A., et al.: Mining the benefits of two-stage and one-stage hoi detection. arXiv preprint arXiv:2108.05077 (2021)
81. Zhang, P., et al.: Vinvl: making visual representations matter in vision-language models. ArXiv arXiv:2101.00529 (2021)
82. Zheng, W., Yan, L., Gou, C., Wang, F.: Webly supervised knowledge embedding model for visual reasoning. 2020 IEEE/CVF Conference on Computer Vision and Pattern Recognition (CVPR) pp. 12442–12451 (2020)

83. Zhong, X., Ding, C., Qu, X., Tao, D.: Polysemy deciphering network for human-object interaction detection. In: Vedaldi, A., Bischof, H., Brox, T., Frahm, J.-M. (eds.) ECCV 2020. LNCS, vol. 12365, pp. 69–85. Springer, Cham (2020). https://doi.org/10.1007/978-3-030-58565-5_5

84. Zou, C., et al.: End-to-end human object interaction detection with hoi transformer. In: Proceedings of the IEEE/CVF Conference on Computer Vision and Pattern Recognition (2021)

FedVLN: Privacy-Preserving Federated Vision-and-Language Navigation

Kaiwen Zhou[✉] and Xin Eric Wang

University of California, Santa Cruz, CA 95064, USA
{kzhou35,xwang366}@ucsc.edu

Abstract. Data privacy is a central problem for embodied agents that can perceive the environment, communicate with humans, and act in the real world. While helping humans complete tasks, the agent may observe and process sensitive information of users, such as house environments, human activities, etc. In this work, we introduce privacy-preserving embodied agent learning for the task of Vision-and-Language Navigation (VLN), where an embodied agent navigates house environments by following natural language instructions. We view each house environment as a local client, which shares nothing other than local updates with the cloud server and other clients, and propose a novel Federated Vision-and-Language Navigation (FedVLN) framework to protect data privacy during both training and pre-exploration. Particularly, we propose a decentralized federated training strategy to limit the data of each client to its local model training and a federated pre-exploration method to do partial model aggregation to improve model generalizability to unseen environments. Extensive results on R2R and RxR datasets show that, decentralized federated training achieve comparable results with centralized training while protecting seen environment privacy, and federated pre-exploration significantly outperforms centralized pre-exploration while preserving unseen environment privacy. Code is available at https://github.com/eric-ai-lab/FedVLN.

Keywords: Privacy-preserving Embodied AI · Vision-and-language navigation · Federated learning

1 Introduction

A long-term goal of AI research is to build embodied agents that can perceive the environment, communicate with humans, and perform real-world tasks to benefit human society. However, since the agent interacts closely with humans and environments, it often receives sensitive information during training and inference. For example, as shown in Fig. 1a, in the task of Vision-and-Language Navigation (VLN) [4], where an agent learns to navigate towards a target location in an indoor environment given natural language instruction, the training

---

Supplementary Information The online version contains supplementary material available at https://doi.org/10.1007/978-3-031-20059-5_39.

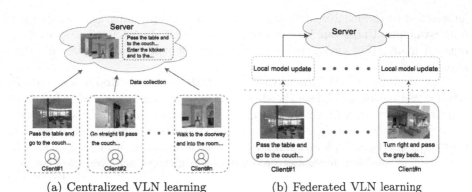

(a) Centralized VLN learning   (b) Federated VLN learning

Fig. 1. Data privacy: centralized VLN learning *vs.* our federated VLN learning. Existing VLN approaches centralize all the client data in a server, including house environments and user instructions, which ignores users' privacy concerns. Our federated VLN framework keeps client data used only locally and the server receives nothing other than local model updates, so the client data privacy is preserved.

and inference data may include private information such as what the user's house looks like, what the user said, and what the user did. Data privacy is a central problem for building trustworthy embodied agents but seldomly studied before [14]. Thus, in this work, we introduce privacy-preserving embodied agent learning for the task of vision-and-language navigation.

VLN models are typically trained on seen environments with ground-truth instruction-trajectory pairs and then deployed to unseen environments without any labeled data. After deployment, the agent may explore the unseen environment and adapt to the new environment for better performance, which is known as pre-exploration. However, as shown in Fig. 1a, most of the existing methods assemble all the data in a server to train a navigation agent for both seen environment training and unseen environment pre-exploration. This is not practical in reality since users may not want to share the data in their own house due to privacy concerns. Privacy-preserving VLN requires the agent to protect the data privacy during both seen environment training and unseen environment pre-exploration while maintaining comparable navigation performance.

In this paper, we propose a novel Federated Vision-and-Language Navigation (FedVLN) framework, to address the aforementioned data privacy issues and improve the adaptation performance on unseen environments at the same time. Specifically, on the seen environment training stage, as shown in Fig. 1b, we treat each house environment as a client. The client's local models (a VLN agent for navigation and a speaker for data augmentation) are trained on private local data, and then the model updates are sent to the server for model aggregation. No private data except the local model updates will be shared with the server and there is no communication between clients. During pre-exploration, we train the client models on seen environments and unseen environments simultaneously under federated learning paradigm—the client models do partial model aggregation (language encoder only) and partial local adaptation, enabling better adaptation to the local visual environment while maintaining general language understanding. Under our FedVLN framework, users do not need to share their data with any other party, thus the privacy of training data and inference data is protected.

Our experiments on Room-to-Room (R2R) [4] and Room-across-Room (RxR) [28][1] datasets validate the effectiveness of our framework. Our federated learning framework achieves comparable results with centralized training while preserving data privacy. More importantly, on the pre-exploration stage, we show that centralized pre-exploration hinders the agent from adapting to each specific environment, and our federated pre-exploration method achieves the best performance among prior pre-exploration methods such as centralized [40,42] and environment-based pre-exploration [11]. Our contributions are three-fold:

- We are the first to discuss data privacy concerns for vision-and-language navigation and define the privacy-preserving embodied AI problem for the two learning stages in VLN.
- We propose a novel federated learning framework for privacy-preserving VLN to ensure that users do not need to share their data to any party.
- Extensive results on R2R and RxR show that our federated learning framework not only achieves comparable results with centralized training, but also outperforms centralized and environment-based pre-exploration methods.

2   Related Work

2.1   Vision-and-Language Navigation

With the development of deep learning and human's vision of more helpful AI agents, embodied AI becomes an emerging research area. Vision-and-language navigation(VLN) [4,25,28,35] is one of the most popular tasks of embodied AI, in which an embodied agent learns to navigation to a goal location in indoor environments following language instruction and given dynamic visual information. Anderson et al. [4] first propose a LSTM-based seq-to-seq model for navigation. For better understanding vision-and-language information, there are works working on vision-and-language pre-training [15,17,19,30,34] and model structures [6,13,19]. Reinforcement learning and navigation planning methods were also introduced into VLN to perform better action decisions [3,27,42,43]. Limited labeled data was another bottleneck to train a better model. To this end, Fried et al. [10] propose a speaker-follower model which can generate pseudo instructions for a sampled path by a trained speaker. Further, to mitigate the gap between seen and unseen environments, pre-exploration was proposed [11,40,42], which can learn and adapt to new environments after deployment. However, most current research ignores the practicality in real-life application scenarios, especially data privacy issues. Fu et al. [11] consider the implementation problem of pre-exploration and proposed environment-based pre-exploration, but they did not consider the privacy issue of training data. Also, we showed that environment-based pre-exploration might suffer from data scarcity and data bias.

---

[1] We conduct experiments on the English data of the RxR dataset.

2.2   Privacy-Preserving Machine Learning

Over the years, researchers propose many methods [7,21,33,41] to address different data privacy problems [9,12,18,39] in machine learning. First, during the training stage, if the training data are from different parties, sharing their data with other parties might leads to privacy concerns. At the inference stage, there are multiple privacy attacks, especially in the scenario of Machine Learning as a Service (MLaaS), in which cloud providers offer machine inference hosted on the cloud [7]. For example, membership inference attack [39] can judge if a specific data sample exists in training data, model inversion attack [9,45] aims to infer training data given white-box or black-box access to the model. Also, in MLaaS, users might not be willing to directly upload their data to the cloud server [7]. Facing these privacy problems for training data and inference data, researchers propose many privacy-preserving methods, including federated learning, homomorphic encryption, differential privacy, etc [29,31,33,41]. However, most of their work focuses on single modality tasks and static data, and seldomly study the data privacy of embodied AI. In embodied AI tasks like vision-and-language navigation, the data contains more human-robot interaction and more complex private information, such as corresponding language-image pairs, dynamic visual information in the indoor environments. VLN also has a unique training stage, pre-exploration. Both of these may make the privacy problems and solutions for VLN more complex. In our work, we elaborate on privacy-preserving VLN training scenarios and propose a solution.

2.3   Federated Learning

Federated learning [41] is a technique that allows client models to train locally and then be sent to the central server for model aggregation. In this way, the clients do not need to send their sensitive data to any party. Thus the privacy of training data is protected. The first federated learning algorithm [41] uses weighted sum for aggregating clients' models. Later, researchers proposed different federated learning algorithms for heterogeneous data distribution and personalization [8,20,22,29]. Especially, Collins et al. [8] proposed to keep classification head locally for personalization. Compared with our framework, they were trying to solve the problem of label heterogeneity and learn a general data representation, and their setting does not have the difference between validation data and training data. Reddi et al. [37] summarized these first-order aggregation methods into one framework as FEDOPT, whose server aggregation is:

$$w_{t+1} = \text{SERVEROPT}(w_t, -\Delta w_t, \eta, t) \tag{1}$$

where SERVEROPT is the aggregation algorithm, η is server learning rate.

Application wise, federated learning framework has been used on various tasks in computer vision [16,20] and natural language processing [23,32]. Recently, there are also some works for federated learning on multi-modal machine learning [1,46]. Zhao, et al. [46] try horizontal federated learning(FL), vertical FL, and Federated Transfer Learning on different multi-modal tasks and datasets, and [1] using semi-supervised FL to extract hidden representations of multi-modality. However, the tasks they discussed is not embodied agent for individual users. In vision-and-language navigation, the training paradigm is different from formerly discussed tasks, which has two different training objectives, training scenarios in two training stages. To solve this, we proposed a novel Federated Vision-and-Language Navigation(FedVLN) framework.

3 Privacy-Preserving Vision-and-Language Navigation

3.1 Vision-and-Language Navigation (VLN)

The goal of the VLN task is to navigate from a given location and reach a destination following natural language instruction. The task can be formally defined as follow: given an language instruction $U = \{u_1, u_2, ..., u_n\}$. At each step, the agent will receive current visual information v_t as input. The agent will need to choose an action a_t at each step based on the instruction U, current/history visual information$\{v_\tau\}_{\tau=1}^t$, and history actions$\{a_\tau\}_{\tau=1}^{t-1}$. The agent's state, which consists of the agent's navigation history and current spatial location, will change according to the agent's action. The navigation terminates when the agent chooses a 'stop' action. The environments that contain labeled training data are seen environments. There are also unseen environments that do not have training data and are invisible during training.

VLN Agents. In general, VLN agents consist of a language encoding module to understand the instruction, a trajectory encoder to encode visual observation and actions, and a multimodal decision module to jointly process multi-modal information including encoded language information L_{enc}, visual information V_{enc}, and action information A_{enc} and predict the next action a_t:

$$L_{enc} = E_L(u_1, u_2, ..., u_n) \tag{2}$$

$$V_{enc}, A_{enc} = E_T(v_1, v_2, ..., v_t, a_1, a_2, ..., a_{t-1}) \tag{3}$$

$$a_t = M(L_{enc}, V_{enc}, A_{enc}) \tag{4}$$

Speaker-Based Data Augmentation. To tackle the problem of data scarcity, Fried et al. [10] propose a back-translation speaker model which can generate corresponding instructions U from the visual information and action sequence of sampled routes in the environment:

$$U = Speaker(v_1, v_2, ..., v_t, a_1, a_2, ..., a_t) \tag{5}$$

The speaker is trained by original labeled route-instruction pairs, which takes the visual and actions information of routes as input and predict the instructions. The generated pseudo instructions along with sampled routes can be the augmented training data for better agent learning.

Pre-exploration. After training on seen environments and deploying on unseen environment, the agent can adapt to the new environment via pre-exploration [11,40,42]. There are different variants of pre-exploration includes

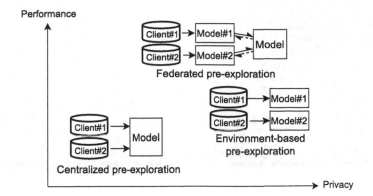

Performance

Privacy

Federated pre-exploration

Environment-based
pre-exploration

Centralized pre-exploration

Fig. 2. Comparison between different pre-exploration strategies on performance-privacy trade-off. Federated pre-exploration achieves the best navigation performance while maintaining good inference data privacy protection.

self-imitation learning [42], graph-based methods [5,47], etc. In our work, we consider the paradigm that sampling routes R' from a new environment and generate instructions I' using the trained speaker mentioned before. Then the agent can be trained on the new environment using sampled routes and pseudo instructions(R', I').

3.2 Privacy-Preserving VLN

Considering the data may have sensitive information, users may have different levels of concern about the privacy of their data. In our work, we consider the case that the users do not want their data to be directly shared with the server (e.g., companies) and any other parties. Based on this, we define privacy-preserving vision-and-language navigation learning setting on two training stages: seen environment training and unseen environment pre-exploration. For seen environment training, including the training of navigation agent, speaker model and data augmentation process, no labeled data within the house environment will be directly shared with the server or any other client to prevent the leak of private information. And our primary purpose is to train a model that can generalize well on unseen environments. Thus, we need to utilize all the data indirectly to train one model.

For pre-exploration, the unlabeled data in unseen environments also can not be shared with others. However, the purpose in this stage is to adapt the model to a specific environment. Thus, training on data in one environment (environment-based pre-exploration) might not be a bad choice. In fact, our experiments show that environment-based pre-exploration performs better than centralized pre-exploration. Nevertheless, as elaborated in Sect. 4.2, we can indirectly utilize all the data in pre-exploration to boost the performance and preserve privacy. As in Fig. 2, we aim to achieve the best performance-privacy trade-off in pre-exploration.

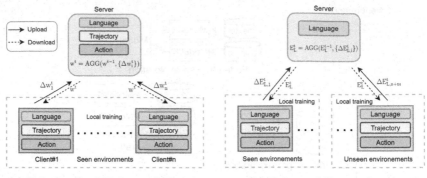

(a) Decentralized Federated Training   (b) Federated Pre-exploration

Fig. 3. The FedVLN framework. In the first stage (a), agents in seen environments will be trained on local data and upload the model updates to the server for aggregation (AGG), then download the global model from the server. In the second stage (b), all the agents in seen and unseen environments join the federated training. During local training, all the modules will be optimized, while only the language encoder will be uploaded/downloaded.

4   The FedVLN Approach

We propose a federated vision-and-language navigation framework (FedVLN) as shown in Fig. 3, in which user's data can be kept locally during both training and pre-exploration. In this section, we will introduce our FedVLN framework for two training stages: Decentralized Federated Training and Federated Pre-exploration. In decentralized federated training, each environment has a local agent, which will be trained on local data, then uploaded to the server. Then the global model on the server will be updated by the aggregation of local model updates and sent to all the environments. In federated pre-exploration, to enable the agent to both adapt to the new environment and maintain the ability to understand language, only the language encoder will be shared with the server after local training, instead of sharing the full model. All the agents from seen and unseen environments will join the federated pre-exploration process.

4.1   Decentralized Federated Training

Original Training Data. When training on the original training data, we first divide the VLN dataset by environments. We treat each environment as a client, then assign a local navigation agent w_i^0 on each environment, which is initialized as the same as global navigation agent w^0. At each communication round between clients and server, a certain percentage of clients will be randomly selected for training, the local agent on each selected client will be trained for a certain number of epochs on their own data d_i:

$$w_i^t = \text{ClientUpdate}(w^{t-1}, d_i) \tag{6}$$

Table 1. Comparison between ground-truth (GT) and speaker generated instructions on seen validation. NoS means the average number of sentences.

Statistics	GT	Speaker
Length	29.58	21.89
Var(Length)	155.70	20.88
NoS	2.44	2.42
Var(NoS)	1.21	0.47

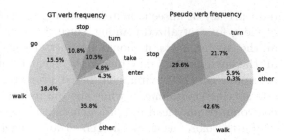

Fig. 4. Comparison of verb frequency between ground truth instructions and generated pseudo instructions.

where ClientUpdate is the local training process. Then each selected client will send the update $\Delta w_{i,t} = w_i^t - w^{t-1}$ of their model to the server, and the server will aggregate all the models with a server learning rate η:

$$w^t = w^{t-1} + \eta \sum_{i \in \phi_t} \frac{n_j}{\sum_{j \in \phi_t} n_j} \Delta w_i^t \tag{7}$$

Here the weight of each local model $\frac{n_j}{\sum_{j \in \phi_t} n_j}$ is the proportion of the use's sample in the total training sample of this communication round.

Augmentation. For data augmentation, we will assign each client a local speaker. Following the federated learning paradigm mentioned above and the training procedure of speaker from Sect. 3.1, at each communication round, each speaker from the selected clients will be trained on the labeled route-instruction pairs in its environment.

The best global model (according to BLUE score) during the training process will be sent to all clients. Each client can use the speaker model to generate pseudo instructions I_i^{aug} for sampled routes within the environment. Then the augmented training of the agent will also follow the federated training process mentioned above, except the local data will be the combination of original data and augmented data $\{(d_i, d_i^{aug})\}_{i=1}^n$.

Notice that during the whole training process, including original data training, speaker training, and augmented data training, no client share their data to other clients or the server. Thus the training data privacy is preserved.

4.2   Federated Pre-exploration

Pre-exploration allows the agent to explore the newly deployed environment and update itself based on the new information. From the perspective of data privacy, centralized pre-exploration is impractical here, since it assumes one navigation agent can get access to data from all the unseen environments. Fu et al. [11] proposed environment-based pre-exploration, which allows each agent to train on only one environment. Thus no data will be shared with other parties, and the data privacy in unseen environments is preserved. From the performance point of view, for centralized training, since the agent is trained on all the data from all the environments, it should have better generalizability. However, training in all the environments may hinder the agent from better adapting to one specific environment. For environment-based pre-exploration, the agent can focus on one specific environment, while the limited data amount and data bias in one environment may lead to a less generalized agent.

Furthermore, as shown in Table 1 and Fig. 4, we found that the instructions generated by the speaker are statistically significantly different from human-generated instructions. Moreover, the language pattern is much simpler than human language. Since current methods only use augmented data with speaker-generated instructions for training during pre-exploration, the agent might suffer from the huge distribution shift between instructions in augmented data and validation data, and can not understand instructions in validation data well. This problem could be even worse on environment-based pre-exploration since the data for one agent is of a smaller amount and from a single environment.

What is more, according to former research [44], the agent will perform better on seen paths or environments. Thus, the best solution is to maintain the generalizability to understand language and adapt to a specific visual environment. To this end, as in Fig. 3a, we propose federated pre-exploration. In federated pre-exploration, The server will only maintain a global language encoder, which is initialized with the global encoder after decentralized federated VLN training. During each communication round, the server will send the global language encoder E^{t-1} to the selected clients. Then the selected clients will update its language encoder with E^{t-1}, and train the full agent on its local data:

$$E_{L,i}^t, E_{T,i}^t, M_i^t = \text{ClientUpdate}(E_{L,i}^{t-1}, E_{T,i}^{t-1}, M_i^{t-1}, \tau, \lambda) \qquad (8)$$

After local training, the model will send only the language encoder $E_{L,i}^t$ to the server for aggregation as lines 9,11 in Algorithm 1. In this way, the language encoder will be jointly updated on data from all the participated environments, thus being more generalized. Meanwhile, to further improve the generalizability of the language encoder, we randomly sample a fraction of seen environments at each communication round, where agents will also follow the training process above. The trajectory encoding module $E_{T,i}$ and multi-modal decision module M_i will keep training locally, which can help local agents adapt to their own environments. For validation, we used the local models after local training. The whole training procedure is in Algorithm 1.

5   Experimental Setup

5.1   Datasets

We implement our federated learning framework on two datasets: Room-to-Room (R2R) [4] and Room-across-Room (RxR)(en) [28]. Both datasets are developed on the Matterport3D Simulator [4], a photorealistic 3D environment for embodied AI research.

Algorithm 1. Federated Pre-exploration

1: Parameters: Seen participation rate r_1, unseen participation rate r_2; local learning rate λ; server learning rate η; number of communication rounds T; number of seen environments n; number of unseen environments m; local training epochs τ.

2: Initialize: $E_{L,i}^0 = E_L^0$, $E_{T,i}^0 = E_T^0$, $M_i^0 = M^0$, for i in {1,2,...,n+m}

3: **for** t in [1,T] **do**

4:     Server sample $r_1 n$ seen environments and $r_2 m$ unseen environments as ϕ_t

5:     Server send global language encoder to selected environments E^{t-1}

6:     **for** client in ϕ_t **do**

7:         Client update language encoder: $E_i^{t-1} = E^{t-1}$

8:         Client local training: $E_{L,i}^t, E_{T,i}^t, M_i^t = \text{ClientUpdate}(E_{L,i}^{t-1}, E_{T,i}^{t-1}, M_i^{t-1}, \tau, \lambda)$

9:         Client upload delta of the language encoder $\Delta E_i^t = E_i^t - E^{t-1}$ to the server

10:     **end for**

11:     Server update language encoder: $E_i^t = E^{t-1} + \eta \sum_{i \in \phi_t} \frac{n_j}{\sum_{j \in \phi_t} n_j} \Delta E_i^t$

12: **end for**

R2R [4] is constructed by generating the shortest paths from sampled start and end points. Then collect three associated navigation instructions for each path using Amazon Mechanical Turk (AMT). The dataset contains 7,189 paths from 90 environments, and each path contains 3 instructions. The environments are split into 61 environments for training and seen validation, 11 for unseen validation, and 18 for testing. The environments in unseen validation and unseen test set do not appear in the training environments.

RxR [28] is proposed to mitigate shortcomings of former VLN datasets. Specifically, it is a large-scale dataset with multilingual instructions. It contains 16,522 paths and 126,069 instructions, among which 42,002 instructions are in English. RxR also ensures spatiotemporal alignments between instructions, visual percepts, and actions for agent training. The RxR dataset samples arbitrary paths from point to point (not necessarily shortest paths) to avoid data bias.

5.2   Evaluation Metrics

For both datasets, we report Success Rate (SR), Success Rate weighted by Path Length (SPL), Oracle Success Rate (OSR), and navigation Error (NE) as goal-oriented metrics. SR is calculated as the percentage of the agent stop within 3 m from the end point. SPL [2] is defined as Success weighted by normalized inverse Path Length, which considers both navigation effectiveness and efficiency. OSR is the percentage of the agent visiting a point within 3 m from the end point. NE is the average distance between the agent's final location and the end point. We also report Coverage weighted by Length Score (CLS) [26] and normalized Dynamic Time Warping (nDTW) [24] to validate the fidelity of navigation paths, which penalize the deviation from the reference path. SR and SPL are often considered as the primary metrics for VLN evaluation.

5.3   Baselines

Currently, we do not consider pre-training privacy, and VLN data pre-training infringes on data privacy. Thus, we choose two strong VLN baselines without VLN pre-training for experiments:

1. **Envdrop** [40]: the environment dropout model uses Bi-directional LSTM as the language encoder and attentive LSTM as the action decoder, a mixed learning objective of imitation learning and reinforcement learning.
2. **CLIP-ViL** [38]: the CLIP-ViL model adapts CLIP [36] visual encoder to improve vision and language encoding and matching for vision-and-language navigation.

5.4   Implementation Details

When training on seen environments, the total number of training steps of local models is the same as centralized training steps. At each communication round, we use the participation rate of $r = 0.2$, and train each local agent for $\tau = 5$ epochs on local data. For federated speaker training, we select the best model on seen validation data according to BLEU2 score to generate instructions.

During pre-exploration, we use the participation rate of $r_1 = 0.6$ for unseen environments. And we train each agent for $\tau_1 = 1$ epoch over unseen local dataset. When training across seen and unseen environments, we use the participation rate of $r_2 = 0.18$ for seen environments. To validate the effectiveness of our framework, for centralized pre-exploration, environment-based pre-exploration and federated pre-exploration, we use federated trained speaker to generate pseudo-instruction and train from federated trained navigation agent.

6   Results

6.1   Decentralized Federated Training

Seen Environment Training. In Table 2 and Table 3, we report the results for seen environment training on R2R and RxR datasets for both baselines.

First, federated learning performs worse than centralized training on seen environments with an average of 2.43% SR gap. This is reasonable, as centralized training can easily overfit to the seen training data for better performance on seen environments, while for federated learning, because of the decentralized optimization over protected local data, the global model can not overfit to the seen environments as well as centralized training.

The performance on unseen environments tests the generalization ability of VLN models and is used for VLN evaluation. As seen in Table 2 and Table 3, on unseen environments, decentralized federated training achieves comparable results with centralized training, on both original data training and augmented data training across different VLN models. For example, FedEnvdrop performs better than Envdrop on R2R and nearly the same on RxR, and FedCLIP-ViL obtains comparable results with CLIP-ViL on both R2R and RxR. Thus, in

Table 2. R2R results of seen environment training. Envdrop is the centralized Envdrop model, and FedEnvdrop is the federated Envdrop model. Envdrop$_{aug}$ means the Envdrop model trained with augmented data. Our decentralized federated training outpeforms centralized training with Envdrop and achieves comparable results with CLIP-ViL on unseen environments.

Model	Val-Seen						Val-Unseen					
	NE↓	OSR↑	SPL↑	SR↑	CLS↑	nDTW↑	NE↓	OSR↑	SPL↑	SR↑	CLS↑	nDTW↑
Envdrop	4.71	65.6	53.2	56.1	66.8	55.0	5.87	52.7	40.9	44.5	57.1	42.3
FedEnvdrop	4.69	63.1	52.4	55.0	66.4	55.1	5.66	53.0	43.4	46.5	59.0	45.5
Envdrop$_{aug}$	3.81	73.1	56.5	62.4	65.4	55.2	5.37	61.7	40.9	50.0	50.5	38.1
FedEnvdrop$_{aug}$	4.00	69.3	53.8	61.8	70.9	60.9	5.41	56.9	46.3	49.8	60.3	47.1
CLIP-ViL	4.07	70.7	57.9	62.9	67.7	55.8	5.02	63.1	47.5	53.6	58.1	44.5
FedCLIP-ViL	4.28	67.2	55.8	60.4	65.7	53.3	4.91	61.9	47.6	53.4	57.9	44.4
CLIP-ViL$_{aug}$	3.52	75.0	61.7	66.8	69.3	58.6	4.59	67.4	50.7	57.0	59.2	46.4
FedCLIP-ViL$_{aug}$	4.13	69.8	58.2	62.6	67.3	56.7	4.80	65.9	49.8	56.3	59.2	46.1

Table 3. RxR results of seen environment training. Decentralized federated training obtains comparable results with centralized training on unseen environments (e.g., only 0.1% SPL difference with the CLIP-ViL model).

Model	Val-Seen						Val-Unseen					
	NE↓	OSR↑	SPL↑	SR↑	CLS↑	nDTW↑	NE↓	OSR↑	SPL↑	SR↑	CLS↑	nDTW↑
Envdrop	7.97	51.6	38.0	40.7	58.8	54.0	8.42	45.1	31.8	35.0	55.6	50.6
FedEnvdrop	8.60	49.2	33.8	36.8	56.2	51.0	8.59	44.3	31.0	34.2	55.1	49.7
CLIP-ViL	6.92	56.8	42.3	46.5	60.0	56.2	7.38	50.6	34.9	39.5	55.6	51.2
FedCLIP-ViL	7.18	54.6	40.0	44.2	59.0	54.7	8.54	50.1	35.0	39.4	56.0	51.5

terms of generalization ability, our decentralized federated training method is comparable with centralized training while protecting the training data privacy.

Federated Speaker *vs.* Centralized Speaker. From Table 2, we notice that when training with augmented data, federated learning has an average gap of 0.45% on unseen SR compared with centralized training, which is slightly worse than results without augmented data. We suspect that it's because the federated speaker produce slightly worse augmented data than the centralized speaker. So we compare the BLEU score between federated speaker and centralized speaker in Table 4. Results show that federated speaker performs 1.15 worse than centralized speaker on seen validation on BLEU2 score, but is 0.65 better on unseen validation data, which is quite aligned with the navigation results. Since we do data augmentation on seen environments, federated speaker generates slightly lower-quality pseudo instructions.

To further validate this, we replace federated speaker with centralized speaker to generate the augmented data. Results are on Table 5, when trained with the same augmented data by centralized speaker, whose quality is still worse than original data, decentralized federated training also obtains comparable performance with centralized training. Thus, federated learning can train a generalized model on both original data and pseudo data.

Table 4. Comparison of BLUE2 score between federated speaker and centralized speaker based on the CLIP encoder and the ResNet encoder on R2R.

Speaker	Val-seen	Val-unseen
CLIP Cent	33.5	30.2
CLIP Fed	32.7	31.5
ResNet Cent	33.6	30.7
ResNet Fed	32.1	30.7

Table 5. Comparison of SR between two baselines on data generated by centralized speaker and federated speaker on R2R validation unseen averaged on two runs. Using centralized speaker improves the navigation performance.

Speaker	Envdrop	CLIP-ViT
Centralized	49.9	56.6
Federated	49.7	55.9

6.2 Federated Pre-exploration

To validate the effectiveness of federated pre-exploration on unseen environments, we compare centralized pre-exploration, environment-based pre-exploration, and different federated pre-exploration methods: full model sharing (Fed-Full), sharing language encoder only (Fed-Lan), and sharing language encoder across seen and unseen environments (Fed-Lan+seen). Results are shown in Table 6.

Navigation Performance. For centralized pre-exploration and Fed-Full, in which one agent is optimized on data from all the environments, the agent can not adapt very well on one specific environment. For example, there is a gap of 3.85% on SR between centralized training and environment-based pre-exploration. When sharing only the language encoder during federated learning, the validation results improve significantly comparing with full model sharing (e.g. 4.6% on SR) since the agents can adapt to each environment better. Also, the generalization ability of language encoder is better than environment-based pre-exploration, since it is trained on more data across different environments. Thus sharing only the encoder in federated pre-exploration achieves better results comparing with environment-based pre-exploration. Federated pre-exploration with seen environments further improves the performance benefiting from human labeled data, and achieves around 1.8% SR improvement than environment-based pre-exploration.

Degree of Privacy. From the perspective of privacy preserving, environment-based pre-exploration is the best, where nothing in the unseen environments will be shared with others. Centralized training is clearly the worse, where all the observable data from unseen environments will be directly shared with the server. Federated pre-exploration only uploads the model updates to the server. Among federated methods, sharing only the language encoder protects data privacy better than full model sharing: it only shares the updates of language encoder, which accounts for only 24.6% of the parameters and keeps other modules completely local. Training with seen environments will not make the training process less private, as seen environments already shared their parameter updates with the server in decentralized federated training process.

Table 6. Comparison between different pre-exploration methods on R2R unseen validation. Fed-Full means full model sharing federated learning, Fed-Lan means sharing only language encoder in federated learning, Fed-Enc+seen means federated training with seen environments and sharing encoder only.

Model	Method	NE↓	OSR↑	SPL↑	SR↑	CLS↑	nDTW↑	Privacy↑
Envdrop	Centralized	3.81	75.8	61.2	64.6	71.4	64.6	0 - sharing data
	Env-based	3.63	77.2	62.0	65.9	72.3	66.5	**3** - no sharing
	Fed-Full	3.94	74.9	59.4	62.9	70.8	63.0	1 - model sharing (100%)
	Fed-Lan	3.56	78.4	63.0	66.7	**73.1**	<u>67.1</u>	<u>2</u> - model sharing (24.6%)
	Fed-Lan+seen	**3.51**	**78.5**	**63.6**	**67.6**	**73.1**	**67.3**	<u>2</u> - model sharing (24.6%)
CLIP-ViT	Centralized	3.66	75.4	61.7	66.1	70.1	62.5	0 - sharing data
	Env-based	3.45	78.0	65.2	69.2	72.5	65.8	**3** - no sharing
	Fed-Full	3.78	74.9	60.5	64.8	69.2	61.0	1 - model sharing (100%)
	Fed-Lan	3.27	**79.8**	66.4	70.1	**74.4**	**69.3**	<u>2</u> - model sharing (24.6%)
	Fed-Lan+seen	**3.21**	**79.8**	**67.3**	**71.0**	**74.4**	<u>68.7</u>	<u>2</u> - model sharing (24.6%)

Overall, our federated pre-exploration method achieves a good performance-privacy trade-off. Centralized training is both worst in terms of navigation ability and privacy protection. Environment-based pre-exploration has the best privacy protection of unseen environment data. Federated pre-exploration achieves the best navigation results with little privacy cost by keeping all client data locally, and sharing only the language encoder model updates with the server.

7   Conclusion and Future Work

In this paper, we study the data privacy problems in vision-and-language navigation with respect to two learning scenarios: seen environment training and unseen environment pre-exploration. We propose a novel federated vision-and-language navigation (FedVLN) framework to preserve data privacy in both learning stages while maintaining comparable navigation performance. Furthermore, we present that federated pre-exploration can even outperform all previous pre-exploration methods and achieves the best performance-privacy trade-off. As the first work along this direction, our work does not consider adversarial attacks that can potentially recover data information from shared local model updates, and we believe future work can consider more embodied AI tasks and defend against privacy attacks for more data security.

Acknowledgement. We thank Jing Gu, Eliana Stefani, Winson Chen, Yang Liu, Hao Tan, Pengchuan Zhang, and anonymous reviewers for their valuable feedback. This work is partially supported by the PI's UCSC start-up funding.

References

1. Federated learning for vision-and-language grounding problems. In: Proceedings of the AAAI Conference on Artificial Intelligence, pp. 11572–11579 (2020)
2. Anderson, P., et al.: On evaluation of embodied navigation agents. CoRR arXiv:1807.06757 (2018)
3. Anderson, P., Shrivastava, A., Parikh, D., Batra, D., Lee, S.: Chasing ghosts: instruction following as Bayesian state tracking. In: Wallach, H., Larochelle, H., Beygelzimer, A., d'Alché-Buc, F., Fox, E., Garnett, R. (eds.) Advances in Neural Information Processing Systems, vol. 32. Curran Associates, Inc. (2019)
4. Anderson, P., et al.: Vision-and-language navigation: interpreting visually-grounded navigation instructions in real environments. In: Proceedings of the IEEE Conference on Computer Vision and Pattern Recognition (CVPR) (2018)
5. Chen, K., Chen, J.K., Chuang, J., Vazquez, M., Savarese, S.: Topological planning with transformers for vision-and-language navigation. In: Proceedings of the IEEE/CVF Conference on Computer Vision and Pattern Recognition (CVPR), pp. 11276–11286 (2021)
6. Chen, S., Guhur, P.L., Schmid, C., Laptev, I.: History aware multimodal transformer for vision-and-language navigation. In: NeurIPS (2021)
7. Chou, E., Beal, J., Levy, D., Yeung, S., Haque, A., Fei-Fei, L.: Faster cryptonets: leveraging sparsity for real-world encrypted inference. CoRR (2018)
8. Collins, L., Hassani, H., Mokhtari, A., Shakkottai, S.: Exploiting shared representations for personalized federated learning. In: Meila, M., Zhang, T. (eds.) Proceedings of the 38th International Conference on Machine Learning, ICML 2021, 18–24 July 2021, Virtual Event. Proceedings of Machine Learning Research, vol. 139, pp. 2089–2099. PMLR (2021)
9. Fredrikson, M., Jha, S., Ristenpart, T.: Model inversion attacks that exploit confidence information and basic countermeasures. In: Proceedings of the 22nd ACM SIGSAC Conference on Computer and Communications Security, pp. 1322–1333. CCS 2015 (2015)
10. Fried, D., et al.: Speaker-follower models for vision-and-language navigation. In: NeurIPS (2018)
11. Fu, T.J., Wang, X.E., Peterson, M.F., Grafton, S.T., Eckstein, M.P., Wang, W.Y.: Counterfactual vision-and-language navigation via adversarial path sampler. In: Proceedings of the European Conference on Computer Vision (ECCV), pp. 71–86 (2020)
12. Ganju, K., Wang, Q., Yang, W., Gunter, C.A., Borisov, N.: Property inference attacks on fully connected neural networks using permutation invariant representations. In: Proceedings of the 2018 ACM SIGSAC Conference on Computer and Communications Security, pp. 619–633. CCS 2018 (2018)
13. Gao, C., Chen, J., Liu, S., Wang, L., Zhang, Q., Wu, Q.: Room-and-object aware knowledge reasoning for remote embodied referring expression. In: Proceedings of the IEEE/CVF Conference on Computer Vision and Pattern Recognition (CVPR), pp. 3064–3073 (2021)
14. Gu, J., Stefani, E., Wu, Q., Thomason, J., Wang, X.: Vision-and-language navigation: a survey of tasks, methods, and future directions. In: Proceedings of the 60th Annual Meeting of the Association for Computational Linguistics (Volume 1: Long Papers), pp. 7606–7623. Association for Computational Linguistics, Dublin, Ireland (2022). https://doi.org/10.18653/v1/2022.acl-long.524

15. Guhur, P.L., Tapaswi, M., Chen, S., Laptev, I., Schmid, C.: Airbert: in-domain pretraining for vision-and-language navigation. In: Proceedings of the IEEE/CVF International Conference on Computer Vision (ICCV), pp. 1634–1643 (2021)

16. Guo, P., Wang, P., Zhou, J., Jiang, S., Patel, V.M.: Multi-institutional collaborations for improving deep learning-based magnetic resonance image reconstruction using federated learning. In: Proceedings of the IEEE/CVF Conference on Computer Vision and Pattern Recognition (CVPR), pp. 2423–2432 (2021)

17. Hao, W., Li, C., Li, X., Carin, L., Gao, J.: Towards learning a generic agent for vision-and-language navigation via pre-training. In: IEEE/CVF Conference on Computer Vision and Pattern Recognition (CVPR) (2020)

18. Hisamoto, S., Post, M., Duh, K.: Membership inference attacks on sequence-to-sequence models: is my data in your machine translation system? Trans. Assoc. Comput. Linguist. **8**, 49–63 (2020)

19. Hong, Y., Wu, Q., Qi, Y., Rodriguez-Opazo, C., Gould, S.: Vln bert: a recurrent vision-and-language Bert for navigation. In: Proceedings of the IEEE/CVF Conference on Computer Vision and Pattern Recognition (CVPR), pp. 1643–1653 (2021)

20. Hsu, T.M.H., Qi, H., Brown, M.: Federated visual classification with real-world data distribution. In: Computer Vision - ECCV 2020: 16th European Conference, Glasgow, UK, 23–28 August 2020, Proceedings, Part X, pp. 76–92 (2020)

21. Huang, Y., Song, Z., Chen, D., Li, K., Arora, S.: TextHide: tackling data privacy in language understanding tasks. In: Findings of the Association for Computational Linguistics: EMNLP 2020, pp. 1368–1382 (2020)

22. Huang, Y., et al.: Personalized cross-silo federated learning on non-iid data. In: Proceedings of the AAAI Conference on Artificial Intelligence, vol. 35, no. 9, pp. 7865–7873 (2021). https://ojs.aaai.org/index.php/AAAI/article/view/16960

23. Huang, Z., Liu, F., Zou, Y.: Federated learning for spoken language understanding. In: Proceedings of the 28th International Conference on Computational Linguistics, pp. 3467–3478. International Committee on Computational Linguistics, Barcelona, Spain (2020)

24. Ilharco, G., Jain, V., Ku, A., Ie, E., Baldridge, J.: General evaluation for instruction conditioned navigation using dynamic time warping (2019)

25. Jain, V., Magalhaes, G., Ku, A., Vaswani, A., Ie, E., Baldridge, J.: Stay on the path: instruction fidelity in vision-and-language navigation. In: Proceedings of the 57th Annual Meeting of the Association for Computational Linguistics, pp. 1862–1872. Association for Computational Linguistics (2019)

26. Jain, V., Magalhaes, G., Ku, A., Vaswani, A., Ie, E., Baldridge, J.: Stay on the path: instruction fidelity in vision-and-language navigation. In: Proceedings of the 57th Annual Meeting of the Association for Computational Linguistics, pp. 1862–1872. Association for Computational Linguistics, Florence, Italy (2019)

27. Krantz, J., Gokaslan, A., Batra, D., Lee, S., Maksymets, O.: Waypoint models for instruction-guided navigation in continuous environments. In: Proceedings of the IEEE/CVF International Conference on Computer Vision (ICCV), pp. 15162–15171 (2021)

28. Ku, A., Anderson, P., Patel, R., Ie, E., Baldridge, J.: Room-across-room: multilingual vision-and-language navigation with dense spatiotemporal grounding. In: Proceedings of the 2020 Conference on Empirical Methods in Natural Language Processing (EMNLP), pp. 4392–4412 (2020)

29. Li, Q., He, B., Song, D.: Model-contrastive federated learning. In: Proceedings of the IEEE/CVF Conference on Computer Vision and Pattern Recognition (CVPR), pp. 10713–10722 (2021)

30. Li, X., Yin, X., Li, C., Zhang, P., Hu, X., Zhang, L., Wang, L., Hu, H., Dong, L., Wei, F., Choi, Y., Gao, J.: OSCAR: object-semantics aligned pre-training for vision-language tasks. In: Vedaldi, A., Bischof, H., Brox, T., Frahm, J.-M. (eds.) ECCV 2020. LNCS, vol. 12375, pp. 121–137. Springer, Cham (2020). https://doi.org/10.1007/978-3-030-58577-8_8

31. Lou, Q., Jiang, L.: She: a fast and accurate deep neural network for encrypted data. In: Wallach, H., Larochelle, H., Beygelzimer, A., dAlché-Buc, F., Fox, E., Garnett, R. (eds.) Advances in Neural Information Processing Systems, vol. 32 (2019)

32. Lu, Y., Huang, C., Zhan, H., Zhuang, Y.: Federated natural language generation for personalized dialogue system (2021)

33. Papernot, N., Song, S., Mironov, I., Raghunathan, A., Talwar, K., Erlingsson, Ú.: Scalable private learning with PATE. In: 6th International Conference on Learning Representations, ICLR 2018, Vancouver, BC, Canada, April 30 - May 3, 2018, Conference Track Proceedings (2018)

34. Qi, Y., Pan, Z., Hong, Y., Yang, M.H., van den Hengel, A., Wu, Q.: The road to know-where: an object-and-room informed sequential Bert for indoor vision-language navigation. In: Proceedings of the IEEE/CVF International Conference on Computer Vision (ICCV), pp. 1655–1664 (2021)

35. Qi, Y., et al.: REVERIE: remote embodied visual referring expression in real indoor environments. In: 2020 IEEE/CVF Conference on Computer Vision and Pattern Recognition, CVPR 2020, Seattle, WA, USA, 13–19 June 2020, pp. 9979–9988. Computer Vision Foundation / IEEE (2020)

36. Radford, A., et al.: Learning transferable visual models from natural language supervision. In: Meila, M., Zhang, T. (eds.) Proceedings of the 38th International Conference on Machine Learning, ICML 2021, 18–24 July 2021, Virtual Event. Proceedings of Machine Learning Research, vol. 139, pp. 8748–8763. PMLR (2021)

37. Reddi, S.J., et al.: Adaptive federated optimization. In: International Conference on Learning Representations (2021)

38. Shen, S., et al.: How much can CLIP benefit vision-and-language tasks? CoRR arXiv:2107.06383 (2021)

39. Shokri, R., Stronati, M., Song, C., Shmatikov, V.: Membership inference attacks against machine learning models. In: 2017 IEEE Symposium on Security and Privacy (SP), pp. 3–18 (2017)

40. Tan, H., Yu, L., Bansal, M.: Learning to navigate unseen environments: back translation with environmental dropout. In: Proceedings of the 2019 Conference of the North American Chapter of the Association for Computational Linguistics: Human Language Technologies, Volume 1 (Long and Short Papers), pp. 2610–2621 (2019)

41. Vanhaesebrouck, P., Bellet, A., Tommasi, M.: Decentralized collaborative learning of personalized models over networks. In: Proceedings of the 20th International Conference on Artificial Intelligence and Statistics, AISTATS 2017, 20–22 April 2017, Fort Lauderdale, FL, USA, pp. 509–517. Proceedings of Machine Learning Research (2017)

42. Wang, X., et al.: Reinforced cross-modal matching and self-supervised imitation learning for vision-language navigation. In: Proceedings of the IEEE/CVF Conference on Computer Vision and Pattern Recognition (CVPR) (June 2019)

43. Wang, X., Xiong, W., Wang, H., Wang, W.Y.: Look before you leap: bridging model-free and model-based reinforcement learning for planned-ahead vision-and-language navigation. In: Proceedings of the European Conference on Computer Vision (ECCV) (2018)

44. Zhang, Y., Tan, H., Bansal, M.: Diagnosing the environment bias in vision-and-language navigation. In: Proceedings of the Twenty-Ninth International Joint Conference on Artificial Intelligence. IJCAI 2020 (2021)
45. Zhang, Y., Jia, R., Pei, H., Wang, W., Li, B., Song, D.: The secret revealer: generative model-inversion attacks against deep neural networks. In: Proceedings of the IEEE/CVF Conference on Computer Vision and Pattern Recognition (CVPR) (2020)
46. Zhao, Y., Barnaghi, P., Haddadi, H.: Multimodal federated learning on IoT data (2022)
47. Zhou, X., Liu, W., Mu, Y.: Rethinking the spatial route prior in vision-and-language navigation. CoRR arXiv:2110.05728 (2021)

CODER: Coupled Diversity-Sensitive Momentum Contrastive Learning for Image-Text Retrieval

Haoran Wang[1], Dongliang He[1(✉)], Wenhao Wu[1,5], Boyang Xia[2], Min Yang[1], Fu Li[1], Yunlong Yu[3], Zhong Ji[4], Errui Ding[1], and Jingdong Wang[1]

[1] Department of Computer Vision Technology (VIS), Baidu Inc., Beijing, China
{wanghaoran09,hedongliang01,yangmin09,lifu,
dingerrui,wangjingdong}@baidu.com
[2] Key Lab of Intelligent Information Processing of Chinese Academy of Sciences (CAS), Institute of Computing Technology, CAS, Beijing, China
xiaboyang20@mails.ucas.ac.cn
[3] College of Information Science & Electronic Engineering, Zhejiang University, Hangzhou, China
yuyunlong@zju.edu.cn
[4] School of Electrical and Information Engineering, Tianjin University, Tianjin, China
jizhong@tju.edu.cn
[5] The University of Sydney, Sydney, Australia

Abstract. Image-Text Retrieval (ITR) is challenging in bridging visual and lingual modalities. Contrastive learning has been adopted by most prior arts. Except for limited amount of negative image-text pairs, the capability of constrastive learning is restricted by manually weighting negative pairs as well as unawareness of external knowledge. In this paper, we propose our novel Coupled Diversity-Sensitive Momentum Constrastive Learning (CODER) for improving cross-modal representation. Firstly, a novel diversity-sensitive contrastive learning (DCL) architecture is invented. We introduce dynamic dictionaries for both modalities to enlarge the scale of image-text pairs, and diversity-sensitiveness is achieved by adaptive negative pair weighting. Furthermore, two branches are designed in CODER. One learns instance-level embeddings from image/text, and it also generates pseudo online clustering labels for its input image/text based on their embeddings. Meanwhile, the other branch learns to query from commonsense knowledge graph to form concept-level descriptors for both modalities. Afterwards, both branches leverage DCL to align the cross-modal embedding spaces while an extra pseudo clustering label prediction loss is utilized to promote concept-level representation learning for the second branch. Extensive experiments conducted on two popular benchmarks, *i.e.* MSCOCO and Flicker30K, validate CODER remarkably outperforms the state-of-the-art approaches.

Supplementary Information The online version contains supplementary material available at https://doi.org/10.1007/978-3-031-20059-5_40.

1   Introduction

Image-text retrieval (ITR) refers to searching for the semantically similar instance from visual (textual) modality with the query instance from textual (visual) modality. Nowadays, it has become a compelling topic from both industrial and research community and is of potential value to benefit extensive relevant applications [2, 3, 16, 21, 22, 37, 47, 48, 57–60, 62]. In the past decade, tremendous progresses have been made with the prevalence of deep learning [27]. Early works typically associate image with text via learning global [10, 26, 50] or local cross-modal alignment [4, 28]. Follow-up studies attempt to introduce external knowledge information, including commonsense knowledge [45, 49] or scene graph [51] information, into visual-semantic embedding models. It remains challenging due to heterogeneous multi-modal data distributions, which requires pretty precise cross-modal alignment.

Loss functions play the central role in aligning multi-modal data. The prevailing bi-directional triplet ranking (BTR) loss used in [10, 11] can be regarded as one special case of contrastive loss [14], where only one negative sample is considered. Then, bidirectional Info-NCE loss [39] (BIN), as a typical contrastive loss, has been widely adopted in many tasks [7, 35, 43]. It exploits the whole paired relationships among a mini-batch of image-text samples when applied to the ITR task. Meanwhile, constrastive learning is well-known in limited negative sample scale [15], which acts as the bottleneck of its capability.

Another notable issue is both aforementioned contrastive losses manually design the weighting strategy for negative image-text pairs. They both enforce

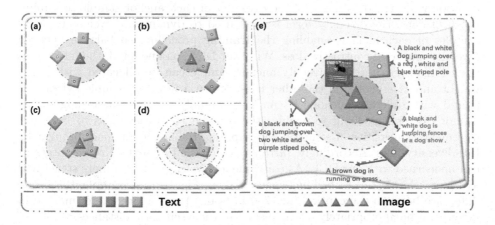

Fig. 1. Conceptual illustration of our proposed Diversity-sensitive Contrastive Learning (DCL) loss. Sub-figure (a), (b) and (c) depict three exemplary distributions of negative samples which are undesired because they do not show much similarity variations, respectively. Sub-figure (d) shows desired negative sample distribution given an anchor, where different negative samples are not equally pushed away. It demonstrate the joint space can well distinguish fine-grained semantic difference among negative samples. Sub-figure (e) illustrates the ideal joint embedding space affected by DCL.

the negatives and anchor samples to be separated far away enough, whilst ignoring the relative differences between them. Consequently, the fine-grained discrepancies among negative pairs are hard to be fully captured.

In fact, the importance of each image/text instance is unequal [6] in contrastive learning. A critical factor determining the importance of instance is its semantic ambiguity [46]. In particular, the samples with high semantic ambiguity refers to those with multiple meanings/concepts. Oppositely, the samples with simple and clear meanings usually have low semantic ambiguity. To explicitly model the semantic ambiguity of sample, we present a term called "**Diversity**". Concretely, the diversity of one sample is defined based on the distribution of cross-modal negatives around it. For example, as depicted in three typical cases in Fig. 1(a-c), if a sample has multiple negatives with similar distances to it, we call this sample as low-diversity one. Obviously, the existence of low-diversity samples are undesirable, which will weaken the discrimination ability of the learned joint space. Conversely, if the data distribution around an anchor instance is well-spaced (see 1(d), this sample has high diversity), it could better measure the difference among different negative samples, which is more ideal.

To address the aforementioned limitations and questions, first of all, inspired by Momentum Contrastive Learning (MCL) paradigm [15], dynamic dictionaries of memory banks are introduced in coupled form for both visual and textual modality to enlarge interactions among image-text pairs. Furthermore, in this paper, we propose to extend constrastive learning to a novel **D**iversity-sensitive **C**ontrastive **L**earning (**DCL**) paradigm. To achieve it, a novel diversity-sensitive contrastive loss is presented, which incorporates our defined diversity into contrastive loss. Specifically, in contrastive loss, a simple yet effective estimation function is designed to quantify the diversity of each anchor sample in a mini-batch of data, the diversity term is then used to dynamically weight negative samples of each anchor, enabling the training procedure to balance between diversity and total contrastive loss. With our DCL, on one hand, the image-text pairs built based on low diversity anchor sample can be allocated with larger weight and *vice versa*; on the other hand, given a negative sample, when it is paired with different anchors, it can be unequally weighted according to the anchor's diversity. Doing so enables the original contrastive loss to be aware of semantic diversities of samples, and suppress the adverse impact brought by low-diversity ones. Accordingly, *instance-level* visual or textual representations can be learned with our DCL. As consequence, we can obtain a more structured and hierarchical joint embedding space. Taking Fig. 1(e) as example, the subtle difference between the caption (marked in orange) and another one (marked in green) can be appropriately distinguished in their semantic distances.

Furthermore, how to leverage external knowledge into contrastive learning framework is worth exploring. To be complementary to the *instance-level* alignment, we achieve *concept-level* cross-modal feature alignment via exploiting commonsense knowledge. Different from the former, *concept-level* alignment is built by firstly learning to extract homogeneous concept-level visual and textual embeddings from commonsense graph, followed by aligning the cross-modal embeddings via adopting DCL along with a **P**rototype-**G**uided **C**lassification loss (**PGC**). In order to enable PGC, an online clustering procedure is performed on *instance-level* representations and each cluster id is treated as a prototype, then a prediction head based on the *concept-level* image/text embedding is employed for classifying the cluster id of the input image/text. The final image-text matching score is a combination of similarities obtained from both instance-level and concept-level alignment. Extensive experiments conducted on MSCOCO [31] and Flicker30K [41] verify the superiority of our framework and show that our Coupled Diversity-Sensitive Contrastive Learning (CODER) method significantly outperforms recent state-of-the-art solutions.

To sum up, the main contributions are listed as follows:

- We incorporate coupled Momentum Contrastive learning (MCL) into image-text representation learning and further extend contrastive learning to a novel Diversity-Sensitive Contrastive Learning (DCL) paradigm, which can adaptively weight negative image-text pairs to further boost the performance.
- A Coupled Diversity-Sensitive Contrastive Learning (CODER) framework is proposed to exploit not only instance-level image-text representations but also concept-level embeddings with the aid of external knowledge as well as on-line clustering based prototype-guided classification loss.
- Extensive experimental results on two benchmarks demonstrate our approach considerably outperforms state-of-the-art methods by a large margin.

2 Related Work

2.1 Contrastive Learning

Recently, Contrastive Learning [7,13,15,39,43] has made remarkable progress in unsupervised representation learning. Chen *at el.* [7] shows that contrastive learning in unsupervised visual representation learning benefits from large batch size negatives and stronger data augmentation. He *at el.* [15] proposed Momentum Contrastive Learning (MCL) paradigm that obtains the new key representation on-the-fly by a momentum-updated key encoder, and maintains a dictionary as a queue to allow the training process to reuse the encoded key representations from the immediate preceding mini-batches. Recently, more Contrastive Learning based vision-language understanding studies [18,30,43,61] are emerging. For video-text retrieval, Liu *at el.* [34] first introduces the vanilla info-NCE loss based MCL mechanism to enhance the cross-modal discrimination. Distinct from them, we integrate coupled MCL into our proposed Diversity-sensitive contrastive learning (DCL) paradigm for tackling ITR.

2.2 Image-Text Retrieval

Along with the renaissance of deep learning, a surge of works have been proposed for ITR. Early attempts [11,36,38,50] typically employ global features to represent both image and text in a common semantic space. For instance, Kiros *at el.* [26] encoded image and text by CNN and RNN respectively, utilizing BTR loss to train the model. Afterwards, another line of research [4,9,28,53,55] employed multi-modal attention mechanism [4,20,28,56] or knowledge aided representation learning [12,17,32,45,49] to achieve cross-modal alignment by exploiting more fine-grained associations. For instance, Lee *et al.* [28] developed Stacked Cross Attention Network that aligns image regions and textual words.

Except for focusing on representation architecture designing, some studies [6,10,33,54] endeavored to improve the learning objectives. As a seminal work, Faghri [10] *et al.* proposed to introduce one on-line hard negative mining (OHNM) strategy into BTR loss, which is very prevailing for ITR. Liu *et al.* [33] proposed to tackle hubness problem by imposing heavy punishment on the hard negatives in triplets. Afterwards, Chen *et al.* [6] further improved the BTR loss by searching for more hard negatives in off-line way to constitute the quintuplet. Overall, the common character of above works is designing constraint strategy for pairwise multi-modal data, whilst our DCL additionally performs diversity estimation especially for each sample. Moreover, we introduce MCL to promote large-scale negative interaction, which leads to more comprehensive diversity estimation in DCL.

3   Methodology

3.1   Overall Framework

The overall framework of our proposed CODER model is illustrated in Fig. 2. In our model, two branches are designed for instance-level and concept-level representation learning. In the instance-level branch (Fig. 2(a)), image and text features are encoded and aggregated to be $\mathbf{v}^I$ and $\mathbf{w}^I$, momentum encodes are used for the two modalities to serve as coupled memory banks. Instance-level alignment is achieved via employing our proposed diversity-sensitive contrastive loss L_{DCL}^I as well as memory-aided DCL loss $L_{M\_DCL}^I$ (Fig. 2(c)). As for the concept-level branch (Fig. 2(b)), statistical commonsense representation (SCC) [49] denoted as $\mathbf{Y}$, is adopted as homogeneous feature basis. Query features $\mathbf{v}_C^q$ and $\mathbf{w}_C^q$ are obtained from image and text, respectively. Then concept-level features $\mathbf{v}^C$ and $\mathbf{w}^C$ are obtained by learning to query from feature basis $\mathbf{Y}$. For concept-level alignment (Fig. 2(d)), except for DCL loss L_{DCL}^C, an online-clustering based prototype-guided classification loss L_{PGC} is additionally leveraged.

3.2   Instance and Concept Level Representations

Instance-Level Representation. For image encoding, we adopt Faster-RCNN [1,44] to obtain L region-level features $\{\mathbf{o}_l\}_{l=1}^L$ and then aggregate these features to be a instance-level visual embedding $\mathbf{v}^I \in \mathbb{R}^F$. Pre-trained BERT [8] is our textual encoder and N word-level embeddings $\{\mathbf{e}_t\}_{t=1}^T$ are also aggregated to instance-level textual embedding $\mathbf{w}^I \in \mathbb{R}^F$.

$$\mathbf{v}^I = g_{vis}(\{\mathbf{o}_l\}_{n=1}^L), \quad \mathbf{w}^I = g_{text}(\{\mathbf{e}_t\}_{t=1}^T), \tag{1}$$

where $g_{vis}(\cdot)$ and $g_{text}(\cdot)$ are visual and textual aggregators.

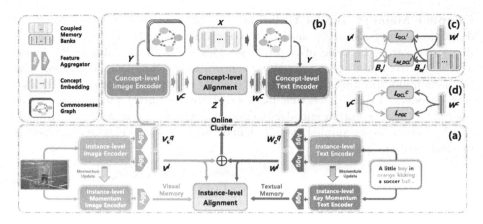

Fig. 2. The overall architecture of our proposed CODER model for image-text retrieval. It is composed of an instance-level representation branch (a) and an concept-level one which leverages external knowledge (b). The former branch is optimized by minimizing instance-level DCL loss and memory-based DCL loss (denoted as L_{DCL}^I and $L_{M\_DCL}^I$, respectively) (c). The other one is learned by employing concept-level DCL loss L_{DCL}^C and online clustering based prototype-guided classification L_{PGC} as objectives (d).

Concept-Level Representation. The concept-level representations for both modalities are built based on a group of *concepts*. Firstly, we extract g representative concepts from the the texts over the whole image-caption dataset. Afterwards, the GloVE [40] is employed to instantiate these concepts as $\mathbf{X}$. Following [49], graph convolution network (GCN) [25] is utilized to process to produce the statistical commonsense aided concept (SCC) representations $\mathbf{Y} = \{\mathbf{y}_1, ..., \mathbf{y}_g\}$. Please refer to the supplementary materials for more details.

To generate concept-level representations, we generate representations ($\mathbf{v}_C^q$ and $\mathbf{w}_C^q$) by using another group of feature aggregators ($g_{vis}(\cdot)$ and $g_{text}(\cdot)$) to combine local features $\{\mathbf{o}_l\}_{l=1}^L$ and $\{\mathbf{e}_t\}_{t=1}^T$, respectively. Then, as depicted in Fig. 2, $\mathbf{v}_C^q$ and $\mathbf{w}_C^q$ are fed into concept-level feature encoders, which are taken as input vectors to query from the SCC representations $\mathbf{Y}$. The output scores for different concepts allow us to uniformly utilize the linear combination of the SCC representations to represent both modalities. Mathematically, the concept-level representation $\mathbf{v}^C$ and $\mathbf{w}^C$ can be calculated as:

$$\mathbf{v}^C = \sum_{i=1}^g a_i^v \mathbf{y}_i; \; a_i^v = \frac{e^{\lambda \mathbf{v}_C^I \mathbf{W}^v \mathbf{y}_i^\top}}{\sum_{i=1}^q e^{\lambda \mathbf{v}_C^I \mathbf{W}^v \mathbf{y}_i^\top}}.$$

$$\mathbf{w}^C = \sum_{j=1}^g a_j^w \mathbf{y}_j; \; a_j^w = \frac{e^{\lambda \mathbf{w}_C^I \mathbf{W}^w \mathbf{y}_j^\top}}{\sum_{j=1}^q e^{\lambda \mathbf{w}_C^I \mathbf{W}^w \mathbf{y}_j^\top}}$$

(2)

where $\mathbf{W}^v \in \mathbb{R}^{F \times F}$ and $\mathbf{W}^w \in \mathbb{R}^{F \times F}$ denote the learnable parameter matrix, a_i^v and a_j^w denote the visual and textual score corresponding to the concept $\mathbf{z}_i$, respectively. λ controls the smoothness of the softmax function.

Coupled Memory Banks Building. We propose to leverage a couple of dynamic memory banks B_v^I and B_w^I to restore more visual and textual embeddings to enlarge the scale of negative samples for both modalities. We follow MoCo [15] to obtain instance-level momentum image encoder and text encoder by momentum updating their weights according to the corresponding image and text encoders. Visual or textual instances from the latest training iterations are fed to the momentum encoders to generate visual and textual embeddings, which are restored in coupled memory banks. Such a process can be conveniently implemented via queues.

3.3 Diversity-Sensitive Contrastive Loss

Estimating the semantic Diversity of instance plays important role in enhancing cross-modal discrimination. Specifically, to describe our diversity-sensitive contrastive loss, we start from diversity estimation, and then introduce our *explicit* diversity-sensitive loss.

Diversity Estimation. For simplicity, we take as example that visual feature $\mathbf{v}_i$ is an anchor sample and Q text features $\mathbf{W} = \{\mathbf{w}_i, \mathbf{w}_2, ..., \mathbf{w}_Q\}$ are to be compared (among which only $\mathbf{w}_i$ is a matching sample for $\mathbf{v}_i$), to illustrate how we estimate diversity of an anchor sample. The cosine similarity of $cosine(\mathbf{v}_i, \mathbf{w}_j)$ is defined as S_{ij}. We propose a simple but effective metric to estimate the semantic diversity explicitly.

In joint embedding space, if an anchor sample with low diversity indicates the close similarities between it and numerous negatives, this case is undesired. By contrast, an ideal data distribution space should be more structured and consistent with text-image pair annotations. Intuitively, we propose to quantify the diversity of anchor sample via employing one statistical variable, *i.e.* standard deviation (SD). Concretely, a low-diversity anchor sample has multiple negatives with close distances to it, implying the SD value of cross-modal similarities between it and them will be small. Conversely, the high SD value means an anchor sample has high diversity. Since the SD value between negative cross-modal similarities are proportional to the diversity of anchor, we propose to estimate the semantic diversity explicitly based on SD value. Taking image sample $\mathbf{v}_i$ for instance, the computation process of its diversity value is defined as:

$$SD(\mathbf{v}_i) = \sqrt{E(S_{ij}^2) - [E(S_{ij})]^2}, i \neq j;$$
$$div(\mathbf{v}_i) = 1/\sigma(\epsilon/SD); \tag{3}$$
$$div(\mathbf{v}_i) = div(\mathbf{v}_i)/\max\{div(\mathbf{v}_1), ..., div(\mathbf{v}_Q)\},$$

where $E(\cdot)$ is the mathematical expectation function and $\sigma(\cdot)$ denotes the Sigmoid function that normalizes the reciprocal of SD value to a uniform scale, assuring it vary in a relatively stable range. $div(\mathbf{v}_i)$ denotes the diversity score of $\mathbf{v}_i$ calculated from the candidate textual samples to be compared with. $\epsilon = 0.1$ is a tunning parameter. Finally, we divide each diversity score $div_{std}(\mathbf{v}_i)$ by the maximum value of them in mini-batch for normalization. Likewise, the diversity of text sample can be calculated in similar manner.

Diversity-Sensitive Loss. As mentioned in Sect.1, we aim to highlight the discrepancy among the anchor sample with low-diversity and its negatives. To achieve it, we need to allocate more attention to such cases in order for an optimal alignment model. To begin with, let us term the contrastive objective that insensitive to diversity as L_{DCL_I}. Given $\mathbf{V} = \{\mathbf{v}_1, ..., \mathbf{v}_N\}$ and $\mathbf{W} = \{\mathbf{w}_1, ..., \mathbf{w}_Q\}$, $L_{DCL\_I}(\mathbf{V}, \mathbf{W})$ can be formulated as:

$$l_{DCL\_I}(\mathbf{V}, \mathbf{W}) = \frac{\mu}{N} \sum_{n=1}^{N} [log(\sum_{q \neq n} \exp(\frac{(S_{nq}-\gamma)}{\mu})) + 1) - log(S_{nn} + 1)];$$

$$l_{DCL\_I}(\mathbf{W}, \mathbf{V}) = \frac{\mu}{Q} \sum_{q=1}^{Q} [log(\sum_{n \neq q} \exp(\frac{(S_{qn}-\gamma)}{\mu})) + 1) - log(S_{qq} + 1)]; \qquad (4)$$

$$L_{DCL\_I}(\mathbf{W}, \mathbf{V}) = l_{DCL\_I}(\mathbf{W}, \mathbf{V}) + l_{DCL\_I}(\mathbf{V}, \mathbf{W})$$

where μ is a temperature scalar; γ is a margin parameter; N is the number of samples within the mini-batch; $S_{nq} = cosine(\mathbf{v}_n, \mathbf{w}_q), S_{qn} = cosine(\mathbf{w}_q, \mathbf{v}_n), S_{nn} = cosine(\mathbf{v}_n, \mathbf{w}_n)$ and $S_{qq} = cosine(\mathbf{w}_q, \mathbf{v}_q)$ denote the cosine similarities.

To *explicitly* introduce diversity awareness, we extend the above loss to DCL loss L_{DCL}. Mathematically,

$$L_{DCL}(\mathbf{V}, \mathbf{W}) = l_{DCL}(\mathbf{W}, \mathbf{V}) + l_{DCL}(\mathbf{V}, \mathbf{W})$$

$$l_{DCL}(\mathbf{V}, \mathbf{W}) = \frac{\mu}{N} \sum_{n=1}^{N} [log(\sum_{q \neq n} \exp(\frac{(S_{nq}-\gamma)}{\mu \cdot div(\mathbf{v}_n)})) + 1) - log(S_{nn} + 1)]; \qquad (5)$$

$$l_{DCL}(\mathbf{W}, \mathbf{V}) = \frac{\mu}{Q} \sum_{q=1}^{Q} [log(\sum_{n \neq q} \exp(\frac{(S_{qn}-\gamma)}{\mu \cdot div(\mathbf{w}_q)})) + 1) - log(S_{qq} + 1)];$$

where $div(\mathbf{v}_n)$ and $div(\mathbf{w}_q)$ denotes the diversity of $\mathbf{v}_n$ and $\mathbf{w}_q$, respectively and they are used to adaptively weight the negative samples.

DCL Loss Based Cross-Modal Alignment Instance-level DCL Loss. For instance-level representation, two items of DCL loss is employed. First, it is imposed on data pairs in mini-batch, named as L_{DCL}^I. Secondly, it is imposed on anchor sample in mini-batch and items from coupled memory banks, namely Memory-aided Diversity-sensitive Contrastive Learning (M-DCL) and abbreviated as $L_{M\_DCL}^I$. Formally, using $\mathbf{V}^I$ and $\mathbf{W}^I$ to denote a mini-batch of embeddings $\mathbf{v}^I$ and $\mathbf{w}^I$, these loss items are defined as:

$$L_{DCL}^I = L_{DCL}(\mathbf{V}^I, \mathbf{W}^I),$$

$$L_{M\_DCL}^I = L_{DCL}(\mathbf{V}^I, B_w^I) + L_{DCL}(\mathbf{W}^I, B_v^I). \qquad (6)$$

Please note that in Eq. 6, because the presence of memory banks, diversity estimation is processed as the average of diversity values at mini-batch level and memory bank level.

Concept-Level DCL Loss. For concept-level representation, we only impose DCL Loss on data pairs in a mini-batch, the concept-level DCL loss is represented as: $L_{DCL}^C = L_{DCL}(\mathbf{V}^C, \mathbf{W}^C) + L_{DCL}(\mathbf{W}^C, \mathbf{V}^C)$.

3.4   Prototype-Guided Classification Loss

In this section, we present a novel Prototype-guided Classification (PGC) loss, which aims to enhance cross-modal discrimination by leveraging the complementary semantics between instance-level and concept-level representations. In particular, we perform K-means [19] clustering in an on-line manner during training based on the summation of instance-level representations $\mathbf{v}^I$ and $\mathbf{w}^I$, which contains more individual information. We name the output clusters as *prototypes* that are able to capture the shared semantic information between semantically related samples. Accordingly, The prototype ids of image/text instances serve as the pseudo class ids and are taken as supervision $\mathbf{Z} = \{z_1, ..., z_K\}$ for concept-level representation learning. Specifically, the PGC loss is formally defined as:

$$\mathbf{P}_v = softmax(\mathbf{P}^C\mathbf{v}^C), \mathbf{P}_w = softmax(\mathbf{P}^C\mathbf{w}^C),$$
$$L_{PGC} = L_{PGC}^v + L_{PGC}^w = L_{cls}(\mathbf{P}_w, \mathbf{Z}) + L_{cls}(\mathbf{P}_v, \mathbf{Z}) \tag{7}$$

where $\mathbf{P}^C \in \mathbb{R}^{K \times F}$ is one learnable parameter matrix that outputs distributions over the K category labels for both $\mathbf{v}^C$ and $\mathbf{w}^C$. $\mathbf{P}_v \in \mathbb{R}^K$ and $\mathbf{P}_w \in \mathbb{R}^K$ denote probabilities over all labels. L_{cls} denotes the cross-entropy classification loss.

3.5   Training and Inference

Training Objective. We deploy the summation of instance-level and concept-level aligning losses as overall training objectives:

$$L = \lambda L_{DCL}^I + L_{M\_DCL}^I + L_{DCL}^C + L_{PGC}, \tag{8}$$

Inference Scheme. For inference, we use the weighted summation of instance-level and concept-level cosine similarities to measure the overall cross-modal similarity $S = \beta S(\mathbf{v}^I, \mathbf{w}^I) + (1-\beta)S(\mathbf{v}^C, \mathbf{w}^C)$, where β is a balancing parameter.

4   Experiments

4.1   Datasets and Evaluation Metrics

Datasets. Flickr30K [41] is an image-caption dataset containing 31,783 images, where each image annotated with five sentences. Following [38], we split the dataset into 29,783 training, 1000 validation, and 1000 testing images. The performance evaluation is reported on 1000 testing set. MSCOCO [31] is another image-caption dataset, totally including 123,287 images with each image roughly

Table 1. Comparisons of experimental results on MSCOCO 1K test set and Flickr30K test set. Note that DSRAN [56], GPO [5] and DIME [42] employ BERT as we use, the rest use inferior text encoders.

Methods	Image encoder	MSCOCO Text retrieval			Image retrieval			R@sum	Flickr30K Text retrieval			Image retrieval			R@sum
		R@1	R@5	R@10	R@1	R@5	R@10		R@1	R@5	R@10	R@1	R@5	R@10	
DVSA [23] (2015)	R-CNN	38.4	69.9	80.5	27.4	60.2	74.8	351.2	22.2	48.2	61.4	15.2	37.7	50.5	235.2
m-CNN [36] (2015)	VGG-19	42.8	73.1	84.1	32.6	68.6	82.8	384.0	33.6	64.1	74.9	26.2	56.3	69.6	324.7
DSPE [50] (2016)	VGG-19	50.1	79.7	89.2	39.6	75.2	86.9	420.7	40.3	68.9	79.9	29.7	60.1	72.1	351.0
VSE++ [10] (2018)	ResNet-152	64.7	–	95.9	52.0	–	92.0	–	52.9	–	87.2	39.6	–	79.5	–
SCAN [28] (2018)	Faster-RCNN	72.7	94.8	98.4	58.8	88.4	94.8	507.9	67.4	90.3	95.8	48.6	77.7	85.2	465.0
PVSE [46] (2019)	Faster-RCNN	69.2	91.6	96.6	55.2	86.5	93.7	492.8	–	–	–	–	–	–	–
VSRN [29] (2019)	Faster-RCNN	76.2	94.8	98.2	62.8	89.7	95.1	516.8	71.3	90.6	96.0	54.7	81.8	88.2	482.6
CVSE [49] (2020)	Faster-RCNN	74.8	95.1	98.3	59.9	89.4	95.2	512.7	73.5	92.1	95.8	52.9	80.4	87.8	482.5
IMRAM [4] (2020)	Faster-RCNN	76.7	95.6	98.5	61.7	89.1	95.0	516.6	74.1	93.0	96.6	53.9	79.4	87.2	484.2
WCGL [52] (2021)	Faster-RCNN	75.4	95.5	98.6	60.8	89.3	95.3	514.9	74.8	93.3	96.8	54.8	80.6	87.5	487.8
SHAN [20] (2021)	Faster-RCNN	76.8	96.3	98.7	62.6	89.6	95.8	519.5	74.6	93.5	96.9	55.3	81.3	88.4	490.0
DSRAN [56] (2021)	Faster-RCNN	77.1	95.3	98.1	62.9	89.9	95.3	518.6	75.3	94.4	97.6	57.3	84.8	90.9	500.3
GPO [5] (2021)	Faster-RCNN	78.6	96.2	98.7	62.9	90.8	96.1	523.3	78.1	94.1	97.8	57.4	84.5	90.4	502.3
DIME (i-t) [42] (2021)	Faster-RCNN	77.9	95.9	98.3	63.0	90.5	**96.2**	521.8	77.4	95.0	97.4	60.1	85.5	91.8	507.2
SGRAF [9] (2021)	Faster-RCNN	79.6	96.2	98.5	63.2	90.7	96.1	524.3	77.8	94.1	97.4	58.5	83.0	88.8	499.6
CODER	Faster-RCNN	**82.1**	**96.6**	**98.8**	**65.5**	**91.5**	**96.2**	**530.6**	**83.2**	**96.5**	**98.0**	**63.1**	**87.1**	**93.0**	**520.9**

annotated with five textual descriptions. We follow the public split of [23], including 113,287 training images, 1000 validation images, and 5000 testing images. The result is reported by averaging the results over 5-folds of 1K testing images.

Evaluation Metrics. We utilize two commonly used evaluation metrics, *i.e.*, R@K and "R@sum". Specifically, R@K refers to the percentage of queries in which the ground-truth matchings appear in the top K retrieved results. "R@sum" is the summation of all six recall rates of R@K, which provides a more comprehensive evaluation to testify the overall retrieval performance.

4.2 Implementation Details

For visual feature encoding, the amount of regions is $L = 36$ and the dimension of region embeddings is 2048. For text encoding, a BERT-base [8] model is used to extract 768-dimension textual embeddings. The dimension of joint space is set to $F=1024$. For concept-level representation, we adopt 300-dim GloVe [40] trained on the Wikipedia dataset to initialize the semantic concepts. The volume of the concept vocabulary is $g = 400$. The size of couple memory banks is set to 4096 and the momentum coefficient is 0.995. The cluster number K of PGC loss is set to 10000 and 20000 for Flickr30K and MSCOCO dataset, respectively. For the training objective, we empirically set $\mu = 0.1$ and $\gamma = 0.3$ in Eq. (5). Our CODER model is trained by Adam optimizer [24] with mini-batch size of 128. The learning rate is set to be 0.0002 for the first 15 epochs and 0.00002 for the next 15 epochs for both datasets. The balancing parameter in Eq. (8) is set to $\lambda = 3$. For inference, the controlling parameter β is equal to 0.9. All our experiments are conducted on a NVIDIA Tesla P40 GPU.

4.3   Comparisons with State-of-the-art Methods

The experimental results on two benchmark datasets are listed in Table 1[1]. As for MSCOCO, we can observe that our CODER is obviously superior to the competitors in most evaluation metrics, which yields a result of 82.1% and 65.5% on R@1 for text retrieval and image retrieval, respectively. Specifically, compared with the best competitor SGRAF method, it achieves absolute boost (2.5%, 0.4%, 0.3%) on (R@1, R@5, R@10) for text retrieval. For image retrieval, our method also outperforms other algorithms. Moreover, on Flickr30K dataset, as for the most persuasive criteria, the "R@sum" achieved by our model exceeds the second best performance by 13.7%. These results solidly validate the advance of our method.

4.4   Ablation Study

In this section, we perform a series of ablation studies to explore the impact of the main modules in our CODER method. All the comparative experiments are conducted on the Flickr30K dataset.

To begin with, we first investigate the effect of each module for instance-level representation. In Table 2, we employ a framework without adopting coupled memory banks for M-DCL as the baseline (#1), which utilizes the traditionally prevailing BTR loss [10] to perform instance-level alignment instead of our DCL loss. From Table 2, Comparing #1 with #2 based on R@1, the DCL loss brings about 3.2% improvement for text retrieval and 2.9% for image retrieval. Moreover, when the coupled memory banks is exploited for M-DCL, Comparing #3 with #2, we can obtain additional performance improvement. These results confirm the effectiveness of our proposed DCL learning paradigm for enhancing instance-level discrimination.

In addition, we explore how the modules for concept-level representation affects the retrieval performance. As shown in Table 2, comparing #4 with #3 based on R@1, the L_{DCL}^C loss leads to 0.2% improvement for text retrieval and 0.2% for image retrieval. It validates our DCL loss is also effective for concept-level representation learning. Furthermore, when our presented PGC loss is leveraged, comparing #5 with #4, it achieves (0.4%, 0.4%) boost on (R@1, R@5) for text retrieval and (0.3%, 0.3%) boost on (R@1, R@5) for image retrieval. The above results prove our designed concept-level representation learning module can provides more complementary semantics for instance-level one thereby enhancing cross-modal discrimination.

Impact of Different Configurations of DCL. In this part, we perform ablation studies to explore the impact of different configurations for the DCL module.

---

[1] We report our replicated results of [5] by using its official code without changing, more discussions are given in the supplementary materials.

Table 2. Performance comparison of our CODER with different main components on Flickr30K test set. "Instance-level Alignment" is abbreviated as "IA". "Concept-level Alignment" is abbreviated as "CA".

Models	IA		CA		Text retrieval			Image retrieval		
	$L^I_{M\_DCL}$	L^I_{DCL}	L_{PGC}	L^C_{DCL}	R@1	R@5	R@10	R@1	R@5	R@10
1					78.7	94.5	97.0	58.6	84.8	90.1
2		✓			81.9	95.6	97.9	61.5	85.8	91.8
3	✓	✓			82.6	96.1	98.0	62.6	86.7	92.3
4	✓	✓		✓	82.8	96.1	98.0	62.8	86.8	92.6
5	✓	✓	✓	✓	**83.2**	**96.5**	**98.0**	**63.1**	**87.1**	**93.0**

Table 3. Effect of different configurations of DCL module on Flickr30K test set. Implicit Diversity estimation is abbreviated as "IE". Explicit Diversity estimation is abbreviated as "EE". "MB" means using memory banks for Explicit Diversity estimation.

Models	$L^I_{M\_DCL}$	L^I_{DCL}			Text retrieval			Image retrieval		
		IE	EE	MB	R@1	R@5	R@10	R@1	R@5	R@10
1		✓			80.3	94.8	97.3	60.2	85.3	91.1
2		✓	✓		81.5	95.6	97.5	61.2	85.6	91.2
3		✓	✓	✓	81.9	95.6	97.7	61.5	85.8	91.4
4	✓	✓			82.0	95.8	97.7	61.6	86.2	92.2
5	✓	✓	✓		82.8	96.3	97.9	62.6	87.0	92.7
6	✓	✓	✓	✓	**83.2**	**96.5**	**98.0**	**63.1**	**87.1**	**93.0**

To analyze the impacts of various components in DCL module, we perform a group of experiments and present the results in Table 3. We take the model adopting L_{DCL_I} loss in Eq. 4 as baseline, named implicit Diversity contrastive loss and abbreviated as "IE". As shown in Table 3, comparing #2 with #1 based on R@1, the explicit Diversity estimation additionally leads to 1.2% improvement for text retrieval and 1.0% for image retrieval. Moreover, the comparison between #3 and #2 validates the introduce of memory bank items in Diversity estimation really matters for alleviating semantic ambiguity. Furthermore, comparing (#4, #5, #6) with (#1, #2, #3), we find the combination of L_{M_DCL} and L^I_{DCL} loss can lead to significant retrieval performance boost, which validates they are mutually beneficial to each other and collaborate to promote discriminative cross-modal embedding learning.

Impact of Size in Mini-Batch. Then, we investigate the impact of size in mini-batch on performance. From Fig. 3, we can see that when mini-batch size decreases from 128 to 32, the R@1 metric of the model "w/o M-DCL" falls from 61.5% to 59.3% for image retrieval, meanwhile falls from 81.9% to 79.3% for text retrieval. By contrast, in the same setting, the R@1 metric of the model "w

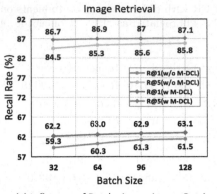
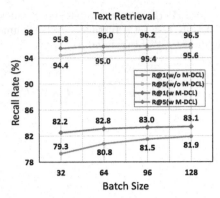

(a) Influence of Batch-size on Image Retrieval   (b) Influence of Batch-size on Text Retrieval

Fig. 3. Performance comparison of CODER model with M-DCL and without M-DCL. The model with M-DCL is abbreviated as "w M-DCL" and that without M-DCL is abbreviated as "w/o M-DCL".

Table 4. Impact of different clustering number K in PGC loss on Flickr30K test set.

K	Text retrieval			Image retrieval		
	R@1	R@5	R@10	R@1	R@5	R@10
5000	82.9	96.3	98.0	**63.1**	87.0	92.7
10000	**83.2**	**96.5**	98.0	**63.1**	**87.1**	**93.0**
15000	**83.2**	96.3	**98.2**	63.0	**87.1**	92.8
20000	82.8	96.2	97.9	62.8	87.0	92.5

M-DCL" only degrades by 0.9% and 0.9% for image retrieval and text retrieval, respectively. These results reveal that, even though the mini-batch size decreases sharply, our CODER with M-DCL can still achieve stable and superior performance, which is achieved by leveraging the coupled memory banks to enlarge interaction with negative samples. Additionally, the insensitivity to mini-batch size indicates our method is able to remain competitive even if the available computation resource is limited.

Impact of Different Configurations of PGC Loss. In this part, we explore the influence of the clustering number K in PGC loss. The corresponding experimental results are listed in Table 4. It can be seen that the performance is not obviously affected by clustering number, archiving best results at $K = 10000$. Afterwards, the performance degrades slightly accompanied by the increase of clustering number, which implies the deceasing samples of one prototypical class may weaken the general semantics conveyed by concept-level representations.

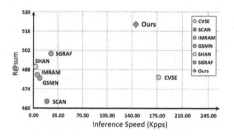

Fig. 4. Performance comparison of inference speed and recall between different methods. The Kpps on the horizontal axis denote the similarities of how many image-text pairs are calculated per second, the higher the better.

Fig. 5. The qualitative bi-directional retrieval results on Flickr30K dataset. For text retrieval, the ground-truth and non ground-truth descriptions are marked in red and black, respectively. For image retrieval, the number in the upper left corner denotes the ranking order, and the ground-truth images are annotated with green check mark. (Color figure online)

4.5   Analysis on Accuracy and Efficiency of Model

The retrieval latency is also very important in real application scenario, whereas was seldom investigated in previous works. Thus, we report both retrieval recall and consuming time for more comprehensive performance comparisons. To achieve that, we compare our CODER with six leading methods [4,9,20,28,32,49]. Note that the inference time of them are reported by re-implementing their open-sourced codes in the same environment. As shown in Fig. 4, we can see that the inference speed of our method is comparable to CVSE, but its retrieval recall surpasses the latter by a large margin. Besides, in comparison to the best competitor SGRAF [9], our method surpasses it up to nearly 6× faster for inference, meanwhile achieves considerable advantage over it on "R@sum" recall metric. Therefore, our method is superior to these approaches from both perspectives of effectiveness and efficiency.

4.6   Retrieval Result Visualization

To further qualitatively show the performance of our model, in Fig. 5, we select several images and texts as queries to display their retrieval results on Flickr30K dataset. The bidirectional ITR results demonstrate our CODER model can return reasonable retrieval results.

5   Conclusions

In this paper, we proposed a Coupled Diversity-Sensitive Momentum Contrastive Learning (CODER) model for image-text retrieval. Specifically, Momentum

Contrastive Learning (MCL) is extended to coupled form with dual dynamic modality-specific memory banks to enlarge interactions among instance pairs for cross-modal representation learning. Meanwhile, a novel diversity-sensitive contrastive loss is designed to take semantic ambiguity of sample embedding into account, which flexibly and dynamically allocate attention weights to negative pairs. In parallel, we devise an on-line clustering based strategy to exploit complementary knowledge between hierarchical semantics to promote discriminative feature learning. Furthermore, we systematically studied the impact of multiple components in our model, and its superiority is validated via substantially surpassing state-of-the-art approaches on two benchmarks with very low latency. In the near future, we plan to integrate our proposed learning paradigm into more large-scale vision-language pre-training models.

References

1. Anderson, P., et al.: Bottom-up and top-down attention for image captioning and vqa. In: CVPR (2018)
2. Antol, S., et al.: Vqa: visual question answering. In: ICCV (2015)
3. Bai, Y., Fu, J., Zhao, T., Mei, T.: Deep attention neural tensor network for visual question answering. In: ECCV (2018)
4. Chen, H., Ding, G., Liu, X., Lin, Z., Liu, J., Han, J.: Imram: iterative matching with recurrent attention memory for cross-modal image-text retrieval. In: CVPR (2020)
5. Chen, J., Hu, H., Wu, H., Jiang, Y., Wang, C.: Learning the best pooling strategy for visual semantic embedding. In: CVPR (2021)
6. Chen, T., Deng, J., Luo, J.: Adaptive offline quintuplet loss for image-text matching. In: Vedaldi, A., Bischof, H., Brox, T., Frahm, J.-M. (eds.) ECCV 2020. LNCS, vol. 12358, pp. 549–565. Springer, Cham (2020). https://doi.org/10.1007/978-3-030-58601-0_33
7. Chen, T., Kornblith, S., Norouzi, M., Hinton, G.: A simple framework for contrastive learning of visual representations. In: ICML (2020)
8. Devlin, J., Chang, M.W., Lee, K., Toutanova, K.: Bert: pre-training of deep bidirectional transformers for language understanding. In: NAACL (2019)
9. Diao, H., Zhang, Y., Ma, L., Lu, H.: Similarity reasoning and filtration for image-text matching. In: AAAI (2021)
10. Faghri, F., Fleet, D.J., Kiros, J., Fidler, S.: Vse++: improved visual-semantic embeddings. In: BMVC (2018)
11. Frome, A., et al.: Devise: a deep visual-semantic embedding model. In: NeurIPS (2013)
12. Ge, X., Chen, F., Jose, J.M., Ji, Z., Wu, Z., Liu, X.: Structured multi-modal feature embedding and alignment for image-sentence retrieval. In: ACMMM (2021)
13. Grill, J.B., et al.: Bootstrap your own latent-a new approach to self-supervised learning. In: NeurIPS (2020)
14. Hadsell, R., Chopra, S., LeCun, Y.: Dimensionality reduction by learning an invariant mapping. In: CVPR (2006)
15. He, K., Fan, H., Wu, Y., Xie, S., Girshick, R.: Momentum contrast for unsupervised visual representation learning. In: CVPR, pp. 9729–9738 (2020)
16. Hua, T., Zheng, H., Bai, Y., Zhang, W., Zhang, X.P., Mei, T.: Exploiting relationship for complex-scene image generation. In: AAAI (2021)

17. Huang, Y., Wu, Q., Song, C., Wang, L.: Learning semantic concepts and order for image and sentence matching. In: CVPR (2018)
18. Huo, Y., et al.: Wenlan: bridging vision and language by large-scale multi-modal pre-training. arXiv preprint arXiv:2103.06561 (2021)
19. Jain, A.: Data clustering: 50 years beyond K-means. Pattern Recogn. Lett. **31**(8), 651–666 (2010)
20. Ji, Z., Chen, K., Wang, H.: Step-wise hierarchical alignment network for image-text matching. In: IJCAI (2021)
21. Jiao, Y., Jie, Z., Chen, J., Ma, L., Jiang, Y.G.: Suspected object matters: rethinking model's prediction for one-stage visual grounding. ArXiv:2203.05186 (2022)
22. Jiao, Y., et al.: Two-stage visual cues enhancement network for referring image segmentation. In: ACM MM (2021)
23. Karpathy, A., Li, F.F.: Deep visual-semantic alignments for generating image descriptions. In: CVPR (2015)
24. Kingma, D., Ba, J.: Adam: a method for stochastic optimization. In: ICLR (2014)
25. Kipf, T.N., Welling, M.: Semi-supervised classification with graph convolutional networks. In: ICLR (2016)
26. Kiros, R., Salakhutdinov, R., Zemel, R.: Unifying visual-semantic embeddings with multimodal neural language models. In: NeurIPS Workshop (2014)
27. LeCun, Y., Bengio, Y., Hinton, G.: Deep learning. Nature **521**(7553), 436–444 (2015)
28. Lee, K.H., Chen, X., Hua, G., Hu, H., He, X.: Stacked cross attention for image-text matching. In: ECCV (2018)
29. Li, K., Zhang, Y., Li, K., Li, Y., Fu, Y.: Visual semantic reasoning for image-text matching. In: ICCV (2019)
30. Li, W., et al.: Unimo: towards unified-modal understanding and generation via cross-modal contrastive learning. In: ACL (2021)
31. Lin, T.-Y., et al.: Microsoft COCO: common objects in context. In: Fleet, D., Pajdla, T., Schiele, B., Tuytelaars, T. (eds.) ECCV 2014. LNCS, vol. 8693, pp. 740–755. Springer, Cham (2014). https://doi.org/10.1007/978-3-319-10602-1_48
32. Liu, C., Mao, Z., Zhang, T., Xie, H., Wang, B., Zhang, Y.: Graph structured network for image-text matching. In: CVPR (2020)
33. Liu, F., Ye, R., Wang, X., Li, S.: Hal: improved text-image matching by mitigating visual semantic hubs. In: AAAI (2020)
34. Liu, S., Fan, H., Qian, S., Chen, Y., Ding, W., Wang, Z.: Hit: hierarchical transformer with momentum contrast for video-text retrieval. arXiv preprint arXiv:2103.15049 (2021)
35. Luo, H., et al.: Clip4clip: an empirical study of clip for end to end video clip retrieval. ArXiv arXiv:abs/2104.08860 (2021)
36. Ma, L., Lu, Z., Shang, L., Li, H.: Multimodal convolutional neural networks for matching image and sentence. In: ICCV (2015)
37. Ma, L., Lu, Z., Li, H.: Learning to answer questions from image using convolutional neural network. In: AAAI (2016)
38. Mao, J., Xu, W., Yang, Y., Wang, J., Yuille, A.: Deep captioning with multimodal recurrent neural networks (m-rnn). In: ICLR (2015)
39. Oord, A.V.D., Li, Y., Vinyals, O.: Representation learning with contrastive predictive coding. arXiv preprint arXiv:1807.03748 (2018)
40. Pennington, J., Socher, R., Manning, C.D.: Glove: global vectors for word representation. In: EMNLP (2014)

41. Plummer, B.A., Wang, L., Cervantes, C., Caicedo, J.C., Hockenmaier, J., Lazebnik, S.: Flickr30k entities: collecting region-to-phrase correspondences for richer image-to-sentence models. In: ICCV (2015)
42. Qu, L., Liu, M., Wu, J., Gao, Z., Nie, L.: Dynamic modality interaction modeling for image-text retrieval. In: SIGIR (2021)
43. Radford, A., et al.: Learning transferable visual models from natural language supervision. arXiv preprint arXiv:2103.00020 (2021)
44. Ren, S., He, K., Girshick, R.B., Sun, J.: Faster r-cnn: towards real-time object detection with region proposal networks. In: NeurIPS (2015)
45. Shi, B., Ji, L., Lu, P., Niu, Z., Duan, N.: Knowledge aware semantic concept expansion for image-text matching. In: IJCAI (2019)
46. Song, Y., Soleymani, M.: Polysemous visual-semantic embedding for cross-modal retrieval (2019)
47. Tanmay, G., Alexander, G.S., Derek, H.: Vico: word embeddings from visual co-occurrences. In: ICCV (2019)
48. Wang, B., Ma, L., Zhang, W., Liu, W.: Reconstruction network for video captioning. In: CVPR (2018)
49. Wang, H., Zhang, Y., Ji, Z., Pang, Y., Ma, L.: Consensus-aware visual-semantic embedding for image-text matching. In: Vedaldi, A., Bischof, H., Brox, T., Frahm, J.-M. (eds.) ECCV 2020. LNCS, vol. 12369, pp. 18–34. Springer, Cham (2020). https://doi.org/10.1007/978-3-030-58586-0_2
50. Wang, L., Li, Y., Lazebnik, S.: Learning deep structure-preserving image-text embeddings. In: CVPR (2016)
51. Wang, S., Wang, R., Yao, Z., Shan, S., Chen, X.: Cross-modal scene graph matching for relationship-aware image-text retrieval. In: WACV (2020)
52. Wang, Y., et al.: Wasserstein coupled graph learning for cross-modal retrieval. In: ICCV (2021)
53. Wehrmann, J., Kolling, C., Barros, R.C.: Adaptive cross-modal embeddings for image-text alignment. In: AAAI (2020)
54. Wei, J., Xu, X., Yang, Y., Ji, Y., Wang, Z., Shen, H.T.: Universal weighting metric learning for cross-modal matching. In: CVPR (2020)
55. Wei, X., Zhang, T., Li, Y., Zhang, Y., Wu, F.: Multi-modality cross attention network for image and sentence matching. In: CVPR (2020)
56. Wen, K., Gu, X., Cheng, Q.: Learning dual semantic relations with graph attention for image-text matching. IEEE Trans. Circ. Syst. Video Technol. 31, 2866–2879 (2021)
57. Wu, W., Sun, Z., Ouyang, W.: Transferring textual knowledge for visual recognition. ArXiv:2207.01297 (2022)
58. Xu, D., Zhu, Y., Choy, C.B., Fei-Fei, L.: Scene graph generation by iterative message passing. In: CVPR (2017)
59. Xu, K., et al.: Show, attend and tell: neural image caption generation with visual attention. In: ICML (2015)
60. Yang, J., et al.: Unified contrastive learning in image-text-label space. ArXiv arXiv:2204.03610 (2022)
61. Zhang, L., et al.: Vldeformer: learning visual-semantic embeddings by vision-language transformer decomposing. ArXiv arXiv:2110.11338 (2021)
62. Zhao, D., Wang, A., Russakovsky, O.: Understanding and evaluating racial biases in image captioning (2021)

Language-Driven Artistic Style Transfer

Tsu-Jui Fu[1]([⊠]), Xin Eric Wang[2], and William Yang Wang[1]

[1] UC Santa Barbara, Santa Barbara, USA
{tsu-juifu,william}@cs.ucsb.edu
[2] UC Santa Cruz, Santa Cruz, USA
xwang366@ucsc.edu

Abstract. Despite having promising results, style transfer, which requires preparing style images in advance, may result in lack of creativity and accessibility. Following human instruction, on the other hand, is the most natural way to perform artistic style transfer that can significantly improve controllability for visual effect applications. We introduce a new task—language-driven artistic style transfer (LDAST)—to manipulate the style of a content image, guided by a text. We propose contrastive language visual artist (CLVA) that learns to extract visual semantics from style instructions and accomplish LDAST by the patch-wise style discriminator. The discriminator considers the correlation between language and patches of style images or transferred results to jointly embed style instructions. CLVA further compares contrastive pairs of content images and style instructions to improve the mutual relativeness. The results from the same content image can preserve consistent content structures. Besides, they should present analogous style patterns from style instructions that contain similar visual semantics. The experiments show that our CLVA is effective and achieves superb transferred results on LDAST.

1 Introduction

Style transfer [14,20,21,27,28,35] adopts appearances and visual patterns from another reference style images to manipulate a content image. Artistic style transfer has a considerable application value for creative visual design, such as image stylization and video effect [13,19,45,59]. However, it requires preparing collections of style image in advance. It even needs to redraw new references first if there is no expected style images, which is impractical due to an additional overhead. In contrast, language is the most natural way for humans to communicate. If a system can follow textual descriptions and automatically perform style transfer, we can significantly improve accessibility and controllability.

In this paper, we introduce Language-driven Artistic Style Transfer (LDAST). As illustrated in Fig. 1, LDAST treats a content image and a text as the input,

Supplementary Information The online version contains supplementary material available at https://doi.org/10.1007/978-3-031-20059-5_41.

Content ($\mathcal{C}$)   Instruction ($\mathcal{X}$)   Language-Driven Artistic Style Transfer (LDAST)

Fig. 1. Language-driven Artistic Style Transfer (LDAST). LDAST performs style transfer for a content image $\mathcal{C}$, guided by the visual attribute (the lower row) or even the visual content and emotional effect (the upper row) from a style instruction $\mathcal{X}$.

and the style transferred result is manipulated based on the style description. It should preserve the structure of the content yet simultaneously modifies the style pattern that corresponds to the instruction. LDAST is different from the general language-based image-editing (LBIE) [9,26,31,33] that aims at altering objects or properties of objects. The main challenge of LDAST is to extract visual semantics from language. Humans use not only explicit visual attributes but also visual content or emotional effects to describe style feelings. For example, it requires connecting *"water, sketching, and painting"* or *"peaceful, feel content"* with their visual concepts and further carrying out correlated style transfer.

We present contrastive language visual artist (CLVA), including language visual artist (LVA) and contrastive reasoning (CR), to perform style transfer conditioning on guided texts. LVA preserves content structures from content images $\mathcal{C}$ and extracts visual semantics from style instructions $\mathcal{X}$. LVA learns the latent style pattern based on the distinguishment between patches of style imags or transferred results from the patch-wise style discriminator. Furthermore, CR boosts by comparing contrastive pairs where relative content images or style instructions should present similar content structures or style patterns.

To evaluate LDAST, we conduct experiments upon DTD^2 [50] and ArtEmis [1]. DTD^2 provides texture images with its colors or texture patterns in text. ArtEmis collects explanations of visual contents and emotional effects for artworks. We treat these annotations as style instructions for the challenging LDAST concerning visual attributes or human style feelings. The experiments show that our CLVA is effective for LDAST and achieves superb yet efficient transferred results on both automatic metrics and human evaluation. Our contributions are four-fold:

- We introduce LDAST that follows natural language for artistic style transfer;
- We present CLVA, which learns to extract explicit visual semantics from style instructions and provide sufficient style patterns for LDAST;
- We conduct the evaluation on DTD^2 and ArtEmis to consider diverse style instructions with visual attributes and emotional effects;
- Extensive experiments and qualitative examples demonstrate that our CLVA outperforms baselines regarding both effectiveness and efficiency.

2   Related Work

Artistic Style Transfer. Style transfer [6,14,16,21,22,43,47] redraws an image with a specific style. Since being a popular form of art, incorporating painting with digital design can produce attractive visual effect (VFX). In general, style transfer can be divided into two categories: *photorealistic* and *artistic*. Photorealistic style transfer [29,32,36,56] aims at applying reference styles on scenes without hurting details and satisfying contradictory objectives. By contrast, artistic style transfer [4,14,20,27,28,30,35] captures style concepts from reference and modifies color distributions and texture patterns of content images. However, it requires preparing numerous style images in advance, which limits practicality of style transfer. To tackle this issue, LDAST allows following textual descriptions to perform *artistic* style transfer and improves the accessibility of VFX design.

Language-Based Image Editing. The general task of LDAST is language-based image editing (LBIE), which also uses language to edit input images. With rule-based instructions and predefined semantic labels, they [7,25] first carry out LBIE but under limited practicality. Inspired by text-to-image generation [40, 54,58], previous works [5,9–11,26,31,33,52] perform LBIE by conditional GAN, which modifies the properties of objects in the image. In contrast, LDAST aims at preserving the scene structure from the content image and performing stylization guided by the style instruction.

CLIP-Guided Optimization. Recently, based on the powerful visual-linguistic connection of CLIP [44], CLIP-guided image synthesis [34,39] has shown exciting results. StyleCLIP [37] and NADA [12] tweak the latent code of a pre-trained StyleGAN [23] for image editing. Since heavily relying on a pre-trained generator, both are confined to the training domain, and the results can only present limited stylization. CLIPstyler [24] updates the style transfer network for target style patterns from the CLIP alignment. Though supporting arbitrary content images, CLIPstyler still requires hundreds of iterations and takes lots of time with considerable GPU memory, suffering from the efficiency and practicality overhead. Moreover, our experiments show that CLIP poorly captures detailed style patterns from instructions, which is intractable to perform explicit LDAST.

3   Language-Driven Artistic Style Transfer

3.1   Overview of CLVA

We introduce language-driven artistic style transfer (LDAST) to manipulate the style of a content image C, guided by a style instruction X, as illustrated in Fig. 1. For training, we have pairs of style images S with style instructions X to learn the mutual correlation. During testing, only X are provided for LDAST to carry out artistic style transfer purely relied on language. We present contrastive language visual artist (CLVA) in Fig. 2. Language visual artist (LVA) extracts content

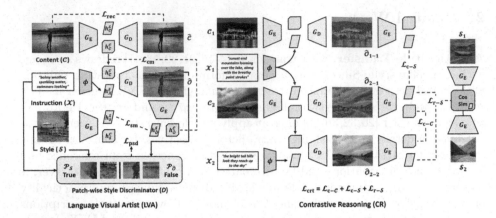

Fig. 2. Contrastive language visual artist (CLVA). Language Visual Artist (LVA) learns to jointly embed style images $\mathcal{S}$ and style instructions $\mathcal{X}$ by the patch-wise style discriminator D and perform LDAST for content images $\mathcal{C}$. Contrastive Reasoning (CR) compares contrasitve pairs to improve the relativeness between transferred results $\hat{\mathcal{O}}$.

structures from $\mathcal{C}$ and visual patterns from $\mathcal{X}$ to perform LDAST. LVA adopts the patch-wise style discriminator D to connect extracted visual semantics to patches of paired style image ($\mathcal{P}_S$ in Fig. 2). Contrastive reasoning (CR) allows comparing contrastive pairs $\mathcal{C}_1$-$\mathcal{X}_1$, $\mathcal{C}_2$-$\mathcal{X}_1$, and $\mathcal{C}_2$-$\mathcal{X}_2$ of content image and style instruction. In this way, it should present consistent content structures from the same content image $\mathcal{C}_2$ or analogous style patterns from related style images $\mathcal{S}_1$ and $\mathcal{S}_2$, despite using different style instructions.

3.2 Language Visual Artist (LVA)

To tackle LDAST, language visual artist (LVA) first adopts visual encoder G_E to extract the content feature h^C and the style feature h^S for an image. Text encoder ϕ also extracts the style instruction feature $h_{\mathcal{X}}^S$ from an instruction. h^C is a spatial tensor containing the content structure feature, and h^S represents the global style pattern. $\mathcal{S}_{\mathcal{X}}^S$ embeds into the same space of h^S to reflect the extracted visual semantic. Then, visual decoder G_D produces transferred results $\hat{\mathcal{O}}$ from h_C^C and $h_{\mathcal{X}}^S$, which performs style transfer by style instructions:

$$h_C^C, h_C^S = G_E(\mathcal{C}), \quad h_{\mathcal{X}}^S = \phi(\mathcal{X}), \tag{1}$$
$$\hat{\mathcal{O}} = G_D(h_C^C, h_{\mathcal{X}}^S).$$

In particular, G_D applies self-attention [35,57] to fuse h^C and h^S over the global spatial dimension. There are two goals to train LVA for LDAST: (i) preserving *content structures* from content images; (ii) presenting *style patterns* correlated with visual semantics of style instructions.

Structure Reconstruction. To preserve content structures, we consider that visual decoder G_D should be able to reconstruct input content images using extracted content features h_C^C and style features h_C^S from visual encoder G_E:

$$\hat{\mathcal{C}} = G_{\mathrm{D}}(h_{\hat{\mathcal{C}}}^{\mathcal{C}}, h_{\hat{\mathcal{C}}}^{\mathcal{S}}),$$
$$\mathcal{L}_{\mathrm{rec}} = ||\hat{\mathcal{C}} - \mathcal{C}||_2, \tag{2}$$

where the reconstruction loss $\mathcal{L}_{\mathrm{rec}}$ is computed as the mean L2 difference between reconstructed content images $\hat{\mathcal{C}}$ and input content images $\mathcal{C}$.

Patch-Wise Style Discriminator (D). Regarding style patterns, results $\hat{\mathcal{O}}$ guided by style instructions $\mathcal{X}$ are expected to present analogously to reference style images $\mathcal{S}$. To address the connection between linguistic from $\mathcal{X}$ and visual semantics from $\mathcal{S}$, we introduce the patch-wise style discriminator D. Inspired by texture synthesis [15,53], images with analogous patch patterns should appear perceptually similar texture patterns. D tries to recognize the correspondence between an image patch $\mathcal{P}$ and a style instruction $\mathcal{X}$:

$$\mathcal{P}_{\hat{\mathcal{O}}}, \mathcal{P}_{\mathcal{S}} = \mathrm{Crop}(\hat{\mathcal{O}}), \mathrm{Crop}(\mathcal{S}),$$
$$\mathcal{L}_{\mathrm{psd}} = \log(1 - D(\mathcal{P}_{\hat{\mathcal{O}}}, \mathcal{X})),$$
$$\mathcal{L}_D = \log(1 - D(\mathcal{P}_{\hat{\mathcal{O}}}, \mathcal{X})) + \log(D(\mathcal{P}_{\mathcal{S}}, \mathcal{X})), \tag{3}$$

where Crop is to randomly crop an image into patches. The patch-wise style loss $\mathcal{L}_{\mathrm{psd}}$ aims at generating transferred results that are correlated with $\mathcal{X}$. Contrarily, by the discriminator loss $\mathcal{L}_D$, D learns to distinguish that a patch $\mathcal{P}$ is from style images ($\mathcal{P}_{\mathcal{S}}$) or transferred results ($\mathcal{P}_{\hat{\mathcal{O}}}$). This adversarial loss [17,41] encourages that transferred results from style instructions are presented similarly with style images, which jointly embeds the extracted visual semantics.

Content Matching and Style Matching. To further enhance the alignment with inputs, inspired by cycle consistency [38,51,55,60], we consider the content matching loss $\mathcal{L}_{\mathrm{cm}}$ and the style matching loss $\mathcal{L}_{\mathrm{sm}}$ of transferred results $\hat{\mathcal{O}}$. We adopt G_{E} again to extract content features $h_{\hat{\mathcal{O}}}^{\mathcal{C}}$ and style features $h_{\hat{\mathcal{O}}}^{\mathcal{S}}$ for $\hat{\mathcal{O}}$, where $h_{\hat{\mathcal{O}}}^{\mathcal{C}}$ and $h_{\hat{\mathcal{O}}}^{\mathcal{S}}$ should correlate with $h_{\mathcal{C}}^{\mathcal{C}}$ from $\mathcal{C}$ and $h_{\mathcal{S}}^{\mathcal{S}}$ from $\mathcal{S}$:

$$(h_{\hat{\mathcal{O}}}^{\mathcal{C}}, h_{\hat{\mathcal{O}}}^{\mathcal{S}}), (h_{\mathcal{S}}^{\mathcal{C}}, h_{\mathcal{S}}^{\mathcal{S}}) = G_{\mathrm{E}}(\hat{\mathcal{O}}), G_{\mathrm{E}}(S),$$
$$\mathcal{L}_{\mathrm{cm}}, \mathcal{L}_{\mathrm{sm}} = ||h_{\hat{\mathcal{O}}}^{\mathcal{C}} - h_{\mathcal{C}}^{\mathcal{C}}||_2, ||h_{\hat{\mathcal{O}}}^{\mathcal{S}} - h_{\mathcal{S}}^{\mathcal{S}}||_2. \tag{4}$$

Therefore, transferred results are required to align with content structures and style patterns from inputs, which meets the goal of LDAST.

3.3 Contrastive Reasoning (CR)

The content image should transfer to various styles while preserving the same structure. Related style instructions can apply analogous style patterns to arbitrary content images. As shown in Fig. 2, contrastive reasoning (CR) compares content structures or style patterns from transferred results of contrastive pairs. The contrastive pair consists of two different content images $\mathcal{C}_1$ and $\mathcal{C}_2$ with two

Algorithm 1. Training Process of Language Visual Artist (LVA)

1: G_E, G_D: Visual Encoder, Visual Decoder
2: ϕ: Text Encoder
3: D: Patch-wise Style Discriminator
4: **while** TRAIN_VLA **do**
5:     $\mathcal{C}$, $\{\mathcal{S}, \mathcal{X}\}$ $\leftarrow$ Sampled content/style
6:
7:     $h_{\mathcal{C}}^{\mathcal{C}}$, $h_{\mathcal{C}}^{\mathcal{S}}$ $\leftarrow$ $G_E(\mathcal{C})$ $\hat{\mathcal{C}}$ $\leftarrow$ $G_D(h_{\mathcal{C}}^{\mathcal{C}}, h_{\mathcal{C}}^{\mathcal{S}})$
8:     $\mathcal{L}_{\text{rec}}$ $\leftarrow$ Reconstruction loss   ▷ Eq. 2
9:     $h_{\mathcal{X}}^{\mathcal{S}}$ $\leftarrow$ $\phi(\mathcal{X})$ $\hat{\mathcal{O}}$ $\leftarrow$ $G_D(h_{\mathcal{C}}^{\mathcal{C}}, h_{\mathcal{X}}^{\mathcal{S}})$
10:     $\mathcal{P}_{\mathcal{S}}$, $\mathcal{P}_{\hat{\mathcal{O}}}$ $\leftarrow$ Crop($\mathcal{S}$), Crop($\hat{\mathcal{O}}$)
11:     $\mathcal{L}_{\text{psd}}$ $\leftarrow$ Patch-wise style loss   ▷ Eq. 3
12:     $(h_{\hat{\mathcal{O}}}^{\mathcal{C}}, h_{\hat{\mathcal{O}}}^{\mathcal{S}})$, $(h_{\mathcal{S}}^{\mathcal{C}}, h_{\mathcal{S}}^{\mathcal{S}})$ $\leftarrow$ $G_E(\hat{\mathcal{O}})$, $G_E(\mathcal{S})$
13:     $\mathcal{L}_{\text{cm}}$ $\leftarrow$ Content matching loss   ▷ Eq. 4
14:     $\mathcal{L}_{\text{sm}}$ $\leftarrow$ Style matching loss   ▷ Eq. 4
15:
16:     $\mathcal{L}_G$ $\leftarrow$ $\mathcal{L}_{\text{rec}} + \mathcal{L}_{\text{psd}} + \mathcal{L}_{\text{cm}} + \mathcal{L}_{\text{sm}}$
17:     $\mathcal{L}_D$ $\leftarrow$ Discriminator loss for D   ▷ Eq. 3
18:     Update G_E, G_D, ϕ by minimizing $\mathcal{L}_G$
19:     Update D by maximizing $\mathcal{L}_D$
20: **end while**

reference styles $\{\mathcal{S}_1, \mathcal{X}_1\}$ and $\{\mathcal{S}_2, \mathcal{X}_2\}$. We follow the LVA inference to acquire cross results for pairs of content images and style instructions:

$$(h_{\mathcal{C}_1}^{\mathcal{C}}, h_{\mathcal{C}_1}^{\mathcal{S}}), (h_{\mathcal{C}_2}^{\mathcal{C}}, h_{\mathcal{C}_2}^{\mathcal{S}}) = G_E(\mathcal{C}_1), G_E(\mathcal{C}_2),$$

$$h_{\mathcal{X}_1}^{\mathcal{S}}, h_{\mathcal{X}_2}^{\mathcal{S}} = \phi(\mathcal{X}_1), \phi(\mathcal{X}_2),$$

$$\hat{\mathcal{O}}_{\mathcal{C}_1\text{-}\mathcal{X}_1}, \hat{\mathcal{O}}_{\mathcal{C}_1\text{-}\mathcal{X}_2} = G_D(h_{\mathcal{C}_1}^{\mathcal{C}}, h_{\mathcal{X}_1}^{\mathcal{S}}), G_D(h_{\mathcal{C}_1}^{\mathcal{C}}, h_{\mathcal{X}_2}^{\mathcal{S}}),$$

$$\hat{\mathcal{O}}_{\mathcal{C}_2\text{-}\mathcal{X}_1}, \hat{\mathcal{O}}_{\mathcal{C}_2\text{-}\mathcal{X}_2} = G_D(h_{\mathcal{C}_2}^{\mathcal{C}}, h_{\mathcal{X}_1}^{\mathcal{S}}), G_D(h_{\mathcal{C}_2}^{\mathcal{C}}, h_{\mathcal{X}_2}^{\mathcal{S}}). \tag{5}$$

Consistent Matching. Transferred results should present similar content structures ($\hat{\mathcal{O}}_{\mathcal{C}_2\text{-}\mathcal{X}_1}$ and $\hat{\mathcal{O}}_{\mathcal{C}_2\text{-}\mathcal{X}_2}$) or analogous style patterns ($\hat{\mathcal{O}}_{\mathcal{C}_1\text{-}\mathcal{X}_1}$ and $\hat{\mathcal{O}}_{\mathcal{C}_2\text{-}\mathcal{X}_1}$) if using the same content image ($\mathcal{C}_2$) or the same style instruction ($\mathcal{X}_1$):

$$h_{\hat{\mathcal{O}}_{\mathcal{C}_i\text{-}\mathcal{X}_j}}^{\mathcal{C}} = G_E(\hat{\mathcal{O}}_{\mathcal{C}_i\text{-}\mathcal{X}_j}),$$

$$\mathcal{L}_{\text{c-c}} = ||h_{\hat{\mathcal{O}}_{\mathcal{C}_1\text{-}\mathcal{X}_1}}^{\mathcal{C}} - h_{\hat{\mathcal{O}}_{\mathcal{C}_1\text{-}\mathcal{X}_2}}^{\mathcal{C}}||_2 + ||h_{\hat{\mathcal{O}}_{\mathcal{C}_2\text{-}\mathcal{X}_1}}^{\mathcal{C}} - h_{\hat{\mathcal{O}}_{\mathcal{C}_2\text{-}\mathcal{X}_2}}^{\mathcal{C}}||_2,$$

$$\mathcal{L}_{\text{c-s}} = ||h_{\hat{\mathcal{O}}_{\mathcal{C}_1\text{-}\mathcal{X}_1}}^{\mathcal{S}} - h_{\hat{\mathcal{S}}_{2-1}}^{\mathcal{S}}||_2 + ||h_{\hat{\mathcal{O}}_{\mathcal{C}_1\text{-}\mathcal{X}_2}}^{\mathcal{S}} - h_{\hat{\mathcal{O}}_{\mathcal{C}_2\text{-}\mathcal{X}_2}}^{\mathcal{S}}||_2, \tag{6}$$

where *consistent matching* of content structure $\mathcal{L}_{\text{c-c}}$ or style pattern $\mathcal{L}_{\text{c-s}}$ is aligned by content features or style features, extracted by G_E.

Relative Matching. Apart from consistent matching, distinct style instructions, which imply corresponding visual semantics, should still present relative patterns. For example, we can only discover *"reach up to the sky"* literally from $\mathcal{X}_2$. If comparing reference style images $\mathcal{S}_1$ and $\mathcal{S}_2$, we can perceive the sharing of a similar style pattern and link the visual concept of *"bright tall hills"* in $\mathcal{X}_2$ to *"mountains looming over the lake"* in $\mathcal{X}_1$. We define *relative matching* $\mathcal{L}_{\text{r-s}}$ with the cosine similarity (CosSim) between reference style images:

$$(h^{\mathcal{C}}_{\mathcal{S}_i}, h^{\mathcal{S}}_{\mathcal{S}_i}) = G_{\mathrm{E}}(\mathcal{S}_i),$$
$$r = \mathrm{CosSim}(h^{\mathcal{S}}_{\mathcal{S}_1}, h^{\mathcal{S}}_{\mathcal{S}_2}),$$
$$\mathcal{L}_{\mathrm{r}-\mathcal{S}} = (\|h^{\mathcal{S}}_{\hat{\mathcal{O}}_{C_1 \cdot \mathcal{X}_1}} - h^{\mathcal{S}}_{\hat{\mathcal{O}}_{C_1 \cdot \mathcal{X}_2}} \|_2 + \tag{7}$$
$$\|h^{\mathcal{S}}_{\hat{\mathcal{O}}_{C_2 \cdot \mathcal{X}_1}} - h^{\mathcal{S}}_{\hat{\mathcal{O}}_{C_2 \cdot \mathcal{X}_2}} \|_2) \cdot r.$$

When style images are related, it has to align style features to certain extent even if paired style instructions are different. Otherwise, $\mathcal{L}_{\mathrm{r}-\mathcal{S}}$ will be close to 0 and ignore this unrelated style pair. The overall contrastive reasoning loss $\mathcal{L}_{\mathrm{ctr}}$ considers both consistent matching and relative matching:

$$\mathcal{L}_{\mathrm{ctr}} = \mathcal{L}_{\mathrm{c}-\mathcal{C}} + \mathcal{L}_{\mathrm{c}-\mathcal{S}} + \mathcal{L}_{\mathrm{r}-\mathcal{S}}. \tag{8}$$

3.4 Learning of CLVA

For each epoch of CLVA training, we first train with the LVA process and then CR. As Algorithm 1, we consider reconstruction loss $\mathcal{L}_{\mathrm{rec}}$ to preserve content structure and patch-wise style loss $\mathcal{L}_{\mathrm{psd}}$ between style instruction and visual pattern of transferred results. Both content matching loss $\mathcal{L}_{\mathrm{cm}}$ and style matching loss $\mathcal{L}_{\mathrm{sm}}$ enhance the matching with the inputs. Simultaneously, we update D by maximizing discriminator loss $\mathcal{L}_D$ to distinguish between true patches $\mathcal{P}_{\mathcal{S}}$ or false patches $\mathcal{P}_{\hat{\mathcal{O}}}$, concerning style instructions. During CR, contrastive pairs of content images and style instructions are randomly sampled, and the transferred results are across produced. We further update by minimizing contrastive reasoning loss $\mathcal{L}_{\mathrm{ctr}}$ to allow considering content consistency and mutual style relativeness. The overall optimization of CLVA is summarized as:

$$\mathcal{L}_G = \mathcal{L}_{\mathrm{rec}} + \mathcal{L}_{\mathrm{psd}} + \mathcal{L}_{\mathrm{cm}} + \mathcal{L}_{\mathrm{sm}},$$
$$\min_{G,\phi} \max_{D} \ \mathcal{L}_G + \mathcal{L}_D + \mathcal{L}_{\mathrm{ctr}}. \tag{9}$$

4 Experiments

4.1 Experimental Setup

Dataset. To evaluate our CLVA, we consider DTD[2] [8] and ArtEmis [1] as reference style instructions. DTD[2] contains 5K texture images with its natural descriptions for visual attributes such as colors and texture patterns. ArtEmis provides 80K artworks from WikiArt[1] with annotations of visual contents and emotional effects as human style feelings. We also collect 15K wallpapers from WallpapersCraft[2], which presents diverse scenes as content images. Each content

---

[1] WikiArt: https://www.wikiart.org.
[2] WallpapersCraft: https://wallpaperscraft.com/.

image is resized to 256 × 192 in our experiment. We randomly sample 100 unseen content images and 100 testing reference styles to evaluate the generalizability of LDAST. Note that both style images and style instructions appear for training, but only style instructions are accessible during testing.

Evaluation Metrics. To support large-scale evaluation, we treat transferred results directly from style images as semi-groundtruth (Semi-GT) [2, 3, 42] by the SOTA style transfer AdaAttn [30]. We apply the following metrics:

- **SSIM** [48] compares images in the luminance, contrast, and structure aspects. A higher SSIM has a higher structural similarity;
- **Percept** [22] computes from the gram matrix of visual features. A lower Percept loss shows that two images share a similar style pattern;
- **FAD** [18] is computed by the mean L2 distance of the activations from the InceptionV3 [46] feature. As a distance metric, a lower FAD represents that LDAST results and Semi-GT are more relevant.

Note that we consider SSIM and FAD to compare with Semi-GT and calculate Percept loss directly with reference style images. Apart from visual similarity, we consider the correlation between style instructions and LDAST results:

- **VLS** [49] calculates the cosine similarity between each other from CLIP [44].

Since each metric has different deficiencies, we also conduct a comprehensive human evaluation from aspects of content, instruction, and style matching. We randomly sample 75 LDAST results and adopt MTurk[3] to rank over all methods. We also hire 3 MTurkers for each task to avoid the potential ranking bias.

Baselines. We conduct baselines for LDAST from various aspects:

- **Style Transfer**: We consider previous artistic style transfer methods NST [14], WCT [28], AdaIn [20], SANet [35], and LST [27] that support arbitrary contetn images. We use the same style (instruction and image) encoding from our CLVA as style features and follow their own training process to perform LDAST upon them. Due to the space issue, we only show the comparison with more recent SANet and LST. Please refer to Appendix for the complete results.
- **Language-based Image Editing**: We adopt ManiGAN [26] with affine combination module (ACM) as the general language-based editing baseline, where it modifies the content image by the style instruction. We treat normal style transferred results as groundtruth for ManiGAN to learn from.
- **CLIP-based Optimization**: StyleCLIP [37], NADA [12], and CLIP-styler [24] manipulate the content image based on the CLIP alignment of the guided instruction. Since StyleCLIP and NADA are restricted by the pre-trained generator, we compare them with the training domains of car and church. Differently, CLIPstyler can carry out arbitrary content images for LDAST.

---

[3] Amazon Mechanical Turk: https://www.mturk.com.

Table 1. Testing results of LDAST using visual attribute instructions on DTD[2].

Method	Automatic metrics				Human evaluation			
	SSIM↑	Percept↓	FAD↓	VLS↑	Content↑	Instruction↑	Style↑	Semi-GT↑
SANet [35]	35.50	0.2129	0.1627	23.57	2.701	2.477	2.738	2.630
LST [27]	34.84	0.2129	0.1533	23.16	2.743	2.831	2.651	2.528
ManiGAN [26]	32.70	0.2401	0.1663	23.25	2.757	2.562	2.937	2.922
CLIPstyler [24]	25.24	0.2598	0.1818	**24.62**	2.948	3.388	3.073	3.265
CLVA	**36.65**	**0.2033**	**0.1493**	24.00	**3.852**	**3.742**	**3.603**	**3.655**

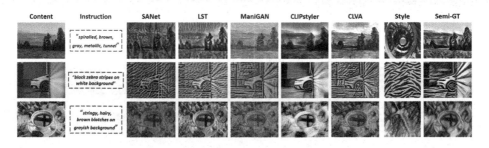

Fig. 3. Visualized comparison using visual attribute instructions on DTD[2].

4.2 Quantitative Results

Instruction with Visual Attributes. Table 1 illustrates the comparison of LDAST with baselines on DTD[2]. As regards automatic metrics, CLVA preserves content structures (highest 36.65 SSIM) and stylizes with related visual attributes to style images (lowest 0.2033 Percept loss). Furthermore, CLVA brings out the highest overall similarity as Semi-GT (lowest 0.1493 FAD). Since CLIPstyler directly optimizes by CLIP [44], it makes the highest VLS. Through the patch-wise discriminator, our CLVA can still produce style patterns correlated to given instructions (competitive 24.00 VLS) even without the pre-trained CLIP.

The human evaluation investigates the matching between transferred results with content images (Content), style instructions (Instruction), style images (Style), and Semi-GT (Semi-GT). In particular, content and instruction matching are the two most crucial, which concern the goal of LDAST: *content structure preservation* and *style pattern presentation*; style image and semi-gt matching are provided for different comparing targets from a human aspect. The results are calculated by the mean ranking score (from 1 to 5, the higher is better) of each method. In general, MTurkers indicate that our CLVA has an apparent advantage in preserving content structures (highest 3.852 Content) and presenting aligned style patterns (highest 3.742 Instruction). Though with the aid of CLIP, CLIPstyler is still behind CLVA (-0.4 Instruction), with an even higher gap in style image matching (−0.5 Style). Contributed by contrastive reasoning that compares the mutual relativeness between pairs of contents and instructions, CLVA

Table 2. Testing results of LDAST using emotional effect instructions on ArtEmis.

Method	Automatic metrics				Human evaluation			
	SSIM↑	Percept↓	FAD↓	VLS↑	Content↑	Instruction↑	Style↑	Semi-GT↑
SANet [35]	38.36	**0.0352**	0.1548	19.30	3.170	2.978	2.980	2.890
LST [27]	**42.13**	0.0386	0.1595	19.92	2.967	2.714	2.614	2.757
ManiGAN [26]	38.46	0.0500	0.1554	19.69	2.729	2.583	2.879	3.192
CLIPstyler [24]	24.17	0.0659	0.1759	**21.04**	2.777	3.140	2.998	2.952
CLVA	40.32	0.0357	**0.1418**	20.11	**3.357**	**3.586**	**3.530**	**3.208**

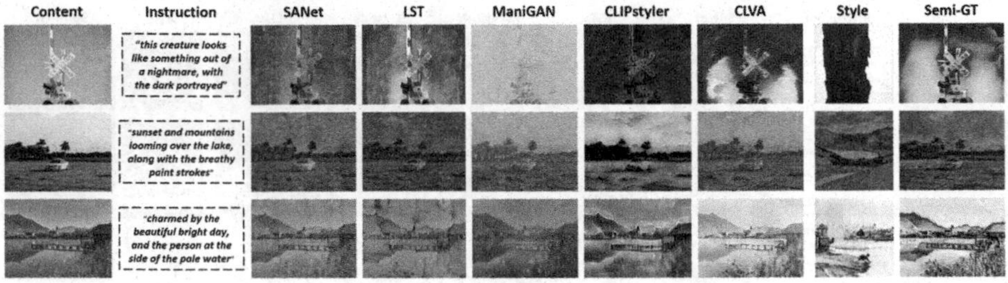

Fig. 4. Visualized comparison using emotional effect instructions on ArtEmis.

can stylize with the captured visual attributes. We adopt Pearson correlation and investigate the coefficients between automatic metrics and human evaluation as 77.2 (FAD→Instruction), 84.5 (FAD→Semi-GT), 81.3 (VLS→Instruction), and 77.8 (VLS→Semi-GT). This high correlation indicates that our metric design is adequate for evaluating large-scale LDAST experiments. The even higher 88.2 correlation (Instruction→Semi-GT) between instruction and Semi-GT matching in human evaluation further supports the usage of Semi-GT.

From the aspect of visualized comparison in Fig. 3, previous SANet and LST only produce repetitive and disorder textures in their transferred results. Mani-GAN modifies the style directly over pixels, suffering from blurring objects; this deficiency can also be found in Table 1 (lower SSIM and lower Content matching). CLIPstyler is sometimes misguided by CLIP, making irrelevant patterns, such as the bright white background in the third case. Contrary to baselines, CLVA extracts a more detailed style from different kinds of guidance (*"brown metallic"* in the first row and *"stringy hairy"* in the third case), leading to superior LDAST results that correspond to style instructions.

Instruction with Emotional Effects. Unlike visual attributes, emotional effect instructions are more challenging as connecting to visual semantics of described objects or style patterns from human feelings. For example, *"yellowish and green"* from *"sunset and mountains"* or *"scaring charcoal grey"* from *"nightmare"*. We consider this human style feeling on ArtEmis [1], where the model has to express the latent visual concepts of emotional effect instructions. CLVA performs with more balance (both second-highest SSIM and second-lowest Per-

Table 3. Testing results of LDAST on specific content domain (Car and Church).

Method	Automatic metrics				Human evaluation			
	SSIM↑	Percept↓	FAD↓	VLS↑	Content↑	Instruction↑	Style↑	Semi-GT↑
ManiGAN [26]	26.45	0.2329	0.1672	23.44	2.861	2.894	2.978	2.893
StyleCLIP [37]	28.03	0.2609	0.1812	21.55	**3.459**	2.845	2.930	2.829
NADA [12]	16.98	0.2733	0.1876	23.38	2.542	2.798	2.846	2.932
CLIPstyler [24]	18.43	0.2493	0.1826	**24.16**	2.986	3.067	3.003	3.032
CLVA	**30.98**	**0.1957**	**0.1544**	23.68	3.153	**3.465**	**3.344**	**3.315**

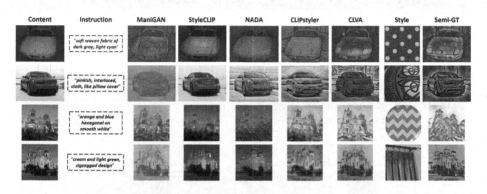

Fig. 5. Visualized comparison on specific content domain (Car and Church).

cept) from Table 2, especially the lowest 0.1418 FAD, making the most similar transferred results to Semi-GT. Though CLIPstyler [24] achieves higher VLS by optimizing over CLIP, from human aspects, CLVA can preserve more concrete contents and present more correlated style patterns (higher 3.357 content and 3.586 instruction matching). The visualized comparison in Fig. 4 illustrates that previous SANet [35] and LST [27] contain unsmooth and fragmentary patterns with blurring contents. Without a style transformation process, ManiGAN [26] modifies with only monotonous colors. CLIPstyler is failed to capture human style feelings well, suffering from weird and unpleasant results. Different from them, our CLVA learns the visual semantic during contrastive reasoning by comparing mutual relativeness between literal instructions and style images, leading to a more colorful and corresponding stylization as human emotion. More surprisingly, despite not instructed literally, CLVA perceives *"side of the water"* and reveals the latent yet correlated *"grassland"* precisely in the third row.

Specific Content Domain. To compare with StyleCLIP [37] and NADA [12] that are restricted by the pre-trained generator, we evaluate LDAST on the specific content domain. We consider the same domain images in StyleGAN2 [23] and visual attribute instructions on DTD[2]. Table 3 indicates the numerical comparison on Car and Church. Our CLVA still produces superior results and is the most admirable by human. Since StyleCLIP and NADA rely on StyleGAN, they can only preserve content (highest 3.459 Content by StyleCLIP) but with

Table 4. Ablation study of CLVA using visual attribute instructions on DTD^2.

	Ablation settings				Automatic metrics			
	$\mathcal{L}_{rec} + \mathcal{L}_{psd}$	$\mathcal{L}_{cm}$	$\mathcal{L}_{sm}$	$\mathcal{L}_{ctr}$	SSIM↑	Percept↓	FAD↓	VLS↑
(a)	✓	✗	✗	✗	34.73	0.2290	0.1568	23.29
(b)	✓	✓	✗	✗	<u>36.05</u>	0.2304	0.1512	23.27
(c)	✓	✗	✓	✗	35.73	<u>0.2049</u>	<u>0.1508</u>	<u>23.69</u>
(d)	✓	✓	✓	✗	35.86	0.2100	0.1499	23.54
(e)	✓	✓	✓	✓	**36.65**	**0.2033**	**0.1493**	**24.00**

Table 5. Instruction-to-style retrieval on DTD^2 and ArtEmis.

Method	DTD^2		ArtEmis	
	R@1	R@5	R@1	R@5
CLIP [44]	13.9	30.7	9.8	20.7
CLVA	**19.3**	**45.1**	**13.9**	**30.7**

Table 6. Human comparison between CLVA and CLIPstyle with fine-tuned CLIP on DTD^2.

Method	Human evaluation			
	Content↑	Instruction↑	Style↑	Semi-GT↑
CLIPstyler (ft.)	1.208	1.347	1.292	1.333
CLVA	**1.792**	**1.653**	**1.708**	**1.667**

Fig. 6. Visualization examples of instruction-to-style retrieval by CLIP and CLVA.

limited stylization (lower Instruction and Style). Similar observations can be found in Fig. 5, where StyleCLIP shows almost no modification for the second car. They can neither deal with the background; NADA even destroys the scene in the third row. In contrast to CLIPstyler [24] that only contains abstractive and obscure styles, CLVA presents the detailed *"read interplaced cloth"* behind the car and the color *"cream"* precisely on the surface of the church.

4.3   Ablation Study

We conduct an ablation study of each component effect on DTD^2 in Table 4. At row (a), with the reconstruction $\mathcal{L}_{rec}$ and the patch-wise style $\mathcal{L}_{psd}$, CLVA achieves feasible LDAST results by concrete structures and extracted style semantics. Row (b)–(d) shows the strength of content matching $\mathcal{L}_{cm}$ and style matching $\mathcal{L}_{sm}$. In particular, content matching helps the structure similarity to content images (higher 36.05 SSIM). Style matching aims at analogous visual patterns

Table 7. Time and GPU cost when performing LDAST on TITAN X with content image size 256 × 192. * means this method can only run one input at a time.

Method	Time (sec)			GPU (MB)		
	BS = 1	32	50	BS = 1	32	50
ManiGAN [26]	0.079	0.533	1.148	3312	6572	8129
StyleCLIP [37]	32.38	*	*	4149	*	*
NADA [12]	63.49	*	*	6413	*	*
CLIPstyler [24]	99.98	*	*	5429	*	*
CLVA	**0.029**	**0.246**	**0.405**	**1525**	**3207**	**4441**

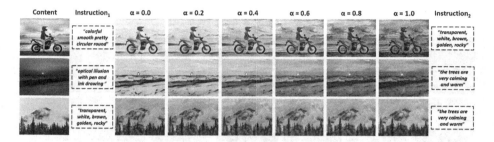

Fig. 7. Style interpolation results of LDAST over instructions.

to style images, which leads to better stylization quality (lower 0.2049 Percept and higher 23.69 VLS). If considering altogether, it can benefit and strike a balance between both. Finally, contrastive reasoning $\mathcal{L}_{ctr}$ further enables CLVA to consider contrastive pairs, making a comprehensive improvement at row (e).

Why CLVA is Better than CLIP-Based? Despite no CLIP optimized, CLVA demonstrates superior results on LDAST with all aspects of automatic metrics and human evaluation. To investigate it, we conduct instruction-to-style retrieval based on the similarity between features of style instructions and style images. Table 5 shows that our learned CLVA performs higher Recall@k on both DTD[2] and ArtEmis, leading to a better instruction-style alignment than the used CLIP. The visualization in Fig. 6 also indicates the flaw of CLIP on detailed style patterns. For example, in the first row, CLIP only presents either *"bright color"* or *"town"* in the retrieval results. In contrast, CLVA can capture both and present more related LDAST to *"happy place to live"*. From Table 6, even CLIP has been fine-tuned ahead; our CLVA still produces preferrable LDAST results from all human aspects of content, instruction, and style matching. This observation supports that contrastive reasoning, which considers contrastive pairs of content images and style instructions, is required to benefit from mutual relativeness.

Apart from transfer quality, CLVA also holds a higher efficiency than CLIP-based methods. Table 7 illustrates the time and GPU cost on a single TITAN X (12GB) with content image size 256 × 192. All CLIP-based methods take more

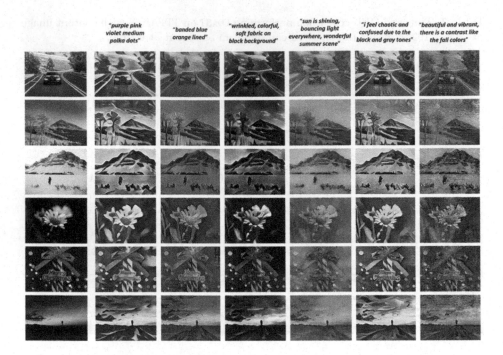

Fig. 8. CLVA results on diverse pairs of content images and style instructions.

than 30 s for only one pair of content images and style instructions. Instead of numerous iterations to align with CLIP, we extract style semantics and carry out **LDAST** in one shot, taking merely 0.03 s for one input. Without updating the model during inference, CLVA supports parallelization and can accomplish 50 pairs in half a second. Besides, as a lightweight style transfer network, CLVA requires the least GPU memory for **LDAST**. In summary, our CLVA surpasses those CLIP-based methods on both quality and efficiency because of the detailed style deficiency and the required optimizing iteration from CLIP.

Qualitative Results. As shown in Fig. 7, we investigate the linear interpolation of extracted style patterns by CLVA. Considering style features $h_{\mathcal{X}_1}^{\mathcal{S}}$ and $h_{\mathcal{X}_2}^{\mathcal{S}}$ of instructions $\mathcal{X}_1$ and $\mathcal{X}_2$, the interpolated $h_{\mathrm{p}}^{\mathcal{S}}$ should be:

$$h_{\mathrm{p}}^{\mathcal{S}} = (1 - \alpha)h_{\mathcal{X}_1}^{\mathcal{S}} + \alpha h_{\mathcal{X}_2}^{\mathcal{S}}, \tag{10}$$

where α is the style ratio between the two. Figure 7 presents a smooth transformation from one style instruction to another. By training on DTD[2] and ArtEmis altogether, CLVA even performs interpolated stylization by both visual attribute and emotional effect instructions in the third row. Figure 8 illustrates diverse **LDAST** results by our CLVA. Since CLVA supports arbitrary content images, we can also modify the style detail for high-resolution inputs in Fig. 9.

Fig. 9. High-resolution (1920 × 1080) LDAST results by CLVA with upper right: *"the lonely world makes me feel scared and nostalgic how sky and sea merge together"*; lower left: *"the snow and lights in the shop windows looks like a winter scene"*; lower right: *"ink painting, black dotted line, whiteboard"*.

5   Conclusion

We introduce language-driven artistic style transfer (LDAST) to do stylization for a content image by a style instruction. We propose contrastive language visual artist (CLVA) that adopts the patch-wise style discriminator and contrastive reasoning to jointly learn between style images and style instructions. We demonstrate that CLVA can express various style patterns of visual attributes as well as emotional effects and perform LDAST efficiently. CLVA also outperforms baselines on both automatic metrics and human evaluation. We believe that LDAST can make visual applications like image/video effect more controllable for humans.

Acknowledgments. Research was sponsored by the U.S. Army Research Office and was accomplished under Contract Number W911NF-19-D-0001 for the Institute for Collaborative Biotechnologies. The views and conclusions contained in this document are those of the authors and should not be interpreted as representing the official policies, either expressed or implied, of the U.S. Government. The U.S. Government is authorized to reproduce and distribute reprints for Government purposes notwithstanding any copyright notation herein.

References

1. Achlioptas, P., Ovsjanikov, M., Haydarov, K., Elhoseiny, M., Guibas, L.: ArtEmis: affective language for visual art. In: CVPR (2021)

2. Al-Sarraf, A., Shin, B.-S., Xu, Z., Klette, R.: Ground truth and performance evaluation of lane border detection. In: Chmielewski, L.J., Kozera, R., Shin, B.-S., Wojciechowski, K. (eds.) ICCVG 2014. LNCS, vol. 8671, pp. 66–74. Springer, Cham (2014). https://doi.org/10.1007/978-3-319-11331-9_9

3. Borkar, A., Hayes, M., Smith, M.T.: An efficient method to generate ground truth for evaluating lane detection systems. In: ICASSP (2010)

4. Chen, H., et al.: DualAST: dual style-learning networks for artistic style transfer. In: CVPR (2021)

5. Chen, J., Shen, Y., Gao, J., Liu, J., Liu, X.: Language-based image editing with recurrent attentive models. In: CVPR (2018)

6. Chen, Y.L., Hsu, C.T.: Towards deep style transfer: a content-aware perspective. In: BMVC (2016)

7. Cheng, M.M., et al.: ImageSpirit: verbal guided image parsing. In: ACM Transactions on Graphics (2013)

8. Cimpoi, M., Maji, S., Kokkinos, I., Mohamed, S., Vedaldi, A.: Describing textures in the wild. In: CVPR (2014)

9. El-Nouby, A., et al.: Tell, draw, and repeat: generating and modifying images based on continual linguistic instruction. In: ICCV (2019)

10. Fu, T.J., Wang, X.E., Grafton, S., Eckstein, M., Wang, W.Y.: SSCR: iterative language-based image editing via self-supervised counterfactual reasoning. In: EMNLP (2020)

11. Fu, T.J., Wang, X.E., Grafton, S., Eckstein, M., Wang, W.Y.: M3L: language-based video editing via multi-modal multi-level transformer. In: CVPR (2022)

12. Gal, R., Patashnik, O., Maron, H., Chechik, G., Cohen-Or, D.: StyleGAN-NADA: CLIP-guided domain adaptation of image generators. arXiv:2108.00946 (2021)

13. Gao, C., Gu, D., Zhang, F., Yu, Y.: ReCoNet: real-time coherent video style transfer network. arXiv:1807.01197 (2018)

14. Gatys, L.A., Ecker, A.S., Bethge, M.: A neural algorithm of artistic style. arXiv:1508.06576 (2015)

15. Gatys, L.A., Ecker, A.S., Bethge, M.: Texture synthesis using convolutional neural networks. In: NeurIPS (2015)

16. Gatys, L.A., Ecker, A.S., Bethge, M., Hertzmann, A., Shechtman, E.: Controlling perceptual factors in neural style transfer. In: CVPR (2017)

17. Goodfellow, I.J., et al.: Generative adversarial networks. In: NeurIPS (2014)

18. Heusel, M., Ramsauer, H., Unterthiner, T., Nessler, B., Hochreiter, S.: GANs trained by a two time-scale update rule converge to a local nash equilibrium. In: NeurIPS (2017)

19. Huang, H., et al.: Real-time neural style transfer for videos. In: CVPR (2017)

20. Huang, X., Belongie, S.: Arbitrary style transfer in real-time with adaptive instance normalization. In: ICCV (2017)

21. Jing, Y., Yang, Y., Feng, Z., Ye, J., Yu, Y., Song, M.: Neural style transfer: a review. arXiv:1705.04058 (2017)

22. Johnson, J., Alahi, A., Fei-Fei, L.: Perceptual losses for real-time style transfer and super-resolution. In: ECCV (2016)

23. Karras, T., Laine, S., Aittala, M., Hellsten, J., Lehtinen, J., Aila, T.: Analyzing and improving the image quality of StyleGAN. In: CVPR (2020)

24. Kwon, G., Ye, J.C.: CLIPstyler: image style transfer with a single text condition. In: CVPR (2022)

25. Laput, G., et al.: PixelTone: a multimodal interface for image editing. In: CHI (2013)

26. Li, B., Qi, X., Lukasiewicz, T., Torr, P.H.S.: ManiGAN: text-guided image manipulation. In: CVPR (2020)
27. Li, X., Liu, S., Kautz, J., Yang, M.H.: Learning linear transformations for fast arbitrary style transfer. In: CVPR (2019)
28. Li, Y., Fang, C., Yang, J., Wang, Z., Lu, X., Yang, M.H.: Universal style transfer via feature transforms. In: NeurIPS (2017)
29. Li, Y., Liu, M.Y., Li, X., Yang, M.H., Kautz, J.: A closed-form solution to photorealistic image stylization. In: ECCV (2018)
30. Liu, S., et al.: AdaAttN: revisit attention mechanism in arbitrary neural style transfer. In: ICCV (2021)
31. Liu, X., et al.: Open-edit: open-domain image manipulation with open-vocabulary instructions. In: Vedaldi, A., Bischof, H., Brox, T., Frahm, J.-M. (eds.) ECCV 2020. LNCS, vol. 12356, pp. 89–106. Springer, Cham (2020). https://doi.org/10.1007/978-3-030-58621-8_6
32. Luan, F., Paris, S., Shechtman, E., Bala, K.: Deep photo style transfer. In: CVPR (2017)
33. Nam, S., Kim, Y., Kim, S.J.: Text-adaptive generative adversarial networks: manipulating images with natural language. In: NeurIPS (2018)
34. Nichol, A., et al.: GLIDE: towards photorealistic image generation and editing with text-guided diffusion models. In: arXiv:2112.10741 (2021)
35. Park, D.Y., Lee, K.H.: Arbitrary style transfer with style-attentional networks. In: CVPR (2019)
36. Park, T., et al.: Swapping autoencoder for deep image manipulation. In: NeurIPS (2020)
37. Patashnik, O., Wu, Z., Shechtman, E., Cohen-Or, D., Lischinski, D.: StyleCLIP: text-driven manipulation of StyleGAN imagery. In: ICCV (2021)
38. Qiao, T., Zhang, J., Xu, D., Tao, D.: MirrorGAN: Learning Text-to-image Generation by Redescription. In: CVPR (2019)
39. Ramesh, A., et al.: Zero-shot text-to-image generation. In: arXiv:2102.12092 (2021)
40. Reed, S., Akata, Z., Yan, X., Logeswaran, L., Schiele, B., Lee, H.: Generative adversarial text to image synthesis. In: ICML (2016)
41. Salehi, P., Chalechale, A., Taghizadeh, M.: Generative adversarial networks (GANs): an overview of theoretical model, evaluation metrics, and recent developments. arXiv:2005.13178 (2020)
42. Salvo, R.D.: Large scale ground truth generation for performance evaluation of computer vision methods. In: VIGTA (2013)
43. Sanakoyeu, A., Kotovenko, D., Lang, S., Ommer, B.: A style-aware content loss for real-time HD style transfer. In: ECCV (2018)
44. Shi, L., et al.: Contrastive visual-linguistic pretraining. arXiv:2007.13135 (2020)
45. Somavarapu, N., Ma, C.Y., Kira, Z.: Frustratingly simple domain generalization via image stylization. arXiv:2006.11207 (2020)
46. Szegedy, C., Vanhoucke, V., Ioffe, S., Shlens, J., Wojna, Z.: Rethinking the inception architecture for computer vision. In: CVPR (2016)
47. Wang, P., Li, Y., Vasconcelos, N.: Rethinking and improving the robustness of image style transfer. In: CVPR (2021)
48. Wang, Z., Bovik, A.C., Sheikh, H.R., Simoncel, E.P.: Image quality assessment: from error visibility to structural similarity. In: TIP (2004)
49. Wu, C., et al.: GODIVA: generating open-DomaIn videos from nAtural descriptions. arXiv:2104.14806 (2021)

50. Wu, C., Timm, M., Maji, S.: Describing textures using natural language. In: Vedaldi, A., Bischof, H., Brox, T., Frahm, J.-M. (eds.) ECCV 2020. LNCS, vol. 12346, pp. 52–70. Springer, Cham (2020). https://doi.org/10.1007/978-3-030-58452-8_4

51. Wu, L., Wang, Y., Shao, L.: Cycle-consistent deep generative hashing for cross-modal retrieval. In: TIP (2018)

52. Xia, W., Yang, Y., Xue, J.H., Wu, B.: TediGAN: text-guided diverse face image generation and manipulation. In: CVPR (2021)

53. Xian, W., et al.: TextureGAN: controlling deep image synthesis with texture patches. In: CVPR (2018)

54. Xu, T., et al.: AttnGAN: fine-grained text to image generation with attentional generative adversarial networks. In: CVPR (2018)

55. Yi, Z., Zhang, H., Tan, P., Gong, M.: DualGAN: unsupervised dual learning for image-to-image translation. In: ICCV (2017)

56. Yoo, J., Uh, Y., Chun, S., Kang, B., Ha, J.W.: Photorealistic style transfer via wavelet transforms. In: ICCV (2019)

57. Zhang, H., Goodfellow, I., Metaxas, D., Odena, A.: Self-attention generative adversarial networks. In: PMLR (2019)

58. Zhang, H., et al.: StackGAN: text to photo-realistic image synthesis with stacked generative adversarial networks. In: ICCV (2017)

59. Zhang, Z., Wang, Z., Lin, Z., Qi, H.: Image super-resolution by neural texture transfer. In: CVPR (2019)

60. Zhu, J.Y., Park, T., Isola, P., Efros, A.A.: Unpaired image-to-image translation using cycle-consistent adversarial networks. In: ICCV (2017)

Single-Stream Multi-level Alignment
for Vision-Language Pretraining

Zaid Khan[1]([⊠])(iD), B. G. Vijay Kumar[2](iD), Xiang Yu[2](iD), Samuel Schulter[2](iD),
Manmohan Chandraker[2,3](iD), and Yun Fu[1](iD)

[1] Northeastern University, Kenner, USA
`khan.za@northeastern.edu, yunfu@ece.neu.edu`
[2] NEC Labs America, Princeton, USA
`{vijay.kumar,xiangyu,samuel}@nec-labs.com, mkchandraker@eng.ucsd.edu`
[3] UC San Diego, San Diego, USA

Abstract. Self-supervised vision-language pretraining from pure images
and text with a contrastive loss is effective, but ignores fine-grained alignment due to a dual-stream architecture that aligns image and text representations only on a global level. Earlier, supervised, non-contrastive
methods were capable of finer-grained alignment, but required dense
annotations that were not scalable. We propose a single stream architecture that aligns images and language at multiple levels: global, fine-
grained patch-token, and conceptual/semantic, using two novel tasks:
symmetric cross-modality reconstruction (XMM) and a pseudo-labeled
key word prediction (PSL). In XMM, we mask input tokens from one
modality and use cross-modal information to reconstruct the masked
token, thus improving fine-grained alignment between the two modalities. In PSL, we use attention to select keywords in a caption, use a
momentum encoder to recommend other important keywords that are
missing from the caption but represented in the image, and then train
the visual encoder to predict the presence of those keywords, helping
it learn semantic concepts that are essential for grounding a textual
token to an image region. We demonstrate competitive performance and
improved data efficiency on image-text retrieval, grounding, visual question answering/reasoning against larger models and models trained on
more data. Code and models available at zaidkhan.me/SIMLA.

Keywords: Vision-language modeling · Cross-modality learning

1 Introduction

To learn a join representation of images and language, early work [6,33,48]
follows a supervised approach, using a pre-trained object detector to extract
image regions, which are then aligned with corresponding image captions or

Supplementary Information The online version contains supplementary material
available at https://doi.org/10.1007/978-3-031-20059-5_42.

dense annotations. Such approaches are limited by the amount of available densely annotated data and the semantic concepts the pretrained object detector can represent. A recent alternative approach is to directly align image representations with the corresponding text representations using a contrastive loss [14,17,29,35,42,55], sidestepping the need for a pretrained object detector or dense annotations. Such approaches can learn from image-text pairs alone, which can be scraped from the web at large scales. However, the image-text contrastive learning paradigm is data hungry, using 1b+ [17,57] or 100m+ [42,62] pairs to overcome the noisiness of web-scraped image-text pairs. Second, the standard image-text contrastive learning architecture and objective uses a dual-stream architecture that aligns the global image and text representations, making it difficult to learn fine-grained details [56]. Third, contrastive learning does not explicitly align visual and language *concepts*, only features. Because the data complexity of images is greater than that of short captions, it can be challenging for the vision model to learn a representation that captures modality-invariant instance information corresponding to coherent natural language concepts rather than vision-specific semantics irrelevant to the modality-invariant image content.

We propose an approach that aligns image and language representations on multiple levels using a single stream transformer-only architecture that enables early, local interactions between image regions and language tokens, without the need for a pretrained object detector or dense annotations. We design a a symmetric cross-modality reconstruction task to teach fine-grained alignment between image patches and language tokens, and construct a concept prediction task that extracts pseudo labels for each image without supervision and trains the visual encoder to detect concepts that are missing from the caption but present in the image. This allows us to align vision and language on multiple levels: fine-grained (cross-modality reconstruction), coarse (contrastive learning) and discrete (concept-level supervision). We empirically evaluate our proposed model, SIMLA (**SI**ngle-Stream **M**ulti-**L**evel **A**lignment) on several downstream tasks, following prior work [24]. The entirely self-supervised SIMLA achieves state-of-the-art results on image-text retrieval and grounding, while outperforming larger models trained with supervision on downstream vision-language tasks, and demonstrates greater data efficiency compared to prior work in an ablation study. Our contributions, summarized:

1. A symmetric cross-modality reconstruction task to learn fine-grained alignment between image patches and language tokens.
2. A natural language, pseudo-labeling approach to align concept-level semantics without dense annotations.
3. A single-stream architecture to enable the proposed multi-level alignment.
4. Extensive experiments on image-text retrieval, vision-language reasoning, and visual grounding to demonstrate effectiveness of the proposed modules.

2   Method

Images are dense, unstructured, and require significant processing to extract useful semantic information. In contrast, language is highly structured, and contains directly available semantic information. Because of this asymmetry, attempting to align image features with language features too early will be futile, because the image features are too low-level to be matched with the more abstract language features. Contemporary architectures thus employ a symmetric encoder design, in which both image and text are processed by equally deep encoders before late fusion through alignment of global image and text representations. This approach wastes model capacity, as high-level image semantics often correspond directly to low-level language semantics, so processing language to same depth as images is wasteful. In addition, both language and images contain a semantic pyramid of concepts, with some concepts being highly localized (e.g. a small image patch/single word) while other concepts are highly abstract (e.g multiple interrelated image patches/multi-token sequences). Cross-modal concepts can exist at different levels of the semantic pyramid for each modality (e.g the singular token 'throwing' describes a complex spatial scene/the phrase 'bird walking on rocky ground' may describe a small local image region). Thus, the problems in vision-language learning are twofold:

1. Asymmetry in inherent semantic abstraction between image and text data.
2. Semantic concepts appear at disparate levels in the abstraction hierarchy across modalities.

We propose an asymmetric architecture with a multi-task loss to address the above issues. Concretely, our architecture consists of a deep stack of transformer encoder layers that can be interpreted as a transformer language model [50] stacked atop a visual transformer [11]. During the forward pass, an image is fed through the bottom of the stack, while language tokens are injected at the middle of the stack, into the bottom of the language model. This design allows processing of the image to an appropriate level of semantic abstraction before fusion with language. Our multi-task loss consists of four tasks, engineered to align vision and language representations at multiple levels. We begin with an image-text matching task for very coarse instance-level alignment, and add a contrastive loss for global feature-level alignment. Next, we add a patch-level reconstruction task for fine-grained region-level alignment. Finally, we add a pseudo-label supervision task to the visual encoder to explicitly ensure the level of abstraction between the visual and language tokens is synchronized prior to fine-grained fusion.

2.1 Preliminary Architectures

Our model is a 24-deep stack of transformer [50] layers that can be decomposed into a vision encoder E_v, a language encoder E_l, and a multimodal encoder E_{mm}. Specifically, we stack the language encoder E_l atop the vision encoder E_v. We then add cross-attention layers after each self-attention layer in the language encoder E_l, allowing us to use it as a multimodal encoder E_{mm} when an image-text pair is passed in, and as a unimodal language encoder when language tokens are passed in. To obtain a multimodal embedding, we first use the bottom half of the transformer encoder stack (E_v) to encode an input image I into a sequence

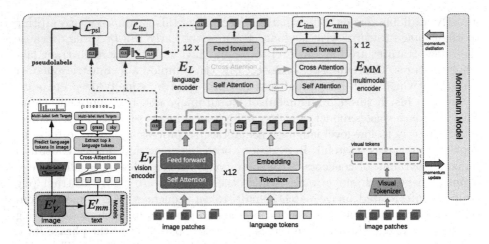

Fig. 1. SIMLA architecture. A language encoder E_l is stacked atop a vision encoder E_v. We add cross attention to E_l, allowing us to reuse it as a multimodal encoder E_{mm} by consuming image embeddings from E_v. Four tasks align images and language at multiple levels, exploiting a momentum model for additional supervision. A D-VAE tokenizes image patches for the cross-modality reconstruction task.

of embeddings $E_v(I) = \{\vec{v}_{\text{cls}}, \vec{v}_1, ..., \vec{v}_N\}$ where v_{cls} is the embedding of the [CLS] token. We then pass the sequence of image embeddings $\{\vec{v}_{\text{cls}}, \vec{v}_1, ..., \vec{v}_N\}$ into the top half of the transformer encoder stack, corresponding to the language model with cross-attention, while concurrently injecting the associated caption, so the image embeddings $\{\vec{v}_{\text{cls}}, \vec{v}_1, ..., \vec{v}_N\}$ from bottom half of the stack and the input *tokens* $\{[\text{cls}], t_1, ..., t_N\}$ are consumed simultaneously and fused through cross-attention after each self attention layer to yield a sequence of multimodal embeddings $\{\vec{m}_{\text{cls}}, \vec{m}_1, ..., \vec{m}_N\} = E_{mm}(\{\vec{v}_{\text{cls}}, \vec{v}_1, ..., \vec{v}_N\}, \{[\text{cls}], t_1, ..., t_N\})$ (Fig. 1).

2.2   Coarse Cross-Modality Alignment

Image-Text Contrastive Learning. The simplest level of alignment is coarse, global alignment between image and text representations. Global alignment is useful training signal for two reasons: (i) it is robust to mismatches in fine-grained details between an image and caption (ii) it is an easier task than fine-grained alignment and enables faster learning during the earlier stages of training, when fine-grained alignment is infeasible due to the large domain gap between images and text. Coarse, global alignment requires learning image and text representations which capture modality-invariant information. A simple, effective and scalable [17,42] approach to learning modality invariant representations is multi-view contrastive learning [49]. The multi-view contrastive objective pushes embeddings of matched image-text pairs together while pulling those of unmatched image-text pairs apart. Our contrastive loss follows the InfoNCE [37] formulation. Contrastive losses benefit from larger batch sizes, but batch sizes are bounded by GPU memory. To increase effective batch size, we follow MoCo [15] by using memory queues of size M for the unimodal image (Q^{img}) and text (Q^{txt}) features, as well as maintaining momentum (time-averaged) versions of the text and image encoders. The normalized image-to-text and text-to-image similarity are calculated as

$$p_m^{\text{i2t}}(I, Q^{\text{txt}}) = \frac{\exp(S(I, Q_m^{\text{txt}})/\tau)}{\sum_{m=1}^{M} \exp(S(I, Q_m^{\text{txt}})/\tau)}$$
$$p_m^{\text{t2i}}(T, Q^{\text{img}}) = \frac{\exp(S(T, Q_m^{\text{img}})/\tau)}{\sum_{m=1}^{M} \exp(S(T, Q_m^{\text{img}})/\tau)} \tag{1}$$

where τ is a learnable temperature parameter, $S(I,T) = g_v(\vec{v}_{\text{cls}})g'_l(\vec{l}_{\text{cls}})$ and $S(T,I) = g_l(\vec{l}_{\text{cls}})^T g'_v(\vec{v}_{\text{cls}})$ are raw similarity scores between image and text [CLS] tokens, obtained by $E_v(I)$ and $E_l(T)$ respectively. The functions g_v and g_l are linear transformations that project the unimodal [CLS] embeddings of the image and text, respectively, to lower-dimensional representations, followed by normalization to unit length. We use $g'_v(\vec{v}'_{\text{cls}})$ and $g'_l(\vec{l}'_{\text{cls}})$ to denote the momentum features, retrieved from the memory queues. The boolean one-hot vectors $\vec{y}^{\text{i2t}}(I)$ and $\vec{y}^{\text{t2i}}(T)$ represent the ground-truth similarity, with the positive pair indicated by a 1 and a 0 for all negatives. Then, the image-text contrastive loss is defined as the cross-entropy H between $\vec{p}$ and $\vec{y}$:

$$\mathcal{L}_{\text{itc}} = \frac{1}{2}\mathbb{E}_{(I,T)\sim D}\left[\text{H}(\vec{y}^{\text{i2t}}(I), \vec{p}^{\text{i2t}}(I)) + \text{H}(\vec{y}^{\text{t2i}}(T), \vec{p}^{\text{t2i}}(T))\right] \tag{2}$$

The one-hot labels $\vec{y}^{\text{i2t}}(I)$ and $\vec{y}^{\text{t2i}}(T)$ penalize all predictions which do not match each image to the text it came paired with, and vice versa. However, one caption can potentially describe many different images, and similarly, many captions may match an image. To avoid this noisy penalization, we soften the hard targets with soft targets generated by the momentum model, corresponding to knowledge distillation [16] with the momentum model as a teacher. The complete loss can then be written as

$$\mathcal{L}_{\text{itc}}^{\text{mod}} = (1-\alpha)\mathcal{L}_{\text{itc}} + \alpha\mathcal{L}'_{\text{itc}} \tag{3}$$

$$\mathcal{L}'_{\text{itc}} = \frac{1}{2}\mathbb{E}_{(I,T)\sim D}\left[\text{H}\left(p_m^{\text{i2t}}(I), p^{\text{i2t}}(I)\right) + \text{H}\left(p_m^{\text{t2i}}(T), p^{\text{t2i}}(T)\right)\right] \tag{4}$$

where $p_m^{\text{i2t}}(I)$ and $p_m^{\text{t2i}}(T)$ is Eq. 1 using only the momentum encoders.

Image-Text Matching is a binary classification task to predict if an image-text pair is matched. We define the ITM loss to be

$$\mathcal{L}_{\text{itm}} = \mathbb{E}_{(I,T)\sim D}\text{H}\left(\boldsymbol{y}^{\text{itm}}, \boldsymbol{p}^{\text{itm}}(I,T)\right) \tag{5}$$

where $\boldsymbol{y}^{\text{itm}}$ is a one-hot vector indicating whether the pair is matched or not, and p^{itm} is a two-class probability vector predicted by a single fully connected layer on top of the multimodal [CLS] token. We mine in-batch hard negatives for each image and text in a pair following ALBEF [24].

2.3   Finer-Grained Cross-Modality Alignment

A contrastive loss such as $\mathcal{L}_{\text{itc}}$ aligns the global image and text representations. However, solely aligning the global representations while simultaneously fusing the image and text at the last possible opportunity makes it difficult to learn fine-grained correspondences, such as those between subregions of an image and subsequences of a caption. We design a reconstruction task to teach a model fine-grained alignment between images and patches. We mask the image, and force the model to reconstruct the masked image region from the remaining portion of the image using the caption as context. We then reverse the reconstruction task, forcing the model to reconstruct masked language tokens from the remaining portion of the caption using the image as context.

Concretely, (I, T) be an image text pair. Let $\mathcal{M}_I$ be a mask for the image, generated following the masking strategy of BEiT [4], and let $\mathcal{M}_T$ be the mask for the language tokens, generated following the masking strategy of BERT [9]. We then generate[1] a masked image as $\hat{I} = I \odot \mathcal{M}_I$ and masked text as $\hat{T} = T \odot \mathcal{M}_T$. Then, the loss to be minimized is

$$\mathcal{L}_{\text{xmm}} = \mathbb{E}_{(I,\hat{T})\sim D}\text{H}\left(\boldsymbol{y}^{\text{MLM}}, \boldsymbol{p}^{\text{MLM}}(I,\hat{T})\right) + \mathbb{E}_{(\hat{I},T)\sim D}\text{H}\left(\boldsymbol{y}^{\text{MIM}}, \boldsymbol{p}^{\text{MIM}}(\hat{I},T)\right) \quad (6)$$

The cross-modality masked language modeling loss $\mathcal{L}_{\text{xmm}}$ is a sum of two cross-entropy losses, where $\boldsymbol{y}^{\text{MLM}}$ and $\boldsymbol{y}^{\text{MIM}}$ indicate the ground-truth value of the masked language token and masked image token respectively, and $\boldsymbol{p}^{\text{MLM}}(I,\hat{T})$, $\boldsymbol{p}^{\text{MIM}}(I,\hat{T})$ represents the model's probability estimates of the masked language and image tokens respectively. Because images are continuous, use the strategy of [4] to discretize the images into a sequence of tokens and mask them. We divide each image into patches and tokenize each patch with a discrete VAE [38] that maps each patch to one of 8192 visual tokens from a learned codebook.

In many cases, the ground-truth visual or language token can be plausibly replaced with an alternative. However, the ground truth target vectors are one-hot encoded and penalize any predictions that do not exactly match for the ground truth, even if they are plausible. Furthermore, the image masking and language masking are random, so it is possible for non-content tokens (e.g. *the, it*) or tokens that cannot be predicted well based on context to be masked. To allow the model to learn even when the ground-truth target for the masked token cannot be reasonably predicted from context, we again use the momentum distillation strategy. Specifically, we decompose $\mathcal{L}_{\text{xmm}}$ into

$$\mathcal{L}_{\text{xmm}}^{\text{mod}} = (1-\alpha)\mathcal{L}_{\text{MIM}} + \alpha\mathcal{L}'_{\text{MIM}} + (1-\alpha)\mathcal{L}_{\text{MLM}} + \alpha\mathcal{L}'_{\text{MLM}} \quad (7)$$

where $\mathcal{L}'_{\text{MIM}} = \text{H}\left(\boldsymbol{p}_m^{\text{MIM}}, \boldsymbol{p}^{\text{MIM}}(I,\hat{T})\right)$, $\mathcal{L}'_{\text{MLM}} = \text{H}\left(\boldsymbol{p}_m^{\text{MLM}}, \boldsymbol{p}^{\text{MLM}}(I,\hat{T})\right)$ and $\boldsymbol{p}_m^{\text{MLM}}, \boldsymbol{p}_m^{\text{MLM}}$ are the softmax-normalized outputs of the MIM and MLM momentum prediction heads over the visual and language token distributions, respectively.

---

[1] We depict the masking as a boolean operation for notational simplicity. The implementation follows the strategy of BEiT [4] and BERT [9] for I, T respectively.

2.4 Concept-Level Alignment

Semantic concepts may appear at disparate levels in the abstraction hierarchy across modalities. A concept may be highly complex in the visual modality, while being expressible with a single token in the language modality, and vice versa. This results in a concept-level mismatch between images and text. Although an asymmetric architecture that subjects image inputs to greater processing than text inputs prior to fusion addresses the intrinsic disparity in the semantic abstraction between image and text data, it does not guarantee that the visual embeddings $E_v(I) = \{v_{\text{cls}}, v_1, \ldots, v_N\}$ express concepts that are commonly described with language, or even possible to describe with language. Furthermore, it is possible that during the alignment process, the *unimodal* representations may degrade, because the emphasis is only on alignment.

To address this, we design a high-level alignment task in which the visual representation is aligned to represent concepts expressible by the language encoder by teaching it to label images with language concepts associated to the image, which also maintains the quality of the unimodal visual representation. We use the self-attention map of the multimodal [CLS] token to determine which language tokens within the text are most salient to the image-text pair. We choose k of the most salient tokens as pseudo-labels for the image, and generate a "hard" 2-D binary target vector $\mathbf{y}^{\text{PSL}} \in \mathbb{R}^V$, where V is the number of tokens known to the language model, and a 1 in the $[0][i]$-th position indicates the i-th token is a target pseudo-label and a 1 in the $[1][j]$-th position indicates the j-th token is not a target. We seek to minimize

$$\mathcal{L}_{\text{PSL}} = -\frac{1}{V} \sum_{i=1}^{V} \mathbf{y}_i^{\text{PSL}} \cdot \log\left(\sigma(\mathbf{p}_i^{\text{PSL}})\right) + \left(1 - \mathbf{y}_i^{\text{PSL}}\right) \cdot \log\left(1 - \sigma(\mathbf{p}_i^{\text{PSL}})\right) \quad (8)$$

where $\mathbf{p}^{\text{PSL}}$ is the output of a single fully-connected layer placed atop the unimodal image [CLS] token, $\sigma(\cdot)$ is a sigmoid function used the clamp the output of the fully-connected layer between 0 and 1, and V is the number of tokens in the vocabulary of the tokenizer. This corresponds to multi-label loss where the model is trained to predict which language concepts (corresponding to tokens) are present in the image, using only the image context. However, the binary pseudolabels $\mathbf{y}^{\text{PSL}}$ may fail to capture relevant concepts in the image, because the caption typically only describes a small number of aspects of an image. To provide a stronger self-supervisory signal, we use the momentum model as a teacher and minimize the K-L divergence between the predicted pseudolabels and the momentum pseudolabels. This can be expressed as a distillation loss where $\mathbf{p}'^{\text{PSL}}$ is the vector of momentum pseudolabel predictions.

$$\mathcal{L}_{\text{PSL}}^{\text{mod}} = (1-\alpha)\mathcal{L}_{\text{PSL}} - \frac{\alpha}{V} \sum_{i=1}^{V} \mathbf{p}_i'^{\text{PSL}} \cdot \log\left(\sigma(\mathbf{p}_i^{\text{PSL}})\right) + \left(1 - \mathbf{p}_i'^{\text{PSL}}\right) \cdot \log\left(1 - \sigma(\mathbf{p}_i^{\text{PSL}})\right)$$

$$(9)$$

The full pre-training objective can be expressed as

$$\mathcal{L} = \mathcal{L}_{\text{itc}}^{\text{mod}} + \mathcal{L}_{\text{xmm}}^{\text{mod}} + \mathcal{L}_{\text{itm}} + \mathcal{L}_{\text{PSL}}^{\text{mod}} \quad (10)$$

2.5   Implementation Details

We initialize the bottom 12 layers of the transformer encoder stack dedicated to vision (corresponding to the visual encoder) with the weights and architecture ViT/B-16 vision transformer [11], which is equipped with self-attention only. We initialize the top 12 multimodal layers of the transformer encoder stack (corresponding to the shared text/multimodal encoder) with the weights and architecture of BERT [9], with cross-attention. We pre-train the model for 30 epochs on 8 NVIDIA A100 GPUs with a batch size of 512. During pre-training, random 256×256 crops of images are used and input, and RandAugment [8] is applied to the images with color changes removed, following [24]. We set the momentum coefficient to 0.995, and linearly scale the distillation coefficient α from $0 \rightarrow 0.4$ in the first epoch. We use an $M = 65,536$ length memory queue. The AdamW [32] optimizer is used to train the model, with a weight decay of 0.02 and a cosine learning rate scheduler with a linear warmup to $1e^{-4}$ followed by a decay to $1e^{-5}$ in the subsequent epochs.

3   Experiments

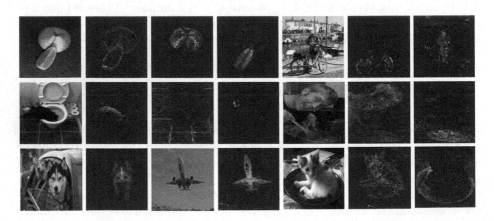

Fig. 2. Self-attention maps of the visual [CLS] token from different heads.

3.1   Experimental Setup

Pretraining Data is constructed by concatenating four image-text datasets: Conceptual Captions [45], SBU Captions [39], COCO [30] and Visual Genome [22], for a total of 4M image-text pairs, identical to [6,24].

Image-Text Retrieval. The goal of text retrieval (TR) is to retrieve texts matching a query image. Image retrieval (IR) reverses the roles of the modalities. We evaluate retrieval on MSCOCO [30] and Flickr30k [41]. We use the Karpathy [18] train/val/test splits for finetuning: 113k/5k/5k for MSCOCO and 29k/1k/1k for Flickr. For 0-shot retrieval on Flickr30k, we use the model fine-tuned on COCO, following [24]. We use ITC (Eq. 2) and ITM losses (Eq. 5) during fine-tuning. We finetune using a learning rate of $1e-5$ for 10 epochs. For fashion image retrieval, we use FashionGen [43], following the protocol of [13]. Fashion retrieval results and evaluation details are in the appendix.

Visual Question Answering (VQA) requires predicting an answer from an (image, question) pair. Following [24], we treat the task as an text generation problem using a auto-regressive decoder atop the multimodal encoder. For answer generation, we use [CLS] as the start of sequence token and [SEP] as the end of sequence token. The decoder is initialized from the multimodal encoder's weights and finetuned with a language modeling loss. We restrict the decoder to generate answers from a predefined set $3k$ of candidate answers [20].

Visual Entailment is a visual reasoning task where a model must decide whether an image (the premise) entails a sentence (hypothesis), contradicts it, or is neutral. We stack a multi-layer perceptron atop the [CLS] token of the multi-modal encoder and treat the task as a 3-way classification problem.

Visual Grounding requires localizing the image region corresponding to a text description (referring expression). We use the RefCOCO+ dataset [58] with 141k referring expressions for 20k images from the COCO dataset. Following [24], we simulate a weakly supervised setting where the bounding box annotations are not used during finetuning. The model is finetuned for 5 epochs in manner similar to image-text retrieval.

Table 1. An ablation study on the components of the proposed approach. ITM: image-text matching. ITC: image-text contrastive learning. MLM: masked language modeling. MIM: masked image modeling. PLS: pseudo-label supervision.

| | Components | | | | | Flickr30k True 0-shot (1k test set) | | | | | |
	ITM	ITC	MLM	MIM	PLS	TR@1	TR@5	TR@10	IR@1	IR@5	IR@10
(a)	✓					6.1	9.3	11.6	7.3	10.4	11.7
(b)	✓	✓				73.1	85.9	88.5	56.6	79.0	83.6
(c)	✓	✓	✓			84.0	96.4	97.8	69.5	89.2	93.9
(d)	✓	✓	✓	✓		85.1	97.1	99.2	70.1	89.3	94.6
(d)	✓	✓	✓	✓	✓	86.2	97.2	98.7	69.5	90.2	94.7

3.2   Results and Discussion

We run each fine-tuning experiment five times with different random seeds, and report the mean and standard deviation in the following tables.

Zero-Shot Retrieval. Table 2 reports results on zero-shot image-text retrieval. Our SIMLA model outperforms both CLIP [42] and ALIGN [17], which were trained on 100x and 300x more pairs respectively. We achieve better Rank-1 performance on both text and image retrieval compared to ALBEF [24].

Table 2. Zero-shot image-text retrieval results on Flickr30K.

Method	# Pre-train Images	Flickr30K (1K test set)					
		TR			IR		
		R@1	R@5	R@10	R@1	R@5	R@10
UNITER	4M	83.6	95.7	97.7	68.7	89.2	93.9
CLIP	400M	88.0	98.7	99.4	68.7	90.6	95.2
ALIGN	1.2B	88.6	98.7	99.7	75.7	93.8	96.8
ALBEF	4M	90.5	**98.8**	**99.7**	76.8	93.7	**96.7**
SIMLA	4M	**91.9**	98.6	99.1	**78.1**	**93.9**	96.7
Std. Dev		±0.4	±0.4	±0.2	±0.4	±0.3	±0.2

3.3   Image-Text Retrieval

Table 3 reports results on fine-tuned image-text retrieval. Our SIMLA model outperforms all other approaches on Rank-1 retrieval across both modalities and dataset, with a substantial (3%) increase over ALBEF [24] and a (6%) increase over OSCAR [28] on Rank-1 MSCOCO text retrieval.

3.4   VQA/NLVR/SNLI-VE

Table 4 compares the performance of SIMLA to existing methods on vision-language understanding tasks. SIMLA achieves state of the art performance, outperforming methods that use object annotations [28] adversarial training [12], and dual stream architectures [24].

3.5   Weakly-Supervised Visual Grounding

We show results on RefCOCO+ in Table 5. We outperform ALBEF [24], which itself outperforms existing methods by $\approx 10\% - 30\%$, by 1.5% and 1.2% on TestA and TestB respectively. We ground a referring expression in an image using Grad-CAM [44] on the cross-attention maps in the 8th layer of the multimodal encoder, using the gradients of the image-text matching score $p^{\text{itm}}(I, T)$ for a text-image pair (I, T). In Fig. 3, we visualize the Grad-CAM to show the grounding and fine-grained alignment ability of the model.

Data Efficiency. The additional pretraining tasks of SIMLA result in a stronger training signal that allow the model to learn faster with fewer training steps. In Fig. 4, we show zero-shot image-text retrieval accuracy as both ALBEF and SIMLA train. SIMLA's zero-shot accuracy smoothly and quickly rises in the beginning stages of training, compared to the more gradual and rocky climb of ALBEF.

Table 3. Fine-tuned image-text retrieval results on Flickr30K and MSCOCO.

Method	Pairs	Flickr30K (1k test set)						MSCOCO (5k test set)					
		TR			IR			TR			IR		
		R@1	R@5	R@10	R@1	R@5	R@10	R@1	R@5	R@10	R@1	R@5	R@10
UNITER	4M	87.3	98.0	99.2	75.6	94.1	96.8	65.7	88.6	93.8	52.9	79.9	88.0
VILLA	4M	87.9	97.5	98.8	76.3	94.2	96.8	–	–	–	–	–	–
OSCAR	4M	–	–	–	–	–	–	70.0	91.1	95.5	54.0	80.8	88.5
ALBEF	4M	94.3	99.4	**99.8**	82.8	**96.7**	**98.4**	73.1	91.4	96.0	56.8	81.5	**89.2**
SIMLA	4M	**94.7**	**99.5**	99.7	**83.3**	96.5	98.2	**75.8**	**92.9**	**96.2**	**57.7**	81.9	**92.0**
Std. Dev		±0.2	±0.1	±0.1	±0.2	±0.2	±0.1	±0.3	±0.3	±0.1	±0.2	±0.4	±0.55

Table 4. Comparison with state-of-the-art methods on downstream vision-language tasks. ALBEF results are from our reproduction, due to expired URLs in NLVR. SNLI-VE results may be noisy due to label errors [10].

Model	VQA		NLVR^2		SNLI-VE	
	test-dev	test-std	dev	test-P	val	test
VisualBERT [25]	70.8	71.0	67.4	67.0	-	-
VL-BERT [47]	71.16	-	-	-	-	-
LXMERT [48]	72.4	72.5	74.9	74.5	-	-
12-in-1 [34]	73.2	-	-	78.9	-	77.0
UNITER [6]	72.7	72.9	77.2	77.9	78.6	78.3
VL-BART/T5 [7]	-	71.3	-	73.6	-	-
ViLT [21]	70.9	-	75.2	76.2	-	-
OSCAR [28]	73.2	73.4	78.1	78.4	-	-
VILLA [12]	73.6	73.7	78.4	79.3	79.5	79.0
ALBEF [24]	74.5	74.7	79.2	**80.0**	79.1	80.1
SIMLA	**74.5**	**74.8**	**79.8**	79.5	**79.6**	**80.2**
Std. Dev	±0.1	±0.1	±0.4	±0.5	±0.2	±0.3

Table 5. Weakly-supervised visual grounding on RefCOCO+ [59] dataset.

Method	Val	TestA	TestB
ARN [31]	32.8	34.4	32.1
CCL [63]	34.3	36.9	33.6
ALBEF [24]	**58.5**	65.9	46.3
SIMLA	58.1	**67.4**	**47.5**
Std. Dev	±0.5	±0.29	±0.33

Ablation Study. In Table 1, we study the effect of the various losses on image-text retrieval performance. Training with only the image-text matching (ITM) loss provides only a weak supervisory signal. Explicit alignment is crucial, and

"shoe"   "sky"   "face"   "woman in blue shirt" "metal flying object" "soft fluffy clouds"

Fig. 3. Examples of fine-grained alignment learned by SIMLA. The model can ground abstract concepts (e.g. metal flying object) in addition to simple concepts (e.g. shoe).

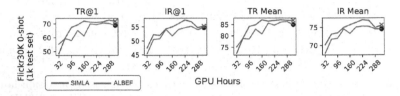

Fig. 4. True zero-shot fast retrieval accuracy on the Flickr30K test set as a function of training time. SIMLA achieves higher accuracy in less training time than ALBEF.

each level of alignment provides an increase in performance. Global alignment ($\mathcal{L}_{itc}$) provides the largest boost in performance, but fine-grained alignment ($\mathcal{L}_{mim} + \mathcal{L}_{mlm}$) is crucial for increasing performance, and pseudo-label supervision ($\mathcal{L}_{psl}$) successfully exploits additional supervisory signals to learn a better-aligned representation.

Qualitative Results. In Fig. 5, we show examples of pseudolabels generated by the momentum models. When the captions are nondescriptive, the pseudolabels provide a strong surrogate supervisory signal that grounds the content of the image in natural language concepts. Even when the captions *are* descriptive (bottom middle of Fig. 5), the pseudolabels provide additional supervision by requiring the visual representation to reflect concepts present in the image but not in the caption. We show self-attention maps obtained from the [CLS] token of the visual encoder in Fig. 2. Different heads of the visual encoder work together to decompose a scene, with heads focusing on various parts of the scene. The subjects of attention correspond to the visual concepts humans are most likely to notice, even in cluttered or dense scenes. The attention map segments objects well, despite having no access to object-level annotations and receiving supervision from oftentimes noisy captions.

3.6 Parameter Count and Inference Speed

In Tables 2, 3 and 4, we report results against the `large` sized versions of UNITER [6], OSCAR [28] and VILLA [12], which have $\approx$ 335M parameters and a depth of 24 transformer encoder layers. SIMLA has equivalent depth (24 layers) with fewer parameters (223M) due to parameter sharing. SIMLA is also substantially faster at inference time (7.2 pairs / second vs $\approx$ 1.1 pairs / second for UNITER/VILLA/OSCAR) due to the dual-encoder design shared with ALBEF [24], in which the text/image encoders can be used separately to quickly

Fig. 5. Examples of pseudolabels used for pseudolabel supervision, obtained by decoding high-probability concept head logits from the momentum encoders.

retrieve the top-k candidates matching a query, and re-ranking them using the slower multimodal encoder.

4   Related Work

4.1   Vision Language Pretraining

Early transformer-based [9,50] vision language pretraining techniques [6,25,33, 48] required an pretrained object detector and were limited to visual categories the object detector could identify. Recent contrastive-image text learners such as CLIP [42] do not rely on object detectors and understand a far wider range of visual concepts. However, CLIP relies on a massive dataset (400m pairs) to overcome label noise. Several methods [14,24,29,55,62] have been proposed for data-efficient pretraining. DeCLIP [29] exploits inter/intra-modality supervision to train a CLIP-like model with less data, similar to [55]. ALBEF [24] proposes a contrastive alignment followed by deeper fusion with a multimodal encoder. Methods such as BLIP [23], CoCa [57], SimVLM [52], UNIMO [26,27] incorporate a decoder and add image-to-text generation as an auxillary task. Other lines of work on vision-language foundation models [5] are multi-task models [1,46,51,60] or foundation model ensembles [5,54,61]. We propose a data-efficient, detector-free pretraining approach, architecturally similar to [24], but with additional supervision for the visual encoder to learn key words (high level concepts) that are present in the image, as well as a symmetric cross-modality reconstruction task inspired by the masked image modeling techniques of [4,64].

4.2 Fusion Methods

Existing fusion techniques can be broadly classified into three categories: early [40], [53], middle [19,36,36], and late fusion [3,17,33,42]. Late fusion (e.g. CLIP) is the dominant approach due to its scalability and encodes input modalities separately using unimodal encoders and fuses the resulting representations at the end. However, each modality can have different levels of information density. For example, [2] shows audio and video to have fine-grained information while text has coarse-grained information, and [62] draws the conclusion that in dual-stream contrastive architectures, the strength of the visual encoder matters more than that of the language encoder. It is thus essential to consider the information density of the input modalities for fusion. Compared to language, images require significant processing to extract useful semantic information, but current dual-stream approaches [29,42,62] apply the same amount of of processing to both. In contrast, we use a single stream architecture where the input modalities undergo asymmetric processing before fusion. OSCAR [28], UNITER [6] and ViLBERT [33] also include a similar patch-level concept prediction task, but they use region labels produced by a pretrained object detector as prediction targets. SIMLA is fully self-supervised, and needs no labels, bounding boxes, or object detectors.

5   Conclusion

We propose SIMLA, a framework for vision-language pretraining. In contrast to contemporary dual-stream approaches that employ symmetric encoders and introduce multimodal interactions after unimodal representation learning, SIMLA uses a single-stream architecture with asymmetric depth of processing for each modality and enables earlier multimodal interactions. SIMLA aligns images and text on multiple levels, and explicitly enriches the visual modality with pseudo-label supervision to ensure similar levels of conceptual abstraction in the representations before fusion. We empirically verify the strength of the approach and achieve state-of-the-art results on image-text retrieval, natural language visual grounding, and vision language reasoning tasks. Finally, we show that the additional training tasks provide additional supervision that increases the data efficiency of SIMLA relative to other state-of-the-art approaches.

References

1. Alayrac, J.B., et al.: Flamingo: a visual language model for few-shot learning. ArXiv arXiv:2204.14198 (2022)
2. Alayrac, J., et al.: Self-supervised multimodal versatile networks. CoRR arXiv:2006.16228 (2020)
3. Alwassel, H., Mahajan, D., Torresani, L., Ghanem, B., Tran, D.: Self-supervised learning by cross-modal audio-video clustering. CoRR arXiv:1911.12667 (2019)
4. Bao, H., Dong, L., Wei, F.: Beit: BERT pre-training of image transformers. CoRR arXiv:2106.08254 (2021)

5. Bommasani, R., et al.: On the opportunities and risks of foundation models. ArXiv arXiv:2108.07258 (2021)
6. Chen, Y.-C., et al.: UNITER: UNiversal image-TExt representation learning. In: Vedaldi, A., Bischof, H., Brox, T., Frahm, J.-M. (eds.) ECCV 2020. LNCS, vol. 12375, pp. 104–120. Springer, Cham (2020). https://doi.org/10.1007/978-3-030-58577-8_7
7. Cho, J., Lei, J., Tan, H., Bansal, M.: Unifying vision-and-language tasks via text generation. arXiv preprint arXiv:2102.02779 (2021)
8. Cubuk, E.D., Zoph, B., Shlens, J., Le, Q.V.: Randaugment: practical automated data augmentation with a reduced search space. In: CVPR Workshops, pp. 702–703 (2020)
9. Devlin, J., Chang, M., Lee, K., Toutanova, K.: BERT: pre-training of deep bidirectional transformers for language understanding. In: Burstein, J., Doran, C., Solorio, T. (eds.) NAACL, pp. 4171–4186 (2019)
10. Do, V., Camburu, O.M., Akata, Z., Lukasiewicz, T.: e-snli-ve-2.0: corrected visual-textual entailment with natural language explanations. ArXiv arXiv:2004.03744 (2020)
11. Dosovitskiy, A., et al.: An image is worth 16 × 16 words: transformers for image recognition at scale. In: ICLR (2021)
12. Gan, Z., Chen, Y., Li, L., Zhu, C., Cheng, Y., Liu, J.: Large-scale adversarial training for vision-and-language representation learning. In: Larochelle, H., Ranzato, M., Hadsell, R., Balcan, M., Lin, H. (eds.) NeurIPS (2020)
13. Gao, D., et al.: Fashionbert: text and image matching with adaptive loss for cross-modal retrieval. In: Proceedings of the 43rd International ACM SIGIR Conference on Research and Development in Information Retrieval (2020)
14. Goel, S., Bansal, H., Bhatia, S.K., Rossi, R.A., Vinay, V., Grover, A.: Cyclip: cyclic contrastive language-image pretraining. ArXiv arXiv:2205.14459 (2022)
15. He, K., Fan, H., Wu, Y., Xie, S., Girshick, R.: Momentum contrast for unsupervised visual representation learning. In: CVPR (2020)
16. Hinton, G., Vinyals, O., Dean, J.: Distilling the knowledge in a neural network. arXiv preprint arXiv:1503.02531 (2015)
17. Jia, C., et al.: Scaling up visual and vision-language representation learning with noisy text supervision. arXiv preprint arXiv:2102.05918 (2021)
18. Karpathy, A., Li, F.: Deep visual-semantic alignments for generating image descriptions. In: CVPR, pp. 3128–3137 (2015)
19. Kazakos, E., Nagrani, A., Zisserman, A., Damen, D.: Epic-fusion: audio-visual temporal binding for egocentric action recognition. CoRR arXiv:1908.08498 (2019)
20. Kim, J., Jun, J., Zhang, B.: Bilinear attention networks. In: Bengio, S., Wallach, H.M., Larochelle, H., Grauman, K., Cesa-Bianchi, N., Garnett, R. (eds.) NIPS, pp. 1571–1581 (2018)
21. Kim, W., Son, B., Kim, I.: Vilt: vision-and-language transformer without convolution or region supervision. arXiv preprint arXiv:2102.03334 (2021)
22. Krishna, R., et al.: Visual genome: connecting language and vision using crowd-sourced dense image annotations. IJCV **123**(1), 32–73 (2017)
23. Li, J., Li, D., Xiong, C., Hoi, S.C.H.: Blip: bootstrapping language-image pre-training for unified vision-language understanding and generation. In: ICML (2022)
24. Li, J., Selvaraju, R.R., Gotmare, A.D., Joty, S., Xiong, C., Hoi, S.: Align before fuse: vision and language representation learning with momentum distillation. In: NeurIPS (2021)
25. Li, L.H., Yatskar, M., Yin, D., Hsieh, C., Chang, K.: Visualbert: a simple and performant baseline for vision and language. arXiv preprint arXiv:1908.03557 (2019)

26. Li, W., et al.: Unimo: towards unified-modal understanding and generation via cross-modal contrastive learning. ArXiv arXiv:2012.15409 (2021)
27. Li, W., et al.: UNIMO-2: end-to-end unified vision-language grounded learning. In: Findings of the Association for Computational Linguistics: ACL 2022, pp. 3187–3201. Association for Computational Linguistics, Dublin, Ireland (2022). https://doi.org/10.18653/v1/2022.findings-acl.251
28. Li, X., et al.: OSCAR: object-semantics aligned pre-training for vision-language tasks. In: Vedaldi, A., Bischof, H., Brox, T., Frahm, J.-M. (eds.) ECCV 2020. LNCS, vol. 12375, pp. 121–137. Springer, Cham (2020). https://doi.org/10.1007/978-3-030-58577-8_8
29. Li, Y., et al.: Supervision exists everywhere: a data efficient contrastive language-image pre-training paradigm. In: International Conference on Learning Representations (2022). https://openreview.net/forum?id=zq1iJkNk3uN
30. Lin, T.-Y., et al.: Microsoft COCO: common objects in context. In: Fleet, D., Pajdla, T., Schiele, B., Tuytelaars, T. (eds.) ECCV 2014. LNCS, vol. 8693, pp. 740–755. Springer, Cham (2014). https://doi.org/10.1007/978-3-319-10602-1_48
31. Liu, X., Li, L., Wang, S., Zha, Z., Meng, D., Huang, Q.: Adaptive reconstruction network for weakly supervised referring expression grounding. In: ICCV, pp. 2611–2620 (2019)
32. Loshchilov, I., Hutter, F.: Decoupled weight decay regularization. arXiv preprint arXiv:1711.05101 (2017)
33. Lu, J., Batra, D., Parikh, D., Lee, S.: Vilbert: pretraining task-agnostic visiolinguistic representations for vision-and-language tasks. In: Wallach, H.M., Larochelle, H., Beygelzimer, A., d'Alché-Buc, F., Fox, E.B., Garnett, R. (eds.) NeurIPS, pp. 13–23 (2019)
34. Lu, J., Goswami, V., Rohrbach, M., Parikh, D., Lee, S.: 12-in-1: multi-task vision and language representation learning. In: CVPR, pp. 10434–10443 (2020)
35. Mu, N., Kirillov, A., Wagner, D.A., Xie, S.: Slip: self-supervision meets language-image pre-training. ArXiv arXiv:2112.12750 (2021)
36. Nagrani, A., Yang, S., Arnab, A., Jansen, A., Schmid, C., Sun, C.: Attention bottlenecks for multimodal fusion. CoRR arXiv:2107.00135 (2021)
37. van den Oord, A., Li, Y., Vinyals, O.: Representation learning with contrastive predictive coding. CoRR arXiv:1807.03748 (2018)
38. van den Oord, A., Vinyals, O., Kavukcuoglu, K.: Neural discrete representation learning. CoRR arXiv:1711.00937 (2017)
39. Ordonez, V., Kulkarni, G., Berg, T.L.: Im2text: describing images using 1 million captioned photographs. In: Shawe-Taylor, J., Zemel, R.S., Bartlett, P.L., Pereira, F.C.N., Weinberger, K.Q. (eds.) NIPS, pp. 1143–1151 (2011)
40. Owens, A., Efros, A.A.: Audio-visual scene analysis with self-supervised multisensory features. CoRR arXiv:1804.03641 (2018)
41. Plummer, B.A., Wang, L., Cervantes, C.M., Caicedo, J.C., Hockenmaier, J., Lazebnik, S.: Flickr30k entities: collecting region-to-phrase correspondences for richer image-to-sentence models. In: ICCV, pp. 2641–2649 (2015)
42. Radford, A., et al.: Learning transferable visual models from natural language supervision. arXiv preprint arXiv:2103.00020 (2021)
43. Rostamzadeh, N., et al.: Fashion-gen: the generative fashion dataset and challenge. ArXiv arXiv:1806.08317 (2018)
44. Selvaraju, R.R., Das, A., Vedantam, R., Cogswell, M., Parikh, D., Batra, D.: Gradcam: visual explanations from deep networks via gradient-based localization. Int. J. Comput. Vision **128**, 336–359 (2017)

45. Sharma, P., Ding, N., Goodman, S., Soricut, R.: Conceptual captions: a cleaned, hypernymed, image alt-text dataset for automatic image captioning. In: Gurevych, I., Miyao, Y. (eds.) ACL, pp. 2556–2565 (2018)
46. Singh, A., et al.: Flava: a foundational language and vision alignment model. ArXiv arXiv:2112.04482 (2021)
47. Su, W., et al.: Vl-bert: pre-training of generic visual-linguistic representations. In: ICLR (2020)
48. Tan, H., Bansal, M.: LXMERT: learning cross-modality encoder representations from transformers. In: Inui, K., Jiang, J., Ng, V., Wan, X. (eds.) EMNLP, pp. 5099–5110 (2019)
49. Tian, Y., Krishnan, D., Isola, P.: Contrastive multiview coding. CoRR arXiv:1906.05849 (2019)
50. Vaswani, A., et al.: Attention is all you need. In: Guyon, I., von Luxburg, U., Bengio, S., Wallach, H.M., Fergus, R., Vishwanathan, S.V.N., Garnett, R. (eds.) NIPS, pp. 5998–6008 (2017)
51. Wang, P., et al.: Ofa: unifying architectures, tasks, and modalities through a simple sequence-to-sequence learning framework. CoRR arXiv:2202.03052 (2022)
52. Wang, Z., Yu, J., Yu, A.W., Dai, Z., Tsvetkov, Y., Cao, Y.: Simvlm: simple visual language model pretraining with weak supervision. ArXiv arXiv:2108.10904 (2021)
53. Xiao, F., Lee, Y.J., Grauman, K., Malik, J., Feichtenhofer, C.: Audiovisual slowfast networks for video recognition. CoRR arXiv:2001.08740 (2020)
54. Xie, Y., et al.: Visual clues: bridging vision and language foundations for image paragraph captioning. ArXiv arXiv:2206.01843 (2022)
55. Yang, J., et al.: Vision-language pre-training with triple contrastive learning. In: CVPR 2022 (2022). https://www.amazon.science/publications/vision-language-pre-training-with-triple-contrastive-learning
56. Yao, L., et al.: Filip: fine-grained interactive language-image pre-training. ArXiv arXiv:2111.07783 (2021)
57. Yu, J., Wang, Z., Vasudevan, V., Yeung, L., Seyedhosseini, M., Wu, Y.: Coca: contrastive captioners are image-text foundation models. ArXiv arXiv:2205.01917 (2022)
58. Yu, L., Poirson, P., Yang, S., Berg, A.C., Berg, T.L.: Modeling context in referring expressions. ArXiv arXiv:1608.00272 (2016)
59. Yu, L., Poirson, P., Yang, S., Berg, A.C., Berg, T.L.: Modeling context in referring expressions. In: Leibe, B., Matas, J., Sebe, N., Welling, M. (eds.) ECCV 2016. LNCS, vol. 9906, pp. 69–85. Springer, Cham (2016). https://doi.org/10.1007/978-3-319-46475-6_5
60. Yuan, L., et al.: Florence: a new foundation model for computer vision. ArXiv arXiv:2111.11432 (2021)
61. Zeng, A., et al.: Socratic models: composing zero-shot multimodal reasoning with language. ArXiv arXiv:2204.00598 (2022)
62. Zhai, X., et al.: Lit: Zero-shot transfer with locked-image text tuning. In: Proceedings of the IEEE/CVF Conference on Computer Vision and Pattern Recognition (CVPR), pp. 18123–18133 (June 2022)
63. Zhang, Z., Zhao, Z., Lin, Z., Zhu, J., He, X.: Counterfactual contrastive learning for weakly-supervised vision-language grounding. In: Larochelle, H., Ranzato, M., Hadsell, R., Balcan, M., Lin, H. (eds.) NeurIPS (2020)
64. Zhou, J., Wei, C., Wang, H., Shen, W., Xie, C., Yuille, A., Kong, T.: ibot: image Bert pre-training with online tokenizer. In: International Conference on Learning Representations (ICLR) (2022)

Author Index

Printed in the United States
by Baker & Taylor Publisher Services